W9-CXK-488

# BEDFORD INTEGRATED MEDIA

## You've got access to LearningCurve!

## Everyone's got a learning curve — what's yours?

Be smart: get ready for class and tests by using LearningCurve's game-like online quizzing to discover what you know and learn what you don't. Quiz feedback tells you why answers are right or wrong and links you to your book for review — with a chance to try again! Try it today and find out why students across the country rave about the LearningCurve advantage.

## For access to LearningCurve

1. Go to **bedfordstmartins.com/highschool/henretta8e**.

2. Click to enter your student access code. Enter it exactly as it appears on the access card that comes with this book, including any dashes, and follow the on-screen instructions.

**For technical support,** visit **macmillanhighered.com/techsupport**.

**Teachers:** For instructor access, visit **bedfordstmartins.com/highschool /henretta8e** and register as an instructor.

If an access card is not attached, visit the following site for more information: bedfordstmartins.com/highschool/henretta8e

bedfordstmartins.com/highschool/henretta8e

# Bedford Integrated Media for *America's History*, Eighth Edition, For the AP® Course

Henretta • Hinderaker • Edwards • Self

## STUDENT ACCESS CODE

a4d-i8x-g74tdw9z

Scratch off to reveal code. Do not peel.

**6-USE CARD:** This student access code is valid for six users. Each user is granted access for a time period of up to one year.

**TEACHERS:** To get instructor access, go to bedfordstmartins.com/highschool/henretta8e.

**For technical support:**
• macmillanhighered.com/techsupport

AP® is a trademark registered by the College Board, which was not involved in the production of, and does not endorse, this product.

**bedfordstmartins.com/highschool/henretta8e**

# Bedford Integrated Media for *America's History*, Eighth Edition, For the AP® Course

Henretta • Hinderaker • Edwards • Self

**RECORD THE INFORMATION YOU NEED TO ACCESS THE INTEGRATED MEDIA. KEEP THIS INFORMATION SECURE.**

| | |
|---|---|
| Student's name: | Student's name: |
| Student's e-mail: | Student's e-mail: |
| Password: | Password: |
| Teacher's name: | Teacher's name: |
| Date activated: | Date activated: |
| | |
| Student's name: | Student's name: |
| Student's e-mail: | Student's e-mail: |
| Password: | Password: |
| Teacher's name: | Teacher's name: |
| Date activated: | Date activated: |
| | |
| Student's name: | Student's name: |
| Student's e-mail: | Student's e-mail: |
| Password: | Password: |
| Teacher's name: | Teacher's name: |
| Date activated: | Date activated: |

AP® is a trademark registered by the College Board, which was not involved in the production of, and does not endorse, this product.

If an access card is not attached, visit the following site for more information: bedfordstmartins.com/highschool/henretta8e

# About the cover image

## *The Sources of Country Music*

In painting this vibrant work, artist Thomas Hart Benton captured many of the forces that shaped America. A preacher and hymn singers emphasize the importance of religious faith to both women and men. Fiddle players—with a decidedly less sacred outlook—keep a jug of whiskey on hand. A man playing the African-derived banjo represents the profound influence of African Americans on the nation's culture. In the background, a steamboat and locomotive show the transformative role of technology and economic change.

# AMERICA'S HISTORY

FOR THE AP® COURSE

# AMERICA'S HISTORY

EIGHTH EDITION

## FOR THE AP® COURSE

**James A. Henretta**
University of Maryland

**Eric Hinderaker**
University of Utah

**Rebecca Edwards**
Vassar College

**Robert O. Self**
Brown University

**BEDFORD / ST. MARTIN'S**
Boston • New York

**For Bedford/St. Martin's**

Publisher for History: *Mary V. Dougherty*
Executive Editor for History: *William J. Lombardo*
Director of Development for History: *Jane Knetzger*
Senior Developmental Editor: *Laura Arcari*
Production Editor: *Annette Pagliaro Sweeney*
Senior Production Supervisor: *Jennifer Peterson*
Senior Marketing Manager: *Janie Pierce-Bratcher*
Associate Editor: *Robin Soule*
Editorial Assistant: *Victoria Royal*
Copyeditor: *Susan Zorn*
Indexer: *Leoni Z. McVey, McVey & Associates, Inc.*
Cartography: *Mapping Specialists, Ltd.*
Photo Researchers: *Pembroke Herbert and Sandi Rygiel, Picture Research Consultants, Inc.*
Senior Art Director: *Anna Palchik*
Text Designer: *Maureen McCutcheon*
Cover Designer: *Marine Miller*
Cover Art: *Thomas Hart Benton,* The Sources of Country Music, *courtesy of Country Music Hall of Fame® and Museum*
Composition: *Jouve*
Printing and Binding: *RR Donnelley and Sons*

President, Bedford/St. Martin's: *Denise B. Wydra*
Director of Marketing: *Karen R. Soeltz*
Production Director: *Susan W. Brown*
Director of Rights and Permissions: *Hilary Newman*

Copyright © 2014, 2011, 2008, 2004 by Bedford/St. Martin's

All rights reserved. No part of this book may be reproduced, stored in a retrieval system, or transmitted in any form or by any means, electronic, mechanical, photocopying, recording, or otherwise, except as may be expressly permitted by the applicable copyright statutes or in writing by the Publisher.

Manufactured in the United States of America.

4   5   6      17   16   15   14

*For information, write:* Bedford/St. Martin's, 75 Arlington Street, Boston, MA 02116    (617-399-4000)

ISBN: 978–1–4576–7382–5
ISBN: 978–1–4576–2893–1 (with Bedford Integrated Media)

AP® is a trademark registered by the College Board, which was not involved in the production of, and does not endorse, this product.

# Preface
## Why This Book This Way

The new College Board standards for AP U.S. History present exciting opportunities and big challenges. As the authors of *America's History*, we have closely followed College Board changes by attending and participating in numerous AP workshops, webinars for teachers, and the AP Annual Conference. We believe the new exam, with its focus on themes and Historical Thinking Skills, represents a positive direction. But we know it means major changes for you, so we're here to help.

The AP U.S. History classroom presents a unique dilemma. How do we offer our students a basic understanding of key events and facts while inviting them to see the past not as a rote list of names and dates but as the fascinating, conflicted prelude to their lives today? How do we teach our students to think like historians? As scholars and teachers who go into the classroom every day, we know these challenges well and have composed the eighth edition of *America's History* to help instructors meet them. *America's History* has long had a reputation in the AP community for its balanced coverage, attention to AP themes and content, and ability to explain to students not just what happened, but *why*. The latest edition both preserves and substantially builds upon those strengths.

The foundation of our approach lies in our commitment to an integrated history. *America's History* combines traditional "top down" narratives of political and economic affairs with "bottom up" narratives of the lived experiences of ordinary people. Our goal is to help students achieve a richer understanding of politics, diplomacy, war, economics, intellectual and cultural life, and gender, class, and race relations by exploring how developments in all these areas were interconnected. Our analysis is fueled by a passion for exploring big, consequential questions. How did a colonial slave society settled by people from four continents become a pluralist democracy? How have liberty and equality informed the American experience? Questions like these help students understand what's at stake as we study the past. In *America's History*, we provide an integrated historical approach and bring a dedication to *why history matters* to bear on the full sweep of America's past.

One of the most exciting developments in this edition is the arrival of a new author, Eric Hinderaker. An expert in native and early American history, Eric brings a fresh interpretation of native and colonial European societies and the revolutionary Atlantic World of the eighteenth century that enlivens and enriches our narrative. Eric joins James Henretta, long the intellectual anchor of the book, whose scholarly work now focuses on law, citizenship, and the state in early America; Rebecca Edwards, an expert in women's and gender history and nineteenth-century electoral politics; and Robert Self, whose work explores the relationship between urban and suburban politics, social movements, and the state. Together, we strive to ensure that energy and creativity, as well as our wide experience in the study of history, infuse every page that follows.

The core of a textbook is its narrative, and we have endeavored to make ours clear, accessible, and lively. In it, we focus not only on the marvelous diversity of peoples who came to call themselves Americans, but also on the institutions that have forged a common national identity. More than ever, we daily confront the collision of our past with the demands of the future and the shrinking distance between Americans and others around the globe. To help students meet these challenges, we call attention to connections with the histories of Canada, Latin America, Europe, Africa, and Asia, drawing links between events in the United States and those elsewhere. In our contemporary digital world, facts and data are everywhere. What students crave is analysis. As it has since its inception, *America's History* provides students with a comprehensive explanation and interpretation of events, a guide to why history unfolded as it did and a roadmap for understanding the world in which we live.

Of course, the contents of this book are only helpful if students read and assimilate the material before coming to class. So that students will come to class prepared, they now receive access to **LearningCurve**—an adaptive, gamelike online learning tool that helps them master content—when they purchase a new copy of *America's History*. And because we know that your classroom needs are changing rapidly, we are excited to announce that *America's History* is available with **LaunchPad**, a new robust interactive e-book built into its own course space that makes customizing and assigning the book and its resources easy and efficient.

To learn more about the benefits of LearningCurve and LaunchPad, see the "Versions and Supplements" section on page xii.

## A Nine-Part Framework Highlights Key Developments

One of the greatest strengths of *America's History* is its part structure, which helps students identify the key forces and major developments that shaped each era. A four-page part opener introduces each part, using analysis, striking images, and a detailed **thematic timeline** to orient students to the major developments and themes of the period covered. New **Thematic Understanding** questions ask students to consider periodization and make connections among chapters while reinforcing AP themes and Thematic Learning Objectives. By organizing U.S. history into nine distinct periods, rather than just thirty-one successive chapters, we encourage students to trace changes and continuities over time and to grasp connections between political, economic, social, and cultural events.

In this edition, we have closely aligned the book's part structure to the redesigned AP U.S. History course to make the transition to the new exam seamless. From beginning to end, you'll find that our nine-part organization corresponds to the College Board's nine periods. To help your students prepare for the new exam's expanded attention to Native Americans, precontact native societies and European colonization are now covered in two distinct parts, allowing us to devote comprehensive attention to the whole of North America before the 1760s. In the modern period, our final two parts offer expanded coverage of the period after 1945, mirroring the AP exam's increased attention to the recent past. Throughout, our part introductions give students the tools to understand *why* the periodization looks the way it does, helping them build the Historical Thinking Skills the course demands. The nine parts organize the complex history of North America and the United States into comprehensible sections with distinct themes, a structure that provides instructors with the crucial historical backbone while allowing them the freedom to adapt specific examples from their classroom.

**Part 1, "Transformations of North America, 1450–1700,"** highlights the diversity and complexity of Native Americans prior to European contact, examines the transformative impact of European intrusions and the Columbian Exchange, and emphasizes the experimental quality of colonial ventures. **Part 2, "British North America and the Atlantic World, 1660–1763,"** explains the diversification of British North America and the rise of the British Atlantic World and emphasizes the importance of contact between colonists and Native Americans and imperial rivalries among European powers. **Part 3, "Revolution and Republican Culture, 1763–1820,"** traces the rise of colonial protest against British imperial reform, outlines the ways that the American Revolution challenged the social order, and explores the processes of conquest, competition, and consolidation that followed it.

**Part 4, "Overlapping Revolutions, 1800–1860,"** traces the transformation of the economy, society, and culture of the new nation; the creation of a democratic polity; and growing sectional divisions. **Part 5, "Creating and Preserving a Continental Nation, 1844–1877,"** covers the conflicts generated by America's empire building in the West, including sectional political struggles that led to the Civil War and national consolidation of power during and after Reconstruction. **Part 6, "Industrializing America: Upheavals and Experiments, 1877–1917,"** examines the transformations brought about by the rise of corporations and a powerhouse industrial economy; immigration and a diverse, urbanizing society; and movements for progressive reform.

**Part 7, "Domestic and Global Challenges, 1890–1945,"** explores America's rise to world power, the cultural transformations and political conflicts of the 1920s, the Great Depression, and the creation of the welfare state. **Part 8, "The Modern State and the Age of Liberalism, 1945–1980,"** addresses the postwar period, including America's new global leadership role during the Cold War; the expansion of federal responsibility during a new "age of liberalism"; and the growth of mass consumption and the middle class. Finally, **Part 9, "Global Capitalism and the End of the American Century, 1980 to the Present,"** discusses the conservative political ascendancy of the 1980s; the end of the Cold War and rising conflict in the Middle East; and globalization and increasing social inequality.

## Hundreds of Sources Encourage Comparative and Critical Thinking

*America's History* has long emphasized primary sources. In addition to weaving lively quotations throughout the narrative, we offer students substantial excerpts from historical documents — letters, diaries, autobiographies, public testimony, and more — and numerous figures that give students practice working with data. These documents allow students to experience the past through the words and perspectives of those who lived it, to understand how historians make sense of the past using data, and to gain skill in interpreting historical evidence. Each chapter contains three source-based features that prepare students for the rigor of the Document-Based Question (DBQ).

**American Voices**, a two-page feature in each chapter, helps students learn to think critically by comparing texts written from two or more perspectives. New topics include "The Debate over Free and Slave Labor," "Jewish Immigrants in the Industrial Economy," "Theodore Roosevelt: From Anti-Populist to New Nationalist," and "Immigration After 1965: Its Defenders and Critics."

New **America Compared** features use primary sources and data to situate U.S. history in a global context while giving students practice in comparison and data analysis. Retooled from the Voices from America feature from the last edition to include data in addition to primary sources, these features appear in every chapter on topics as diverse as the fight for women's rights in France and the United States, an examination of labor laws after emancipation in Haiti and the United States, the loss of human life in World War I, and an analysis of the worldwide economic malaise of the 1970s.

Finally, we are excited to introduce a brand-new feature to aid you in teaching Historical Thinking Skills. A **Thinking Like a Historian** feature in every chapter includes five to eight brief sources organized around a central theme, such as "Beyond the Proclamation Line," "Making Modern Presidents," and "The Suburban Landscape of Cold War America." In this DBQ-like environment, students are asked to analyze the documents and complete a Putting It All Together assignment that asks them to synthesize and use the evidence to create an argument. Because we understand how important primary sources are to the study of history, we are also pleased to offer an all-new companion reader, *Sources for America's History*, featuring a wealth of additional documents, including unique part sets tied to AP Thematic Learning Objectives.

As in past editions, an outstanding **visual program** engages students' attention and gives them practice in working with visual sources. The eighth edition features over 425 paintings, cartoons, illustrations, photographs, and charts, most of them in full color and more

than a quarter new to this edition. Informative captions set the illustrations in context and provide students with background for making their own analysis of the images in the book. Keenly aware that students lack geographic literacy, we have included dozens of **maps** that show major developments in the narrative, each with a caption to help students interpret what they see.

Taken together, these documents, figures, maps, and illustrations provide instructors with a trove of teaching materials, so that *America's History* offers not only a compelling narrative, but also — right in the text — the rich documentary materials that instructors need to bring the past alive and introduce students to historical analysis.

## Study Aids Support Understanding and Teach Historical Thinking Skills

The study aids in the eighth edition have been completely revised to better support students in their understanding of the material and in their development of Historical Thinking Skills. New **Identify the Big Idea** questions at the start of every chapter guide students' reading and focus their attention on identifying not just what happened, but why. A variety of learning tools from the beginning to the end of each chapter support this big idea focus, which is in line with the new AP exam's emphasis on Thematic Learning Objectives. As they read, students will gain proficiency in Historical Thinking Skills via **marginal review questions** that ask them to "Identify Causes," "Trace Change over Time," and "Understand Points of View," among other skills. Where students are likely to stumble over a key concept, we boldface it in the text where it is first mentioned and provide a **glossary** that defines each term.

In the Chapter Review section, a set of **Review Questions** is given for the chapter as a whole that includes a new **Thematic Understanding** question, along with **Making Connections** questions that ask students to consider broader historical issues, developments, and continuities and changes over time. A brief list of **More to Explore** sources directs students to accessible print and Web resources for additional reading. Lastly, a **Timeline** with a new **Key Turning Points** question reminds students of important events and asks them to consider periodization.

# New Scholarship Includes Latest Research and Interpretations

In the new edition, we continue to offer instructors a bold account of U.S. history that reflects the latest, most exciting scholarship in the field. Throughout the book, we have given increased attention to political culture and political economy, including the history of capitalism, using this analysis to help students understand how society, culture, politics, and the economy informed one another.

With new author Eric Hinderaker aboard, we have taken the opportunity to reconceptualize much of the pre-1800 material. This edition opens with two dramatically revised chapters marked by closer and more sustained attention to the way Native Americans shaped, and were shaped by, the contact experience and highlighting the tenuous and varied nature of colonial experimentation. These changes carry through the edition in a sharpened continental perspective and expanded coverage of Native Americans, the environment, and the West in every era. We have also brought closer attention to the patterns and varieties of colonial enterprise and new attention to the Atlantic World and the many revolutions — in print, consumption, and politics — that transformed the eighteenth century.

In our coverage of the nineteenth century, the discussion of slavery now includes material on African American childhood and the impact of hired-out slaves on black identity. The spiritual life of Joseph Smith also receives greater attention, as do the complex attitudes of Mormons toward slavery. New findings have also deepened the analysis of the war with Mexico and its impact on domestic politics. But the really new feature of these chapters is their heightened international, indeed global, perspective.

In the post–Civil War chapters, enhanced coverage of gender, ethnicity, and race includes greater emphasis on gay and lesbian history and Asian and Latino immigration, alongside the entire chapter devoted to the civil rights movement, a major addition to the last edition. Finally, we have kept up with recent developments with an expanded section on the Obama presidency and the elections of 2008 and 2012.

# Acknowledgments

We are grateful to the following scholars and teachers who reported on their experiences with the seventh edition or reviewed features of the new edition. Their comments often challenged us to rethink or justify our interpretations and always provided a check on accuracy down to the smallest detail.

*High School Reviewers:*

Christine Bond-Curtright, *Edmond Memorial High School*
Matthew Ellington, *Ruben S. Ayala High School*
Jason George, *The Bryn Mawr School*
Geri Hastings, *Catonsville High School*
Susan Ikenberry, *Georgetown Day School*
John Irish, *John Paul II High School*
Jocelyn Miner, *Mercy High School*
Louisa Bond Moffitt, *Marist School*
Caren R. B. Saunders, *Kent County High School*
Nancy Schick, *Los Alamos High School*
William A. Shelton, *Trinity Valley School*

*College Reviewers:*

Jeffrey S. Adler, *University of Florida*
Jennifer L. Bertolet, *The George Washington University*
Vicki Black, *Blinn College*
Stefan Bosworth, *Hostos Community College*
Tammy K. Byron, *Dalton State College*
Jessica Cannon, *University of Central Missouri*
Rose Darrough, *Palomar College*
Petra DeWitt, *Missouri University of Science & Technology*
Nancy J. Duke, *Daytona State College*
Richard M. Filipink, *Western Illinois University*
Matthew Garrett, *Bakersfield College*
Benjamin H. Hampton, *Manchester Community College and Great Bay Community College*
Isadora Helfgott, *University of Wyoming*
Stephanie Jannenga, *Muskegon Community College*
Antoine Joseph, *Bryant University*
Lorraine M. Lees, *Old Dominion University*
John S. Leiby, *Paradise Valley Community College*
Karen Ward Mahar, *Siena College*

Timothy R. Mahoney, *University of Nebraska–Lincoln*

Eric Mayer, *Victor Valley College*

Glenn Melancon, *Southeastern Oklahoma State University*

James Mills, *University of Texas, Brownsville*

Frances Mitilineos, *Oakton Community College*

Anne Paulet, *Humboldt State University*

Thomas Ratliff, *Central Connecticut State University*

LeeAnn Reynolds, *Samford University*

Jenny Shaw, *University of Alabama*

Courtney Smith, *Cabrini College*

Timothy Thurber, *Virginia Commonwealth University*

Sarah E. Vandament, *North Lake College of the Dallas County Community College District*

Julio Vasquez, *University of Kansas*

Louis Williams, *St. Louis Community College–Forest Park*

As the authors of *America's History*, we know better than anyone else how much this book is the work of other hands and minds. We are indebted to Mary Dougherty, William J. Lombardo, Dan McDonough, and Jane Knetzger, who oversaw this edition, and Laura Arcari, who asked the right questions, suggested a multitude of improvements, and expertly guided the manuscript to completion. As usual, Denise B. Wydra and Joan E. Feinberg generously provided the resources we needed to produce an outstanding volume. Annette Pagliaro Sweeney did a masterful job consulting with the authors and seeing the book through the production process. Karen R. Soeltz, Sandi McGuire, and Janie Pierce-Bratcher in the marketing department understood how to communicate our vision to teachers; they and the members of college and high school sales forces did wonderful work in helping this edition reach the classroom. We also thank the rest of our editorial and production team for their dedicated efforts: Associate Editors Robin Soule and Jen Jovin; Editorial Assistant Victoria Royal; Susan Zorn, who copyedited the manuscript; proofreaders Arthur Johnson and Lindsay DiGianvittorio; art researchers Pembroke Herbert and Sandi Rygiel at Picture Research Consultants, Inc.; text permissions researcher Eve Lehmann; and Kalina Ingham and Hilary Newman, who oversaw permissions. Finally, we want to express our appreciation for the invaluable assistance of Patricia Deveneau, who expertly suggested topics and sources for the Thinking Like a Historian features in Chapters 8–14; Kendra Kennedy, for crucial research aid; and Eliza Blanchard and Erin Boss, and especially Michelle Whalen and the U.S. historians — Robert Brigham, Miriam Cohen, James Merrell, and Quincy Mills — for their invaluable help and advice at Vassar. Many thanks to all of you for your contributions to this new edition of *America's History*.

James A. Henretta
Eric Hinderaker
Rebecca Edwards
Robert O. Self

# Versions and Supplements

Adopters of *America's History* and their students have access to abundant extra resources, including documents, presentation and testing materials, the acclaimed Bedford Series in History and Culture volumes, and much more. See below for more information, visit the book's catalog site at **highschool.bfwpub.com/henretta8e**, or contact your local Bedford, Freeman, and Worth sales representative.

## New Assign LaunchPad—the Online, Interactive e-Book in a Course Space Enriched with Integrated Assets

The new standard in digital history, LaunchPad course tools are so intuitive to use that teachers find it's easy to create assignments, track students' work, and access a wealth of relevant learning and teaching resources. It is the ideal learning environment for students to work with the text, maps, documents, video, and assessment. LaunchPad is loaded with the full interactive e-book and the *Sources for America's History* documents collection—plus LearningCurve, short author video chapter previews, additional primary sources, videos, guided reading exercises designed to help students read actively for key concepts, boxed feature reading quizzes, chapter summative quizzes, and more. LaunchPad can be used as is or customized, and it easily integrates with course management systems. And with fast ways to build assignments, rearrange chapters, and add new pages, sections, or links, it lets teachers build the course materials they need and hold students accountable.

## ✓ New Assign LearningCurve So You Know What Your Students Know and They Come to Class Prepared

Assigning LearningCurve in place of reading quizzes is easy for instructors, and the reporting features help instructors track overall class trends and spot topics that are giving students trouble so they can adjust their lectures and class activities. This online learning tool is popular with students because it was designed to help them rehearse content at their own pace in a non-threatening, gamelike environment. The feedback for wrong answers provides instructional coaching and sends students back to the book for review. Students answer as many questions as necessary to reach a target score, with repeated chances to revisit material they haven't mastered. When LearningCurve is assigned, students come to class better prepared.

## New *Annotated Teacher's Edition for America's History*

The Annotated Teacher's Edition provides a wealth of guidance and support for AP teachers. Developed for the AP U.S. History exam redesign, annotations include model answers for questions in the book, teaching tips, Historical Thinking Skills practice, pacing guides, exam alerts, and more. The teacher's edition helps teachers at all levels build the most successful AP U.S. History course they can. Authors Matthew J. Ellington of Ruben S. Ayala Senior High School, Jason George of the Bryn Mawr School, and George W. Henry Jr. of East High School are all experienced AP instructors, exam readers, and workshop leaders with a deep familiarity with the AP U.S. History redesign.

## *Strive for a 5: Preparing for the AP U.S. History Examination*

Revised for the redesigned course, this print guide provides students with narrative and thematic overviews of each historical period, chapter reviews organized around AP key concepts, and AP-style practice exams, including source-based multiple-choice and document-based questions as well as short- and long-answer essay questions. The guide is authored by Warren Hierl of the Career Center, Winston-Salem, NC (retired), Louisa Moffitt of Marist School, Atlanta, GA, and Nancy Schick of Los Alamos High School, NM (retired), all experienced AP teachers, exam readers, and workshop leaders.

## Take Advantage of Instructor Resources

Bedford/St. Martin's has developed a rich array of teaching resources for this book and for this course. They range from lecture and presentation materials and assessment tools to course management options. Most can be downloaded or ordered at **highschool.bfwpub.com/henretta8e**.

**Computerized Test Bank.** The test bank includes a mix of fresh, carefully crafted multiple-choice, short-answer, and essay questions for each chapter. It also contains brand new source-based multiple-choice questions and partwide essay questions. All questions appear in Microsoft Word format and in easy-to-use test bank software that allows instructors to add, edit, re-sequence, and print questions and answers. Instructors can also export questions into a variety of formats, including Blackboard, Desire2Learn, and Moodle.

**NEW** *Teacher's Survival Guide.* Created for teachers, by teachers, this unique set of resources — a test bank and a roundtable — offers APUSH teachers assessment tools, help with redesigning their U.S. history courses, and thoughtful advice from veteran teachers and college professors.

Created by Matthew J. Ellington, James Bokern, Michael A. Smith, and William Polasky III — veteran AP U.S. history teachers, exam readers, and workshop leaders — the ExamView **U.S. History Test Bank for the New AP® Course** allows teachers to create and edit tests and quizzes for in-class or at-home use. Organized according to the redesigned curriculum framework, the test bank's nine parts include 250 formative multiple-choice questions focused on key concepts, more than 300 stimulus-based multiple-choice questions, numerous short-answer and long-essay questions, and 8 complete DBQs.

The test bank is accompanied by **Teaching U.S. History: A Roundtable Discussion** focused on teaching the new AP U.S. History course with insights from experienced AP teachers into the redesign of the U.S. history survey, including teaching with themes, emphasizing historical thinking skills, and balancing breadth and depth in the course.

*The Bedford Lecture Kit* **Instructor's Resource CD-ROM.** This resource provides ready-made and fully customizable PowerPoint multimedia presentations that include lecture outlines with embedded maps, figures, and selected images from the textbook and extra background for instructors. Also available are maps and selected images in JPEG and PowerPoint formats; content for i>clicker, a classroom response system, in Microsoft Word and PowerPoint formats; the Instructor's Resource Manual in Microsoft Word format; and outline maps in PDF format for quizzing or handing out. All files are suitable for copying onto transparency acetates.

**NEW** *Teaching Ideas for AP History: A Video Resource.* This DVD is a new professional resource for teachers of AP United States, European, and World History. In three hours of interviews with thirty AP history experts, teachers, and college professors, this video offers a wealth of advice on varied topics, including creating a syllabus, reading and writing strategies, and specific assignments to help students develop their Historical Thinking Skills while learning historical content. The disc also includes dozens of files — from lesson plans to graphic organizers — that can be downloaded and used in class, as well as a series of downloadable discussion questions for teachers that allow the DVD to be used effectively in a formal professional development setting.

*America in Motion: Video Clips for U.S. History.* Set history in motion with *America in Motion*, an instructor DVD containing dozens of short digital movie files of events in twentieth-century American history. From the wreckage of the battleship *Maine* to FDR's fireside chats to Oliver North testifying before Congress, *America in Motion* engages students with dynamic scenes from key events and challenges them to think critically. All files are classroom-ready, edited for brevity, and easily integrated with PowerPoint or other presentation software for electronic lectures or assignments. An accompanying guide provides each clip's historical context, ideas for use, and suggested questions.

**Videos and Multimedia.** A wide assortment of videos and multimedia CD-ROMs on various topics in U.S. history is available to qualified adopters through your Bedford/St. Martin's sales representative.

## Package and Give Your Students Even More

Stretch your budget and package your favorite text with more! Many of the following resources can be packaged at minimal additional cost. For information on packages, discounts, and class sets, contact your local Bedford, Freeman, and Worth sales representative.

**NEW** *Sources for America's History.* Edited by Kevin B. Sheets of SUNY Cortland, and designed to complement the textbook, *Sources for America's History* provides a broad selection of over 225 primary-source documents as well as editorial apparatus to help students understand the sources. Unique part sets that support Thematic Learning Objectives are closely aligned to the new AP periodization. Available at a discount when packaged with the print text and included in the

LaunchPad e-book. Also available on its own as a downloadable PDF e-book or with the main text's e-Book to Go.

**NEW Bedford Digital Collections @ bedfordstmartins .com/bdc/catalog.** This source collection provides a flexible and affordable online repository of discovery-oriented primary-source projects and single primary sources that you can easily customize and link to from your course management system or Web site.

**The Bedford Series in History and Culture.** More than 120 titles in this highly praised series combine first-rate scholarship, historical narrative, and important primary documents for undergraduate courses. Each book is brief, inexpensive, and focused on a specific topic or period. For a complete list of titles, visit **bedfordstmartins.com/history/series**.

*Rand McNally Atlas of American History.* This collection of over eighty full-color maps illustrates key events and eras, from early exploration, settlement, expansion, and immigration to U.S. involvement in wars abroad and on U.S. soil. Introductory pages for each section include a brief overview, timelines, graphs, and photos to quickly establish a historical context.

*Maps in Context: A Workbook for American History.* Written by historical cartography expert Gerald A. Danzer (University of Illinois at Chicago), this skill-building workbook helps students comprehend essential connections between geographic literacy and historical understanding. Organized to correspond to the typical U.S. history survey course, *Maps in Context* presents a wealth of map-centered projects and convenient pop quizzes that give students hands-on experience working with maps.

*The Bedford Glossary for U.S. History.* This handy supplement for the survey course gives students historically contextualized definitions for hundreds of terms — from *abolitionism* to *zoot suit* — that they will encounter in lectures, reading, and exams.

*U.S. History Matters: A Student Guide to U.S. History Online.* This resource, written by Alan Gevinson, Kelly Shrum, and the late Roy Rosenzweig (all of George Mason University), provides an illustrated and annotated guide to 250 of the most useful Web sites for student research in U.S. history as well as advice on evaluating and using Internet sources. This essential guide is based on the acclaimed "History Matters" Web site developed by the American Social History Project and the Center for History and New Media.

**Trade Books.** Titles published by sister companies Hill and Wang; Farrar, Straus and Giroux; Henry Holt and Company; St. Martin's Press; Picador; and Palgrave Macmillan are available at a discount when packaged with Bedford/St. Martin's textbooks. For more information, visit **bedfordstmartins.com/tradeup**.

*A Pocket Guide to Writing in History.* This portable and affordable reference tool by Mary Lynn Rampolla provides reading, writing, and research advice useful to students in all history courses. Concise yet comprehensive advice on approaching typical history assignments, developing critical reading skills, writing effective history papers, conducting research, using and documenting sources, and avoiding plagiarism — enhanced with practical tips and examples throughout — has made this slim reference a best-seller.

*A Student's Guide to History.* This complete guide to success in any history course provides the practical help students need to be successful. In addition to introducing students to the nature of the discipline, author Jules Benjamin teaches a wide range of skills, from preparing for exams to approaching common writing assignments, and explains the research and documentation process with plentiful examples.

*Going to the Source: The Bedford Reader in American History.* Developed by Victoria Bissell Brown and Timothy J. Shannon, this reader's strong pedagogical framework helps students learn how to ask fruitful questions in order to evaluate documents effectively and develop critical reading skills. The reader's wide variety of chapter topics that complement the survey course and its rich diversity of sources — from personal letters to political cartoons — provoke students' interest while teaching them the skills they need to successfully interrogate historical sources.

*America Firsthand.* With its distinctive focus on ordinary people, this primary documents reader, by Anthony Marcus, John M. Giggie, and David Burner, offers a remarkable range of perspectives on America's history from those who lived it. Popular Points of View sections expose students to different perspectives on a specific event or topic, and Visual Portfolios invite analysis of the visual record.

# Brief Contents

# Contents

---

## PART 1 Transformations of North America, 1450–1700   *2*

### Chapter 1
### Colliding Worlds, 1450–1600   *6*

How did the political, economic, and religious systems of Native Americans, Europeans, and Africans compare, and how did things change as a result of contacts among them?

**AMERICA COMPARED**
Altered Landscapes   *14*

**THINKING LIKE A HISTORIAN**
Colliding Cultures   *26*

**AMERICA VOICES**
The Spanish Conquest of Mexico   *32*

### Chapter 2
### American Experiments, 1521–1700   *40*

In what ways did European migrants transfer familiar patterns and institutions to their colonies in the Americas, and in what ways did they create new American worlds? How did Native Americans adapt to the growing presence of Europeans among them?

**THINKING LIKE A HISTORIAN**
Who Was Pocahontas?   *50*

**AMERICA COMPARED**
Plantation Colonies Versus Neo-Europes   *57*

**AMERICA VOICES**
The Causes of Metacom's War   *68*

## Chapter 19
## "Civilization's Inferno": The Rise and Reform of Industrial Cities, 1880–1917 *606*

How did the rise of large cities shape American society and politics?

## Chapter 20
## Whose Government? Politics, Populists, and Progressives, 1880–1917 *636*

In the Progressive Era, how and why did reformers seek to address the problems of industrial America? To what extent did they succeed?

## Chapter 21
## An Emerging World Power, 1890–1918 *672*

As the United States became a major power on the world stage, what ideas and interests did policymakers seek to promote in international affairs?

## Chapter 22
## Cultural Conflict, Bubble, and Bust, 1919–1932 *704*

What conflicts in culture and politics arose in the 1920s, and how did economic developments in that decade help cause the Great Depression?

# Maps, Figures, and Tables

# Special Features

# Historical Thinking, Reading, and Writing Skills for AP U.S. History

**DAVE NEUMANN,** *Director*
**The History Project at California State University–Long Beach**

Students and adults alike often grumble that history is just a bunch of facts to memorize. While it's true that studying history requires data, information, and yes, facts, that's not the essence of what history is. History is a way of thinking about the world by looking at the past. It is a reconstruction of the past, drawing on both imagination and interpretation. In this effort historians use a number of skills. This skills primer will help you develop the Historical Thinking Skills you need to succeed in any Advanced Placement history course and on the exams. It will also enable you to improve critical-thinking, reading, and writing skills that will be useful in college or whatever endeavor you pursue after high school.

## Historical Thinking Skills

Historical thinking requires understanding and evaluating change and continuity over time. It also involves making appropriate use of historical evidence in answering questions and developing arguments about the past. Each historian would describe the various skills needed for this complex task slightly differently, but for AP history courses, they have been organized into four major skills that represent the ways historians study the past. These skills have been described as "habits of mind." This useful phrase should remind you that a skill needs to be practiced repeatedly until it becomes second nature. Because practice is an integral part of learning to think historically, the sections below include exercises to help you develop these "habits of mind." Like shooting free throws, rehearsing dance moves, or playing scales, Historical Thinking Skills need to be exercised regularly until you can use them easily and almost effortlessly.

As we discuss each skill separately below, keep in mind that these skills overlap in many ways. For example, you can't make a historical argument without also evaluating evidence. So as you develop one Historical Thinking Skill, you will also be practicing other skills. The first three skills are all necessary to move on to the fourth — interpretation and synthesis — in which you will bring what you have learned together.

## Chronological Reasoning

"Chronological reasoning" means thinking logically about how and why the world changes — or, sometimes, stays the same — over time. While all fields of knowledge offer arguments based on evidence or make comparisons, historians are uniquely concerned about the past and its relationship to the present. How is the world different now than it was 50 years ago, 500 years ago, or 5,000 years ago? Why did the world change? How have some aspects of the world remained relatively the same over long periods of time? On what basis do historians simplify the long and complicated past by breaking it into smaller eras?

**Historical Causation** Causation has to do with explanations about how or why changes take place in history. Sometimes there is an obvious connection between an event and its consequence, like a cue ball striking the eight ball and making it move. And some events *are* fairly straightforward: the attack on Pearl Harbor prompted President Roosevelt to ask Congress for a declaration of war against Japan. But even this seemingly simple example soon becomes more complicated. *Why* did Japan attack the United States? What role did the American embargo on the sale of oil have on Japan's decision? Why did the United States enact this embargo? All of these other events took place just a few years before the Pearl Harbor attack. If we go even further back, we'll gain additional insight about the larger context of the Japanese government's decision. A longer-term analysis might lead, for example, to an understanding of Japanese imperial aggression as an outgrowth of their rapid industrialization during the Meiji Restoration of the late nineteenth century.

Just as there were many factors behind the attack on Pearl Harbor, most examples of historical causation involve multiple causes and effects. Events and processes often result from developments in many realms of life, including social, political, economic, and cultural.

## Historical Causation involves:

| | |
|---|---|
| **Large processes** | Many changes take place through major processes that are larger than any one person and occur over a long period of time. Urbanization, for example, is a complex set of changes resulting from the actions of countless different individuals that became an underlying cause of many other developments. |
| **Multiple causes** | Most events or developments occur from a combination of factors, not just one. The protests of the late 1960s, for example, had multiple causes, including movements for civil rights and decolonization, the rise of the New Left, the Vietnam War, and the postwar baby boom that produced a new youth culture. |
| **Unintended consequences** | Many changes take place accidentally, like the large-scale deaths of Native Americans during the Columbian Exchange due to diseases Europeans weren't aware they were carrying. |
| **Contingency** | Events are not preordained, and history could have turned out differently. This is known as contingency. Because we read major events in history already knowing their outcome, we have a tendency to think they were bound to happen, but that is not the case. For example, the initial Spanish conquest of the Incas was very precarious, and early on they might have been defeated. |

Historians cannot test these in laboratories the way scientists can, but they can use historical evidence and reasoning to determine which of these are probable causes and effects. Historical causation also involves large processes, complex causes, unintended consequences, and contingencies, as the chart above describes.

You can begin to develop the skill of determining causation by asking yourself, whenever some significant change in history is described, what reasons explain the development. If the answer seems simple, keep digging, because there's bound to be a more complicated (and longer-term) explanation.

**EXERCISE:** One major controversy in U.S. history (and in European and world history as well) regarding causation has to do with why the Great Depression of the 1930s became so severe and lasted so long. How do the authors explain the causes of the Great Depression on pages 726–729 in Chapter 22? Which of the types of explanations from the box above do they use in their explanation about why this particular economic depression became so bad that it is still known as the "Great Depression"?

### Patterns of Continuity and Change over Time

Historians are interested in both historical changes and persisting patterns, or "continuities." Change is easier to see: when one country conquers another one, that event often becomes part of the historical record. But some things stay relatively the same for long periods of time. Because continuity (such as a network of trade that remains in existence for hundreds of years) is less dramatic than change, it can be harder to spot.

What counts as continuity depends on the scale of time you're working with. The Soviet Union was continuous throughout most of the twentieth century. However, in the time frame of Russia's history since the formation of Kievan Rus in the ninth century, the Soviet era looks more like a short-lived exception to tsarist rule.

When historians talk about continuity, they're not implying that a particular pattern applied to everyone in the world or even in a particular country or region. Nor are they claiming that absolutely nothing changed in the pattern they're describing. For example, agricultural production has been continuous for thousands of years. But there are exceptions to this broad statement: on the one hand, some people have continued to be foragers; on the other hand, methods of farming have changed substantially with technology. So the continuity of agriculture is a generalization but not a completely unchanging pattern or a pattern that applies to everyone on the planet.

To work on developing this skill, look for places in your text where the authors directly indicate that a historical pattern persisted over time and explain *why* that pattern persisted. But even when an author focuses on change in history, you can still find continuity by inference, since few things ever change completely. When the text describes a new development, ask yourself what *didn't* change. For example, employing the ideas of the European Enlightenment, Thomas Jefferson in the Declaration of Independence proclaimed "that all men are created equal." But many of the thinkers of the early republic used custom and biology to justify limiting suffrage to white men only. In this way, they continued to defend traditional stereotypes about the inferiority of women and non-Europeans that had existed for centuries.

> **EXERCISE:** Look at the authors' discussion of "Neo-European Colonies" on pages 56–66 in Chapter 2. How did the different colonies of the North American Atlantic coast seek to replicate European patterns of economic and social organization?

**Periodization**    Periodization refers to the ways that historians break the past into separate periods of time. Historians look for major turning points in history — places where the world looked very different *before* some event than it did *after* — to decide how to break the past into chunks. They then give a label to each period to convey the key characteristics and developments of that era.

Because the past is complex, any attempt to create eras and give those eras labels can provoke disagreement. For example, the word *Renaissance*, which means "rebirth," was first used in the later sixteenth century by the Italian art historian Giorgio Vasari to describe artists such as his contemporary Michelangelo whom Vasari regarded as geniuses even greater than those of the ancient world. Over time, the word's meaning was broadened to include many aspects of life, expanded geographically to include developments in many countries, and extended chronologically to include several centuries. But scholars do not agree about when exactly the Renaissance began and when it ended, and they debate whether certain artists and writers should be considered "Renaissance" figures. Many note that along with significant changes during the Renaissance, there were also striking continuities with the medieval period that preceded it. Others have questioned whether the word *Renaissance* should be used at all to describe an era in which many social groups saw decline rather than advance. These debates remind us that all periodization is done by people after the fact, and it all involves value judgments. No Delaware or Shawnee soldier in the Ohio Valley in the mid-eighteenth century, for example, knew he was fighting what would later be called "The French and Indian War," or that he was living in a period of time that would later be referred to as "colonial America."

As you develop this skill, pay attention to the labels for various periods that are used in the chapter you're reading. Sometimes chapter titles themselves contain a period label, which can give you an idea of what the authors have decided is the main story for that era. Chapter 3, for example, is titled "The British Atlantic World," and Chapter 25 is titled "Cold War America."

> **EXERCISE:** Chapter 26, which discusses society and culture in the postwar period, is titled "Triumph of the Middle Class." Read the chapter introduction and Big Idea question on page 838. What words do the authors use to convey their judgment that this was a period of triumph? From other history courses you have had, or from history you have learned on your own, you might know that this era occurred in the midst of other periods to which labels have also been given, including the "Red Scare" and the "Cold War." Consider why these labels were given to their respective periods. How do they complicate the idea that this was an era of "triumph"?

## Comparison and Contextualization

People don't learn things in isolation, but in relationship. Historians are no different. The third category of Historical Thinking Skills reflects the ways historians make sense of the past by placing particulars in some larger framework. For example, they understand historical events and processes by comparing them to related events and processes to see how they're similar and different. Second, historians recognize that historical evidence, including artifacts, photographs, and speeches, can only be adequately understood by knowing something about their context, that is, the time and place when they came into existence.

**Comparison**    Comparisons help historians understand how a development in the past was similar to or different from another development and in this way determine what was distinctive. For example, some scholars have concluded that the reform spanning the Progressive and New Deal eras shared key features that led to the development of a welfare state. Other scholars have argued that the New Deal represented a radical break from the progressive policies of the past. Through the tool of comparison we can see how leaders and ordinary people handled common problems in unique ways.

As you develop this skill, practice comparing two social justice movements, such as the African American and women's suffrage movements — and also compare the same movement at two different points in time. For example, how was the women's suffrage movement of the nineteenth century similar to that of the women's suffrage movement of the early twentieth century? How was it different? What had happened to lead to these differences?

> **EXERCISE:** Look at the authors' comparison of slavery in the Chesapeake, South Carolina, and the West Indies in the eighteenth century in Chapter 3. How was the institution of slavery similar from place to place? Why? What key features do the authors say are different? Why are they different?

**Contextualization**  Just as historical events make more sense when they're studied alongside similar events, historians know that any event can only be understood in "context." Context refers to the historical circumstances surrounding a particular event. Historians look for major developments in any era to help determine context. They typically think in terms of two levels of context: an *immediate* (or short-term) context and a *broad* (or long-term) context.

The easiest way to begin thinking about context is to figure out when a particular event took place or when a document was created. Then brainstorm the major developments of the era. Ask yourself, "How might these larger events have shaped this event (or document)?"

For example, European Enlightenment ideas — among them John Locke's revolutionary idea that political authority was not given by God to monarchs and that the people should have the power to change government policies, or even their form of government — had been carried over to the Americas by European colonists. These ideas added a secular dimension to colonial cultural life, but it wouldn't be until the Revolutionary era that these ideas would be embraced by American intellectuals such as John Adams, James Madison, and Thomas Jefferson in their formulation of republican political theory.

To understand why these ideas had such dramatic effects, you need to consider the larger context. That context, as Chapter 4 indicates, includes both the immediate context of the political and social situation in the colonies in the eighteenth century and the long-term context of the print revolution. The context sometimes includes things that might at first seem unrelated. In this case, after 1700 improved transportation networks facilitated the spread of people, goods, and information in the colonies. Around the same time, in 1695 the British government let the Licensing Act lapse, which had given it the right to censor all printed materials, further opening the floodgates for the spread of books, newspapers, letters, and pamphlets. In 1704, the first colonial newspaper was founded. By 1776, the thirteen colonies that united in declaring independence had thirty-seven newspapers among them. The transportation and print revolution thus allowed revolutionary ideas to be communicated far more widely and quickly than they would have without it.

> **EXERCISE:** Look at the "kitchen debate" between U.S. vice president Richard Nixon and Soviet premier Nikita Khrushchev on page 838 in Chapter 26. Note that it occurred in 1959, in a model kitchen the Americans set up in Moscow as part of the American National Exhibition. What immediate developments (including the location) might have shaped the arguments presented by the two leaders for the merits of their political systems? How do the broad context of the Cold War and the even broader context of U.S.-Soviet relations in the twentieth century help you understand the debate?

## Crafting Historical Arguments from Historical Evidence

This Historical Thinking Skill focuses our attention on using evidence to make historical arguments. The word *argument* reminds us that any attempt to explain the past requires interpretation, since our understanding of the past is limited. Arguing means making a logical — rather than an emotional — case for your interpretation of a particular historical question or controversy. To be convincing, your interpretation has to present supporting evidence. This evidence consists of information you have gathered from primary sources, which are materials produced during the period being studied, as well as from existing historical studies, which are called secondary sources.

**Historical Argumentation**  Historians make arguments about what life was like in the past, how or why things changed, and why those changes matter. Their arguments are informed by their deep knowledge about the subject and careful reading of primary and secondary sources. But because evidence from the past is often incomplete or difficult to understand, historians inevitably make inferences to fill the gaps in their knowledge. Not all historians make the same inferences, so there are often a variety of interpretations about most historical events.

For example, all scholars agree that the growth of industry first in England and then in America and elsewhere in the eighteenth and nineteenth centuries was a major historical development. It was so important, in fact, that we call it a revolution: the Industrial Revolution. But historians disagree about the most significant causes for the way industry developed. Some highlight the coal deposits located near English rivers, which provided a source of power far greater than human or animal power. Others point to a culture of innovation that developed in England, in which artisans and inventors read scientific works and looked for solutions to practical problems. Still others emphasize the role of England's overseas colonies, which provided raw materials and markets for manufactured products.

To develop this Historical Thinking Skill, ask yourself how historians think they know what they know about a particular event. What evidence do they provide? Does their language suggest hesitancy or uncertainty about their interpretation? Do they offer alternative explanations?

> **EXERCISE:** On page 11 of Chapter 1 of this text, how do the authors explain the decline of the Mississippian settlement of Cahokia? What inferences do they make?

### Appropriate Use of Relevant Historical Evidence

Historians make arguments about the past based on primary-source evidence. As mentioned earlier, a primary source is something produced *in* the era under investigation. In contrast, a secondary source, also called a secondary interpretation or a secondary work, is something *about* the era under investigation made after the fact. It is usually the result of scholarly research of primary sources, or a distillation of such research. The narrative sections of this textbook, for example, are secondary sources, as are most published works of history, biographies, and encyclopedias. Sometimes a source can be both primary and secondary. Former British prime minister Winston Churchill's history of World War II is a primary source, because he was directly involved in some of the events he describes, and also a secondary source, because he uses a variety of historical sources to tell the story of events during the war in which he was not directly involved.

Traditionally, primary sources have consisted overwhelmingly of written sources. In fact, some historians referred to any time before writing as "pre-historic." In the last few decades, however, historians have increasingly moved beyond relying exclusively on written primary sources by turning to visual sources — paintings, photographs, architecture, artifacts, etc. — and evidence from other fields of knowledge. They even use evidence contained within the human body, such as DNA. For example, using scientific and medical information, historians have come to see the role that disease has played in history, such as the Black Death, which killed about one-third of the European population over just a few years in the middle of the fourteenth century. Since no historian can be an expert in every field, historians increasingly make use of the secondary sources produced by scholars in other fields, including archaeology, art history, biology, and chemistry.

In assessing primary sources, you need to begin with a careful examination of the source itself. But understanding evidence requires more. Primary sources are creations from a particular time and place, so you also have to consider the information that you know or can find out about the broader conditions in which the source was created — that is, the *context* of the source. Primary sources are created by a specific individual or group, called the *maker*, or in the case of written sources, the *author*. Even if they are eyewitnesses, people construct different accounts of the same event, which are shaped by their ideas, attitudes, and beliefs — what is often termed their *perspective* or *point of view*. Primary sources are also often created for someone else, so determining the purpose and intended audience of a source is essential to your understanding of it.

> **EXERCISE:** Take a look at the American Voices feature in Chapter 12, "The Debate over Free and Slave Labor," on page 384. Then review the headnotes and the chapter narrative to determine the context for these documents.

## Historical Interpretation and Synthesis

You first learned about how historians make arguments; now you'll practice evaluating those arguments and making your own. Since history requires making inferences about the past, it's inevitable that scholars will come to different conclusions. It can be very helpful, then, to study different historical interpretations about a particular event or movement over time, as interpretations often change. The final skill component, synthesis, is also related to argumentation. It is the culminating skill because it requires you to integrate all the other skills in creating your own argument.

**Interpretation** Historians interpret both primary and secondary sources, evaluating points of view and considering context to create their own interpretations. Through analyzing different historical interpretations, you will see how historical interpretations change over time. We have already established that formulating a historical argument requires making inferences from evidence. The background of a particular historian (age, gender, nationality, political philosophy, time of writing, etc.) often shapes the way he or she understands or interprets the past. In many cases, knowing something about the context of a historian can help you understand his or her argument better — in the same way that understanding the context of the author of a primary source helps you understand the primary source. Sometimes this information can help you identify the prejudices or limitations of a particular interpretation.

For example, in the early 1960s the British historian Hugh Trevor-Roper claimed that Africa had no history until Europeans took over the continent, an argument that built on the ideas of many earlier European thinkers, especially those of the nineteenth-century German philosopher Georg Hegel. Subsequent scholarship has shown this conclusion to be faulty, and we can assume that several aspects of Trevor-Roper's situation influenced his point of view. For one, he was a historian of early modern and modern Europe who thought, as did many historians of his generation, that history could only be based on written documents. Because there were fewer of these for Africa before colonization than for Europe at the same time, he jumped to the conclusion that Africa had no history. Historians since Trevor-Roper have broadened the source base that they use in their research to incorporate many other types of sources, and they have also demonstrated that there are, in fact, many written documents relating to Africa that Trevor-Roper did not know about or chose to ignore with his comment. His choice to ignore these may have been influenced by the fact that he was a citizen of an imperial nation writing during decolonization.

Be careful when analyzing historical interpretations. You can't simply assume that because a scholar has *x* background he or she will make *y* argument. There are far too many exceptions for such a rule. Instead, begin by finding out what you can about a scholar's background and then make a hunch about how his or her background might shape his or her views. Then, as you read the arguments carefully, look for evidence that the author actually makes the kinds of arguments you anticipated. If you don't find such evidence, discard your hunch.

**Synthesis** Synthesis is a culminating skill that reflects your ability to make persuasive arguments of your own from evidence. It draws on all of the other Historical Thinking Skills — historical argumentation, appropriate use of relevant historical evidence, causation, continuity and change, periodization, comparison, contextualization, and interpretation — along with two other elements. First, you may need to draw on evidence outside the field of history. This might come from the social sciences, such as archaeology, anthropology, economics, or sociology; it might come from the humanities, such as art history or literary studies; or it might even come from the natural sciences, such as biology or chemistry. The other element is the ability to apply insights from historical evidence to a new setting. This is a creative form of comparison. You might link some moment in the past to a more recent issue, for example, the African civil rights movement of the 1960s and 1970s to Reconstruction, or compare how the United States has tended to underestimate the strength of nationalism in other people, as evidenced by the Iraq and Vietnam wars. In so doing, you will be using the past to shed light on the present. You will have taken a major step in historical thinking, as making connections is a key part of what historians do.

# Getting the Most Out of Reading History

Active reading means reading for meaning. The big challenges of reading are length and detail. If you understand the "big picture," you can read much more quickly and effectively, because you can "see the forest for the trees." That is, you can see the main ideas and recognize how specific information is provided to illustrate those big ideas. The three stages of reading described below will help you understand the "big picture" when reading this text and others.

## Before Reading (Prereading)

When approaching a text such as this one, it is helpful to spend a few minutes prereading the material of a chapter. During this stage, you are simply getting prepared for what you will be reading. This involves several steps. First, determine the chronology and major theme(s) by looking at the chapter title and dates. The title often gives you a clue as to what the authors see as the main point, theme, or development of that chapter. Second, read the chapter headings and any focus questions, such as the Identify the Big Idea questions in this book, at the beginning of the chapter. The headings and questions provide a sense of the major topics addressed in the chapter, and the questions may also point toward the Historical Thinking Skills that are especially emphasized in the chapter. Third, page through the chapter, scanning the titles of the subsections and looking at the maps, timelines, illustrations, and primary sources. This will provide you with information about the major events, individuals, comparisons, and connections discussed in the chapter.

> **EXERCISE:** Let's practice by prereading Chapter 1, "Colliding Worlds, 1450–1600." Scan the chapter and answer the following questions without writing anything down.
>
> **Step One:** Look at the chapter title. What is the chronology of this chapter? What is the central theme?
>
> **Step Two:** Look at the headings and Big Idea question in the chapter introduction on page 6. What are the four major topics in this chapter? What Historical Thinking Skills does the Big Idea question focus on?
>
> **Step Three:** Page through each section, looking at the subheadings, maps, and illustrations and keeping the following questions in mind:
>
> In the first section, "The Native American Experience," what were the important empires, chiefdoms, and confederacies prior to 1492? What connections existed between these diverse groups? In the second section, "Western Europe: The Edge of the Old World," what characterized European society? How did the growth of the Christian Church affect events in Europe? In the third section, "West and Central Africa: Origins of the Atlantic Slave Trade," how did trade connect Africa to the wider world? What does Map 1.4 tell you about the types of goods that were exchanged? In the fourth section, "Exploration and Conquest," what countries were especially important in exploration? From the order in which these countries appear in the subheadings, can you get clues about the chronology of the voyages? Which individuals are mentioned in

> subheadings? (You might not always recognize an individual named in a subheading, but you can always count on his or her historical importance.) What commodities are mentioned in subheadings or shown in illustrations?

Remember, there's no need to write this down. The point right now is just to get a clear idea of the "big picture" developments covered in the chapter. You haven't read the chapter yet — and you haven't taken a single note. But by spending 5 to 10 minutes prereading the chapter, you already have a good idea of what the chapter's all about. You have recognized what parts of the story you may have heard about before, and what parts are completely new. By taking this time, you'll be able to read with a clear focus, saving yourself a lot of time later on. Now that you have a good idea of the "big picture," you're ready to begin actually reading the text.

## During Reading

As you read chapters of this text, remember that reading is an active process — so stay focused. The meaning will only become clear as you work at it. The authors have intentionally written an organized textbook and want you to be able to follow along, so take advantage of the clues they have provided, especially the main questions, section titles, and subheadings.

Active readers use four skills to understand texts: *questioning, clarifying, summarizing,* and *predicting.* These steps don't have to happen in a particular order. In fact, once you become comfortable with them, they'll pop up on their own without you trying in whatever order they choose, perhaps several at the same time — that's when you know that they've truly become habits of mind. Use these skills along with note-taking to get the most out of your reading.

**Questioning**   Historians look at the world in a particular way, and they usually organize their writing around the Historical Thinking Skills discussed above: cause and effect, comparison, interpretation, and so on. Many of the questions in each chapter involve one or more of these thinking skills. For example, the marginal question on page 15 of Chapter 1, "How did landscape, climate, and resources influence the development of Native American societies?" is a question about change over time and about causation. As the authors answer that question in the chapter section on pages 8–18, they utilize every other Historical Thinking Skill as well. They *craft a historical argument* using many types of *relevant historical evidence*, including evidence gathered by scholars in other fields, such as archaeologists and anthropologists who study the remains of early native peoples; present a *periodization* of the thousands of years before European contact, when the peoples of the Western Hemisphere were largely isolated from the rest of the world; *compare* the trade networks and religious practices of Native American groups; *contextualize* the different ways that societies developed within the processes of climate and geography; and develop an *interpretation* about the development of diverse groups across the Americas that *synthesizes* information from different sources and fields of inquiry.

Asking questions is thus an essential way to develop Historical Thinking Skills. For every section you read, you might begin with the very basic "reporter questions": Who? What? Where? When? Why?

1. *Who* is the section about? History texts are almost always about people. Is the focus an individual? A social group? A political entity?
2. *What* does the section say about this person or group? Texts usually describe some major event or pattern. Did they do something important? Did something happen to them?
3. *Where* did the subject being described take place? Physical location is often crucial in history. Does this location help make sense of the subject in some way?
4. *When* did the events take place? Like physical location, chronology forms part of the historical context that makes events understandable. Does the text describe something unfolding over a very short period — or a longer one? Are there crucial events that came before that make the description understandable?
5. *Why* did the event or pattern being described take place — and why does it matter? Whether talking about a dramatic development or a continuity that endured for a long period of time, historians always attempt to understand what led to it. What reasons does the text provide for the event or pattern? How is the significance of the development explained?

**Clarifying**   As you read, ask yourself if there are any words you don't understand. Some of these will be included as key terms defined in the margins, but not all will. When it comes to vocabulary, use good judgment. Is the word crucial for understanding the passage? If not, read right past it, as the meaning may become clearer as you read further in the text. If it is a crucial word, you may need to look it up in a dictionary.

When a longer passage throws you off, usually clearing up difficult vocabulary will help make the passage clearer. If it doesn't, simply reread the sentence a few times (slowly!). If you're still unclear, back up — usually to the beginning of the paragraph — and try again. The most common way skilled readers get clarification is simply by rereading.

**Summarizing**   A summary is a brief review of the "big picture" of a particular section or chapter. After reading, briefly explain what each section is about in one sentence — being sure your summary considers all five of the "reporter questions" from the *Questioning* section above. If you are summarizing a section, you might think of this as answering the main question posed in the section. For example, a summary of the first section in Chapter 1, "How did landscape, climate, and resources influence the development of Native American societies?" might be: Native Americans (*who*) in present-day Mexico and Peru (*where*) began raising domesticated crops (*what*) around 6000 B.C. (*when*), and as agriculture spread northward across much of North America, agricultural surpluses led to population growth and facilitated the growth of diverse urban societies (*why*).

**Predicting**   Based on your reading of an entire section or chapter, what do you think will come next in the text? How do you know? You may think predicting what's coming next is a waste of time, but it's a really good test of how well you understand the flow of the text. If you're in a car with your family going to visit your grandmother, you probably know the route to get there. If your mother takes an unanticipated turn, it alerts you that something is different from what you were expecting — and prompts you to ask why. So if your prediction based on reading is wildly off, it may alert you to the fact that your previous idea of the "big picture" of the section was off for some reason. You may need to back up and reread a section, or at least move forward more alert to where the author is going. Again using the first section of Chapter 1 as an example, what do you imagine will happen to native peoples after European contact?

**Note-Taking**   Of course, simply reading the text is not sufficient. You'll never remember everything that's important unless you take notes. Students experience many pitfalls when taking notes. You should only write notes *after* you understand what you have read. Actively *question, clarify, summarize,* and *predict* in your head (or out loud) as you read each chapter, and then go back through the subsections and take brief notes representing the key ideas of that section.

Brief is generally better — don't wear yourself out in the notes themselves. Find some consistent abbreviations for frequent words, and use symbols: an up arrow to indicate growth, a flat arrow to indicate cause/effect, an "=" to indicate a definition, and so on. Don't write everything; ask yourself if a particular point is a main idea or just an example. If you own your textbook, make annotations in the margins. If not, get a stack of sticky notes and place them in the margins for your comments.

> **EXERCISE:** Let's practice these four skills with the section called "Sixteenth-Century Incursions" on pages 30–35 in Chapter 1, "Colliding Worlds, 1450–1600."
>
> - **Questioning:** What were the sixteenth-century incursions? Whom did they affect? Where did they happen? When did they happen? Why and how did they happen? How did people respond? What were their effects and consequences?
>
> - **Clarifying:** Important words like *reconquista* are defined in the text itself, but are there any words that you do not understand? If there were any sentences you didn't understand, did they become clearer as you reread them or as you read on in the text?
>
> - **Summarizing:** Briefly explain what this section is about in one sentence.
>
> - **Predicting:** Based on the section you've just read, what do you think will come next in the text? How do you know?

Now that you know what this section is about, what brief comments are worth writing down in your notes?

## After Reading

Reflecting on what you've read places information you've just learned into long-term memory. This involves doing the same kind of summarizing you've done section by section, but now for the entire chapter. In essence, it is a summary of your summaries. While it might seem enough to summarize the chapter verbally, writing down key ideas helps place them into long-term memory. Read through the notes that you've taken for the chapter, particularly the summary of each section. Then try to write a master summary of the entire chapter using no more than fifty words that captures the key point of each section of the chapter as well as the chapter as a whole.

> **EXERCISE:** Write a master summary of Chapter 1 now.

## Writing About History

This skills primer began by introducing you to the patterns of thinking you need to really understand history. The next section pointed out ways to be smart about reading your textbook. This third and final section turns to the writing skills you need to develop for AP history courses and exams. Our focus shifts away from you *receiving* input toward you *providing* output: sharing your understanding of Historical Thinking Skills through writing.

There are different types of essays on AP history exams, but two essential skills apply to all of the essays you'll encounter. First, to successfully demonstrate what you know, you have to answer the question that has been asked. Sounds simple, but many students get in trouble on the exam by failing to address the question in front of them, which is called the "prompt."

Every prompt contains three elements, and you need to pay attention to all of them as you plan your response. First, each prompt deals with a subject, expressed in two important types of nouns. A *proper noun* refers to a specific historical entity — Puritanism, the Confederacy, the New Deal. A *common noun* typically refers to a historical concept: a key historical idea (republicanism, liberalism) or process (industrialization, western expansion). Sometimes this process is limited in time, but often it is a pattern that occurs over a relatively long period. Your answer must deal with all of the subjects of the prompt, not just some of them. Second, the prompt specifies a periodization or date range expressed in years. Obviously, you need to be sure your response addresses this era. One of the most common problems in student essays is providing historical information from the wrong era. Third, and most importantly, the prompt contains a task expressed as its main verb: *compare, describe, explain, analyze,* and so forth. Pay attention to this task verb, as these tasks are not the same, and your answer must do what the prompt asks you to do.

It doesn't matter how strong your content knowledge and historical skills are if you can't communicate clearly what you know. Every essay needs to have a specific, focused *thesis* in the introductory paragraph that makes an argument addressing the prompt. Your thesis should be as brief as possible while still addressing the complexity of the topic. If your thesis explicitly responds to each of the three prompt elements clearly and accurately—if it includes the subjects, the time period, and the task—you will have a strong thesis. And you'll be on your way to a persuasive essay.

Every essay needs to be organized into distinct *paragraphs*. The number of paragraphs depends on the complexity of the prompt. Typically, however, two body paragraphs won't be sufficient to address the topic thoroughly. What's most important is that you clearly announce the point you're going to make in each paragraph through a *topic sentence* that effectively covers the subject of the paragraph. Any content in the paragraph that doesn't support the topic sentence doesn't belong there.

Finally, every essay requires you to make use of *evidence* to support your claims. The type of evidence also differs depending on the type of essay. The document-based question (DBQ) requires you to reference the documents included with the question, while the other essays require you to draw on information that you know. In every case, however, you need to both discuss relevant historical information you've learned during the course and then *explain how that information supports your claim.*

While many of these writing suggestions would apply equally to essays in other academic subjects, the essay types on AP history exams are all geared to the concerns of historians. Each type of essay requires the use of the Historical Thinking Skills discussed earlier, often in combination with one another. For example, every essay type requires you to discuss the *historical context* of the subject you're writing about and to *appropriately use relevant evidence* to develop an *interpretation* and *argument* about the past. Every essay requires you to go beyond simply listing factual information to *analyze* that information. In fact, "analyze" is commonly used as a question prompt in all types of essays.

## Document-Based Questions

The document-based question, or DBQ, is a defining feature of all AP history exams. Of all the essays, this one tends to make students the most anxious. But much of this anxiety is misplaced. Once you understand the DBQ, you will feel less worried about it—and may even come to find it your favorite essay type. Unlike the other essays, for which you have to call on your memory to provide all the evidence, the documents in the DBQ form the basic evidence you need to use.

To do well on a DBQ, you need to go beyond the content of the documents in order to set the context, make a clear argument, and analyze the documents properly. Using documents as evidence requires the sophisticated analysis skills we discussed in the section "Appropriate Use of Relevant Historical Evidence." That means that you have to consider the perspective or point of view of the documents. Every primary source—textual, visual, or statistical—was created for a specific purpose. Even if the author is an eyewitness or participant, people construct different accounts of the same event, which are shaped by their perspective. That doesn't necessarily mean the author intentionally wrote it to mislead or provide only part of the story, but every document is limited and imperfect in the information it provides.

As with all essay questions, be sure your introductory paragraph includes a clear and focused thesis statement that encapsulates your argument. Use the "reporter questions"—Who? What? When? Where? Why?—to interrogate each document, and then consider the limitations of each document before writing your DBQ. Then be sure to incorporate these insights about document limitations into the essay itself to make your essay more analytical—and therefore stronger.

Consider the photo of men from the Kansas Volunteer Infantry during the Civil War on page 454 in Chapter 14. Students tend to view a document like that as a straightforward factual record. After all, we often hear that "pictures don't lie." But the picture was taken for a particular purpose by someone who decided to arrange the shot so that the soldiers would appear in uniform posed with their rifles. So it's worth asking *why* the photographer took the picture in this way. What purpose might this picture serve? What message might it convey to someone who saw it at the time it was taken? How might it misrepresent—or represent in a limited way—the realities of the soldier experience?

Purposes can be stated explicitly by the maker of a source, or they can be determined later by those analyzing the source, including you as you write your answer to a DBQ. Sometimes the purposes given by the maker and by later historians are different from one another. For example, during the Renaissance, European city governments issued laws limiting what people could spend on clothing or family celebrations such as weddings. The governments stated that the purpose of these laws was to restrict wasteful spending, but later historians studying these laws have determined that their purpose was also to sharpen distinctions between social classes. For many of the documents you will be using to answer a DBQ, you will need to make your best judgment about the purpose, just as historians do.

You also need to corroborate your documents. That means bringing the documents into "conversation" with each other. Since the documents in a DBQ don't directly refer to each other, you have to use your intuition to see connections. This relates to a distinctive task about the DBQ: you need to organize the evidence from the documents into several categories or groups — usually at least three. The categories are sometimes stated or implied in the prompt, but you'll often have to call on your knowledge of history and the content of the documents themselves to determine what categories (and how many) make sense. Please note that because you can use the same document multiple times, you often have flexibility in coming up with categories. You might choose to group the documents according to geography, or the social status of their authors, or the type of document, or what they say about the issue discussed in the question, or according to any number of other lines of connection.

In all of the American Voices and Thinking Like a Historian features in this book, the authors have included multiple primary sources that address the same or related topics, along with questions that allow you to bring the documents in conversation with each other just as you will for a DBQ. For example, in Chapter 5, the feature Thinking Like a Historian, "Beyond the Proclamation Line" includes six brief primary sources of the types that you might encounter on a DBQ that speak to life in "Indian country" between 1763 and 1776. Voices range from the crown's superintendent for Indian affairs in the northern colonies, to a Baptist minister's description of the trading communities of the Ohio Valley, to a list of grievances by a Delaware headman. Comparison is one of the Historical Thinking Skills identified for AP history exams, and it is often a task word in essay questions, so use the document features and questions in this book to practice the skills needed for the DBQ.

Finally, you have to draw on your outside knowledge. To do well, you need to position the DBQ documents within the broader context of the period, drawing on what you've learned from your textbook, from your teacher, and from any outside reading or research that you've done. Feel free to mention other sources that you may have encountered previously, especially if they offer a perspective that is missing or if the addition of outside sources helps to support your argument. In the "Beyond the Proclamation Line" feature, for example, if these were the sources provided for a DBQ, you would use the information in the textbook, especially that in the section "The Problem of the West" on pages 163–166, to provide broader context for your answer.

## Long-Essay Questions

Along with the DBQ, AP history exams contain other essay questions, called "thematic essays," "free response questions," or simply "long essays." This type of essay question tests your ability to use information that you already know to answer a specific question that draws on one or more Historical Thinking Skills. Like the DBQ, essay questions have different task verbs that correspond to different Historical Thinking Skills. Three of the most common of these involve change and continuity, causation, and comparison.

**Change and Continuity Questions**  For questions that focus on change over time, you will have to identify major changes and explain the significance of those changes — that is, why the changes matter — for the topic described in the prompt. You will also have to analyze *why* something changed. If the question prompt asks about both change and continuity, your thesis statement and the essay itself must clearly address both elements. A strong argument must do more than simply *identify* some continuities and changes. It has to *analyze* why both the continuities and changes existed and why they mattered. (The Making Connections questions that appear at the end of each chapter often ask you to analyze continuity and change over time, so they are good practice for this type of essay.) It's a good idea to weigh the relative value of continuities and changes. In other words, do you perceive continuities to have been more powerful than changes on the topic addressed in the prompt, or vice versa? Why do you think so?

In terms of structure, avoid the temptation to organize your essay into two large paragraphs, one for continuities and one for changes. Instead, identify important topics or categories of comparison — governmental structure, immigration patterns, or gender relations — and use those topics as the body paragraphs. Then, in each body paragraph, address *both* continuities *and* changes, being clear to signal your transition from one to the other.

In the same way that identifying change is an easier Historical Thinking Skill than identifying continuity, change is also easier to write about than continuity. U.S. history narratives devote a lot of time to, say, how American Christianity changed as a result of the Great Awakening. So if you're writing an essay about eighteenth-century religion, that information will come to mind more quickly. After brief reflection, however, you'll realize that certain aspects of American Christianity did *not* change with the Great Awakening. Therefore, along with changes, you will want to identify several major continuities, such as Martin Luther's belief in the priesthood of all Christians or the influence of clergy. Then you will need to discuss why these were significant and suggest some reasons why they did not change.

Question prompts about change and continuity may not always be phrased in exactly those words. Often they might ask you to assess the impact of something (or someone) on something else, analyze the influence of something on something else, or analyze the extent to which something shaped something else. Thinking a bit about such questions, you can recognize that they are actually about change and continuity. To assess the impact or influence of A on B, you will need to decide what changed in B as a result of A. To write a good essay about this, you will also need to discuss what did *not* change, and why — in other words, continuities. For example, a question might ask you to assess the impact of World War I on U.S. culture and society in the 1920s and 1930s. You can see that this question is about change and continuity: what changed as a result of the war, and what did not change. As in the example of the Great Awakening, it is often easier to remember what changed than to recall what stayed the same, but a strong essay will consider both. A strong essay might also go beyond the direct impact of World War I to include broader cultural changes that relate more indirectly to the war. If you do this, however, be sure to relate everything you include to the prompt, and do not use the question as an opportunity for a "data dump" of everything you can think of about the 1920s and 1930s. Throwing in a lot of extraneous information to pad your answer will not improve it.

**Causation Questions** Questions about change, or about impact or influence, are also about causation, for any good answer will go beyond *what* happened to *why*. Asking *why* is at the heart of what historians — including the AP history text makers — mean by *analysis*. A quick way to see whether you have provided analysis in your answer is to see whether it includes the word *because*. There are many other ways to analyze, but most sentences containing the word *because* at least attempt to analyze something.

Some question prompts might also address causation directly, asking you to explain the reasons for something or analyze the causes for something. The historical causation chart on page xxxix will provide

you with a good way to structure your answer. Take a question about the causes of Columbus's voyages of exploration, for example. After your thesis statement that directly addresses the prompt of the question, you could begin with *large-scale processes* that developed over centuries. These might include trading networks through which Europeans became familiar with the products of Asia and Africa, such as spices, silk, and ivory; conflicts between Christianity and Islam, which had especially shaped Spanish culture in the many centuries when Christians fought Muslims for control of the Iberian peninsula; and improvements in ship design and navigational instruments. Then you could move to complex causes that were more immediate: the expansion of the Ottoman Empire, which disrupted old trade routes and lessened the direct access of Western Europeans to exotic luxuries; the aims of the Spanish monarchs Ferdinand and Isabella to compete with Portugal in the race for direct access to spices and to continue the expansion of Christianity; the invention of the printing press, which allowed work by earlier geographers and travelers to be cheap and accessible to ship captains and merchants; and Columbus's personal ambition, desire for glory, and religious fervor.

If the question prompt is about consequences as well as causes, you can continue using the chart to discuss the many consequences of Columbus's voyages. Among these were *unintended consequences*, which begin with one that seems almost too obvious: Columbus's voyages made Europeans aware that there were large landmasses in the world other than the ones they already knew about. (This is what we mean by "discovering" — becoming aware of something that is already there.) As you probably know, at first Columbus did not recognize what he had discovered, and even after he did, he spent most of his efforts trying to get around these new lands to reach Asia, his intended destination. Although Columbus claimed the lands that he explored for Spain, he (and the Spanish monarchs who backed him) was primarily looking for trade connections, not lands to conquer. So you might even choose to argue that colonization was an unintended consequence. Beyond this are a range of changes that were truly unintended, such as the widespread exchange of animals, plants, human populations, and diseases across the Atlantic in both directions, later called the "Columbian Exchange."

Again depending on the exact question prompt, you might also want to discuss *contingency*, the fact that things might have turned out differently. One of the most common problems in analyzing cause and effect in the past is that we know the outcome, or at least the outcome up to now. It is thus very tempting to view developments *teleologically*, that is, as leading inevitably to the outcome that we know happened. Immediately after a game is over, for example, commentators often explain why the team that won was destined to win, although if the other team had won, they would have a ready explanation for that as well. Immediately after an election, the loser's strategy is analyzed as faulty and misguided, although if the results had been different, the same strategy would have been praised as brilliant. In this example, all large-scale processes and long- and short-term causes seem to lead to Columbus. It is easy to imagine the story turning out differently, however. An Aztec conquest of Europe would not have been a possibility, but Columbus's ships could have easily sunk on the first voyage. Or Ferdinand and Isabella could have said no. Or John Cabot — like Columbus, an Italian trying to get backing for voyages from a Western European monarch — could have moved to England slightly earlier than he did and convinced Henry VII of England to support him in 1490 instead of 1496. Not every question about causation will lend itself to thinking about possible alternate scenarios so easily, but in every one there are some lines of causation that are coincidental.

**Comparison Questions**   Another Historical Thinking Skill often involved in essay questions is comparison, with questions that might be phrased "compare and contrast . . ." or "analyze similarities and differences . . ." Your thesis statement should focus on major similarities and differences, but it cannot simply be "there were similarities and differences in A and B." Instead it must include some information about *how* A and B were similar or different. When you place two presidents, two ways of thinking, or two revolutions side by side, what do you notice? How are they similar? How are they different? One good way to structure the thesis for a comparative question is: Although A and B were different in C, they were similar in D.

Once you move beyond the most basic level of identifying broad similarities and differences, you need to be more precise. You should begin by teasing out both categories in more detail, providing specific evidence to support your broad generalizations. For example, in broad terms the American, French, and Haitian revolutions all included demands for liberty and equality, and all of them significantly expanded citizenship rights. In all three these rights were limited to men, another similarity among them. But only in the Haitian Revolution, when a massive revolt ended slavery and won Haiti's independence from France,

were those rights extended to men of African descent. Just as with change and continuity, it's often worthwhile to indicate whether you think similarities are more significant than differences, or vice versa, and why.

You need to be careful about the structure of this essay. Many students fall into the trap of simply describing topic 1 in a body paragraph and topic 2 in a separate body paragraph. They assume that readers will be able to recognize the similarities and differences between the two topics on their own. But you'll never earn a high score that way.

After your introductory paragraph and thesis statement, always begin each body paragraph with a topic sentence that introduces the category or topic you want to compare. Your comparisons need to be explicit and concrete. Be sure to use clear signal words that identify that you are shifting from similarity to difference ("Despite these similarities during times of financial crisis, the two presidents differed dramatically.") In the contrast portion of your essay, be clear about the particular difference, making use of contrast words such as *conversely, unlike,* and *however* to signal your point to the reader.

In brainstorming similarities, try to step back and think in more abstract conceptual terms so you don't miss deep similarities that seem different on the surface. For example, students sometimes say that a king is different from an emperor, because they focus on the different titles. But both are hereditary monarchs typically viewed as having divine authority to rule. That makes them very similar in deep ways, despite the different labels. They are much more similar to each other than they are to, say, a democracy or a communist regime.

Students sometimes wonder whether the first body paragraph should focus on similarities or differences. One approach is to deal with the less significant topic first, get it out of the way, and then move on to the more significant topic. But that is really a matter of taste. What *is* important is that you provide a clear transition when you move from the compare to the contrast portion of your essay (or vice versa): "These similarities [that you've just discussed], however, were much less crucial than differences in *x, y,* and *z*." If this sounds like a repeat of your thesis statement, that's because it is. In the body of your essay, you want to echo the road map, your thesis, to help your reader know that you are now making the transition that your introductory paragraph said you would be making.

You might be thinking that the suggestions here about answering comparative questions sound similar to those about answering change-over-time questions, and you would be absolutely right. Embedded (and not very deeply) in change-over-time questions are comparisons, for the only way that you can identify something as a change or continuity, or assess the impact of something on something else, is to compare them. To transform these comparisons into analysis, you will need to provide relevant historical evidence, contextualize the developments you are discussing, and evaluate causes and effects. As we have said all along, all of the Historical Thinking Skills are related, which is why the final thinking skill is synthesis: "the ability to arrive at meaningful and persuasive understandings of the past by applying all of the other Historical Thinking Skills."*

Many students feel anxious about having to write the AP history essays. But once you become familiar with the elements of each prompt and know how to address them effectively, you'll realize that there's no reason to be stressed. In fact, you should feel confident as you approach the writing portion of the test. Unlike the multiple-choice portion of the AP exam, the essay section gives you a lot of freedom to demonstrate what you know in an open-ended way. And if you've been thinking historically, reading the text with that lens, and sharing your ideas in class, you may begin to look forward to an opportunity to show just how developed your Historical Thinking Skills are.

---

*http://advancesinap.collegeboard.org/historical-thinking

# AMERICA'S
# HISTORY

# Transformations of North America
## 1450–1700

In 1450, North America, Europe, and Africa were each home to complex societies with their own distinctive cultures. But their histories were about to collide, bringing vast changes to all three continents. European voyagers sailing in the wake of Christopher Columbus set in motion one of the most momentous developments in world history: sustained contact among Native Americans, Europeans, and Africans in dozens of distinct colonial settings. Before the arrival of Europeans, a wide range of complex Native American societies claimed the continent as their own. Although colonization brought profound change, it did not erase what had come before because Native American societies interacted with colonizers from the beginning. They shaped colonial enterprise in important ways, enabling some forms of colonization while preventing others.

Native Americans, Europeans, and Africans were surprisingly similar in many ways, though the differences among them were important as well. Their distinctive ideas about gods and the spirit world informed their political systems and animated their approaches to trade and warfare. Whether they met in peace or war — or whether peaceful interactions quickly turned violent — Native Americans, Europeans, and Africans viewed one another through lenses that were shaped by these ideas.

In Part 1, we compare Native American, European, and African societies on the eve of colonization and then explore how Europeans experimented with various models of colonization in the first two centuries of sustained transatlantic contacts. The story in Chapters 1 and 2 addresses three main developments that are central to this period:

## Native American Diversity and Complexity

Popular culture can lead us to think of Native American societies as being substantially the same everywhere in North America: they were organized into tribes, with few material possessions and primitive beliefs and cultures, and reliant mostly on hunting for their subsistence. This impression distorts a much more complicated picture. Native American political organization ran the gamut from vast, complex imperial states to kin-based bands of hunters and gatherers. Patterns of political organization varied widely, and the familiar label of *tribe* does more to obscure than to clarify their workings. Native Americans' economic and social systems were adapted to the ecosystems they inhabited. Many were extremely productive farmers, some hunted bison and deer, while others were expert salmon fishermen who plied coastal waters in large oceangoing boats. Native American religions and cultures also varied widely, though they shared some broad characteristics.

These variations in Native American societies shaped colonial enterprise. Europeans conquered and coopted Native American empires with relative ease, but smaller and more decentralized polities were harder to exploit. Mobile hunter-gatherers appeared politically amorphous, but they became especially formidable opponents of colonial expansion.

## Colonial Settlement and the Columbian Exchange

European colonization triggered a series of sweeping changes that historians have labeled the "Columbian Exchange." At the same time that people crossed the Atlantic in large numbers, so too did plants, animals, and germs. Old World grains like wheat and barley were planted in the Americas for the first time, and weeds like dandelions were carried across the ocean as well. Potatoes, maize (corn), and tomatoes, among other foods, crossed the Atlantic in the other direction and transformed dietary practices in Asia as well as Europe. Native Americans domesticated very few animals; the Columbian Exchange introduced horses, pigs, cattle, and a variety of other creatures to the American landscape. Germs also made the voyage, especially the deadly pathogens that had so disordered life in Europe in the centuries prior to colonization. Smallpox, influenza, and bubonic plague, among others, took an enormous toll on Native American populations. Inanimate materials made the voyage as well: enough gold and silver traveled from the Americas to Europe and Asia to transform the world's economies, intensifying competition and empire building in Europe.

Old World diseases devastated Native American peoples. On average, they lost ninety percent of their numbers over the first century of contact, forcing them to cope with European and African newcomers in a weakened and vulnerable state.

## Experimentation and Transformation

The collisions of American, European, and African worlds challenged the beliefs and practices of all three groups. Colonization was, above all, a long and tortured process of experimentation. Over time, Europeans carved out three distinct types of colonies in the Americas, each shaped by the constraints and opportunities presented by American landscapes and peoples. Where Native American societies were organized into densely settled empires, Europeans conquered the ruling class and established tribute-based empires of their own. In tropical and subtropical settings, colonizers created plantation societies that demanded large, imported labor forces—a need that was met through the African slave trade. And in the temperate regions of the mainland North America, where neither the landscape nor the native population yielded easy wealth, European colonists came in large numbers hoping to create familiar societies in unfamiliar settings.

Everywhere in the Americas, core beliefs and worldviews were shaken by contact with radically unfamiliar peoples. Native Americans and Africans struggled to maintain autonomy in their relations with colonizers, while Europeans labored to understand—and profit from—their relations with nonwhite peoples. These transformations are the subject of Part 1.

# Transformations of North America 1450–1700

## Thematic Understanding

This timeline arranges some of the important events of this period into themes. Look at the entries for "Ideas, Beliefs, and Culture" from 1450 to 1700. How did the Protestant Reformation and the response of the Catholic Church influence the colonization of the Americas in these years? In the realm of "Work, Exchange, and Technology," how did colonial economies evolve, and what roles did Native American and African labor play in them?  >

| | WORK, EXCHANGE, & TECHNOLOGY | PEOPLING | POLITICS & POWER | IDEAS, BELIEFS, & CULTURE | IDENTITY |
|---|---|---|---|---|---|
| **1450** | • Diversified economies of Native America<br><br>• Rise of the Ottoman Empire blocks Asian trading routes of the Italian city-states<br><br>• Europeans fish off North American coast<br><br>• Portuguese traders explore African coast | • Christopher Columbus explores the Bahamas and West Indies (1492–1504)<br><br>• Pedro Alvares Cabral makes landfall in Brazil (1500)<br><br>• Spanish conquest of Mexico and Peru (1519–1535) | • Rise of monarchical nation-states in Europe<br><br>• Aztecs and Incas consolidate their empires<br><br>• Probable founding of the Iroquois Confederacy<br><br>• Rise of the Songhai Empire in Africa | • Protestant Reformation (1517) sparks century of religious warfare<br><br>• Henry VIII creates Church of England (1534)<br><br>• Founding of Jesuit order (1540) | • Castile and Aragon joined to create Spain; the Inquisition helps create a sense of Spanishness<br><br>• John Calvin establishes a Protestant commonwealth in Geneva, Switzerland |
| **1550** | • Growth of the outwork system in English textile industry<br><br>• Spanish *encomienda* system organizes native labor in Mexico<br><br>• Inca *mita* system is co-opted by the Spanish in the Andes | • Castilians and Africans arrive in Spanish America in large numbers<br><br>• English colonies in Newfoundland, Maine, and Roanoke fail | • Elizabeth's "sea dogs" plague Spanish shipping<br><br>• English monarchs adopt mercantilist policies<br><br>• Defeat of the Spanish Armada (1588) | • Philip II defends the Roman Catholic Church against Protestantism<br><br>• Elizabeth I adopts Protestant Book of Common Prayer (1559) | • English conquest and persecution of native Irish<br><br>• Growing Protestant movement in England |
| **1600** | • First staple exports from the English mainland colonies: furs and tobacco<br><br>• Subsistence farms in New England<br><br>• Transition to sugar plantation system in the Caribbean islands | • First set of Anglo-Indian wars<br><br>• African servitude begins in Virginia (1619)<br><br>• Caribbean islands move from servitude to slavery | • James I claims divine right to rule England<br><br>• Virginia's House of Burgesses (1619)<br><br>• English Puritan Revolution<br><br>• Native Americans rise up against English invaders (1622, 1640s) | • Persecuted English Puritans and Catholics migrate to America<br><br>• Established churches set up in Puritan New England and Anglican Virginia<br><br>• Dissenters settle in Rhode Island | • Pilgrims and Puritans seek to create godly commonwealths<br><br>• Powhatan and Virginia Company representatives attempt to extract tribute from each other |
| **1700** | • Tobacco trade stagnates<br><br>• Maturing yeoman economy and emerging Atlantic trade in New England | • Growing gentry immigration to Virginia<br><br>• White indentured servitude shapes Chesapeake society<br><br>• Africans defined as property rather than people in the Chesapeake | • Restoration of the English crown (1660)<br><br>• English conquer New Netherland (1664) | • Metacom's War in New England (1675–1676)<br><br>• Bacon's Rebellion calls for removal of Indians and end of elite rule<br><br>• Salem witchcraft crisis (1692) | • Social mobility for Africans ends with collapse of tobacco trade and increased power of gentry |

# Colliding Worlds
## 1450–1600

In April 1493, a Genoese sailor of humble origins appeared at the court of Queen Isabella of Castile and King Ferdinand of Aragon along with six Caribbean natives, numerous colorful parrots, and "samples of finest gold, and many other things never before seen or heard tell of in Spain." The sailor was Christopher Columbus, just returned from his first voyage into the Atlantic. He and his party entered Barcelona's fortress in a solemn procession. The monarchs stood to greet Columbus; he knelt to kiss their hands. They talked for an hour and then adjourned to the royal chapel for a ceremony of thanksgiving. Columbus, now bearing the official title *Admiral of the Ocean Sea*, remained at court for more than a month. The highlight of his stay was the baptism of the six natives, whom Columbus called Indians because he mistakenly believed he had sailed westward all the way to Asia.

•

In the spring of 1540, the Spanish explorer Hernando de Soto met the Lady of Cofachiqui, ruler of a large Native American province in present-day South Carolina. Though an epidemic had carried away many of her people, the lady of the province offered the Spanish expedition as much corn, and as many pearls, as it could carry. As she spoke to de Soto, she unwound "a great rope of pearls as large as hazelnuts" and handed them to the Spaniard; in return he gave her a gold ring set with a ruby. De Soto and his men then visited the temples of Cofachiqui, which were guarded by carved statues and held storehouses of weapons and chest upon chest of pearls. After loading their horses with corn and pearls, they continued on their way.

•

A Portuguese traveler named Duarte Lopez visited the African kingdom of Kongo in 1578. "The men and women are black," he reported, "some approaching olive colour, with black curly hair, and others with red. The men are of middle height, and, excepting the black skin, are like the Portuguese." The royal city of Kongo sat on a high plain that was "entirely cultivated," with a population of more than 100,000. The city included a separate commercial district, a mile around, where Portuguese traders acquired ivory, wax, honey, palm oil, and slaves from the Kongolese.

•

Three glimpses of three lost worlds. Soon these peoples would be transforming one another's societies, often through conflict and exploitation. But at the moment they first met, Europeans, Native Americans, and Africans stood on roughly equal terms. Even a hundred years after Columbus's discovery of the Americas, no one could have foreseen the shape that their interactions would take in the generations to come. To begin, we need to understand the three worlds as distinct places, each home to unique societies and cultures.

**IDENTIFY THE BIG IDEA**

How did the political, economic, and religious systems of Native Americans, Europeans, and Africans compare, and how did things change as a result of contacts among them?

Their greene corne.

Corne newly sprong.

Their sitting at meate.

The place of Solemne prayer.

e house wherin the Tombe of their Herounds standeth.

SECOTON.

A Ceremony in their prayers w
strange iestures and songs dansing
abowt posts carued on the topp's
lyke mens faces.

**Village of Secoton, 1585**   English colonist John White painted this view of an Algonquian village on the outer banks of present-day North Carolina. Its cluster of houses surrounded by fields of crops closely resembled European farming communities of the same era. White captured everyday details of the town's social life, including food preparation and a ceremony or celebration in progress (lower right). Service Historique de la Marine Vincennes, France/Giraudon/The Bridgeman Art Library.

# The Native American Experience

When Europeans arrived, perhaps 60 million people occupied the Americas, 7 million of whom lived north of Mexico. In Mesoamerica (present-day Mexico and Guatemala) and the Andes, empires that rivaled the greatest civilizations in world history ruled over millions of people. At the other end of the political spectrum, hunters and gatherers were organized into kin-based bands. Between these extremes, semisedentary societies planted and tended crops in the spring and summer, fished and hunted, made war, and conducted trade. Though we often see this spectrum as a hierarchy in which the empires are most impressive and important while hunter-gatherers deserve scarcely a mention, this bias toward civilizations that left behind monumental architecture and spawned powerful ruling classes is misplaced. Regardless of size or political complexity, the energies and innovations of Native American societies everywhere profoundly transformed American landscapes. To be fully understood, the Americas must be treated in all their complexity, with an appreciation for their diverse societies and cultures.

## The First Americans

Archaeologists believe that migrants from Asia crossed a 100-mile-wide land bridge connecting Siberia and Alaska during the last Ice Age sometime between 13,000 and 3000 B.C. and thus became the first Americans. The first wave of this migratory stream from Asia lasted from about fifteen thousand to nine thousand years ago. Then the glaciers melted, and the rising ocean submerged the land bridge beneath the Bering Strait (Map 1.1). Around eight thousand years ago, a second movement of peoples, traveling by water across the same narrow strait, brought the ancestors of the Navajos and the Apaches to North America. The forebears of the Aleut and Inuit peoples, the "Eskimos," came in a third wave around five thousand years ago. Then, for three hundred generations, the peoples of the Western Hemisphere were largely cut off from the rest of the world.

During this long era, migrants dispersed through the continents as they hunted and gathered available resources. The predominant flow was southward, and the densest populations developed in central Mexico—home to some 20 million people at the time of first contact with Europeans—and the Andes Mountains, with a population of perhaps 12 million. In North America, a secondary trickle of migration pushed eastward, across the Rockies and into the Mississippi Valley and the eastern woodlands.

Around 6000 B.C., some Native American peoples in present-day Mexico and Peru began raising domesticated crops. Mesoamericans cultivated maize into a nutritious plant with a higher yield per acre than wheat, barley, or rye, the staple cereals of Europe. In Peru they also bred the potato, a root crop of unsurpassed nutritional value. The resulting agricultural surpluses encouraged population growth and laid the foundation for wealthy, urban societies in Mexico and Peru, and later in the Mississippi Valley and the southeastern woodlands of North America (Map 1.2).

## American Empires

In Mesoamerica and the Andes, the two great empires of the Americas—the Aztecs and Incas—dominated the landscape. Dense populations, productive agriculture, and an aggressive bureaucratic state were the keys to their power. Each had an impressive capital city. Tenochtitlán, established in 1325 at the center of the Aztec Empire, had at its height around 1500 a population of about 250,000, at a time when the European cities of London and Seville each had perhaps 50,000. The Aztec state controlled the fertile valleys in the highlands of Mexico, and Aztec merchants forged trading routes that crisscrossed the empire. Trade, along with **tribute** demanded from subject peoples (comparable to taxes in Europe), brought gold, textiles, turquoise, obsidian, tropical bird feathers, and cacao to Tenochtitlán. The Europeans who first encountered this city in 1519 marveled at the city's wealth and beauty. "Some of the soldiers among us who had been in many parts of the world," wrote Spanish conquistador Bernal Díaz del Castillo, "in Constantinople, and all over Italy, and in Rome, said that [they had never seen] so large a market place and so full of people, and so well regulated and arranged" (see American Voices, p. 32).

Ruled by priests and warrior-nobles, the Aztecs subjugated most of central Mexico. Captured enemies were brought to the capital, where Aztec priests brutally sacrificed thousands of them. The Aztecs believed that these ritual murders sustained the cosmos, ensuring fertile fields and the daily return of the sun.

Cuzco, the Inca capital located more than 11,000 feet above sea level, had perhaps 60,000 residents. A dense network of roads, storehouses, and administrative

**IDENTIFY CAUSES**
What factors allowed for the development of empires in central Mexico and the Andes?

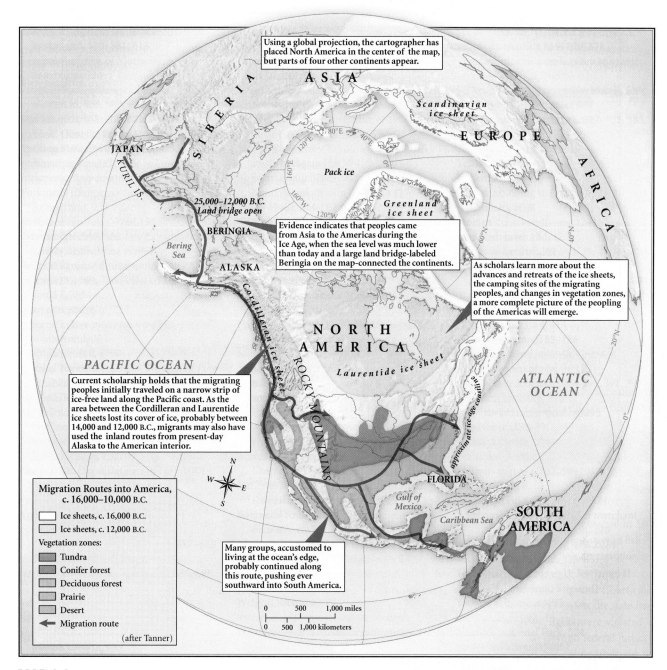

Using a global projection, the cartographer has placed North America in the center of the map, but parts of four other continents appear.

ASIA

SIBERIA

*Scandinavian ice sheet*

EUROPE

AFRICA

JAPAN

KURIL IS.

*Pack ice*

80°E  40°E

120°E

160°E

160°W

120°W

*Greenland ice sheet*

25,000–12,000 B.C.
Land bridge open

BERINGIA

Evidence indicates that peoples came from Asia to the Americas during the Ice Age, when the sea level was much lower than today and a large land bridge-labeled Beringia on the map-connected the continents.

*Bering Sea*

ALASKA

As scholars learn more about the advances and retreats of the ice sheets, the camping sites of the migrating peoples, and changes in vegetation zones, a more complete picture of the peopling of the Americas will emerge.

*Cordilleran ice sheet*

NORTH AMERICA

*Laurentide ice sheet*

60°N

40°N

20°N

*PACIFIC OCEAN*

ROCKY MOUNTAINS

*approximate ice-age coastline*

*ATLANTIC OCEAN*

Current scholarship holds that the migrating peoples initially traveled on a narrow strip of ice-free land along the Pacific coast. As the area between the Cordilleran and Laurentide ice sheets lost its cover of ice, probably between 14,000 and 12,000 B.C., migrants may also have used the inland routes from present-day Alaska to the American interior.

N
W  E
S

FLORIDA

*Gulf of Mexico*

SOUTH AMERICA

*Caribbean Sea*

**Migration Routes into America,
c. 16,000–10,000 B.C.**

☐ Ice sheets, c. 16,000 B.C.
☐ Ice sheets, c. 12,000 B.C.

Vegetation zones:
■ Tundra
■ Conifer forest
■ Deciduous forest
■ Prairie
■ Desert
← Migration route

(after Tanner)

Many groups, accustomed to living at the ocean's edge, probably continued along this route, pushing ever southward into South America.

0    500    1,000 miles
0   500  1,000 kilometers

**MAP 1.1**
**The Ice Age and the Settling of the Americas**

Some sixteen thousand years ago, a sheet of ice covered much of Europe and North America. The ice lowered the level of the world's oceans, which created a broad bridge of land between Siberia and Alaska. Using that land bridge, hunting peoples from Asia migrated to North America as they pursued woolly mammoths and other large game animals and sought ice-free habitats. By 10,000 B.C., the descendants of these migrant peoples had moved south to present-day Florida and central Mexico. In time, they would settle as far south as the tip of South America and as far east as the Atlantic coast of North America.

**MAP 1.2**

**Native American Peoples, 1492**

Having learned to live in many environments, Native Americans populated the entire Western Hemisphere. They created cultures that ranged from centralized empires (the Incas and Aztecs), to societies that combined farming with hunting, fishing, and gathering (the Iroquois and Algonquians), to nomadic tribes of hunter-gatherers (the Micmacs and Shoshones). The great diversity of Native American peoples—in language, tribal identity, and ways of life—and the long-standing rivalries among neighboring peoples usually prevented them from uniting to resist the European invaders.

centers stitched together this improbable high-altitude empire, which ran down the 2,000-mile-long spine of the Andes Mountains. A king claiming divine status ruled the empire through a bureaucracy of nobles. Like the Aztecs, the empire consisted of subordinate kingdoms that had been conquered by the Incas, and tribute flowed from local centers of power to the imperial core.

## Chiefdoms and Confederacies

Nothing on the scale of the Aztec and Inca empires ever developed north of Mexico, but maize agriculture spread from Mesoamerica across much of North America beginning around A.D. 1000, laying a foundation for new ways of life there as well.

**Understanding the Cosmos of the Aztecs**

Using Aztec sources, German geographers drew this map of Tenochtitlán in 1524. Recent scholarship suggests that the Aztecs viewed their city as a cosmic linchpin, where the human world brushed up against the divine. In the center of the city stand two elevated temples that represent Coatepec, the Serpent Mountain and the mythic birth-place of the Aztecs' tribal god Huitzilopochtli. Priests sacrificed thousands of men and women here, a ritual the Aztecs believed transformed the temples into the Sacred Mountain and sustained the cosmos. Bildarchiv Preussischer Kulturbesitz/Art Resource, NY.

**The Mississippi Valley** The spread of maize to the Mississippi River Valley around A.D. 1000 led to the development of a large-scale northern Native American culture. The older Adena and Hopewell cultures had already introduced moundbuilding and distinctive pottery styles to the region. Now residents of the Mississippi River Valley experienced the greater urban density and more complex social organization that agriculture encouraged.

The city of Cahokia, in the fertile bottomlands along the Mississippi River, emerged around 1000 as the foremost center of the new Mississippian culture. At its peak, Cahokia's population exceeded 10,000; smaller satellite communities brought the region's population to 20,000 to 30,000. In an area of 6 square miles, archaeologists have found 120 mounds of varying size,

shape, and function. Some contain extensive burials; others, known as platform mounds, were used as bases for ceremonial buildings or rulers' homes. Cahokia had a powerful ruling class and a priesthood that worshipped the sun. After peaking in size around 1350, it declined rapidly. Scholars speculate that its decline was caused by an era of ruinous warfare, exacerbated by environmental factors that made the site less habitable. It had been abandoned by the time Europeans arrived in the area.

Mississippian culture endured, however, and was still in evidence throughout much of the Southeast at the time of first contact with Europeans. The Lady of Cofachiqui encountered by Hernando de Soto in 1540 ruled over a Mississippian community, and others dotted the landscape between the Carolinas and the lower

Mississippi River. In Florida, sixteenth-century Spanish explorers encountered the Apalachee Indians, who occupied a network of towns built around mounds and fields of maize.

**Eastern Woodlands** In the eastern woodlands, the Mississippian-influenced peoples of the Southeast interacted with other groups, many of whom adopted maize agriculture but did not otherwise display Mississippian characteristics. To the north, Algonquian and Iroquoian speakers shared related languages and lifeways but were divided into dozens of distinct societies. Most occupied villages built around fields of maize, beans, and squash during the summer months; at other times of the year, they dispersed in smaller groups to hunt, fish, and gather. Throughout the eastern woodlands, as in most of North America, women tended crops, gathered plants, and oversaw affairs within the community, while men were responsible for activities beyond it, especially hunting, fishing, and warfare.

In this densely forested region, Indians regularly set fires — in New England, twice a year, in spring and fall — to clear away underbrush, open fields, and make it easier to hunt big game. The catastrophic population decline accompanying European colonization quickly put an end to seasonal burning, but in the years before Europeans arrived in North America bison roamed east as far as modern-day New York and Georgia. Early European colonists remarked upon landscapes that "resemble[d] a stately Parke," where men could ride among widely spaced trees on horseback and even a "large army" could pass unimpeded (America Compared, p. 14).

Algonquian and Iroquoian peoples had no single style of political organization. Many were chiefdoms, with one individual claiming preeminent power in a community. Some were paramount chiefdoms, in which numerous communities with their own local chiefs banded together under a single, more powerful ruler. For example, the Powhatan Chiefdom, which

**The Great Serpent Mound**

Scholars long believed that this mound was the work of the Adena peoples (500 B.C.–A.D. 200) because of its proximity to an Adena burial site in present-day southern Ohio. Recent research places the mound at a much later date (A.D. 950–1200) and, because of the serpent imagery, ties it to the Fort Ancient culture, which is closely related to the Mississippian complex. The head of the serpent is aligned with the sunset of the summer solstice (June 20 or 21 in the Northern Hemisphere), an event of great religious significance to a sun-worshipping culture. © Bettmann/Corbis.

**The Kincaid Site**

Located on the north bank of the Ohio River 140 miles from Cahokia, the Kincaid site was a Mississippian town from c. A.D. 1050 to 1450. It contains at least nineteen mounds topped by large buildings thought to have been temples or council houses. Now a state historic site in Illinois, it has been studied by anthropologists and archaeologists since the 1930s. Artist Herb Roe depicts the town as it may have looked at its peak. Herb Roe, Chromesun Productions.

dominated the Chesapeake Bay region, embraced more than thirty subordinate chiefdoms, and some 20,000 people, by the time Englishmen established the colony of Virginia in Powhatan territory. Powhatan himself, according to the English colonist John Smith, was attended by "a guard of 40 or 50 of the tallest men his Country affords."

Elsewhere, especially in the Mid-Atlantic region, the power of chiefs was strictly local. Along the Delaware and Hudson rivers, Lenni Lenape (or Delaware) and Munsee Indians lived in small, independent communities without overarching political organizations. Early European maps of this region show a landscape dotted with a bewildering profusion of Indian names. European colonization would soon

drive many of these groups into oblivion and force survivors to coalesce into larger groups.

Some Native American groups were not chiefdoms at all, but instead granted political authority to councils of sachems, or leaders. This was the case with the Iroquois Confederacy. Sometime shortly before the arrival of Europeans, probably around 1500, five nations occupying the region between the Hudson River and Lake Erie—the Mohawks, Oneidas, Onondagas, Cayugas, and Senecas—banded together to form the Iroquois.

These groups had been fighting among themselves for years, caught in a destructive cycle of wars of retribution. Then, according to Iroquois legend, a Mohawk man named Hiawatha lost his family in one of these

## Altered Landscapes

In the eastern woodlands, Native Americans set fires once or twice a year to clear underbrush and open up landscapes that would otherwise have been densely wooded. The burnings made it easier to plant corn, beans, and squash and drew big game animals into the clearings, where hunters could fell them. As European colonization displaced Indian populations, this practice ended. Some scholars have even suggested that the decline in burning caused a drop of carbon in the atmosphere large enough to account for the Little Ice Age, an episode of global cooling that lasted from about 1550 to 1850, though the claim is controversial.

### Thomas Morton, Of the Custome in burning the Country, and the reason thereof (1637)

The Savages are accustomed to set fire of the Country in all places where they come, and to burne it twize a yeare, viz: at the Spring, and the fall of the leafe. The reason that mooves them to doe so, is because it would other wise be so overgrowne with underweedes that it would be all a coppice wood, and the people would not be able in any wise to passe through the Country out of a beaten path.

The meanes that they do it with, is with certaine minerall stones, that they carry about them in baggs made for that purpose of the skinnes of little beastes, which they convert into good lether, carrying in the same a peece of touch wood, very excellent for that purpose, of their owne making. These minerall stones they have from the Piquenteenes, (which is to the Southward of all the plantations in New England,) by trade and trafficke with those people.

The burning of the grasse destroyes the underwoods, and so scorcheth the elder trees that it shrinkes them, and hinders their grouth very much: so that hee that will looke to finde large trees and good tymber, must not depend upon the help of a wooden prospect to finde them on the uplandground; but must seeke for them, (as I and others have done,) in the lower grounds, where the grounds are wett, when the Country is fired, by reason of the snow water that remaines there for a time, untill the Sunne by continuance of that hath exhaled the vapoures of the earth, and dried up those places where the fire, (by reason of the moisture,) can have no power to doe them any hurt: and if he would endevoure to finde out any goodly Cedars, hee must not seeke for them on the higher grounds, but make his inquest for them in the vallies, for the Savages,

by this custome of theirs, have spoiled all the rest: for this custome hath bin continued from the beginninge.

And least their firing of the Country in this manner should be an occasion of damnifying us, and indaingering our habitations, wee our selves have used carefully about the same times to observe the winds, and fire the grounds about our owne habitations; to prevent the Dammage that might happen by any neglect thereof, if the fire should come neere those howses in our absence.

For, when the fire is once kindled, it dilates and spreads it selfe as well against, as with the winde; burning continually night and day, untill a shower of raine falls to quench it.

And this custome of firing the Country is the meanes to make it passable; and by that meanes the trees growe here and there as in our parks: and makes the Country very beautifull and commodious.

Source: Thomas Morton, *The New English Canaan* (Boston: John Wilson and Son, 1883 [orig. pub. 1637]), 172–173.

### QUESTIONS FOR ANALYSIS

1. What benefits and dangers does Morton attribute to the practice of Indian burning? How did he and his fellow colonists respond to the practice?

2. Since Europeans did not practice widespread burning in the Indian manner, they achieved deforestation only slowly, through many years of backbreaking labor. Thinking comparatively about European and Native American approaches to landscape management, how would you assess the benefits and challenges of each approach?

wars. Stricken by grief, he met a spirit who taught him a series of condolence rituals. He returned to his people preaching a new gospel of peace and power, and the condolence rituals he taught became the foundation for the Iroquois Confederacy.

Once bound by these rituals, the Five Nations began acting together as a political confederacy. They avoided violence among themselves and became one of the most powerful Native American groups in the Northeast. The Iroquois did not recognize chiefs; instead, councils of sachems made decisions. These were **matriarchal** societies, with power inherited through female lines of authority. Women were influential in local councils, though men served as sachems, made war, and conducted diplomacy.

Along the southern coast of the region that would soon be called New England, a dense network of powerful chiefdoms—including the Narragansetts, Wampanoags, Mohegans, Pequots, and others—competed for resources and dominance. When the Dutch and English arrived, they were able to exploit these rivalries and play Indian groups against one another. Farther north, in northern New England and much of present-day Canada, the short growing season and thin, rocky soil were inhospitable to maize agriculture. Here the native peoples were hunters and gatherers and therefore had smaller and more mobile communities, though they were no less complex than their agriculturally oriented cousins.

### The Great Lakes

To the west, Algonquian-speaking peoples dominated the Great Lakes. The tribal groups recognized by Europeans in this region included the Ottawas, Ojibwas, and Potawatomis. But collectively they thought of themselves as a single people: the Anishinaabe. Clan identities—beaver, otter, sturgeon, deer, and others—crosscut tribal affiliations and were in some ways more fundamental. The result was a social landscape that could be bewildering to outsiders. Here lived, one French official remarked, "an infinity of undiscovered nations."

The extensive network of lakes and rivers, and the use of birchbark canoes, made Great Lakes peoples especially mobile. "They seem to have as many abodes as the year has seasons," wrote one observer. They traveled long distances to hunt and fish, to trade, or to join in important ceremonies or military alliances. Groups negotiated access to resources and travel routes. Instead of a map with clearly delineated tribal territories, it is best to imagine the Great Lakes as a porous region, where "political power and social identity took on multiple forms," as one scholar has written.

### The Great Plains and Rockies

Farther west lies the vast, arid steppe region known as the Great Plains, which was dominated by the hunting and gathering activities of small, dispersed groups. The geopolitics of the Plains Indians was transformed by a European import—the horse—long before Europeans themselves arrived. Livestock was introduced in the Spanish colony of New Mexico in the late sixteenth century, and from there horses gradually dispersed across the plains. Bison hunters who had previously relied on stealth became much more successful on horseback.

Indians on horseback were also more formidable opponents than their counterparts on foot, and some Plains peoples leveraged their control of horses to gain power over their neighbors. The Comanches were a small Shoshonean band on the northern plains that migrated south in pursuit of horses. They became expert raiders, capturing people and horses alike and trading them for weapons, food, clothing, and other necessities. Eventually they controlled a vast territory. From their humble origins, their skill in making war on horseback made the Comanches one of the region's most formidable peoples.

> **EXPLAIN CONSEQUENCES**
> How did landscape, climate, and resources influence the development of Native American societies?

Similarly, horses allowed the Sioux, a confederation of seven distinct peoples who originated in present-day Minnesota, to move west and dominate a vast territory ranging from the Mississippi River to the Black Hills. The Crow Indians moved from the Missouri River to the eastern slope of the Rocky Mountains, where they became nomadic bison hunters. Beginning in the mid-eighteenth century, they became horse breeders and traders as well.

In some places, farming communities were embedded within the much wider geographical range of hunter-gatherers. Thus the Hidatsa and Mandan Indians maintained settled agricultural villages along the Missouri River, while the more mobile Sioux dominated the region around them. Similarly, the Caddo Indians, who lived on the edge of the southern plains, inhabited agricultural communities that were like islands in a sea of more mobile peoples.

Three broad swaths of Numic-speaking peoples occupied the Great Basin that separated the Rockies from the Sierra Mountains: Bannocks and Northern Paiutes in the north, Shoshones in the central basin, and Utes and Southern Paiutes in the south. Resources were varied and spread thin on the land. Kin-based bands traveled great distances to hunt bison along the

Yellowstone River (where they shared territory with the Crows) and bighorn sheep in high altitudes, to fish for salmon, and to gather pine nuts when they were in season. Throughout the Great Basin, some groups adopted horses and became relatively powerful, while others remained foot-borne and impoverished in comparison with their more mobile neighbors.

**The Arid Southwest** In the part of North America that appears to be most hostile to agriculture—the canyon-laced country of the arid Southwest—surprisingly large farming settlements developed. Anasazi peoples were growing maize by the first century A.D., earlier than anywhere else north of Mexico, and Pueblo cultures emerged around A.D. 600. By A.D. 1000, the Hohokams, Mogollons, and Anasazis (all Pueblo peoples) had developed irrigation systems to manage scarce water, enabling them to build sizable villages and towns of adobe and rock that were often molded to sheer canyon walls. Chaco Canyon, in modern New Mexico, supported a dozen large Anasazi towns, while beyond the canyon a network of roads tied these settlements together with hundreds of small Anasazi villages.

Extended droughts and soil exhaustion caused the abandonment of Chaco Canyon and other large settlements in the Southwest after 1150, but smaller communities still dotted the landscape when the first Europeans arrived. It was the Spanish who called these groups Pueblo Indians: *pueblo* means "town" in Spanish, and the name refers to their distinctive building style. When Europeans arrived, Pueblo peoples, including the Acomas, Zuñis, Tewas, and Hopis, were found throughout much of modern New Mexico, Arizona, and western Texas.

**The Pacific Coast** Hunter-gatherers inhabited the Pacific coast. Before the arrival of the Spanish, California was home to more than 300,000 people, subdivided into dozens of small, localized groups and speaking at least a hundred distinct languages. This diversity of languages and cultures discouraged intermarriage and kept these societies independent. Despite these differences, many groups did share common characteristics, including clearly defined social hierarchies separating elites from commoners. They gathered acorns and other nuts and seeds, caught fish and shellfish, and hunted game.

The Pacific Northwest also supported a dense population that was divided into many distinct groups who controlled small territories and spoke different languages. Their stratified societies were ruled by wealthy families. To maintain control of their territories, the more powerful nations, including the Chinooks, Coast Salishes, Haidas, and Tlingits, nurtured strong warrior traditions. They developed sophisticated fishing technologies and crafted oceangoing dugout canoes, made from enormous cedar trees, that ranged up to 60 feet in length. Their distinctive material culture included large longhouses that were home to dozens of people and totem poles representing clan lineages or local legends.

## Patterns of Trade

Expansive trade networks tied together regions and carried valuable goods hundreds and even thousands of miles. Trade goods included food and raw materials, tools, ritual artifacts, and decorative goods. Trade enriched diets, enhanced economies, and allowed the powerful to set themselves apart with luxury items.

**Anasazi Ladle**

Crafted between A.D. 1300 and 1600 and found in a site in central Arizona, this Anasazi dipper was coiled and molded by hand and painted with a geometric motif. Anasazi pottery is abundant in archaeological sites, thanks in part to the Southwest's dry climate. Clay vessels and ladles helped Anasazi peoples handle water—one of their most precious resources—with care. National Museum of the American Indian, Smithsonian Institution.

**Chilkat Tlingit Bowl**

This bowl in the form of a brown bear, which dates to the mid-nineteenth century, is made of alder wood and inlaid with snail shells. The brown bear is a Tlingit clan totem. Animal-form bowls like this one, which express an affinity with nonhuman creatures, are a common feature of Tlingit culture. National Museum of the American Indian, Smithsonian Institution.

In areas where Indians specialized in a particular economic activity, regional trade networks allowed them to share resources. Thus nomadic hunters of the southern plains, including the Navajos and Apaches, conducted annual trade fairs with Pueblo farmers, exchanging hides and meat for maize, pottery, and cotton blankets. Similar patterns of exchange occurred throughout the Great Plains, wherever hunters and farmers coexisted. In some parts of North America, a regional trade in war captives who were offered as slaves helped to sustain friendly relations among neighboring groups. One such network developed in the Upper Mississippi River basin, where Plains Indian captives were traded, or given as diplomatic gifts, to Ottawas and other Great Lakes and eastern woodlands peoples.

Across longer distances, rare and valuable objects traveled through networks that spanned much of the continent. Great Lakes copper, Rocky Mountain mica, jasper from Pennsylvania, obsidian from New Mexico and Wyoming, and pipestone from the Midwest have all been found in archaeological sites hundreds of miles from their points of origin. Seashells — often shaped and polished into beads and other artifacts — traveled hundreds of miles inland. Grizzly bear claws and eagle feathers were prized, high-status objects. After European contact, Indian hunters often traveled long distances to European trading posts to trade for cloth, iron tools, and weapons.

Within Native American groups, powerful leaders controlled a disproportionate share of wealth and redistributed it to prove their generosity and strengthen their authority. In small, kin-based bands, the strongest hunters possessed the most food, and sharing it was essential. In chiefdoms, rulers filled the same role, often collecting the wealth of a community and then redistributing it to their followers. Powhatan, the powerful Chesapeake Bay chief, reportedly collected nine-tenths of the produce of the communities he oversaw — "skins, beads, copper, pearls, deer, turkeys, wild beasts, and corn" — but then gave much of it back to his subordinates. His generosity was considered a mark of good leadership. In the Pacific Northwest, the Chinook word *potlatch* refers to periodic festivals in which wealthy residents gave away belongings to friends, family, and followers.

## Sacred Power

Most Native North Americans were **animists** who believed that the natural world was suffused with spiritual power. They sought to understand the world by interpreting dreams and visions, and their rituals appeased guardian spirits that could ensure successful hunts and other forms of good fortune. Although their views were subject to countless local variations, certain patterns were widespread.

Women and men interacted differently with these spiritual forces. In agricultural communities, women grew crops and maintained hearth, home, and village. Native American conceptions of female power linked their bodies' generative functions with the earth's fertility, and rituals like the Green Corn Ceremony — a summer ritual of purification and renewal — helped to sustain the life-giving properties of the world around them.

For men, spiritual power was invoked in hunting and war. To ensure success in hunting, men took care

**UNDERSTAND POINTS OF VIEW**
How did Native Americans' conceptions of the spiritual world influence their daily lives?

not to offend the spirits of the animals they killed. They performed rituals before, during, and after a hunt to acknowledge the power of those guardian spirits, and they believed that, when an animal had been killed properly, its spirit would rise from the earth unharmed. Success in hunting and prowess in war were both interpreted as signs of sacred protection and power.

Ideas about war varied widely. War could be fought for geopolitical reasons — to gain ground against an enemy — but for many groups, warfare was a crucial rite of passage for young men, and raids were conducted to allow warriors to prove themselves in battle. Motives for war could be highly personal; war was often more like a blood feud between families than a contest between nations. If a community lost warriors in battle, it often retaliated by capturing or killing a like number of warriors in response — a so-called mourning war. Some captives were adopted into new communities, while others were enslaved or tortured.

# Western Europe: The Edge of the Old World

In 1450, Western Europe lay at the far fringe of the Eurasian and African continents. It had neither the powerful centralized empires nor the hunter-gatherer bands and semisedentary societies of the Americas; it was, instead, a patchwork of roughly equivalent kingdoms, duchies, and republics vying with one another and struggling to reach out effectively to the rest of the world. No one would have predicted that Europeans would soon become overlords of the Western Hemisphere. A thousand years after the fall of the Roman Empire, Europe's populations still relied on subsistence agriculture and were never far from the specter of famine. Moreover, around 1350, a deadly plague introduced from Central Asia — the Black Death — had killed one-third of Europe's population. The lives of ordinary people were afflicted by poverty, disease, and uncertainty, and the future looked as difficult and dark as the past.

## Hierarchy and Authority

In traditional hierarchical societies — American or European — authority came from above. In Europe, kings and princes owned vast tracts of land, forcibly conscripted men for military service, and lived off the peasantry's labor. Yet monarchs were far from supreme: local nobles also owned large estates and controlled hundreds of peasant families. Collectively, these nobles challenged royal authority with both their military power and their legislative institutions, such as the French *parlements* and the English House of Lords.

Just as kings and nobles ruled society, men governed families. These were **patriarchies**, in which property and social identity descended in male family lines. Rich or poor, the man was the head of the house, his power justified by the teachings of the Christian Church. As one English clergyman put it, "The woman is a weak creature not embued with like strength and constancy of mind"; law and custom "subjected her to the power of man." Once married, an Englishwoman assumed her husband's surname, submitted to his orders, and surrendered the right to her property. When he died, she received a dower, usually the use during her lifetime of one-third of the family's land and goods.

Men also controlled the lives of their children, who usually worked for their father into their middle or late twenties. Then landowning peasants would give land to their sons and dowries to their daughters and choose marriage partners of appropriate wealth and status. In many regions, fathers bestowed all their land on their eldest son — a practice known as **primogeniture** — forcing many younger children to join the ranks of the roaming poor. Few men and even fewer women had much personal freedom.

Hierarchy and authority prevailed in traditional European society because of the power held by established institutions — nobility, church, and village — and because, in a violent and unpredictable world, they offered ordinary people a measure of security. Carried by migrants to America, these security-conscious institutions would shape the character of family and society well into the eighteenth century.

## Peasant Society

In 1450, most Europeans were **peasants**, farmworkers who lived in small villages surrounded by fields farmed cooperatively by different families. On manorial lands, farming rights were given in exchange for labor on the lord's estate, an arrangement that turned peasants into serfs. Gradually, obligatory manorial services gave way to paying rent, or, as in France, landownership. Once freed from the obligation to labor for their farming rights, European farmers began to produce surpluses and created local market economies.

As with Native Americans, the rhythm of life followed the seasons. In March, villagers began the exhausting work of plowing and then planting wheat, rye, and oats. During the spring, the men sheared wool, which the women washed and spun into yarn. In June, peasants cut hay and stored it as winter fodder for their livestock. During the summer, life was more relaxed, and families repaired their houses and barns. Fall brought the harvest, followed by solemn feasts of thanksgiving and riotous bouts of merrymaking. As winter approached, peasants slaughtered excess livestock and salted or smoked the meat. During the cold months, they threshed grain and wove textiles, visited friends and relatives, and celebrated the winter solstice or the birth of Christ. Just before the cycle began again in the spring, they held carnivals, celebrating with drink and dance the end of the long winter (Figure 1.1).

For most peasants, survival meant constant labor, and poverty corroded family relationships. Malnourished mothers fed their babies sparingly, calling them "greedy and gluttonous," and many newborn girls were "helped to die" so that their brothers would have enough to eat. Half of all peasant children died before the age of twenty-one, victims of malnourishment and disease. Many peasants drew on strong religious beliefs, "counting blessings" and accepting their harsh existence. Others hoped for a better life. It was the peasants of Spain, Germany, and Britain who would supply the majority of white migrants to the Western Hemisphere.

## Expanding Trade Networks

In the millennium before contact with the Americas, Western Europe was the barbarian fringe of the civilized world. In the Mediterranean basin, Arab scholars carried on the legacy of Byzantine civilization, which had preserved the achievements of the Greeks and Romans in medicine, philosophy, mathematics, astronomy, and geography, while merchants controlled trade in the Mediterranean, Africa, and the Near East. This control gave them access to spices from India and silks, magnetic compasses, water-powered mills, and mechanical clocks from China.

> **COMPARE AND CONTRAST**
> In what ways were the lives of Europeans similar to and different from those of Native Americans?

In the twelfth century, merchants from the Italian city-states of Genoa, Florence, Pisa, and especially Venice began to push their way into the Arab-dominated trade routes of the Mediterranean. Trading in Alexandria, Beirut, and other eastern Mediterranean ports, they carried the luxuries of Asia into European markets. At its peak, Venice had a merchant fleet of more than three thousand ships. This enormously profitable commerce created wealthy merchants, bankers, and textile manufacturers who expanded trade, lent vast sums of money, and spurred technological innovation in silk and wool production.

Italian moneyed elites ruled their city-states as **republics**, states that had no prince or king but instead

**FIGURE 1.1**

**The Yearly Rhythm of Rural Life and Death**

The annual cycle of nature profoundly affected life in the traditional agricultural world. The death rate soared by 20 percent in February (from viruses) and September (from fly-borne dysentery). Summer was the healthiest season, with the fewest deaths and the most successful conceptions (as measured by births nine months later). A value of 100 indicates an equal number of deaths and conceptions.

**Procession in St. Mark's Square in Venice, 1496**
Venice was one of the world's great trading centers in the fifteenth century. Its merchant houses connected Europe to Asia and the Middle East, while its complex republican government aroused both admiration and mistrust. Here, Venetian painter Gentile Bellini (c. 1429–1507) depicts a diplomatic procession celebrating the League of Venice, a union of European states opposed to French expansion into Italy. Galleria dell 'Accademia, Venice, Italy/Giraudon/The Bridgeman Art Library.

were governed by merchant coalitions. They celebrated **civic humanism**, an ideology that praised public virtue and service to the state and in time profoundly influenced European and American conceptions of government. They sponsored great artists—Michelangelo, Leonardo da Vinci, and others—who produced an unprecedented flowering of genius. Historians have labeled the arts and learning associated with this cultural transformation from 1300 to 1450 the **Renaissance**.

The economic revolution that began in Italy spread slowly to northern and western Europe. England's principal export was woolen cloth, which was prized in the colder parts of the continent but had less appeal in southern Europe and beyond. Northern Europe had its own trade system, controlled by an alliance of merchant communities called the Hanseatic League centered on the Baltic and North seas, which dealt in timber, furs, wheat and rye, honey, wax, and amber.

As trade picked up in Europe, merchants and artisans came to dominate its growing cities and towns. While the Italian city-states ruled themselves without having a powerful monarch to contend with, in much of Europe the power of merchants stood in tension with that of kings and nobles. In general, the rise of commerce favored the power of kings at the expense of the landed nobility. The kings of Western Europe established royal law courts that gradually eclipsed the manorial courts controlled by nobles; they also built bureaucracies that helped them centralize power while they forged alliances with merchants and urban artisans. Monarchs allowed merchants to trade throughout their realms; granted privileges to **guilds**, or artisan organizations that regulated trades; and safeguarded commercial transactions, thereby encouraging domestic manufacturing and foreign trade. In return, they extracted taxes from towns and loans from merchants to support their armies and officials.

## Myths, Religions, and Holy Warriors

The oldest European religious beliefs drew on a form of animism similar to that of Native Americans, which held that the natural world—the sun, wind, stones, animals—was animated by spiritual forces. As in North America, such beliefs led ancient European peoples to develop localized cults of knowledge and spiritual practice. Wise men and women developed rituals to protect their communities, ensure abundant harvests, heal illnesses, and bring misfortunes to their enemies.

**TRACE CHANGE OVER TIME**
How did the growth of commerce shift the structure of power in European societies?

The pagan traditions of Greece and Rome overlaid animism with elaborate myths about gods interacting directly with the affairs of human beings. As the Roman Empire expanded, it built temples to its gods wherever it planted new settlements. Thus peoples throughout Europe, North Africa, and the Near East were exposed to the Roman pantheon. Soon the teachings of Christianity began to flow in these same channels.

**The Rise of Christianity**  **Christianity**, which grew out of Jewish monotheism (the belief in one god), held that Jesus Christ was himself divine. As an institution, Christianity benefitted enormously from the conversion of the Roman emperor Constantine in A.D. 312. Prior to that time, Christians were an underground sect at odds with the Roman Empire. After Constantine's conversion, Christianity became Rome's official religion, temples were abandoned or remade into churches, and noblemen who hoped to retain their influence converted to the new state religion. For centuries, the Roman Catholic Church was the great unifying institution in Western Europe. The pope in Rome headed a vast hierarchy of cardinals, bishops, and priests. Catholic theologians preserved Latin, the language of classical scholarship, and imbued kingship with divine power. Christian dogma provided a common understanding of God and human history, and the authority of the Church buttressed state institutions. Every village had a church, and holy shrines served as points of contact with the sacred world. Often those shrines had their origins in older, animist practices, now largely forgotten and replaced with Christian ritual.

Christian doctrine penetrated deeply into the everyday lives of peasants. While animist traditions held that spiritual forces were alive in the natural world, Christian priests taught that the natural world was flawed and fallen. Spiritual power came from outside nature, from a supernatural God who had sent his divine son, Jesus

*The Last Judgment,* **1467–1471**

Death—and their fate in the after-life—loomed large in the minds of fifteenth-century Christians, and artists depicted their hopes and fears in vividly rendered scenes. In this painting by the German-Flemish artist Hans Memling (c. 1433–1494), Christ and his apostles sit in judgment as the world ends and the dead rise from their graves. The archangel Michael weighs the souls of the dead in a balance to determine their final fate: either eternal life with God in heaven or everlasting punishment in hell. Erich Lessing/Art Resource, NY.

Christ, into the world to save humanity from its sins. The Christian Church devised a religious calendar that transformed animist festivals into holy days. The winter solstice, which had for millennia marked the return of the sun, became the feast of Christmas.

The Church also taught that Satan, a wicked supernatural being, was constantly challenging God by tempting people to sin. People who spread **heresies** — doctrines that were inconsistent with the teachings of the Church — were seen as the tools of Satan, and suppressing false doctrines became an obligation of Christian rulers.

**The Crusades**    In their work suppressing false doctrines, Christian rulers were also obliged to combat **Islam**, the religion whose followers considered Muhammad to be God's last prophet. Islam's reach expanded until it threatened European Christendom. Following the death of Muhammad in A.D. 632, the newly converted Arab peoples of North Africa used force and fervor to spread the Muslim faith into sub-Saharan Africa, India, and Indonesia, as well as deep into Spain and the Balkan regions of Europe. Between A.D. 1096 and 1291, Christian armies undertook a series of **Crusades** to reverse the Muslim advance in Europe and win back the holy lands where Christ had lived. Under the banner of the pope and led by Europe's Christian monarchs, crusading armies aroused great waves of popular piety as they marched off to combat. New orders of knights, like the Knights Templar and the Teutonic Knights, were created to support them.

The crusaders had some military successes, but their most profound impact was on European society. Religious warfare intensified Europe's Christian identity and prompted the persecution of Jews and their expulsion from many European countries. The Crusades also introduced Western European merchants to the trade routes that stretched from Constantinople to China along the Silk Road and from the Mediterranean Sea through the Persian Gulf to the Indian Ocean. And crusaders encountered sugar for the first time. Returning soldiers brought it back from the Middle East, and as Europeans began to conquer territory in the eastern Mediterranean, they experimented with raising it themselves. These early experiments with sugar would have a profound impact on European enterprise in the Americas — and European involvement with the African slave trade — in the centuries to come. By 1450, Western Europe remained relatively isolated from the centers of civilization in Eurasia and Africa, but the Crusades and the rise of Italian merchant houses had introduced it to a wider world.

**The Reformation**    In 1517, Martin Luther, a German monk and professor at the university in Wittenberg, took up the cause of reform in the Catholic Church. Luther's *Ninety-five Theses* condemned the Church for many corrupt practices. More radically, Luther downplayed the role of the clergy as mediators between God and believers and said that Christians must look to the Bible, not to the Church, as the ultimate authority in matters of faith. So that every literate German could read the Bible, previously available only in Latin, Luther translated it into German.

Meanwhile, in Geneva, Switzerland, French theologian John Calvin established a rigorous Protestant regime. Even more than Luther, Calvin stressed human weakness and God's omnipotence. His *Institutes of the Christian Religion* (1536) depicted God as an absolute sovereign. Calvin preached the doctrine of **predestination**, the idea that God chooses certain people for salvation before they are born and condemns the rest to eternal damnation. In Geneva, he set up a model Christian community and placed spiritual authority in ministers who ruled the city, prohibiting frivolity and luxury. "We know," wrote Calvin, "that man is of so perverse and crooked a nature, that everyone would scratch out his neighbor's eyes if there were no bridle to hold them in." Calvin's authoritarian doctrine won converts all over Europe, including the Puritans in Scotland and England.

Luther's criticisms triggered a war between the Holy Roman Empire and the northern principalities in Germany, and soon the controversy between the Roman Catholic Church and radical reformers like Luther and Calvin spread throughout much of Western Europe. The **Protestant Reformation**, as this movement came to be called, triggered a **Counter-Reformation** in the Catholic Church that sought change from within and created new monastic and missionary orders, including the Jesuits (founded in 1540), who saw themselves as soldiers of Christ. The competition between these divergent Christian traditions did much to shape European colonization of the Americas. Roman Catholic powers — Spain, Portugal, and France — sought to win souls in the Americas for the Church, while Protestant nations — England and the Netherlands — viewed the Catholic Church as corrupt and exploitative and hoped instead to create godly communities attuned to the true gospel of Christianity.

**TRACE CHANGE OVER TIME**
How did the growing influence of the Christian Church affect events in Europe?

# West and Central Africa: Origins of the Atlantic Slave Trade

*Homo sapiens* originated in Africa. Numerous civilizations had already risen and fallen there, and contacts with the Near East and the Mediterranean were millennia old, when Western Europeans began sailing down its Atlantic coast. Home to perhaps 100 million in 1400, Africa was divided by the vast expanse of the Sahara. North Africa bordered on the Mediterranean, and its peoples fell under the domination of Christian Byzantium until the seventh century, when Muslim conquests brought the region under Islamic influence. In its coastal seaports, the merchandise of Asia, the Near East, Africa, and Europe converged. South of the Sahara, by contrast, the societies of West and Central Africa bordering on the Atlantic were relatively isolated. After 1400, that would quickly change.

## Empires, Kingdoms, and Ministates

West Africa—the part of the continent that bulges into the Atlantic—can be visualized as a broad horizontal swath divided into three climatic zones. The Sahel is the mostly flat, semiarid zone immediately south of the Sahara. Below it lies the savanna, a grassland region dotted with trees and shrubs. South of the savanna, in a band 200 to 300 miles wide along the West African coast, lies a tropical rain forest. A series of four major watersheds—the Senegal, Gambia, Volta, and Niger—dominate West Africa (Map 1.3).

Sudanic civilization took root at the eastern end of West Africa beginning around 9000 B.C. and traveled westward. Sudanic peoples domesticated cattle (8500–7500 B.C.) and cultivated sorghum and millet (7500–7000 B.C.). Over several thousand years, these peoples developed a distinctive style of pottery, began to cultivate and weave cotton (6500–3500 B.C.), and invented techniques for working copper and iron (2500–1000 B.C.). Sudanic civilization had its own tradition of monotheism distinct from that of Christians, Muslims, and Jews. Most Sudanic peoples in West Africa lived in stratified states ruled by kings and princes who were regarded as divine.

From these cultural origins, three great empires arose in succession in the northern savanna. The first, the Ghana Empire, appeared sometime around A.D. 800. Ghana capitalized on the recently domesticated camel to pioneer trade routes across the Sahara to North Africa, where Ghana traders carried the wealth of West Africa. The Ghana Empire gave way to the Mali Empire in the thirteenth century, which was eclipsed in turn by the Songhai Empire in the fifteenth century. All three empires were composed of smaller vassal kingdoms, not unlike the Aztec and Inca empires, and relied on military might to control their valuable trade routes.

Gold, abundant in West Africa, was the cornerstone of power and an indispensable medium of international trade. By 1450, West African traders had carried so much of it across the Sahara that it constituted one-half to two-thirds of all the gold in circulation in Europe, North Africa, and Asia. Mansa Musa, the tenth emperor of Mali, was a devout Muslim famed for his construction projects and his support of mosques and schools. In 1326, he embarked on a pilgrimage to Mecca with a vast retinue that crossed the Sahara and passed through Egypt. They spent so much gold along the way that the region's money supply was devalued for more than a decade after their visit.

To the south of these empires, the lower savanna and tropical rain forest of West Africa were home to a complex mosaic of kingdoms that traded among themselves and with the empires to the north. In such a densely populated, resource-rich region, they also fought frequently in a competition for local power. A few of these coastal kingdoms were quite large in size, but most were small enough that they have been termed ministates by historians. Comparable to the city-states of Italy, they were often about the size of a modern-day county in the United States. The tropical ecosystem prevented them from raising livestock, since the tsetse fly (which carries a parasite deadly to livestock) was endemic to the region, as was malaria. In place of the grain crops of the savanna, these peoples pioneered the cultivation of yams; they also gathered resources from the rivers and seacoast.

**COMPARE AND CONTRAST**
How do the states of the savanna compare to those of the Americas and Europe?

## Trans-Saharan and Coastal Trade

For centuries, the primary avenue of trade for West Africans passed through the Ghana, Mali, and Songhai empires, whose power was based on the monopoly they enjoyed over the **trans-Saharan trade**. Their caravans carried West African goods—including gold, copper, salt, and slaves—from the south to the north across the Sahara, then returned with textiles and other foreign goods. For the smaller states clustered

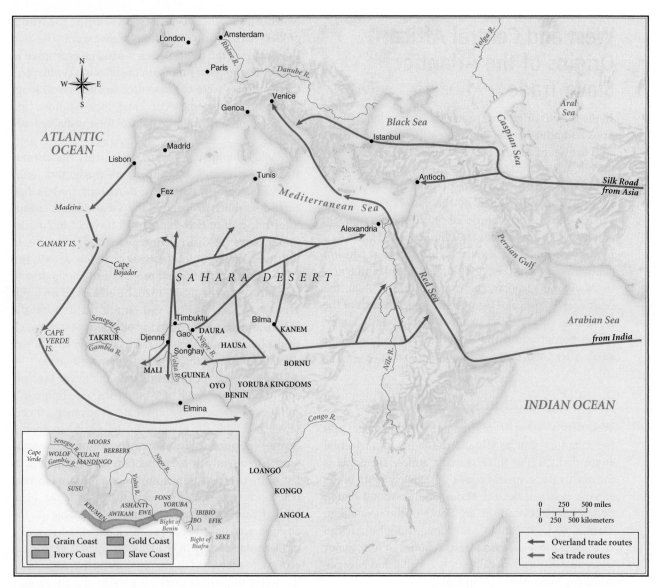

**MAP 1.3**

**West Africa and the Mediterranean in the Fifteenth Century**

Trade routes across the Sahara had long connected West Africa with the Mediterranean region. Gold, ivory, and slaves moved north and east; fine textiles, spices, and the Muslim faith traveled south. Beginning in the 1430s, the Portuguese opened up maritime trade with the coastal regions of West Africa, which were home to many peoples and dozens of large and small states. Over the next century, the movement of gold and slaves into the Atlantic would surpass that across the Sahara.

along the West African coast, merchandise originating in the world beyond the Sahara was scarce and expensive, while markets for their own products were limited.

Beginning in the mid-fifteenth century, a newly opening coastal trade with Europeans offered many West African peoples a welcome alternative. As European sailors made their way along the coast of West and then Central Africa, they encountered a bewilderingly complicated political landscape. Around

the mouths of the Senegal and Gambia rivers, numerous Mande-speaking states controlled access to the trade routes into the interior. Proceeding farther along the coast, they encountered the Akan states, a region of several dozen independent but culturally linked peoples. The Akan states had goldfields of their own, and this region soon became known to Europeans as the Gold Coast. East of the Akan states lay the Bight of Benin, which became an early center of the slave trade and thus came to be called the Slave Coast. Bending

**Terracotta Figure from Mali**
Dating to the thirteenth or fourteenth century, this terracotta figure came from an archaeological site near Djenna. The rider wears a large, ornate necklace, while the horse has a decorative covering on its head. The Mali Empire relied on a large cavalry to expand and defend its borders, and the horse was an important symbol of Mali's wealth and power. Werner Forman/Art Resource, NY.

south, fifteenth-century sailors encountered the Kingdom of Kongo in Central Africa, the largest state on the Atlantic seaboard, with a coastline that ran for some 250 miles. It was here in 1578 that Duarte Lopez visited the capital city of more than 100,000 residents. Wherever they went ashore along this route, European traders had to negotiate contacts on local terms (Thinking Like a Historian, p. 26).

## The Spirit World

Some West Africans who lived immediately south of the Sahara — the Fulanis in Senegal, the Mande-speakers in Mali, and the Hausas in northern Nigeria — learned about Islam from Arab merchants and Muslim leaders called imams. Converts to Islam knew the Koran and worshipped only a single God. Some of their cities, like Timbuktu, the legendary commercial center on the Niger River, became centers of Islamic learning and instruction. But most West

Africans acknowledged multiple gods, as well as spirits that lived in the earth, animals, and plants.

Like animists in the Americas and Europe, African communities had wise men and women adept at manipulating these forces for good or ill. The Sudanic tradition of divine kingship persisted, and many people believed that their kings could contact the spirit world. West Africans treated their ancestors with great respect, believing that the dead resided in a nearby spiritual realm and interceded in their lives. Most West African peoples had secret societies, such as the Poro for men and the Sande for women, that united people from different lineages and clans. These societies conducted rituals that celebrated male virility and female fertility. "Without children you are naked," said a Yoruba proverb. Happy was the man with a big household, many wives, many children, and many relatives — and, in a not very different vein, many slaves.

> **PLACE EVENTS IN CONTEXT**
> Why were West African leaders eager to engage in trade with Europeans?

## Exploration and Conquest

European engagement with the wider Atlantic world began around 1400, when the Portuguese monarchy propelled Europe into overseas expansion. Portugal soon took a leading role in the African slave trade, while the newly unified kingdom of Spain undertook Europe's first conquests in the Americas. These two ventures, though not initially linked, eventually became cornerstones in the creation of the "Atlantic World."

### Portuguese Expansion

As a young soldier fighting North African Moors with the Crusading Order of Christ, Prince Henry of Portugal (1394–1460) learned of Arab merchants' rich trade in gold and slaves across the Sahara. Seeking a maritime route to the source of this trade in West Africa, Henry founded a center for oceanic navigation. Henry's mariners, challenged to find a way through the treacherous waters off the northwest African coast, designed a better-handling vessel, the caravel, rigged with a lateen (triangular) sail that enabled the ship to tack into the wind. This innovation allowed them to sail far into the Atlantic, where they discovered and colonized the Madeira and Azore islands. From there, they sailed in 1435 to sub-Saharan Sierra Leone, where they exchanged salt, wine, and fish for African ivory and gold.

## Colliding Cultures

Carefully consider each of the objects or texts below. What meanings might you—thinking like a historian—impart to them?

1. **Mississippian warrior gorget (neck guard), A.D. 1250–1350.**

Source: The National Museum of the American Indian/George Gustav Heye Center/New York, NY William E. Meyer Collection 15/853.

2. **Portuguese officer's account of de Soto's expedition, 1557.** *This excerpt describes Indian resistance in the face of de Soto's campaign of conquest against Indians in the southeastern United States.*

[Spanish soldiers] went over a swampy land where the horsemen could not go. A half league from camp they came upon some Indian huts near the river; [but] the people who were inside them plunged into the river. They captured four Indian women, and twenty Indians came at us and attacked us so stoutly that we had to retreat to the camp, because of their being (as they are) so skillful with their weapons. Those people are so warlike and so quick that they make no account of foot soldiers; for if these go for them, they flee, and when their adversaries turn their backs they are immediately on them. The farthest they flee is the distance of an arrow shot. They are never quiet but always running and crossing from one side to another so that the crossbows or the arquebuses can not be aimed at them; and before a crossbowman can fire a shot, an Indian can shoot three or four arrows, and very seldom does he miss what he shoots at. If the arrow does not find armor, it penetrates as deeply as a crossbow. The bows are very long and the arrows are made of certain reeds like canes, very heavy and so tough that a sharpened cane passes through a shield. Some are pointed with a fish bone, as sharp as an awl, and others with a certain stone like a diamond point.

3. **Duarte Lopez, *A Report on the Kingdom of Kongo*, 1591.** *A Portuguese explorer's account of his travels in southern Africa in the sixteenth century.*

[T]he Kingdom of Sofala lies between the two rivers, Magnice and Cuama, on the sea-coast. It is small in size, and has but few villages and towns. . . . It is peopled by Mohammedans, and the king himself belongs to the same sect. He pays allegiance to the crown of Portugal, in order not to be subject to the government of Monomotapa [Mutapa]. On this account the Portuguese have a fortress at the mouth of the River Cuama, trading with those countries in gold, amber, and ivory, all found on that coast, as well as in slaves, and giving in exchange silk stuffs and taffetas. . . . It is said, that from these regions the gold was brought by sea which served for Solomon's Temple at Jerusalem, a fact by no means improbable, for in these countries of Monomotapa are found several ancient buildings of stone, brick, and wood, and of such wonderful workmanship, and architecture, as is nowhere seen in the surrounding provinces.

The Kingdom of Monomotapa is extensive, and has a large population of Pagan heathens, who are black, of middle stature, swift of foot, and in battle fight with great bravery, their weapons being bows and arrows, and light darts. There are numerous kings tributary to Monomotapa, who constantly rebel and wage war against it. The Emperor maintains large armies, which in the provinces are divided into legions, after the manner of the Romans, for, being a great ruler, he must be at constant warfare in order to maintain his dominion. Amongst his warriors, those most renowned for bravery, are the female legions, greatly valued by the Emperor, being the sinews of his military strength.

**4. Benin figurine of a Portuguese soldier from the seventeenth century.** *This brass figure would have been kept on an altar or on the roof of the royal palace of Benin.*

Source: © The Trustees of the British Museum/Art Resource, NY.

**6. Sixteenth- or seventeenth-century Spanish silver real.** *Spain minted enormous quantities of American silver; much of it was shipped to Manila, where it was exchanged for Asian luxury goods.*

Source: © RMN-Grand Palais/Art Resource, NY.

Sources: (2) John E. Worth, "Account of the Northern Conquest and Discovery of Hernando de Soto by Rodrigo Rangel," trans. John E. Worth, in Lawrence A. Clayton et al., eds., *The De Soto Chronicles: The Expedition of Hernando de Soto to North America in 1539–1543* (University of Alabama Press, 1993), 59; (3) Filippo Pigafetta, *A Report of the Kingdom of Congo,* trans. Margarite Hutchinson (London: John Murray, 1881), 117–119.

**5. Sixteenth-century Portuguese coin made from African gold.** *Before the discovery of the Americas, half of the Old World's gold came from sub-Saharan Africa.*

Source: © The Trustees of the British Museum/Art Resource, NY.

## ANALYZING THE EVIDENCE

1. What can you infer about cultural values among Mississippian peoples from source 1? About the cultural values of the Spanish and Portuguese from sources 5 and 6? What *can't* you infer from these objects?

2. How does de Soto describe the native peoples he encounters in Florida (source 2)? How does that compare to the traits of the African kingdoms that Lopez comments upon in source 3? Why might the king of Sofala prefer a Portuguese alliance to subjection to Monomotapa?

3. What does source 4 suggest about Benin relations with the Portuguese?

## PUTTING IT ALL TOGETHER

What do these sources tell us about the ways Native Americans, Europeans, and Africans thought about themselves, perceived one another, and capitalized on cross-cultural exchanges as they came into sustained contact? Write a short essay that considers the connection between the impulses of warfare and commerce, which appear again and again in contact settings.

**Banza in the Kingdom of Kongo, c. 1670**

The city of Banza, or Mbanza Kongo, was the capital of the Kingdom of Kongo when Portuguese traders first arrived in 1483. Kongo's king, Nzinga a Nkuwu, chose to be baptized to cement an alliance with Portugal and took the name João I. Kongo became officially Christian and Banza came to be known as São Salvador. Duarte Lopez visited and described the city in 1578; this engraving shows the city as it appeared a century later. Banza in the Kingdom of Kongo, San Salvador, from Olfert Dapper, ca. 1668.

Henry's efforts were soon joined to those of Italian merchants, who were being forced out of eastern Mediterranean trade routes by the rising power of the Ottoman Empire. Cut off from Asia, Genoese traders sought an Atlantic route to the lucrative markets of the Indian Ocean. They began to work with Portuguese and Castilian mariners and monarchs to finance trading voyages, and the African coast and its offshore islands opened to their efforts. European voyagers discovered the Canaries, the Cape Verde Islands, and São Tomé; all of them became laboratories for the expansion of Mediterranean agriculture.

On these Atlantic islands, planters transformed local ecosystems to experiment with a variety of familiar cash crops: wheat, wine grapes, and woad, a blue dye plant; livestock and honeybees; and, where the climate permitted, sugar. By 1500,

**IDENTIFY CAUSES**
How did Europe's desire for an ocean route to Asia shape its contacts with Africa?

Madeira was producing 2,500 metric tons a year, and Madeira sugar was available — in small, expensive quantities — in London, Paris, Rome, and Constantinople. Most of the islands were unpopulated. The Canaries were the exception; it took Castilian adventurers decades to conquer the Guanches who lived there. Once defeated, they were enslaved to labor in the Canaries or on Madeira, where they carved irrigation canals into the island's steep rock cliffs.

Europeans made no such inroads on the continent of Africa itself. The coastal kingdoms were well defended, and yellow fever, malaria, and dysentery quickly struck down Europeans who spent any time in the interior of West Africa. Instead they maintained small, fortified trading posts on offshore islands or along the coast, usually as guests of the local king.

Portuguese mariners continued to look for an Atlantic route to Asia. In 1488, Bartolomeu Dias rounded the Cape of Good Hope, the southern tip of

Africa. Vasco da Gama reached East Africa in 1497 and India in the following year; his ships were mistaken for those of Chinese traders, the last pale-skinned men to arrive by sea. Although da Gama's inferior goods — tin basins, coarse cloth, honey, and coral beads — were snubbed by the Arab and Indian merchants along India's Malabar Coast, he managed to acquire a highly profitable cargo of cinnamon and pepper. Da Gama returned to India in 1502 with twenty-one fighting vessels, which outmaneuvered and outgunned the Arab fleets. Soon the Portuguese government set up fortified trading posts for its merchants at key points around the Indian Ocean, in Indonesia, and along the coast of China (Map 1.4). In a transition that sparked the momentous growth of European wealth and power, the Portuguese and then the Dutch replaced the Arabs as the leaders in Asian commerce.

## The African Slave Trade

Portuguese traders likewise ousted Arab merchants as the prime purveyors of African slaves. Coerced labor — through slavery, serfdom, or indentured servitude — was the norm in most premodern societies, and in Africa slavery was widespread. Some Africans were held in bondage as security for debts; others were sold into servitude by their kin in exchange for food in times of famine; many others were war captives. Slaves were a key commodity of exchange, sold as agricultural laborers, concubines, or military recruits. Sometimes their descendants were freed, but others endured hereditary bondage. Sonni Ali (r. 1464–1492),

**TRACE CHANGE OVER TIME**
How was the African slave trade adapted to European needs?

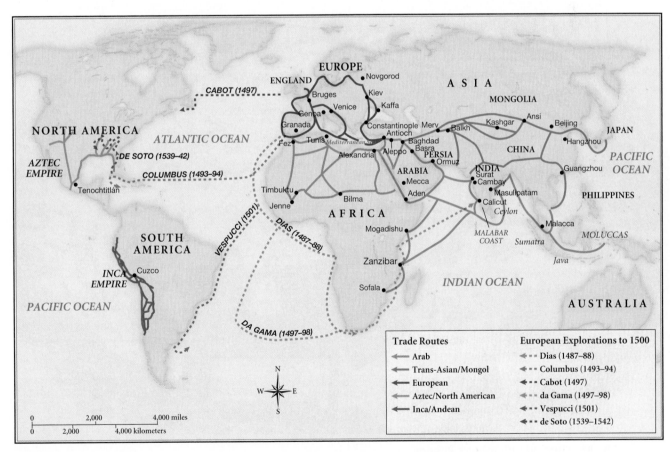

**MAP 1.4**
**The Eurasian Trade System and European Maritime Ventures, c. 1500**
For centuries, the Mediterranean Sea was the meeting point for the commerce of Europe, North Africa, and Asia — via the Silk Road from China and the Spice Route from India. Beginning in the 1490s, Portuguese, Spanish, and Dutch rulers and merchants subsidized Christian maritime explorers who discovered new trade routes around Africa and new sources of wealth in the Americas. These initiatives undermined the commercial primacy of the Arab Muslim–dominated Mediterranean.

the ruler of the powerful Songhai Empire, personally owned twelve "tribes" of hereditary agricultural slaves, many of them seized in raids against stateless peoples.

Slaves were also central to the trans-Saharan trade. When the renowned Tunisian adventurer Ibn Battuta crossed the Sahara from the Kingdom of Mali around 1350, he traveled with a caravan of six hundred female slaves, destined for domestic service or concubinage in North Africa, Egypt, and the Ottoman Empire. Between A.D. 700 and 1900, it is estimated that as many as nine million Africans were sold in the trans-Saharan slave trade.

Europeans initially were much more interested in trading for gold and other commodities than in trading for human beings, but gradually they discovered the enormous value of human trafficking. To exploit and redirect the existing African slave trade, Portuguese merchants established fortified trading posts like those in the Indian Ocean beginning at Elmina in 1482,

where they bought gold and slaves from African princes and warlords. First they enslaved a few thousand Africans each year to work on sugar plantations on São Tomé, Cape Verde, the Azores, and Madeira; they also sold slaves in Lisbon, which soon had an African population of 9,000. After 1550, the Atlantic slave trade, a forced diaspora of African peoples, expanded enormously as Europeans set up sugar plantations in Brazil and the West Indies.

## Sixteenth-Century Incursions

As Portuguese traders sailed south and east, the Spanish monarchs Ferdinand II of Aragon and Isabella I of Castile financed an explorer who looked to the west. As Renaissance rulers, Ferdinand (r. 1474–1516) and Isabella (r. 1474–1504) saw national unity and foreign commerce as the keys to power and prosperity. Married in an arranged match to combine their Christian

**The Map Behind Columbus's Voyage**

In 1489, Henricus Martellus, a German cartographer living in Florence, produced this huge (4 feet by 6 feet) view of the known world, probably working from a map devised by Christopher Columbus's brother, Bartholomew. The map uses the spatial projection of the ancient Greek philosopher Claudius Ptolemy (A.D. 90–168) and incorporates information from Marco Polo's explorations in Asia and Bartolomeu Dias's recent voyage around the tip of Africa. Most important, it greatly exaggerates the width of Eurasia, thereby suggesting that Asia lies only 5,000 miles west of Europe (rather than the actual distance of 15,000 miles). Using Martellus's map, Columbus persuaded the Spanish monarchs to support his westward voyage. Bildarchiv Preussischer Kulturbesitz/Art Resource, NY.

kingdoms, the young rulers completed the centuries-long *reconquista*, the campaign by Spanish Catholics to drive Muslim Arabs from the European mainland, by capturing Granada, the last Islamic territory in Western Europe, in 1492. Using Catholicism to build a sense of "Spanishness," they launched the brutal Inquisition against suspected Christian heretics and expelled or forcibly converted thousands of Jews and Muslims.

**Columbus and the Caribbean**   Simultaneously, Ferdinand and Isabella sought trade and empire by subsidizing the voyages of Christopher Columbus, an ambitious and daring mariner from Genoa. Columbus believed that the Atlantic Ocean, long feared by Arab merchants as a 10,000-mile-wide "green sea of darkness," was a much narrower channel of water separating Europe from Asia. After cajoling and lobbying for six years, Columbus persuaded Genoese investors in Seville; influential courtiers; and, finally, Ferdinand and Isabella to accept his dubious theories and finance a western voyage to Asia.

Columbus set sail in three small ships in August 1492. Six weeks later, after a perilous voyage of 3,000 miles, he disembarked on an island in the present-day Bahamas. Believing that he had reached Asia — "the Indies," in fifteenth-century parlance — Columbus called the native inhabitants Indians and the islands the West Indies. He was surprised by the crude living conditions but expected the native peoples "easily [to] be made Christians." He claimed the islands for Spain and then explored the neighboring Caribbean islands and demanded tribute from the local Taino, Arawak, and Carib peoples. Buoyed by stories of rivers of gold lying "to the west," Columbus left forty men on the island of Hispaniola (present-day Haiti and the Dominican Republic) and returned triumphantly to Spain (Map 1.5).

 To see a longer excerpt of Columbus's views of the West Indies, along with other primary sources from this period, see *Sources for America's History.*

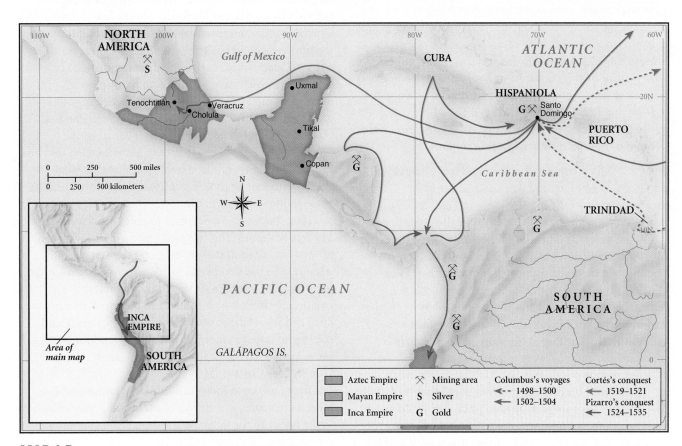

**MAP 1.5**

**The Spanish Conquest of America's Great Empires**

The Spanish first invaded the islands of the Caribbean, largely wiping out the native peoples. Rumors of a gold-rich civilization led to Cortés's invasion of the Aztec Empire in 1519. By 1535, other Spanish conquistadors had conquered the Mayan temple cities and the Inca empire in Peru, completing one of the great conquests in world history.

## The Spanish Conquest of Mexico

How could a Spanish force of 600 men take control of an empire of 20 million people? That the Spanish had steel swords, armor, some guns, horses, and attack dogs certainly gave them a military advantage. Still, concerted attack by the armies of the Aztecs and their allies would have overwhelmed the invaders before they reached the capital of Tenochtitlán. Why was there no such attack? One reason was that Cortés's force was bolstered by a sizable army from Tlaxcala, an independent kingdom hostile to the Aztecs. A later tradition also suggests that some Aztecs, including Moctezuma, thought that Cortés might be an emissary of their god Quetzalcoatl.

These documents come from people who experienced the conquest. Consider them first as *sources*: How trustworthy are they? Are they biased in any way? Then think about their *contents*: Do their accounts agree? Do they explain why the Spaniards reached the city unmolested?

### Bernal Díaz del Castillo

### Cortés and Moctezuma Meet

Bernal Díaz was an unlikely chronicler of great events. Born poor, he went to America as a common soldier in 1514 and served under conquistadors in Panama and Cuba. In 1519, Bernal Díaz joined Cortés's expedition, fought in many battles, and as a reward received an estate in present-day Guatemala. In his old age, Díaz wrote *The True History of the Conquest of New Spain*, a compelling memoir written from the perspective of a common soldier. In fresh and straightforward prose, it depicts the conquest as a divinely blessed event that saved the non-Aztec peoples of Mexico from a barbarous regime.

The Great Moctezuma had sent these great Caciques in advance to receive us, and when they came before Cortés they bade us welcome in their language, and as a sign of peace, they touched their hands against the ground. . . .

When we arrived near to [Tenochtitlán], . . . the Great Moctezuma got down from his litter, and those great Caciques [aristocrats] supported him with their arms beneath a marvelously rich canopy of green coloured feathers with much gold and silver embroidery . . . which was wonderful to look at. The Great Moctezuma was richly attired according to his usage, and he was shod with sandals, the soles were of gold and the upper part adorned with precious stones. . . .

Many other Lords walked before the Great Moctezuma, sweeping the ground where he would tread and spreading cloths on it, so that he should not tread on the earth. Not one of these chieftains dared even to think of looking him in the face, but kept their eyes lowered with great reverence. . . .

When Cortés was told that the Great Moctezuma was approaching, and he saw him coming, he dismounted from his horse, and when he was near Moctezuma, they simultaneously paid great reverence to one another. Moctezuma bade him welcome and our Cortés replied through Doña Marina [Malinali, also called Malinche, Cortés's Indian interpreter who bore him a child] wishing him very good health. . . . And then Cortés brought out a necklace which he had ready at hand, made of glass stones, . . . which have within them many patterns of diverse colours, these were strung on a cord of gold and with musk so that it should have a sweet scent, and he placed it round the neck of the Great Moctezuma. . . . Then Cortés through the mouth of Doña Marina told him that now his heart rejoiced having seen such a great Prince, and that he took it as a great honour that he had come in person to meet him. . . .

Thus space was made for us to enter the streets of Mexico, without being so much crowded. But who could now count the multitude of men and women and boys who were in the streets and in canoes on the canals, who had come out to see us. It was indeed wonderful. . . . Coming to think it over it seems to be a great mercy that our Lord Jesus Christ was pleased to give us grace and courage to dare to enter into such a city; and for the many times He has saved me from danger of death . . . I give Him sincere thanks. . . .

They took us to lodge in some large houses, where there were apartments for all of us, for they had belonged to the father of the Great Moctezuma, who was named Axayaca. . . .

Cortés thanked Moctezuma through our interpreters, and Moctezuma replied, "Malinche, you and your brethren are in your own house, rest awhile," and then he went to his palaces, which were not far away, and we divided our lodgings by companies, and placed the artillery pointing in a convenient direction, and the order which we had to keep was clearly explained to us, and that we were to be much on the alert, both the cavalry and all of us soldiers. A sumptuous dinner was provided for us according to their use and custom, and we ate it at once. So this was our lucky and daring entry into the great city of Tenochtitlan Mexico on the 8th day of November the year of our Saviour Jesus Christ, 1519.

Source: Bernal Díaz del Castillo, *The True History of the Conquest of New Spain*, trans. A. P. Maudslay (1632; London: Routledge, 1928), 272–275.

### Friar Bernardino de Sahagún

## Aztec Elders Describe the Behavior of Moctezuma

During the 1550s, Friar Bernardino de Sahagún published *General History of the Things of New Spain*. His *History* compiled the stories of Aztec elders who lived through the conquest. They told their stories to Sahagún in a repetitive style, according to the conventions of Aztec oral histories, and he translated them into Spanish.

Moctezuma enjoyed no sleep, no food, no one spoke to him. Whatsoever he did, it was as if he were in torment. Ofttimes it was as if he sighed, became weak, felt weak. . . . Wherefore he said, "What will now befall us? Who indeed stands [in charge]? Alas, until now, I. In great torment is my heart; as if it were washed in chili water it indeed burns." And when he had so heard what the messengers reported, he was terrified, he was astounded. . . . Especially did it cause him to faint away when he heard how the gun, at [the Spaniards'] command, discharged: how it resounded as if it thundered when it went off. It indeed bereft one of strength; it shut off one's ears. And when it discharged, something like a round pebble came forth from within. Fire went showering forth; sparks went blazing forth. And its smoke smelled very foul; it had a fetid odor which verily wounded the head. And when [the shot] struck a mountain, it was as if it were destroyed, dissolved . . . as if someone blew it away.

All iron was their war array. In iron they clothed themselves. With iron they covered their heads. Iron were their swords. Iron were their crossbows. Iron were their shields. Iron were their lances. And those which bore them upon their backs, their deer [horses], were as tall as roof terraces.

And their bodies were everywhere covered; only their faces appeared. They were very white; they had chalky faces; they had yellow hair, though the hair of some was black. . . . And when Moctezuma so heard, he was much terrified. It was as if he fainted away. His heart saddened; his heart failed him. . . . [but] he made himself resolute; he put forth great effort; he quieted, he controlled his heart; he submitted himself entirely to whatsoever he was to see, at which he was to marvel. . . . [He then greeted Cortés, as described above.]

And when [the Spaniards] were well settled, they thereupon inquired of Moctezuma as to all the city's treasure . . . the devices, the shields. Much did they importune him; with great zeal they sought gold. . . . Thereupon were brought forth all the brilliant things; the shields, the golden discs, the devils' necklaces, the golden nose crescents, the golden leg bands, the golden arm bands, the golden forehead bands.

Source: From Friar Bernardino de Sahagún, *Florentine Codex: General History of New Spain*, translated by Arthur O. Anderson and Charles E. Dibble. Copyright © 1975. Reprinted by permission of Utah Press.

### QUESTIONS FOR ANALYSIS

1. Both Díaz's account and that of the Aztec elders were written in retrospect, and both reflect their authors' awareness of the impending conquest. Compare the tone of these accounts. How does each reflect the author's knowledge of what is to come?

2. Why does Moctezuma pay "great reverence" to Cortés? Why does Cortés return the honor? What is the strategy of each leader?

3. What is Díaz's explanation for the easy entry of the Spanish into the city? What explanation is suggested by the elders' account?

Although Columbus brought back no gold, the Spanish monarchs supported three more of his voyages. Columbus colonized the West Indies with more than 1,000 Spanish settlers — all men — and hundreds of domestic animals. But he failed to find either golden treasures or great kingdoms, and his death in 1506 went virtually unnoticed.

A German geographer soon labeled the newly found continents America in honor of a Florentine explorer, Amerigo Vespucci. Vespucci, who had explored the coast of present-day South America around 1500, denied that the region was part of Asia. He called it a *nuevo mundo*, a "new world." The Spanish crown called the two continents *Las Indias* ("the Indies") and wanted to make them a new Spanish world.

**The Spanish Invasion**    After brutally subduing the Arawaks and Tainos on Hispaniola, the Spanish probed the mainland for gold and slaves. In 1513, Juan Ponce de León explored the coast of Florida and gave that peninsula its name. In the same year, Vasco Núñez de Balboa crossed the Isthmus of Darien (Panama) and became the first European to see the Pacific Ocean. Rumors of rich Indian kingdoms encouraged other Spaniards, including hardened veterans of the *reconquista*, to invade the mainland. The Spanish monarchs offered successful conquistadors noble titles, vast estates, and Indian laborers.

With these inducements before him, in 1519 Hernán Cortés (1485–1547) led an army of 600 men to the Yucatán Peninsula. Gathering allies among native peoples who chafed under Aztec rule, he marched on Tenochtitlán and challenged its ruler, Moctezuma. Awed by the Spanish invaders, Moctezuma received Cortés with great ceremony (American Voices, p. 32). However, Cortés soon took the emperor captive, and following a prolonged siege, he and his men captured the city. The conquest took a devastating toll: the

**Mexican Counterattack**

This image, which comes from a history of the Aztecs written in 1570 by the Spanish Dominican monk Diego Durán, illustrates a successful counterattack by Mexica warriors against Spanish soldiers prior to the final conquest of Tenochtitlán. The Spaniards try to hold their position as the Mexicans prepare to strike. Institut Amatller d'Art Hispanic/Arxiu Mas.

conquerors cut off the city's supply of food and water, and the residents of Tenochtitlán suffered spectacularly. By 1521, Cortés and his men had toppled the Aztec Empire.

The Spanish had a silent ally: disease. Having been separated from Eurasia for thousands of years, the inhabitants of the Americas had no immunities to common European diseases. After the Spaniards arrived, a massive smallpox epidemic ravaged Tenochtitlán, "striking everywhere in the city," according to an Aztec source, and killing Moctezuma's brother and thousands more. "They could not move, they could not stir. . . . Covered, mantled with pustules, very many people died of them." Subsequent outbreaks of smallpox, influenza, and measles killed hundreds of thousands of Indians and sapped the survivors' morale. Exploiting this demographic weakness, Cortés quickly extended Spanish rule over the Aztec Empire. His lieutenants then moved against the Mayan city-states of the Yucatán Peninsula, eventually conquering them as well.

In 1524, Francisco Pizarro set out to accomplish the same feat in Peru. By the time he and his small force of 168 men and 67 horses finally reached their destination in 1532, half of the Inca population had already died from European diseases. Weakened militarily and divided between rival claimants to the throne, the Inca nobility was easy prey. Pizarro killed Atahualpa, the last Inca emperor, and seized his enormous wealth. Although Inca resistance continued for a generation, the conquest was complete by 1535, and Spain was now the master of the wealthiest and most populous regions of the Western Hemisphere.

The Spanish invasion changed life forever in the Americas. Disease and warfare wiped out virtually all of the Indians of Hispaniola — at least 300,000 people. In Peru, the population of 9 million in 1530 plummeted to fewer than 500,000 a century later. Mesoamerica suffered the greatest losses: In one of the great demographic disasters in world history, its population of 20 million Native Americans in 1500 had dwindled to just 3 million in 1650.

**Cabral and Brazil**   At the same time, Portuguese efforts to find a sailing route around the southern tip of Africa led to a surprising find. As Vasco da Gama and his contemporaries experimented with winds and currents, their voyages carried them ever farther away from the African coast and into the Atlantic. On one such voyage in 1500, the Portuguese commander Pedro Alvares Cabral and his fleet were surprised to see land loom up in the west. Cabral named his discovery Ihla da Vera Cruz — the Island of the True Cross — and continued on his way toward India. Others soon followed and changed the region's name to Brazil after the indigenous tree that yielded a valuable red dye; for several decades, Portuguese sailors traded with the Tupi Indians for brazilwood. Then in the 1530s, to secure Portugal's claim, King Dom João III sent settlers who began the long, painstaking process of carving out sugar plantations in the coastal lowlands. For several decades, Native Americans supplied most of the labor for these operations, but African slaves gradually replaced them. Brazil would soon become the world's leading producer of sugar; it would also devour African lives. By introducing the plantation system to the Americas — a form of estate agriculture using slave labor that was pioneered by Italian merchants and crusading knights in the twelfth century and transplanted to the islands off the coast of Africa in the fifteenth century — the Portuguese set in motion one of the most significant developments of the early modern era.

By the end of the sixteenth century, the European colonization of the Americas had barely begun. Yet several of its most important elements were already taking shape. Spanish efforts demonstrated that densely populated empires were especially vulnerable to conquest and were also especially valuable sources of wealth. The Portuguese had discovered the viability of sugar plantations in the tropical regions of the Americas and pioneered the transatlantic slave trade as a way of manning them. And contacts with native peoples revealed their devastating vulnerabilities to Eurasian diseases — one part of the larger phenomenon of the Columbian Exchange (discussed in Chapter 2).

# SUMMARY

Native American, European, and African societies developed independently over thousands of years before they experienced direct contacts with one another. In the Americas, residents of Mesoamerica and the Andes were fully sedentary (with individual ownership of land and intensive agriculture), but elsewhere societies were semisedentary (with central fields and villages that were occupied seasonally) or nonsedentary (hunter-gatherers). West and Central Africa also had a mix of sedentary, semisedentary, and nonsedentary settlements. Western Europe, by contrast, was predominantly sedentary. All three continents had a complex patchwork of political organization, from empires, to kingdoms and chiefdoms, to principalities, duchies, and ministates; everywhere, rulership was imbued with notions of spiritual power. Ruling classes relied on warfare, trade, and tribute (or taxes) to dominate those around them and accumulate precious goods that helped to set them apart from ordinary laborers, but they also bore responsibility for the well-being of their subjects and offered them various forms of protection.

As Portuguese and Castilian (later Spanish) seafarers pushed into the Atlantic, they set in motion a chain of events whose consequences they could scarcely imagine. From a coastal trade with Africa that was secondary to their efforts to reach the Indian Ocean, from the miscalculations of Columbus and the happy accident of Cabral, developed a pattern of transatlantic exploration, conquest, and exploitation that no one could have foretold or planned. In the tropical zones of the Caribbean and coastal Brazil, invading Europeans enslaved Native Americans and quickly drove them into extinction or exile. The demands of plantation agriculture soon led Europeans to import slaves from Africa, initiating a transatlantic trade that would destroy African lives on both sides of the ocean. And two of the greatest empires in the world — the Aztec and Incan empires — collapsed in response to unseen biological forces that acted in concert with small invading armies.

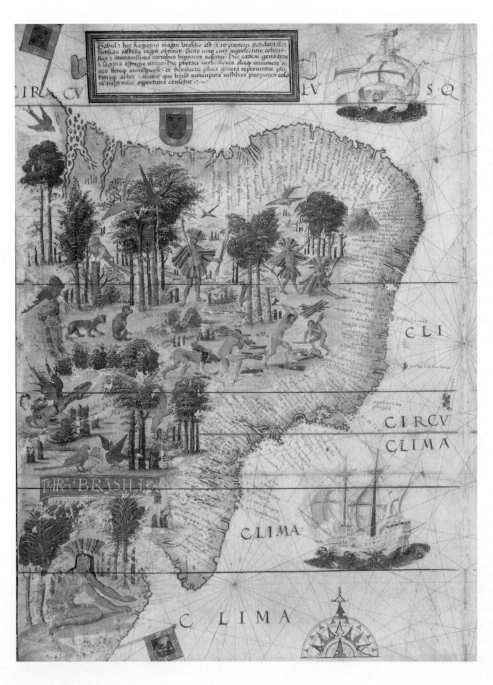

**European Map of Brazil, c. 1519**

This lavishly illustrated map of Brazil is drawn from the Miller Atlas, made by order of King Manuel I of Portugal around 1519. It features images of Indians harvesting brazilwood; macaws and other colorful birds; a monkey; and—improbably—a fire-breathing dragon. Note, too, the dense annotations and place names along the coast—a reminder that Portuguese familiarity with Brazil was confined almost entirely to the seaboard. Bibliotheque Nationale de France.

# CHAPTER REVIEW

**MAKE IT STICK**   Go to **LearningCurve** to retain what you've read.

## TERMS TO KNOW   Identify and explain the significance of each term below.

### Key Concepts and Events

tribute (p. 8)

matriarchy (p. 15)

animism (p. 17)

patriarchy (p. 18)

primogeniture (p. 18)

peasants (p. 18)

republic (p. 19)

civic humanism (p. 20)

Renaissance (p. 20)

guilds (p. 20)

Christianity (p. 21)

heresy (p. 22)

Islam (p. 22)

Crusades (p. 22)

predestination (p. 22)

Protestant Reformation (p. 22)

Counter-Reformation (p. 22)

trans-Saharan trade (p. 23)

*reconquista* (p. 31)

### Key People

Hiawatha (p. 13)

Martin Luther (p. 22)

Mansa Musa (p. 23)

Vasco da Gama (p. 29)

Christopher Columbus (p. 31)

Hernán Cortés (p. 34)

Moctezuma (p. 34)

Pedro Alvares Cabral (p. 35)

## REVIEW QUESTIONS   Answer these questions to demonstrate your understanding of the chapter's main ideas.

1. How did the rulers of Native American, European, and African empires and kingdoms secure and sustain their power? How did ordinary people benefit from, or suffer under, their rule?

2. What role did religious and spiritual ideas play in shaping the experience of ordinary people on the three continents?

3. Why was long-distance trade in exotic goods such an important phenomenon in North America, Europe, and Africa?

4. Compare the societies of the eastern woodlands of North America with the kingdoms of Western Europe. What similarities do you see? Differences? How do you weigh their relative importance?

5. **THEMATIC UNDERSTANDING**  Review the events listed under "Peopling" and "Work, Exchange, and Technology" on the thematic timeline on page 5. How did contacts among Europeans, Native Americans, and Africans alter the economies of the three continents?

## MAKING CONNECTIONS

Recognize the larger developments and continuities within and across chapters by answering these questions.

1. **ACROSS TIME AND PLACE** The century following the first contacts among Europe, sub-Saharan Africa, and the Americas brought some of the most momentous changes in world history: a dramatic reconfiguration of human populations across the globe, new patterns of trade and warfare, and immense challenges to peoples' worldviews. Thinking about our contemporary world, what monumental changes are currently affecting our lives? How would you compare them with the events described in this chapter?

2. **VISUAL EVIDENCE** Return to the image of *The Last Judgment* on page 21. How does the emphasis on universal truth and everlasting punishment and reward make Christianity different from animism? How might faith in such a religious system shape the values and priorities of believers?

## MORE TO EXPLORE

Start here to learn more about the events discussed in this chapter.

Philip D. Curtin, *The Rise and Fall of the Plantation Complex,* 2nd ed. (1998). Traces the long evolution of plantations and slavery in world history.

Peter C. Mancall, ed., *Travel Narratives from the Age of Discovery* (2006). Travelers' accounts from Asia, Africa, the Americas, and Europe.

Charles C. Mann, *1491* (2005) and *1493* (2011). These two books explore the Americas before Columbus and the global changes unleashed by his voyages.

David Northrup, *Africa's Discovery of Europe: 1450–1850,* 2nd ed. (2008). European-African interactions from an African perspective.

Timothy R. Pauketat, *Cahokia* (2009). An evocative account of North America's great city and archaeologists' efforts to unearth it.

"1492: An Ongoing Voyage" (**loc.gov/exhibits/1492/intro.html**). Offers images and analysis of the native cultures of the Western Hemisphere.

## TIMELINE

Ask yourself why this chapter begins and ends with these dates and then identify the links among related events.

| | |
|---|---|
| c. 13,000–3000 B.C. | • Asian migrants reach North America |
| c. 6000 B.C. | • Domestication of maize begins in Mesoamerica |
| 312 | • Roman emperor Constantine converts to Christianity |
| c. 600 | • Pueblo cultures emerge |
| 632 | • Death of Muhammad |
| 632–1100 | • Arab people adopt Islam and spread its influence |
| c. 800 | • Ghana Empire emerges |
| c. 1000 | • Irrigation developed by Hohokam, Mogollon, and Anasazi peoples |
| c. 1000–1350 | • Development of Mississippian culture |
| c. 1050 | • The founding of Cahokia |
| 1096–1291 | • Crusades link Europe with Arab trade routes |
| c. 1150 | • Chaco Canyon abandoned |
| c. 1200 | • Mali Empire emerges |
| 1300–1450 | • The Renaissance in Italy |
| c. 1325 | • Aztecs establish capital at Tenochtitlán |
| 1326 | • Mansa Musa's pilgrimage to Mecca |
| c. 1350 | • The Black Death sweeps Europe; Cahokia goes into rapid decline |
| c. 1400 | • Songhai Empire emerges |
| 1435 | • Portuguese trade begins along West and Central African coasts |
| 1492 | • Christopher Columbus makes first voyage to America |
| 1497–1498 | • Portugal's Vasco da Gama reaches East Africa and India |
| 1500 | • Pedro Alvares Cabral encounters Brazil |
| c. 1500 | • Founding of the Iroquois Confederacy |
| 1513 | • Juan Ponce de León explores Florida |
| 1517 | • Martin Luther sparks Protestant Reformation |
| 1519–1521 | • Hernán Cortés conquers Aztec Empire |
| 1532–1535 | • Francisco Pizarro vanquishes Incas |
| 1536 | • John Calvin publishes *Institutes of the Christian Religion* |
| 1540 | • De Soto meets the Lady of Cofachiqui; founding of the Jesuit order |
| 1578 | • Duarte Lopez visits the Kongo capital |

**KEY TURNING POINTS:** The domestication of maize (6000 B.C.), the founding of Tenochtitlán (1325), and the conquest of the Aztec empire (1519–1521). How did the domestication of maize make the city of Tenochtitlán possible? What characteristics of the Aztec empire and its capital city made it vulnerable to conquest?

# 2 American Experiments 1521–1700

Beginning in the 1660s, legislators in Virginia and Maryland hammered out the legal definition of **chattel slavery**: the ownership of human beings as property. The institution of slavery — which would profoundly affect African Americans and shape much of American history — had been obsolete in England for centuries, and articulating its logic required lawmakers to reverse some of the most basic presumptions of English law. For example, in 1662 a Virginia statute declared, "all children borne in this country shalbe held bond or free only according to the condition of the mother." This idea — that a child's legal status derived from the mother, rather than the father — ran contrary to the patriarchal foundations of English law. The men who sat in Virginia's House of Burgesses would not propose such a thing lightly. Why would they decide that the principle of patriarchal descent, which was so fundamental to their own worlds, was inappropriate for their slaves?

The question needed to be addressed, according to the statute's preamble, since "doubts have arisen whether children got by an Englishman upon a negro woman should be slave or free." One such case involved Elizabeth Key, a woman whose father was a free Englishman and mother was an African slave. She petitioned for her freedom in 1656, based on her father's status. Her lawyer was an Englishman named William Greensted. He not only took Key's case, but he also fathered two of her children and, eventually, married her. Key won her case and her freedom from bondage. Elizabeth Key escaped her mother's fate — a life in slavery — because her father and her husband were both free Englishmen. The 1662 statute aimed to close Key's avenue to freedom.

The process by which the institution of chattel slavery was molded to the needs of colonial planters is just one example of the way Europeans adapted the principles they brought with them to the unfamiliar demands of their new surroundings. In the showdown between people like Elizabeth Key and William Greensted, on the one hand, and the members of Virginia's House of Burgesses on the other, we see how people in disorienting circumstances — some in positions in power, others in various states of subjection to their social and political superiors — scrambled to make sense of their world and bend its rules to their advantage. Through countless contests of power and authority like this one, the outlines of a new world gradually began to emerge from the collision of cultures.

By 1700, three distinct types of colonies had developed in the Americas: the tribute colonies created in Mexico and Peru, which relied initially on the wealth and labor of indigenous peoples; plantation colonies, where sugar and other tropical and subtropical crops could be produced with bound labor; and **neo-Europes**, where colonists sought to replicate, or at least approximate, economies and social structures they knew at home.

## IDENTIFY THE BIG IDEA

In what ways did European migrants transfer familiar patterns and institutions to their colonies in the Americas, and in what ways did they create new American worlds? How did Native Americans adapt to the growing presence of Europeans among them?

**Power and Race in the Chesapeake** In this 1670 painting by Gerard Soest, proprietor Lord Baltimore holds a map of Maryland, the colony he owned and which would soon belong to his grandson Cecil Calvert, shown in the painting as already grasping his magnificent inheritance. The presence of a young African servant foretells the importance of slave labor in the post-1700 economy of the Chesapeake colonies. Enoch Pratt Free Library, Maryland's State Library Resource Center. All Rights reserved.

# Spain's Tribute Colonies

European interest in the Americas took shape under the influence of Spain's conquest of the Aztec and Inca empires. There, Spanish colonizers capitalized on pre-existing systems of tribute and labor discipline to tap the enormous wealth of Mesoamerica and the Andes. Once native rulers were overthrown, the Spanish monarchs transferred their institutions — municipal councils, the legal code, the Catholic Church — to America; the empire was centrally controlled to protect the crown's immensely valuable holdings. The Spanish conquest also set in motion a global ecological transformation through a vast intercontinental movement of plants, animals, and diseases that historians call the Columbian Exchange. And the conquest triggered hostile responses from Spain's European rivals, especially the Protestant Dutch and English (Figure 2.1).

## A New American World

After Cortés toppled Moctezuma and Pizarro defeated Atahualpa (see pages 34–35), leading conquistadors received *encomiendas* from the crown, which allowed them to claim tribute in labor and goods from Indian communities. Later these grants were repartitioned, but the pattern was set early: prominent men controlled vast resources and monopolized Indian labor. The value of these grants was dramatically enhanced by the discovery of gold and, especially, silver deposits in both Mexico and the Andes. In the decades after the conquest, mines were developed in Zacatecas, in Guanajuato, and — most famously — at Potosí, high in the Andes. Spanish officials co-opted the *mita* system, which made laborers available to the Inca Empire, to force Indian workers into the mines. At its peak, Potosí

alone produced 200 tons of silver per year, accounting for half the world's supply.

The two great indigenous empires of the Americas thus became the core of an astonishingly wealthy European empire. Vast amounts of silver poured across the Pacific Ocean to China, where it was minted into money; in exchange, Spain received valuable Chinese silks, spices, and ceramics. In Europe, the gold that had formerly honored Aztec and Inca gods now flowed into the countinghouses of Spain and gilded the Catholic churches of Europe. The Spanish crown benefitted enormously from all this wealth — at least initially. In the long run, it triggered ruinous inflation. As a French traveler noted in 1603: "Everything is dear [expensive] in Spain, except silver."

A new society took shape on the conquered lands. Between 1500 and 1650, at least 350,000 Spaniards migrated to Mesoamerica and the Andes. About two-thirds were males drawn from a cross section of Spanish society, many of them skilled tradesmen. Also arriving were 250,000–300,000 Africans. Racial mixture was widespread, and such groups as mestizos (Spaniard-Indian) and mulattos (Spaniard-African) grew rapidly. Zambo (Indian-African) populations developed gradually as well. Over time, a system of increasingly complex racial categories developed — the "casta system" — buttressed by a legal code that differentiated among the principal groups.

Indians were always in the majority in Mexico and Peru, but profound changes came as their numbers declined and peoples of Spanish and mixed-race descent grew in number. Spaniards initially congregated in cities, but gradually they moved into the countryside, creating large estates (known as haciendas) and regional networks of market exchange. Most Indians remained in their native communities, under the authority of native rulers and speaking native

**FIGURE 2.1**
**Chronology of European Colonies in the Americas**

languages. However, Spanish priests suppressed religious ceremonies and texts and converted natives to Christianity *en masse*. Catholicism was transformed in the process: Catholic parishes took their form from Indian communities; indigenous ideas and expectations reshaped Church practices; and new forms of Native American Christianity emerged in both regions.

## The Columbian Exchange

The Spanish invasion permanently altered the natural as well as the human environment. Smallpox, influenza, measles, yellow fever, and other silent killers carried from Europe and Africa ravaged Indian communities, whose inhabitants had never encountered these diseases before and thus had no immunity to them. In the densely populated core areas, populations declined by 90 percent or more in the first century of contact with Europeans. On islands and in the tropical lowlands, the toll was even heavier; native populations were often wiped out altogether. Syphilis was the only significant illness that traveled in the opposite direction: Columbus's sailors carried a virulent strain of the sexually transmitted disease back to Europe with them.

The movement of diseases and peoples across the Atlantic was part of a larger pattern of biological transformation that historians call the **Columbian Exchange** (Map 2.1). Foods of the Western Hemisphere—especially maize, potatoes, manioc, sweet potatoes, and tomatoes—

significantly increased agricultural yields and population growth in other continents. Maize and potatoes, for example, reached China around 1700; in the following century, the Chinese population tripled from 100 million to 300 million. At the same time, many animals, plants, and germs were carried to the Americas. European livestock transformed American landscapes. While Native Americans domesticated very few animals—dogs and llamas were the principal exceptions—Europeans brought an enormous Old World bestiary to the Americas, including cattle, swine, horses, oxen, chickens, and honeybees. Eurasian grain crops—wheat, barley, rye, and rice—made the transatlantic voyage along with inadvertent imports like dandelions and other weeds.

**PLACE EVENTS IN CONTEXT**
How did the ecological context of colonization shape interactions between Europeans and Native Americans?

## The Protestant Challenge to Spain

Beyond the core regions of its empire, Spain claimed vast American dominions but struggled to hold them. Controlling the Caribbean basin, which was essential for Spain's transatlantic shipping routes, was especially difficult, since the net of tiny islands spanning the eastern Caribbean—the Lesser Antilles—provided many safe harbors for pirates and privateers. Fortified outposts in Havana and St. Augustine provided some

**Smallpox Victims**

Hans Staden, a German soldier who was shipwrecked in Brazil in 1552, was captured by a Tupinambá Indian named Jeppipo Wasu. Shortly thereafter, Wasu and his family traveled to a neighboring village as smallpox ravaged the population; when they returned, they were very sick. Wasu recovered, but he lost his mother, two brothers, and two children. This engraving, which depicts Wasu's return amid his townspeople's grief, appeared in the third volume of Theodor de Bry's monumental *America*, published in Frankfurt in 1593. Courtesy of the John Carter Brown Library at Brown University.

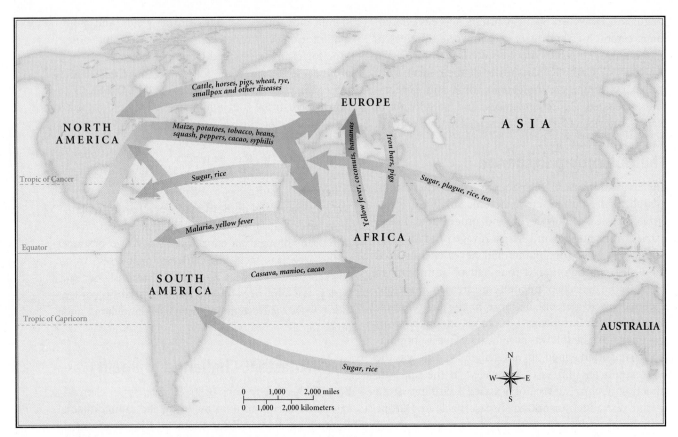

**MAP 2.1**

**The Columbian Exchange**

As European traders and adventurers traversed the world between 1430 and 1600, they began what historians call the Columbian Exchange, a vast intercontinental movement of plants, animals, and diseases that changed the course of historical development. The nutritious, high-yielding American crops of corn and potatoes enriched the diets of Europeans, Africans, and Asians. However, the Eurasian and African diseases of smallpox, diphtheria, malaria, and yellow fever nearly wiped out the native inhabitants of the Western Hemisphere and virtually ensured that they would lose control of their lands.

protection, but they were never sufficient to keep enemies at bay.

And Spain had powerful enemies, their animosity sharpened by the Protestant Reformation and the resulting split in European Christendom (see p. 22). In the wake of Martin Luther's attack on the Catholic Church, the Protestant critique of Catholicism broadened and deepened. Gold and silver from Mexico and Peru made Spain the wealthiest nation in Europe, and King Philip II (r. 1556–1598)—an ardent Catholic—its most powerful ruler. Philip was determined to root out challenges to the Catholic Church wherever they appeared. One such place was in the Spanish Netherlands, a collection of Dutch- and Flemish-speaking provinces that had grown wealthy from textile manufacturing and trade with Portuguese outposts in Africa and Asia. To protect their Calvinist faith and political liberties, they revolted against Spanish rule in

1566. After fifteen years of war, the seven northern provinces declared their independence, becoming the Dutch Republic (or Holland) in 1581.

The English king Henry VIII (r. 1509–1547) initially opposed Protestantism. However, when the pope refused to annul his marriage to the Spanish princess Catherine of Aragon in 1534, Henry broke with Rome and placed himself at the head of the new Church of England, which promptly granted an annulment. Although Henry's new church maintained most Catholic doctrines and practices, Protestant teachings continued to spread. Faced with popular pressure for reform, Henry's daughter and successor, Queen Elizabeth I (r. 1558–1603), approved a Protestant confession of faith. At the same time, however, Elizabeth retained the Catholic ritual of Holy Communion and left the Church in the hands of Anglican bishops and archbishops. Elizabeth's compromises angered radical

**Queen Elizabeth Receiving Dutch Ambassadors**

This sixteenth-century Dutch painting by an anonymous artist depicts a pair of Dutch ambassadors being received by England's Queen Elizabeth I. The seventeen provinces that constituted the Dutch Republic were in rebellion against Spanish rule in the later decades of the sixteenth century and hoped for Elizabeth's support. In 1585 she signed the Treaty of Nonsuch, pledging her support for the Dutch cause. An undeclared war with Spain ensued, punctuated by the defeat of the Spanish Armada in 1588. © Museumslandschaft Hessen Kassel/ The Bridgeman Art Library.

Protestants, but the independent Anglican Church was anathema to the Spanish king, Philip II.

Elizabeth supported a generation of English seafarers who took increasingly aggressive actions against Spanish control of American wealth. The most famous of these Elizabethan "sea dogs" was Francis Drake, a rough-hewn, devoutly Protestant farmer's son from Devon who took to the sea and became a scourge to Philip's American interests. In 1577, he ventured into the Pacific to disrupt Spanish shipping to Manila. Drake's fleet lost three ships and a hundred men, but the survivors completed the first English circumnavigation of the globe and captured two Spanish treasure ships. When Drake's flagship, the *Golden Hind,* returned to England in 1580, it brought enough silver, gold, silk, and spices to bring his investors a 4,700 percent return on their investment.

At the same time, Elizabeth supported military expeditions that imposed English rule over Gaelic-speaking Catholic Ireland. Calling the Irish "wild savages" who were "more barbarous and more brutish in their customs . . . than in any other part of the world," English soldiers brutally massacred thousands, prefiguring the treatment of Indians in North America. To meet Elizabeth's challenges, Philip sent a Spanish Armada — 130 ships and 30,000 men — against England in 1588. Philip intended to restore the Roman Church in England and then to wipe out Calvinism in Holland. But he failed utterly: a fierce storm and English ships destroyed the Spanish fleet.

Philip continued to spend his American gold and silver on religious wars, an ill-advised policy that diverted workers and resources from Spain's fledgling industries. The gold was like a "shewer of Raine," complained one critic, that left "no benefite behind." Oppressed by high taxes on agriculture and fearful of military service, more than 200,000 residents of Castile, once the most prosperous region of Spain, migrated to America. By the time of Philip's death in 1598, Spain was in serious economic decline.

By contrast, England grew significantly during the sixteenth century, its economy stimulated, as colonial advocate Richard Hakluyt noted, by a "wounderful increase of our people." As England's population soared from 3 million in 1500 to 5 million in 1630, its monarchs supported the expansion of commerce and manufacturing. English merchants had long supplied European weavers with high-quality wool; around 1500, they created their own **outwork** textile industry. Merchants bought wool from the owners of great estates and sent it "out" to landless peasants in small cottages to spin and weave into cloth. The government aided textile entrepreneurs by setting low wage rates and helped merchants by giving them monopolies in foreign markets.

This system of state-assisted manufacturing and trade became known as **mercantilism**. By encouraging textile production, Elizabeth reduced imports and increased exports. The resulting favorable balance of trade caused gold and silver to flow into England and stimulated further economic expansion. Increased trade

**TRACE CHANGE OVER TIME**

Why did Spain's economy deteriorate and England's economy improve in the sixteenth century?

with Turkey and India also boosted import duties, which swelled the royal treasury and the monarch's power. By 1600, Elizabeth's mercantile policies had laid the foundations for overseas colonization. Now the English had the merchant fleet and wealth needed to challenge Spain's control of the Western Hemisphere.

# Plantation Colonies

As Spain hammered out its American empire and struggled against its Protestant rivals, Portugal, England, France, and the Netherlands created successful plantation settlements in Brazil, Jamestown, Maryland, and the Caribbean islands (Map 2.2). Worldwide demand for sugar and tobacco fuelled the growth of these new colonies, and the resulting influx of colonists diminished Spain's dominance in the New World. At the same time, they imposed dramatic new pressures on native populations, who scrambled, in turn, to survive the present and carve out pathways to the future.

## Brazil's Sugar Plantations

Portuguese colonists transformed the tropical lowlands of coastal Brazil into a sugar plantation zone like the ones they had recently created on Madeira, the Azores, the Cape Verdes, and São Tomé. The work proceeded slowly, but by 1590 more than a thousand sugar mills had been established in Pernambuco and Bahia. Each large plantation had its own milling operation: because sugarcane is extremely heavy and rots quickly, it must be processed on site. Thus sugar plantations combined backbreaking agricultural labor with milling, extracting, and refining processes that made sugar plantations look like Industrial Revolution–era factories.

Initially, Portuguese planters hoped that Brazil's indigenous peoples would supply the labor required to

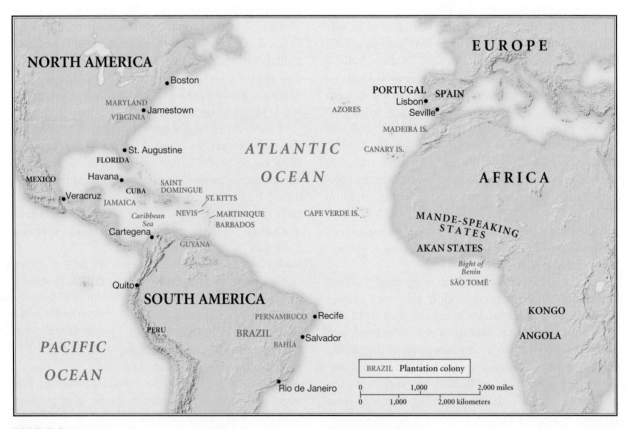

**MAP 2.2**
**The Plantation Colonies**
The plantation zone in the Americas extended from the tropical coast of Brazil northwestward through the West Indies and into the tropical and subtropical lowlands of southeastern North America. Sugar was the most important plantation crop in the Americas, but where the soil or climate could not support it planters experimented with a wide variety of other possibilities, including tobacco, indigo, cotton, cacao, and rice.

operate their sugar plantations. But, beginning with a wave of smallpox in 1559, unfamiliar diseases soon ravaged the coastal Indian population. As a result, planters turned to African slaves in ever-growing numbers; by 1620, the switch was complete. While Spanish colonies in Mexico and Peru took shape with astonishing speed following conquest, Brazil's occupation and development progressed more gradually; it required both trial and error and hard work to build a paying colony.

## England's Tobacco Colonies

England was slow to embrace the prospect of planting colonies in the Americas. There were fumbling attempts in the 1580s in Newfoundland and Maine, privately organized and poorly funded. Sir Walter Raleigh's three expeditions to North Carolina likewise ended in

disaster when 117 settlers on Roanoke Island, left unsupplied for several years, vanished. The fate of Roanoke—the "lost colony"—remains a compelling puzzle for modern historians.

**The Jamestown Settlement**  Merchants then took charge of English expansion. In 1606, King James I (r. 1603–1625) granted to the Virginia Company of London all the lands stretching from present-day North Carolina to southern New York. To honor the memory of Elizabeth I, the never-married "Virgin Queen," the company's directors named the region Virginia (Map 2.3). Influenced by the Spanish example, in 1607 the Virginia Company dispatched an all-male group with no ability to support itself—no women, farmers, or ministers were among the first arrivals—that expected to extract tribute from the region's Indian

**Carolina Indians Fishing, 1585**

Though maize was a mainstay of the Indian diet, native peoples along the Atlantic coast also harvested protein-rich fish, crabs, and oysters. In this watercolor by the English adventurer John White, Indians gather fish (in their "cannow," or dugout canoe) in the shallow waters of the Albemarle Sound, off present-day North Carolina. On the left, note the weir used both to catch fish and to store them live for later consumption.
© Trustees of the British Museum/Art Resource, NY.

**John White's Map of Virginia**

This map, drawn by Roanoke colonist John White, may hold a clue to the fate of the so-called lost colony. The island of Roanoke is right of center, just off the mainland and within the barrier islands. Directly west, on the point where the Roanoke and Chowan rivers join, is a (barely visible) paper patch. When lit from behind, a red fort is clearly visible beneath the patch, suggesting that the Roanoke colonists may already have identified a settlement site there: when he left the colony, John White wrote that the remaining colonists "were prepared to remove from Roanoak 50 miles into the maine[land]." Archaeologists and historians plan to use this discovery to guide further explorations in the area. The Art Archive at Art Resource, NY.

population while it searched out valuable commodities like pearls and gold. Some were young gentlemen with personal ties to the company's shareholders: a bunch of "unruly Sparks, packed off by their Friends to escape worse Destinies at home." Others hoped to make a quick profit. All they wanted, one of them said, was to "dig gold, refine gold, load gold."

But there was no gold, and the men fared poorly in their new environment. Arriving in Virginia after an exhausting four-month voyage, they settled on a swampy peninsula, which they named Jamestown to honor the king. There the adventurers lacked access to fresh water, refused to plant crops, and quickly died off; only

**MAP 2.3**

**Eastern North America, 1650**

By 1650, four European nations had permanent settlements along the eastern coast of North America, but only England had substantial numbers of settlers, some 25,000 in New England and another 15,000 in the Chesapeake region. French, Dutch, Swedish, and English colonists were also trading European manufactures to Native Americans in exchange for animal furs and skins, with far-reaching implications for Indian societies.

**John Smith and Opechancanough**

The powerful Indian warrior Opechancanough towers over English explorer John Smith in this engraving. In December 1607, Smith led a party of Jamestown colonists upriver in search of Indian food supplies. Two hundred warriors intercepted them, captured Smith, and took him to the Powhatan village of Werowacomoco. It was on this occasion that Pocahontas supposedly interceded to save his life (see Thinking Like a Historian, p. 50). The note at the bottom of the engraving is doubly mistaken, as it was Opechancanough (not Powhatan) who took Smith captive. Library of Congress.

C Smith taketh the King of Pamaunkee prisoner  1608

38 of the 120 men were alive nine months later. Death rates remained high: by 1611, the Virginia Company had dispatched 1,200 colonists to Jamestown, but fewer than half remained alive. "Our men were destroyed with cruell diseases, as Swellings, Fluxes, Burning Fevers, and by warres," reported one of the settlement's leaders, "but for the most part they died of meere famine."

Their plan to dominate the local Indian population ran up against the presence of Powhatan, the powerful chief who oversaw some thirty tribal chiefdoms between the James and Potomac rivers. He was willing to treat the English traders as potential allies who could provide valuable goods, but — just as the Englishmen expected tribute from the Indians — Powhatan expected tribute from the English. He provided the hungry English adventurers with corn; in return, he demanded "hatchets . . . bells, beads, and copper" as well as "two great guns" and expected Jamestown to become a dependent community within his chiefdom. Subsequently, Powhatan arranged a marriage between his daughter Pocahontas and John Rolfe, an English colonist (Thinking Like a Historian, p. 50). But these tactics failed. The inability to decide who would pay tribute to whom led to more than a decade of uneasy relations, followed by a long era of ruinous warfare.

The war was precipitated by the discovery of a cash crop that — like sugar in Brazil — offered colonists a way to turn a profit but required steady expansion onto Indian lands. Tobacco was a plant native to the Americas, long used by Indians as a medicine and a stimulant. John Rolfe found a West Indian strain that could flourish in Virginia soil and produced a small crop — "pleasant, sweet, and strong" — that fetched a high price in England and spurred the migration of thousands of new settlers. The English soon came to crave the nicotine that tobacco contained. James I initially condemned the plant as a "vile Weed" whose "black stinking fumes" were "baleful to the nose, harmful to the brain, and dangerous to the lungs." But the king's attitude changed as taxes on imported tobacco

## Who Was Pocahontas?

Matoaka—nicknamed Pocahontas—was born around 1596 in the region the English would soon name Virginia. A daughter of Chief Powhatan, her interactions with colonists were important at the time and have been mythologized ever since. Pocahontas left no writings, so what we know of her comes from others. From these accounts, we know that she acted as a mediator with the Jamestown settlers; she was the first Native American to marry an Englishman; and she traveled to England with her husband and son. Pocahontas fell ill and died in Gravesend, England, in June 1617.

1. **John Smith, *Generall Historie of Virginia*, 1624.**
*Smith's description of being a captive of Powhatan in 1607.*

Having feasted [Smith] after their best barbarous manner they could, a long consultation was held, but the conclusion was, two great stones were brought before Powhatan: then as many as could layd hands on him, dragged him to them, and thereon laid his head, and being ready with their clubs, to beate out his braines, Pocahontas the Kings dearest daughter, when no entreaty could prevaile, got his head in her armes, and laid her owne upon his to save him from death: whereat the Emperour was contented he should live to make him hatchets, and her bells, beads, and copper.

2. **Robert Vaughn's engraving of Pocahontas saving Smith's life, from John Smith's *Generall Historie of Virginia*, 1624.**

Source: © British Library Board / Robana / Art Resource, NY.

3. **John Smith, *Generall Historie of Virginia*, 1624.**
*Pocahontas visited Jamestown regularly in the years following Smith's capture. Smith returned to England in 1609; four years later Captain Samuel Argall kidnapped Pocahontas and held her captive in Jamestown.*

[S]he too James towne [was brought.] A messenger forthwith was sent to her father, that his daughter Pocahontas he loved so dearely, he must ransome with our men, swords, peeces, tooles, &c. he treacherously had stolen. . . . [H]e . . . sent us word, that when we would deliver his daughter, he would make us satisfaction for all injuries done to us, and give us five hundred bushels of Corne, and for ever be friends with us. . . . [W]e could not believe the rest of our armes were either lost or stolen from him, and therefore till he sent them, we would keep his daughter. . . . [W]e heard no more from him a long time after. . . . .

[Long before this, Master John Rolfe, an honest Gentleman of good behavior had been in love with Pocahontas, and she with him. . . . T]his marriage came soone to the knowledge of Powhatan, a thing acceptable to him, as appeared by his sudden consent, for within ten daies he sent Opachisco, an old Uncle of hers, and two of his sons, to see the manner of the marriage, and to do in that behalf what they were requested . . . which was accordingly done about the first of April: And ever since we have had friendly trade and commerce.

4. **John Rolfe, Letter to Sir Thomas Dale, 1614.**
*Pocahontas and John Rolfe married in April 1614. In June, Rolfe defended his motives in this letter to Virginia's deputy-governor.*

I freely subject my selfe to your grave and mature judgment, deliberation, approbation and determination. . . . [I am not led by] the unbridled desire of carnal affection: but for the good of this plantation, for the honour of our countrie, for the glory of God, for my owne salvation, and for the converting to the true knowledge of God and Jesus

Christ, an unbeleeving creature, namely Pocahontas. To whom my hartie and best thoughts are, and have [for] a long time bin so intangled, and inthralled in so intricate a labyrinth, that I was even awearied to unwinde my selfe thereout. . . . [I have often thought]: surely these are wicked instigations, hatched by him who seeketh and delighteth in man's destruction[.]

I say the holy spirit of God has often demanded of me, why I was created . . . but to labour in the Lord's vine-yard. . . . Likewise adding hereunto her great appearance of love to me, her desire to be taught and instructed in the knowledge of God, her capableness of understanding, her aptness and willingness to receive any good impression, and also the spirituall, besides her owne incitements stirring me up hereunto. . . .

Now if the vulgar sort, who square all men's actions by the base rule of their owne filthiness, shall tax or taunt me in this my godly labour: let them know, it is not any hungry appetite, to gorge my selfe with incontinency; sure (if I would, and were so sensually inclined) I might satisfy such desire, though not without a seared conscience.

5. **Portrait of Pocahontas by Simon Van De Pass, 1616.** *In 1616, the Virginia Company of London sent Pocahontas, John Rolfe, and their son Thomas to England, where she met King James and sat for this portrait, the only surviving image of Pocahontas.*

Source: National Portrait Gallery, Smithsonian Institution/Art Resource, NY.

6. **John Smith, *Generall Historie of Virginia*, 1624.** *In 1624, John Smith recalled a meeting he had with Pocahontas during her 1616 tour of England.*

[H]earing shee was at Branford with divers of my friends, I went to see her: After a modest salutation, without any word, she turned about, obscured her face, as not seeming well contented; and in that humour her husband, with divers others, we all left her two or three houres. . . . But not long after, she began to talke, and remembred mee well what courtesies she had done: saying, ["]You did promise Powhatan what was yours should bee his, and he the like to you; you called him father being in his land a stranger, and by the same reason so must I doe you:["] which though I would have excused, I durst not allow of that title, because she was a Kings daughter; with a well set countenance she said, ["]Were you not afraid to come into my fathers Countrie, and caused feare in him and all his people (but mee) and feare you here I should call you father; I tell you then I will, and you shall call mee childe, and so I will bee for ever and ever your Countrieman. They did tell us [always] you were dead, and I knew no other till I came to [Plymouth]; yet Powhatan did command Uttamatomakkin to seeke you, and know the truth, because your Countriemen will lie much.["]

Sources: (1, 3, 6) John Smith, *Generall Historie of Virginia* (Glasgow: James MacLehose and Sons, 1907), 101, 218, 220, 238–239; (4) J. Franklin Jameson, *Narratives of Early Virginia* (New York: Charles Scribner's Sons, 1907), 237–244.

## ANALYZING THE EVIDENCE

1. Most historians now believe that the event described and shown in sources 1 and 2 was a Powhatan ritual to make Smith an ally and that his life was not actually in danger. What elements of these sources suggest the validity of this interpretation? Why would Pocahontas—a child of eleven or twelve at the time—have had a role in such a ritual?

2. How does Vaughn (source 2) depict power relations and social hierarchy among the Powhatans? Where does Pocahontas fit within this hierarchy? What messages about Pocahontas do you think Van De Pass (source 5) intended to convey? How do these images contribute to the Pocahontas myth?

3. How does Rolfe explain his interest in Pocahontas (source 4)? What is his view of her? How do you interpret the letter?

4. Assess the reliability of sources 1, 3, and 6 and consider Smith's motive in including them in his *Historie*. Source 6 purports to record an actual conversation between Pocahontas and Smith. What is the tone of this encounter, and what might explain Pocahontas's remarks?

## PUTTING IT ALL TOGETHER

Imagine the various encounters Pocahontas experienced with the Jamestown Englishmen from her point of view. Reflect on who Pocahontas was as described in these documents—savior and friend, captive, baptized wife, Virginia Company prize, and betrayed ally—and in a brief essay, use Pocahontas's experience to explore the uncertain nature of English-Powhatan relations in the first decade of contact.

bolstered the royal treasury. Powhatan, however, now accused the English of coming "not to trade but to invade my people and possess my country."

To foster the flow of migrants, the Virginia Company allowed individual settlers to own land, granting 100 acres to every freeman and more to those who imported servants. The company also created a system of representative government: the **House of Burgesses**, first convened in 1619, could make laws and levy taxes, although the governor and the company council in England could veto its acts. By 1622, land-ownership, self-government, and a judicial system based on "the lawes of the realme of England" had attracted some 4,500 new recruits. To encourage the transition to a settler colony, the Virginia Company recruited dozens of "Maides young and uncorrupt to make wifes to the Inhabitants."

**The Indian War of 1622**    The influx of migrants sparked an all-out conflict with the neighboring Indians. The struggle began with an assault led by Opechancanough, Powhatan's younger brother and successor. In 1607, Opechancanough had attacked some of the first English invaders; subsequently, he "stood aloof" from the English settlers and "would not be drawn to any Treaty." In particular, he resisted English proposals to place Indian children in schools to be "brought upp in Christianytie." Upon becoming the paramount chief in 1621, Opechancanough told the leader of the neighboring Potomack Indians: "Before the end of two moons, there should not be an Englishman in all their Countries."

Opechancanough almost succeeded. In 1622, he coordinated a surprise attack by twelve Indian chief-doms that killed 347 English settlers, nearly one-third of the population. The English fought back by seizing the fields and food of those they now called "naked, tanned, deformed Savages" and declared "a per-petual war without peace or truce" that lasted for a decade. They sold captured warriors into slavery, "destroy[ing] them who sought to destroy us" and taking control of "their cultivated places."

Shocked by the Indian uprising, James I revoked the Virginia Company's charter and, in 1624, made Virginia a **royal colony**. Now the king and his ministers appointed the governor and a small advisory council, retaining the locally elected House of Burgesses but stipulating that the king's Privy Council (a committee of political advisors) must ratify all legislation. The king

**EXPLAIN CONSEQUENCES**
How did the proximity of the Powhatan Chiefdom affect developments in early Virginia?

also decreed the legal establishment of the Church of England in the colony, which meant that residents had to pay taxes to support its clergy. These institutions — an appointed governor, an elected assembly, a formal legal system, and an established Anglican Church — became the model for royal colonies throughout English America.

**Lord Baltimore Settles Catholics in Maryland**    A second tobacco-growing colony developed in neighboring Maryland. King Charles I (r. 1625–1649), James's successor, was secretly sympathetic toward Catholicism, and in 1632 he granted lands bordering the vast Chesapeake Bay to Catholic aristocrat Cecilius Calvert, Lord Baltimore. Thus Maryland became a refuge for Catholics, who were subject to persecution in England. In 1634, twenty gentlemen, mostly Catholics, and 200 artisans and laborers, mostly Protestants, established St. Mary's City at the mouth of the Potomac River. To minimize religious confrontations, the proprietor instructed the governor to allow "no scandall nor offence to be given to any of the Protestants" and to "cause All Acts of Romane Catholicque Religion to be done as privately as may be."

Maryland grew quickly because Baltimore imported many artisans and offered ample lands to wealthy migrants. But political conflict threatened the colony's stability. Disputing Baltimore's powers, settlers elected a representative assembly and insisted on the right to initiate legislation, which Baltimore grudgingly granted. Anti-Catholic agitation by Protestants also threatened his religious goals. To protect his coreligionists, Lord Baltimore persuaded the assembly to enact the Toleration Act (1649), which granted all Christians the right to follow their beliefs and hold church services. In Maryland, as in Virginia, tobacco quickly became the main crop, and that similarity, rather than any religious difference, ultimately made the two colonies very much alike in their economic and social systems.

## The Caribbean Islands

Virginia's experiment with a cash crop that created a land-intensive plantation society ran parallel to developments in the Caribbean, where English, French, and Dutch sailors began looking for a permanent toehold. In 1624, a small English party under the command of Sir Thomas Warner established a settlement on St. Christopher (St. Kitts). A year later, Warner allowed a French group to settle the other end of the island so they could better defend their position from the Spanish.

**A Sugar Mill in the French West Indies, 1655**

Making sugar required both hard labor and considerable expertise. Field slaves labored strenuously in the hot tropical sun to cut the sugarcane and carry or cart it to an oxen- or wind-powered mill, where it was pressed to yield the juice. Then skilled slave artisans took over. They carefully heated the juice and, at the proper moment, added ingredients that granulated the sugar and separated it from the molasses, which was later distilled into rum. The Granger Collection, New York.

Within a few years, the English and French colonists on St. Kitts had driven the native Caribs from the island, weathered a Spanish attack, and created a common set of bylaws for mutual occupation of the island.

After St. Kitts, a dozen or so colonies were founded in the Lesser Antilles, including the French islands of Martinique, Guadeloupe, and St. Bart's; the English outposts of Nevis, Antigua, Montserrat, Anguilla, Tortola, and Barbados; and the Dutch colony of St. Eustatius. In 1655, an English fleet captured the Spanish island of Jamaica — one of the large islands of the Greater Antilles — and opened it to settlement as well. A few of these islands were unpopulated before Europeans settled there; elsewhere, native populations were displaced, and often wiped out, within a decade or so. Only on the largest islands did native populations hold out longer.

Colonists experimented with a wide variety of cash crops, including tobacco, indigo, cotton, cacao, and ginger. Beginning in the 1640s — and drawing on the example of Brazil — planters on many of the islands shifted to sugar cultivation. Where conditions were right, as they were in Barbados, Jamaica, Nevis, and Martinique, these colonies were soon producing substantial crops of sugar and, as a consequence, claimed some of the world's most valuable real estate.

## Plantation Life

In North America and the Caribbean, plantations were initially small **freeholds**, farms of 30 to 50 acres owned and farmed by families or male partners. But the logic of plantation agriculture soon encouraged consolidation: large planters engrossed as much land as they could and experimented with new forms of labor discipline that maximized their control over production. In Virginia, the **headright system** guaranteed 50 acres of land to anyone who paid the passage of a new immigrant to the colony; thus, by buying additional indentured servants and slaves, the colony's largest planters also amassed ever-greater claims to land.

European demand for tobacco set off a forty-year economic boom in the Chesapeake. "All our riches for the present do consist in tobacco," a planter remarked in 1630. Exports rose from 3 million pounds in 1640 to 10 million pounds in 1660. After 1650, wealthy migrants from gentry or noble families established large estates along the coastal rivers. Coming primarily from southern England, where tenants and wage laborers farmed large manors, they copied that hierarchical system by buying English indentured servants and enslaved Africans to work their lands. At about the same time, the switch to sugar production in Barbados caused the price of land there to quadruple, driving small landowners out.

For rich and poor alike, life in the plantation colonies of North America and the Caribbean was harsh. The scarcity of towns deprived settlers of community (Map 2.4). Families were equally scarce because there were few women, and marriages often ended with the early death of a spouse. Pregnant women were especially vulnerable to malaria, spread by mosquitoes that flourished in tropical and subtropical climates. Many mothers died after bearing a first or second child, so orphaned children (along with unmarried young men)

formed a large segment of the society. Sixty percent of the children born in Middlesex County, Virginia, before 1680 lost one or both parents before they were thirteen. Death was pervasive. Although 15,000 English migrants arrived in Virginia between 1622 and 1640, the population rose only from 2,000 to 8,000. It was even harsher in the islands, where yellow fever epidemics killed indiscriminately. On Barbados, burials outnumbered baptisms in the second half of the seventeenth century by four to one.

**Indentured Servitude**    Still, the prospect of owning land continued to lure settlers. By 1700, more than 100,000 English migrants had come to Virginia and Maryland and over 200,000 had migrated to the islands of the West Indies, principally to Barbados; the vast majority to both destinations traveled as indentured servants (Figure 2.2). Shipping registers from the English port of Bristol reveal the backgrounds of 5,000 servants embarking for the Chesapeake. Three-quarters were young men. They came to Bristol searching for work; once there, merchants persuaded them to sign contracts to labor in America. **Indentured servitude** contracts bound the men — and the quarter who were women — to work for a master for four or five years, after which they would be free to marry and work for themselves.

For merchants, servants were valuable cargo: their contracts fetched high prices from Chesapeake and West Indian planters. For the plantation owners, indentured servants were a bargain if they survived the

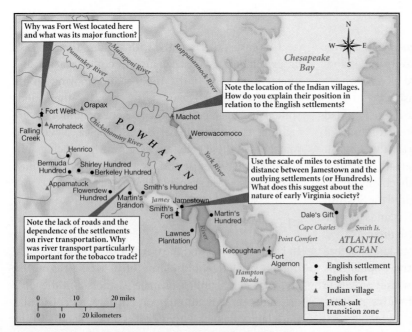

**MAP 2.4**

**River Plantations in Virginia, c. 1640**

The first migrants settled in widely dispersed plantations along the James River, a settlement pattern promoted by the tobacco economy. From their riverfront plantations wealthy planter-merchants could easily load heavy hogsheads of tobacco onto oceangoing ships and offload supplies that they then sold to smallholding planters. Consequently, few substantial towns or trading centers developed in the Chesapeake region.

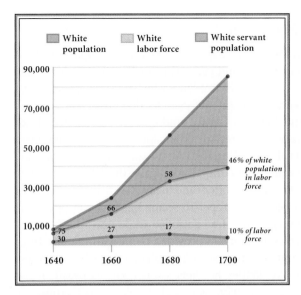

**FIGURE 2.2**

**Chesapeake Whites: Workers, Dependents, and Indentured Servants, 1640–1700**

The Chesapeake's white population grew tenfold in the years after 1640, and it also changed significantly in character. As more women migrated to Virginia and Maryland and bore children, the percentage of the population who worked in the fields daily fell dramatically, from 75 percent to 46 percent. The proportion of indentured servants in the labor force likewise declined, from 30 percent to 10 percent.

voyage and their first year in a harsh new disease environment, a process called "seasoning." During the Chesapeake's tobacco boom, a male servant could produce five times his purchase price in a single year. To maximize their gains, many masters ruthlessly exploited servants, forcing them to work long hours, beating them without cause, and withholding permission to marry. If servants ran away or became pregnant, masters went to court to increase the term of their service. Female servants were especially vulnerable to abuse. A Virginia law of 1692 stated that "dissolute masters have gotten their maids with child; and yet claim the benefit of their service." Planters got rid of uncooperative servants by selling their contracts. In Virginia, an Englishman remarked in disgust that "servants were sold up and down like horses."

Few indentured servants escaped poverty. In the Chesapeake, half the men died before completing the term of their contract, and another quarter remained landless. Only one-quarter achieved their quest for property and respectability. Female servants generally fared better. Because men had grown "very sensible of the Misfortune of Wanting Wives," many propertied planters married female servants. Thus a few — very

fortunate — men and women escaped a life of landless poverty.

**African Laborers**    The rigors of indentured servitude paled before the brutality that accompanied the large-scale shift to African slave labor. In Barbados and the other English islands, sugar production devoured laborers, and the supply of indentured servants quickly became inadequate to planters' needs. By 1690, blacks outnumbered whites on Barbados nearly three to one, and white slave owners were developing a code of force and terror to keep sugar flowing and maintain control of the black majority that surrounded them. The first comprehensive slave legislation for the island, adopted in 1661, was called an "Act for the better ordering and governing of Negroes."

In the Chesapeake, the shift to slave labor was more gradual. In 1619, John Rolfe noted that "a Dutch man of warre . . . sold us twenty Negars" — slaves originally shipped by the Portuguese from the port of Luanda in Angola. For a generation, the number of Africans remained small. About 400 Africans lived in the Chesapeake colonies in 1649, just 2 percent of the population. By 1670, that figure had reached 5 percent. Most Africans served their English masters for life. However, since English common law did not acknowledge chattel slavery, it was possible for some Africans to escape bondage. Some were freed as a result of Christian baptism; some purchased their freedom from their owners; some — like Elizabeth Key, whose story was related at the beginning of the chapter — won their freedom in the courts. Once free, some ambitious Africans became landowners and purchased slaves or the labor contracts of English servants for themselves.

Social mobility for Africans ended in the 1660s with the collapse of the tobacco boom and the increasing political power of the gentry. Tobacco had once sold for 30 pence a pound; now it fetched less than one-tenth of that. The "low price of Tobacco requires it should bee made as cheap as possible," declared Virginia planter-politician Nicholas Spencer, and "blacks can make it cheaper than whites." As they imported more African workers, the English-born political elite grew more race-conscious. Increasingly, Spencer and other leading legislators distinguished English from African residents by color (white-black) rather than by religion (Christian-pagan). By 1671, the Virginia House of Burgesses had forbidden Africans to

**COMPARE AND CONTRAST**

How were the experiences of indentured servants and slaves in the Chesapeake and the Caribbean similar? In what ways were they different?

own guns or join the militia. It also barred them — "tho baptized and enjoying their own Freedom" — from owning English servants. Being black was increasingly a mark of inferior legal status, and slavery was fast becoming a permanent and hereditary condition. As an English clergyman observed, "These two words, Negro and Slave had by custom grown Homogeneous and convertible."

# Neo-European Colonies

While Mesoamerica and the Andes emerged at the heart of a tribute-based empire in Latin America, and tropical and subtropical environments were transformed into plantation societies, a series of colonies that more closely replicated European patterns of economic and social organization developed in the temperate zone along North America's Atlantic coast (America Compared, opposite page). Dutch, French, and English sailors probed the continent's northern coastline, initially searching for a Northwest Passage through the continent to Asia. Gradually, they developed an interest in the region on its own terms. They traded for furs with coastal Native American populations, fished for cod on the Grand Banks off the coast of Newfoundland, and established freehold family farms and larger manors where they reproduced European patterns of agricultural life. Many migrants also came with aspirations to create godly communities, places of refuge where they could put religious ideals into practice. New France, New Netherland, and New England were the three pillars of neo-European colonization in the early seventeenth century.

## New France

In the 1530s, Jacques Cartier ventured up the St. Lawrence River and claimed it for France. Cartier's claim to the St. Lawrence languished for three-quarters of a century, but in 1608 Samuel de Champlain returned and founded the fur-trading post of Quebec. Trade with the Cree-speaking Montagnais; Algonquian-speaking Micmacs, Ottawas, and Ojibwas; and Iroquois-speaking Hurons gave the French access to furs — mink, otter, and beaver — that were in great demand in Europe. To secure plush beaver pelts from the Hurons, who controlled trade north of the Great Lakes, Champlain provided them with manufactured goods. Selling pelts, an Indian told a French priest, "makes kettles, hatchets, swords, knives, bread." It also made guns, which Champlain sold to the Hurons.

The Hurons also became the first focus of French Catholic missionary activity. Hundreds of priests, most of them Jesuits, fanned out to live in Indian communities. They mastered Indian languages and came to understand, and sometimes respect, their values. Many Indian peoples initially welcomed the French "Black Robes" as spiritually powerful beings, but when prayers to the Christian god did not protect them from disease, the Indians grew skeptical. A Peoria chief charged that a priest's "fables are good only in his own country; we have our own [beliefs], which do not make us die as his do." When a drought struck, Indians blamed the missionaries. "If you cannot make rain, they speak of nothing less than making away with you," lamented one Jesuit.

While New France became an expansive center of fur trading and missionary work, it languished as a

*Caftor de 26 pouces de longueur entre tefte et queue*

*Tom. Prem. pag.*

### The Fur Trade

Luxuriant pelts like ermine and silver fox were always desirable, but the humble beaver dominated the early trade between Europeans and Indians in the Northeast. It had thick, coarse hair, but beneath that outer layer was soft "underfur." Those fine hairs were covered in microscopic barbs that allowed them to mat into a dense mass. European hatmakers pressed this fur into felt so strong and pliable that even broad-brimmed hats would hold their shape. As such hats became fashionable in Europe and the colonies, beavers were hunted to near-extinction in North America. National Archives of Canada.

## Plantation Colonies Versus Neo-Europes

The prospects for Europeans who traveled to tropical plantations like Barbados differed dramatically from those traveling to neo-European colonies like Massachusetts Bay. In the former, planters employed small armies of servants and slaves; in the latter, the first generation of colonists worked hard, often in cold climates and rocky soils, to eke out a living.

### Henry Whistler's Journal, 1655

This Island [Barbados] is one of the Richest Spots of ground in the world and fully inhabited. . . . The gentry here doth Hue [appear] far better than ours do in England : they have most of them 100 or 2 or 3 of slaves[,] apes who they command as they please. . . . This Island is inhabited with all sorts : with English, French, Dutch, Scots, Irish, Spaniards they being Jews : with Indians and miserable Negroes borne to perpetual slavery they and their seed : these Negroes they do allow as many wives as they will have, some will have 3 or 4, according as they find their body able : our English here doth think a negro child the first day it is born to be worth £5, they cost them nothing the bringing up, they go all ways naked : some planters will have 30 more or les about 4 or 5 years old : they sell them from one to the other as we do sheep. This Island is the Dunghill whereon England doth cast forth its rubbish. . . . A rogue in England will hardly make a cheater here : a Bawd brought over puts on a demure comportment, a whore if handsome makes a wife for some rich planter.

Source: *The Narrative of General Venables* (New York: Longmans, Green, and Co., 1900), 145–146.

### William Wood, *New England's Prospect*, 1634

But it may be objected that it is too cold a country for our English men, who have been accustomed to a warmer climate. To which it may be answered . . . , there is wood good store and better cheap to build warm houses and make good fires, which makes the winter less tedious. . . . [T]rue it is that some venturing too nakedly in extremity of cold, being more foolhardy than wise, have for a time lost the use of their feet, others the use of their fingers; but time and surgery afterwards recovered them. Some have had their overgrown beards so frozen together that they could not get their strong-water bottles into their mouths. . . . [W]hereas many do disparage the land, saying a man cannot live without labor, in that they more disparage and discredit themselves in giving the world occasion to take notice of their dronish disposition that would live off the sweat of another man's brows. . . . For all in New England must be workers of some kind. . . . And howsoever they are accounted poor, they are well contented and look not so much at abundance as at competency.

Source: William Wood, *New England's Prospect* (Boston: The University of Massachusetts Press, 1993), 28–29, 68.

### QUESTIONS FOR ANALYSIS

1. Henry Whistler was a soldier who briefly visited Barbados on a military expedition to the West Indies, while William Wood lived for four years in Massachusetts Bay. How might that difference influence the tone of these two descriptions?

2. What core values does each author ascribe to the colony he writes about? What kinds of people are most likely to end up in each of these two colonies?

farming settlement. In 1662, King Louis XIV (r. 1643–1714) turned New France into a royal colony and subsidized the migration of indentured servants. French servants labored under contract for three years, received a salary, and could eventually lease a farm — far more generous terms than those for indentured servants in the English colonies.

Nonetheless, few people moved to New France, a cold and forbidding country "at the end of the world," as one migrant put it. And some state policies discouraged migration. Louis XIV drafted tens of thousands of men into military service and barred Huguenots (French Calvinist Protestants) from migrating to New France, fearing they might win converts and take control of the colony. Moreover, the French legal system gave peasants strong rights to their village lands, whereas migrants to New France faced an oppressive, aristocracy- and church-dominated feudal system. In the village of Saint Ours in Quebec, for example, peasants paid 45 percent of their wheat crop to nobles and the Catholic Church. By 1698, only 15,200 Europeans lived in New France, compared to 100,000 in England's North American colonies.

Despite this small population, France eventually claimed a vast inland arc, from the St. Lawrence Valley through the Great Lakes and down the course of the Ohio and Mississippi rivers. Explorers and fur traders drove this expansion. In 1673, Jacques Marquette reached the Mississippi River in present-day Wisconsin; then, in 1681, Robert de La Salle traveled down the majestic river to the Gulf of Mexico. To honor Louis XIV, La Salle named the region Louisiana. By 1718, French merchants had founded the port of New Orleans at the mouth of the Mississippi. Eventually a network of about two dozen forts grew up in the Great Lakes and Mississippi. Soldiers and missionaries used them as bases of operations, while Indians, traders, and their métis (mixed-race) offspring created trading communities alongside them.

## New Netherland

By 1600, Amsterdam had become the financial and commercial hub of northern Europe, and Dutch financiers dominated the European banking, insurance, and textile industries. Dutch merchants owned more ships and employed more sailors than did the combined fleets of England, France, and Spain. Indeed, the Dutch managed much of the world's commerce. During their struggle for independence from Spain and Portugal (ruled by Spanish monarchs, 1580–1640), the Dutch seized Portuguese forts in Africa and Indonesia and sugar plantations in Brazil. These conquests gave the Dutch control of the Atlantic trade in slaves and sugar and the Indian Ocean commerce in East Indian spices and Chinese silks and ceramics (Map 2.5).

In 1609, Dutch merchants dispatched the English mariner Henry Hudson to locate a navigable route to the riches of the East Indies. What he found as he probed the rivers of northeast America was a fur bonanza. Following Hudson's exploration of the river that now bears his name, the merchants built Fort Orange (Albany) in 1614 to trade for furs with the Munsee and Iroquois Indians. Then, in 1621, the Dutch government chartered the West India Company, which founded the colony of New Netherland, set up New Amsterdam (on Manhattan Island) as its capital, and brought in farmers and artisans to make the enterprise self-sustaining. The new colony did not thrive. The population of the Dutch Republic was too small to support much emigration—just 1.5 million people, compared to 5 million in Britain and 20 million in France—and its migrants sought riches in Southeast Asia rather than fur-trading profits in America. To protect its colony from rival European nations, the West India Company granted huge estates along the Hudson River to wealthy Dutchmen who promised to populate them. But by 1664, New Netherland had only 5,000 residents, and fewer than half of them were Dutch.

**New Amsterdam, c. 1640**

As the wooden palisade suggests, New Amsterdam was a fortlike trading post at the edge of a vast land populated by alien Indian peoples feared by the Dutch. The city was also a pale miniature imitation of Amsterdam, with its many canals. The first settlers built their houses in the Dutch style, with gable ends facing the street (note the two middle houses), and excavated a canal across lower Manhattan Island (New York City's Canal Street today). Library of Congress.

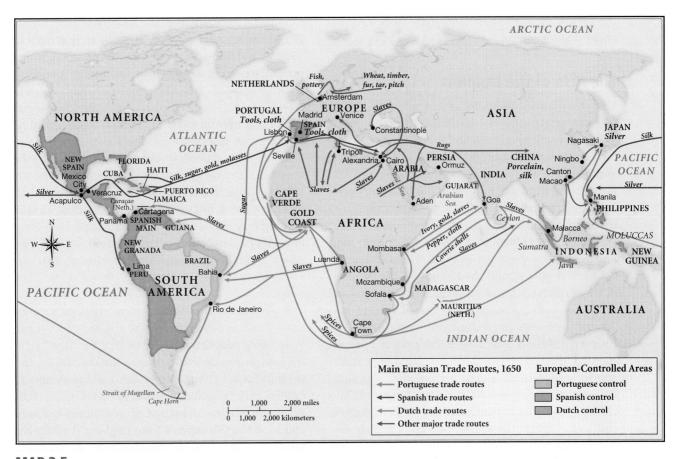

**MAP 2.5**

**The Eurasian Trade System and European Spheres of Influence, 1650**

Between 1550 and 1650, Spanish, Portuguese, and Dutch merchants took control of the maritime trade routes between Europe and India, Indonesia, and China. They also created two new trading connections. The South Atlantic System carried slaves, sugar, and manufactured goods between Europe, Africa, and the valuable plantation settlements in Brazil and the Caribbean islands. And a transpacific trade carried Spanish American silver to China in exchange for silks, ceramics, and other manufactures. (To trace long-term changes in trade and empires, see Map 1.4 on p. 24 and Map 5.1 on p. 154.)

Like New France, New Netherland flourished as a fur-trading enterprise. Trade with the powerful Iroquois, though rocky at first, gradually improved. But Dutch settlers had less respect for their Algonquian-speaking neighbors. They seized prime farming land from the Algonquian peoples and took over their trading network, which exchanged corn and wampum from Long Island for furs from Maine. In response, in 1643 the Algonquians launched attacks that nearly destroyed the colony. "Almost every place is abandoned," a settler lamented, "whilst the Indians daily threaten to overwhelm us." To defeat the Algonquians, the Dutch waged vicious warfare — maiming, burning, and killing hundreds of men, women, and children — and formed an alliance with the Mohawks, who were no less brutal. The grim progression of Euro-Indian relations — an uneasy welcome, followed by rising tensions and war — afflicted even the Dutch, who had few designs on Indian lands or on their "unregenerate" souls and were only looking to do business.

After the crippling Indian war, the West India Company ignored New Netherland and expanded its profitable trade in African slaves and Brazilian sugar. In New Amsterdam, Governor Peter Stuyvesant ruled in an authoritarian fashion, rejecting demands for a representative system of government and alienating the colony's diverse Dutch, English, and Swedish residents. Consequently, the residents of New Netherland offered little resistance when England invaded the colony in

**IDENTIFY CAUSES**

Why did New France and New Netherland struggle to attract colonists?

1664. New Netherland became New York and fell under English control.

## The Rise of the Iroquois

Like other native groups decimated by European diseases and warfare, the Five Nations of the Iroquois suffered as a result of colonization, but they were able to capitalize on their strategic location in central New York to dominate the region between the French and Dutch colonies. Obtaining guns and goods from Dutch merchants at Fort Orange, Iroquois warriors inflicted terror on their neighbors. Partly in response to a virulent smallpox epidemic in 1633, which cut their number by one-third, the Iroquois waged a series of devastating wars against the Hurons (1649), Neutrals (1651), Eries (1657), and Susquehannocks (1660) — all Iroquoian-speaking peoples. They razed villages, killing many residents and taking many more captive. The conquered Hurons ceased to exist as a distinct people; survivors trekked westward with displaced Algonquian peoples and formed a new nation, the Wyandots. Iroquois warriors pressed still farther — eastward into New England, south to the Carolinas, north to Quebec, and west via the Great Lakes to the Mississippi — dominating Indian groups along the way. Collectively known as the Beaver Wars, these Iroquois campaigns dramatically altered the map of northeastern North America.

Many Iroquois raids came at the expense of French-allied Algonquian Indians, and in the 1660s New France committed to all-out war against the Iroquois. In 1667, the Mohawks were the last of the Five Nations to admit defeat. As part of the peace settlement, the Five Nations accepted Jesuit missionaries into their communities. A minority of Iroquois — perhaps 20 percent of the population — converted to Catholicism and moved to the St. Lawrence Valley, where they settled in mission communities near Montreal (where their descendants still live today).

The Iroquois who remained in New York did not collapse, however. Forging a new alliance with the Englishmen who had taken over New Netherland, they would continue to be a dominant force in the politics of the Northeast for generations to come.

## New England

In 1620, 102 English Protestants landed at a place they called Plymouth, near Cape Cod. A decade later, a much larger group began to arrive just north of Plymouth, in the newly chartered Massachusetts Bay Colony. By 1640, the region had attracted more than 20,000 migrants (Map 2.6). Unlike the early arrivals in Virginia and Barbados, these were not parties of young male adventurers seeking their fortunes or bound to labor for someone else. They came in family groups to create communities like the ones they left behind, except that they intended to establish them according to Protestant principles, as John Calvin had done in Geneva. Their numbers were small compared to the Caribbean and the Chesapeake, but their balanced sex ratio and organized approach to community formation allowed them to multiply quickly. By distributing land broadly, they built a society of independent farm families. And by establishing a "holy commonwealth," they gave a moral dimension to American history that survives today.

**The Pilgrims**    The **Pilgrims** were religious separatists — Puritans who had left the Church of England. When King James I threatened to drive Puritans "out of the land, or else do worse," some Puritans chose to live among Dutch Calvinists in Holland. Subsequently, 35 of these exiles resolved to maintain their English identity by moving to America. Led by William Bradford and joined by 67 migrants from England, the Pilgrims sailed to America aboard the *Mayflower*. Because they lacked a royal charter, they combined themselves "together into a civill body politick," as their leader explained. This Mayflower Compact used the Puritans' self-governing religious congregation as the model for their political structure.

Only half of the first migrant group survived until spring, but thereafter Plymouth thrived; the cold climate inhibited the spread of mosquito-borne disease, and the Pilgrims' religious discipline encouraged a strong work ethic. Moreover, a smallpox epidemic in 1618 devastated the local Wampanoags, minimizing the danger they posed. By 1640, there were 3,000 settlers in Plymouth. To ensure political stability, they established representative self-government, broad political rights, property ownership, and religious freedom of conscience.

Meanwhile, England plunged deeper into religious turmoil. When King Charles I repudiated certain Protestant doctrines, including the role of grace in salvation, English Puritans, now powerful in Parliament, accused the king of "popery" — of holding Catholic beliefs. In 1629, Charles dissolved Parliament, claimed the authority to rule by "divine right," and raised money through royal edicts and the sale of monopolies. When Charles's Archbishop William Laud began to purge dissident ministers, thousands of

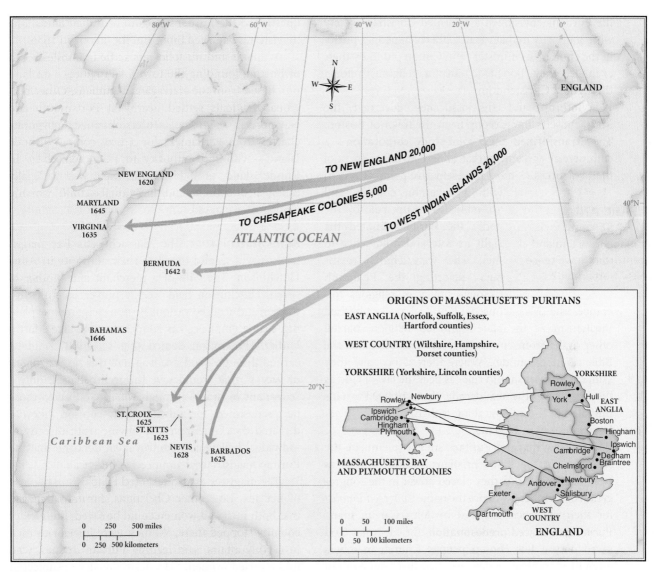

**MAP 2.6**

**The Puritan Migration to America, 1620–1640**

Forty-five thousand Puritans left England for America and the West Indies between 1620 and 1640. About half traveled to the New England colonies of Plymouth, Massachusetts Bay, and Connecticut, where they created durable societies with deep religious identities. Migrants from the three major centers of Puritanism in England — Yorkshire, East Anglia, and the West Country — commonly settled among those from their own region. Often they named American communities after their English towns of origin and tried to live as they had in Old England. For example, settlers from Rowley in Yorkshire transplanted their customary system of open-field agriculture to Rowley in Massachusetts Bay.

**Puritans** — Protestants who did not separate from the Church of England but hoped to purify it of its ceremony and hierarchy — fled to America.

**John Winthrop and Massachusetts Bay**    The Puritan exodus began in 1630 with the departure of 900 migrants led by John Winthrop, a well-educated country squire who became the first governor of the Massachusetts Bay Colony. Calling England morally

corrupt and "overburdened with people," Winthrop sought land for his children and a place in Christian history for his people. "We must consider that we shall be as a City upon a Hill," Winthrop told the migrants. "The eyes of all people are upon us." Like the Pilgrims,

 To see a longer excerpt of Winthrop's "City Upon a Hill" sermon, along with other primary sources from this period, see *Sources for America's History*.

the Puritans envisioned a reformed Christian society with "authority in magistrates, liberty in people, purity in the church," as minister John Cotton put it. By their example, they hoped to inspire religious reform throughout Christendom.

Winthrop and his associates governed the Massachusetts Bay Colony from the town of Boston. They transformed their **joint-stock corporation**—a commercial agreement that allows investors to pool their resources—into a representative political system with a governor, council, and assembly. To ensure rule by the godly, the Puritans limited the right to vote and hold office to men who were church members. Rejecting the Plymouth Colony's policy of religious toleration, the Massachusetts Bay Colony established Puritanism as the state-supported religion, barred other faiths from conducting services, and used the Bible as a legal guide. "Where there is no Law," they said, magistrates should rule "as near the law of God as they can." Over the next decade, about 10,000 Puritans migrated to the colony, along with 10,000 others fleeing hard times in England.

**COMPARE AND CONTRAST**
What made New England different from New France and New Netherland?

The New England Puritans sought to emulate the simplicity of the first Christians. Seeing bishops as "traitours unto God," they placed power in the congregation of members—hence the name *Congregationalist* for their churches. Inspired by John Calvin, many Puritans embraced **predestination**, the idea that God saved only a few chosen people. Church members often lived in great anxiety, worried that God had not placed them among the "elect." Some hoped for a conversion experience, the intense sensation of receiving God's grace and being "born again." Other Puritans relied on "preparation," the confidence in salvation that came from spiritual guidance by their ministers. Still others believed that they were God's chosen people, the new Israelites, and would be saved if they obeyed his laws.

**Roger Williams and Rhode Island**    To maintain God's favor, the Massachusetts Bay magistrates purged their society of religious dissidents. One target was Roger Williams, the Puritan minister in Salem, a coastal town north of Boston. Williams opposed the decision to establish an official religion and praised the Pilgrims' separation of church and state. He advocated **toleration**, arguing that political magistrates had authority over only the "bodies, goods, and outward estates of men," not their spiritual lives. Williams also

questioned the Puritans' seizure of Indian lands. The magistrates banished him from the colony in 1636.

Williams and his followers settled 50 miles south of Boston, founding the town of Providence on land purchased from the Narragansett Indians. Other religious dissidents settled nearby at Portsmouth and Newport. In 1644, these settlers obtained a corporate charter from Parliament for a new colony—Rhode Island—with full authority to rule themselves. In Rhode Island, as in Plymouth, there was no legally established church, and individuals could worship God as they pleased.

**Anne Hutchinson**    The Massachusetts Bay magistrates saw a second threat to their authority in Anne Hutchinson. The wife of a merchant and mother of seven, Hutchinson held weekly prayer meetings for women and accused various Boston clergymen of placing undue emphasis on good behavior. Like Martin Luther, Hutchinson denied that salvation could be earned through good deeds. There was no "**covenant of works**" that would save the well-behaved; only a "**covenant of grace**" through which God saved those he predestined for salvation. Hutchinson likewise declared that God "revealed" divine truth directly to individual believers, a controversial doctrine that the Puritan magistrates denounced as heretical.

The magistrates also resented Hutchinson because of her sex. Like other Christians, Puritans believed that both men and women could be saved. But gender equality stopped there. Women were inferior to men in earthly affairs, said leading Puritan divines, who told married women: "Thy desires shall bee subject to thy husband, and he shall rule over thee." Puritan women could not be ministers or lay preachers, nor could they vote in church affairs. In 1637, the magistrates accused Hutchinson of teaching that inward grace freed an individual from the rules of the Church and found her guilty of holding heretical views. Banished, she followed Roger Williams into exile in Rhode Island.

Other Puritan groups moved out from Massachusetts Bay in the 1630s and settled on or near the Connecticut River. For several decades, the colonies of Connecticut, New Haven, and Saybrook were independent of one another; in 1660, they secured a charter from King Charles II (r. 1660–1685) for the self-governing colony of Connecticut. Like Massachusetts Bay, Connecticut had a legally established church and an elected governor and assembly; however, it granted voting rights to most property-owning men, not just to church members as in the original Puritan colony.

**The Puritan Revolution in England**  Meanwhile, a religious civil war engulfed England. Archbishop Laud had imposed the Church of England prayer book on Presbyterian Scotland in 1637; five years later, a rebel Scottish army invaded England. Thousands of English Puritans (and hundreds of American Puritans) joined the Scots, demanding religious reform and parliamentary power. After years of civil war, parliamentary forces led by Oliver Cromwell emerged victorious. In 1649, Parliament beheaded King Charles I, proclaimed a republican Commonwealth, and banished bishops and elaborate rituals from the Church of England.

The Puritan triumph in England was short-lived. Popular support for the Commonwealth ebbed after Cromwell took dictatorial control in 1653. Following his death in 1658, moderate Protestants and a resurgent aristocracy restored the monarchy and the hierarchy of bishops. With Charles II (r. 1660–1685) on the throne, England's experiment in radical Protestant government came to an end.

For the Puritans in America, the restoration of the monarchy began a new phase of their "errand into the wilderness." They had come to New England expecting to return to Europe in triumph. When the failure of the English Revolution dashed that sacred mission, ministers exhorted congregations to create a godly republican society in America. The Puritan colonies now stood as outposts of Calvinism and the Atlantic republican tradition.

**Puritanism and Witchcraft**  Like Native Americans, Puritans believed that the physical world was full of supernatural forces. Devout Christians saw signs of God's (or Satan's) power in blazing stars, birth defects, and other unusual events. Noting after a storm that the houses of many ministers "had been smitten with Lightning," Cotton Mather, a prominent Puritan theologian, wondered "what the meaning of God should be in it."

Puritans were hostile toward people who they believed tried to manipulate these forces, and many were willing to condemn neighbors as Satan's "wizards" or "witches." People in the town of Andover "were much addicted to sorcery," claimed one observer, and "there were forty men in it that could raise the Devil as well as any astrologer." Between 1647 and 1662, civil authorities in New England hanged fourteen people for witchcraft, most of them older women accused of being "double-tongued" or of having "an unruly spirit."

The most dramatic episode of witch-hunting occurred in Salem in 1692. Several girls who had experienced strange seizures accused neighbors of bewitching them. When judges at the accused witches' trials allowed the use of "spectral" evidence — visions of evil beings and marks seen only by the girls — the accusations spun out of control. Eventually, Massachusetts Bay authorities tried 175 people for witchcraft and executed 19 of them. The causes of this mass hysteria were complex and are still debated. Some historians point to group rivalries: many accusers were the daughters or servants of poor farmers, whereas many of the alleged witches were wealthier church members or their friends. Because 18 of those put to death were women, other historians see the episode as part of a broader

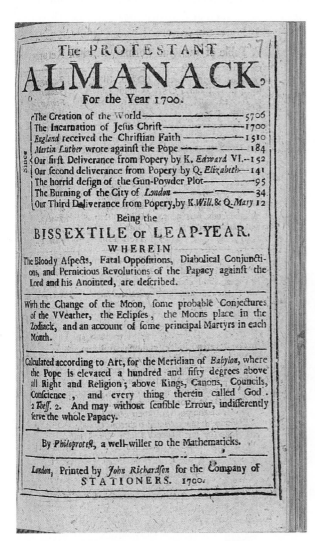

**The Protestant Almanack, 1700**
The conflict between Protestants and Catholics took many forms. To reinforce the religious identity of English Protestants, a writer using the pseudonym *Philopretes* published this almanac that charted not only the passage of the seasons (and the influence of the pagan signs of the "Zodiack") but also the "Pernicious Revolutions of the Papacy against the Lord and his Anointed." Cambridge University Library.

Puritan effort to subordinate women. Still others focus on political instability in Massachusetts Bay in the early 1690s and on fears raised by recent Indian attacks in nearby Maine, which had killed the parents of some of the young accusers. It is likely that all of these causes played some role in the executions.

Whatever the cause, the Salem episode marked a major turning point. Shaken by the number of deaths, government officials now discouraged legal prosecutions for witchcraft. Moreover, many influential people embraced the outlook of the European Enlightenment, a major intellectual movement that began around 1675 and promoted a rational, scientific view of the world. Increasingly, educated men and women explained strange happenings and sudden deaths by reference to "natural causes," not witchcraft. Unlike Cotton Mather (1663–1728), who believed that lightning was a supernatural sign, Benjamin Franklin (1706–1790) and other well-read men of his generation would investigate it as a natural phenomenon.

**A Yeoman Society, 1630–1700**   In building their communities, New England Puritans consciously rejected the feudal practices of English society. Many Puritans came from middling families in East Anglia, a region of pasture lands and few manors, and had no desire to live as tenants of wealthy aristocrats or submit to oppressive taxation by a distant government. They

had "escaped out of the pollutions of the world," the settlers of Watertown in Massachusetts Bay declared, and vowed to live "close togither" in self-governing communities. Accordingly, the General Courts of Massachusetts Bay and Connecticut bestowed land on groups of settlers, who then distributed it among the male heads of families.

Widespread ownership of land did not mean equality of wealth or status. "God had Ordained different degrees and orders of men," proclaimed Boston merchant John Saffin, "some to be Masters and Commanders, others to be Subjects, and to be commanded." Town proprietors normally awarded the largest plots to men of high social status who often became selectmen and justices of the peace. However, all families received some land, and most adult men had a vote in the **town meeting**, the main institution of local government (Map 2.7).

In this society of independent households and self-governing communities, ordinary farmers had much more political power than Chesapeake yeomen and European peasants did. Although Nathaniel Fish was one of the poorest men in the town of Barnstable — he owned just a two-room cottage, 8 acres of land, an ox, and a cow — he was a voting member of the town meeting. Each year, Fish and other Barnstable farmers levied taxes; enacted ordinances governing fencing, roadbuilding, and the use of common fields; and chose

**The Mason Children**

This 1670 portrait of David, Joanna, and Abigail Mason by an unknown painter illustrates the growing prosperity of well-to-do Boston households. All three wear white linen edged with fine lace and expensive ribbons. Eight-year-old David is dressed like a gentleman; his slashed sleeves, kid gloves, and silver-tipped walking stick represent the height of English fashion. Puritans, with their plain style, were uneasy about such finery. As minister Samuel Torrey complained, "a spirit of worldliness, a spirit of sensuality" was gaining strength in the younger generation. The Fine Arts Museums of San Francisco, M. H. de Young Memorial Museum, Gift of Mr. and Mrs. John D. Rockefeller III, 1979.7.3. © Fine Arts Museums of San Francisco.

Andover, 1650–1692
Nucleated to dispersed in fifty years

New houses
- By 1650
- By 1692
▲ Meeting House

(after Vaughn)

The key to the right indicates that a central purpose of this map is to show the geographic distribution of nucleated and dispersed villages. Why are there so many nucleated towns in the Connecticut River Valley and so many dispersed settlements in eastern Massachusetts?

Village types
● Nucleated
◉ Initially nucleated, dispersed by 1700
○ Dispersed
◆ Indian settlements
▨ Continuous English settlements by 1700
── Roads
── Field boundaries

The map of Andover shows how an originally nucleated settlement changed over time into a dispersed town. New farms tended to be located farther and farther from the meeting house and town center, represented by a triangle on the town plan.

Wethersfield in 1640 is an example of a nucleated village, with house lots clustered around the meeting house and fields arranged in geometric patterns in the surrounding countryside.

Wethersfield, 1640
Meeting House
(after Andrews)

The field boundaries in Wethersfield indicate that the land is flat in the Connecticut River Valley. In contrast, the pattern of roads and paths in Andover suggests a hilly topography. These uplands gave the Merrimack River a strong current and many rapids, which were later harnessed for industrial development. (See Map 9.1 on page 288.)

(after Wood)

**MAP 2.7**

**Settlement Patterns in New England Towns, 1630–1700**

Throughout New England, colonists pressed onto desirable Indian lands. Initially, most Puritan towns were compact: families lived close to one another in village centers and traveled daily to work in the surrounding fields. This 1640 map of Wethersfield, Connecticut, a town situated on the broad plains of the Connecticut River Valley, shows this pattern clearly. The first settlers in Andover, Massachusetts, also chose to live in the village center. However, the rugged topography of eastern Massachusetts encouraged the townspeople to disperse. By 1692 (as the varied location of new houses shows), many Andover residents were living on farms distant from the village center.

the selectmen who managed town affairs. The farmers also selected the town's representatives to the General Court, which gradually displaced the governor as the center of political authority. For Fish and thousands of other ordinary settlers, New England had proved to be a new world of opportunity.

# Instability, War, and Rebellion

Everywhere in the colonies, conflicts arose over the control of resources, the legitimacy of colonial leaders' claims to power, and attempts to define social and cultural norms. Periodically, these conflicts flared spectacularly into episodes of violence. Each episode has its own story — its own unique logic and narrative — but taken together, they also illustrate the way that, in their formative stages, colonial societies pressured people to accept new patterns of authority and new claims to power. When these claims were contested, the results could quickly turn deadly.

## New England's Indian Wars

Relations between colonists and Indians in early New England were bewilderingly complex. Many rival Indian groups lived there before Europeans arrived; by the 1630s, these groups were bordered by the Dutch colony of New Netherland to their west and the various English settlements to the east: Plymouth, Massachusetts Bay, Rhode Island, Connecticut, New Haven, and Saybrook. The region's Indian leaders created various alliances for the purposes of trade and defense: Wampanoags with Plymouth; Mohegans with Massachusetts and Connecticut; Pequots with New Netherland; Narragansetts with Rhode Island.

**Puritan-Pequot War** Because of their alliance with the Dutch, the Pequots became a thorn in the side of English traders. A series of violent encounters began in July 1636 with the killing of English trader John Oldham and escalated until May 1637, when a combined force of Massachusetts and Connecticut

**The Hurons' Feast of the Dead**

Hurons buried their dead in temporary raised tombs so they could easily care for their spirits. When they moved their villages in search of fertile soil and better hunting, the Hurons held a Feast of the Dead and reburied the bones of their own deceased (and often bones from other villages) in a common pit lined with beaver robes. This solemn ceremony united living as well as dead clan members, strengthening the bonds of the Huron Confederacy. It also was believed to release the spirits of the dead, allowing them to travel to the land where the first Huron, Aataentsic, fell from the sky, "made earth and man," and lived with her son and assistant, Iouskeha. Library of Congress.

militiamen, accompanied by Narragansett and Mohegan warriors, attacked a Pequot village and massacred some five hundred men, women, and children. In the months that followed, the New Englanders drove the surviving Pequots into oblivion and divided their lands.

Believing they were God's chosen people, Puritans considered their presence to be divinely ordained. Initially, they pondered the morality of acquiring Native American lands. "By what right or warrant can we enter into the land of the Savages?" they asked themselves. Responding to such concerns, John Winthrop detected God's hand in a recent smallpox epidemic: "If God were not pleased with our inheriting these parts," he asked, "why doth he still make roome for us by diminishing them as we increase?" Experiences like the Pequot War confirmed New Englanders' confidence in their enterprise. "God laughed at the Enemies of his People," one soldier boasted after the 1637 massacre, "filling the Place with Dead Bodies."

Like Catholic missionaries, Puritans believed that their church should embrace all peoples. However, their strong emphasis on predestination — the idea that God saved only a few chosen people — made it hard for them to accept that Indians could be counted among the elect. "Probably the devil" delivered these "miserable savages" to America, Cotton Mather suggested, "in hopes that the gospel of the Lord Jesus Christ would never come here." A few Puritan ministers committed themselves to the effort to convert Indians. On Martha's Vineyard, Jonathan Mayhew helped to create an Indian-led community of Wampanoag Christians. John Eliot translated the Bible into Algonquian and created fourteen Indian praying towns. By 1670, more than 1,000 Indians lived in these settlements, but relatively few Native Americans were ever permitted to become full members of Puritan congregations.

### Metacom's War, 1675–1676

By the 1670s, Europeans in New England outnumbered Indians by three to one. The English population had multiplied to 55,000, while native peoples had diminished from an estimated 120,000 in 1570 to barely 16,000. To the Wampanoag leader Metacom (also known as King Philip), the prospects for coexistence looked dim. When his people copied English ways by raising hogs and selling pork in Boston, Puritan officials accused them of selling at "an under rate" and restricted their trade. When Indians killed wandering hogs that devastated their cornfields, authorities prosecuted them for violating English property rights (American Voices, p. 68).

Metacom concluded that the English colonists had to be expelled. In 1675, the Wampanoags' leader forged

**Metacom (King Philip), Chief of the Wampanoags**
The Indian War of 1675–1676 left an indelible mark on the history of New England. This painting from the 1850s, done on semitransparent cloth and lit from behind for effect, was used by traveling performers to tell the story of King Philip's War. Notice that Metacom is pictured not as a savage but as a dignified man. No longer in danger of Indian attack, nineteenth-century whites in New England adopted a romanticized version of their region's often brutal history.
© Shelburne Museum, Shelburne, Vermont.

a military alliance with the Narragansetts and Nipmucks and attacked white settlements throughout New England. Almost every day, settler William Harris fearfully reported, he heard new reports of the Indians' "burneing houses, takeing cattell, killing men & women & Children: & carrying others captive." Bitter fighting continued into 1676, ending only when the Indian warriors ran short of gunpowder and the Massachusetts Bay government hired Mohegan and Mohawk warriors, who killed Metacom.

Metacom's War of 1675–1676 (which English settlers called King Philip's War) was a deadly affair. Indians destroyed one-fifth of the English towns in

> **UNDERSTAND POINTS OF VIEW**
> How did New Englanders' religious ideas influence their relations with neighboring Native American peoples?

## The Causes of
## Metacom's War

The causes of—and responsibility for—every American war are much debated, and the war of 1675–1676 between Puritans and Native Americans is no exception. The English settlers called it King Philip's War, suggesting that the Wampanoag chief Metacom (King Philip) instigated it. Was that the case? We have no firsthand Indian accounts of its origins, but three English accounts offer different versions of events. Given the variation among the accounts and their fragmentary character, how can historians reconstruct what "really happened"?

### John Easton
### A Relacion of the Indyan Warre

John Easton was the deputy governor of Rhode Island and a Quaker. Like many Quakers, Easton was a pacifist and tried to prevent the war. He wrote this "Relacion" shortly after the conflict ended.

In [January 1675], an Indian was found dead; and by a coroner inquest of Plymouth Colony judged murdered. . . . The dead Indian was called Sassamon, and a Christian that could read and write. . . .

The report came that . . . three Indians had confessed and accused Philip [of employing them to kill Sassamon, and that consequently] . . . the English would hang Philip. So the Indians were afraid, and reported that . . . Philip [believed that the English] . . . might kill him to have his land. . . . So Philip kept his men in arms.

Plymouth governor [Josiah Winslow] required him to disband his men, and informed him his jealousy [his worry about land seizure] was false. Philip answered he would do no harm, and thanked the Governor for his information. The three Indians were hung [on June 8, 1675]. . . . And it was reported [that] Sassamon, before his death had informed [the English] of the Indian plot, and that if the Indians knew it they would kill him, and that the heathen might destroy the English for their wickedness as God had permitted the heathen to destroy the Israelites of old.

So the English were afraid and Philip was afraid and both increased in arms; but for forty years' time reports and jealousies of war had been very frequent that we did not think that now a war was breaking forth. But about a week before it did we had cause to think it would; then to endeavor to prevent it, we sent a man to Philip. . . .

He called his council and agreed to come to us; [Philip] came himself, unarmed, and about forty of his men, armed. Then five of us went over [to speak to the Indians]. Three were magistrates. We sat very friendly together [June 14–18]. We told him our business was to endeavor that they might not . . . do wrong. They said that was well; they had done no wrong; the English wronged them. We said we knew the English said that the Indians wronged them, and the Indians said the English wronged them, but our desire was the quarrel might rightly be decided in the best way, and not as dogs decide their quarrels.

The Indians owned that fighting was the worst way; then they propounded how right might take place; we said by arbitration. They said all English agreed against them; and so by arbitration they had had much wrong, many square miles of land so taken from them, for the English would have English arbitrators. . . .

Another grievance [of the Indians]: the English cattle and horses still increased [and that] . . . they could not keep their corn from being spoiled [by the English livestock]. . . .

So we departed without any discourtesies; and suddenly [c. June 25] had [a] letter from [the] Plymouth governor, [that] they intended in arms to [subjugate] Philip . . . and in a week's time after we had been with the Indians the war thus begun.

Source: John Easton, "A Relacion of the Indyan Warre, by Mr. Easton, of Roade Isld., 1675," in *Narratives of the Indian Wars, 1675–1699*, ed. Charles H. Lincoln (New York: Charles Scribner's Sons, 1913), 7–17.

### Edward Randolph
### Short Narrative of My Proceedings

Edward Randolph, an English customs official in Boston, denounced the independent policies of the Puritan colonies and tried to subject them to English control. His "Short Narrative," written in 1675, was a report to his superiors in London.

Various are the reports and conjectures of the causes of the present Indian war. Some impute it to an impudent zeal in the magistrates of Boston to Christianize those heathen before they were civilized and enjoining them the strict observation of their laws, which, to a people so rude and licentious, hath proved even intolerable. . . . While the magistrates, for their profit, put the laws severely in execution against the Indians, the people, on the other side, for lucre and gain, entice and provoke the Indians . . . to drunkenness, to which those people are so generally addicted that they will strip themselves to their skin to have their fill of rum and brandy. . . .

Some believe there have been vagrant and jesuitical [French] priests, who have made it their business, for some years past, to go from Sachem to Sachem [chief to chief], to exasperate the Indians against the English and to bring them into a confederacy, and that they were promised supplies from France and other parts to extirpate the English nation out of the continent of America. . . . Others impute the cause to some injuries offered to the Sachem Philip; for he being possessed of a tract of land called Mount Hope . . . some English had a mind to dispossess him thereof, who never wanting one pretence or other to attain their end, complained of injuries done by Philip and his Indians to their stock and cattle, whereupon Philip was often summoned before the magistrate, sometimes imprisoned, and never released but upon parting with a considerable part of his land.

But the government of the Massachusetts . . . do declare [that because of the sins of the people] . . . God hath given the heathen commission to rise against them. . . . For men wearing long hair and periwigs made of women's hair; for women . . . cutting, curling and laying out the hair. . . . For profaneness in the people not frequenting their [church] meetings.

Source: Albert B. Hart, ed., *American History Told by Contemporaries* (New York: Macmillan, 1897), 1: 458–460.

## Benjamin Church
## Entertaining Passages

Captain Benjamin Church fought in the war and helped end it by capturing Metacom's wife and son and leading the expedition that killed the Indian chieftain. Forty years later, in 1716, Church's son Thomas wrote an account of the war based on his father's notes and recollections.

While Mr. Church was diligently settling his new farm . . . Behold! The rumor of a war between the English and the natives gave a check to his projects. . . . Philip, according to his promise to his people, permitted them to march out of the neck [of the Mount Hope peninsula, where they lived]. . . . They plundered the nearest houses that the inhabitants had deserted [on the rumor of a war], but as yet offered no violence to the people, at least none were killed. . . . However, the alarm was given by their numbers, and hostile equipage, and by the prey they made of what they could find in the forsaken houses.

An express came the same day to the governor [c. June 25], who immediately gave orders to the captains of the towns to march the greatest part of their companies [of militia], and to rendezvous at Taunton. . . .

The enemy, who began their hostilities with plundering and destroying cattle, did not long content themselves with that game. They thirsted for English blood, and they soon broached it; killing two men in the way not far from Mr. Miles's garrison. And soon after, eight more at Mattapoisett, upon whose bodies they exercised more than brutish barbarities. . . .

These provocations drew out the resentment of some of Capt. Prentice's troop, who desired they might have liberty to go out and seek the enemy in their own quarters [c. June 26].

Source: Benjamin Church, *Entertaining Passages Relating to Philip's War Which Began in the Month of June, 1675*, ed. Thomas Church (Boston: B. Green, 1716).

---

### QUESTIONS FOR ANALYSIS

1. Compare what these documents say about the causes of the war. Where do the documents agree and disagree about these causes?

2. According to Randolph, what did the magistrates of Massachusetts Bay believe to be a major cause of the war? Could historians verify or disprove their explanation? How? What additional sources of evidence might be useful?

3. Drawing from these sources, who was the prime instigator of the war? Which documents provide the most compelling evidence for your conclusion? Why?

Massachusetts and Rhode Island and killed 1,000 set-tlers, nearly 5 percent of the adult population; for a time the Puritan experiment hung in the balance. But the natives' losses — from famine and disease, death in battle, and sale into slavery — were much larger: about 4,500 Indians died, one-quarter of an already dimin-ished population. Many of the surviving Wampanoag, Narragansett, and Nipmuck peoples moved west, inter-marrying with Algonquian tribes allied to the French. Over the next century, these displaced Indian peoples would take their revenge, joining with French Catholics to attack their Puritan enemies. Metacom's War did not eliminate the presence of Native Americans in south-ern New England, but it effectively destroyed their existence as independent peoples.

## Bacon's Rebellion

At the same time that New England fought its war with Metacom, Virginia was wracked by a rebellion that nearly toppled its government. It, too, grew out of a conflict with neighboring Indians, but this one inspired a popular uprising against the colony's royal governor. Like Metacom's War, it highlighted the way that a land-intensive settler colony created friction with Native American populations; in addition, it dramatized the way that ordinary colonists could challenge the right of a new planter elite to rule over them.

By the 1670s, economic and political power in Virginia was in the hands of a small circle of men who amassed land, slaves, and political offices. Through headrights and royal grants, they controlled nearly half of all the settled land in Virginia; what they could not plant themselves, they leased to tenants. Freed inden-tured servants found it ever harder to get land of their own; many were forced to lease lands, or even sign new indentures, to make ends meet. To make matters worse, the price of tobacco fell until planters received only a penny a pound for their crops in the 1670s.

At the top of Virginia's narrow social pyramid was William Berkeley, governor between 1642 and 1652 and again after 1660. To consolidate power, Berkeley bestowed large land grants on members of his council. The councilors exempted these lands from taxation and appointed friends as justices of the peace and county judges. To win support in the House of Burgesses, Berkeley bought off legislators with land grants and lucrative appointments as sheriffs and tax collectors. But social unrest erupted when the Burgesses took the vote away from landless freemen, who by now constituted half the adult white men. Although property-

holding yeomen retained their voting rights, they were angered by falling tobacco prices, political corruption, and "grievous taxations" that threatened the "utter ruin of us the poor commonalty." Berkeley and his allies were living on borrowed time.

**Frontier War**    An Indian conflict ignited the flame of social rebellion. In 1607, when the English intruded, 30,000 Native Americans resided in Virginia; by 1675, the native population had dwindled to only 3,500. By then, Europeans numbered some 38,000 and Africans another 2,500. Most Indians lived on treaty-guaranteed territory along the frontier, where poor freeholders and landless former servants now wanted to settle, demanding that the natives be expelled or extermi-nated. Their demands were ignored by wealthy plant-ers, who wanted a ready supply of tenants and laborers, and by Governor Berkeley and the planter-merchants, who traded with the Occaneechee Indians for beaver pelts and deerskins.

Fighting broke out late in 1675, when a vigilante band of Virginia militiamen murdered thirty Indians. Defying Berkeley's orders, a larger force then sur-rounded a fortified Susquehannock village and killed five leaders who came out to negotiate. The Susquehan-nocks retaliated by attacking outlying plantations and killing three hundred whites. In response, Berkeley proposed a defensive strategy: a series of frontier forts to deter Indian intrusions. The settlers dismissed this scheme as a militarily useless plot by planter-merchants to impose high taxes and take "all our tobacco into their own hands."

**Challenging the Government**    Enter Nathaniel Bacon, a young, well-connected migrant from England who emerged as the leader of the rebels. Bacon held a position on the governor's council, but he was shut out of Berkeley's inner circle and differed with Berkeley on Indian policy. When the governor refused to grant him a military commission, Bacon mobilized his neighbors and attacked any Indians he could find. Condemning the frontiersmen as "rebels and mutineers," Berkeley expelled Bacon from the council and had him arrested. But Bacon's army forced the governor to release their leader and hold legislative elections. The newly elected House of Burgesses enacted far-reaching reforms that curbed the powers of the governor and council and restored voting rights to landless freemen.

These much-needed reforms came too late. Poor farmers and servants resented years of exploitation by wealthy planters, arrogant justices of the peace, and

**Nathaniel Bacon**
Condemned as a rebel and a traitor in his own time, Nathaniel Bacon emerged in the late nineteenth century as a southern hero, a harbinger of the Confederate rebels of 1860–1865. The Association for the Preservation of Virginia Antiquities, founded in 1888, commissioned this stained-glass window depicting Bacon in dual guises of a well-dressed gentleman and a rebel in body armor. Installing Bacon's portrait in a window of the Powder Magazine in Williamsburg (built by Governor Alexander Spotswood in 1715), explained a leading member of the association, would connect "present Virginia with her great and noble past" and commemorate those who shed their "blood for Virginia and the South." Preservation Virginia.

"wicked & pernicious Counsellors." As one yeoman rebel complained, "A poor man who has only his labour to maintain himself and his family pays as much [in taxes] as a man who has 20,000 acres." Backed by 400 armed men, Bacon issued a "Manifesto and Declaration of the People" that demanded the removal of Indians and an end to the rule of wealthy "parasites." "All the power and sway is got into the hands of the rich," Bacon proclaimed as his army burned Jamestown to the ground and plundered the plantations of Berkeley's allies. When Bacon died suddenly of dysentery in October 1676, the governor took revenge, dispersing the rebel army, seizing the estates of well-to-do rebels, and hanging 23 men.

In the wake of Bacon's Rebellion, Virginia's leaders worked harder to appease their humble neighbors. But the rebellion also coincided with the time when Virginia planters were switching from indentured servants, who became free after four years, to slaves, who labored for life. In the eighteenth century, wealthy planters would make common cause with poorer whites, while slaves became the colony's most exploited workers. That fateful change eased tensions within the free population but committed subsequent generations of Americans to a labor system based on racial exploitation. Bacon's Rebellion, like Metacom's War, reminds us that these colonies were unfinished worlds, still searching for viable foundations.

> **PLACE EVENTS IN CONTEXT**
> In what ways was Bacon's Rebellion symptomatic of social tensions in the colony of Virginia?

## SUMMARY

During the sixteenth and seventeenth centuries, three types of colonies took shape in the Americas. In Mesoamerica and the Andes, Spanish colonists made indigenous empires their own, capitalizing on pre-existing labor systems and using tribute and the discovery of precious metals to generate enormous wealth, which Philip II used to defend the interests of the Catholic Church in Europe. In tropical and subtropical regions, colonizers transferred the plantation complex—a centuries-old form of production and labor discipline—to places suited to growing exotic crops like sugar, tobacco, and indigo. The rigors of plantation agriculture demanded a large supply of labor, which was first filled in English colonies by indentured servitude and later supplemented and eclipsed by African slavery. The third type of colony, neo-European settlement, developed in North America's temperate zone, where European migrants adapted familiar systems of social and economic organization in new settings.

Everywhere in the Americas, colonization was, first and foremost, a process of experimentation. As resources from the Americas flowed to Europe, monarchies were strengthened and the competition among them — sharpened by the schism between Protestants and Catholics — gained new force and energy. Establishing colonies demanded political, social, and cultural innovations that threw Europeans, Native Americans, and Africans together in bewildering circumstances, triggered massive ecological change through the Columbian Exchange, and demanded radical adjustments. In the Chesapeake and New England — the two earliest regions of English settlement on mainland North America — the adjustment to new circumstances sparked conflict with neighboring Indians and waves of instability within the colonies. These external and internal crises were products of the struggle to adapt to the rigors of colonization.

# CHAPTER REVIEW

 **MAKE IT STICK**   Go to **LearningCurve** to retain what you've read.

## TERMS TO KNOW   Identify and explain the significance of each term below.

### Key Concepts and Events

chattel slavery (p. 40)

neo-Europes (p. 40)

*encomienda* (p. 42)

Columbian Exchange (p. 43)

outwork (p. 45)

mercantilism (p. 45)

House of Burgesses (p. 52)

royal colony (p. 52)

freeholds (p. 53)

headright system (p. 54)

indentured servitude (p. 54)

Pilgrims (p. 60)

Puritans (p. 61)

joint-stock corporation (p. 62)

predestination (p. 62)

toleration (p. 62)

covenant of works (p. 62)

covenant of grace (p. 62)

town meeting (p. 64)

### Key People

Philip II (p. 44)

Francis Drake (p. 45)

Opechancanough (p. 52)

Lord Baltimore (p. 52)

John Winthrop (p. 61)

Roger Williams (p. 62)

Anne Hutchinson (p. 62)

Metacom (p. 67)

## REVIEW QUESTIONS   Answer these questions to demonstrate your understanding of the chapter's main ideas.

1. How did Spain's conquest of central Mexico and the Andes shape European competition in the Americas? How did the Protestant Reformation affect this competition?

2. How did environmental and ecological factors shape colonial enterprise, and how did the process of colonization impact American ecology and environments?

3. What "push factors" caused people to leave England for its colonies in the seventeenth century? What "pull factors" drew them to particular colonies or regions?

4. **THEMATIC UNDERSTANDING**   Review the events listed under "Politics and Power" and "Ideas, Beliefs, and Culture" on the thematic timeline on page 5. How did political developments in seventeenth-century England impact the development of its American colonies?

## MAKING CONNECTIONS

Recognize the larger developments and continuities within and across chapters by answering these questions.

1. **ACROSS TIME AND PLACE**   In Chapter 1, we saw that there were many parallels between Native American, European, and African societies on the eve of contact. Yet Europeans ended up dominating both Native American and African populations in colonial American settings. Based on what you learned in Chapter 2, what factors help to explain that dominance?

2. **VISUAL EVIDENCE**   Take another look at the image of John Smith and Opechancanough on page 49. It is taken from Smith's *Generall Historie of Virginia, New-England, and the Summer Isles*, which was first published in 1624. What is the dominant theme of the image? How might recent events in Virginia have colored the emphases in the book's illustrations?

## MORE TO EXPLORE

Start here to learn more about the events discussed in this chapter.

Virginia DeJohn Anderson, *Creatures of Empire* (2004). Explores the significance of animal domestication in early New England and Chesapeake colonies.

Kathleen Brown, *Good Wives, Nasty Wenches, and Anxious Patriarchs* (1996). Examines the interrelationship of gender and race in early Virginia.

Alfred W. Crosby, *Ecological Imperialism* (1986). Introduces the term *neo-Europes* and asks why there are so many of them.

Jenny Hale Pulsipher, *Subjects unto the Same King* (2005). Considers the multifaceted contest for power in seventeenth-century New England.

"The Plymouth Colony Archive Project" (**histarch .uiuc.edu/plymouth/**). A rich array of fully searchable texts and material culture resources.

"Salem Witch Trials" (**etext.virginia.edu/salem /witchcraft/home.html**). Extensive materials on the Salem witchcraft trials, including a fascinating interactive map feature.

## TIMELINE

Ask yourself why this chapter begins and ends with these dates and then identify the links among related events.

| | |
|---|---|
| **1550–1630** | • English crown supports mercantilism |
| **1556–1598** | • Reign of Philip II, king of Spain |
| **1558–1603** | • Reign of Elizabeth I, queen of England |
| **1577–1580** | • Francis Drake's *Golden Hind* circles the globe, captures Spanish treasure fleet |
| **1560–1620** | • Growth of English Puritan movement |
| **1588** | • Storms and English ships destroy Spanish Armada |
| **1603–1625** | • Reign of James I, king of England |
| **1607** | • English traders settle Jamestown (Virginia) |
| **1608** | • Samuel de Champlain founds Quebec |
| **1609** | • Henry Hudson explores North America for the Dutch |
| **1614** | • Dutch set up fur-trading post at Fort Orange (Albany) |
| **1619** | • First Africans arrive in Chesapeake region<br>• House of Burgesses convenes in Virginia |
| **1620** | • Pilgrims found Plymouth Colony |
| **1620–1660** | • Chesapeake colonies enjoy tobacco boom |
| **1621** | • Dutch West India Company chartered |
| **1622** | • Opechancanough's uprising |
| **1624** | • Virginia becomes royal colony |
| **1625–1649** | • Reign of Charles I, king of England |
| **1630** | • Puritans found Massachusetts Bay Colony |
| **1634** | • Colonists arrive in Maryland |
| **1636** | • Beginning of Puritan-Pequot War<br>• Roger Williams founds Providence |
| **1637** | • Anne Hutchinson banished from Massachusetts Bay |
| **1640s** | • Iroquois initiate wars over fur trade |
| **1642–1659** | • Puritan Revolution in England |
| **1660** | • Restoration of the English monarchy<br>• tobacco prices fall and remain low |
| **1664** | • English conquer New Netherland |
| **1675** | • Bacon's Rebellion in Virginia |
| **1675–1676** | • Metacom's War in New England |
| **1692** | • Salem witchcraft trials |

**KEY TURNING POINTS:** The Chesapeake tobacco boom (1620–1660), Opechancanough's uprising (1622), and the takeover of Virginia by the crown (1624). How were these events related to each other? What was their cumulative result?

# British North America and the Atlantic World

## 1660–1763

By 1660, the patterns of colonial enterprise in the Americas were becoming clear. For the colonies of England — which became Britain after the 1707 Act of Union with Scotland — the period from 1660 to 1763 was one of growth and diversification. Slave imports to plantation colonies exploded, while a wide array of European peoples — coming from Ireland and continental Europe as well as England, Wales, and Scotland — jostled together in rapidly growing regions of neo-European settlement. Yet a coherent imperial vision for these American holdings emerged slowly, and the colonies remained largely independent of crown control.

After 1689, Europe plunged into a century of warfare that had an enormous impact on the Americas. As wars spilled over into North America, British, French, and Spanish colonies all engaged more deeply with neighboring Indians, whom they often sought to employ as allies in their struggles to control North American territory. Native American polities were undergoing dramatic transformations in these same years, reshaping themselves to function more effectively in relation to their European neighbors. At the same time, warfare, immigration, and trade laid the foundation for more intensive interactions across the Atlantic. These interactions, and the cultural movements they supported, helped to knit together the increasingly diverse colonies of British North America.

Part 2 addresses these developments, giving particular attention to the following three main concepts:

## The Diversification of British North America

The American colonies of the various European nations gradually diverged from each other in character. The tribute-based societies at the core of Spain's empire developed into complex multiracial societies; Portuguese Brazil was dominated by its plantation and mining enterprises; the Dutch largely withdrew their energies from the Americas, except for a few plantation colonies; the French, too, developed several important plantation colonies in the West Indies but struggled to populate their vast North American holdings. The population of Britain's colonies, by contrast, grew and diversified after 1660. Britain came to dominate the Atlantic slave trade and brought more than two million slaves to its American colonies. The great majority went to Jamaica, Barbados, and the other sugar islands, but half a million found their way to the mainland, where, by 1763, they constituted nearly 20 percent of the mainland colonies' populations. Slavery was a growing and thriving institution in British North America.

Non-English Europeans also crossed the Atlantic in very large numbers. The ethnic landscape of Britain's mainland colonies was dramatically altered by 115,000 migrants from Ireland (most of them Scots-Irish Presbyterians) and 100,000 Germans. Most immigrated to Pennsylvania, which soon had the most ethnically diverse population of Europeans on the continent. Relations among these groups were often divisive, as each struggled to maintain its identity and autonomy in a rapidly changing landscape.

## Rise of the British Atlantic World

These population movements were part of the larger growth and development of the Atlantic World, a phrase historians use to refer to the quickening pace of contacts and exchanges connecting Europe, Africa, and the Americas. The rise of the British Atlantic was a layered phenomenon that began with the strength of Britain's transatlantic shipping networks, which in turn laid the foundation for large-scale population flows, rising economic productivity, and dramatic cultural transformations. The growing power of its navy, merchant marine, and manufacturing sector allowed Britain to dominate the eighteenth-century Atlantic. Much of the cultural impact of its maritime power derived from two further developments: the print revolution, which brought a vast array of ideas into circulation; and the consumer revolution, which flooded the Atlantic World with a wide array of newly available merchandise.

The British Atlantic World gave rise to four critically important cultural developments. It spread Enlightenment ideas and helped to create a transatlantic community of literati interested in science and rationalism; it supported communities of Pietists who promoted the revival and expansion of Christianity; it gave well-to-do colonists access to genteel values and the finery needed to put them into action; and, by making such an abundance of consumer goods available, it encouraged colonists to go further into debt than they ever had before.

## Contact and Conflict

Alongside the diversification of colonial populations and the rise of the British Atlantic, the eighteenth century was shaped by contact and conflict: between colonies and their Native American neighbors, and also among rival European empires. In Europe, the period after 1689 has sometimes been called the Second Hundred Years' War, when Britain, France, and their European allies went to war against each other repeatedly. As these conflicts came to the North American theater, they decisively influenced Indian relations. Native American populations shrank dramatically or disappeared altogether during the seventeenth century, devastated by the effects of the Columbian Exchange (Chapter 2). The rise of imperial warfare encouraged the process of "tribalization," whereby Indians regrouped into political structures—called "tribes" by Europeans—that could deal more effectively with their colonial neighbors and strike alliances in times of war. Europeans, in turn, employed Indian allies as proxy warriors in their conflicts over North American territory.

This pattern culminated in the Great War for Empire, which began in the North American backcountry, engaged thousands of provincial soldiers and Native American warriors, and reshaped the map of North America. The Treaty of Paris of 1763 gave Britain control of the entire continent east of the Mississippi. Events would soon show what a mixed blessing that outcome would turn out to be.

# British North America and the Atlantic World 1660–1763

## Thematic Understanding

This timeline organizes some of the important developments of this period into themes. How did the demographic changes outlined under the theme "Peopling" impact the developments that are listed under "Work, Exchange, and Technology"?  **>**

| | WORK, EXCHANGE, & TECHNOLOGY | PEOPLING | POLITICS & POWER | IDEAS, BELIEFS, & CULTURE | IDENTITY |
|---|---|---|---|---|---|
| **1660** | • South Atlantic System links plantation and neo-European colonies<br><br>• Mercantilist legislation in England: Navigation Acts (1651, 1660, 1663)<br><br>• New York inherits Hudson River Valley manors from the Dutch; Carolina proprietors try but fail to institute a manorial system<br><br>• Migrants to Pennsylvania seek freehold lands<br><br>• Rapid expansion of African slave imports undergirds sugar, tobacco, and rice plantation systems | • The Middle Passage shapes Africans' experiences of arrival<br><br>• Indian slave trade emerges in South Carolina<br><br>• First Mennonites arrive in Pennsylvania (1683) | • Dominion of New England (1686–1689)<br><br>• Glorious Revolution (1688–1689)<br><br>• War of the League of Augsburg (1689–1697)<br><br>• Founding of the Restoration Colonies: the Carolinas (1663), New York (1664), Pennsylvania (1681) | • Collapse of the Puritan Commonwealth leads to toleration in England<br><br>• Isaac Newton publishes *Principia Mathematica* (1687) | • Restoration makes England a monarchy again; royalist revival<br><br>• The Glorious Revolution makes England a constitutional monarchy<br><br>• Massachusetts loses its charter (1684) and gains a new one (1691) |
| **1690** | • New England shipbuilding industry and merchant community come to dominate the coastal trade<br><br>• Agricultural labor and artisanal skills in high demand in the Middle colonies | • Quakers emigrate to Pennsylvania and New Jersey<br><br>• Second wave of Germans arrives in Pennsylvania, Shenandoah Valley | • Parliament creates Board of Trade (1696)<br><br>• War of the Spanish Succession (1702–1713) | • John Locke publishes *Two Treatises on Government* (1690)<br><br>• Rise of toleration among colonial Protestants<br><br>• Print revolution begins | • Colonists gain autonomy in the post–Glorious Revolution era<br><br>• Tribalization developing among Native American peoples |
| **1720** | • The price of wheat rises (doubles in Philadelphia, 1720–1770)<br><br>• British trade dominates the Atlantic<br><br>• Opportunity and inequality in the Middle colonies<br><br>• Ohio Company of Virginia receives 200,000 acres (1749) | • Scots-Irish begin migrating to Pennsylvania (c. 1720)<br><br>• Parliament charters Georgia (1732)<br><br>• Penns make Walking Purchase from the Delawares (1737) | • Robert Walpole is prime minister (1720–1742)<br><br>• Stono Rebellion (1739)<br><br>• War of Jenkins's Ear (1739–1741)<br><br>• War of the Austrian Succession (1740–1748) | • George Whitefield's visit to America sparks the Great Awakening (1739)<br><br>• Benjamin Franklin founds American Philosophical Society (1743)<br><br>• New colleges, newspapers, magazines | • African American community forms in the Chesapeake<br><br>• Planter aristocracy emerges in the Chesapeake and South Carolina<br><br>• Culture of gentility spreads among well-to-do |
| **1750** | • Freehold society in crisis in New England<br><br>• Half of Middle colonies' white men landless<br><br>• Conflicts over western lands and political power (1750–1775)<br><br>• British industry being mechanized; colonial debt crisis | • 40,000 Germans and Swiss emigrate to Pennsylvania (1749–1756)<br><br>• Anglo-Americans pushing onto backcountry lands | • French and Indian War/Seven Years' War (1754–1763)<br><br>• The Albany Congress (1754)<br><br>• The Treaty of Paris (1763)<br><br>• Pontiac's Rebellion (1763) | • At least twelve religious denominations in Philadelphia<br><br>• Neolin promotes nativist revival among Ohio Indians (1763) | • Victory in the Great War for Empire sparks pro-British pride in the colonies<br><br>• Desire for political autonomy and economic independence strong |

# 3
## CHAPTER

# The British Atlantic World
# 1660–1750

For two weeks in June 1744, the town of Lancaster, Pennsylvania, hosted more than 250 Iroquois men, women, and children for a diplomatic conference with representatives from Pennsylvania, Maryland, and Virginia. Crowds of curious observers thronged Lancaster's streets and courthouse. The conference grew out of a diplomatic system between the colonies and the Iroquois designed to air grievances and resolve conflict: the Covenant Chain. Participants welcomed each other, exchanged speeches, and negotiated agreements in public ceremonies whose minutes became part of the official record of the colonies.

At Lancaster, the colonies had much to ask of their Iroquois allies. For one thing, they wanted them to confirm a land agreement. The Iroquois often began such conferences by resisting land deals; as the Cayuga orator Gachradodon said, "You know very well, when the White people came first here they were poor; but now they have got our Lands, and are by them become rich, and we are now poor; what little we have had for the Land goes soon away, but the Land lasts forever." In the end, however, they had little choice but to accept merchandise in exchange for land, since colonial officials were unwilling to take no for an answer. The colonists also announced that Britain was once again going to war with France, and they requested military support from their Iroquois allies. Canassatego—a tall, commanding Onondaga orator, about sixty years old, renowned for his eloquence—replied, "We shall never forget that you and we have but one Heart, one Head, one Eye, one Ear, and one Hand. We shall have all your Country under our Eye, and take all the Care we can to prevent any Enemy from coming into it."

**IDENTIFY THE BIG IDEA**
How did the South Atlantic System create an interconnected Atlantic World, and how did this system impact development in the British colonies?

To see a longer excerpt of the Canassatego document, along with other primary sources from this period, see *Sources for America's History*.

The Lancaster conference—and dozens of others like it that occurred between 1660 and 1750—demonstrates that the British colonies, like those of France and Spain, relied ever more heavily on alliances with Native Americans as they sought to extend their power in North America. Indian nations remade themselves in these same years, creating political structures—called "tribes" by Europeans—that allowed them to regroup in the face of population decline and function more effectively alongside neighboring colonies. The colonies, meanwhile, were drawn together into an integrated economic sphere—the South Atlantic System—that brought prosperity to British North America, while they achieved a measure of political autonomy that became essential to their understanding of what it meant to be British subjects.

**English Tobacco Label, c. 1700** This label, which was used to advertise Virginia tobacco to London consumers, illustrates the growth of plantation economies in North America. Three well-to-do planters, bewigged and dressed in fashionable, colorful coats, take their ease with pipes of tobacco and glasses of liquor while slaves labor for them in the fields. The product's name—London's Virginia—highlights the relationship between production on colonial plantations and consumption in the English metropolis. The Granger Collection, New York.

81

# Colonies to Empire, 1660–1713

Before 1660, England governed its New England and Chesapeake colonies haphazardly. Taking advantage of that laxness and the English civil war, local "big men" (Puritan magistrates and tobacco planters) ran their societies as they wished. Following the restoration of the monarchy in 1660, royal bureaucrats tried to impose order on the unruly settlements and, enlisting the aid of Indian allies, warred with rival European powers.

## The Restoration Colonies and Imperial Expansion

Charles II (r. 1660–1685) expanded English power in Asia and America. In 1662, he married the Portuguese princess Catherine of Braganza, whose dowry included the islands of Bombay (present-day Mumbai). Then, in 1663, Charles initiated new outposts in America by authorizing eight loyal noblemen to settle Carolina, an area that had long been claimed by Spain and populated by thousands of Indians. The following year, he awarded the just-conquered Dutch colony of New Netherland to his brother James, the Duke of York, who renamed the colony New York and then re-granted a portion of it, called New Jersey, to another group of proprietors. Finally, in 1681, Charles granted a vast track to William Penn: Pennsylvania, or "Penn's Woods." In a great land grab, England had ousted the Dutch from North America, intruded into Spain's northern empire, and claimed all the land in between.

**The Carolinas**   In 1660, English settlement was concentrated in New England and the Chesapeake. Five corporate colonies coexisted in New England: Massachusetts Bay, Plymouth, Connecticut, New Haven, and Rhode Island. (Connecticut absorbed New Haven in 1662, while Massachusetts Bay became a royal colony and absorbed Plymouth in 1692.) In the Chesapeake, Virginia was controlled by the crown while Maryland was in the hands of a Lord Proprietor. Like Lord Baltimore's Maryland, the new settlements in Carolina, New York, New Jersey, and Pennsylvania — the Restoration Colonies, as historians call them — were **proprietorships**: the Carolina and Jersey grantees, the Duke of York, and William Penn owned all the land in their new colonies and could rule them as they wished, provided that their laws conformed broadly to those of England (Table 3.1). Indeed, in New York, James II refused to allow an elective assembly and ruled by decree. The Carolina proprietors envisioned a traditional European society; there the Fundamental Constitutions of Carolina (1669) legally established the Church of England and prescribed a manorial system, with a mass of serfs governed by a handful of powerful nobles.

The manorial system proved a fantasy. The first North Carolina settlers were a mixture of poor families and runaway servants from Virginia and English Quakers, an equality-minded Protestant sect (also known as the Society of Friends). Quakers "think there is no difference between a Gentleman and a labourer," complained an Anglican clergyman. Refusing to work on large manors, the settlers raised corn, hogs, and tobacco on modest family farms. Inspired by Bacon's Rebellion, they rebelled in 1677 against taxes on tobacco and again in 1708 against taxes to support the Anglican Church. Through their stubborn independence, residents forced the proprietors to abandon their dreams of a feudal society.

In South Carolina, the colonists also went their own way. The leading white settlers there were migrants from overcrowded Barbados. Hoping to re-create that island's hierarchical slave society, they used enslaved workers — both Africans and Native Americans — to raise cattle and food crops for export to the West Indies. Carolina merchants opened a lucrative trade in deerskins and Indian slaves with neighboring peoples. Then, around 1700, South Carolina planters hit upon rice cultivation. The swampy estuaries of the coastal low country could be modified with sluices, floodgates, and check dams to create ideal rice-growing conditions, and slaves could do the backbreaking work. By 1708, white Carolinians relied upon a few thousand slaves to work their coastal plantations; thereafter, the African population exploded. Blacks outnumbered whites by 1710 and constituted two-thirds of the population by 1740.

**William Penn and Pennsylvania**   In contrast to the Carolinas, which languished for decades with proprietors and colonists at odds, William Penn's colony was marked by unity of purpose: all who came hoped to create a prosperous neo-European settlement that approximated the social and economic systems they knew at home. In 1681, Charles II bestowed Pennsylvania (which included present-day Delaware) on William Penn as payment for a large debt owed to Penn's father. The younger Penn, though born to wealth — he owned substantial estates in Ireland and England and lived lavishly — joined the **Quakers**, who condemned extravagance. Penn designed Pennsylvania as a refuge for his fellow Quakers, who were persecuted in England because they refused to serve in the military or pay taxes to support the Church of England. Penn

## TABLE 3.1

### English Colonies Established in North America, 1660–1750

| Colony | Date | Original Colony Type | Religion | Status in 1775 | Chief Export/ Economic Activity |
|---|---|---|---|---|---|
| Carolina | 1663 | Proprietary | Church of England | Royal | |
| North | 1691 | | | | Farming, naval stores |
| South | 1691 | | | | Rice, indigo |
| New Jersey | 1664 | Proprietary | Church of England | Royal | Wheat |
| New York | 1664 | Proprietary | Church of England | Royal | Wheat |
| Pennsylvania | 1681 | Proprietary | Quaker | Proprietary | Wheat |
| Georgia | 1732 | Trustees | Church of England | Royal | Rice |
| New Hampshire (separated from Massachusetts) | 1741 | Royal | Congregationalist | Royal | Mixed farming, lumber, naval stores |
| Nova Scotia | 1749 | Royal | Church of England | Royal | Fishing, mixed farming, naval stores |

himself had spent more than two years in jail in England for preaching his beliefs.

Like the Puritans, the Quakers sought to restore Christianity to its early simple spirituality. But they rejected the Puritans' pessimistic Calvinist doctrines, which restricted salvation to a small elect. The Quakers followed the teachings of two English visionaries, George Fox and Margaret Fell, who argued that God had imbued all men — and women — with an "inner light" of grace or understanding. Reflecting the sect's emphasis on gender equality, 350 Quaker women would serve as ministers in the colonies.

Mindful of the catastrophic history of Indian relations in the Chesapeake and New England, Penn exhorted colonists to "sit downe Lovingly" alongside the Native American inhabitants of the Delaware and Susquehanna valleys. He wrote a letter to the leaders of the Iroquois Confederacy alerting them to his intention to settle a colony, and in 1682 he arranged a public treaty with the Delaware Indians to purchase the lands that Philadelphia and the surrounding settlements would soon occupy.

Penn's Frame of Government (1681) applied the Quakers' radical beliefs to politics. It ensured religious freedom by prohibiting a legally established church, and it promoted political equality by allowing all property-owning men to vote and hold office.

Cheered by these provisions, thousands of Quakers, mostly yeoman families from the northwest Midland region of England, flocked to Pennsylvania. To attract European Protestants, Penn published pamphlets in Germany promising cheap land and religious toleration. In 1683, migrants from Saxony founded Germantown (just outside Philadelphia), and thousands of other Germans soon followed. Ethnic diversity, pacifism, and freedom of conscience made Pennsylvania the most open and democratic of the Restoration Colonies.

## From Mercantilism to Imperial Dominion

As Charles II distributed American land, his ministers devised policies to keep colonial trade in English hands. Since the 1560s, the English crown had pursued mercantilist policies, using government subsidies and charters to stimulate English manufacturing and foreign trade. Now it extended these mercantilist strategies to the American settlements through the **Navigation Acts** (Table 3.2).

**The Navigation Acts**   Believing they had to control trade with the colonies to reap their economic benefits, English ministers wanted agricultural goods and raw materials to be carried to English ports in English

**William Penn's Treaty with the Indians, 1771**

Benjamin West executed this famous picture of William Penn's 1683 meeting with the Lenni-Lenapes, who called themselves the Common People. A Quaker pacifist, Penn refused to seize Indian lands by force and negotiated their purchase. But his son, Thomas Penn, probably had a political purpose when he commissioned the painting in 1771. By evoking a peaceful past, West's work reinforced the Penn family's proprietary claims, which were under strong attack by the Pennsylvania assembly. Pennsylvania Academy of the Fine Arts, Philadelphia, USA / The Bridgeman Art Library.

vessels. In reality, Dutch and French shippers were often buying sugar and other colonial products from English colonies and carrying them directly into foreign markets. To counter this practice, the Navigation Act of 1651 required that goods be carried on ships owned by English or colonial merchants. New parliamentary acts in 1660 and 1663 strengthened the ban on foreign traders: colonists could export sugar and tobacco only to England and import European goods only through England; moreover, three-quarters of the crew on English vessels had to be English. To pay the customs officials who enforced these laws, the Revenue Act of 1673 imposed a "plantation duty" on American exports of sugar and tobacco.

**PLACE EVENTS IN CONTEXT**
How did the ambitions of Charles II and James II remake English North America?

The English government backed these policies with military force. In three wars between 1652 and 1674, the English navy drove the Dutch from New Netherland and contested Holland's control of the Atlantic slave trade by attacking Dutch forts and ships along the West African coast. Meanwhile, English merchants expanded their fleets, which increased in capacity from 150,000 tons in 1640 to 340,000 tons in 1690. This growth occurred on both sides of the Atlantic; by 1702, only London and Bristol had more ships registered in port than did the town of Boston.

Though colonial ports benefitted from the growth of English shipping, many colonists violated the Navigation Acts. Planters continued to trade with Dutch shippers, and New England merchants imported sugar and molasses from the French West Indies. The Massachusetts Bay assembly boldly declared: "The laws of

| TABLE 3.2 | | |
|---|---|---|
| **Navigation Acts, 1651–1751** | | |
| | **Purpose** | **Compliance** |
| Act of 1651 | Cut Dutch trade | Mostly ignored |
| Act of 1660 | Ban foreign shipping; enumerate goods that go only to England | Partially obeyed |
| Act of 1663 | Allow European imports only through England | Partially obeyed |
| Staple Act (1673) | Ensure enumerated goods go only to England | Mostly obeyed |
| Act of 1696 | Prevent frauds; create vice-admiralty courts | Mostly obeyed |
| Woolen Act (1699) | Prevent export or intercolonial sale of textiles | Partially obeyed |
| Hat Act (1732) | Prevent export or intercolonial sale of hats | Partially obeyed |
| Molasses Act (1733) | Cut American imports of molasses from French West Indies | Extensively violated |
| Iron Act (1750) | Prevent manufacture of finished iron products | Extensively violated |
| Currency Act (1751) | End use of paper currency as legal tender in New England | Mostly obeyed |

England are bounded within the seas [surrounding it] and do not reach America." Outraged by this insolence, customs official Edward Randolph called for troops to "reduce Massachusetts to obedience." Instead, the Lords of Trade — the administrative body charged with colonial affairs — chose a less violent, but no less confrontational, strategy. In 1679, it denied the claim of Massachusetts Bay to New Hampshire and eventually established a separate royal colony there. Then, in 1684, the Lords of Trade persuaded an English court to annul the Massachusetts Bay charter by charging the Puritan government with violating the Navigation Acts and virtually outlawing the Church of England.

**The Dominion of New England**   The Puritans' troubles had only begun, thanks to the accession of King James II (r. 1685–1688), an aggressive and inflexible ruler. During the reign of Oliver Cromwell, James had grown up in exile in France, and he admired its authoritarian king, Louis XIV. James wanted stricter control over the colonies and targeted New England for his reforms. In 1686, the Lords of Trade revoked the charters of Connecticut and Rhode Island and merged them with Massachusetts Bay and Plymouth to form a new royal province, the **Dominion of New England**. As governor of the Dominion, James II appointed Sir Edmund Andros, a hard-edged former military officer. Two years later, James II added New York and New Jersey to the Dominion, creating a vast colony that stretched from Maine to Pennsylvania (Map 3.1).

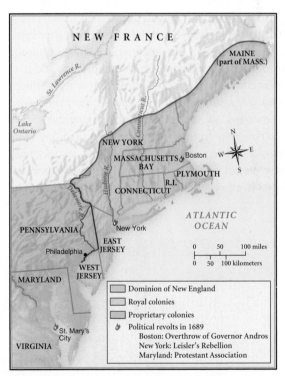

**MAP 3.1**

**The Dominion of New England, 1686–1689**

In the Dominion, James II created a vast royal colony that stretched nearly 500 miles along the Atlantic coast. During the Glorious Revolution in England, politicians and ministers in Boston and New York City led revolts that ousted Dominion officials and repudiated their authority. King William and Queen Mary replaced the Dominion with governments that balanced the power held by imperial authorities and local political institutions.

The Dominion extended to America the authoritarian model of colonial rule that the English government had imposed on Catholic Ireland. James II ordered Governor Andros to abolish the existing legislative assemblies. In Massachusetts, Andros banned town meetings, angering villagers who prized local self-rule, and advocated public worship in the Church of England, offending Puritan Congregationalists. Even worse, from the colonists' perspective, the governor invalidated all land titles granted under the original Massachusetts Bay charter. Andros offered to provide new deeds, but only if the colonists would pay an annual fee.

## The Glorious Revolution in England and America

Fortunately for the colonists, James II angered English political leaders as much as Andros alienated colonists. The king revoked the charters of English towns, rejected the advice of Parliament, and aroused popular opposition by openly practicing Roman Catholicism. Then, in 1688, James's Spanish Catholic wife gave birth to a son. To forestall the outcome of having a Catholic heir to the English throne, Protestant bishops and parliamentary leaders in the Whig Party invited William of Orange, a staunchly Protestant Dutch prince who was married to James's Protestant daughter, Mary Stuart, to come to England at the head of an invading army. With their support, William led a quick and nearly bloodless coup, and King James II was overthrown in an event dubbed the **Glorious Revolution** by

its supporters. Whig politicians forced King William and Queen Mary to accept the Declaration of Rights, creating a constitutional monarchy that enhanced the powers of the House of Commons at the expense of the crown. The Whigs wanted political power, especially the power to levy taxes, to reside in the hands of the gentry, merchants, and other substantial property owners.

To justify their coup, the members of Parliament relied on political philosopher John Locke. In his *Two Treatises on Government* (1690), Locke rejected the divine-right monarchy celebrated by James II, arguing that the legitimacy of government rests on the consent of the governed and that individuals have inalienable natural rights to life, liberty, and property. Locke's celebration of individual rights and representative government had a lasting influence in America, where many political leaders wanted to expand the powers of colonial assemblies.

**Rebellions in America**   The Glorious Revolution sparked rebellions by Protestant colonists in Massachusetts, Maryland, and New York. When news of the coup reached Boston in April 1689, Puritan leaders and 2,000 militiamen seized Governor Andros and shipped him back to England. Heeding American complaints of authoritarian rule, the new monarchs broke up the Dominion of New England. However, they refused to restore the old Puritan-dominated government of Massachusetts Bay, instead creating in 1692 a new royal colony (which included Plymouth and Maine). The new charter empowered the king to

**The Leviathan Absolutist State**

This detail from the title-page engraving of Thomas Hobbes's *Leviathan* (1651) conveys Hobbes's belief that peace and security required submission to a powerful sovereign. In this image, a giant king looms over his domain, his staff and sword symbolizing his civil and religious powers. He is the head of a body made up of the multitudes of his faceless and voiceless subjects, as they carry out his commands. What Hobbes celebrated, a majority of English politicians and people rejected. Fearing the claims of absolute power by Stuart kings, they revolted twice, executing Charles I in 1649 and deposing James II in 1688. Title page from the first edition of Thomas Hobbes's *Leviathan*, published in 1651.

appoint the governor and customs officials, gave the vote to all male property owners (not just Puritan church members), and eliminated Puritan restrictions on the Church of England.

In Maryland, the uprising had economic as well as religious causes. Since 1660, falling tobacco prices had hurt poorer farmers, who were overwhelmingly Protestant, while taxes and fees paid to mostly Catholic proprietary officials continued to rise. When Parliament ousted James II, a Protestant association mustered 700 men and forcibly removed the Catholic governor. The Lords of Trade supported this Protestant initiative: they suspended Lord Baltimore's proprietorship, imposed royal government, and made the Church of England the legal religion in the colony. This arrangement lasted until 1715, when Benedict Calvert, the fourth Lord Baltimore, converted to the Anglican faith and the king restored the proprietorship to the Calvert family.

In New York, a Dutchman named Jacob Leisler led the rebellion against the Dominion of New England. Initially he enjoyed broad support, but he soon alienated many English-speaking New Yorkers and well-to-do Dutch residents. Leisler's heavy-handed tactics made him vulnerable; when William and Mary appointed Henry Sloughter as governor in 1691, Leisler was indicted for treason, hanged, and decapitated—an act of ethnic vengeance that corrupted New York politics for a generation.

The Glorious Revolution of 1688–1689 began a new era in the politics of both England and its American colonies. In England, William and Mary ruled as **constitutional monarchs**; overseas, they promoted an empire based on commerce. They accepted the overthrow of James's disastrous Dominion of New England and allowed Massachusetts (under its new charter) and New York to resume self-government. In 1696, Parliament created a new body, the Board of Trade, to oversee

**EXPLAIN CONSEQUENCES**
How did the Glorious Revolution affect relations between England and its colonies?

**King William III and Mary II**

Rejecting Hobbes's vision of Leviathan and James II's attempts to impose absolutism, a group of England's most powerful politicians invited William of Orange—a prince of the Dutch Republic—to invade England, depose James II, and occupy the throne jointly with his wife Mary. William's army quickly overthrew James in the so-called Glorious Revolution of 1688, an event that reverberated across the Atlantic in rebellions in Massachusetts, Maryland, and New York. This portrait, from the Guild Book of the Barber Surgeons of York, was probably painted to celebrate the coronation of William and Mary in 1689.
HIP/Art Resource, NY.

colonial affairs. While the Board of Trade continued to pursue the mercantilist policies that made the colonies economically beneficial, otherwise it permitted local elites to maintain a strong hand in colonial affairs. As England plunged into a new era of European warfare, its leaders had little choice but to allow its colonies substantial autonomy.

## Imperial Wars and Native Peoples

The price that England paid for bringing William of Orange to the throne was a new commitment to warfare on the continent. England wanted William because of his unambiguous Protestant commitments; William wanted England because of the resources it could bring to bear in European wars. Beginning with the War of the League of Augsburg in 1689, England embarked on an era sometimes called the **Second Hundred Years' War**, which lasted until the defeat of Napoleon at Waterloo in 1815. In that time, England (Britain after 1707) fought in seven major wars; the longest era of peace lasted only twenty-six years (Table 3.3).

Imperial wars transformed North America. Prior to 1689, American affairs were distant from those of Europe, but the recurrent wars of the eighteenth century spilled over repeatedly into the colonies. Governments were forced to arm themselves and create new

alliances with neighboring Native Americans, who tried to turn the fighting to their own advantage. Although war brought money to the American colonies in the form of war contracts, it also placed new demands on colonial governments to support the increasingly militant British Empire. To win wars in Western Europe, the Caribbean, and far-flung oceans, British leaders created a powerful central state that spent three-quarters of its revenue on military and naval expenses.

## Tribalization

For Native Americans, the rise of war intersected with a process scholars have called **tribalization**: the adaptation of stateless peoples to the demands imposed on them by neighboring states. In North America, tribalization occurred in catastrophic circumstances. Eurasian diseases rapidly killed off broad swaths of native communities, disproportionately victimizing the old and the very young. In oral cultures, old people were irreplaceable repositories of knowledge, while the young were quite literally the future. With populations in free fall, many polities disappeared altogether. By the eighteenth century, the groups that survived had all been transformed. Many were polyglot peoples: Some new tribes, like the Catawbas, had not existed before and were pieced together from remnants of formerly large groups. Other nations, like the Iroquois, declined in numbers but sustained themselves by adopting many

| TABLE 3.3 | | | |
|---|---|---|---|
| **English Wars, 1650–1750** | | | |
| **War** | **Date** | **Purpose** | **Result** |
| Anglo-Dutch | 1652–1654 | Control markets and African slave trade | Stalemate |
| Anglo-Dutch | 1664 | Markets; conquest | England takes New Amsterdam |
| Anglo-Dutch | 1673 | Commercial markets | England makes maritime gains |
| King William's | 1689–1697 | Maintain European balance of power | Stalemate in North America |
| Queen Anne's | 1702–1713 | Maintain European balance of power | British acquire Hudson Bay and Nova Scotia |
| Jenkins's Ear | 1739–1741 | Expand markets in Spanish America | English merchants expand influence |
| King George's | 1740–1748 | Maintain European balance of power | Capture and return of Louisbourg |

war captives. In the Carolina borderlands, a large number of Muskogean-speaking communities came together as a nation known to the British as the "Creek" Indians, so named because some of them lived on Ochese Creek. Similarly, the Cherokees, the Delawares, and other groups that were culturally linked but politically fragmented became coherent "tribes" to deal more effectively with their European neighbors.

The rise of imperial warfare exposed Native American communities to danger, but it also gave them newfound leverage. The Iroquois were radically endangered by imperial conflict: a promised English alliance failed them, and in 1693 a combined force of French soldiers, militiamen, and their Indian allies burned all three Mohawk villages to the ground. Thereafter, the Iroquois devised a strategy for playing French and English interests off against each other. In 1701, they made alliances with both empires, declaring their intention to remain neutral in future conflicts between them. This did not mean that the Iroquois stayed on the sideline: Iroquois warriors often participated in raids during wartime, and Iroquois spokesmen met regularly with representatives of New York and New France to affirm their alliances and receive diplomatic gifts that included guns, powder, lead, clothing, and rum (from the British) or brandy (from the French). Their neutrality, paradoxically, made them more sought after as allies. For example, their alliance with New York, known as the **Covenant Chain**, soon became a model for relations between the British Empire and other Native American peoples.

Imperial warfare also reshaped Indian relations in the Southeast. During the War of the Spanish Succession (1702–1713), which pitted Britain against France and Spain, English settlers in the Carolinas armed the Creeks, whose 15,000 members farmed the fertile lands along the present-day border of Georgia and Alabama. A joint English-Creek expedition attacked Spanish

### The "Four Indian Kings" in London, 1710

After a failed invasion of Canada in 1709, a colonial delegation went to London to ask the queen to try again. They brought four Indians with them—three Mohawks and a Mahican—and presented them in London as the "Four Indian Kings" of the Iroquois. The four kings met Queen Anne, dined with nobility, attended the theater, and toured the sites. They sat for several portraits, which were engraved for prints like this one. The queen agreed to make another try for Canada, but the 1711 invasion failed again. Albany Institute of History and Art, Gift of the Estate of Cornelia Cogswell (Mrs. Henry M. Sage) 1972.65.7.

Florida, burning the town of St. Augustine but failing to capture the fort. To protect Havana in nearby Cuba, the Spanish reinforced St. Augustine and unsuccessfully attacked Charleston, South Carolina.

## Indian Goals

The Creeks had their own agenda: to become the dominant tribe in the region, they needed to vanquish their longtime enemies, the pro-French Choctaws to the west and the Spanish-allied Apalachees to the south. Beginning in 1704, a force of Creek and Yamasee warriors destroyed the remaining Franciscan missions in northern Florida, attacked the Spanish settlement at Pensacola, and captured a thousand Apalachees, whom they sold to South Carolinian slave traders for sale in the West Indies. Simultaneously, a Carolina-supported Creek expedition attacked the Iroquois-speaking Tuscarora people of North Carolina, killing hundreds, executing 160 male captives, and sending 400 women and children into slavery. The surviving Tuscaroras joined the Iroquois in New York (who now became the Six Nations of the Iroquois). The Carolinians, having used the Creeks to kill Spaniards, now died at the hands of their former allies: when English traders demanded payment for trade debts in 1715, the Creeks and Yamasees revolted, killing 400 colonists before being overwhelmed by the Carolinians and their new Indian allies, the Cherokees.

Native Americans also joined in the warfare between French Catholics in Canada and English Protestants in New England. With French aid, Catholic Mohawk and Abenaki warriors took revenge on their Puritan enemies. They destroyed English settlements in Maine and, in 1704, attacked the western Massachusetts town of Deerfield, where they killed 48 residents and carried 112 into captivity. In response, New England militia attacked French settlements and, in 1710, joined with British naval forces to seize Port Royal in French Acadia (Nova Scotia). However, a major British–New England expedition against the French stronghold at Quebec, inspired in part by the visit of four Indian "kings" to London, failed miserably.

Stalemated militarily in America, Britain won major territorial and commercial concessions through its victories in Europe. In the Treaty of Utrecht (1713), Britain obtained Newfoundland, Acadia, and the Hudson Bay region of northern Canada from France, as well as access through Albany to the western Indian trade. From Spain, Britain acquired the strategic fortress of Gibraltar at the entrance to the Mediterranean and a thirty-year contract to supply slaves to Spanish America. These gains advanced Britain's quest for commercial supremacy and brought peace to eastern North America for a generation (Map 3.2).

**UNDERSTAND POINTS OF VIEW**
What did Native Americans have to gain by participating in imperial wars?

# The Imperial Slave Economy

Britain's focus on America reflected the growth of a new agricultural and commercial order — the **South Atlantic System** — that produced sugar, tobacco, rice, and other tropical and subtropical products for an international market. Its plantation societies were ruled by European planter-merchants and worked by hundreds of thousands of enslaved Africans (Figure 3.1).

## The South Atlantic System

The South Atlantic System had its center in Brazil and the West Indies, and sugar was its primary product. Before 1500, there were few sweet foods in Europe — mostly honey and fruits — so when European planters developed vast sugarcane plantations in America, they found a ready market for their crop. (The craving for the potent new sweet food was so intense that, by 1900, sugar accounted for an astonishing 20 percent of the calories consumed by the world's people.)

European merchants, investors, and planters garnered the profits of the South Atlantic System. Following mercantilist principles, they provided the plantations with tools and equipment to grow and process the sugarcane and ships to carry it to Europe. But it was the Atlantic slave trade that made the system run. Between 1520 and 1650, Portuguese traders carried about 820,000 Africans across the Atlantic — about 4,000 slaves a year before 1600 and 10,000 annually thereafter. Over the next half century, the Dutch dominated the Atlantic slave trade; then, between 1700 and 1800, the British transported about 2.5 million of the total of 6.1 million Africans carried to the Americas.

**England and the West Indies**    England was a latecomer to the plantation economy, but from the beginning the prospect of a lucrative cash crop drew large numbers of migrants. On St. Kitts, Nevis, Montserrat, and Barbados, most early settlers were small-scale English farmers (and their indentured servants) who exported tobacco and livestock hides; on this basis, they created small but thriving colonies. In 1650, there were more English residents in the West Indies (some 44,000) than in the Chesapeake (20,000) and New England (23,000) colonies combined.

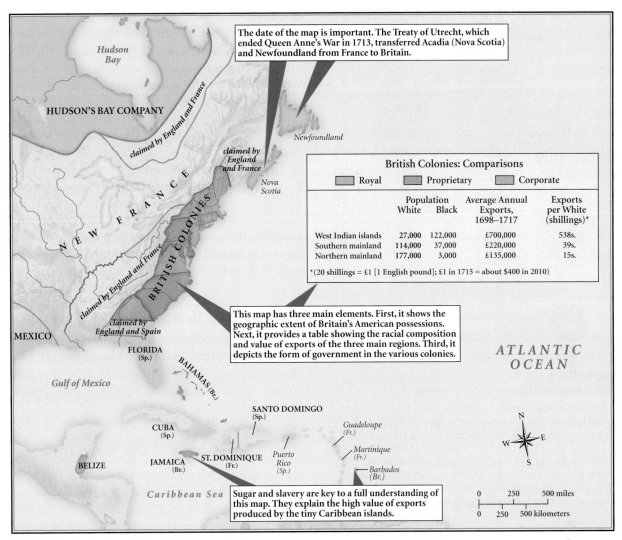

The date of the map is important. The Treaty of Utrecht, which ended Queen Anne's War in 1713, transferred Acadia (Nova Scotia) and Newfoundland from France to Britain.

This map has three main elements. First, it shows the geographic extent of Britain's American possessions. Next, it provides a table showing the racial composition and value of exports of the three main regions. Third, it depicts the form of government in the various colonies.

Sugar and slavery are key to a full understanding of this map. They explain the high value of exports produced by the tiny Caribbean islands.

**British Colonies: Comparisons**

Royal    Proprietary    Corporate

| | Population | | Average Annual Exports, 1698–1717 | Exports per White (shillings)* |
|---|---|---|---|---|
| | White | Black | | |
| West Indian islands | 27,000 | 122,000 | £700,000 | 538s. |
| Southern mainland | 114,000 | 37,000 | £220,000 | 39s. |
| Northern mainland | 177,000 | 3,000 | £135,000 | 15s. |

*(20 shillings = £1 [1 English pound]; £1 in 1715 = about $400 in 2010)

**MAP 3.2**

**Britain's American Empire, 1713**

Many of Britain's possessions in the West Indies were tiny islands, mere dots on the Caribbean Sea. However, in 1713, these small pieces of land were by far the most valuable parts of the empire. Their sugar crops brought wealth to English merchants, commerce to the northern colonies, and a brutal life and early death to the hundreds of thousands of African slaves working on the plantations.

After 1650, sugar transformed Barbados and the other islands into slave-based plantation societies, a change facilitated by English capital combined with the knowledge and experience of Dutch merchants. By 1680, an elite group of 175 planters, described by one antislavery writer of the time as "inhumane and barbarous," dominated Barbados's economy; they owned more than half of the island, thousands of indentured servants, and half of its more than 50,000 slaves. In 1692, exploited Irish servants and island-born African slaves staged a major uprising, which was brutally suppressed. The "leading principle" in a slave society, declared one West Indian planter, was to instill "fear" among workers and a commitment to "absolute coercive" force among masters. As social inequality and racial conflict increased, hundreds of English farmers fled to South Carolina and the large island of Jamaica. But the days of Caribbean smallholders were numbered. English sugar merchants soon invested heavily in Jamaica; by 1750, it had seven hundred large sugar plantations, worked by more than 105,000 slaves, and had become the wealthiest British colony.

Sugar was a rich man's crop because it could be produced most efficiently on large plantations. Scores of slaves planted and cut the sugarcane, which was then processed by expensive equipment—crushing mills,

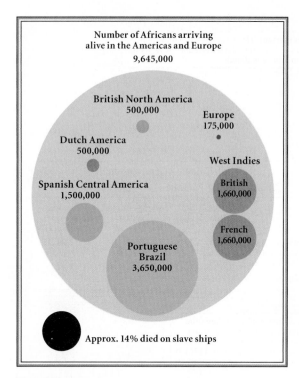

**Number of Africans arriving alive in the Americas and Europe**
**9,645,000**

British North America
500,000

Europe
175,000

Dutch America
500,000

West Indies

Spanish Central America
1,500,000

British
1,660,000

French
1,660,000

Portuguese Brazil
3,650,000

Approx. 14% died on slave ships

**FIGURE 3.1**

**The Transit of Africans to the Americas**

Though approximately 11 million enslaved Africans boarded ships to the Americas, about 1.5 million (14 percent) of them died en route. Two-thirds of the survivors ended up in Brazil (3.65 million) and the West Indies (3.32 million), where they worked primarily on sugar plantations. Half a million arrived directly from Africa in the present-day United States, while many thousands more were traded to the mainland from the West Indies.

and tobacco to Europe accounted for half of British exports. Enormous profits also flowed into Britain from the slave trade. The value of the guns, iron, rum, and cloth that were used to buy slaves was only about one-tenth (in the 1680s) to one-third (by the 1780s) of the value of the crops those slaves produced in America, allowing English traders to sell slaves in the West Indies for three to five times what they paid for them in Africa.

These massive profits drove the slave trade. At its height in the 1790s, Britain annually exported three hundred thousand guns to Africa, and a British ship carrying 300 to 350 slaves left an African port every other day. This commerce stimulated the entire British economy. English, Scottish, and American shipyards built hundreds of vessels, and thousands of people worked in trade-related industries: building port facilities and warehouses, refining sugar and tobacco, distilling rum from molasses, and manufacturing textiles and iron products for the growing markets in Africa and America. More than one thousand British merchant ships were plying the Atlantic by 1750, providing a supply of experienced sailors and laying the foundation for the supremacy of the Royal Navy.

## Africa, Africans, and the Slave Trade

As the South Atlantic System enhanced European prosperity, it imposed enormous costs on West and Central Africa. Between 1550 and 1870, the Atlantic slave trade uprooted 11 million Africans, draining lands south of the Sahara of people and wealth and changing African society (Map 3.3). By directing commerce away from the savannas and the Islamic world on the other side of the Sahara, the Atlantic slave trade changed the economic and religious dynamics of the African interior. It also fostered militaristic, centralized states in the coastal areas.

**Africans and the Slave Trade**   Warfare and slaving had been part of African life for centuries, but the South Atlantic System made slaving a favorite tactic of ambitious kings and plundering warlords. "Whenever the King of Barsally wants Goods or Brandy," an observer noted, "the King goes and ransacks some of his enemies' towns, seizing the people and selling them." Supplying slaves became a way of life in the West African state of Dahomey, where the royal house monopolized the sale of slaves and used European guns to create a military despotism. Dahomey's army, which included a contingent of 5,000 women, raided the interior for captives; between 1680 and 1730, Dahomey annually exported 20,000 slaves from the

boiling houses, distilling apparatus — into raw sugar, molasses, and rum. The affluent planter-merchants who controlled the sugar industry drew annual profits of more than 10 percent on their investment. As Scottish economist Adam Smith noted in his famous treatise *The Wealth of Nations* (1776), sugar was the most profitable crop grown in America or Europe.

**The Impact on Britain**   The South Atlantic System brought wealth to the entire British and European economy and helped Europeans achieve world economic leadership. Most British West Indian plantations belonged to absentee owners who lived in England, where they spent their profits and formed a powerful sugar lobby. The Navigation Acts kept the British sugar trade in the hands of British merchants, who exported it to foreign markets, and by 1750 reshipments of American sugar

**EXPLAIN CONSEQUENCES**
How did the South Atlantic System affect the British economy?

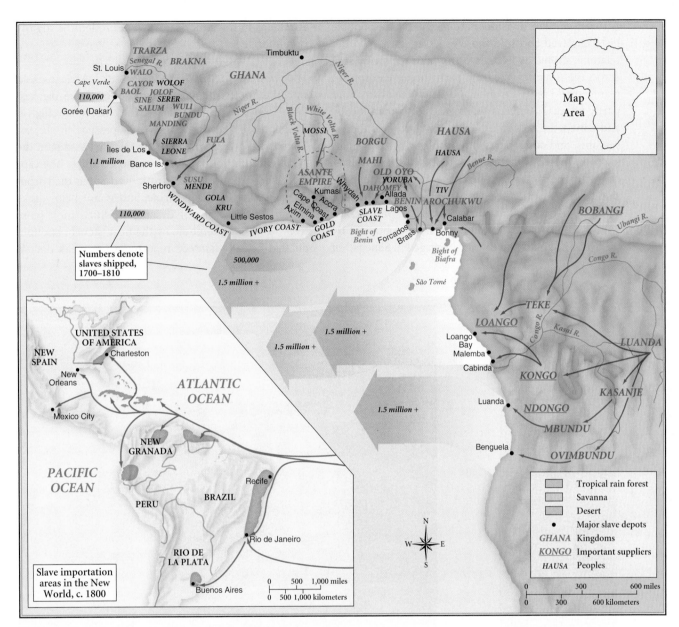

**MAP 3.3**

**Africa and the Atlantic Slave Trade, 1700–1810**

The tropical rain forest of West Africa was home to scores of peoples and dozens of kingdoms. With the rise of the slave trade, some of these kingdoms became aggressive slavers. Dahomey's army, for example, seized tens of thousands of captives in wars with neighboring peoples and sold them to European traders. About 14 percent of the captives died during the grueling Middle Passage, the transatlantic voyage between Africa and the Americas. Most of the survivors labored on sugar plantations in Brazil and the British and French West Indies.

ports of Allada and Whydah. The Asante kings likewise used slaving to conquer states along the Gold Coast as well as Muslim kingdoms in the savanna. By the 1720s, they had created a prosperous empire of 3 to 5 million people. Yet participation in the transatlantic slave trade remained a choice for Africans, not a necessity. The powerful kingdom of Benin, famous for its cast bronzes

and carved ivory, prohibited for decades the export of all slaves, male and female. Other Africans atoned for their guilt for selling neighbors into slavery by building hidden shrines, often in the household granary.

The trade in humans produced untold misery. Hundreds of thousands of young Africans died, and millions more endured a brutal life in the Americas. In

Africa itself, class divisions hardened as people of noble birth enslaved and sold those of lesser status. Gender relations shifted as well. Two-thirds of the slaves sent across the Atlantic were men, partly because European planters paid more for men and "stout men boys" and partly because Africans sold enslaved women locally and across the Sahara as agricultural workers, house servants, and concubines. The resulting sexual imbalance prompted African men to take several wives, changing the meaning of marriage. Finally, the expansion of the Atlantic slave trade increased the extent of slavery in Africa. Sultan Mawlay Ismail of Morocco (r. 1672–1727) owned 150,000 black slaves, obtained by trade in Timbuktu and in wars he waged in Senegal. In

Africa, as in the Americas, slavery eroded the dignity of human life.

**The Middle Passage and Beyond**    Africans sold into the South Atlantic System suffered the bleakest fate. Torn from their villages, they were marched in chains to coastal ports, their first passage in slavery. Then they endured the perilous **Middle Passage** to the New World in hideously overcrowded ships. The captives had little to eat or drink, and some died from dehydration. The feces, urine, and vomit belowdecks prompted outbreaks of dysentery, which took more lives. "I was so overcome by the heat, stench, and foul air that I nearly fainted," reported a European doctor.

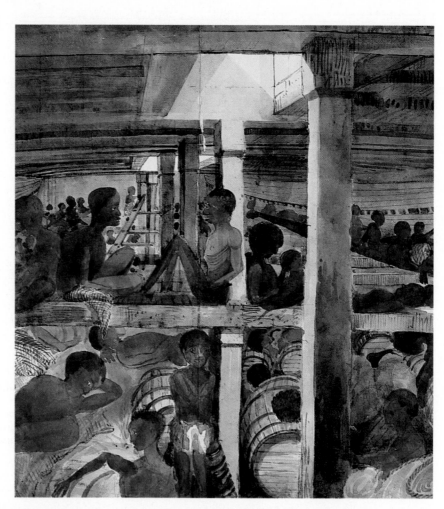

**Two Views of the Middle Passage**

An 1846 watercolor (on the right) shows the cargo hold of a slave ship en route to Brazil, which imported large numbers of African slaves until the 1860s. Painted by a ship's officer, the work minimizes the brutality of the Middle Passage—none of the slaves are in chains—and captures the Africans' humanity and dignity. The illustration on the left, which was printed by England's Abolitionist Society, shows the plan of a Liverpool slave ship designed to hold 482 Africans, packed in with no more respect than that given to hogsheads of sugar and tobacco. Records indicate that the ship actually carried as many as 609 Africans at once. Private Collection/© Michael Graham-Stewart/The Bridgeman Art Library / © National Maritime Museum, London.

## Olaudah Equiano: The Brutal "Middle Passage"

Olaudah Equiano claimed to have been born in Igboland (present-day southern Nigeria). But Vincent Carretta of the University of Maryland has discovered strong evidence that Equiano was born in South Carolina. He suggests that Equiano drew on conversations with African-born slaves to create a fictitious account of his kidnapping at the age of eleven and a traumatic passage across the Atlantic. After being purchased by an English sea captain, Equiano bought his freedom in 1766. In London, he became an antislavery activist, and in 1789 he published the memoir from which the following selections are drawn.

My father, besides many slaves, had a numerous family. . . . I was trained up from my earliest years in the art of war, . . . and my mother adorned me with emblems after the manner of our greatest warriors. One day, when all our people were gone out to their works as usual and only I and my dear sister were left to mind the house, two men and a woman got over our walls, and in a moment seized us both. . . .

I was . . . sold and carried through a number of places till . . . at the end of six or seven months after I had been kidnapped I arrived at the sea coast.

. . . I now saw myself deprived of all chance of returning to my native country. . . . I was soon put down under the decks, and there I received such a salutation in my nostrils as I had never experienced in my life; so that with the loathsomeness of the stench and crying together, I became so sick and low that I was not able to eat, nor had I the least desire to taste anything. I now wished for the last friend, death, to relieve me; but soon, to my grief, two of the white men offered me eatables, and on my refusing to eat, one of them held me fast by the hands and . . . tied my feet while the other flogged me severely. I had never experienced anything of this kind before, and . . . could I have got over the nettings, I would have jumped over the side. . . . One day, when we had a smooth sea and moderate wind, two of my wearied countrymen who were chained together . . . , preferring death to such a life of misery, somehow made it through the nettings and jumped into the sea. . . .

At last we came in sight of the island of Barbados; the white people got some old slaves from the land to pacify us. They told us we were not to be eaten but to work, and were soon to go on land where we should see many of our country people. This report eased us much; and sure enough soon after we were landed there came to us Africans of all languages.

Source: *The Interesting Narrative of the Life of Olaudah Equiano, or Gustavus Vassa, the African, Written by Himself* (London, 1789), 15, 22–23, 28–29.

### QUESTIONS FOR ANALYSIS

1. What elements of Equiano's account might explain the average slave mortality rate of about 14 percent during the Atlantic crossing?
2. Assuming that Carretta is correct, and Equiano was not born in Africa, why do you think he composed this fictitious narrative of his childhood instead of describing his own childhood in slavery?

Some slaves jumped overboard to drown rather than endure more suffering. Others staged violent shipboard revolts. Slave uprisings occurred on two thousand voyages, roughly one of every ten Atlantic passages. Nearly 100,000 slaves died in these insurrections, and nearly 1.5 million others — about 14 percent of those who were transported — died of disease or illness on the month-long journey (America Compared, above).

For those who survived the Atlantic crossing, things only got worse as they passed into endless slavery. Life on the sugar plantations of northwestern Brazil and the West Indies was one of relentless exploitation. Slaves worked ten hours a day under the hot tropical sun; slept in flimsy huts; and lived on a starchy diet of corn, yams, and dried fish. They were subjected to brutal discipline: "The fear of punishment is the principle [we use] . . . to keep them in awe and order," one planter declared. When punishments came, they were brutal. Flogging was commonplace; some planters rubbed salt, lemon juice, or urine into the resulting wounds.

Planters often took advantage of their power by raping enslaved women. Sexual exploitation was a largely unacknowledged but ubiquitous feature of master-slave relations: something that many slave masters considered to be an unquestioned privilege of their position. "It was almost a constant practice with our clerks, and other whites," Olaudah Equiano wrote, "to commit violent depredations on the chastity of the female slaves." Thomas Thistlewood was a Jamaica planter who kept an unusually detailed journal in which he noted every act of sexual exploitation he committed. In thirty-seven years as a Jamaica planter, Thistlewood recorded 3,852 sex acts with 138 enslaved women.

With sugar prices high and the cost of slaves low, many planters simply worked their slaves to death and then bought more. Between 1708 and 1735, British planters on Barbados imported about 85,000 Africans; however, in that same time the island's black population increased by only 4,000 (from 42,000 to 46,000). The constant influx of new slaves kept the population thoroughly "African" in its languages, religions, and culture. "Here," wrote a Jamaican observer, "each different nation of Africa meet and dance after the manner of their own country . . . [and] retain most of their native customs."

## Slavery in the Chesapeake and South Carolina

West Indian–style slavery came to Virginia and Maryland following Bacon's Rebellion. Taking advantage of the expansion of the British slave trade (following the end of the Royal African Company's monopoly in 1698), elite planter-politicians led a "tobacco revolution" and bought more Africans, putting these slaves to work on ever-larger plantations. By 1720, Africans made up 20 percent of the Chesapeake population; by 1740, nearly 40 percent. Slavery had become a core institution, no longer just one of several forms of unfree labor. Moreover, slavery was now defined in racial terms. Virginia legislators prohibited sexual intercourse between English and Africans and defined virtually all resident Africans as slaves: "All servants imported or brought into this country by sea or land who were not Christians in their native country shall be accounted and be slaves."

On the mainland as in the islands, slavery was a system of brutal exploitation. Violence was common, and the threat of violence always hung over master-slave relationships. In 1669, Virginia's House of Burgesses decreed that a master who killed a slave in the process of "correcting" him could not be charged with a felony, since it would be irrational to destroy his own property. From that point forward, even the most extreme punishments were permitted by law. Slaves

could not carry weapons or gather in large numbers. Slaveholders were especially concerned to discourage slaves from running away. Punishments for runaways commonly included not only brutal whipping but also branding or scarring to make recalcitrant slaves easier to identify. Virginia laws spelled out the procedures for capturing and returning runaway slaves in detail. If a runaway slave was killed in the process of recapturing him, the county would reimburse the slave's owner for his full value. In some cases, slave owners could choose to put runaway slaves up for trial; if they were found guilty and executed, the owner would be compensated for his loss (Thinking Like a Historian, p. 98).

Despite the inherent brutality of the institution, slaves in Virginia and Maryland worked under better conditions than those in the West Indies. Many lived relatively long lives. Unlike sugar and rice, which were "killer crops" that demanded strenuous labor in a tropical climate, tobacco cultivation required steadier and less demanding labor in a more temperate environment. Workers planted young tobacco seedlings in spring, hoed and weeded the crop in summer, and in fall picked and hung the leaves to cure over the winter. Nor did diseases spread as easily in the Chesapeake, because plantation quarters were less crowded and more dispersed than those in the West Indies. Finally, because tobacco profits were lower than those from sugar, planters treated their slaves less harshly than West Indian planters did.

Many tobacco planters increased their workforce by buying female slaves and encouraging them to have children. In 1720, women made up more than one-third of the Africans in Maryland, and the black population had begun to increase naturally. "Be kind and indulgent to the breeding wenches," one slave owner told his overseer, "[and do not] force them when with child upon any service or hardship that will be injurious to them." By midcentury, more than three-quarters of the enslaved workers in the Chesapeake were American-born.

Slaves in South Carolina labored under much more oppressive conditions. The colony grew slowly until 1700, when planters began to plant and export rice to southern Europe, where it was in great demand. Between 1720 and 1750, rice production increased fivefold. To expand production, planters imported thousands of Africans, some of them from rice-growing societies. By 1710, Africans formed a majority of the total population, eventually rising to 80 percent in rice-growing areas (Figure 3.2).

Most rice plantations lay in inland swamps, and the work was dangerous and exhausting. Slaves planted, weeded, and harvested the rice in ankle-deep mud.

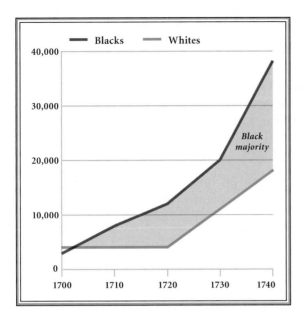

**FIGURE 3.2**

**A Black Majority Emerges in South Carolina, 1700–1740**

Between disease and the toll taken by the Indian wars, South Carolina's white population hardly grew at all between 1690 and 1720. But white planters imported thousands of enslaved Africans to grow rice, an extremely profitable plantation crop. As early as 1705, the colony had a black majority, which allowed the development among slaves of a strongly African-influenced language and culture.

Pools of stagnant water bred mosquitoes, which transmitted diseases that claimed hundreds of African lives. Other slaves, forced to move tons of dirt to build irrigation works, died from exhaustion. "The labour required [for growing rice] is only fit for slaves," a Scottish traveler remarked, "and I think the hardest work I have seen them engaged in." In South Carolina, as in the West Indies and Brazil, there were many slave deaths and few births, and the arrival of new slaves continually "re-Africanized" the black population.

## An African American Community Emerges

Slaves came from many peoples in West Africa and the Central African regions of Kongo and Angola. White planters welcomed ethnic diversity to deter slave revolts. "The safety of the Plantations," declared a widely read English pamphlet, "depends upon having Negroes from all parts of Guiny, who do not understand each other's languages and Customs and cannot agree to Rebel." By accident or design, most plantations drew laborers of many languages, including Kwa, Mande, and Kikongo. Among Africans imported after

1730 into the upper James River region of Virginia, 41 percent came from ethnic groups in present-day Nigeria, and another 25 percent from West-Central Africa. The rest hailed from the Windward and Gold coasts, Senegambia, and Sierra Leone. In South Carolina, plantation owners preferred laborers from the Gold Coast and Gambia, who had a reputation as hardworking farmers. But as African sources of slaves shifted southward after 1730, more than 30 percent of the colony's workers later came from Kongo and Angola.

Initially, the slaves did not think of themselves as Africans or blacks but as members of a specific family, clan, or people — Wolof, Hausa, Ibo, Yoruba, Teke, Ngola — and they sought out those who shared their language and customs. In the upper James River region, Ibo men and women arrived in equal numbers, married each other, and maintained their Ibo culture. In most places, though, this was impossible. Slaves from varying backgrounds were thrown together and only gradually discovered common ground.

**Building Community**   Through painful trial and error, slaves eventually discovered what limited freedoms their owners would allow them. Those who were not too rebellious or too recalcitrant were able to carve out precarious family lives — though they were always in danger of being disrupted by sale or life-threatening punishment — and build the rudiments of a slave community.

One key to the development of families and communities was a more or less balanced sex ratio that encouraged marriage and family formation. In South Carolina, the high death rate among slaves undermined ties of family and kinship; but in the Chesapeake, after 1725 some slaves, especially on larger plantations, were able to create strong nuclear families and extended kin relations. On one of Charles Carroll's estates in Maryland, 98 of the 128 slaves were members of two extended families. These African American kin groups passed on family names, traditions, and knowledge to the next generation, and thus a distinct culture gradually developed. As one observer suggested, blacks had created a separate world, "a Nation within a Nation."

As the slaves forged a new identity, they carried on certain African practices but let others go. Many Africans arrived in America with ritual scars that white planters called "country markings"; these signs of ethnic identity fell into disuse on culturally diverse plantations. (Ironically, on some plantations these African markings were replaced by

**COMPARE AND CONTRAST**

How did the experiences of slaves in the Chesapeake differ from their experiences in South Carolina?

## Servitude and Slavery

Britain's American colonies relied heavily on bound labor. Two forms predominated: indentured servitude and African slavery. The idea of being bound to a master is alien to most of us today; the following texts allow us to glimpse some aspects of the experience. In what ways were these two institutions similar, and how did they differ?

1. **Slave advertisement from Charlestown, Virginia, July 24, 1769.**

Source: Courtesy American Antiquarian Society.

2. **Indentured servant advertisement from the *Pennsylvania Gazette*, 1770.** *This advertisement offers to sell the remainder of a servant girl's indenture.*

TO BE SOLD, A HEALTHY servant GIRL'S Time, about 17 Years old, who has between 3 and 4 years to serve. She is sold for no other Reason, only there being more Servants than are needful in the family where she is.

N. B. She has had the Small pox, can wash, and do all Sorts of Housework. Enquire of the Printers.

3. **Poem by James Revel, c. 1680.** *James Revel was an Englishman convicted of theft and transported to Virginia, where he served fourteen years as an indentured servant. Upon returning he published*

A Poor Unhappy Transported Felon's Sorrowful Account of His Fourteen Years' Transportation at Virginia, in America *(1680).*

At last to my new master's house I came,
At the town of Wicocc[o]moco call'd by name,
Where my Europian clothes were took from me,
Which never after I again could see.

   A canvas shirt and trowsers then they gave,
With a hop-sack frock in which I was to slave:
No shoes nor stockings had I for to wear,
Nor hat, nor cap, both head and feet were bare.

   Thus dress'd into the Field I nex[t] must go,
Amongst tobacco plants all day to hoe,
At day break in the morn our work began,
And so held to the setting of the Sun.

   My fellow slaves were just five Transports more,
With eighteen Negroes, which is twenty four . . .
   We and the Negroes both alike did fare,
Of work and food we had an equal share.

4. **Mechanisms used to control slaves, from Thomas Branagan, *The Penitential Tyrant; or, slave trader reformed*, 1807.** *The shackles and spurs (lower left) were intended to prevent escape; the faceguard with spiked collar (top and lower right) kept its wearer from either eating or lying down.*

Source: Library of Congress.

## 5. Court deposition of Joseph Mulders, July 31, 1649.
*In a court case in Lower Norfolk County, Virginia indentured servant Joseph Mulders testified that his mistress, Deborah Fernehaugh, brutally beat her maidservant, Charity Dallen.*

[Mulders testified] That Deborah Fernehaugh, the Mistress of this deponent, did beate her mayd Sarvant in the quartering house before the dresser more Liken a dogge then a Christian, and that at a Certaine time, I felt her head, which was beaten as soft as a sponge, in one place, and that as there shee was a weeding, shee complained and sayd, her backe bone as shee thought was broken with beating, and that I did see the mayds arme naked which was full of blacke and blew bruises and pinches, and her necke Likewise and that after wards, I tould my Mistress of it and said, that two or three blowes, could not make her in such a Case, and after this my speeches shee Chidge [i.e., chided] the said mayd, for shewing her body to the men, and very often afterwards she [the maid] would have shoen mee, how shee had been beaten, but I refused to have seene it, saying it concernes me not, I will doe my worke and if my Mistress abuse you; you may complaine, and about 8 dayes since, being about the time shee last went to Complaine, I knew of her goeing, but would not tell my mistress of it, although shee asked mee, and sayd I could not chuse but know of it.

## 6. Runaway slave advertisement, Chestertown, Maryland, March 12, 1755.
*Absconding from their masters was a common method of resistance for both slaves and servants, and masters frequently posted runaway advertisements in local newspapers.*

Chestertown, Maryland, March 12, 1755. TEN PISTOLES Reward. RAN away last night, from James Ringgold, of Eastern Neck, in Kent county, in the province of Maryland, the two following servant men; one named James Francis, an indented servant for five years, a middle siz'd young fellow, about 26 years of age, of a smooth fair complexion, his hair cut off, is an Englishman, and speaks a little in the west country dialect; was brought up to farming and husbandry: Had on, a country kersey jacket and breeches, blue fearnought jacket, and an old dark colour'd coat. The other a lusty young Mulatto fellow, named Toby, a slave about the same age, he is a well set, clean limb'd, stout fellow neither a very bright or very dark Mulatto, has large nostrils, is a likely fellow, and when he talks drawls his words out in a very slow manner, is no other way remarkable; he had on the same sort of clothes with the other servant, and one of them has a check or striped green and red everlasting jacket on or with them; and perhaps the Mulatto may set up for a cooper or carpenter, having work at both those business, and also understands plantation affairs. Whoever takes up and secures the above persons, and gives notice, so as their master gets them again, shall have Four Pistoles reward for the white servant, and Six Pistoles for the Mulatto. . . . That this slave should runaway, and attempt getting his liberty, is very alarming, as he has always been too kindly used, if any thing by his master, and one in whom his master has put great confidence, and depended on him to overlook the rest of his slaves, and he had no kind of provocation to go off. It seems to be the interest at least of every gentleman that has slaves, to be active in the beginning of these attempts . . . THOMAS RINGGOLD.

---

Sources: (2) *Pennsylvania Gazette*, May 3, 1770; (3) John Melville Jennings, ed., *The Virginia Magazine of History and Biography* 56 (April 1948), 187–194; (5) *Second to None: A Documentary History of American Women*, Vol. 1 (University of Nebraska Press, 1993), 67–68; (6) *Pennsylvania Gazette*, March 12, 1755.

### ANALYZING THE EVIDENCE

1. What information do the traders in sources 1 and 2 want to convey to prospective buyers, and why? What similarities and differences do you see in the way sellers might choose to market servants and slaves?

2. What aspects of servitude did James Revel object to (source 3)? How did he compare the experiences of servants and slaves?

3. Source 4 appeared in an abolitionist work published in New York in 1807. How does that fact influence your interpretation of the images?

4. How does Mulders grapple with his position as a fellow servant as he testifies against his mistress (source 5)? Based on Mulders's testimony, the court removed Dallen from Fernehaugh's household. How might things have worked differently if either Mulders or Dallen had been a slave?

5. In source 6, what characteristics of each man does the ad emphasize? How does Ringgold view himself as a master, and what does his special plea to other slaveholders tell us about slaveholding culture?

### PUTTING IT ALL TOGETHER

Using the sources above, along with what you learned in class and in Chapter 3, write a short essay that compares servitude and slavery. In what ways did African slavery in the British colonies grow out of servitude and bear close similarities to it, and in what ways were slaves set apart and treated fundamentally differently than their servant counterparts?

**Hulling Rice in West Africa and Georgia**
Cultural practices often extend over time and space. The eighteenth-century engraving on the left shows
West African women using huge wooden mortars and pestles to strip the tough outer hull from rice kernels.
In the photo on the right, taken a century and a half later, African American women in Georgia use similar
tools to prepare rice for their families. Library of Congress. / Courtesy Georgia Vanishing Archives Collection, sap093.

brands or scars that identified them with their owners.)
But other tangible markers of African heritage persisted, including hairstyles, motifs used in wood carv-
ings and pottery, the large wooden mortars and pestles
used to hull rice, and the design of houses, in which
rooms were arranged from front to back in a distinctive "I" pattern, not side by side as was common in
English dwellings. Musical instruments—especially
drums, gourd rattles, and a stringed instrument called
a "molo," forerunner to the banjo—helped Africans
preserve cultural traditions and, eventually, shape
American musical styles.

African values also persisted. Some slaves passed
down Muslim beliefs, and many more told their children of the spiritual powers of conjurers, called *obeah*
or *ifa*, who knew the ways of the African gods. Enslaved
Yorubas consulted Orunmila, the god of fate, and other
Africans (a Jamaican planter noted) relied on *obeah* "to
revenge injuries and insults, discover and punish
thieves and adulterers; [and] to predict the future."

**Resistance and Accommodation** Slaves' freedom
of action was always dramatically circumscribed. It
became illegal to teach slaves to read and write, and
most slaves owned no property of their own. Because
the institution of slavery rested on fear, planters had to
learn a ferocious form of cruelty. Slaves might be
whipped, restrained, or maimed for any infraction,
large or small. A female cook in a Virginia household
"was cruelly loaded with various kinds of iron
machines; she had one particularly on her head, which
locked her mouth so fast that she could scarcely speak;
and could not eat nor drink." Thomas Jefferson, who
witnessed such punishments on his father's Virginia
plantation, noted that each generation of whites was
"nursed, educated, and daily exercised in tyranny," and
he concluded that the relationship "between master
and slave is a perpetual exercise of the most unremitting despotism on the one part, and degrading submission on the other." A fellow Virginian, planter George
Mason, agreed: "Every Master is born a petty tyrant."

*Virginian Luxuries*, c. 1810

This painting by an unknown artist depicts the brutality and sexual exploitation inherent in a slave society. On the right, an owner chastises a male slave by beating him with a cane; on the left, a white master asserts his sexual prerogative with a female slave. Abby Aldrich Rockefeller Folk Art Museum, Williamsburg, VA.

The extent of white violence often depended on the size and density of the slave population. As Virginia planter William Byrd II complained of his slaves in 1736, "Numbers make them insolent." In the northern colonies, where slaves were few, white violence was sporadic. But plantation owners and overseers in the sugar- and rice-growing areas, where Africans outnumbered Europeans eight or more to one, routinely whipped assertive slaves. They also prohibited their workers from leaving the plantation without special passes and called on their poor white neighbors to patrol the countryside at night.

Despite the constant threat of violence, some slaves ran away, a very small number of them successfully. In some parts of the Americas—for example, in Jamaica—runaway slaves were able to form large, independent Maroon communities. But on the mainland, planters had the resources necessary to reclaim runaways, and such communities were unusual and precarious. More often, slaves who spoke English and possessed artisanal skills fled to colonial towns, where they tried to pass as free; occasionally they succeeded. Slaves who did not run away were engaged in a constant tug-of-war with their owners over the terms of their enslavement. Some blacks bartered extra work for better food and clothes; others seized a small privilege and dared the master to revoke it. In this way, Sundays gradually became a day of rest—asserted as a right, rather than granted as a privilege. When bargaining failed, slaves protested silently by working slowly or stealing.

Slave owners' greatest fear was that their regime of terror would fail and slaves would rise up to murder them in their beds. Occasionally that fear was realized. In the 1760s, in Amherst County, Virginia, a slave killed four whites; in Elizabeth City County, eight slaves strangled their master in bed. But the circumstances of slavery made any larger-scale uprising all but impossible. To rebel against their masters, slaves would have to be able to communicate secretly but effectively across long distances; choose leaders they could trust; formulate and disseminate strategy; accumulate large numbers of weapons; and ensure that no one betrayed their plans. This was all but impossible: in plantation slavery, the preponderance of force was on the side of the slave owners, and blacks who chose to rise up did so at their peril.

**The Stono Rebellion**   The largest slave uprising in the mainland colonies, South Carolina's **Stono Rebellion** of 1739, illustrates the impossibility of success. The Catholic governor of Spanish Florida instigated the revolt by promising freedom to fugitive slaves. By February 1739, at least 69 slaves had escaped to St. Augustine, and rumors circulated "that a Conspiracy was formed by Negroes in Carolina to rise and make their way out of the province." When war between England and Spain broke out in September, 75 Africans rose in revolt and killed a number of whites near the

> **TRACE CHANGE OVER TIME**
> How much autonomy could slaves attain, and what did slave owners do to control them?

Stono River. According to one account, some of the rebels were Portuguese-speaking Catholics from the Kingdom of Kongo who hoped to escape to Florida. Displaying their skills as soldiers—decades of brutal slave raiding in Kongo had militarized the society there—the rebels marched toward Florida "with Colours displayed and two Drums beating."

Though their numbers and organization were impressive, the Stono rebels were soon met by a well-armed, mounted force of South Carolina militia. In the ensuing battle, 44 slaves were killed and the rebellion was suppressed, preventing any general uprising. In response, frightened South Carolinians cut slave imports and tightened plantation discipline.

## The Rise of the Southern Gentry

As the southern colonies became full-fledged slave societies, life changed for whites as well as for blacks. Consider the career of William Byrd II (1674–1744). Byrd's father, a successful planter-merchant in Virginia, hoped to marry his children into the English gentry. To smooth his son's entry into landed society, Byrd sent him to England for his education. But his status-conscious classmates shunned young Byrd, calling him a "colonial," a first bitter taste of the gradations of rank in English society.

**IDENTIFY CAUSES**
How did the planter elite maintain alliances with their smallholder neighbors?

Other English rejections followed. Lacking aristocratic connections, Byrd was denied a post with the Board of Trade, passed over three times for the royal governorship of Virginia, and rejected as a suitor by a rich Englishwoman. In 1726, at age fifty-two, Byrd finally gave up and moved back to Virginia, where he sometimes felt he was "being buried alive." Accepting his lesser destiny as a member of the colony's elite, Byrd built an elegant brick mansion on the family's estate at Westover, sat in "the best pew in the church," and won an appointment to the governor's council.

William Byrd II's experience mirrored that of many planter-merchants, trapped in Virginia and South Carolina by their inferior colonial status. They used their wealth to rule over white yeomen families and tenant farmers and relied on violence to exploit enslaved blacks. Planters used Africans to grow food, as well as tobacco; to build houses, wagons, and tobacco casks; and to make shoes and clothes. By making their plantations self-sufficient, the Chesapeake elite survived the depressed tobacco market between 1670 and 1720.

**White Identity and Equality**    To prevent uprisings like Bacon's Rebellion, the Chesapeake gentry found ways to assist middling and poor whites. They gradually lowered taxes; in Virginia, for example, the annual head tax (on each adult man) fell from 45 pounds of tobacco in 1675 to just 5 pounds in 1750. They also encouraged smallholders to improve their economic lot by using slave labor, and many did so. By 1770, 60 percent of English families in the Chesapeake owned at least one slave. On the political front, planters now allowed poor yeomen and some tenants to vote. The strategy of the leading families—the Carters, Lees, Randolphs, and Robinsons—was to bribe these voters with rum, money, and the promise of minor offices in county governments. In return, they expected the yeomen and tenants to elect them to office and defer to their rule. This horse-trading solidified the authority of the planter elite, which used its control of the House of Burgesses to limit the power of the royal governor. Hundreds of yeomen farmers benefitted as well, tasting political power and garnering substantial fees and salaries as deputy sheriffs, road surveyors, estate appraisers, and grand jurymen.

Even as wealthy Chesapeake gentlemen formed political ties with smallholders, they took measures to set themselves apart culturally. As late as the 1720s, leading planters were boisterous, aggressive men who lived much like the common folk—hunting, drinking, gambling on horse races, and demonstrating their manly prowess by forcing themselves on female servants and slaves. As time passed, however, the planters began, like William Byrd II, to model themselves on the English aristocracy, remaining sexual predators but learning from advice books how to act like gentlemen in other regards: "I must not sit in others' places; Nor sneeze, nor cough in people's faces. Nor with my fingers pick my nose, Nor wipe my hands upon my clothes." Cultivating **gentility**—a refined but elaborate lifestyle—they replaced their modest wooden houses with mansions of brick and mortar. Planters educated their sons in London as lawyers and gentlemen. But unlike Byrd's father, they expected them to return to America, marry local heiresses, and assume their fathers' roles: managing plantations, socializing with fellow gentry, and running the political system.

Wealthy Chesapeake and South Carolina women likewise emulated the English elite. They read English newspapers and fashionable magazines, wore the finest English clothes, and dined in the English fashion, including an elaborate afternoon tea. To enhance their daughters' gentility (and improve their marriage prospects), parents hired English tutors. Once married, planter women deferred to their husbands, reared pious children, and maintained elaborate social networks, in time creating a new ideal: the southern gentlewoman. Using the profits generated by enslaved Africans in the South Atlantic System of commerce, wealthy planters formed an increasingly well-educated, refined, and stable ruling class.

# The Northern Maritime Economy

The South Atlantic System had a broad geographical reach. As early as the 1640s, New England farmers supplied the sugar islands with bread, lumber, fish, and meat. As a West Indian explained, planters "had rather buy foode at very deare rates than produce it by labour, soe infinite is the profitt of sugar works." By 1700, the economies of the West Indies and New England were closely interwoven. Soon farmers and merchants in New York, New Jersey, and Pennsylvania were also shipping wheat, corn, and bread to the Caribbean. By the 1750s, about two-thirds of New England's exports and half of those from the Middle Atlantic colonies went to the British and French sugar islands.

The sugar economy linked Britain's entire Atlantic empire. In return for the sugar they sent to England, West Indian planters received credit, in the form of bills of exchange, from London merchants. The planters used these bills to buy slaves from Africa and to pay North American farmers and merchants for their provisions and shipping services. The mainland colonists then exchanged the bills for British manufactures, primarily textiles and iron goods.

## The Urban Economy

The West Indian trade created the first American merchant fortunes and the first urban industries. Merchants in Boston, Newport, Providence, Philadelphia, and New York invested their profits in new ships; some set up manufacturing enterprises, including twenty-six refineries that processed raw sugar into finished loaves. Mainland distilleries turned West Indian molasses into rum, producing more than 2.5 million gallons in Massachusetts alone by the 1770s. Merchants in Salem, Marblehead, and smaller New England ports built a major fishing industry by selling salted mackerel and cod to the sugar islands and to southern Europe. Baltimore merchants transformed their town into a major

port by developing a bustling export business in wheat, while traders in Charleston shipped deerskins, indigo, and rice to European markets (Map 3.4).

As transatlantic commerce expanded—from five hundred voyages a year in the 1680s to fifteen hundred annually in the 1730s—American port cities grew in size and complexity. By 1750, the populations of Newport and Charleston were nearly 10,000; Boston had 15,000 residents; and New York had almost 18,000. The largest port was Philadelphia, whose population by 1776 had reached 30,000, the size of a large European provincial city. Smaller coastal towns emerged as centers of the lumber and shipbuilding industries. Seventy sawmills lined the Piscataqua River in New Hampshire, providing low-cost wood for homes, warehouses, and especially shipbuilding. Hundreds of shipwrights turned out oceangoing vessels, while other artisans made ropes, sails, and metal fittings for the new fleet. By the 1770s, colonial-built ships made up one-third of the British merchant fleet.

The South Atlantic System extended far into the interior. A fleet of small vessels sailed back and forth on the Hudson and Delaware rivers, delivering cargoes of European manufactures and picking up barrels of flour and wheat to carry to New York and Philadelphia for export to the

> **EXPLAIN CONSEQUENCES**
> How did the rise of the South Atlantic System impact economic development in the northern colonies?

West Indies and Europe. By the 1750s, hundreds of professional teamsters in Maryland were transporting 370,000 bushels of wheat and corn and 16,000 barrels of flour to urban markets each year—more than 10,000 wagon trips. To service this traffic, entrepreneurs and artisans set up taverns, horse stables, and barrel-making shops in towns along the wagon roads. Lancaster (the town that hosted the Iroquois conference described in the chapter opening), in a prosperous wheat-growing area of Pennsylvania, boasted more than 200 German and English artisans and a dozen merchants.

## Urban Society

Wealthy merchants dominated the social life of seaport cities. In 1750, about 40 merchants controlled more than 50 percent of Philadelphia's trade. Like the Chesapeake gentry, urban merchants imitated the British upper classes, importing architectural design books from England and building Georgian-style mansions to display their wealth. Their wives strove to create a genteel culture by buying fine furniture and entertaining guests at elegant dinners.

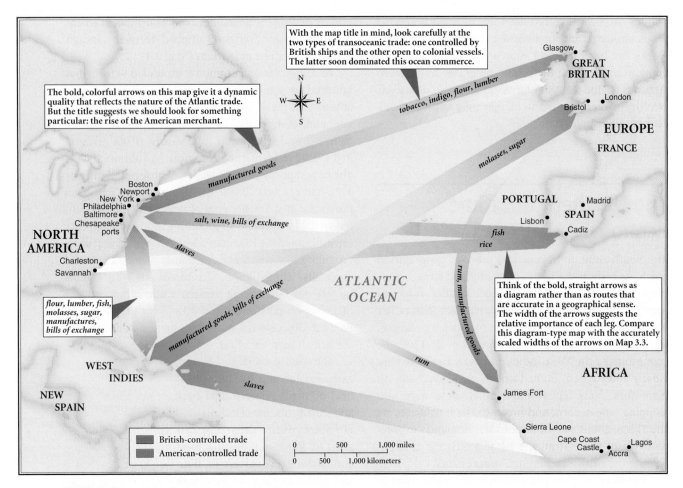

**MAP 3.4**

**The Growing Power of American Merchants, 1750**

Throughout the colonial era, British merchant houses dominated the transatlantic trade in manufactures, sugar, tobacco, and slaves. However, by 1750, American-born merchants in Boston, New York, and Philadelphia had seized control of the commerce between the mainland and the West Indies. In addition, Newport traders played a small role in the slave trade from Africa, and Boston and Charleston merchants grew rich carrying fish and rice to southern Europe.

Artisan and shopkeeper families, the middle ranks of seaport society, made up nearly half the population. Innkeepers, butchers, seamstresses, shoemakers, weavers, bakers, carpenters, masons, and dozens of other skilled workers toiled to gain an income sufficient to maintain their families in modest comfort. Wives and husbands often worked as a team and taught the "mysteries of the craft" to their children. Some artisans aspired to wealth and status, an entrepreneurial ethic that prompted them to hire apprentices and expand production. However, most artisans were not well-to-do. During his working life, a tailor was lucky to accumulate £30 worth of property, far less than the £2,000 owned at death by an ordinary merchant or the £300 listed in the probate inventory of a successful blacksmith.

Laboring men and women formed the lowest ranks of urban society. Merchants needed hundreds of dockworkers to unload manufactured goods and molasses from inbound ships and reload them with barrels of wheat, fish, and rice. For these demanding jobs, merchants used enslaved blacks and indentured servants, who together made up 30 percent of the workforce in Philadelphia and New York City until the 1750s; otherwise, they hired unskilled wageworkers. Poor white and black women eked out a living by washing clothes, spinning wool, or working as servants or prostitutes. To make ends meet, laboring families sent their children out to work.

Periods of stagnant commerce threatened the financial security of merchants and artisans alike. For laborers, seamen, and seamstresses—whose

**The Greenwood-Lee Family, 1747**

Born in Massachusetts and apprenticed as an engraver, John Greenwood (1727–1792) painted dozens of commissioned works there before moving to Surinam in 1752. He painted this scene of his own family at the age of twenty. Group portraits with so many people were rare in the colonies, and it is a technically impressive composition. Greenwood himself is at the right rear, wigless (he wears a velvet cap to keep his head warm) and holding a palette and brushes. The table displays a basket of needlework and a volume of *The Spectator,* the popular London periodical published by Joseph Addison and Richard Steele. Photograph © 2014 Museum of Fine Arts, Boston. Bequest of Henry Lee Shattuck in memory of the late Morris Gray, 1983.34.

household budgets left no margin for sickness or unemployment — depressed trade meant hunger, dependence on public charity, and (for the most desperate) petty thievery or prostitution. The sugar- and slave-based South Atlantic System, and cycles of imperial warfare, brought economic uncertainty as well as opportunity to the people of the northern colonies.

# The New Politics of Empire, 1713–1750

The South Atlantic System also changed the politics of empire. British ministers, pleased with the wealth produced by the trade in slaves, sugar, rice, and tobacco, ruled the colonies with a gentle hand. The colonists took advantage of that leniency to strengthen their political institutions and eventually to challenge the rules of the mercantilist system.

## The Rise of Colonial Assemblies

After the Glorious Revolution, representative assemblies in America copied the English Whigs and limited the powers of crown officials. In Massachusetts during the 1720s, the assembly repeatedly ignored the king's instructions to provide the royal governor with a permanent salary, and legislatures in North Carolina,

New Jersey, and Pennsylvania did the same. Using such tactics, the legislatures gradually took control of taxation and appointments, angering imperial bureaucrats and absentee proprietors. "The people in power in America," complained William Penn during a struggle with the Pennsylvania assembly, "think nothing taller than themselves but the Trees."

Leading the increasingly powerful assemblies were members of the colonial elite. Although most property-owning white men had the right to vote, only men of wealth and status stood for election. In New Jersey in 1750, 90 percent of assemblymen came from influential political families (Figure 3.3). In Virginia, seven members of the wealthy Lee family sat in the House of Burgesses and, along with other powerful families, dominated its major committees. In New England, affluent descendants of the original Puritans formed a core of political leaders. "Go into every village in New England," John Adams wrote in 1765, "and you will find that the office of justice of the peace, and even the place of representative, have generally descended from generation to generation, in three or four families at most."

However, neither elitist assemblies nor wealthy property owners could impose unpopular edicts on the people. Purposeful crowd actions were a fact of colonial life. An uprising of ordinary citizens overthrew the

> **IDENTIFY CAUSES**
> What explains the increasing political autonomy of the colonies in the eighteenth century?

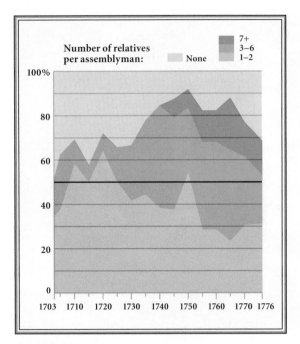

**FIGURE 3.3**
**Family Connections and Political Power, New Jersey, 1700–1776**

As early as 1700, more than 50 percent of the members of the New Jersey assembly came from families with a history of political leadership. By 1750, the percentage whose fathers or other relatives had served in the assembly reached 90 percent; indeed, some members had seven relatives who were (or had been) political leaders, clear testimony of the emergence of powerful political families and an experienced governing elite. However, as the conflict with Britain increased after 1765, voters in New Jersey and elsewhere ousted lukewarm patriots, and new families entered the political ranks.

Dominion of New England in 1689. In New York, mobs closed houses of prostitution; in Salem, Massachusetts, they ran people with infectious diseases out of town; and in New Jersey in the 1730s and 1740s, mobs of farmers battled with proprietors who were forcing tenants off disputed lands. When officials in Boston restricted the sale of farm produce to a single public market, a crowd destroyed the building, and its members defied the authorities to arrest them. "If you touch One you shall touch All," an anonymous letter warned the sheriff, "and we will show you a Hundred Men where you can show one." These expressions of popular discontent, combined with the growing authority of the assemblies, created a political system that was broadly responsive to popular pressure and increasingly resistant to British control.

## Salutary Neglect

British colonial policy during the reigns of George I (r. 1714–1727) and George II (r. 1727–1760) allowed for this rise of American self-government as royal bureaucrats, pleased by growing trade and import duties, relaxed their supervision of internal colonial affairs. In 1775, British political philosopher Edmund Burke would praise this strategy as **salutary neglect**.

Salutary neglect was a by-product of the political system developed by Sir Robert Walpole, the Whig leader in the House of Commons from 1720 to 1742. By providing supporters with appointments and pensions, Walpole won parliamentary approval for his policies. However, his patronage appointments filled the British government, including the Board of Trade and the colonial bureaucracy, with do-nothing political hacks. When Governor Gabriel Johnson arrived in North Carolina in the 1730s, he vowed to curb the powers of the assembly and "make a mighty change in the face of affairs." Receiving little support from the Board of Trade, Johnson renounced reform and decided "to do nothing which can be reasonably blamed, and leave the rest to time, and a new set of inhabitants."

Walpole's tactics also weakened the empire by undermining the legitimacy of the political system. Radical Whigs protested that Walpole had betrayed the Glorious Revolution by using **patronage**—the practice of giving offices and salaries to political allies—and bribery to create a strong Court (or Kingly) Party. The Country Party, whose members were landed gentlemen, likewise warned that Walpole's policies of high taxes and a bloated royal bureaucracy threatened British liberties. Heeding these arguments, colonial legislators complained that royal governors abused their patronage powers. To preserve American liberty, the colonists strengthened the powers of the representative assemblies, unintentionally laying the foundation for the American independence movement (American Voices, p. 108).

## Protecting the Mercantile System

In 1732, Walpole provided a parliamentary subsidy for the new colony of Georgia. While Georgia's reform-minded trustees envisioned the colony as a refuge for Britain's poor, Walpole had little interest in social reform; he subsidized Georgia to protect the valuable rice-growing colony of South Carolina. The subsidy, however, did exactly the opposite. Britain's expansion into Georgia outraged Spanish officials, who were

**Sir Robert Walpole, the King's Minister**

All eyes are on the secretary of the Treasury, Sir Robert Walpole (left), as he offers advice to the Speaker of the House of Commons. A brilliant politician, Walpole used patronage to command a majority in the Commons and also won the confidence of George I and George II, the German-speaking monarchs from the duchy of Hanover. Walpole's personal motto, "Let sleeping dogs lie," helps explain his colonial policy of salutary neglect. Clandon Park, Surrey, UK/National Trust Photographic Library/Hawksley Studios/The Bridgeman Art Library.

already angry about the rising tide of smuggled British manufactures in New Spain. To counter Britain's commercial imperialism, Spanish naval forces stepped up their seizure of illegal traders, in the process mutilating an English sea captain, Robert Jenkins.

Yielding to parliamentary pressure, Walpole declared war on Spain in 1739. The so-called War of Jenkins's Ear (1739–1741) was a fiasco for Britain. In 1740, British regulars failed to capture St. Augustine because South Carolina whites, still shaken by the Stono Rebellion, refused to commit militia units to the expedition. A year later, an assault on the prosperous seaport of Cartagena (in present-day Colombia) also failed; 20,000 British sailors and soldiers and 2,500 colonial troops died in the attack, mostly from tropical diseases.

The War of Jenkins's Ear quickly became part of a general European conflict, the War of the Austrian Succession (1740–1748). Massive French armies battled British-subsidized German forces in Europe, and French naval forces roamed the West Indies, vainly trying to conquer a British sugar island. Three thousand New England militiamen, supported by a British naval squadron, in 1745 captured Louisbourg, the French fort guarding the entrance to the St. Lawrence River. To the dismay of New England Puritans, who feared invasion from Catholic Quebec, the Treaty of Aix-la-Chapelle (1748) returned Louisbourg to France. The treaty made it clear to colonial leaders that England would act in its own interests, not theirs.

## Mercantilism and the American Colonies

Though Parliament prohibited Americans from manufacturing textiles (Woolen Act, 1699), hats (Hat Act, 1732), and iron products such as plows, axes, and skillets (Iron Act, 1750), it could not prevent the colonies from maturing economically. American merchants soon controlled over 75 percent of the transatlantic trade in manufactures and 95 percent of the commerce between the mainland and the British West Indies (see Map 3.4, p. 104).

Moreover, by the 1720s, the British sugar islands could not absorb all the flour, fish, and meat produced by mainland settlers. So, ignoring Britain's intense rivalry with France, colonial merchants sold their produce to the French sugar islands. When American rum distillers began to buy cheap molasses from the French islands, the West Indian sugar lobby in London persuaded Parliament to pass the Molasses Act of 1733. The act placed a high tariff on French molasses, so high that it would no longer be profitable for American merchants to import it. Colonists protested that the Molasses Act would cripple the distilling industry; cut farm exports; and, by slashing colonial income, reduce the mainland's purchases of British goods. When Parliament ignored these arguments, American merchants smuggled in French molasses by bribing customs officials.

The lack of currency in the colonies prompted another conflict with British officials. To pay for British manufactures, American merchants used the bills of exchange and the gold and silver coins earned in the West Indian trade. These payments drained the colonial economy of money, making it difficult for Americans to borrow funds or to buy and sell goods among themselves. To remedy the problem, ten colonial assemblies established public **land banks**, which lent paper money

## The Rise of Colonial Self-Government

Between 1700 and 1760, members of the representative assemblies in British North America gradually expanded their authority and power. Their success was the result of greater popular participation in politics and their own political skills. However, the shift in power from imperial appointees to colonial legislators occurred in a piecemeal fashion, as the almost unconscious product of a series of small, seemingly inconsequential struggles. As you read the following correspondence among legislators, governors, and British officials, look closely at the character of the disputes and how they were resolved.

### Alexander Spotswood
### Confronting the House of Burgesses

As a reward for his military service fighting the forces of Louis XIV of France, Alexander Spotswood became governor of Virginia in 1710. A contentious man, Spotswood was a controversial governor. He told the House of Burgesses to its face that the voters had mistakenly chosen "a set of representatives whom heaven has not generally endowed with the ordinary [intellectual or social] qualifications requisite to legislators." Spotswood set out to reform the voting system that, in his judgment, produced such mediocre representatives. His efforts to oust popular members of the gentry from the House of Burgesses created few friends; in 1722, his enemies in Virginia used their influence in London to have him removed from office.

To ye Council of Trade, Virginia, October 15, 1712
MY LORDS:

. . . The Indians continue their Incursions in North Carolina, and the Death of Colo. Hyde, their Gov'r, which happened the beginning of last Month, increases the misery of that province. . . .

This Unhappy State of her Maj't's Subjects in my Neighbourhood is ye more Affecting to me because I have very little hopes of being enabled to relieve them by our Assembly, which I have called to meet next Week; for the Mob of this Country, having tried their Strength in the late Election and finding themselves able to carry whom they please, have generally chosen representatives of their own Class, who as their principal Recommendation have declared their resolution to raise no Tax on the people, let the occasion be what it will. This is owing to a defect in the Constitution, which allows to every one, tho' but just out of the Condition of a Servant, and that can but purchase half an acre of Land, an equal Vote with the Man of the best Estate in the Country.

The Militia of this Colony is perfectly useless without Arms or ammunition, and by an unaccountable infatuation, no arguments I have used can prevail on these people to make their Militia more Serviceable, or to fall into any other measures for the Defence of their Country. [From the Journal of the Virginia Council]
December the 17th, 1714

The Governor this day laying before the Council a letter from the Right Honorable the Lords Commissioners for Trade dated the 23d of April 1713 directing him to advise with the Council & to recommend to the Generall Assembly to pass a law for qualifying the Electors & the persons Elected Burgesses to serve in the Generall Assembly of this Colony in a more just & equal manner than the Laws now in force do direct. . . . The Council declare that they cannot advise the Governor to move for any alteration in the present method of Electing of Burgesses, some being of opinion that this is not a proper time, & others that the present manner of electing of Burgesses & the qualifications of the elected is sufficiently provided for by the Laws now in force.

To Mr. Secretary James Stanhope, July 15, 1715

. . . I cannot forbear regretting yt I must always have to do with ye Representatives of ye Vulgar People, and mostly with such members as are of their Stamp and Understanding, for so long as half an Acre of Land (which is of small value in this Country) qualifys a man to be an Elector, the meaner sort of People will ever carry ye Elections, and the humour generally runs to choose such men as are their most familiar Companions, who very eagerly seek to be Burgesses merely for the lucre of the Salary, and who, for fear of not being chosen again, dare in Assembly do nothing that may be disrelished [disapproved] out of the House by ye Common People. Hence it often happens yt what appears prudent and feasible to his Majesty's Governors and Council here will not pass with the House of Burgesses, upon whom they must depend for the means of putting their designs in Execution.

To the Lords Commissioners of Trade, May 23, 1716

. . . The behaviour of this Gentleman [Philip Ludwell Jr., the colony's Auditor] in constantly opposing whatever I have offered for ye due collecting the Quitt rents [annual feudal dues on land] and regulating the Acc'ts; his stirring up ye humours of the people before the last election of Burgesses; tampering with the most mutinous of that house, and betraying to them the measures resolved on in Council for his Majesty's Service, would have made me likewise suspend him from ye Council, but I find by the late Instructions I have received from his Majesty that Power is taken from ye Governor and transferred upon the majority of that Board [of Councilors], and while there are no less than seven of his Relations there, it is impossible to get a Majority to consent to the Suspension of him.

Sources: R. A. Brock, ed., *The Official Letters of Alexander Spotswood* (Richmond: Virginia Historical Society, 1885), 2: 1–2, 124, 154–155; H. R. MacIlwaine, ed., *Executive Journals of the Council of Colonial Virginia* (Richmond: Virginia State Library, 1928), 3: 392.

## George Clinton
## A Plea for Assistance

George Clinton served as governor of New York from 1744 to 1752. Like many governors during the era of salutary neglect, Clinton owed his appointment to political connections in England. As the second son of the seventh Earl of Lincoln, he would inherit neither the family's estate nor his father's position in the House of Lords; those went to his elder brother. To provide an income for Clinton, his family traded its votes in Parliament for patronage appointments. However, once Clinton was installed as governor of New York, he found himself dependent on the assembly for the payment of his salary—and the salaries of all members of his administration.

My Lords,

I have in my former letters inform'd Your Lordships what Incroachments the Assemblys of this province have from time to time made on His Majesty's Prerogative & Authority in this Province in drawing an absolute dependence of all the Officers upon them for their Saleries & Reward of their services, & by their taking in effect the Nomination to all Officers. . . .

1stly, That the Assembly refuse to admit of any amendment to any money bill, in any part of the Bill; so that the Bill must pass as it comes from the Assembly, or all the Supplies granted for the support of Government, & the most urgent services must be lost.

2ndly, It appears that they take the Payment of the [military] Forces, passing of Muster Rolls into their own hands by naming the Commissaries for those purposes in the Act.

3rdly, They by granting the Saleries to the Officers personally by name & not to the Officer for the time being, intimate that if any person be appointed to any Office his Salery must depend upon their approbation of the Appointment. . . .

I must now refer it to Your Lordships' consideration whether it be not high time to put a stop to these usurpations of the Assembly on His Majesty's Authority in this Province and for that purpose may it not be proper that His Majesty signify his Disallowance of the Act at least for the payment of Saleries.

Source: E. B. O'Callaghan, ed., *Documents Relative to the Colonial History of the State of New York* (Albany, 1860 on), 2: 211.

### QUESTIONS FOR ANALYSIS

1. What policies does Spotswood wish to pursue? Why can't he persuade the House of Burgesses to implement them? According to Spotswood, what is wrong with Virginia's political system? How does he propose to reform it?

2. Unlike the House of Burgesses, which was elected by qualified voters, the members of the Governor's Council in Virginia were appointed by the king, usually on the governor's recommendation. What is the council's response to the plan to reform the political system? Given Spotswood's description of the incident involving Philip Ludwell, where did the political sympathies of the council lie?

3. What were Clinton's complaints about the actions of the New York assembly? Did these actions represent a more or less serious threat to imperial power than the activities of the Virginia Burgesses? Based on their correspondence with the Board of Trade, which governor—Spotswood or Clinton—was the stronger representative of the interests of the crown?

**The Siege and Capture of Louisbourg, 1745**

In 1760, as British and colonial troops moved toward victory in the French and Indian War (1754–1763), the London artist J. Stevens sought to bolster imperial pride by celebrating an earlier Anglo-American triumph. In 1745, a British naval squadron led a flotilla of colonial ships and thousands of New England militiamen in an attack on the French fort at Louisbourg, on Cape Breton Island, near the mouth of the St. Lawrence River. After a siege of forty days, the Anglo-American force captured the fort, long considered impregnable. The victory was bittersweet because the Treaty of Aix-la-Chapelle (1748) returned the island to France. Anne S. K. Brown Military Collection, Brown University Library.

to farmers who pledged their land as collateral for the loans. Farmers used the currency to buy tools or livestock or to pay creditors, thereby stimulating trade. However, some assemblies, particularly the legislature in Rhode Island, issued huge quantities of paper money (which consequently decreased in value) and required merchants to accept it as legal tender. English merchants and other creditors rightly complained about being forced to accept devalued money. So in 1751, Parliament passed the Currency Act, which barred the New England colonies from establishing new land banks and prohibited the use of publicly issued paper money to pay private debts.

These conflicts over trade and paper money angered a new generation of English political leaders. In 1749, Charles Townshend of the Board of Trade charged that the American assemblies had assumed many of the "ancient and established prerogatives wisely preserved in the Crown," and he vowed to replace salutary neglect with more rigorous imperial control.

The wheel of empire had come full circle. In the 1650s, England had set out to create a centrally managed Atlantic empire and, over the course of a century, achieved the military and economic aspects of that goal. Mercantilist legislation, maritime warfare, commercial expansion, and the forced labor of a million African slaves brought prosperity to Britain. However, internal unrest (the Glorious Revolution) and a policy of salutary neglect had weakened Britain's political

authority over its American colonies. Recognizing the threat self-government posed to the empire, British officials in the late 1740s vowed to reassert their power in America — an initiative with disastrous results.

## SUMMARY

In this chapter, we examined processes of change in politics and society. The political story began in the 1660s as Britain imposed controls on its American possessions. Parliament passed the Acts of Trade and Navigation to keep colonial products and trade in English hands. Then King James II abolished representative institutions in the northern colonies and created the authoritarian Dominion of New England. Following the Glorious Revolution, the Navigation Acts remained in place and tied the American economy to that of Britain. But the uprisings of 1688–1689 overturned James II's policy of strict imperial control, restored colonial self-government, and ushered in an era of salutary political neglect. It also initiated a long era of imperial warfare, in which Native American peoples allied themselves to the colonies and often served as proxy warriors against French- and Spanish-allied peoples, pursuing their own goals in the process.

The social story centers on the development of the South Atlantic System of production and trade, which involved an enormous expansion in African slave raiding; the Atlantic slave trade; and the cultivation of sugar, rice, and tobacco in America. This complex system created an exploited African American labor force in the southern mainland and West Indian colonies, while it allowed European American farmers, merchants, and artisans on the North American mainland to prosper. How would the two stories play out? In 1750, slavery and the South Atlantic System seemed firmly entrenched, but the days of salutary neglect appeared numbered.

# CHAPTER REVIEW

**MAKE IT STICK**   Go to **LearningCurve** to retain what you've read.

## TERMS TO KNOW   Identify and explain the significance of each term below.

### Key Concepts and Events

proprietorship (p. 82)

Quakers (p. 82)

Navigation Acts (p. 83)

Dominion of New England (p. 85)

Glorious Revolution (p. 86)

constitutional monarchy (p. 87)

Second Hundred Years' War (p. 88)

tribalization (p. 88)

Covenant Chain (p. 89)

South Atlantic System (p. 90)

Middle Passage (p. 94)

Stono Rebellion (p. 101)

gentility (p. 102)

salutary neglect (p. 106)

patronage (p. 106)

land banks (p. 110)

### Key People

William Penn (p. 82)

Edmund Andros (p. 85)

William of Orange (p. 86)

John Locke (p. 86)

Jacob Leisler (p. 87)

William Byrd II (p. 102)

Robert Walpole (p. 106)

## REVIEW QUESTIONS   Answer these questions to demonstrate your understanding of the chapter's main ideas.

**1.** What strategies did Charles II and James II employ to try to gain more centralized control over England's American colonies? What did James hope to accomplish by creating the Dominion of New England?

**2.** How did the long era of imperial warfare beginning in 1689 affect the colonies, Native Americans, and relations between them?

**3.** What was the South Atlantic System, and how did it shape colonial society?

**4.** How did the institution of slavery develop, and why did it develop differently in the Chesapeake, the Carolina low country, and the West Indies?

**5. THEMATIC UNDERSTANDING** Trace the developments outlined in the section entitled "Politics and Power" from 1660 to 1750 on the thematic timeline on page 79. What pattern of political evolution do you see in colonial interactions with Britain?

# MAKING CONNECTIONS

Recognize the larger developments and continuities within and across chapters by answering these questions.

1. **ACROSS TIME AND PLACE**   In Chapter 2, we traced the emergence of three distinct colonial types in the Americas during the sixteenth and seventeenth centuries: tribute, plantation, and neo-European colonies. In Chapter 3, we have seen how Britain's plantation and neo-European colonies became more closely interconnected after 1700. What developments caused them to become more closely tied to each other? How did they benefit from these ties? Can you see any disadvantages to the colonies in a more fully integrated Atlantic system?

2. **VISUAL EVIDENCE**   Consider the illustrations of women hulling rice in West Africa and Georgia on page 100. Historians have long debated the role Africans played in developing rice cultivation in the South Carolina and Georgia low country. These debates have focused primarily on methods of cultivation: Did Africans who had prior experience with rice teach English planters how to grow it? How can these two images contribute to the debate and expand our perspective on the question of African influences in American rice production?

## MORE TO EXPLORE

Start here to learn more about the events discussed in this chapter.

Ira Berlin, *Many Thousands Gone* (2000). Explores the varieties of slave experience in North America.

Olaudah Equiano, *The Interesting Narrative of the Life of Olaudah Equiano* (1789; reprint 2006). A compelling and influential eighteenth-century slave autobiography.

Paul Mapp, *The Elusive West and the Contest for Empire, 1713–1763* (2011). Offers a continental perspective on the contest for European control of North America.

Owen Stanwood, *The Empire Reformed* (2011). Tells the story of the Glorious Revolution in the American colonies.

*Africans in America, Part 1: Terrible Transformation, 1450–1750* (PBS video, 1998) and the related Web site (**pbs.org/wgbh/aia/part1/title.html**). Treats the early African American experience.

"The Atlantic Slave Trade and Slave Life in the Americas: A Visual Record" (**hitchcock.itc.virginia.edu/Slavery**). An extensive collection of slave images.

## TIMELINE

Ask yourself why this chapter begins and ends with these dates and then identify the links among related events.

| | |
|---|---|
| **1651** | • First Navigation Act |
| **1660–1685** | • Reign of Charles II, king of England |
| **1663** | • Charles II grants Carolina proprietorship |
| **1664** | • English capture New Netherland, rename it New York |
| **1669** | • Virginia law declares that the murder of a slave cannot be treated as a felony |
| **1681** | • William Penn founds Pennsylvania |
| **1685–1688** | • Reign of James II, king of England |
| **1686–1689** | • Dominion of New England |
| **1688–1689** | • Glorious Revolution in England |
| **1689** | • William and Mary ascend throne in England <br> • Revolts in Massachusetts, Maryland, and New York |
| **1689–1713** | • England, France, and Spain at war |
| **1696** | • Parliament creates Board of Trade |
| **1714–1750** | • British policy of salutary neglect <br> • American assemblies gain power |
| **1720–1742** | • Robert Walpole leads Parliament |
| **1720–1750** | • African American communities form <br> • Rice exports from South Carolina soar <br> • Planter aristocracy emerges <br> • Seaport cities expand |
| **1732** | • Parliament charters Georgia, challenging Spain <br> • Hat Act limits colonial enterprise |
| **1733** | • Molasses Act threatens distillers |
| **1739** | • Stono Rebellion in South Carolina |
| **1739–1748** | • War with Spain in the Caribbean and France in Canada and Europe |
| **1750** | • Iron Act restricts colonial iron production |
| **1751** | • Currency Act prohibits land banks and paper money |

**KEY TURNING POINTS:** The Glorious Revolution (1688–1689), salutary neglect and the rise of the assemblies (1714–1750), and the Hat, Molasses, Iron, and Currency Acts (1732–1751). How do these developments reflect Britain's new attitude toward its colonies? In what matters did Parliament seek to control the colonies, and in what did it grant them autonomy?

# 4

**CHAPTER**

# Growth, Diversity, and Conflict
## 1720–1763

In 1736, Alexander MacAllister left the Highlands of Scotland for the back-country of North Carolina, where his wife and three sisters soon joined him. MacAllister prospered as a landowner and mill proprietor and had only praise for his new home. Carolina was "the best poor man's country," he wrote to his brother Hector, urging him to "advise all poor people . . . to take courage and come." In North Carolina, there were no landlords to keep "the face of the poor . . . to the grinding stone," and so many Highlanders were arriving that "it will soon be a new Scotland." Here, on the far margins of the British Empire, people could "breathe the air of liberty, and not want the necessarys of life." Some 300,000 European migrants—primarily Highland Scots, Scots-Irish, and Germans—heeded MacAllister's advice and helped swell the population of Britain's North American settlements from 400,000 in 1720 to almost 2 million by 1765.

MacAllister's "air of liberty" did not last forever, as the rapid increase in white settlers and the arrival of nearly 300,000 enslaved Africans transformed life throughout mainland British North America. Long-settled towns in New England became overcrowded, and antagonistic ethnic and religious communities jostled uneasily with one another in the Middle Atlantic colonies; in 1748, there were more than a hundred German Lutheran and Reformed congregations in Quaker-led Pennsylvania. By then, the MacAllisters and thousands of other Celtic and German migrants had altered the social landscape and introduced religious conflict into the southern backcountry.

Everywhere, two European cultural movements, the Enlightenment and Pietism, changed the tone of intellectual and spiritual life. Advocates of "rational thought" viewed human beings as agents of moral self-determination and urged Americans to fashion a better social order. Religious Pietists outnumbered them and had more influence. Convinced of the weakness of human nature, evangelical ministers told their followers to seek regeneration through divine grace. Amidst this intellectual and religious ferment, migrants and the landless children of long-settled families moved inland and sparked wars with the native peoples and with France and Spain. A generation of dynamic growth produced a decade of deadly warfare that would set the stage for a new era in American history.

**IDENTIFY THE BIG IDEA**

In what ways were Britain's American colonies affected by events across the Atlantic, and how were their societies taking on a life of their own?

**John Collet,** *George Whitefield Preaching*   No painting could capture English minister George Whitefield's charismatic appeal, although this image conveys his open demeanor and religious intensity. When Whitefield spoke to a crowd near Philadelphia, an observer noted that his words were "sharper than a two-edged sword. . . . Some of the people were pale as death; others were wringing their hands . . . and most lifting their eyes to heaven and crying to God for mercy." An astute businessman as well as a charismatic preacher, Whitefield tirelessly promoted the sale of his sermons and books. © Private Collection/The Bridgeman Art Library.

# New England's Freehold Society

In the 1630s, the Puritans had fled England, where a small elite of nobles and gentry owned 75 percent of the arable land, while **tenants** (renters) and property-less workers farmed it. In New England, the Puritans created a yeoman society of relatively equal landowning farm families. But by 1750, the migrants' numerous descendants had parceled out the best farmland, threatening the future of the freehold ideal.

## Farm Families: Women in the Household Economy

The Puritans' vision of social equality did not extend to women, and their ideology placed the husband firmly at the head of the household. In *The Well-Ordered Family* (1712), the Reverend Benjamin Wadsworth of Boston advised women, "Since he is thy Husband, God has made him the head and set him above thee." It was a wife's duty "to love and reverence" her husband.

Women learned this subordinate role throughout their lives. Small girls watched their mothers defer to their fathers, and as young women, they were told to be "silent in company." They saw the courts prosecute more women than men for the crime of fornication (sex outside of marriage), and they found that their marriage portions would be inferior to those of their brothers. Thus Ebenezer Chittendon of Guilford, Connecticut, left his land to his sons, decreeing that "Each Daughter [shall] have half so much as Each Son, one half in money and the other half in Cattle."

**UNDERSTAND POINTS OF VIEW**

What ideas, institutions, and responsibilities shaped New England farm women's lives?

Throughout the colonies, women assumed the role of dutiful helpmeets (helpmates) to their husbands. In addition to tending gardens, farmwives spun thread and yarn from flax and wool and then wove it into cloth for shirts and gowns. They knitted sweaters and stockings, made candles and soap, churned milk into butter, fermented malt for beer, preserved meats, and mastered dozens of other household tasks. "Notable women"—those who excelled at domestic arts—won praise and high status (Thinking Like a Historian, p. 118).

Bearing and rearing children were equally important tasks. Most women in New England married in their early twenties and by their early forties had given birth to six or seven children, delivered with the help of a female neighbor or a midwife. One Massachusetts mother confessed that she had little time for religious activities because "the care of my Babes takes up so large a portion of my time and attention." Yet most Puritan congregations were filled with women: "In a Church of between *Three* and *Four* Hundred *Communicants*," the eminent minister Cotton Mather noted, "there are but few more than *One* Hundred *Men*; all the Rest are Women."

Women's lives remained tightly bound by a web of legal and cultural restrictions. Ministers praised women for their piety but excluded them from an equal role in the church. When Hannah Heaton, a Connecticut farmwife, grew dissatisfied with her

**Prudence Punderson (1758–1784),** *The First, Second and Last Scenes of Mortality*

This powerful image reveals both the artistic skills of colonial women in the traditional medium of needlework and the Puritans' continuing cultural concern with the inevitability of death. Prudence Punderson, the Connecticut woman who embroidered this scene, rejected a marriage proposal and followed her Loyalist father into exile on Long Island in 1778. Sometime later, she married a cousin, Timothy Rossiter, and bore a daughter, Sophia, who may well be the baby in the cradle being rocked by "Jenny," a slave owned by Prudence's father. Long worried by "my ill state of health" and perhaps now anticipating her own death, Prudence has inscribed her initials on the coffin—and, in creating this embroidery, transformed her personal experience into a broader meditation on the progression from birth, to motherhood, to death. Connecticut Historical Society.

*The First, Second, and Last Scene of Mortality. Prudence Punderson.*

Congregationalist minister, thinking him unconverted and a "blind guide," she sought out equality-minded Quaker and evangelist Baptist churches that welcomed questioning women such as herself and treated "saved" women equally with men. However, by the 1760s, many evangelical congregations had reinstituted men's dominance over women. "The government of Church and State must be . . . family government" controlled by its "king," declared the Danbury (Connecticut) Baptist Association.

## Farm Property: Inheritance

By contrast, European men who migrated to the colonies escaped many traditional constraints, including the curse of landlessness. "The hope of having land of their own & becoming independent of Landlords is what chiefly induces people into America," an official noted in the 1730s. Owning property gave formerly dependent peasants a new social identity.

Unlike the adventurers seeking riches in other parts of the Americas, most New England migrants wanted farms that would provide a living for themselves and ample land for their children. In this way, they hoped to secure a **competency** for their families: the ability to keep their households solvent and independent and to pass that ability on to the next generation. Parents who could not give their offspring land placed these children as indentured servants in more prosperous households. When the indentures ended at age eighteen or twenty-one, propertyless sons faced a decades-long climb up the agricultural ladder, from laborer to tenant and finally to freeholder.

Sons and daughters in well-to-do farm families were luckier: they received a marriage portion when they were in their early twenties. That portion — land, livestock, or farm equipment — repaid them for their past labor and allowed parents to choose their marriage partners. Parents' security during old age depended on a wise choice of son- or daughter-in-law. Although the young people could refuse an unacceptable match, they did not have the luxury of falling in love with and marrying whomever they pleased.

Marriage under eighteenth-century English common law was not a contract between equals. A bride relinquished to her husband the legal ownership of all her property. After his death, she received a dower right, the right to use (though not sell) one-third of the family's property. On the widow's death or remarriage, her portion was divided among the children. Thus the widow's property rights were subordinate to those of the family line, which stretched across the generations.

A father's duty was to provide inheritances for his children so that one day they could "be for themselves." Men who failed to do so lost status in the community. Some fathers willed the family farm to a single son and provided other children with money, an apprenticeship, or uncleared frontier tracts. Other yeomen moved their families to the frontier, where life was hard but land was cheap and abundant. "The Squire's House stands on the Bank of the Susquehannah," traveler Philip Fithian reported from the Pennsylvania backcountry in the early 1760s. "He tells me that he will be able to settle all his sons and his fair Daughter Betsy on the Fat of the Earth."

## Freehold Society in Crisis

Because of rapid natural increase, New England's population doubled each generation, from 100,000 in 1700, to nearly 200,000 in 1725, to almost 400,000 in 1750. Farms had been divided and then subdivided, making them so small — 50 acres or less — that parents could provide only one child with an adequate inheritance. In the 1740s, the Reverend Samuel Chandler of Andover, Massachusetts, was "much distressed for land for his children," seven of them young boys. A decade later, in nearby Concord, about 60 percent of the farmers owned less land than their fathers had.

Because parents had less to give their sons and daughters, they had less control over their children's lives. The traditional system of arranged marriages broke down, as young people engaged in premarital sex and then used the urgency of pregnancy to win permission to marry. Throughout New England, premarital conceptions rose dramatically, from about 10 percent of firstborn children in the 1710s to more than 30 percent in the 1740s. Given another chance, young people "would do the same again," an Anglican minister observed, "because otherwise they could not obtain their parents' consent to marry."

Even as New England families changed, they maintained the freeholder ideal. Some parents chose to have smaller families and used birth control to do so: abstention, coitus interruptus, or primitive condoms. Other families petitioned the provincial government for frontier land grants and hacked new farms out of the forests of central Massachusetts, western Connecticut, and eventually New Hampshire and Vermont. Still others improved their farms' productivity by replacing the traditional English crops of wheat and barley with high-yielding potatoes

> **IDENTIFY CAUSES**
> What factors threatened the freeholder ideal in midcentury New England, and what strategies did farming families use to preserve this ideal?

## Women's Labor

As these documents show, women bore the responsibility for a wide variety of work, from keeping up households to supporting themselves independently.

1. **Thomas Tusser, *Five Hundred Pointes of Good Husbandrie*, 1557.** *Advice manuals like Tusser's circulated for generations and offered guidance on household management. In this couplet, Tusser stresses the virtues of a wife's economy and hard work.*

Wife, make thine own candle,
Spare penny to handle.
Provide for thy tallow ere frost cometh in,
And make thine own candle ere winter begin.

2. **Eliza Lucas, letters, 1740–1742.** *George Lucas owned three South Carolina plantations, but, as lieutenant governor of Antigua, he was frequently absent. When his daughter was sixteen, he gave her responsibility for managing them. She introduced indigo cultivation in South Carolina, and it soon became the colony's second-leading cash crop. These letters were written when she was between the ages of eighteen and twenty.*

May 2, 1740

"I have the business of 3 plantations to transact, which requires much writing and more business and fatigue of other sorts than you can imagine. But least you should imagine it too burthensom to a girl at my early time of life, give me leave to answer you: I assure you I think myself happy that I can be useful to so good a father, and by rising very early I find I can go through much business."

July 1740

"Wrote my Father a very long letter on his plantation affairs and on . . . the pains I had taken to bring the Indigo, Ginger, Cotton and Lucerne and Casada to perfection, and had greater hopes from the Indigo . . . than any of the rest of the things I tried."

February 6, 1741

". . . I have a Sister to instruct and a parcel of little Negroes whom I have undertaken to teach to read."

April 23, 1741

"Wrote to my Father informing him of the loss of a Negro man — also the boat being overset in Santilina [Saint Helena] Sound and 20 barrels of Rice lost."

[1742]

"Wont you laugh at me if I tell you I am so busey in providing for Posterity I hardly allow my self time to Eat or sleep. . . . I am making a large plantation of Oaks which I look upon as my own property, whether my father gives me the land or not; and therefore I design many years hence when oaks are more valueable than they are now — which you know they will be when we come to build fleets."

[c. June 1742]

"I am engaged with the rudiments of the law to which I am yet but a stranger. . . . If You will not laugh too immoderately at me I'll Trust you with a secrett. I have made two wills already."

3. **Mary Vial Holyoke, diary excerpts, 1761.** *Mary Vial Holyoke, wife of a prominent physician in Salem, Massachusetts, kept a diary that offers a glimpse of the range of household tasks women faced.*

[1761]
Jan. 16: Began upon the firkin of butter of 40 lb. . . .
22: Bo't hog, weighed 182 pounds, at 2/5. Salted hog with half Lisbon & half saltertudas [Tortugas] salt. . . .
Mar. 4: Ironing. . . .
7: Scower'd pewter. . . .
17: Made the Dr. six Cravats marked H. . . .
Apr. 17: Made soap. . . .
23: Dressed a Calves Head turtle fashion. . . .
May 20: Began to whitewash. . . .
28: Ironed. . . .
30: Scower'd pewter. . . .
July 7: Scowered rooms. . . .

4. **Colonial house interiors in Germantown, Pennsylvania, and Augusta, Maine.** *These images show the dining room of Benjamin Chew, a wealthy Philadelphia lawyer (below), and the kitchen of the Howards, an extended family of soldiers and merchants on the Maine frontier (opposite).*

Source: Photo by Ron Blunt, Courtesy of Cliveden, a National Trust Historic Site, Philadelphia, PA.

Source: Old Fort Western, Augusta, Maine.

MOLL PLACKET-HOLE was born in a *Bawdy House* in a *Lane* in the City of *Brotherly Love*. . . . [A]t the Age of twelve (Shocking to consider!) . . . [her] Mother *sold* her Virginity — *sold* it for the Trifling Consideration of *Ten Pounds*. Her Purchaser was soon cloyed and abandoned her. Virtue lost and good Reputation (if ever she had it) gone, she commenced open Prostitute and dealt out her Favours to the highest Bidder. . . . [S]he understood the Trade and set up a *Bawdy-House*. . . . It was necessary, however, that a Man should live with her, that they might appear to the Publick, as *honest* Housekeepers. . . . The Trade became at last so publick, that it gave Offence to her sober Neighbours. . . . [T]he Town tired out with her Insolence, and her Escape from Justice in a regular Manner, set a Mob (many of whom had been her Beneficiaries) upon her. They pulled down her House, and destroyed her Furniture &c. She stormed and raged and swore if her Customers would not build her a better House, she would expose them. . . . They opened a Subscription, and a hundred Pounds were subscribed in one Day.

Sources: (1) Alice Morse Earle, *Home Life in the Colonial Days* (New York: The Macmillan Company, 1898), 35; (2) From *The Letterbook of Eliza Lucas Pinckney, 1739–1762*, edited by Elise Pinckney, University of North Carolina Press, 1972. Based on original documents from the South Carolina Historical Society. Courtesy of the South Carolina Historical Society; (3) George Francis Dow, ed., *The Holyoke Diaries, 1709–1856* (Salem, MA: The Essex Institute, 1911), 49–51; (6) *Hilliad Magna: Being the Life and Adventures of Moll Placket-Hole* ([Philadelphia]: Printed [by Anthony Armbruster], 1765).

**5. Business advertisement in the *Pennsylvania Gazette*, 1758.** *Not all women's work was done in the home. Hannah Breintnall, a Philadelphia widow, ran a tavern before opening a shop specializing in eyeglasses.*

Source: Library Company of Philadelphia.

**6. *Hilliad Magna: Being the Life and Adventures of Moll Placket-Hole*, 1765.** *Moll Placket-Hole was a satirical, seven-page pamphlet that purported to describe the life of a Philadelphia prostitute.* Moll *was an eighteenth-century term for a loose woman or prostitute, while* placket-hole *referred to a slit that might be found in a woman's skirt.*

## ANALYZING THE EVIDENCE

1. Compare the advice manual (source 1) with Eliza Lucas's letters and Mary Vial Holyoke's diary. What themes do they share in common, and how do these women's experiences deviate from the expectations of the advice book authors?

2. Eliza Lucas supervised slave labor, and Mary Vial Holyoke very likely employed servants. How do these facts affect the way you interpret sources 2 and 3?

3. Compare the two house interiors (source 4). What work would women have done in these spaces? The Chews were a slaveholding family, and the Howards probably employed servants. With that in mind, consider the relationship between supervisory and manual labor.

4. Hannah Breintnall was a well-to-do widow, while Moll Placket-Hole was a fictional stereotype. What does Breintnall's experience tell us about the prospects of a woman living without a male protector? How does Moll Placket-Hole shed light on popular attitudes toward such women?

## PUTTING IT ALL TOGETHER

With all these sources in mind, write a short essay that considers the role of hierarchy and social power in women's work. How did economic and social status affect the work that was expected of women? How did the women whose lives are documented here navigate the challenges and opportunities they faced? And how does the satire of Moll Placket-Hole illuminate popular attitudes toward women's work and its place in colonial society?

and maize (Indian corn). Corn was an especially wise choice: good for human consumption, as well as for feeding cattle and pigs, which provided milk and meat. Gradually, New England changed from a grain to a livestock economy, becoming a major exporter of salted meat to the plantations of the West Indies.

As the population swelled, New England farmers developed the full potential of what one historian has called the "**household mode of production**," in which families swapped labor and goods. Women and children worked in groups to spin yarn, sew quilts, and shuck corn. Men loaned neighbors tools, draft animals, and grazing land. Farmers plowed fields owned by artisans and shopkeepers, who repaid them with shoes, furniture, or store credit. Partly because currency was in short supply, no cash changed hands. Instead, farmers, artisans, and shopkeepers recorded debits and credits and "balanced" the books every few years. This system helped New Englanders to maximize agricultural output and preserve the freehold ideal.

# Diversity in the Middle Colonies

The Middle colonies—New York, New Jersey, and Pennsylvania—became home to peoples of differing origins, languages, and religions. Scots-Irish Presbyterians, English and Welsh Quakers, German Lutherans and Moravians, Dutch Reformed Protestants, and others all sought to preserve their cultural and religious identities as they pursued economic opportunity. At the same time, rapid population growth throughout the region strained public institutions, pressured Indian lands, and created a dynamic but unstable society.

## Economic Growth, Opportunity, and Conflict

Previously home to New Netherland and New Sweden, the Mid-Atlantic region was already ethnically diverse before England gained control of it. The founding of Pennsylvania and New Jersey amplified this pattern. Fertile land seemed abundant, and grain exports to Europe and the West Indies financed the colonies' rapid settlement (America Compared, p. 121). Between 1720 and 1770, a growing demand for wheat, corn, and flour doubled their prices and brought people and prosperity to the region. Yet that very growth led to conflict, both within the Middle colonies and in their relations with Native American neighbors.

**Tenancy in New York**   In New York's fertile Hudson River Valley, wealthy Dutch and English families presided over the huge manors created by the Dutch West India Company and English governors (Map 4.1). Like Chesapeake planters, the New York landlords aspired to live in the manner of the European gentry but found that few migrants wanted to labor as peasants. To

**MAP 4.1**

**The Hudson River Manors**

Dutch and English manorial lords owned much of the fertile east bank of the Hudson River, where they leased farms on perpetual contracts to German tenants and refused to sell land to freehold-seeking migrants from overcrowded New England. This powerful landed elite produced aristocratic-minded Patriot leaders such as Gouverneur Morris and Robert Livingston, as well as prominent American families such as the Roosevelts.

## Transatlantic Migration, 1500–1760

The following graph compares the number of European and African migrants who arrived in the American colonies of Spain, Portugal, Britain, France, and the Netherlands. It also charts change over time: while immigrants in the sixteenth and early seventeenth centuries went predominantly to the colonies of Spain and Portugal, Britain's colonies became the principal destination for both Europeans and Africans between 1640 and 1760.

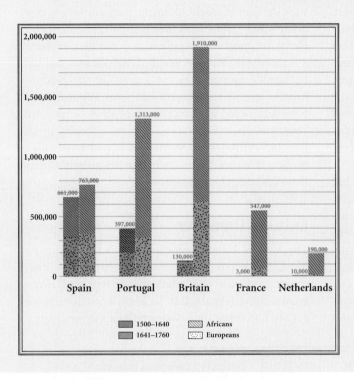

**FIGURE 4.1**

**Transatlantic Migration**

Source of data: Stanley L. Engerman and Kenneth L. Sokoloff, "Factor Endowments, Institutions, and Differential Paths of Growth Among New World Economies: A View from Economic Historians of the United States," in *How Latin America Fell Behind: Economic Histories of Brazil and Mexico, 1800–1914*, ed. Stephen Haber (Palo Alto, CA: Stanford University Press, 1997), 264.

### QUESTIONS FOR ANALYSIS

1. What relationship do you see between the number of European emigrants and the importation of African slaves? Which nation's colonies had the highest percentage of Africans relative to Europeans? Which had the lowest? Which time periods had the highest and lowest percentages of Africans?

2. Compare France and the Netherlands to Spain, Portugal, and Britain. Why do you suppose that the ratio of Africans to Europeans is so much higher in French and Dutch colonies than in the other nations? Which type of colony—tribute, plantation, or neo-European—was likely to have been most important to the French and Dutch?

attract tenants, the manorial lords granted long leases, with the right to sell improvements such as houses and barns to the next tenant. They nevertheless struggled to populate their estates.

Most tenant families hoped that with hard work and ample sales they could eventually buy their own farmsteads. But preindustrial technology limited output. A worker with a hand sickle could reap only half an acre of wheat, rye, or oats a day. The cradle scythe, a tool introduced during the 1750s, doubled or tripled the amount of grain one worker could cut. Even so, a family with two adult workers could reap only about 12 acres of grain, or roughly 150 to 180 bushels of wheat. After saving enough grain for food and seed, the surplus might be worth £15 — enough to buy salt and sugar, tools, and cloth, but little else. The road to land-ownership was not an easy one.

**Conflict in the Quaker Colonies** In Quaker-dominated Pennsylvania and New Jersey, wealth was initially distributed more evenly than in New York,

but the proprietors of each colony, like the manor lords of New York, had enormous land claims. The first migrants lived simply in small, one- or two-room houses with a sleeping loft, a few benches or stools, and some wooden platters and cups. Economic growth brought greater prosperity, along with conflicts between ordinary settlers and the proprietors who tried to control their access to land, resources, and political power.

William Penn's early appeals to British Quakers and continental Protestants led to a boom in immigrants. When these first arrivals reported that Pennsylvania and New Jersey were "the best poor man's country in the world," thousands more followed. Soon the proprietors of both colonies were overwhelmed by the demand for land. By the 1720s, many new migrants were forced to become **squatters**, settling illegally on land they hoped eventually to be able to acquire on legal terms.

Frustration over the lack of land led the Penn family to perpetrate one of the most infamous land frauds of the eighteenth century, the so-called Walking Purchase of 1737, in which they exploited an old (and probably fraudulent) Indian deed to claim more than a million acres of prime farmland north of Philadelphia. This purchase, while opening new lands to settlement, poisoned Indian relations in the colony. Delaware and Shawnee migration to western Pennsylvania and the Ohio Valley, which was already under way, accelerated rapidly in response.

Immigrants flooded into Philadelphia, which grew from 2,000 people in 1700 to 25,000 by 1760. Many families came in search of land; for them, Philadelphia was only a temporary way station. Other migrants came as laborers, including a large number of indentured servants. Some were young, unskilled men, but the colony's explosive growth also created a strong demand for all kinds of skilled laborers, especially in the construction trades.

**EXPLAIN CONSEQUENCES**
How did rapid immigration and economic growth trigger conflict in the Middle colonies?

Pennsylvania and New Jersey grew prosperous but contentious. New Jersey was plagued by contested land titles, and ordinary settlers rioted against the proprietors in the 1740s and the 1760s. By the 1760s, eastern Pennsylvania landowners with large farms were using slaves and poor Scots-Irish migrants to grow wheat. Other ambitious men were buying up land and dividing it into small tenancies, which they lent out on profitable leases. Still others sold farming equipment and

manufactured goods or ran mills. These large-scale farmers, rural landlords, speculators, storekeepers, and gristmill operators formed a distinct class of agricultural capitalists. They built large stone houses for their families, furnishing them with four-poster beds and expensive mahogany tables, on which they laid elegant linen and imported Dutch dinnerware.

By contrast, one-half of the Middle colonies' white men owned no land and little personal property. Some were the sons of smallholding farmers and would eventually inherit some land. But many were Scots-Irish or German "inmates" — single men or families, explained a tax assessor, "such as live in small cottages and have no taxable property, except a cow." In the predominantly German township of Lancaster, Pennsylvania, a merchant noted an "abundance of Poor people" who "maintain their Families with great difficulty by day Labour." Although these workers hoped eventually to become landowners, rising land prices prevented many from realizing their dreams.

## Cultural Diversity

The Middle Atlantic colonies were not a melting pot. Most European migrants held tightly to their traditions, creating a patchwork of ethnically and religiously diverse communities (Figure 4.2). In 1748, a Swedish traveler counted no fewer than twelve religious denominations

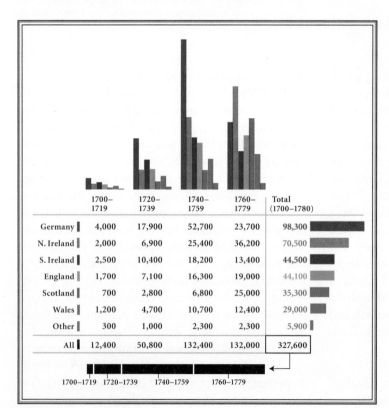

**FIGURE 4.2**
**Estimated European Migration to the British Mainland Colonies, 1700–1780**
After 1720, European migration to British North America increased dramatically, peaking between 1740 and 1780, when more than 264,000 settlers arrived in the mainland colonies. Emigration from Germany peaked in the 1740s, but the number of migrants from Ireland, Scotland, England, and Wales continued to increase during the 1760s and early 1770s. Most migrants, including those from Ireland, were Protestants.

|  | 1700–1719 | 1720–1739 | 1740–1759 | 1760–1779 | Total (1700–1780) |
|---|---|---|---|---|---|
| Germany | 4,000 | 17,900 | 52,700 | 23,700 | 98,300 |
| N. Ireland | 2,000 | 6,900 | 25,400 | 36,200 | 70,500 |
| S. Ireland | 2,500 | 10,400 | 18,200 | 13,400 | 44,500 |
| England | 1,700 | 7,100 | 16,300 | 19,000 | 44,100 |
| Scotland | 700 | 2,800 | 6,800 | 25,000 | 35,300 |
| Wales | 1,200 | 4,700 | 10,700 | 12,400 | 29,000 |
| Other | 300 | 1,000 | 2,300 | 2,300 | 5,900 |
| All | 12,400 | 50,800 | 132,400 | 132,000 | 327,600 |

1700–1719   1720–1739   1740–1759   1760–1779

in Philadelphia, including Anglicans, Baptists, Quakers, Swedish and German Lutherans, Mennonites, Scots-Irish Presbyterians, and Roman Catholics.

Migrants preserved their cultural identity by marrying within their ethnic groups. A major exception was the Huguenots, Calvinists who had been expelled from Catholic France in the 1680s and resettled in Holland, England, and the British colonies. Huguenots in American port cities such as Boston, New York, and Charleston quickly lost their French identities by intermarrying with other Protestants. More typical were the Welsh Quakers in Chester County, Pennsylvania: 70 percent of the children of the original Welsh migrants married other Welsh Quakers, as did 60 percent of the third generation.

In Pennsylvania and western New Jersey, Quakers shaped the culture because of their numbers, wealth, and social cohesion. Most Quakers came from English counties with few landlords and brought with them traditions of local village governance, popular participation in politics, and social equality. But after 1720, the growth of German and Scots-Irish populations challenged their dominance.

**The German Influx**    The Quaker vision of a "peaceable kingdom" attracted 100,000 German migrants who had fled their homelands because of military conscription, religious persecution, and high taxes. First to arrive, in 1683, were the Mennonites, religious dissenters drawn by the promise of freedom of worship. In the 1720s, a larger wave of German migrants arrived from the overcrowded villages of southwestern Germany and Switzerland. "Wages were far better" in Pennsylvania, Heinrich Schneebeli reported to his friends in Zurich, and "one also enjoyed there a free unhindered exercise of religion." A third wave of Germans and Swiss — nearly 40,000 strong — landed in Philadelphia between 1749 and 1756. To help pay

**A Quaker Meeting for Worship**

Quakers dressed plainly and met for worship in unadorned buildings, sitting in silence until inspired by an "inner light." Women spoke during meetings on terms of near-equality to men, a tradition that prepared Quaker women to take a leading part in the nineteenth-century women's rights movement. In this English work, titled *Quaker Meeting*, an elder (his hat on a peg above his head) conveys his thoughts to the congregation. Museum of Fine Arts, Boston. M. and M. Karolik Collection.

**The Demory House, c. 1780**

The Demory House lies near the Shenandoah Valley in northwestern Virginia and was probably built by a migrant from Pennsylvania according to a German design used by both German and Scots-Irish settlers. The house is small but sturdy. It measures 20 feet by 14 feet deep and has one and a half stories. The two first-floor rooms, a kitchen and a parlor, are separated by an 18 × 18–inch square chimney set in the center of the house, as well as the stairs leading up to the sleeping chamber. Clay and small stones fill the gaps in the exterior walls, which consist of timber planking about 12 inches tall and 6 to 8 inches wide. © 2003 Copyright and All Rights Reserved by Christopher C. Fennell.

the costs of the expensive trip from the Rhine Valley, German immigrants pioneered the **redemptioner** system, a flexible form of indentured servitude that allowed families to negotiate their own terms upon arrival. Families often indentured one or more children while their parents set up a household of their own.

Germans soon dominated many districts in eastern Pennsylvania, and thousands more moved down the fertile Shenandoah Valley into the western backcountry of Maryland, Virginia, and the Carolinas (Map 4.2). Many migrants preserved their cultural identity by settling in German-speaking Lutheran and Reformed communities that endured well beyond 1800. A minister in North Carolina admonished young people "not to contract any marriages with the English or Irish," arguing that "we owe it to our native country to do our part that German blood and the German language be preserved in America."

These settlers were willing colonial subjects of Britain's German-born and German-speaking Protestant monarchs, George I (r. 1714–1727) and George II (r. 1727–1760). They generally avoided politics except to protect their cultural practices; for example, they insisted that married women have the legal right to hold property and write wills, as they did in Germany.

**Scots-Irish Settlers**   Migrants from Ireland, who numbered about 115,000, were the most numerous of the incoming Europeans. Some were Irish and Catholic, but most were Scots and Presbyterian, the descendants of the Calvinist Protestants sent to Ireland during the

**IDENTIFY CAUSES**
What attracted German and Scots-Irish migrants to Pennsylvania in such large numbers?

seventeenth century to solidify English rule there. Once in Ireland, the Scots faced hostility from both Irish Catholics and English officials and landlords. The Irish Test Act of 1704 restricted voting and office holding to members of the Church of England, English mercantilist regulations placed heavy import duties on linens made by Scots-Irish weavers, and farmers paid heavy taxes. This persecution made America seem desirable. "Read this letter, Rev. Baptist Boyd," a migrant to New York wrote back to his minister, "and tell all the poor folk of ye place that God has opened a door for their deliverance . . . all that a man works for is his own; there are no revenue hounds to take it from us here."

Lured by such reports, thousands of Scots-Irish families sailed for the colonies. By 1720, most migrated to Philadelphia, attracted by the religious tolerance there. Seeking cheap land, they moved to central Pennsylvania and to the fertile Shenandoah Valley to the south. Governor William Gooch of Virginia welcomed the Scots-Irish presence to secure "the Country against the Indians." An Anglican planter, however, thought them as dangerous as "the Goths and Vandals of old" had been to the Roman Empire. Like the Germans, the Scots-Irish retained their culture, living in ethnic communities and holding firm to the Presbyterian Church.

## Religion and Politics

In Western Europe, the leaders of church and state condemned religious diversity. "To tolerate all [religions] without controul is the way to have none at all," declared an Anglican clergyman. Orthodox church

**MAP 4.2**

**Ethnic and Racial Diversity in the British Colonies, 1775**

In 1700, most colonists in British North America were of English origin; by 1775, settlers of English descent constituted only about 50 percent of the total population. African Americans now accounted for one-third of the residents of the South, while tens of thousands of German and Scots-Irish migrants added ethnic and religious diversity in the Middle colonies, the southern backcountry, and northern New England (see Figure 4.2).

Scots and Scots Irish made up 15 percent of the population.

Those of German ancestry made up about 7 percent of the population.

People of African origin accounted for 20 percent of the total population and were particularly numerous in the South.

Predominant Ethnic Group
- African
- Dutch
- English
- German
- Scots-Irish
- Scots
- Swedish
- Welsh

officials carried such sentiments to Pennsylvania. "The preachers do not have the power to punish anyone, or to force anyone to go to church," complained Gottlieb Mittelberger, an influential German minister. As a result, "Sunday is very badly kept. Many people plough, reap, thresh, hew or split wood and the like." He concluded: "Liberty in Pennsylvania does more harm than good to many people, both in soul and body."

Mittelberger was mistaken. Although ministers in Pennsylvania could not invoke government authority to uphold religious values, the result was not social anarchy. Instead, religious sects enforced moral behavior through communal self-discipline. Quaker families attended a weekly meeting for worship and a monthly meeting for business; every three months, a committee reminded parents to provide proper religious instruction. The committee also supervised adult behavior; a Chester County meeting, for example, disciplined a member "to reclaim him from drinking to excess and keeping vain company." Significantly, Quaker meetings allowed couples to marry only if they had land and livestock sufficient to support a family. As a result, the children of well-to-do Friends usually married within the sect, while poor Quakers remained unmarried, wed later in life, or married without permission — in which case they were often ousted from the meeting. These marriage rules helped the Quakers build a self-contained and prosperous community.

In the 1740s, the flood of new migrants reduced Quakers to a minority — a mere 30 percent of Pennsylvanians. Moreover, Scots-Irish settlers in central Pennsylvania demanded an aggressive Indian policy, challenging the pacifism of the assembly. To retain power, Quaker politicians sought an alliance with those German religious groups that also embraced pacifism and voluntary (not compulsory) militia service. In response, German leaders demanded more seats in the assembly and laws that respected their inheritance customs. Other Germans — Lutherans and Baptists — tried to gain control of the assembly by forming a "general confederacy"

**UNDERSTAND POINTS OF VIEW**

What issues divided the various ethnic and religious groups of the Middle colonies? What core values did they agree upon?

with Scots-Irish Presbyterians. An observer predicted that the scheme was doomed to failure because of "mutual jealousy" (Map 4.3).

By the 1750s, politics throughout the Middle colonies roiled with conflict. In New York, a Dutchman declared that he "Valued English Law no more than a Turd," while in Pennsylvania, Benjamin Franklin disparaged the "boorish" character and "swarthy complexion" of German migrants. Yet there was broad agreement on the importance of economic opportunity and liberty of conscience. The unstable balance between shared values and mutual mistrust prefigured tensions that would pervade an increasingly diverse American society in the centuries to come.

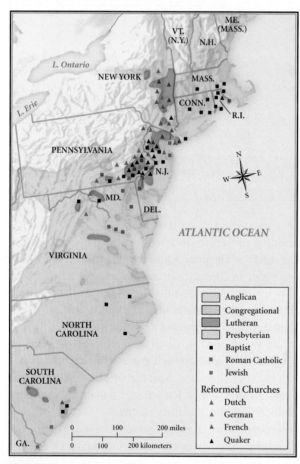

**MAP 4.3**

**Religious Diversity in 1750**

By 1750, religious diversity was on the rise, not only in the multiethnic Middle colonies but also in all of British North America. Baptists had increased their numbers in New England, long the stronghold of Congregationalists, and would soon become important in Virginia. Already there were considerable numbers of Presbyterians, Lutherans, and German Reformed in the South, where Anglicanism was the established religion.

# Commerce, Culture, and Identity

After 1720, transatlantic shipping grew more frequent and Britain and its colonies more closely connected, while a burgeoning print culture flooded the colonies with information and ideas. Two great European cultural movements — the **Enlightenment**, which emphasized the power of human reason to understand and shape the world; and **Pietism**, an evangelical Christian movement that stressed the individual's personal relationship with God — reached America as a result. At the same time, an abundance of imported goods began to reshape material culture, bringing new comforts into the lives of the middling sort while allowing prosperous merchants and landowners to set themselves apart from their neighbors in new ways.

## Transportation and the Print Revolution

In the eighteenth century, improved transportation networks opened Britain's colonies in new ways, and British shipping came to dominate the north Atlantic. In 1700, Britain had 40,000 sailors; by 1750, the number had grown to 60,000, while many more hailed from the colonies. An enormous number of vessels plied Atlantic waters: in the late 1730s, more than 550 ships arrived in Boston annually. About a tenth came directly from Britain or Ireland; the rest came mostly from other British colonies, either on the mainland or in the West Indies.

A road network slowly took shape as well, though roadbuilding was expensive and difficult. In 1704, Sarah Kemble Knight traveled from Boston to New York on horseback. The road was "smooth and even" in some places, treacherous in others; it took eight days of hard riding to cover 200 miles. Forty years later, a physician from Annapolis, Maryland, traveled along much better roads to Portsmouth, New Hampshire, and back — more than 1,600 miles in all. He spent four months on the road, stopping frequently to meet the locals and satisfy his curiosity. By the mid-eighteenth century, the "Great Wagon Road" carried migrating families down the Shenandoah Valley as far as the Carolina backcountry.

All of these water and land routes carried people, produce, and finished merchandise. They also carried information, as letters, newspapers, pamphlets, and crates of books began to circulate widely. The trip across the Atlantic took seven to eight weeks on average, so the news arriving in colonial ports was not fresh by our standard, but compared to earlier years, the colonies were awash in information.

Until 1695, the British government had the power to censor all printed materials. In that year, Parliament let the Licensing Act lapse, and the floodgates opened. Dozens of new printshops opened in London and Britain's provincial cities. They printed newspapers and pamphlets; poetry, ballads, and sermons; and hand-bills, tradesman's cards, and advertisements. Larger booksellers also printed scientific treatises, histories, travelers' accounts, and novels. The result was a print revolution. In Britain and throughout Europe, print was essential to the transmission of new ideas, and both the Enlightenment and Pietism took shape in part through its growing influence.

All this material crossed the Atlantic and filled the shops of colonial booksellers. The colonies also began printing their own newspapers. In 1704, the *Boston Newsletter* was founded; by 1720, Boston had five print-ing presses and three newspapers; and by 1776, the thirteen colonies that united in declaring indepen-dence had thirty-seven newspapers among them. This world of print was essential to their ability to share grievances and join in common cause.

## The Enlightenment in America

To explain the workings of the natural world, some col-onists relied on folk wisdom. Swedish migrants in Pennsylvania attributed magical powers to the great white mullein, a common wildflower, and treated fevers by tying the plant's leaves around their feet and arms. Traditionally, Christians believed that the earth stood at the center of the universe, and God (and Satan) intervened directly and continuously in human affairs. The scientific revolution of the sixteenth and seven-teenth centuries challenged these ideas, and educated people — most of them Christians — began to modify their views accordingly.

**The European Enlightenment**  In 1543, the Polish astronomer Copernicus published his observation that the earth traveled around the sun, not vice versa. Copernicus's discovery suggested that humans occupied a more modest place in the universe than Christian theology assumed. In the next century, Isaac Newton, in his *Principia Mathematica* (1687), used the sciences of mathematics and physics to explain the movement of the planets around the sun (and invented calculus in the process). Though Newton was himself profoundly religious, in the long run his work undermined the traditional Christian understanding of the cosmos.

In the century between the *Principia Mathematica* and the French Revolution of 1789, the philosophers of the European Enlightenment used empirical research and scientific reasoning to study all aspects of life, including social institutions and human behavior. Enlightenment thinkers advanced four fundamental principles: the lawlike order of the natural world, the power of human reason, the "natural rights" of individ-uals (including the right to self-government), and the progressive improvement of society.

English philosopher John Locke was a major contributor to the Enlightenment. In his *Essay Con-cerning Human Understanding* (1690), Locke stressed the impact of environment and experience on human behavior and beliefs, arguing that the character of individuals and societies was not fixed but could be changed through edu-cation, rational thought, and purposeful action. Locke's *Two Treatises of Government* (1690) advanced the revolutionary the-ory that political authority was not given by God to monarchs, as James II had insisted (see Chapter 3). Instead, it derived from social compacts that people made to preserve their **natural rights** to life, liberty, and property. In Locke's view, the people should have the power to change government policies — or even their form of government.

> **PLACE EVENTS IN CONTEXT**
> What conditions and ideas lay behind the emergence of the Enlightenment in America?

Some clergymen responded to these developments by devising a rational form of Christianity. Rejecting supernatural interventions and a vengeful Calvinist God, Congregationalist minister Andrew Eliot main-tained that "there is nothing in Christianity that is contrary to reason." The Reverend John Wise of Ipswich, Massachusetts, used Locke's philosophy to defend giving power to ordinary church members. Just as the social compact formed the basis of political soci-ety, Wise argued, so the religious covenant among the lay members of a congregation made them — not the bishops of the Church of England or even ministers like himself — the proper interpreters of religious truth. The Enlightenment influenced Puritan minister Cotton Mather as well. When a measles epidemic ravaged Boston in the 1710s, Mather thought that only God could end it; but when smallpox struck a decade later, he used his newly acquired knowledge of inoculation — gained in part from a slave, who told him of the practice's success in Africa — to advocate this scientific preventive for the disease.

**Enlightenment Philanthropy: Pennsylvania Hospital, Philadelphia**

Using public funds and private donations, Philadelphia reformers built this imposing structure in 1753. The new hospital embodied two principles of the Enlightenment: that purposeful actions could improve society, and that the products of these actions should express reason and order, exhibited here in the building's symmetrical facade. Etchings like this one from the 1760s (*A Perspective View of the Pennsylvania Hospital*, by John Streeper and Henry Dawkins) circulated widely and bolstered Philadelphia's reputation as the center of the American Enlightenment. Historical Society of Pennsylvania.

**Franklin's Contributions**   Benjamin Franklin was the exemplar of the American Enlightenment. Born in Boston in 1706 to devout Calvinists, he grew to manhood during the print revolution. Apprenticed to his brother, a Boston printer, Franklin educated himself through voracious reading. At seventeen, he fled to Philadelphia, where he became a prominent printer, and in 1729 he founded the *Pennsylvania Gazette*, which became one of the colonies' most influential newspapers. Franklin also formed a "club of mutual improvement" that met weekly to discuss "Morals, Politics, or Natural Philosophy." These discussions, as well as Enlightenment literature, shaped his thinking. As Franklin explained in his *Autobiography* (1771), "From the different books I read, I began to doubt of Revelation [God-revealed truth]."

Like a small number of urban artisans, wealthy Virginia planters, and affluent seaport merchants, Franklin became a deist. **Deism** was a way of thinking, not an established religion. "My own mind is my own church," said deist Thomas Paine. "I am of a sect by myself," added Thomas Jefferson. Influenced by Enlightenment science, deists such as Jefferson believed that a Supreme Being (or Grand Architect) created the world and then allowed it to operate by natural laws but did not intervene in people's lives. Rejecting the divinity of Christ and the authority of the Bible, deists relied on "natural reason," their innate moral sense, to define right and wrong. Thus Franklin, a onetime slave owner, came to question the morality of slavery, repudiating it once he recognized the parallels between racial bondage and the colonies' political bondage to Britain.

Franklin popularized the practical outlook of the Enlightenment in *Poor Richard's Almanack* (1732–1757), an annual publication that was read by thousands. He also founded the American Philosophical Society (1743–present) to promote "useful knowledge." Adopting this goal in his own life, Franklin invented bifocal lenses for eyeglasses, the Franklin stove, and the lightning rod. His book on electricity, published in England in 1751, won praise as the greatest contribution to science since Newton's discoveries. Inspired by

**Benjamin Franklin's Rise**

This portrait of Benjamin Franklin, attributed to Robert Feke and executed around 1746, portrays Franklin as a successful businessman. His ruffled collar and cuffs, his fashionably curly wig, and his sober but expensive suit reveal his social ambitions. In later portraits, after he gained fame as an Enlightenment sage, he dispensed with the wig and chose more unaffected poses; but in 1746, he was still establishing his credentials as a young Philadelphia gentleman on the rise. Harvard University Art Museum, Fogg Art Museum, Bequest of Dr. John Collins Warren, 1856, H47 Photo: Imaging Department © President and Fellows of Harvard College.

Franklin, ambitious printers in America's seaport cities published newspapers and gentlemen's magazines, the first significant nonreligious periodicals to appear in the colonies. The European Enlightenment, then, added a secular dimension to colonial cultural life, foreshadowing the great contributions to republican political theory by American intellectuals of the Revolutionary era: John Adams, James Madison, and Thomas Jefferson.

## American Pietism and the Great Awakening

As some colonists turned to deism, thousands of others embraced Pietism, a Christian movement originating in Germany around 1700 and emphasizing pious behavior (hence the name). In its emotional worship services and individual striving for a mystical union with God, Pietism appealed to believers' hearts rather than their minds (American Voices, p. 130). In the 1720s, German migrants carried Pietism to America, sparking a religious **revival** (or renewal of religious enthusiasm) in Pennsylvania and New Jersey, where Dutch minister Theodore Jacob Frelinghuysen preached passionate sermons to German settlers and encouraged church members to spread the message of spiritual urgency. A decade later, William Tennent and his son Gilbert copied Frelinghuysen's approach and led revivals among Scots-Irish Presbyterians throughout the Middle Atlantic region.

**New England Revivalism**  Simultaneously, an American-born Pietist movement appeared in New England. Revivals of Christian zeal were built into the logic of Puritanism. In the 1730s, Jonathan Edwards, a minister in Northampton, Massachusetts, encouraged a revival there that spread to towns throughout the Connecticut River Valley. Edwards guided and observed the process and then published an account entitled *A Faithful Narrative of the Surprising Work of God*, printed first in London (1737), then in Boston (1738), and then in German and Dutch translations. Its publication history highlights the transatlantic network of correspondents that gave Pietism much of its vitality.

**Whitefield's Great Awakening**  English minister George Whitefield transformed the local revivals of Edwards and the Tennents into a Great Awakening. After Whitefield had his personal awakening upon reading the German Pietists, he became a follower of John Wesley, the founder of English Methodism. In 1739, Whitefield carried Wesley's fervent message to America, where he attracted huge crowds from Georgia to Massachusetts.

Whitefield had a compelling presence. "He looked almost angelical; a young, slim, slender youth . . . cloathed with authority from the Great God," wrote a Connecticut farmer. Like most evangelical preachers, Whitefield did not read his sermons but spoke from memory. More like an actor than a theologian, he gestured eloquently, raised his voice for dramatic effect, and at times assumed a female persona — as a woman in labor struggling to deliver the word of God. When the young preacher told his spellbound listeners that they had sinned and must seek salvation, some suddenly felt a "new light" within them. As "the power of god come down," Hannah Heaton recalled, "my knees smote together . . . [and] it seemed to me I was a sinking down into hell . . . but then I resigned my distress and was perfectly easy quiet and calm . . . [and] it seemed as

# Evangelical Religion and Enlightenment Rationalism

Two great historical movements, Enlightenment thought and Pietistic religion, swept across British North America in the eighteenth century and offered radically different—indeed, almost completely contradictory—worldviews. Pietism sparked religious revivals based on passion and emotion, while Enlightenment rationalism encouraged personal restraint and intellectual logic. Both movements shaped American cultural development: Pietism transformed American religious life, and Enlightenment thinking influenced the principles of the American government.

## Sarah Lippet
### Death as a Passage to Life

Sarah Lippet was a longtime member of the Baptist church of Middletown in eastern New Jersey. She died in October 1767 at the age of sixty-one; fellow parishioners reported her sentiments as she lay, for four days, on her deathbed.

All my lifetime I have been in fears and doubts, but now am delivered. He hath delivered them who through fear of death were all their lifetime subject to bondage. For the love I have for Christ I am willing to part with all my friends to be with Him, for I love Him above all; yet it is nothing in me, for I know if I had my desert I should be in Hell. I believe in Christ, and I know that I put my whole trust in Him, and he that believeth in Him shall not be ashamed nor be confounded. . . .

Why do you mourn when I rejoice? You should not; it is no more for me to die and leave my friends for the great love I have for Christ than for me to go to sleep. I have no fears of death in my mind. Christ has the keys of death and hell, and blessed are the dead that die in the Lord. I can't bear to see a tear shed. You should not mourn.

Source: "The Triumphant Christian," in *Historical and Genealogical Miscellany*, ed. John E. Stillwell (New York, 1964), 3: 465–466.

## Nathan Cole
### The Struggle for Salvation

Connecticut farmer Nathan Cole found God after listening to a sermon by George Whitefield, the great English evangelist. But Cole's spiritual quest was not easy. He struggled for two years before coming to believe that he was saved.

[After hearing Whitefield] I began to think I was not Elected, and that God made some for heaven and me for hell. And I thought God was not Just in so doing. . . . My heart then rose against God exceedingly, for his making me for hell; Now this distress lasted Almost two years—

Poor Me—Miserable me. . . . I was loaded with the guilt of Sin. . . .

Hell fire was most always in my mind; and I have hundreds of times put my fingers into my pipe when I have been smoking to feel how fire felt: And to see how my Body could bear to lye in Hell fire for ever and ever. . . . And while these thoughts were in my mind God appeared unto me and made me Skringe: before whose face the heavens and the earth fled away; and I was Shrinked into nothing; I knew not whether I was in the body or out, I seemed to hang in open Air before God, and he seemed to Speak to me in an angry and Sovereign way[:] What? Won't you trust your Soul with God?; My heart answered O yes, yes, yes. . . .

When God disappeared or in some measure withdrew, every thing was in its place again and I was on my Bed. . . . I was set free, my distress was gone, and I was filled with a pineing desire to see Christs own words in the bible; . . . I got the bible up under my Chin and hugged it; it was sweet and lovely; the word was nigh [near] me in my hand, then I began to pray and to praise God.

Source: "The Spiritual Travels of Nathan Cole, 1741" in *The Great Awakening: Documents on the Revival of Religion, 1740–1745*, ed. Richard L. Bushman (New York: Atheneum, 1970), 68–70.

## Benjamin Franklin
### The Importance of a Virtuous Life

Franklin stood at the center of the American Enlightenment. In his *Autobiography*, he outlined his religious views and his human-centered moral principles.

My Parents had early given me religious Impressions, and brought me through my Childhood piously in the Dissenting Way. But I was scarce 15 when, after doubting by turns of several Points as I found them disputed in the different Books I read, I began to doubt of Revelation itself. Some Books against Deism fell into my Hands. . . . It happened that they wrought an Effect on me quite contrary to what was intended by them: For the Arguments of the Deists [that were quoted in those books] appeared to me much Stronger than the Refutations. In short I soon became a thorough Deist. . . .

I grew convinc'd that Truth, Sincerity & Integrity in Dealings between Man & Man, were of the utmost Importance to the Felicity of Life, and I form'd written Resolutions, (which still remain in my Journal Book) to practice them ever while I lived. . . .

About the Year 1734. There arrived among us from Ireland, a young Presbyterian Preacher named Hemphill, who delivered with a good Voice, & apparently extempore, most excellent Discourses, which drew together considerable Numbers of different Persuasions, who join'd in admiring them. Among the rest I became one of his constant Hearers, his Sermons pleasing me as they had little of the dogmatical kind, but inculcated strongly the Practice of Virtue, or what in the religious Stile are called Good Works. Those however, of our Congregation, who considered themselves as orthodox Presbyterians, disapprov'd his Doctrine, and were join'd by most of the old Clergy, who arraign'd him of Heterodoxy before the Synod, in order to have him silenc'd. I became his zealous Partisan. . . .

I never was without some religious Principles; I never doubted, for instance, the Existance of the Deity, that he made the World, & govern'd it by his Providence; that the most acceptable Service of God was the doing Good to Man; that our Souls are immortal; and that all Crime will be punished & Virtue rewarded either here or hereafter; these I esteem'd the Essentials of every Religion.

Source: Louis P. Masur, ed., *The Autobiography of Benjamin Franklin, with Related Documents*, 2nd ed. (Boston: Bedford/St. Martin's, 2003), 73–74, 93–94, 108.

## John Wise
## The Primacy of Human Reason and Natural Laws

Reverend John Wise (1652–1725) served for many years as a pastor in Ipswich, Massachusetts. A graduate of Harvard College, Wise used the Enlightenment doctrines of John Locke and Samuel von Pufendorf to justify the democratic structure of New England Congregational churches.

I Shall disclose several Principles of Natural Knowledge; plainly discovering the Law of Nature; or the true sentiments of Natural Reason, with Respect to Mans Being and Government. . . . I shall consider Man in a state of Natural Being, as a Free-Born Subject under the Crown of Heaven, and owing Homage to none but God himself. It is certain Civil Government in General, is a very Admirable Result of Providence, and an Incomparable Benefit to Mankind, yet must needs be acknowledged to be the Effect of Humane Free-Compacts and not of Divine Institution; it is the Produce of Mans Reason, of Humane and Rational Combinations, and not from any direct Orders of Infinite Wisdom. . . .

The Prime Immunity in Mans State, is that he is most properly the Subject of the Law of Nature. He is the Favourite Animal on Earth; in that this Part of Gods Image, viz. Reason is Congenate with his Nature, wherein by a Law Immutable, Instampt upon his Frame, God has provided a Rule for Men in all their Actions; obliging each one to the performance of that which is Right, not only as to Justice, but likewise as to all other Moral Vertues, which is nothing but the Dictate of Right Reason founded in the Soul of Man. . . .

The Second Great Immunity of Man is an Original Liberty Instampt upon his Rational Nature. He that intrudes upon this Liberty, Violates the Law of Nature. . . .

The Third Capital Immunity belonging to Mans Nature, is an equality amongst Men; Which is not to be denied by the Law of Nature, till Man has Resigned himself with all his Rights for the sake of a Civil State; and then his Personal Liberty and Equality is to be cherished, and preserved to the highest degree.

Source: John Wise, *A Vindication of the Government of New England Churches* (Boston: J. Allen, for N. Boone, 1717), 32–40.

---

### QUESTIONS FOR ANALYSIS

1. All of these writers declare a belief in God. How do their beliefs and outlooks differ?

2. These writers were variously influenced by the Great Awakening, the Enlightenment, and rational Christianity. How are these movements reflected in the passages above?

3. What roles do fear and anxiety play in the experiences of Sarah Lippet and Nathan Cole? What difference does it make that neither Franklin nor Wise expresses fear, either of God or of his own sinfulness?

4. Benjamin Franklin and John Wise stress the importance of reason and virtue as guides to human conduct. How would Nathan Cole and Sarah Lippet react to that emphasis?

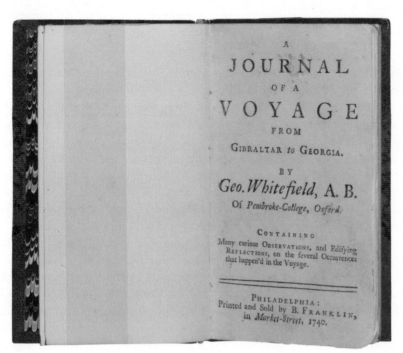

**The Print Revolution and the Great Awakening**

George Whitefield made his first trip to North America in 1738, when he traveled to Savannah, Georgia. Benjamin Franklin published the first edition of this journal of his voyage in Philadelphia in 1739; the copy pictured here was printed a year later. Texts like this one highlight the importance of the print revolution to eighteenth-century culture: Whitefield was utterly unknown in North America until he began publicizing his ministry and his travels through such works. Enlightenment ideas, too, were conveyed to large and far-flung audiences in books, magazines, and newspapers. Library Company of Philadelphia.

if I had a new soul & body both." Strengthened and self-confident, these converts, the so-called New Lights, were eager to spread Whitefield's message.

The rise of print intersected with this enthusiasm. "Religion is become the Subject of most Conversations," the *Pennsylvania Gazette* reported. "No books are in Request but those of Piety and Devotion." Whitefield and his circle did their best to answer the demand for devotional reading. As he traveled, Whitefield regularly sent excerpts of his journal to be printed in newspapers. Franklin printed Whitefield's sermons and journals by subscription and found them to be among his best-selling titles. Printed accounts of Whitefield's travels, conversion narratives, sermons, and other devotional literature helped to confirm Pietists in their faith and strengthen the communication networks that sustained them.

## Religious Upheaval in the North

Like all cultural explosions, the Great Awakening was controversial. Conservative ministers—passionless **Old Lights**, according to the evangelists—condemned the "cryings out, faintings and convulsions" in revivalist meetings and the New Lights' claims of "working Miracles or speaking with Tongues." Boston minister Charles Chauncy attacked the Pietist **New Lights**

**COMPARE AND CONTRAST**

In what ways was the spread of ideas during the Enlightenment and the Great Awakening similar, and how did it differ?

for allowing women to speak in public: it was "a plain breach of that commandment of the lord, where it is said, Let your women keep silence in the churches." In Connecticut, Old Lights persuaded the legislature to prohibit evangelists from speaking to a congregation without the minister's permission. But the New Lights refused to be silenced. Dozens of farmers, women, and artisans roamed the countryside, condemning the Old Lights as "unconverted" and willingly accepting imprisonment: "I shall bring glory to God in my bonds," a dissident preacher wrote from jail.

The Great Awakening undermined legally established churches and their tax-supported ministers. In New England, New Lights left the Congregational Church and founded 125 "separatist" churches that supported their ministers through voluntary contributions (Figure 4.3). Other religious dissidents joined Baptist congregations, which also condemned government support of churches: "God never allowed any civil state upon earth to impose religious taxes," declared Baptist preacher Isaac Backus. In New York and New Jersey, the Dutch Reformed Church split in two as New Lights refused to accept doctrines imposed by conservative church authorities in Holland.

The Great Awakening also appealed to Christians whose established churches could not serve their needs. By 1740, Pennsylvania's German Reformed and Lutheran congregations suffered from a severe lack of university-trained pastors. In the colony's Dutch Reformed, Dutch and Swedish Lutheran, and even its

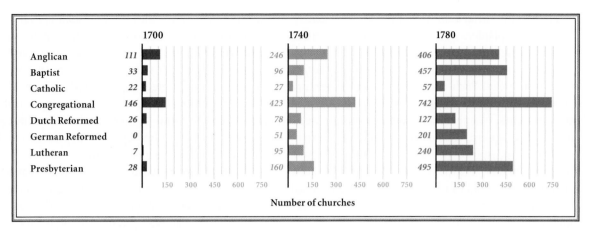

**FIGURE 4.3**
**Church Growth by Denomination, 1700–1780**
In 1700, and again in 1740, the Congregationalist and Anglican churches had the most members. By 1780, however, largely because of their enthusiastic evangelical message, Presbyterian and Baptist congregations outnumbered those of the Anglicans. The growth of immigrant denominations, such as the German Reformed and Lutheran, was equally impressive.

Anglican congregations, half the pulpits were empty. In this circumstance, itinerant preachers who stressed the power of "heart religion" and downplayed the importance of formal ministerial training found a ready audience.

The Great Awakening challenged the authority of all ministers, whose status rested on respect for their education and knowledge of the Bible. In an influential pamphlet, *The Dangers of an Unconverted Ministry* (1740), Gilbert Tennent asserted that ministers' authority should come not from theological knowledge but from the conversion experience. Reaffirming Martin Luther's belief in the priesthood of all Christians, Tennent suggested that anyone who had felt God's redeeming grace could speak with ministerial authority. Sarah Harrah Osborn, a New Light "exhorter" in Rhode Island, refused "to shut up my mouth . . . and creep into obscurity" when silenced by her minister.

As religious enthusiasm spread, churches founded new colleges to educate their young men and to train ministers. New Light Presbyterians established the College of New Jersey (Princeton) in 1746, and New York Anglicans founded King's College (Columbia) in 1754. Baptists set up the College of Rhode Island (Brown) in 1764; two years later, the Dutch Reformed Church subsidized Queen's College (Rutgers) in New Jersey. However, the main intellectual legacy of the Great Awakening was not education for the privileged few but a new sense of authority among the many. A European visitor to Philadelphia remarked in surprise, "The poorest day-laborer . . . holds it his right to advance his opinion, in religious as well as political matters, with as much freedom as the gentleman."

## Social and Religious Conflict in the South

In the southern colonies, where the Church of England was legally established, religious enthusiasm triggered social conflict. Anglican ministers generally ignored the spiritual needs of African Americans and landless whites, who numbered 40 percent and 20 percent of the population, respectively. Middling white freeholders (35 percent of the residents) formed the core of most Church of England congregations. But prominent planters (just 5 percent) held the real power, using their control of parish finances to discipline ministers. One clergyman complained that dismissal awaited any minister who "had the courage to preach against any Vices taken into favor by the leading Men of his Parish."

**The Presbyterian Revival**   Soon, a democratization of religion challenged the dominance of both the Anglican Church and the planter elite. In 1743, bricklayer Samuel Morris, inspired by reading George Whitefield's sermons, led a group of Virginia Anglicans out of their congregation. Seeking a deeper religious experience, Morris invited New Light Presbyterian Samuel Davies to lead their prayer meetings. Davies's sermons, filled with erotic devotional imagery and urging Christians to feel "ardent Passion," sparked Presbyterian revivals across the Tidewater region, threatening the social authority of the Virginia gentry. Traditionally, planters and their well-dressed families arrived at Anglican services in fancy carriages drawn by well-bred horses and flaunted their power by sitting in the front pews. Such ritual displays of the gentry's superiority were meaningless if freeholders attended other churches. Moreover, religious pluralism threatened the tax-supported status of the Anglican Church.

To halt the spread of New Light ideas, Virginia governor William Gooch denounced them as "false teachings," and Anglican justices of the peace closed Presbyterian churches. This harassment kept most white yeomen and poor tenant families in the Church of England.

**The Baptist Insurgency**   During the 1760s, the vigorous preaching and democratic message of New Light Baptist ministers converted thousands of white farm families. The Baptists were radical Protestants whose central ritual was adult (rather than infant) baptism. Once men and women had experienced the infusion of grace — had been "born again" — they were baptized in an emotional public ceremony, often involving complete immersion in water.

Slaves were welcome at Baptist revivals. During the 1740s, George Whitefield had urged Carolina planters to bring their slaves into the Christian fold, but white opposition and the Africans' commitment to their ancestral religions kept the number of converts low. However, in the 1760s, native-born African Americans in Virginia welcomed the Baptists' message that all people were equal in God's eyes. Sensing a threat to the system of racial slavery, the House of Burgesses imposed heavy fines on Baptists who preached to slaves without their owners' permission.

Baptists threatened gentry authority because they repudiated social distinctions and urged followers to call one another "brother" and "sister." They also condemned the planters' decadent lifestyle. As planter Landon Carter complained, the Baptists were "destroying pleasure in the Country; for they encourage ardent Prayer . . . & an intire Banishment of *Gaming*, *Dancing*, & *Sabbath-Day Diversions*." The gentry responded with violence. In Caroline County, an Anglican posse attacked Brother John Waller at a prayer meeting. Waller "was violently jerked off the stage; they caught him by the back part of his neck, beat his head against the ground, and a gentleman gave him twenty lashes with his horsewhip."

Despite these attacks, Baptist congregations multiplied. By 1775, about 15 percent of Virginia's whites and hundreds of enslaved blacks had joined Baptist

**Baptism in the Schuylkill River**

The Baptist movement, which made adult baptism central to its religious practice, gained enormous influence during the Great Awakening. Baptists presented a challenge to the social order in New England, where Isaac Backus and other leaders vigorously opposed the power of established Congregationalist churches. They presented an even graver threat to established authority in Virginia, where they ministered to African American slaves and ridiculed the pretensions of the gentry. This woodcut, from an eighteenth-century history of the Baptist movement, shows a congregation gathered on the banks of the Schuylkill River in Pennsylvania to witness the baptism of a new convert. Historical Society of Pennsylvania.

churches. To signify their state of grace, some Baptist men "cut off their hair, like Cromwell's round-headed chaplains." Others forged a new evangelical masculinity, "crying, weeping, lifting up the eyes, groaning" when touched by the Holy Spirit.

The Baptist revival in the Chesapeake challenged customary authority in families and society but did not overturn it. Rejecting the pleas of evangelical women, Baptist men kept church authority in the hands of "free born male members"; and Anglican slaveholders retained control of the political system. Still, the Baptist insurgency infused the lives of poor tenant families with spiritual meaning and empowered yeomen to defend their economic interests. Moreover, as Baptist ministers spread Christianity among slaves, the cultural gulf between blacks and whites shrank, undermining one justification for slavery and giving some blacks a new religious identity. Within a generation, African Americans would develop distinctive versions of Protestant Christianity.

# The Midcentury Challenge: War, Trade, and Social Conflict, 1750–1763

Between 1750 and 1763, three significant events transformed colonial life. First, Britain went to war against the French in America, sparking a worldwide conflict: the Great War for Empire. Second, a surge in trade boosted colonial consumption but caused Americans to become deeply indebted to British creditors. Third, westward migration sparked warfare with Indian peoples, violent disputes between settlers and land speculators, and backcountry rebellions against eastern-controlled governments.

## The French and Indian War

In 1754, overlapping French and British claims in North America came to a head (Map 4.4). The French maintained their vast claims through a network of forts and trading posts that sustained alliances with neighboring Indians. The soft underbelly of this sprawling empire was the Ohio Valley, where French claims were tenuous. Native peoples were driven out of the valley by Iroquois attacks in the seventeenth century, but after 1720 displaced Indian populations — especially Delawares and Shawnees from Pennsylvania — resettled there in large numbers. In the 1740s, British traders from Pennsylvania began traveling down the Ohio

River. They traded with Delawares and Shawnees in the upper valley and began to draw French-allied Indians into their orbit and away from French posts. Then, in 1748, the Ohio Company of Virginia, a partnership of prominent colonial planters and London merchants, received a 200,000-acre grant from the crown to establish a new settlement on the upper Ohio, threatening French claims to the region.

**Conflict in the Ohio Valley**   By midcentury, Britain relied on the Iroquois Confederacy as its partner in Indian relations throughout the Northeast. By extending the Covenant Chain, the Iroquois had become a kind of Indian empire in their own right, claiming to speak for other groups throughout the region based on their seventeenth-century conquests. The Delawares, Shawnees, and other groups who repopulated the Ohio Valley did so in part to escape the Iroquois yoke. To maintain influence on the Ohio, the Iroquois sent two "half-kings," Tanaghrisson (an adopted Seneca) and Scarouady (an Oneida), to the native settlement of Logstown, a trading town on the upper Ohio, where Britain recognized them as leaders.

French authorities, alarmed by British inroads, built a string of forts from Lake Erie to the headwaters of the Ohio, culminating with Fort Duquesne on the site of present-day Pittsburgh. To reassert British claims, Governor Dinwiddie dispatched an expedition led by Colonel George Washington, a twenty-two-year-old Virginian whose half-brothers were Ohio Company stockholders. Washington discovered that most of the Ohio Indians had decided to side with the French; only the Iroquois half-kings and a few of their followers supported his efforts. After Washington's party fired on a French detachment, Tanaghrisson rushed in and killed a French officer to ensure war — a prospect that would force British arms to support Iroquois interests in the valley.

Washington's party was soon defeated by a larger French force. The result was an international incident that prompted Virginian and British expansionists to demand war. But war in North America was a worrisome prospect: the colonies were notoriously incapable of cooperating in their own defense, and the Covenant Chain was badly in need of repair.

**The Albany Congress**   The Iroquois Confederacy was unhappy with its British alliance and believed that the British were neglecting the Iroquois while settlers from New York pressed onto their lands. Moreover, the Ohio Indians, France, and Britain were all acting in the Ohio Valley without consulting them. To mend

**MAP 4.4**

**European Spheres of Influence in North America, 1754**

In the mid-eighteenth century, France, Spain, and the British-owned Hudson Bay Company laid claim to the vast areas of North America still inhabited primarily by Indian peoples. British settlers had already occupied much of the land east of the Appalachian Mountains. To safeguard their lands west of the mountains, Native Americans played off one European power against another. As a British official remarked: "To preserve the Ballance between us and the French is the great ruling Principle of Modern Indian Politics." When Britain expelled France from North America in 1763, Indians had to face encroaching Anglo-American settlers on their own.

continental assembly to manage trade, Indian policy, and the colonies' defense. Though it was attractive to a few reform-minded colonists and administrators, the plan would have compromised the independence of colonial assemblies and the authority of Parliament. It never received serious consideration, but that did not stop the push toward war.

 To see a longer excerpt of the Albany Plan of Union, along with other primary sources from this period, see *Sources for America's History*.

**The War Hawks Win**   In Parliament, the fight for the Ohio prompted a debate over war with France. Henry Pelham, the British prime minister, urged calm: "There is such a load of debt, and such heavy taxes already laid upon the people, that nothing but an absolute necessity can justifie our engaging in a new War." But two expansionist-minded war hawks — rising British statesman William Pitt and Lord Halifax, the new head of the Board of Trade — persuaded Pelham to launch an American war. In June 1755, British and New England troops captured Fort Beauséjour in the disputed territory of Nova Scotia (which the French called Acadia). Soldiers from Puritan Massachusetts then forced nearly 10,000 French settlers from their lands, arguing they were "rebels" without property rights, and deported them to France, the West Indies, and Louisiana (where "Acadians" became "Cajuns"). English and Scottish Protestants took over the farms the French Catholics left behind.

This Anglo-American triumph was quickly offset by a stunning defeat. In July 1755, General Edward Braddock advanced on Fort Duquesne with a force of 1,500 British regulars and Virginia militiamen. Braddock alienated potential allies by treating Indians (including Tanaghrisson) dismissively and denying the privilege of rank to colonial officers like George Washington. Persuaded that British arms could easily triumph in the American backcountry, he was instead routed by a French and Indian force. Braddock was killed, and more than half his troops were killed or wounded. "We have been beaten, most shamefully beaten, by a handfull of Men," George Washington complained bitterly as he led the survivors back to Virginia.

## The Great War for Empire

By 1756, the American conflict had spread to Europe, where it was known as the Seven Years' War, and pitted Britain and Prussia against France, Spain, and Austria.

**Hendrick Peters Theyanoguin, Chief of the Mohawks**

Great Britain's alliance with the Iroquois Confederacy — the Covenant Chain — was central to its Indian policy in the mid-eighteenth century, and the Mohawk warrior and sachem Hendrick Peters Theyanoguin emerged as its most powerful spokesman. His speech at the Albany Congress of 1754, in which he urged Great Britain toward war, was reported in newspapers in Britain and the colonies and made him a transatlantic celebrity. This print was advertised for sale in London bookstalls just as his death at the Battle of Lake George (1755) was being reported in newspapers there. Hendrick wears a rich silk waistcoat, an overcoat trimmed with gold lace, a ruffled shirt, and a tricorn hat — gifts from his British allies — while he holds a wampum belt in one hand and a tomahawk in the other. Courtesy of the John Carter Brown Library at Brown University.

relations with the Iroquois, the British Board of Trade called a meeting at Albany in June 1754. There, a prominent Mohawk leader named Hendrick Peters Theyanoguin challenged Britain to defend its interests more vigorously, while Benjamin Franklin proposed a "Plan of Union" among the colonies to counter French expansion.

The Albany Plan of Union proposed that "one general government . . . be formed in America, including all the said colonies." It would have created a

**Braddock's Defeat and Death, July 1755**

In May 1755 General Edward Braddock led a force of 1,500 British regulars and Virginia militiamen out of Fort Cumberland in western Maryland, intending to oust the French from Fort Duquesne, 50 miles to the west. As Braddock neared the fort, the French garrison of 200 troops and about 600 Indian allies—mostly Potawatomis, Ottawas, Shawnees, and Delawares—set out to ambush his force. Instead, they unexpectedly met the British along a narrow roadway. As the French and Indians fanned out to attack from the woods, the British troops (George Washington reported) "were struck with such a panic that they behaved with more cowardice than it is possible to conceive. The officers behaved gallantly, in order to encourage their men, for which they suffered greatly." The British casualties—450 killed, 500 wounded—included General Braddock, pictured above, who later died from his wounds. © Chicago History Museum, USA/The Bridgeman Art Library.

When Britain mounted major offensives in India, West Africa, and the West Indies as well as in North America, the conflict became the Great War for Empire.

William Pitt emerged as the architect of the British war effort. Pitt was a committed expansionist with a touch of arrogance. "I know that I can save this country and that I alone can," he boasted. A master strategist, he planned to cripple France by seizing its colonies. In North America, he enjoyed a decisive demographic advantage, since George II's 2 million subjects outnumbered the French 14 to 1. To mobilize the colonists, Pitt paid half the cost of their troops and supplied them with arms and equipment, at a cost of £1 million a year. He also committed a fleet of British ships and 30,000 British soldiers to the conflict in America.

Beginning in 1758, the powerful Anglo-American forces moved from one triumph to the next, in part because they brought Indian allies back into the fold. They forced the French to abandon Fort Duquesne (renamed Fort Pitt) and then captured Fort Louisbourg, a stronghold at the mouth of the St. Lawrence. In 1759, an armada led by British general James Wolfe sailed down the St. Lawrence and took Quebec, the heart of France's American empire. The Royal Navy prevented French reinforcements from crossing the Atlantic, allowing British forces to complete the conquest of Canada in 1760 by capturing Montreal (Map 4.5).

Elsewhere, the British likewise had great success. From Spain, the British won Cuba and the Philippine Islands. Fulfilling Pitt's dream, the East India Company

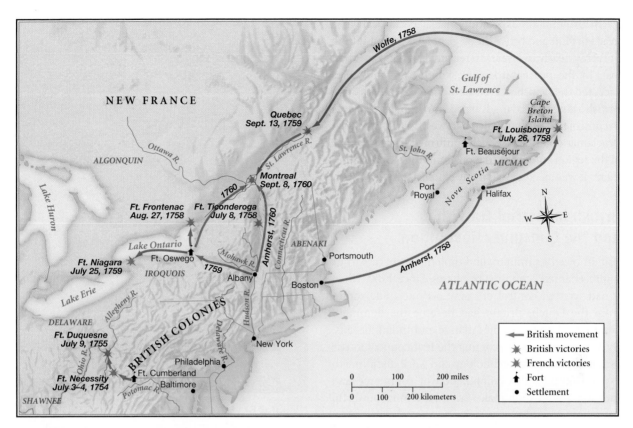

**MAP 4.5**
**The Anglo-American Conquest of New France**

After full-scale war with France began in 1756, it took almost three years for the British ministry to equip colonial forces and dispatch a sizable army to far-off America. In 1758, British and colonial troops attacked the heartland of New France, capturing Quebec in 1759 and Montreal in 1760. This conquest both united and divided the allies. Colonists celebrated the great victory: "The Illuminations and Fireworks exceeded any that had been exhibited before," reported the *South Carolina Gazette*. However, British officers had little respect for colonial soldiers. Said one, "[They are] the dirtiest, most contemptible, cowardly dogs you can conceive."

ousted French traders from India, and British forces seized French Senegal in West Africa. They also captured the rich sugar islands of Martinique and Guadeloupe in the French West Indies, but at the insistence of the West Indian sugar lobby (which wanted to protect its monopoly), the ministry returned the islands to France in the Treaty of Paris of 1763. Despite that controversial decision, the treaty confirmed Britain's triumph. It granted Britain sovereignty over half of North America, including French Canada, all French territory east of the Mississippi River, Spanish Florida, and the recent conquests in Africa and India. Britain had forged a commercial and colonial empire that was nearly worldwide.

Though Britain had won cautious support from some Native American groups in the late stages of the war, its territorial acquisitions alarmed many native peoples from New York to the Mississippi, who preferred the presence of a few French traders to an influx of thousands of Anglo-American settlers. To encourage the French to return, the Ottawa chief Pontiac declared, "I am French, and I want to die French." Neolin, a Delaware prophet, went further, calling for the expulsion of all white-skinned invaders: "If you suffer the English among you, you are dead men. Sickness, smallpox, and their poison [rum] will destroy you entirely." In 1763, inspired by Neolin's nativist vision, Pontiac led a major uprising at Detroit. Following his example, Indians throughout the Great Lakes and Ohio Valley seized nearly every British military garrison west of Fort Niagara, besieged Fort Pitt, and killed or captured more than 2,000 settlers.

**EXPLAIN CONSEQUENCES**

How did the Seven Years' War reshape Britain's empire in North America and affect native peoples?

British military expeditions defeated the Delawares near Fort Pitt and broke the siege of Detroit, but it took the army nearly two years to reclaim all the posts it had lost. In the peace settlement, Pontiac and his allies accepted the British as their new political "fathers." The British ministry, having learned how expensive it was to control the trans-Appalachian west, issued the Royal Proclamation of 1763, which confirmed Indian control of the region and declared it off-limits to colonial settlement. It was an edict that many colonists would ignore.

## British Industrial Growth and the Consumer Revolution

Britain owed its military and diplomatic success to its unprecedented economic resources. Since 1700, when it had wrested control of many oceanic trade routes from the Dutch, Britain had become the dominant commercial power in the Atlantic and Indian oceans. By 1750, it was also becoming the first country to use new manufacturing technology and work discipline to expand output. This combination of commerce and industry would soon make Britain the most powerful nation in the world.

Mechanical power was key to Britain's Industrial Revolution. British artisans designed and built water mills and steam engines that efficiently powered a wide array of machines: lathes for shaping wood, jennies and looms for spinning and weaving textiles, and hammers for forging iron. Compared with traditional manufacturing methods, the new power-driven machinery produced woolen and linen textiles, iron tools, furniture, and chinaware in greater quantities—and at lower cost. Moreover, the entrepreneurs running the new workshops drove their employees hard, forcing them to keep pace with the machines and work long hours. To market the abundant factory-produced goods, English and Scottish merchants extended credit to colonial shopkeepers for a full year instead of the traditional six months. Americans soon were purchasing 30 percent of all British exports.

To pay for British manufactures, mainland colonists increased their exports of tobacco, rice, indigo, and wheat. Using credit advanced by Scottish merchants, planters in Virginia bought land, slaves, and equipment to grow tobacco, which they exported to expanding markets in France and central Europe. In South Carolina, rice planters used British government subsidies to develop indigo and rice plantations. New York, Pennsylvania, Maryland, and Virginia became the breadbasket of the Atlantic World, supplying Europe's exploding population with wheat.

Americans used their profits and the generous credit extended from overseas to buy English manufactures. When he was practicing law in Boston, John Adams visited the home of Nicholas Boylston, one of the city's wealthiest merchants, "to view the Furniture, which alone cost a thousand Pounds sterling," he wrote. "[T]he Marble Tables, the rich Beds with Crimson Damask Curtains and Counterpins, the Beautiful Chimny Clock, the Spacious Garden, are the most magnificent of any Thing I have ever seen." Through their possessions, well-to-do colonists set themselves apart from their humbler—or, as they might have said, more vulgar—neighbors.

**EXPLAIN CONSEQUENCES**

How did the prosperity of the British Empire improve and endanger the lives and interests of colonists?

**Nicholas Boylston, c. 1769**

Merchants in the coastal and transatlantic trades gained enormous wealth in the mid-eighteenth century and displayed it in new ways. Among the most flamboyant was Nicholas Boylston. Of Boylston's home John Adams wrote, "A Seat it is for a noble Man, a Prince." In this portrait, painted by John Singleton Copley in 1769, Boylston flaunts his exotic possessions. In place of the wig he would have worn outside his home, Boylston wears a red velvet turban to keep his shaved head warm. His morning gown of heavy silk damask covers a rich waistcoat, casually unbuttoned in the middle to reveal his elegant ruffled shirt. Boylston rests his left elbow on two thick account books, an unmistakable reminder of the source of his wealth. Photograph © 2014 Museum of Fine Arts, Boston. Bequest of David P. Kimball, 23.504.

Although Britain's **consumer revolution** raised living standards, it landed many consumers—and the colonies as a whole—in debt (Figure 4.4). Even during the wartime boom of the 1750s, exports paid for only 80 percent of British imports. Britain financed the remaining 20 percent—the Americans' trade deficit—through the extension of credit and Pitt's military expenditures. When the military subsidies ended in 1763, the colonies fell into an economic recession. Merchants looked anxiously at their overstocked warehouses and feared bankruptcy. "I think we have a gloomy prospect before us," a Philadelphia trader noted in 1765. The increase in transatlantic trade had made Americans more dependent on overseas credit and markets.

## The Struggle for Land in the East

In good times and bad, the population continued to grow, intensifying the demand for arable land. Consider the experience of Kent, Connecticut. Like earlier generations, Kent's residents had moved inland to establish new farms, but Kent stood at the colony's western boundary. To provide for the next generation, many Kent families joined the Susquehanna Company (1749), which speculated in lands in the Wyoming Valley in present-day northeastern Pennsylvania. As settlers took up farmsteads there, the company urged the Connecticut legislature to claim the region on the

basis of Connecticut's "sea-to-sea" royal charter of 1662. However, Charles II had also granted the Wyoming Valley to William Penn, and the Penn family had sold farms there to Pennsylvania residents. By the late 1750s, settlers from Connecticut and Pennsylvania were at war, burning down their rivals' houses and barns. Delawares with their own claim to the valley were caught in the crossfire. In April 1763, the Delaware headman Teedyuscung was burned to death in his cabin; in retaliation, Teedyuscung's son Captain Bull led a war party that destroyed a community of Connecticut settlers.

Simultaneously, three distinct but related land disputes broke out in the Hudson River Valley (Map 4.6). Dutch tenant farmers, Wappinger Indians, and migrants from Massachusetts asserted ownership rights to lands long claimed by manorial families such as the Van Rensselaers and the Livingstons. When the manor lords turned to the legal system to uphold their claims, Dutch and English farmers in Westchester, Dutchess, and Albany counties rioted to close the courts. In response, New York's royal governor ordered British troops to assist local sheriffs and manorial bailiffs: they suppressed the tenant uprisings, intimidated the Wappingers, and evicted the Massachusetts squatters.

Other land disputes erupted in New Jersey and the southern colonies, where landlords and English aristocrats had successfully revived legal claims based on long-dormant seventeenth-century charters. One

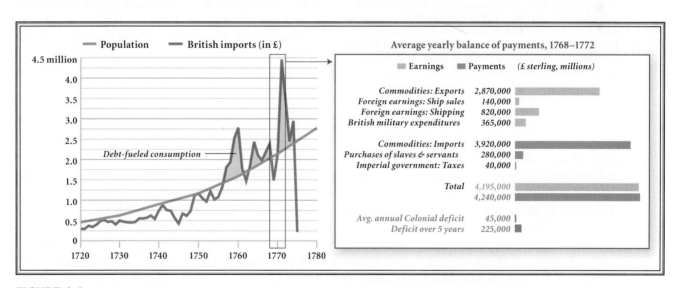

**FIGURE 4.4**

**Mainland Population and British Imports**

Around 1750, British imports were growing at a faster rate than the American population, indicating that the colonists were consuming more per capita. But Americans went into debt to pay for these goods, running an annual trade deficit with their British suppliers that by 1772 had created a cumulative debt of £2 million.

**MAP 4.6**
**Westward Expansion and Land Conflicts, 1750–1775**
Between 1750 and 1775, the mainland colonial population more than doubled—from 1.2 million to 2.5 million—triggering westward migrations and legal battles over land, which had become increasingly valuable. Violence broke out in eastern areas, where tenant farmers and smallholders contested landlords' property claims based on ancient titles; and in the backcountry, where migrating settlers fought with Indians, rival claimants, and the officials of eastern-dominated governments.

court decision allowed Lord Granville, the heir of an original Carolina proprietor, to collect an annual tax on land in North Carolina; another decision awarded ownership of the entire northern neck of Virginia (along the Potomac River) to Lord Fairfax.

The revival of these proprietary claims by manorial lords and English nobles testified to the rising value of land along the Atlantic coastal plain. It also underscored the increasing similarities between rural societies in Europe and America. To avoid the status of European peasants, native-born yeomen and tenant families joined the stream of European migrants searching for cheap land near the Appalachian Mountains.

# Western Rebels and Regulators

As would-be landowners moved west, they sparked conflicts over Indian policy, political representation, and debts. During the war with France, Delaware and Shawnee warriors had exacted revenge for Thomas Penn's land swindle of 1737 by destroying frontier farms in Pennsylvania and killing hundreds of residents. Scots-Irish settlers demanded the expulsion of all Indians, but Quaker leaders refused. So in 1763, a group of Scots-Irish frontiersmen called the Paxton Boys massacred twenty Conestoga Indians, an assimilated community that had lived alongside their colonist neighbors peacefully for many years. When Governor John Penn tried to bring the murderers to justice, 250 armed Scots-Irishmen advanced on Philadelphia. Benjamin Franklin intercepted the angry mob at Lancaster and arranged a truce, averting a battle with the militia. Prosecution of the Paxton Boys failed for lack of witnesses, and the episode gave their defenders the opportunity to excoriate Pennsylvania's government for protecting Indians while it neglected the interests of backcountry colonists.

**The South Carolina Regulators**   Violence also broke out in the backcountry of South Carolina, where land-hungry Scottish and Anglo-American settlers clashed repeatedly with Cherokees during the war with France. After the fighting ended in 1763, a group of landowning vigilantes known as the **Regulators** demanded that the eastern-controlled government provide western districts with more courts, fairer taxation, and greater representation in the assembly. "We are *Free-Men* — British Subjects — Not Born *Slaves*," declared a Regulator manifesto. Fearing slave revolts, the lowland rice planters who ran the South Carolina assembly compromised. In 1767, the assembly created western courts and reduced the fees for legal documents; but it refused to reapportion the legislature or lower western taxes. Like the Paxton Boys in Pennsylvania, the South Carolina Regulators won attention to backcountry needs but failed to wrest power from the eastern elite.

**Civil Strife in North Carolina**   In 1766, a more radical Regulator movement arose in North Carolina. When the economic recession of the early 1760s brought a sharp fall in tobacco prices, many farmers could not pay their debts. When creditors sued these farmers for payment, judges directed sheriffs to seize the debtors' property. Many backcountry farmers lost their property or ended up in jail for resisting court orders.

To save their farms, North Carolina's debtors defied the government's authority. Disciplined mobs intimidated judges, closed courts, and freed their comrades from jail. The Regulators proposed a series of reforms, including lower legal fees and tax payments in the "produce of the country" rather than in cash. They also demanded greater representation in the assembly and a just revenue system that would tax each person "in proportion to the profits arising from his estate." All to no avail. In May 1771, Royal Governor William Tryon mobilized British troops and the eastern militia, which defeated a large Regulator force at the Alamance River. When the fighting ended, thirty men lay dead, and Tryon summarily executed seven insurgent leaders. Not since Bacon's Rebellion in Virginia in 1675 and the colonial uprisings during the Glorious Revolution of 1688 (see Chapter 2) had a colonial dispute caused so much political agitation.

In 1771, as in 1675 and 1688, colonial conflicts became linked with imperial politics. In Connecticut, the Reverend Ezra Stiles defended the North Carolina Regulators. "What shall an injured & oppressed people do," he asked, "[when faced with] Oppression and tyranny?" Stiles's remarks reflected growing resistance to recently imposed British policies of taxation and control. The American colonies still depended primarily on Britain for their trade and military defense. However, by the 1760s, the mainland settlements had evolved into complex societies with the potential to exist independently. British policies would play a crucial role in determining the direction the maturing colonies would take.

## SUMMARY

In this chapter, we observed dramatic changes in British North America between 1720 and 1765. An astonishing surge in population—from 400,000 to almost 2 million—was the combined result of natural increase, European migration, and the African slave trade. The print revolution and the rise of the British Atlantic brought important new influences: the European Enlightenment and European Pietism transformed the world of ideas, while a flood of British consumer goods and the genteel aspirations of wealthy colonists reshaped the colonies' material culture.

Colonists confronted three major regional challenges. In New England, crowded towns and ever-smaller farms threatened the yeoman ideal of independent farming, prompting families to limit births, move to the frontier, or participate in an "exchange" economy. In the Middle Atlantic colonies, Dutch, English, German, and Scots-Irish residents maintained their religious and cultural identities while they competed for access to land and political power. Across the backcountry, new interest in western lands triggered conflicts with Indian peoples, civil unrest among whites, and, ultimately, the Great War for Empire. In the aftermath of the fighting, Britain stood triumphant in Europe and America.

# CHAPTER REVIEW

**MAKE IT STICK**   Go to **LearningCurve** to retain what you've read.

## TERMS TO KNOW   Identify and explain the significance of each term below.

### Key Concepts and Events

tenancy (p. 116)

competency (p. 117)

household mode of production (p. 120)

squatters (p. 121)

redemptioner (p. 124)

Enlightenment (p. 126)

Pietism (p. 126)

natural rights (p. 127)

deism (p. 128)

revival (p. 129)

Old Lights (p. 132)

New Lights (p. 132)

consumer revolution (p. 141)

Regulators (p. 142)

### Key People

Isaac Newton (p. 127)

John Locke (p. 127)

Benjamin Franklin (p. 128)

Jonathan Edwards (p. 129)

George Whitefield (p. 129)

Tanaghrisson (p. 135)

William Pitt (p. 138)

Pontiac (p. 139)

## REVIEW QUESTIONS
Answer these questions to demonstrate your understanding of the chapter's main ideas.

1. Compare colonists' "pursuits of happiness" in New England, the Middle colonies, the backcountry, and the South. How did poorer colonists in each of these regions seek to maintain their autonomy from powerful landlords and institutions, and how did this effort shape the formation of regional identities?

2. How did the print and transportation revolutions transform colonial culture and the economy in the eighteenth century?

3. The Great War for Empire delivered the eastern half of North America into British hands. How did that massive territorial acquisition affect ordinary colonists? What impact did it have on Native Americans' strategies for coexisting with their European neighbors?

4. **THEMATIC UNDERSTANDING** Review the events listed under "Work, Exchange, and Technology" and "Identity" for the period 1720–1750 on the thematic timeline on page 79. How did economic developments in the colonies influence the formation of new cultural identities in this era?

## MAKING CONNECTIONS
Recognize the larger developments and continuities within and across chapters by answering these questions.

1. **ACROSS TIME AND PLACE** In Chapter 3 we saw the rise of the South Atlantic System, an engine of economic growth that tied Britain's colonies more closely together and generated prosperity throughout the British Atlantic world. What consequences of that integration and prosperity are evident in the topics discussed in this chapter? How was the Great War for Empire grounded in earlier economic developments? And how did the postwar debt crisis grow out of the South Atlantic System?

2. **VISUAL EVIDENCE** Return to the John Collet painting of George Whitefield that opened the chapter (p. 115). How does Collet portray Whitefield's audience? Consider the postures and facial expressions of individual members of the crowd and imagine what might have been running through their minds as they listened. What do the various elements of this painting (the crowd, tankard of ale, sleeping dog, setting) suggest about the Great Awakening's appeal? About Collet's attitude toward evangelical preaching?

## MORE TO EXPLORE
Start here to learn more about the events discussed in this chapter.

Fred Anderson, *The War That Made America* (2005). A compelling narrative of the Seven Years' War in America. Also see *The War That Made America* (PBS video) and its Web site: **thewarthatmadeamerica.org**.

Colin G. Calloway, *White People, Indians, and Highlanders* (2008). Makes suggestive comparisons between Britain's encounters in Scotland and America.

Aaron Spencer Fogleman, *Hopeful Journeys* (1996). Covers German migrations to America.

Patrick Griffin, *The People with No Name* (2001). Treats the experience of the Scots-Irish in Ireland and America.

Susan E. Klepp and Billy G. Smith, eds., *The Infortunate* (1992). A compelling narrative of one indentured servant immigrant's experience in the Middle colonies.

Laurel Thatcher Ulrich, *A Midwife's Tale* (1990). A vivid account of one woman's experiences on the Maine frontier. See also *A Midwife's Tale* (PBS video) and two related Web sites: **pbs.org/wgbh/amex /midwife** and **DoHistory.org**.

TIMELINE    Ask yourself why this chapter begins and ends with these dates
and then identify the links among related events.

| 1695 | • Licensing Act lapses in England, triggering the print revolution |
|---|---|
| 1710s–1730s | • Enlightenment ideas spread from Europe to America<br>• Germans and Scots-Irish settle in Middle colonies<br>• Theodore Jacob Frelinghuysen preaches Pietism to German migrants |
| 1720s–1730s | • William and Gilbert Tennent lead Presbyterian revivals among Scots-Irish<br>• Jonathan Edwards preaches in New England |
| 1729 | • Benjamin Franklin founds the *Pennsylvania Gazette* |
| 1739 | • George Whitefield sparks Great Awakening |
| 1740s–1760s | • Conflict between Old Lights and New Lights<br>• Shortage of farmland in New England threatens freehold ideal<br>• Growing ethnic and religious pluralism in Middle Atlantic colonies<br>• Religious denominations establish colleges |
| 1743 | • Benjamin Franklin founds American Philosophical Society<br>• Samuel Morris starts Presbyterian revivals in Virginia |
| 1748 | • Ohio Company receives grant of 200,000 acres from the crown |
| 1749 | • Connecticut farmers form Susquehanna Company |
| 1750s | • Industrial Revolution begins in England<br>• British shipping dominates North Atlantic<br>• Consumer purchases increase American imports and debt |
| 1754 | • French and Indian War begins<br>• Iroquois and colonists meet at Albany Congress<br>• Franklin's Plan of Union |
| 1756 | • Britain begins Great War for Empire |
| 1759–1760 | • Britain completes conquest of Canada |
| 1760s | • Land conflict along New York and New England border<br>• Baptist revivals win converts in Virginia |
| 1763 | • Pontiac's Rebellion leads to Proclamation of 1763<br>• Treaty of Paris ends Great War for Empire<br>• Scots-Irish Paxton Boys massacre Indians in Pennsylvania |
| 1771 | • Royal governor puts down Regulator revolt in North Carolina |

**KEY TURNING POINTS:** The Ohio Company grant (1748), the formation of the Susquehanna Company (1749), land conflict along New York and New England border (1760s), and the defeat of the North Carolina Regulators (1771). How do these events reveal tensions over the question of who would control the development of frontier lands in Britain's mainland North American colonies? What were the effects of these conflicts on Native American populations?

# 3

**P A R T**

# Revolution and Republican Culture
## 1763–1820

"The American war is over," Philadelphia Patriot Benjamin Rush declared in 1787, "but this is far from being the case with the American Revolution. On the contrary, nothing but the first act of the great drama is closed. It remains yet to establish and perfect our new forms of government." The changes that had already unfolded since 1763 were revolutionary in themselves: Britain had triumphed in the Great War for Empire, only to see its American empire unravel and descend into war. Against all odds, the thirteen rebelling colonies had pulled together and won their independence; now they were forming a federal republic that would take its place among the nations of the world.

The republican revolution extended far beyond politics. It challenged many of the values and institutions that had prevailed for centuries in Europe and the Atlantic World. After 1776, Americans reconsidered basic assumptions that structured their societies, cultures, families, and communities. Here, in summary, are the three principal developments discussed in Part 3:

## From British North America to the United States of America

After violently rejecting attempts to reform the British Empire, the Patriots won independence and began constructing republican governments. Their experiments extended across an entire generation, and it took still longer to decide how much power the federal republic should wield over the states. The political culture spawned by the Revolution was similarly unformed and slow to develop. Political parties, for example, were unanticipated by the founders and, at first, widely regarded as illegitimate. However, by 1820, they had become central to the adjudication of political conflict, heightening some forms of competition while blunting others. The United States also fought wars with Native Americans in the trans-Appalachian west to gain new territory, and with Great Britain to ensure its independence. Across three generations, American political culture was transformed, national borders were secured, and republican national and state governments commanded the allegiance of their citizens.

## Challenges to the Social Order

As Patriots articulated values they associated with independence, they aligned their movement with currents of reform eddying through the Atlantic World: antislavery; women's rights; religious liberty; social equality. Each of these ideas was controversial, and the American Revolution endorsed none of them in an unqualified way. But its idealism—the sense that the Revolution marked "a memorable epoch in the annals of the human race," as John Adams put it—made the era malleable and full of possibility.

Legislatures abolished slavery in the North, broadened religious liberty by allowing freedom of conscience, and, except in New England, ended the system of legally established churches. Postwar evangelicalism gave enormous energy to a new wave of innovative religious developments. However, Americans continued to argue over social equality, in part because their republican creed placed family authority in the hands of men and political power in the hands of propertied individuals: this arrangement denied power and status not only to slaves but also to free blacks, women, and middling and poor white men. Though the Revolution's legacy was mixed, its meaning would be debated for decades in American public life.

## Conquest, Competition, and Consolidation

One uncontested value of the Revolutionary era was a commitment to economic opportunity. To achieve this, people migrated in large numbers, and the United States dramatically expanded its boundaries: first, by conquest, pushing west to the Mississippi River; then, by purchase, all the way to the Pacific Ocean. Northern merchants created a banking system and organized rural manufacturing. State governments used charters and other privileges to assist businesses and to improve infrastructure. Southern planters used slaves to grow a new staple crop—cotton. Many yeomen farm families moved west to farm; and Eastern laborers worked in burgeoning manufacturing enterprises. By 1820, the young American republic was on the verge of achieving economic as well as political independence.

Even as the borders of the United States expanded, its diversity inhibited the effort to define an American culture and identity. Native Americans still lived in their own clans and nations; black Americans were developing a distinct African American culture; and White Americans were enmeshed in vigorous regional ethnic communities. Over time, political institutions began to unite Americans of diverse backgrounds, as did increasing participation in the market economy and in evangelical Protestant churches. By 1820, to be an American meant, for many members of the dominant white population, to be a republican, a Protestant, and an enterprising individual.

# Revolution and Republican Culture 1763–1820

## Thematic Understanding

This timeline arranges some of the important events of this period into themes. Consider the items listed under the theme "Ideas, Beliefs, and Culture." How did the American Revolution challenge existing social arrangements? Consider the role of religion in American life, the status of women, and the institution of slavery. What tensions developed as a result of those challenges? **>**

| | WORK, EXCHANGE, & TECHNOLOGY | PEOPLING | POLITICS & POWER | IDEAS, BELIEFS, & CULTURE | IDENTITY |
|---|---|---|---|---|---|
| **1763** | • Merchants defy Sugar and Stamp Acts<br>• Patriots mount three boycotts of British goods, in 1765, 1767, and 1774<br>• Boycotts spur Patriot women to make textiles | • Migration into the Ohio Valley after Pontiac's Rebellion<br>• Quebec Act (1774) allows Catholicism | • Stamp Act Congress (1765)<br>• First Continental Congress (1774)<br>• Second Continental Congress (1775) | • Patriots call for American unity<br>• The idea of natural rights poses a challenge to the institution of chattel slavery | • Concept of popular sovereignty gains force in the colonies<br>• Colonists lay claim to rights of Englishmen |
| **1776** | • Manufacturing expands during the war<br>• Cutoff of trade and severe inflation threaten economy<br>• War debt grows | • Declining immigration from Europe (1775–1820) enhances American identity<br>• African American slaves seek freedom through military service | • The Declaration of Independence (1776)<br>• States adopt republican constitutions (1776 on)<br>• Articles of Confederation ratified (1781)<br>• Treaty of Paris (1783) | • Judith Sargent Murray publishes "On the Equality of the Sexes" (1779)<br>• Emancipation of slaves begins in the North<br>• Virginia enacts religious freedom (1786) | • Thomas Paine's *Common Sense* (1776) causes colonists to rethink political loyalties<br>• States rely on property qualifications to define citizenship rights in their new constitutions |
| **1787** | • Bank of North America founded (1781)<br>• Land speculation increases in the West | • State cessions, land ordinances, and Indian wars create national domain in the West<br>• The Alien Act makes it harder for immigrants to become citizens and allow for deporting aliens (1798) | • U.S. Constitution drafted (1787)<br>• Conflict over Alexander Hamilton's economic policies<br>• First national parties: Federalists and Republicans | • Politicians and ministers deny vote to women; praise republican motherhood<br>• Bill of Rights ratified (1791)<br>• Sedition Act limits freedom of the press (1798) | • Indians form Western Confederacy (1790)<br>• Second Great Awakening (1790–1860)<br>• Emerging political divide between South and North |
| **1800** | • Cotton output and demand for African labor expands<br>• Farm productivity improves<br>• Embargo encourages U.S. manufacturing<br>• Second Bank of the United States chartered (1816–1836)<br>• Supreme Court guards property | • Suffrage for white men expands; New Jersey retracts suffrage for propertied women (1807)<br>• Atlantic slave trade ends (1808)<br>• American Colonization Society founded (1817) | • Jefferson reduces activism of national government<br>• Chief Justice Marshall asserts federal judicial powers<br>• Triumph of Republican Party and end of Federalist Party | • Free blacks enhance sense of African American identity<br>• Religious benevolence engenders social reform movements | • Tenskwatawa and Tecumseh revive Western Indian Confederacy<br>• War of 1812 tests national unity<br>• State constitutions democratized |

# 5
## CHAPTER

# The Problem of Empire
## 1763–1776

In June 1775, the city of New York faced a perplexing dilemma. Word arrived that George Washington, who had just been named commander in chief of the newly formed Continental army, was coming to town. But on the same day, William Tryon, the colony's crown-appointed governor, was scheduled to return from Britain. Local leaders orchestrated a delicate dance. Though the Provincial Congress was operating illegally in the eyes of the crown, it did not wish to offend Governor Tryon. It instructed the city's newly raised volunteer battalion to divide in two. One company awaited Washington's arrival, while another prepared to greet the governor. The "residue of the Battalion" was to be "ready to receive either the General or Governour *Tryon*, which ever shall first arrive." Washington arrived first. He was met by nine companies of the volunteer battalion and a throng of well-wishers, who escorted him to his rooms in a local tavern. Many of this same crowd then crossed town to join the large group assembled to greet the governor, whose ship was just landing. The crowd met him with "universal shouts of applause" and accompanied him home.

This awkward moment in the history of one American city reflects a larger crisis of loyalty that plagued colonists throughout British North America in the years between 1763 and 1776. The outcome of the Great War for Empire left Great Britain the undisputed master of eastern North America. But that success pointed the way to catastrophe. Convinced of the need to reform the empire and tighten its administration, British policymakers imposed a series of new administrative measures on the colonies. Accustomed as they were to governing their own affairs, colonists could not accept these changes. Yet the bonds of loyalty were strong, and the unraveling of British authority was tortuous and complex. Only gradually—as militancy slowly mounted on both sides—were the ties of empire broken and independence declared.

## IDENTIFY THE BIG IDEA
Consider whether the collapse of British authority in the thirteen rebellious colonies might have been avoided through compromise measures and more astute leadership. Was colonial independence inevitable, and was war the only way to achieve it?

**The Great New York Fire of 1776** In the wake of the Declaration of Independence, General William Howe's first objective was to capture New York, with its strategic location and excellent harbor. Patriot forces under George Washington's command attempted to defend the city but were forced into retreat and abandoned it to the British in September 1776. Early in the morning of September 21, a fire broke out near the southern tip of Manhattan and burned northwestward, driven by a strong wind. As many as a quarter of the town's buildings were destroyed; residents, already distressed by the fighting, fled into the streets with whatever possessions they could carry. Each side accused the other of arson, but that charge was never proven. Miriam and Ira D. Wallach Division of Art, Prints and Photographs, The New York Public Library. Astor, Lenox and Tilden Foundations.

# An Empire Transformed

The Great War for Empire of 1756–1763 (Chapter 4) transformed the British Empire in North America. The British ministry could no longer let the colonies manage their own affairs while it contented itself with minimal oversight of the Atlantic trade. Its interests and responsibilities now extended far into the continental interior — a much more costly and complicated proposition than it had ever faced before. And neither its American colonies nor their Native American neighbors were inclined to cooperate in the transformation.

British administrators worried about their American colonists, who, according to former Georgia governor Henry Ellis, felt themselves "entitled to a greater measure of Liberty than is enjoyed by the people of England." Ireland had been closely ruled for decades, and recently the East India Company set up dominion over millions of non-British peoples (Map 5.1 and America Compared, p. 153). Britain's American possessions were likewise filled with aliens and "undesirables": "French, Dutch, Germans innumerable, Indians, Africans, and a multitude of felons from this country," as one member of Parliament put it. Consequently, declared Lord Halifax, "The people of England" considered Americans "as foreigners."

Contesting that status, wealthy Philadelphia lawyer John Dickinson argued that his fellow colonists were "not [East Indian] Sea Poys, nor Marattas, but *British subjects* who are born to liberty, who know its worth, and who prize it high." Thus was the stage set for a struggle between the conceptions of identity — and empire — held by British ministers, on the one hand, and many American colonists on the other.

**EXPLAIN CONSEQUENCES**

What was the impact of the Great War for Empire on British policymakers and the colonies?

## The Costs of Empire

The Great War for Empire imposed enormous costs on Great Britain. The national debt soared from £75 million to £133 million and was, an observer noted, "becoming the alarming object of every British subject." By war's end, interest on the debt alone consumed 60 percent of the nation's budget, and the ministry had to raise taxes. During the eighteenth century, taxes were shifting from land — owned by the gentry and aristocracy — to consumables, and successive ministries became ever more ingenious in devising new ways to raise money. Excise (or sales) taxes were levied on all kinds of ordinary goods — salt and beer, bricks and candles, paper (in the form of a stamp tax) — that were consumed by middling and poor Britons. In the 1760s, the per capita tax burden was 20 percent of income.

To collect the taxes, the government doubled the size of the tax bureaucracy (Figure 5.1). Customs agents patrolled the coasts of southern Britain, seizing tons of contraband French wines, Dutch tea, and Flemish textiles. Convicted smugglers faced heavy penalties, including death or forced "transportation" to America as indentured servants. (Despite colonial protests, nearly fifty thousand English criminals had already been shipped to America to be sold as indentured servants.)

The price of empire abroad was thus larger government and higher taxes at home. Members of two British opposition parties, the Radical Whigs and the Country Party, complained that the huge war debt placed the nation at the mercy of the "monied interests," the banks and financiers who reaped millions of pounds' interest from government bonds. To reverse the growth of government and the threat to personal liberty and property rights, British reformers demanded that Parliament represent a broader spectrum of the property-owning classes. The Radical Whig John Wilkes condemned rotten boroughs — sparsely populated, aristocratic-controlled electoral districts — and demanded greater representation for rapidly growing commercial and manufacturing cities. The war thus transformed British politics.

The war also revealed how little power Britain wielded in its American colonies. In theory, royal governors had extensive political powers, including command of the provincial militia; in reality, they shared power with the colonial assemblies, which outraged British officials. The Board of Trade complained that in Massachusetts "almost every act of executive and legislative power is ordered and directed by votes and resolves of the General Court." To enforce the collection of trade duties, which colonial merchants had evaded for decades by bribing customs officials, Parliament passed the Revenue Act of 1762. The ministry also instructed the Royal Navy to seize American vessels carrying food crops from the mainland colonies to the French West Indies. It was absurd, declared a British politician, that French armies attempting "to Destroy one English province . . . are actually supported by Bread raised in another."

Britain's military victory brought another fundamental shift in policy: a new peacetime deployment of 15 royal battalions — some 7,500 troops — in North

## Britain's Atlantic and Asian Empires

The following table enumerates the economic benefits derived by Great Britain from its various colonies, which sent a wide variety of goods to Britain and also served as markets for British exports.

### TABLE 5.1

**English/British Imports and Exports (annual averages in pounds sterling)**

| | England* | | Britain* | |
|---|---|---|---|---|
| | 1700–01 | 1750–51 | 1772–73 | 1789–90 |
| **Imports from Asia, Africa, and America** | | | | |
| North America | 372,000 | 877,000 | 1,997,000 | 1,351,000 |
| The Fisheries** | 0 | 7,000 | 27,000 | 188,000 |
| West Indies | 785,000 | 1,484,000 | 3,222,000 | 4,045,000 |
| Africa | 24,000 | 43,000 | 80,000 | 87,000 |
| East Indies | 775,000 | 1,101,000 | 2,203,000 | 3,256,000 |
| Total | 1,956,000 | 3,512,000 | 7,529,000 | 8,927,000 |
| **Exports to America, Asia, and Africa** | | | | |
| North America | 362,000 | 1,355,000 | 3,254,000 | 3,763,000 |
| West Indies | 336,000 | 589,000 | 1,402,000 | 1,892,000 |
| Africa | 145,000 | 188,000 | 777,000 | 799,000 |
| East India | 125,000 | 653,000 | 893,000 | 2,173,000 |
| Total | 968,000 | 2,785,000 | 6,326,000 | 8,627,000 |

*The "England" column shows data for England and Wales; "Britain" includes Scotland as well.
**Includes Massachusetts Bay, Maine, and Newfoundland; by the 1760s more than £500,000 worth of fish was being sent annually to the West Indies and southern Europe.

Source: Adapted from *The Oxford History of the British Empire*, vol. 2, ed. P. J. Marshall (Oxford: Oxford University Press, 1998), 101.

---

### QUESTIONS FOR ANALYSIS

1. Compare Britain's colonies in their roles as producers of British imports to their roles as consumers of British exports. Why are the mainland colonies of North America a distant third as producers of imports, but ranked first as consumers of exports?

2. How did the American Revolution (1776–1783) impact the economic relationship between Great Britain and its mainland colonies? Is it reasonable to conclude that political independence did not bring economic independence?

---

America. The ministers who served under George III (r. 1760–1820) feared a possible rebellion by the 60,000 French residents of Canada, Britain's newly conquered colony (Map 5.2). Native Americans were also a concern: Pontiac's Rebellion had nearly overwhelmed Britain's frontier forts. Moreover, only a substantial military force would deter land-hungry whites from defying the Proclamation of 1763 and settling west of the Appalachian Mountains (see Chapter 4). Finally, British politicians worried about the colonists' loyalty

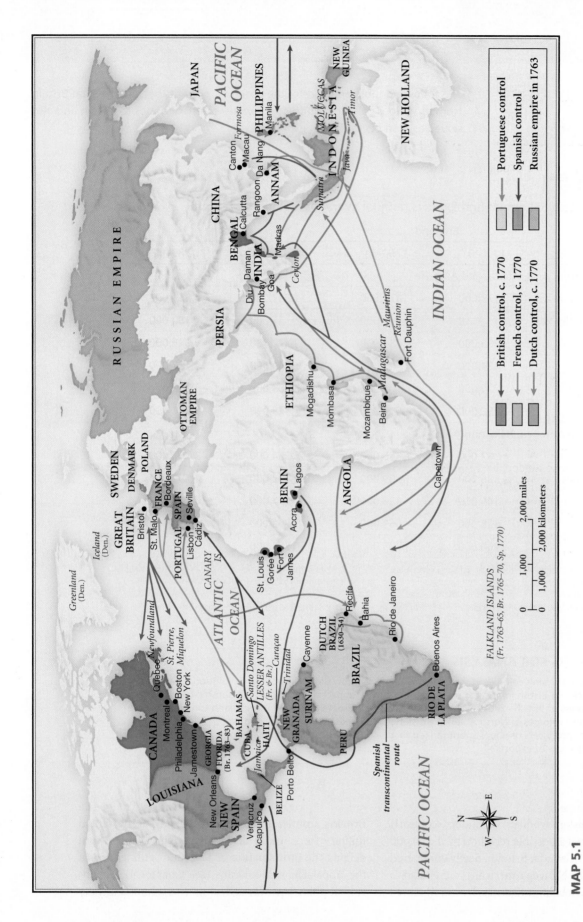

**MAP 5.1**

**Eurasian Trade and European Colonies, c. 1770**

By 1770, the Western European nations that had long dominated maritime trade had created vast colonial empires and spheres of influence. Spain controlled the western halves of North and South America, Portugal owned Brazil, and Holland ruled Indonesia. Britain, a newer imperial power, boasted settler societies in North America, rich sugar islands in the West Indies, slave ports in West Africa, and a growing presence on the Indian subcontinent. Only France had failed to acquire and hold on to a significant colonial empire. (To trace changes in empire and trade routes, see Map 1.4 on p. 24 and Map 2.2 on p. 46.)

**FIGURE 5.1**

**The Cost of Empire, 1690–1790**

It cost money to build and maintain an empire. As Britain built a great navy, subsidized the armies of European allies, and fought four wars against France and Spain between 1702 and 1783, military expenditures soared. Tax revenues did not keep pace, so the government created a large national debt by issuing bonds for millions of pounds. This policy created a class of wealthy financiers, led to political protests, and eventually prompted attempts to tax the American colonists.

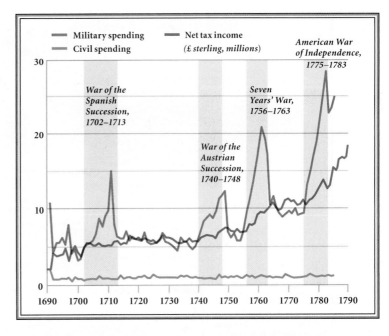

now that they no longer faced a threat from French Canada.

The cost of stationing these troops, estimated at £225,000 per year, compounded Britain's fiscal crisis, and it seemed clear that the burden had to be shared by the colonies. They had always managed their own finances, but the king's ministers agreed that Parliament could no longer let them off the hook for the costs of empire. The greatest gains from the war had come in North America, where the specter of French encirclement had finally been lifted, and the greatest new postwar expenses were being incurred in North America as well.

## George Grenville and the Reform Impulse

The challenge of raising revenue from the colonies fell first to George Grenville. Widely regarded as "one of the ablest men in Great Britain," Grenville understood the need for far-reaching imperial reform. He first passed the Currency Act of 1764, which banned the American colonies from using paper money as legal tender. Colonial shopkeepers, planters, and farmers had used local currency, which was worth less than British pounds sterling, to pay their debts to British merchants. The Currency Act ensured that merchants would no longer be paid in money printed in the colonies, boosting their profits and British wealth.

**The Sugar Act**   Grenville also won parliamentary approval of the **Sugar Act of 1764** to replace the widely ignored Molasses Act of 1733 (see Chapter 3). The earlier act had set a tax rate of 6 pence per gallon on French molasses — a rate so high that it made the trade unprofitable. Rather than pay it, colonial merchants bribed customs officials at the going rate of 1.5 pence per gallon. Grenville settled on a duty of 3 pence per gallon, which merchants could pay and still turn a profit, and then tightened customs enforcement so that it could actually be collected.

This carefully crafted policy garnered little support in America. New England merchants, among them John Hancock of Boston, had made their fortunes smuggling French molasses. In 1754, Boston merchants paid customs duties on a mere 400 hogsheads of molasses, yet they imported 40,000 hogsheads for use by 63 Massachusetts rum distilleries. Publicly, the merchants claimed that the Sugar Act would ruin the distilling industry; privately, they vowed to evade the duty by smuggling or by bribing officials.

**The End of Salutary Neglect**   More important, colonists raised constitutional objections to the Sugar Act. In Massachusetts, the leader of the assembly argued that the new legislation was "contrary to a fundamental Principall of our Constitution: That all Taxes ought to originate with the people." In Rhode Island, Governor Stephen Hopkins warned: "They who are taxed at

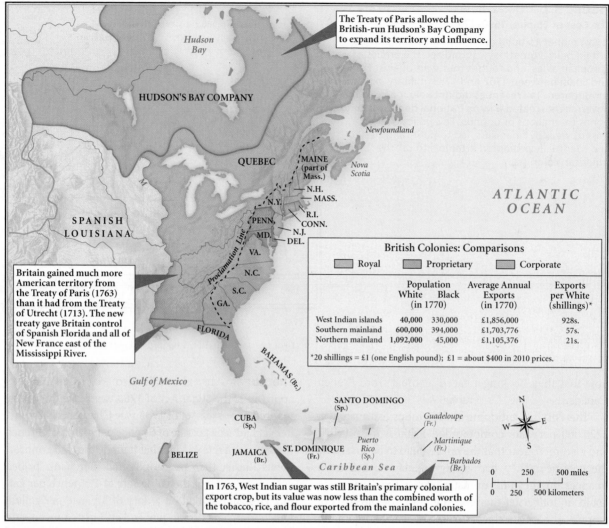

The Treaty of Paris allowed the British-run Hudson's Bay Company to expand its territory and influence.

Britain gained much more American territory from the Treaty of Paris (1763) than it had from the Treaty of Utrecht (1713). The new treaty gave Britain control of Spanish Florida and all of New France east of the Mississippi River.

In 1763, West Indian sugar was still Britain's primary colonial export crop, but its value was now less than the combined worth of the tobacco, rice, and flour exported from the mainland colonies.

### British Colonies: Comparisons

Royal    Proprietary    Corporate

| | Population White Black (in 1770) | | Average Annual Exports (in 1770) | Exports per White (shillings)* |
|---|---|---|---|---|
| West Indian islands | 40,000 | 330,000 | £1,856,000 | 928s. |
| Southern mainland | 600,000 | 394,000 | £1,703,776 | 57s. |
| Northern mainland | 1,092,000 | 45,000 | £1,105,376 | 21s. |

*20 shillings = £1 (one English pound); £1 = about $400 in 2010 prices.

**MAP 5.2**

**Britain's American Empire in 1763**

The Treaty of Paris gave Britain control of the eastern half of North America and returned a few captured sugar islands in the West Indies to France. To protect the empire's new mainland territories, British ministers dispatched troops to Florida and Quebec. They also sent troops to uphold the terms of the Proclamation of 1763, which prohibited Anglo-American settlement west of the Appalachian Mountains.

pleasure by others cannot possibly have any property, and they who have no property, can have no freedom." The Sugar Act raised other constitutional issues as well. Merchants prosecuted under the act would be tried in **vice-admiralty courts**, tribunals governing the high seas and run by British-appointed judges. Previously, merchants accused of Navigation Acts violations were tried by local common-law courts, where friendly juries often acquitted them. The Sugar Act closed this legal loophole by extending the jurisdiction of the vice-admiralty courts to all customs offenses.

The Sugar Act revived old American fears. The influential Virginia planter Richard Bland emphasized that the American colonists "were not sent out to be the Slaves but to be the Equals of those that remained behind." John Adams, the young Massachusetts lawyer defending John Hancock on a charge of smuggling,

 To see a longer excerpt of the Richard Bland document, along with other primary sources from this period, see *Sources for America's History*.

argued that the vice-admiralty courts diminished this equality by "degrad[ing] every American . . . below the rank of an Englishman."

In fact, accused smugglers in Britain were also tried in vice-admiralty courts, so there was no discrimination against Americans. The real issue was the growing power of the British state. Americans had lived for decades under an administrative policy of salutary neglect. Now they saw that the new imperial regime would deprive them "of some of their most essential Rights as British subjects," as a committee of the Massachusetts assembly put it. In response, Royal Governor Francis Bernard replied: "The rule that a British subject shall not be bound by laws or liable to taxes, but what he has consented to by his representatives must be confined to the inhabitants of Great Britain only." To Bernard, Grenville, and other imperial reformers, Americans were second-class subjects of the king, with rights limited by the Navigation Acts, parliamentary laws, and British interests.

## An Open Challenge: The Stamp Act

Another new tax, the **Stamp Act of 1765**, sparked the first great imperial crisis. The new levy was to cover part of the cost of keeping British troops in America—which turned out to be £385,000 a year (about $150 million today), 70 percent more than the initial estimate. Grenville hoped the Stamp Act would raise £60,000 per year. The act would require a tax stamp on all printed items, from college diplomas, court documents, land titles, and contracts to newspapers, almanacs, and playing cards. It was ingeniously designed. Like its counterpart in England, it bore more heavily on the rich, since it charged only a penny a sheet for newspapers and other common items but up to £10 for a lawyer's license. It also required no new bureaucracy; stamped paper would be delivered to colonial ports and sold to printers in lieu of unstamped stock.

Benjamin Franklin, agent of the Pennsylvania assembly, proposed a different solution: American representation in Parliament. "If you chuse to tax us," he wrote, "give us Members in your Legislature, and let us be one People." With the exception of William Pitt, British politicians rejected Franklin's idea as too radical. They argued that the colonists already had **virtual representation** in Parliament because some of its members were transatlantic merchants and West Indian sugar planters. Colonial leaders were equally skeptical of Franklin's plan. Americans were "situate at a great Distance from their Mother Country," the Connecticut assembly declared, and therefore "cannot participate in the general Legislature of the Nation."

Asserting "the Right of Parliament to lay an internal Tax upon the Colonies," the House of Commons ignored American opposition and passed the act by an overwhelming majority of 205 to 49. At the request of General Thomas Gage, the British military commander in America, Parliament also passed the **Quartering Act of 1765**, which required colonial governments to provide barracks and food for British troops. Finally, Parliament approved Grenville's proposal that violations of the Stamp Act be tried in vice-admiralty courts.

Using the doctrine of parliamentary supremacy, Grenville had begun to fashion a centralized imperial system in America much like that already in place in Ireland: British officials would govern the colonies with little regard for the local assemblies. Consequently, the prime minister's plan provoked a constitutional confrontation on the specific issues of taxation, jury trials, and military quartering as well as on the general question of representative self-government.

**UNDERSTAND POINTS OF VIEW**
Why did most British and colonial leaders reject the idea that the colonies should be represented in Parliament?

# The Dynamics of Rebellion, 1765–1770

In the name of reform, Grenville had thrown down the gauntlet to the Americans. The colonists had often resisted unpopular laws and aggressive governors, but they had faced an all-out attack on their institutions only once before—in 1686, when James II had unilaterally imposed the Dominion of New England. Now the danger to colonial autonomy was even greater because both the king and Parliament backed reform. But the Patriots, as the defenders of American rights came to be called, met the challenge posed by Grenville and his successor, Charles Townshend. They organized protests—formal and informal, violent as well as peaceful—and fashioned a compelling ideology of resistance.

## Formal Protests and the Politics of the Crowd

Virginia's House of Burgesses was the first formal body to complain. In May 1765, hotheaded young Patrick Henry denounced Grenville's legislation and attacked

**Protesting the Stamp Act in Portsmouth, New Hampshire**
Throughout the colonies, disciplined mobs protesting the Stamp Act forced stamp distributors to resign their offices. In this engraving, protesters in the small city of Portsmouth, New Hampshire, stone an effigy of the distributor as other members of the mob carry off a coffin representing the death of American "Liberty." Illustration from "Interesting Events in the History of the U.S." by J. W. Barber, 1829/Picture Research Consultants & Archives.

George III for supporting it. He compared the king to Charles I, whose tyranny had led to his overthrow and execution in the 1640s. These remarks, which bordered on treason, frightened the Burgesses; nonetheless, they condemned the Stamp Act's "manifest Tendency to Destroy American freedom." In Massachusetts, James Otis, another republican-minded firebrand, persuaded the House of Representatives to call a meeting of all the mainland colonies "to implore Relief" from the act.

**The Stamp Act Congress**    Nine assemblies sent delegates to the **Stamp Act Congress**, which met in New York City in October 1765. The congress protested the loss of American "rights and liberties," especially the right to trial by jury. And it challenged the constitutionality of both the Stamp and Sugar Acts by declaring that only the colonists' elected representatives could tax them. Still, moderate-minded delegates wanted compromise, not confrontation. They assured Parliament that Americans "glory in being subjects of the best of Kings" and humbly petitioned for repeal of the Stamp Act. Other influential Americans favored active (but peaceful) resistance; they organized a boycott of British goods.

**Crowd Actions**    Popular opposition also took a violent form, however. When the Stamp Act went into effect on November 1, 1765, disciplined mobs demanded the resignation of stamp-tax collectors. In Boston, a group calling itself the **Sons of Liberty** burned an effigy of collector Andrew Oliver and then destroyed Oliver's new brick warehouse. Two weeks later, Bostonians attacked the house of Lieutenant Governor Thomas Hutchinson, Oliver's brother-in-law and a prominent defender of imperial authority, breaking his furniture, looting his wine cellar, and setting fire to his library.

Wealthy merchants and Patriot lawyers, such as John Hancock and John Adams, encouraged the mobs, which were usually led by middling artisans and minor merchants. In New York City, nearly three thousand shopkeepers, artisans, laborers, and seamen marched through the streets breaking windows and crying "Liberty!" Resistance to the Stamp Act spread far beyond the port cities: in nearly every colony, angry crowds—the "rabble," their detractors called them—intimidated royal officials. Near Wethersfield, Connecticut, five hundred farmers seized tax collector Jared Ingersoll and forced him to resign his office in "the Cause of the People."

**The Motives of the Crowd**    Such crowd actions were common in both Britain and America, and protesters had many motives. Roused by the Great Awakening, evangelical Protestants resented arrogant British military officers and corrupt royal bureaucrats. In New England, where rioters invoked the anti-monarchy sentiments of their great-grandparents, an anonymous letter sent to a Boston newspaper promising to save "all the Freeborn Sons of America" was signed "Oliver Cromwell," the English republican revolutionary of the 1650s. In New York City, Sons of Liberty leaders Isaac Sears and Alexander McDougall were minor merchants and Radical Whigs who feared

**COMPARE AND CONTRAST**
Why did the Stamp Act arouse so much more resistance than the Sugar Act?

that imperial reform would undermine political liberty. The mobs also included apprentices, day laborers, and unemployed sailors: young men with their own notions of liberty who—especially if they had been drinking—were quick to resort to violence.

Nearly everywhere popular resistance nullified the Stamp Act. Fearing an assault on Fort George, New York lieutenant governor Cadwallader Colden called on General Gage to use his small military force to protect the stamps. Gage refused. "Fire from the Fort might disperse the Mob, but it would not quell them," he told Colden, and the result would be "an Insurrection, the Commencement of Civil War." The tax was collected in Barbados and Jamaica, but frightened collectors resigned their offices in all thirteen colonies that would eventually join in the Declaration of Independence. This popular insurrection gave a democratic cast to the emerging Patriot movement. "Nothing is wanting but your own Resolution," declared a New York rioter, "for great is the Authority and Power of the People."

## The Ideological Roots of Resistance

Some Americans couched their resistance in constitutional terms. Many were lawyers or well-educated merchants and planters. Composing pamphlets of remarkable political sophistication, they gave the resistance movement its rationale, its political agenda, and its leaders.

Patriot writers drew on three intellectual traditions. The first was **English common law**, the centuries-old body of legal rules and procedures that protected the lives and property of the monarch's subjects. In the famous *Writs of Assistance* case of 1761, Boston lawyer James Otis invoked English legal precedents to challenge open-ended search warrants. In demanding a jury trial for John Hancock in the late 1760s, John Adams appealed to the Magna Carta (1215), the ancient document that, said Adams, "has for many Centuries been esteemed by Englishmen, as one of the . . . firmest Bulwarks of their Liberties." Other lawyers protested that new strictures violated specific "liberties and privileges" granted in colonial charters or embodied in Britain's "ancient constitution."

Enlightenment rationalism provided Patriots with a second important intellectual resource. Virginia planter Thomas Jefferson and other Patriots drew on the writings of John Locke, who had argued that all individuals possessed certain "**natural rights**"—life, liberty, and property—that governments must protect (see Chapter 4). And they turned to the works of

French philosopher Montesquieu, who had maintained that a "separation of powers" among government departments prevented arbitrary rule.

The republican and Whig strands of the English political tradition provided a third ideological source for American Patriots. Puritan New England had long venerated the Commonwealth era (1649–1660), when England had been a republic (see Chapter 2). After the Glorious Revolution of 1688–1689, many colonists praised the English Whigs for creating a constitutional monarchy that prevented the king from imposing taxes and other measures. Joseph Warren, a physician and a Radical Whig Patriot, suggested that the Stamp Act was part of a ministerial plot "to force the colonies into rebellion" and justify the use of "military power to reduce them to servitude." John Dickinson's *Letters from a Farmer in Pennsylvania* (1768) urged colonists to "remember your ancestors and your posterity" and oppose parliamentary taxes. The letters circulated widely and served as an early call to resistance. If Parliament could tax the colonies without their consent, he wrote, "our boasted liberty is but A sound and nothing else."

Such arguments, widely publicized in newspapers and pamphlets, gave intellectual substance to the Patriot movement and turned a series of impromptu riots, tax protests, and boycotts of British manufactures into a formidable political force.

## Another Kind of Freedom

"We are taxed without our own consent," Dickinson wrote in one of his *Letters*. "We are therefore—SLAVES." As Patriot writers argued that taxation without representation made colonists the slaves of Parliament, many, including Benjamin Franklin in Philadelphia and James Otis in Massachusetts, also began to condemn the institution of chattel slavery itself as a violation of slaves' natural rights. African Americans made the connection as well. In Massachusetts, slaves submitted at least four petitions to the legislature asking that slavery be abolished. As one petition noted, slaves "have in common with other men, a natural right to be free, and without molestation, to enjoy such property, as they may acquire by their industry."

In the southern colonies, where slaves constituted half or more of the population and the economy depended on their servitude, the quest for freedom

**COMPARE AND CONTRAST**
Why were southerners more threatened by challenges to the institution of slavery than northerners?

**Phillis Wheatley**

Born in West Africa and enslaved as a child, Phillis Wheatley was purchased by Boston merchant and tailor John Wheatley when she was eight. Tutored by Wheatley's children, Phillis learned to read English, Greek, and Latin by the age of twelve. This engraving, which pictures her at a writing desk, was the frontispiece for her *Poems on Various Subjects, Religious and Moral* (1773), which was praised by George Washington and gained attention in both Britain and the colonies. Freed upon the death of her master, Wheatley married John Peters, a free black man. He was later imprisoned for debt, forcing Wheatley to take employment as a maid. She died in 1784 at age thirty-one; none of her three children survived infancy. Library of Congress.

---

**TABLE 5.2**

**Ministerial Instability in Britain, 1760–1782**

| Leading Minister | Dates of Ministry | American Policy |
|---|---|---|
| Lord Bute | 1760–1763 | Mildly reformist |
| George Grenville | 1763–1765 | Ardently reformist |
| Lord Rockingham | 1765–1766 | Accommodationist |
| William Pitt / Charles Townshend | 1766–1770 | Ardently reformist |
| Lord North | 1770–1782 | Coercive |

---

alarmed slaveholders. In November 1773, a group of Virginia slaves hoped to win their freedom by supporting British troops that, they heard, would soon arrive in the colony. Their plan was uncovered, and, as James Madison wrote, "proper precautions" were taken "to prevent the Infection" from spreading. He fully understood how important it was to defend the colonists' liberties without allowing the idea of natural rights to undermine the institution of slavery. "It is prudent," he wrote, "such things should be concealed as well as suppressed." Throughout the Revolution, the quest for African American rights and liberties would play out alongside that of the colonies, but unlike national independence, the liberation of African Americans would not be fulfilled for many generations.

## Parliament and Patriots Square Off Again

When news of the Stamp Act riots and the boycott reached Britain, Parliament was already in turmoil. Disputes over domestic policy had led George III to dismiss Grenville as prime minister (Table 5.2). However, Grenville's allies demanded that imperial reform continue, if necessary at gunpoint. "The British legislature," declared Chief Justice Sir James Mansfield, "has authority to bind every part and every subject, whether such subjects have a right to vote or not."

Yet a majority in Parliament was persuaded that the Stamp Act was cutting deeply into British exports and thus doing more harm than good. "The Avenues of Trade are all shut up," a Bristol merchant told Parliament: "We have no Remittances and are at our Witts End for want of Money to fulfill our Engagements with our Tradesmen." Grenville's successor, the Earl of Rockingham, forged a compromise. To mollify the colonists and help British merchants, he repealed the Stamp Act and reduced the duty on molasses imposed by the Sugar Act to a penny a gallon. Then he pacified imperial reformers and hard-liners with the **Declaratory Act of 1766**, which explicitly reaffirmed Parliament's "full power and authority to make laws and statutes . . . to bind the colonies and people of America . . . in all cases whatsoever." By swiftly ending the Stamp Act crisis, Rockingham hoped it would be forgotten just as quickly.

**Charles Townshend Steps In**  Often the course of history is changed by a small event — an illness, a personal grudge, a chance remark. That was the case in 1767, when George III named William Pitt to head a new government. Pitt, chronically ill and often absent

**Celebrating Repeal**

This British cartoon mocking supporters of the Stamp Act—"The Repeal, or the Funeral Procession of Miss Americ-Stamp"—was probably commissioned by merchants trading with America. Preceded by two flag bearers, George Grenville, the author of the legislation, carries a miniature coffin (representing the act) to a tomb, as a dog urinates on the leader of the procession. Two bales on the wharf, labeled "Stamps from America" and "Black cloth return'd from America," testify to the failure of the act. The Granger Collection, New York.

THE REPEAL. — or the Funeral Procession, of MISS AMERIC-STAMP.

from parliamentary debates, left chancellor of the exchequer Charles Townshend in command. Pitt was sympathetic toward America; Townshend was not. As a member of the Board of Trade, Townshend had sought restrictions on the colonial assemblies and strongly supported the Stamp Act. In 1767, he promised to find a new source of revenue in America.

The new tax legislation, the **Townshend Act of 1767**, had both fiscal and political goals. It imposed duties on colonial imports of paper, paint, glass, and tea that were expected to raise about £40,000 a year. Though Townshend did allocate some of this revenue for American military expenses, he earmarked most of it to pay the salaries of royal governors, judges, and other imperial officials, who had always previously been paid by colonial assemblies. Now, he hoped, royal appointees could better enforce parliamentary laws and carry out the king's instructions. Townshend next devised the Revenue Act of 1767, which created a board of customs commissioners in Boston and vice-admiralty courts in Halifax, Boston, Philadelphia, and Charleston. By using parliamentary taxes to finance imperial administration, Townshend intended to undermine American political institutions.

The Townshend duties revived the constitutional debate over taxation. During the Stamp Act crisis, some Americans, including Benjamin Franklin, distinguished between external and internal taxes. They suggested that external duties on trade (such as those long mandated by the Navigation Acts) were acceptable to Americans, but that direct, or internal, taxes were not.

Townshend thought this distinction was "perfect nonsense," but he indulged the Americans and laid duties only on trade.

**A Second Boycott and the Daughters of Liberty**  Even so, most colonial leaders rejected the legitimacy of Townshend's measures. In February 1768, the Massachusetts assembly condemned the Townshend Act, and Boston and New York merchants began a new boycott of British goods. Throughout Puritan New England, ministers and public officials discouraged the purchase of "foreign superfluities" and promoted the domestic manufacture of cloth and other necessities.

American women, ordinarily excluded from public affairs, became crucial to the **nonimportation movement**. They reduced their households' consumption of imported goods and produced large quantities of homespun cloth. Pious farmwives spun yarn at their ministers' homes. In Berwick, Maine, "true Daughters of Liberty" celebrated American products by "drinking rye coffee and dining on bear venison." Other women's groups supported the boycott with charitable work, spinning flax and wool for the needy. Just as Patriot men followed tradition by joining crowd actions, so women's protests reflected their customary concern for the well-being of the community.

Newspapers celebrated these exploits of the Daughters of Liberty. One Massachusetts town proudly claimed an annual output of 30,000 yards of cloth; East Hartford, Connecticut, reported 17,000 yards. This surge in domestic production did not offset the loss of British imports, which had averaged about 10 million yards of cloth annually, but it brought thousands of women into the public arena.

The boycott mobilized many American men as well. In the seaport cities, the Sons of Liberty published the names of merchants who imported British goods and harassed their employees and customers. By March 1769, the nonimportation movement had spread to Philadelphia; two months later, the members of the Virginia House of Burgesses vowed not to buy dutied articles, luxury goods, or imported slaves. Reflecting colonial self-confidence, Benjamin Franklin called for a return to the pre-1763 mercantilist system: "Repeal the laws, renounce the right, recall the troops, refund the money, and return to the old method of requisition."

Despite the enthusiasm of Patriots, nonimportation—accompanied by pressure on merchants and consumers who resisted it—opened fissures in colonial society. Not only royal officials, but also merchants, farmers, and ordinary folk, were subject to new forms of surveillance and coercion—a pattern that would only become more pronounced as the imperial crisis unfolded.

**Troops to Boston** American resistance only increased British determination. When the Massachusetts assembly's letter opposing the Townshend duties reached London, Lord Hillsborough, the secretary of state for American affairs, branded it "unjustifiable opposition to the constitutional authority of Parliament." To strengthen the "Hand of Government" in Massachusetts, Hillsborough dispatched General Thomas Gage and 2,000 British troops to Boston (Map 5.3). Once in Massachusetts, Gage accused its leaders of "Treasonable and desperate Resolves" and

**Edenton Ladies' Tea Party**

In October 1774, a group of fifty-one women from Edenton, North Carolina, led by Penelope Barker created a local association to support a boycott of British goods. Patriots in the colonies praised the Edenton Tea Party, which was one of the first formal female political associations in North America, but it was ridiculed in Britain, where this cartoon appeared in March 1775. The women are given a mannish appearance, and the themes of promiscuity and neglect to their female duties are suggested by the presence of a slave and an amorous man, the neglected child, and the urinating dog. Library of Congress.

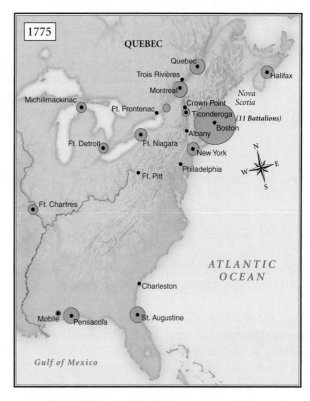

**MAP 5.3**

**British Troop Deployments, 1763 and 1775**

As the imperial crisis deepened, British military priorities changed. In 1763, most British battalions were stationed in Canada to deter Indian uprisings and French Canadian revolts. After the Stamp Act riots of 1765, the British placed large garrisons in New York and Philadelphia. By 1775, eleven battalions of British regulars occupied Boston, the center of the Patriot movement.

advised the ministry to "Quash this Spirit at a Blow." In 1765, American resistance to the Stamp Act had sparked a parliamentary debate; in 1768, it provoked a plan for military coercion.

## The Problem of the West

At the same time that successive ministries addressed the problem of raising a colonial revenue, they quarreled over how to manage the vast new inland territory — about half a billion acres — acquired in the Treaty of Paris in 1763 (see Chapter 4). The Proclamation Line had drawn a boundary between the colonies and Indian country. The line was originally intended as a temporary barrier. It prohibited settlement "for the present, and until our further Pleasure be known." The Proclamation also created three new mainland colonies — Quebec, East Florida, and West Florida — and thus opened new opportunities at the northern and southern extremities of British North America.

But many colonists looked west rather than north or south. Four groups in the colonies were especially interested in westward expansion. First, gentlemen who had invested in numerous land speculation companies were petitioning the crown for large land grants in the Ohio country. Second, officers who served in the Seven Years' War were paid in land warrants — up to 5,000 acres for field officers — and some, led by George Washington, were exploring possible sites beyond the Appalachians. Third, Indian traders who had received large grants from the Ohio Indians hoped to sell land titles. And fourth, thousands of squatters were following the roads cut to the Ohio by the Braddock and Forbes campaigns during the Seven Years' War to take up lands in the hope that they could later receive a title to them. "The roads are . . . alive with Men, Women, Children, and Cattle from Jersey, Pennsylvania, and Maryland," wrote one astonished observer (Thinking Like a Historian, p. 164).

All of this activity antagonized the Ohio Indians. In 1770, Shawnees invited hundreds of Indian leaders to

**IDENTIFY CAUSES**
What groups were most interested in western lands, and why did Hillsborough oppose them?

## Beyond the Proclamation Line

Though the Royal Proclamation of 1763 called the territory between the Appalachian Mountains and the Mississippi River "Indian country," the reality was more complex than this phrase indicates. The following documents illustrate some of the patterns that shaped life beyond the Proclamation Line between 1763 and 1776.

---

1. **Colonel John Bradstreet's Thoughts on Indian Affairs, 1764.** *Colonel John Bradstreet led a force of British redcoats to Fort Niagara in response to Pontiac's Rebellion. He drafted these remarks shortly afterward.*

Of all the Savages upon the continent, the most knowing, the most intriguing, the less useful, and the greatest Villains, are those most conversant with the Europeans, and deserve most the attention of Govern[men]t by way of correction, and these are the Six Nations, Shawanese and Delawares; they are well acquainted with the defenceless state of the Inhabitants, who live on the Frontiers, and think they will ever have it in their power to distress and plunder them, and never cease raising the jealousy of the Upper Nations against us, by propagating amongst them such stories, as make them believe the English have nothing so much at heart as the extirpation of all Savages. The apparent design of the Six Nations, is to keep us at war with all Savages, but themselves, that they may be employed as mediators between us and them.

2. **William Johnson to the British Lords of Trade, 1763.** *William Johnson, a New Yorker with extensive experience in Indian relations, was the crown's superintendent for Indian affairs in the northern colonies.*

[T]he Colonies, had all along neglected to cultivate a proper understanding with the Indians, and from a mistaken notion, have greatly dispised them, without considering, that it is in their power at pleasure to lay waste and destroy the Frontiers. . . . Without any exageration, I look upon the Northern Indians to be the most formidable of any uncivilized body of people in the World. Hunting and War are their sole occupations, and the one qualifies them for the other, they have few wants, and those are easily supplied, their properties of little value, consequently, expeditions against them however successful, cannot distress them, and they have courage sufficient for their manner of fighting, the nature and situation of their Countrys, require not more.

3. **"Indians Giving a Talk to Colonel Bouquet," 1766.** *Based on a painting by Benjamin West, this engraving from a book about Bouquet's campaign to the Ohio following Pontiac's Rebellion depicts a meeting with Delaware, Seneca, and Shawnee representatives in October 1764.*

Source: The Granger Collection, New York.

4. **David Jones's journal, 1773.** *David Jones was a Baptist minister who traveled down the Ohio River in 1772 and 1773. His journal offers a compelling glimpse of life in the valley's trading communities.*

FRIDAY [January] 22, in company with Mr. Irwine, set out for Chillicaathee. . . . Here Mr. Irwine kept an assortment of goods, and for that purpose rented an house from an Indian whose name is *Waappee Monneeto*, often called the White Devil. . . . Went to see Mr. Moses Henry a gunsmith and trader from Lancaster. This gentleman has lived for some years in this town, and is lawfully married to a white woman, who was captivated so young that she speaks the language as well as any Indian. . . . Mr. Henry lives in a comfortable manner, having plenty of good beef, pork, milk, &c. . . . Chillicaathee is the chief town of the Shawannee Indians — it is situated north of a large plain adjacent to a branch of Paint Creek. This plain is their corn-field, which supplies great part of their town. Their houses are made of logs. . . .

WEDNESDAY [February] 10. . . . This is a small town consisting of Delawares and Shawanees. The chief is a Shawanee woman, who is esteemed very rich — she entertains travelers — there were four of us in company, and for our use, her negro quarter was evacuated this night, which had a fire in the middle without any chimney. This woman has a large stock, and supplied us with milk. Here we also got corn for our horses at a very expensive price. . . .

FRIDAY [February] 12 . . . We passed [the Delaware chief] Captain White Eye's Town. . . . He told me that he intended to be religious, and have his children educated. He saw that their way of living would not answer much longer — game grew scarce — they could not much longer pretend to live by hunting, but must farm, &c. — But said, he could not attend to matters of religion now, for he intended to make a great *hunt* down Ohio, and take the skins himself to Philadelphia.

**5. Killbuck to the governors of Pennsylvania, Maryland, and Virginia, December 1771.** *John Killbuck Jr., or Gelelemend, a Delaware headman, aired grievances on behalf of Ohio Delaware, Munsie, and Mahican Indians.*

Great numbers more of your people have come over the Great Mountains and settled throughout this country, and we are sorry to tell you, that several quarrels have happened between your people and ours, in which people have been killed on both sides, and that we now see the nations round us and your people ready to embroil in a quarrel, which gives our nations great concerns, as we, on our parts, want to live in friendship with you. As you have always told us, you have laws to govern your people by, -- but we do not see that you have; therefore, brethren, unless you can fall upon some method of governing your people who live between the Great Mountains and the Ohio River and who are now very numerous, it will be out of the Indians' power to govern their young men, for we assure you the black clouds begin to gather fast in this country. . . . We find your people are very fond of our rich land. We see them quarrelling every day about land and burning one another's houses, so that we do not know how soon they may come over the river Ohio and drive us from our villages, nor do we see you, brothers, take any care to stop them.

**6. Aeneas MacKay to Pennsylvania governor John Penn, April 4, 1774.** *MacKay, a magistrate of Pennsylvania's Westmoreland County, reported on Virginia's effort to create a competing jurisdiction in the vicinity of Pittsburgh. Dr. John Connolly, appointed by Governor Dunmore as commander of the militia in Pittsburgh, was at the center of the controversy.*

Since the return of the Celebrated Doctor Connelly from Virginia last to this place, which he did on the 28th of March, our village is become the scene of anarchy and Confusion. . . .

The Doctor now is in actual possession of the Fort, with a Body Guard of Militia about him, Invested, as we are told, with both Civil & military power, to put the Virginia Law in Force in these parts, and a considerable Number of the Inhabitants of these back Parts of this Country, Ready to join him on any emergency, every artifice are used to seduce the people, some by being promoted to Civil or military employments, and others with the promises of grants of Lands, on easy Terms, & the giddy headed mobs are so Infatuated as to suffer themselves to be carried away by these Insinuating Delusions. . . .

The Indians are greatly alarmed at seeing parties of armed men patrolling through our streets Daily, not knowing but there is hostility intended against them and their country.

Sources: (1, 2) E. B. O'Callaghan and Berthold Fernow, eds., *Documents Relative to the Colonial History of the State of New York*, 15 vols. (Albany, 1856–1887), 7: 690–694, 574; (4) David Jones, *A Journal of Two Visits Made to Some Nations of Indians on the West Side of the River Ohio, in the Years 1772 and 1773* (Burlington, 1774 [rep. NY, 1971]); (5) K. G. Davies, ed., *Documents of the American Revolution, 1770–1783*, 19 vols. (Shannon and Dublin, 1972–1981), 3: 254–255; (6) Samuel Hazard, ed., *Pennsylvania Archives*, series 1, 12 vols. (Philadelphia: Joseph Severns & Co., 1856), 4: 484–486.

## ANALYZING THE EVIDENCE

1. John Bradstreet, a career British army officer, based his observations (source 1) on his wartime experiences in the West. William Johnson (source 2) had lived in close proximity to Iroquois Indians for many years. Compare their views: what do they agree upon, and where do they differ?

2. Charles Grignion's engraving (source 3) appeared in print a short time after Pontiac's Rebellion. How does it portray the Ohio Indians? Compare Grignion's image with the descriptions in sources 1 and 2 and John Killbuck's speech (source 5). What parallels or differences do you see?

3. What do you find most surprising about source 4? What evidence of European influence do you see in the Indian towns Jones describes?

4. Sources 5 and 6 describe the state of affairs on the upper Ohio shortly before the outbreak of Dunmore's War. What concerns does Killbuck express? Why was Virginia's willingness to organize a militia so important to the residents of the region?

## PUTTING IT ALL TOGETHER

Using these documents and what you have learned in Chapter 5, write a short essay that surveys British and Anglo-American attitudes toward the Ohio Indians and explores the contradictions between these attitudes and the reality of life in the Ohio country.

gather at the town of Chillicothe on the Scioto River. There they formed the Scioto Confederacy, which pledged to oppose any further expansion into the Ohio country.

Meanwhile, in London, the idea that the Proclamation Line was only temporary gave way to the view that it should be permanent. Hillsborough, who became colonial secretary in 1768, adamantly opposed westward expansion, believing it would antagonize the Indians without benefitting the empire. Moreover, he owned vast Irish estates, and he was alarmed by the number of tenants who were leaving Ireland for America. To preserve Britain's laboring class, as well as control costs, Hillsborough wanted to make the Proclamation Line permanent.

For colonists who were already moving west to settle in large numbers, this shift in policy caused confusion and frustration. Eventually, like the Patriots along the seaboard, they would take matters into their own hands.

## Parliament Wavers

In Britain, the colonies' nonimportation agreement was taking its toll. In 1768, the colonies had cut imports of British manufactures in half; by 1769, the mainland colonies had a trade surplus with Britain of £816,000. Hard-hit by these developments, British merchants and manufacturers petitioned Parliament to repeal the Townshend duties. Early in 1770, Lord North became prime minister. A witty man and a skillful politician, North designed a new compromise. Arguing that it was foolish to tax British exports to America (thereby raising their price and decreasing consumption), he persuaded Parliament to repeal most of the Townshend

duties. However, North retained the tax on tea as a symbol of Parliament's supremacy (Figure 5.2).

**The Boston Massacre**   Even as Parliament was debating North's repeal, events in Boston guaranteed that reconciliation between Patriots and Parliament would be hard to achieve. Between 1,200 and 2,000 troops had been stationed in Boston for a year and a half. Soldiers were also stationed in New York, Philadelphia, several towns in New Jersey, and various frontier outposts in these years, with a minimum of conflict or violence. But in Boston — a small port town on a tiny peninsula — the troops numbered 10 percent of the local population, and their presence wore on the locals. On the night of March 5, 1770, a group of nine British redcoats fired into a crowd and killed five townspeople. A subsequent trial exonerated the soldiers, but Boston's Radical Whigs, convinced of a ministerial conspiracy against liberty, labeled the incident a "massacre" and used it to rally sentiment against imperial power.

**Sovereignty Debated**   When news of North's compromise arrived in the colonies in the wake of the Boston Massacre, the reaction was mixed. Most of Britain's colonists remained loyal to the empire, but five years of conflict had taken their toll. In 1765, American leaders had accepted Parliament's authority; the Stamp Act Resolves had opposed only certain "unconstitutional" legislation. By 1770, the most outspoken Patriots — Benjamin Franklin in Pennsylvania, Patrick Henry in Virginia, and Samuel Adams in Massachusetts — repudiated parliamentary supremacy and claimed equality for the American assemblies within the empire. Franklin suggested that the colonies

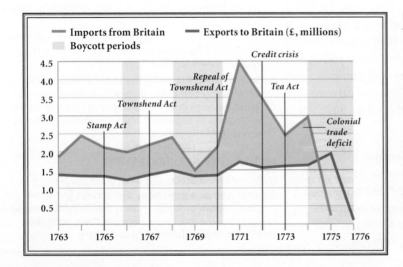

**FIGURE 5.2**

**Trade as a Political Weapon, 1763–1776**

Political upheaval did not affect the mainland colonies' exports to Britain, which rose slightly over the period, but imports fluctuated greatly. The American boycott of 1765–1766 prompted a dip in imports, but the second boycott of 1768–1770 led to a sharp drop in imports of British textiles, metal goods, and ceramics. Imports of manufactures soared after the repeal of the Townshend duties, only to plummet when the First Continental Congress proclaimed a third boycott in 1774.

**Patriot Propaganda**
Silversmith Paul Revere issued this engraving of the confrontation between British redcoats and snowball-throwing Bostonians in the days after it occurred. To whip up opposition to the military occupation of their town, Revere and other Patriots labeled the incident "The Boston Massacre." The shooting confirmed their Radical Whig belief that "standing armies" were instruments of tyranny. Library of Congress.

were now "distinct and separate states" with "the same Head, or Sovereign, the King."

Franklin's suggestion outraged Thomas Hutchinson, the American-born royal governor of Massachusetts. Hutchinson emphatically rejected the idea of "two independent legislatures in one and the same state." He told the Massachusetts assembly, "I know of no line that can be drawn between the supreme authority of Parliament and the total independence of the colonies."

There the matter rested. The British had twice imposed revenue acts on the colonies, and American Patriots had twice forced a retreat. If Parliament

insisted on a policy of constitutional absolutism by imposing taxes a third time, some Americans were prepared to pursue violent resistance. Nor did they flinch when reminded that George III condemned their agitation. As the Massachusetts House replied to Hutchinson, "There is more reason to dread the consequences of absolute uncontrolled supreme power, whether of a nation or a monarch, than those of total independence." Fearful of civil war, Lord North's ministry hesitated to force the issue.

**TRACE CHANGE OVER TIME**
What was Benjamin Franklin's position on colonial representation in 1765, and why had his view changed by 1770?

# The Road to Independence, 1771–1776

Repeal of the Townshend duties in 1770 restored harmony to the British Empire, but strong feelings and mutual distrust lay just below the surface. In 1773, those emotions erupted, destroying any hope of compromise. Within two years, the Americans and the British clashed in armed conflict. Despite widespread resistance among loyal colonists, Patriot legislators created provisional governments and military forces, the two essentials for independence.

## A Compromise Repudiated

Once aroused, political passions are not easily quieted. In Boston, Samuel Adams and other radical Patriots continued to warn Americans of imperial domination and, late in 1772, persuaded the town meeting to set up a committee of correspondence "to state the Rights of the Colonists of this Province." Soon, eighty Massachusetts towns had similar committees. When British officials threatened to seize the Americans responsible for the burning of the customs vessel *Gaspée* and prosecute them in Britain, the Virginia House of Burgesses and several other assemblies set up their own **committees of correspondence**. These standing committees allowed Patriots to communicate with leaders in other colonies when new threats to liberty occurred. By 1774, among the colonies that would later declare independence, only Pennsylvania was without one.

**The East India Company and the Tea Act**   These committees sprang into action when Parliament passed the **Tea Act of May 1773**. The act provided financial relief for the East India Company, a royally chartered private corporation that served as the instrument of British imperialism. The company was deeply in debt; it also had a huge surplus of tea as a result of high import duties, which led Britons and colonists alike to drink smuggled Dutch tea instead. The Tea Act gave the company a government loan and, to boost its revenue, canceled the import duties on tea the company exported to Ireland and the American colonies. Now even with the Townshend duty of 3 pence a pound on tea, high-quality East India Company tea would cost less than the Dutch tea smuggled into the colonies by American merchants.

**UNDERSTAND POINTS OF VIEW**
Why did colonists react so strongly against the Tea Act, which imposed a small tax and actually lowered the price of tea?

Radical Patriots accused the British ministry of bribing Americans with the cheaper East India Company's tea so they would give up their principled opposition to the tea tax. As an anonymous woman wrote to the *Massachusetts Spy*, "The use of [British] tea is considered not as a private but as a public evil . . . a handle to introduce a variety of . . . oppressions amongst us." Merchants joined the protest because the East India Company planned to distribute its tea directly to shopkeepers, excluding American wholesalers from the trade's profits. "The fear of an Introduction of a Monopoly in this Country," British general Frederick Haldimand reported from New York, "has induced the mercantile part of the Inhabitants to be very industrious in opposing this Step and added Strength to a Spirit of Independence already too prevalent."

**The Tea Party and the Coercive Acts**   The Sons of Liberty prevented East India Company ships from delivering their cargoes in New York, Philadelphia, and Charleston. In Massachusetts, Royal Governor Hutchinson was determined to land the tea and collect the tax. To foil the governor's plan, artisans and laborers disguised as Indians boarded three ships—the *Dartmouth*, the *Eleanor*, and the *Beaver*—on December 16, 1773, broke open 342 chests of tea (valued at about £10,000, or about $900,000 today), and threw them into the harbor. "This destruction of the Tea . . . must have so important Consequences," John Adams wrote in his diary, "that I cannot but consider it as an Epoch in History."

The king was outraged. "Concessions have made matters worse," George III declared. "The time has come for compulsion." Early in 1774, Parliament passed four **Coercive Acts** to force Massachusetts to pay for the tea and to submit to imperial authority. The Boston Port Bill closed Boston Harbor to shipping; the Massachusetts Government Act annulled the colony's charter and prohibited most town meetings; a new Quartering Act mandated new barracks for British troops; and the Justice Act allowed trials for capital crimes to be transferred to other colonies or to Britain.

Patriot leaders throughout the colonies branded the measures "Intolerable" and rallied support for Massachusetts. In Georgia, a Patriot warned the "Freemen of the Province" that "every privilege you at present claim as a birthright, may be wrested from you by the same authority that blockades the town of Boston." "The cause of Boston," George Washington declared in Virginia, "now is and ever will be considered as the cause of America." The committees of correspondence had created a firm sense of Patriot unity.

**The Boston Tea Party**
Led by radical Patriots disguised as Mohawk Indians, Bostonians dumped the East India Company's taxed tea into the harbor. The rioters made clear their "pure" political motives by punishing those who sought personal gain: one Son of Liberty who stole some of the tea was "stripped of his booty and his clothes together, and sent home naked." Library of Congress.

In 1774, Parliament also passed the Quebec Act, which allowed the practice of Roman Catholicism in Quebec. This concession to Quebec's predominantly Catholic population reignited religious passions in New England, where Protestants associated Catholicism with arbitrary royal government. Because the act extended Quebec's boundaries into the Ohio River Valley, it likewise angered influential land speculators in Virginia and Pennsylvania and ordinary settlers by the thousands (Map 5.4). Although the ministry did not intend the Quebec Act as a coercive measure, many colonists saw it as further proof of Parliament's intention to control American affairs.

## The Continental Congress Responds

In response to the Coercive Acts, Patriot leaders convened a new continent-wide body, the **Continental Congress**. Twelve mainland colonies sent representatives. Four recently acquired colonies — Florida, Quebec, Nova Scotia, and Newfoundland — refused to send delegates, as did Georgia, where the royal governor controlled the legislature. The assemblies of Barbados, Jamaica, and the other sugar islands, although wary of British domination, were even more fearful of revolts by their predominantly African populations and therefore declined to attend.

The delegates who met in Philadelphia in September 1774 had different agendas. Southern representatives, fearing a British plot "to overturn the constitution and introduce a system of arbitrary government," advocated a new economic boycott. Independence-minded representatives from New England demanded political union and defensive military preparations. Many delegates from the Middle Atlantic colonies favored compromise.

Led by Joseph Galloway of Pennsylvania, these men of "loyal principles" proposed a new political system similar to Benjamin Franklin's proposal at the Albany Congress of 1754: each colony would retain its assembly to legislate on local matters, and a new continent-wide body would handle general American affairs. The king would appoint a president-general to preside over a legislative council selected by the colonial assemblies. Galloway's plan failed by a single vote; a bare majority thought it was too conciliatory (American Voices, p. 172).

Instead, the delegates demanded the repeal of the Coercive Acts and stipulated that British control

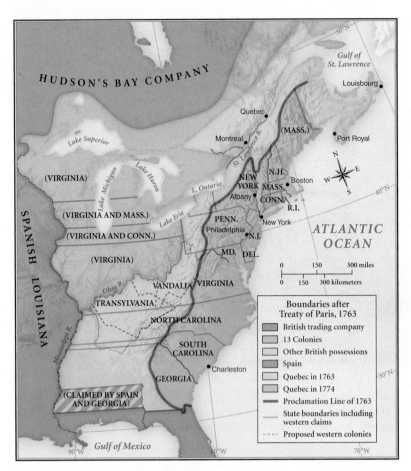

**MAP 5.4**

**British Western Policy, 1763–1774**

The Proclamation of 1763 prohibited white settlement west of the Appalachian Mountains. Nonetheless, Anglo-American settlers and land speculators proposed the new colonies of Vandalia and Transylvania to the west of Virginia and North Carolina. The Quebec Act of 1774 designated most western lands as Indian reserves and vastly enlarged the boundaries of Quebec, dashing speculators' hopes and eliminating the old sea-to-sea land claims of many seaboard colonies. The act especially angered New England Protestants, who condemned it for allowing French residents to practice Catholicism, and colonial political leaders, who protested its failure to provide Quebec with a representative assembly.

be limited to matters of trade. It also approved a program of economic retaliation: Americans would stop importing British goods in December 1774. If Parliament did not repeal the Coercive Acts by September 1775, the Congress vowed to cut off virtually all colonial exports to Britain, Ireland, and the British West Indies. Ten years of constitutional conflict had culminated in a threat of all-out commercial warfare.

A few British leaders still hoped for compromise. In January 1775, William Pitt, now sitting in the House of Lords as the Earl of Chatham, asked Parliament to renounce its power to tax the colonies and to recognize the Continental Congress as a lawful body. In return, he suggested, the Congress should acknowledge parliamentary supremacy and provide a permanent source of revenue to help defray the national debt.

The British ministry rejected Pitt's plan. Twice it had backed down in the face of colonial resistance; a third retreat was impossible. Branding the Continental Congress an illegal assembly, the ministry rejected

**COMPARE AND CONTRAST**
Why did Parliament prefer North's solution to the Boston Tea Party to William Pitt's?

Lord Dartmouth's proposal to send commissioners to negotiate a settlement. Instead, Lord North set stringent terms: Americans must pay for their own defense and administration and acknowledge Parliament's authority to tax them. To put teeth in these demands, North imposed a naval blockade on American trade with foreign nations and ordered General Gage to suppress dissent in Massachusetts. "Now the case seemed desperate," the prime minister told Thomas Hutchinson, whom the Patriots had forced into exile in London. "Parliament would not — could not — concede. For aught he could see it must come to violence."

## The Rising of the Countryside

The fate of the urban-led Patriot movement would depend on the colonies' large rural population. Most farmers had little interest in imperial affairs. Their lives were deeply rooted in the soil, and their prime allegiance was to family and community. But imperial policies had increasingly intruded into the lives of farm families by sending their sons to war and raising their taxes. In 1754, farmers on Long Island, New York, had paid an average tax of 10 shillings; by 1756, thanks to the Great War for Empire, their taxes had jumped to 30 shillings.

**The Continental Association**  The boycotts of 1765 and 1768 raised the political consciousness of rural Americans. When the First Continental Congress established the **Continental Association** in 1774 to enforce a third boycott of British goods, it quickly set up a rural network of committees to do its work. In Concord, Massachusetts, 80 percent of the male heads of families and a number of single women signed a "Solemn League and Covenant" supporting nonimportation. In other farm towns, men blacked their faces, disguised themselves in blankets "like Indians," and threatened violence against shopkeepers who traded "in rum, molasses, & Sugar, &c." in violation of the boycott.

Patriots likewise warned that British measures threatened the yeoman tradition of landownership. In Petersham, Massachusetts, the town meeting worried that new British taxes would drain "this People of the Fruits of their Toil." Arable land was now scarce and expensive in older communities, and in new settlements merchants were seizing farmsteads for delinquent

debts. By the 1770s, many northern yeomen felt personally threatened by British policies, which, a Patriot pamphlet warned, were "paving the way for reducing the country to lordships" (Table 5.3).

**Southern Planters Fear Dependency**  Despite their higher standard of living, southern slave owners had similar fears. Many Chesapeake planters were deeply in debt to British merchants. Accustomed to being absolute masters on their slave-labor plantations and seeing themselves as guardians of English liberties, planters resented their financial dependence on British creditors and dreaded the prospect of political subservience to British officials.

That danger now seemed real. If Parliament used the Coercive Acts to subdue Massachusetts, then it might turn next to Virginia, dissolving its representative assembly and assisting British merchants to seize debt-burdened properties. Consequently, the Virginia gentry supported demands by indebted yeomen farmers to close the law courts so that they could bargain with merchants over debts without the threat of legal action. "The spark of liberty is not yet extinct among our people," declared one planter, "and if properly

| TABLE 5.3 | | |
|---|---|---|
| **Patriot Resistance, 1762–1776** | | |
| **Date** | **British Action** | **Patriot Response** |
| 1762 | Revenue Act | Merchants complain privately |
| 1763 | Proclamation Line | Land speculators voice discontent |
| 1764 | Sugar Act | Merchants and Massachusetts legislature protest |
| 1765 | Stamp Act | Sons of Liberty riot; Stamp Act Congress; first boycott of British goods |
| 1765 | Quartering Act | New York assembly refuses to fund until 1767 |
| 1767–1768 | Townshend Act; military occupation of Boston | Second boycott of British goods; harassment of pro-British merchants |
| 1772 | Royal commission to investigate *Gaspée* affair | Committees of correspondence form |
| 1773 | Tea Act | Widespread resistance; Boston Tea Party |
| 1774 | Coercive Acts; Quebec Act | First Continental Congress; third boycott of British goods |
| 1775 | British raids near Boston; king's Proclamation for Suppressing Rebellion and Sedition | Armed resistance; Second Continental Congress; invasion of Canada; cutoff of colonial exports |
| 1776 | Military attacks led by royal governors in South | Paine's *Common Sense*; Declaration of Independence |

## The Debate over Representation and Sovereignty

Speaking before the House of Commons, Benjamin Franklin declared that before 1763 Americans had paid little attention to the question of Parliament's "right to lay taxes and duties" in the colonies. The reason was simple, Franklin said: "A right to lay internal taxes was never supposed to be in Parliament, as we are not represented there." Franklin recognized that representation was central to the imperial debate. As the following selections show, the failure to solve the problem of representation, and the closely related issue of parliamentary sovereignty, led to the American rebellion.

### Jared Ingersoll
### Report on the Debates in Parliament (1765)

Connecticut lawyer Jared Ingersoll (1722–1781) served as his colony's agent, or lobbyist, in Britain. In this 1765 letter to the governor of Connecticut, Ingersoll summarizes the debate then under way in Parliament over the Stamp Act. When the act passed, he returned home to become the stamp distributor in Connecticut. A mob forced him to resign that post. Ingersoll later served as a vice-admiralty judge in Philadelphia and, during the Revolution, remained loyal to Britain.

The principal Attention has been to the Stamp bill that has been preparing to Lay before Parliament for taxing America. The Point of the Authority of Parliament to impose such Tax I found on my Arrival here was so fully and Universally yielded [accepted], that there was not the least hopes of making any impressions that way. . . .

I beg leave to give you a Summary of the Arguments which are made use of in favour of such Authority. The House of Commons, say they, is a branch of the supreme legislature of the Nation, and which in its Nature is supposed to represent, or rather to stand in the place of, the Commons, that is, of the great body of the people. . . .

That this house of Commons, therefore, is now . . . a part of the Supreme unlimited power of the Nation, as in every State there must be some unlimited Power and Authority. . . .

They say a Power to tax is a necessary part of every Supreme Legislative Authority, and that if they have not that Power over America, they have none, and then America is at once a Kingdom of itself.

On the other hand those who oppose the bill say, it is true the Parliament have a supreme unlimited Authority over every Part and Branch of the Kings dominions and as well over Ireland as any other place.

Yet [they say] we believe a British parliament will never think it prudent to tax Ireland [or America]. Tis true they say, that the Commons of England and of the British Empire are all represented in and by the house of Commons, but this representation is confessedly on all hands by Construction and Virtual [because most British subjects] . . . have no hand in choosing the representatives. . . .

[They say further] that the Effects of this implied Representation here and in America must be infinitely different in the Article of Taxation. . . . By any Mistake an act of Parliament is made that prove injurious and hard the Member of Parliament here [in Britain] sees with his own Eyes and is moreover very accessible to the people. . . . [Also,] the taxes are laid equally by one Rule and fall as well on the Member himself as on the people. But as to America, from the great distance in point of Situation [they are not represented in the same way]. . . .

[Finally, the opponents of the Act say] we already by the Regulations upon their trade draw from the Americans all that they can spare. . . . This Step [of taxation] should not take place until or unless the Americans are allowed to send Members to Parliament.

Thus I have given you, I think, the Substance of the Arguments on both sides of that great and important Question of the right and also of the Expediency of taxing America by Authority of Parliament. . . . [But] upon a Division of the house upon the Question, there was about 250 to about 50 in favour of the Bill.

Source: New Haven Colony Historical Society, *Papers* (1918), 9: 306–315.

### Joseph Galloway
### Plan of Union (1775)

Speaker of the Pennsylvania assembly Joseph Galloway was a delegate to the First Continental Congress, where he proposed a plan that addressed the issue of representation. The colonies would remain British but operate under a continental government with the power to veto parliamentary laws that affected America. Radical Patriots in the Congress, who favored independence, prevented a vote on Galloway's plan and suppressed mention of it in the records. Galloway remained loyal to the crown, fought on the British side in the War for Independence, and moved to England in 1778.

If we sincerely mean to accommodate the difference between the two countries, . . . we must take into consideration a number of facts which led the Parliament to pass the acts complained of. . . . [You will recall] the dangerous situation of the Colonies from the intrigues of France, and the incursions of the Canadians and their Indian allies, at the commencement of the last war. . . . Great-Britain sent over her fleets and armies for their protection. . . .

In this state of the Colonies, it was not unreasonable to expect that Parliament would have levied a tax on them proportionate to their wealth, . . . Parliament was naturally led to exercise the power which had been, by its predecessors, so often exercised over the Colonies, and to pass the Stamp Act. Against this act, the Colonies petitioned Parliament, and denied its authority . . . [declaring] that the Colonies could not be represented in that body. This justly alarmed the British Senate. It was thought and called by the ablest men [in] Britain, a clear and explicit declaration of the American Independence, and compelled the Parliament to pass the Declaratory Act, in order to save its ancient and incontrovertible right of supremacy over all the parts of the empire. . . .

Having thus briefly stated the arguments in favour of parliamentary authority, . . . I am free to confess that the exercise of that authority is not perfectly constitutional in respect to the Colonies. We know that the whole landed interest of Britain is represented in that body, while neither the land nor the people of America hold the least participation in the legislative authority of the State. . . . Representation, or a participation in the supreme councils of the State, is the great principle upon which the freedom of the British Government is established and secured.

I wish to see . . . the right to participate in the supreme councils of the State extended, in some form . . . to America . . . [and therefore] have prepared the draught of a plan for uniting America more intimately, in constitutional policy, with Great-Britain. . . . I am certain when dispassionately considered, it will be found to be the most perfect union in power and liberty with the Parent State, next to a representation in Parliament, and I trust it will be approved of by both countries.

*The Plan*

That the several [colonial] assemblies shall [form an American union and] choose members for the grand council. . . .

That the Grand Council . . . shall hold and exercise all the like rights, liberties and privileges, as are held and exercised by and in the House of Commons of Great-Britain. . . .

That the President-General shall hold his office during the pleasure of the King, and his assent shall be requisite to all acts of the Grand Council, and it shall be his office and duty to cause them to be carried into execution. . . .

That the President-General, by and with the advice and consent of the Grand-Council, hold and exercise all the legislative rights, powers, and authorities, necessary for regulating and administering all the general police and affairs of the colonies. . . .

That the said President-General and the Grand Council, be an inferior and distinct branch of the British legislature, united and incorporated with it, . . . and that the assent of both [Parliament and the Grand Council] shall be requisite to the validity of all such general acts or statutes [that affect the colonies].

Source: Joseph Galloway, *Historical and Political Reflections on the Rise and Progress of the American Rebellion* (London, 1780), 70.

## ANALYZING THE EVIDENCE

1. According to Ingersoll, what were the main arguments of those in Parliament who opposed the Stamp Act? Did those opposing the Stamp Act agree with the act's supporters that Parliament had the right to tax the colonies?

2. How did Galloway's plan solve the problem of colonial representation in Parliament? How would the British ministers who advocated parliamentary supremacy have reacted to the plan?

3. The framers of the U.S. Constitution addressed the problem of dividing authority between state governments and the national government by allowing the states to retain legal authority over most matters and delegating limited powers to the national government. Could such a solution have been implemented in the British Empire? Why or why not?

fanned by the Gentlemen of influence will, I make no doubt, burst out again into a flame."

## Loyalists and Neutrals

Yet in many places, the Patriot movement was a hard sell. In Virginia, Patriot leaders were nearly all wealthy planters, and many of their poorer neighbors regarded the movement with suspicion. In regions where great landowners became Patriots — the Hudson River Valley of New York, for example — many tenant farmers supported the king because they hated their landlords. Similar social conflicts prompted some Regulators in the North Carolina backcountry and many farmers in eastern Maryland to oppose the Patriots there.

There were many reasons to resist the Patriot movement. Skeptics believed that Patriot leaders were subverting British rule only to advance their own selfish interests. Peter Oliver wrote of Samuel Adams, for example, "He was so thorough a Machiavilian, that he divested himself of every worthy Principle, & would stick at no Crime to accomplish his Ends." Some "Gentlemen of influence" worried that resistance to Britain would undermine all political institutions and "introduce Anarchy and disorder and render life and property here precarious." Their fears increased when the Sons of Liberty used intimidation and violence to uphold the boycotts. One well-to-do New Yorker complained, "No man can be in a more abject state of bondage than he whose Reputation, Property and Life are exposed to the discretionary violence . . . of the community." As the crisis deepened, such men became Loyalists — so called because they remained loyal to the British crown.

Many other colonists simply hoped to stay out of the fray. Some did so on principle: in New Jersey and Pennsylvania, thousands of pacifist Quakers and Germans resisted conscription and violence out of religious conviction. Others were ambivalent or confused about the political crisis unfolding around them. The delegate elected to New York's Provincial Congress from Queen's County, on Long Island, chose not to attend since "the people [he represented] seemed to be much inclined to remain peaceable and quiet." More than three-fourths of Queen's County voters, in fact, opposed sending any delegate at all. Many loyal or neutral colonists hoped, above all, to preserve their families' property and independence, whatever the outcome of the imperial crisis.

Historians estimate that some 15 to 20 percent of the white population — perhaps as many as 400,000

colonists — were loyal to the crown. Some managed to avoid persecution, but many were pressured by their neighbors to join the boycotts and subjected to violence and humiliation if they refused. As Patriots took over the reins of local government throughout the colonies, Loyalists were driven out of their homes or forced into silence. At this crucial juncture, Patriots commanded the allegiance, or at least the acquiescence, of the majority of white Americans.

# Violence East and West

By 1774, British authority was wavering. At the headwaters of the Ohio, the abandonment of Fort Pitt left a power vacuum that was filled by opportunistic men, led by a royally appointed governor acting in defiance of his commission. In Massachusetts, the attempt to isolate and punish Boston and the surrounding countryside backfired as Patriots resisted military coercion. Violence resulted in both places, and with it the collapse of imperial control.

## Lord Dunmore's War

In the years since the end of Pontiac's Rebellion, at least 10,000 people had traveled along Braddock's and Forbes's Roads to the headwaters of the Ohio River, where Fort Pitt had replaced Fort Duquesne during the Great War for Empire, and staked claims to land around Pittsburgh (Map 5.5). They relied for protection on Fort Pitt, which remained one of Britain's most important frontier outposts. But the revenue crisis forced General Gage to cut expenses, and in October 1772, the army pulled down the fort's log walls and left the site to the local population. Settler relations with the neighboring Ohio Indians were tenuous and ill-defined, and the fort's abandonment left them exposed and vulnerable.

In the ensuing power vacuum, Pennsylvania and Virginia both claimed the region. Pennsylvania had the better claim on paper. It had organized county governments, established courts, and collected taxes there. But — in keeping with its pacifist Quaker roots — it did not organize a militia. In this decision, Virginia's royal governor, the Earl of Dunmore, recognized an opportunity. Appointed to his post in 1771, Dunmore was an irascible and unscrupulous man who clashed repeatedly with the House of Burgesses. But when it suited him, he was just as willing to defy the crown. In 1773, he traveled to Pittsburgh, where, he later wrote, "the people flocked about me and beseeched me . . . to

**MAP 5.5**

### The Ohio Country, 1774–1775

The erosion of British imperial authority caused chaos in the Ohio country. Pennsylvania and Virginia each claimed Pittsburgh and the surrounding countryside, while the Indian communities on the upper Ohio increasingly feared colonist aggression. Their fears were realized in the summer of 1774, when Lord Dunmore led a force of Virginia militia into the valley. After defeating a Shawnee force in the Battle of Point Pleasant, many Virginians began surveying and staking claims to land in the Kentucky bluegrass. In the summer of 1775, perhaps a dozen new towns were settled there, in violation of the Royal Proclamation of 1763 and the Quebec Act of 1774.

appoint magistrates and officers of militia." He organized a local militia; soon, men armed by Virginia were drilling near the ruins of Fort Pitt.

In the summer of 1774, Dunmore took the next step. In defiance of both his royal instructions and the House of Burgesses, he called out Virginia's militia and led a force of 2,400 men against the Ohio Shawnees, who had a long-standing claim to Kentucky as a hunting ground. They fought a single battle, at Point Pleasant; the Shawnees were defeated, and Dunmore and his militia forces claimed Kentucky as their own. A participant justified his actions shortly afterward: "When without a king," he wrote, "[one] doeth according to the freedom of his own will." Years of neglect left many colonists in the backcountry feeling abandoned by the crown. **Dunmore's War** was their declaration of independence.

## Armed Resistance in Massachusetts

Meanwhile, as the Continental Congress gathered in Philadelphia in September 1774, Massachusetts was also defying British authority. In August, a Middlesex County Congress had urged Patriots to close the existing royal courts and to transfer their political allegiance to the popularly elected House of Representatives. Subsequently, armed crowds harassed Loyalists and ensured Patriot rule in most of New England.

In response, General Thomas Gage, now the military governor of Massachusetts, ordered British troops in Boston in September 1774 to seize Patriot armories in nearby Charlestown and Cambridge. An army of 20,000 militiamen quickly mobilized to safeguard other Massachusetts military depots. The Concord town meeting raised a defensive force, the famous **Minutemen**, to "Stand at a minutes warning in Case of alarm." Increasingly, Gage's authority was limited to Boston, where it rested on the bayonets of his 3,500 troops. Meanwhile, the Patriot-controlled Massachusetts assembly met in nearby Salem in open defiance of Parliament, collecting taxes, bolstering the militia, and assuming the responsibilities of government.

In London, the colonial secretary, Lord Dartmouth, proclaimed Massachusetts to be in "open rebellion" and ordered Gage to march against the "rude rabble." On the night of April 18, 1775, Gage dispatched 700 soldiers to capture colonial leaders and supplies at Concord. However, Paul Revere and a series of other riders warned Patriots in many towns, and at dawn, militiamen confronted the British regulars first at Lexington and then at Concord. Those first skirmishes took a handful of lives, but as the British retreated to Boston, militia from neighboring towns repeatedly ambushed them. By the end of the day, 73 British soldiers were dead, 174 wounded, and 26 missing. British fire had killed 49 Massachusetts militiamen and wounded 39. Twelve years of economic and constitutional conflict had ended in violence.

> **PLACE EVENTS IN CONTEXT**
> What led to Dunmore's War, and why did western settlers support it?

## The Second Continental Congress Organizes for War

A month later, in May 1775, Patriot leaders gathered in Philadelphia for the **Second Continental Congress**. As the Congress opened, 3,000 British troops attacked American fortifications on Breed's Hill and Bunker Hill overlooking Boston. After three assaults and 1,000 casualties, they finally dislodged the Patriot militia. Inspired by his countrymen's valor, John Adams exhorted the Congress to rise to the "defense of American liberty" by creating a continental army. He nominated George Washington to lead it. After bitter debate, the Congress approved the proposals, but, Adams lamented, only "by bare majorities."

**Congress Versus King George**   Despite the bloodshed in Massachusetts, a majority in the Congress still hoped for reconciliation. Led by John Dickinson of Pennsylvania, these moderates won approval of a petition expressing loyalty to George III and asking for repeal of oppressive parliamentary legislation. But Samuel Adams, Patrick Henry, and other zealous Patriots drummed up support for a Declaration of the Causes and Necessities of Taking Up Arms. Americans dreaded the "calamities of civil war," the declaration asserted, but were "resolved to die Freemen rather than to live [as] slaves." George III failed to exploit the divisions among the Patriots; instead, in August 1775, he issued a Proclamation for Suppressing Rebellion and Sedition.

Before the king's proclamation reached America, the radicals in the Congress had won support for an invasion of Canada to prevent a British attack from the north. Patriot forces easily defeated the British at Montreal; but in December 1775, they failed to capture Quebec City and withdrew. Meanwhile, American merchants waged the financial warfare promised at the First Continental Congress by cutting off exports to Britain and its West Indian sugar islands. Parliament retaliated with the Prohibitory Act, which outlawed all trade with the rebellious colonies.

**George III, 1771**

King George III was a young man of twenty-seven when the American troubles began in 1765. Six years later, as this portrait by Johann Zoffany suggests, the king had aged. Initially, George had been headstrong and tried to impose his will on Parliament, but he succeeded only in generating political confusion and inept policy. He strongly supported Parliament's attempts to tax the colonies and continued the war in America long after most of his ministers agreed that it had been lost. The Royal Collection © 2011 Her Majesty Queen Elizabeth II/The Bridgeman Art Library.

> **EXPLAIN CONSEQUENCES**
> How did the violence around Boston in the spring of 1775 affect proceedings in the Second Continental Congress?

**Fighting in the South**   Skirmishes between Patriot and Loyalist forces now broke out in the southern colonies. In Virginia, Patriots ousted Governor Dunmore and forced him to take refuge on a British warship in Chesapeake Bay. Branding the rebels "traitors," the governor organized two military forces: one white, the Queen's Own Loyal Virginians; and one black, the Ethiopian Regiment, which enlisted 1,000 slaves who had fled their Patriot owners. In November 1775, Dunmore issued a controversial proclamation promising freedom to black slaves and white indentured servants who joined the Loyalist cause. White planters denounced this "Diabolical scheme," claiming it "point[ed] a dagger to their Throats." A new rising of the black and white underclasses, as in Bacon's Rebellion in the 1670s, seemed a possibility. In Fincastle County in southwestern Virginia, Loyalist planter John Hiell urged workers to support the king, promising "a Servant man" that soon "he and all the negroes would get their freedom." Frightened by Dunmore's aggressive tactics, Patriot yeomen and tenants called for a final break with Britain.

In North Carolina, too, military clashes prompted demands for independence. Early in 1776, Josiah Martin, the colony's royal governor, raised a Loyalist force of 1,500 Scottish Highlanders in the backcountry. In response, Patriots mobilized the lowcountry militia and, in February, defeated Martin's army at the Battle of Moore's Creek Bridge, capturing more than 800 Highlanders. Following this victory, radical Patriots in the North Carolina assembly told its representatives to the Continental Congress to join with "other Colonies in declaring Independence, and forming foreign alliances." In May, the Virginia gentry followed suit: led by James Madison, Edmund Pendleton, and Patrick Henry, the Patriots met in convention and resolved unanimously to support independence.

**Occupying Kentucky**   Beginning in the spring of 1775, in the wake of Dunmore's War, independent parties of adventurers began to occupy the newly won lands of Kentucky. Daniel Boone led one group to the banks of the Kentucky River, where they established the town of Boonesborough; nearby was Lexington, named in honor of the Massachusetts town that had resisted the redcoats a few months earlier. The Shawnees and other Ohio Indians opposed the settlers, and colonists built their tiny towns in the form of stations to protect themselves — groups of cabins connected by palisades to form small forts.

These western settlers had confused political loyalties. Many had marched under Dunmore and hoped to receive recognition for their claims from the crown. But as the rebellion unfolded, most recognized that the Patriots' emphasis on liberty and equality squared with their view of the world. They soon petitioned Virginia's rebel government, asking it to create a new county that would include the Kentucky settlements. They had "Fought and bled" for the land in Dunmore's War and now wanted to fight against the crown and its Indian allies in the Ohio country. Virginia agreed: in 1776, it organized six new frontier counties and sent arms and ammunition to Kentucky. In July, the Continental Congress followed suit, dispatching troops and arms to the Ohio River as well.

## Thomas Paine's *Common Sense*

As military conflicts escalated, Americans were divided in their opinions of King George III. Many blamed him for supporting oppressive legislation and ordering armed retaliation, but other influential colonists held out the hope that he might mediate their conflict with Parliament. John Dickinson, whose *Letters* did so much to arouse Patriot resistance in 1768, nevertheless believed that war with Great Britain would be folly. In July 1775, he persuaded Congress to send George III the Olive Branch Petition, which pleaded with the king to negotiate. John Adams, a staunch supporter of independence, was infuriated by Dickinson's waffling. But Dickinson had many supporters, both inside and outside of Congress. For example, many of Philadelphia's Quaker and Anglican merchants were neutrals or Loyalists. In response to their passivity, Patriot artisans in the city organized a Mechanics' Association to protect America's "just Rights and Privileges."

**Daniel Boone Escorting Settlers Through the Cumberland Gap**

In 1775 Daniel Boone led a group of prospective settlers into Kentucky on behalf of Richard Henderson, a North Carolina judge and self-appointed proprietor of a land speculation venture called the Transylvania Colony. Henderson's venture soon collapsed, but Boonesborough was one of perhaps a dozen towns founded in Kentucky in violation of crown policy that summer. Boone became a folk hero, and in the mid-nineteenth century George Caleb Bingham painted this memorable scene. Using biblical imagery (the woman on horseback recalls Mary riding into Bethlehem on a donkey) and dramatic lighting, Bingham portrays Boone as an agent of progress bringing civilization to a howling and dangerous wilderness. George Caleb Bingham, *Daniel Boone Escorting Settlers Through the Cumberland Gap*, 1851–52. Oil on Canvas, 36½ x 50¼". Mildred Lane Kemper Art Museum, Washington University in St. Louis. Gift of Nathanial Phillips, 1890.

With popular sentiment in flux, a single brief pamphlet helped tip the balance. In January 1776, Thomas Paine published *Common Sense*, a rousing call for independence and a republican form of government. Paine had served as a minor customs official in England until he was fired for joining a protest against low wages. In 1774, Paine migrated to Philadelphia, where he met Benjamin Rush and other Patriots who shared his republican sentiments.

In *Common Sense*, Paine assaulted the traditional monarchical order in stirring language. "Monarchy and hereditary succession have laid the world in blood and ashes," Paine proclaimed, leveling a personal attack at George III, "the hard hearted sullen Pharaoh of England." Mixing insults with biblical quotations, Paine blasted the British system of "mixed government" that balanced power among the three estates of king, lords, and commoners. Paine granted that the system "was noble for the dark and slavish times" of the past, but now it yielded only "monarchical tyranny in the person of the king" and "aristocratical tyranny in the persons of the peers."

Paine argued for American independence by turning the traditional metaphor of patriarchal authority on its head: "Is it the interest of a man to be a boy all his life?" he asked. Within six months, *Common Sense* had gone through twenty-five editions and reached hundreds of thousands of people. "There is great talk of independence," a worried New York Loyalist noted, "the unthinking multitude are mad for it. . . . A pamphlet called Common Sense has carried off . . .

thousands." Paine urged Americans to create independent republican states: "A government of our own is our natural right, 'tis time to part."

## Independence Declared

Inspired by Paine's arguments and beset by armed Loyalists, Patriot conventions urged a break from Britain. In June 1776, Richard Henry Lee presented Virginia's resolution to the Continental Congress: "That these United Colonies are, and of right ought to be, free and independent states." Faced with certain defeat, staunch Loyalists and anti-independence moderates withdrew from the Congress, leaving committed Patriots to take the fateful step. On July 4, 1776, the Congress approved the **Declaration of Independence** (see Documents, p. D-1).

The Declaration's main author, Thomas Jefferson of Virginia, had mobilized resistance to the Coercive Acts with the pamphlet *A Summary View of the Rights of British America* (1774). Now, in the Declaration, he justified independence and republicanism to Americans and the world by vilifying George III: "He has plundered our seas, ravaged our coasts, burned our towns, and destroyed the lives of our people." Such a prince was a "tyrant," Jefferson concluded, and "is unfit to be the ruler of a free people."

Employing the ideas of the European Enlightenment, Jefferson proclaimed a series of "self-evident" truths: "that all men are created equal"; that they possess the "unalienable rights" of "Life, Liberty, and the pursuit

**Independence Declared**

In this painting by John Trumbull, Thomas Jefferson and the other drafters of the Declaration (John Adams of Massachusetts, Roger Sherman of Connecticut, Robert Livingston of New York, and Benjamin Franklin of Pennsylvania) present the document to John Hancock, the president of the Second Continental Congress. One Patriot observer reported that when the Declaration was read at a public meeting in New York City on July 10, a massive statue of George III was "pulled down by the Populace" and its 4,000 pounds of lead melted down to make "Musquet balls" for use against the British troops massed on Staten Island. Yale University Art Gallery/Art Resource, NY.

of Happiness"; that government derives its "just powers from the consent of the governed" and can rightly be overthrown if it "becomes destructive of these ends." By linking these doctrines of individual liberty, **popular sovereignty** (the principle that ultimate power lies in the hands of the electorate), and republican government with American independence, Jefferson established them as the defining political values of the new nation.

For Jefferson, as for Paine, the pen proved mightier than the sword. The Declaration won wide support in France and Germany; at home, it sparked celebrations in rural hamlets and seaport cities, as crowds burned effigies and toppled statues of the king. On July 8, 1776, in Easton, Pennsylvania, a "great number of spectators" heard a reading of the Declaration, "gave their hearty assent with three loud huzzahs, and cried out, 'May God long preserve and unite the Free and Independent States of America.'"

## SUMMARY

Chapters 4 and 5 have focused on a short span of time — a mere two decades — and outlined the plot of a political drama. Act I of that drama, the Great War

for Empire discussed in Chapter 4, prompted British political leaders to implement a program of imperial reform and taxation. Act II, discussed in this chapter, is full of dramatic action, as colonial mobs riot, colonists chafe against restrictions on western lands, Patriot pamphleteers articulate ideologies of resistance, and British ministers search for compromise between claims of parliamentary sovereignty and assertions of colonial autonomy. Act III takes the form of tragedy: the once-proud British Empire dissolves into civil war, an imminent nightmare of death and destruction.

Why did this happen? More than two centuries later, the answers still are not clear. Certainly, the lack of astute leadership in Britain was a major factor. But British leaders faced circumstances that limited their actions: a huge national debt and deep commitments to both a powerful fiscal-military state and the absolute supremacy of Parliament. Moreover, in America, decades of salutary neglect strengthened Patriots' demands for political autonomy and economic opportunity. Artisans, farmers, and aspiring western settlers all feared an oppressive new era in imperial relations. The trajectories of their conflicting intentions and ideas placed Britain and its American possessions on course for a disastrous and fatal collision.

# C H A P T E R   R E V I E W

**MAKE IT STICK**   Go to **LearningCurve** to retain what you've read.

## TERMS TO KNOW   Identify and explain the significance of each term below.

### Key Concepts and Events

Sugar Act of 1764 (p. 155)
vice-admiralty courts (p. 156)
Stamp Act of 1765 (p. 157)
virtual representation (p. 157)
Quartering Act of 1765 (p. 157)
Stamp Act Congress (p. 158)
Sons of Liberty (p. 158)
English common law (p. 159)
natural rights (p. 159)
Declaratory Act of 1766 (p. 160)
Townshend Act of 1767 (p. 161)
nonimportation movement
  (p. 161)

committees of correspondence
  (p. 168)
Tea Act of May 1773 (p. 168)
Coercive Acts (p. 168)
Continental Congress (p. 169)
Continental Association (p. 171)
Dunmore's War (p. 175)
Minutemen (p. 175)
Second Continental Congress
  (p. 176)
Declaration of Independence
  (p. 178)
popular sovereignty (p. 179)

### Key People

George Grenville (p. 155)
John Dickinson (p. 159)
Charles Townshend (p. 160)
Lord North (p. 166)
Samuel Adams (p. 166)
Lord Dunmore (p. 174)
Thomas Paine (p. 178)
Thomas Jefferson (p. 178)

## REVIEW QUESTIONS
Answer these questions to demonstrate your understanding of the chapter's main ideas.

1. As British administrators sought to increase colonial revenues and tighten administrative control, what might have led them to pursue a less confrontational course with the colonies? What factors do you think are most important in explaining the failure of compromise?

2. What kinds of provocation caused colonists to riot or otherwise act directly, even violently, in defense of their interests? How did common law, Enlightenment, and republican ideas shape their thinking as they took action?

3. What compromises were proposed in the colonies as alternatives to independence? Why did Patriots reject them?

4. **THEMATIC UNDERSTANDING** Consider the events listed under "Work, Exchange, and Technology" and "Politics and Power" for the period 1763–1776 on the thematic timeline on page 149. How important were the linkages between economic developments and political ones in these years?

## MAKING CONNECTIONS
Recognize the larger developments and continuities within and across chapters by answering these questions.

1. **ACROSS TIME AND PLACE** Chapter 4 presented a turbulent era, marked by social and cultural conflict and imperial warfare, during which the regions of British North America were disparate and without unity. Yet by 1776 — only thirteen years after the Treaty of Paris ending the Great War for Empire — thirteen of Britain's mainland colonies were prepared to unite in a Declaration of Independence. What happened in that intervening time to strengthen and deepen colonists' sense of common cause? As they drew together to resist imperial authority, what political and cultural resources did they have in common?

2. **VISUAL EVIDENCE** Return to the Paul Revere engraving of the Boston Massacre on page 167. This image was an instrument of political propaganda. What features of the image are most important to its political purpose? Consider his depiction of both the soldiers and the townspeople. Look, too, at the buildings surrounding the crowd, especially the Custom House on the right. List the ways in which Revere invokes the idea of tyranny in this image.

## MORE TO EXPLORE
Start here to learn more about the events discussed in this chapter.

David Armitage, *The Declaration of Independence: A Global History* (2007). Traces the international impact of the Declaration.

Jack P. Greene and J. R. Pole, eds., *A Companion to the American Revolution* (2000). A useful compendium of short essays on topics related to the Revolution.

Woody Holton, *Forced Founders* (1999). Considers the coming of the Revolution in Virginia.

Maya Jasanoff, *Liberty's Exiles* (2011). A compelling narrative of Loyalist experiences in the Revolution.

Andrew O'Shaughnessy, *The Men Who Lost America* (2013). A British view of the crisis.

*Liberty! The American Revolution* (PBS video) and its companion Web site: **pbs.org/ktca/liberty/**. A useful overview of the Revolutionary movement.

**TIMELINE**    Ask yourself why this chapter begins and ends with these dates
and then identify the links among related events.

| | |
|---|---|
| **1763** | • Proclamation Line limits white settlement |
| **1764** | • Sugar Act and Currency Act<br>• Colonists oppose vice-admiralty courts |
| **1765** | • Stamp Act imposes direct tax<br>• Quartering Act requires barracks for British troops<br>• Stamp Act Congress meets<br>• Americans boycott British goods |
| **1766** | • First compromise: Stamp Act repealed<br>• Declaratory Act passed |
| **1767** | • Townshend duties |
| **1768** | • Second American boycott |
| **1770** | • Second compromise: partial repeal of Townshend Act<br>• Boston Massacre |
| **1772** | • Committees of correspondence form |
| **1773** | • Tea Act leads to Boston Tea Party |
| **1774** | • Coercive Acts punish Massachusetts<br>• Dunmore's War against the Shawnees<br>• Continental Congress meets<br>• Third American boycott |
| **1775** | • General Gage marches to Lexington and Concord<br>• Second Continental Congress creates Continental army<br>• Lord Dunmore recruits Loyalist slaves<br>• Patriots invade Canada and skirmish with Loyalists in South<br>• Western settlers occupy Kentucky |
| **1776** | • Thomas Paine's *Common Sense*<br>• Declaration of Independence |

**KEY TURNING POINTS:** The Boston Tea Party (1773), the Coercive Acts (1774), and the first
Continental Congress (1774). What did Parliament hope to achieve with the Coercive Acts?
How did the decision to convene a continent-wide congress demonstrate the failure of Parliament's efforts?

# 6

**CHAPTER**

# Making War and Republican Governments 1776–1789

When Patriots in Frederick County, Maryland, demanded his allegiance to their cause in 1776, Robert Gassaway would have none of it. "It was better for the poor people to lay down their arms and pay the duties and taxes laid upon them by King and Parliament than to be brought into slavery and commanded and ordered about [by you]," he told them. The story was much the same in Farmington, Connecticut, where Patriot officials imprisoned Nathaniel Jones and seventeen other men for "remaining neutral." In Pennsylvania, Quakers accused of Loyalism were rounded up, jailed, and charged with treason, and some were hanged for aiding the British cause. Everywhere, the outbreak of fighting in 1776 forced families to choose the Loyalist or the Patriot side.

The Patriots' control of most local governments gave them an edge in this battle. Patriot leaders organized militia units and recruited volunteers for the Continental army, a ragtag force that surprisingly held its own on the battlefield. "I admire the American troops tremendously!" exclaimed a French officer. "It is incredible that soldiers composed of every age, even children of fifteen, of whites and blacks, almost naked, unpaid, and rather poorly fed, can march so well and withstand fire so steadfastly."

Military service created political commitment, and vice versa. Many Patriot leaders encouraged Americans not only to support the war but also to take an active role in government. As more people did so, their political identities changed. Previously, Americans had lived within a social world dominated by the links of family, kinship, and locality. Now, the abstract bonds of citizenship connected them directly to more distant institutions of government. "From subjects to citizens the difference is immense," remarked South Carolina Patriot David Ramsay. By repudiating monarchical rule and raising a democratic army, the Patriots launched the age of republican revolutions.

Soon republicanism would throw France into turmoil and inspire revolutionaries in Spain's American colonies. The independence of the Anglo-American colonies, remarked the Venezuelan political leader Francisco de Miranda, who had been in New York and Philadelphia at the end of the American Revolution, "was bound to be . . . the infallible preliminary to our own [independence movement]." The Patriot uprising of 1776 set in motion a process that gradually replaced an Atlantic colonial system that spanned the Americas with an American system of new nations.

**IDENTIFY THE BIG IDEA**

How revolutionary was the American Revolution? What political, social, and economic changes did it produce, and what stayed the same?

**General Washington, 1780**   By war's end, George Washington was a hero on both sides of the Atlantic. This engraving, printed in Paris in 1780, shows him with various British bills and declarations in tatters at his feet while he holds copies of the Declaration of Independence and the Treaty of Alliance with France. In the background of this vaguely Orientalized scene, a black slave—presumably William Lee, Washington's valet and constant companion during the Revolution—saddles his horse. Anne S. K. Brown Military Collection, Brown University Library.

# The Trials of War, 1776–1778

The Declaration of Independence appeared just as the British launched a full-scale military assault. For two years, British troops manhandled the Continental army. A few inspiring American victories kept the rebellion alive, but during the winters of 1776 and 1777, the Patriot cause hung in the balance.

## War in the North

Once the British resorted to military force, few Europeans gave the rebels a chance. The population of Great Britain was 11 million; the colonies, 2.5 million, 20 percent of whom were enslaved Africans. Moreover, the British government had access to the immense wealth generated by the South Atlantic System and the emerging Industrial Revolution. Britain also had the most powerful navy in the world, a standing army of 48,000 Britons plus thousands of German (Hessian) soldiers, and the support of thousands of American Loyalists and powerful Indian coalitions. In the Carolinas, the Cherokees resisted colonists' demands for their lands by allying with the British, as did four of the six Iroquois nations of New York (Map 6.1). In the Ohio country, Shawnees and their allies, armed by the British, attacked the new Kentucky settlements.

By contrast, the Americans were economically and militarily weak. They lacked a strong central government and a reliable source of tax revenue. Their new Continental army, commanded by General George Washington, consisted of 18,000 poorly trained and inexperienced recruits.

To demonstrate Britain's military superiority, the prime minister, Lord North, ordered General William Howe to capture New York City. His strategy was to seize control of the Hudson River and thereby isolate the radical Patriots in New England from the colonies to the south. As the Second Continental Congress declared independence in Philadelphia in July 1776, Howe landed 32,000 troops — British regulars and German mercenaries — outside New York City. In August 1776, Howe defeated the Americans in the **Battle of Long Island** and forced their retreat to Manhattan Island. There, Howe outflanked Washington's troops and nearly trapped them. Outgunned and outmaneuvered, the Continental army again retreated, eventually crossing the Hudson River to New Jersey.

**UNDERSTAND POINTS OF VIEW**

Why was control of New York City Britain's first military objective in the emerging war?

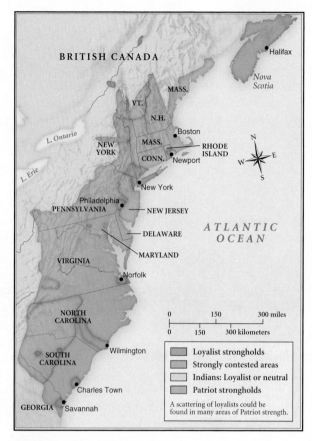

**MAP 6.1**

**Patriot and Loyalist Strongholds**

Patriots were in the majority in most of the thirteen mainland colonies and used their control of local governments to funnel men, money, and supplies to the rebel cause. Although Loyalists could be found in every colony, their strongholds were limited to Nova Scotia, eastern New York, New Jersey, and certain areas in the South. However, most Native American peoples favored the British cause and bolstered the power of Loyalist militias in central New York (see Map 6.3) and in the Carolina backcountry.

By December, the British army had pushed the rebels across New Jersey and over the Delaware River into Pennsylvania.

From the Patriots' perspective, winter came just in time. Following eighteenth-century custom, the British halted their military campaign for the cold months, allowing the Americans to catch them off guard. On Christmas night 1776, Washington crossed the Delaware River and staged a successful surprise attack on Trenton, New Jersey, where he forced the surrender of 1,000 German soldiers. In early January 1777, the Continental army won a small victory at nearby Princeton (Map 6.2). But these minor triumphs could

**MAP 6.2**

**The War in the North, 1776–1777**

In 1776, the British army drove Washington's forces across New Jersey into Pennsylvania. The Americans counterattacked successfully at Trenton and Princeton and then set up winter headquarters in Morristown. In 1777, British forces stayed on the offensive. General Howe attacked the Patriot capital, Philadelphia, from the south and captured it in early October. Meanwhile, General Burgoyne and Colonel St. Leger launched simultaneous invasions from Canada. With the help of thousands of New England militiamen, American troops commanded by General Horatio Gates defeated Burgoyne in August at Bennington, Vermont, and in October at Saratoga, New York, the military turning point in the war.

not mask British military superiority. "These are the times," wrote Thomas Paine, "that try men's souls."

## Armies and Strategies

Thanks in part to General Howe, the rebellion survived. Howe had opposed the Coercive Acts of 1774 and still hoped for a political compromise. So he did not try to destroy the American army but instead tried to show its weakness and persuade the Continental

Congress to give up the struggle. Howe's restrained tactics cost Britain the opportunity to nip the rebellion in the bud. For his part, Washington acted cautiously to avoid a major defeat: "On our Side the War should be defensive," he told Congress. His strategy was to draw the British away from the seacoast, extend their lines of supply, and sap their morale.

Congress had promised Washington a regular force of 75,000 men, but the Continental army never reached even a third of that number. Yeomen, refusing to be

**The Battle of Princeton**

Black smoke from burning buildings partially obscures the sun as the muzzle flash from an American cannon lights up the battlefield. Pursued by Cornwallis after his surprise attack and victory at nearby Trenton, Washington (on horseback to the right of the flag) confronted three regiments of redcoats at Princeton. The Americans had an advantage in numbers and put the British to flight, but only after withstanding the bayonet charge depicted in the right-center of William Mercer's painting. Courtesy of the Historical Society of Pennsylvania Collection Atwater Kent Museum of Philadelphia.

"Haras'd with callouts" that took them away from their families and farms, would serve only in local militias. When the Virginia gentry imposed a military draft and three years of service on propertyless men — the "Lazy fellows who lurk about and are pests to Society" — they resisted so fiercely that the legislature had to pay them substantial bounties and agree to shorter terms of service. The Continental soldiers recruited in Maryland by General William Smallwood were poor American youths and older foreign-born men, often British ex-convicts and former indentured servants. Most enlisted for the $20 cash bonus (about $2,000 today) and the promise of 100 acres of land.

Molding such recruits into an effective fighting force was nearly impossible. Inexperienced soldiers panicked in the face of British attacks; thousands deserted, unwilling to submit to the discipline of military life. The soldiers who stayed resented the contempt their officers had for the "camp followers," the women who made do with the meager supplies provided to feed and care for the troops. General Philip Schuyler of New York complained that his troops were "destitute of provisions, without camp equipage, with little ammunition, and not a single piece of cannon."

The Continental army was not only poorly supplied but was also held in suspicion by Radical Whig Patriots, who believed that a standing army was a threat to liberty. Even in wartime, they preferred militias to a professional fighting force. Given these handicaps, Washington and his army were fortunate to have escaped an overwhelming defeat.

## Victory at Saratoga

After Howe failed to achieve an overwhelming victory, Lord North and his colonial secretary, Lord George Germain, launched another major military campaign in 1777. Isolating New England remained the primary goal. To achieve it, Germain planned a three-pronged

**IDENTIFY CAUSES**

What factors made it difficult for the Continental Congress to create an effective army?

attack converging on Albany, New York. General John Burgoyne would lead a large contingent of regulars south from Quebec, Colonel Barry St. Leger and a force of Iroquois would attack from the west, and General Howe would lead troops north from New York City.

Howe instead decided to attack Philadelphia, the home of the Continental Congress, hoping to end the rebellion with a single decisive blow. But instead of marching quickly across New Jersey, Howe loaded his troops onto boats and sailed up the Chesapeake Bay to attack Philadelphia from the south. The plan worked. Howe's troops easily outflanked the American positions along Brandywine Creek in Delaware and, in late September, marched triumphantly into Philadelphia. However, the capture of the rebels' capital did not end the uprising; the Continental Congress, determined to continue the struggle, fled to the countryside.

Howe's slow campaign against Philadelphia contributed to the defeat of Burgoyne's army at **Saratoga**. Burgoyne's troops had at first advanced quickly, overwhelming the American defenses at Fort Ticonderoga in early July and driving south toward the Hudson River. Then they stalled. Burgoyne — nicknamed "Gentleman Johnny" — was used to high living and had fought in Europe in a leisurely fashion; believing his large army would easily dominate the rebels, he stopped early each day to pitch comfortable tents and eat elaborate dinners with his officers. The American troops led by General Horatio Gates also slowed Burgoyne's progress by felling huge trees in his path and raiding British supply lines to Canada.

At summer's end, Burgoyne's army of 6,000 British and German troops and 600 Loyalists and Indians was stuck near Saratoga, New York. Desperate for food and horses, in August the British raided nearby Bennington, Vermont, but were beaten back by 2,000 American militiamen. Patriot forces in the Mohawk Valley also threw St. Leger and the Iroquois into retreat. Making matters worse, the British commander in New York City recalled 4,000 troops he had sent toward Albany and ordered them to Philadelphia to bolster Howe's force. While Burgoyne waited in vain for help, thousands of Patriot militiamen from Massachusetts, New Hampshire, and New York joined Gates, blocking Burgoyne in a series of skirmishes that finally gave the British no avenue of escape. The Patriots "swarmed around the army like birds of prey," reported an English sergeant, and in October 1777, they forced Burgoyne to surrender.

The victory at Saratoga was the turning point of the war. The Patriots captured more than 5,000 British

**Joseph Brant**

Mohawk chief Thayendanegea, known to whites as Joseph Brant, was a devout member of the Church of England and helped to translate the Bible into the Mohawk language. Brant persuaded four of the six Iroquois nations to support Britain in the war. In 1778 and 1779, he led Iroquois warriors and Tory rangers in devastating attacks on American settlements in the Wyoming Valley of Pennsylvania and Cherry Valley in New York. In this 1797 portrait, artist Charles Willson Peale has portrayed Brant with European features. Independence National Historic Park.

troops and ensured the diplomatic success of American representatives in Paris, who won a military alliance with France.

## The Perils of War

The Patriots' triumph at Saratoga was tempered by wartime difficulties. A British naval blockade cut off supplies of European manufactures and disrupted the New England fishing industry; meanwhile, the British occupation of Boston, New York, and Philadelphia reduced trade. As Patriots, along with unemployed artisans and laborers, moved to the countryside, New York City's population declined from 21,000 to 10,000. The British blockade cut tobacco exports in the Chesapeake, so planters grew grain to sell to the contending armies. All across the land, farmers and artisans adapted to a war economy.

With goods now scarce, governments requisitioned military supplies directly from the people. In 1776, Connecticut officials asked the citizens of Hartford to

**American Militiamen**

Beset by continuing shortages of cloth, the Patriot army dressed in a variety of uniforms and fabrics. This German engraving, taken from a drawing by a Hessian officer, shows two American militiamen (one of them barefoot) wearing hunting shirts and trousers made of ticking, the strong linen fabric often used to cover mattresses and pillows. Anne S. K. Brown Military Collection, Brown University.

provide 1,000 coats and 1,600 shirts, and soldiers echoed their pleas. After losing all his shirts "except the one on my back" in the Battle of Long Island, Captain Edward Rogers told his wife that "the making of Cloath . . . must go on." Patriot women responded; in Elizabeth, New Jersey, they promised "upwards of 100,000 yards of linnen and woolen cloth." Other women assumed the burdens of farmwork while their men were away at war and acquired a taste for decision making. "We have sow'd our oats as you desired," Sarah Cobb Paine wrote to her absent husband. "Had I been master I should have planted it to Corn." Their self-esteem boosted by wartime activities, some women expected greater legal rights in the new republican society.

Still, goods remained scarce and pricey. Hard-pressed consumers assailed shopkeepers as "enemies, extortioners, and monopolizers" and called for government regulation. But when the New England states imposed price ceilings in 1777, many farmers and artisans refused to sell their goods. Ultimately, a government official admitted, consumers had to pay the higher market prices "or submit to starving."

The fighting endangered tens of thousands of civilians. A British officer, Lord Rawdon, favored giving "free liberty to the soldiers to ravage [the country] at will, that these infatuated creatures may feel what a calamity war is." As British and American armies marched back and forth across New Jersey, they forced Patriot and Loyalist families to flee their homes to escape arrest — or worse. Soldiers and partisans looted farms, and disorderly troops harassed and raped women and girls. "An army, even a friendly one, are a dreadful scourge to any people," wrote one Connecticut soldier. "You cannot imagine what devastation and distress mark their steps."

The war divided many farm communities. Patriots formed committees of safety to collect taxes and seized the property of those who refused to pay. "Every Body submitted to our Sovereign Lord the Mob," lamented a Loyalist preacher. In parts of Maryland, the number of "nonassociators" — those who refused to join either side — was so large that they successfully defied Patriot mobs. "Stand off you dammed rebel sons of bitches," shouted Robert Davis of Anne Arundel County, "I will shoot you if you come any nearer."

## Financial Crisis

Such defiance exposed the weakness of Patriot governments. Most states were afraid to raise taxes, so officials issued bonds to secure gold or silver from wealthy individuals. When those funds ran out, individual states financed the war by issuing so much paper money — some $260 million all told — that it lost worth, and most people refused to accept it at face value. In North Carolina, even tax collectors eventually rejected the state's currency.

The finances of the Continental Congress collapsed, too, despite the efforts of Philadelphia merchant Robert Morris, the government's chief treasury official. Because the Congress lacked the authority to impose taxes, Morris relied on funds requisitioned from the states, but the states paid late or not at all. So Morris secured loans from France and Holland and sold Continental loan certificates to some thirteen thousand firms and individuals. All the while, the Congress was issuing paper money — some $200 million between 1776 and 1779 — which, like state currencies, quickly fell in value. In 1778, a family needed $7 in Continental bills to buy goods worth $1 in gold or silver. As the exchange rate deteriorated — to 42 to 1 in

## Paper Currency

Testifying to their independent status, the new state governments printed their own currencies. Rejecting the English system of pounds and shillings, Virginia used the Spanish gold dollar as its basic unit of currency, although the equivalent in English pounds is also shown. Initially, $1,200 was equal to £360 — a ratio of 3.3 to 1. By 1781, Virginia had printed so much paper money to pay its soldiers and wartime expenses that the value of its currency had depreciated. It now took $40 in Virginia currency to buy the same amount of goods as £1 sterling. The American Numismatic Society.

1779, 100 to 1 in 1780, and 146 to 1 in 1781 — it sparked social upheaval. In Boston, a mob of women accosted merchant Thomas Boyleston, "seazd him by his Neck," and forced him to sell his wares at traditional prices. In rural Ulster County, New York, women told the committee of safety to lower food prices or "their husbands and sons shall fight no more." As morale crumbled, Patriot leaders feared the rebellion would collapse.

## Valley Forge

Fears reached their peak during the winter of 1777. While Howe's army lived comfortably in Philadelphia, Washington's army retreated 20 miles to **Valley Forge**, where 12,000 soldiers and hundreds of camp followers suffered horribly. "The army . . . now begins to grow sickly," a surgeon confided to his diary. "Poor food — hard lodging — cold weather — fatigue — nasty clothes — nasty cookery. . . . Why are we sent here to starve and freeze?" Nearby farmers refused to help. Some were pacifists, Quakers and German sectarians unwilling to support either side. Others looked out for their own families, selling grain for gold from British quartermasters but refusing depreciated Continental currency. "Such a dearth of public spirit, and want of public virtue," lamented Washington. By spring, more than 200 officers had resigned, 1,000 hungry soldiers had deserted, and another 3,000 had died from malnutrition and disease. That winter at Valley Forge took as many American lives as had two years of fighting.

In this dark hour, Baron von Steuben raised the readiness of the American army. A former Prussian military officer, von Steuben was one of a handful of republican-minded foreign aristocrats who joined the American cause. Appointed as inspector general of the

Continental army, he instituted a strict drill system and encouraged officers to become more professional. Thanks to von Steuben, the smaller army that emerged from Valley Forge in the spring of 1778 was a much tougher and better-disciplined force.

# The Path to Victory, 1778–1783

Wars are often won by astute diplomacy, and so it was with the War of Independence. The Patriots' prospects improved dramatically in 1778, when the Continental Congress concluded a military alliance with France, the most powerful nation in Europe. The alliance gave the Americans desperately needed money, supplies, and, eventually, troops. And it confronted Britain with an international war that challenged its domination of the Atlantic and Indian oceans.

## The French Alliance

France and America were unlikely partners. France was Catholic and a monarchy; the United States was Protestant and a federation of republics. From 1689 to 1763, the two peoples had been enemies: New Englanders had brutally uprooted the French population from Acadia (Nova Scotia) in 1755, and the French and their Indian allies had raided British settlements. But the Comte de Vergennes, the French foreign minister, was determined to avenge the loss of Canada during the Great War for Empire (see Chapter 4) and persuaded King Louis XVI to provide the rebellious colonies with a secret loan and much-needed gunpowder. When news of the rebel victory at Saratoga reached Paris in December 1777, Vergennes sought a formal alliance.

Benjamin Franklin and other American diplomats craftily exploited France's rivalry with Britain to win an explicit commitment to American independence. The Treaty of Alliance of February 1778 specified that once France entered the war, neither partner would sign a separate peace without the "liberty, sovereignty, and independence" of the United States. In return, the Continental Congress agreed to recognize any French conquests in the West Indies. "France and America," warned Britain's Lord Stormont, "were indissolubly leagued for our destruction."

The alliance gave new life to the Patriots' cause. "There has been a great change in this state since the news from France," a Patriot soldier reported from Pennsylvania. Farmers — "mercenary wretches," he called them — "were as eager for Continental Money now as they were a few weeks ago for British gold." Its confidence bolstered, the Continental Congress addressed the demands of the officer corps. Most officers were gentlemen who equipped themselves and raised volunteers; in return, they insisted on lifetime military pensions at half pay. John Adams condemned the officers for "scrambling for rank and pay like apes for nuts," but General Washington urged the Congress to grant the pensions: "The salvation of the cause depends upon it." The Congress reluctantly granted the officers half pay, but only for seven years.

Meanwhile, the war had become unpopular in Britain. At first, George III was determined to crush the rebellion. If America won independence, he warned Lord North, "the West Indies must follow them. Ireland would soon follow the same plan and be a separate state, then this island would be reduced to itself, and soon would be a poor island indeed." Stunned by the defeat at Saratoga, however, the king changed his mind. To thwart an American alliance with France, he authorized North to seek a negotiated settlement. In February 1778, North persuaded Parliament to repeal the Tea and Prohibitory Acts and, amazingly, to renounce its power to tax the colonies. But the Patriots, now allied with France and committed to independence, rejected North's overture.

**EXPLAIN CONSEQUENCES**
What were the most important results of the Patriot victory at Saratoga?

## War in the South

The French alliance did not bring a rapid end to the war. When France entered the conflict in June 1778, it hoped to seize all of Britain's sugar islands. Spain, which joined the war against Britain in 1779, aimed to regain Florida and the fortress of Gibraltar at the entrance to the Mediterranean Sea.

**Britain's Southern Strategy**    For its part, the British government revised its military strategy to defend the West Indies and capture the rich tobacco- and rice-growing colonies: Virginia, the Carolinas, and Georgia. Once conquered, the ministry planned to use the Scottish Highlanders in the Carolinas and other Loyalists to hold them. It had already mobilized the Cherokees and Delawares against the land-hungry Americans and knew that the Patriots' fears of slave uprisings weakened them militarily (Map 6.3). As South Carolina Patriots admitted to the Continental Congress, they could raise only a few recruits "by reason of the great proportion of citizens necessary to remain at home to prevent insurrection among the Negroes."

The large number of slaves in the South made the Revolution a "triangular war," in which African Americans constituted a strategic problem for Patriots and a tempting, if dangerous, opportunity for the British. Britain actively recruited slaves to its cause. The effort began with Dunmore's controversial proclamation in November 1775 recruiting slaves to his Ethiopian Regiment (see Chapter 5). In 1779, the **Philipsburg Proclamation** declared that any slave who deserted a rebel master would receive protection, freedom, and land from Great Britain. Together, these proclamations led some 30,000 African Americans to take refuge behind British lines. George Washington initially barred blacks from the Continental army, but he relented in 1777. By war's end, African Americans could enlist in every state but South Carolina and Georgia, and some 5,000 — slave and free — fought for the Patriot cause (Thinking Like a Historian, p. 192).

It fell to Sir Henry Clinton — acutely aware of the role slaves might play — to implement Britain's southern strategy. From the British army's main base in New York City, Clinton launched a seaborne attack on Savannah, Georgia. Troops commanded by Colonel Archibald Campbell captured the town in December 1778. Mobilizing hundreds of blacks to transport supplies, Campbell moved inland and captured Augusta early in 1779. By year's end, Clinton's forces and local Loyalists controlled coastal Georgia and had 10,000 troops poised for an assault on South Carolina.

In 1780, British forces marched from victory to victory (Map 6.4). In May, Clinton forced the surrender of Charleston, South Carolina, and its garrison of 5,000 troops. Then Lord Charles Cornwallis assumed control of the British forces and, at Camden, defeated an

**MAP 6.3**

**Native Americans and the War in the West, 1778–1779**

Many Indian peoples remained neutral, but others, fearing land-hungry Patriot farmers, used British-supplied guns to raid American settlements. To thwart attacks by militant Shawnees, Cherokees, and Delawares, a Patriot militia led by George Rogers Clark captured the British fort and supply depot at Vincennes on the Wabash River in February 1779. To the north, Patriot generals John Sullivan and James Clinton defeated pro-British Indian forces near Tioga (on the New York–Pennsylvania border) in August 1779 and then systematically destroyed villages and crops throughout the lands of the Iroquois.

American force commanded by General Horatio Gates, the hero of Saratoga. Only 1,200 Patriot militiamen joined Gates at Camden, a fifth of the number at Saratoga. Cornwallis took control of South Carolina, and hundreds of African Americans fled to freedom behind British lines. The southern strategy was working.

Then the tide of battle turned. Thanks to another republican-minded European aristocrat, the Marquis de Lafayette, France finally dispatched troops to the American mainland. A longtime supporter of the American cause, Lafayette persuaded King Louis XVI to send General Comte de Rochambeau and 5,500 men

to Newport, Rhode Island, in 1780. There, they threatened the British forces holding New York City.

**Guerrilla Warfare in the Carolinas**  Meanwhile, Washington dispatched General Nathanael Greene to recapture the Carolinas, where he found "a country that has been ravaged and plundered by both friends and enemies." Greene put local militiamen, who had been "without discipline and addicted to plundering," under strong leaders and unleashed them on less mobile British forces. In October 1780, Patriot militia defeated a regiment of Loyalists at King's Mountain, South Carolina, taking about one thousand prisoners.

## The Black Soldier's Dilemma

For African American slaves, the Revolution offered no clear path to freedom. Some slaves agreed to fight for Britain because of its promise to liberate slaves who fought against their masters. While some were freed, many others died fighting, were forced into servitude in the army, or even sold into slavery in the West Indies. Patriots at first refused the service of black soldiers, then enlisted them in small numbers, but always upheld the property rights of masters.

---

1. **Dunmore's Proclamation, 1775.** *Virginia's Governor Dunmore issued this proclamation in response to the emerging rebellion and formed his recruits into the so-called Ethiopian Regiment.*

To defeat such unreasonable Purposes . . . that the Peace, and good Order of this Colony may be again restored . . . I have thought fit to issue this my Proclamation, hereby declaring, that until the aforesaid good Purposes can be obtained, I do in Virtue of the Power and Authority to me given, by His majesty, determine to execute Martial Law, and cause the same to be executed throughout this Colony: and to the end that Peace and good Order may the sooner be [effected], I do require every Person capable of bearing Arms, to [resort] to His majesty's standard, or be looked upon as Traitors to His [majesty] . . . I do hereby further declare all indentured Servants, Negroes, or others, (appertaining to Rebels,) free that are able and willing to bear Arms, they joining His majesty's Troops as soon as may be, for the more speedily reducing this Colony to a proper Sense of their Duty.

2. **Virginia's response to Dunmore's Proclamation, 1775.** *A month later, Virginia's General Assembly issued the following response.*

WHEREAS lord Dunmore, by his proclamation, dated on board the ship William, off Norfolk, the 7th day of November 1775, hath offered freedom to such able-bodied slaves as are willing to join him, and take up arms, against the good people of this colony, giving thereby encouragement to a general insurrection . . . it is enacted, that all negro or other slaves, conspiring to rebel or make insurrection, shall suffer death. . . . We think it proper to declare, that all slaves who have been, or shall be seduced, by his lordship's proclamation, or other arts, to desert their masters' service, and take up arms against the inhabitants of this colony, shall be liable to such punishment as shall hereafter be directed by the General Convention. . . . [A]ll such, who have taken this unlawful and wicked step, may return in safety to their duty, and escape the punishment due their crimes. . . . And we do

farther earnestly recommend it to all humane and benevolent persons in this colony to explain and make known this our offer of mercy to those unfortunate people.

3. **Runaway advertisement, 1775.** *Titus—or, as he was later known, Captain Tye of the Ethiopian Regiment—abandoned his Delaware master in response to Dunmore's Proclamation.*

**THREE POUNDS Reward.**
RUN away from the subscriber, living in Shrewsbury, in the county of Monmouth, New-Jersey, a NEGROE man, named TITUS, but may probably change his name; he is about 21 years of age, not very black, near 6 feet high; had on a grey homespun coat, brown breeches, blue and white stockings, and took with him a wallet, drawn up at one end with a string, in which was a quantity of clothes. Whoever takes up said Negroe, and secures him in any goal, or brings him to me, shall be entitled to the above reward of *Three Pounds* proc. and all reasonable charges, paid by
Nov. 8, 1775. § JOHN CORLIS.

Source: Courtesy American Antiquarian Society.

4. **Report of Bernardo de Gálvez, 1780.** *Fighting against the British in support of the Patriots, Louisiana governor Bernardo de Gálvez raised a mixed regiment, almost half of whom were slaves and free people of color from New Orleans. He praised their efforts in this report of his campaign.*

No less deserving of eulogy are the companies of Negroes and free Mulattoes who were continually occupied in the outposts, in false attacks, and discoveries, exchanging shots with the enemy . . . conduct[ing] themselves with as much valor and generosity as the whites.

5. **Boston King gains his freedom, 1783.** *In 1780, Boston King, like many other southern slaves, escaped to the British army. Here he describes his experiences at war's end.*

About this time, peace was restored between America and Great Britain which diffused universal joy among all parties except us, who had escaped slavery and taken refuge in the English army; for a report prevailed at New-York that all the slaves, in number two thousand, were to be delivered up to their masters, altho' some of them had been three or four years among the English. This dreadful rumour filled us with inexpressible anguish and terror, especially when we saw our old masters coming from Virginia, North-Carolina and other parts and seizing upon slaves in the streets of New-York, or even dragging them out of their beds. Many of the slaves had very cruel masters, so that the thought of returning home with them embittered life to us. For some days we lost our appetite for food, and sleep departed from our eyes. The English had compassion upon us in the day of our distress, and issued out a Proclamation importing "That all slaves should be free who had taken refuge in the British lines and claimed the sanction and privileges of the Proclamations respecting the security and protection of Negroes." In consequence of this, each of us received a certificate from the commanding officer at New-York, which dispelled our fears and filled us with joy and gratitude.

6. **Jehu Grant is re-enslaved, 1778.** *Jehu Grant of Narragansett, Rhode Island, was owned by a Loyalist. In August 1777 he escaped and joined the Patriot side; ten months later, his master tracked him down and reclaimed him. In 1837 Grant applied for a pension from the U.S. government and supplied the following narrative of his experience. His application was denied.*

[I] enlisted as a soldier but was put to the service of a teamster in the summer and a waiter in the winter . . . I was then grown to manhood, in the full vigor and strength of life, and heard much about the cruel and arbitrary things done by the British. Their ships lay within a few miles of my master's house, which stood near the shore, and I was confident that my master traded with them, and I suffered much from fear that I should be sent aboard a ship of war. This I disliked. But when I saw liberty poles and the people all engaged for the support of freedom, I could not but like and be pleased with such thing (God forgive me if I sinned in so feeling). And living on the borders of Rhode Island, where whole companies of colored people enlisted, it added to my fears and dread of being sold to the British. These considerations induced me to enlist into the American army, where I served faithful about ten months, when my master found and took me home. Had I been taught to read or understand the precepts of the Gospel, "Servants obey your master," I might have done otherwise, notwithstanding the songs of liberty that saluted my ear, thrilled through my heart.

Sources: (1) Lord Dunmore's Proclamation, Learn NC, North Carolina Digital History "Revolutionary North Carolina," www.learnnc.org; (2) J. N. Brenaman, *A History of Virginia Conventions* (Richmond: J. L. Hill Printing Company, 1902), p. 30; (4) Thomas Truxtun Moebs, *Black Soldiers-Black Sailors-Black Ink: Research Guide on African-Americans in U. S. Military History, 1526–1900* (Chesapeake Bay, Paris: Moebs Publishing Company, 1994), 1125; (5) Boston King, *Book of Negroes* (New York, 1783), in Simon Schama, *Rough Crossings: Britain, the Slaves and the American Revolution* (New York: HarperCollins, 2006), 107, 150; (6) Jehu Grant, To Hon. J. L. Edwards, Commissioner of Pension, 1836, in *The Revolution Remembered: Eyewitness Accounts of the War for Independence,* ed. John C. Dann (Chicago: University of Chicago Press, 1980), 27–28.

## ANALYZING THE EVIDENCE

1. Why was Dunmore willing to offer freedom to slaves (source 1) when they were a recognized form of property under the British Empire? What assumptions about the loyalties of slaves underlie the response of the Virginia assembly (source 2)?

2. Why might Louisiana governor Bernardo de Gálvez (source 4) have made a point of praising the contributions of black soldiers to the Patriot cause?

3. Compare the runaway ad for Titus (source 3) and the narratives of Boston King and Jehu Grant (sources 5 and 6). What goals did British officers hope to achieve in their relations with slaves? What Patriot values trumped slaves' individual liberties during and after the war?

## PUTTING IT ALL TOGETHER

Considering these sources along with the chapter contents and what you've learned in class, write a short essay that explains how the presence of slaves created a "triangular war" in the South, assesses the choices that individual slaves had to make during the Revolution, and considers how the differences in the institution of slavery between northern and southern colonies shaped slaves' experiences in the war.

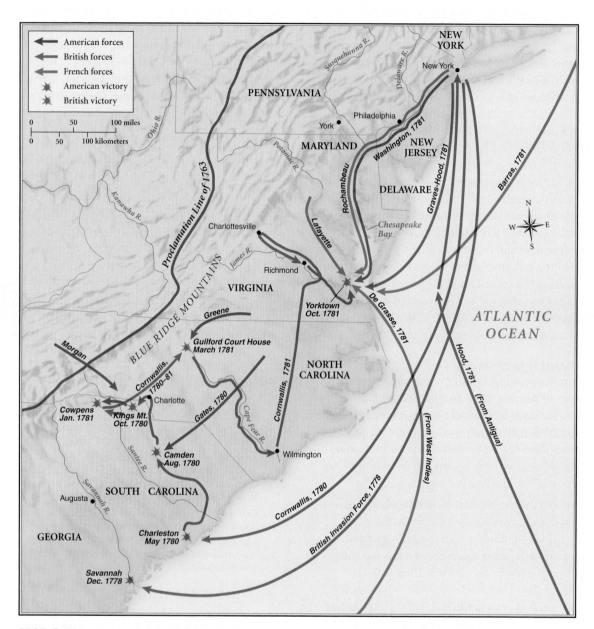

**MAP 6.4**

**The War in the South, 1778–1781**

Britain's southern military strategy started well. British forces captured Savannah in December 1778, took control of Georgia during 1779, and vanquished Charleston in May 1780. Over the next eighteen months, brutal warfare between the British troops and Loyalist units and the Continental army and militia raged in the interior of the Carolinas and ended in a stalemate. Hoping to break the deadlock, British general Charles Cornwallis carried the battle into Virginia in 1781. A Franco-American army led by Washington and Lafayette, with the help of the French fleet under Admiral de Grasse, surrounded Cornwallis's forces on the Yorktown Peninsula and forced their surrender.

American guerrillas commanded by the "Swamp Fox," General Francis Marion, also won a series of small but fierce battles. Then, in January 1781, General Daniel Morgan led an American force to a bloody victory at Cowpens, South Carolina. In March, Greene's soldiers fought Cornwallis's seasoned army to a draw at North Carolina's Guilford Court House. Weakened by this war of attrition, the British general decided to concede the Carolinas to Greene and seek a decisive victory in Virginia. There, many Patriot militiamen had refused to take up arms, claiming that "the Rich wanted the Poor to fight for them."

Exploiting these social divisions, Cornwallis moved easily through the Tidewater region of Virginia in the

**Francis Marion Crossing the Pedee River**

Francis Marion was a master of the ferocious guerrilla fighting that characterized the war in South Carolina. Though Patriot general Horatio Gates had little confidence in him, Marion led an irregular militia brigade in several successful attacks. After chasing Marion into a swamp, British general Banastre Tarleton declared, "As for this damned old fox, the Devil himself could not catch him." Soon Patriots began calling Marion the Swamp Fox. In 1851, William T. Ranney painted Marion (on horseback in a white shirt and blue coat) and his men crossing the Pedee River in flatboats. Ranney included an unidentified (and possibly fictionalized) black oarsman. Amon Carter Museum, Fort Worth, Texas, William T. Ranney (1813–1857). Marion Crossing the Peedee, oil on canvas, 1850.

early summer of 1781. Reinforcements sent from New York and commanded by General Benedict Arnold, the infamous Patriot traitor, bolstered his ranks. As Arnold and Cornwallis sparred with an American force led by Lafayette near the York Peninsula, Washington was informed that France had finally sent its powerful West Indian fleet to North America, and he devised an audacious plan. Feigning an assault on New York City, he secretly marched General Rochambeau's army from Rhode Island to Virginia. Simultaneously, the French fleet took control of Chesapeake Bay. By the time the British discovered Washington's scheme, Cornwallis was surrounded, his 9,500-man army outnumbered 2 to 1 on land and cut off from reinforcement or retreat by sea. In a hopeless position, Cornwallis surrendered at **Yorktown** in October 1781.

The Franco-American victory broke the resolve of the British government. "Oh God! It is all over!" Lord North exclaimed. Isolated diplomatically in Europe, stymied militarily in America, and lacking public support at home, the British ministry gave up active prosecution of the war on the American mainland.

## The Patriot Advantage

How could mighty Britain, victorious in the Great War for Empire, lose to a motley rebel army? The British ministry pointed to a series of blunders by the military leadership. Why had Howe not ruthlessly pursued Washington's army in 1776? Why had Howe and Burgoyne failed to coordinate their attacks in 1777? Why had Cornwallis marched deep into the Patriot-dominated state of Virginia in 1781?

**IDENTIFY CAUSES**

What were the keys to the Patriot victory in the South?

Historians acknowledge British mistakes, but they also attribute the rebels' victory to French aid and the inspired leadership of George Washington. Astutely deferring to elected officials, Washington won the support of the Continental Congress and the state governments. Confident of his military abilities, he pursued a defensive strategy that minimized casualties and maintained the morale of his officers and soldiers through five difficult years of war. Moreover, the Patriots' control of local governments gave Washington a greater margin for error than the British generals had. Local militiamen provided the edge in the 1777 victory at Saratoga and forced Cornwallis from the Carolinas in 1781.

**TRACE CHANGE OVER TIME**
Despite being at a clear disadvantage at the start of the war, the American Patriots won. Why?

In the end, it was the American people who decided the outcome, especially the one-third of the white colonists who were zealous Patriots. Tens of thousands of these farmers and artisans accepted Continental bills in payment for supplies, and thousands of soldiers took them as pay, even as the currency literally depreciated in their pockets. Rampant inflation meant that every paper dollar held for a week lost value, imposing a hidden "**currency tax**" on those who accepted the paper currency. Each individual tax was small—a few pennies on each dollar. But as millions of dollars changed hands multiple times, the currency taxes paid by ordinary citizens financed the American military victory.

## Diplomatic Triumph

After Yorktown, diplomats took two years to conclude a peace treaty. Talks began in Paris in April 1782, but the French and Spanish, still hoping to seize a West Indian island or Gibraltar, stalled for time. Their tactics infuriated American diplomats Benjamin Franklin, John Adams, and John Jay. So the Americans negotiated secretly with the British, prepared if necessary to ignore the Treaty of Alliance and sign a separate peace. British ministers were equally eager: Parliament wanted peace, and they feared the loss of a rich sugar island.

Consequently, the American diplomats secured extremely favorable terms. In the **Treaty of Paris**, signed in September 1783, Great Britain formally recognized American independence and relinquished its claims to lands south of the Great Lakes and east of the Mississippi River. The British negotiators did not insist on a separate territory for their Indian allies. "In endeavouring to assist you," a Wea Indian complained to a British general, "it seems we have wrought our own ruin." The Cherokees were forced to relinquish claims to 5 million acres—three-quarters of their territory—in treaties with Georgia, the Carolinas, and Virginia, while New York and the Continental Congress pressed the Iroquois and Ohio Indians to cede much of their land as well. British officials, like those of other early modern empires, found it easy to abandon allies they had never really understood (America Compared, p. 197).

The Paris treaty also granted Americans fishing rights off Newfoundland and Nova Scotia, prohibited the British from "carrying away any negroes or other property," and guaranteed freedom of navigation on the Mississippi to American citizens "forever." In return, the American government allowed British merchants to pursue legal claims for prewar debts and encouraged the state legislatures to return confiscated property to Loyalists and grant them citizenship.

In the Treaty of Versailles, signed simultaneously, Britain made peace with France and Spain. Neither American ally gained very much. Spain reclaimed Florida from Britain, but not the strategic fortress at Gibraltar. France received the Caribbean island of Tobago, small consolation for a war that had sharply raised taxes and quadrupled France's national debt. Just six years later, cries for tax relief and political liberty would spark the French Revolution. Only Americans profited handsomely; the treaties gave them independence and access to the trans-Appalachian west.

# Creating Republican Institutions, 1776–1787

When the Patriots declared independence, they confronted the issue of political authority. "Which of us shall be the rulers?" asked a Philadelphia newspaper. The question was multifaceted. Would power reside in the national government or the states? Who would control the new republican institutions: traditional elites or average citizens? Would women have greater political and legal rights? What would be the status of slaves in the new republic?

## The State Constitutions: How Much Democracy?

In May 1776, the Second Continental Congress urged Americans to reject royal authority and establish republican governments. Most states quickly complied. "Constitutions employ every pen," an observer noted. Within six months, Virginia, Maryland, North Carolina, New Jersey, Delaware, and Pennsylvania had all ratified

## China's Growing Empire

As Britain was losing control of its multiethnic empire in North America, China's Qing [pronounced Ching] dynasty was consolidating its authority over borderlands peoples during the eighteenth century. And just as Europeans relied on ethnographic descriptions of Native Americans to understand the peoples and territories they hoped to control, Chinese authorities used ethnographic manuals that included prose, poetry, and illustrations to make sense of their new subjects. These excerpts from a set of "Miao albums" illustrate the cultural characteristics they observed in, or ascribed to, one such group of these non-Chinese (or non-Han) peoples.

### Bulong (Basket-Repairing) Zhongjia

The Bulong Zhongjia are located in Dinfan and Guangshun Districts. Their customs are similar to those of the Kayou. For them, the New Year begins in the twelfth month. They greet it by striking a bronze drum. When they dig in the ground and find a drum, they consider it to be the legacy of Zhuge Liang [an ancient Chinese hero claimed as a forebear]. The rich must pay a high price to buy the drum. At funerals, cattle are butchered and dressed, and relatives and friends are invited. Drinking from the "ox horn of happiness," the guests often get drunk and sometimes even wind up killing each other. The host does not usually eat meat but only fish and shrimp. After burial, the grave is covered by an umbrella. By nature the Bulong are alert and fierce. When coming and going they carry sharp knives. They will avenge even an angry look.

### Nong (Agricultural) Miao

The Nong Miao are located in the Zhenfeng District, which once belonged to Guangxi. . . . Men shave their heads and dress just like Han people. Women wear short tunics and long skirts, and cover their heads with colorful scarves. They still follow Miao customs. Their nature is fierce and cruel; they enjoy killing.

### Gedou Miao

The Gedou Miao are found in Zhenyuan, Shibing, and Huangping. They are as good at hunting as the Turen. Women wear their hair up, inclined toward one side, with a comb inserted. Their short tunics are collarless, and their skirts do not reach beyond the knee. They embroider in five colors on the bust and the sleeves, and ornament themselves with seashells [shaped] like silkworm cocoons, stringing them together like real pearls. If a man is injured by one of their poisoned arrows he will die immediately. They are not, however, given to thievery.

Source: From *The Art of Ethnography: A Chinese "Miao Album,"* translated by David M. Deal and Laura Hostetler (Seattle: University of Washington Press, 2006). Reprinted by permission of the University of Washington Press.

### QUESTIONS FOR ANALYSIS

1. What attributes seemed especially meaningful to the authors of these descriptions?
2. Why would the authors have singled out the particular qualities that are remarked upon here? How does this compare to the ways in which the British viewed their Native Americans?

new constitutions, and Connecticut and Rhode Island had revised their colonial charters to delete references to the king.

Republicanism meant more than ousting the king. The Declaration of Independence stated the principle of popular sovereignty: governments derive "their just powers from the consent of the governed." In the heat of revolution, many Patriots gave this clause a further democratic twist. In North Carolina, the backcountry farmers of Mecklenburg County told their delegates to the state's constitutional convention to "oppose everything that leans to aristocracy or power in the hands of the rich." In Virginia, voters elected a new assembly in 1776 that, an eyewitness remarked, "was composed of men not quite so well dressed, nor so politely educated, nor so highly born" as colonial-era legislatures (Figure 6.1).

To see a longer excerpt of the Mecklenburg delegates' document, along with other primary sources from this period, see *Sources for America's History*.

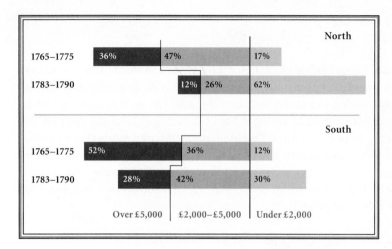

**FIGURE 6.1**

**Middling Men Enter the Halls of Government, 1765–1790**

Before the Revolution, wealthy men (with assets of £2,000 or more, as measured by tax lists and probate records) dominated most colonial assemblies. The power of money was especially apparent in the southern colonies, where representatives worth at least £5,000 formed a majority of the legislators. However, in the new American republic, the proportion of middling legislators (yeomen farmers and others worth less than £2,000) increased dramatically, especially in the northern states. Adapted from Jackson T. Main, "Government by the People: The American Revolution and the Democratization of the Legislatures," by Jackson T. Main in *William and Mary Quarterly*, series 3, 23 (1966). Used by permission of *William and Mary Quarterly*, Omohundro Institute of Early History and Culture.

**Pennsylvania's Controversial Constitution**   This democratic impulse flowered in Pennsylvania, thanks to a coalition of Scots-Irish farmers, Philadelphia artisans, and Enlightenment-influenced intellectuals. In 1776, these insurgents ousted every officeholder of the Penn family's proprietary government, abolished property ownership as a qualification for voting, and granted all taxpaying men the right to vote and hold office. The **Pennsylvania constitution of 1776** also created a unicameral (one-house) legislature with complete power; there was no governor to exercise a veto. Other provisions mandated a system of elementary education and protected citizens from imprisonment for debt.

Pennsylvania's democratic constitution alarmed many leading Patriots. From Boston, John Adams denounced the unicameral legislature as "so democratical that it must produce confusion and every evil work." Along with other conservative Patriots, Adams wanted to restrict office holding to "men of learning, leisure and easy circumstances" and warned of oppression under majority rule: "If you give [ordinary citizens] the command or preponderance in the . . . legislature, they will vote all property out of the hands of you aristocrats."

**COMPARE AND CONTRAST**
What aspects of the Pennsylvania constitution were most objectionable to Adams, and what did he advocate instead?

**Tempering Democracy**   To counter the appeal of the Pennsylvania constitution, Adams published *Thoughts on Government* (1776). In that treatise, he adapted the British Whig theory of **mixed government** (a sharing of power among the monarch, the House of Lords, and the Commons) to a republican society. To disperse authority and preserve liberty, he insisted on separate institutions: legislatures would make laws, the executive would administer them, and the judiciary would enforce them. Adams also demanded a bicameral (two-house) legislature with an upper house of substantial property owners to offset the popular majorities in the lower one. As further curbs on democracy, he proposed an elected governor with veto power and an appointed — not elected — judiciary.

Conservative Patriots endorsed Adams's governmental system. In New York's constitution of 1777, property qualifications for voting excluded 20 percent of white men from assembly elections and 60 percent from casting ballots for the governor and the upper house. In South Carolina, elite planters used property rules to disqualify about 90 percent of white men from office holding. The 1778 constitution required candidates for governor to have a debt-free estate of £10,000 (about $700,000 today), senators to be worth £2,000, and assemblymen to own property valued at £1,000. Even in traditionally democratic Massachusetts, the 1780 constitution, authored primarily by Adams, raised property qualifications for voting and office holding and skewed the lower house toward eastern, mercantile interests.

The political legacy of the Revolution was complex. Only in Pennsylvania and Vermont were radical Patriots able to create truly democratic institutions. Yet in all the new states, representative legislatures had acquired more power, and average citizens now had greater power at the polls and greater influence in the halls of government.

## Women Seek a Public Voice

The extraordinary excitement of the Revolutionary era tested the dictum that only men could engage in politics. Men controlled all public institutions — legislatures, juries, government offices — but upper-class women engaged in political debate and, defying men's scorn, filled their letters, diaries, and conversations with opinions on public issues. "The men say we have no business [with politics]," Eliza Wilkinson of South Carolina complained in 1783. "They won't even allow us liberty of thought, and that is all I want."

As Wilkinson's remark suggests, most women did not insist on civic equality with men; many sought only an end to restrictive customs and laws. Abigail Adams demanded equal legal rights for married women, who under common law could not own property, enter into contracts, or initiate lawsuits. The war bonds she purchased had to be held in a trust run by a male relative. "Men would be tyrants" if they continued to hold such power over women, Adams declared to her husband, John, criticizing him and other Patriots for "emancipating all nations" from monarchical despotism while "retaining absolute power over Wives."

Most politicians ignored women's requests, and most men insisted on traditional sexual and political prerogatives. Long-married husbands remained patriarchs who dominated their households, and even young men who embraced the republican ideal of "companionate marriage" did not support legal equality for their wives and daughters. Except in New Jersey, which until 1807 allowed unmarried and widowed female property holders to vote, women remained disenfranchised. In the new American republic, only white men enjoyed full citizenship.

Nevertheless, the republican belief in an educated citizenry created opportunities for some women. In her 1779 essay "On the Equality of the Sexes," Judith Sargent Murray argued that men and women had equal capacities for memory and that women had superior imaginations. She conceded that most women were inferior to men in judgment and reasoning, but only from lack of training: "We can only reason from what we know," she argued, and most women had been denied "the opportunity of acquiring knowledge." That situation changed in the 1790s, when the attorney general of Massachusetts declared that girls had an equal right to schooling under the state constitution. By 1850, the literacy rates of women and men in the northeastern states were equal, and educated women again challenged their subordinate legal and political status.

## The War's Losers: Loyalists, Native Americans, and Slaves

The success of republican institutions was assisted by the departure of as many as 100,000 Loyalists, many of whom suffered severe financial losses. Some Patriots demanded revolutionary justice: the seizure of

**Judith Sargent Murray**

Judith Sargent Murray was perhaps the most accomplished female essayist of the Revolutionary era. Publishing under various pen names, she advocated for economic independence and better educational opportunities for women. Two years before Mary Wollstonecraft's *A Vindication of the Rights of Woman* (1792), she published "On the Equality of the Sexes" in the *Massachusetts Magazine*. Her letter books, which run to twenty volumes, were discovered only in 1984; the Judith Sargent Murray Society (**jsmsociety.com**) is now transcribing and indexing them for publication. This striking portrait by John Singleton Copley hints at her intelligence and sardonic wit. Terra Foundation for American Art, Chicago/Art Resource, NY.

all Loyalist property and its distribution to needy Americans. But most officials were unwilling to go so far. When state governments did seize Loyalist property, they often auctioned it to the highest bidders; only rarely did small-scale farmers benefit. In the cities, Patriot merchants replaced Loyalists at the top of the economic ladder, supplanting a traditional economic elite — who often invested profits from trade in real estate — with republican entrepreneurs who tended to promote new trading ventures and domestic manufacturing. This shift facilitated America's economic development in the years to come.

**IDENTIFY CAUSES**
What impact did republican ideals have on gender roles and expectations during the Revolutionary era?

Though the Revolution did not result in widespread property redistribution, it did encourage yeomen, middling planters, and small-time entrepreneurs to believe that their new republican governments would protect their property and ensure widespread access to land. In western counties, former Regulators demanded that the new governments be more responsive to their needs; beyond the Appalachians, thousands of squatters who had occupied lands in Kentucky and Tennessee expected their claims to be recognized and lands to be made available on easy terms. If the United States were to secure the loyalty of westerners, it would have to meet their needs more effectively than the British Empire had.

This meant, among other things, extinguishing Native American claims to land as quickly as possible.

**EXPLAIN CONSEQUENCES**

How did the Revolutionary commitment to liberty and the protection of property affect enslaved African Americans and western Indians?

**A Black Loyalist Pass, 1783**

White Patriots claimed their freedom by fighting *against* the British; thousands of black slaves won their liberty by fighting *for* them. This pass certifies that Cato Rammsay (actually Ramsey), "a Negro, resorted to the British Lines" in search of the freedom promised by Virginia royal governor Dunmore and British commander Henry Clinton to slaves who escaped from Patriot owners. Now age forty-five and a "slim fellow," Ramsey had escaped from his owner, John Ramsey of Norfolk, Virginia, in 1776, probably fleeing to Dunmore's ships. Seven years later, he ended up in New York, reunited with his wife, China Godfrey (thirty-five), and their three children: James (twenty), Betsey (fifteen), and Nelly Ramsey (ten), who had fled subsequently from other owners. As the British evacuated New York in 1783, Ramsey and his family were free "to go to Nova-Scotia," where they worked as farmers. Nova Scotia Archives and Records Management.

At war's end, George Washington commented on the "rage for speculating" in Ohio Valley lands. "Men in these times, talk with as much facility of fifty, a hundred, and even 500,000 Acres as a Gentleman formerly would do of 1000 acres." "If we make a right use of our natural advantages," a Fourth of July orator observed, "we soon must be a truly great and happy people." Native American land claims stood as a conspicuous barrier to the "natural advantages" he imagined.

For southern slaveholders, the Revolution was fought to protect property rights, and any sentiment favoring slave emancipation met with violent objections. When Virginia Methodists called for general emancipation in 1785, slaveholders used Revolutionary principles to defend their right to human property. They "risked [their] Lives and Fortunes, and waded through Seas of Blood" to secure "the Possession of [their] Rights of Liberty and Property," only to hear of "a very subtle and daring Attempt" to "dispossess us of a very important Part of our Property." Emancipation would bring "Want, Poverty, Distress, and Ruin to the Free Citizen." The liberties coveted by ordinary white Americans bore hard on the interests of Native Americans and slaves.

## The Articles of Confederation

As Patriots embraced independence in 1776, they envisioned a central government with limited powers. Carter Braxton of Virginia thought the Continental Congress should "regulate the affairs of trade, war, peace, alliances, &c." but "should by no means have authority to interfere with the internal police [governance] or domestic concerns of any Colony."

That idea informed the **Articles of Confederation**, which were approved by the Continental Congress in November 1777. The Articles provided for a loose union in which "each state retains its sovereignty, freedom, and independence." As an association of equals, each state had one vote regardless of its size, population, or wealth. Important laws needed the approval of nine of the thirteen states, and changes in the Articles required unanimous consent. Though the Confederation had significant powers on paper — it could declare war, make treaties with foreign nations, adjudicate disputes between the states, borrow and print money, and requisition funds from the states "for the common defense or general welfare" — it had major weaknesses as well. It had neither a chief executive nor a judiciary. Though it could make treaties, it could not enforce their provisions, since the states remained sovereign. Most important, it lacked the power to tax either the states or the people.

Although the Congress exercised authority from 1776 — raising the Continental army, negotiating the treaty with France, and financing the war — the Articles won formal ratification only in 1781. The delay stemmed from conflicts over western lands. The royal charters of Virginia, Massachusetts, Connecticut, and other states set boundaries stretching to the Pacific Ocean. States without western lands — Maryland and Pennsylvania — refused to accept the Articles until the land-rich states relinquished these claims to the Confederation. Threatened by Cornwallis's army in 1781, Virginia gave up its claims, and Maryland, the last holdout, finally ratified the Articles (Map 6.5).

**Continuing Fiscal Crisis**   By 1780, the central government was nearly bankrupt, and General Washington called urgently for a national tax system; without one, he warned, "our cause is lost." Led by Robert Morris, who became superintendent of finance in 1781, nationalist-minded Patriots tried to expand the Confederation's authority. They persuaded Congress to charter the Bank of North America, a private institution in Philadelphia, arguing that its notes would stabilize the inflated Continental currency. Morris also created a central bureaucracy to manage the Confederation's finances and urged Congress to enact a 5 percent import tax. Rhode Island and New York rejected the tax proposal. His state had opposed British import duties, New York's representative declared, and it would not accept them from Congress. To raise revenue, Congress looked to the sale of western lands. In 1783, it asserted that the recently signed Treaty of Paris had extinguished the Indians' rights to those lands and made them the property of the United States.

**The Northwest Ordinance**   By 1784, more than thirty thousand settlers had already moved to Kentucky and Tennessee, despite the uncertainties of frontier warfare, and after the war their numbers grew rapidly. In that year, the residents of what is now eastern Tennessee organized a new state, called it Franklin, and sought admission to the Confederation. To preserve its authority over the West, Congress refused to recognize Franklin. Subsequently, Congress created the Southwest and Mississippi Territories (the future states of Tennessee, Alabama, and Mississippi) from lands ceded by North Carolina and Georgia. Because these cessions carried the stipulation that "no regulation . . . shall tend to emancipate slaves," these states and all those south of the Ohio River allowed human bondage.

However, the Confederation Congress banned slavery north of the Ohio River. Between 1784 and 1787, it issued three important ordinances organizing the "Old Northwest." The Ordinance of 1784, written by Thomas Jefferson, established the principle that territories could become states as their populations grew. The Land Ordinance of 1785 mandated a rectangular-grid system of surveying and specified a minimum price of $1 an acre. It also required that half of the townships be sold in single blocks of 23,040 acres each, which only large-scale speculators could afford, and the rest in parcels of 640 acres each, which restricted their sale to well-to-do farmers (Map 6.6).

Finally, the **Northwest Ordinance of 1787** created the territories that would eventually become the states of Ohio, Indiana, Illinois, Michigan, and Wisconsin. The ordinance prohibited slavery and earmarked funds from land sales for the support of schools. It also specified that Congress would appoint a governor and judges to administer each new territory until the population reached 5,000 free adult men, at which point the citizens could elect a territorial legislature. When the population reached 60,000, the legislature could devise a republican constitution and apply to join the Confederation.

The land ordinances of the 1780s were a great and enduring achievement of the Confederation Congress. They provided for orderly settlement and the admission of new states on the basis of equality; there would be no politically dependent "colonies" in the West. But they also extended the geographical division between slave and free areas that would haunt the nation in the coming decades. And they implicitly invalidated Native American claims to an enormous swath of territory — a corollary that would soon lead the newly independent nation, once again, into war.

**COMPARE AND CONTRAST**
In what ways did the Confederation function effectively, and what were its greatest failings?

## Shays's Rebellion

Though many national leaders were optimistic about the long-term prospects of the United States, postwar economic conditions were grim. The Revolution had crippled American shipping and cut exports of tobacco, rice, and wheat. The British Navigation Acts, which had nurtured colonial commerce, now barred Americans from legal trade with the British West Indies. Moreover, low-priced British manufactures (and some from India as well) were flooding American markets, driving urban artisans and wartime textile firms out of business.

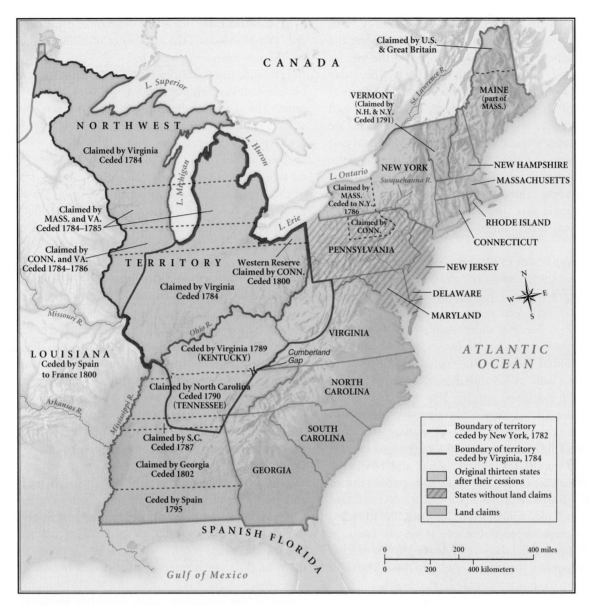

**MAP 6.5**

**The Confederation and Western Land Claims, 1781–1802**

The Congress formed by the Articles of Confederation had to resolve conflicting state claims to western lands. For example, the territories claimed by New York and Virginia on the basis of their royal charters overlapped extensively. Beginning in 1781, the Confederation Congress and, after 1789, the U.S. Congress persuaded all of the states to cede their western claims, creating a "national domain" open to all citizens. In the Northwest Ordinance (1787), the Congress divided the domain north of the Ohio River into territories and set up democratic procedures by which they could eventually join the Union as states. South of the Ohio River, the Congress allowed the existing southern states to play a substantial role in settling the ceded lands.

The fiscal condition of the state governments was dire, primarily because of war debts. Well-to-do merchants and landowners (including Abigail Adams) had invested in state bonds during the war; others had speculated in debt certificates, buying them on the cheap from hard-pressed farmers and soldiers. Now creditors and speculators demanded that the state governments redeem the bonds and certificates quickly and at full value, a policy that would require tax increases and a decrease in the amount of paper currency. Most legislatures — now including substantial numbers of middling farmers and artisans — refused. Instead they

**MAP 6.6**

**Land Division in the Northwest Territory**

Throughout the Northwest Territory, government surveyors imposed a rectangular grid on the landscape, regardless of the local topography, so that farmers bought neatly defined tracts of land. The right-angled property lines in Muskingum County, Ohio (lower left), contrasted sharply with those in Baltimore County, Maryland (lower right), where—as in most of the eastern and southern states—boundaries followed the contours of the land.

authorized new issues of paper currency and allowed debtors to pay private creditors in installments. Although wealthy men deplored these measures as "intoxicating Draughts of Liberty" that destroyed "the just rights of creditors," such political intervention prevented social upheaval.

In Massachusetts, however, the new constitution placed power in the hands of a mercantile elite that owned the bulk of the state's war bonds. Ignoring the interests of ordinary citizens, the legislature increased taxes fivefold to pay off wartime debts—and it stipulated that they be paid in hard currency. Even for substantial farmers, this was a crushing burden. When cash-strapped farmers could not pay both their taxes and their debts, creditors threatened lawsuits. Debtor Ephraim Wetmore heard a rumor that merchant Stephan Salisbury "would have my Body Dead or Alive in case I did not pay." To protect their livelihoods, farmers called extralegal conventions to protest high taxes and property seizures. Then mobs of angry farmers, including men of high status, closed the courts by force. "[I] had no Intensions to Destroy the Publick Government," declared Captain Adam Wheeler, a former town selectman; his goal was simply to prevent "Valuable and Industrious members of Society [being] dragged from their families to prison" because of their debts. These crowd actions grew into a full-scale revolt led by Captain Daniel Shays, a Continental army veteran.

As a revolt against taxes imposed by an unresponsive government, **Shays's Rebellion** resembled American resistance to the British Stamp Act. Consciously linking themselves to the Patriot movement, Shays's men placed pine twigs in their hats just as Continental troops had done. "The people have turned against their teachers the doctrines which were inculcated to effect the late revolution," complained Fisher Ames, a conservative Massachusetts lawmaker. Some of the radical Patriots of 1776 likewise condemned the Shaysites: "[Men who] would lessen the Weight of Government lawfully exercised must be Enemies to our happy Revolution and Common Liberty," charged Samuel Adams. To put down the rebellion, the Massachusetts legislature passed the Riot Act, and wealthy bondholders equipped a formidable fighting force, which Governor James Bowdoin used to disperse Shays's ragtag army during the winter of 1786–1787.

Although Shays's Rebellion failed, it showed that many middling Patriot families felt that American oppressors had replaced British tyrants. Massachusetts voters turned Governor Bowdoin out of office, and debt-ridden farmers in New York, northern Pennsylvania, Connecticut, and New Hampshire closed courthouses and forced their governments to provide economic relief. British officials in Canada predicted the imminent demise of the United States; and American leaders urged purposeful action to save their republican experiment. Events in Massachusetts, declared nationalist Henry Knox, formed "the strongest arguments possible" for the creation of "a strong general government."

# The Constitution of 1787

These issues ultimately led to the drafting of a national constitution. From its creation, the U.S. Constitution was a controversial document, both acclaimed for solving the nation's woes and condemned for perverting its republican principles. Critics charged that republican institutions worked only in small political units—the states. Advocates replied that the Constitution extended republicanism by adding another level of government elected by the people. In the new two-level political federation created by the Constitution, the national government would exercise limited, delegated powers, and the existing state governments would retain authority over all other matters.

## The Rise of a Nationalist Faction

Money questions—debts, taxes, and tariffs—dominated the postwar political agenda. Americans who had served the Confederation as military officers, officials, and diplomats viewed these issues from a national perspective and advocated a stronger central government. George Washington, Robert Morris, Benjamin Franklin, John Jay, and John Adams wanted Congress to control foreign and interstate commerce and tariff policy. However, lawmakers in Massachusetts, New York, and Pennsylvania—states with strong commercial traditions—insisted on controlling their own tariffs, both to protect their artisans from low-cost imports and to assist their merchants. Most southern states opposed tariffs because planters wanted to import British textiles and ironware at the lowest possible prices.

Nonetheless, some southern leaders became nationalists because their state legislatures had cut taxes and refused to redeem state war bonds. Such policies, lamented wealthy bondholder Charles Lee of Virginia, led taxpayers to believe they would "never be compelled

**PLACE EVENTS IN CONTEXT**

How did the Shaysites draw on the Revolution for inspiration?

to pay" the public debt. Creditors also condemned state laws that "stayed" (delayed) the payment of mortgages and other private debts. "While men are madly accumulating enormous debts, their legislators are making provisions for their nonpayment," complained a South Carolina merchant. To undercut the democratic majorities in the state legislatures, creditors joined the movement for a stronger central government.

Spurred on by Shays's Rebellion, nationalists in Congress secured a resolution calling for a convention to revise the Articles of Confederation. Only an "efficient plan from the Convention," a fellow nationalist wrote to James Madison, "can prevent anarchy first & civil convulsions afterwards."

## The Philadelphia Convention

In May 1787, fifty-five delegates arrived in Philadelphia. They came from every state except Rhode Island, where the legislature opposed increasing central authority. Most were strong nationalists; forty-two had served in the Confederation Congress. They were also educated and propertied: merchants, slaveholding planters, and "monied men." There were no artisans, backcountry settlers, or tenants, and only a single yeoman farmer.

Some influential Patriots missed the convention. John Adams and Thomas Jefferson were serving as American ministers to Britain and France, respectively. The Massachusetts General Court rejected Sam Adams as a delegate because he opposed a stronger national government, and his fellow firebrand from Virginia, Patrick Henry, refused to attend because he "smelt a rat."

The absence of experienced leaders and contrary-minded delegates allowed capable younger nationalists to set the agenda. Declaring that the convention would "decide for ever the fate of Republican Government," James Madison insisted on increased national authority. Alexander Hamilton of New York likewise demanded a strong central government to protect the republic from "the imprudence of democracy."

**The Virginia and New Jersey Plans**   The delegates elected George Washington as their presiding officer and voted to meet behind closed doors. Then — momentously — they decided not to revise the Articles of Confederation but rather to consider the so-called **Virginia Plan**, a scheme for a powerful national government devised by James Madison. Just thirty-six years old, Madison was determined to fashion national political institutions run by men of high character. A graduate of Princeton, he had read classical and modern political theory and served in both the Confederation Congress and the Virginia assembly. Once an optimistic Patriot, Madison had grown discouraged because of the "narrow ambition" and outlook of state legislators.

Madison's Virginia Plan differed from the Articles of Confederation in three crucial respects. First, the plan rejected state sovereignty in favor of the "supremacy of national authority," including the power to overturn state laws. Second, it called for the national government to be established by the people (not the states) and for national laws to operate directly on citizens of the various states. Third, the plan proposed a three-tier election system in which ordinary voters would elect only the lower house of the national legislature. This lower house would then select the upper house, and both houses would appoint the executive and judiciary.

From a political perspective, Madison's plan had two fatal flaws. First, most state politicians and

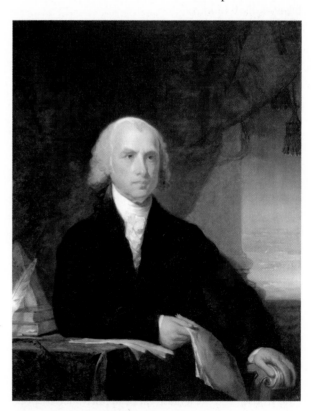

**James Madison, Statesman**
Throughout his long public life, Madison kept the details of his private life to himself. His biography, he believed, should be a record of his public accomplishments, not his private affairs. Future generations celebrated him not as a great man (like Hamilton or Jefferson) or as a great president (like Washington), but as an original and incisive political thinker. The chief architect of the U.S. Constitution and the Bill of Rights, Madison was the preeminent republican political theorist of his generation. Mead Art Museum, Amherst College, Amherst, Massachusetts, Bequest of Herbert L. Pratt (Class of 1895) # 1945.82.

citizens resolutely opposed allowing the national government to veto state laws. Second, the plan based representation in the lower house on population; this provision, a Delaware delegate warned, would allow the populous states to "crush the small ones whenever they stand in the way of their ambitious or interested views."

So delegates from Delaware and other small states rallied behind a plan devised by William Paterson of New Jersey. The **New Jersey Plan** gave the Confederation the power to raise revenue, control commerce, and make binding requisitions on the states. But it preserved the states' control of their own laws and guaranteed their equality: as in the Confederation Congress, each state would have one vote in a unicameral legislature. Delegates from the more populous states vigorously opposed this provision. After a month-long debate on the two plans, a bare majority of the states agreed to use Madison's Virginia Plan as the basis of discussion.

This decision raised the odds that the convention would create a more powerful national government. Outraged by this prospect, two New York delegates, Robert Yates and John Lansing, accused their colleagues of exceeding their mandate to revise the Articles and left the convention. The remaining delegates met six days a week during the summer of 1787, debating both high principles and practical details. Experienced politicians, they looked for a plan that would be acceptable to most citizens and existing political interests. Pierce Butler of South Carolina invoked a classical Greek precedent: "We must follow the example of Solon, who gave the Athenians not the best government he could devise but the best they would receive."

**The Great Compromise**    As the convention grappled with the central problem of the representation of large and small states, the Connecticut delegates suggested a possible solution. They proposed that the national legislature's upper chamber (the Senate) have two members from each state, while seats in the lower chamber (the House of Representatives) be apportioned by population (determined every ten years by a national census). After bitter debate, delegates from the populous states reluctantly accepted this "Great Compromise."

Other state-related issues were quickly settled by restricting (or leaving ambiguous) the extent of central authority. Some delegates opposed a national system of courts, predicting that "the states will revolt at such encroachments" on their judicial authority.

This danger led the convention to vest the judicial power "in one supreme Court" and allow the new national legislature to decide whether to establish lower courts within the states. The convention also refused to set a property requirement for voting in national elections. "Eight or nine states have extended the right of suffrage beyond the freeholders," George Mason of Virginia pointed out. "What will people there say if they should be disfranchised?" Finally, the convention specified that state legislatures would elect members of the upper house, or Senate, and the states would select the electors who would choose the president. By allowing states to have important roles in the new constitutional system, the delegates hoped that their citizens would accept limits on state sovereignty.

**Negotiations over Slavery**    The shadow of slavery hovered over many debates, and Gouverneur Morris of New York brought it into view. To safeguard property rights, Morris wanted life terms for senators, a property qualification for voting in national elections, and a strong president with veto power. Nonetheless, he rejected the legitimacy of two traditional types of property: the feudal dues claimed by aristocratic landowners and the ownership of slaves. An advocate of free markets and personal liberty, Morris condemned slavery as "a nefarious institution."

Many slave-owning delegates from the Chesapeake region, including Madison and George Mason, recognized that slavery contradicted republican principles and hoped for its eventual demise. They supported an end to American participation in the Atlantic slave trade, a proposal the South Carolina and Georgia delegates angrily rejected. Unless the importation of African slaves continued, these rice planters and merchants declared, their states "shall not be parties to the Union." At their insistence, the convention denied Congress the power to regulate immigration—and so the slave trade—until 1808 (American Voices, p. 208).

The delegates devised other slavery-related compromises. To mollify southern planters, they wrote a "fugitive clause" that allowed masters to reclaim enslaved blacks (or white indentured servants) who fled to other states. But in acknowledgment of the antislavery sentiments of Morris and other northerners, the delegates excluded the words *slavery* and *slave* from the Constitution; it spoke only of citizens and "all other Persons." Because slaves lacked the vote, antislavery delegates wanted their census numbers excluded when apportioning seats in Congress.

Southerners—ironically, given that they considered slaves property—demanded that slaves be counted in the census the same as full citizens, to increase the South's representation. Ultimately, the delegates agreed that each slave would count as three-fifths of a free person for purposes of representation and taxation, a compromise that helped southern planters dominate the national government until 1860.

**National Authority**   Having addressed the concerns of small states and slave states, the convention created a powerful national government. The Constitution declared that congressional legislation was the "supreme" law of the land. It gave the new government the power to tax, raise an army and a navy, and regulate foreign and interstate commerce, with the authority to make all laws "necessary and proper" to implement those and other provisions. To assist creditors and establish the new government's fiscal integrity, the Constitution required the United States to honor the existing national debt and prohibited the states from issuing paper money or enacting "any Law impairing the Obligation of Contracts."

The proposed constitution was not a "perfect production," Benjamin Franklin admitted, as he urged the delegates to sign it in September 1787. But the great statesman confessed his astonishment at finding "this system approaching so near to perfection." His colleagues apparently agreed; all but three signed the document.

## The People Debate Ratification

The procedure for ratifying the new constitution was as controversial as its contents. Knowing that Rhode Island (and perhaps other states) would reject it, the delegates did not submit the Constitution to the state legislatures for their unanimous consent, as required by the Articles of Confederation. Instead, they arbitrarily—and cleverly—declared that it would take effect when ratified by conventions in nine of the thirteen states.

As the constitutional debate began in early 1788, the nationalists seized the initiative with two bold moves. First, they called themselves **Federalists**, suggesting that they supported a federal union—a loose, decentralized system—and obscuring their commitment to a strong national government. Second, they launched a coordinated campaign in pamphlets and newspapers to explain and justify the Philadelphia constitution.

**The Antifederalists**   The opponents of the Constitution, called by default the **Antifederalists**, had diverse backgrounds and motives. Some, like Governor George Clinton of New York, feared that state governments would lose power. Rural democrats protested that the proposed document, unlike most state constitutions, lacked a declaration of individual rights; they also feared that the central government would be run by wealthy men. "Lawyers and men of learning and monied men expect to be managers of this Constitution," worried a Massachusetts farmer. "[T]hey will swallow up all of us little folks . . . just as the whale swallowed up Jonah." Giving political substance to these fears, Melancton Smith of New York argued that the large electoral districts prescribed by the Constitution would restrict office holding to wealthy men, whereas the smaller districts used in state elections usually produced legislatures "composed principally of respectable yeomanry." John Quincy Adams agreed: if only "*eight* men" would represent Massachusetts, "they will infallibly be chosen from the aristocratic part of the community."

**COMPARE AND CONTRAST**
How did the Constitution, in its final form, differ from the plan that James Madison originally proposed?

Smith summed up the views of Americans who held traditional republican values. To keep government "close to the people," they wanted the states to remain small sovereign republics tied together only for trade and defense—not the "United States" but the "States United." Citing the French political philosopher Montesquieu, Antifederalists argued that republican institutions were best suited to small polities. "No extensive empire can be governed on republican principles," declared James Winthrop of Massachusetts. Patrick Henry worried that the Constitution would recreate British rule: high taxes, an oppressive bureaucracy, a standing army, and a "great and mighty President . . . supported in extravagant munificence." As another Antifederalist put it, "I had rather be a free citizen of the small republic of Massachusetts than an oppressed subject of the great American empire."

**Federalists Respond**   In New York, where ratification was hotly contested, James Madison, John Jay, and Alexander Hamilton defended the proposed constitution in a series of eighty-five essays written in 1787 and 1788, collectively titled *The Federalist*. This work influenced political leaders throughout the country and subsequently won acclaim as an important treatise of practical republicanism. Its authors denied that a

## The First National Debate over Slavery

In this part of the text, we trace the impact of republican ideology on American politics and society. What happened when republicanism collided head-on with the well-established practice of slavery? After the Revolution, the Massachusetts courts abolished slavery, but in 1787, slavery was legal in the rest of the Union and was the bedrock of social order and agricultural production in the southern states. A look at the debates on the issue of the African slave trade at the Philadelphia convention and in a state ratifying convention shows that slavery was an extremely divisive issue at the birth of the nation—a dark cloud threatening the bright future of the young republic.

### The Constitutional Convention

Slavery was not a major topic of discussion at the Philadelphia convention, but it surfaced a number of times, notably in the important debate over representation (which produced the three-fifths clause). A discussion of the Atlantic slave trade began when Luther Martin, a delegate from Maryland, proposed a clause allowing Congress to impose a tax on or prohibit the importation of slaves.

Mr. Martin proposed to vary article 7, sect. 4 so as to allow a prohibition or tax on the importation of slaves. . . . [He believed] it was inconsistent with the principles of the Revolution, and dishonorable to the American character, to have such a feature [promoting the slave trade] in the Constitution.

Mr. [John] Rutledge [of South Carolina declared that] religion and humanity had nothing to do with this question. Interest alone is the governing principle with nations. The true question at present is whether the Southern states shall or shall not be parties to the Union. . . .

Mr. [Oliver] Ellsworth [of Connecticut] was for leaving the clause as it stands. Let every state import what it pleases. The morality or wisdom of slavery are considerations belonging to the states themselves. . . . The old Confederation had not meddled with this point, and he did not see any greater necessity for bringing it within the policy of the new one.

Mr. [Charles C.] Pinckney [said] South Carolina can never receive the plan [for a new constitution] if it prohibits the slave trade. In every proposed extension of the powers of Congress, that state has expressly and watchfully excepted that of meddling with the importation of Negroes. . . .

Mr. [Roger] Sherman [of Connecticut] was for leaving the clause as it stands. He disapproved of the slave trade; yet, as the states were now possessed of the right

to import slaves, . . . and as it was expedient to have as few objections as possible to the proposed scheme of government, he thought it best to leave the matter as we find it.

Col. [George] Mason [of Virginia stated that] this infernal trade originated in the avarice of British merchants. The British government constantly checked the attempts of Virginia to put a stop to it. The present question concerns not the importing states alone, but the whole Union. . . . Maryland and Virginia, he said, had already prohibited the importation of slaves expressly. North Carolina had done the same in substance. All this would be in vain if South Carolina and Georgia be at liberty to import. The Western people are already calling out for slaves for their new lands, and will fill that country with slaves, if they can be got through South Carolina and Georgia. Slavery discourages arts and manufactures. The poor despise labor when performed by slaves. They prevent the immigration of whites, who really enrich and strengthen a country. . . .

Every master of slaves is born a petty tyrant. They bring the judgment of Heaven on a country. As nations cannot be rewarded or punished in the next world, they must be in this. By an inevitable chain of causes and effects, Providence punishes national sins by national calamities. . . . He held it essential, in every point of view, that the general government should have power to prevent the increase of slavery.

Mr. Ellsworth, as he had never owned a slave, could not judge of the effects of slavery on character. He said, however, that if it was to be considered in a moral light, we ought to go further, and free those already in the country. . . . Let us not intermeddle. As population increases, poor laborers will be so plenty as to render slaves useless. Slavery, in time, will not be a speck in our country. . . .

Gen. [Charles C.] Pinckney [argued that] South Carolina and Georgia cannot do without slaves. As to

Virginia, she will gain by stopping the importations. Her slaves will rise in value, and she has more than she wants. It would be unequal to require South Carolina and Georgia to confederate on such unequal terms. . . . He contended that the importation of slaves would be for the interest of the whole Union. The more slaves, the more produce to employ the carrying trade; the more consumption also; and the more of this, the more revenue for the common treasury. . . . [He] should consider a rejection of the [present] clause as an exclusion of South Carolina from the Union.

Source: Max Farrand, ed., *The Records of the Federal Convention of 1787* (New Haven: Yale University Press, 1911), 2: 364–365, 369–372.

## The Massachusetts Ratifying Convention

In Philadelphia, the delegates agreed on a compromise: they gave Congress the power to tax or prohibit slave imports, as Luther Martin had proposed, but withheld that power for twenty years. In the Massachusetts convention, the delegates split on this issue and on many others. They ratified the Constitution by a narrow margin, 187 to 168.

Mr. Neal (from Kittery) [an Antifederalist] went over the ground of objection to . . . the idea that slave trade was allowed to be continued for 20 years. His profession, he said, obliged him to bear witness against any thing that should favor the making merchandize of the bodies of men, and unless his objection was removed, he could not put his hand to the constitution. Other gentlemen said, in addition to this idea, that there was not even a proposition that the negroes ever shall be free: and Gen. Thompson exclaimed — "Mr. President, shall it be said, that after we have established our own independence and freedom, we make slaves of others? Oh! Washington . . . he has immortalized himself! but he holds those in slavery who have a good right to be free as he is. . . ."

On the other side, gentlemen said, that the step taken in this article, towards the abolition of slavery, was one of the beauties of the constitution. They observed, that in the confederation there was no provision whatever for its ever being abolished; but this constitution provides, that Congress may after twenty years, totally annihilate the slave trade. . . .

Mr. Heath (Federalist): . . . I apprehend that it is not in our power to do any thing for or against those who are in slavery in the southern states. No gentleman within these walls detests every idea of slavery more than I do: it is generally detested by the people of this commonwealth, and I ardently hope that the time will soon come, when our brethren in the southern states will view it as we do, and put a stop to it; but to this we have no right to compel them.

Two questions naturally arise: if we ratify the Constitution, shall we do any thing by our act to hold the blacks in slavery or shall we become the partakers of other men's sins? I think neither of them: each state is sovereign and independent to a certain degree, and they have a right, and will regulate their own internal affairs, as to themselves appears proper. . . . We are not in this case partakers of other men's sins. . . .

The federal convention went as far as they could; the migration or immigration &c. is confined to the states, now existing only, new states cannot claim it. Congress, by their ordnance for erecting new states, some time since, declared that there shall be no slavery in them. But whether those in slavery in the southern states, will be emancipated after the year 1808, I do not pretend to determine: I rather doubt it.

Source: Jonathan Elliot, ed., *The Debates . . . on the Adoption of the Federal Constitution* (Philadelphia: J. B. Lippincott, 1836), 1: 103–105, 107, 112, 117.

---

### QUESTIONS FOR ANALYSIS

1. At the Constitutional Convention in Philadelphia, what were the main arguments for and against federal restrictions on the Atlantic slave trade? How do you explain the position taken by the Connecticut delegates in Philadelphia and Mr. Heath in the Massachusetts debate?

2. What argument does George Mason, a Virginia slave owner, make in favor of prohibiting the Atlantic slave trade?

3. What evidence of regional tensions appears in the documents? Several men from different states—Mason from Virginia, Ellsworth from Connecticut, and Heath from Massachusetts—offered predictions about the future of slavery. How accurate were they?

centralized government would lead to domestic tyranny. Drawing on Montesquieu's theories and John Adams's *Thoughts on Government*, Madison, Jay, and Hamilton pointed out that authority would be divided among the president, a bicameral legislature, and a judiciary. Each branch of government would "check and balance" the others and so preserve liberty.

In "**Federalist No. 10**," Madison challenged the view that republican governments only worked in small polities, arguing that a large state would better protect republican liberty. It was "sown in the nature of man," Madison wrote, for individuals to seek power and form factions. Indeed, "a landed interest, a manufacturing interest, a mercantile interest, a moneyed interest, with many lesser interests, grow up of necessity in civilized nations." A free society should welcome all factions but keep any one of them from becoming dominant—something best achieved in a large republic. "Extend the sphere and you take in a greater variety of parties and interests," Madison concluded, inhibiting the formation of a majority eager "to invade the rights of other citizens."

**The Constitution Ratified**    The delegates debating these issues in the state ratification conventions included untutored farmers and middling artisans as well as educated gentlemen. Generally, backcountry delegates were Antifederalists, while those from coastal areas were Federalists. In Pennsylvania, Philadelphia merchants and artisans joined commercial farmers to ratify the Constitution. Other early Federalist successes came in four less populous states—Delaware, New Jersey, Georgia, and Connecticut—where delegates hoped that a strong national government would offset the power of large neighboring states (Map 6.7).

The Constitution's first real test came in January 1788 in Massachusetts, a hotbed of Antifederalist sentiment. Influential Patriots, including Samuel Adams and Governor John Hancock, opposed the new constitution, as did many followers of Daniel Shays. But Boston artisans, who wanted tariff protection from British imports, supported ratification. To win over other delegates, Federalist leaders assured the convention that they would recommend a national bill of

**MAP 6.7**
**Ratifying the Constitution of 1787**

In 1907, geographer Owen Libby mapped the votes of members of the state conventions that ratified the Constitution. His map showed that most delegates from seaboard or commercial farming districts (which sent many delegates to the conventions) supported the Constitution, while those from sparsely represented, subsistence-oriented backcountry areas opposed it. Subsequent research has confirmed Libby's socioeconomic interpretation of the voting patterns in North and South Carolina and in Massachusetts. However, other states' delegates were influenced by different factors. For example, in Georgia, delegates from all regions voted for ratification.

Votes at District Level
With date of ratification
by state convention

- Delegates in support of ratification
- Delegates opposed to ratification
- Districts evenly divided
- No returns

rights. By a close vote of 187 to 168, the Federalists carried the day.

Spring brought Federalist victories in Maryland, South Carolina, and New Hampshire, reaching the nine-state quota required for ratification. But it took the powerful arguments advanced in *The Federalist* and more promises of a bill of rights to secure the Constitution's adoption in the essential states of Virginia and New York. The votes were again close: 89 to 79 in Virginia and 30 to 27 in New York.

Testifying to their respect for popular sovereignty and majority rule, most Americans accepted the verdict of the ratifying conventions. "A decided majority" of the New Hampshire assembly had opposed the "new system," reported Joshua Atherton, but now they said, "It is adopted, let us try it." In Virginia, Patrick Henry vowed to "submit as a quiet citizen" and fight for amendments "in a constitutional way."

Unlike in France, where the Revolution of 1789 divided the society into irreconcilable factions for generations, the American Constitutional Revolution of 1787 created a national republic that enjoyed broad popular support. Federalists celebrated their triumph by organizing great processions in the seaport cities. By marching in an orderly fashion — in conscious contrast to the riotous Revolutionary mobs — Federalist-minded citizens affirmed their allegiance to a self-governing but elite-ruled republican nation.

## SUMMARY

In this chapter, we examined the unfolding of two related sets of events. The first was the war between Britain and its rebellious colonies that began in 1776 and ended in 1783. The two great battles of Saratoga (1777) and Yorktown (1781) determined the outcome of that conflict. Surprisingly, given the military might of the British Empire, both were American victories. These triumphs testify to the determination of George Washington, the resilience of the Continental army, and support for the Patriot cause from hundreds of local militias and tens of thousands of taxpaying citizens.

This popular support reflected the Patriots' second success: building effective institutions of republican government. These elected institutions of local and state governance evolved out of colonial-era town meetings and representative assemblies. They were defined in the state constitutions written between 1776 and 1781, and their principles informed the first national constitution, the Articles of Confederation. Despite the challenges posed by conflicts over suffrage, women's rights, and fiscal policy, these self-governing political institutions carried the new republic successfully through the war-torn era and laid the foundation for the Constitution of 1787, the national charter that endures today.

# CHAPTER REVIEW

**MAKE IT STICK**   Go to **LearningCurve** to retain what you've read.

## KEY TERMS    Identify and explain the significance of each term below.

### Key Concepts and Events

**Battle of Long Island (1776)** (p. 184)

**Battle of Saratoga (1777)** (p. 187)

**Valley Forge** (p. 189)

**Philipsburg Proclamation** (p. 190)

**Battle of Yorktown (1781)** (p. 195)

**currency tax** (p. 196)

**Treaty of Paris of 1783** (p. 196)

**Pennsylvania constitution of 1776** (p. 198)

**mixed government** (p. 198)

**Articles of Confederation** (p. 200)

**Northwest Ordinance of 1787** (p. 201)

**Shays's Rebellion** (p. 204)

**Virginia Plan** (p. 205)

**New Jersey Plan** (p. 206)

**Federalists** (p. 207)

**Antifederalists** (p. 207)

**Federalist No. 10** (p. 210)

### KEY PEOPLE

**General George Washington** (p. 184)

**General William Howe** (p. 184)

**General Horatio Gates** (p. 187)

**Robert Morris** (p. 188)

**Baron von Steuben** (p. 189)

**Judith Sargent Murray** (p. 199)

**James Madison** (p. 205)

## REVIEW QUESTIONS
Answer these questions to demonstrate your understanding of the chapter's main ideas.

**1.** What were the principal reasons that Great Britain, despite its enormous military advantages, lost the War for Independence?

**2.** The war had wrenching effects on the American economy. What economic problems became especially acute during wartime? How did the states and the Second Continental Congress attempt to address them?

**3.** Federalists and Antifederalists both claimed to represent the true spirit of the American Revolution. Which of these competing visions of national identity do you think was right? Why?

**4.** **THEMATIC UNDERSTANDING**   Consider the events listed under "Work, Exchange, and Technology" and "Politics and Power" for the period 1776–1787 on the thematic timeline on page 149. How did war debt and inflation influence the development of political institutions during these years?

## MAKING CONNECTIONS
Recognize the larger developments and continuities within and across chapters by answering these questions.

**1.** **ACROSS TIME AND PLACE**   In Chapter 5, we saw the way that protests against imperial policy grew until colonists chose to declare their independence rather than submit to Parliament's authority. By 1787, the problems created by the Revolutionary War forced leaders of the newly independent states to consider plans for their own powerful central government. What problems led nationalists to believe such a step was necessary? How did Antifederalists draw on Revolutionary ideas to make their case against the Constitution? What claims did nationalists make in response to dampen Antifederalist fears?

**2.** **VISUAL EVIDENCE**   Look again at Map 6.5 on page 202 showing western land claims in the 1780s. If these claims had not been ceded to the Continental Congress, what would have been the likely result? Why was it so important to the survival of the Confederation that individual states give up their claims to these western lands?

## MORE TO EXPLORE
Start here to learn more about the events discussed in this chapter.

Colin G. Calloway, *The American Revolution in Indian Country* (1995). Tracks the experiences of numerous Native American communities in the Revolution.

Saul Cornell, *The Other Founders* (1999). Explores the ideas and legacy of the Antifederalists.

John C. Dann, ed., *The Revolution Remembered* (1980). Contains vivid eyewitness accounts of the Revolution.

Pauline Maier, *Ratification* (2010). A compelling narrative of the debate over the Constitution.

Michael McDonnell, *The Politics of War* (2007). A penetrating account of Virginia's mobilization for war.

Leonard Richards, *Shays's Rebellion* (2003). A persuasive interpretation of the rebellion's participants and motives.

# TIMELINE

Ask yourself why this chapter begins and ends with these dates and then identify the links among related events.

| | |
|---|---|
| **1776** | • Second Continental Congress declares independence<br>• Howe forces Washington to retreat from New York and New Jersey<br>• Pennsylvania approves democratic state constitution<br>• John Adams publishes *Thoughts on Government* |
| **1777** | • Articles of Confederation create central government<br>• Howe occupies Philadelphia (September)<br>• Gates defeats Burgoyne at Saratoga (October) |
| **1778** | • Franco-American alliance (February)<br>• Lord North seeks political settlement<br>• Congress rejects negotiations<br>• British adopt southern strategy<br>• British capture Savannah (December) |
| **1778–1781** | • Severe inflation of Continental currency |
| **1779** | • British and American forces battle in Georgia |
| **1780** | • Clinton seizes Charleston (May)<br>• French troops land in Rhode Island |
| **1781** | • Cornwallis invades Virginia (April), surrenders at Yorktown (October)<br>• States finally ratify Articles of Confederation |
| **1783** | • Treaty of Paris (September 3) officially ends war |
| **1784–1785** | • Congress enacts political and land ordinances for new states |
| **1786** | • Nationalists hold convention in Annapolis, Maryland<br>• Shays's Rebellion roils Massachusetts |
| **1787** | • Congress passes Northwest Ordinance<br>• Constitutional Convention in Philadelphia |
| **1787–1788** | • Jay, Madison, and Hamilton write *The Federalist*<br>• Eleven states ratify U.S. Constitution |

**KEY TURNING POINTS:** Gates defeats Burgoyne at Saratoga (1777), the Franco-American alliance (1778), and Cornwallis surrenders at Yorktown (1781). How were these three events linked? How important was the French alliance to the Patriot victory?

# 7

**CHAPTER**

# Hammering Out a Federal Republic
## 1787–1820

Like an earthquake, the American Revolution shook the European monarchical order, and its aftershocks reverberated for decades. By "creating a new republic based on the rights of the individual, the North Americans introduced a new force into the world," the eminent German historian Leopold von Ranke warned the king of Bavaria in 1854, a force that might cost the monarch his throne. Before 1776, "a king who ruled by the grace of God had been the center around which everything turned. Now the idea emerged that power should come from below [from the people]."

Other republican-inspired upheavals—England's Puritan Revolution of the 1640s and the French Revolution of 1789—ended in political chaos and military rule. Similar fates befell many Latin American republics that won independence from Spain in the early nineteenth century. But the American states escaped both anarchy and dictatorship. Having been raised in a Radical Whig political culture that viewed standing armies and powerful generals as instruments of tyranny, General George Washington left public life in 1783 to manage his plantation, astonishing European observers but bolstering the authority of elected Patriot leaders. "'Tis a Conduct so novel," American painter John Trumbull reported from London, that it is "inconceivable to People [here]."

The great task of fashioning representative republican governments absorbed the energy and intellect of an entire generation and was rife with conflict. Seeking to perpetuate the elite-led polity of the colonial era, Federalists celebrated "natural aristocrats" such as Washington and condemned the radical republicanism of the French Revolution. In response, Jefferson and his Republican followers claimed the Fourth of July as their holiday and "we the people" as their political language. "There was a grand democrat procession in Town on the 4th of July," came a report from Baltimore: "All the farmers, tanners, black-smiths, shoemakers, etc. were there . . . and afterwards they went to a grand feast."

Many people of high status worried that the new state governments were too attentive to the demands of such ordinary workers and their families. When considering a bill, Connecticut conservative Ezra Stiles grumbled, every elected official "instantly thinks how it will affect his constituents" rather than how it would enhance the general welfare. What Stiles criticized as irresponsible, however, most Americans welcomed. The concerns of ordinary citizens were now paramount, and traditional elites trembled.

**IDENTIFY THE BIG IDEA**

What was required to make the United States a strong, viable, independent republic in its early years, and how did debates over the Constitution shape relations between the national government and the states?

**An Emblem of America, 1800**   In the first years of independence, citizens of the United States searched for a symbolic representation of their new nation. This engraving shows many of the choices: Should the symbol of "America" have an ideological meaning, as in the Goddess of Liberty? Or should it enshrine national heroes, as in the stone Memorial to Washington? Or should America's symbol be found among its unique features, such as Niagara Falls (pictured in the background) or the presence of Africans and Indians (as represented by the black youth to the right and the spear-brandishing figure in front of the falls)? Or, finally, should its symbol be the national flag? Courtesy of the John Carter Brown Library at Brown University.

# The Political Crisis of the 1790s

The final decade of the eighteenth century brought fresh challenges for American politics. The Federalists split into two factions over financial policy and the French Revolution, and their leaders, Alexander Hamilton and Thomas Jefferson, offered contrasting visions of the future. Would the United States remain an agricultural nation governed by local officials, as Jefferson hoped? Or would Hamilton's vision of a strong national government and an economy based on manufacturing become reality?

## The Federalists Implement the Constitution

The Constitution expanded the dimensions of political life by allowing voters to choose national leaders as well as local and state officials. The Federalists swept the election of 1788, winning forty-four seats in the House of Representatives; only eight Antifederalists won election. As expected, members of the electoral college chose George Washington as president. John Adams received the second-highest number of electoral votes and became vice president.

**Devising the New Government**   Once the military savior of his country, Washington now became its political father. At age fifty-seven, the first president possessed great personal dignity and a cautious personality. To maintain continuity, he adopted many of the administrative practices of the Confederation and asked Congress to reestablish the existing executive departments: Foreign Affairs (State), Finance (Treasury), and War. To head the Department of State, Washington chose Thomas Jefferson, a fellow Virginian and an experienced diplomat. For secretary of the treasury, he turned to Alexander Hamilton, a lawyer and his former military aide. The president designated Jefferson, Hamilton, and Secretary of War Henry Knox as his cabinet, or advisory body.

The Constitution mandated a supreme court, but the Philadelphia convention gave Congress the task of creating a national court system. The Federalists wanted strong national institutions, and the **Judiciary Act of 1789** reflected their vision. The act established a federal district court in each state and three circuit courts to hear appeals from the districts, with the Supreme Court having the final say. The Judiciary Act also specified that cases arising in state courts that involved federal laws could be appealed to the Supreme Court. This provision ensured that federal judges would have the final say on the meaning of the Constitution.

**The Bill of Rights**   The Federalists kept their promise to add a declaration of rights to the Constitution. James Madison, now a member of the House of Representatives, submitted nineteen amendments to the First Congress; by 1791, ten had been approved by Congress and ratified by the states. These ten amendments, known as the **Bill of Rights**, safeguard fundamental personal rights, including freedom of speech and religion, and mandate legal procedures, such as trial by jury. By protecting individual citizens, the amendments eased Antifederalists' fears of an oppressive national government and secured the legitimacy of the Constitution. They also addressed the issue of federalism: the proper balance between the authority of the national and state governments. But that question was constantly contested until the Civil War and remains important today.

## Hamilton's Financial Program

George Washington's most important decision was choosing Alexander Hamilton as secretary of the treasury. An ambitious self-made man of great intelligence, Hamilton married into the Schuyler family, influential Hudson River Valley landowners, and was a prominent lawyer in New York City. At the Philadelphia convention, he condemned the "democratic spirit" and called for an authoritarian government and a president with near-monarchical powers.

As treasury secretary, Hamilton devised bold policies to enhance national authority and to assist financiers and merchants. He outlined his plans in three pathbreaking reports to Congress: on public credit (January 1790), on a national bank (December 1790), and on manufactures (December 1791). These reports outlined a coherent program of national mercantilism — government-assisted economic development.

**Public Credit: Redemption and Assumption**   The financial and social implications of Hamilton's "**Report on the Public Credit**" made it instantly controversial. Hamilton asked Congress to redeem at face value the $55 million in Confederation securities held by foreign and domestic investors (Figure 7.1). His reasons were simple: As an underdeveloped nation, the United States needed good credit to secure loans from Dutch and

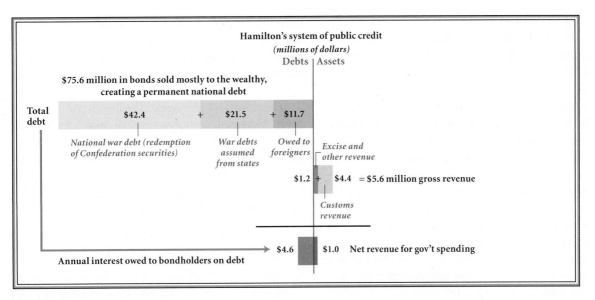

**FIGURE 7.1**

**Hamilton's Fiscal Structure, 1792**

As treasury secretary, Alexander Hamilton established a national debt by issuing government bonds and using the proceeds to redeem Confederation securities and assume the war debts of the states. To pay the annual interest due on the bonds, he used the revenue from excise taxes and customs duties. Hamilton deliberately did not attempt to redeem the bonds because he wanted to tie the interests of the wealthy Americans who owned them to the new national government.

British financiers. However, Hamilton's redemption plan would give enormous profits to speculators, who had bought up depreciated securities. For example, the Massachusetts firm of Burrell & Burrell had paid $600 for Confederation notes with a face value of $2,500; it stood to reap a profit of $1,900. Such windfall gains offended a majority of Americans, who condemned the speculative practices of capitalist financiers. Equally controversial was Hamilton's proposal to pay the Burrells and other note holders with new interest-bearing securities, thereby creating a permanent national debt.

Patrick Henry condemned this plan "to erect, and concentrate, and perpetuate a large monied interest" and warned that it would prove "fatal to the existence of American liberty." James Madison demanded that Congress recompense those who originally owned Confederation securities: the thousands of shopkeepers, farmers, and soldiers who had bought or accepted them during the dark days of the war. However, it would have been difficult to trace the original owners; moreover, nearly half the members of the House of Representatives owned Confederation securities and would profit personally from Hamilton's plan. Melding practicality with self-interest, the House rejected Madison's suggestion.

Hamilton then proposed that the national government further enhance public credit by assuming the war debts of the states. This assumption plan, costing $22 million, also favored well-to-do creditors such as Abigail Adams, who had bought depreciated Massachusetts government bonds with a face value of $2,400 for only a few hundred dollars and would reap a windfall profit. Still, Adams was a long-term investor, not a speculator like Assistant Secretary of the Treasury William Duer. Knowing Hamilton's intentions in advance, Duer and his associates secretly bought up $4.6 million of the war bonds of southern states at bargain rates. Congressional critics condemned Duer's speculation. They also pointed out that some states had already paid off their war debts; in response, Hamilton promised to reimburse those states. To win the votes of congressmen from Virginia and Maryland, the treasury chief arranged another deal: he agreed that the permanent national capital would be built along the Potomac River, where suspicious southerners could easily watch its operations. Such astute bargaining gave Hamilton the votes he needed to enact his redemption and assumption plans.

**UNDERSTAND POINTS OF VIEW**

Why did Hamilton believe a national debt would strengthen the United States and help to ensure its survival?

**Creating a National Bank**  In December 1790, Hamilton asked Congress to charter the **Bank of the United States**, which would be jointly owned by private stockholders and the national government. Hamilton argued that the bank would provide stability to the specie-starved American economy by making loans to merchants, handling government funds, and issuing bills of credit — much as the Bank of England had done in Great Britain. These potential benefits persuaded Congress to grant Hamilton's bank a twenty-year charter and to send the legislation to the president for his approval.

At this critical juncture, Secretary of State Thomas Jefferson joined with James Madison to oppose Hamilton's financial initiatives. Jefferson charged that Hamilton's national bank was unconstitutional. "The incorporation of a Bank," Jefferson told President Washington, was not a power expressly "delegated to the United States by the Constitution." Jefferson's argument rested on a *strict* interpretation of the Constitution. Hamilton preferred a *loose* interpretation; he told Washington that Article 1, Section 8, empowered Congress to make "all Laws which shall be necessary and proper" to carry out the provisions of the Constitution. Agreeing with Hamilton, the president signed the legislation.

**Raising Revenue Through Tariffs**  Hamilton now sought revenue to pay the annual interest on the national debt. At his insistence, Congress imposed excise taxes, including a duty on whiskey distilled in the United States. These taxes would yield $1 million a year. To raise another $4 million to $5 million, the treasury secretary proposed higher tariffs on foreign imports. Although Hamilton's "**Report on Manufactures**" (1791)

urged the expansion of American manufacturing, he did not support high protective tariffs that would exclude foreign products. Rather, he advocated moderate revenue tariffs that would pay the interest on the debt and other government expenses.

Hamilton's scheme worked brilliantly. As American trade increased, customs revenue rose steadily and paid down the national debt. Controversies notwithstanding, the treasury secretary had devised a strikingly modern and successful fiscal system; as entrepreneur Samuel Blodget Jr. declared in 1801, "the country prospered beyond all former example."

## Jefferson's Agrarian Vision

Hamilton paid a high political price for his success. As Washington began his second four-year term in 1793, Hamilton's financial measures had split the Federalists into bitterly opposed factions. Most northern Federalists supported the treasury secretary, while most southern Federalists joined a group headed by Madison and Jefferson. By 1794, the two factions had acquired names. Hamiltonians remained Federalists; the allies of Madison and Jefferson called themselves Democratic Republicans or simply Republicans.

Thomas Jefferson spoke for southern planters and western farmers. Well-read in architecture, natural history, agricultural science, and political theory, Jefferson embraced the optimism of the Enlightenment. He believed in the "improvability of the human race" and deplored the corruption and social divisions that threatened its progress. Having seen the poverty of laborers in British factories, Jefferson doubted that wageworkers had the economic and political independence needed to sustain a republican polity.

**Two Visions of America**

Thomas Jefferson (left) and Alexander Hamilton confront each other in these portraits, as they did in the political battles of the 1790s. Jefferson was pro-French, Hamilton pro-British. Jefferson favored farmers and artisans; Hamilton supported merchants and financiers. Jefferson believed in democracy and rule by legislative majorities; Hamilton argued for strong executives and judges. Still, in the contested presidential election of 1800, Hamilton (who detested candidate Aaron Burr) threw his support to Jefferson and secured the presidency for his longtime political foe. The White House Historical Association (White House Collection). / Yale University Art Gallery/Art Resource, NY.

Jefferson therefore set his democratic vision of America in a society of independent yeomen farm families. "Those who labor in the earth are the chosen people of God," he wrote. The grain and meat from their homesteads would feed European nations, which "would manufacture and send us in exchange our clothes and other comforts." Jefferson's notion of an international division of labor resembled that proposed by Scottish economist Adam Smith in *The Wealth of Nations* (1776).

 To see a longer excerpt of Jefferson's *Notes on the State of Virginia,* along with other primary sources from this period, see *Sources for America's History*.

Turmoil in Europe brought Jefferson's vision closer to reality. The French Revolution began in 1789; four years later, the First French Republic (1792–1804) went to war against a British-led coalition of monarchies. As fighting disrupted European farming, wheat prices leaped from 5 to 8 shillings a bushel and remained high for twenty years, bringing substantial profits to Chesapeake and Middle Atlantic farmers. "Our farmers have never experienced such prosperity," remarked one observer. Simultaneously, a boom in the export of raw cotton, fueled by the invention of the cotton gin and the mechanization of cloth production in Britain, boosted the economies of Georgia and South Carolina. As Jefferson had hoped, European markets brought prosperity to American agriculture.

## The French Revolution Divides Americans

American merchants profited even more handsomely from the European war. In 1793, President Washington issued a **Proclamation of Neutrality**, allowing U.S. citizens to trade with all belligerents. As neutral carriers, American merchant ships claimed a right to pass through Britain's naval blockade of French ports, and American firms quickly took over the lucrative sugar trade between France and its West Indian islands. Commercial earnings rose spectacularly, averaging $20 million annually in the 1790s — twice the value of cotton and tobacco exports. As the American merchant fleet increased from 355,000 tons in 1790 to 1.1 million tons in 1808, northern shipbuilders and merchants provided work for thousands of shipwrights, sailmakers, dockhands, and seamen. Carpenters, masons, and cabinetmakers in Boston, New York, and Philadelphia easily found work building warehouses and fashionable "Federal-style" town houses for newly affluent merchants.

**Ideological Politics**   As Americans profited from Europe's struggles, they argued passionately over its ideologies. Most Americans had welcomed the **French Revolution** (1789–1799) because it abolished feudalism and established a constitutional monarchy. The creation of the First French Republic was more controversial. Many applauded the end of the monarchy and embraced the democratic ideology of the radical **Jacobins**. Like the Jacobins, they formed political clubs and began to address one another as "citizen." However, Americans with strong religious beliefs condemned the new French government for closing Christian churches and promoting a rational religion based on "natural morality." Fearing social revolution at home, wealthy Americans condemned revolutionary leader Robespierre and his followers for executing King Louis XVI and three thousand aristocrats.

Their fears were well founded, because Hamilton's economic policies quickly sparked a domestic insurgency. In 1794, western Pennsylvania farmers mounted the so-called **Whiskey Rebellion** to protest Hamilton's excise tax on spirits (Thinking Like a Historian, p. 220). This tax had cut demand for the corn whiskey the farmers distilled and bartered for eastern manufactures. Like the Sons of Liberty in 1765 and the Shaysites in 1786, the Whiskey Rebels assailed the tax collectors who sent the farmers' hard-earned money to a distant government. Protesters waved banners proclaiming the French revolutionary slogan "Liberty, Equality, Fraternity!" To deter popular rebellion and uphold national authority, President Washington raised a militia force of 12,000 troops and dispersed the Whiskey Rebels.

**COMPARE AND CONTRAST**
How did Jefferson's idea of an agrarian republic differ from the economic vision put forward by Alexander Hamilton?

**Jay's Treaty**   Britain's maritime strategy intensified political divisions in America. Beginning in late 1793, the British navy seized 250 American ships carrying French sugar and other goods. Hoping to protect merchant property through diplomacy, Washington dispatched John Jay to Britain. But Jay returned with a controversial treaty that ignored the American claim that "free ships make free goods" and accepted Britain's right to stop neutral ships. The treaty also required the U.S. government to make "full and complete compensation" to British merchants for pre–Revolutionary War debts owed by American citizens. In return, the

## The Social Life of Alcohol

Alcohol was ubiquitous in post-Revolutionary America. Expensive wines and distilled spirits traveled through the channels of Atlantic trade; molasses was imported from the West Indies and distilled into rum in American port towns; and cider, beer, and whiskey were produced on a small scale everywhere in the countryside. Taverns were centers of social and political activity. Alcohol both mirrored and reinforced the economic and geographical divisions in American life.

**1. James Newport's ad in the *Pennsylvania Gazette*, 1790.**

JAMES NEWPORT, At his *Wine, Spirit and Cordial Stores*, in Second street, at the upper corner of Carter's alley, has, by Wholesale and Retail,

MADEIRA, Sherry, Lisbon, Teneriffe, Malaga, Fayal, and Port Wines, Jamaica spirits, Antigua rum, Philadelphia ditto, Holland gin, Philadelphia ditto, very excellent, in cases, Coniac [sic] brandy, American ditto, good flavor, choice shrub. CORDIALS, &c. Anniseed water, clove water, all-fours, Cinnamon water, prime wine and rum colouring, wine bitters. Spirits of wine. Retail Stores and Tavern-keepers will in particular, find their interest in buying here, the articles being all the best in their kind, and selling at the most reduced prices. Philadelphia, April 30, 1790.

**2. Benjamin Chew on providing alcohol to his slaves, 1794.** *The instructions of a prominent Philadelphia lawyer and landowner to his overseer about giving rum to his slaves during the harvest.*

I have written . . . to let you have [illegible] Rum & other necessaries for the Harvest. But as these articles are so [illegible] dear I must recommend it to you to be as sparing of them as possible. . . . I must rely on you good man [to conduct] the Business. . . . I would have you let the People have a little Rum — let them be cautious in using too much Spirits during Harvest — it will be well to mix some molasses with water to drink — it is very wholesome & much recommended. . . . I need not caution you that a great deal depends upon your own proper attention to yourself and that you are careful of good Conduct during Harvest.

**3. Anonymous, *The Toast*, c. 1810–1815.**

Source: John Nugent Collection, Newburgh, Indiana.

**4. John Lewis Krimmel, *Village Tavern*, 1814.** *This painting of a postman arriving at a Pennsylvania tavern with letters and newspapers reminds us that taverns were not merely places to drink.*

Source: John Lewis Krimmel (American, 1786–1821) Village Tavern, 1813–1814, oil on canvas, 16⅞ x 22½ inches, Toledo Museum of Art (Toledo, Ohio) Purchased with funds from the Florence Scott Libbey Bequest in Memory of her Father, Maurice A. Scott. 1954.13. Photo Credit: Photography Incorporated, Toledo.

execution and obtaining a repeal of the excise law, he or they will be deemed as enemies and stand opposed to virtuous principles of republican liberty, and shall receive punishment according to the nature of the offense.

And whereas, a certain John Reed, now resident in Washington, and being at his place near Pittsburgh, called Reedsburgh, and having a set of stills employed at said Reedsburgh, entered on the excise docket, contrary to the will and good pleasure of his fellow citizens, and came not forth to assist in the suppression of the execution of said law, by aiding and assisting in the late expedition, have, by delinquency, manifested his approbation to the execution of the aforesaid law, is hereby charged forthwith to cause the contents of this paper, without adding or diminishing, to be published in the Pittsburgh Gazette, the ensuing week, under the no less penalty than the consumption of his distillery.

Given under my hand, this 19th day of July, one thousand seven hundred and ninety-four.

Sources: (1) James Newport, *Pennsylvania Gazette*, May 5, 1790; (2) Chew Family Papers, Box 773, ff. 25, 10, Historical Society of Pennsylvania; (5) *Pennsylvania Gazette*, October 1, 1794; (6) *Pennsylvania Archives*, 2nd ser., 4:61–62 (Harrisburg: E. K. Meyers, State Printer, 1890).

**5. Public notice from the *Pennsylvania Gazette*, 1794.** *Here, a tavern serves as the gathering place for citizens interested in nominating candidates for election to office.*

THE INHABITANTS of the County of Chester, are hereby requested to meet at the Centre house, kept by Abraham Marshall, in West Bradford, on FRIDAY the 10th Day of October next, at 10 o'clock, A. M. in order to form a TICKET for the ensuing Election.

**6. Tom the Tinker demands compliance, July 23, 1794.** *During the Whiskey Rebellion, "Tom the Tinker" pinned this notice to a tree near John Reed's distillery. Reed had it published in a Pittsburgh newspaper.*

In taking a survey of the troops under my direction in the late expedition against that insolent exciseman, John Neville, I find there were a great number of delinquents, even among those who carry on distilling. It will, therefore, be observed that I, Tom the Tinker, will not suffer any certain class or set of men to be excluded [from] the service of this my district, when notified to attend on any expedition carried on in order to obstruct the execution of the excise law, and obtain a repeal thereof.

And I do declare on my solemn word, that if such delinquents do not come forth on the next alarm, with equipments, and give their assistance in opposing the

---

### ANALYZING THE EVIDENCE

1. Who is the intended audience for an advertisement like James Newport's (source 1)? How many Atlantic ports of call are represented in the products he advertises?

2. The two paintings (sources 3 and 4), set in the interiors of a private home and a tavern, depict mostly men. What have they gathered for in each case? *Village Tavern* is set during the War of 1812. How does that fact influence your interpretation of the scene? What do you think the woman and child are doing in the tavern?

3. *Village Tavern* (source 4) and the ad calling for a political gathering (source 5) both suggest the way that politics and drinking often mixed. How might the fact that taverns were gathering places for political discussion and decision making have influenced outcomes?

4. What concerns does Benjamin Chew express in his correspondence with his overseer (source 2)? Given those worries, why do you think he provides rum to his slaves at all?

5. Tom the Tinker expressed the collective will of whiskey distillers in western Pennsylvania during the Whiskey Rebellion (source 6). Why would it have been important to enforce unanimous action during the uprising?

### PUTTING IT ALL TOGETHER

Considering everything you know about the trade and consumption of alcohol, social stratification in the early republic, and differences between urban and rural communities, write a short essay that considers the ways in which taverns and alcohol helped unite people in some ways while differentiating or dividing them in others.

**The Whiskey Rebellion, 1794**

This painting of Washington reviewing the militia forces that would march against the Whiskey Rebels in western Pennsylvania expresses a Federalist vision of hierarchy (in the form of officers on horseback) and order (represented by the ranks of troops). The reality was messier: militia was called up from four states, but when volunteers were too few the states resorted to a draft, which prompted protests and riots. In the end, the militia force of more than 12,000 men was larger than the Continental army itself through much of the Revolution. Upon its approach, the rebellion evaporated. Twenty-four men were indicted for treason; two were sentenced to hang, but Washington pardoned them to encourage peaceful reconciliation. The Granger Collection, New York.

agreement allowed Americans to submit claims for illegal seizures and required the British to remove their troops and Indian agents from the Northwest Territory. Despite Republican charges that **Jay's Treaty** was too conciliatory, the Senate ratified it in 1795, but only by the two-thirds majority required by the Constitution. As long as the Federalists were in power, the United States would have a pro-British foreign policy.

**The Haitian Revolution**   The French Revolution inspired a revolution closer to home that would also impact the United States. The wealthy French plantation colony of Saint-Domingue in the West Indies was deeply divided: a small class of elite planters stood atop the population of 40,000 free whites and dominated the island's half million slaves. In

**IDENTIFY CAUSES**
How did events abroad during the 1790s sharpen political divisions in the United States?

between, some 28,000 *gens de couleur*—free men of color—were excluded from most professions, forbidden from taking the names of their white relatives, and prevented from dressing and carrying themselves like whites. The French Revolution intensified conflict between planters and free blacks, giving way to a massive slave uprising in 1791 that aimed to abolish slavery. The uprising touched off years of civil war, along with Spanish and British invasions. In 1798, black Haitians led by Toussaint L'Ouverture—himself a former slave-owning planter—seized control of the country. After five more years of fighting, in 1803 Saint-Domingue became the independent nation of Haiti: the first black republic in the Atlantic World.

The **Haitian Revolution** profoundly impacted the United States. In 1793, thousands of refugees—planters, slaves, and free blacks alike—fled the island and traveled to Charleston, Norfolk, Baltimore,

**Toussaint L'Ouverture, Haitian Revolutionary and Statesman**

The American Revolution of 1776 constituted a victory for republicanism; the Haitian revolt of the 1790s represented a triumph of liberty over slavery and a demand for racial equality. After leading the black army that ousted French planters and British invaders from Haiti, Toussaint formed a constitutional government in 1801. A year later, when French troops invaded the island, he negotiated a treaty that halted Haitian resistance in exchange for a pledge that the French would not reinstate slavery. Subsequently, the French seized Toussaint and imprisoned him in France, where he died in 1803. Snark/Art Resource, NY.

Philadelphia, and New York, while newspapers detailed the horrors of the unfolding war. Many slaveholders panicked, fearful that the "contagion" of black liberation would undermine their own slave regimes. U.S. policy toward the rebellion presented a knotty problem. The first instinct of the Washington administration was to supply aid to the island's white population. Adams — strongly antislavery and no friend of France — changed course, aiding the rebels and strengthening commercial ties. Jefferson, though sympathetic to moral arguments against slavery, was himself a southern slaveholder; he was, moreover, an ardent supporter of France. When he became president, he cut off aid to the rebels, imposed a trade embargo, and refused to recognize an independent Haiti. For many Americans, an independent nation of liberated citizen-slaves was a horrifying paradox, a perversion of the republican ideal (America Compared, p. 224).

## The Rise of Political Parties

The appearance of Federalists and Republicans marked a new stage in American politics — what historians call the First Party System. Colonial legislatures had factions based on family, ethnicity, or region, but they did not have organized political parties. Nor did the new state and national constitutions make any provision for political societies. Indeed, most Americans believed that parties were dangerous because they looked out for themselves rather than serving the public interest.

But a shared understanding of the public interest collapsed in the face of sharp conflicts over Hamilton's fiscal policies. Most merchants and creditors supported the Federalist Party, as did wheat-exporting slaveholders in the Tidewater districts of the Chesapeake. The emerging Republican coalition included southern tobacco and rice planters, debt-conscious western farmers, Germans and Scots-Irish in the southern backcountry, and subsistence farmers in the Northeast.

Party identity crystallized in 1796. To prepare for the presidential election, Federalist and Republican leaders called caucuses in Congress and conventions in the states. They also mobilized popular support by organizing public festivals and processions: the Federalists held banquets in February to celebrate Washington's birthday, and the Republicans marched through the streets on July 4 to honor the Declaration of Independence.

In the election, voters gave Federalists a majority in Congress and made John Adams president. Adams continued Hamilton's pro-British foreign policy and strongly criticized French seizures of American merchant ships. When the French foreign minister Talleyrand solicited a loan and a bribe from American diplomats to stop the seizures, Adams charged that Talleyrand's agents, whom he dubbed X, Y, and Z, had insulted America's honor. In response to the **XYZ Affair**, Congress cut off trade with France in 1798 and authorized American privateering (licensing private ships to seize French vessels). This undeclared maritime war curtailed American trade with the French West Indies and resulted in the capture of nearly two hundred French and American merchant vessels.

### The Naturalization, Alien, and Sedition Acts of 1798
As Federalists became more hostile to the French Republic, they also took a harder line against their Republican critics. When Republican-minded

## The Haitian Revolution and the Problem of Race

The slave uprising on the French island of Saint-Domingue triggered international war, created a refugee crisis, and ended with the creation of a new republic. The American Revolution did all these things as well, yet the United States did not support either the rebellion or the republic of Haiti.

### Savannah City Council's Resolution in Response to the Haitian Uprising, 1795

Whereas, from the mischiefs which the people of St. Domingo, and other French islands, have experienced, from the insurrection of their Negroes and People of Colour, the precautions taken by the people of South Carolina . . . to prevent the importation or landing of any such Negroes or Mulattoes amongst them, and the information the Citizens now assembled have received, that a vessel is now lying at Cockspur, recently from Kingston, with near one hundred Negroes on board, whose landing may be dangerous to the inhabitants of this state, with the daily expectation of many more; therefore, to prevent the evils that may arise from suffering people of this description, under any pretense whatever, from being introduced amongst us, the Citizens pledge themselves unanimously to support the City Council in any salutary measures they may adopt[.]

Source: Schomburg Center for Research in Black Culture, Manuscripts, Archives and Rare Books Division, Image ID 1243998, digitalgallery.nypl.org.

### Excerpts from the Constitution of 1801 Established by the Central Assembly of Saint-Domingue

**Article 1.** – Saint-Domingue in its entire expanse, and Samana, La Tortue, La Gonave, Les Cayemites, L'Ile-a-Vache, La Saone and other adjacent islands form the territory of a single colony, which is part of the French Empire, but ruled under particular laws. . . .

**Article 3.** – There cannot exist slaves on this territory, servitude is therein forever abolished. All men are born, live and die free and French.

**Article 4.** – All men, regardless of color, are eligible to all employment.

**Article 5.** – There shall exist no distinction other than those based on virtue and talent, and other superiority afforded by law in the exercise of a public function.

The law is the same for all whether in punishment or in protection.

Source: *Haitian Constitution of 1801* (English), The Louverture Project, thelouvertureproject.org.

---

### QUESTIONS FOR ANALYSIS

1. How does the first document express the fears of American slaveholders? Why do you suppose the Savannah City Council perceived Haitian refugees to be a danger?

2. How does the excerpt from the 1801 Constitution echo themes of the American Revolution? What differences do you see? Comparing the second document to the first, how would you say that the two revolutions impacted views of race in Georgia and in Haiti?

---

immigrants from Ireland vehemently attacked Adams's policies, a Federalist pamphleteer responded in kind: "Were I president, I would hang them for otherwise they would murder me." To silence the critics, the Federalists enacted three coercive laws limiting individual rights and threatening the fledgling party system. The **Naturalization Act** lengthened the residency requirement for American citizenship from five to fourteen years, the **Alien Act** authorized the deportation of foreigners, and the **Sedition Act** prohibited the publication of insults or malicious attacks on the president

or members of Congress. "He that is not for us is against us," thundered the Federalist *Gazette of the United States*. Using the Sedition Act, Federalist prosecutors arrested more than twenty Republican newspaper editors and politicians, accused them of sedition, and convicted and jailed a number of them.

This repression sparked a constitutional crisis. Republicans charged that the Sedition Act violated the First Amendment's prohibition against "abridging the freedom of speech, or of the press." However, they did not appeal to the Supreme Court because the Court's power to review congressional legislation was uncertain and because most of the justices were Federalists. Instead, Madison and Jefferson looked to the state legislatures. At their urging, the Kentucky and Virginia legislatures issued resolutions in 1798 declaring the Alien and Sedition Acts to be "unauthoritative, void, and of no force." The **Virginia and Kentucky Resolutions** set forth a states' rights interpretation of the Constitution, asserting that the states had a "right to judge" the legitimacy of national laws.

The conflict over the Sedition Act set the stage for the presidential election of 1800. Jefferson, once opposed on principle to political parties, now asserted that they could "watch and relate to the people" the activities of an oppressive government. Meanwhile, John Adams reevaluated his foreign policy. Rejecting Hamilton's advice to declare war against France (and benefit from the resulting upsurge in patriotism), Adams put country ahead of party and used diplomacy to end the maritime conflict.

**The "Revolution of 1800"**   The campaign of 1800 degenerated into a bitter, no-holds-barred contest. The Federalists launched personal attacks on Jefferson, branding him an irresponsible pro-French radical and, because he opposed state support of religion in Virginia, "the arch-apostle of irreligion and free thought." Both parties changed state election laws to favor their candidates, and rumors circulated of a Federalist plot to stage a military coup.

The election did not end these worries. Thanks to a low Federalist turnout in Virginia and Pennsylvania and the three-fifths rule (which boosted electoral votes in the southern states), Jefferson won a narrow 73-to-65 victory over Adams in the electoral college. However, the Republican electors also gave 73 votes to Aaron Burr of New York, who was Jefferson's vice-presidential running mate (Map 7.1). The Constitution specified that in the case of a tie vote, the House of Representatives would choose between the candidates. For thirty-five rounds of balloting, Federalists in the House blocked Jefferson's election, prompting rumors that Virginia would raise a military force to put him into office.

Ironically, arch-Federalist Alexander Hamilton ushered in a more democratic era by supporting Jefferson. Calling Burr an "embryo Caesar" and the "most unfit man in the United States for the office of president," Hamilton persuaded key Federalists to allow Jefferson's election. The Federalists' concern for political stability also played a role. As Senator James Bayard of Delaware explained, "It was admitted on all

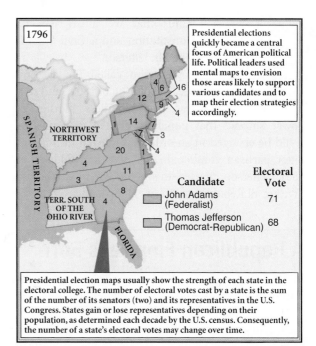

Presidential elections quickly became a central focus of American political life. Political leaders used mental maps to envision those areas likely to support various candidates and to map their election strategies accordingly.

| Candidate | Electoral Vote |
|---|---|
| John Adams (Federalist) | 71 |
| Thomas Jefferson (Democrat-Republican) | 68 |

Presidential election maps usually show the strength of each state in the electoral college. The number of electoral votes cast by a state is the sum of the number of its senators (two) and its representatives in the U.S. Congress. States gain or lose representatives depending on their population, as determined each decade by the U.S. census. Consequently, the number of a state's electoral votes may change over time.

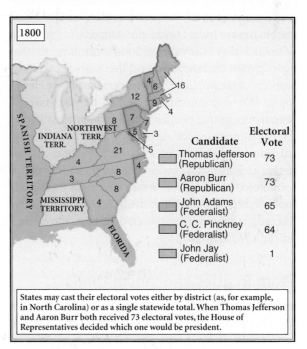

| Candidate | Electoral Vote |
|---|---|
| Thomas Jefferson (Republican) | 73 |
| Aaron Burr (Republican) | 73 |
| John Adams (Federalist) | 65 |
| C. C. Pinckney (Federalist) | 64 |
| John Jay (Federalist) | 1 |

States may cast their electoral votes either by district (as, for example, in North Carolina) or as a single statewide total. When Thomas Jefferson and Aaron Burr both received 73 electoral votes, the House of Representatives decided which one would be president.

**MAP 7.1**

**The Presidential Elections of 1796 and 1800**

Both elections pitted Federalist John Adams of Massachusetts against Republican Thomas Jefferson of Virginia, and both saw voters split along regional lines. Adams carried every New England state and, reflecting Federalist strength in maritime and commercial areas, the eastern districts of the Middle Atlantic states; Jefferson won most of the agricultural-based states of the South and West (Kentucky and Tennessee). New York was the pivotal swing state. It gave its 12 electoral votes to Adams in 1796 and, thanks to the presence of Aaron Burr on the Republican ticket, bestowed them on Jefferson in 1800.

UNDERSTAND
POINTS OF VIEW
Why did Jefferson consider
his election in 1800 to be
revolutionary?

hands that we must risk the Constitution and a Civil War or take Mr. Jefferson."

Jefferson called the election the "Revolution of 1800," and so it was. The bloodless transfer of power showed that popularly elected governments could be changed in an orderly way, even in times of bitter partisan conflict. In his inaugural address in 1801, Jefferson praised this achievement, declaring, "We are all Republicans, we are all Federalists."

# A Republican Empire Is Born

In the Treaty of Paris of 1783, Great Britain gave up its claims to the trans-Appalachian region and, said one British diplomat, left the Indian nations "to the care of their [American] neighbours." *Care* was hardly the right word: many white Americans wanted to destroy native communities. "Cut up every Indian Cornfield and burn every Indian town," proclaimed Congressman William Henry Drayton of South Carolina, so that their "nation be extirpated and the lands become the property of the public." Other leaders, including Henry Knox, Washington's first secretary of war, favored assimilating native peoples into Euro-American society. Knox proposed the division of tribal lands among individual Indian families, who would become citizens of the various states. Indians resisted both forms of domination and fought to retain control of their lands and cultures. In the ensuing struggle, the United States emerged as an expansive power, determined to control the future of the continent.

## Sham Treaties and Indian Lands

As in the past, the major struggle between natives and Europeans centered on land rights. Invoking the Paris treaty and regarding Britain's Indian allies as conquered peoples, the U.S. government asserted both sovereignty over and ownership of the trans-Appalachian west. Indian nations rejected both claims, pointing out they had not been conquered and had not signed the Paris treaty. "Our lands are our life and our breath," declared Creek chief Hallowing King; "if we part with them, we part with our blood." Brushing aside such objections and threatening military action, U.S. commissioners forced the pro-British Iroquois

PLACE EVENTS
IN CONTEXT
Why did the United States
go to war against western
Indians so quickly after the
Revolution?

peoples—Mohawks, Onondagas, Cayugas, and Senecas—to cede huge tracts in New York and Pennsylvania in the Treaty of Fort Stanwix (1784). New York land speculators used liquor and bribes to take a million more acres, confining the once powerful Iroquois to reservations—essentially colonies of subordinate peoples.

American negotiators used similar tactics to grab Ohio Valley lands. At the Treaties of Fort McIntosh (1785) and Fort Finney (1786), they pushed the Chippewas, Delawares, Ottawas, Wyandots, and Shawnees to cede most of the future state of Ohio. The tribes quickly repudiated the agreements, justifiably claiming they were made under duress. Recognizing the failure of these agreements, American negotiators arranged for a comprehensive agreement at Fort Harmar (1789), but it, too, failed. To defend their lands, these tribes joined with the Miami and Potawatomi Indians to form the Western Confederacy. Led by Miami chief Little Turtle, confederacy warriors crushed American expeditionary forces sent by President Washington in 1790 and 1791.

**The Treaty of Greenville** Fearing an alliance between the Western Confederacy and the British in Canada, Washington doubled the size of the U.S. Army and ordered General "Mad Anthony" Wayne to lead a new expedition. In August 1794, Wayne defeated the confederacy in the Battle of Fallen Timbers (near present-day Toledo, Ohio). However, continuing Indian resistance forced a compromise. In the **Treaty of Greenville** (1795), American negotiators acknowledged Indian ownership of the land, and, in return for various payments, the Western Confederacy ceded most of Ohio (Map 7.2). The Indian peoples also agreed to accept American sovereignty, placing themselves "under the protection of the United States, and no other Power whatever." These American advances caused Britain to agree, in Jay's Treaty (1795), to reduce its trade and military aid to Indians in the trans-Appalachian region.

The Greenville treaty sparked a wave of white migration. Kentucky already had a population of 73,000 in 1790, and in 1792 it was admitted to the Union as the fifteenth state (Vermont entered a year earlier). By 1800, more than 375,000 people had moved into the Ohio and Tennessee valleys; in 1805, the new state of Ohio alone had more than 100,000 residents. Thousands more farm families moved into the future states of Indiana and Illinois, sparking new conflicts with native peoples over land and hunting rights. Between 1790 and 1810, farm families settled as much

**MAP 7.2**

**Indian Cessions and State Formation, 1776–1840**

By virtue of the Treaty of Paris (1783) with Britain, the United States claimed sovereignty over the entire trans-Appalachian west. The Western Confederacy contested this claim, but the U.S. government upheld it with military force. By 1840, armed diplomacy had forced most Native American peoples to move west of the Mississippi River. White settlers occupied their lands, formed territorial governments, and eventually entered the Union as members of separate—and equal—states. By 1860, the trans-Appalachian region constituted an important economic and political force in American national life.

land as they had during the entire colonial period. The United States "is a country in flux," a visiting French aristocrat observed in 1799, and "that which is true today as regards its population, its establishments, its prices, its commerce will not be true six months from now."

**Assimilation Rejected**  To dampen further conflicts, the U.S. government encouraged Native Americans to assimilate into white society. The goal, as one Kentucky Protestant minister put it, was to make the Indian "a farmer, a citizen of the United States, and a Christian." Most Indians rejected wholesale assimilation; even those who joined Christian churches retained many ancestral values and religious beliefs. To think of themselves as individuals or members of a nuclear family, as white Americans were demanding, meant repudiating the clan, the very essence of Indian life. To preserve "the old Indian way," many native communities expelled white missionaries and forced Christianized Indians to participate in tribal rites. As a Munsee prophet declared, "There are two ways to God, one for the whites and one for the Indians."

A few Indian leaders sought a middle path in which new beliefs overlapped with old practices. Among the Senecas, the prophet Handsome Lake encouraged traditional animistic rituals that gave thanks to the sun, the earth, water, plants, and animals. But he included Christian elements in his teachings—the concepts of heaven and hell and an emphasis on personal morality—to deter his followers from alcohol, gambling, and witchcraft. Handsome Lake's teachings divided the Senecas into hostile factions. Led by Chief Red Jacket, traditionalists condemned European culture as evil and demanded a complete return to ancestral ways.

Most Indians also rejected the efforts of American missionaries to turn warriors into farmers and women into domestic helpmates. Among eastern woodland peoples, women grew corn, beans, and squash—the mainstays of the Indians' diet—and land cultivation rights passed through the female line. Consequently, women exercised considerable political influence, which they were eager to retain. Nor were Indian men interested in becoming farmers. When war raiding and hunting were no longer possible, many turned to grazing cattle and sheep.

**Treaty Negotiations at Greenville, 1795**

In 1785, Indian tribes in the Northwest Territory formed the Western Confederacy to prevent white settle-ment north of the Ohio River. After Indian triumphs in battles in the early 1790s, an American victory at the Battle of Fallen Timbers (1794) and the subsequent Treaty of Greenville (1795) opened up the region for white farmers. However, the treaty recognized many Indian rights because it was negotiated between relative equals on the battlefield. The artist suggests this equality: notice the height and stately bearing of the Indian leaders—ninety of whom signed the document—and their placement slightly in front of General Anthony Wayne and his officers. Chicago History Museum.

## Migration and the Changing Farm Economy

Native American resistance slowed the advance of white settlers but did not stop it. Nothing "short of a Chinese Wall, or a line of Troops," Washington declared, "will restrain . . . the Incroachment of Settlers, upon the Indian Territory." During the 1790s, two great streams of migrants moved out of the southern states (Map 7.3).

**Southern Migrants**    One stream, composed primar-ily of white tenant farmers and struggling yeomen families, flocked through the Cumberland Gap into

Kentucky and Tennessee. "Boundless settlements open a door for our citizens to run off and leave us," a wor-ried Maryland landlord lamented, "depreciating all our landed property and disabling us from paying taxes." In fact, many migrants were fleeing from this planter-controlled society. They wanted more freedom and hoped to prosper by growing cotton and hemp, which were in great demand.

Many settlers in Kentucky and Tennessee lacked ready cash to buy land. Like the North Carolina Regulators in the 1770s, poorer migrants claimed a customary right to occupy "back waste vacant Lands" sufficient "to provide a subsistence to themselves and their Posterity." Virginia legislators, who administered

**MAP 7.3**

**Regional Cultures Move West, 1790–1820**

By 1790, four core cultures had developed in the long-settled states along the Atlantic seaboard. Between 1790 and 1820, migrants from these four regions carried their cultures into the trans-Appalachian west. New England customs and institutions were a dominant influence in upstate New York and along the Great Lakes, while the Lower South's hierarchical system of slavery and heavy concentration of African Americans shaped the character of the new states along the Gulf of Mexico. The pattern of cultural diffusion was more complex in the Ohio and Tennessee river valleys, which were settled by migrants from various core regions.

Cultural Core Areas
- New England
- Mid-Atlantic
- Chesapeake
- Lower South
- Direction of cultural diffusion

the Kentucky Territory, had a more elitist vision. Although they allowed poor settlers to buy up to 1,400 acres of land at reduced prices, they sold or granted huge tracts of 100,000 acres to twenty-one groups of speculators and leading men. In 1792, this landed elite owned one-fourth of the state, while half the white men owned no land and lived as quasi-legal squatters or tenant farmers.

Widespread landlessness—and opposition to slavery—prompted a new migration across the Ohio River into the future states of Ohio, Indiana, and Illinois. In a free community, thought Peter Cartwright, a Methodist lay preacher from southwestern Kentucky who moved to Illinois, "I would be entirely clear of the evil of slavery . . . [and] could raise my children to work where work was not thought a degradation." Yet land distribution in Ohio was almost exactly as unequal as in Kentucky: in 1810, a quarter of its real estate was owned by 1 percent of the population, while more than half of its white men were landless.

Meanwhile, a second stream of southern planters and slaves from the Carolinas moved along the coastal plain toward the Gulf of Mexico. Some set up new estates in the interior of Georgia and South Carolina, while others moved into the future states of Alabama, Mississippi, and Louisiana. "The Alabama Feaver rages here with great violence," a North Carolina planter remarked, "and has carried off vast numbers of our Citizens."

Cotton was the key to this migratory surge. Around 1750, the demand for raw wool and cotton increased dramatically as water-powered spinning jennies, weaving mules, and other technological innovations of the Industrial Revolution boosted textile production in England. South Carolina and Georgia planters began growing cotton, and American inventors, including Connecticut-born Eli Whitney, built machines (called gins) that efficiently extracted seeds from its strands. To grow more cotton, white planters imported about 115,000 Africans between 1776 and 1808, when Congress cut off the Atlantic slave trade. The cotton boom financed the rapid settlement of Mississippi and Alabama—in a

**IDENTIFY CAUSES**

Why were westward migration and agricultural improvement so widespread in the late eighteenth and early nineteenth centuries?

**An Indian Log House in Georgia, 1791**

The Indian peoples of the southeastern United States—the Cherokees, Creeks, Choctaws, and Chickasaws—quickly adopted European practices that fit easily into their relatively settled, agricultural-based way of life. This sturdy Creek log cabin was based on a Scots-Irish or German design and sat adjacent to the family's cornfields, visible in the background. Library of Congress.

single year, a government land office in Huntsville, Alabama, sold $7 million of uncleared land—and the two states entered the Union in 1817 and 1819, respectively.

**Exodus from New England**    As southerners moved across the Appalachians and along the Gulf Coast, a third stream of migrants flowed out of the overcrowded communities of New England. Previous generations of Massachusetts and Connecticut farm families had moved north and east, settling New Hampshire, Vermont, and Maine. Now New England farmers moved west. Seeking land for their children, thousands of parents migrated to New York. "The town of Herkimer," noted one traveler, "is entirely populated by families come from Connecticut." By 1820, almost 800,000 New Englanders lived in a string of settlements stretching from Albany to Buffalo, and many others had traveled on to Ohio and Indiana. Soon, much of the Northwest Territory consisted of New England communities that had moved inland.

In New York, as in Kentucky and Ohio, well-connected speculators snapped up much of the best land, leasing farms to tenants for a fee. Imbued with the "homestead" ethic, many New England families

preferred to buy farms. They signed contracts with the Holland Land Company, a Dutch-owned syndicate of speculators, that allowed settlers to pay for their farms as they worked them, or moved west again in an elusive search for land on easy terms.

**Innovation on Eastern Farms**    The new farm economy in New York, Ohio, and Kentucky forced major changes in eastern agriculture. Unable to compete with lower-priced western grains, farmers in New England switched to potatoes, which were high yielding and nutritious. To make up for the labor of sons and daughters who had moved inland, Middle Atlantic farmers bought more efficient farm equipment. They replaced metal-tipped wooden plows with cast-iron models that dug deeper and required a single yoke of oxen instead of two. Such changes in crop mix and technology kept production high.

Easterners also adopted the progressive farming methods touted by British agricultural reformers. "Improvers" in Pennsylvania doubled their average yield per acre by rotating their crops. Yeomen farmers raised sheep and sold the wool to textile manufacturers. Many farmers adopted a year-round planting cycle, sowing corn in the spring for animal fodder and then planting winter wheat in September for market sale. Women and girls milked the family cows and made butter and cheese to sell in the growing towns and cities.

Whether hacking fields out of western forests or carting manure to replenish eastern soils, farmers now worked harder and longer, but their increased productivity brought them a better standard of living. European demand for American produce was high in these years, and westward migration — the settlement and exploitation of Indian lands — boosted the farming economy throughout the country.

## The Jefferson Presidency

From 1801 to 1825, three Republicans from Virginia — Thomas Jefferson, James Madison, and James Monroe — each served two terms as president. Supported by farmers in the South and West and strong Republican majorities in Congress, this "Virginia Dynasty" completed what Jefferson had called the Revolution of 1800. It reversed many Federalist policies and actively supported westward expansion.

When Jefferson took office in 1801, he inherited an old international conflict. Beginning in the 1780s, the Barbary States of North Africa had raided merchant ships in the Mediterranean, and like many European nations, the United States had paid an annual bribe — massive in relation to the size of the federal budget — to protect its vessels. Initially Jefferson refused to pay this "tribute" and ordered the U.S. Navy to attack the pirates' home ports. After four years of intermittent fighting, in which the United States bombarded Tripoli and captured the city of Derna, the Jefferson administration cut its costs. It signed a peace treaty that included a ransom for returned prisoners, and Algerian ships were soon taking American sailors hostage again.

At home, Jefferson inherited a national judiciary filled with Federalist appointees, including the formidable John Marshall of Virginia, the new chief justice of the Supreme Court. To add more Federalist judges, the outgoing Federalist Congress had passed the Judiciary Act of 1801. The act created sixteen new judgeships and various other positions, which President Adams filled at the last moment with "midnight appointees." The Federalists "have retired into the judiciary as a stronghold," Jefferson complained, "and from that battery all the works of Republicanism are to be beaten down and destroyed."

Jefferson's fears were soon realized. When Republican legislatures in Kentucky and Virginia repudiated the Alien and Sedition Acts as unconstitutional,

Marshall declared that only the Supreme Court held the power of constitutional review. The Court claimed this authority for itself when James Madison, the new secretary of state, refused to deliver the commission of William Marbury, one of Adams's midnight appointees. In ***Marbury v. Madison* (1803)**, Marshall asserted that Marbury had the right to the appointment but that the Court did not have the constitutional power to enforce it. In defining the Court's powers, Marshall voided a section of the Judiciary Act of 1789, in effect asserting the Court's authority to review congressional legislation and interpret the Constitution. "It is emphatically the province and duty of the judicial department to say what the law is," the chief justice declared, directly challenging the Republican view that the state legislatures had that power.

Ignoring this setback, Jefferson and the Republicans reversed other Federalist policies. When the Alien and Sedition Acts expired in 1801, Congress branded them unconstitutional and refused to extend them. It also amended the Naturalization Act, restoring the original waiting period of five years for resident aliens to become citizens. Charging the Federalists with grossly expanding the national government's size and power, Jefferson had the Republican Congress shrink it. He abolished all internal taxes, including the excise tax that had sparked the Whiskey Rebellion of 1794. To quiet Republican fears of a military coup, Jefferson reduced the size of the permanent army. He also secured repeal of the Judiciary Act of 1801, ousting forty of Adams's midnight appointees. Still, Jefferson retained competent Federalist officeholders, removing only 69 of 433 properly appointed Federalists during his eight years as president.

Jefferson likewise governed tactfully in fiscal affairs. He tolerated the economically important Bank of the United States, which he had once condemned as unconstitutional. But he chose as his secretary of the treasury Albert Gallatin, a fiscal conservative who believed that the national debt was "an evil of the first magnitude." By limiting expenditures and using customs revenue to redeem government bonds, Gallatin reduced the debt from $83 million in 1801 to $45 million in 1812. With Jefferson and Gallatin at the helm, the nation's fiscal affairs were no longer run in the interests of northeastern creditors and merchants.

## Jefferson and the West

Jefferson had long championed settlement of the West. He celebrated the yeoman farmer in *Notes on the State of Virginia* (1785); wrote one of the Confederation's

BOMBARDMENT OF TRIPOLI.

AUGUST 1804.

**America in the Middle East, 1804**

To protect American merchants from capture and captivity in the Barbary States, President Thomas Jefferson sent in the U.S. Navy. This 1846 lithograph, created by the famous firm of Currier & Ives, depicts one of the three attacks on the North African port of Tripoli by Commodore Edward Preble in August 1804. As the USS *Constitution* and other large warships lob shells into the city, small American gunboats defend the fleet from Tripolitan gunboats. "Our loss in Killed & Wounded has been considerable," Preble reported, and "the Enemy must have suffered very much . . . among their Shipping and on shore." The Granger Collection, New York.

western land ordinances; and supported Pinckney's Treaty (1795), the agreement between the United States and Spain that reopened the Mississippi River to American trade and allowed settlers to export crops via the Spanish-held port of New Orleans.

As president, Jefferson pursued policies that made it easier for farm families to acquire land. In 1796, a Federalist-dominated Congress had set the price of land in the national domain at $2 per acre; by the 1830s, Jefferson-inspired Republican Congresses had enacted more than three hundred laws that cut the cost to $1.25, eased credit terms, and allowed illegal squatters to buy their farms. Eventually, in the Homestead Act of 1862, Congress gave farmsteads to settlers for free.

**The Louisiana Purchase**   International events challenged Jefferson's vision of westward expansion. In

1799, Napoleon Bonaparte seized power in France and sought to reestablish France's American empire. In 1801, he coerced Spain into signing a secret treaty that returned Louisiana to France and restricted American access to New Orleans, violating Pinckney's Treaty. Napoleon also launched an invasion to restore French rule in Saint-Domingue. It was once the richest sugar colony in the Americas, but its civil war had ruined the economy and cost France a fortune. Napoleon wanted to crush the rebellion, restore its planter class, and "destroy the new Algiers that has been growing up in the middle of America."

Napoleon's actions in Haiti and Louisiana prompted Jefferson to question his pro-French foreign policy. "The day that France takes possession of New Orleans, we must marry ourselves to the British fleet and nation," the president warned, dispatching James Monroe to

Britain to negotiate an alliance. To keep the Mississippi River open to western farmers, Jefferson told Robert Livingston, the American minister in Paris, to negotiate the purchase of New Orleans.

Jefferson's diplomacy yielded a magnificent prize: the entire territory of Louisiana. By 1802, the French invasion of Saint-Domingue was faltering in the face of disease and determined black resistance, a new war threatened in Europe, and Napoleon feared an American invasion of Louisiana. Acting with characteristic decisiveness, the French ruler offered to sell the entire territory of Louisiana for $15 million (about $500 million today). "We have lived long," Livingston remarked to Monroe as they concluded the **Louisiana Purchase** in 1803, "but this is the noblest work of our lives."

The Louisiana Purchase forced Jefferson to reconsider his strict interpretation of the Constitution. He had long believed that the national government possessed only the powers expressly delegated to it in the Constitution, but there was no provision for adding new territory. So Jefferson pragmatically accepted a loose interpretation of the Constitution and used its treaty-making powers to complete the deal with France. The new western lands, Jefferson wrote, would be "a means of tempting all our Indians on the East side of the Mississippi to remove to the West."

**Secessionist Schemes**   The acquisition of Louisiana brought new political problems. Some New England Federalists, fearing that western expansion would hurt their region and party, talked openly of leaving the Union and forming a confederacy of northeastern states. The secessionists won the support of Aaron Burr, the ambitious vice president. After Alexander Hamilton accused Burr of planning to destroy the Union, the two fought an illegal pistol duel that led to Hamilton's death.

This tragedy propelled Burr into another secessionist scheme, this time in the Southwest. When his term as vice president ended in 1805, Burr moved west to avoid prosecution. There, he conspired with General James Wilkinson, the military governor of the Louisiana Territory, either to seize territory in New Spain or to establish Louisiana as a separate nation. But Wilkinson, himself a Spanish spy and incipient traitor, betrayed Burr and arrested him. In a highly politicized trial presided over by Chief Justice John Marshall, the jury acquitted Burr of treason.

The Louisiana Purchase had increased party conflict and generated secessionist schemes in both New England and the Southwest. Such sectional differences

would continue, challenging Madison's argument in "Federalist No. 10" that a large and diverse republic was more stable than a small one.

**Lewis and Clark Meet the Mandans and Sioux**   A scientist as well as a statesman, Jefferson wanted information about Louisiana: its physical features, plant and animal life, and native peoples. He was also worried about intruders: the British-run Hudson's Bay Company and Northwest Company were actively trading for furs on the upper Missouri River. So in 1804, Jefferson sent his personal secretary, Meriwether Lewis, to explore the region with William Clark, an army officer. From St. Louis, Lewis, Clark, and their party of American soldiers and frontiersmen traveled up the Missouri for 1,000 miles to the fortified, earth-lodge towns of the Mandan and Hidatsa peoples (near present-day Bismarck, North Dakota), where they spent the winter.

The Mandans lived primarily by horticulture, growing corn, beans, and squash. They had acquired horses by supplying food to nomadic Plains Indians and secured guns, iron goods, and textiles by selling buffalo hides and dried meat to European traders. However, the Mandans (and neighboring Arikaras) had been hit hard by the smallpox epidemics that swept across the Great Plains in 1779–1781 and 1801–1802. Now they were threatened by Sioux peoples: Tetons, Yanktonais, and Oglalas. Originally, the Sioux had lived in the prairie and lake region of northern Minnesota. As their numbers rose and fish and game grew scarce, the Sioux moved westward, acquired horses, and hunted buffalo, living as nomads in portable skin tepees. The Sioux became ferocious fighters who tried to reduce the Mandans and other farming tribes to subject peoples. According to Lewis and Clark, they were the "pirates of the Missouri." Soon the Sioux would dominate the buffalo trade throughout the upper Missouri region.

In the spring of 1805, Lewis and Clark began an epic 1,300-mile trek into unknown country. Their party now included Toussaint Charbonneau, a French Canadian fur trader, and his Shoshone wife, Sacagawea, who served as a guide and translator. After following the Missouri River to its source on the Idaho-Montana border, they crossed the Rocky Mountains, and — venturing far beyond the Louisiana Purchase — traveled down the Columbia River to the Pacific Ocean. Nearly everywhere, Indian peoples asked for guns so they could defend themselves from other armed tribes.

> **EXPLAIN CONSEQUENCES**
> How was Jefferson's agrarian vision reflected in his policies affecting western lands?

**A Mandan Village**
This Mandan settlement in North Dakota, painted by George Catlin around 1837, resembled those in which the Lewis and Clark expedition spent the winter of 1804–1805. Note the palisade of logs that surrounds the village, as protection from the Sioux and other marauding Plains peoples, and the solidly built mud lodges that provided warm shelter from the bitter cold of winter. Smithsonian American Art Museum, Washington, D.C./Art Resource, NY.

In 1806, Lewis and Clark capped off their pathbreaking expedition by providing Jefferson with the first maps of the immense wilderness and a detailed account of its natural resources and inhabitants (Map 7.4). Their report prompted some Americans to envision a nation that would span the continent.

# The War of 1812 and the Transformation of Politics

The Napoleonic Wars that ravaged Europe after 1802 brought new attacks on American merchant ships. American leaders struggled desperately to protect the nation's commerce while avoiding war. When this effort finally failed, it sparked dramatic political changes that destroyed the Federalist Party and split the Republicans into National and Jeffersonian factions.

## Conflict in the Atlantic and the West

As Napoleon conquered European countries, he cut off their commerce with Britain and seized American merchant ships that stopped in British ports. The British ministry responded with a naval blockade and seized American vessels carrying sugar and molasses from the French West Indies. The British navy also searched American merchant ships for British deserters and used these raids to replenish its crews, a practice

known as impressment. Between 1802 and 1811, British naval officers impressed nearly 8,000 sailors, including many U.S. citizens. In 1807, American anger boiled over when a British warship attacked the U.S. Navy vessel *Chesapeake*, killing three, wounding eighteen, and seizing four alleged deserters. "Never since the battle of Lexington have I seen this country in such a state of exasperation as at present," Jefferson declared.

**The Embargo of 1807**  To protect American interests, Jefferson pursued a policy of peaceful coercion. **The Embargo Act of 1807** prohibited American ships from leaving their home ports until Britain and France stopped restricting U.S. trade. A drastic maneuver, the embargo overestimated the reliance of Britain and France on American shipping and underestimated the resistance of merchants, who feared the embargo would ruin them. In fact, the embargo cut the American gross national product by 5 percent and weakened the entire economy. Exports plunged from $108 million in 1806 to $22 million in 1808, hurting farmers as well as merchants. "All was noise and bustle" in New York City before the embargo, one visitor remarked; afterward, everything was closed up as if "a malignant fever was raging in the place."

Despite popular discontent over the embargo, voters elected Republican James Madison to the presidency in 1808. A powerful advocate for the Constitution, the architect of the Bill of Rights, and a prominent congressman and party leader, Madison

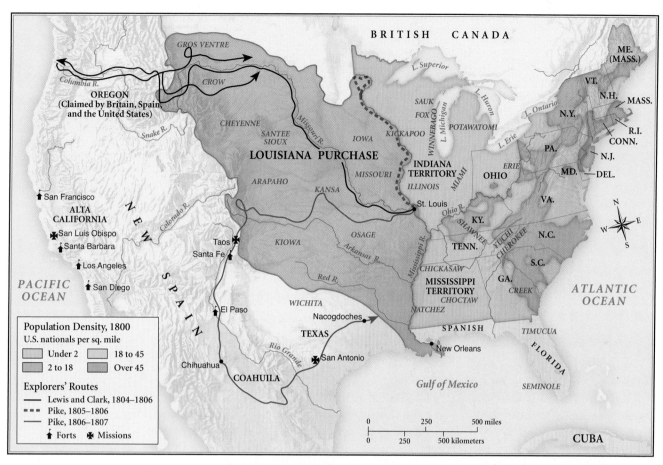

**MAP 7.4**

**U.S. Population Density in 1803 and the Louisiana Purchase**

When the United States purchased Louisiana from France in 1803, much of the land to its east—the vast territory between the Appalachian Mountains and the Mississippi River—remained in Indian hands. The equally vast lands beyond the Mississippi were virtually unknown to Anglo-Americans, even after the epic explorations of Meriwether Lewis and William Clark. Still, President Jefferson predicted quite accurately that the huge Mississippi River Valley "from its fertility . . . will ere long yield half of our whole produce, and contain half of our whole population."

had served the nation well. But John Beckley, a loyal Republican, worried that Madison would be "too timid and indecisive as a statesman," and events proved him right. Acknowledging the embargo's failure, Madison replaced it with new economic restrictions, which also failed to protect American commerce.

**Western War Hawks**   Republican congressmen from the West were certain that Britain was the primary offender. They pointed to its trade with Indians in the Ohio River Valley in violation of the Treaty of Paris and Jay's Treaty. Bolstered by British guns and supplies, the Shawnee war chief Tecumseh revived the Western Confederacy in 1809. His brother, the prophet Tenskwatawa, provided the confederacy with a powerful nativist ideology. He urged Indian peoples to shun

Americans, "the children of the Evil Spirit . . . who have taken away your lands"; renounce alcohol; and return to traditional ways. The Shawnee leaders found their greatest support among Kickapoo, Potawatomi, Winnebago, Ottawa, and Chippewa warriors: Indians of the western Great Lakes who had so far been largely shielded from the direct effects of U.S. westward expansion. They flocked to Tenskwatawa's holy village, Prophetstown, in the Indiana Territory.

As Tecumseh mobilized the western Indian peoples for war, William Henry Harrison, the governor of the Indiana Territory, decided on a preemptive strike. In November 1811, when Tecumseh went south to seek support from the Chickasaws, Choctaws, and Creeks, Harrison took advantage of his absence and attacked Prophetstown. The governor's 1,000 troops

**Tenskwatawa, "The Prophet," 1830**
Tenskwatawa added a spiritual dimension to Native American resistance by urging a holy war against the invading whites and calling for a return to sacred ancestral ways. His dress reflects his teachings: note the animal-skin shirt and the heavily ornamented ears. However, some of Tenskwatawa's religious rituals reflected the influence of French Jesuits; he urged his followers to finger a sacred string of beads (such as those in his left hand) that were similar to the Catholic rosary, thereby "shaking hands with the Prophet." Whatever its origins, Tenskwatawa's message transcended the cultural differences among Indian peoples and helped his brother Tecumseh create a formidable political and military alliance. Smithsonian American Art Museum, Washington, D.C./Art Resource.

and militiamen traded heavy casualties with the confederacy's warriors at the **Battle of Tippecanoe** and then destroyed the holy village.

With Britain assisting Indians in the western territories and seizing American ships in the Atlantic, Henry Clay of Kentucky, the new Speaker of the House of Representatives, and John C. Calhoun, a rising young congressman from South Carolina, pushed Madison toward war. Like other Republican "war hawks" from the West and South, they wanted to seize territory in British Canada and Spanish Florida. With national elections approaching, Madison issued an ultimatum to Britain. When Britain failed to respond quickly, the president asked Congress for a declaration of war. In June 1812, a sharply divided Senate voted 19 to 13 for war, and the House of Representatives concurred, 79 to 49.

The causes of the War of 1812 have been much debated. Officially, the United States went to war because Britain had violated its commercial rights as a neutral nation. But the Federalists in Congress who represented the New England and Middle Atlantic merchants voted against the war; and in the election of 1812, those regions cast their 89 electoral votes for the Federalist presidential candidate, De Witt Clinton of New York. Madison amassed most of his 128 electoral votes in the South and West, where voters and congressmen strongly supported the war. Many historians therefore argue that the conflict was actually "a western war with eastern labels" (American Voices, p. 238).

## The War of 1812

The War of 1812 was a near disaster for the United States. An invasion of British Canada in 1812 quickly ended in a retreat to Detroit. Nonetheless, the United States stayed on the offensive in the West. In 1813, American raiders burned the Canadian capital of York (present-day Toronto), Commodore Oliver Hazard Perry defeated a small British flotilla on Lake Erie, and

**Counting Scalps**

Effective propaganda usually contains a grain of truth, in this case the Indian warriors' practice of scalping their wartime victims. Entitled "A scene on the frontiers as practiced by the humane British and their worthy allies!", this cartoon by Philadelphia artist William Charles accuses the British of paying Indians to kill—and then mutilate—American soldiers. "Bring me the scalps, and the King our master will reward you," says the British officer in the cartoon. The verse at the bottom urges "Columbia's Sons" to press forward their attacks; otherwise, "The Savage Indian with his Scalping knife, / Or Tomahawk may seek to take your life." Library of Congress.

General William Henry Harrison overcame a British and Indian force at the Battle of the Thames, taking the life of Tecumseh, now a British general.

In the East, political divisions prevented a wider war. New England Federalists opposed the war and prohibited their states' militias from attacking Canada. Boston merchants and banks refused to lend money to the federal government, making the war difficult to finance. In Congress, Daniel Webster, a dynamic young politician from New Hampshire, led Federalists opposed to higher tariffs and national conscription of state militiamen.

Gradually, the tide of battle turned in Britain's favor. When the war began, American privateers had captured scores of British merchant vessels, but by 1813 British warships were disrupting American commerce and threatening seaports along the Atlantic coast. In 1814, a British fleet sailed up the Chesapeake Bay, and troops stormed ashore to attack Washington City. Retaliating for the destruction of York, the invaders burned the U.S. Capitol and government buildings. After two years of fighting, the United States was stalemated along the Canadian frontier and on the defensive in the Atlantic, and its new capital city lay in ruins. The only U.S. victories came in the Southwest. There, a rugged slave-owning planter named Andrew Jackson and a force of Tennessee militiamen defeated British- and Spanish-supported Creek Indians in the Battle of Horseshoe Bend (1814) and forced the Indians to cede 23 million acres of land (Map 7.5).

**Federalists Oppose the War**   American military setbacks increased opposition to the war in New England. In 1814, Massachusetts Federalists called for a convention "to lay the foundation for a radical reform in the National Compact." When New England Federalists met in Hartford, Connecticut, some delegates proposed secession, but most wanted to revise the Constitution. To end Virginia's domination of the presidency, the Hartford Convention proposed a constitutional amendment limiting the office to a single

**IDENTIFY CAUSES**
What do you think is the most persuasive explanation for the United States's decision to declare war on Great Britain in 1812?

## Factional Politics and the War of 1812

In the quarter-century following the ratification of the U.S. Constitution, American leaders had to deal with the wars of the French Revolution and Napoleon. These European conflicts posed two dangers to the United States. First, the naval blockades imposed by the British and the French hurt American commerce and prompted calls for a military response. Second, European ideological and political struggles intensified party conflicts in the United States. On three occasions, the American republic faced danger from the combination of an external military threat and internal political turmoil. In 1798, the Federalist administration of John Adams almost went to war with France to help American merchants and to undermine the Republican Party. In 1807, Thomas Jefferson's embargo on American commerce shocked Federalists and sharply increased political tensions. And, as the following selections show, the political divisions during the War of 1812 threatened the very existence of the American republic.

### George Washington
### Farewell Address, 1796

Washington's support for Alexander Hamilton's economic policies promoted political factionalism. Ignoring his own role in creating that political divide, Washington condemned factionalism and, as his presidency proceeded, tried to stand above party conflicts. In his farewell address, Washington warned Americans to stand united and avoid the "Spirit of Party."

A solicitude for your welfare [prompts me] . . . to offer . . . the disinterested warnings of a parting friend, who can possibly have no personal motive to bias his counsels. . . .

The Unity of Government which constitutes you one people . . . is a main Pillar in the Edifice of your real independence . . . your tranquility at home; your peace abroad. . . . But it is easy to foresee, that, from different causes, and from different quarters, much pains will be taken, many artifices employed, to weaken in your minds the conviction of this truth. . . .

I have already intimated to you the danger of parties in the State, with particular reference to founding them on geographical discriminations. Let me now take a more comprehensive view, and warn you, in the most solemn manner, against the baneful effects of the Spirit of Party, generally.

This spirit, unfortunately, is inseparable from our nature, having its root in the strongest passions of the human mind. It exists under different shapes, in all governments, more or less stifled, controlled or repressed; but in those of the popular form, it is seen in its greatest rankness, and is truly their worst enemy.

The alternate dominion of one faction over another, sharpened by the spirit of revenge . . . , is itself a frightful despotism; but this leads at length to a more formal and permanent despotism.

Source: James D. Richardson, ed., *A Compilation of the Messages and Papers of the Presidents, 1789–1896* (Washington, D.C.: U.S. Government Printing Office, 1896), 1: 213–215.

### Josiah Quincy et al.
### Federalists Protest "Mr. Madison's War"

The United States—and its two political parties—divided sharply over the War of 1812. As Congress debated the issue of going to war against Great Britain, Josiah Quincy and other antiwar Federalist congressmen published a manifesto that questioned the justifications for the war offered by President Madison and the military strategy proposed by Republican war hawks.

How will war upon the land [an invasion of British Canada] protect commerce upon the ocean? What balm has Canada for wounded honor? How are our mariners benefited by a war which exposes those who are free, without promising release to those who are impressed?

But it is said that war is demanded by honor. Is national honor a principle which thirsts after vengeance, and is appeased only by blood? . . . If honor demands a war with England, what opiate lulls that honor to sleep over the wrongs done us by France? On land, robberies, seizures, imprisonments, by French authority; at sea, pillage, sinkings, burnings, under French orders. These are notorious. Are they unfelt because they are French? . . .

There is . . . a headlong rushing into difficulties, with little calculation about the means, and little concern about the consequences. With a navy comparatively [small], we are about to enter into the lists against the greatest marine [power] on the globe. With a commerce unprotected and spread over every ocean, we propose to make a profit by privateering, and for this endanger the wealth of which we are honest proprietors. An invasion is threatened of the [British colonies in Canada, but Britain] . . . without putting a new ship into commission, or taking another soldier into pay, can spread alarm or desolation along the extensive range of our seaboard. . . .

What are the United States to gain by this war? Will the gratification of some privateersmen compensate the nation for that sweep of our legitimate commerce by the extended marine of our enemy which this desperate act invites? Will Canada compensate the Middle states for [the loss of] New York; or the Western states for [the loss of] New Orleans?

Let us not be deceived. A war of invasion may invite a retort of invasion. When we visit the peaceable, and as to us innocent, colonies of Great Britain with the horrors of war, can we be assured that our own coast will not be visited with like horrors?

Source: *Annals of Congress*, 12th Cong., 1st sess., vol. 2, cols. 2219–2221.

## Hezekiah Niles
## A Republican Defends the War

In 1814, what the Federalists feared had come to pass: British ships blockaded American ports, and British troops invaded American territory. In January 1815, Republican editor Hezekiah Niles used the pages of his influential Baltimore newspaper, *Niles' Weekly Register*, to explain current Republican policies and blame the Federalists for American reverses.

It is universally known that the causes for which we declared war are no obstruction to peace. The practice of blockade and impressment having ceased by the general pacification of Europe, our government is content to leave the principle as it was. . . .

We have no further business in hostility, than such as is purely defensive; while that of Great Britain is to humble or subdue us. The war, on our part, has become a contest for life, liberty and property — on the part of our enemy, of revenge or ambition. . . .

What then are we to do? Are we to encourage him by divisions among ourselves — to hold out the hope of a separation of the states and a civil war — to refuse to bring forth the resources of the country against him? . . . I did think that in a defensive war — a struggle for all that is valuable — that all parties would have united. But it is not so — every measure calculated to replenish the treasury or raise men is opposed [by Federalists] as though it were determined to strike the "star spangled banner" and exalt the bloody cross. Look at the votes and proceedings of congress — and mark the late spirit [to secede from the Union] . . . that existed in Massachusetts, and see with what unity of action every thing has been done [by New England Federalists] to harass and embarrass the government. Our loans have failed; and our soldiers have wanted their pay, because those [New England merchants] who had the greater part of the monied capital covenanted with each other to refuse its aid to the country. They had a right, legally, to do this; and perhaps, also, by all the artifices of trade or power that money gave them, to oppress others not of their "stamp" and depress the national credit — but history will shock posterity by detailing the length to which they went to bankrupt the republic. . . .

To conclude — why does the war continue? It is not the fault of the government — we demand no extravagant thing. I answer the question, and say — *it lasts because Great Britain depends on the exertions of her "party" in this country to destroy our resources, and compel "unconditional submission."*

Thus the war began, and is continued, by our divisions.

Source: *Niles' Weekly Register*, January 28, 1815.

---

### QUESTIONS FOR ANALYSIS

1. According to Washington, what is the ultimate cause of political factionalism? Why does Washington believe that factionalism is most dangerous in "popular" — that is, republican — governments?

2. Compare and contrast the Quincy and Niles documents. What specific dangers did Josiah Quincy and the Federalists foresee with regard to Republican war policies? According to Hezekiah Niles, what were the war goals of the Republican administration?

3. Read the section on the War of 1812 on pages 236–241, and then discuss the accuracy of the Federalists' predictions.

4. How had Republican war goals changed since the start of the war? Niles charged the Federalists and their supporters with impeding the American war effort. What were his specific charges? Did they have any merit? How might the Federalists have defended their stance with respect to the war?

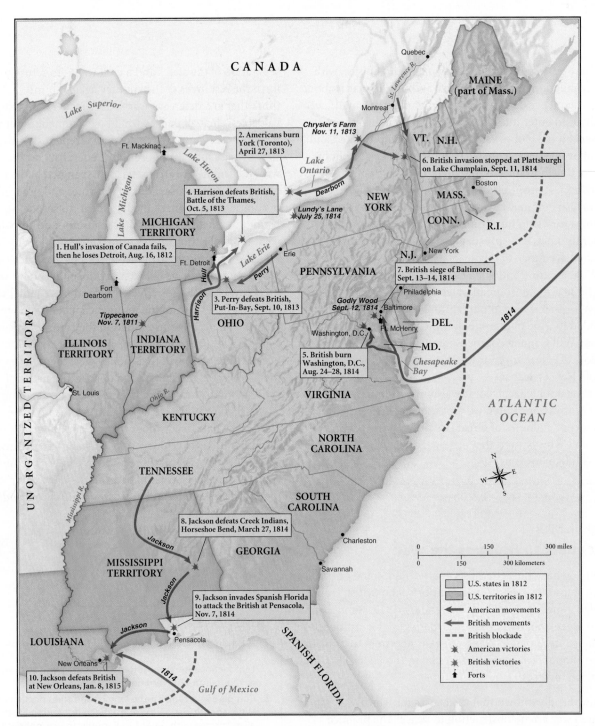

The following labels appear on the map:

**CANADA**

**MAINE (part of Mass.)**

Quebec

Montreal

Lake Superior

Lake Huron

Lake Michigan

Ft. Mackinac

**2. Americans burn York (Toronto), April 27, 1813**

*Chrysler's Farm Nov. 11, 1813*

Lake Ontario

*Dearborn*

VT.  N.H.

**6. British invasion stopped at Plattsburgh on Lake Champlain, Sept. 11, 1814**

Boston

MASS.

CONN.  R.I.

**4. Harrison defeats British, Battle of the Thames, Oct. 5, 1813**

*Lundy's Lane July 25, 1814*

**NEW YORK**

**1. Hull's invasion of Canada fails, then he loses Detroit, Aug. 16, 1812**

**MICHIGAN TERRITORY**

Ft. Detroit

*Hull*

*Perry*

Lake Erie

Erie

N.J.  New York

**PENNSYLVANIA**

**7. British siege of Baltimore, Sept. 13–14, 1814**

Philadelphia

*Godly Wood Sept. 12, 1814*  Baltimore

Ft. McHenry  DEL.

Fort Dearborn

*Harrison*

**3. Perry defeats British, Put-In-Bay, Sept. 10, 1813**

**OHIO**

Washington, D.C.

MD.

*Tippecanoe Nov. 7, 1811*

**ILLINOIS TERRITORY**

**INDIANA TERRITORY**

*Ohio R.*

**5. British burn Washington, D.C., Aug. 24–28, 1814**

*Chesapeake Bay*

*1814*

**U N O R G A N I Z E D   T E R R I T O R Y**

St. Louis

**VIRGINIA**

**ATLANTIC OCEAN**

*Mississippi R.*

**KENTUCKY**

**NORTH CAROLINA**

**TENNESSEE**

**SOUTH CAROLINA**

Charleston

**8. Jackson defeats Creek Indians, Horseshoe Bend, March 27, 1814**

**GEORGIA**

*Jackson*

**MISSISSIPPI TERRITORY**

Savannah

**9. Jackson invades Spanish Florida to attack the British at Pensacola, Nov. 7, 1814**

*Jackson*

*Jackson*

**LOUISIANA**

Pensacola

New Orleans

**10. Jackson defeats British at New Orleans, Jan. 8, 1815**

*1814*

*Gulf of Mexico*

**SPANISH FLORIDA**

0    150    300 miles

0    150    300 kilometers

Legend:
- U.S. states in 1812
- U.S. territories in 1812
- American movements
- British movements
- British blockade
- American victories
- British victories
- Forts

## MAP 7.5
### The War of 1812

Unlike the War of Independence, the War of 1812 had few large-scale military campaigns. In 1812 and 1813, most of the fighting took place along the Canadian border, as small American military forces attacked British targets with mixed success (nos. 1–4). The British took the offensive in 1814, launching a successful raid on Washington, but their attack on Baltimore failed, and they suffered heavy losses when they invaded the United States along Lake Champlain (nos. 5–7). Near the Gulf of Mexico, American forces moved from one success to another: General Andrew Jackson defeated the pro-British Creek Indians at the Battle of Horseshoe Bend, won a victory in Pensacola, and, in the single major battle of the war, routed an invading British army at New Orleans (nos. 8–10).

four-year term and rotating it among citizens from different states. The convention also suggested amendments restricting commercial embargoes to sixty days and requiring a two-thirds majority in Congress to declare war, prohibit trade, or admit a new state to the Union.

As a minority party, the Federalists could prevail only if the war continued to go badly — a very real prospect. The war had cost $88 million, raising the national debt to $127 million. And now, as Albert Gallatin warned Henry Clay in May 1814, Britain's triumph over Napoleon in Europe meant that a "well organized and large army is [now ready] . . . to act immediately against us." When an attack from Canada came in the late summer of 1814, only an American naval victory on Lake Champlain stopped the British from marching down the Hudson River Valley. A few months later, thousands of seasoned British troops landed outside New Orleans, threatening American control of the Mississippi River. With the nation politically divided and under attack from north and south, Gallatin feared that "the war might prove vitally fatal to the United States."

**Peace Overtures and a Final Victory**  Fortunately for the young American republic, by 1815 Britain wanted peace. The twenty-year war with France had sapped its wealth and energy, so it began negotiations with the United States in Ghent, Belgium. At first, the American commissioners — John Quincy Adams, Gallatin, and Clay — demanded territory in Canada and Florida, while British diplomats sought an Indian buffer state between the United States and Canada. Both sides quickly realized that these objectives were not worth the cost of prolonged warfare. The **Treaty of Ghent**, signed on Christmas Eve 1814, retained the prewar borders of the United States.

That result hardly justified three years of war, but before news of the treaty reached the United States, a final military victory lifted Americans' morale. On January 8, 1815, General Jackson's troops crushed the British forces attacking New Orleans. Fighting from carefully constructed breastworks, the Americans rained "grapeshot and cannister bombs" on the massed British formations. The British lost 700 men, and 2,000 more were wounded or taken prisoner; just 13 Americans died, and only 58 suffered wounds. A newspaper headline proclaimed: "Almost Incredible Victory!! Glorious News." The victory made Jackson a national hero, redeemed the nation's battered pride, and undercut the Hartford Convention's demands for constitutional revision.

## The Federalist Legacy

The War of 1812 ushered in a new phase of the Republican political revolution. Before the conflict, Federalists had strongly supported Alexander Hamilton's program of national mercantilism — a funded debt, a central bank, and tariffs — while Jeffersonian Republicans had opposed it. After the war, the Republicans split into two camps. Led by Henry Clay, National Republicans pursued Federalist-like policies. In 1816, Clay pushed legislation through Congress creating the Second Bank of the United States and persuaded President Madison to sign it. In 1817, Clay won passage of the Bonus Bill, which created a national fund for roads and other internal improvements. Madison vetoed it. Reaffirming traditional Jeffersonian Republican principles, he argued that the national government lacked the constitutional authority to fund internal improvements.

Meanwhile, the Federalist Party crumbled. As one supporter explained, the National Republicans in the eastern states had "destroyed the Federalist party by the adoption of its principles" while the favorable farm policies of Jeffersonians maintained the Republican Party's dominance in the South and West. "No Federal character can run with success," Gouverneur Morris of New York lamented, and the election of 1818 proved him right: Republicans outnumbered Federalists 37 to 7 in the Senate and 156 to 27 in the House. Westward expansion and the success of Jefferson's Revolution of 1800 had shattered the First Party System.

**Marshall's Federalist Law**  However, Federalist policies lived on thanks to John Marshall's long tenure on the Supreme Court. Appointed chief justice by President John Adams in January 1801, Marshall had a personality and intellect that allowed him to dominate the Court until 1822 and strongly influence its decisions until his death in 1835.

Three principles informed Marshall's jurisprudence: judicial authority, the supremacy of national laws, and traditional property rights (Table 7.1). Marshall claimed the right of judicial review for the Supreme Court in *Marbury v. Madison* (1803), and the Court frequently used that power to overturn state laws that, in its judgment, violated the Constitution.

**Asserting National Supremacy**  The important case of ***McCulloch v. Maryland*** **(1819)** involved one such law. When Congress created the Second Bank of the United States in 1816, it allowed the bank to set up state branches that competed with state-chartered banks. In response, the Maryland legislature imposed a

**TABLE 7.1**

**Major Decisions of the Marshall Court**

|  | Date | Case | Significance of Decision |
|---|---|---|---|
| Judicial Authority | 1803 | *Marbury v. Madison* | Asserts principle of judicial review |
| Property Rights | 1810 | *Fletcher v. Peck* | Protects property rights through broad reading of Constitution's contract clause |
|  | 1819 | *Dartmouth College v. Woodward* | Safeguards property rights, especially of chartered corporations |
| Supremacy of National Law | 1819 | *McCulloch v. Maryland* | Interprets Constitution to give broad powers to national government |
|  | 1824 | *Gibbons v. Ogden* | Gives national government jurisdiction over interstate commerce |

tax on notes issued by the Baltimore branch of the Second Bank. The Second Bank refused to pay, claiming that the tax infringed on national powers and was therefore unconstitutional. The state's lawyers then invoked Jefferson's argument: that Congress lacked the constitutional authority to charter a national bank. Even if a national bank was legitimate, the lawyers argued, Maryland could tax its activities within the state.

Marshall and the nationalist-minded Republicans on the Court firmly rejected both arguments. The Second Bank was constitutional, said the chief justice, because it was "necessary and proper," given the national government's control over currency and credit, and Maryland did not have the power to tax it.

The Marshall Court again asserted the dominance of national over state statutes in *Gibbons v. Ogden* (1824). The decision struck down a New York law granting a monopoly to Aaron Ogden for steamboat passenger service across the Hudson River to New Jersey. Asserting that the Constitution gave the federal government authority over interstate commerce, the chief justice sided with Thomas Gibbons, who held a federal license to run steamboats between the two states.

**Upholding Vested Property Rights** Finally, Marshall used the Constitution to uphold Federalist notions of property rights. During the 1790s, Jefferson Republicans had celebrated "the will of the people," prompting Federalists to worry that popular sovereignty would result in a "tyranny of the majority." If

**UNDERSTAND POINTS OF VIEW**
Why do historians think the decisions of the Marshall Court constitute a Federalist legacy?

state legislatures enacted statutes infringing on the property rights of wealthy citizens, Federalist judges vowed to void them.

Marshall was no exception. Determined to protect individual property rights, he invoked the contract clause of the Constitution to do it. The contract clause (in Article I, Section 10) prohibits the states from passing any law "impairing the obligation of contracts." Economic conservatives at the Philadelphia convention had inserted the clause to prevent "stay" laws, which kept creditors from seizing the lands and goods of delinquent debtors. In *Fletcher v. Peck* (1810), Marshall greatly expanded its scope. The Georgia legislature had granted a huge tract of land to the Yazoo Land Company. When a new legislature cancelled the grant, alleging fraud and bribery, speculators who had purchased Yazoo lands appealed to the Supreme Court to uphold their titles. Marshall did so by ruling that the legislative grant was a contract that could not be revoked. His decision was controversial and far-reaching. It limited state power; bolstered vested property rights; and, by protecting out-of-state investors, promoted the development of a national capitalist economy.

The Court extended its defense of vested property rights in *Dartmouth College v. Woodward* (1819). Dartmouth College was a private institution created by a royal charter issued by King George III. In 1816, New Hampshire's Republican legislature enacted a statute converting the school into a public university. The Dartmouth trustees opposed the legislation and hired Daniel Webster to plead their case. A renowned constitutional lawyer and a leading Federalist, Webster cited the Court's decision in *Fletcher v. Peck* and argued that the royal charter was an unalterable contract. The Marshall Court agreed and upheld Dartmouth's claims.

*John Marshall*, **by Chester Harding, c. 1830**

Even at the age of seventy-five, John Marshall (1755–1835) had a commanding personal presence. After he became chief justice of the U.S. Supreme Court in 1801, Marshall elevated the Court from a minor department of the national government to a major institution in American legal and political life. His decisions on judicial review, contract rights, the regulation of commerce, and national banking permanently shaped the character of American constitutional law. © Boston Athenaeum, USA/The Bridgeman Art Library.

**The Diplomacy of John Quincy Adams**   Even as John Marshall incorporated important Federalist principles into the American legal system, voting citizens and political leaders embraced the outlook of the Republican Party. The political career of John Quincy Adams was a case in point. Although he was the son of Federalist president John Adams, John Quincy Adams had joined the Republican Party before the War of 1812. He came to national attention for his role in negotiating the Treaty of Ghent, which ended the war.

Adams then served brilliantly as secretary of state for two terms under James Monroe (1817–1825). Ignoring Republican antagonism toward Great Britain,

in 1817 Adams negotiated the Rush-Bagot Treaty, which limited American and British naval forces on the Great Lakes. In 1818, he concluded another agreement with Britain setting the forty-ninth parallel as the border between Canada and the lands of the Louisiana Purchase. Then, in the **Adams-Onís Treaty** of 1819, Adams persuaded Spain to cede the Florida territory to the United States (Map 7.6). In return, the American government accepted Spain's claim to Texas and agreed to a compromise on the western boundary for the state of Louisiana, which had entered the Union in 1812.

Finally, Adams persuaded President Monroe to declare American national policy with respect to the

**MAP 7.6**
**Defining the National Boundaries, 1800–1820**
After the War of 1812, American diplomats negotiated treaties with Great Britain and Spain that defined the boundaries of the Louisiana Purchase, with British Canada to the north and New Spain (which in 1821 became the independent nation of Mexico) to the south and west. These treaties eliminated the threat of border wars with neighboring states for a generation, giving the United States a much-needed period of peace and security.

Western Hemisphere. At Adams's behest, Monroe warned Spain and other European powers to keep their hands off the newly independent republics in Latin America. The American continents were not "subject for further colonization," the president declared in 1823 — a policy that thirty years later became known as the **Monroe Doctrine**. In return, Monroe pledged that the United States would not "interfere in the internal concerns" of European nations. Thanks to John Quincy Adams, the United States had successfully asserted its diplomatic leadership in the Western Hemisphere and won international acceptance of its northern and western boundaries.

The appearance of political consensus after two decades of bitter party conflict prompted observers to dub James Monroe's presidency (1817–1825) the "Era of Good Feeling." This harmony was real but transitory. The Republican Party was now split between the National faction, led by Clay and Adams, and the Jeffersonian faction, soon to be led by Martin Van

Buren and Andrew Jackson. The two groups differed sharply over federal support for roads and canals and many other issues. As the aging Jefferson himself complained, "You see so many of these new [National] republicans maintaining in Congress the rankest doctrines of the old federalists." This division in the Republican Party would soon produce the Second Party System, in which national-minded Whigs and state-focused Democrats would confront each other. By the early 1820s, one cycle of American politics and economic debate had ended, and another was about to begin.

# SUMMARY

In this chapter, we traced three interrelated themes: public policy, westward expansion, and party politics. We began by examining the contrasting public policies advocated by Alexander Hamilton and Thomas

Jefferson. A Federalist, Hamilton supported a strong national government and created a fiscal infrastructure (the national debt, tariffs, and a national bank) to spur trade and manufacturing. By contrast, Jefferson wanted to preserve the authority of state governments, and he envisioned an America enriched by farming rather than industry.

Jefferson and the Republicans promoted a westward movement that transformed the agricultural economy and sparked new wars with Indian peoples. Expansion westward also shaped American diplomatic and military policy, leading to the Louisiana Purchase, the War of 1812, and the treaties negotiated by John Quincy Adams.

Finally, there was the unexpected rise of the First Party System. As Hamilton's policies split the political elite, the French Revolution divided Americans into hostile ideological groups. The result was two decades of bitter conflict and controversial measures: the Federalists' Sedition Act, the Republicans' Embargo Act, and Madison's decision to go to war with Britain. Although the Federalist Party faded away, it left as its enduring legacy Hamilton's financial innovations and John Marshall's constitutional jurisprudence.

# CHAPTER REVIEW

**MAKE IT STICK**   Go to **LearningCurve** to retain what you've read.

## TERMS TO KNOW   Identify and explain the significance of each term below.

### Key Concepts and Events

Judiciary Act of 1789 (p. 216)

Bill of Rights (p. 216)

Report on the Public Credit (p. 216)

Bank of the United States (p. 218)

Report on Manufactures (p. 218)

Proclamation of Neutrality (p. 219)

French Revolution (p. 219)

Jacobins (p. 219)

Whiskey Rebellion (p. 219)

Jay's Treaty (p. 222)

Haitian Revolution (p. 222)

XYZ Affair (p. 223)

Naturalization, Alien, and Sedition Acts (p. 224)

Virginia and Kentucky Resolutions (p. 225)

Treaty of Greenville (p. 226)

*Marbury v. Madison* (1803) (p. 231)

Louisiana Purchase (p. 233)

Embargo Act of 1807 (p. 234)

Battle of Tippecanoe (p. 236)

Treaty of Ghent (p. 241)

*McCulloch v. Maryland* (1819) (p. 241)

Adams-Onís Treaty (p. 243)

Monroe Doctrine (p. 244)

### Key People

Alexander Hamilton (p. 216)

Thomas Jefferson (p. 218)

John Adams (p. 223)

Little Turtle (p. 226)

John Marshall (p. 231)

Tecumseh (p. 235)

Henry Clay (p. 241)

John Quincy Adams (p. 243)

## REVIEW QUESTIONS   Answer these questions to demonstrate your understanding of the chapter's main ideas.

1. Why did Alexander Hamilton, as Washington's first secretary of the treasury, advocate the creation of a permanent national debt and a national bank? What fears did his economic plans arouse in his Republican opponents?

2. What were the principal effects of the French and Haitian Revolutions in the United States? How did they influence the development of the American economy, American politics, and westward development?

**3.** What forces — ideological, political, and economic — led the United States to gain dominance over eastern North America in these years?

**4.** Explain the rise and fall of the First Party System. How did the policies implemented by Republican presidents between 1801 and 1825 differ from those implemented during the 1790s? Why did the Federalists fall out of favor? What legacy did the Federalists leave?

**5. THEMATIC UNDERSTANDING**   Look at the events listed under "Work, Exchange, and Technology" and "Politics and Power" for the period 1800–1820 on the thematic timeline on page 149. What was the relationship in these years between the activism of the national government and developments in the American economy?

# MAKING CONNECTIONS

Recognize the larger developments and continuities within and across chapters by answering these questions.

**1. ACROSS TIME AND PLACE**   In Chapter 6, thirteen former British colonies cooperated in war and established new republican institutions of self-government. After 1789, unforeseen divisions developed in American politics. Why did Hamiltonians and Jeffersonians disagree so sharply on key questions of national policy? Which of the factions in the First Party System — Federalists or Republicans — best embodied the principles of the Revolution? How did westward expansion and international relations force the United States to modify its Revolutionary republican ideals?

**2. VISUAL EVIDENCE**   Return to the Currier & Ives print depicting the bombardment of Tripoli on page 232. What message does it convey about America's position in the world? How well does that message square with the actual outcome of the First Barbary War? What does this suggest about the artist's purpose?

# MORE TO EXPLORE   Start here to learn more about the events discussed in this chapter.

Gregory Dowd, *A Spirited Resistance* (1993). A penetrating account of Indian resistance to American expansion.

Joanne B. Freeman, *Affairs of Honor* (2002). A cultural analysis of the politics of the 1790s.

Jon Kukla, *A Wilderness So Immense* (2004). A sweeping account of the contexts for the Louisiana Purchase.

Alan Taylor, *The Civil War of 1812* (2010). Presents the contest for Canada as a multiethnic civil war.

Ashli White, *Encountering Revolution* (2012). Considers the impact of the Haitian Revolution on the United States.

*The War of 1812* (PBS video, 2011) and its accompanying Web site (**pbs.org/wned/war-of-1812/home/**) offer reenactments, animations, interpretive essays, and historical site analyses.

## TIMELINE

Ask yourself why this chapter begins and ends with these dates and then identify the links among related events.

| | |
|---|---|
| **1784–1789** | • Contested Indian treaties: Fort Stanwix (1784), Fort McIntosh (1785), Fort Finney (1786), and Fort Harmar (1789) |
| **1789–1799** | • French Revolution |
| **1789** | • Judiciary Act establishes federal courts |
| **1790** | • Hamilton's public credit system approved |
| **1790–1791** | • Western Confederacy defeats U.S. armies |
| **1791–1803** | • Haitian Revolution |
| **1791** | • Bill of Rights ratified<br>• Bank of the United States chartered |
| **1792** | • Kentucky joins Union |
| **1793** | • War between Britain and France |
| **1794** | • Madison and Jefferson found Republican Party<br>• Whiskey Rebellion<br>• Battle of Fallen Timbers |
| **1795** | • Jay's Treaty with Great Britain<br>• Pinckney's Treaty with Spain<br>• Treaty of Greenville accepts Indian land rights |
| **1798** | • XYZ Affair<br>• Alien, Sedition, and Naturalization Acts<br>• Virginia and Kentucky Resolutions |
| **1800** | • Jefferson elected president |
| **1801–1812** | • Gallatin reduces national debt |
| **1803** | • Louisiana Purchase<br>• *Marbury v. Madison* asserts judicial review |
| **1804–1806** | • Lewis and Clark explore West |
| **1807** | • Embargo Act cripples American shipping |
| **1808** | • Madison elected president |
| **1809** | • Tecumseh and Tenskwatawa revive Western Confederacy |
| **1812–1815** | • War of 1812 |
| **1817–1825** | • Era of Good Feeling |
| **1819** | • Adams-Onís Treaty<br>• *McCulloch v. Maryland; Dartmouth College v. Woodward* |

**KEY TURNING POINTS:** The Northwest Ordinance (1787; Chapter 6), Kentucky and Tennessee join the Union (1792, 1796), and Jefferson is elected president (1800). How were developments in the West tied into national politics in the 1790s? Why did the Federalists steadily lose ground to the Republicans?

# 8

**CHAPTER**

# Creating a Republican Culture
# 1790–1820

B y the 1820s, America's white citizenry had embraced the republican political order. Their nation stood forth as a "promised land of civil liberty, and of institutions designed to liberate and exalt the human race," declared a Kentucky judge. White Americans were indeed fortunate. They lived under a representative republican government, free from arbitrary taxation and from domination by an established church. The timing of the deaths of aging political leaders John Adams and Thomas Jefferson seemed to many Americans to confirm that God looked with favor on their experiment in self-government. What other than divine intervention could explain their nearly simultaneous deaths on July 4, 1826, the fiftieth anniversary of the Declaration of Independence?

Inspired by their political freedom, many citizens sought to extend republican principles throughout their society. But what were those principles? For entrepreneurial-minded merchants, farmers, and political leaders, republicanism meant a dynamic market economy based on the private ownership of property and capital. However, they welcomed legislative policies that assisted private business and, they claimed, enhanced the "common wealth" of the society. Other Americans in the northern states championed democratic republican cultural values, such as equality in the family and in social relationships. In the southern states, sharply divided by class and race, politicians and pamphleteers endorsed aristocratic republicanism. It stressed liberty for whites rather than equality for all.

Yet another vision of American republicanism emerged from the Second Great Awakening, religious revivals that swept the nation between 1790 and 1850. As Alexis de Tocqueville reported in *Democracy in America* (1835), the Second Great Awakening gave "the Christian religion . . . a greater influence over the souls of men" than in any other country. Moreover, religious enthusiasm—what Methodist bishop McIlvaine praised as "the quickening of the people of God to a spirit and walk becoming the gospel"—prompted social reform on many fronts. For those who embraced the Awakening, the United States was both a great experiment in republican government and a Christian civilization destined to redeem the world—a moral mission that would inform American diplomacy in the centuries to come.

## IDENTIFY THE BIG IDEA

In eighteenth-century Europe, the leading principles were aristocracy, patriarchy, mercantilism, arranged marriages, legal privilege, and established churches. What principles would replace those societal rules in America's new republican society?

**Mrs. Hugh McCurdy and Her Daughters**   This 1806 portrait of Grace Allison McCurdy and her daughters, Mary Jane and Letitia Grace, excludes her husband, the Baltimore merchant Hugh McCurdy, suggesting the increased cultural focus on mothers and children in the early republic. A few years earlier, the artist, Joshua Johnson (or Johnston, c. 1763–c. 1824), had painted a solo portrait of Letitia Grace. Here Johnson links Mrs. McCurdy and her elder daughter visually with a splash of vibrant red fruit near their laps, which probably also serves as a symbol of their fertility. Corcoran Gallery of Art, Washington D.C., USA/Museum Purchase through the gifts of William Wilson Corcoran, Elizabeth Donner Norment, Francis Biddle, Erich Cohn, Hardinge Scholle and the William A. Clark Fund/The Bridgeman Art Library.

# The Capitalist Commonwealth

What did republicanism mean for economic life? In early-nineteenth-century America, it meant private property, market exchange, individual opportunity, and activist governments. Throughout the nation, and especially in the Northeast, republican state legislatures embraced a **"neomercantilist"** system of government-assisted economic development. And it worked. Beginning around 1800, the average per capita income of Americans increased by more than 1 percent a year — more than 30 percent in a single generation.

## Banks, Manufacturing, and Markets

America was "a Nation of Merchants," a British visitor reported from Philadelphia in 1798, "keen in the pursuit of wealth in all the various modes of acquiring it." Acquire it they did, making spectacular profits as the wars of the French Revolution and Napoleon (1793–1815) crippled European firms. Merchants John Jacob Astor and Robert Oliver became the nation's first millionaires. After working for an Irish-owned linen firm in Baltimore, Oliver struck out on his own, achieving affluence by trading West Indian sugar and coffee. Astor, who migrated from Germany to New York in 1784, began by selling dry-goods in western New York and became wealthy by carrying furs from the Pacific Northwest to China and investing in New York City real estate (Thinking Like a Historian, p. 252).

**Banking and Credit**    To finance their ventures, Oliver, Astor, and other merchants needed capital, from either their own savings or loans. Before the Revolution, farmers relied on government-sponsored land banks for loans, while merchants arranged partnerships or obtained credit from British suppliers. Then, in 1781, Philadelphia merchants persuaded the Confederation Congress to charter the Bank of North America, and traders in Boston and New York soon founded similar institutions that raised funds and lent them out. "Our monied capital has so much increased from the Introduction of Banks, & the Circulation of the Funds," Philadelphia merchant William Bingham boasted in 1791, "that the Necessity of Soliciting Credits from England will no longer exist."

That same year, Federalists in Congress chartered the Bank of the United States to issue notes and make commercial loans (Chapter 7, p. 218). By 1805, the bank had branches in eight seaport cities, profits that averaged a handsome 8 percent annually, and clients

**A Cloth Merchant, 1789**
Originally a prosperous storekeeper in New Milford, Connecticut, Elijah Boardman (1760–1832) eventually became a U.S. senator. Like other American traders during the 1780s, he imported huge quantities of cloth from Britain. When the wars of the 1790s cut off trade, some merchants financed the domestic production of textiles. Others, including Boardman, turned to land speculation. In 1795, he joined the Connecticut Land Company and bought huge tracts in Connecticut's Western Reserve, including the present towns of Medina, Palmyra, and Boardman, Ohio. Ralph Earl painted this portrait in 1789.
© The Metropolitan Museum of Art. Image Source: Art Resource/NY.

with easy access to capital. As trader Jesse Atwater noted, "the foundations of our [merchant] houses are laid in bank paper."

However, Jeffersonians attacked the bank as an unconstitutional expansion of federal power. Moreover, they claimed it promoted "a consolidated, energetic government supported by public creditors, speculators, and other insidious men." When the bank's twenty-year charter expired in 1811, the Jeffersonian Republican–dominated Congress refused to renew it.

**The China Trade**

Following the Revolution, New England merchants traded actively with the major Asian manufacturing centers of China and India. In this painting by George Chinnery (1774–1852), the American flag flies prominently, alongside other national banners, in front of the warehouse district in Canton (modern Guangzhou). There, merchants exchanged bundles of American furs for cargoes of Chinese tea, silks, and porcelain plates, cups, and serving dishes. © Peabody Essex Museum, Salem, Massachusetts, USA/The Bridgeman Art Library.

Merchants, artisans, and farmers quickly persuaded state legislatures to charter banks — in Pennsylvania, no fewer than 41. By 1816, when Congress (now run by National Republicans) chartered a new national bank (known as the Second Bank of the United States), there were 246 state-chartered banks with tens of thousands of stockholders and $68 million in banknotes in circulation. These state banks were often shady operations that issued notes without adequate specie reserves, made loans to insiders, and lent generously to farmers buying overpriced land.

Dubious banking policies helped bring on the **Panic of 1819** (just as they caused the financial crisis of 2008), but broader forces were equally important. As the Napoleonic Wars ended in 1815, Americans sharply increased their consumption of English woolen and cotton goods. However, in 1818, farmers and planters faced an abrupt 30 percent drop in world agricultural prices. The price of raw cotton in South Carolina fell from 34 to 15 cents a pound, and as Britain closed the West Indies to American trade, wheat prices plummeted as well. As farmers' income declined, they could not pay debts owed to stores and banks, many of which went bankrupt. "A deep shadow has passed over our land," lamented one New Yorker, as land prices dropped by 50 percent. The panic gave Americans their first taste of a business cycle, the periodic boom and bust inherent to an unregulated market economy.

**Rural Manufacturing**   The Panic of 1819 devastated artisans and farmers who sold goods in regional or national markets. Before 1800, many artisans worked part-time and bartered their handicrafts locally. A French traveler in Massachusetts found many "men who are both cultivators and artisans," while in Lancaster, Pennsylvania, clockmaker John Hoff exchanged

## The Entrepreneur and the Community

Americans of the early republic believed that with hard work and virtue, even the lowliest of white men might rise to economic and political respectability, if not prominence. In the Revolutionary generation, Benjamin Franklin, born into a large and impoverished Boston family, had become a successful businessman and an international celebrity. Franklin's success reflected the optimism that laboring men felt when contemplating the new nation's seemingly boundless opportunity.

---

1. **Banner of the Society of Pewterers of the City of New York, carried in the Federal Procession, July 23, 1788, celebrating the ratification of the U.S. Constitution.** *The ribbon at top right reads "The Federal Plan Most Solid & Secure/Americans Their Freedom Will Endure/All Art Shall Flourish in Columbia's Land/And All her Sons Join as One Social Band."*

Source: © Collection of the New York Historical Society, USA/The Bridgeman Art Library.

2. **John Jacob Astor quoted in Elbert Hubbard, *Little Journeys to the Homes of Great Business Men*, 1909.** *John Jacob Astor's (1763–1848) story is a parable of American entrepreneurial triumph. Arriving in America in 1783 from Germany, Astor worked in the fur industry treating pelts and, with capital borrowed from his brother, started up a musical instrument shop and fur business in 1786. Over the next three decades, Astor's American Fur Company prospered by trading furs in China, making Astor America's first millionaire. Apparently influenced by Benjamin*

*Franklin's aphorism "Early to bed and early to rise, makes a man healthy wealthy and wise," Astor wrote:*

The man who makes it the habit of his life to go to bed at nine o'clock, usually gets rich and is always reliable. Of course, going to bed does not make him rich — I merely mean that such a man will in all probability be up early in the morning and do a big day's work . . . good habits in America make any man rich.

3. **Anonymous, "A Working Man's Recollections of America," *Knight's Penny Magazine*, 1846.** *A cabinetmaker penned this account after returning to England following an unsuccessful stint seeking success in New York.*

I was a cabinet-maker by trade, and one of the many who, between the years 1825–35, expatriated themselves in countless thousands, drawn by the promise of fair wages for faithful work, and driven by the scanty remuneration offered to unceasing toil at home. . . . On landing in New York I made up my mind to lose none of the advantages it uttered by want of diligence on my part. During the first two years I took but one holiday. . . . In summer we began work at six; at eight took half an hour for breakfast, and then worked till twelve, when one an hour for dinner; after which we kept on till six, seven, or eight. . . . A relative who arrived from England held out to me bright prospects of advantages to be realized by the employment of a little capital, combined with a removal to some inland town. I sold off nearly the whole of our moveables . . . [and committed all my savings to this enterprise. However,] our scheme . . . completely failed, and I had no resources but my industry and chest of tools to meet the impending difficulties.

4. **Diary entry by Philip Hone, March 29, 1848.** *Philip Hone (1780–1851), a conservative Whig, was a successful merchant and entrepreneur and mayor of New York City from 1826 to 1827.*

*Hone's marvelous diary (1828–1851) records the changing character of New York City, as well as his contempt for Jacksonian Democracy and its Irish immigrant supporters.*

John Jacob Astor died this morning, at nine o'clock, in the eighty-fifth year of his age . . . and left reluctantly his unbounded wealth. His property is estimated at $20,000,000, some judicious persons say $30,000,000; but, at any rate, he was the richest man in the United States in productive and valuable property; and this immense, gigantic fortune was the fruit of his own labor, unerring sagacity, and far-seeing penetration. He came to this country at twenty years of age; penniless, friendless, without inheritance, without education . . . but with a determination to be rich, and ability to carry it into effect. His capital consisted of a few trifling musical instruments, which he got from his brother, George Astor, in London, a dealer in music. . . . The fur trade was the philosopher's stone of this modern Croesus; beaver-skins and musk-rats furnished the oil for the supply of Aladdin's lamp. His traffic was the shipment of furs to China, where they brought immense prices, for he monopolized the business; and the return cargoes of teas, silks, and rich productions of China brought further large profits. . . . My brother and I found in Mr. Astor a valuable customer. . . . All he touched turned to gold.

**5. Editorial in the *New York Herald*, April 5, 1848.**
*John Jacob Astor's will included a bequest of $400,000 for the establishment of what became the New York Public Library. This editorial questioned whether this relatively meager bequest adequately repaid residents.*

If we had been an associate of John Jacob Astor the first idea that we should have put into his head would have been that one-half of his immense property — ten million at least — belonged to the people of the city of New York. During the last fifty years of the life of John Jacob Astor, his property has been augmented and increased in the value by the aggregate intelligence, industry, enterprise and commerce of New York, fully to the amount of one-half its value. The farms and lots of ground which he

bought forty, twenty and ten and five years ago, have all increased in value entirely by the industry of the citizens of New York . . . half of his immense estate, in its actual value, has accrued to him by the industry of the community.

Sources: (2) Elbert Hubbard, *Little Journeys to the Homes of Great Business Men* (New York: Wm. H. Wise & Co., 1916), 201; (3) *Knight's Penny Magazine*, Vol. 1 (London: Charles Knight & Co., 1846), 97, 107, 108; (4) Philip Hone, *The Diary of Philip Hone, 1828–1851*, Vol. 2 (New York: Dodd, Mead and Company, 1889), 347–348; (5) Gustavus Myers, *History of the Great American Fortunes*, Vol. 1 (Chicago: Charles H. Kerr & Company, 1910), 199–200.

## ANALYZING THE EVIDENCE

1. What does the Pewterer's Banner (source 1) suggest about personal and by extension national success in the post-Revolutionary era? What can you infer about artisan entrepreneurs in the new republic from this source?

2. According to John Jacob Astor (source 2) and the cabinetmaker (source 3), what traits are important in work? Based on the sources included here, do you agree with Astor that good habits make any man rich? Why or why not?

3. Sources 2, 4, and 5 all deal with John Jacob Astor. What do these sources suggest about the road to wealth in America?

4. Compare and contrast Hone's view of Astor (source 4) with that of the *Herald*'s editorial (source 5). Then apply the *Herald*'s critique to contemporary entrepreneurs such as Bill Gates of Microsoft or Steve Jobs of Apple. Are their fortunes also the product, in part, of "the industry of the community"?

## PUTTING IT ALL TOGETHER

John Jacob Astor initially made money by trading furs in local and then in international markets. Next, he speculated in land in booming cities. Finally, he became a *rentier*, crafting long-term property leases that guaranteed wealth to future generations of his family. Using the material in Chapter 8, explain how a pewterer or a cabinetmaker might follow a somewhat similar path to wealth in the market economy of nineteenth-century America. Noting also the statement "All her Sons Join as One Social Band" (source 1), explain why other Americans were critical of the rise of such ambitious capitalist entrepreneurs.

his clocks for a dining table, a bedstead, and labor on his small farm. Then various artisans — shipbuilders in seacoast towns, ironworkers in Pennsylvania and Maryland, clockmakers in Connecticut, and shoemakers in Massachusetts — expanded their output and sold their products in wider markets.

American entrepreneurs drove this expansion of rural manufacturing. Beginning in the 1790s, enterprising merchants bought raw materials, hired farm families to process them, and distributed the finished manufactures. "Straw hats and Bonnets are manufactured by many families," a Maine census-taker noted in the 1810s. Merchants shipped rural manufactures — shoes, brooms, and palm-leaf hats as well as cups, baking pans, and other tin utensils — to stores in seaport cities. New England peddlers, who quickly acquired repute as hard-bargaining "Yankees," sold them throughout the rural South.

New technology initially played only a minor role in producing this boom in consumer goods. Take the case of textile production. During the 1780s, New England and Middle Atlantic merchants built water-powered mills to run machines that combed wool — and later cotton — into long strands. However, until the 1810s, they used the household-based outwork system for the next steps: farm women and children spun the machine-combed strands into thread and yarn on foot-driven spinning wheels, and men in other households used foot-powered looms to weave the yarn into cloth. In 1820, more than 12,000 household workers labored full-time weaving woolen cloth, which water-powered fulling mills then pounded flat, giving the cloth a smooth finish. By then, the transfer of textile production to factories was gaining speed; the number of water-driven cotton spindles soared from 8,000 in 1809 to 333,000 in 1817.

**TRACE CHANGE OVER TIME**

How did governments, banks, and merchants expand American commerce and manufacturing between 1780 and 1820?

**The Yankee Peddler, c. 1830**
Even in 1830, many Americans lived too far from a market town to go there regularly to buy goods. Instead, they purchased their tinware, clocks, textiles, and other manufactures from peddlers, often from New England, who traveled far and wide in small horse-drawn vans like the one visible through the doorway.
Collection IBM Corporation, Armonk, New York.

The growth of manufacturing offered farm families new opportunities — and new risks. Ambitious New England farmers switched from subsistence crops of wheat and potatoes to raising livestock. They sold meat, butter, and cheese to city markets and cattle hides to the booming shoe industry. "Along the whole road from Boston, we saw women engaged in making cheese," a Polish traveler reported. Other families raised sheep and sold raw wool to textile manufacturers. Processing these raw materials brought new jobs and income to stagnating farming towns. In 1792, Concord, Massachusetts, had one slaughterhouse and five small tanneries; a decade later, the town boasted eleven slaughterhouses and six large tanneries.

As the rural economy churned out more goods, it altered the environment. Foul odors from stockyards and tanning pits wafted over Concord and other leather-producing towns. Nor was that all. Tanners cut down thousands of acres of hemlock trees, using the bark to process stiff cow hides into pliable leather. More trees fell to the ax to create pasturelands for huge herds of livestock — dairy cows, cattle, and especially sheep. By 1850, most of the ancient forests in southern New England and eastern New York were gone: "The hills had been stripped of their timber," New York's *Catskill Messenger* reported, "so as to present their huge, rocky projections." Moreover, scores of textile milldams dotted New England's rivers, altering their flow and preventing fish — already severely depleted from decades of overfishing — from reaching upriver spawning grounds. Even as the income of farmers rose, the quality of their natural environment declined.

In the new capitalist-driven market economy, rural parents and their children worked longer and harder. They made yarn, hats, and brooms during the winter and returned to their regular farming chores during the warmer seasons. More important, these farm families now depended on their wage labor or market sales to purchase the textiles, shoes, and hats they had once made for themselves. The new productive system made families and communities more efficient and prosperous — and more dependent on a market they could not control.

**New Transportation Systems**   The expansion of the market depended on improvements in transportation, where governments also played a crucial role. Between 1793 and 1812, the Massachusetts legislature granted charters to more than one hundred private turnpike corporations. These charters gave the companies special legal status and often included monopoly rights to a transportation route. Pennsylvania issued fifty-five charters, including one to the Lancaster Turnpike Company, which built a 65-mile graded and graveled toll road to Philadelphia. The road quickly boosted the regional economy. Although turnpike investors received only about "three percent annually," Henry Clay estimated, society as a whole "actually reap[ed] fifteen or twenty percent." A farm woman agreed: "The turnpike is finished and we can now go to town at all times and in all weather." New turnpikes soon connected dozens of inland market centers to seaport cities.

Water transport was even quicker and cheaper, so state governments and private entrepreneurs dredged shallow rivers and constructed canals to bypass waterfalls and rapids. For their part, farmers in Kentucky and Tennessee and in southern Ohio, Indiana, and Illinois settled near the Ohio River and its many tributaries, so they could easily get goods to market. Similarly, speculators hoping to capitalize on the expansion of commerce bought up property in the cities along the banks of major rivers: Cincinnati, Louisville, Chattanooga, and St. Louis. Farmers and merchants built barges to carry cotton, grain, and meat downstream to New Orleans, which by 1815 was exporting about $5 million in agricultural products yearly.

## Public Enterprise: The Commonwealth System

Legislative charters for banks, turnpikes, and canal companies reflected the ideology of mercantilism: government-assisted economic development. Just as Parliament had used the Navigation Acts to spur British prosperity, so American legislatures enacted laws "of great public utility" to increase the "common wealth." These statutes generally took the form of special charters that bestowed legal privileges, such as the power of eminent domain, that allowed turnpike, bridge, and canal corporations to force the sale of privately owned land along their routes. State legislatures also aided capital-intensive flour millers and textile manufacturers, who flooded adjacent farmland as they built dams to power their water-driven machinery. In Massachusetts, the Mill Dam Act of 1795 deprived farmers of their traditional common-law right to stop the flooding and forced them to accept "fair compensation" for their lost acreage. Judges approved this state-ordered shift in property rights. "The establishment of a great mill-power for manufacturing purposes," Justice Lemuel Shaw intoned, was "one of the great industrial pursuits of the commonwealth."

> **UNDERSTAND POINTS OF VIEW**
> Did state mercantilism (the grant of privileges and charters) embody republican ideology or violate it?

***View of Cincinnati,* by John Caspar Wild, c. 1835**

Thanks to its location on the Ohio River (a tributary of the Mississippi), Cincinnati quickly became one of the major processing centers for grain and hogs in the trans-Appalachian west. By the 1820s, passenger steamboats and freight barges connected the city with Pittsburgh to the north and the ocean port of New Orleans far to the south. Museum of Fine Arts, Boston, M. and M. Karolik Collection.

Critics condemned the legal privileges given to private enterprises as "Scheme[s] of an evident anti-republican tendency," as some "freeholder citizens" in Putney, Vermont, put it. Such grants to business corporations, they argued, violated the "equal rights" of citizens and infringed on the sovereignty of the governments. "Whatever power is given to a corporation, is just so much power taken from the State," argued a Pennsylvanian. Nonetheless, judges in state courts, following the lead of John Marshall's Supreme Court (Chapter 7), consistently upheld corporate charters and grants of eminent domain to private transportation companies. "The opening of good and easy internal communications is one of the highest duties of government," declared a New Jersey judge.

State mercantilism soon spread beyond transportation. Following Jefferson's embargo of 1807, which cut off goods and credit from Europe, the New England

states awarded charters to two hundred iron-mining, textile-manufacturing, and banking companies, while Pennsylvania granted more than eleven hundred. By 1820, state governments had created a republican political economy: a **Commonwealth System** that funneled state aid to private businesses whose projects would improve the general welfare.

# Toward a Democratic Republican Culture

After independence, many Americans in the northern states embraced a democratic republicanism that celebrated political equality and social mobility. These citizens, primarily members of the emerging middle class, redefined the nature of the family and of education by seeking egalitarian marriages and affectionate ways of rearing their children.

## Opportunity and Equality— for White Men

Between 1780 and 1820, hundreds of well-educated visitors agreed that the American social order was different from that of Europe. In his famous *Letters from an American Farmer* (1782), French-born essayist J. Hector St. Jean de Crèvecoeur wrote that European society was composed "of great lords who possess everything, and of a herd of people who have nothing." By contrast, the United States had "no aristocratical families, no courts, no kings, no bishops."

The absence of a hereditary aristocracy encouraged Americans to condemn inherited social privilege and to extol legal equality. "The law is the same for everyone," noted one European traveler. Yet citizens of the new republic willingly accepted social divisions that reflected personal achievement, a phenomenon that astounded many Europeans. "In Europe to say of someone that he rose from nothing is a disgrace and a reproach," remarked a Polish aristocrat. "It is the opposite here. To be the architect of your own fortune is honorable. It is the highest recommendation."

Some Americans from long-distinguished families felt threatened by the ideology of wealth-driven social mobility. "Man is estimated by dollars," complained Nathaniel Booth, whose high-status family had once dominated the small Hudson River port town of Kingston, New York. However, for most white men, a merit-based system meant the chance to better themselves (Map 8.1).

Old cultural rules—and new laws—denied such chances to most women and African American men. When women and free blacks asked for voting rights, male legislators wrote explicit race and gender restrictions into the law. In 1802, Ohio disenfranchised African Americans, and the New York constitution of 1821 imposed a property-holding requirement on black voters. A striking case of sexual discrimination occurred in New Jersey, where the state constitution of 1776 had granted the voting franchise to all property

> **IDENTIFY CAUSES**
> What factors encouraged— and inhibited—equality and democracy in early-nineteenth-century American life?

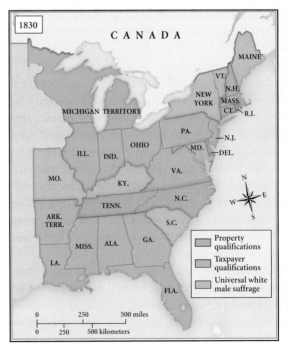

**MAP 8.1**

**The Expansion of Voting Rights for White Men, 1800 and 1830**

Between 1800 and 1830, the United States moved steadily toward political equality for white men. Many existing states revised their constitutions and replaced a property qualification for voting with less restrictive criteria, such as paying taxes or serving in the militia. Some new states in the West extended the suffrage to all adult white men. As parties sought votes from a broader electorate, the tone of politics became more open and competitive—swayed by the interests and values of ordinary people.

holders. As Federalists and Republicans competed for power, they ignored customary gender rules and urged property-owning single women and widows to vote. Sensing a threat to men's monopoly on politics, the New Jersey legislature in 1807 invoked both biology and custom to limit voting to men only: "Women, generally, are neither by nature, nor habit, nor education, nor by their necessary condition in society fitted to perform this duty with credit to themselves or advantage to the public."

## Toward Republican Families

The controversy over women's political rights mirrored a debate over authority within the household. British and American husbands had long claimed patriarchal power and legal control of the family's property. However, as John Adams lamented in 1776, the republican principle of equality had "spread where it was not intended," encouraging his wife and other women to demand legal and financial rights. Patriot author and historian Mercy Otis Warren argued that patriarchy was not a "natural" rule but a social contrivance and could be justified only "for the sake of order in families."

 To see a longer excerpt of the Mercy Otis Warren document, along with other primary sources from this period, see *Sources for America's History*.

**Republican Marriages**  Economic and cultural changes also eroded customary paternal authority. In colonial America, most property-owning parents had arranged their children's marriages. They looked for a morally upright son- or daughter-in-law with financial resources; physical attraction and emotional compatibility between the young people were secondary considerations. As landholdings shrank in long-settled communities, many yeomen fathers has less control over their children's marriages because they had fewer resources to give them.

Increasingly, young men and women chose their own partners, influenced by a new cultural attitude: **sentimentalism**. Sentimentalism originated in Europe as part of the Romantic movement and, after 1800, spread quickly through all classes of American society. Rejecting the Enlightenment's emphasis on rational thought, sentimentalism celebrated the importance of "feeling"—a physical, sensuous appreciation of God, nature, and fellow humans. This new emphasis on deeply felt emotions pervaded literary works, popular theatrical melodramas, and the passionate rhetoric of revivalist preachers.

As the passions of the heart overwhelmed the logic of the mind, magazines praised **companionate marriages**: marriages "contracted from motives of affection, rather than of interest." Many young people looked for a relationship based on intimacy and a spouse who was, as Eliza Southgate of Maine put it, "calculated to promote my happiness." As young people "fell in love" and married, many fathers changed from authoritarian patriarchs to watchful paternalists. To guard against free-spending sons-in-law, wealthy fathers often placed their daughters' inheritance in a legal trust. One Virginia planter told his lawyer "to see the property settlement properly drawn before the marriage, for I by no means consent that Polly shall be left to the Vicissitudes of Life."

As voluntary contracts between individuals, love marriages conformed more closely to republican principles than did arranged matches. In theory, such marriages would be companionate, giving wives and husbands "true equality," as one Boston man suggested. In practice, husbands dominated most marriages, because male authority was deeply ingrained in cultural mores and because American common law gave husbands control of the family's property. Moreover, the new love-based marriage system discouraged parents from protecting young wives, and governments refused to prevent domestic tyranny. The marriage contract "is so much more important in its consequences to females than to males," a young man at the Litchfield Law School in Connecticut astutely observed in 1820, for "they subject themselves to his authority. He is their all—their only relative—their only hope" (American Voices, p. 260).

Young adults who chose partners unwisely were severely disappointed when their spouses failed as providers or faithful companions. Before 1800, unhappy wives and husbands could do little; officials granted divorces infrequently and then only in cases of neglect, abandonment, or adultery—serious offenses against the moral order of society. After 1800, most divorce petitions cited emotional issues. One woman complained that her husband had "ceased to cherish her," while a man grieved that his wife had "almost broke his heart." Responding to changing cultural values, several states expanded the legal grounds for divorce to include drunkenness and personal cruelty.

**Republican Motherhood**  Traditionally, most American women had spent their active adult years working as farmwives and bearing and nurturing children. However, after 1800, the birthrate in the northern states dropped significantly. In the farming village of

**The Wedding, 1805**
Bride and groom stare intently into each other's eyes as they exchange vows, suggesting that their union was a love match, not an arranged marriage based on economic calculation. The plain costumes of the guests and the sparse furnishings of the room suggest that the unknown artist may have provided us with a picture of a rural Quaker wedding. The Granger Collection, NYC.

Sturbridge in central Massachusetts, women now bore an average of six children; their grandmothers had usually given birth to eight or nine. In the growing seaport cities, native-born white women now bore an average of only four children.

The United States was among the first nations to experience this sharp decline in the birthrate — what historians call the **demographic transition**. There were several causes. Beginning in the 1790s, thousands of young men migrated to the trans-Appalachian west, which increased the number of never-married women in the East and delayed marriage for many more. Women who married in their late twenties had fewer children. In addition, white urban middle-class couples deliberately limited the size of their families. Fathers wanted to leave children an adequate inheritance, while mothers, influenced by new ideas of individualism and self-achievement, refused to spend their entire adulthood rearing children. After having four or five children, these couples used birth control or abstained from sexual intercourse.

Even as women bore fewer children, they accepted greater responsibility for the welfare of the family. In his *Thoughts on Female Education* (1787), Philadelphia physician Benjamin Rush argued that young women should ensure their husbands' "perseverance in the paths of rectitude" and called for loyal "republican mothers" who would instruct "their sons in the principles of liberty and government."

 To see a longer excerpt of *Thoughts on Female Education*, along with other primary sources from this period, see *Sources for America's History*.

Christian ministers readily embraced this idea of **republican motherhood**. "Preserving virtue and instructing the young are not the fancied, but the real 'Rights of Women,'" the Reverend Thomas Bernard told the Female Charitable Society of Salem, Massachusetts. He urged his audience to dismiss public roles for women, such as voting or serving on juries, that English feminist Mary Wollstonecraft had advocated in *A Vindication of the Rights of Woman* (1792). Instead, women should care for their children, a responsibility that gave

**IDENTIFY CAUSES**
How did republican ideals, new economic circumstances, and changing cultural values affect marriage practices?

## The Trials of Married Life

As the text explains, the ideal American marriage of the early nineteenth century was republican (a contract between equals) and romantic (a match in which mutual love was foremost). Were these ideals attainable, given the social authority of men and the volatility of human passions? Letters, memoirs, and diaries are excellent sources for answering these questions. These selections from the personal writings of a variety of American women offer insights into the new system of marriage and how changes in cultural values intersected with individual lives.

### Emma Hart Willard
### The Danger of High Expectations

Born in Connecticut in 1787, Emma Hart married John Willard in 1809. An early proponent of advanced education for women, she founded female academies in Middlebury, Vermont (1814), and Waterford and Troy, New York (1821). She wrote this letter to her sister, Almira Hart, in 1815.

You think it strange that I should consider a period of happiness as more likely than any other to produce future misery. I know I did not sufficiently explain myself. Those tender and delicious sensations which accompany successful love, while they soothe and soften the mind, diminish its strength to bear or to conquer difficulties. It is the luxury of the soul; and luxury always enervates. . . . This life is a life of vicissitude. . . .

[Suppose] you are secured to each other for life. It will be natural that, at first, he should be much devoted to you; but, after a while, his business must occupy his attention. While absorbed in that he will perhaps neglect some of those little tokens of affection which have become necessary to your happiness. His affairs will sometimes go wrong, . . . and he may sometimes hastily give you a harsh word or a frown.

But where is the use, say you, of diminishing my present enjoyment by such gloomy apprehensions? Its use is this, that, if you enter the marriage state believing such things to be absolutely impossible, if you should meet them, they would come upon you with double force.

### Caroline Howard Gilman
### Female Submission in Marriage

Born in Boston in 1794, Caroline Howard married in 1819 and moved to Charleston, South Carolina, with her husband, Samuel Gilman, a Unitarian minister. A novelist, she published *Recollections of a Housekeeper* (1835), a portrait of domestic life in New England, and *Recollections of a Southern Matron* (1838), a fictional account that includes this selection.

The planter's bride, who leaves a numerous and cheerful family in her paternal home, little imagines the change which awaits her in her own retired residence. She dreams of an independent sway over her household, devoted love and unbroken intercourse with her husband, and indeed longs to be released from the eyes of others, that she may dwell only beneath the sunbeam of his. And so it was with me. . . .

There we were together, asking for nothing but each other's presence and love. At length it was necessary for him to tear himself away to superintend his interests. . . . But the period of absence was gradually protracted; then a friend sometimes came home with him, and their talk was of crops and politics, draining the fields and draining the revenue. . . . A growing discomfort began to work upon my mind. I had undefined forebodings; I mused about past days; my views of life became slowly disorganized; my physical powers enfeebled; a nervous excitement followed: I nursed a moody discontent. . . .

If the reign of romance was really waning, I resolved not to chill his noble confidence, but to make a steadier light rise on his affections. . . . This task of self-government was not easy. To repress a harsh answer, to confess a fault . . . in gentle submission, sometimes requires a struggle like life and death; but these . . . efforts are the golden threads with which domestic happiness is woven. . . . How clear is it, then, that woman loses by petulance and recrimination! Her first study must be self-control, almost to hypocrisy. A good wife must smile amid a thousand perplexities.

### Martha Hunter Hitchcock
### Isolation, Unmentionable Sorrows, and Suffering

Martha Hunter Hitchcock married a doctor in the U.S. Army. These excerpts from letters, in the Virginia Historical

Society, to her cousins Martha and Sarah Hunter describe her emotional dependence on her husband and her unhappy life.

To Martha Hunter, 1840:

If I had never married how much of pain, and dissatisfaction, should I have escaped — at all events I should never have known what jealousy is. You must not betray me, dear cousin, for despite all my good resolutions, I find it impossible always to struggle against my nature — the school of indulgence, in which I was educated, was little calculated to teach me, those lessons of forbearance, which I have had to practice so frequently, since my marriage — it is ungrateful in me to murmur, if perchance a little bitter is mingled in my cup of life.

To Sarah Hunter, 1841:

I have lived so long among strangers since my marriage, that when I contrast it with the old warm affection, in which I was nurtured, the contrast is so terrible, that I cannot refrain from weeping at the thought of it — I hope my dear cousin, that yours, will be a happier destiny than mine, in that respect — only think of it! Nearly a year and a half have passed away, since I have seen, a single relation!

To Martha Hunter, 1845:

Uneasiness about [my daughter] Lillie, and very great sorrows of my own, which I cannot commit to paper, have almost weighed me down to the grave; and indeed, without any affectation, I look forward to that, as the only real rest, I shall ever know.

To Martha Hunter, 1846:

Lillie had the scarlet fever, during our visit to Alabama, and she has never recovered from the effects of it — My life is a constant vigil — and there is nothing which wearies mind, and body, so much, as watching a sickly child. . . . All this I have to endure, and may have to suffer more for I know not, what Fate may have in store for me.

## Elizabeth Scott Neblett
## My Seasons of Gloom and Despondency

Elizabeth Scott Neblett lived with her husband and children in Navarro County, Texas. In 1860, she reflected in her diary on her bouts of depression and the difficulties of wives and husbands in understanding each other's inner lives.

It has now been almost eight years since I became a married woman. Eight years of checkered good and ill, and yet thro' all it seems the most of the ill has fallen to my lot, until now my poor weak cowardly heart sighs only for its final resting place, where sorrow grief nor pain can never reach it more.

I feel that I have faithfully discharged my duty towards you and my children, but for this I know that I deserve no credit nor aspire to none; my affection has been my prompter, and the task has proven a labor of love. You have not rightly understood me at all times, and being naturally very hopeful you could in no measure sympathize with me during my seasons of gloom and despondency. . . . But marriage is a lottery and that your draw proved an unfortunate one on your part is not less a subject of regret with me than you. . . .

It is useless to say that during these eight years I have suffered ten times more than you have and ten times more than I can begin to make you conceive of, but of course you can not help the past, nor by knowing my suffering relieve it, but it might induce you to look with more kindness upon [my] faults. . . . The 17th of this month I was 27 years old and I think my face looks older than that, perhaps I'll never see an other birth day and I don't grieve at the idea.

Source: These selections are abridged versions of materials in Anya Jabour, ed., *Major Problems in the History of American Families and Children* (Boston: Houghton Mifflin, 2005), 108–113.

### QUESTIONS FOR ANALYSIS

1. What problems do these women share? How might their problems reflect larger social and economic issues in nineteenth-century America?

2. How would you characterize the unhappiness of these women? In what ways is it related to their expectations about love-based marriage?

3. What was Caroline Gilman's advice to wives? How does it apply to the other women in this section?

4. Do these selections suggest that most American women had unfulfilled marriages? Or were these isolated cases? Would you expect to find more records of happy or unhappy marriages?

them "an extensive power over the fortunes of man in every generation."

## Raising Republican Children

Republican values changed assumptions about inheritance and child rearing. English common law encouraged primogeniture, the bequest of the family's property to the eldest son (Chapter 1). After the Revolution, most state legislatures enacted statutes specifying equal division of the estate among all children, when there was no will. Most American parents applauded these statutes because they were already treating their children equally and with respect.

**Two Modes of Parenting**    Indeed, many European visitors believed that republican parents gave their children too much respect and freedom. Because of the "general ideas of Liberty and Equality engraved on their hearts," a Polish aristocrat suggested around 1800, American children had "scant respect" for their parents. Several decades later, a British traveler stood dumbfounded when an American father excused his son's "resolute disobedience" with a smile and the remark, "A sturdy republican, sir." The traveler speculated that American parents encouraged such independence to prepare youth to "go their own way" in the world.

Permissive child rearing was not universal. Foreign visitors interacted primarily with well-to-do Episcopalians and Presbyterians who held an Enlightenment conception of children. This outlook, transmitted by religious authors influenced by John Locke, viewed children as "rational creatures" best trained by means of advice and praise. The parents' role was to develop their child's conscience, self-discipline, and sense of responsibility. Families in the rapidly expanding middle class widely adopted this rationalist method of child rearing.

By contrast, many yeomen and tenant farmers, influenced by the Second Great Awakening, raised their children in an authoritarian fashion. Evangelical Baptist and Methodist writers insisted that children were "full of the stains and pollution of sin" and needed strict rules and harsh discipline. Fear was a "useful and necessary principle in family government," minister John Abbott advised parents; a child "should submit to your authority, not to your arguments or persuasions." Abbott told parents to instill humility in children and to teach them to subordinate their personal desires to God's will.

**The Battle over Education**

Here an unknown artist pokes fun at a tyrannical schoolmaster and, indirectly, at the strict approach to child rearing taken by evangelical authors, parents, and teachers. The students' faces reflect the artist's own rationalist outlook. One Enlightenment-minded minister suggested that we see in young children's eyes "the first dawn of reason, beaming forth its immortal rays." Picture Research Consultants & Archives.

**Women's Education**
Even in education-conscious New England, before 1800 few girls attended free public primary schools for more than a few years. Subsequently, as this detail from *Scenes from a Seminary for Young Ladies* (c. 1810–1820) indicates, some girls stayed in school into their teenage years and studied a wide variety of subjects, including geography. Many graduates of these female academies became teachers, a new field of employment for women. The St. Louis Art Museum, Missouri, USA/The Bridgeman Art Library.

**Debates over Education**   Although families provided most moral and intellectual training, republican ideology encouraged publicly supported schooling. Bostonian Caleb Bingham, an influential textbook author, called for "an equal distribution of knowledge to make us emphatically a 'republic of letters.'" Both Thomas Jefferson and Benjamin Rush proposed ambitious schemes for a comprehensive system of primary and secondary schooling, followed by college training for bright young men. They also envisioned a university in which distinguished scholars would lecture on law, medicine, theology, and political economy.

To ordinary citizens, whose teenage children had to labor in the fields or workshops, talk of secondary and college education smacked of elitism. Farmers, artisans, and laborers wanted elementary schools that would instruct their children in the "three Rs" — reading, 'riting, and 'rithmetic — and make them literate enough to read the Bible. In New England, locally funded public schools offered basic instruction to most boys and some girls. In other regions, there were few publicly supported schools, and only 25 percent of the boys and perhaps 10 percent of the girls attended private institutions or had personal tutors. Even in New England, only a few young men and almost no young women went on to grammar school (high school), and less than 1 percent of men attended college. "Let anybody show what advantage the poor man receives from colleges," an anonymous "Old Soldier" wrote to the *Maryland Gazette*. "Why should they support them, unless it is to serve those who are in affluent circumstances, whose children can be spared from labor, and receive the benefits?"

Although many state constitutions encouraged support for education, few legislatures acted until the 1820s. Then a new generation of educational

reformers, influenced by merchants and manufacturers, raised standards by certifying qualified teachers and appointing statewide superintendents of schools. To encourage students, the reformers chose textbooks such as Parson Mason Weems's *The Life of George Washington* (c. 1800), which praised honesty and hard work and condemned gambling, drinking, and laziness. To bolster patriotism and shared cultural ideals, reformers required the study of American history. As a New Hampshire schoolboy, Thomas Low recalled: "We were taught every day and in every way that ours was the freest, the happiest, and soon to be the greatest and most powerful country of the world."

**UNDERSTAND POINTS OF VIEW**
Which form of child rearing—the rationalist or the authoritarian—was the most compatible with republican values and why?

**Promoting Cultural Independence**   Like Caleb Bingham, writer Noah Webster wanted to raise the nation's intellectual prowess. Asserting that "America must be as independent in literature as she is in politics," he called on his fellow citizens to free themselves "from the dependence on foreign opinions and manners, which is fatal to the efforts of genius in this country." Webster's *Dissertation on the English Language* (1789) celebrated language as a marker of national identity by defining words according to American usage. With less success, it proposed that words be spelled as they were pronounced, that *labour* (British spelling), for example, be spelled *labur*. Still, Webster's famous "blue-back speller," a compact textbook first published in 1783, sold 60 million copies over the next half century and served the needs of Americans of all backgrounds. "None of us was 'lowed to see a book," an enslaved African American recalled, "but we gits hold of that Webster's old blue-back speller and we . . . studies [it]."

Despite Webster's efforts, a republican literary culture developed slowly. Ironically, the most successful writer in the new republic was Washington Irving, an elitist-minded Federalist. His whimsical essay and story collections — which included the tales of "Rip Van Winkle" and "The Legend of Sleepy Hollow" — sold well in America and won praise abroad. Frustrated by the immaturity of American cultural life, Irving lived for seventeen years in Europe, reveling in its aristocratic culture and intense intellectuality.

Apart from Irving, no American author was well known in Europe or, indeed, in the United States. "Literature is not yet a distinct profession with us," Thomas Jefferson told an English friend. "Now and then a strong mind arises, and at its intervals from business emits a flash of light. But the first object of young societies is bread and covering." Not until the 1830s and 1840s would American authors achieve a professional identity and make a significant contribution to Western literature (Chapter 11).

## Aristocratic Republicanism and Slavery

Republicanism in the South differed significantly from that in the North. Enslaved Africans constituted one-third of the South's population; their bondage contradicted the new nation's professed ideology of freedom and equality. "How is it that we hear the loudest yelps for liberty among the drivers of Negroes?" British author Samuel Johnson had chided the American rebels in 1775, a point that some Patriots took to heart. "I wish most sincerely there was not a Slave in the province," Abigail Adams confessed to her husband, John. "It always appeared a most iniquitous Scheme to me — to fight ourselves for what we are daily robbing and plundering from those who have as good a right to freedom as we have."

### The Revolution and Slavery, 1776–1800

In fact, the whites' struggle for independence had raised the prospect of freedom for blacks. As the Revolutionary War began, a black preacher in Georgia told his fellow slaves that King George III "came up with the Book [the Bible], and was about to alter the World, and set the Negroes free." Similar rumors, probably

prompted by Royal Governor Lord Dunmore's proclamation of 1775 (Chapter 5), circulated among slaves in Virginia and the Carolinas, prompting thousands of African Americans to flee behind British lines. Two neighbors of Virginia Patriot Richard Henry Lee lost "every slave they had in the world," as did many other planters. In 1781, when the British army evacuated Charleston, more than 6,000 former slaves went with them; another 4,000 left from Savannah. All told, 30,000 blacks may have fled their owners. Hundreds of freed black Loyalists settled permanently in Canada. More than 1,000 others, poorly treated in British Nova Scotia, sought a better life in Sierra Leone, West

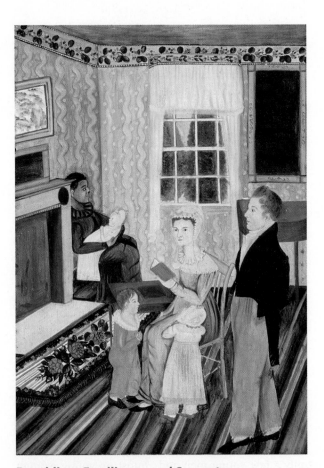

**Republican Families . . . and Servants**
Around 1828, an unidentified artist painted this York, Pennsylvania, family with an African American servant. The artist gives equal emphasis to the wife and the husband, suggesting they enjoyed a companionate-style marriage. Reflecting the outlook of republican motherhood, the mother takes the leading role in educating the children. The family, probably of upper-middle-class status given their attire and furnishings, employs an African American woman as a domestic servant and nanny — common occupations among free black women of the time. The Saint Louis Art Museum, Missouri, USA/The Bridgeman Art Library.

Africa, a settlement founded by English antislavery organizations.

**Manumission and Gradual Emancipation** Yet thousands of African Americans supported the Patriot cause. Eager to raise their social status, free blacks in New England volunteered for military service in the First Rhode Island Company and the Massachusetts "Bucks." In Maryland, some slaves took up arms for the rebels in return for the promise of freedom. Enslaved Virginians struck informal bargains with their Patriot owners, trading loyalty in wartime for the hope of liberty. Following the Virginia legislature's passage of a **manumission** act in 1782, allowing owners to free their slaves, 10,000 slaves won their freedom.

Two other developments — one religious, the other intellectual — encouraged manumission. Beginning in the 1750s, Quaker evangelist John Woolman urged Friends to free their slaves, and many did so. Rapidly growing evangelical churches, especially Methodists and Baptists, initially advocated slave emancipation; in 1784, a conference of Virginia Methodists declared

that slavery was "contrary to the Golden Law of God on which hang all the Law and Prophets."

Meanwhile, Enlightenment philosophy challenged the widespread belief among whites that Africans were inherently inferior to Europeans. According to John Locke, ideas were not innate but stemmed from a person's experiences in the world. Pointing out the obvious — "A state of slavery has a mighty tendency to shrink and contract the minds of men" — Enlightenment-influenced Americans suggested that the debased condition of blacks reflected their oppressive captivity. Quaker philanthropist Anthony Benezet declared that African Americans were "as capable of improvement as White People" and funded a Philadelphia school for their education.

Swept along by these religious and intellectual currents, legislators in northern states enacted gradual emancipation statutes (Map 8.2). These laws recognized white property rights by requiring slaves to buy their freedom by years — even decades — of additional

**IDENTIFY CAUSES**
Why did aristocratic republicanism develop in the South, and what were its defining features?

**MAP 8.2**

**The Status of Slavery, 1800**

In 1775, racial slavery was legal in all of the British colonies in North America. By the time the confederated states achieved their independence in 1783, the New England region was mostly free of slavery. By 1800, all of the states north of Maryland had provided for the gradual abolition of slavery, but the process of gradual emancipation dragged on until the 1830s. Some slave owners in the Chesapeake region manumitted a number of their slaves, leaving only the whites of the Lower South firmly committed to racial bondage.

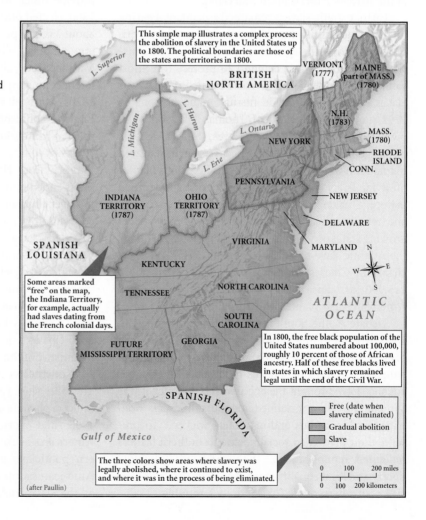

This simple map illustrates a complex process: the abolition of slavery in the United States up to 1800. The political boundaries are those of the states and territories in 1800.

Some areas marked "free" on the map, the Indiana Territory, for example, actually had slaves dating from the French colonial days.

In 1800, the free black population of the United States numbered about 100,000, roughly 10 percent of those of African ancestry. Half of these free blacks lived in states in which slavery remained legal until the end of the Civil War.

The three colors show areas where slavery was legally abolished, where it continued to exist, and where it was in the process of being eliminated.

Free (date when slavery eliminated)

Gradual abolition

Slave

(after Paullin)

labor. For example, the New York Emancipation Act of 1799 allowed slavery to continue until 1828 and freed slave children only at the age of twenty-five. Consequently, as late as 1810, almost 30,000 blacks in the northern states—nearly one-fourth of the African Americans living there—were still enslaved. Freed blacks faced severe prejudice from whites who feared job competition and racial melding. When Massachusetts judges abolished slavery through case law in 1784, the legislature reenacted an old statute that prohibited whites from marrying blacks, mulattos, or Indians. For African Americans in the North, freedom meant second-class citizenship.

**Slavery Defended**   The southern states faced the most glaring contradiction between liberty and property rights, because enslaved blacks represented a huge financial investment. Some Chesapeake tobacco planters, moved by evangelical religion or an oversupply of workers, manumitted their slaves or allowed them to buy their freedom by working as artisans or laborers. Such measures gradually brought freedom to one-third of the African Americans in Maryland.

Farther south, slavery remained ascendant. Fearing total emancipation, hundreds of slave owners petitioned the Virginia legislature to repeal the manumission act. Heeding this demand to protect "the most valuable and indispensible Article of our Property, our Slaves," legislators forbade further manumissions in 1792. Following the lead of Thomas Jefferson, who owned more than a hundred slaves, political leaders now argued that slavery was a "necessary evil" required to maintain white supremacy and the luxurious planter lifestyle. In North Carolina, legislators condemned private Quaker manumissions as "highly criminal and reprehensible." Moreover, the slave-hungry rice-growing states of South Carolina and Georgia reopened the Atlantic slave trade. Between 1790 and 1808, merchants in Charleston and Savannah imported about 115,000 Africans, selling thousands to French and American sugar planters in Louisiana.

Debate in the South over emancipation ended in 1800, when Virginia authorities thwarted an uprising planned by Gabriel Prosser, an enslaved artisan, and hanged him and thirty of his followers. "Liberty and equality have brought the evil upon us," a letter to the *Virginia Herald* proclaimed, denouncing such doctrines as "dangerous and extremely wicked." To preserve their privileged social position, southern leaders redefined republicanism. They restricted individual liberty and legal equality to whites, creating what historians call a **herrenvolk** ("master race") **republic**.

## The North and South Grow Apart

European visitors to the United States agreed that North and South had distinct characters. A British observer labeled New England the home to religious "fanaticism" but added that "the lower orders of citizens" there had "a better education, [and were] more intelligent" than those he met in the South. "The state of poverty in which a great number of white people live in Virginia" surprised the Marquis de Chastellux. Other visitors to the South likewise commented on the rude manners, heavy drinking, and weak work ethic of its residents. White tenants and smallholding farmers seemed only to have a "passion for gaming at the billiard table, a cock-fight or cards," and rich planters squandered their wealth on extravagant lifestyles while their slaves endured bitter poverty.

Some southerners worried that human bondage had corrupted white society. "Where there are Negroes a White Man despises to work," one South Carolina merchant commented. Moreover, well-to-do planters, able to hire tutors for their own children, did little to provide other whites with elementary schooling. In 1800, elected officials in Essex County, Virginia, spent about 25 cents per person for local government, including schools, while their counterparts in Acton, Massachusetts, allocated about $1 per person. This difference in support for education mattered: by the 1820s, nearly all native-born men and women in New England could read and write, while more than one-third of white southerners could not.

**Slavery and National Politics**   As the northern states ended human bondage, the South's commitment to slavery became a political issue. At the Philadelphia convention in 1787, northern delegates had reluctantly accepted clauses allowing slave imports for twenty years and guaranteeing the return of fugitive slaves (Chapter 6). Seeking even more protection for their "peculiar institution," southerners in the new national legislature won approval of James Madison's resolution that "Congress have no authority to interfere in the emancipation of slaves, or in the treatment of them within any of the States."

Nonetheless, slavery remained a contested issue. The black slave revolt in Haiti brought 6,000 white and mulatto planters and their slaves to the United States in 1793, and stories of Haitian atrocities frightened American slave owners (Chapter 7). Meanwhile, northern politicians assailed the British impressment of American sailors as just "as oppressive and tyrannical as the slave trade" and demanded the end of both.

### Aristocratic Republicanism in South Carolina

The money that paid for Drayton Hall came originally from raising cattle in South Carolina for sale in the West Indies. At his death in 1717, Thomas Drayton left an estate that included 1,300 cattle and 46 slaves (both Native American and African). His third son, John (1715–1779), used his inheritance to buy slaves and to create a rice-growing plantation along the Ashley River. The home he erected on the site, Drayton Hall (built 1738–1742), reflected the designs of Andrea Palladio, the Italian Renaissance architect who celebrated the concepts of classical Roman proportion and decoration in his widely read *The Four Books of Architecture* (1516). Photo courtesy of Drayton Hall.

When Congress outlawed the Atlantic slave trade in 1808, some northern representatives demanded an end to the trade in slaves between states. Southern leaders responded with a forceful defense of their labor system. "A large majority of people in the Southern states do not consider slavery as even an evil," declared one congressman. The South's political clout — its domination of the presidency and the Senate — ensured that the national government would protect slavery. American diplomats vigorously demanded compensation for slaves freed by British troops during the War of 1812, and Congress enacted legislation upholding slavery in the District of Columbia.

**African Americans Speak Out**   Heartened by the end of the Atlantic slave trade, black abolitionists spoke out. In speeches and pamphlets, Henry Sipkins and Henry Johnson pointed out that slavery — "relentless tyranny," they called it — was a central legacy of America's colonial history. For inspiration, they looked to the Haitian Revolution; for collective support, they joined in secret societies, such as Prince Hall's African Lodge of Freemasons in Boston. Initially, black (and white) antislavery advocates hoped that slavery would die out naturally as the tobacco economy declined. However, a boom in cotton planting dramatically increased the demand for slaves, and Louisiana (1812), Mississippi (1817), and Alabama (1819) joined the Union with state constitutions permitting slavery.

As some Americans redefined slavery as a problem rather than a centuries-old social condition, a group of prominent citizens founded the **American Colonization Society** in 1817. According to Henry Clay — a society member, Speaker of the House of Representatives, and a slave owner — racial bondage hindered economic progress. It had placed his state of Kentucky "in the rear of our neighbors . . . in the state of agriculture, the progress of manufactures, the advance of improvement, and the general prosperity of society." Clay and other colonizationists argued that slaves had to be freed and then resettled, in Africa or elsewhere; emancipation without removal would lead to chaos — "a civil war that would end in the extermination or subjugation of the one race or the other." Given the cotton boom, few planters responded to the society's plea. It resettled only about 6,000 African Americans in Liberia, its colony on the west coast of Africa.

Most free blacks strongly opposed such colonization schemes because they saw themselves as Americans. As Bishop Richard Allen of the African Methodist Episcopal Church put it, "[T]his land which we have watered with our tears and our blood is now our mother country." Allen spoke from experience. Born into slavery in Philadelphia in 1760 and sold to a farmer in Delaware, Allen grew up in bondage. In 1777, Freeborn Garretson, an itinerant preacher, converted Allen to Methodism and convinced Allen's owner that on Judgment Day, slaveholders would be "weighted in the balance, and . . . found wanting." Allowed to buy his freedom, Allen enlisted in the Methodist cause, becoming a "licensed exhorter" and then a regular minister in

**EXPLAIN CONSEQUENCES**
Why did the colonization movement of the 1810s fail?

**The Reverend Richard Allen and the African Methodist Episcopal Church**

One of the best-known African Americans in the early republic, Richard Allen founded a separate congregation for Philadelphia's black Methodists, the Bethel Church. Working with other ministers in 1816, he created the first independent black religious domination in the United States—the African Methodist Episcopal (AME) Church—and became its first bishop. Library of Congress / Picture Research Consultants & Archives.

Philadelphia. In 1795, Allen formed a separate black congregation, the Bethel Church; in 1816, he became the first bishop of a new denomination: the African Methodist Episcopal Church. Two years later, 3,000 African Americans met in Allen's church to condemn colonization and to claim American citizenship. Sounding the principles of democratic republicanism, they vowed to defy racial prejudice and advance in American society using "those opportunities . . . which the Constitution and the laws allow to all."

## The Missouri Crisis, 1819–1821

The abject failure of colonization set the stage for a major battle over slavery. In 1818, Congressman Nathaniel Macon of North Carolina warned that radical members of the "bible and peace societies" intended to place "the question of emancipation" on the national political agenda. When Missouri applied for admission to the Union in 1819, Congressman James Tallmadge of New York did so: he would support statehood for Missouri only if its constitution banned the entry of new slaves and provided for the emancipation of existing bonds-people. Missouri whites rejected Tallmadge's proposals, and the northern majority in the House of Representatives blocked the territory's admission.

White southerners were horrified. "It is believed by some, & feared by others," Alabama senator John

Walker reported from Washington, that Tallmadge's amendment was "merely the entering wedge and that it points already to a total emancipation of the blacks." Mississippi congressman Christopher Rankin accused his northern colleagues of brinksmanship: "You conduct us to an awful precipice, and hold us over it." Underlining their commitment to slavery, southerners used their power in the Senate—where they held half the seats—to withhold statehood from Maine, which was seeking to separate itself from Massachusetts.

**Constitutional Issues**   In the ensuing debate, southerners advanced three constitutional arguments. First, they invoked the principle of "equal rights," arguing that Congress could not impose conditions on Missouri that it had not imposed on other territories. Second, they maintained that the Constitution guaranteed a state's sovereignty with respect to its internal affairs and domestic institutions, such as slavery and marriage. Finally, they insisted that Congress had no authority to infringe on the property rights of individual slaveholders. Beyond those arguments, southern leaders defended human bondage. Downplaying the proposition that slavery was a "necessary evil," they now justified slavery on religious grounds. "Christ himself gave a sanction to slavery," declared Senator William Smith of South Carolina. "If it be offensive and sinful to own slaves," a prominent Mississippi Methodist added, "I wish someone would just put his finger on the place in Holy Writ."

Controversy raged in Congress and the press for two years before Henry Clay devised a series of political agreements known collectively as the **Missouri Compromise**. Faced with unwavering southern opposition to Tallmadge's amendment, a group of northern congressmen deserted the antislavery coalition. They accepted a deal that allowed Maine to enter the Union as a free state in 1820 and Missouri to follow as a slave state in 1821. This bargain preserved a balance in the Senate between North and South and set a precedent for future admissions to the Union. For their part, southern senators accepted the prohibition of slavery in most of the Louisiana Purchase, all the lands north of latitude 36°30' except for the state of Missouri (Map 8.3).

As they had in the Philadelphia convention of 1787, white politicians preserved the Union by compromising over slavery. However, the delegates in Philadelphia had resolved their sectional differences in two months; it took Congress two years to work out the Missouri Compromise, which even then did not command universal support. "[B]eware," the *Richmond Enquirer* protested sharply as southern representatives agreed to exclude slavery from most of the Louisiana Purchase: "What is a territorial restriction to-day becomes a state restriction tomorrow." The fate of the western lands, enslaved blacks, and the Union itself were now intertwined, raising the specter of civil war and the end of the American republican experiment. As the aging Thomas Jefferson exclaimed during the Missouri crisis, "This momentous question, like a fire-bell in the night, awakened and filled me with terror."

**PLACE EVENTS IN CONTEXT**
What compromises over slavery did Congress make to settle the Missouri crisis?

# Protestant Christianity as a Social Force

Throughout the colonial era, religion played a significant role in American life but not an overwhelming one. Then, beginning around 1790, religious revivals planted the values of Protestant Christianity deep in the national character and gave a spiritual dimension to American republicanism. These revivals especially changed the lives of blacks and of women. Thousands of African Americans became Baptists and Methodists and created a powerful institution: the black Christian Church. Evangelical Christianity also gave rise to new public roles for white women, especially in the North, and set in motion long-lasting movements for social reform.

**MAP 8.3**

**The Missouri Compromise, 1820–1821**

The Missouri Compromise resolved for a generation the issue of slavery in the lands of the Louisiana Purchase. The agreement prohibited slavery north of the Missouri Compromise line (36°30' north latitude), with the exception of the state of Missouri. To maintain an equal number of senators from free and slave states in the U.S. Congress, the compromise provided for the nearly simultaneous admission to the Union of Missouri and Maine.

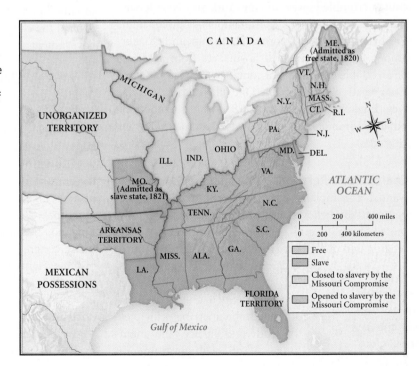

## A Republican Religious Order

The republican revolution of 1776 forced American lawmakers to devise new relationships between church and state. Previously, only the Quaker- and Baptist-controlled governments of Pennsylvania and Rhode Island had rejected a legally established church that claimed everyone as a member and collected compulsory religious taxes. Then, a convergence of factors — Enlightenment principles, wartime needs, and Baptist ideology — eliminated most state support for religion and allowed voluntary church membership.

**Religious Freedom**     Events in Virginia revealed the dynamics of change. In 1776, James Madison and George Mason advanced Enlightenment ideas of religious toleration as they persuaded the state's constitutional convention to guarantee all Christians the "free exercise of religion." This measure, which ended the privileged legal status of the Anglican Church, won Presbyterian and Baptist support for the independence struggle. Baptists, who also opposed public support of religion, convinced lawmakers to reject a tax bill (supported by George Washington and Patrick Henry) that would have funded all Christian churches. Instead, in 1786, the Virginia legislature enacted Thomas Jefferson's bill for Establishing Religious Freedom, which made all churches equal in the eyes of the law and granted direct financial support to none.

Elsewhere, the old order of a single **established church** crumbled away. In New York and New Jersey, the sheer number of denominations — Episcopalian, Presbyterian, Dutch Reformed, Lutheran, and Quaker, among others — prevented lawmakers from agreeing on an established church or compulsory religious taxes. Congregationalism remained the official church in the New England states until the 1830s, but members of other denominations could now pay taxes to their own churches.

**Church-State Relations**     Few influential Americans wanted a complete separation of church and state because they believed that religious institutions promoted morality and governmental authority. "Pure religion and civil liberty are inseparable companions," a group of North Carolinians advised their minister. "It is your particular duty to enlighten mankind with the unerring principles of truth and justice, the main props of all civil government." Accepting this premise, most state governments indirectly supported churches by exempting their property and ministers from taxation.

Freedom of conscience also came with sharp cultural limits. In Virginia, Jefferson's Religious Freedom act prohibited religious requirements for holding public office, but other states discriminated against those who were not Protestant Christians. The North Carolina Constitution of 1776 disqualified from public office any citizen "who shall deny the being of God, or the Truth of the Protestant Religion, or the Divine Authority of the Old or New Testament." New Hampshire's constitution contained a similar provision until 1868.

Americans influenced by Enlightenment deism and by evangelical Protestantism condemned these religious restrictions. Jefferson, Franklin, and other American intellectuals maintained that God had given humans the power of reason so that they could determine moral truths for themselves. To protect society from "ecclesiastical tyranny," they demanded complete freedom of conscience. The "truth is great and will prevail if left to herself," Jefferson declared; "religion is a matter which lies solely between man and his God." Many evangelical Protestants likewise demanded religious liberty to protect their churches from an oppressive government. Isaac Backus, a New England minister, warned Baptists not to incorporate their churches or accept public funds because that might lead to state control. In Connecticut, a devout Congregationalist welcomed "**voluntarism**," the funding of churches by their members; it allowed the laity to control the clergy, he said, while also supporting self-government and "the principles of republicanism."

**Republican Church Institutions**     Following independence, Americans embraced churches that preached spiritual equality and governed themselves democratically while ignoring those with hierarchical and authoritarian institutions. Preferring Luther's doctrine of the priesthood of all believers, few citizens accepted the authority claimed by Roman Catholic priests and bishops. Likewise, few Americans joined the Protestant Episcopal Church, the successor to the Church of England, because wealthy lay members dominated many congregations and it, too, had a hierarchy of bishops (Figure 8.1). The Presbyterian Church attracted more adherents, in part because its churches elected lay members to synods, the congresses that determined doctrine and practice.

Evangelical Methodist and Baptist churches were by far the most successful institutions in attracting new members, especially from the "**unchurched**" — the

**UNDERSTAND POINTS OF VIEW**
What were the main principles of the new republican religious regime?

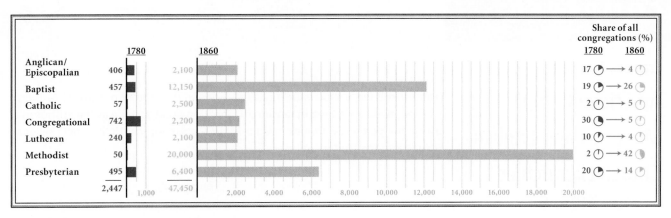

**FIGURE 8.1**

**Number of Church Congregations by Denomination, 1780 and 1860**

The growth of evangelical churches, Methodist and Baptist, transformed American Christianity during the first half of the nineteenth century. Also noteworthy was the surge in the number of Roman Catholic congregations, the result of Catholic immigration from Ireland and Germany after 1830.

great number of irreligious Americans. The Baptists boasted a thoroughly republican church organization, with self-governing congregations. Also, Baptists (and Methodists as well) developed an egalitarian religious culture marked by communal singing and emotional services. These denominations formed a dynamic new force in American religion.

## The Second Great Awakening

As Americans adopted new religious principles, a decades-long series of religious revivals—the **Second Great Awakening**—made the United States a genuinely Christian society. Evangelical denominations began the revival in the 1790s, as they spread their message in seacoast cities and the backcountry of New England. A new sect of Universalists, who repudiated Calvinism and preached universal salvation, also gained tens of thousands of converts, especially in Massachusetts and northern New England. After 1800, enthusiastic camp meetings swept the frontier regions of South Carolina, Tennessee, Ohio, and Kentucky. The largest gathering, at Cane Ridge in Kentucky in 1801, lasted for nine electrifying days and nights and attracted almost 20,000 people (Map 8.4). With these revivals, Baptist and Methodist preachers reshaped the spiritual landscape throughout the South. Offering a powerful emotional message and the promise of religious fellowship, revivalists attracted both unchurched individuals and pious families searching for social ties as they migrated to new communities (America Compared, p. 272).

**A New Religious Landscape** The Second Great Awakening transformed the denominational makeup of American religion. The main colonial-period churches—the Congregationalists, Episcopalians, and Quakers—grew slowly through natural increase, while Methodist and Baptist churches expanded spectacularly by winning converts. In rural areas, their preachers followed a regular circuit, "riding a hardy pony or horse" with their "Bible, hymn-book, and Discipline" to visit existing congregations. They began new churches by searching out devout families, bringing them together for worship, and then appointing lay elders to lead the congregation and enforce moral discipline. Soon, Baptists and Methodists were the largest denominations.

To attract converts, evangelical ministers copied the "practical preaching" techniques of George Whitefield and other eighteenth-century revivalists (Chapter 4). They spoke from memory in plain language, raised their voice to make important points, and punctuated their words with theatrical gestures. "Preach without papers," advised one minister. "[S]eem earnest & serious; & you will be listened to with Patience, & Wonder."

In the South, evangelical religion was initially a disruptive force because many ministers spoke of spiritual equality and criticized slavery. Husbands and planters grew angry when their wives became more assertive and when blacks joined evangelical congregations. To retain white men in their churches, Methodist and Baptist preachers gradually adapted their religious

## Frances Trollope

## American Camp Meetings and English Church Hierarchies

Frances Trollope, a successful English author and the mother of novelist Anthony Trollope, lived for a time in Cincinnati. She won great acclaim as the author of a critical-minded study, *Domestic Manners of the Americans* (1832), a best-seller in Europe and the United States.

I found the opportunity I had long wished for, of attending a camp-meeting, . . . in a wild district on the confines of Indiana. . . .

One of the preachers began in a low nasal tone, and, like all other Methodist preachers, assured us of the enormous depravity of man as he comes from the hands of his Maker, and of his perfect sanctification after he had wrestled sufficiently with the Lord. . . . The admiration of the crowd was evinced by almost constant cries of "Amen! Amen!" "Jesus! Jesus!" "Glory! Glory!" and the like. . . . [T]he preacher told them that "this night was the time fixed upon for anxious sinners to wrestle with the Lord" . . . and that such as needed their help were to come forward. . . .

[A]bove a hundred persons, nearly all females, came forward, uttering howlings and groans, so terrible that I shall never cease to shudder when I recall them. They appeared to drag each other forward, and on the word being given, "let us pray," they all fell on their knees; but this posture was soon changed for others that permitted greater scope for the convulsive movements of their limbs. . . .

Many of these wretched creatures were beautiful young females. The preachers moved about among them, at once exciting and soothing their agonies. . . . I watched their tormentors breathing into their ears consolations that tinged the pale cheek with red. Had I been a man, I am sure I should have been guilty of some rash act of interference; nor do I believe that such a scene could have been acted in the presence of Englishmen, without instant punishment being inflicted . . . to check so turbulent and vicious a scene.

\*\*　　\*\*　　\*\*

The critics who have from time to time reproached me with undue severity in my strictures on the domestic manners of the Americans have said that a candid examination of matters at home would have shown me that what I reprobated might be found in England, as well as in the United States. In most cases I have felt that this might be rebutted . . . by showing that what I complained of in the Union as indicative of imperfect civilisation, [whereas] if existing at all with us, could only be met with among persons in a much lower station of life. . . .

But on the subject treated in the present chapter, justice compels me to avow that no such pleading can avail me. That such fearful profanation of the holy name of religion has rapidly increased among us since the year 1827, in which I quitted England for America, is most sadly certain. . . . [Yet, the bishops of the Church of England protect us from many excesses, while in America the lack of an established] national church, and of that guardian protection which its episcopal authority seems to promise against its desecration by the ever-varying innovations of sectarian licence, appeared to account for all the profanations I witnessed.

Source: Frances Trollope, *Domestic Manners of the Americans* (London: Whittaker, Treacher, 1832), 139, 142–144; the material following the asterisks comes from ibid., 5th ed. (London: R. Bentley, 1839), chapter 8.

### QUESTIONS FOR ANALYSIS

1. According to Trollope, what accounts for the frequency of "profane" religious services in America and their relative absence in England?
2. How does Trollope use "social class" to analyze the differences between England and America?

message to justify the authority of yeomen patriarchs and slave-owning planters. Man was naturally at "the head of the woman," declared one Baptist minister, while a Methodist conference told Christian slaves to be "submissive, faithful, and obedient."

**Black Christianity** Other evangelists persuaded planters to spread Protestant Christianity among their African American slaves. During the eighteenth century, most blacks had maintained the religious practices of their African homelands, giving homage to

**MAP 8.4**

**The Second Great Awakening, 1790–1860**

The Second Great Awakening lasted for decades and invigorated churches in every part of the nation. The revivals in Kentucky and New York State were particularly influential. As thousands of farm families migrated to the West, they carried with them the religious excitement generated by the Cane Ridge revival in Kentucky in 1801. And, between 1825 and 1835, the area along the Erie Canal in New York witnessed such fervor that it came to be known as the Burned-over District.

In the 1820s an intense wave of revivals ignited religious fervor in communities along the Erie Canal, and this region became known as the "burned-over district."

As devout farmers moved west, they established new Protestant churches throughout the Upper South and Midwest.

Student revivals at Yale College and Andover Seminary around 1800 led to the expansion of Protestant missions in the West and also in Africa, India, and Hawaii. Societies supporting the missions combined into the American Home Missionary Society in 1826.

The Second Great Awakening started in the 1790s as Baptists, Methodists, and a new sect called Universalists proselytized in New England. After 1800 the Awakening continued in Kentucky in camp meetings of pioneer farmers, who carried evangelical religion back to their communities.

← Paths of settlement, 1790–1830
▲ Camp meeting, 1801
Kentucky revival
New York's "burned-over district"
← Paths of revival

African gods and spirits or practicing Islam. "At the time I first went to Carolina," remembered former slave Charles Ball, "there were a great many African slaves in the country. . . . Many of them believed there were several gods [and] I knew several . . . Mohamedans." Beginning in the mid-1780s, Baptist and Methodist preachers converted hundreds of African Americans along the James River in Virginia and throughout the Chesapeake and the Carolinas.

Subsequently, black Christians adapted Protestant teachings to their own needs. They generally ignored the doctrines of original sin and Calvinist predestination as well as biblical passages that prescribed unthinking obedience to authority. Some African American converts envisioned the Christian God as a warrior who had liberated the Jews. Their own "cause was similar to the Israelites," preacher Martin Prosser told his fellow slaves as he and his brother Gabriel plotted rebellion in Virginia in 1800. "I have read in my Bible where God says, if we worship him, . . . five of you shall conquer a hundred and a hundred of you a hundred thousand of our enemies." Confident of a special relationship with God, Christian slaves prepared themselves spiritually for emancipation, the first step in their journey to the Promised Land.

## Religion and Reform

Many whites also rejected the Calvinists' emphasis on human depravity and weakness; instead, they celebrated human reason and free will. In New England, educated Congregationalists discarded the mysterious concept of the Trinity — Father, Son, and Holy Spirit — and, taking the name *Unitarians*, worshipped a "united" God and promoted rational thought. "The ultimate reliance of a human being is, and must be, on his own mind," argued William Ellery Channing, a famous Unitarian minister. A children's catechism conveyed the denomination's optimistic message: "If I am good, God will love me, and make me happy."

Other New England Congregationalists softened Calvinist doctrines. Lyman Beecher, the preeminent Congregationalist clergyman, accepted the traditional Christian belief that people had a natural tendency to

**COMPARE AND CONTRAST**

How did evangelical and African American churches differ from other Protestant denominations?

**Women in the Awakening**

The Second Great Awakening was a pivotal moment in the history of American women. In this detail from *Religious Camp Meeting*, painted by J. Maze Burbank in 1839, male preachers inspire religious frenzy, mostly among young women. In fact, most women embraced evangelical Christianity in a calm and measured manner, becoming dedicated workers, teachers, and morality-minded mothers. When tens of thousands of these women also joined movements for temperance, abolition, and women's rights, they spurred a great wave of social reform. Old Dartmouth Historical Society/New Bedford Whaling Museum.

sin; but, rejecting predestination, he affirmed the capacity of all men and women to choose God. By embracing the doctrine of free will, Beecher — along with "Free Will" Baptists — testified to the growing belief that people could shape their destiny.

Reflecting this optimism, the Reverend Samuel Hopkins linked individual salvation to religious benevolence — the practice of disinterested virtue. As the Presbyterian minister John Rodgers explained, fortunate individuals who had received God's grace or bounty had a duty "to dole out charity to their poorer brothers and sisters." Heeding this message, pious

merchants in New York City founded the Humane Society and other charitable organizations. Devout women aided their ministers by holding prayer meetings and distributing charity. By the 1820s, so many Protestant men and women had embraced benevolent reform that conservative church leaders warned them not to neglect spiritual matters. Still, improving society was a key element of the new religious sensibility. The mark of a true church, declared the devout Christian social reformer Lydia Maria Child, is when members' "heads and hearts unite in working for the welfare of the human-race."

By the 1820s, many Protestant Christians had embraced that goal. Unlike the First Great Awakening, which split churches into warring factions, the Second Great Awakening fostered cooperation among denominations. Religious leaders founded five interdenominational societies: the American Education Society (1815), the Bible Society (1816), the Sunday School Union (1824), the Tract Society (1825), and the Home Missionary Society (1826). Based in eastern cities— New York, Boston, and Philadelphia—these societies dispatched hundreds of missionaries to the West and distributed thousands of religious pamphlets.

Increasingly, American Protestants saw themselves as a movement that could change the course of history. "I want to see our state evangelized," declared a churchgoer near the Erie Canal: "Suppose the great State of New York in all its physical, political, moral, commercial, and pecuniary resources should come over to the Lord's side. Why it would turn the scale and could convert the world. I shall have no rest until it is done."

Because the Second Great Awakening aroused such enthusiasm, religion became an important new force in political life. On July 4, 1827, the Reverend Ezra Stiles Ely called on the Philadelphia Presbyterians to begin a "Christian party in politics." Ely's sermon, "The Duty of Christian Freemen to Elect Christian Rulers," proclaimed a religious agenda for the American republic that Thomas Jefferson and John Adams would have found strange and troubling. The two founders had gone to their graves the previous year believing that America's mission was to spread political republicanism. In contrast, Ely urged the United States to become an evangelical Christian nation dedicated to religious conversion at home and abroad: "All our rulers ought in their official capacity to serve the Lord Jesus Christ." Evangelical Christians would issue similar calls during the Third (1880–1900) and Fourth (1970–present) Great Awakenings.

## Women's New Religious Roles

The upsurge in religious enthusiasm allowed women to demonstrate their piety and even to found new sects. Mother Ann Lee organized the Shakers in Britain and in 1774 migrated to America, where she attracted numerous recruits; by the 1820s, Shaker communities dotted the American countryside from New Hampshire to Indiana. Jemima Wilkinson, a young Quaker woman in Rhode Island, found inspiration by reading George Whitefield's sermons. After experiencing a vision that she had died and been reincarnated as Christ, Wilkinson declared herself the "Publick Universal Friend," dressed in masculine attire, and preached a new gospel. Her teachings blended the Calvinist warning of "a lost and guilty, gossiping, dying World" with Quaker-inspired plain dress, pacifism, and abolitionism. Wilkinson's charisma initially won scores of converts, but her radical lifestyle and ambiguous gender aroused hostility, and her sect dwindled away.

**A Growing Public Presence**  Female-led sects had far less impact than thousands of women in mainstream churches. For example, women in New Hampshire churches managed more than fifty local

**Mrs. Juliann Jane Tillman, 1844**

In 1837, Mrs. Tillman explained in a newspaper article that she "was strangely wrought upon" and "went to God" for help. Soon, "what seemed to be an angel made his sudden appearance, and in his hand was a roll . . . on which was written, 'Thee I have chosen to preach my gospel without delay.'" After much anguish and more supernatural visitations, Mrs. Tillman overcame strong personal doubts—and the equally strong opposition of male ministers and laity—and began to preach in the African Methodist Episcopal Church. Library of Congress.

**COMPARE AND CONTRAST**
How was the Second Great Awakening similar to, and different from, the First Great Awakening of the 1740s (Chapter 4)?

"cent" societies to raise funds for the Society for Promoting Christian Knowledge, New York City women founded the Society for the Relief of Poor Widows, and young Quaker women in Philadelphia ran the Society for the Free Instruction of African Females.

Women took charge of religious and charitable enterprises because of their exclusion from other public roles and because of their numbers. After 1800, more than 70 percent of the members of New England Congregational churches were women. The predominance of women prompted Congregational ministers to end traditional gender-segregated prayer meetings, and evangelical Methodist and Baptist preachers actively promoted mixed-sex praying. "Our prayer meetings have been one of the greatest means of the conversion of souls," a minister in central New York reported in the 1820s, "especially those in which brothers and sisters have prayed together."

Far from leading to sexual promiscuity, as critics feared, mixing men and women in religious activities promoted greater self-discipline. Believing in female virtue, young women and the men who courted them postponed sexual intercourse until after marriage—previously a much rarer form of self-restraint. In Hingham, Massachusetts, and many other New England towns, more than 30 percent of the women who married between 1750 and 1800 bore a child within eight months of their wedding day; by the 1820s, the rate had dropped to 15 percent.

As women claimed spiritual authority, men tried to curb their power. In both the North and the South, evangelical Baptist churches that had once advocated spiritual equality now prevented women from voting on church matters or offering public testimonies of faith. Testimonies by women, one layman declared, were "directly opposite to the apostolic command in [Corinthians] xiv, 34, 35, 'Let your women learn to keep silence in the churches.'" Another man claimed, "Women have a different calling. That they be chaste, keepers at home is the Apostle's direction." Such injunctions merely changed the focus of women's religious activism. Embracing the idea of republican motherhood, Christian women throughout the United States founded maternal associations to encourage proper child rearing. By the 1820s, *Mother's Magazine* and other newsletters, widely read in hundreds of small towns and villages, were giving women a sense of shared identity and purpose.

**IDENTIFY CAUSES**
Why did Protestant Christianity and Protestant women emerge as forces for social change?

Religious activism also advanced female education, as churches sponsored academies where girls from the middling classes received intellectual and moral instruction. Emma Willard, the first American advocate of higher education for women, opened the Middlebury Female Seminary in Vermont in 1814 and later founded girls' academies in Waterford and Troy, New York. Beginning in the 1820s, women educated in these seminaries and academies displaced men as public-school teachers, in part because they accepted lower pay than men would. Female schoolteachers earned from $12 to $14 a month with room and board—less than a farm laborer. However, as schoolteachers, women had an acknowledged place in public life—a status that previously had been beyond their reach. Just as the ideology of democratic republicanism had expanded voting rights and the political influence of ordinary white men in the North, so the values of Christian republicanism had bolstered the public authority of middling women.

The Second Great Awakening made Americans a fervently Protestant people. Along with the values of republicanism and capitalism, this religious impulse formed the core of an emerging national identity.

## SUMMARY

Like all important ideologies, republicanism has many facets. We have explored three of them in this chapter. We saw how state legislatures used government-granted charters and monopolies to support private businesses, with the goal of enhancing the commonwealth of society. This republican-inspired "commonwealth" policy of state mercantilism remained dominant until the 1840s, when classical liberal doctrines partially replaced it.

We also saw how republicanism influenced social and family values. The principle of legal equality encouraged social mobility among white men and prompted men and women to seek companionate marriages. Republicanism likewise encouraged parents to provide their children with equal inheritances and to allow them to choose their marriage partners. In the South, republican doctrines of liberty and equality coexisted uneasily with racial slavery and class divisions, and ultimately they benefitted only a minority of the white population.

Finally, we observed the complex interaction of republicanism and religion. Stirred by republican principles, many citizens joined democratic and egalitarian denominations, particularly Methodist and Baptist churches. Inspired by "benevolent" ideas and the enthusiastic preachers of the Second Great Awakening, many women devoted their energies to religious purposes and social reform organizations. The result of all these initiatives — in economic policy, social relations, and religious institutions — was the creation of a distinctive American republican culture.

# CHAPTER REVIEW

**MAKE IT STICK**  Go to **LearningCurve** to retain what you've read.

## TERMS TO KNOW  Identify and explain the significance of each term below.

### Key Concepts and Events

"neomercantilist" (p. 250)
Panic of 1819 (p. 251)
Commonwealth System (p. 256)
sentimentalism (p. 258)
companionate marriages (p. 258)
demographic transition (p. 259)
republican motherhood (p. 259)
manumission (p. 265)

*herrenvolk* republic (p. 266)
American Colonization Society (p. 267)
Missouri Compromise (p. 269)
established church (p. 270)
voluntarism (p. 270)
"unchurched" (p. 270)
Second Great Awakening (p. 271)

### Key People

John Jacob Astor (p. 250)
Benjamin Rush (p. 259)
Henry Clay (p. 267)
Richard Allen (p. 267)
Lyman Beecher (p. 273)
Emma Willard (p. 276)

## REVIEW QUESTIONS  Answer these questions to demonstrate your understanding of the chapter's main ideas.

1. How important were the regional differences in the social aspects of republicanism, given the national scope of other republican-inspired developments such as state mercantilism and religious revivalism?

2. Trace the relationship between America's republican culture and the surge of evangelism called the Second Great Awakening. In what ways are the goals of the two movements similar? How are they different?

3. In what ways did women's private and public lives change during the years between 1790 and 1820, and what were the motive forces behind those changes?

4. **THEMATIC UNDERSTANDING** Review the events listed under "Work, Exchange, and Technology," "Ideas, Beliefs, and Culture," and "Identity" on the thematic timeline on page 149. How did the emerging economic and social order of early-nineteenth-century America represent an advance upon, or a retreat from, the republican ideology articulated during the decades of the independence struggle?

## MAKING CONNECTIONS

Recognize the larger developments and continuities within and across chapters by answering these questions.

1. **ACROSS TIME AND PLACE**  The text argues that a distinct American identity had begun to emerge by 1820. How would you describe this identity, and how did it differ from the sense of identity in the American mainland colonies in 1750 (Chapter 4)? What forces might account for the changes?

2. **VISUAL EVIDENCE**  The painting of "Republican Families . . . and Servants" (p. 264) addresses many of the themes of this chapter. What are those themes, and what position does the artist take in presenting them?

## MORE TO EXPLORE    Start here to learn more about the events discussed in this chapter.

Nancy Cott, *Public Vows: A History of Marriage and the Nation* (2000). Analyzes the cultural and legal aspects of marriage.

Jan Lewis, *The Pursuit of Happiness* (1983). Discusses the paternalistic slave-owning gentry of the Upper South.

Jeffrey L. Pasley et al., eds., *Beyond the Founders* (2004). Shows how ordinary citizens promoted a democratic polity.

Randolph Ferguson Scully, *Religion and the Making of Nat Turner's Virginia* (2008). Links the rise of evangelical Christianity in the South to the slave revolt led by Nat Turner.

Bernard Weisberger, *They Gathered at the River* (1958). A classic study of the revivalists who led America's Great Awakenings.

Rosemarie Zagarri, *Revolutionary Backlash* (2007). Demonstrates the limited inclusion of women in politics.

## TIMELINE

Ask yourself why this chapter begins and ends with these dates and then identify the links among related events.

| | |
|---|---|
| **1782** | • St. Jean de Crèvecoeur publishes *Letters from an American Farmer* |
| | • Virginia manumission law (repealed 1792) |
| **1783** | • Noah Webster publishes his "blue-back speller" |
| **1784** | • Slavery ends in Massachusetts |
| | • Northern states begin gradual emancipation |
| **1787** | • Benjamin Rush writes *Thoughts on Female Education* |
| **1790s** | • States grant corporations charters and special privileges |
| | • Private companies build roads and canals to facilitate trade |
| | • Merchants expand rural outwork system |
| | • Chesapeake blacks adopt Protestant beliefs |
| | • Parents limit family size as farms shrink |
| | • Second Great Awakening expands church membership |
| **1791** | • Congress charters first Bank of the United States |
| **1792** | • Mary Wollstonecraft publishes *A Vindication of the Rights of Woman* |
| **1795** | • Massachusetts Mill Dam Act |
| **1800** | • Gabriel Prosser plots slave rebellion in Virginia |
| **1800s** | • Rise of sentimentalism and of companionate marriages |
| | • Women's religious activism |
| | • Founding of female academies |
| | • Religious benevolence sparks social reform |
| **1801** | • Cane Ridge revival in Kentucky |
| **1816** | • Congress charters Second Bank of the United States |
| **1817** | • Prominent whites create American Colonization Society |
| **1819** | • Plummeting agricultural prices set off financial panic |
| **1819–1821** | • Missouri Compromise |
| **1820s** | • States reform education |
| | • Women become schoolteachers |

**KEY TURNING POINTS:** The timeline mentions books by four authors (Crèvecoeur, Webster, Rush, and Wollstonecraft) and two other entries relating to education. Based on the materials in Chapter 8, what might account for this blossoming of American literary and educational life?

# Overlapping Revolutions

## 1800–1860

"The procession was nearly a mile long . . . [and] the democrats marched in good order to the glare of torches," a French visitor remarked in amazement during the U.S. presidential election of 1832. "These scenes belong to history . . . the wondrous epic of the coming of democracy." As Part 4 shows, Americans were making history in many ways between 1800 and 1860. Indeed, these decades constitute a distinct period precisely because the pace of historical change accelerated, especially between 1820 and 1860, as overlapping revolutions transformed American life. One revolution was political: the creation of a genuinely democratic polity. A second was economic: in 1800, the United States was predominantly an agricultural nation; by 1860, the northern states boasted one of the world's foremost industrial economies. Third, these years witnessed far-reaching cultural changes. Beginning about 1800, the Second Great Awakening swept across the nation, sparking great movements of social reform and intellectual ferment that revolutionized the culture of the North and Midwest. Finally, sectionalism increased in intensity, as the South extended its slave-labor system and the North developed a free-labor society. The overall result by 1860 was striking and alarming: now more politically democratic, economically prosperous, and deeply religious, the United States stood divided into antagonistic sections. Here, in brief, are the key aspects of those transformations.

## Transforming the Economy, Society, and Culture

Impressive advances in industrial production, transportation, and commerce transformed the nation's economy. Factory owners used water- and steam-powered machines and a new system of labor discipline to boost the output of goods. Manufacturers produced 5 percent of the country's wealth in 1820 but nearly 25 percent by 1860. As enterprising merchants, entrepreneurs, and government officials developed a network of canals and markets, manufacturers sold these products throughout an expanding nation. The new economy created a class-based, urban society in the North and Midwest. A wealthy elite of merchants, manufacturers, bankers, and entrepreneurs rose to the top of the society. To preserve social stability, this elite embraced benevolent reform, preaching the gospel of temperance, Sunday observance, and universal elementary education. Simultaneously, an expanding urban middle class created a distinct material and religious culture and promoted its ideology of individual responsibility and social mobility. Some middle-class Americans advocated radical causes: joining utopian socialist communities and demanding equal rights for women and the immediate end of racial slavery. A mass of propertyless wage-earning workers, including poor immigrants from Germany and Ireland, devised a vibrant popular culture of their own. This complex story of economic change and social fragmentation is the focus of Chapter 9 and Chapter 11.

## Creating a Democratic Polity

Beginning in the 1810s, the rapid expansion of white male suffrage and political parties created a competitive and responsive democratic polity. Pressure came from ordinary citizens who organized political movements, such as the Anti-Masonic, Working Men's, and Liberty parties, to advance their interests and beliefs. Farmers, workers, and entrepreneurs persuaded state legislatures to improve transportation, shorten workdays, and award valuable charters to banks and business corporations. Catholic immigrants from Ireland and Germany entered the political arena to protect their cultural habits and religious institutions from restrictive legislation advocated by Protestant nativists and reformers. Then, during the 1830s, Andrew Jackson and the Democratic Party led a political and constitutional revolution that cut federal and state government aid to financiers, merchants, and corporations. To contend with the Democrats, the Whig Party devised a competing program that stressed state-sponsored economic development, moral reform, and individual social mobility. This party competition engaged the energies of the electorate, helped to unify a fragmented social order, and, during the 1830s and 1840s, lessened sectional tensions. Chapters 10 and 12 analyze this story of political change and party politics.

## Growing Sectional Divisions

However, the party system could not overcome the increasingly sharp sectional divisions. As the North developed into an urban industrial society based on free labor, the South increasingly defended white supremacy and slavery as a "positive good" and expanded its plantation-based agricultural society. Beginning in the 1820s, the two sections had differed over economic issues and Indian policy. Georgia and other southeastern states demanded and won—over the objections of northeastern reformers—the Indian Removal Act of 1830, which resettled native peoples west of the Mississippi River. Concurrently, between 1816 and 1832, northern manufacturers, workers, and farmers won high protective tariffs, which southern planters bitterly opposed. Eventually, party politicians negotiated a compromise, with the North accepting tariff reductions. The sections had clashed again over the expansion of slavery, into Missouri and the Louisiana Purchase in the 1820s and into Texas and the Southwest in the 1840s, and political leaders again devised compromises. However, by the 1850s, slavery—and the social system it symbolized—increasingly divided the nation. Moreover, because the democratic political revolution had engaged the passions of millions of ordinary Americans, the political system had become more volatile and resistant to compromise. Chapters 10 and 12 explain how national expansion led to increasing sectional struggle.

# Overlapping Revolutions 1800–1860

## Thematic Understanding

This timeline arranges some of the important events of this period into themes. Look at the entries under "Identity": what identities emerged in this period, and which issues shaped these developments? In the "Work, Exchange, and Technology" theme, how did industrial output and the transportation system change over time?   **>**

| | WORK, EXCHANGE, & TECHNOLOGY | PEOPLING | POLITICS & POWER | IDEAS, BELIEFS, & CULTURE | IDENTITY |
|---|---|---|---|---|---|
| **1810** | • Congress approves funds for a National Road (1806)<br><br>• First American textile factory opens in Waltham, Massachusetts (1814) | • Congress outlaws Atlantic slave trade (1776–1809)<br><br>• Andrew Jackson forces Creeks to relinquish millions of acres during War of 1812 | • Struggle to expand the suffrage begins with Maryland reformers<br><br>• Martin Van Buren creates first statewide political machine (1817–1821)<br><br>• Missouri crisis (1819–1821) over slavery | • In rural areas, people of different ranks share a common culture<br><br>• Upper-class women sponsor charitable organizations | • American Colonization Society (1817)<br><br>• Benjamin Franklin's *Autobiography* (1818) spreads notion of the self-made man |
| **1820** | • New England shoe industry expands<br><br>• Erie Canal completed (1825)<br><br>• Henry Clay's "American System" of government-assisted development<br><br>• Market economy expands nationwide | • Slave trade moves African Americans west<br><br>• Rural women take factory work, alter gender roles | • Rise of Andrew Jackson and Democratic Party<br><br>• Anti-Masonic Party and Working Men's Party rise and decline | • Benevolent reform movements<br><br>• Emerson champions transcendentalism<br><br>• Charles Finney and others advance revivalist religion<br><br>• Industrialism fragments society into more distinct classes and cultures | • David Walker's *Appeal . . . to the Colored Citizens* (1829) attacks slavery<br><br>• Rise of southern sectionalism |
| **1830** | • U.S. textiles compete with British goods<br><br>• Canal systems expand trade in eastern U.S.<br><br>• Financial panic of 1837 begins six-year depression<br><br>• Boom in cotton output<br><br>• Increase in waged work sparks conflict between labor and capital | • Indian Removal Act (1830) forces native peoples west<br><br>• Cherokees' "Trail of Tears" (1838) | • Tariff battles (1828, 1832) and nullification<br><br>• Whig Party forms (1834)<br><br>• Jackson destroys Second Bank, expands executive power | • Temperance crusade expands<br><br>• Joseph Smith and Mormonism<br><br>• Middle-class culture spreads<br><br>• Slavery defended as a "positive good"<br><br>• Urban popular culture (sex trade and minstrelsy) | • W. L. Garrison's American Anti-Slavery Society (1833)<br><br>• Female Moral Reform Society (1834) defines gender identity<br><br>• Texas gains independence (1836) |
| **1840** | • American machine tool industry expands<br><br>• Walker Tariff moves U.S. toward "free trade" system and principles of "classical liberalism" | • Working-class districts emerge in cities<br><br>• German and Irish immigrants spark nativist movement<br><br>• Mormons resettle in Utah | • Log cabin campaign (1840)<br><br>• Second Party System flourishes<br><br>• Lawyers emerge as political leaders | • Fourierist and other communal settlements<br><br>• Seneca Falls Convention (1848) calls for women's rights | • Antislavery Liberty Party (1840)<br><br>• New African American culture develops in Mississippi Valley |
| **1850** | • Severe recession cuts industrial jobs (1858)<br><br>• Railroads connect Midwest and eastern ports<br><br>• Cotton production and prices rise, as does the cost of enslaved laborers | • Immigrants replace native-born women in textile mills<br><br>• White farm families settle trans-Mississippi west | • Reform becomes political: states enact Maine-style temperance laws (1851 on)<br><br>• "Mormon War" over polygamy (1858) | • American Renaissance: Melville, Whitman, and Hawthorne<br><br>• Harriet Beecher Stowe's *Uncle Tom's Cabin* (1852) | • Black and white preachers promote Christianity among slaves<br><br>• Free blacks in North become politically active |

# 9
## CHAPTER

# Transforming the Economy
## 1800–1860

I n 1804, life turned grim for eleven-year-old Chauncey Jerome. His father died suddenly, and Jerome became an indentured servant on a Connecticut farm. Quickly learning that few farmers "would treat a poor boy like a human being," Jerome bought out his indenture by making dials for clocks and then found a job with clockmaker Eli Terry. A manufacturing wizard, Terry used water power to drive precision saws and woodworking lathes. Soon his shop, and dozens of outworkers, were turning out thousands of tall clocks with wooden works. Then, in 1816, Terry patented an enormously popular desk clock with brass parts, an innovation that turned Waterbury, Connecticut, into the clockmaking center of the United States.

In 1822, Chauncey Jerome set up his own clock factory. By organizing work more efficiently and using new machines that stamped out interchangeable metal parts, he drove down the price of a simple clock from $20 to $5 and then to less than $2. By the 1840s, Jerome was selling his clocks in England, the hub of the Industrial Revolution; a decade later, his workers were turning out 400,000 clocks a year, clear testimony to American industrial enterprise. By 1860, the United States was not only the world's leading exporter of cotton and wheat but also the third-ranked manufacturing nation behind Britain and France.

"Business is the very soul of an American: the fountain of all human felicity," author Francis Grund observed shortly after arriving from Europe. "It is as if all America were but one gigantic workshop, over the entrance of which there is the blazing inscription, 'No admission here, except on business.'" Stimulated by the entrepreneurial culture of early-nineteenth-century America, thousands of artisan-inventors like Chauncey Jerome propelled the country into the Industrial Revolution, a new system of production based on water and steam power and machine technology. Simultaneously, thousands of traders fashioned a second great economic advance, a Market Revolution that exploited advances in transportation and business organization to expand trade in farm products and manufactured goods.

Not all Americans embraced the new business-dominated society, and many failed to share in the new prosperity. Moreover, the increase in manufacturing, commerce, and finance created class divisions that challenged the founders' vision of an agricultural republic with few distinctions of wealth. As the philosopher Ralph Waldo Emerson warned in 1839: "The invasion of Nature by Trade with its Money, its Credit, its Steam, [and] its Railroad threatens to . . . establish a new, universal Monarchy."

## IDENTIFY THE BIG IDEA

What were the causes and consequences of the Industrial and Market revolutions, and how did they change the way ordinary Americans lived?

**Women Weavers from Maine, c. 1860** Nineteenth-century workers were proud of their skills and, like these textiles operatives from Winthrop, Maine, often posed for photographs with the tools of their craft. This small tintype, 3 by 4 inches and printed on thin metal, dates from the mid-nineteenth century. Beginning in the 1830s, cotton textile entrepreneurs built factories in rural Maine, attracted by its abundant water power and the inexpensive labor of young farm women. The women wear striped dresses of cotton fabric, which they probably helped to manufacture. American Textile History Museum.

# The American Industrial Revolution

The **Industrial Revolution** came to the United States between 1790 and 1860, as merchants and manufacturers reorganized work routines, built factories, and exploited a wide range of natural resources. As output increased, goods that once had been luxury items became part of everyday life (Figure 9.1). The rapid construction of turnpikes, canals, and railroads by state governments and private entrepreneurs, working together in the Commonwealth System (Chapter 8), distributed manufactures throughout the nation.

## The Division of Labor and the Factory

Increased output stemmed initially from changes in the organization of work that turned independent artisans into wage laborers. Traditionally, New England shoemakers had turned leather hides into finished shoes and boots in small wooden shacks called "ten-footers," where they worked at their own pace. During the 1820s and 1830s, merchants in Lynn, Massachusetts, destroyed the businesses of these artisans by introducing an outwork system and a **division of labor**. The merchants

**IDENTIFY CAUSES**
How did the division of labor increase output, and what was its impact on workers?

hired semiskilled journeymen and set them up in large shops cutting leather into soles and uppers. They sent out the upper sections to rural Massachusetts towns, where women binders sewed in fabric linings. The manufacturers then had other journeymen attach the uppers to the soles and return the shoes to the central shop for inspection, packing, and sale. This more efficient system increased output and cut the price of shoes and boots, even as it turned employers into powerful "shoe bosses" and eroded workers' wages and independence.

For products not suited to the outwork system, manufacturers created the modern factory, which concentrated production under one roof. For example, in the 1830s, Cincinnati merchants built large slaughterhouses that processed thousands of hogs every month. The technology remained simple, but a division of labor increased output. As a system of overhead rails moved the hog carcasses along a "disassembly" line, one worker split the animals, another removed the organs, and others trimmed the carcasses into pieces. Packers then stuffed the pork into barrels and salted it to prevent spoilage. Reported landscape architect and journalist Frederick Law Olmsted:

> We entered an immense low-ceiling room and followed a vista of dead swine, upon their backs, their paws stretching mutely toward heaven. Walking down to the vanishing point, we found there a sort of human chopping-machine where the hogs were

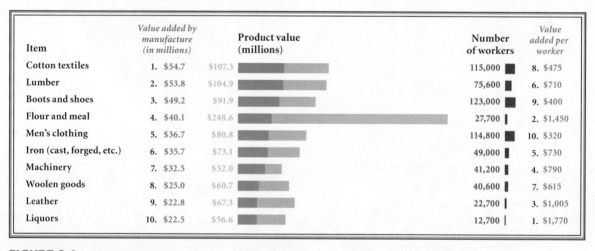

| Item | Value added by manufacture (in millions) | Product value (millions) | | Number of workers | Value added per worker |
|---|---|---|---|---|---|
| Cotton textiles | 1. $54.7 | $107.3 | | 115,000 | 8. $475 |
| Lumber | 2. $53.8 | $104.9 | | 75,600 | 6. $710 |
| Boots and shoes | 3. $49.2 | $91.9 | | 123,000 | 9. $400 |
| Flour and meal | 4. $40.1 | $248.6 | | 27,700 | 2. $1,450 |
| Men's clothing | 5. $36.7 | $80.8 | | 114,800 | 10. $320 |
| Iron (cast, forged, etc.) | 6. $35.7 | $73.1 | | 49,000 | 5. $730 |
| Machinery | 7. $32.5 | $52.0 | | 41,200 | 4. $790 |
| Woolen goods | 8. $25.0 | $60.7 | | 40,600 | 7. $615 |
| Leather | 9. $22.8 | $67.3 | | 22,700 | 3. $1,005 |
| Liquors | 10. $22.5 | $56.6 | | 12,700 | 1. $1,770 |

**FIGURE 9.1**

**Leading Branches of Manufacture, 1860**

This chart shows clearly that in 1860, three industries—boots and shoes, cotton textiles, and men's clothing—each employed more than 100,000 workers. However, the workers in three other industries had the highest productivity, with each worker adding more than $1,000 in value to the finished goods. What were these industries? Why were their workers more productive? Adapted from Douglass C. North, *Growth and Welfare in the American Past*, Second Edition. Copyright © 1974. Reprinted with permission of the author.

converted into commercial pork. . . . Plump falls the hog upon the table, chop, chop; chop, chop; chop, chop, fall the cleavers. . . . We took out our watches and counted thirty-five seconds, from the moment when one hog touched the table until the next occupied its place.

The Cincinnati system was so efficient—processing sixty hogs an hour—that by the 1840s the city was known as "Porkopolis." By 1850, factories were slaughtering 334,000 hogs a year, and 400,000 by 1860.

Other factories boasted impressive new technology. In 1782, Oliver Evans, a prolific Delaware inventor, built a highly automated flour mill driven by water power. His machinery lifted the wheat to the top of the mill, cleaned the grain as it fell into hoppers, ground it into flour, and then cooled the flour as it was funneled into barrels. Evans's factory, remarked one observer, "was as full of machinery as the case of a watch." It needed only six men to mill 100,000 bushels of wheat a year—perhaps ten times as much as they could grind in a traditional mill.

By the 1830s, a new "**mineral-based economy**" of coal and metal began to emerge. Manufacturers increasingly ran their machinery with coal-burning stationary steam engines rather than with water power. And they now fabricated metal products—iron, brass, copper, and tinplate (tin-coated rolled iron)—as well as pork, leather, wool, cotton, and other agricultural goods. In Chicago, Cyrus McCormick used steam-driven machines to make parts for farm reapers, which workers assembled on a conveyor belt. In Hartford, Connecticut, Samuel Colt built an assembly line to produce his invention, the six-shooter revolver. Other New England artisans designed machines that fabricated tinplate into pails, pans, pots, and dozens of other inexpensive and useful household items. These advances in technology and factory organization alarmed British observers: "The contriving and making of machinery has become so common in this country . . . [that] it is to be feared that American manufacturers will become exporters not only to foreign countries, but even to England."

## The Textile Industry and British Competition

To protect the British textile industry from American competition, the British government prohibited the export of textile machinery and the emigration of **mechanics** (skilled craftsmen who invented and improved tools for industry). Lured by the prospect of higher wages, though, thousands of British mechanics

disguised themselves as laborers and sailed to the United States. By 1812, at least three hundred British mechanics worked in the Philadelphia area alone.

Samuel Slater, the most important émigré mechanic, came to America in 1789 after working for Richard Arkwright, who had invented the most advanced British machinery for spinning cotton. A year later, Slater reproduced Arkwright's innovations in merchant Moses Brown's cotton mill in Providence, Rhode Island.

In competing with British mills, American manufacturers had the advantage of an abundance of natural resources. The nation's farmers produced huge amounts of cotton and wool, and the fast-flowing rivers that cascaded down from the Appalachian foothills to the Atlantic coastal plain provided a cheap source of energy. From Massachusetts to Delaware, these waterways were soon lined with industrial villages and textile mills as large as 150 feet long, 40 feet wide, and four stories high (Map 9.1).

**American and British Advantages**   Still, British producers easily undersold their American competitors. Thanks to cheap transatlantic shipping and low interest rates in Britain, they could import raw cotton from the United States, manufacture it into cloth, and sell it in America at a bargain price. (As they did in India; see America Compared p. 289.) The most important British advantage was cheap labor: Britain had a larger population—about 12.6 million in 1810 compared to 7.3 million Americans—and thousands of landless laborers prepared to accept low-paying factory jobs. To offset these advantages, American entrepreneurs relied on help from the federal government: in 1816, 1824, and 1828, Congress passed tariff bills that taxed imported cotton and woolen cloth. However, in the 1830s, Congress reduced tariffs because southern planters, western farmers, and urban consumers demanded inexpensive imports.

**Better Machines, Cheaper Workers**   American producers used two other strategies to compete with their British rivals. First, they improved on British technology. In 1811, Francis Cabot Lowell, a wealthy Boston merchant, toured British textile mills, secretly making detailed drawings of their power machinery. Paul Moody, an experienced American mechanic, then copied the machines and improved their design. In 1814, Lowell joined with merchants Nathan Appleton and Patrick

> **COMPARE AND CONTRAST**
> What were the advantages and strategies of British and American textile manufacturers?

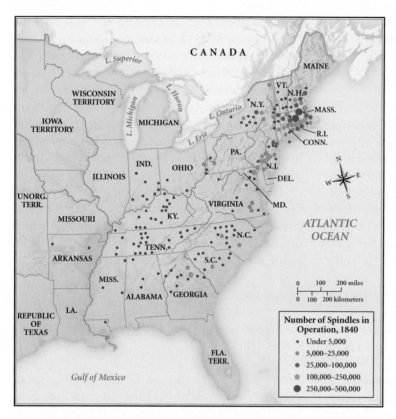

**MAP 9.1**

**New England's Dominance in Cotton Spinning, 1840**

Although the South grew the nation's cotton, it did not process it. Prior to the Civil War, entrepreneurs in Massachusetts and Rhode Island built most of the factories that spun and wove raw cotton into cloth. Their factories made use of the abundant water power available in New England and the region's surplus labor force. Initially, factory managers hired young farm women to work the machines; later, they relied on immigrants from Ireland and the French-speaking Canadian province of Quebec.

Tracy Jackson to form the Boston Manufacturing Company. Having raised the staggering sum of $400,000, they built a textile plant in Waltham, Massachusetts — the first American factory to perform all clothmaking operations under one roof. Thanks to Moody's improvements, Waltham's power looms operated at higher speeds than British looms and needed fewer workers.

The second strategy was to tap a cheaper source of labor. In the 1820s, the Boston Manufacturing Company recruited thousands of young women from farm families, providing them with rooms in boardinghouses and with evening lectures and other cultural activities. To reassure parents about their daughters' moral welfare, the mill owners enforced strict curfews, prohibited alcoholic beverages, and required regular church attendance. At Lowell (1822), Chicopee (1823), and other sites in Massachusetts and New Hampshire, the company built new factories that used this labor system, known as the **Waltham-Lowell System**.

By the early 1830s, more than 40,000 New England women were working in textile mills. As an observer noted, the wages were "more than could be obtained by the hitherto ordinary occupation of housework," the living conditions were better than those in crowded farmhouses, and the women had greater independence.

Lucy Larcom became a Lowell textile operative at age eleven to avoid being "a trouble or burden or expense" to her widowed mother. Other women operatives used wages to pay off their father's farm mortgages, send brothers to school, or accumulate a marriage dowry for themselves.

 To see a longer excerpt of the Lucy Larcom document, along with other primary sources from this period, see *Sources for America's History*.

Some operatives just had a good time. Susan Brown, who worked as a Lowell weaver for eight months, spent half her earnings on food and lodging and the rest on plays, concerts, lectures, and a two-day excursion to Boston. Like most textile workers, Brown soon tired of the rigors of factory work and the never-ceasing clatter of the machinery, which ran twelve hours a day, six days a week. After she quit, she lived at home for a time and then moved to another mill. Whatever the hardships, waged work gave young women a sense of freedom. "Don't I feel independent!" a woman mill worker wrote to her sister. "The thought that I am living on no one is a happy one indeed to me." The owners of the Boston Manufacturing Company were even happier. By combining tariff protection with improved technology

## The Fate of the American and Indian Textile Industries

In 1776, the United States declared its independence from the British Empire. About the same time, Britain began to create in India what historians call the Second British Empire. By 1860, Britain had become the world's leading industrial economy and dominated the princely states and peoples of the Indian subcontinent. The following tables trace the impact of political decisions on the American and Indian textile industries. As the legislature of an independent republic, the U.S. Congress could impose tariffs (taxes on imported goods) on British textiles; as colonies, Indian governments could not do so.

### TABLE 9.1

**Cotton Textile Production and Consumption in India**

| Year | Population (millions) | Imports from Britain (mill. yds.) | Production for Domestic Consumption (mill. yds.) | Exports to Britain (pieces, ave./year) |
|---|---|---|---|---|
| 1751 | 190 | 0 | 1,598 | 632,000 (1750–1754) |
| 1801 | 207 | 0 | 1,741 | 1,355,304 (1800–1804) |
| 1821 | 205 | 20 | 1,704 | 542,117 (1820–1824) |
| 1841 | 212 | 141 | 1,642 | 192,965 (1830–1834) |
| 1861 | 242 | 514 | 1,538 | Data not available |

### TABLE 9.2

**Textile Production in the United States**

| Year | Number of Cotton Mill Workers | Number of Spindles (ave./decade)[1] | Imports from Britain (mill. yds.) | Average U.S. Tariff (as % of item's value) |
|---|---|---|---|---|
| 1810 | | 215,000 | | |
| 1815 | | | 70.81 | 25.0% |
| 1820 | 12,000 | 936,000 | | |
| 1827 | | | 52.86 | 53.8% |
| 1830 | 55,000 | 1,038,000 | | |
| 1835 | | | 74.96 | 40.4% |
| 1840 | 72,000 | 1,243,000 | | |
| 1850 | 92,000 | 1,709,000 | 104.23 | 27.1% |
| 1859 | | | 225.15 | 19.6% |
| 1860 | 122,000 | | | |

[1]Entries in Spindle column are the average per year across the decade; i.e., there were perhaps 100,000 spindles in 1810 and 350,000 in 1820, yielding an average of 215,000 between 1810 and 1819.

### QUESTIONS FOR ANALYSIS

1. Compare changes in Indian production ("Production for Domestic Consumption" and "Exports to Britain") with changes in American production ("Number of Cotton Mill Workers" and "Number of Spindles") between 1800 and 1861. Which country is "industrializing," and which is "deindustrializing"?

2. How do American tariffs change over time? (Chapter 10 will explain the reasons for these changes.) What is the impact of American tariff rates on the import of British textiles?

3. What insights does this material provide into the political and economic aspects of American industrialization?

and cheap female labor, they could undersell their British rivals. Their textiles were also cheaper than those made in New York and Pennsylvania, where farmworkers were paid more than in New England and textile wages consequently were higher. Manufacturers in those states garnered profits by using advanced technology to produce higher-quality cloth. Even Thomas Jefferson, the great champion of yeoman farming, was impressed. "Our manufacturers are now very nearly on a footing with those of England," he boasted in 1825.

## American Mechanics and Technological Innovation

By the 1820s, American-born artisans had replaced British immigrants at the cutting edge of technological innovation. Though few mechanics had a formal education, they commanded respect as "men professing an ingenious art." In the Philadelphia region, the remarkable Sellars family produced the most important inventors. Samuel Sellars Jr. invented a machine for twisting worsted woolen yarn to give it an especially smooth surface. His son John improved the efficiency of the waterwheels powering the family's sawmills and built a machine to weave wire sieves. John's sons and grandsons ran machine shops that turned out riveted leather fire hoses, papermaking equipment, and eventually locomotives. In 1824, the Sellars and other mechanics founded the Franklin Institute in Philadelphia. Named after Benjamin Franklin, whom the mechanics admired for his work ethic and scientific accomplishments, the institute published a journal; provided high-school-level instruction in chemistry, mathematics, and mechanical design; and organized exhibits of new products. Craftsmen in Ohio and other states established similar institutes to disseminate technical knowledge and encourage innovation. Between 1820 and 1860, the number of patents issued by the U.S. Patent Office rose from two hundred to four thousand a year.

American craftsmen pioneered the development of **machine tools** — machines that made parts for other machines. A key innovator was Eli Whitney (1765–1825), the son of a middling New England farm family. At the age of fourteen, Whitney began fashioning nails and knife blades; later, he made women's hatpins. Aspiring to wealth and status, Whitney won admission to Yale College and subsequently worked as a tutor on a Georgia cotton plantation. Using his expertise in making hatpins, he built a simple machine in 1793 that separated

**Eli Whitney**

Eli Whitney posed for this portrait in the 1820s, when he had achieved prosperity and social standing as the inventor of the cotton gin and other machines. Whitney's success prompted the artist — his young New Haven, Connecticut, neighbor Samuel F. B. Morse — to turn his creative energies from painting to industrial technology. By the 1840s, Morse had devised the hardware for the first successful commercial telegraph and the software — the "Morse Code" — that it transmitted. Yale University Art Gallery/Art Resource, NY.

the seeds in a cotton boll from the delicate fibers, work previously done slowly by hand. Although Whitney patented his cotton engine (or "gin," as it became known), other manufacturers improved on his design and captured the market.

Still seeking his fortune, Whitney decided in 1798 to manufacture military weapons. He eventually designed and built machine tools that could rapidly produce interchangeable musket parts, bringing him the wealth and fame he had long craved. After Whitney's death in 1825, his partner John H. Hall built an array of metalworking machine tools, such as turret lathes, milling machines, and precision grinders.

Technological innovation now swept through American manufacturing. Mechanics in the textile industry invented lathes, planers, and boring machines that turned out standardized parts for new spinning jennies and weaving looms. Despite being mass-produced, these jennies and looms were precisely made and operated at higher speeds than British equipment.

**TRACE CHANGE OVER TIME**

What new types of products came out of American factories by the 1840s and 1850s?

The leading inventor was Richard Garsed: he nearly doubled the speed of the power looms in his father's Delaware factory and patented a cam-and-harness device that allowed damask and other elaborately designed fabrics to be machine-woven. Meanwhile, the mechanics employed by Samuel W. Collins built a machine for pressing and hammering hot metal into dies (cutting forms). Using this machine, a worker could make three hundred ax heads a day—compared to twelve using traditional methods. In Richmond, Virginia, Welsh- and American-born mechanics at the Tredegar Iron Works produced great quantities of low-cost parts for complicated manufacturing equipment. As a group of British observers noted admiringly, many American products were made "with machinery applied to almost every process . . . all reduced to an almost perfect system of manufacture."

As mass production spread, the American Industrial Revolution came of age. Reasonably priced products such as Remington rifles, Singer sewing machines, and Yale locks became household names in the United States and abroad. After winning praise at the Crystal Palace Exhibition in London in 1851—the first major international display of industrial goods—Remington, Singer, and other American firms became multinational businesses, building factories in Great Britain and selling goods throughout Europe. By 1877, the Singer Manufacturing Company controlled 75 percent of the world market for sewing machines.

## Wageworkers and the Labor Movement

As the Industrial Revolution gathered momentum, it changed the nature of workers' lives. Following the American Revolution, many craft workers espoused **artisan republicanism**, an ideology of production based on liberty and equality. They saw themselves as small-scale producers, equal to one another and free to work for themselves. The poet Walt Whitman summed up their outlook: "Men must be masters, under themselves."

**Free Workers Form Unions** However, as the outwork and factory systems spread, more and more workers became wage earners who labored under the control of an employer. Unlike young women, who embraced factory work because it freed them from parental control and domestic service, men bridled at their status as supervised wageworkers. To assert their independent status, male wageworkers rejected the traditional terms of *master* and *servant* and used the Dutch word *boss* to refer to their employer. Likewise, lowly apprentices refused to allow masters to control their private (nonwork) lives and joined their mates in building a robust plebeian culture. Still, as hired hands, they received meager wages and had little job security. The artisan-republican ideal of "self-ownership" confronted the harsh reality of waged work in an industrializing capitalist society. Labor had become a commodity, to be bought and sold.

Some wage earners worked in carpentry, stonecutting, masonry, and cabinetmaking—traditional crafts that required specialized skills. Their strong sense of identity, or trade consciousness, enabled these workers to form **unions** and bargain with their master-artisan employers. They resented low wages and long hours, which restricted their family life and educational opportunities. In Boston, six hundred carpenters went on strike in 1825. That protest failed, but in 1840, craft

> **UNDERSTAND POINTS OF VIEW**
> How did the capitalist-run industrial economy conflict with artisan republicanism, and how did workers respond?

**Diagram of McCormick's Reaper**

The economic revolution was the result, in part, of increased output created by power-driven machinery used in factories. However, machines also increased farm productivity. Using McCormick's Reaper and a horse, a farmer and his son could cut as much grain in a day as seven men with scythes. They could now plant more acres and not worry about the wheat sprouting (and becoming worthless) before it could be harvested. Moreover, as this advertisement from the May 1846 issue of the *Cultivator* indicates, farmers could easily repair their new reapers by providing McCormick with the letter denoting a broken part. Wisconsin Historical Society.

M'CORMICK'S REAPER.

**Woodworker, c. 1850**

Skilled makers took great pride in their furniture, which was often intricately designed and beautifully executed. To underline the dignity of his occupation, this woodworker poses in formal dress and proudly displays the tools of his craft. A belief in the value of their labor was an important ingredient of the artisan-republican ideology held by many workers. Library of Congress.

workers in St. Louis secured a ten-hour day, and President Van Buren issued an executive order setting a similar workday for federal workers.

Artisans in other occupations were less successful in preserving their pay and working conditions. As aggressive entrepreneurs and machine technology took command, shoemakers, hatters, printers, furniture makers, and weavers faced the regimentation of low-paid factory work. In response, some artisans in these trades moved to small towns, while in New York City, 800 highly skilled cabinetmakers made fashionable furniture. In status and income, these cabinetmakers outranked a group of 3,200 semitrained, wage-earning workers — disparagingly called "botches" — who made cheaper tables and chairs in factories. Thus the new industrial system split the traditional artisan class into self-employed craftsmen and wage-earning workers.

When wage earners banded together to form unions, they faced a legal hurdle: English and American common law branded such groups as illegal "combinations." As a Philadelphia judge put it, unions were "a government unto themselves" and unlawfully interfered with a "master's" authority over his "servant." Other lawsuits accused unions of "conspiring" to raise wages and thereby injure employers. "It is important to the best interests of society that the price of labor be left to regulate itself," the New York Supreme Court declared in 1835, while excluding employers from this rule. Clothing manufacturers in New York City collectively agreed to set wage rates and to dismiss members of the Society of Journeymen Tailors.

**Labor Ideology**   Despite such obstacles, during the 1830s journeymen shoemakers founded mutual benefit societies in Lynn, Massachusetts, and other shoe-making centers. As the workers explained, "The capitalist has no other interest in us, than to get as much labor out of us as possible. We are hired men, and hired men, like hired horses, have no souls." To exert more pressure on their employers, in 1834 local unions from Boston to Philadelphia formed the National Trades Union, the first regional union of different trades.

Workers found considerable popular support for their cause. When a New York City court upheld a conspiracy verdict against their union, tailors warned that the "Freemen of the North are now on a level with the slaves of the South," and organized a mass meeting of 27,000 people to denounce the decision. In 1836, local juries hearing conspiracy cases acquitted shoemakers in Hudson, New York; carpet makers in Thompsonville, Connecticut; and plasterers in Philadelphia. Even when juries convicted workers, judges imposed only light fines, so labor organizers were not deterred. Then, in *Commonwealth v. Hunt* (1842), Chief Justice Lemuel Shaw of the Massachusetts Supreme Judicial Court overturned common-law precedents and upheld the right of workers to form unions and call strikes to enforce closed-shop agreements that limited employment to union members. But many judges continued to resist unions by issuing injunctions forbidding strikes.

Union leaders expanded artisan republicanism to include wageworkers. Arguing that wage earners were becoming "slaves to a monied aristocracy," they condemned the new factory system in which "capital and labor stand opposed." To create a just society in which workers could "live as comfortably as others," they advanced a **labor theory of value**. Under this theory, the price of goods should reflect the labor required to make them, and the income from their sale should go primarily to the producers, not to factory owners, middlemen, or storekeepers. "The poor who perform the work, ought to receive at least half of that sum which is charged" to the consumer, declared minister

Ezra Stiles Ely. Union activists agreed, organizing nearly fifty strikes for higher wages in 1836. Appealing to the spirit of the American Revolution, which had destroyed the aristocracy of birth, they called for a new revolution to demolish the aristocracy of capital.

Women textile operatives were equally active. Competition in the woolen and cotton textile industries was fierce because mechanization caused output to grow faster than consumer demand. As textile prices fell, manufacturers' revenues declined. To maintain profits, employers reduced workers' wages and imposed tougher work rules. In 1828 and again in 1834, women mill workers in Dover, New Hampshire, went on strike and won some relief. In Lowell, two thousand women operatives backed a strike by withdrawing their savings from an employer-owned bank. "One of the leaders mounted a pump," the *Boston Transcript* reported, "and made a flaming . . . speech on the rights of women and the iniquities of the 'monied aristocracy.' " Increasingly, young New England women refused to enter the mills, and impoverished Irish (and later French Canadian) immigrants took their places.

In 1857, the new economic system faltered, as overproduction and a financial panic sparked by the bankruptcies of several railroads pushed the economy into a recession. Urban unemployment soared to 10 percent and reminded Americans of the social costs of industrial production.

# The Market Revolution

As American factories and farms churned out more goods, legislators and businessmen created faster and cheaper ways to get those products to consumers. Around 1820, they began constructing a massive system of canals and roads linking states along the Atlantic coast with new states in the trans-Appalachian west. This transportation system set in motion both a crucial **Market Revolution** and a massive migration of people to the Greater Mississippi River basin. This huge area, drained by six river systems (the Missouri, Arkansas, Red, Ohio, Tennessee, and Mississippi), contains the largest and most productive contiguous acreage of arable land in the world. By 1860, nearly one-third of the nation's citizens lived in eight of its states — the "Midwest," consisting of the five states carved out of the Northwest Territory (Ohio, Indiana, Illinois, Michigan, and Wisconsin) along with Missouri, Iowa, and Minnesota. There they created a rich agricultural economy and an industrializing society similar to that of the Northeast.

## The Transportation Revolution Forges Regional Ties

With the Indian peoples in retreat, slave-owning planters from the Lower South settled in Missouri (admitted to the Union in 1821) and pushed on to Arkansas (admitted in 1836). Simultaneously, yeomen families from the Upper South joined migrants from New England and New York in farming the fertile lands near the Great Lakes. Once Indiana and Illinois were settled, land-hungry farmers poured into Michigan (1837), Iowa (1846), and Wisconsin (1848) — where they resided among tens of thousands of hardworking immigrants from Germany. To meet the demand for cheap farmsteads, Congress in 1820 reduced the price of federal land from $2.00 an acre to $1.25. For $100, a farmer could buy 80 acres, the minimum required under federal law. By the 1840s, this generous policy had enticed about 5 million people to states and territories west of the Appalachians (Map 9.2).

To link the midwestern settlers to the seaboard states, Congress approved funds for a National Road constructed of compacted gravel. The project began in 1811 at Cumberland in western Maryland, at the head of navigation of the Potomac River; reached Wheeling, Virginia (now West Virginia), on the Ohio River in 1818; and ended in Vandalia, Illinois, in 1839. The National Road and other interregional highways carried migrants and their heavily loaded wagons westward; these migrants passed livestock herds heading in the opposite direction, destined for eastern markets. To link the settler communities with each other, state legislatures chartered private companies to build toll roads, or turnpikes.

**Canals and Steamboats Shrink Distance**   Even on well-built gravel roads, overland travel was slow and expensive. To carry people, crops, and manufactures to and from the great Mississippi River basin, public money and private businesses developed a water-borne transportation system of unprecedented size, complexity, and cost. The key event was the New York legislature's 1817 financing of the **Erie Canal**, a 364-mile waterway connecting the Hudson River and Lake Erie. Previously, the longest canal in the United States was just 28 miles long — reflecting the huge capital cost of canals and the lack of American engineering expertise. New York's ambitious project had three things working in its favor: the vigorous support of New York City's merchants, who wanted access to western markets; the backing of New York's governor, De Witt Clinton, who proposed to finance the waterway from tax revenues,

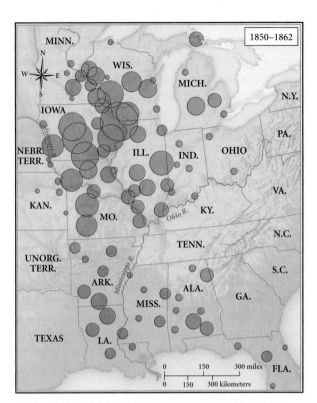

## MAP 9.2
### Western Land Sales, 1830–1839 and 1850–1862

The federal government set up local offices to sell land in the national domain to settlers. During the 1830s, the offices sold huge amounts of land in the corn and wheat belt of the Midwest (Ohio, Indiana, Illinois, and Michigan) and the cotton belt to the south (especially Alabama and Mississippi). As settlers moved westward in the 1850s, most sales were in the Upper Mississippi River Valley (particularly Iowa and Wisconsin). Each circle indicates the relative amount of land sold at a local office.

tolls, and bond sales to foreign investors; and the relatively gentle terrain west of Albany. Even so, the task was enormous. Workers—many of them Irish immigrants—dug out millions of cubic yards of soil, quarried thousands of tons of rock for the huge locks that raised and lowered the boats, and constructed vast reservoirs to ensure a steady supply of water.

The first great engineering project in American history, the Erie Canal altered the ecology of an entire region. As farming communities and market towns sprang up along the waterway, settlers cut down millions of trees to provide wood for houses and barns and to open the land for growing crops and grazing animals. Cows and sheep foraged in pastures that had recently been forests occupied by deer and bears, and spring rains caused massive erosion of the denuded landscape.

Whatever its environmental consequences, the Erie Canal was an instant economic success. The first 75-mile section opened in 1819 and quickly yielded enough revenue to repay its construction cost. When workers finished the canal in 1825, a 40-foot-wide ribbon of water stretched from Buffalo, on the eastern shore of Lake Erie, to Albany, where it joined the Hudson River for the 150-mile trip to New York City. The canal's water "must be the most fertilizing of all fluids," suggested novelist Nathaniel Hawthorne, "for it causes towns with their masses of brick and stone, their churches and theaters, their business and hubbub, their luxury and refinement, their gay dames and polished citizens, to spring up."

The Erie Canal brought prosperity to the farmers of central and western New York and the entire Great Lakes region. Northeastern manufacturers shipped clothing, boots, and agricultural equipment to farm families; in return, farmers sent grain, cattle, and hogs as well as raw materials (leather, wool, and hemp, for example) to eastern cities and foreign markets. One-hundred-ton freight barges, each pulled by two horses,

**IDENTIFY CAUSES**

Which was more important in the Market Revolution, government support for transportation or technological innovations, and why was that the case?

***View of the Erie Canal***

This pastoral view of the Erie Canal near Lockport, New York, painted by artist John William Hill, hints at this waterway's profound impact on American life. Without the canal, the town in the background would not exist and farmers such as the man in the foreground would not have a regional market for their cattle and grain. The success of the Erie Canal had led to the construction of a vast system of canals by 1860. This infrastructure was as important to the nation as the railroad network of the late nineteenth century and the interstate highway and airport transportation systems of the late twentieth century. © Bettmann/Corbis.

moved along the canal at a steady 30 miles a day, cutting transportation costs and accelerating the flow of goods. In 1818, the mills in Rochester, New York, processed 26,000 barrels of flour for export east (and north to Montreal, for sale as "Canadian" produce to the West Indies); ten years later, their output soared to 200,000 barrels; and by 1840, it was at 500,000 barrels.

The spectacular benefits of the Erie Canal prompted a national canal boom. Civic and business leaders in Philadelphia and Baltimore proposed waterways to link their cities to the Midwest. Copying New York's fiscal innovations, they persuaded their state legislatures to invest directly in canal companies or to force state-chartered banks to do so. They also won state guarantees that encouraged British and Dutch investors; as one observer noted in 1844, "The prosperity of America, her railroads, canals, steam navigation, and banks, are the fruit of English capital." Soon, artificial waterways connected Philadelphia and Baltimore, via the Pennsylvania Canal and the Chesapeake and Ohio Canal, to the Great Lakes region.

Equally important was the vast network of navigable rivers that drained into the Mississippi. Every year, 25,000 farmer-built flatboats used these waterways to carry produce to New Orleans. In 1848, the completion of the Michigan and Illinois Canal, which linked Chicago to the Mississippi River, completed an inland all-water route from New York City to New Orleans, the two most important port cities in North America (Map 9.3).

The steamboat, another product of the industrial age, added crucial flexibility to the Mississippi basin's river-based transportation system. In 1807, engineer-inventor Robert Fulton built the first American steamboat, the *Clermont*, which he piloted up the Hudson River. To navigate shallow western rivers, engineers broadened steamboats' hulls to reduce their draft and enlarge their cargo capacity. These improved vessels halved the cost of upstream river transport along the Mississippi River and its tributaries and dramatically increased the flow of goods, people, and news. In 1830, a traveler or a letter from New York could reach Buffalo or Pittsburgh by water in less than a week and Detroit, Chicago, or St. Louis in two weeks. In 1800, the same journeys had taken twice as long.

The state and national governments played key roles in developing this interregional network of trade and travel. State legislatures subsidized canals, while the national government created a vast postal system, the first network for the exchange of information. Thanks to the Post Office Act of 1792, there were more than eight thousand post offices by 1830, and they safely delivered thousands of letters and banknotes worth millions of dollars. The U.S. Supreme Court, headed by John Marshall, likewise encouraged interstate trade by firmly establishing federal authority over

**MAP 9.3**

**The Transportation Revolution: Roads and Canals, 1820–1850**

By 1850, the United States had an efficient system of water-borne transportation with three distinct parts. Short canals and navigable rivers carried cotton, tobacco, and other products from the countryside of the southern seaboard states into the Atlantic commercial system. A second system, centered on the Erie, Chesapeake and Ohio, and Pennsylvania Mainline canals, linked northeastern seaports to the vast trans-Appalachian region. Finally, a set of regional canals in the Midwest connected most of the Great Lakes region to the Ohio and Mississippi rivers and the port of New Orleans.

interstate commerce (Chapter 7). In *Gibbons v. Ogden* (1824), the Court voided a New York law that created a monopoly on steamboat travel into New York City. That decision prevented local or state monopolies — or tariffs — from impeding the flow of goods, people, and news across the nation.

**Railroads Link the North and Midwest**    In the 1850s, railroads, another technological innovation, joined canals as the core of the national transportation system (Map 9.4). In 1852, canals carried twice the tonnage transported by railroads. Then, capitalists in Boston, New York, and London secured state charters for railroads and invested heavily in new lines, which by 1860 had become the main carriers of wheat and freight from the Midwest to the Northeast. Serviced by a vast network of locomotive and freight-car repair shops, the Erie, Pennsylvania, New York Central, and the Baltimore and Ohio railroads connected the Atlantic ports — New York, Philadelphia, and Baltimore — with the rapidly expanding Great Lakes cities of Cleveland and Chicago (Thinking Like a Historian, p. 298).

The railroad boom also linked these western cities to adjacent states. Chicago-based railroads carried huge quantities of lumber from Michigan to the treeless prairies of Indiana, Illinois, Iowa, and Missouri, where settlers built 250,000 new farms (covering 19 million acres) and hundreds of small towns. On their

return journey, the trains moved millions of bushels of wheat to Chicago for transport to eastern markets. Increasingly, they also carried livestock to Chicago's slaughterhouses. In Jacksonville, Illinois, a farmer decided to feed his entire corn crop of 1,500 bushels "to hogs & cattle, as we think it is more profitable than to sell the corn." A Chicago newspaper boasted, "In ancient times all roads led to Rome; in modern times all roads lead to Chicago."

Initially, midwestern settlers relied on manufactured goods imported from the Northeast. They bought high-quality shovels and spades fabricated at the Delaware Iron Works and the Oliver Ames Company in Easton, Massachusetts; axes forged in Connecticut factories; and steel horseshoes manufactured in Troy, New York. However, by the 1840s, midwestern entrepreneurs were also producing machine tools, hardware, furniture, and especially agricultural implements. Working as a blacksmith in Grand Detour, Illinois, John Deere made his first steel plow out of old saws in 1837; ten years later, he opened a factory in Moline, Illinois, that mass-produced the plows. Stronger than the existing cast-iron models built in New York, Deere's steel plows allowed farmers to cut through the thick sod of the prairies. Other midwestern companies — such as McCormick and Hussey — mass-produced self-raking reapers that harvested 12 acres of grain a day (rather than the 2 acres that an adult worker could

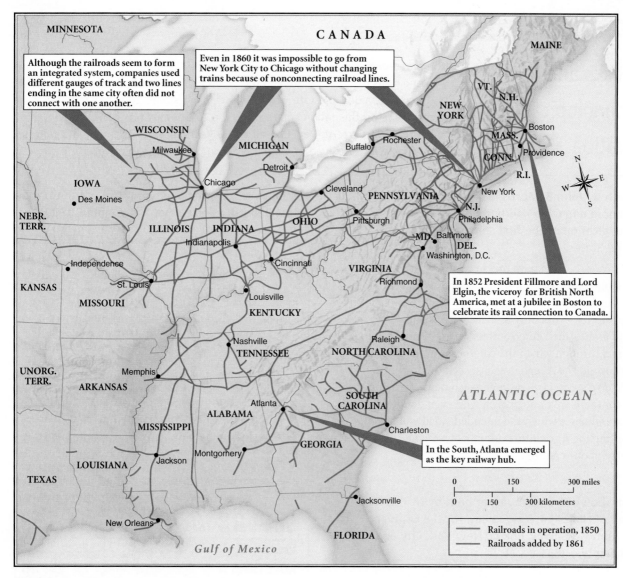

Although the railroads seem to form an integrated system, companies used different gauges of track and two lines ending in the same city often did not connect with one another.

Even in 1860 it was impossible to go from New York City to Chicago without changing trains because of nonconnecting railroad lines.

In 1852 President Fillmore and Lord Elgin, the viceroy for British North America, met at a jubilee in Boston to celebrate its rail connection to Canada.

In the South, Atlanta emerged as the key railway hub.

—— Railroads in operation, 1850
—— Railroads added by 1861

**MAP 9.4**

**Railroads of the North and South, 1850 and 1861**

In the decade before the Civil War, entrepreneurs in the Northeast and the Midwest financed thousands of miles of new railroad lines, creating an extensive and dense transportation system that stimulated economic development. The South built a more limited railroad system. In all regions, railroad companies used different track gauges, which prevented the efficient flow of traffic.

cut by hand). With the harvest bottleneck removed, farmers planted more acres and grew even more wheat. Flour soon accounted for 10 percent of all American exports to foreign markets.

Interregional trade also linked southern cotton planters to northeastern textile plants and foreign markets. This commerce in raw cotton bolstered the wealth of white southerners but did not transform their economic and social order as it did in the Midwest. With the exception of Richmond, Virginia, and a few other places, southern planters did not invest their

profits in manufacturing. Lacking cities, factories, and highly trained workers, the South remained tied to agriculture, even as the commerce in wheat, corn, and livestock promoted diversified economies in the Northeast and Midwest.

## The Growth of Cities and Towns

The expansion of industry and trade dramatically increased America's urban population. In 1820, there were 58 towns with more than 2,500 inhabitants; by

## The Risks and Rewards of Technological Innovation

The nineteenth century was the Age of Progress, and improved transportation was one of its hallmarks. Between the 1830s and the 1860s, American capitalists and workers, aided by state governments, built steam-powered railroads that stretched across the nation and reduced the cost of moving goods and people by more than 90 percent. Yet, like all major technological changes, the railroad revolution was controversial, expensive, and politically explosive.

1. **Speech by John B. Morris, a director of the Baltimore and Ohio Railroad, July 4, 1828, at the dedication of the first steam railway in the United States.**

*Fellow-Citizens.* . . . We have met to celebrate the laying of the first stone of the Baltimore and Ohio Railroad. . . . The result of our labors will be felt, not only by ourselves, but also by posterity, — not only by Baltimore, but also by Maryland and by the United States. We are about opening the channel through which the commerce of the mighty country beyond the Alleghany must seek the [Atlantic] ocean. . . . We are in fact commencing a new era in our history; for there are none present who even doubt the beneficial influence which the intended Road will have in promoting the Agriculture, Manufactures and Inland Commerce of our country.

2. **Illustration of a passenger car built by M. P. & M. E. Green of Hoboken, New Jersey, for the Camden and Amboy Railway, linking New York City and Philadelphia, 1831.**

Source: Division of Work & Industry, National Museum of American History, Smithsonian Institution.

3. **Poster protesting the laying of tracks through the "most Beautiful Streets" of Philadelphia, 1839.**

Source: National Archives.

4. **Opposition to the state financing of railroads from the *Republican Compiler*, Gettysburg, Pennsylvania, October 6, 1851.** *As American track mileage grew from 3,000 miles in 1840 to 30,000 miles by 1860, entrepreneurs in Pennsylvania, assisted by the state legislature, led the nation in laying rail.*

The Governor's organ [newspaper] is still harping about the Governor having paid off the State debt, and reducing the taxes. If the taxes have been reduced, why is it that every farmer finds that he has paid MORE TAXES the last year than he has ever paid in a single year before? . . . The true issue is that Gov. Johnston and his friends created the [huge state] debt. . . .

The people remember that Gov. Johnston voted $405,000 to the Gettysburg railroad. . . .

They remember that he voted $150,000 to the Danville and Pottsville railroad.

They remember that he voted $140,000 to the Laughlintown and Pittsburg railroad, that never was incorporated.

They remember that he voted $120,000 to the Norristown railroad.

They remember that he voted for a bill appropriating over THREE MILLIONS OF DOLLARS to State and company improvements in one year, and that Gov. Ritner said that such appropriations would increase the State debt, in four years, to $45,000,000.

### 5. Lyrics to "The Waggoner's Curse," c. 1850.

Come all ye bold wagoners turn out man by man
That's opposed to the railroad or any such a plan;
'Tis once I made money by driving my team
But the goods are now hauled on the railroad by steam. . . .

If we go to Philadelphia, inquiring for a load,
They'll tell us quite directly it's gone out on the railroad.
The rich folks, the plan they may justly admire,
But it ruins us poor wag'ners and it makes our taxes
    higher . . .

It ruins wheelwrights, blacksmiths, and every other trade,
So damned be all the railroads that ever was made.
It ruins our mechanics, what think you of it, then?
And it fills our country full of just a lot of great rich men.

The ships they will be coming with Irishmen by loads,
All with their picks and shovels, to work on the railroads;
When they get on the railroad, it is then that they are fixed
They'll fight just like the devil with their cudgels and their
    sticks.

The American with safety can scarcely ever pass,
For they will blacken both his eyes for one word of his sass
If it wasn't for the torment I as life would be in hell,
As upon the cursed railroad, or upon the canal.

### 6. Henry David Thoreau, *Walden, or, Life in the Woods*, 1854. *The workers who built and ran the railroads suffered high rates of injury and death—facts noted by Henry David Thoreau, a critic of the market, transportation, and industrial revolutions of his day.*

We do not ride on the railroad; it rides upon us. Did you ever think what those sleepers are that underlie the railroad? Each one is a man. . . . The rails are laid

on them, and they are covered with sand, and the cars run smoothly over them . . . ; so that, if some have the pleasure of riding on a rail, others have the misfortune to be ridden upon.

### 7. Senator L. J. Rose, from *Testimony Taken by the United States Pacific Railway Commission*, 1887.

The railroads have made Southern California what it is to-day. Before the completion of the . . . Union and Central Pacific roads the southern half of California, which is now famous the world over as the most favored quarter in America in point of climate and soil conditions, was no more nor less than a barren sheep pasture. . . . Our redemption came in 1869, when the railroad people completed that gigantic and wonderful work . . . , giving California a direct rail connection with the East. The effect was marvelous and immediate. . . . We beheld ourselves in a day, as it were, surrounded by possibilities which made us a new and different people, in a new and completely changed land.

---

Sources: (1) Eli Bowen, *Rambles in the Path of the Steam-Horse* (Philadelphia: Wm. Bromwell and Wm. White Smith, 1855), 37; (4) Adapted from ExplorePAhistory.com; (5) George Korson, ed., *Pennsylvania Songs and Legends* (Philadelphia: University of Pennsylvania Press, 1949), 255–257; (6) Henry David Thoreau, *Walden, or, Life in the Woods*, 1854 (Boston, 1910), 102; (7) *Testimony Taken by the United States Pacific Railway Commission*, Vol. 5 (Washington, D.C.: Government Printing Office, 1887), 2505.

### ANALYZING THE EVIDENCE

1. What does source 1 tell us about the hopes of steam railroad pioneers? Do the other sources suggest their hopes were achieved?

2. What does source 2 suggest about early railroad design and marketing? How does this image contrast with source 3? What threats does source 3 highlight? What audiences were the targets of these illustrations, and how successful are their respective messages?

3. According to source 4, how did Pennsylvania raise the money for these subsidies? Who was left holding the bag? Why would governments fund such private enterprises?

4. What social tensions do the lyrics to source 5 reveal? What other conflicts are manifest in the documents presented here?

5. Who are the "sleepers" in source 6? How does Thoreau calculate the cost of progress? How are these costs similar to or different from the ones described by the author of source 5?

### PUTTING IT ALL TOGETHER

After re-reading the section in this chapter on the transportation revolution, answer the following questions: Why did the transportation revolution take place? What roles in the spread of the railway, canals, and turnpikes were played by entrepreneurs and capitalists? By governments, taxpayers, and various groups of workers? What were some of the unintended consequences? Who won? Lost? Using these documents and your answers, write an essay assessing the benefits and costs of the transition to new transportation technologies.

1840, there were 126 such towns, located mostly in the Northeast and Midwest. During those two decades, the total number of city dwellers grew more than fourfold, from 443,000 to 1,844,000.

The fastest growth occurred in the new industrial towns that sprouted along the "fall line," where rivers descended rapidly from the Appalachian Mountains to the coastal plain. In 1822, the Boston Manufacturing Company built a complex of mills in a sleepy Merrimack River village that quickly became the bustling textile factory town of Lowell, Massachusetts. The towns of Hartford, Connecticut; Trenton, New Jersey; and Wilmington, Delaware, also became urban centers as mill owners exploited the water power of their rivers and recruited workers from the countryside.

**COMPARE AND CONTRAST**

What different types of cities emerged between 1820 and 1860, and what caused their growth?

Western commercial cities such as Pittsburgh, Cincinnati, and New Orleans grew almost as rapidly. These cities expanded initially as transit centers, where workers transferred goods from farmers' rafts and wagons to steamboats or railroads. As the midwestern population grew during the 1830s and 1840s, St. Louis, Detroit, and especially Buffalo and Chicago also emerged as dynamic centers of commerce. "There can

be no two places in the world," journalist Margaret Fuller wrote from Chicago in 1843, "more completely thoroughfares than this place and Buffalo. . . . The life-blood [of commerce] rushes from east to west, and back again from west to east." To a German visitor, Chicago seemed "for the most part to consist of shops . . . [as if] people came here merely to trade, to make money, and not to live." Chicago's merchants and bankers developed the marketing, provisioning, and financial services essential to farmers and small-town shopkeepers in its vast hinterland. "There can be no better [market] any where in the Union," declared a farmer in Paw Paw, Illinois.

These midwestern hubs quickly became manufacturing centers. Capitalizing on the cities' links to rivers, canals, and railroads, entrepreneurs built warehouses, flour mills, packing plants, and machine shops, creating work for hundreds of artisans and factory laborers. In 1846, Cyrus McCormick moved his reaper factory from western Virginia to Chicago to be closer to his midwestern customers. By 1860, St. Louis and Chicago had become the nation's eighth- and ninth-largest cities; by 1870, they were the fourth and fifth, behind New York, Philadelphia, and Brooklyn (Map 9.5).

The old Atlantic seaports—Boston, Philadelphia, Baltimore, Charleston, and especially New York City—

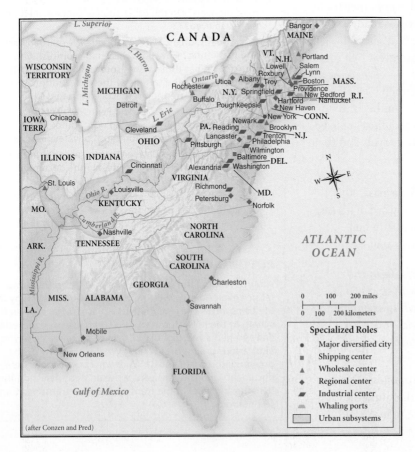

**MAP 9.5**

**The Nation's Major Cities, 1840**

By 1840, the United States boasted three major conglomerations of cities. The long-settled ports on the Atlantic—from Boston to Baltimore—served as centers for import merchants, banks, insurance companies, and manufacturers of ready-made clothing, and their financial reach extended far into the interior—nationwide in the case of New York City. A second group of cities stretched along the Great Lakes and included the commercial hubs of Buffalo, Detroit, and Chicago, as well as the manufacturing center of Cleveland. A third urban system extended along the Ohio River, comprising the industrial cities of Pittsburgh and Cincinnati and the wholesale centers of Louisville and St. Louis.

remained important for their foreign commerce and, increasingly, as centers of finance and small-scale manufacturing. New York City and nearby Brooklyn grew at a phenomenal rate: between 1820 and 1860, their combined populations increased nearly tenfold to 1 million people, thanks to the arrival of hundreds of thousands of German and Irish immigrants. Drawing on these workers, New York became a center of the ready-made clothing industry, which relied on thousands of low-paid seamstresses. "The wholesale clothing establishments are . . . absorbing the business of the country," a "Country Tailor" complained to the *New York Tribune*, "casting many an honest and hardworking man out of employment [and helping] . . . the large cities to swallow up the small towns."

New York City's growth stemmed primarily from its dominant position in foreign and domestic trade. It had the best harbor in the United States and, thanks to the Erie Canal, was the best gateway to the Midwest and the best outlet for western grain. Recognizing the city's advantages, in 1818 four English Quaker merchants founded the Black Ball Line to carry cargo, people, and mail between New York and London, Liverpool, and Le Havre, establishing the first regularly scheduled transatlantic shipping service. By 1840, its port handled almost two-thirds of foreign imports into the United States, almost half of all foreign trade, and much of the immigrant traffic. New York likewise monopolized trade with the newly independent South American nations of Brazil, Peru, and Venezuela, and its merchants took over the trade in cotton by offering finance, insurance, and shipping to southern planters and merchants.

# New Social Classes and Cultures

The Industrial Revolution and the Market Revolution improved the lives of many Americans, who now lived in larger houses, cooked on iron stoves, and wore better-made clothes. Yet in the booming cities, the new economic order spawned distinct social classes: a small but wealthy business elite, a substantial middle class, and a mass of propertyless wage earners. By creating a class-divided society, industrialization posed a momentous challenge to America's republican ideals.

## The Business Elite

Before industrialization, white Americans thought of their society in terms of rank: "notable" families had higher status than those from the "lower orders." Yet in rural areas, people of different ranks often shared a common culture. Gentlemen farmers talked easily with yeomen about crop yields, while their wives conversed about the art of quilting. In the South, humble tenants and aristocratic slave owners enjoyed the same amusements: gambling, cockfighting, and horse racing. Rich and poor attended the same Quaker meetinghouse or Presbyterian church. "Almost everyone eats, drinks, and dresses in the same way," a European visitor to Hartford, Connecticut, reported in 1798, "and one can see the most obvious inequality only in the dwellings."

The Industrial Revolution shattered this agrarian social order and fragmented society into distinct classes and cultures. The urban economy made a few city residents — the merchants, manufacturers, bankers, and landlords who made up the business elite — very rich. In 1800, the richest 10 percent of the nation's families owned about 40 percent of the wealth; by 1860, they held nearly 70 percent. In New York, Chicago, Baltimore, and New Orleans, the super-rich — the top 1 percent — owned more than 40 percent of the land, buildings, and other tangible property and an even higher share of intangible property, such as stocks and bonds.

Government tax policies facilitated the accumulation of wealth. There were no federal taxes on individual and corporate income. Rather, the U.S. Treasury raised most of its revenue from tariffs: regressive taxes on textiles and other imported goods purchased mostly by ordinary citizens. State and local governments also favored the wealthy. They taxed real estate (farms, city lots, and buildings) and tangible personal property (furniture, tools, and machinery), but almost never taxed stocks and bonds or the inheritances the rich passed on to their children.

As cities expanded in size and wealth, affluent families consciously set themselves apart. They dressed in well-tailored clothes, rode in fancy carriages, and bought expensively furnished houses tended by butlers, cooks, and other servants. The women no longer socialized with those of lesser wealth, and the men no longer labored side by side with their employees. Instead, they became managers and directors and relied on trusted subordinates to supervise hundreds of factory operatives. Increasingly, merchants, manufacturers, and bankers placed a premium on privacy and lived in separate neighborhoods, often in exclusive central areas or at the city's edge. The geographic isolation of privileged families and the massive flow of immigrants into separate districts

**TRACE CHANGE OVER TIME**
How and why did elite families change between 1800 and 1860?

**Hartford Family**
Completely at home in their elegant drawing room, this elite family in Hartford, Connecticut, enjoys the fruits of the father's business success. As the father lounges in his silk robe, his eldest son (and presumptive heir) adopts an air of studied nonchalance, and his daughter fingers a piano, signaling her musical accomplishments and the family's gentility. A diminutive African American servant (her size suggesting her status) serves fruit to the lavishly attired woman of the house. The sumptuously appointed drawing room reflects the owners' prosperity and their aesthetic and cultural interests. © White House Historical Association/Photo by National Geographic Society.

divided cities spatially along lines of class, race, and ethnicity.

## The Middle Class

Standing between wealthy owners and propertyless wage earners was a growing **middle class** — the social product of increased commerce. The "middling class," a Boston printer explained, was made up of "the farmers, the mechanics, the manufacturers, the traders, who carry on professionally the ordinary operations of buying, selling, and exchanging merchandize." Professionals with other skills — building contractors, lawyers, surveyors, and so on — were suddenly in great demand and well compensated, as were middling business owners and white-collar clerks. In the Northeast, men with these qualifications numbered about 30 percent of the population in the 1840s. But they also could be found in small towns of the agrarian Midwest and South. In 1854, the cotton boomtown of Oglethorpe, Georgia (population 2,500), boasted eighty "business houses" and eight hotels.

The emergence of the middle class reflected a dramatic rise in prosperity. Between 1830 and 1857, the per capita income of Americans increased by about 2.5 percent a year, a remarkable rate that has never since

**The Social Dimensions of Whaling**

Whale oil fueled the lamps that illuminated the houses of well-to-do Americans in the early nineteenth century, and bright spermaceti candles made from the waxy substance in the heads of sperm whales graced their dining tables. To provide these luxuries, five hundred ships from New Bedford, Massachusetts, and the nearby island of Nantucket roamed the world on voyages lasting up to three years. Ten thousand workers—young men seeking adventure and veteran white and black sailors—manned the ships. As this painting, *Capturing a Sperm Whale* by William Page (1835, from a sketch by whaler C. B. Hulsart), suggests, whaling was a dangerous trade that took the lives of many men. © Peabody Essex Museum, Salem, Massachusetts, USA/The Bridgeman Art Library.

been matched. This surge in income, along with an abundance of inexpensive mass-produced goods, fostered a distinct middle-class urban culture. Middle-class husbands earned enough to save about 15 percent of their income, which they used to buy well-built houses in a "respectable part of town." They purchased handsome clothes and drove to work and play in smart carriages. Middle-class wives became purveyors of genteel culture, buying books, pianos, lithographs, and comfortable furniture for their front parlors. Upper-middle-class families hired Irish or African American domestic servants, while less prosperous folk enjoyed the comforts provided by new industrial goods. The middle class outfitted their residences with furnaces (to warm the entire house and heat water for bathing), cooking stoves with ovens, and Singer's treadle-operated sewing machines. Some urban families now kept their perishable food in iceboxes, which

ice-company wagons periodically refilled, and bought many varieties of packaged goods. As early as 1825, the Underwood Company of Boston was marketing jars of well-preserved Atlantic salmon.

If material comfort was one distinguishing mark of the middle class, moral and mental discipline was another. Middle-class writers denounced raucous carnivals and festivals as a "chaos of sin and folly, of misery and fun" and, by the 1830s, had largely suppressed them. Ambitious parents were equally concerned with their children's moral and intellectual development. To help their offspring succeed in life, middle-class parents often provided them with a high school education (in an era when most white children received only five years of schooling) and stressed the importance of discipline and hard work. American Protestants had long

**UNDERSTAND POINTS OF VIEW**

What were the moral values and material culture of the urban middle class?

[Fig. 130. Plain Timber Cottage-Villa.]

[Fig. 131. Principal Floor.]

**Architecture for the Emergent Middle Class**

This dwelling was well suited for a "farmer of wealth" or a middle-class suburbanite, according to Andrew Downing, author of *The Architecture of Country Houses* (1850). The exterior of the house exhibited "a considerable degree of elegance," while the interior boasted a substantial drawing room and dining room, for the entertainment of guests, and a parlor for more intimate conversations among family and friends. Downing's books helped to define the culture of the growing middle class and diffuse it across the nation. Andrew J. Downing, *The Architecture of Country Houses*, 1850.

believed that diligent work in an earthly "calling" was a duty owed to God. Now the business elite and the middle class gave this idea a secular twist by celebrating work as the key to individual social mobility and national prosperity.

Benjamin Franklin gave the classic expression of this secular work ethic in his *Autobiography*, which was published in full in 1818 (thirty years after his death) and immediately found a huge audience. Heeding Franklin's

**PLACE EVENTS IN CONTEXT**
How did the increasingly urban, capitalist economy of the northeastern states affect the lives of poor workers?

suggestion that an industrious man would become a rich one, tens of thousands of young American men saved their money, adopted temperate habits, and aimed to rise in the world. There was an "almost universal ambition to get forward," observed Hezekiah Niles, editor of *Niles' Weekly Register*. Warner Myers, a Philadelphia housepainter, rose from poverty by saving his wages, borrowing from his family and friends, and becoming a builder, eventually constructing and selling sixty houses. Countless children's books, magazine stories, self-help manuals, and novels recounted the tales of similar individuals. The **self-made man** became a central theme of American popular culture and inspired many men (and a few women) to seek success. Just as the yeoman ethic had served as a unifying ideal in pre-1800 agrarian America, so the gospel of personal achievement linked the middle and business classes of the new industrializing society.

## Urban Workers and the Poor

As thoughtful business leaders surveyed their society, they concluded that the yeoman farmer and artisan-republican ideal—a social order of independent producers—was no longer possible. "Entire independence ought not to be wished for," Ithamar A. Beard, the paymaster of the Hamilton Manufacturing Company (in Lowell, Massachusetts), told a mechanics' association in 1827. "In large manufacturing towns, many more must fill subordinate stations and must be under the immediate direction and control of a master or superintendent, than in the farming towns."

Beard had a point. In 1840, all of the nation's slaves, some 2.5 million people, and about half of its adult white workers, another 3 million, were laboring for others. The bottom 10 percent of white wage earners consisted of casual workers hired on a short-term basis for arduous jobs. Poor women washed clothes; their husbands and sons carried lumber and bricks for construction projects, loaded ships, and dug out dirt and stones to build canals. When they could find jobs, these men earned "their dollar per diem," a longtime resident told readers of the *Baltimore American*, but they could never save enough "to pay rent, buy fire wood and eatables" when the job market or the harbor froze up. During business depressions, casual laborers suffered and died; in good times, their jobs were temporary and dangerous.

Other laborers had greater security of employment, but few were prospering. In Massachusetts in 1825, an unskilled worker earned about two-thirds as much as a mechanic did; two decades later, it was less than half as much. A journeyman carpenter in Philadelphia reported that he was about "even with the World" after several years of work but that many of his coworkers were in debt. The 18,000 women who sewed men's ready-made clothing in New York City in the 1850s earned just a few pennies a day, less than $100 a year (about $3,000 today). Such meager wages barely paid for food and rent, so poorer workers could not take advantage of the rapidly falling prices of manufactured goods. Only the most fortunate working-class families could afford to educate their children, buy apprenticeships for their sons, or accumulate small dowries for their daughters. Most families sent ten-year-old children out to work, and the death of a parent often threw the survivors into dire poverty. As a charity worker noted, "What can a bereaved widow do, with 5 or 6 little children, destitute of every means of support but what her own hands can furnish (which in a general way does not amount to more than 25 cents a day)?"

Impoverished workers congregated in dilapidated housing in bad neighborhoods. Single men and women lived in crowded boardinghouses, while families jammed themselves into tiny apartments in the basements and attics of small houses. As immigrants poured in after 1840, urban populations soared, and developers squeezed more and more dwellings and foul-smelling outhouses onto a single lot. Venturing into the New York City slums in the 1850s, shocked state legislators found gaunt, shivering people with "wild ghastly faces" living amid "hideous squalor and deadly effluvia, the dim, undrained courts oozing with pollution, the dark, narrow stairways, decayed with age, reeking with filth, overrun with vermin." Many wage earners sought solace in alcohol, leading to fistfights, brawls, and robberies. The urban police, mostly low-paid watchmen and untrained constables, were unable to contain the lawlessness.

## The Benevolent Empire

The disorder among wage earners alarmed the rising middle classes, who wanted safe cities and a disciplined workforce. To improve the world around them, many upwardly mobile men and women embraced religious benevolence. Led by Congregational and Presbyterian ministers, they created organizations of conservative social reform that historians call the **Benevolent Empire**, which became prominent in the 1820s. The reformers' goal was to restore "the moral government of God" by reducing the consumption of alcohol and other vices that resulted in poverty, explained Presbyterian minister Lyman Beecher. Reform-minded

individuals had regulated their own behavior; now they tried to control the lives of working people — by persuasion if possible, by law if necessary.

The Benevolent Empire targeted age-old evils such as drunkenness, adultery, prostitution, and crime, but its methods were new. Instead of relying on church sermons and admonitions from community leaders to combat evil, the reformers created large-scale organizations: the Prison Discipline Society and the American Society for the Promotion of Temperance, among many others. Each organization had a managing staff, a network of hundreds of chapters, thousands of volunteer members, and a newspaper.

**IDENTIFY CAUSES**
What was the Benevolent Empire, and why did it emerge at this specific historical moment?

Often acting in concert, these benevolent groups worked to improve society. First, they encouraged people to lead disciplined lives and acquire "regular habits." They persuaded local governments to ban carnivals of drink and dancing, such as Negro Election Day (festivities in which African Americans symbolically took control of the government), which had been enjoyed by whites as well as blacks. Second, they devised new institutions to help the needy and control the unruly. Reformers provided homes of refuge for abandoned children and asylums for the insane, who previously had been confined by their families in attics and cellars. They campaigned to end corporal punishment of criminals and to rehabilitate them in specially designed penitentiaries.

Women formed a crucial part of the Benevolent Empire. Since the 1790s, upper-class women had sponsored charitable organizations such as the Society for the Relief of Poor Widows with Small Children, founded in 1797 in New York by Isabella Graham, a devout Presbyterian widow. Her daughter Joanna Bethune set up other charitable institutions, including the Orphan Asylum Society and the Society for the Promotion of Industry, which found jobs for hundreds of poor women as spinners and seamstresses.

Some reformers believed that declining observance by Christians of the Sabbath (Sunday) as a day devoted to religion was the greatest threat to the "moral government of God." As the Market Revolution spread, merchants and storekeepers conducted business on Sundays, and urban saloons provided drink and entertainment. To halt these profane activities, Lyman Beecher and other ministers founded the General Union for Promoting the Observance of the Christian Sabbath in 1828. General Union chapters, replete with women's auxiliaries, sprang up from Maine to

Cincinnati and beyond. The General Union demanded that Congress repeal an 1810 law allowing mail to be transported — though not delivered — on Sundays. Members boycotted shipping companies that did business on the Sabbath and campaigned for municipal laws forbidding games and festivals on the Lord's day.

The Benevolent Empire's efforts to impose its **Sabbatarian values** provoked opposition from workers and freethinkers. Men who labored twelve to fourteen hours a day, six days a week, wanted the freedom to spend their one day of leisure as they wished. To keep goods moving, shipping company managers demanded that the Erie Canal provide lockkeepers on Sundays; using laws to enforce a particular set of moral beliefs was "contrary to the free spirit of our institutions," they said. When evangelical reformers proposed teaching Christianity to slaves, they aroused hostility among white southerners. This popular resistance by workers and planters limited the success of the Benevolent Empire.

**IDENTIFY CAUSES**
Who opposed the work of the Benevolent Empire and why?

## Charles Grandison Finney: Revivalism and Reform

Presbyterian minister Charles Grandison Finney found a new way to propagate religious values. Finney was not part of the traditional religious elite. Born into a poor farming family in Connecticut, he had planned to become a lawyer and rise into the middle class. But in 1823, Finney underwent an intense religious experience and chose the ministry as his career. Beginning in towns along the Erie Canal, the young minister conducted emotional revival meetings that stressed conversion rather than doctrine. Repudiating Calvinist beliefs, he preached that God would welcome any sinner who submitted to the Holy Spirit. Finney's ministry drew on — and greatly accelerated — the Second Great Awakening, the wave of Protestant revivalism that had begun after the Revolution (Chapter 8).

**Evangelical Beliefs** Finney's central message was that "God has made man a **moral free agent**" who could choose salvation. This doctrine of free will was particularly attractive to members of the new middle class, who had accepted personal responsibility for their lives, improved their material condition, and welcomed Finney's assurance that heaven was also within their grasp. But Finney also had great success in converting people at both ends of the social spectrum, from the haughty rich who had placed themselves

**Charles Grandison Finney, Evangelist (1792–1875)**
When an unknown artist painted this flattering portrait in 1834, Finney was forty-two years old and at the height of his career as an evangelist. Handsome and charismatic, Finney had just led a series of enormously successful revivals in Rochester, New York, and other cities along the Erie Canal. In 1835, he established a theology department at newly founded Oberlin College in Ohio, where he trained a generation of ministers and served as president from 1851 to 1866. Oberlin College Archives.

above God, to the abject poor who seemed lost to drink and sloth. Finney celebrated their common fellowship in Christ and identified them spiritually with pious middle-class respectability.

Finney's most spectacular triumph came in 1830, when he moved his revivals from small towns to Rochester, New York, now a major milling and commercial city on the Erie Canal. Preaching every day for six months and promoting group prayer meetings in family homes, Finney won over the influential merchants and manufacturers of Rochester. They promised to attend church, give up intoxicating beverages, and work hard. To encourage their employees to do the same, wealthy businessmen founded a Free Presbyterian Church — "free" because members did not have to pay for pew space. Other evangelical Protestants founded churches to serve transient canal laborers, and pious businessmen set up a savings bank to encourage thrift among the working classes. Meanwhile, Finney's wife,

Lydia, and other middle-class women carried the Christian message to the wives of the unconverted, set up Sunday schools for poor children, and formed the Female Charitable Society to assist the unemployed.

Finney's efforts to create a spiritual Christian community were not completely successful. Skilled workers in strong craft organizations — boot makers, carpenters, stonemasons, and boatbuilders — protested that they needed higher wages and better schools more urgently than sermons and prayers. Poor people ignored Finney's revival, as did Irish Catholic immigrants, many of whom hated Protestants as religious heretics and political oppressors.

Nonetheless, revivalists from New England to the Midwest copied Finney's evangelical message and techniques. In New York City, wealthy silk merchants Arthur and Lewis Tappan founded a magazine, *The Christian Evangelist*, that promoted Finney's ideas. The revivals swept through Pennsylvania, North Carolina, Tennessee, and Indiana, where, a convert reported, "you could not go upon the street and hear any conversation,

except upon religion." The success of the revivals "has been so general and thorough," concluded a Presbyterian general assembly, "that the whole customs of society have changed."

**Temperance** The temperance movement was the most successful social reform. Beer and rum had long been standard fare in American rituals: patriotic ceremonies, work breaks, barn raisings, and games. Long before the arrival of spirit-drinking Irish and beer-drinking German immigrants, grogshops dotted almost every block in working-class districts and were centers of disorder. During the 1820s and 1830s, alcohol consumption reached new heights, even among the elite; alcoholism killed Daniel Tompkins, vice president under James Monroe, and undermined Henry Clay's bid for the presidency. Heavy drinking was especially devastating for wage earners, who could ill afford its costs. Although Methodist artisans and ambitious

> **EXPLAIN CONSEQUENCES**
> What was Finney's central message, and how did it influence the work of reform movements?

**The Drunkard's Progress: From the First Glass to the Grave**

This 1846 lithograph, published by N. Currier, suggests the inevitable fate of those who drink. The drunkard's descent into "Poverty and Disease" ends with "Death by suicide," leaving a grieving and destitute wife and child. Temperance reformers urged Americans to take "The Cold Water Cure" by drinking water instead of alcoholic beverages. To promote abstinence among the young, in 1836 revivalist preacher Reverend Thomas Poage Hunt founded the Cold Water Army, an organization that grew to embrace several hundred thousand children, all of whom pledged "perpetual hate to all that can Intoxicate." Library of Congress.

## A Debate over Catholic Immigration

Between 1776 and 1830, few immigrants came to the United States. Then, increasing population and poverty in Europe prompted the migration of hundreds of thousands of Germans (both Catholics and Protestants) and Irish Catholics. The sudden arrival of foreign Catholics amidst the intense Protestantism of the Second Great Awakening led to religious riots, the formation of the nativist American Party, and sharp debates in the public press. Contemporary pamphlets and books offer historians access to the public rhetoric (and the private passions) of the time.

### Lyman Beecher

### Catholicism Is Incompatible with Republicanism

Lyman Beecher (1775–1863) was a leading Protestant minister and the father of a remarkable family: the influential minister Henry Ward Beecher and authors Harriet Beecher Stowe (*Uncle Tom's Cabin*) and Catharine Beecher (*A Treatise on Domestic Economy*). In *A Plea for the West* (1835), Lyman Beecher warned Protestants of the powerful priestly hierarchy of the Roman Catholic Church and its opposition to republicanism. Papal encyclicals issued by Pope Gregory XVI (*Mirari Vos*, 1832) and Pope Pius IX (*Quanta Cura*, 1864) condemned republicanism, freedom of conscience, and the separation of church and state as false political ideologies.

Since the irruption of the northern barbarians, the world has never witnessed such a rush of dark-minded population from one country to another, as is now leaving Europe, and dashing upon our shores. . . . They come, also, not undirected. . . . [They] are led or followed quickly by a Catholic priesthood, who maintain over them in the land of strangers and unknown tongues an [absolute] ascendancy. . . .

The ministers of no Protestant sect could or would dare to attempt to regulate the votes of their people as the Catholic priests can do, who . . . have almost unlimited power over the conscience as it respects the performance of every civil or social duty.

There is another point of dissimilarity. . . . The opinions of the Protestant clergy are congenial with liberty — they are chosen by the people who have been educated as freemen, and they are dependent on them for patronage and support. The Catholic system is adverse to liberty, and the clergy to a great extent are dependent on foreigners [the pope and European bishops] opposed to the principles of our government.

Nor is this all. . . . How many mechanics, merchants, lawyers, physicians, in any political crisis, might [the priests] reach and render timid . . . ? A tenth part of the suffrage of the nation, thus condensed and wielded by the Catholic powers of Europe, might decide our elections, perplex our policy, inflame and divide the nation, break the bond of our union, and throw down our free institutions. . . .

[Catholicism is] a religion which never prospered but in alliance with despotic governments, has always been and still is the inflexible enemy of Liberty of conscience and free inquiry, and at this moment is the main stay of the battle against republican institutions.

Source: Lyman Beecher, *A Plea for the West* (Cincinnati: Truman & Smith, 1835), 72–73, 126, 59–63, 85–86, 59.

### Orestes Brownson

### Catholicism as a Necessity for Popular Government

Like Lyman Beecher, Orestes Brownson was born into the Presbyterian Church, but he quickly grew dissatisfied with its doctrines. After experimenting with Unitarianism, communalism, socialism, and transcendentalism, Brownson converted to Catholicism in 1844. A zealous convert, Brownson defended Catholicism with rigorous, provocative arguments in this article, "Catholicity Necessary to Sustain Popular Liberty" (1845).

Without the Roman Catholic religion it is impossible to preserve a democratic government, and secure its free, orderly, and wholesome action. . . . The theory of democracy is, Construct your government and commit it to the people to be taken care of . . . as they shall think proper.

It is a beautiful theory, and would work admirably, if it were not for one little difficulty, namely, the people are fallible, both individually and collectively, and governed by their passions and interests, which not unfrequently lead them far astray, and produce much mischief.

We know of but one solution of the difficulty, and that is in RELIGION. There is no foundation for virtue but in religion, and it is only religion that can command the degree of popular virtue and intelligence requisite to insure to popular government the right direction. . . . But what religion? It must be a religion which is above the people and controls them, or it will not answer the purpose. It cannot be Protestantism, [because] . . . the faith and discipline of a [Protestant] sect take any and every direction the public opinion of that sect demands. All is loose, floating, — is here to-day, is there tomorrow, and, next day, may be nowhere . . . according to the prejudices, interests, or habits of the people. . . .

Here, then, is the reason why Protestantism, though it may institute, cannot sustain popular liberty. It is itself subject to popular control, and must follow in all things the popular will, passion, interest, ignorance, prejudice, or caprice.

If Protestantism will not answer the purpose, what religion will? The Roman Catholic, or none. The Roman Catholic religion assumes, as its point of departure, that it is instituted not to be taken care of by the people, but to take care of the people; not to be governed by them, but to govern them. The word is harsh in democratic ears, we admit; but it is not the office of religion to say soft or pleasing words. . . . The people need governing, and must be governed, or nothing but anarchy and destruction await them. They must have a master. . . .

Quote our expression, THE PEOPLE MUST HAVE A MASTER, as you doubtless will; hold it up in glaring capitals, to excite the unthinking and unreasoning multitude, and to doubly fortify their prejudices against Catholicity . . . [even as you] seek to bring the people into subjection to your banks or moneyed corporations. . . .

The Roman Catholic religion, then, is necessary to sustain popular liberty, because popular liberty can be sustained only by a religion free from popular control, above the people, speaking from above and able to command them.

Source: Orestes A. Brownson, *Essays and Reviews, Chiefly on Theology, Politics, and Socialism* (New York: D. & J. Sadlier, 1852), 368–370, 372–373, 376, 379–381.

### QUESTIONS FOR ANALYSIS

1. According to Beecher, what specific dangers does Catholicism pose to American republican institutions? Why do Protestant churches not pose the same dangers?

2. Compare and contrast Brownson's and Beecher's views of the social and political impact of Catholicism. How does Brownson defend the values and practices of the Catholic Church?

3. Given Brownson's statement that "the people must have a master," what would be his view of popular democratic government? Would the leaders of the Protestant Benevolent Empire agree with any aspects of Brownson's social and political philosophy?

craft workers swore off liquor to protect their work skills, health, and finances, other workers drank heavily on the job — and not just during the traditional 11 A.M. and 4 P.M. "refreshers." A baker recalled how "one man was stationed at the window to watch, while the rest drank."

The evangelical Protestants who took over the **American Temperance Society** in 1832 set out to curb the consumption of alcoholic beverages. The society grew quickly to two thousand chapters and more than 200,000 members. Its nationwide campaign employed revivalist methods — group confession and prayer, using women as spiritual guides, and sudden emotional conversion — and was a stunning success. On one day in New York City in 1841, more than 4,000 people took the temperance "pledge." The annual consumption of spirits fell dramatically, from an average of 5 gallons per person in 1830 to 2 gallons in 1845.

Evangelical reformers celebrated religion as the key to moral improvement. Laziness and drinking might be cured by self-discipline, as Benjamin Franklin had argued, but religious conversion would ensure a profound change of heart. Religious discipline and the ideology of social mobility thus served as powerful cements, bonding middle-class Americans and wage-earning citizens as they grappled with the economic divisions created by industrialization, market expansion, and increasing cultural diversity.

## Immigration and Cultural Conflict

Cultural diversity was the result of a vast wave of immigration. Between 1840 and 1860, about 2 million Irish, 1.5 million Germans, and 750,000 Britons poured into the United States. The British migrants were primarily Protestants and relatively prosperous — trained professionals, propertied farmers, and skilled workers. Many German immigrants also came from propertied farming and artisan families and had sufficient resources to move to the midwestern states of Wisconsin, Iowa, and Missouri. Poorer Germans and most of the Irish settled in the Northeast, where by 1860 they numbered nearly one-third of white adults. Most immigrants avoided the South because they feared competition from enslaved workers.

**Irish Poverty** The poorest migrants, Irish peasants and laborers, were fleeing a famine caused by severe overpopulation and a devastating blight that destroyed much of the Irish potato crop. They settled mostly in the cities of New England and New York. The men took low-paying jobs as factory hands, construction workers, and canal diggers, while the women became washerwomen and domestic servants. Irish families crowded into cheap tenement buildings with primitive sanitation systems and were the first to die when disease struck a city. In the summer of 1849, cholera epidemics took the lives of thousands of poor immigrants in St. Louis and New York City.

In times of hardship and sorrow, immigrants turned to their churches. Many Germans and virtually all the Irish were Catholics, and they fueled the growth of the American Catholic Church. In 1840, there were 16 Catholic dioceses and 700 churches; by 1860, there were 45 dioceses and 2,500 churches. Guided by their priests and bishops, Catholics built an impressive network of institutions — charitable societies, orphanages, militia companies, parochial schools, and political organizations — that maintained both their religion and their German or Irish identity.

**Nativism** Confronted by Catholic and German-speaking immigrants, some American-born citizens formed **nativist movements** that condemned immigration and asserted the superiority of Protestant religious and cultural values. In 1834, artist and inventor Samuel F. B. Morse published *Foreign Conspiracy Against the Liberties of the United States*, which warned of a Catholic threat to American republican institutions. Morse argued that Catholic immigrants would obey the dictates of Pope Gregory XVI (1831–1846), who urged Catholics to repudiate republicanism and acknowledge the "submission due to princes" and to the papacy. Republican-minded Protestants of many denominations shared Morse's fears of papal interference in American life and politics, and *Foreign Conspiracy* became their handbook (American Voices, p. 308).

The social tensions stemming from industrialization intensified nativist and anti-Catholic attitudes. Unemployed Protestant mechanics and factory workers joined mobs that attacked Catholic immigrants, accusing them of taking jobs and driving down wages. These cultural conflicts undercut trade unionism, because many Protestant wage earners sided more with their Protestant employers than with their Catholic coworkers. Benevolent-minded Protestants supported the anti-Catholic movement for reasons of public policy. As crusaders for public education, they opposed the use of tax resources for Catholic schools; as advocates of temperance and civilized manners, they condemned the rowdyism of drunken Irish men.

**UNDERSTAND POINTS OF VIEW**
Why did the Catholic hierarchy consider republicanism a threat? Why did Morse think the same of Catholicism?

Religious and cultural tensions led to violence. In 1834, in Charlestown, Massachusetts, a quarrel between Catholic laborers repairing a convent and Protestant workers in a neighboring brickyard led to a full-scale riot and the convent's destruction. In 1844, in Philadelphia, riots erupted when the Catholic bishop persuaded public-school officials to use both Catholic and Protestant versions of the Bible. Anti-Irish violence incited by the city's nativist clubs eventually escalated into open warfare between Protestants and the Pennsylvania militia. Thus even as the American economic revolution attracted millions of European immigrants, it divided society along lines of ethnicity and religion as well as class.

## SUMMARY

This chapter examined the causes of the economic transformation of the first half of the nineteenth century. That transformation had two facets: a major increase in production—the Industrial Revolution—and the expansion of commerce—the Market Revolution. Water, steam, and minerals such as coal and iron were crucial ingredients in both revolutions—driving factory machinery, carrying goods to market on canals and rivers, and propelling steamboats and railroad engines.

We also explored the consequences of that transformation: the rise of an urban society, the increasing similarity between the Northeast and Midwest and their growing difference from the South, and the creation of a society divided by class and ethnicity. To shape this emerging society, benevolent reformers and evangelical revivalists worked to instill moral discipline and Christian values. However, artisan republicans, unionized workers, and Irish and German immigrants had their own cultural values and economic interests. The result was a fragmented society. As the next chapter suggests, Americans looked to their political system, which was becoming increasingly democratic, to address these social divisions. In fact, the tensions among economic inequality, cultural diversity, and political democracy became a troubling—and enduring—part of American life.

# C H A P T E R   R E V I E W

**MAKE IT STICK**   Go to **LearningCurve** to retain what you've read.

**TERMS TO KNOW**   Identify and explain the significance of each term below.

## Key Concepts & Events

**Industrial Revolution** (p. 286)
**division of labor** (p. 286)
**mineral-based economy** (p. 287)
**mechanics** (p. 287)
**Waltham-Lowell System** (p. 288)
**machine tools** (p. 290)
**artisan republicanism** (p. 291)
**unions** (p. 291)
**labor theory of value** (p. 292)
**Market Revolution** (p. 293)

**Erie Canal** (p. 293)
**middle class** (p. 302)
**self-made man** (p. 304)
**Benevolent Empire** (p. 305)
**Sabbatarian values** (p. 306)
**moral free agency** (p. 306)
**American Temperance Society** (p. 310)
**nativist movements** (p. 310)

## Key People

**Samuel Slater** (p. 287)
**Francis Cabot Lowell** (p. 287)
**Sellars Family** (p. 290)
**Eli Whitney** (p. 290)
**Cyrus McCormick** (p. 300)
**Lyman Beecher** (p. 305)
**Charles Grandison Finney and Lydia Finney** (p. 305)

## REVIEW QUESTIONS
Answer these questions to demonstrate your understanding of the chapter's main ideas.

1. What was the impact of the economic revolution on the various social groups and classes?

2. What different types of reform movements arose during this period, and what types of change did they advocate? What strategies did they use, and how successful were they in their efforts?

3. Did the Industrial and Market revolutions make America a more "republican" society? Or did they undermine republicanism? Defend your interpretation by reference to specific events and developments.

4. **THEMATIC UNDERSTANDING** Review the events listed under "Work, Exchange, and Technology" on the thematic timeline on page 283. In what ways was the economy different in 1860 from what it had been in 1800? Which factors listed in the thematic timeline best explain the changes?

## MAKING CONNECTIONS
Recognize the larger developments and continuities within and across chapters by answering these questions.

1. **ACROSS TIME AND PLACE** How did the economic revolution described in Chapter 9 affect the lives of women in various social groups, and how did it make their experiences different from those of their mothers, whose political and social lives were explored in Chapter 6 on the American Revolution, and their grandmothers, whose work lives and cultural experiences were considered in Chapter 4?

2. **VISUAL EVIDENCE** Look again at three images, the women weavers from Maine (p. 285), the woodworker (p. 292), and the Hartford family (p. 302). Taken together, what insights do they provide into the different aspects and social consequences of the Economic Revolution?

## MORE TO EXPLORE
Start here to learn more about the events discussed in this chapter.

Stuart M. Blumin, *The Emergence of the Middle Class* (1989). Discusses urban class formation during the nineteenth century.

Stephen P. Rice, *Minding the Machine* (2004). Analyzes the ways in which language reflects and undergirds changing social and cultural relationships.

Scott A. Sandage, *Born Losers: A History of Failure in America* (2005). Focuses on failed entrepreneurs and the changing cultural meaning of failure.

Charles G. Sellers, *The Market Revolution: Jacksonian America, 1815–1846* (1991). Explores the social impact of economic change.

Laurel Thatcher Ulrich, *The Age of Homespun* (2001). Uses objects of early craft production to tell absorbing stories that reveal broad historical developments.

For a textile operative's account of mill life, see **fordham.edu/halsall/mod/robinson-lowell.html**. For religion and benevolent societies, consult **loc.gov /exhibits/religion/rel07.html**.

## TIMELINE

Ask yourself why this chapter begins and ends with these dates and then identify the links among related events.

| | |
|---|---|
| **1782** | • Oliver Evans builds automated flour mill |
| **1790** | • Samuel Slater opens spinning mill in Providence, Rhode Island |
| **1792** | • Congress passes Post Office Act |
| **1793** | • Eli Whitney devises cotton gin |
| **1814** | • Boston Manufacturing Company opens factory in Waltham, Massachusetts |
| **1816–1828** | • Congress levies protective tariffs |
| **1817** | • Erie Canal begun (completed in 1825) |
| **1820–1840** | • Urban population surges in Northeast and Midwest; shoe entrepreneurs adopt division of labor |
| **1820s** | • New England women take textile jobs<br>• Rise of Benevolent Empire spurs conservative social reforms |
| **1824** | • *Gibbons v. Ogden* promotes interstate trade |
| **1830s** | • Emergence of western commercial cities<br>• Labor movement gains strength<br>• Middle-class culture emerges<br>• Growth of temperance movement |
| **1830** | • Charles G. Finney begins Rochester revivals |
| **1840s** | • Irish and German immigration sparks ethnic riots<br>• Maturation of machine-tool industry |
| **1842** | • *Commonwealth v. Hunt* legitimizes trade unions |
| **1850s** | • Expansion of railroads in Northeast and Midwest |
| **1857** | • Overproduction and speculation trigger a business recession |

**KEY TURNING POINT:** Many of the early timeline entries concern economic matters, while later entries refer to other subjects. Based on your reading of the chapter, when and why does this change in emphasis occur?

# 10

## CHAPTER

# A Democratic Revolution
# 1800–1844

Europeans who visited the United States in the 1830s mostly praised its republican society but not its political parties and politicians. "The gentlemen spit, talk of elections and the price of produce, and spit again," Frances Trollope reported in *Domestic Manners of the Americans* (1832). In her view, American politics was the sport of self-serving party politicians who reeked of "whiskey and onions." Other Europeans lamented the low intellectual level of American political debate. The "clap-trap of praise and pathos" from a Massachusetts politician "deeply disgusted" Harriet Martineau, while the shallow arguments advanced by the inept "farmers, shopkeepers, and country lawyers" who sat in the New York assembly astonished Basil Hall.

The negative verdict was nearly unanimous. "The most able men in the United States are very rarely placed at the head of affairs," French aristocrat Alexis de Tocqueville concluded in *Democracy in America* (1835). The reason, said Tocqueville, lay in the character of democracy itself. Most citizens ignored important policy issues, jealously refused to elect their intellectual superiors, and listened in awe to "the clamor of a mountebank [a charismatic fraud] who knows the secret of stimulating their tastes."

These Europeans were witnessing the American Democratic Revolution. Before 1815, men of ability had sat in the seats of government, and the prevailing ideology had been republicanism, or rule by "men of TALENTS and VIRTUE," as a newspaper put it. Many of those leaders feared popular rule, so they wrote constitutions with Bills of Rights, bicameral legislatures, and independent judiciaries, and they censured overambitious men who campaigned for public office. But history took a different course. By the 1820s and 1830s, the watchwords were *democracy* and *party politics*, a system run by men who avidly sought office and rallied supporters through newspapers, broadsides, and great public processions. Politics became a sport—a competitive contest for the votes of ordinary men. "That the majority should govern was a fundamental maxim in all free governments," declared Martin Van Buren, the most talented of the new breed of professional politicians. A republican-minded Virginian condemned Van Buren as "too great an intriguer," but by encouraging ordinary Americans to burn with "election fever" and support party principles, he and other politicians redefined the meaning of democratic government and made it work.

**IDENTIFY THE BIG IDEA**

What were the main features of the Democratic Revolution, and what role did Andrew Jackson play in its outcome?

**The Politics of Democracy**   As ordinary American men asserted a claim to a voice in government affairs, politicians catered to their preferences and prejudices. Aspiring candidates took their messages to voters, in rural hamlets as well as large towns. This detail from George Caleb Bingham's *Stump Speaking* (1855) shows a swanky, tail-coated politician on an improvised stage seeking the votes of an audience of well-dressed gentlemen and local farmers—identified by their broad-brimmed hats and casual attire.
Private Collection/The Bridgeman Art Library.

# The Rise of Popular Politics, 1810–1828

Expansion of the **franchise** (the right to vote) dramatically symbolized the Democratic Revolution. By the 1830s, most states allowed nearly all white men to vote. Nowhere else in the world did ordinary farmers and wage earners exercise such political influence; in England, the Reform Bill of 1832 extended the vote to only 600,000 out of 6 million men — a mere 10 percent. Equally important, political parties provided voters with the means to express their preferences.

## The Decline of the Notables and the Rise of Parties

The American Revolution weakened the elite-run society of the colonial era but did not overthrow it. Only two states — Pennsylvania and Vermont — gave the vote to all male taxpayers, and many families of low rank continued to defer to their social "betters." Consequently, wealthy **notables** — northern landlords, slave-owning planters, and seaport merchants — dominated the political system in the new republic. And rightly so, said John Jay, the first chief justice of the Supreme Court: "Those who own the country are the most fit persons to participate in the government of it." Jay and other notables managed local elections by building up an "interest": lending money to small farmers, giving business to storekeepers, and treating their tenants to rum. An outlay of $20 for refreshments, remarked one poll watcher, "may produce about 100 votes." This gentry-dominated system kept men who lacked wealth and powerful family connections from seeking office.

**The Rise of Democracy**    To expand the suffrage, Maryland reformers in the 1810s invoked the equal-rights rhetoric of republicanism. They charged that property qualifications for voting were a "tyranny" because they endowed "one class of men with privileges which are denied to another." To defuse such arguments and deter migration to the West, legislators in Maryland and other seaboard states grudgingly accepted a broader franchise and its democratic results. The new voters often rejected candidates who wore "top boots, breeches, and shoe buckles," their hair in "powder and queues." Instead, they elected men who dressed simply and endorsed popular rule.

Smallholding farmers and ambitious laborers in the Midwest and Southwest likewise challenged the old hierarchical order. In Ohio, a traveler reported, "no white man or woman will bear being called a servant." The constitutions of the new states of Indiana (1816), Illinois (1818), and Alabama (1819) prescribed a broad male franchise, and voters usually elected middling men to local and state offices. A well-to-do migrant in Illinois was surprised to learn that the man who plowed his fields "was a colonel of militia, and a member of the legislature." Once in public office, men from modest backgrounds restricted imprisonment for debt, kept taxes low, and allowed farmers to claim squatters' rights to unoccupied land.

By the mid-1820s, many state legislatures had given the vote to all white men or to all men who paid taxes or served in the militia. Only a few — North Carolina, Virginia, and Rhode Island — still required the possession of freehold property. Equally significant, between 1818 and 1821, Connecticut, Massachusetts, and New York wrote more democratic constitutions that reapportioned legislative districts on the basis of population and mandated the popular election (rather than the appointment) of judges and justices of the peace.

Democratic politics was contentious and, because it attracted ambitious men, often corrupt. Powerful entrepreneurs and speculators — both notables and self-made men — demanded government assistance and paid bribes to get it. Speculators won land grants by paying off the members of important committees, and bankers distributed shares of stock to key legislators. When the Seventh Ward Bank of New York City received a legislative charter in 1833, the bank's officials set aside one-third of the 3,700 shares of stock for themselves and their friends and almost two-thirds for state legislators and bureaucrats, leaving just 40 shares for public sale (America Compared, p. 317).

More political disputes broke out when religious reformers sought laws to enforce the cultural agenda of the Benevolent Empire. In Utica, New York, evangelical Presbyterians insisted upon a town ordinance restricting Sunday entertainment. In response, a member of the local Universalist church — a freethinking Protestant denomination — denounced the measure as coercive and called for "Religious Liberty."

**Parties Take Command**    The appearance of political parties encouraged such debates over government policy. Revolutionary-era Americans had condemned political "factions" as antirepublican, and the new state

**IDENTIFY CAUSES**
What was the relationship between the growth of democracy and the emergence of political parties?

## Alexis de Tocqueville

## Letter to Louis de Kergorlay, June 29, 1831

In 1831, the French aristocrat Alexis de Tocqueville (1805–1859) came to the United States to report on its innovative penal system. Instead, he produced a brilliant analysis of the new republican society and politics, *Democracy in America* (1835, 1840). This letter to a French friend reveals his thinking and insights.

Do you know what, in this country's political realm, makes the most vivid impression on me? The effect of laws governing inheritance. . . . The English had exported their laws of primogeniture, according to which the eldest acquired three-quarters of the father's fortune. This resulted in a host of vast territorial domains passing from father to son and wealth remaining in families. My American informants tell me that there was no aristocracy but, instead, a class of great landowners leading a simple, rather intellectual life characterized by its air of good breeding, its manners, and a strong sense of family pride. . . . Since then, inheritance laws have been revised.

Primogeniture gave way to equal division, with almost magical results. Domains split up, passing into other hands. Family spirit disappeared. The aristocratic bias that marked the republic's early years was replaced by a democratic thrust of irresistible force. . . . I've seen several members of these old families. . . . They regret the loss of everything aristocratic: patronage, family pride, high tone. . . .

There can be no doubt that the inheritance law is responsible in some considerable measure for this complete triumph of democratic principles. The Americans . . . agree that "it has made us what we are, it is the foundation of our republic." . . .

When I apply these ideas to France, I cannot resist the thought that Louis XVIII's charter [of 1814 sought to restore the pre-Revolutionary regime by creating] . . . aristocratic institutions in political law, but [by mandating equality before the law and retaining the Revolutionary-era inheritance laws giving all children, irrespective of sex, an equal share of the parental estate] within the domain of civil law gave shelter to a democratic principle

so vigorous that it was bound before long to destroy the foundations of the edifice it raised. . . . We are moving toward an unrestricted democracy . . . that . . . would not suit France at all. . . . [However,] there is no human power capable of changing the law of inheritance, and with this change our families will disappear, possessions will pass into other hands, wealth will be increasingly equalized, the upper class will melt into the middle, the latter will become immense and shape everything to its level. . . .

What I see in America leaves me doubting that government by the multitude, even under the most favorable circumstances — and they exist here — is a good thing. There is general agreement that in the early days of the republic, statesmen and members of the two legislative houses were much more distinguished than they are today. They almost all belonged to that class of landowners I mentioned above. The populace no longer chooses with such a sure hand. It generally favors those who flatter its passions and descend to its level.

Source: From *Letters from America: Alexis de Tocqueville*, edited, translated, and with an introduction by Frederick Brown, Yale University Press, 2010. Copyright © 2010 by Frederick Brown. Used by permission of Yale University Press.

### QUESTIONS FOR ANALYSIS

1. According to Tocqueville, what is the legal basis of American social equality and political democracy? What is the comparable situation in France?

2. Why does Tocqueville doubt that democratic rule is a good thing, even in the United States, and "would not suit France at all"?

and national constitutions made no mention of political parties. However, as the power of notables waned in the 1820s, disciplined political parties appeared in a number of states. Usually they were run by professional politicians, often middle-class lawyers and journalists. One observer called the new parties **political machines** because, like the new power-driven textile looms, they

efficiently wove together the interests of diverse social and economic groups.

Martin Van Buren of New York was the chief architect of the emerging system of party government. The ambitious son of a Jeffersonian tavern keeper, Van Buren grew up in the landlord-dominated society of the Hudson River Valley. To get training as a lawyer, he

**Martin Van Buren**

Martin Van Buren's skills as a lawyer and a politician won him many admirers, as did his personal charm, sharp intellect, and imperturbable composure. "Little Van"—a mere 5 feet 6 inches in height—had almost as many detractors. Davy Crockett, Kentucky frontiersman, land speculator, and congressman, labeled him "an artful, cunning, intriguing, selfish lawyer," concerned only with "office and money." In truth, Van Buren was a complex man, a middle-class lawyer with republican values and aristocratic tastes who nonetheless created a democratic political party. National Portrait Gallery, Smithsonian Institution/Art Resource, NY.

relied on the Van Ness clan, a powerful local gentry family. Then, determined not to become their dependent "tool," Van Buren repudiated their tutelage and set out to create a political order based on party identity, not family connections. In justifying party governments, Van Buren rejected the traditional republican belief that political factions were dangerous and claimed that the opposite was true: "All men of sense know that political parties are inseparable from free government," because they checked an elected official's inherent "disposition to abuse power."

 To see a longer excerpt of Martin Van Buren's autobiography, along with other primary sources from this period, see *Sources for America's History.*

Between 1817 and 1821 in New York, Van Buren turned his "Bucktail" supporters (who wore a deer's tail on their hats) into the first statewide political machine. He purchased a newspaper, the *Albany Argus*, and used it to promote his policies and get out the vote. Patronage was an even more important tool. When Van Buren's Bucktails won control of the New York legislature in 1821, they acquired the power to appoint some six thousand of their friends to positions in New York's legal bureaucracy of judges, justices of the peace, sheriffs, deed commissioners, and coroners. Critics called this ruthless distribution of offices a **spoils system**, but Van Buren argued it was fair, operating "sometimes in favour of one party, and sometimes of another." Party government was thoroughly republican, he added, because it reflected the preferences of a majority of the citizenry. To ensure the passage of the party's legislative program, Van Buren insisted on disciplined voting as determined by a **caucus**, a meeting of party leaders. On one crucial occasion, the "Little Magician"—a nickname reflecting Van Buren's short stature and political dexterity—honored seventeen New York legislators for sacrificing "individual preferences for the general good" of the party.

## The Election of 1824

The advance of political democracy in the states undermined the traditional notable-dominated system of national politics. After the War of 1812, the aristocratic Federalist Party virtually disappeared, and the Republican Party splintered into competing factions (Chapter 7). As the election of 1824 approached, five Republican candidates campaigned for the presidency. Three were veterans of President James Monroe's cabinet: Secretary of State John Quincy Adams, the son of former president John Adams; Secretary of War John C. Calhoun; and Secretary of the Treasury William H. Crawford. The other candidates were Henry Clay of Kentucky, the hard-drinking, dynamic Speaker of the House of Representatives; and General Andrew Jackson, now a senator from Tennessee. When the Republican caucus in Congress selected Crawford as the party's official nominee, the other candidates took their case to the voters. Thanks to democratic reforms, eighteen of the twenty-four states required popular elections (rather than a vote of the state legislature) to choose their representatives to the electoral college.

Each candidate had strengths. Thanks to his diplomatic successes as secretary of state, John Quincy

Adams enjoyed national recognition; and his family's prestige in Massachusetts ensured him the electoral votes of New England. Henry Clay based his candidacy on the **American System**, his integrated mercantilist program of national economic development similar to the Commonwealth System of the state governments. Clay wanted to strengthen the Second Bank of the United States, raise tariffs, and use tariff revenues to finance **internal improvements**, that is, public works such as roads and canals. His nationalistic program won praise in the West, which needed better transportation, but elicited sharp criticism in the South, which relied on rivers to market its cotton and had few manufacturing industries to protect. William Crawford of Georgia, an ideological heir of Thomas Jefferson, denounced Clay's American System as a scheme to "consolidate" political power in Washington. Recognizing Crawford's appeal in the South, John C. Calhoun of South Carolina withdrew from the race and endorsed Andrew Jackson.

As the hero of the Battle of New Orleans, Jackson benefitted from the surge of patriotism after the War of 1812. Born in the Carolina backcountry, Jackson settled in Nashville, Tennessee, where he formed ties to influential families through marriage and a career as an attorney and a slave-owning cotton planter. His rise from common origins symbolized the new democratic age, and his reputation as a "plain solid republican" attracted voters in all regions. Still, Jackson's strong showing in the electoral college surprised most political leaders. The Tennessee senator received 99 electoral votes; Adams garnered 84 votes; Crawford, struck down by a stroke during the campaign, won 41; and Clay finished with 37 (Map 10.1).

Because no candidate received an absolute majority, the Twelfth Amendment to the Constitution (ratified in 1804) set the rules: the House of Representatives would choose the president from among the three highest vote-getters. This procedure hurt Jackson because many congressmen feared that the rough-hewn "military chieftain" might become a tyrant. Excluded from the race, Henry Clay used his influence as Speaker to thwart Jackson's election. Clay assembled a coalition of representatives from New England and the Ohio River Valley that voted Adams into the presidency in 1825. Adams showed his gratitude by appointing Clay his secretary of state, the traditional stepping-stone to the presidency. Clay's appointment was politically fatal for both men: Jackson's supporters accused Clay and Adams of making a **corrupt bargain**, and they vowed to oppose Adams's policies and to prevent Clay's rise to the presidency.

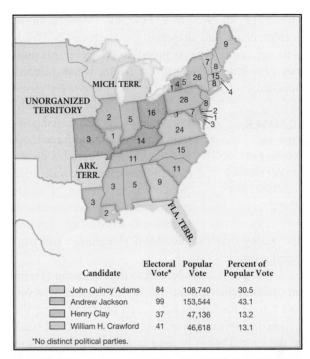

| Candidate | Electoral Vote* | Popular Vote | Percent of Popular Vote |
|---|---|---|---|
| John Quincy Adams | 84 | 108,740 | 30.5 |
| Andrew Jackson | 99 | 153,544 | 43.1 |
| Henry Clay | 37 | 47,136 | 13.2 |
| William H. Crawford | 41 | 46,618 | 13.1 |

*No distinct political parties.

**MAP 10.1**

**The Presidential Election of 1824**

Regional voting was the dominant pattern in 1824. John Quincy Adams captured every electoral vote in New England and most of those in New York; Henry Clay carried Ohio and Kentucky, the most populous trans-Appalachian states; and William Crawford took the southern states of Virginia and Georgia. Only Andrew Jackson claimed a national constituency, winning Pennsylvania and New Jersey in the East, Indiana and most of Illinois in the Midwest, and much of the South. Only 356,000 Americans voted, about 27 percent of the eligible electorate.

## The Last Notable President: John Quincy Adams

As president, Adams called for bold national action. "The moral purpose of the Creator," he told Congress, was to use the president to "improve the conditions of himself and his fellow men." Adams called for the establishment of a national university in Washington, scientific explorations in the Far West, and a uniform standard of weights and measures. Most important, he endorsed Henry Clay's American System and its three key elements: protective tariffs to stimulate manufacturing, federally subsidized roads and canals to facilitate commerce, and a national bank to control credit and provide a uniform currency.

**UNDERSTAND POINTS OF VIEW**

Why did Jacksonians consider the political deal between Adams and Clay "corrupt"?

**The Fate of Adams's Policies** Manufacturers, entrepreneurs, and farmers in the Northeast and Midwest welcomed Adams's proposals. However, his policies won little support in the South, where planters opposed protective tariffs because these taxes raised the price of manufactures. Southern smallholders also feared powerful banks that could force them into bankruptcy. From his deathbed, Thomas Jefferson condemned Adams for promoting "a single and splendid government of [a monied] aristocracy . . . riding and ruling over the plundered ploughman and beggared yeomanry."

EXPLAIN CAUSES
What were the successes and failures of John Adams's presidency, and what accounted for those outcomes?

Other politicians objected to the American System on constitutional grounds. In 1817, President Madison had vetoed the Bonus Bill, which proposed using the national government's income from the Second Bank of the United States to fund improvement projects in the states. Such projects, Madison argued, were the sole responsibility of the states, a sentiment shared by the Republican followers of Thomas Jefferson. In 1824, Martin Van Buren likewise declared his allegiance to the constitutional "doctrines of the Jefferson School" and his opposition to **"consolidated government,"** a powerful and potentially oppressive national administration. Now a member of the U.S. Senate, Van Buren helped to defeat most of Adams's proposed subsidies for roads and canals.

**The Tariff Battle** The major battle of the Adams administration came over tariffs. The Tariff of 1816 had placed relatively high duties on imports of cheap English cotton cloth, allowing New England textile producers to control that segment of the market. In 1824, Adams and Clay secured a new tariff that protected New England and Pennsylvania manufacturers from more expensive woolen and cotton textiles and also English iron goods. Without these tariffs, British imports would have dominated the market and significantly inhibited American industrial development (Chapter 9, America Compared, p. 289).

Recognizing the appeal of tariffs, Van Buren and his Jacksonian allies hopped on the bandwagon. By increasing duties on wool, hemp, and other imported raw materials, they hoped to win the support of farmers in New York, Ohio, and Kentucky for Jackson's presidential candidacy in 1828. The tariff had become a political weapon. "I fear this tariff thing," remarked Thomas Cooper, the president of the College of South

Carolina and an advocate of free trade. "[B]y some strange mechanical contrivance [it has become] . . . a machine for manufacturing Presidents, instead of broadcloths, and bed blankets." Disregarding southern protests, northern Jacksonians joined with supporters of Adams and Clay to enact the Tariff of 1828, which raised duties significantly on raw materials, textiles, and iron goods.

The new tariff enraged the South, which produced the world's cheapest raw cotton and did not need to protect its main industry. Moreover, the tariff cost southern planters about $100 million a year. Planters had to buy either higher-cost American textiles and iron goods, thus enriching northeastern businesses and workers, or highly dutied British imports, thus paying the expenses of the national government. The new tariff was "little less than legalized pillage," an Alabama legislator declared, calling it a **Tariff of Abominations**. Ignoring the Jacksonians' support for the Tariff of 1828, most southerners heaped blame on President Adams.

Southern governments also criticized Adams's Indian policy. A deeply moral man, the president supported the treaty-guaranteed land rights of Native

A CARTOON COMPARING CONDITIONS UNDER FREE TRADE AND PROTECTIVE TARIFF
From "The United States Weekly Telegram," November 5, 1832.

**The "Tariff of Abominations"**

Political cartoons enjoyed wide use in eighteenth-century England and became popular in the United States during the political battles of the First Party System (1794–1815). By the 1820s, American newspapers, the mouthpiece of political parties, published cartoons daily. This cartoon attacks the tariffs of 1828 and 1832 as hostile to the prosperity of the South. The gaunt figure on the left represents a southern planter, starved by high tariff duties, while the northern textile manufacturer has grown stout feasting on the bounty of protectionism. © Bettmann/Corbis.

Americans against expansion-minded whites. In 1825, U.S. commissioners had secured a treaty from one faction of Creeks ceding its lands in Georgia to the United States for eventual sale to the state's citizens. When the Creek National Council repudiated the treaty, claiming that it was fraudulent, Adams called for new negotiations. In response, Georgia governor George M. Troup attacked the president as a "public enemy . . . the unblushing ally of the savages." Mobilizing Georgia's congressional delegation, Troup persuaded Congress to extinguish the Creeks' land titles, forcing most Creeks to leave the state.

Elsewhere, Adams's primary weakness was his out-of-date political style. The last notable to serve in the White House, he acted the part: aloof, inflexible, and paternalistic. When Congress rejected his activist economic policies, Adams accused its members of following the whims of public opinion and told them not to be enfeebled "by the will of our constituents." Ignoring his waning popularity, the president refused to dismiss hostile federal bureaucrats or to award offices to his supporters. Rather than "run" for reelection in 1828, Adams "stood" for it, telling friends, "If my country wants my services, she must ask for them."

## "The Democracy" and the Election of 1828

Martin Van Buren and the politicians handling Andrew Jackson's campaign for the presidency had no reservations about running for office. To put Jackson in the White House, Van Buren revived the political coalition created by Thomas Jefferson, championing policies that appealed to both southern planters and northern farmers and artisans, the "plain Republicans of the North." John C. Calhoun, Jackson's running mate, brought his South Carolina allies into Van Buren's party, and Jackson's close friends in Tennessee rallied voters throughout the Old Southwest. The Little Magician hoped that a national party would reconcile the diverse "interests" that, as James Madison suggested in "Federalist No. 10" (Chapter 6), inevitably existed in a large republic. Equally important, added Jackson's ally Duff Green, it would put the "anti-slave party in the North . . . to sleep for twenty years to come."

At Van Buren's direction, the Jacksonians orchestrated a massive publicity campaign. In New York, fifty Democrat-funded newspapers declared their support for Jackson. Elsewhere, Jacksonians used mass meetings, torchlight parades, and barbecues to celebrate the candidate's frontier origin and rise to fame. They praised "Old Hickory" as a "natural" aristocrat, a self-made man.

The Jacksonians called themselves Democrats or "the Democracy" to convey their egalitarian message. As Thomas Morris told the Ohio legislature, Democrats were fighting for equality: the republic had been corrupted by legislative charters that gave "a few individuals rights and privileges not enjoyed by the citizens at large." Morris promised that the Democracy would destroy such "artificial distinction." Jackson himself declared that "equality among the people in the rights conferred by government" was the "great radical principle of freedom."

Jackson's message appealed to many social groups. His hostility to corporations and to Clay's American System won support from northeastern artisans and workers who felt threatened by industrialization. Jackson also captured the votes of Pennsylvania ironworkers and New York farmers who had benefitted from the controversial Tariff of Abominations. Yet, by astutely declaring his support for a "judicious" tariff that would balance regional interests, Jackson remained popular in the South. Old Hickory likewise garnered votes in the Southeast and Midwest, where his well-known hostility toward Native Americans reassured white farmers seeking Indian removal.

The Democrats' celebration of popular rule carried Jackson into office. In 1824, about one-quarter of the electorate had voted; in 1828, more than one-half went to the polls, and 56 percent voted for the Tennessee senator (Figure 10.1 and Map 10.2). The first president from a trans-Appalachian state, Jackson cut a dignified figure as he traveled to Washington. He "wore his hair carelessly but not ungracefully arranged," an English observer noted, "and in spite of his harsh, gaunt features looked like a gentleman and a soldier." Still, Jackson's popularity and sharp temper frightened men of wealth. Senator Daniel Webster of Massachusetts, a former Federalist and now a corporate lawyer, warned his clients that the new president would "bring a breeze with him. Which way it will blow, I cannot tell [but] . . . my fear is stronger than my hope." Supreme Court justice Joseph Story shared Webster's apprehensions. Watching an unruly Inauguration Day crowd climb over the elegant White House furniture to congratulate Jackson, Story lamented that "the reign of King 'Mob' seemed triumphant."

> ## TRACE CHANGE OVER TIME
> Jackson lost the presidential election of 1824 and won in 1828: what changes explain these different outcomes?

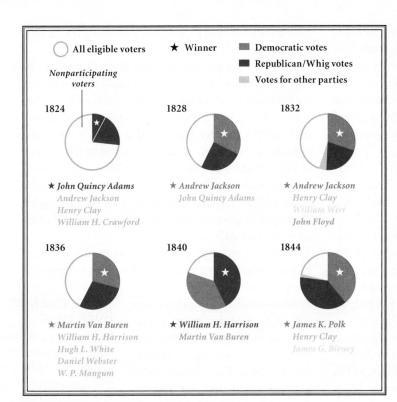

**FIGURE 10.1**

**The Rise of Voter Turnout, 1824–1844**

As the shrinking white sections of these pie graphs indicate, the proportion of eligible voters who cast ballots in presidential elections increased dramatically over time. In 1824, 27 percent voted; in 1840 and thereafter, about 80 percent went to the polls. Voter participation soared first in 1828, when Andrew Jackson and John Quincy Adams contested for the White House, and again in 1840, as competition heated up between Democrats and Whigs, who advocated different policies and philosophies of government. Democrats won most of these contests because their policies had greater appeal to ordinary citizens.

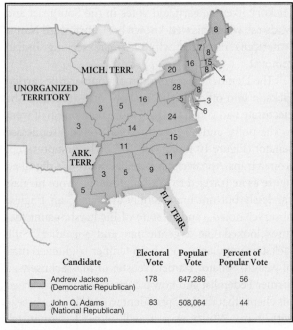

| Candidate | Electoral Vote | Popular Vote | Percent of Popular Vote |
|---|---|---|---|
| Andrew Jackson (Democratic Republican) | 178 | 647,286 | 56 |
| John Q. Adams (National Republican) | 83 | 508,064 | 44 |

**MAP 10.2**

**The Presidential Election of 1828**

As in 1824, John Quincy Adams carried all of New England and some of the Mid-Atlantic states. However, Andrew Jackson swept the rest of the nation and won a resounding victory in the electoral college. Over 1.1 million American men cast ballots in 1828, more than three times the number who voted in 1824.

# The Jacksonian Presidency, 1829–1837

American-style political democracy—a broad franchise, a disciplined political party, and policies favoring specific interests—ushered Andrew Jackson into office. Jackson used his popular mandate to transform the policies of the national government and the definition of the presidency. During his two terms, he enhanced presidential authority, destroyed the mercantilist and nationalist American System, and established a new ideology of limited government. An Ohio supporter summed up Jackson's vision: "the Sovereignty of the People, the Rights of the States, and a Light and Simple Government."

## Jackson's Agenda: Rotation and Decentralization

To make policy, Jackson relied primarily on his so-called Kitchen Cabinet. Its most influential members were two Kentuckians, Francis Preston Blair, who edited the *Washington Globe*, and Amos Kendall, who wrote Jackson's speeches; Roger B. Taney of Maryland, who became attorney general, treasury secretary, and

**President Andrew Jackson, 1830**

The new president came to Washington with a well-deserved reputation as an aggressive Indian fighter and unpredictable military leader. In this official portrait, Jackson looks "presidential"—his dress and posture, and the artist's composition, conveyed an image of a calm, deliberate statesman. Subsequent events would show that Jackson had not lost his hard-edged authoritarian personality. Library of Congress.

Jackson's highest priority was to destroy the American System. He believed that Henry Clay's system—and all government-sponsored plans for national economic development—were contrary to the Constitution, encouraged "consolidated government," and, through higher tariffs, increased the burden of taxation. As Clay noted apprehensively, the new president wanted "to cry down old [expansive, Hamiltonian] constructions of the Constitution . . . to make all Jefferson's opinions the articles of faith of the new Church." Declaring that the "voice of the people" called for "economy in the expenditures of the Government," Jackson rejected national subsidies for transportation projects. Invoking constitutional arguments, he vetoed four internal improvement bills in 1830, including an extension of the National Road, arguing that they infringed on "the reserved powers of states." By eliminating potential expenditures by the federal government, these vetoes also undermined the case for protective tariffs. As Jacksonian senator William Smith of South Carolina pointed out, "[D]estroy internal improvements and you leave no motive for the tariff."

> **IDENTIFY CAUSES**
> Jackson cut the national budget and the national debt but increased the number of federal employees. How do you explain this paradox?

## The Tariff and Nullification

The Tariff of 1828 had helped Jackson win the presidency, but it saddled him with a major political crisis. There was fierce opposition to high tariffs throughout the South and especially in South Carolina. That state was the only one with an African American majority—56 percent of the population in 1830—and its slave owners, like the white sugar planters in the West Indies, feared a black rebellion. Even more, they worried about the legal abolition of slavery. The British Parliament had declared that slavery in its West Indian colonies would end in 1833; South Carolina planters, vividly recalling northern efforts to end slavery in Missouri (Chapter 8), worried that the U.S. Congress would follow the British lead. So they attacked the tariff, both to lower rates and to discourage the use of federal power to attack slavery.

The crisis began in 1832, when high-tariff congressmen ignored southern warnings that they were "endangering the Union" and reenacted the Tariff of Abominations. In response, leading South Carolinians called a state convention, which in November boldly adopted an Ordinance of Nullification declaring the tariffs of 1828 and 1832 to be null and void. The ordinance

then chief justice of the Supreme Court; and Martin Van Buren, whom Jackson named secretary of state.

Following Van Buren's example in New York, Jackson used patronage to create a disciplined national party. He rejected the idea of "property in office" (that a qualified official held a position permanently) and insisted on a rotation of officeholders when a new administration took power. Rotation would not lessen expertise, Jackson insisted, because public duties were "so plain and simple that men of intelligence may readily qualify themselves for their performance." William L. Marcy, a New York Jacksonian, offered a more realistic explanation for rotation: government jobs were like the spoils of war, and "to the victor belong the spoils of the enemy." Jackson used those spoils to reward his allies and win backing for his policies.

CAPITOL.

The rejected Minister,
*We never can make him President,*
*without first making him Vice-president.*
This webb.
*Pub. by H. Anshea N.º 214 Broadway N.Y*

### Who Will Be Jackson's Heir?

Elected vice president in 1828, John C. Calhoun hoped to succeed Jackson in the White House. He failed to account for the ambition of Martin Van Buren, who managed Jackson's campaign and claimed the prized office of secretary of state. When Van Buren resigned as secretary in 1831 and Jackson nominated him as minister to Britain, Calhoun sought to destroy his rival by blocking his confirmation in the Senate. The "Little Magician" pounced on this miscalculation, persuading Jackson, already disillusioned by Calhoun's support for nullification, to oust him from the ticket. Van Buren took his place as vice president in 1832, carried into the office—as the cartoonist tells the tale—on Jackson's back, and succeeded to the presidency in 1836. © Collection of the New-York Historical Society.

### UNDERSTAND POINTS OF VIEW
How did South Carolina justify nullification on constitutional grounds?

prohibited the collection of those duties in South Carolina after February 1, 1833, and threatened secession if federal officials tried to collect them.

South Carolina's act of **nullification**—the argument that a state has the right to void, within its borders, a law passed by Congress—rested on the constitutional arguments developed in *The South Carolina Exposition and Protest* (1828). Written anonymously by Vice President John C. Calhoun, the *Exposition* gave a localist (or sectional) interpretation to the federal union. Because each state or geographic region had distinct interests, localists argued, protective tariffs and other national legislation that operated unequally on the various states lacked fairness and legitimacy—in fact, they were unconstitutional. An obsessive defender of the interests of southern slave owners, Calhoun exaggerated the frequency and severity of such legislation, declaring, "Constitutional government and the government of a majority are utterly incompatible."

Calhoun's constitutional doctrines reflected the arguments advanced by Jefferson and Madison in the Kentucky and Virginia Resolutions of 1798. Those

resolutions asserted that, because state-based conventions had ratified the Constitution, sovereignty lay in the states, not in the people. Beginning from this premise, Calhoun argued that a state convention could declare a congressional law to be void within the state's borders. Replying to this **states' rights** interpretation of the Constitution, which had little support in the text of the document, Senator Daniel Webster of Massachusetts presented a nationalist interpretation that celebrated popular sovereignty and Congress's responsibility to secure the "general welfare."

Jackson hoped to find a middle path between Webster's strident nationalism and Calhoun's radical doctrine of localist federalism. The Constitution clearly gave the federal government the authority to establish tariffs, and Jackson vowed to enforce it. He declared that South Carolina's Ordinance of Nullification violated the letter of the Constitution and was "destructive of the great object for which it was formed." More pointedly, he warned, "Disunion by armed force is treason." At Jackson's request, Congress in early 1833 passed a military Force Bill, authorizing the president to compel South Carolina's obedience to national laws. Simultaneously, Jackson addressed the South's objections to high import duties with a new tariff act that,

**The Great Webster-Hayne Debate, 1830**

The "Tariff of Abominations" sparked one of the great debates in American history. When Senator Robert Y. Hayne of South Carolina (seated in the middle of the picture, with his legs crossed) opposed the federal tariffs by invoking the doctrines of states' rights and nullification, Daniel Webster rose to the defense of the Union. Speaking for two days to a spellbound Senate, Webster delivered an impassioned oration that celebrated the unity of the American people as the key to their freedom. His parting words—"Liberty and Union, now and forever, one and inseparable!"—quickly became part of the national memory. "Webster's Reply to Haynes," by G.P.A. Healy, City of Boston Art Commission.

over the course of a decade, reduced rates to the modest levels of 1816. Subsequently, export-hungry midwestern wheat farmers joined southern planters in advocating low duties to avoid retaliatory tariffs by foreign nations. "Illinois wants a market for her agricultural products," declared Senator Sidney Breese in 1846. "[S]he wants the market of the world."

Having won the political battle by securing a tariff reduction, the South Carolina convention did not press its constitutional stance on nullification. Jackson was satisfied. He had assisted the South economically while upholding the constitutional principle of national authority—a principle that Abraham Lincoln would embrace to defend the Union during the secession crisis of 1861.

## The Bank War

In the midst of the tariff crisis, Jackson faced a major challenge from politicians who supported the **Second Bank of the United States**. Founded in Philadelphia in 1816 (Chapter 7), the bank was privately managed and operated under a twenty-year charter from the federal government, which owned 20 percent of its stock. The bank's most important role was to stabilize the nation's money supply, which consisted primarily of notes and bills of credit—in effect, paper money—issued by state-chartered banks. Those banks promised to redeem the notes on demand with "hard" money (or "specie")—that is, gold or silver coins minted by the U.S. or foreign governments—but there were few coins in circulation. By collecting those notes and regularly demanding specie, the Second Bank kept the state banks from issuing too much paper money and depreciating its value.

This cautious monetary policy pleased creditors—the bankers and entrepreneurs in Boston, New York, and Philadelphia, whose capital investments were underwriting economic development. However, expansion-minded bankers, including friends of Jackson's in Nashville, demanded an end to central oversight. Moreover, many ordinary Americans worried that the

Second Bank would force weak banks to close, leaving them holding worthless paper notes. Many politicians resented the arrogance of the bank's president, Nicholas Biddle. "As to mere power," Biddle boasted, "I have been for years in the daily exercise of more personal authority than any President habitually enjoys."

**Jackson's Bank Veto**   Although the Second Bank had many enemies, a political miscalculation by its friends brought its downfall. In 1832, Henry Clay and Daniel Webster persuaded Biddle to seek an early extension of the bank's charter (which still had four years to run). They had the votes in Congress to enact the required legislation and hoped to lure Jackson into a veto that would split the Democrats just before the 1832 elections.

Jackson turned the tables on Clay and Webster. He vetoed the rechartering bill with a masterful message that blended constitutional arguments with class rhetoric and patriotic fervor. Adopting the position taken by Thomas Jefferson in 1793, Jackson declared that Congress had no constitutional authority to charter a national bank. He condemned the bank as "subversive of the rights of the States," "dangerous to the liberties of the people," and a privileged monopoly that promoted "the advancement of the few at the expense of . . . farmers, mechanics, and laborers." Finally, the president noted that British aristocrats owned much of the bank's stock. Such a powerful institution should be "purely American," Jackson declared with patriotic zeal.

Jackson's attack on the bank carried him to victory in 1832. Old Hickory and Martin Van Buren, his new running mate, overwhelmed Henry Clay, who headed the National Republican ticket, by 219 to 49 electoral votes. Jackson's most fervent supporters were eastern workers and western farmers, who blamed the Second Bank for high urban prices and stagnant farm income. "All the flourishing cities of the West are mortgaged to this money power," charged Senator Thomas Hart Benton, a Jacksonian from Missouri. Still, many of Jackson's supporters had prospered during a decade of strong economic growth. Thousands of middle-class Americans — lawyers, clerks, shopkeepers, and artisans — had used the opportunity to rise in the world and cheered Jackson's attack on privileged corporations.

**PLACE EVENTS IN CONTEXT**
Why — and how — did Jackson destroy the Second National Bank?

**The Bank Destroyed**   Early in 1833, Jackson met their wishes by appointing Roger B. Taney, a strong opponent of corporate privilege, as head of the Treasury Department. Taney promptly transferred the federal government's gold and silver from the Second Bank to various state banks, which critics labeled Jackson's "pet banks." To justify this abrupt (and probably illegal) transfer, Jackson declared that his reelection represented "the decision of the people against the bank" and gave him a mandate to destroy it. This sweeping claim of presidential power was new and radical. Never before had a president claimed that victory at the polls allowed him to pursue a controversial policy or to act independently of Congress (American Voices, p. 328).

The "bank war" escalated into an all-out political battle. In March 1834, Jackson's opponents in the Senate passed a resolution composed by Henry Clay that censured the president and warned of executive tyranny: "We are in the midst of a revolution, hitherto bloodless, but rapidly descending towards a total change of the pure republican character of the Government, and the concentration of all power in the hands of one man." Clay's charges and Congress's censure did not deter Jackson. "The Bank is trying to kill me but I will kill it," he vowed to Van Buren. And so he did. When the Second Bank's national charter expired in 1836, Jackson prevented its renewal.

Jackson had destroyed both national banking — the handiwork of Alexander Hamilton — and the American System of protective tariffs and public works created by Henry Clay and John Quincy Adams. The result was a profound check on economic activism and innovative policymaking by the national government. "All is gone," observed a Washington newspaper correspondent. "All is gone, which the General Government was instituted to create and preserve."

## Indian Removal

The status of Native American peoples posed an equally complex political problem. By the late 1820s, white voices throughout the South and Midwest demanded the resettlement of Indian peoples west of the Mississippi River. Many whites who were sympathetic to Native Americans also favored resettlement. Removal to the West seemed the only way to protect Indians from alcoholism, financial exploitation, and cultural decline.

However, most Indians did not want to leave their ancestral lands. For centuries, Cherokees and Creeks had lived in Georgia, Tennessee, and Alabama; Chickasaws and Choctaws in Mississippi and Alabama; and Seminoles in Florida. During the War of 1812, Andrew Jackson had forced the Creeks to relinquish millions of acres, but Indian tribes still controlled vast tracts and wanted to keep them.

### Cherokee Resistance

But on what terms? Some Indians had adopted white ways. An 1825 census revealed that various Cherokees owned 33 gristmills, 13 sawmills, 2,400 spinning wheels, 760 looms, and 2,900 plows. Many of these owners were mixed-race, the offspring of white traders and Indian women. They had grown up in a bicultural world, knew the political and economic ways of whites, and often favored assimilation into white society. Indeed, some of these mixed-race people were indistinguishable from southern planters. At his death in 1809, Georgia Cherokee James Vann owned one hundred black slaves, two trading posts, and a gristmill. Three decades later, forty other mixed-blood Cherokee families each owned ten or more African American workers.

Prominent mixed-race Cherokees believed that integration into American life was the best way to protect their property and the lands of their people. In 1821, Sequoyah, a part-Cherokee silversmith, perfected a system of writing for the Cherokee language; six years later, mixed-race Cherokees devised a new charter of Cherokee government modeled directly on the U.S. Constitution. "You asked us to throw off the hunter and warrior state," Cherokee John Ridge told a Philadelphia audience in 1832. "We did so. You asked us to form a republican government: We did so. . . . You asked us to learn to read: We did so. You asked us to cast away our idols, and worship your God: We did so." Full-blood Cherokees, who made up 90 percent of the population, resisted many of these cultural and political innovations but were equally determined to retain their ancestral lands. "We would not receive money for land in which our fathers and friends are buried," one full-blood chief declared. "We love our land; it is our mother."

What the Cherokees did or wanted carried no weight with the Georgia legislature. In 1802, Georgia had given up its western land claims in return for a federal promise to extinguish Indian landholdings in the state. Now it demanded fulfillment of that pledge. Having spent his military career fighting Indians and seizing their lands, Andrew Jackson gave full support to Georgia. On assuming the presidency, he withdrew the federal troops that had protected Indian enclaves there and in Alabama and Mississippi. The states, he declared, were sovereign within their borders.

### The Removal Act and Its Aftermath

Jackson then pushed the **Indian Removal Act of 1830** through Congress over the determined opposition of evangelical Protestant men—and women. To block removal, Catharine Beecher and Lydia Sigourney composed a Ladies Circular, which urged "benevolent ladies" to use "prayers and exertions to avert the calamity of removal." Women from across the nation flooded Congress with petitions. Nonetheless, Jackson's bill squeaked through the House of Representatives by a vote of 102 to 97.

The Removal Act created the Indian Territory on national lands acquired in the Louisiana Purchase and located in present-day Oklahoma and Kansas. It promised money and reserved land to Native American peoples who would give up their ancestral holdings east of the Mississippi River. Government officials promised the Indians that they could live on their new land, "they and all their children, as long as grass grows and water runs." However, as one Indian leader noted, on the Great Plains "water and timber are scarcely to be seen." When Chief Black Hawk and his Sauk and Fox

***Blackhawk***

This portrait of Black Hawk (1767–1838), by George Catlin, shows the Indian leader holding his namesake, a black hawk and its feathers. When Congress approved Andrew Jackson's Indian Removal Act in 1830, Black Hawk mobilized Sauk and Fox warriors to protect their ancestral lands in Illinois. "It was here, that I was born—and here lie the bones of many friends and relatives," the aging chief declared. "I . . . never could consent to leave it." Courtesy Warner Collection of Gulf States Paper Corporation, Tuscaloosa, AL.

## The Character and Goals of Andrew Jackson

From the start of his career, Andrew Jackson was a controversial figure. "Hot-tempered," "Indian-hater," "military despot," said his critics, while his friends praised him as a forthright statesman. His contemporary biographer, the journalist James Parton, found him a man of many faces, an enigma. Others thought they understood his personality and policies: James Hamilton, a loyal Jacksonian congressman, recalled Jackson's volatile temper. Henry Clay, his archrival, warned that Jackson's quest for power threatened American republicanism, while wealthy New York Whig Philip Hone accused him of inciting class warfare. After talking with dozens of Americans, Frenchman Alexis de Tocqueville offered a balanced interpretation of the man and his goals.

### James Parton
### Preface to *The Life of Andrew Jackson* (1860)

If any one . . . had asked what I had yet discovered respecting General Jackson, I might have answered thus: "Andrew Jackson, I am given to understand, was a patriot and a traitor. He was one of the greatest of generals, and wholly ignorant of the art of war. . . . The first of statesmen, he never devised, he never framed a measure. He was the most candid of men, and was capable of the profoundest dissimulation. A most law-defying, law-obeying citizen. A stickler for discipline, he never hesitated to disobey his superior. A democratic autocrat. An urbane savage. An atrocious saint."

### James Hamilton Jr.
### Recalling an Event in 1827, as Jackson Campaigns for the Presidency

The steamer Pocahontas was chartered by citizens of New Orleans to convey the General and his party from Nashville to that city. She was fitted out in the most sumptuous manner. The party was General and Mrs. Jackson, . . . Governor Samuel Houston, Wm. B. Lewis, Robert Armstrong, and others. . . . The only freight was the General's cotton-crop. . . .

In the course of the voyage an event occurred, which I repeat, as it is suggestive of [his] character. A steamer of greater speed than ours, going in the same direction, passed us, crossed our bow; then stopped and let us pass her and then passed us again in triumph. This was repeated again and again, until the General, being excited by the offensive course, ordered a rifle to be brought to him; hailed the pilot of the other steamer, and swore that if he did the same thing again he would shoot him.

### Philip Hone
### Ruminating in His Diary on the Jacksonians' Victory in the New York Elections of 1834

I apprehend that Mr. Van Buren [Jackson's vice president] and his friends have no permanent cause of triumph in their victory. They . . . have mounted a vicious horse, who, taking the bit in his mouth, will run away with [them]. . . . This battle had been fought upon the ground of the poor against the rich, and this unworthy prejudice, this dangerous delusion, has been encouraged by the leaders of the triumphant party, and fanned into a flame by the polluted breath of the hireling press in their employ. . . .

The cry of "Down with the aristocracy!" mingled with the shouts of victory. . . . They have succeeded in raising this dangerous spirit [of the mob], and have gladly availed themselves of its support to accomplish a temporary object; but can they allay it at pleasure? . . . Eighteen thousand men in New York have voted for the high-priest of the party whose professed design is to bring down the property, the talents, the industry, the steady habits of that class which constituted the real strength of the Commonwealth, to the common level of the idle, the worthless, and the unenlightened. Look to it, ye men of respectability in the Jackson party, are ye not afraid of the weapons ye have used in this warfare?

### Henry Clay
### Introducing a Senate Resolution Censuring Jackson, December 26, 1833

We are in the midst of a revolution, hitherto bloodless, but rapidly tending toward a total change of the pure republican character of the government, and to the concentration of all power in the hands of one man. The powers of Congress are paralyzed, except when exerted in conformity with his will, by frequent and an extraordinary exercise of the executive veto, not anticipated by the founders of our Constitution, and not practiced by any of the predecessors of the present chief magistrate. . . .

The judiciary has not been exempt from the prevailing rage for innovation. Decisions of the tribunals, deliberately pronounced, have been contemptuously disregarded. . . . Our Indian relations, coeval with the existence of the government, and recognized and established by numerous laws and treaties, have been subverted. . . . The system of protection of improvement lies crushed beneath the veto. The system of protection of American industry [will soon meet a similar fate]. . . . In a term of eight years, a little more than equal to that which was required to establish our liberties [as an independent republic between 1776 and 1783], the government will have been transformed into an elective monarchy — the worst of all forms of government.

### Alexis de Tocqueville
## Analysis of Jackson in *Democracy in America* (1835)

We have been told that General Jackson has won battles; that he is an energetic man, prone by nature and habit to the use of force, covetous of power and a despot by inclination.

All this may be true; but the inferences which have been drawn from these truths are very erroneous. It has been imagined that General Jackson is bent on establishing a dictatorship in America, introducing a military spirit, and giving a degree of influence to the central authority that cannot but be dangerous to provincial [state] liberties. . . .

Far from wishing to extend the Federal power, the President belongs to the party which is desirous of limiting that power to the clear and precise letter of the Constitution and which never puts a construction upon that act favorable to the government of the Union; far from standing forth as the champion of centralization, General Jackson is the agent of the state jealousies; and he was placed in his lofty station by the passions that are most opposed to the central government.

Sources: James Parton, *The Life of Andrew Jackson. In Three Volumes* (New York: Mason Brothers, 1860), vol. 1, vii–viii; Sean Wilentz, ed., *Major Problems in the Early Republic, 1787–1848* (Lexington, MA: D. C. Heath, 1991), 374 (Hamilton) and 392–393 (Hone); Calvin Colton, ed., *The Life . . . of Henry Clay*, 6 vols. (New York: A. Barnes, 1857), 576–580; Alexis de Tocqueville, *Democracy in America*, abr. by Thomas Bender (New York: Modern Library, 1981), 271–273.

### QUESTIONS FOR ANALYSIS

1. Was Jackson a "democratic autocrat," as Parton puts it? Would the authors of the other excerpts agree? Did Jackson instigate class warfare, as Hone suggests?

2. In your judgment, which writer, Clay or Tocqueville, offers the more accurate assessment of Jackson and his policies?

3. Do you agree with Philip Hone's view that the Jacksonian Democrats mobilized "poor against the rich"? What evidence would support or contradict Hone's assertion?

**COMPARE AND CONTRAST**
How did the views of Jackson and John Marshall differ regarding the status and rights of Indian peoples?

followers refused to leave rich, well-watered farmland in western Illinois in 1832, Jackson sent troops to expel them by force. Eventually, the U.S. Army pursued Black Hawk into the Wisconsin Territory and, in the brutal eight-hour Bad Axe Massacre, killed 850 of his 1,000 warriors. Over the next five years, American diplomatic pressure and military power forced seventy Indian peoples to sign treaties and move west of the Mississippi (Map 10.3).

In the meantime, the Cherokees had carried the defense of their lands to the Supreme Court, where they claimed the status of a "foreign nation." In *Cherokee Nation v. Georgia* (1831), Chief Justice John Marshall denied that claim and declared that Indian peoples were "domestic dependent nations." However, in *Worcester v. Georgia* (1832), Marshall and the Court sided with the Cherokees against Georgia. Voiding Georgia's extension of state law over the Cherokees, the Court held that Indian nations were "distinct political communities, having territorial boundaries, within which their authority is exclusive [and is] guaranteed by the United States."

Instead of guaranteeing the Cherokees' territory, the U.S. government took it from them. In 1835, American officials and a minority Cherokee faction

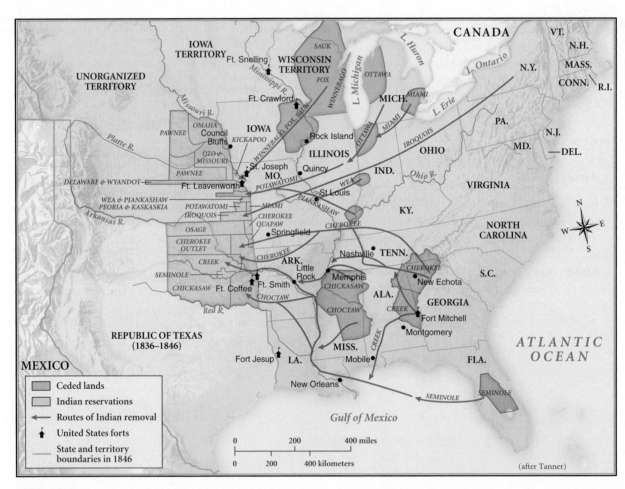

**MAP 10.3**

**The Removal of Native Americans, 1820–1846**

As white settlers moved west, the U.S. government forced scores of Native American peoples to leave their ancestral lands. Andrew Jackson's Indian Removal Act of 1830 formalized this policy. Subsequently, scores of Indian peoples signed treaties that exchanged their lands in the East, Midwest, and Southeast for money and designated reservations in an Indian Territory west of the Mississippi River. When the Sauk, Fox, Cherokees, and Seminoles resisted resettlement, the government used the U.S. Army to enforce the removal policy.

**Raising Public Opinion Against the Seminoles**

During the eighteenth century, hundreds of enslaved Africans fled South Carolina and Georgia and found refuge in Spanish Florida, where they lived among and intermarried with the Seminole people. This color engraving from the 1830s—showing red and black Seminoles butchering respectable white families—sought to bolster political support for the removal of the Seminoles to Indian Territory. By the mid-1840s, after a decade of warfare, the U.S. Army had forced 2,500 Seminoles to migrate to Oklahoma. However, another 2,500 Seminoles continued to fight and eventually won a new treaty allowing them to live in Florida. The Granger Collection, New York.

negotiated the Treaty of New Echota, which specified that Cherokees would resettle in Indian Territory. When only 2,000 of 17,000 Cherokees had moved by the May 1838 deadline, President Martin Van Buren ordered General Winfield Scott to enforce the treaty. Scott's army rounded up 14,000 Cherokees (including mixed-race African Cherokees) and marched them 1,200 miles, an arduous journey that became known as the **Trail of Tears**. Along the way, 3,000 Indians died of starvation and exposure. Once in Oklahoma, the Cherokees excluded anyone of "negro or mulatto parentage" from governmental office, thereby affirming that full citizenship in their nation was racially defined. Just as the United States was a "white man's country," so Indian Territory would be defined as a "red man's country."

Encouraged by generous gifts of land, the Creeks, Chickasaws, and Choctaws moved west of the Mississippi, leaving the Seminoles in Florida as the only numerically significant Indian people remaining in the Southeast. Government pressure persuaded about half of the Seminoles to migrate to Indian Territory, but families whose ancestors had intermarried with runaway slaves feared the emphasis on "blood purity" there. During the 1840s, they fought a successful guerrilla war against the U.S. Army and retained their lands in central Florida. These Seminoles were the exception: the Jacksonians had forced the removal of most eastern Indian peoples.

## The Jacksonian Impact

Jackson's legacy, like that of every other great president, is complex and rich. On the institutional level, he expanded the authority of the nation's chief executive. As Jackson put it, "The President is the direct representative of the American people." Assuming that role during the nullification crisis, he upheld national authority by threatening the use of military force, laying the foundation for Lincoln's defense of the Union a generation later. At the same time (and somewhat contradictorily), Jackson curbed the reach of the national government. By undermining Henry Clay's American System of national banking, protective tariffs, and internal improvements, Jackson reinvigorated the Jeffersonian tradition of a limited and frugal central government.

**The Taney Court**    Jackson also undermined the constitutional jurisprudence of John Marshall by appointing Roger B. Taney as his successor in 1835. During his long tenure as chief justice (1835–1864), Taney partially reversed the nationalist and vested-property-rights decisions of the Marshall Court and gave constitutional legitimacy to Jackson's policies of states' rights and free enterprise. In the landmark case *Charles River Bridge Co. v. Warren Bridge Co.* (1837), Taney declared that a legislative charter—in this case, to build and operate a toll bridge—did not necessarily bestow a monopoly, and that a legislature could charter a competing bridge to promote the general welfare: "While the rights of private property are sacredly guarded, we must not forget that the community also has rights." This decision directly challenged Marshall's interpretation of the contract clause of the Constitution in *Dartmouth College v. Woodward* (1819), which had stressed the binding nature of public charters and the sanctity of "vested rights" (Chapter 7). By limiting the property claims of existing canal and turnpike companies, Taney's decision allowed legislatures to charter competing railroads that would provide cheaper and more efficient transportation.

The Taney Court also limited Marshall's nationalistic interpretation of the commerce clause by enhancing the regulatory role of state governments. For example, in *Mayor of New York v. Miln* (1837), the Taney Court ruled that New York State could use its "police power" to inspect the health of arriving immigrants. The Court also restored to the states some of the economic powers they had exercised prior to the Constitution of 1787. In *Briscoe v. Bank of Kentucky* (1837), the justices allowed a bank owned by the state of Kentucky to issue currency, despite the wording of Article 1, Section 10 of the Constitution, which prohibits states from issuing "bills of credit."

**EXPLAIN CONSEQUENCES**
How did the Taney Court and the Jacksonian state constitutions alter the American legal and constitutional system?

**States Revise Their Constitutions** Inspired by Jackson and Taney, Democrats in the various states mounted their own constitutional revolutions. Between 1830 and 1860, twenty states called conventions that furthered democratic principles by reapportioning state legislatures on the basis of population and giving the vote to all white men. Voters also had more power because the new documents mandated the election, rather than the appointment, of most public officials, including sheriffs, justices of the peace, and judges.

The new constitutions also embodied the principles of **classical liberalism**, or **laissez-faire**, by limiting the government's role in the economy. (Twentieth-century social-welfare liberalism endorses the opposite principle: that government should intervene in economic and social life.) As president, Jackson had destroyed the American System, and his disciples now attacked the state-based Commonwealth System, which used chartered corporations and state funds to promote economic development. Most Jackson-era constitutions prohibited states from granting special charters to corporations and extending loans and credit guarantees to private businesses. "If there is any danger to be feared

in . . . government," declared a New Jersey Democrat, "it is the danger of associated wealth, with special privileges." The revised constitutions also protected taxpayers by setting strict limits on state debt and encouraging judges to enforce them. Said New York reformer Michael Hoffman, "We will not trust the legislature with the power of creating indefinite mortgages on the people's property."

"The world is governed too much," the Jacksonians proclaimed as they embraced a small-government, laissez-faire outlook and celebrated the power of ordinary people to make decisions in the voting booth and the marketplace.

# Class, Culture, and the Second Party System

The rise of the Democracy and Jackson's tumultuous presidency sparked the creation in the mid-1830s of a second national party: the **Whigs**. For the next two decades, Whigs and Democrats competed fiercely for votes and appealed to different cultural groups. Many evangelical Protestants became Whigs, while most Catholic immigrants and traditional Protestants joined the Democrats. By debating issues of economic policy, class power, and moral reform, party politicians offered Americans a choice between competing programs and political leaders. "Of the two great parties," remarked philosopher Ralph Waldo Emerson, "[the Democracy] has the best cause . . . for free trade, for wide suffrage, [but the Whig Party] has the best men."

## The Whig Worldview

The Whig Party arose in 1834, when a group of congressmen contested Andrew Jackson's policies and his high-handed, "kinglike" conduct. They took the name *Whigs* to identify themselves with the pre-Revolutionary American and British parties — also called Whigs — that had opposed the arbitrary actions of British monarchs. The Whigs accused "King Andrew I" of violating the Constitution by creating a spoils system and undermining elected legislators, whom they saw as the true representatives of the sovereign people. One Whig accused Jackson of ruling in a manner "more absolute than that of any absolute monarchy of Europe."

Initially, the Whigs consisted of political factions with distinct points of view. However, guided by Senators Webster of Massachusetts, Clay of Kentucky, and Calhoun of South Carolina, they gradually coalesced into a party with a distinctive stance and coherent ideology. Like the Federalists of the 1790s, the Whigs wanted a political world dominated by men of ability and wealth; unlike the Federalists, they advocated an elite based on talent, not birth.

The Whigs celebrated the entrepreneur and the enterprising individual: "This is a country of self-made men," they boasted, pointing to the relative absence of permanent distinctions of class and status among white citizens. Embracing the Industrial Revolution, northern Whigs welcomed the investments of "moneyed capitalists," which provided workers with jobs and "bread, clothing and homes." Indeed, Whig congressman Edward Everett championed a "holy alliance" among laborers, owners, and governments and called for a return to Henry Clay's American System. Many New England and Pennsylvania textile and iron workers shared Everett's vision because they benefitted directly from protective tariffs.

**Calhoun's Dissent**  Support for the Whigs in the South — less widespread than that in the North — rested on the appeal of specific policies and politicians. Some southern Whigs were wealthy planters who invested in railroads and banks or sold their cotton to New York merchants. But the majority were yeomen whites who resented the power and policies of low-country planters, most of whom were Democrats. In addition, some Virginia and South Carolina Democrats, such as John Taylor, became Whigs because they condemned Andrew Jackson's crusade against nullification.

Southern Whigs rejected their party's enthusiasm for high tariffs and social mobility, and John C. Calhoun was their spokesman. Extremely conscious of class divisions in society, Calhoun believed that northern Whigs' rhetoric of equal opportunity was contradicted not only by slavery, which he considered a fundamental American institution, but also by the wage-labor system of industrial capitalism. "There is and always has been in an advanced state of wealth and civilization a conflict between labor and capital," Calhoun declared in 1837. He urged slave owners and factory owners to unite against their common foe: the working class of enslaved blacks and propertyless whites.

Most northern Whigs rejected Calhoun's class-conscious social ideology. "A clear and well-defined line between capital and labor" might fit the slave South or class-ridden Europe, Daniel Webster conceded, but in the North "this distinction grows less and less definite as commerce advances." Ignoring the ever-increasing numbers of propertyless immigrants and native-born wageworkers, Webster focused on the growing size of the middle class, whose members generally favored Whig candidates. In the election of 1834, the Whigs

**John C. Calhoun (1782–1850)**
This daguerreotype, made close to the time of Calhoun's death, suggests his emotional intensity and thwarted ambition. The prime advocate of the doctrines of nullification and states' rights, a founder of the Whig Party, and a steadfast defender of slavery, Calhoun found his lifelong pursuit of the presidency frustrated by Martin Van Buren's political skills and sectional divisions over tariffs and slavery. © Image courtesy of the Gibbes Museum of Art/Carolina Art Association.

took control of the House of Representatives by appealing to evangelical Protestants and upwardly mobile families — prosperous farmers, small-town merchants, and skilled industrial workers in New England, New York, and the new communities along the Great Lakes.

> **COMPARE AND CONTRAST**
> How did the ideology of the Whigs differ from that of the Jacksonian Democrats?

**Anti-Masons Become Whigs**  Many Whig voters in 1834 had previously supported the Anti-Masons, a powerful but short-lived party that formed in the late 1820s. As its name implies, Anti-Masons opposed the Order of Freemasonry. Freemasonry began in Europe as an organization of men seeking moral improvement by promoting the welfare and unity of humanity. Many Masons espoused republicanism, and the Order spread rapidly in America after the Revolution. Its ideology, mysterious symbols, and semisecret character gave the Order an air of exclusivity that attracted ambitious businessmen and political leaders, including George Washington, Henry Clay, and Andrew Jackson. In New

York State alone by the mid-1820s, there were more than 20,000 Masons, organized into 450 local lodges. However, after the kidnapping and murder in 1826 of William Morgan, a New York Mason who had threatened to reveal the Order's secrets, the Freemasons fell into disrepute. Thurlow Weed, a newspaper editor in Rochester, New York, spearheaded an Anti-Masonic Party, which condemned the Order as a secret aristocratic fraternity. The new party quickly ousted Freemasons from local and state offices, and just as quickly ran out of political steam.

Because many Anti-Masons espoused temperance, equality of opportunity, and evangelical morality, they gravitated to the Whig Party. Throughout the Northeast and Midwest, Whig politicians won election by proposing legal curbs on the sale of alcohol and local ordinances that preserved Sunday as a day of worship. The Whigs also secured the votes of farmers, bankers, and shopkeepers, who favored Henry Clay's American System. For these citizens of the growing Midwest, the Whigs' program of government subsidies for roads, canals, and bridges was as important as their moral agenda.

In the election of 1836, the Whig Party faced Martin Van Buren, the architect of the Democratic Party and Jackson's handpicked successor. Like Jackson, Van Buren denounced the American System and warned that its revival would create a "consolidated government." Positioning himself as a defender of individual rights, Van Buren also condemned the efforts of Whigs and moral reformers to enact state laws imposing temperance and national laws abolishing slavery. "The government is best which governs least" became his motto in economic, cultural, and racial matters.

To oppose Van Buren, the Whigs ran four candidates, each with a strong regional reputation. They hoped to garner enough electoral votes to throw the contest into the House of Representatives. However, the Whig tally — 73 electoral votes collected by William Henry Harrison of Ohio, 26 by Hugh L. White of Tennessee, 14 by Daniel Webster of Massachusetts, and 11 by W. P. Mangum of Georgia — fell far short of Van Buren's 170 votes. Still, the four Whigs won 49 percent of the popular vote, showing that the party's message of economic and moral improvement had broad appeal.

## Labor Politics and the Depression of 1837–1843

As the Democrats battled Whigs on the national level, they faced challenges from urban artisans and workers. Between 1828 and 1833, artisans and laborers in fifteen states formed Working Men's Parties. "Past experience teaches us that we have nothing to hope from the aristocratic orders of society," declared the New York Working Men's Party. It vowed "to send men of our own description, if we can, to the Legislature at Albany."

The new parties' agenda reflected the values and interests of ordinary urban workers. The Philadelphia Working Men's Party set out to secure "a just balance of power . . . between all the various classes." It called for the abolition of private banks, chartered monopolies, and debtors' prisons, and it demanded universal public education and a fair system of taxation (Thinking Like a Historian, p. 336). It won some victories, electing a number of assemblymen and persuading the Pennsylvania legislature in 1834 to authorize tax-supported schools. Elsewhere, Working Men's candidates won office in many cities, but their parties' weakness in statewide contests soon took a toll. By the mid-1830s, most politically active workers had joined the Democratic Party.

The Working Men's Parties left a mixed legacy. They mobilized craft workers and gave political expression to their ideology of artisan republicanism. As labor intellectual Orestes Brownson defined their distinctive vision, "All men will be independent proprietors, working on their own capitals, on their own farms, or in their own shops." However, this emphasis on proprietorship inhibited alliances between the artisan-based Working Men's Parties and the rapidly increasing class of dependent wage earners. As Joseph Weydemeyer, a close friend of Karl Marx, reported from New York in the early 1850s, many American craft workers "are incipient bourgeois, and feel themselves to be such."

Moreover, the **Panic of 1837** threw the American economy — and the workers' movement — into disarray. The panic began when the Bank of England tried to boost the faltering British economy by sharply curtailing the flow of money and credit to the United States. Since 1822, British manufacturers had extended credit to southern planters to expand cotton production, and British investors had purchased millions of dollars of the canal bonds from the northern states. Suddenly deprived of British funds, American planters, merchants, and canal corporations had to withdraw gold from domestic banks to pay their foreign debts. Moreover, British textile mills drastically reduced their purchases of raw cotton, causing its price to plummet from 20 cents a pound to 10 cents or less.

Falling cotton prices and the drain of specie to Britain set off a financial panic. On May 8, the Dry Dock Bank of New York City ran out of specie, prompting worried depositors to withdraw gold and silver coins from other banks. Within two weeks, every American bank had stopped trading specie and called in its loans, turning a financial panic into an economic crisis. "This sudden overthrow of the commercial credit" had a "stunning effect," observed Henry Fox, the British minister in Washington. "The conquest of the land by a foreign power could hardly have produced a more general sense of humiliation and grief."

To stimulate the economy, state governments increased their investments in canals and railroads. However, as governments issued (or guaranteed) more and more bonds to finance these ventures, they were unable to pay the interest charges, sparking a severe financial crisis on both sides of the Atlantic in 1839. Nine state governments defaulted on their debts, and hard-pressed European lenders cut the flow of new capital to the United States.

The American economy fell into a deep depression. By 1843, canal construction had dropped by 90 percent, prices and wages had fallen by 50 percent, and unemployment in seaports and industrial centers had reached 20 percent. Bumper crops drove down cotton prices, pushing hundreds of planters and merchants into bankruptcy. Minister Henry Ward Beecher described a land "filled with lamentation . . . its inhabitants wandering like bereaved citizens among the ruins of an earthquake, mourning for children, for houses crushed, and property buried forever."

By creating a surplus of unemployed workers, the depression completed the decline of the union movement and the Working Men's Parties. In 1837, six thousand masons, carpenters, and other building-trades workers lost their jobs in New York City, destroying their unions' bargaining power. By 1843, most local unions, all the national labor organizations, and all the workers' parties had disappeared.

## "Tippecanoe and Tyler Too!"

Many Americans blamed the Democrats for the depression of 1837–1843. They criticized Jackson for destroying the Second Bank and directing the Treasury

**IDENTIFY CAUSES**
What factors led to the demise of the Anti-Masonic and Working Men's political parties?

**Hard Times**
The Panic of 1837 struck hard at Americans of all social ranks. This anti-Democratic cartoon shows unemployed workers turning to drink; women and children begging in the streets; and fearful depositors withdrawing funds as their banks collapse. As the plummeting hot-air balloon in the background symbolizes, the rising "Glory" of an independent America was crashing to earth. © Museum of the City of New York, USA/The Bridgeman Art Library.

## Becoming Literate: Public Education and Democracy

The struggle for a genuinely *democratic* polity—"government of the people, by the people, and for the people," as Lincoln put it—played out at the local and state level in battles over who should participate in the political arena. As legislators argued over extending the franchise, they considered the knowledge that citizens needed to participate responsibly in politics. Although primary education was publicly supported in most New England towns (giving that region nearly universal literacy), it received only spotty funding in the other northern states and almost none in the South (restricting literacy there to one-third of the white population). The following documents address the resulting debate over publicly supported education and citizenship.

1. **Editorial from the *Philadelphia National Gazette*, 1830.** *Pennsylvania was one of the first states to debate legislation regarding universal free public education.*

The scheme of Universal Equal Education . . . is virtually "Agrarianism" [redistribution of land from rich to poor]. It would be a compulsory application of the means of the richer, for the direct use of the poorer classes. . . . One of the chief excitements to industry . . . is the hope of earning the means of educating their children respectably . . . that incentive would be removed, and the scheme of state and equal education be a premium for comparative idleness, to be taken out of the pockets of the laborious and conscientious.

2. **Thaddeus Stevens, speech before the Pennsylvania General Assembly, February 1835.** *Pennsylvania's Free Public School Act of 1834 was the handiwork of the Working Men's Party of Philadelphia (see p. 334). When over half of Pennsylvania's school districts refused to implement the law, the legislature threatened to repeal it. Thaddeus Stevens, later a leading antislavery advocate, turned back that threat through this speech to the Pennsylvania General Assembly.*

It would seem to be humiliating to be under the necessity, in the nineteenth century, of entering into a formal argument to prove the utility, and to free governments, the absolute necessity of education. . . . Such necessity would be degrading to a Christian age and a free republic. If an elective republic is to endure for any great length of time, every elector must have sufficient information, not only to accumulate wealth and take care of his pecuniary concerns, but to direct wisely the Legislatures, the Ambassadors, and the Executive of the nation; for some part of all these things, some agency in approving or disapproving of them, falls to every freeman. If,

then, the permanency of our government depends upon such knowledge, it is the duty of government to see that the means of information be diffused to every citizen. This is a sufficient answer to those who deem education a private and not a public duty—who argue that they are willing to educate their own children, but not their neighbor's children.

3. **"Letter from a Teacher" in Catharine E. Beecher, *The True Remedy for the Wrongs of Women*, 1851.** *The public school movement created new opportunities not just for children of middle and lower classes but also for the young Protestant women who contributed to the "Benevolent Empire" as professional educators. Beecher's academy (see p. 369) in Hartford, Connecticut, sent out dozens of young women to establish schools.*

I am now located in this place, which is the county-town of a newly organized county [in a midwestern state]. . . . The Sabbath is little regarded, and is more a day for diversion than devotion. . . . My school embraces both sexes and all ages from five to seventeen, and not one can read intelligibly.

4. **"Popular Education," 1833.** *This piece appeared in the* North American Review, *the nation's first literary and cultural journal and the mouthpiece of New England's intellectual elite.*

[T]he mind of a people, in proportion as it is educated, will not only feel its own value, but will also perceive its rights. We speak now of those palpable rights which are recognised by all free states. . . . [T]he palpable rights of men, those of personal security, of property and of the free and unembarrassed pursuit of individual welfare, it is obviously impossible to conceal from an educated and reading people. Such a people rises at once above the condition of feudal tenants. . . . It directs its attention to the laws and institutions that govern it. It compels public office to give an account of itself. It strips off the veil of secrecy from the machinery of power. . . . And when all this is spread abroad in newspaper details . . . of a people that can read; when the estimate is freely made, of what the government tax levies upon the daily hoard, and upon apparel, and upon every comfort of life, can it be doubted that such a people will demand and obtain an influence in affairs that so vitally concern it? This would be freedom.

5. **Judge Baker, sentencing hearing in the court case against Mrs. Margaret Douglass of Norfolk, Virginia, January 10, 1854.** *Southern whites considered the acquisition of literacy by blacks, whether slave or free, as a public danger, especially after the Nat Turner uprising in Southampton County, Virginia, in 1831 (Chapter 11, p. 362). A Virginia court sent Mrs. Margaret Douglass to jail for a month "as an example to all others" for teaching free black children to read so they might have access to books on religion and morality.*

There are persons, I believe, in our community, opposed to the policy of the law in question. They profess to believe that universal intellectual culture is necessary to religious instruction and education, and that such culture is suitable to a state of slavery. . . .

Such opinions in the present state of our society I regard as manifestly mischievous. It is not true that our slaves cannot be taught religious and moral duty, without being able to read the Bible and use the pen. Intellectual and religious instruction often go hand in hand, but the latter may well be exist without the former; . . . among the whites one-fou[r]th or more are entirely without a knowledge of letters, [nonetheless,] respect for the law, and for moral and religious conduct and behavior, are justly and prope[r]ly appreciated and practiced. . . .

The first legislative provision upon this subject was introduced in the year 1831, immediately succeeding the bloody scenes of the memorable Southampton insurrection; and . . . was re-enacted with additional penalties in the year 1848. . . . After these several and repeated recognitions of the wisdom and propriety of the said act, it may well be said that bold and open opposition to it [must be condemned] . . . as a measure of self-preservation and protection.

Sources: (1) "Religion and Social Reform," the Gilder Lehrman Institute of American History, gilderlehrman.org; (2) *New York Legislature Documents*, Vol. 34, No. 65, Part 1 (Albany, NY: J. B. Lyon Company, 1919), 60; (3) Catharine E. Beecher, *Educational Reminiscences and Suggestions* (New York: J. D. Ford & Company, 1874), 127; (4) *The North American Review* 36, no. 58 (January 1833); (5) "The Case of Mrs. Margaret Douglass," *Africans in America*, pbs.org.

6. **Working Men's Party poster for immigrant voters, New York, 1830.**

Source: Joshua R. Greenberg, Advocating the Man.

## ANALYZING THE EVIDENCE

1. What arguments does the editorial in the *Philadelphia National Gazette* (source 1) advance? How does Stevens (source 2) reframe this argument?

2. What does the letter from a former student of Beecher's (source 3) tell us about the links between educational reform and other social movements, such as Sabbatarianism (p. 305)? How does it help us to understand the fate of the "notables" and the "log cabin campaign" of 1840?

3. What is the larger agenda of the author of source 4? How is the argument here similar to, or different from, that in sources 1 and 2?

4. How does Judge Baker (source 5) justify the denial of education to African Americans?

5. What do the occupations of the Working Men's Party candidates suggest about its definition of "worker" (source 6)? How does the political agenda of the party relate to the arguments advanced in sources 2 and 4? To present-day debates regarding the education of illegal immigrants?

## PUTTING IT ALL TOGETHER

As these selections indicate, the debate over education had many facets. Did the power traditionally held by "notables" rest on their access to private schooling? Should a democratic society ensure the literacy of citizen voters? Was religious instruction a telling argument for slave literacy? Using these documents, your answers to the questions above, and materials in Chapters 8 and 10, write an essay that discusses public education, responsible citizenship, and social reform in America between 1820 and 1860.

Department in 1836 to issue the **Specie Circular**, an executive order that required the Treasury Department to accept only gold and silver in payment for lands in the national domain. Critics charged — mistakenly — that the Circular drained so much specie from the economy that it sparked the Panic of 1837. In fact (as noted above), the curtailing of credit by the Bank of England was the main cause of the panic.

Nonetheless, the public turned its anger on Van Buren, who took office just before the panic struck. Ignoring the pleas of influential bankers, the new president refused to revoke the Specie Circular or take actions to stimulate the economy. Holding to his philosophy of limited government, Van Buren advised Congress that "the less government interferes with private pursuits the better for the general prosperity." As the depression deepened in 1839, this laissez-faire outlook commanded less and less political support. Worse, Van Buren's major piece of fiscal legislation, the Independent Treasury Act of 1840, delayed recovery by pulling federal specie out of Jackson's pet banks (where it had backed loans) and placing it in government vaults, where it had little economic impact.

**The Log Cabin Campaign** The Whigs exploited Van Buren's weakness. In 1840, they organized their first national convention and nominated William Henry Harrison of Ohio for president and John Tyler of Virginia for vice president. A military hero of the Battle of Tippecanoe and the War of 1812, Harrison was well advanced in age (sixty-eight) and had little political experience. However, the Whig leaders in Congress, Henry Clay and Daniel Webster, wanted a president who would rubber-stamp their program for protective tariffs and a national bank. An unpretentious, amiable man, Harrison told voters that Whig policies were "the only means, under Heaven, by which a poor industrious man may become a rich man without bowing to colossal wealth."

The depression stacked the political cards against Van Buren, but the election turned as much on style as on substance. It became the great "log cabin campaign" — the first time two well-organized parties competed for votes through a new style of campaigning. Whig songfests, parades, and well-orchestrated mass meetings drew new voters into politics. Whig speakers assailed "Martin Van Ruin" as a manipulative politician with aristocratic tastes — a devotee of fancy wines, elegant clothes, and polite refinement, as indeed he was. Less truthfully, they portrayed Harrison as a self-made man who lived contentedly in a log cabin and quaffed hard cider, a drink of the common people. In fact, Harrison's father was a wealthy Virginia planter who

### The Whigs Boost Harrison and Tyler for the White House

In their quest for victory in 1840, Whig political strategists advanced a wide-ranging (and misleading) set of policies. This poster celebrates William Henry Harrison and John Tyler as candidates who would secure protective tariffs for American manufacturers — a policy that appealed to northern voters but one that Tyler opposed. It also promises to cut the size of the U.S. Army, which General Harrison did not favor. However, denouncing a large "Standing Army" would win votes in Virginia, where it recalled the fears of Radical Whig Patriots of 1776 and remained central to the states' rights ideology espoused by Senator Tyler and other "Old Republicans." Grouseland Foundation, Inc./Photo courtesy of "Fords the Art of Photography," Vincennes, IN.

**President John Tyler (1790–1862)**
Both as an "accidental" president and as a man, John Tyler left his mark on the world. His initiative to annex Texas made the election of 1844 into a pivotal contest and led to the war with Mexico in 1846. Tyler's first wife, Letitia, give birth to eight children before dying in the White House in 1842. Two years later, he married twenty-four-year-old Julia Gardiner, who bore him seven more children. White House Historical Association (White House Collection).

had signed the Declaration of Independence, and Harrison himself lived in a series of elegant mansions.

The Whigs boosted their electoral hopes by welcoming women to campaign festivities — a "first" for American politics. Many Jacksonian Democrats had long embraced an ideology of aggressive manhood, likening politically minded females to "public" women, prostitutes who plied their trade in theaters and other public places. Whigs took a more restrained view of masculinity and recognized that Christian women had already entered American public life through the temperance movement and other benevolent activities. In October 1840, Daniel Webster celebrated moral reform to an audience of twelve hundred women and urged them to back Whig candidates. "This way of making politicians of their women is something new under the sun," exclaimed one Democrat, worried that it would bring more Whig men to the polls. And it did: more than 80 percent of the eligible male voters cast ballots in 1840, up from fewer than 60 percent in 1832 and 1836 (see Figure 10.1). Heeding the Whigs' campaign slogan "Tippecanoe and Tyler Too," they voted Harrison into the White House with 53 percent of the popular vote and gave the party a majority in Congress.

**Tyler Subverts the Whig Agenda**   Led by Clay and Webster, the Whigs in Congress prepared to reverse the Jacksonian revolution. Their hopes were short-lived; barely a month after his inauguration in 1841, Harrison died of pneumonia, and the nation got "Tyler Too." But in what capacity: as acting president or as president? The Constitution was vague on the issue. Ignoring his Whig associates in Congress, who wanted a weak chief executive, Tyler took the presidential oath of office and declared his intention to govern as he pleased. As it turned out, that would not be like a Whig.

Tyler had served in the House and the Senate as a Jeffersonian Democrat, firmly committed to slavery and states' rights. He had joined the Whigs only to protest Jackson's stance against nullification. On economic issues, Tyler shared Jackson's hostility to the Second Bank and the American System. He therefore vetoed Whig bills that would have raised tariffs and created a new national bank. Outraged by this betrayal, most of Tyler's cabinet resigned in 1842, and the Whigs expelled Tyler from their party. "His Accidency," as he

> **UNDERSTAND POINTS OF VIEW**
> How did Whigs and Democrats view women in politics, and why did they hold those views?

was called by his critics, was now a president without a party.

The split between Tyler and the Whigs allowed the Democrats to regroup. The party vigorously recruited subsistence farmers in the North, smallholding planters in the South, and former members of the Working Men's Parties in the cities. It also won support among Irish and German Catholic immigrants — whose numbers had increased during the 1830s — by backing their demands for religious and cultural liberty, such as the freedom to drink beer and whiskey. A pattern of **ethnocultural politics**, as historians refer to the practice of voting along ethnic and religious lines, now became a prominent feature of American life. Thanks to these urban and rural recruits, the Democrats remained the majority party in most parts of the nation. Their program of equal rights, states' rights, and cultural liberty was attractive to more white Americans than the Whig platform of economic nationalism, moral reform, temperance laws, and individual mobility.

## SUMMARY

In this chapter, we examined the causes and the consequences of the democratic political revolution. We saw that the expansion of the franchise weakened the political system run by notables of high status and encouraged the transfer of power to professional politicians — men like Martin Van Buren, who were mostly of middle-class origin.

We also witnessed a revolution in government policy, as Andrew Jackson and his Democratic Party dismantled the mercantilist economic system of government-supported economic development. On the national level, Jackson destroyed Henry Clay's American System; on the state level, Democrats wrote new constitutions that ended the Commonwealth System of government charters and subsidies to private businesses. Jackson's treatment of Native Americans was equally revolutionary; the Removal Act of 1830 forcefully resettled eastern Indian peoples west of the Mississippi River, opening their ancestral lands to white settlement.

Finally, we watched the emergence of the Second Party System. Following the split in the Republican Party during the election of 1824, two new parties — the Democrats and the Whigs — developed on the national level and eventually absorbed the members of the Anti-Masonic and Working Men's parties. The new party system established universal suffrage for white men and a mode of representative government that was responsive to ordinary citizens. In their scope and significance, these political innovations matched the economic advances of both the Industrial Revolution and the Market Revolution.

# CHAPTER REVIEW

**MAKE IT STICK** Go to **LearningCurve** to retain what you've read.

## TERMS TO KNOW    Identify and explain the significance of each term below.

### Key Concepts and Events

franchise (p. 316)

notables (p. 316)

political machine (p. 317)

spoils system (p. 318)

caucus (p. 318)

American System (p. 319)

internal improvements (p. 319)

corrupt bargain (p. 319)

"consolidated government"
   (p. 320)

Tariff of Abominations (p. 320)

nullification (p. 324)

states' rights (p. 324)

Second Bank of the United States
   (p. 325)

Indian Removal Act of 1830
   (p. 327)

Trail of Tears (p. 331)

classical liberalism, or laissez-
   faire (p. 332)

Whigs (p. 332)

Panic of 1837 (p. 334)

Specie Circular (p. 338)

ethnocultural politics (p. 340)

### Key People

Martin Van Buren (p. 317)

John Quincy Adams (p. 318)

Henry Clay (p. 319)

Andrew Jackson (p. 319)

John C. Calhoun (p. 324)

Daniel Webster (p. 324)

Nicholas Biddle (p. 326)

Roger B. Taney (p. 331)

John Tyler (p. 339)

## REVIEW QUESTIONS    Answer these questions to demonstrate your understanding of the chapter's main ideas.

1. How did Andrew Jackson and the Democratic Party fundamentally change public policy? Illustrate your argument with specific examples.

2. What were the various constitutional arguments underlying the debates over internal improvements, the tariff, and nullification?

3. How and why did the policies of the federal and state governments toward Native Americans change between the 1790s (Chapter 7) and the 1850s, and what were the reactions of Indian peoples to those policies?

4. **THEMATIC UNDERSTANDING** Review the events listed under "Politics and Power" on the thematic timeline on page 283. As the timeline indicates, the Working Men's and Anti-Masonic parties rose and declined between 1827 and 1834, and then the Whig Party emerged. How do you explain the timing of these events?

## MAKING CONNECTIONS

Recognize the larger developments and continuities within and across chapters by answering these questions.

1. **ACROSS TIME AND PLACE** The chapter argues that a democratic revolution swept America in the decades after 1820 and uprooted the old system of politics. After reviewing the discussions of politics in Chapters 6 and 7, explain how party systems and political alignments changed over time and then assess the strength of this argument.

2. **VISUAL EVIDENCE** Look again at the political cartoons on the tariff (p. 320) and the vice-presidency (p. 324). What point of view does the cartoonist support, and how effective are the cartoons in championing that view? How are today's negative political advertisements on television similar or different?

## MORE TO EXPLORE

Start here to learn more about the events discussed in this chapter.

Robert J. Conley, *Mountain Windsongs: A Novel of the Trail of Tears* (1992). Captures the human impact of Jackson's removal policy.

Richard Hofstadter, *The Idea of a Party System* (1969). Lucidly explains the triumph of party politics.

Thomas N. Ingersoll, *To Intermix with Our White Brothers* (2005). Argues that fear of racial intermixture shaped popular thought and government policy toward Indians.

Robert V. Remini, *The Life of Andrew Jackson* (1988). Highlights Jackson's triumphs and shortcomings.

Alexis de Tocqueville, *Democracy in America* (1835). A classic that is still worth dipping into; also available at **xroads.virginia.edu/~hyper/detoc/home.html**.

Sean Wilentz, *Chants Democratic* (1986). Covers the ideology of working men.

## TIMELINE    Ask yourself why this chapter begins and ends with these dates and then identify the links among related events.

| | |
|---|---|
| **1810s** | • States expand white male voting rights<br>• Martin Van Buren creates disciplined party in New York |
| **1825** | • House of Representatives selects John Quincy Adams as president<br>• Adams endorses Henry Clay's American System |
| **1828** | • Working Men's Parties win support<br>• Tariff of Abominations raises duties<br>• Andrew Jackson elected president<br>• John C. Calhoun's *South Carolina Exposition and Protest* |
| **1830** | • Jackson vetoes National Road bill<br>• Congress enacts Jackson's Indian Removal Act |
| **1831** | • *Cherokee Nation v. Georgia* denies Indians' independence, but *Worcester v. Georgia* (1832) upholds their political autonomy |
| **1832** | • Massacre of 850 Sauk and Fox warriors at Bad Axe<br>• Jackson vetoes renewal of Second Bank<br>• South Carolina adopts Ordinance of Nullification |
| **1833** | • Congress enacts compromise tariff |
| **1834** | • Whig Party formed by Clay, Calhoun, and Daniel Webster |
| **1835** | • Roger Taney named Supreme Court chief justice |
| **1836** | • Van Buren elected president |
| **1837** | • *Charles River Bridge* case weakens chartered monopolies<br>• Panic of 1837 derails economy and labor movement |
| **1838** | • Many Cherokees die in Trail of Tears march to Indian Territory |
| **1839–1843** | • Defaults on bonds by state governments spark international financial crisis and depression |
| **1840** | • Whigs win "log cabin campaign" |
| **1841** | • John Tyler succeeds William Henry Harrison as president |

**KEY TURNING POINTS:** Based on the events in the timeline (and your reading in Chapter 10), which five-year period brought more significant changes to American political and economic life: 1829–1833, Andrew Jackson's first term as president, or 1837–1842, the years of panic and depression? Explain and defend your choice.

# 11
## CHAPTER

# Religion and Reform
# 1800–1860

T he spirit of reform is in every place," declared the children of legal reformer David Dudley Field in their handwritten monthly *Gazette* in 1842:

> The labourer with a family says "reform the common schools," the merchant and the planter say, "reform the tariff," the lawyer "reform the laws," the politician "reform the government," the abolitionist "reform the slave laws," the moralist "reform intemperance," . . . the ladies wish their legal privileges extended, and in short, the whole country is wanting reform.

Like many Americans, the Field children sensed that the political whirlwind of the 1830s had transformed the way people thought about themselves and about society. Suddenly, thousands of men and women took inspiration from the economic progress and democratic spirit of the age. Drawing on the religious optimism of the Second Great Awakening, they felt that they could improve their personal lives and society as a whole. Some activists dedicated themselves to the cause of reform. William Lloyd Garrison began as an antislavery advocate and foe of Indian removal and then went on to campaign for women's rights, pacifism, and the abolition of prisons. Susan B. Anthony embraced antislavery, temperance, and female suffrage. Such obsessively reform-minded individuals, warned Unitarian minister Henry W. Bellows, were pursuing "an object, which in its very nature is unattainable—the perpetual improvement of [people's] outward condition." In Bellows's view, human progress depended on inner character, the "regeneration of man" through Christian precepts.

Such debates reveal the multifaceted character of the reform impulse. Like Bellows, the first wave of American reformers, the benevolent religious improvers of the 1820s, hoped to promote morality and enforce social discipline. They championed regular church attendance, temperance, and a strict moral code. Their zeal offended many upright citizens: "A peaceable man can hardly venture to eat or drink, . . . to correct his child or kiss his wife, without obtaining the permission . . . of some moral or other reform society," said one.

A second wave of reformers—Garrison, Anthony, and other activists of the 1830s and 1840s—undertook to liberate people from archaic customs and traditional lifestyles. Mostly middle-class northerners and midwesterners, these activists promoted a bewildering assortment of radical ideals: extreme individualism, common ownership of property, the immediate emancipation of slaves, and sexual equality. Although their numbers were small, second-wave reformers challenged deeply rooted cultural practices and elicited horrified opposition among the majority of Americans. As one fearful southerner saw it, radical reformers favored a chaotic world with "No-Marriage, No-Religion, No-Private Property, No-Law and No-Government."

## IDENTIFY THE BIG IDEA
To what extent did individualism, new religious sects, abolitionism, and women's rights (as the movement was called in the nineteenth century) change American culture between 1820 and 1860?

**A Middle-Class Marriage** During the 1830s, Joseph H. Davis used bright watercolors to paint scores of family portraits—150 still survive—that capture the comfortable lives of New England's middle classes. This double portrait commemorates the marriage of Hannah Roberts and Lewis Tebbets of Berwick, Maine. To emphasize their romantic love, Davis shows them gazing into each other's eyes, their hands linked by a prayer book, a symbol of their education and piety. Such respectable couples—Lewis Tebbets became a minister of the Methodist Episcopal Church—flocked to hear Ralph Waldo Emerson and other lecturers on the lyceum circuit. Terra Foundation for American Art, Chicago/Art Resource, NY.

# Individualism: The Ethic of the Middle Class

Those fears were not exaggerated. Rapid economic growth and geographical expansion had weakened traditional institutions, forcing individuals to fend for themselves. In 1835, Alexis de Tocqueville coined the word *individualism* to describe the result. Native-born white Americans were "no longer attached to each other by any tie of caste, class, association, or family," the French aristocrat lamented, and so lived in social isolation. As Tocqueville mourned the loss of social ties, the New England essayist and philosopher Ralph Waldo Emerson (1803–1882) celebrated the liberation of the individual. Emerson's vision influenced thousands of ordinary Americans and a generation of important artists, who, in the **American Renaissance**, a mid-nineteenth-century flourishing of literature and philosophy, wrote a remarkable number of first-class novels, poems, and essays.

## Ralph Waldo Emerson and Transcendentalism

Emerson was the leading voice of **transcendentalism**, an intellectual movement rooted in the religious soil of New England. Its first advocates were Unitarian ministers from well-to-do New England families who questioned the constraints of their Puritan heritage (Chapter 8). For inspiration, they turned to European romanticism, a new conception of self and society. Romantic thinkers, such as German philosopher Immanuel Kant and English poet Samuel Taylor Coleridge, rejected the ordered, rational world of the eighteenth-century Enlightenment. They embraced human passion and sought deeper insight into the mysteries of existence. By tapping their intuitive powers, the young Unitarians believed, people could come to know the infinite and the eternal.

As a Unitarian, Emerson stood outside the mainstream of American Protestantism. Unlike most Christians, Unitarians believed that God was a single being, not a trinity of Father, Son, and Holy Spirit. In 1832, Emerson took a more radical step by resigning his Boston pulpit and rejecting all organized religion. He moved to Concord, Massachusetts, and wrote influential essays probing what he called "the infinitude of the private man," the radically free person.

The young philosopher argued that people were trapped by inherited customs and institutions. They

**The Founder of Transcendentalism**
As this painting of Ralph Waldo Emerson by an unknown artist indicates, the young philosopher was an attractive man, his face brimming with confidence and optimism. With his radiant personality and incisive intellect, Emerson deeply influenced dozens of influential writers, artists, and scholars and enjoyed great success as a lecturer to the emerging middle class. © The Metropolitan Museum of Art. Image source: Art Resource, NY.

wore the ideas of earlier times — New England Calvinism, for example — as a kind of "faded masquerade," and they needed to shed those values. "What is a man born for but to be a Reformer, a Remaker of what man has made?" Emerson asked. In his view, individuals could be remade only by discovering their "original relation with Nature" and entering into a mystical union with the "currents of Universal Being." The ideal setting for this transcendent discovery was under an open sky, in solitary communion with nature. The revivalist Charles Grandison Finney described his religious conversion in Emersonian terms: an individual in the woods, alone, joining with God in a mystical union.

The transcendentalist message of individual self-realization reached hundreds of thousands of people through Emerson's writings and lectures. Public lectures had become a spectacularly successful way of spreading information and fostering discussion among the middle classes. Beginning in 1826, the lyceum movement—modeled on the public forum of the ancient Greek philosopher Aristotle—arranged lecture tours by hundreds of poets, preachers, scientists, and reformers. The lyceum became an important cultural institution in the North and Midwest, but not in the South, where the middle class was smaller and popular education had a lower priority. In 1839, nearly 150 lyceums in Massachusetts invited lecturers to address more than 33,000 subscribers. Emerson was the most popular speaker, eventually delivering fifteen hundred lectures in more than three hundred towns in twenty states.

Emerson celebrated those who rejected tradition and practiced self-discipline and civic responsibility. His individualistic ethos spoke directly to the experiences of many middle-class Americans, who had left family farms to make their way in the urban world. His pantheistic view of nature—that it was saturated with the presence of God—encouraged Unitarians in Boston to create the Mount Auburn Cemetery, a beautiful planned landscape of trees and bushes and burial markers for the dead of all faiths; soon there were similar rural cemeteries in many American cities. Emerson's optimism also inspired many religious preachers of the Second Great Awakening, such as Finney, who told believers to transcend old doctrines and constraints. "God has made man a moral free agent," Finney declared.

Emerson worried that the new market society—the focus on work, profits, and consumption—was debasing Americans' spiritual lives. "Things are in the saddle," he wrote, "and ride mankind." Seeking to revive intellectual life, transcendentalists created communal experiments. The most important was Brook Farm, just outside Boston, where Emerson, Henry David Thoreau, and Margaret Fuller were residents or frequent visitors. Members recalled that they "inspired the young with a passion for study, and the middle-aged with deference and admiration." Whatever its intellectual excitement and spiritual rewards, Brook Farm was an economic failure. The residents planned to produce their own food and exchange their surplus milk, vegetables, and hay for manufactures. However, most members were ministers, teachers, writers, and students who had few farming skills; only the cash of affluent residents kept the enterprise afloat for five years. After a devastating fire in 1846, the organizers disbanded the community and sold the farm.

With the failure of Brook Farm, the Emersonians abandoned their quest for new social institutions. They accepted the brute reality of the emergent commercial and industrial order and tried to reform it, especially through the education of workers and the movement to abolish slavery.

**UNDERSTAND POINTS OF VIEW**
What were the main principles of transcendentalism, and how did they differ from the beliefs of most Protestant Christians?

## Emerson's Literary Influence

Even as Emerson urged his fellow citizens to break free from tradition and expand their spiritual awareness, he issued a declaration of literary independence. In "The American Scholar" (1837), Emerson urged American authors to free themselves from the "courtly muse" of Old Europe and find inspiration in the experiences of ordinary Americans: "the ballad in the street; the news of the boat; the glance of the eye; the form and gait of the body."

**Thoreau, Fuller, and Whitman**   One young New England intellectual, Henry David Thoreau (1817–1862), heeded Emerson's call and sought inspiration from the natural world. In 1845, depressed by his beloved brother's death, Thoreau built a cabin near Walden Pond in Concord, Massachusetts, and lived alone there for two years. In 1854, he published *Walden, or Life in the Woods*, an account of his search for meaning beyond the artificiality of civilized society:

> I went to the woods because I wished to live deliberately, to front only the essential facts of life, and see if I could not learn what it had to teach, and not, when I came to die, discover that I had not lived.

*Walden's* most famous metaphor provides an enduring justification for independent thinking: "If a man does not keep pace with his companions, perhaps it is because he hears a different drummer." Beginning from this premise, Thoreau advocated a thoroughgoing individuality, urging readers to avoid unthinking conformity to social norms and peacefully to resist unjust laws.

As Thoreau was seeking self-realization for men, Margaret Fuller (1810–1850) was exploring the possibilities of freedom for women. Born into a wealthy Boston family, Fuller mastered six languages and read broadly in classic literature. Embracing Emerson's ideas, she started a transcendental "conversation," or discussion group, for educated Boston women in 1839. While editing *The Dial*, the leading transcendentalist journal, Fuller published *Woman in the Nineteenth Century* (1844).

***Margaret Fuller,* 1848**

At the age of thirty-eight, the American transcendentalist author Margaret Fuller moved to Italy, where she reported on the Revolution of 1848 for the *New York Tribune.* There she fell in love with Thomas Hicks (1823–1890), a much younger American artist. Hicks rebuffed Fuller's romantic advances but painted this flattering portrait, softening her features and giving her a pensive look. Fuller took as a lover a petty noble and republican revolutionary, Giovanni Angelo, Marchese d'Ossoli, and gave birth to a son in September 1848. Two years later, the entire family died in a shipwreck while en route to the United States. Constance Fuller Threinen.

To see a longer excerpt of *Woman in the Nineteenth Century,* along with other primary sources from this period, see ***Sources for America's History.***

The poet Walt Whitman (1819–1892) also responded to Emerson's call. He had been "simmering, simmering," he recalled, and then Emerson "brought me to a boil." Whitman worked as a printer, a teacher, a journalist, an editor of the *Brooklyn Eagle,* and an influential publicist for the Democratic Party. However, poetry was the "direction of his dreams." In *Leaves of Grass,* a collection of wild, exuberant poems first published in 1855 and constantly revised and expanded, Whitman recorded in verse his efforts to transcend various "invisible boundaries": between solitude and community, between prose and poetry, even between the living and the dead. At the center of *Leaves of Grass* is the individual — "I, Walt." He begins alone: "I celebrate myself, and sing myself." Because he has an Emersonian "original relation" with nature, Whitman claims perfect communion with others: "For every atom belonging to me as good belongs to you." For Emerson, Thoreau, and Fuller, the individual had a divine spark; for Whitman, the collective democracy assumed a sacred character.

The transcendentalists were optimistic but not naive. Whitman wrote about human suffering with passion, and Emerson laced his accounts of transcendence with twinges of anxiety. "I am glad," he once said, "to the brink of fear." Thoreau was gloomy about everyday life: "The mass of men lead lives of quiet desperation." Nonetheless, dark murmurings remain muted in their work, overshadowed by assertions that nothing was impossible for the individual who could break free from tradition.

Fuller embraced the transcendental principle that all people could develop a life-affirming mystical relationship with God. Every woman therefore deserved psychological and social independence: the ability "to grow, as an intellect to discern, as a soul to live freely and unimpeded." She wrote: "We would have every arbitrary barrier thrown down [and] every path laid open to Woman as freely as to Man." Fuller became the literary critic of the *New York Tribune* and traveled to Italy to report on the Revolution of 1848, only to drown in a shipwreck en route home to the United States. Fuller's life and writings inspired a rising generation of women writers and reformers.

**EXPLAIN CONSEQUENCES**
How did authors of the American Renaissance incorporate transcendentalist ideas into their work?

**Darker Visions**    Emerson's writings also influenced two great novelists, Nathaniel Hawthorne and Herman Melville, who had more pessimistic worldviews. Both sounded powerful warnings that unfettered egoism could destroy individuals and those around them. Hawthorne brilliantly explored the theme of excessive individualism in his novel *The Scarlet Letter* (1850). The two main characters, Hester Prynne and Arthur Dimmesdale, blatantly challenge their seventeenth-century New England community by committing adultery and producing a child. Their decision to ignore social restraints results not in liberation but in degradation: a profound sense of guilt and condemnation by the community.

Herman Melville explored the limits of individualism in even more extreme and tragic terms and emerged as a scathing critic of transcendentalism. His most powerful statement was *Moby Dick* (1851), the story of Captain Ahab's obsessive hunt for a mysterious white whale that ends in death for Ahab and all but one member of his crew. Here, the quest for spiritual meaning in nature brings death, not transcendence, because Ahab, the liberated individual, lacks inner discipline and self-restraint.

*Moby Dick* was a commercial failure. The middle-class audience that devoured sentimental American fiction refused to follow Melville into the dark, dangerous realm of individualism gone mad. What middle-class readers emphatically preferred were the more modest examples of individualism offered by Emerson and Finney: personal improvement and religious piety through spiritual awareness and self-discipline.

# Rural Communalism and Urban Popular Culture

Between 1820 and 1860, thousands of Americans grew dissatisfied with life in America's emerging market society and retreated into rural areas of the Northeast and Midwest (Map 11.1). There they sought to create ideal communities, or **utopias**, that would allow people to live differently and realize their spiritual potential.

Simultaneously, tens of thousands of rural Americans and European immigrants poured into the larger cities of the United States. There, they created a popular culture that challenged some sexual norms, reinforced traditional racist feelings, and encouraged new styles of dress and behavior.

## The Utopian Impulse

Many rural communalists were farmers and artisans seeking refuge from the economic depression of 1837–1843. Others were religious idealists. Whatever their origins, these rural utopias were symbols of social protest and experimentation. By advocating the common ownership of property (socialism) and unconventional forms of marriage and family life, the communalists challenged traditional property rights and gender roles.

### Mother Ann and the Shakers
The United Society of Believers in Christ's Second Appearing, known as the Shakers because of the ecstatic dances that were part of their worship, was the first successful American communal movement. In 1770, Ann Lee Stanley (Mother Ann), a young cook in Manchester, England, had a vision that she was an incarnation of Christ. Four years later, she led a few followers to America and established a church near Albany, New York.

After Mother Ann's death in 1784, the Shakers honored her as the Second Coming of Christ, withdrew from the profane world, and formed disciplined

**MAP 11.1**

**Major Communal Experiments Before 1860**

Some experimental communities settled along the frontier, but the vast majority chose rural areas in settled regions of the North and Midwest. Because they opposed slavery, communalists usually avoided the South. Most secular experiments failed within a few decades, as the founders lost their reformist enthusiasm or died off; tightly knit religious communities, such as the Shakers and the Mormons, were longer-lived.

**Shakers at Prayer**

Most Americans viewed the Shakers with a mixture of fascination and suspicion. They feared the sect's radical aspects, such as a commitment to celibacy and communal property, and considered the Shakers' dancing more an invitation to debauchery than a form of prayer. Those apprehensions surfaced in this engraving, *The Shakers of New Lebanon* (New York), which expresses both the powerful intensity and the menacing character of this Shaker spiritual ritual. The work of the journalist-engraver Joseph Becker, the picture appeared in Frank Leslie's *Illustrated Newspaper* in 1873. © Bettmann.

religious communities. Members embraced the common ownership of property; accepted strict oversight by church leaders; and pledged to abstain from alcohol, tobacco, politics, and war. Shakers also repudiated sexual pleasure and marriage. Their commitment to celibacy followed Mother Ann's testimony against "the lustful gratifications of the flesh as the source and foundation of human corruption." The Shakers' theology was as radical as their social thought. They held that God was "a dual person, male and female." This doctrine prompted Shakers to repudiate male leadership and to place community governance in the hands of both women and men — the Eldresses and the Elders.

**IDENTIFY CAUSES**
What factors led to the proliferation of rural utopian communities in nineteenth-century America?

Shakers founded twenty communities, mostly in New England, New York, and Ohio. Their agriculture and crafts, especially furniture making, acquired a reputation for quality that made most Shaker communities self-sustaining and even comfortable. Because the Shakers disdained sexual intercourse, they relied on conversions and the adoption of thousands of young orphans to increase their numbers. During the 1830s, three thousand adults, mostly women, joined the Shakers, attracted by their communal intimacy and sexual equality. To Rebecca Cox Jackson, an African American seamstress from Philadelphia, the Shakers seemed to be "loving to live forever." However, with the proliferation of public and private orphanages during the 1840s and 1850s, Shaker communities began to decline and, by 1900, had virtually disappeared. They left as a material legacy a plain but elegant style of wood furniture.

**Albert Brisbane and Fourierism** As the Shakers' growth slowed during the 1840s, the American Fourierist movement mushroomed. Charles Fourier (1777–1837) was a French reformer who devised an eight-stage theory of social evolution that predicted the imminent decline of individual property rights and capitalist values. Fourier's leading disciple in America was Albert Brisbane. Just as republicanism had freed Americans from slavish monarchical government, Brisbane argued, so Fourierist **socialism** would liberate workers from capitalist employers and the "menial and slavish system of Hired Labor or Labor for Wages." Members would work for the community, in cooperative groups called phalanxes; they would own its property in common, including stores and a bank, a school, and a library.

Fourier and Brisbane saw the phalanx as a humane system that would liberate women as well as men. "In society as it is now constituted," Brisbane wrote, individual freedom was possible only for men, while "woman is subjected to unremitting and slavish domestic duties." In the "new Social Order . . . based upon Associated households," men would share women's domestic labor and thereby increase sexual equality.

Brisbane skillfully promoted Fourier's ideas in his influential book *The Social Destiny of Man* (1840), a regular column in Horace Greeley's *New York Tribune*, and hundreds of lectures. Fourierist ideas found a receptive audience among educated farmers and craftsmen, who yearned for economic stability and communal solidarity following the Panic of 1837. During the 1840s, Fourierists started nearly one hundred cooperative communities, mostly in western New York and the Midwest. Most communities quickly collapsed as members fought over work responsibilities and social policies. Fourierism's rapid decline revealed the difficulty of maintaining a utopian community in the absence of a charismatic leader or a compelling religious vision.

**John Humphrey Noyes and Oneida** John Humphrey Noyes (1811–1886) was both charismatic and religious. He ascribed the Fourierists' failure to their secular outlook and embraced the pious Shakers as the true "pioneers of modern Socialism." The Shakers' marriageless society also inspired Noyes to create a community that defined sexuality and gender roles in radically new ways.

**Attacking the Women's Rights Movement**

Amelia Jenks Bloomer (1818–1894) wrote for her husband's newspaper, the *County Courier* of Seneca Falls, New York. In 1848 she attended the women's convention there and began her own biweekly newspaper, *The Lily*, focusing on temperance and women's rights. In 1851, Bloomer enthusiastically promoted—and serendipitously gave her name to—the comfortable women's costume devised by another temperance activist: loose trousers gathered at the ankles topped by a short skirt. Fearing women's quest for equal dress and equal rights, humorists such as John Leech ridiculed the new female attire. Here, bloomer-attired women smoke away and belittle the male proprietor as "one of the 'inferior animals,'" a thinly veiled effort by Leech to reassert men's "natural" claim as the dominant sex. From *Punch* 1851, John Leech Archive.

No. VI.—*SOMETHING MORE OF BLOOMERISM.*
(BEHIND THE COUNTER THERE IS ONE OF THE "INFERIOR ANIMALS.")

Noyes was a well-to-do graduate of Dartmouth College who joined the ministry after hearing a sermon by Charles Grandison Finney. Dismissed as the pastor of a Congregational church for holding unorthodox beliefs, Noyes turned to **perfectionism**, an evangelical Protestant movement of the 1830s that attracted thousands of New Englanders who had migrated to New York and Ohio. Perfectionists believed that Christ had already returned to earth (the Second Coming) and therefore people could aspire to sinless perfection in their earthly lives. Unlike most perfectionists, who lived conventional personal lives, Noyes rejected marriage, calling it a major barrier to perfection. "Exclusiveness, jealousy, quarreling have no place at the marriage supper of the Lamb," Noyes wrote. Instead of the Shakers' celibacy, Noyes embraced "complex marriage," in which all members of the community were married to one another. He rejected monogamy partly to free women from their status as the property of their husbands, as they were by custom and by common law. Symbolizing the quest for equality, Noyes's women followers cut their hair short and wore pantaloons under calf-length skirts.

In 1839, Noyes set up a perfectionist community near his hometown of Putney, Vermont. However, local outrage over the practice of complex marriage forced Noyes to relocate the community in 1848 to an isolated area near Oneida, New York, where the members could follow his precepts. To give women the time and energy to participate fully in community affairs, Noyes urged them to avoid multiple pregnancies. He asked men to help by avoiding orgasm during intercourse. Less positively, he encouraged sexual relations at a very early age and used his position of power to manipulate the sexual lives of his followers.

By the mid-1850s, the Oneida settlement had two hundred residents and became self-sustaining when the inventor of a highly successful steel animal trap joined the community. With the profits from trap making, the Oneidians diversified into the production of silverware. When Noyes fled to Canada in 1879 to avoid prosecution for adultery, the community abandoned complex marriage but retained its cooperative spirit. The Oneida Community, Ltd., a jointly owned silverware-manufacturing company, remained a successful communal venture until the middle of the twentieth century.

The historical significance of the Oneidians, Shakers, and Fourierists does not lie in their numbers, which were small, or in their fine crafts. Rather, it stems from their radical questioning of traditional sexual norms and of the capitalist values and class divisions of the emerging market society. Their utopian communities stood as countercultural blueprints of a more egalitarian social and economic order.

## Joseph Smith and the Mormon Experience

The Mormons, members of the Church of Jesus Christ of Latter-day Saints, were religious utopians with a conservative social agenda: to perpetuate close-knit communities and patriarchal power. Because of their cohesiveness, authoritarian leadership, and size, the Mormons provoked more animosity than the radical utopians did.

**Joseph Smith**    Like many social movements of the era, **Mormonism** emerged from religious ferment among families of Puritan descent who lived along the

**A Mormon Man and His Wives**

The practice of polygamy split the Mormon community and, because it deviated from Christian religious principles, enraged Protestant denominations. This Mormon household, pictured in the late 1840s, was unusually prosperous, partly because of the labor of the husband's multiple wives. Although the cabin provides cramped quarters for a large polygamous family, it boasts a brick chimney and—a luxury for any pioneer home—a glass window. Library of Congress.

Erie Canal and who were heirs to a religious tradition that believed in a world of wonders, supernatural powers, and visions of the divine.

The founder of the Latter-day Church, Joseph Smith Jr. (1805–1844), was born in Vermont to a poor farming and shop-keeping family that migrated to Palmyra in central New York. In 1820, Smith began to have religious experiences similar to those described in conversion narratives: "[A] pillar of light above the brightness of the sun at noonday came down from above and rested upon me and I was filled with the spirit of God." Smith came to believe that God had singled him out to receive a special revelation of divine truth. In 1830, he published *The Book of Mormon*, which he claimed to have translated from ancient hieroglyphics on gold plates shown to him by an angel named Moroni. *The Book of Mormon* told the story of an ancient Jewish civilization from the Middle East that had migrated to the Western Hemisphere and of the visit of Jesus Christ, soon after his Resurrection, to those descendants of Israel. Smith's account explained the presence of native peoples in the Americas and integrated them into the Judeo-Christian tradition.

Smith proceeded to organize the Church of Jesus Christ of Latter-day Saints. Seeing himself as a prophet in a sinful, excessively individualistic society, Smith revived traditional social doctrines, including patriarchal authority. Like many Protestant ministers, he encouraged practices that led to individual success in the age of capitalist markets and factories: frugality, hard work, and enterprise. Smith also stressed communal discipline to safeguard the Mormon "New Jerusalem." His goal was a church-directed society that would restore primitive Christianity and encourage moral perfection.

Constantly harassed by anti-Mormons, Smith struggled to find a secure home for his new religion. At one point, he identified Jackson County in Missouri as the site of the sacred "City of Zion," and his followers began to settle there. Agitation led by Protestant ministers quickly forced them out: "Mormons were the common enemies of mankind and ought to be destroyed," said one cleric. Smith and his growing congregation eventually settled in Nauvoo, Illinois, a town they founded on the Mississippi River (Map 11.2). By the early 1840s, Nauvoo had 30,000 residents. The Mormons' rigid discipline and secret rituals — along with their prosperity, hostility toward other sects, and bloc voting in Illinois elections — fueled resentment among their neighbors. That resentment increased when Smith refused to accept Illinois laws of which he disapproved, asked Congress to make Nauvoo a separate federal territory, and declared himself a candidate for president of the United States.

Moreover, Smith claimed to have received a new revelation justifying polygamy, the practice of a man having multiple wives. When leading Mormon men took several wives — "plural celestial marriage" — they threw the Mormon community into turmoil and enraged nearby Christians. In 1844, Illinois officials arrested Smith and charged him with treason for allegedly conspiring to create a Mormon colony in Mexican territory. An anti-Mormon mob stormed the jail in Carthage, Illinois, where Smith and his brother were being held and murdered them.

**Brigham Young and Utah**  Led by Brigham Young, Smith's leading disciple and now the sect's "prophet, seer and revelator," about 6,500 Mormons fled the United States. Beginning in 1846, they crossed the

**COMPARE AND CONTRAST**

In what ways were Mormons similar to, and different from, other communal movements of the era?

**MAP 11.2**

**The Mormon Trek, 1830–1848**

Because of their unorthodox religious views and communal solidarity, Mormons faced hostility first in New York and then in Missouri and Illinois. After founder Joseph Smith Jr. was murdered, Brigham Young led the polygamist faction of Mormons into lands claimed by Mexico and thinly populated by Native Americans. From Omaha, the migrants followed the path of the Oregon Trail to Fort Bridger and then struck off to the southwest. They settled along the Wasatch Range in the basin of the Great Salt Lake in present-day Utah.

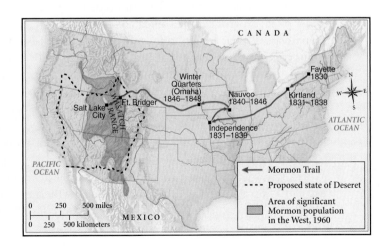

Great Plains into Mexican territory and settled in the Great Salt Lake Valley in present-day Utah. Using cooperative labor and an irrigation system based on communal water rights, the Mormon pioneers quickly spread agricultural communities along the base of the Wasatch Range. Many Mormons who rejected polygamy remained in the United States. Led by Smith's son, Joseph Smith III, they formed the Reorganized Church of Jesus Christ of Latter-day Saints and settled throughout the Midwest.

When the United States acquired Mexico's northern territories in 1848, the Salt Lake Mormons petitioned Congress to create a vast new state, Deseret, stretching from Utah to the Pacific coast. Instead, Congress set up the much smaller Utah Territory in 1850 and named Brigham Young its governor. Young and his associates ruled in an authoritarian fashion, determined to ensure the ascendancy of the Mormon Church and its practices. By 1856, Young and the Utah territorial legislature were openly vowing to resist federal laws. Pressed by Protestant church leaders to end polygamy and considering the Mormons' threat of nullification "a declaration of war," President James Buchanan dispatched a small army to Utah. As the "Nauvoo Legion" resisted the army's advance, aggressive Mormon militia massacred a party of 120 California-bound emigrants and murdered suspicious travelers and Mormons seeking to flee Young's regime. Despite this bloodshed, the "Mormon War" ended quietly in June 1858. President Buchanan, a longtime supporter of the white South, feared that the forced abolition of polygamy would serve as a precedent for ending slavery and offered a pardon to Utah citizens who would acknowledge federal authority. (To enable Utah to win admission to the Union in 1896, its citizens ratified a constitution that "forever" banned the practice of polygamy. However, the state government has never strictly enforced that ban.)

The Salt Lake Mormons had succeeded even as other social experiments had failed. Reaffirming traditional values, their leaders resolutely used strict religious controls to perpetuate patriarchy and communal discipline. However, by endorsing private property and individual enterprise, Mormons became prosperous contributors to the new market society. This blend of economic innovation, social conservatism, and hierarchical leadership, in combination with a strong missionary impulse, created a wealthy and expansive church that now claims a worldwide membership of about 12 million people.

## Urban Popular Culture

As utopians organized communities in the countryside, rural migrants and foreign immigrants created a new urban culture. In 1800, American cities were overgrown towns with rising death rates: New York had only 60,000 residents, Philadelphia had 41,000, and life expectancy at birth was a mere twenty-five years. Then urban growth accelerated as a huge in-migration outweighed the high death rates. By 1840, New York's population had ballooned to 312,000; Philadelphia and its suburbs had 150,000 residents; and three other cities — New Orleans, Boston, and Baltimore — each had about 100,000. By 1860, New York had become a metropolis with more than 1 million residents: 813,000 in Manhattan and another 266,000 in the adjacent community of Brooklyn.

**Sex in the City**    These newly populous cities, particularly New York, generated a new urban culture. Thousands of young men and women flocked to the city searching for adventure and fortune, but many found only a hard life. Young men labored for meager wages building thousands of tenements, warehouses, and workshops. Others worked as low-paid clerks or operatives in hundreds of mercantile and manufacturing firms. The young women had an even harder time. Thousands toiled as live-in domestic servants, ordered about by the mistress of the household and often sexually exploited by the master. Thousands more scraped out a bare living as needlewomen in New York City's booming ready-made clothes industry. Unwilling to endure domestic service or subsistence wages, many young girls turned to prostitution. Dr. William Sanger's careful survey, commissioned in 1855 by worried city officials, found six thousand women engaged in commercial sex. Three-fifths were native-born whites, and the rest were foreign immigrants; most were between fifteen and twenty years old. Half were or had been domestic servants, half had children, and half were infected with syphilis.

Commercialized sex — and sex in general — formed one facet of the new urban culture. "Sporting men" engaged freely in sexual conquests; otherwise respectable married men kept mistresses in handy apartments; and working men frequented bawdy houses. New York City had two hundred brothels in the 1820s and five hundred by the 1850s. Prostitutes — so-called "public" women — openly advertised their wares on Broadway,

**COMPARE AND CONTRAST**
How were the cultures of utopian communalists and urban residents similar to and different from the mainstream culture described in Chapters 8 and 9?

*Night Life in Philadelphia*

This watercolor by Russian painter Pavel Svinin (1787–1839) captures the social diversity and allure of urban America. A respectable gentleman relishes the delicacies sold by a black oysterman. Meanwhile, a young woman—probably a prostitute but perhaps an adventurous working girl—engages the attention of two well-dressed young "swells" outside the Chestnut Street Theatre. Such scenes were new to Americans and marked the beginning of a profound split between the nation's rural and urban cultures. © The Metropolitan Museum of Art. Image source: Art Resource, NY.

the city's most fashionable thoroughfare, and welcomed clients on the infamous "Third Tier" of the theaters. Many men considered illicit sex as a right. "Man is endowed by nature with passions that must be gratified," declared the *Sporting Whip*, a working-class magazine. Even the Reverend William Berrian, pastor of the ultra-respectable Trinity Episcopal Church, remarked from the pulpit that he had resorted ten times to "a house of ill-fame."

Prostitution formed only the tip of the urban sexual volcano. Freed from family oversight, men formed homoerotic friendships and relationships; as early as 1800, the homosexual "Fop" was an acknowledged character in Philadelphia. Young people moved from partner to partner until they chanced on an ideal mate. Middle-class youth strolled along Broadway in the latest fashions: elaborate bonnets and silk dresses for young women; flowing capes, leather boots, and silver-plated walking sticks for young men. Rivaling the elegance on Broadway was the colorful dress on the Bowery, the broad avenue that ran along the east side of lower Manhattan. By day, the "Bowery Boy" worked as an apprentice or journeyman. By night, he prowled the streets as a "consummate dandy," his hair cropped at the back of his head "as close as scissors could cut," with long front locks "matted by a lavish application of *bear's grease*, the ends tucked under so as to form a roll and brushed until they shone like glass bottles." The "B'hoy," as he was called, cut a dashing figure as he walked along with a "Bowery Gal" in a striking dress and shawl: "a light pink contrasting with a deep blue" or "a bright yellow with a brighter red."

**Minstrelsy** Popular entertainment was a central facet of the new urban culture. In New York, working-men could partake of traditional rural blood sports—rat and terrier fights as well as boxing matches—at Sportsmen Hall, or they could seek drink and fun in billiard and bowling saloons. Other workers crowded into the pit of the Bowery Theatre to see the "Mad Tragedian," Junius Brutus Booth, deliver a stirring (abridged) performance of Shakespeare's *Richard III*. Reform-minded couples enjoyed evenings at the huge Broadway Tabernacle, where they could hear an abolitionist lecture, see the renowned Hutchinson Family Singers lead a roof-raising rendition of their antislavery anthem, "Get Off the Track," and sentimentally lament the separation of a slave couple in Stephen Foster's "Oh Susanna," a popular song of the late 1840s. Families could visit the museum of oddities (and hoaxes) created by P. T. Barnum, the great cultural entrepreneur and founder of the Barnum & Bailey Circus.

However, the most popular theatrical entertainments were the minstrel shows, in which white actors in blackface presented comic routines that combined racist caricature and social criticism. **Minstrelsy** began around 1830, when a few actors put on blackface and performed song-and-dance routines (Thinking Like a Historian, p. 358). The most famous was John Dartmouth Rice, whose "Jim Crow" blended a weird shuffle-dance-and-jump with unintelligible lyrics delivered in "Negro dialect." By the 1840s, there were hundreds of minstrel troupes, including a group of black entertainers, Gavitt's Original Ethiopian Serenaders. The actor-singers' rambling lyrics poked racist fun at African Americans, portraying them as lazy, sensual, and irresponsible while simultaneously using them to criticize white society. Minstrels ridiculed the drunkenness of Irish immigrants, parodied the halting English of German immigrants, denounced women's demands for political rights, and mocked the arrogance of upper-class men. Still, by caricaturing blacks, the minstrels declared the importance of being white and spread racist sentiments among Irish and German immigrants.

**Immigrant Masses and Nativist Reaction**   By 1850, immigrants were a major presence throughout the Northeast. Irish men and women in New York City numbered 200,000, and Germans 110,000 (Figure 11.1). German-language shop signs filled entire neighborhoods, and German foods (sausages, hamburgers, sauerkraut) and food customs (such as drinking beer in family *biergärten*) became part of the city's culture. The mass of impoverished Irish migrants found allies in the American Catholic Church, which soon became an Irish-dominated institution, and the Democratic Party, which gave them a foothold in the political process.

Native-born New Yorkers took alarm as hordes of ethnically diverse migrants altered the city's culture. They organized a nativist movement—a final aspect of the new urban world. Beginning in the mid-1830s, nativists called for a halt to immigration and mounted a cultural and political assault on foreign-born residents (Chapter 9). Gangs of B'hoys assaulted Irish youths in the streets, employers restricted Irish workers to the most menial jobs, and temperance reformers denounced the German fondness for beer. In 1844, the American Republican Party, with the endorsement of the Whigs, swept the city elections by focusing on

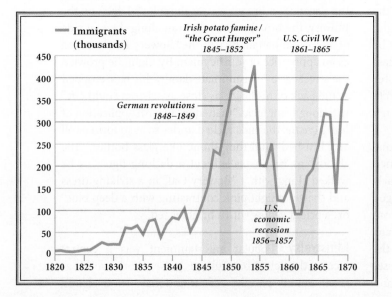

**FIGURE 11.1**

**The Surge in Imigration, 1854–1855**

In 1845, the failure of the potato crop in Ireland prompted the wholesale migration to the United States of peasants from the overcrowded farms of its western counties. Population growth and limited economic prospects likewise spurred the migration of tens of thousands of German peasants, while the failure of the liberal republican political revolution of 1848 prompted hundreds of prominent German politicians and intellectuals to follow them. An American economic recession cut the flow of immigrants, but the booming northern economy during the Civil War again persuaded Europeans to set sail for the United States.

the culturally emotional issues of temperance, anti-Catholicism, and nativism.

In the city, as in the countryside, new values were challenging old beliefs. The sexual freedom celebrated by Noyes at Oneida had its counterpart in commercialized sex and male promiscuity in New York City, where it came under attack from the Female Moral Reform Society. Similarly, the disciplined rejection of tobacco and alcohol by the Shakers and the Mormons found a parallel in the Washington Temperance Society and other urban reform organizations. American society was in ferment, and the outcome was far from clear.

# Abolitionism

Like other reform movements, the **abolitionist** crusade of the 1830s drew on the religious enthusiasm of the Second Great Awakening. Around 1800, antislavery activists had assailed human bondage as contrary to republicanism and liberty. Three decades later, white abolitionists condemned slavery as a sin and demanded immediate, uncompensated emancipation. Their uncompromising stance led to fierce political debates, urban riots, and sectional conflict.

**Rampant Racism**

Minstrel shows and their music were just two facets of the racist culture of mid-nineteenth-century America. Exploiting the market for almanacs among farmers and city-folk alike, the publishing firm of Fisher and Brother produced the *Black Joke Al-Ma-Nig* for 1852. Like other almanacs, it provided astrological charts, weather predictions, and a detailed calendar of events. To boost sales, the almanac included "new an' original nigga' stories, black jokes, puns, parodies" that would "magnetize bofe white an' black." Such racist caricatures of black faces and language influenced white views of African Americans well into the twentieth century. Courtesy: The Library Company of Philadelphia.

## Dance and Social Identity in Antebellum America

Styles of dance and attitudes toward them tell us a great deal about cultural and social norms. When nineteenth-century Americans took to partying, their dances—regardless of the class or ethnic identity of the dancers—focused more on individual couples and allowed more room for improvisation and intimacy than the dance forms of the previous century.

1. **William Sidney Mount, *Rustic Dance After a Sleigh Ride*, 1830.** *In the eighteenth century, wealthy, fashionable Americans danced the French minuet, a ceremonious and graceful dance in which couples executed prescribed steps while barely touching. Ordinary white folks preferred the country dances brought by their ancestors from Europe, which also involved intricate steps, line formations, and limited physical contact. Mount (1807–1868) was self-taught, lived in rural Long Island, and depicted scenes of everyday life. This painting, replete with amorous pursuits, depicts a traditional contra dance in which the lead couple advances a few steps and then sashays to the back of the line, as another couple takes its place.*

Museum of Fine Arts, Boston, Massachusetts, USA/Bequest of Martha C. Karolik for the M. and M. Karolik/Collection of American Paintings, 1815–65/The Bridgeman Art Library.

2. **"The Polka Fashions," from *Godey's Lady's Book*, 1845.** *"A magazine of elegant literature," according to its publisher, Louis A. Godey, the* Lady's Book *was the most widely circulated American periodical prior to the Civil War and an arbiter of good taste among the aspiring middle classes. Each issue contained a sheet of music for the latest dance craze. The* Lady's Book *cautiously endorsed the waltz, a sensuous dance that required a close embrace, but enthusiastically welcomed its cousin, the polka, whose lively tempo and rapid spinning had a wholesome and joyful quality. Introduced from Bohemia, the polka dominated the ballrooms of America's upper and middle classes in the 1840s and 1850s.*

Private Collection/The Bridgeman Art Library.

3. **George Templeton Strong, diary entry, December 23, 1845.**

Well, last night I spent at Mrs. Mary Jones's great ball. Very splendid affair — "the Ball of the Season." . . . Two houses open, standing supper table, "dazzling array of beauty and fashion." "Polka" for the first time brought under my inspection. It's a kind of insane Tartar jig performed to disagreeable music of an uncivilized character.

4. **Description of juba dancing from Charles Dickens,** *American Notes for General Circulation*, **1842.** *In New York's Five Points slum in 1842, Charles Dickens described a challenge dance featuring William Henry Lane, or Master Juba, a young African American who created juba dancing, a blend of Irish jig and African dance moves.*

The corpulent black fiddler, and his friend who plays the tambourine, stamp upon the boarding of the small raised orchestra in which they sit, and play a lively measure. Five or six couples come upon the floor, marshalled by a lively young negro, who is the wit of the assembly, and the greatest dancer known. . . . Instantly the fiddler grins, and goes at it tooth and nail; there is new energy in the tambourine. . . . Single shuffle, double shuffle, cut and cross-cut; snapping his fingers, rolling his eyes, turning in his knees, presenting the backs of his legs in front, spinning about on his toes and heels like nothing but the man's fingers on the tambourine; dancing with two left legs, two right legs, two wooden legs, two wire legs, two spring legs — all sorts of legs and no legs — . . . having danced his partner off her feet, and himself too, he finishes by leaping gloriously on the bar-counter, and calling for something to drink.

5. **Poster advertising Barlow, Wilson, Primrose, and West's "Mammoth Minstrels' Colored Masquerade."** *Unlike slavery, minstrelsy survived the Civil War and remained popular until the early twentieth century, when it evolved into vaudeville. Barlow, Wilson, Primrose, and West's Mammoth*

*Minstrels toured the United States, Europe, and Australia between 1877 and 1882, thrilling audiences with the clog dances that had devolved out of juba.*

Sources: (3) Luther S. Harris, *Around Washington Square: An Illustrated History of Greenwich Village* (Baltimore, 2003), 41; (4) Charles Dickens, *American Notes and Pictures from Italy* (C. Scribner: New York, 1868), 107.

## ANALYZING THE EVIDENCE

1. What do sources 1 and 2 suggest about sexual manners among rural folk and genteel urbanites?
2. What does the polka (sources 3 and 4) reveal about changing cultural practices among the social elite?
3. Compare the juba and minstrelsy dances described above (sources 4 and 5) with the polka and contra dance forms (sources 1 and 2). How were dance forms and popular entertainment evolving? How did those changes relate to broader social developments?
4. The waltz, polka, and juba dances were popular during the Second Great Awakening, when (and long afterward) preachers often complained that "dance is destructive to Christian life." Why might ministers (and priests) take such a view? Would any form of dance be acceptable to them?

## PUTTING IT ALL TOGETHER

Using the material on class, religion, and culture in Chapters 9 and 11, the description of the Quarterons Ball in Chapter 12 (p. 387), and the insights you have gathered by a careful inspection of these sources, write an essay showing how dance and other entertainments reflect or reveal differences among American social groups.

Private Collection/Photo © Barbara Singer/The Bridgeman Art Library.

## Black Social Thought: Uplift, Race Equality, and Rebellion

Beginning in the 1790s, leading African Americans in the North advocated a strategy of social uplift, encouraging free blacks to "elevate" themselves through education, temperance, and hard work. By securing "respectability," they argued, blacks could become the social equals of whites. To promote that goal, black leaders—men such as James Forten, a Philadelphia sailmaker; Prince Hall, a Boston barber; and ministers Hosea Easton and Richard Allen (Chapter 8)—founded an array of churches, schools, and self-help associations. Capping this effort, John Russwurm and Samuel D. Cornish of New York published the first African American newspaper, *Freedom's Journal*, in 1827.

The black quest for respectability elicited a violent response in Boston, Pittsburgh, and other northern cities among whites who refused to accept African Americans as their social equals. "I am Mr. _____'s help," a white maid informed a British visitor. "I am no sarvant; none but negers are sarvants." Motivated by racial contempt, white mobs terrorized black communities. The attacks in Cincinnati were so violent and destructive that several hundred African Americans fled to Canada for safety.

**CHANGE OVER TIME**

How and why did African American efforts to achieve social equality change between 1800 and 1840?

**David Walker's *Appeal***   Responding to the attacks, David Walker published a stirring pamphlet, *An Appeal . . . to the Colored Citizens of the World* (1829), protesting black "wretchedness in this Republican Land of Liberty!!!!!" Walker was a free black from North Carolina who had moved to Boston, where he sold secondhand clothes and copies of *Freedom's Journal*. A self-educated author, Walker ridiculed the religious pretensions of slaveholders, justified slave rebellion, and in biblical language warned of a slave revolt if justice were delayed. "We must and shall be free," he told white Americans. "And woe, woe, will be it to you if we have to obtain our freedom by fighting. . . . Your destruction is at hand, and will be speedily consummated unless you repent." Walker's pamphlet quickly went through three printings and, carried by black merchant seamen, reached free African Americans in the South.

In 1830, Walker and other African American activists called a national convention in Philadelphia. The delegates refused to endorse either Walker's radical call for a slave revolt or the traditional program of uplift for free blacks. Instead, this new generation of activists demanded freedom and "race equality" for those of African descent. They urged free blacks to use every legal means, including petitions and other forms of political protest, to break "the shackles of slavery."

**Nat Turner's Revolt**   As Walker threatened violence in Boston, Nat Turner, a slave in Southampton County,

**A Call for Revolution**

David Walker (1785–1830), who ran a used clothing shop in Boston, spent his hard-earned savings to publish *An Appeal . . . to the Colored Citizens of the World* (1829), a learned and passionate attack on racial slavery. Walker depicted Christ as an avenging "God of justice and of armies" and raised the banner of slave rebellion. A year later, a passerby found Walker in the doorway of his shop, dead from unknown causes. Library of Congress.

Virginia, staged a bloody revolt—a chronological coincidence that had far-reaching consequences. As a child, Turner had taught himself to read and had hoped for emancipation, but one new master forced him into the fields, and another separated him from his wife. Becoming deeply spiritual, Turner had a religious vision in which "the Spirit" explained that "Christ had laid down the yoke he had borne for the sins of men, and that I should take it on and fight against the Serpent, for the time was fast approaching when the first should be last and the last should be first." Taking an eclipse of the sun in August 1831 as an omen, Turner and a handful of relatives and friends rose in rebellion and killed at least 55 white men, women, and children. Turner hoped that hundreds of slaves would rally to his cause, but he mustered only 60 men. The white militia quickly dispersed his poorly armed force and took their revenge. One company of cavalry killed 40 blacks in two days and put 15 of their heads on poles to warn "all those who should undertake a similar plot." Turner died by hanging, still identifying his mission with that of his Savior. "Was not Christ crucified?" he asked.

Deeply shaken by Turner's Rebellion, the Virginia assembly debated a law providing for gradual emancipation and colonization abroad. When the bill failed by a vote of 73 to 58, the possibility that southern planters would voluntarily end slavery was gone forever. Instead, the southern states toughened their slave codes, limited black movement, and prohibited anyone from teaching slaves to read. They would meet Walker's radical *Appeal* with radical measures of their own.

## Evangelical Abolitionism

Rejecting Walker's and Turner's resort to violence, a cadre of northern evangelical Christians launched a moral crusade to abolish the slave regime. If planters did not allow blacks their God-given status as free

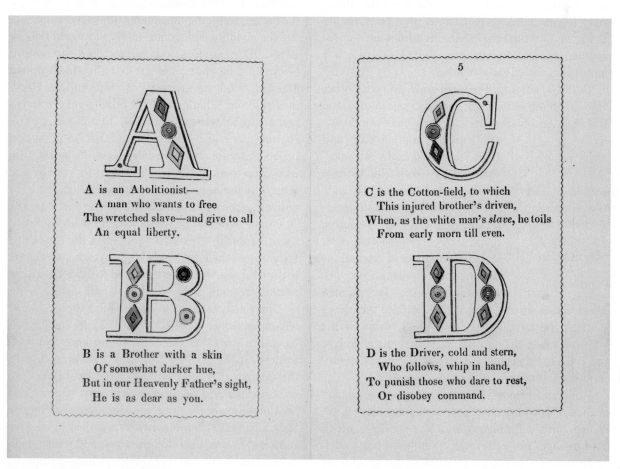

5

A is an Abolitionist—
A man who wants to free
The wretched slave—and give to all
An equal liberty.

B is a Brother with a skin
Of somewhat darker hue,
But in our Heavenly Father's sight,
He is as dear as you.

C is the Cotton-field, to which
This injured brother's driven,
When, as the white man's *slave*, he toils
From early morn till even.

D is the Driver, cold and stern,
Who follows, whip in hand,
To punish those who dare to rest,
Or disobey command.

**The Anti-Slavery Alphabet**
Girding themselves for a long fight, abolitionists conveyed their beliefs to the next generation. This primer, written by Quakers Hannah and Mary Townsend and published in Philadelphia in 1846, taught young children the alphabet by spreading the antislavery message. "A" was for "Abolitionist," and "B" was for a "Brother," an enslaved black who, though of a "darker hue," was considered by God "as dear as you." The Huntington Library & Art Collections, San Marino, CA.

moral agents, these radical Christians warned, they faced eternal damnation at the hands of a just God.

### William Lloyd Garrison, Theodore Weld, and Angelina and Sarah Grimké

The most determined abolitionist was William Lloyd Garrison (1805–1879). A Massachusetts-born printer, Garrison had worked during the 1820s in Baltimore on an antislavery newspaper, the *Genius of Universal Emancipation*. In 1830, Garrison went to jail, convicted of libeling a New England merchant engaged in the domestic slave trade. In 1831, Garrison moved to Boston, where he immediately started his own weekly, *The Liberator* (1831–1865), and founded the New England Anti-Slavery Society.

Influenced by a bold pamphlet, *Immediate, Not Gradual Abolition* (1824), by an English Quaker, Elizabeth Coltman Heyrick, Garrison demanded immediate abolition without compensation to slaveholders. "I will not retreat a single inch," he declared, "AND I WILL BE HEARD." Garrison accused the American Colonization Society (Chapter 8) of perpetuating slavery and assailed the U.S. Constitution as "a covenant with death and an agreement with Hell" because it implicitly accepted racial bondage.

In 1833, Garrison, Theodore Weld, and sixty other religious abolitionists, black and white, established the American Anti-Slavery Society. The society won financial support from Arthur and Lewis Tappan, wealthy silk merchants in New York City. Women abolitionists established separate groups, including the Philadelphia Female Anti-Slavery Society, founded by Lucretia Mott in 1833, and the Anti-Slavery Conventions of American Women, a network of local societies. The women raised money for *The Liberator* and carried the movement to the farm villages and small towns of the Midwest, where they distributed abolitionist literature and collected thousands of signatures on antislavery petitions.

Abolitionist leaders launched a three-pronged plan of attack. To win the support of religious Americans, Weld published *The Bible Against Slavery* (1837), which used passages from Christianity's holiest book to discredit slavery. Two years later, Weld teamed up with the Grimké sisters—Angelina, whom he married, and Sarah. The Grimkés had left their father's plantation in South Carolina, converted to Quakerism, and taken up the abolitionist cause in Philadelphia. In *American*

**COMPARE AND CONTRAST**
How did the ideology and tactics of the Garrisonian abolitionists differ from those of the antislavery movements discussed in Chapters 6 and 8?

*Slavery as It Is: Testimony of a Thousand Witnesses* (1839), Weld and the Grimkés addressed a simple question: "What is the actual condition of the slaves in the United States?" Using reports from southern newspapers and firsthand testimony, they presented incriminating evidence of the inherent violence of slavery. Angelina Grimké told of a treadmill that South Carolina slave owners used for punishment: "One poor girl, [who was] sent there to be flogged, and who was accordingly stripped naked and whipped, showed me the deep gashes on her back—I might have laid my whole finger in them—large pieces of flesh had actually been cut out by the torturing lash." Filled with such images of pain and suffering, the book sold more than 100,000 copies in a single year.

### The American Anti-Slavery Society

To spread their message, the abolitionists turned to mass communication. Using new steam-powered presses to print a million pamphlets, the American Anti-Slavery Society carried out a "great postal campaign" in 1835, flooding the nation, including the South, with its literature.

The abolitionists' second tactic was to aid fugitive slaves. They provided lodging and jobs for escaped blacks in free states and created the **Underground Railroad**, an informal network of whites and free blacks in Richmond, Charleston, and other southern towns that assisted fugitives (Map 11.3). In Baltimore, a free African American sailor loaned his identification papers to future abolitionist Frederick Douglass, who used them to escape to New York. Harriet Tubman and other runaways risked re-enslavement or death by returning repeatedly to the South to help others escape. "I should fight for . . . liberty as long as my strength lasted," Tubman explained, "and when the time came for me to go, the Lord would let them take me." Thanks to the Railroad, about one thousand African Americans reached freedom in the North each year.

There, they faced an uncertain future because most whites continued to reject civic or social equality for African Americans. Voters in six northern and midwestern states adopted constitutional amendments that denied or limited the franchise for free blacks. "We want no masters," declared a New York artisan, "and least of all no negro masters." Moreover, the Fugitive Slave Law (1793) allowed owners and their hired slave catchers to seize suspected runaways and return them to bondage. To thwart these efforts, white abolitionists and free blacks formed mobs that attacked slave catchers, released their captives, and often spirited them off to British-ruled Canada, which refused to extradite fugitive slaves.

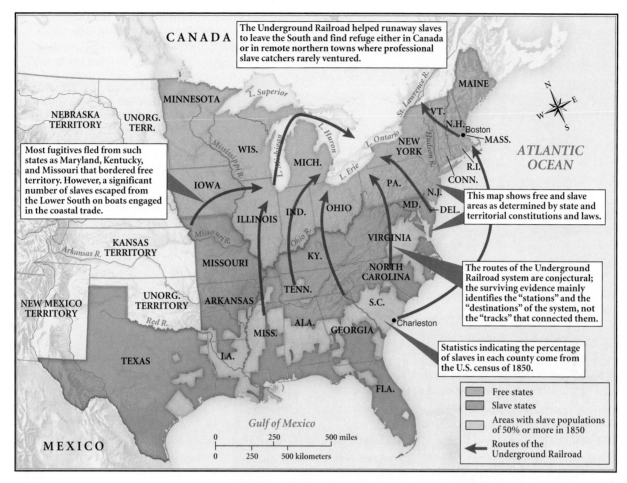

The Underground Railroad helped runaway slaves to leave the South and find refuge either in Canada or in remote northern towns where professional slave catchers rarely ventured.

Most fugitives fled from such states as Maryland, Kentucky, and Missouri that bordered free territory. However, a significant number of slaves escaped from the Lower South on boats engaged in the coastal trade.

This map shows free and slave areas as determined by state and territorial constitutions and laws.

The routes of the Underground Railroad system are conjectural; the surviving evidence mainly identifies the "stations" and the "destinations" of the system, not the "tracks" that connected them.

Statistics indicating the percentage of slaves in each county come from the U.S. census of 1850.

Free states
Slave states
Areas with slave populations of 50% or more in 1850
Routes of the Underground Railroad

**MAP 11.3**

**The Underground Railroad in the 1850s**

Before 1840, most African Americans who fled slavery did so on their own or with the help of family and friends. Thereafter, they could count on support from members of the Underground Railroad. Provided with food and directions by free blacks in the South, fugitive slaves crossed into free states. There, they received protection and shelter from abolitionists who arranged for their transportation to Canada or to "safe" American cities and towns.

A political campaign was the final element of the abolitionists' program. Between 1835 and 1838, the American Anti-Slavery Society bombarded Congress with petitions containing nearly 500,000 signatures. They demanded the abolition of slavery in the District of Columbia, an end to the interstate slave trade, and a ban on admission of new slave states.

Thousands of deeply religious farmers and small-town proprietors supported these efforts. The number of local abolitionist societies grew from two hundred in 1835 to two thousand by 1840, with nearly 200,000 members, including many transcendentalists. Emerson condemned Americans for supporting slavery, and Thoreau, viewing the Mexican War as a naked scheme to extend slavery, refused to pay taxes and submitted to arrest. In 1848, he published "Resistance to Civil Government," an essay urging individuals to follow a higher moral law. The black abolitionist Henry Highland Garnet went further; his *Address to the Slaves of the United States of America* (1841) called for "Liberty or Death" and urged slave "Resistance! Resistance! Resistance!"

## Opposition and Internal Conflict

Still, abolitionists remained a minority, even among churchgoers. Perhaps 10 percent of northerners and midwesterners strongly supported the movement, and only another 20 percent were sympathetic to its goals.

**Attacks on Abolitionism**   Slavery's proponents were more numerous and equally aggressive. The

THE NEGRO IN HIS OWN COUNTRY.

THE NEGRO IN AMERICA.

**"The Negro in His Own Country" Versus "The Negro in America"**

Slave owners and their intellectual and religious allies responded to abolitionists' attacks by defending slavery as a "positive good." These two images, from Josiah Priest's *Bible Defence of Slavery* (1852), support the argument that enslavement saved Africans from a savage, war-ridden life (note the skeleton in the top image) and exposed them to the civilized world. Such publications achieved wide circulation and popularity among the planter classes. Chicago History Museum.

abolitionists' agitation, ministers warned, risked "embroiling neighborhoods and families — setting friend against friend, overthrowing churches and institutions of learning, embittering one portion of the land against the other." Wealthy men feared that the attack on slave property might become an assault on all property rights, conservative clergymen condemned the public roles assumed by abolitionist women, and northern wage earners feared that freed blacks would work for lower wages and take their jobs. Underlining the national "reach" of slavery, northern merchants and textile manufacturers supported the southern planters who supplied them with cotton, as did hog farmers in Ohio, Indiana, and Illinois and pork packers in Cincinnati and

**UNDERSTAND POINTS OF VIEW**
Which groups of Americans opposed the abolitionists, and why did they do so?

Chicago who profited from lucrative sales to slave plantations. Finally, whites almost universally opposed "**amalgamation**," the racial mixing and intermarriage that Garrison seemed to support by holding meetings of blacks and whites of both sexes.

Racial fears and hatreds led to violent mob actions. White workers in northern towns laid waste to taverns and brothels where blacks and whites mixed, and they vandalized "respectable" African American churches, temperance halls, and orphanages. In 1833, a mob of 1,500 New Yorkers stormed a church in search of Garrison and Arthur Tappan. Another white mob swept through Philadelphia's African American neighborhoods, clubbing and stoning residents and destroying homes and churches. In 1835, "gentlemen of property and standing" — lawyers, merchants, and bankers — broke up an abolitionist convention in Utica, New

York. Two years later, a mob in Alton, Illinois, shot and killed Elijah P. Lovejoy, editor of the abolitionist *Alton Observer*. By pressing for emancipation and equality, the abolitionists had revealed the extent of racial prejudice and had heightened race consciousness, as both whites and blacks identified across class lines with members of their own race.

Racial solidarity was especially strong in the South, where whites banned abolitionists. The Georgia legislature offered a $5,000 reward for kidnapping Garrison and bringing him to the South to be tried (or lynched) for inciting rebellion. In Nashville, vigilantes whipped a northern college student for distributing abolitionist pamphlets; in Charleston, a mob attacked the post office and destroyed sacks of abolitionist mail. After 1835, southern postmasters simply refused to deliver mail suspected to be of abolitionist origin.

Politicians joined the fray. President Andrew Jackson, a longtime slave owner, asked Congress in 1835 to restrict the use of the mails by abolitionist groups. Congress refused, but in 1836, the House of Representatives adopted the so-called **gag rule**. Under this informal agreement, which remained in force until 1844, the House automatically tabled antislavery petitions, keeping the explosive issue of slavery off the congressional stage.

**Internal Divisions** Assailed by racists from the outside, evangelical abolitionists fought among themselves over gender issues. Many antislavery clergymen

## AN AFFECTING SCENE IN KENTUCKY.

**The Complexities of Race**

This cartoon takes aim at Richard Mentor Johnson of Kentucky, the distraught man being comforted by abolitionists Frederick Douglass and William Lloyd Garrison. A longtime congressman and senator, Johnson was the Democrats' vice-presidential candidate in 1836. Although the party stood for the South and slavery—and condemned mixed-race unions—Johnson lived openly with an African American woman, Julia Chinn, whose daughters hold her portrait. Future Supreme Court justice John Catron noted with disgust that Johnson tried "to force his daughters into society" and that they and their mother "claimed equality." Racial prejudice cost Johnson some votes, but he won a plurality in the electoral college, and, on a party-line vote, Democrats in the Senate elected him Martin Van Buren's vice president. Library of Congress.

opposed an activist role for women, but Garrison had broadened his reform agenda to include pacifism, the abolition of prisons, and women's rights: "Our object is universal emancipation, to redeem women as well as men from a servile to an equal condition." In 1840, Garrison's demand that the American Anti-Slavery Society support women's rights split the abolitionist movement. Abby Kelley, Lucretia Mott, and Elizabeth Cady Stanton, among others, remained with Garrison in the American Anti-Slavery Society and assailed both the institutions that bound blacks and the customs that constrained free women.

Garrison's opponents founded a new organization, the American and Foreign Anti-Slavery Society, which turned to politics. Its members mobilized their churches to oppose racial bondage and organized the Liberty Party, the first antislavery political party. In 1840, the new party nominated James G. Birney, a former Alabama slave owner, for president. Birney and the Liberty Party argued that the Constitution did not recognize slavery and, consequently, that slaves became free when they entered areas of federal authority, such as the District of Columbia and the national territories. However, Birney won few votes, and the future of political abolitionism appeared dim.

Popular violence in the North, government-aided suppression in the South, and internal schisms stunned the abolitionist movement. By melding the energies and ideas of evangelical Protestants, moral reformers, and transcendentalists, it had raised the banner of antislavery to new heights, only to face a hostile backlash. "When we first unfurled the banner of *The Liberator*,"

Garrison admitted, "it did not occur to us that nearly every religious sect, and every political party would side with the oppressor."

# The Women's Rights Movement

The prominence of women among the abolitionists reflected a broad shift in American culture. By joining religious revivals and reform movements, women entered public life. Their activism caused many gender issues — sexual behavior, marriage, family authority — to become subjects of debate. The debate entered a new phase in 1848, when some reformers focused on women's rights and demanded complete equality with men.

## Origins of the Women's Movement

"Don't be afraid, not afraid, fight Satan; stand up for Christ; don't be afraid." So spoke Mary Walker Ostram on her deathbed in 1859. Her religious convictions were as firm at the age of fifty-eight as they had been in 1816, when she joined the first Sunday school in Utica, New York. Married to a lawyer-politician and childless, Ostram had devoted her life to evangelical Presbyterianism and its program of benevolent social reform. At her funeral, minister Philemon Fowler celebrated Ostram as a "living fountain" of faith, an exemplar of "Women's Sphere of Influence" in the world.

**A Nineteenth-Century Middle-Class Family**

Whereas colonial-era families were large, often with six to eight children, nineteenth-century middle-class couples, such as Azariah and Eliza Caverly, pictured here in 1836 by Joseph H. Davis (1811–1865), consciously limited their fertility, treated their spouses with affection, and carefully supervised the education of their children. The Caverlys' daughter fingers a Bible, suggesting her future moral responsibilities as a mother, while their son holds a square ruler, either indicating Azariah's profession or foreshadowing the son's career as a prosperous architect or engineer. Fenimore Art Museum, Cooperstown, New York.

Although Reverend Fowler heaped praise on Ostram, he rejected a public presence for women. Like men of the Revolutionary era, Fowler thought women should limit their political role to that of "republican mother," instructing "their sons in the principles of liberty and government." Women inhabited a "**separate sphere**" of domestic life, he said, and had no place in "the markets of trade, the scenes of politics and popular agitation, the courts of justice and the halls of legislation. Home is her peculiar sphere."

However, Ostram and many other middle-class women were redefining the notion of the domestic sphere by becoming active in their churches. Their spiritual activism bolstered their authority within the household and gave them new influence over many areas of family life, including the timing of pregnancies. Publications such as *Godey's Lady's Book*, a popular monthly periodical, and Catharine Beecher's *Treatise on Domestic Economy* (1841) taught women how to make their homes examples of middle-class efficiency and domesticity. Women in propertied farm families were equally vigilant and carried domestic issues into the public sphere. To protect their homes and husbands from alcoholic excess, they joined the Independent Order of Good Templars, a temperance group which made women full members (American Voices, p. 368).

**Moral Reform**   Some religious women developed a sharp consciousness of gender and became public actors. In 1834, middle-class women in New York City founded the Female Moral Reform Society and elected Lydia Finney, the wife of revivalist Charles Grandison Finney, as its president. The society tried to curb prostitution and to protect single women from moral corruption. Rejecting the sexual double standard, its members demanded chaste behavior by men. By 1840, the Female Moral Reform Society had blossomed into a national association, with 555 chapters and 40,000 members throughout the North and Midwest. Employing only women as agents, the society provided moral guidance for young women who were working as factory operatives, seamstresses, or servants. Society members visited brothels, where they sang hymns, offered prayers, searched for runaway girls, and noted the names of clients. They also founded homes of refuge for prostitutes and won the passage of laws in Massachusetts and New York that made seduction a crime.

**Improving Prisons, Creating Asylums, Expanding Education**   Other women set out to improve public institutions, and Dorothea Dix (1801–1887) was their model. Dix's paternal grandparents were prominent Bostonians, but her father, a Methodist minister, ended

up an impoverished alcoholic. Emotionally abused as a child, Dix grew into a compassionate young woman with a strong sense of moral purpose. She used money from her grandparents to set up charity schools to "rescue some of America's miserable children from vice" and became a successful author. By 1832, she had published seven books, including *Conversations on Common Things* (1824), an enormously successful treatise on natural science and moral improvement.

> **TRACE CHANGE OVER TIME**
> Using the material on women's lives in Chapters 4, 8, and 11, analyze and explain the changing nature of their "private" and "public" lives.

In 1841, Dix took up a new cause. Discovering that insane women were jailed alongside male criminals, she persuaded Massachusetts lawmakers to enlarge the state hospital to house indigent mental patients. Exhilarated by that success, Dix began a national movement to establish state asylums for the mentally ill. By 1854, she had traveled more than 30,000 miles and had visited eighteen state penitentiaries, three hundred county jails, and more than five hundred almshouses and hospitals. Dix's reports and agitation prompted many states to improve their prisons and public hospitals.

Both as reformers and teachers, other northern women transformed public education. From Maine to Wisconsin, women vigorously supported the movement led by Horace Mann to increase elementary schooling and improve the quality of instruction. As secretary of the Massachusetts Board of Education from 1837 to 1848, Mann lengthened the school year; established teaching standards in reading, writing, and arithmetic; and recruited well-educated women as teachers. The intellectual leader of the new women educators was Catharine Beecher, who founded academies for young women in Hartford, Connecticut, and Cincinnati, Ohio. In widely read publications, Beecher argued that "energetic and benevolent women" were better qualified than men were to impart moral and intellectual instruction to the young. By the 1850s, most teachers were women, both because local school boards heeded Beecher's arguments and because they could hire women at lower salaries than men. As secular educators as well as moral reformers, women were now part of American public life.

## From Black Rights to Women's Rights

As women addressed controversial issues such as moral reform and emancipation, they faced censure over their public presence. Offended by this criticism, which revealed their own social and legal inferiority, some women sought full freedom for their sex.

## Saving the Nation from Drink

The temperance crusade was the most successful antebellum reform movement. It mobilized more than a million supporters in all sections of the nation and significantly lowered the consumption of alcoholic beverages. Nonetheless, like other reform efforts, the antidrinking crusade divided over questions of strategy and tactics. The following passages, taken from the writings of leading temperance advocates, show that some reformers favored legal regulation while others preferred persuasion and voluntary abstinence.

### Lyman Beecher
### "Intemperance Is the Sin of Our Land"

A leading Protestant minister and spokesman for the Benevolent Empire, Lyman Beecher regarded drunkenness as a sin. His *Six Sermons on . . . Intemperance* (1829) condemned the recklessness of working-class drunkards and called on responsible members of the middle class to lead the way to a temperate society.

Intemperance is the sin of our land, and, with our boundless prosperity, is coming in upon us like a flood; and if anything shall defeat the hopes of the world, which hang upon our experiment of civil liberty, it is that river of fire. . . .

In every city and town the poor-tax, created chiefly by intemperance, is [increasing the burden on taxpaying citizens]. . . . The frequency of going upon the town [relying on public welfare] has taken away the reluctance of pride, and destroyed the motives to providence which the fear of poverty and suffering once supplied. The prospect of a destitute old age, or of a suffering family, no longer troubles the vicious portion of our community. They drink up their daily earnings, and bless God for the poor-house, and begin to look upon it as, of right, the drunkard's home. . . . Every intemperate and idle man, whom you behold tottering about the streets and steeping himself at the stores, regards your houses and lands as pledged to take care of him, puts his hands deep, annually, into your pockets. . . .

What then is this universal, natural, and national remedy for intemperance? IT IS THE BANISHMENT OF ARDENT SPIRITS FROM THE LIST OF LAWFUL ARTICLES OF COMMERCE, BY A CORRECT AND EFFICIENT PUBLIC SENTIMENT; SUCH AS HAS TURNED SLAVERY OUT OF HALF OUR LAND, AND WILL YET EXPEL IT FROM THE WORLD.

We are not therefore to come down in wrath upon the distillers, and importers, and venders of ardent spirits. None of us are enough without sin to cast the first stone. . . . It is the buyers who have created the demand for ardent spirits, and made distillation and importation a gainful traffic. . . . Let the temperate cease to buy — and the demand for ardent spirits will fall in the market three fourths, and ultimately will fail wholly. . . .

This however cannot be done effectually so long as the traffic in ardent spirits is regarded as lawful, and is patronized by men of reputation and moral worth in every part of the land. Like slavery, it must be regarded as sinful, impolitic, and dishonorable. That no measures will avail short of rendering ardent spirits a contraband of trade, is nearly self-evident.

### Abraham Lincoln
### "A New Class of Champions"

In Baltimore in 1840, a group of reformed alcoholics formed the Washington Temperance Society, which turned the antidrinking movement in a new direction. By talking publicly about their personal experiences of alcoholic decline and spiritual recovery, they inspired thousands to "sign the pledge" of total abstinence. (Its philosophy exists today in the organization Alcoholics Anonymous.) In 1842, Lincoln, an ambitious lawyer and Illinois legislator who did not drink, praised such "moral suasion" in an address to the Washingtonians of Springfield, Illinois.

Although the temperance cause has been in progress for near twenty years, it is apparent to all that it is just now being crowned with a degree of success hitherto unparalleled. The list of its friends is daily swelled by the additions of fifties, of hundreds, and of thousands.

The warfare heretofore waged against the demon intemperance has somehow or other been erroneous. . . . [Its] champions for the most part have been preachers [such as Beecher], lawyers, and hired agents. Between these and the mass of mankind there is a want of approachability. . . .

But when one who has long been known as a victim of intemperance bursts the fetters that have bound him, and appears before his neighbors "clothed and in his right mind," . . . to tell of the miseries once endured, now to be endured no more . . . there is a logic and an eloquence in it that few with human feelings can resist. . . .

In my judgment, it is to the battles of this new class of champions that our late success is greatly, perhaps chiefly, owing. . . . [Previously,] too much denunciation against dram-sellers and dram-drinkers was indulged in. This I think was both impolitic and unjust. . . . When the dram-seller and drinker were incessantly [condemned] . . . as moral pestilences . . . they were slow [to] . . . join the ranks of their denouncers in a hue and cry against themselves.

By the Washingtonians this system of consigning the habitual drunkard to hopeless ruin is repudiated. . . . They teach hope to all — despair to none. As applying to their cause, they deny the doctrine of unpardonable sin. . . .

If the relative grandeur of revolutions shall be estimated by the great amount of human misery they alleviate, and the small amount they inflict, then indeed will this be the grandest the world shall ever have seen. Of our political revolution of '76 we are all justly proud. It has given us a degree of political freedom far exceeding that of any other nation of the earth. . . . But, with all these glorious results, past, present, and to come, [this freedom] had its evils too. It [was abused by drunken husbands and thereby] breathed forth famine, swam in blood, and rode in fire; and long, long after, the orphan's cry and the widow's wail continued to break the sad silence that ensued. These were the price, the inevitable price, paid for the blessings it brought. . . .

Turn now to the temperance revolution. In it we shall find a stronger bondage broken, a viler slavery manumitted, a greater tyrant deposed; in it, more of want supplied, more disease healed, more sorrow assuaged. By it no orphans starving, no widows weeping.

Glorious consummation! Hail, fall of fury! Reign of reason, all hail!

### American Temperance Magazine
### "You Shall Not Sell"

In 1851, the Maine legislature passed a statute prohibiting the sale of alcoholic beverages in the state. The Maine Supreme Court upheld the statute, arguing that the legislature had the "right to regulate by law the sale of any article, the use of which would be detrimental of the morals of the people." Subsequently, the *American Temperance Magazine* became a strong advocate of legal prohibition and by 1856 had won passage of "Maine Laws" in twelve other states (Chapter 9).

This is a utilitarian age. The speculative has in all things yielded to the practical. Words are mere noise unless they are things [and result in action].

In this sense, moral suasion is moral balderdash. "Words, my lord, words" . . . are a delusion. . . . The drunkard's mental and physical condition pronounces them an absurdity. He is ever in one or other extreme — under the excitement of drink, or in a state of morbid collapse. . . . Reason with a man when all reason has fled, and it is doubtful whether he or you is the greater fool. . . . Moral suasion! Bah!

Place this man we have been describing out of the reach of temptation. He will have time to ponder. His mind and frame recover their native vigor. The public-house does not beset his path. . . . Thus, and thus only, will reformation and temperance be secured. And how is this accomplished? Never except through the instrumentality of the law. If it were possible to reason the drunkard into sobriety, it would not be possible to make the rum-seller forego his filthy gains. Try your moral suasion on him. . . . The only logic he will comprehend, is some such ordinance as this, coming to him in the shape and with the voice of law — you shall not sell.

Source: David Brion Davis, *Antebellum American Culture: An Interpretive Anthology* (University Park: Pennsylvania State University Press, 1997), 395–398, 403–409.

---

### QUESTIONS FOR ANALYSIS
1. What does Lincoln's address suggest about his general political philosophy?
2. Compare Beecher's position to Lincoln's. In what ways are they similar? How are they different? Then compare Beecher's solution to that of the *American Temperance Magazine*. Are they the same? Whose view of personal responsibility versus institutional coercion is closest to the position of Orestes Brownson (Chapter 9, pp. 308–309)?
3. In which of these selections do you see the influence of the Second Great Awakening, especially the evangelical message of Charles Grandison Finney? Where do you see the influence of the Market Revolution and the cultural values of the rising middle class? What positions do these selections take with respect to the appropriate role of government in regulating morality and personal behavior?

**Abolitionist Women**    Women were central to the antislavery movement because they understood the special horrors of slavery for women. In her autobiography, *Incidents in the Life of a Slave Girl*, black abolitionist Harriet Jacobs described forced sexual intercourse with her white owner. "I cannot tell how much I suffered in the presence of these wrongs," she wrote. According to Jacobs and other enslaved women, such sexual assaults incited additional cruelty by their owners' wives, who were enraged by their husbands' promiscuity. In her best-selling novel, *Uncle Tom's Cabin* (1852), Harriet Beecher Stowe pinpointed the sexual abuse of women as a profound moral failing of the slave regime.

As Garrisonian women attacked slavery, they frequently violated social taboos by speaking to mixed audiences of men and women. Maria W. Stewart, an African American, spoke to mixed crowds in Boston in the early 1830s. As abolitionism blossomed, scores of white women delivered lectures condemning slavery, and thousands more made home "visitations" to win converts to their cause (Map 11.4). When Congregationalist clergymen in New England assailed Angelina and Sarah Grimké for such activism in a Pastoral Letter in 1837, Sarah Grimké turned to the Bible for justification: "The Lord Jesus defines the duties of his followers in his Sermon on the Mount . . . without any reference to sex or condition," she replied: "Men and women were CREATED EQUAL; both are moral and accountable beings and whatever is right for man to do, is right for woman." In a pamphlet debate with Catharine Beecher (who believed that women should exercise authority primarily as wives, mothers, and schoolteachers), Angelina Grimké pushed the argument beyond religion by invoking Enlightenment principles to claim equal civic rights:

> It is a woman's right to have a voice in all the laws and regulations by which she is governed, whether in Church or State. . . . The present arrangements of society on these points are a violation of human rights, a rank usurpation of power, a violent seizure and confiscation of what is sacredly and inalienably hers.

By 1840, female abolitionists were asserting that traditional gender roles resulted in the **domestic slavery** of women. "How can we endure our present marriage relations," asked Elizabeth Cady Stanton, "[which give a woman] no charter of rights, no individuality of her own?" As reformer Ernestine Rose put it: "The radical difficulty . . . is that women are considered as belonging to men." Having acquired a public voice and

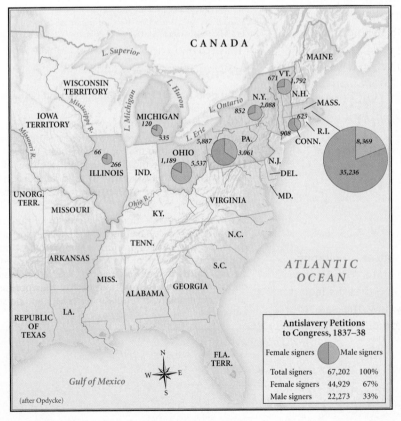

**MAP 11.4**

**Women and Antislavery, 1837–1838**

Beginning in the 1830s, abolitionists and antislavery advocates dispatched dozens of petitions to Congress demanding an end to forced labor. Women accounted for two-thirds of the 67,000 signatures on the petitions submitted in 1837–1838, a fact that suggests not only the influence of women in the antislavery movement but also the extent of female organizations and social networks. Lawmakers, eager to avoid sectional conflict, devised an informal agreement (the "gag rule") to table the petitions without discussion.

Antislavery Petitions to Congress, 1837–38

Female signers / Male signers

| | | |
|---|---|---|
| Total signers | 67,202 | 100% |
| Female signers | 44,929 | 67% |
| Male signers | 22,273 | 33% |

political skills in the crusade for African American freedom, thousands of northern women now advocated greater rights for themselves.

**Seneca Falls and Beyond**    During the 1840s, women's rights activists devised a pragmatic program of reform. Unlike radical utopians, they did not challenge the institution of marriage or the conventional division of labor within the family. Instead, they tried to strengthen the legal rights of married women by seeking legislation that permitted them to own property (America Compared, p. 372). This initiative won crucial support from affluent men, who feared bankruptcy in the volatile market economy and wanted to put

**Crusading Reformers**

Elizabeth Cady Stanton (1815–1902) and Susan B. Anthony (1820–1906) were a dynamic duo. Stanton, the well-educated daughter of a prominent New York judge, was an early abolitionist and the mother of seven children. Anthony came from a Quaker family and became a teacher and a temperance activist. Meeting in 1851, Stanton and Anthony became friends and co-organizers. From 1854 to 1860, they led a successful struggle to expand New York's Married Women's Property Law of 1848. During the Civil War, they formed the Women's Loyal National League, which helped win passage of the Thirteenth Amendment, ending slavery. In 1866, they joined the American Equal Rights Association, which demanded the vote for women and African Americans. © Bettmann/Corbis.

some family assets in their wives' names. Fathers also desired their married daughters to have property rights to protect them (and their paternal inheritances) from financially irresponsible husbands. Such motives prompted legislatures in three states — Mississippi, Maine, and Massachusetts — to enact **married women's property laws** between 1839 and 1845. Then, women activists in New York won a comprehensive statute that became the model for fourteen other states. The New York statute of 1848 gave women full legal control over the property they brought to a marriage.

Also in 1848, Elizabeth Cady Stanton and Lucretia Mott organized a gathering of women's rights activists in the small New York town of Seneca Falls. Seventy women and thirty men attended the **Seneca Falls Convention**, which issued a rousing manifesto extending to women the egalitarian republican ideology of the Declaration of Independence. "All men and women are created equal," the Declaration of Sentiments declared, "[yet] the history of mankind is a history of repeated injuries and usurpations on the part of man toward woman [and] the establishment of an absolute tyranny over her." To persuade Americans to right this long-standing wrong, the activists resolved to "employ agents, circulate tracts, petition the State and National legislatures, and endeavor to enlist the pulpit and the press on our behalf." By staking out claims for equality for women in public life, the Seneca Falls reformers repudiated both the natural inferiority of women and the ideology of separate spheres.

Most men dismissed the Seneca Falls declaration as nonsense, and many women also rejected the activists and their message. In her diary, one small-town mother and housewife lashed out at the female reformer who "aping mannish manners . . . wears absurd and barbarous attire, who talks of her wrongs in harsh tone, who struts and strides, and thinks that she proves herself superior to the rest of her sex."

Still, the women's rights movement grew in strength and purpose. In 1850, delegates to the first national women's rights convention in Worcester, Massachusetts, hammered out a program of action. The women called on churches to eliminate notions of female inferiority in their theology. Addressing state legislatures, they proposed laws to allow married women to institute lawsuits, testify in court, and assume custody of their children in the event of divorce or a husband's death. Finally, they began a concerted campaign to win the vote for women. As delegates to the 1851 convention

**PLACE EVENTS IN CONTEXT**
What was the relationship between the abolitionist and women's rights movements?

## Women's Rights in France and the United States, 1848

During the political uprising in France in 1848, Pauline Roland and Jeanne Deroine unsuccessfully sought voting rights and an equal civil status for French women. However, the two women won election to the Central Committee of the Associative Unions, the umbrella organization of French trade unions. Imprisoned for their activism, they dispatched a letter to the Second Woman's Rights Convention, which met in Worcester, Massachusetts, in 1851.

When their letter was read to the Convention, Ernestine Potowsky Rose (1810–1892) offered the following response, which indicated the different perspective and political strategy of the American women's movement.

### Pauline Roland and Jeanne Deroine
### Letter to the Convention of the Women of America

Dear Sisters: Your courageous declaration of Woman's Rights has resounded even to our prison and has filled our souls with inexpressible joy. In France the [conservative] reaction [to the uprising of 1848] has suppressed the cry of liberty of the women of the future. . . . The Assembly kept silence in regard to the right of one half of humanity. . . . No mention was made of the right of woman in a Constitution framed in the name of Liberty, Equality, and Fraternity. . . .

[However,] the right of woman has been recognized by the laborers and they have consecrated that right by the election of those who had claimed it in vain for both sexes. . . . It is by labor; it is by entering resolutely into the ranks of the working people that women will conquer the civil and political equality on which depends the happiness of the world. . . . Sisters of America! your socialist sisters of France are united with you in the vindication of the right of woman to civil and political equality. . . . [Only] by the union of the working classes of both sexes [can we achieve] . . . the civil and political equality of woman.

### Ernestine Rose
### Speech to the Second Woman's Rights Convention

After having heard the letter read from our poor incarcerated sisters of France, well might we exclaim, Alas poor France! Where is thy glory?

. . . But need we wonder that France, governed as she is by Russian and Austrian despotism, does not recognize . . . the Rights of Woman, when even here, in this far-famed land of freedom . . . woman, the mockingly so-called "better half" of man, has yet to plead for her rights. . . . In the laws of the land, she has no rights; in government she has no voice. . . . From the cradle to the grave she is subject to the power and control of man. Father, guardian, or husband, one conveys her like some piece of merchandise over to the other.

. . . Carry out the republican principle of universal suffrage, or strike it from your banners and substitute "Freedom and Power to one half of society, and Submission and Slavery to the other." Give women the elective franchise. Let married women have the same right to property that their husbands have. . . .

There is no reason against woman's elevation, but . . . prejudices. The main cause is a pernicious falsehood propagated against her being, namely that she is inferior by her nature. Inferior in what? What has man ever done that woman, under the same advantages could not do?

Source: *History of Woman Suffrage*, ed. Elizabeth Cady Stanton, Susan B. Anthony, and Matilda Joslyn Gage (New York: Fowler & Wells, 1887), 1: 234–242.

### QUESTIONS FOR ANALYSIS

1. What strategy to achieve women's rights do Roland and Deroine advocate? What strategy can be detected in Rose's remarks? How are their perspectives similar to, or different from, one another?
2. What does this French-American comparison (and your reading in Chapter 11) suggest about the nature and values of the American women's rights movement?

proclaimed, suffrage was "the corner-stone of this enterprise, since we do not seek to protect woman, but rather to place her in a position to protect herself."

The activists' legislative campaign required talented organizers and lobbyists. The most prominent political operative was Susan B. Anthony (1820–1906), a Quaker who had acquired political skills in the temperance and antislavery movements. Those experiences, Anthony reflected, taught her "the great evil of woman's utter dependence on man." Joining the women's rights movement, she worked closely with Elizabeth Cady Stanton. Anthony created an activist network of political "captains," all women, who relentlessly lobbied state legislatures. In 1860, her efforts secured a New York law granting women the right to control their own wages (which fathers or husbands had previously managed); to own property acquired by "trade, business, labors, or services"; and, if widowed, to assume sole guardianship of their children. Genuine individualism for women, the dream of transcendentalist Margaret Fuller, had advanced a tiny step closer to reality. In such small and much larger ways, the mid-century reform movements had altered the character of American culture.

## SUMMARY

In this chapter, we examined four major cultural movements of the mid-nineteenth century — transcendentalist reform, communalism, abolitionism, and women's rights — as well as the new popular culture in New York City. Our discussion of the transcendentalists highlighted the influence of Ralph Waldo Emerson on the great literary figures of the era and linked transcendentalism to the rise of individualism and the character of middle-class American culture.

Our analysis of communal experiments probed their members' efforts to devise new rules for sexual behavior, gender relationships, and property ownership. We saw that successful communal experiments, such as Mormonism, required a charismatic leader or a religious foundation and endured if they developed strong, even authoritarian, institutions.

We also traced the personal and ideological factors that linked the abolitionist and women's rights movements. Lucretia Mott, Elizabeth Cady Stanton, and the Grimké sisters began as antislavery advocates, but, denied access to lecture platforms by male abolitionists and conservative clergy, they became staunch advocates of women's rights. This transition was a logical one: both enslaved blacks and married women were "owned" by men, either as property or as their legal dependents. Consequently, the efforts to abolish the legal prerogatives of husbands were as controversial as those to end the legal property rights of slave owners. As reformers took aim at such deeply rooted institutions and customs, many Americans feared that their activism would not perfect society but destroy it.

# CHAPTER REVIEW

**MAKE IT STICK**   Go to **LearningCurve** to retain what you've read.   ✓

## TERMS TO KNOW   Identify and explain the significance of each term below.

### Key Concepts and Events

| | |
|---|---|
| individualism (p. 346) | Underground Railroad (p. 362) |
| American Renaissance (p. 346) | amalgamation (p. 364) |
| transcendentalism (p. 346) | gag rule (p. 365) |
| utopias (p. 349) | separate sphere (p. 367) |
| socialism (p. 351) | domestic slavery (p. 370) |
| perfectionism (p. 352) | married women's property laws (p. 371) |
| Mormonism (p. 352) | Seneca Falls Convention (p. 371) |
| minstrelsy (p. 356) | |
| abolitionism (p. 357) | |

### Key People

Ralph Waldo Emerson (p. 346)

Henry David Thoreau (p. 347)

Margaret Fuller (p. 347)

Walt Whitman (p. 348)

Herman Melville (p. 349)

Nat Turner (p. 360)

William Lloyd Garrison (p. 362)

Dorothea Dix (p. 367)

Elizabeth Cady Stanton (p. 371)

Susan B. Anthony (p. 371)

## REVIEW QUESTIONS
Answer these questions to demonstrate your understanding of the chapter's main ideas.

1. Analyze the relationship between religion and reform in the decades from 1800 to 1860. Why did many religious people feel compelled to remake society? How successful were they? Do you see any parallels with social movements today?

2. The word *reform* has a positive connotation, as an effort to make things better. Yet many mid-nineteenth-century Americans viewed some "reforms," such as abolitionism and women's rights, as destructive to the social order, and other "reforms," such as Sabbatarianism and temperance, as threats to individual freedom. What was the apparent conflict among reform, social order, and liberty?

3. **THEMATIC UNDERSTANDING** Review the events listed under "Ideas, Beliefs, and Culture" on the thematic timeline on page 283, paying particular attention to the entries related to individualism and rights on the one hand and to various communal and religious movements on the other. What was the relationship between these somewhat contradictory cultural impulses? How were these two movements related to the social and economic changes in America in the decades after 1800?

## MAKING CONNECTIONS
Recognize the larger developments and continuities within and across chapters by answering these questions.

1. **ACROSS TIME AND PLACE** Did the era of reform (1820–1860) increase or diminish the extent of social and cultural freedom that existed during the Revolutionary era (1770–1820)?

2. **VISUAL EVIDENCE** Compare the cheerful depiction of the young woman in the watercolor depicting "night life in Philadelphia" on page 355 with the thoughtful or intense expression on the faces of the social reformers depicted in this chapter (Emerson, p. 346; Fuller, p. 348; and Stanton and Anthony, p. 371). Given their beliefs, would those reformers have approved or disapproved of the conduct of the young Philadelphia woman? Explain your reasoning.

## MORE TO EXPLORE
Start here to learn more about the events discussed in this chapter.

Patricia Cline Cohen, *The Murder of Helen Jewett: The Life and Death of a Prostitute in New York City* (1998). A gripping murder mystery that probes the nature of the new plebeian culture.

Daniel Walker Howe, *What Hath God Wrought: The Transformation of America, 1815–1848* (2007). A comprehensive history from a cultural perspective.

Paul E. Johnson and Sean Wilentz, *The Kingdom of Matthias* (1995). A compelling story of religious utopianism gone mad.

Stephen B. Oates, *The Fires of Jubilee* (1975). Explores the life and rebellion of Nat Turner.

Mark Perry, *Lift Up Thy Voice* (2001). Offers a study of the Grimké family.

David Roediger, *The Wages of Whiteness* (1995). Shows how racism shaped white working-class culture.

## TIMELINE

Ask yourself why this chapter begins and ends with these dates and then identify the links among related events.

| Year | Event |
|---|---|
| 1826 | • Lyceum movement begins |
| 1829 | • David Walker's *Appeal . . . to the Colored Citizens of the World* |
| 1830 | • Joseph Smith publishes *The Book of Mormon* |
| 1830s | • Emergence of minstrelsy shows |
| 1831 | • William Lloyd Garrison founds *The Liberator*<br>• Nat Turner's uprising in Virginia |
| 1832 | • Ralph Waldo Emerson turns to transcendentalism |
| 1833 | • Garrison organizes American Anti-Slavery Society |
| 1834 | • New York activists create Female Moral Reform Society |
| 1835 | • Abolitionists launch great postal campaign, sparking series of antiabolitionist riots |
| 1836 | • House of Representatives adopts gag rule |
| 1837 | • Grimké sisters defend public roles for women |
| 1840 | • Liberty Party runs James G. Birney for president |
| 1840s | • Fourierist communities arise in Midwest |
| 1841 | • Dorothea Dix promotes hospitals for mentally ill |
| 1844 | • Margaret Fuller publishes *Woman in the Nineteenth Century* |
| 1845 | • Henry David Thoreau goes to Walden Pond |
| 1846 | • Brigham Young leads Mormons to Salt Lake |
| 1848 | • Seneca Falls Convention proposes women's equality |
| 1850 | • Nathaniel Hawthorne's *The Scarlet Letter* |
| 1851 | • Herman Melville publishes *Moby Dick* |
| 1852 | • Harriet Beecher Stowe writes *Uncle Tom's Cabin* |
| 1855 | • Dr. Sanger surveys sex trade in New York City<br>• Walt Whitman's *Leaves of Grass* |
| 1858 | • "Mormon War" over polygamy |

**KEY TURNING POINTS:** Most of the entries here relate to events in the 1830s, 1840s, and 1850s. In your judgment, which is the most important event in each decade? Over all three decades? Write a coherent essay that justifies your choices and, if possible, relates those events to each other.

# 12

# The South Expands: Slavery and Society 1800–1860

L ife in South Carolina had been good to James Lide. A slave-owning planter along the Pee Dee River, Lide and his wife raised twelve children and long resisted the "Alabama Fever" that prompted thousands of Carolinians to move west. Finally, at age sixty-five, probably seeking land for his many offspring, he moved his slaves and family—including six children and six grandchildren—to a plantation near Montgomery, Alabama. There, the family lived initially in a squalid log cabin with air holes but no windows. Even after building a new house, the Lides' life remained unsettled. "Pa is quite in the notion of moving somewhere," his daughter Maria reported. Although James Lide died in Alabama, many of his children moved on. In 1854, at the age of fifty-eight, Eli Lide migrated to Texas, telling his father, "Something within me whispers onward and onward."

The Lides' story was that of southern society. Between 1800 and 1860, white planters moved west and, using the muscles and sweat of a million enslaved African Americans, brought millions of acres into cultivation. By 1840, the South was at the cutting edge of the American Market Revolution (Figure 12.1). It annually produced and exported 1.5 million bales of raw cotton—over two-thirds of the world's supply—and its economy was larger and richer than that of most nations. "Cotton is King," boasted the *Southern Cultivator*.

No matter how rich they were, few cotton planters in Alabama, Mississippi, and Texas lived in elegant houses or led cultured lives. They had forsaken the aristocratic gentility of the Chesapeake and the Carolinas to make money. "To sell cotton in order to buy negroes—to make more cotton to buy more negroes, 'ad infinitum,' is the aim . . . of the thorough-going cotton planter," a traveler reported from Mississippi in 1835. "His whole soul is wrapped up in the pursuit." Plantation women lamented the loss of genteel surroundings and polite society. Raised in North Carolina, where she was "blest with every comfort, & even luxury," Mary Drake found Mississippi and Alabama "a dreary waste."

Enslaved African Americans knew what "dreary waste" really meant: unremitting toil, unrelieved poverty, and profound sadness. Sold south from Maryland, where his family had lived for generations, Charles Ball's father became "gloomy and morose" and ran off and disappeared. With good reason: on new cotton plantations, slaves labored from "sunup to sundown" and from one end of the year to the other, forced to work by the threat of the lash. Always wanting more, southern planters and politicians plotted to extend their plantation economy across the continent.

## IDENTIFY THE BIG IDEA

How did the creation of a cotton-based economy change the lives of whites and blacks in all regions of the South?

**A Slave Family Picking Cotton**   Picking cotton—thousands of small bolls attached to 3-foot-high woody and often prickly stalks—was a tedious and time-consuming task, taking up to four months on many plantations. However, workers of both sexes and all ages could pick cotton, and masters could measure output by weighing the baskets of each picker or family, chastising those who failed to meet their quotas. What does this early photograph of a family of pickers, taken on a plantation near Savannah, Georgia, suggest about women's and children's lives, family relations, and living conditions?

© Collection of the New-York Historical Society.

# The Domestic Slave Trade

In 1817, when the American Colonization Society began to transport a few freed blacks to Africa (Chapter 8), the southern plantation system was expanding rapidly. In 1790, its western boundary ran through the middle of Georgia; by 1830, it stretched through western Louisiana; by 1860, the slave frontier extended far into Texas (Map 12.1). That advance of 900 miles more than doubled the geographical area cultivated by slave labor and increased the number of slave states from eight in 1800 to fifteen by 1850. The federal government played a key role in this expansion. It acquired Louisiana from the French in 1803, welcomed the slave states of Mississippi and Alabama into the Union in 1817 and 1819, removed Native Americans from the southeastern states in the 1830s, and annexed Texas and Mexican lands in the 1840s.

To cultivate this vast area, white planters imported enslaved laborers first from Africa and then from the Chesapeake region. Between 1776 and 1809, when Congress outlawed the Atlantic slave trade, planters purchased about 115,000 Africans. "The Planter will . . . Sacrifice every thing to attain Negroes," declared one slave trader. Despite the influx, the demand for labor far exceeded the supply. Consequently, planters imported new African workers illegally, through the Spanish colony of Florida until 1819 and then through the Mexican province of Texas. Yet these Africans — about 50,000 between 1810 and 1865 — did not satisfy the demand.

## The Upper South Exports Slaves

Planters seeking labor looked to the Chesapeake region, home in 1800 to nearly half of the nation's black population. There, the African American population

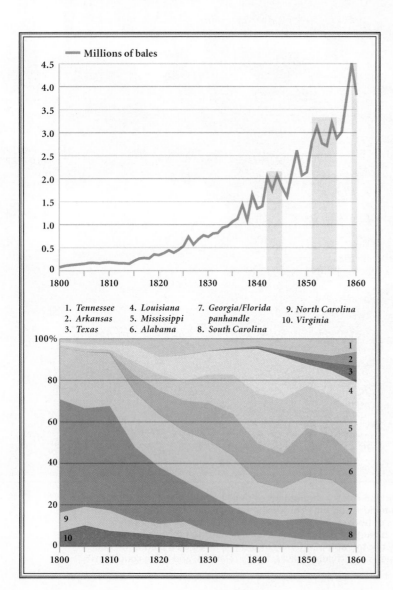

**FIGURE 12.1**

**Cotton Production and Producers, 1800–1860**

Until 1820, Georgia and South Carolina plantations (marked #7 and #8 on the right side of the lower graph) grew more than one-half of American cotton. As output increased significantly between 1820 and 1840 (see the upper graph), the locus of production shifted. By the early 1840s, planters had moved hundreds of thousands of slaves to the Mississippi Valley, and Louisiana, Mississippi, and Alabama (#4, #5, and #6) grew nearly 70 percent of a much larger cotton crop. Simultaneously, production leapt dramatically, reaching (as the red bars show) 2 million bales a year by the mid-1840s, 3 million by the mid-1850s, and 4 million on the eve of the Civil War.

Source: From *Time on the Cross: The Economics of American Negro Slavery*, by Robert W. Fogel and Stanley L. Engerman. Copyright © 1974 Little Brown.

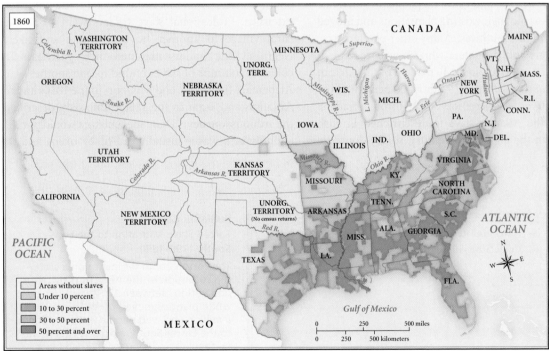

**MAP 12.1**

**Distribution of the Slave Population in 1790, 1830, and 1860**

The cotton boom shifted the African American population to the South and West. In 1790, most slaves lived and worked on Chesapeake tobacco and Carolina rice and indigo plantations. By 1830, those areas were still heavily populated by black families, but hundreds of thousands of slaves also labored on the cotton and sugar lands of the Lower Mississippi Valley and on cotton plantations in Georgia and northern Florida. Three decades later, the majority of blacks lived and worked along the Mississippi River and in an arc of fertile cotton lands—the "black belt"—sweeping from Mississippi through South Carolina.

was growing rapidly from natural increase — an average of 27 percent a decade by the 1810s — and creating a surplus of enslaved workers on many plantations. The result was a growing domestic trade in slaves. Between 1818 and 1829, planters in just one Maryland tobacco-growing county — Frederick — sold at least 952 slaves to traders or cotton planters. Plantation owners in Virginia disposed of 75,000 slaves during the 1810s and again during the 1820s. The number of forced Virginia migrants jumped to nearly 120,000 during the 1830s and then averaged 85,000 during the 1840s and 1850s. In Virginia alone, then, slave owners ripped 440,000 African Americans from communities where their families had lived for three or four generations. By 1860, the "mania for buying negroes" from the Upper South had resulted in a massive transplantation of more than 1 million slaves (Figure 12.2). A majority of African Americans now lived and worked in the Deep South, the lands that stretched from Georgia to Texas.

This African American migration took two forms: transfer and sale. Looking for new opportunities, thousands of Chesapeake and Carolina planters — men like James Lide — sold their existing plantations and moved their slaves to the Southwest. Many other planters gave slaves to sons and daughters who moved west. Such transfers accounted for about 40 percent of the African American migrants. The rest — about 60 percent of the 1 million migrants — were "sold south" through traders.

Just as the Atlantic slave trade enriched English merchants in the eighteenth century, so the domestic market brought wealth to American traders between 1800 and 1860. One set of routes ran to the Atlantic coast and sent thousands of slaves to sugar plantations in Louisiana, the former French territory that entered the Union in 1812. As sugar output soared, slave traders scoured the countryside near the port cities of Baltimore, Alexandria, Richmond, and Charleston — searching, as one of them put it, for "likely young men such as I think would suit the New Orleans market." Each year, hundreds of muscular young slaves passed through auction houses in the port cities bound for the massive trade mart in New Orleans. Because this **coastal trade** in laborers was highly visible, it elicited widespread condemnation by northern abolitionists.

Sugar was a "killer" crop, and Louisiana (like the eighteenth-century West Indies) soon had a well-deserved reputation among African Americans "as a place of slaughter." Hundreds died each year from disease, overwork, and brutal treatment. Maryland farmer John Anthony Munnikhuysen refused to allow his daughter Priscilla to marry a Louisiana sugar planter, declaring: "Mit has never been used to see negroes flayed alive and it would kill her."

The **inland system** that fed slaves to the Cotton South was less visible than the coastal trade but more extensive. Professional slave traders went from one rural village to another buying "young and likely Negroes." The traders marched their purchases in coffles — columns of slaves bound to one another — to Alabama, Mississippi, and Missouri in the 1830s and to Arkansas and Texas in the 1850s. One slave described the arduous journey: "Dem Speculators would put the chilluns in a wagon usually pulled by oxens and de

**IDENTIFY CAUSES**
What factors drove the expansion of the domestic slave trade, and how did it work?

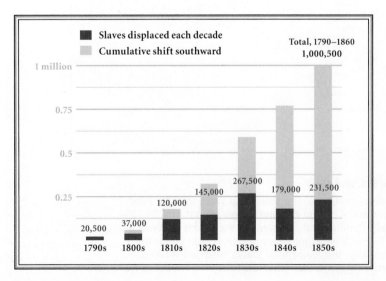

**FIGURE 12.2**
**Forced Slave Migration to the Lower South, 1790–1860**

The cotton boom set in motion a vast redistribution of the African American population. Between 1790 and 1860, white planters moved or sold more than a million enslaved people from the Upper to the Lower South, a process that broke up families and long-established black communities. Based on data in Robert William Fogel and Stanley L. Engerman, *Time on the Cross: The Economics of American Negro Slavery*, by Robert W. Fogel and Stanley L. Engerman. Copyright © 1974 Little Brown and in *Speculators and Slaves: Masters, Traders, and Slaves in the Old South*, by Michael Tadman, University of Wisconsin Press, 1996.

**The Inland Slave Trade**

Mounted whites escort a convoy of slaves from Virginia to Tennessee in Lewis Miller's *Slave Trader, Sold to Tennessee* (1853). For white planters, the interstate trade in slaves was lucrative; it pumped money into the declining Chesapeake economy and provided young workers for the expanding plantations of the cotton belt. For blacks, it was a traumatic journey, a new Middle Passage that broke up their families and communities. "Arise! Arise! and weep no more, dry up your tears, we shall part no more," the slaves sing sorrowfully as they journey to new lives in Tennessee. Abby Aldrich Rockefeller Folk Art Museum, Williamsburg, VA.

older folks was chained or tied together sos dey could not run off." Once a coffle reached its destination, the trader would sell slaves "at every village in the county."

Chesapeake and Carolina planters provided the human cargo. Some planters sold slaves when poor management or their "own extravagances" threw them into debt. "Trouble gathers thicker and thicker around me," Thomas B. Chaplin of South Carolina lamented in his diary. "I will be compelled to send about ten prime Negroes to Town on next Monday, to be sold." Many more planters doubled as slave traders, earning substantial profits by traveling south to sell some of their slaves and those of their neighbors. Thomas Weatherly of South Carolina drove his surplus slaves to Hayneville, Alabama, where he "sold ten negroes." Colonel E. S. Irvine, a member of the South Carolina legislature and "a highly respected gentleman" in white circles, likewise traveled frequently "to sell a drove of Negroes." Prices marched in step with those for cotton; during a boom year in the 1850s, a planter noted that a slave "will fetch $1000, cash, quick."

The domestic slave trade was crucial to the prosperity of the migrating white planters because it provided workers to fell the forests and plant cotton in the Gulf states. Equally important, it sustained the wealth of slave owners in the Upper South. By selling surplus black workers, tobacco, rice, and grain producers in the Chesapeake and Carolinas added about 20 percent to their income. As a Maryland newspaper remarked in 1858, "[The trade serves as] an almost universal resource to raise money. A prime able-bodied slave is worth three times as much to the cotton or sugar planter as to the Maryland agriculturalist."

## The Impact on Blacks

For African American families, the domestic slave trade was a personal disaster that underlined their status — and vulnerability — as chattel slaves. In law, they were the movable personal property of the whites who owned them. As Lewis Clark, a fugitive from slavery, noted: "Many a time i've had 'em say to me, 'You're my property.'" "The being of slavery, its soul and its body, lives and moves in the **chattel principle**, the property principle, the bill of sale principle," declared former slave James W. C. Pennington. As a South Carolina master put it, "[The slave's earnings] belong to me because I bought him."

Slave property underpinned the entire southern economic system. Whig politician Henry Clay noted that the "immense amount of capital which is invested in slave property . . . is owned by widows and orphans, by the aged and infirm, as well as the sound and vigorous. It is the subject of mortgages, deeds of trust, and family settlements." Clay concluded: "I know that there is a visionary dogma, which holds that negro slaves cannot be the subject of property [but] . . . that is property which the law declares to be property."

As a slave owner, Clay also knew that property rights were key to slave discipline. "I govern them . . . without the whip," another master explained, "by stating . . . that I should sell them if they do not conduct themselves as I wish." The threat was effective. "The Negroes here dread nothing on earth so much as this," a Maryland observer noted. "They regard the south with perfect horror, and to be sent there is considered as the worst punishment." Thousands of slaves suffered

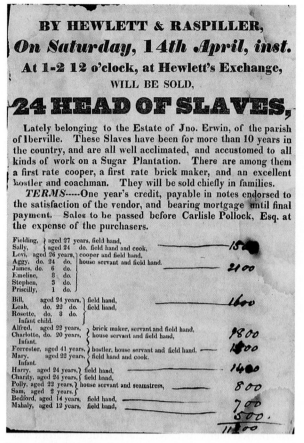

**Slave Auction Notice**

This public notice for a slave auction to be held in Iberville, Louisiana, advertises "24 Head of Slaves" as if they were cattle—a striking commentary on the "chattel principle" and business of slavery. Library of Congress.

that fate, which destroyed about one in every four slave marriages. "Why does the slave ever love?" asked black abolitionist Harriet Jacobs in her autobiography, *Incidents in the Life of a Slave Girl*, when her partner "may at any moment be wrenched away by the hand of violence?" After being sold, one Georgia slave lamented, "My Dear wife for you and my Children my pen cannot Express the griffe I feel to be parted from you all."

The interstate slave trade often focused on young adults. In northern Maryland, planters sold away boys and girls at an average age of seventeen years. "Dey sole my sister Kate," Anna Harris remembered decades later, "and I ain't seed or heard of her since." The trade also separated almost a third of all slave children under the age of fourteen from one or both of their parents. Sarah Grant remembered,

**EXPLAIN CONSEQUENCES**
What were the effects of the slave trade on black families?

"Mamma used to cry when she had to go back to work because she was always scared some of us kids would be sold while she was away." Well might she worry, for slave traders worked quickly. "One night I lay down on de straw mattress wid my mammy," Vinny Baker recalled, "an' de nex' mo'nin I woke up an' she wuz gone." When their owner sold seven-year-old Laura Clark and ten other children from their plantation in North Carolina, Clark sensed that she would see her mother "no mo' in dis life."

Despite these sales, 75 percent of slave marriages remained unbroken, and the majority of children lived with one or both parents until puberty. Consequently, the sense of family among African Americans remained strong. Sold from Virginia to Texas in 1843, Hawkins Wilson carried with him a mental picture of his family. Twenty-five years later and now a freedman, Wilson set out to find his "dearest relatives" in Virginia. "My sister belonged to Peter Coleman in Caroline County and her name was Jane. . . . She had three children, Robert, Charles and Julia, when I left — Sister Martha belonged to Dr. Jefferson. . . . Sister Matilda belonged to Mrs. Botts."

During the decades between sale and freedom, Hawkins Wilson and thousands of other African Americans constructed new lives for themselves in the Mississippi Valley. Undoubtedly, many did so with a sense of foreboding, knowing from personal experience that their owners could disrupt their lives at any moment. Like Charles Ball, some "longed to die, and escape from the bonds of my tormentors." The darkness of slavery shadowed even moments of joy. Knowing that sales often ended slave marriages, a white minister blessed one couple "for so long as God keeps them together."

Many white planters "saw" only the African American marriages that endured and ignored those they had broken. Accordingly, many owners considered themselves **benevolent masters**, committed to the welfare of "my family, black and white." Some masters gave substance to this paternalist ideal by treating kindly "loyal and worthy" slaves — black overseers, the mammy who raised their children, and trusted house servants. By preserving the families of these slaves, many planters could believe that they "sold south" only "coarse" troublemakers and uncivilized slaves who had "little sense of family." Other owners were more honest about the human cost of their pursuit of wealth. "Tomorrow the negroes are to get off [to Kentucky]," a slave-owning woman in Virginia wrote to a friend, "and I expect there will be great crying and moaning, with children Leaving there mothers, mothers there children, and women there husbands."

Whether or not they acknowledged the slaves' pain, few southern whites questioned the morality of the slave trade. Responding to abolitionists' criticism, the city council of Charleston, South Carolina, declared that "the removal of slaves from place to place, and their transfer from master to master, by gift, purchase, or otherwise" was completely consistent "with moral principle and with the highest order of civilization" (American Voices, p. 384).

 To see a longer excerpt of the city council of Charleston, South Carolina, document, along with other primary sources from this period, see *Sources for America's History*.

# The World of Southern Whites

American slavery took root in the early eighteenth century on the tobacco plantations of the Chesapeake and in the rice fields of the Carolina low country. However, it grew to maturity during the first half of the nineteenth century on the cotton fields and sugar plantations of the Mississippi Valley. By then, a small elite of extraordinarily wealthy planter families stood at the top of southern society. These families—about three thousand in number—each owned more than one hundred slaves and huge tracts of the most fertile lands. Their ranks included many of the richest families in the United States. On the eve of the Civil War, southern slave owners accounted for nearly two-thirds of all American men with wealth of $100,000 or more. Other white southerners—backcountry yeomen farmers and cotton-planting tenants in particular—occupied some of the lowest rungs of the nation's social order. The expansion of southern slavery, like the flowering of northern capitalism, increased inequalities of wealth and status.

## The Dual Cultures of the Planter Elite

The westward movement split the plantation elite into two distinct groups: the traditional aristocrats of the Old South, whose families had gained their wealth from tobacco and rice, and the upstart capitalist-inclined planters of the cotton states.

### The Traditional Southern Gentry
The Old South gentry dominated the Tidewater region of the Chesapeake and the low country of South Carolina and Georgia. During the eighteenth century, these planters built impressive mansions and adopted the manners and values of the English landed gentry (Chapter 3). Their aristocratic-oriented culture survived the Revolution of 1776 and soon took on a republican glaze

**Redcliffe Plantation**

In 1857, James Henry Hammond began construction of this house on a 400-acre site in Aiken County, South Carolina. It originally had a double-decked porch in the Greek Revival style, which gave it an even more imposing presence. Fifty enslaved African Americans worked at Redcliffe, and nearly three hundred more on Hammond's other properties, providing the wealth that allowed his family to live in comfort. Hammond lived at Redcliffe until he died in 1864 at the age of fifty-seven, his health undermined by his struggles with Confederate leaders over wartime policies and by mercury poisoning from the laxatives he had taken for nearly forty years. Michael A. Stroud.

## The Debate over Free and Slave Labor

As the abolitionist assault on slavery mounted, its rhetoric shaped the debate over the emergent system of wage labor in the northern states. By the 1850s, New York senator William Seward starkly contrasted the political systems of the South and the North in terms of their labor systems: "the one resting on the basis of servile or slave labor, the other on voluntary labor of freemen." Seward strongly favored the "free-labor system," crediting to it "the strength, wealth, greatness, intelligence, and freedom, which the whole American people now enjoy." As the following documents show, some Americans agreed with Seward, while others, such as *New York Tribune* editor Horace Greeley and South Carolina senator James Henry Hammond (who is quoted often in this chapter and whose house appears on page 383), contested his premises and conclusions.

### South Carolina Senator James Henry Hammond
## Speech to the Senate, March 4, 1858

In response to New York senator Seward, Senator Hammond urged admission of Kansas under the proslavery Lecompton Constitution and, by way of argument, celebrated the success of the South's cotton economy and its political and social institutions.

In all social systems there must be a class to do the menial duties, to perform the drudgery of life. . . . Such a class you must have, or you would not have that other class which leads progress, civilization, and refinement. It constitutes the very mud-sill of society and of political government. . . . Fortunately for the South, she found a race adapted to that purpose to her hand. A race inferior to her own, but eminently qualified in temper, in vigor, in docility, in capacity to stand the climate, to answer all her purposes. We use them for our purpose, and call them slaves. . . .

The Senator from New York said yesterday that the whole world had abolished slavery. Aye, the name, but not the thing; . . . for the man who lives by daily labor, and scarcely lives at that, and who has to put out his labor in the market, and take the best he can get for it; in short, your whole hireling class of manual laborers and "operatives," as you call them, are essentially slaves. The difference between us is, that our slaves are hired for life and well compensated; there is no starvation, no begging, no want of employment among our people, and not too much employment either. Yours are hired by the day, not cared for, and scantily compensated, which may be proved in the most painful manner, at any hour in any street in any of your large towns.

Source: *The Congressional Globe* (Washington, DC, March 6, 1858), 962.

### New York Protestant Episcopal Church Mission Society
## Sixth Annual Report, 1837

This excerpt demonstrates the society's belief that a class-bound social order could be avoided by encouraging "a spirit of independence and self-estimation" among the poor.

In the older countries of Europe, there is a CLASS OF POOR: families born to poverty, living in poverty, dying in poverty. With us there are none such. In our bounteous land individuals alone are poor; but they form no poor class, because with them poverty is but a transient evil . . . save [except] paupers and vagabonds . . . all else form one common class of citizens; some more, others less advanced in the career of honorable independence.

Source: New York Protestant Episcopal Church Mission Society, Sixth Annual Report (New York, 1837), 15–16.

### Horace Greeley
## Public Letter Declining an Invitation to Attend an Antislavery Convention in Cincinnati, Ohio, June 3, 1845

This letter from the editor of the *New York Tribune* explains his broad definition of slavery.

Dear Sir: — I received, weeks since, your letter inviting me to be present at a general convention of opponents of Human Slavery. . . . What is Slavery? You will probably answer; "The legal subjection of one human being to the will and power of another." But this definition appears to me inaccurate. . . .

I understand by Slavery, that condition in which one human being exists mainly as a convenience for other human beings. . . . In short, . . . where the relation [is one] of authority, social ascendency and power over subsistence on the one hand, and of necessity, servility, and degradation on the other — there, in my view, is Slavery. . . . If I am less troubled concerning the Slavery prevalent in Charleston or New-Orleans, it is because I see so much Slavery in New-York. . . .

Wherever Opportunity to Labor is obtained with difficulty, and is so deficient that the Employing class may virtually prescribe their own terms and pay the Laborer only such share as they choose of the produce, there is a strong tendency to Slavery.

---

Source: Horace Greeley, *Hints Toward Reform in Lectures, Addresses, and Other Writings* (New York: Harper & Brothers, 1850), 352–355.

## Editorial in the *Staunton Spectator*, 1859

Entitled "Freedom and Slavery," this editorial argues that "the black man's lot as a slave, is vastly preferable to that of his free brethren at the North."

The intelligent, christian slave-holder at the South is the best friend of the negro. He does not regard his bondsmen as mere chattel property, but as human beings to whom he owes duties. While the Northern Pharisee will not permit a negro to ride on the city railroads, Southern gentlemen and ladies are seen every day, side by side, in cars and coaches, with their faithful servants. Here the honest black man is not only protected by the laws and public sentiment, but he is respected by the community as truly as if his skin were white. Here there are ties of genuine friendship and affection between whites and blacks, leading to an interchange of all the comities of life. The slave nurses his master in sickness, and sheds tears of genuine sorrow at his grave.

---

Source: *Staunton Spectator*, December 6, 1859, p. 2, c. 1.

## James Henry Hammond
## Private Letter to His Son Harry Hammond, 1856

This letter regards the future of Hammond's slave mistress, Sally Johnson, her son Henderson, and her daughter Louisa, who was the common mistress of father and son, and Louisa's children whom they sired.

In the last will I made I left to you . . . Sally Johnson the mother of Louisa & all the children of both. Sally says Henderson is my child. It is possible, but I do not believe it Yet act on her's rather than my opinion. Louisa's first child may be mine. I think not. Her second I believe is mine. Take care of her & her children who are both of your blood if not of mine. . . . The services of the rest will compensate for indulgence to these. I cannot free these people & send them North. It would be cruelty to them. Nor would I like that any but my own blood should own as slaves my own blood or Louisa. I leave them to your charge, believing that you will best appreciate & most independently carry out my wishes in regard to them. Do not let Louisa or any of my children or possible children be the Slaves of Strangers. Slavery in the family will be their happiest earthly condition.

---

Source: James Hammond to Harry Hammond, February 19, 1856, in JHH Papers, SCL, quoted in Drew Gilpin Faust, *James Henry Hammond and the Old South: A Design for Mastery* (Baton Rouge: Louisiana State University Press, 1982), 87.

### QUESTIONS FOR ANALYSIS

1. Which of these documents argue for slave owners as benevolent paternalists and the institution of slavery as a "positive good"? What other points of view are represented?

2. Given the discussion of "class" and "honorable independence" in the Mission Society statement, how would an Episcopalian reply to Hammond's critique of the northern labor system?

3. How can we understand Hammond's treatment of Sally Johnson and her daughter, as well as his refusal to free his and his son's children, in the context of his 1858 speech and the *Staunton Spectator*'s editorial?

4. Using the principles asserted in his letter, how would Horace Greeley analyze the southern labor system, as described by Hammond and the *Staunton Spectator*? Why does Greeley suggest that the northern system has only "a strong tendency to Slavery"?

5. Consider the sources above in the light of this Abraham Lincoln comment: "although volume upon volume is written to prove slavery a very good thing, we never hear of the man who wishes to take the good of it, by being a slave himself."

(Chapter 8). Classical republican theory, which had long identified political tyranny as the major threat to liberty, had its roots in the societies of Greece and Rome, where slavery was part of the natural order of society. That variety of republicanism appealed to wealthy southerners, who feared federal government interference with their slave property. On the state level, planters worried about populist politicians who would mobilize poorer whites, and so they demanded that authority rest in the hands of incorruptible men of "virtue."

Indeed, affluent planters cast themselves as a **republican aristocracy**. "The planters here are essentially what the nobility are in other countries," declared James Henry Hammond of South Carolina. "They stand at the head of society & politics . . . [and form] an aristocracy of talents, of virtue, of generosity and courage." Wealthy planters criticized the democratic polity and middle-class society that was developing in the Northeast and Midwest. "Inequality is the fundamental law of the universe," declared one planter. Others condemned professional politicians as "a set of demagogues" and questioned the legitimacy of universal suffrage. "Times are sadly different now to what they were when I was a boy," lamented David Gavin, a prosperous South Carolinian. Then, the "Sovereign people, alias mob" had little influence; now they vied for power with the elite. "[How can] I rejoice for a freedom," Gavin thundered, "which allows every bankrupt, swindler, thief, and scoundrel, traitor and seller of his vote to be placed on an equality with myself?"

To maintain their privileged identity, aristocratic planters married their sons and daughters to one another and expected them to follow in their footsteps — the men working as planters, merchants, lawyers, newspaper editors, and ministers and the women hosting plantation balls and church bazaars. To confirm their social preeminence, they lived extravagantly and entertained graciously. James Henry Hammond built a Greek Revival mansion with a center hall 53 feet by 20 feet, its floor embellished with stylish Belgian tiles and expensive Brussels carpets. "Once a year, like a great feudal landlord," Hammond's neighbor recounted, "[he] gave a fete or grand dinner to all the country people."

Rice planters remained at the apex of the plantation aristocracy. In 1860, the fifteen proprietors of the vast plantations in All Saints Parish in South Carolina

**TRACE CHANGE OVER TIME**

Between 1800 and 1860, what changes occurred in the South's plantation crops, labor system, defense of slavery, and elite planter lifestyle?

owned 4,383 slaves — nearly 300 apiece — who annually grew and processed 14 million pounds of rice. As inexpensive Asian rice entered the world market in the 1820s and cut their profits, the Carolina rice aristocrats sold some slaves and worked the others harder, sustaining their luxurious lifestyle. The "hospitality and elegance" of Charleston and Savannah impressed savvy English traveler John Silk Buckingham. Buckingham likewise found "polished" families among long-established French Catholic planters in New Orleans and along the Mississippi River: There, the "sugar and cotton planters live in splendid edifices, and enjoy all the luxury that wealth can impart" (America Compared, p. 387).

In tobacco-growing regions, the lives of the planter aristocracy followed a different trajectory, in part because slave ownership was widely diffused. In the 1770s, about 60 percent of white families in the Chesapeake region owned at least one African American. As wealthy tobacco planters moved their estates and slaves to the Cotton South, middling whites (who owned between five and twenty slaves) came to dominate the Chesapeake economy. The descendants of the old tobacco aristocracy remained influential, but increasingly as slave-owning grain farmers, lawyers, merchants, industrialists, and politicians. They hired out surplus slaves, sold them south, or allowed them to purchase their freedom.

**The Ideology and Reality of "Benevolence"**    The planter aristocracy flourished around the periphery of the South's booming Cotton Belt — in Virginia, South Carolina, and Louisiana — but it took the lead in defending slavery. Ignoring the Jeffersonian response to slavery as a "misfortune" or a "necessary evil" (Chapter 8), southern apologists in the 1830s argued that the institution was a **"positive good"** because it subsidized an elegant lifestyle for a white elite and provided tutelage for genetically inferior Africans. "As a race, the African is inferior to the white man," declared Alexander Stephens, the future vice president of the Confederacy. "Subordination to the white man, is his normal condition." Apologists depicted planters and their wives as aristocratic models of "disinterested benevolence," who provided food and housing for their workers and cared for them in old age. One wealthy Georgian declared, "Plantation government should be eminently patriarchal. . . . The pater-familias, or head of the family, should, in one sense, be the father of the whole concern, negroes and all."

Those planters who embraced Christian stewardship tried to shape the religious lives of their chattel.

## Bernhard, Duke of Saxe-Weimar-Eisenach

# The Racial Complexities of Southern Society

In 1825 and 1826, Bernhard, heir to the German principality of Saxe-Weimar-Eisenach, traveled throughout the United States, and in 1828 he published an account of his adventures. After a military career, the duke ruled his principality from 1853 until his death in 1862.

In New Orleans we were invited to a subscription ball. . . . Only good society is invited to these balls. The first to which we came was not very well attended; but most of the ladies were very nice looking and well turned out in the French manner. Their clothing was elegant after the latest Paris fashions. They danced very well and did credit to their French dancing masters. Dancing and some music are the main branches of the education of a Creole [an American-born white] woman. . . .

The native men are far from matching the women in elegance. And they stayed only a short time, preferring to escape to a so-called "Quarterons Ball" which they find more amusing and where they do not have to stand on ceremony. . . .

A "quarteron" [actually an octoroon, a person of one-eighth African ancestry] is the offspring of a mestizo mother and a white father, just as the mestizo is the child of a mulatto and a white man. The "quarterons" are almost completely white. There would be no way of recognizing them by their complexion, for they are often fairer than the Creoles. Black hair and eyes are generally the signs of their status, although some are quite blond. The ball is attended by the free "quarterons." Yet the deepest prejudice reigns against them on account of their colored origin; the white women particularly feel or affect to feel a strong repugnance to them.

Marriage between colored and white people is forbidden by the laws of the state. Yet the "quarterons," for their part, look upon the Negroes and mulattoes as inferiors and are unwilling to mix with them. The girls therefore have no other recourse than to become the mistresses of white men. The "quarterons" regard such attachment as the equivalent of marriage. They would not think of entering upon it other than with a formal contract in which the man engages to pay a stipulated sum to the mother or father of the girl. . . .

Some of these women have inherited from their fathers and lovers, and possess considerable fortunes. Their status is nevertheless always very depressed. They must not ride in the street in coaches, and their lovers can bring them to the balls in their own conveyances only after nightfall. . . . But many of these girls are much more carefully educated than the whites, behave with more polish and more politeness, and make their lovers happier than white wives their husbands. And yet the white ladies speak of these unfortunate depressed creatures with great disdain, even bitterness. Because of the depth of these prejudices, many fathers send their daughters, conceived after this manner, to France where good education and wealth are no impediments to the attainment of a respectable place.

Source: From *Travels by His Highness Duke Bernhard of Saxe-Weimar-Eisenach Through North America in the Years 1825 and 1826*, edited by C. J. Jeronimus and translated by William Jeronimus. Copyright © 2001 University Press of America. Used by permission of the Rowan & Littlefield Publishing Company.

### QUESTIONS FOR ANALYSIS

1. What does this passage suggest about the effect of slavery and the meaning of racial identity on sexual relationships and marriages in America and in France?
2. How does Bernhard's account help to explain the values and outlook of the free black population in the South?

They built churches on their plantations, welcomed evangelical preachers, and required their slaves to attend services. A few encouraged African Americans with spiritual "gifts" to serve as exhorters and deacons. Most of these planters acted from sincere Christian belief, but they also hoped to counter abolitionist criticism and to use religious teachings to control their workers.

Indeed, slavery's defenders increasingly used religious justifications for human bondage. Protestant ministers in the South pointed out that the Hebrews, God's chosen people, had owned slaves and that Jesus Christ had never condemned slavery. As James Henry Hammond told a British abolitionist in 1845: "What God ordains and Christ sanctifies should surely command the respect and toleration of man." However, many aristocratic defenders of slavery were absentee owners or delegated authority to overseers, and they rarely glimpsed the day-to-day brutality of their regime of forced labor. "I was at the plantation last Saturday and the crop was in fine order," an absentee's son wrote to his father, "but the negroes are most brutally scarred & several have run off."

**Cotton Entrepreneurs**   There was much less hypocrisy and far less elegance among the entrepreneurial planters of the Cotton South. "The glare of expensive luxury vanishes" in the black soil regions of Alabama and Mississippi, John Silk Buckingham remarked as he traveled through the Cotton South. Frederick Law Olmsted — the future architect of New York's Central Park, who during the mid-1850s traveled through the South for the *New York Times* — found that the plantations in Mississippi mostly had "but small and mean residences." Aristocratic paternalism vanished as well. A Mississippi planter put it plainly: "Everything has to give way to large crops of cotton, land has to be cultivated wet or dry, negroes [must] work, hot or cold."

Angry at being sold south and pressed to hard labor, many slaves grew "mean" and stubborn. Those who would not labor were subject to the lash. "Whiped all the hoe hands," Alabama planter James Torbert wrote matter-of-factly in his journal. Overseers pushed workers hard because their salaries often depended on the amount of cotton they were able "to make for the market." A Mississippi slave recalled, "When I wuz so tired I cu'dnt hardly stan', I had to spin my cut of cotton befor' I cu'd go to sleep. We had to card, spin, an' reel at nite."

Cotton was a demanding crop because of its long growing season. Slaves plowed the land in March; dropped seeds into the ground in early April; and, once the plants began to grow, continually chopped away the surrounding grasses. In between these tasks, they planted the corn and peas that would provide food for them and the plantation's hogs and chickens. When the cotton bolls ripened in late August, the long four-month picking season began. Slaves in the Cotton South, concluded Olmsted, worked "much harder and more unremittingly" than those in the tobacco regions. Moreover, fewer of them acquired craft skills than in tobacco, sugar, and rice areas, where slave coopers and engineers made casks, processed sugar, and built irrigation systems.

To increase output, profit-seeking cotton planters began during the 1820s to use a rigorous **gang-labor system**. Previously, many planters had supervised their workers sporadically or assigned them specific tasks to complete at their own pace. Now masters with twenty or more slaves organized disciplined teams, or "gangs," supervised by black drivers and white overseers. They instructed the supervisors to work the gangs at a steady pace, clearing and plowing land or hoeing and picking cotton. A traveler in Mississippi described two gangs returning from work:

> First came, led by an old driver carrying a whip, forty of the largest and strongest women I ever saw together; they were all in a simple uniform dress of a bluish check stuff, the skirts reaching little below the knee. . . . They carried themselves loftily, each having a hoe over the shoulder, and walking with a free, powerful swing.

Next marched the plow hands with their mules, "the cavalry, thirty strong, mostly men, but a few of them women." Finally, "a lean and vigilant white overseer, on a brisk pony, brought up the rear."

The gang-labor system enhanced profits by increasing productivity. Because slaves in gangs finished tasks in thirty-five minutes that took a white yeoman planter an hour to complete, gang labor became ever more prevalent. In one Georgia county, the percentage of blacks working in gangs doubled between 1830 and 1850. As the price of raw cotton surged after 1846, the wealth of the planter class skyrocketed. And no wonder: nearly 2 million enslaved African Americans now labored on the plantations of the Cotton South and annually produced 4 million bales of the valuable fiber.

## Planters, Smallholding Yeomen, and Tenants

Although the South was a **slave society** — that is, a society in which the institution of slavery affected all aspects of life — most white southerners did not own slaves. The percentage of white families who held blacks in bondage steadily decreased — from 36 percent in 1830, to 31 percent in 1850, to about 25 percent a decade later. However, slave ownership varied by region. In some cotton-rich counties, 40 percent of the white families owned slaves; in the hill country near the Appalachian Mountains, the proportion dropped to 10 percent.

**The Inherent Brutality of Slavery**
Like all systems of forced labor, American racial slavery relied ultimately on physical coercion. Slave owners and overseers routinely whipped slaves who worked slowly or defied their orders. On occasion, they applied the whip with such ferocity that the slave was permanently injured or killed. This photograph of a Mississippi slave named Gordon, taken after he fled to the Union army in Louisiana in 1863 and published in *Harper's Weekly*, stands as graphic testimony to the inherent brutality of the system. Library of Congress.

**Planter Elites**   A privileged minority of 395,000 southern families owned slaves in 1860, their ranks divided into a strict hierarchy. The top one-fifth of these families owned twenty or more slaves. This elite — just 5 percent of the South's white population — dominated the economy, owning over 50 percent of the entire slave population of 4 million and growing 50 percent of the South's cotton crop. The average wealth of these planters was $56,000 (about $1.6 million in purchasing power today); by contrast, a prosperous southern yeoman or northern farmer owned property worth a mere $3,200.

Substantial proprietors, another fifth of the slave-owning population, held title to six to twenty bondsmen

and -women. These middling planters owned almost 40 percent of the enslaved laborers and produced more than 30 percent of the cotton. Often they pursued dual careers as skilled artisans or professional men. Thus some of the fifteen slaves owned by Georgian Samuel L. Moore worked in his brick factory, while others labored on his farm. Dr. Thomas Gale used the income from his medical practice to buy a Mississippi plantation that annually produced 150 bales of cotton. In Alabama, lawyer Benjamin Fitzpatrick used his legal fees to buy ten slaves.

Like Fitzpatrick, lawyers acquired wealth by managing the affairs of the slave-owning elite, representing planters and merchants in suits for debt, and helping smallholders and tenants register their deeds and contracts. Standing at the legal crossroads of their small towns, they rose to prominence and regularly won election to public office. Less than 1 percent of the male population, in 1828 lawyers made up 16 percent of the Alabama legislature and an astounding 26 percent in 1849.

**Smallholding Planters and Yeomen**   Smallholding slave owners were much less visible than the wealthy grandees and the middling lawyer-planters. These planters held from one to five black laborers in bondage and owned a few hundred acres of land. Some smallholders were well-connected young men who would rise to wealth when their father's death blessed them with more land and slaves. Others were poor but ambitious men trying to pull themselves up by their bootstraps, often encouraged by elite planters and proslavery advocates. "Ours is a proslavery form of Government, and the proslavery element should be increased," declared a Georgia newspaper. "We would like to see every white man at the South the owner of a family of negroes." Some aspiring planters achieved modest prosperity. A German settler reported from Alabama in 1855 that "nearly all his countrymen" who emigrated with him were slaveholders. "They were poor on their arrival in the country; but no sooner did they realize a little money than they invested it in slaves."

Bolstered by the patriarchal ideology of the planter class, yeomen farmers ruled their smallholdings with a firm hand. The male head of the household had legal authority over all the dependents — wives, children, and slaves — and, according to one South Carolina judge, the right on his property "to be as churlish as he pleases." Yeomen wives had little power; like women

> **UNDERSTAND POINTS OF VIEW**
> By 1860, what different groups made up the South's increasingly complex society? How did these groups interact?

in the North, they lost their legal identity when they married. To express their concerns, many southern women joined churches, where they usually outnumbered men by a margin of two to one. Women especially welcomed the message of spiritual equality preached in evangelical Baptist and Methodist churches, and they hoped that the church community would hold their husbands to the same standards of Christian behavior to which they conformed. However, most churches supported patriarchal rule and told female members to remain in "wifely obedience," whatever the actions of their husbands.

Whatever their authority within the household, most southern yeomen lived and died as hardscrabble farmers. They worked alongside their slaves in the fields, struggled to make ends meet as their families grew, and moved regularly in search of opportunity. Thus, in 1847, James Buckner Barry left North Carolina with his new wife and two slaves to settle in Bosque County, Texas. There he worked part-time as an Indian fighter while his slaves toiled on a drought-ridden farm

that barely kept the family in food. In South Carolina, W. J. Simpson struggled for years as a smallholding cotton planter and then gave up. He hired out one of his two slaves and went to work as an overseer on his father's farm.

Less fortunate smallholders fell from the privileged ranks of the slave-owning classes. Selling their land and slaves to pay off debts, they joined the mass of propertyless tenants who farmed the estates of wealthy landlords. In 1860, in Hancock County, Georgia, there were 56 slave-owning planters and 300 propertyless white farm laborers and factory workers; in nearby Hart County, 25 percent of the white farmers were tenants. Across the South, about 40 percent of the white population worked as tenants or farm laborers; as the *Southern Cultivator* observed, they had "no legal right nor interest in the soil [and] no homes of their own."

**Poor Freemen**   Propertyless whites suffered the ill consequences of living in a slave society that accorded little respect to hardworking white laborers. Nor could

***North Carolina Emigrants: Poor White Folks***
Completed in 1845, James Henry Beard's (1811–1893) painting depicts a family moving north to Ohio. Unlike many optimistic scenes of emigration, the picture conveys a sense of resigned despair. The family members, led by a sullen, disheveled father, pause at a water trough while their cow drinks and their dog chews a bone. The mother looks apprehensively toward the future as she cradles a child; two barefoot older children listlessly await their father's command. New York writer Charles Briggs interpreted the painting as an "eloquent sermon on Anti-Slavery . . . , the blight of Slavery has paralyzed the strong arm of the man and destroyed the spirit of the woman." Although primarily a portrait painter, Beard questioned the ethics and optimism of American culture in *Ohio Land Speculator* (1840) and *The Last Victim of the Deluge* (1849), as well as in *Poor White Folks*.
Cincinnati Art Museum, Ohio, USA/Gift of the Proctor & Gamble Company/The Bridgeman Art Library.

they hope for a better life for their children, because slave owners refused to pay taxes to fund public schools. Moreover, wealthy planters bid up the price of African Americans, depriving white laborers and tenants of easy access to the slave labor required to accumulate wealth. Finally, planter-dominated legislatures forced all white men, whether they owned slaves or not, to serve in the patrols and militias that deterred black uprisings. The majority of white southerners, Frederick Law Olmsted concluded, "are poor. They . . . have little — very little — of the common comforts and consolations of civilized life. Their destitution is not material only; it is intellectual and it is moral."

Marking this moral destitution, poor whites enjoyed the psychological satisfaction that they ranked above blacks. As Alfred Iverson, a U.S. senator from Georgia (1855–1861), explained: a white man "walks erect in the dignity of his color and race, and feels that he is a superior being, with the more exalted powers and privileges than others." To reinforce that sense of racial superiority, planter James Henry Hammond told his poor white neighbors, "In a slave country every freeman is an aristocrat."

Rejecting that half-truth, many southern whites fled planter-dominated counties in the 1830s and sought farms in the Appalachian hill country and beyond — in western Virginia, Kentucky, Tennessee, the southern regions of Illinois and Indiana, and Missouri. Living as yeomen farmers, they used family labor to grow foodstuffs for sustenance. To obtain cash or store credit to buy agricultural implements, cloth, shoes, salt, and other necessities, yeomen families sold their surplus crops, raised hogs for market sale, and — when the price of cotton rose sharply — grew a few bales. Their goals were modest: on the family level, they wanted to preserve their holdings and buy enough land to set up their children as small-scale farmers. As citizens, smallholders wanted to control their local government and elect men of their own kind to public office. However, thoughtful yeomen understood that the slave-based cotton economy sentenced family farmers to a subordinate place in the social order. They could hope for a life of independence and dignity only by moving north or farther west, where labor was "free" and hard work was respected.

# Expanding and Governing the South

By the 1830s, settlers from the South had carried both yeoman farming and plantation slavery into Arkansas and Missouri. Between those states and the Rocky Mountains stretched great grasslands. An army explorer, Major Stephen H. Long, thought the plains region "almost wholly unfit for cultivation" and in 1820 labeled it the Great American Desert. The label stuck. Americans looking for land turned south, to Mexican territory. At the same time, elite planters struggled to control state governments in the Cotton South.

## The Settlement of Texas

After winning independence from Spain in 1821, the Mexican government pursued an activist settlement policy. To encourage migration to the refigured state of Coahuila y Tejas, it offered sizable land grants to its citizens and to American emigrants. Moses Austin, an American land speculator, settled smallholding farmers on his large grant, and his son, Stephen F. Austin, acquired even more land — some 180,000 acres — which he sold to newcomers. By 1835, about 27,000 white Americans and their 3,000 African American slaves were raising cotton and cattle in the well-watered plains and hills of eastern and central Texas. They far outnumbered the 3,000 Mexican residents, who lived primarily near the southwestern Texas towns of Goliad and San Antonio.

When Mexico in 1835 adopted a new constitution creating a stronger central government and dissolving state legislatures, the Americans split into two groups. The "war party," led by Sam Houston and recent migrants from Georgia, demanded independence for Texas. Members of the "peace party," led by Stephen Austin, negotiated with the central government in Mexico City for greater political autonomy. They believed Texas could flourish within a decentralized Mexican republic, a "federal" constitutional system favored by the Liberal Party in Mexico (and advocated in the United States by Jacksonian Democrats). Austin won significant concessions for the Texans, including an exemption from a law ending slavery, but in 1835 Mexico's president, General Antonio López de Santa Anna, nullified them. Santa Anna wanted to impose national authority throughout Mexico. Fearing central control, the war party provoked a rebellion that most of the American settlers ultimately supported. On March 2, 1836, the American rebels proclaimed the independence of Texas and adopted a constitution legalizing slavery.

To put down the rebellion, President Santa Anna led an army that wiped out the Texan garrison defending the **Alamo** in San Antonio and then captured Goliad,

> **UNDERSTAND POINTS OF VIEW**
> What issues divided the Mexican government and the Americans in Texas, and what proposals sought to resolve them?

**Starting Out in Texas**
Thousands of white farmers, some owning a few slaves, moved onto small farms in Texas and Arkansas during the 1840s and 1850s. They lived in crudely built log huts; owned a few cows, horses, and oxen; and eked out a meager living by planting a few acres of cotton in addition to their crops of corn. Their aspirations were simple: to achieve modest prosperity during their lives and to assist their children to own farms of their own. Daughters of the Republic of Texas Library.

executing about 350 prisoners of war (Map 12.2). Santa Anna thought that he had crushed the rebellion, but New Orleans and New York newspapers romanticized the deaths at the Alamo of folk heroes Davy Crockett and Jim Bowie. Drawing on anti-Catholic sentiment aroused by Irish immigration and the massacre at Goliad, they urged Americans to "Remember the Alamo" and depicted the Mexicans as tyrannical butchers in the service of the pope. American adventurers, lured by offers of land grants, flocked to Texas to join the rebel forces. Commanded by General Sam Houston, the Texans routed Santa Anna's overconfident army in the Battle of San Jacinto in April 1836, winning de facto independence. The Mexican government refused to recognize the Texas Republic but, for the moment, did not seek to conquer it.

The Texans voted for annexation by the United States, but President Martin Van Buren refused to bring the issue before Congress. As a Texas diplomat reported, the cautious Van Buren and other party politicians feared that annexation would spark a war with Mexico and, beyond that, a "desperate death-struggle . . . between the North and the South [over the extension of slavery]; a struggle involving the probability of a dissolution of the Union."

## The Politics of Democracy

As national leaders refused admission to Texas, elite planters faced political challenges in the Cotton South. Unlike the planter-aristocrats who ruled the colonial world, they lived in a republican society with a

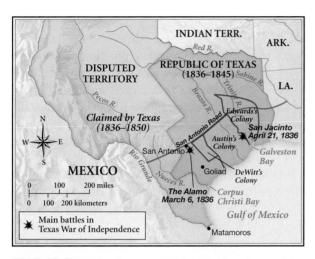

**MAP 12.2**

**American Settlements, the Texas-Mexican War, and Boundary Disputes**

During the 1820s the Mexican government encouraged Americans to settle in the sparsely populated state of Coahuila y Tejas. By 1835 the nearly 30,000 Americans far outnumbered Mexican residents. To put down an American-led revolt, General Santa Anna led 6,000 soldiers into Tejas in 1836. After overwhelming the rebels at the Alamo in March, Santa Anna set out to capture the Texas Provisional Government, which had fled to Galveston. But the Texans' victory at San Jacinto in April ended the war and secured de facto independence for the Republic of Texas (1836–1845). However, the annexation of Texas to the United States sparked a war with Mexico in 1846, and the state's boundaries remained in dispute until the Compromise of 1850.

democratic ethos. The Alabama Constitution of 1819 granted suffrage to all white men; it also provided for a **secret ballot** (rather than voice-voting); apportionment of legislative seats based on population; and the election of county supervisors, sheriffs, and clerks of court. Given these democratic provisions, political factions in Alabama had to compete for votes. When a Whig newspaper sarcastically asked whether the state's policies should "be governed and controlled by the whim and caprice of the majority of the people," Democrats hailed the power of the common folk. They called on "Farmers, Mechanics, laboring men" to repudiate Whig "aristocrats . . . the soft handed and soft headed gentry."

**Taxation Policy**   Whatever the electioneering rhetoric, most Whig and Democrat political candidates were men of substance. In the early 1840s, nearly 90 percent of Alabama's legislators owned slaves, testimony to the political power of the slave-owning minority. Still, relatively few lawmakers — only about 10 percent — were rich planters, a group voters by and large distrusted. "A rich man cannot sympathize with the poor," declared one candidate. Consequently, the majority of elected state officials, and most county officials, in the Cotton South came from the ranks of middle-level planters and planter-lawyers. Astute politicians, they refrained from laying "oppressive" taxes on the people, particularly the white majority who owned no slaves. Between 1830 and 1860, the Alabama legislature obtained about 70 percent of the state's revenue from taxes on slaves and land. Another 10 to 15 percent came from levies on carriages, gold watches, and other luxury goods and on the capital invested in banks, transportation companies, and manufacturing enterprises.

To win the votes of taxpaying slave owners, Alabama Democrats advocated limited government and low taxes. They attacked their Whig opponents for favoring higher taxes and for providing government subsidies for banks, canals, railroads, and other internal improvements. "Voting against appropriations is the safe and popular side," one Democratic legislator declared, and his colleagues agreed; until the 1850s, they rejected most of the bills that would have granted subsidies to transportation companies or banks.

If tax policy in Alabama had a democratic thrust, elsewhere in the South it did not. In some states, wealthy planters used their political muscle to exempt slave property from taxation. Or they shifted the burden to backcountry yeomen, who owned low-quality pasturelands, by taxing farms according to acreage rather than value. Planter-legislators also spared themselves the cost of building fences around their fields by enacting laws that required yeomen to "fence in" their livestock. And, during the 1850s, wealthy legislators throughout the South used public funds to subsidize the canals and railroads in which they had invested, ignoring the protests of yeoman-backed legislators.

**The Paradox of Southern Prosperity**   Even without these internal improvements, the South had a strong economy. Indeed, it ranked fourth in the world in 1860, with a per capita income among whites higher than that of France and Germany. As a contributor to a Georgia newspaper argued in the 1850s, planters and yeomen should not complain about "tariffs, and merchants, and manufacturers" because "the most highly prosperous people now on earth, are to be found in these very [slave] States." Such arguments tell only part of the story. Nearly all African Americans — 40 percent of the population — lived in dire and permanent poverty. And, although the average southern white man was 80 percent richer than the average northerner in

**EXPLAIN CONSEQUENCES**
How did the political power of slave owners affect tax policy and the character of economic development in the southern states?

1860, the southerner's *non-slave* wealth was only 60 percent of the northern average. Moreover, the wealth of the industrializing Northeast was increasing at a faster pace than that of the South. Between 1820 and 1860, slave-related trade across the Atlantic declined from 12.6 percent of world trade to 5.3 percent.

Influential southerners blamed the shortcomings of their plantation-based economy on outsiders: "Purely agricultural people," intoned slave-owning planter-politician James Henry Hammond, "have been in all ages the victims of rapacious tyrants grinding them down." And they steadfastly defended their way of life. "We have no cities—we don't want them," boasted U.S. senator Louis Wigfall of Texas in 1861. "We want no manufactures: we desire no trading, no

mechanical or manufacturing classes. . . . As long as we have our rice, our sugar, our tobacco, and our cotton, we can command wealth to purchase all we want." So wealthy southerners continued to buy land and slaves, a strategy that neglected investments in the great technological innovations of the nineteenth century—water- and steam-powered factories, machine tools, steel plows, and crushed-gravel roads—that would have raised the South's productivity and wealth.

Urban growth, the key to prosperity in Europe and the North, occurred primarily in the commercial cities around the periphery of the South: New Orleans, St. Louis, and Baltimore. Factories—often staffed by slave labor—appeared primarily in the Chesapeake region, which had a diverse agricultural economy and a surplus of bound workers. Within the Cotton South, wealthy planters invested in railroads primarily to grow more cotton; when the Western & Atlantic Railroad reached the Georgia upcountry, the cotton

***Colonel and Mrs. James A. Whiteside, Son Charles and Servants***
James A. Whiteside (1803–1861) was a Tennessee lawyer, politician, land speculator, and entrepreneur, with investments in iron manufacturing, banking, steamboats, and railroads. In 1857, he became vice president of the Nashville, Chattanooga, and St. Louis Railroad. The following year, Whiteside persuaded the Scottish-born painter James Cameron (1817–1882) to move to Chattanooga, where Cameron completed this ambitious portrait of the colonel; his second wife, Harriet; their youngest child, Charles; and two enslaved "servants." The painting shows the family at home, with a view of Chattanooga and of Lookout Mountain, where the colonel had built a hotel. Whiteside died from pneumonia in 1861 after returning home from Virginia with his son James, who had fallen ill while serving in the Confederate army. Hunter Museum of American Art, Chattanooga, Tennessee. Gift of Mr. & Mrs. Thomas B. Whiteside, 1975.7.

crop there quickly doubled. Cotton and agriculture remained King.

Slavery also deterred Europeans from migrating to the South, because they feared competition from bound labor. Their absence deprived the region of skilled artisans and of hardworking laborers to drain swamps, dig canals, smelt iron, and work on railroads. When entrepreneurs tried to hire slaves for these dangerous tasks, planters replied that "a negro's life is too valuable to be risked." Slave owners also feared that hiring out would make their slaves too independent. As a planter told Frederick Law Olmsted, such workers "had too much liberty . . . and got a habit of roaming about and taking care of themselves."

Thus, despite its increasing size and booming exports, the South remained an economic colony: Great Britain and the North bought its staple crops and provided its manufactures, financial services, and shipping facilities. In 1860, some 84 percent of southerners — more than double the percentage in the northern states — still worked in agriculture, and southern factories turned out only 10 percent of the nation's manufactures. The South's fixation on an "exclusive and exhausting" system of cotton monoculture and slave labor filled South Carolina textile entrepreneur William Gregg with "dark forebodings": "It has produced us such an abundant supply of all the luxuries and elegances of life, with so little exertion on our part, that we have become enervated, unfitted for other and more laborious pursuits."

# The African American World

By the 1820s, the cultural life of most slaves reflected both the values and customs of their West African ancestors and the language, laws, and religious beliefs of the South's white population. This mix of African- and European-derived cultural values persisted for decades because whites discouraged blacks from assimilating and because slaves prized their diverse African heritages.

## Evangelical Black Protestantism

The emergence of black Christianity illustrated the synthesis of African and European cultures. From the 1790s to the 1840s, the Second Great Awakening swept over the South, and evangelical Baptist and Methodist preachers converted thousands of white families and hundreds of enslaved blacks (see Chapter 8). Until that time, African-born blacks, often identifiable by their ritual scars, had maintained the religious practices of their homelands.

**African Religions and Christian Conversion**  Africans carried their traditional religious practices to the United States. Some practiced Islam, but the majority relied on African gods and spirits. As late as 1842, Charles C. Jones, a Presbyterian minister, noted that the blacks on his family's plantation in Georgia believed "in second-sight, in apparitions, charms, witchcraft . . . [and other] superstitions brought from Africa." Fearing for their own souls if they withheld "the means of salvation" from African Americans, Jones and other zealous Protestant preachers and planters set out to convert slaves.

Other Protestant crusaders came from the ranks of pious black men and women who had become Christians in the Chesapeake. Swept to the Cotton South by the domestic slave trade, they carried with them the evangelical message of emotional conversion, ritual baptism, and communal spirituality. Equally important, these crusaders adapted Protestant doctrines to black needs. Enslaved Christians pointed out that blacks as well as whites were "children of God" and should be treated accordingly. **Black Protestantism** generally ignored the doctrines of original sin and predestination, and preachers didn't use biblical passages that encouraged unthinking obedience to authority. A white minister in Liberty County, Georgia, reported that when he urged slaves to obey their masters, "one half of my audience deliberately rose up and walked off."

> **PLACE EVENTS IN CONTEXT**
> How did the Second Great Awakening affect the development of black religion?

**Black Worship**  Indeed, some African American converts envisioned the deity as the Old Testament warrior who had liberated the Jews and so would liberate them. Inspired by a vision of Christ, Nat Turner led his bloody rebellion against slavery in Virginia (see Chapter 11). Other black Christians saw themselves as Chosen People: "de people dat is born of God." Charles Davenport, a Mississippi slave, recalled black preachers "exhort[ing] us dat us was de chillun o' Israel in de wilderness an' de Lawd done sont us to take dis lan' o' milk an' honey."

Still, African Americans expressed their Christianity in distinctive ways. The thousands of blacks who joined the Methodist Church respected its ban on profane dancing but praised the Lord in what minister Henry George Spaulding called the "religious dance of the Negroes." Spaulding described the African-derived

**Black Kitchen Ball**

From time to time, festive celebrations punctuated the demanding work routine of slaves' lives. In this 1838 painting, *Kitchen Ball at White Sulphur Springs Virginia*, African Americans dance to the music of a fiddle and a fife (on the right). Note the light complexions and Europeanized features of the most prominent figures, the result of either racial mixing or the cultural perspective of the artist. The painter, Christian Mayr, was born in Germany in 1805 and migrated to the United States in 1833. After working for years as a traveling portrait painter, Mayr settled in New York City in 1845 and died there in 1850. North Carolina Museum of Art, Raleigh. Purchased with funds from the State of North Carolina.

"ring shout" this way: "Three or four, standing still, clapping their hands and beating time with their feet, commence singing in unison one of the peculiar shout melodies, while the others walk around in a ring, in single file, joining also in the song." The songs themselves were usually collective creations, devised spontaneously from bits of old hymns and tunes. Recalled an ex-slave:

> We'd all be at the "prayer house" de Lord's day, and de white preacher he'd splain de word and read whar Esekial done say — Dry bones gwine ter lib ergin. And, honey, de Lord would come a-shinin' thoo dem pages and revive dis ole nigger's heart, and I'd jump up dar and den and holler and shout and sing and pat, and dey would all cotch de words and I'd sing it to some ole shout song I'd heard 'em sing from

Africa, and dey'd all take it up and keep at it, and keep a-addin' to it, and den it would be a spiritual.

By such African-influenced means, black congregations devised a distinctive and joyous brand of Protestant worship to sustain them on the long journey to emancipation and the Promised Land. "O my Lord delivered Daniel," the slaves sang, "O why not deliver me too?"

## Forging Families and Communities

Black Protestantism was one facet of an increasingly homogeneous African American culture in the rural South. Even in South Carolina — a major point of entry for imported slaves — only 20 percent of the black residents in 1820 had been born in Africa. The domestic slave trade mingled blacks from many states, erased regional differences, and prompted the emergence of a core culture in the Lower Mississippi Valley. A prime example was the fate of the Gullah dialect, which combined words from English and a variety of African languages in an African grammatical structure. Spoken by blacks in the Carolina low country well into the twentieth century, Gullah did not take root on the cotton plantations of Alabama and Mississippi. There, slaves from Carolina were far outnumbered by migrants from the Chesapeake, who spoke black English. Like Gullah, black English used double negatives and other African grammatical forms, but it consisted primarily of English words rendered with West African pronunciation (for example, with *th* pronounced as *d* — "de preacher").

Nonetheless, African influences remained significant. At least one-third of the slaves who entered the United States between 1776 and 1809 came from the Congo region of West-Central Africa, and they brought their cultures with them. As traveler Isaac Holmes reported in 1821: "In Louisiana, and the state of Mississippi, the slaves . . . dance for several hours during Sunday afternoon. The general movement is in what they call the Congo dance." Similar descriptions of blacks who "danced the Congo and sang a purely African song to the accompaniment of . . . a drum" appeared as late as 1890.

African Americans also continued to respect African incest taboos by shunning marriages between cousins. On the Good Hope Plantation in South Carolina, nearly half of the slave children born between 1800 and 1857 were related by blood to one another; yet when they married, only one of every forty-one unions took place between cousins. White planters were not the source of this taboo: cousin marriages were frequent among the 440 South Carolina men and women who owned at least one hundred slaves in 1860, in part because such unions kept wealth within an extended family (Thinking Like a Historian, p. 398).

Unlike white marriages, slave unions were not legally binding. According to a Louisiana judge, "slaves have no legal capacity to assent to any contract . . . because slaves are deprived of all civil rights." Nonetheless, many African Americans took marriage vows before Christian ministers or publicly marked their union in ceremonies that included the West African custom of jumping over a broomstick together. Once married, newly arrived young people in the Cotton South often chose older people in their new communities as fictive "aunts" and "uncles." The slave trade had destroyed their family, but not their family values.

The creation of fictive kinship ties was part of a community-building process, a partial substitute for the family ties that sustained whites during periods of crisis. Naming children was another. Recently imported slaves frequently gave their children African names. Males born on Friday, for example, were often called Cuffee — the name of that day in several West African languages. Many American-born parents chose names of British origin, but they usually named sons after fathers, uncles, or grandfathers and daughters after grandmothers. Those transported to the Cotton South often named their children for relatives left behind. Like incest rules and marriage rituals, this intergenerational sharing of names evoked memories of a lost world and bolstered kin ties in the new one.

### UNDERSTAND POINTS OF VIEW

In what respects did African cultural practices affect the lives of enslaved African Americans?

## Negotiating Rights

By forming stable families and communities, African Americans gradually created a sense of order in the harsh and arbitrary world of slavery. In a few regions, slaves won substantial control over their lives.

**Working Lives**   During the Revolutionary era, blacks in the rice-growing lowlands of South Carolina successfully asserted the right to labor by the "task." Under the **task system**, workers had to complete a precisely defined job each day — for example, digging up a quarter-acre of land, hoeing half an acre, or pounding seven mortars of rice. By working hard, many finished their tasks by early afternoon, a Methodist preacher reported, and had "the rest of the day for themselves, which they spend in working their own private fields . . . planting rice, corn, potatoes, tobacco &c. for their own use and profit."

Slaves on sugar and cotton plantations led more regimented lives, thanks to the gang-labor system. As one field hand put it, there was "no time off [between] de change of de seasons. . . . Dey was allus clearin' mo' lan' or sump'." Many slaves faced bans on growing crops on their own. "It gives an excuse for trading," explained one owner, and that encouraged roaming and independence. Still, many masters hired out surplus workers as teamsters, drovers, steamboat workers, turpentine gatherers, and railroad builders; in 1856, no fewer than 435 hired slaves laid track for the Virginia & Tennessee Railroad. Many owners regretted the result. As an overseer remarked about a slave named John, "He is not as good a hand as he was before he went to Alabama."

## Childhood in Black and White

A major theme of Harriet Beecher Stowe's powerful antislavery novel *Uncle Tom's Cabin* is the sin of separating black families and denying parental rights to enslaved mothers and fathers. The following documents reveal the dynamics of plantation family life, and particularly mother-child relations.

1. **Ex-siave Josephine Smith, interviewed at age ninety-four by Mary A. Hicks, Raleigh, North Carolina, 1930s.** *Slave children had loving but limited relationships with their mothers, who worked long hours in the fields and were sometimes sold away from their children.*

I 'members seein' a heap o' slave sales, wid de niggers in chains, an' de spec'ulators sellin' an' buyin' dem off. I also 'members seein' a drove of slaves wid nothin' on but a rag 'twixt dere legs bein' galloped roun' 'fore de buyers. 'Bout de wust thing dat eber I seed do' wuz a slave 'woman at Louisburg who had been sold off from her three weeks old baby, an wuz bein' marched ter New Orleans.

She had walked till she quz give out, an' she wuz weak enough ter fall in de middle o' de road. . . . As I pass by dis 'oman begs me in God's name fer a drink o' water, an' I gives it ter her. I ain't neber be so sorry fer nobody. . . . Dey walk fer a little piece an' dis 'oman fall out. She dies dar side o' de road, an' right dar dey buries her, cussin', dey tells me, 'bout losin' money on her.

2. **"Narrative of James Curry, a Fugitive Slave,"** ***The Liberator*, January 10, 1840.** *The abolitionist newspaper* The Liberator *published heartrending accounts of death and separation in slave families and how "fictive kinship" assisted the survivors.*

My mother's labor was very hard. She would go to the house in the morning, take her pail upon her head, and go away to the cow-pen, and milk fourteen cows. She then put on the bread for the family breakfast, and got the cream ready for churning, and set a little child to churn it, she having the care of from ten to fifteen children, whose mothers worked in the field. . . . Among the slave children, were three little orphans, whose mothers, at their death, committed them to the care of my mother. One of them was a babe. She took them and treated them as her own. The master took no care about them. She always took a share of the cloth she had provided for her own children, to cover these little friendless ones.

3. **Former slave Barney Alford, interview for the Works Progress Administration in Mississippi, 1930s.**

Ole mammy 'Lit' wus mity ole en she lived in one corner of de big yard en she keered fur all de black chilluns while de old folks wurk in de field. Mammy Lit wus good to all de chilluns en I had ter help her wid dem chilluns en keep dem babies on de pallet. Mammy Lit smoked a pipe, en sum times I wuld hide dat pipe, en she wuld slap me fur it, den sum times I wuld run way en go ter de kitchen whar my mammy wus at wurk en mammy Lit wuld hafter cum fur me en den she wuld whip me er gin. She sed I wus bad.

4. **"Mrs. Meriwether Administering Bitters,"** illustration from John Pendleton Kennedy, *Swallow Barn, Or, A Sojourn in the Old Dominion*, **1851.** *Bitters—strong alcoholic beverages flavored with bitter herbs—were administered as medicine in the nineteenth century, as in this depiction of a planter's wife tending to enslaved children. Kennedy's cheerful depictions of Virginia plantation life in this popular book, first published in 1832, reinforced the notion of slavery as a "positive good."*

Source: Picture Research Consultants & Archives.

5. **G. M. J., "Early Culture of Children," 1855.** *This excerpt from a Christian advice manual for mothers reflects the values of the mid-nineteenth-century white Protestant middle class.*

"Train up a child in the way he should go," is a law as imperative in the 19th century, as when first uttered by the lips of the wise man. Mothers are the natural executors of this law to their daughters. Nothing but the most unavoidable and pressing force of circumstances, should wrench this power from their hands. Who will guard with a mother's jealous eye the health, habits, morals, and religion of this most delicate part of creation. . . . How often I have been pained to see mothers place those delicate plants in the nursery with servants, whose tastes, feelings, morals, manners, and language are but a little removed from the lower animals of creation; there to receive impressions, and imbibe habits, which will grow with their growth, and strengthen with their strength, until like the branches of the giant oak, they shall expand and deepen into a shade that will forever conceal the parent stock.

6. **Visiting Cards Created by Philadelphia Portrait Painter and Photographer Peregrine F. Cooper, As We Found Them (left), As They Are Now (right), 1864.** *One of the ways to "train up a child in the way he should go" was to inculcate abolitionist sentiments early and often.*

AS WE FOUND THEM.

These children were owned by Thomas White, of Mathews Co., Va., until Feb. 20th, when Capt. Riley, 6th U. S. C. I., took them and gave them to the Society of Friends to educate at the Orphan's Shelter, Philadelphia.

Profits from sale, for the benefit of the children.

AS THEY ARE NOW.

The Mother of these children was beaten, branded and sold at auction because she was kind to Union Soldiers. As she left for Richmond, Va., Feb. 15th, 1864, bound down in a cart, she prayed "O! God send the Yankees to take my children away."

Profits from sale, for the benefit of the children.

Source: George Eastman House.

Sources: (1) WPA Slave Narrative Project, 1936–38, learnnc.org; (2) "Narrative of James Curry, a Fugitive Slave," *The Liberator*, January 10, 1840, learnnc.org; (3) The MS Gen Web Project, msgw.org/slaves/alford-xslave.htm; (5) *Home Garner; or the Intellectual and Moral Store House*, ed. Mary G. Clarke (Philadelphia: J. P. Lippincott & Co., 1855), 115.

## ANALYZING THE EVIDENCE

1. What do these sources reveal about slave communities? About the extent to which the ideology of "benevolent paternalism" governed the behavior of slave owners?

2. How does the engraving (source 4) compare to the descriptions of the care of slave children (sources 1–3)? What biases, if any, can you detect in these sources?

3. How would a person holding the beliefs described in source 5 react to the engraving of Mrs. Meriwether? To images showing slave "mammies" raising the master's children?

4. How do the images of enslaved children in source 6 pertain to "train[ing] up a child in the way he should go"? How effective are they? What emotions do they play upon?

## PUTTING IT ALL TOGETHER

In the political system, debate over "the peculiar institution" of slavery often focused on property rights and constitutional principles. In the actual world of the plantation, human bondage evoked a range of human emotions—jealousy, resentment, anger, love, fear, tenderness—and human pain. Write an essay that assesses the economic, legal, and political arguments over slavery in light of the experiences of enslaved mothers and children.

**Antebellum Slave Quarters**
During the colonial period, owners often housed their slaves by gender in communal barracks. In the nineteenth century, slaves usually lived in family units in separate cabins. The slave huts on this South Carolina plantation were sturdily built but had few windows. Inside, they were sparsely furnished. Library of Congress.

The planters' greatest fear was that enslaved African Americans—a majority of the population in most cotton-growing counties—would rise in rebellion. Legally speaking, owners had virtually unlimited power over their slaves. "The power of the master must be absolute," intoned Justice Thomas Ruffin of the North Carolina Supreme Court in 1829. But absolute power required brutal coercion, and only hardened or sadistic masters had the stomach for such violence. "These poor negroes, receiving none of the fruits of their labor, do not love work," explained one woman who worked her own farm; "if we had slaves, we should have to . . . beat them to make use of them."

Moreover, passive resistance by African Americans seriously limited their owners' power. Slaves slowed the pace of work by feigning illness and losing or breaking tools. One Maryland slave, faced with transport to Mississippi and separation from his wife, flatly refused "to accompany my people, or to be exchanged or sold," his owner reported. Masters ignored such feelings at their peril. A slave (or a relative) might retaliate by setting fire to the master's house and barns, poisoning his food, or destroying his crops. Fear of resistance, as well as critical scrutiny by abolitionists, prompted many masters to reduce their reliance on the lash and use positive incentives such as food and special privileges. Noted Frederick Law Olmsted: "Men of sense have discovered that it was better to offer them rewards than to whip them." Nonetheless, owners could always resort to violence, and countless masters regularly asserted their power by demanding sex from their female slaves. As ex-slave Bethany Veney lamented in her autobiography, from "the unbridled lust of the slave-owner . . . the law holds . . . no protecting arm" over black women.

**Survival Strategies**    Slavery remained an exploitative system grounded in fear and coercion. Over the decades, hundreds of individual slaves responded by attacking their masters and overseers. But only a few blacks—among them Gabriel and Martin Prosser (1800) and Nat Turner (1831)—plotted mass uprisings. Most slaves recognized that revolt would be futile; they lacked the autonomous institutions such as the communes of European peasants, for example, needed to organize a successful rebellion. Moreover, whites

**PLACE EVENTS IN CONTEXT**
How successful were slaves in securing significant control over their lives?

were numerous, well armed, and determined to maintain their position of racial superiority.

Escape was equally problematic. Blacks in the Upper South could flee to the North, but only by leaving their family and kin. Slaves in the Lower South escaped to sparsely settled regions of Florida, where some intermarried with the Seminole Indians. Elsewhere in the South, escaped slaves eked out a meager existence in inhospitable marshy areas or mountain valleys. Consequently, most African Americans remained on plantations; as Frederick Douglass put it, they were

"pegged down to one single spot, and must take root there or die."

"Taking root" meant building the best possible lives for themselves. Over time, enslaved African Americans pressed their owners for a greater share of the product of their labor, much like unionized workers in the North were doing. Thus slaves insisted on getting paid for "overwork" and on the right to cultivate a garden and sell its produce. "De menfolks tend to de gardens round dey own house," recalled a Louisiana slave. "Dey raise some cotton and sell it to massa and git li'l money dat way." Enslaved women raised poultry and sold chickens and eggs. An Alabama slave remembered buying "Sunday clothes with dat money, sech as hats and pants and shoes and dresses." By the 1850s, thousands of African Americans were reaping the small rewards of this underground economy, and some accumulated sizable property. Enslaved Georgia carpenter Alexander Steele owned four horses, a mule, a silver watch, two cows, a wagon, and large quantities of fodder, hay, and corn.

Whatever their material circumstances, few slaves accepted the legitimacy of their status. Although he was fed well and never whipped, a former slave told an English traveler, "I was cruelly treated because I was kept in slavery."

## The Free Black Population

Some African Americans escaped slavery through flight or a grant of freedom by their owners and, if they lived in the North, through gradual emancipation laws that, by 1840, had virtually ended bound labor. The proportion of free blacks rose from 8 percent of the African American population in 1790 to about 13 percent between 1820 and 1840, and then (because of high birthrates among enslaved blacks) fell to 11 percent. Still, the number of free blacks continued to grow. In the slave state of Maryland in 1860, half of all African Americans were free, and many more were "term" slaves, guaranteed their freedom in exchange for a few more years of work.

**Northern Blacks**    Almost half of free blacks in the United States in 1840 (some 170,000) and again in 1860 (250,000) lived in the free states of the North. However, few of them enjoyed unfettered freedom. Most whites regarded African Americans as their social inferiors and confined them to low-paying jobs. In rural areas, blacks worked as farm laborers or tenant farmers; in

### CLASS No. 1.

*Comprises those prisoners who were found guilty and executed.*

| Prisoners Names. | Owners' Names. | Time of Commit. | How Disposed of. |
|---|---|---|---|
| Peter | James Poyas | June 18 | Hanged on Tuesday the 2d July, 1822, on Blake's lands, near Charleston. |
| Ned | Gov. T. Bennett, | do. | |
| Rolla | do. | do | |
| Batteau | do. | do. | |
| Denmark Vesey | A free black man | 22 | |
| Jessy | Thos. Blackwood | 23 | |
| John | Elias Horry | July 5 | Do on the Lines near Ch.; Friday July 12. |
| Gullah Jack | Paul Pritchard | do. | |
| Mingo | Wm. Harth | June 21 | |
| Lot | Forrester | 27 | |
| Joe | P. L. Jore | July 6 | |
| Julius | Thos. Forrest | 8 | |
| Tom | Mrs. Russell | 10 | |
| Smart | Robt. Anderson | do. | |
| John | John Robertson | 11 | |
| Robert | do. | do. | |
| Adam | do. | do. | |
| Polydore | Mrs. Faber | do. | Hanged on the Lines near Charleston, on Friday, 26th July. |
| Bacchus | Benj. Hammet | do. | |
| Dick | Wm. Sims | 13 | |
| Pharaoh | — Thompson | do. | |
| Jemmy | Mrs. Clement | 18 | |
| Mauidore | Mordecai Cohen | 19 | |
| Dean | — Mitchell | do. | |
| Jack | Mrs. Purcell | 12 | |
| Bellisle | Est. of Jos. Yates | 18 | |
| Naphur | do. | do. | |
| Adam | do. | do. | |
| Jacob | John S. Glen | 16 | |
| Charles | John Billings | 18 | |
| Jack | N. McNeill | 22 | |
| Cæsar | Miss Smith | do. | |
| Jacob Stagg | Jacob Lankester | 23 | Do. Tues. July 30. |
| Tom | Wm. M. Scott | 24 | |
| William | Mrs. Garner | Aug. 2 | Do. Friday, Aug. 9. |

**"An Account of the Late Intended Insurrection, Charleston, South Carolina"**

In 1820, Charleston had a free black population of 1,500 and an array of African American institutions, including the Brown Fellowship Society (for those of mixed racial ancestry) and an African Methodist Episcopal (AME) church. In 1822, Charleston authorities accused a free black, Denmark Vesey, of organizing a revolt to free the city's slaves. Although historians long accepted the truth of that charge, recent scholarship suggests that Vesey's only offense was antagonizing some whites by claiming his rights as a free man and that fearful slave owners conjured up the plot. Regardless, South Carolina officials hanged Vesey and thirty-four alleged co-conspirators and tore down the AME church where they allegedly plotted the uprising. David M. Rubenstein Rare Book & Manuscript Library, Duke University.

**COMPARE AND CONTRAST**
How were the lives of free African Americans different in the northern and southern states?

**A Master Bridge Builder**

Horace King (1807–1885) was a self-made man of color, a rarity in the nineteenth-century South. Born a slave of mixed European, African, and Native American (Catawba) ancestry, King built major bridges in Georgia, Alabama, and Mississippi during the early 1840s. After winning his freedom in 1846, he built and ran a toll bridge across the Chattahoochee River in Alabama. During the Civil War, King worked as a contractor for the Confederacy; during Reconstruction, he served two terms as a Republican in the Alabama House of Representatives. Collection of the Columbus Museum, Columbus, Georgia; Museum Purchase.

towns and cities, they toiled as domestic servants, laundresses, or day laborers. Only a small number of African Americans owned land. "You do not see one out of a hundred . . . that can make a comfortable living, own a cow, or a horse," a traveler in New Jersey noted. In most states, law or custom prohibited northern blacks from voting, attending public schools, or sitting next to whites in churches. They could testify in court against whites only in Massachusetts. The federal government did not allow African Americans to work for the postal service, claim public lands, or hold a U.S. passport. As black activist Martin Delaney remarked in 1852: "We are slaves in the midst of freedom."

Of the few African Americans able to make full use of their talents, several achieved great distinction. Mathematician and surveyor Benjamin Banneker (1731–1806) published an almanac and helped lay out the new capital in the District of Columbia; Joshua Johnston (1765–1832) won praise for his portraiture;

and merchant Paul Cuffee (1759–1817) acquired a small fortune from his business enterprises. More impressive and enduring were the community institutions created by free African Americans. Throughout the North, these largely unknown men and women founded schools, mutual-benefit organizations, and fellowship groups, often called Free African Societies. Discriminated against by white Protestants, they formed their own congregations and a new religious denomination — the African Methodist Episcopal Church, headed by Bishop Richard Allen (see Chapter 8).

These institutions gave African Americans a measure of cultural autonomy, even as they marked sharp social divisions among blacks. "Respectable" blacks tried through their dress, conduct, and attitude to win the "esteem and patronage" of prominent whites — first Federalists and then Whigs and abolitionists — who were sympathetic to their cause. Those efforts separated them from impoverished blacks, who distrusted not only whites but also blacks who "acted white."

**Standing for Freedom in the South**    The free black population in the slave states numbered approximately 94,000 in 1810 and 225,000 in 1860. Most of these men and women lived in coastal cities — Mobile, Memphis, New Orleans — and in the Upper South. Partly because skilled Europeans avoided the South, free blacks formed the backbone of the urban artisan workforce. African American carpenters, blacksmiths, barbers, butchers, and shopkeepers played prominent roles in the economies of Baltimore, Richmond, Charleston, and New Orleans. But whatever their skills, free blacks faced many dangers. White officials often denied jury trials to free blacks accused of crimes, and sometimes they forced those charged with vagrancy back into slavery. Some free blacks were simply kidnapped and sold.

As a privileged minority among African Americans in the South, free blacks had divided loyalties. To advance the welfare of their families, some distanced themselves from plantation slaves and assimilated white culture and values. Indeed, mixed-race individuals sometimes joined the ranks of the planter class. David Barland, one of twelve children born to a white Mississippi planter and his black slave Elizabeth, himself owned no fewer than eighteen slaves. In neighboring Louisiana, some free blacks supported secession because they owned slaves and were "dearly attached to their native land."

Such individuals were exceptions. Most free African Americans acknowledged their ties to the great mass of slaves, some of whom were their relatives. "We's different [from whites] in color, in talk and in 'ligion and

**An African American Clergyman**

This flattering portrait is one of two paintings of African Americans by black artist Joshua Johnson (who also went by the surname Johnston). The son of an enslaved black woman and a white man, who bought his son's freedom in 1782, Johnson described himself in an advertisement in the *Baltimore Intelligence* in 1798 as a "Portrait Painter . . . a self-taught genius deriving from nature and industry his knowledge of the Art." White merchant families in Maryland and Virginia held Johnson's work in high regard and commissioned most of his thirty or so extant works. Bowdoin College Museum of Art, Brunswick, Maine. Museum Purchase, George Otis Hamlin Fund.

beliefs," said one. Calls by white planters in the 1840s to re-enslave free African Americans reinforced black unity. Knowing their own liberty was not secure so long as slavery existed, free blacks celebrated on August 1, the day slaves in the British West Indies won emancipation, and sought a similar goal for enslaved African Americans. As a delegate to the National Convention of Colored People in 1848 put it, "Our souls are yet dark under the pall of slavery." In the rigid American caste system, free blacks stood as symbols of hope to enslaved African Americans and as symbols of danger to most whites.

## SUMMARY

In this chapter, we focused on the theme of an expanding South. Beginning about 1800, planters carried the system of plantation slavery from its traditional home in the Upper South to the Mississippi Valley and

beyond. Powered by cotton, this movement westward involved the forced migration of more than 1 million enslaved African Americans and divided the planter elite into aristocratic paternalists and entrepreneurial capitalists.

We also examined the character of white and black societies in the Cotton South. After 1820, less than a third of white families owned slaves, and another third were yeomen farmers; propertyless tenant farmers and laborers made up the rest. Many whites joined evangelical Protestant churches, as did blacks, who infused their churches with African modes of expression. Indeed, church and family became core institutions of African American society, providing strength and solace amid the tribulations of slavery. Finally, we explored the initiatives taken by the free black population, in both the northern and southern states, to achieve individual mobility and to build community institutions. These efforts resulted in a church-based leadership class and a black abolitionist movement.

# CHAPTER REVIEW

 **MAKE IT STICK**    Go to **LearningCurve** to retain what you've read.

## TERMS TO KNOW    Identify and explain the significance of each term below.

### Key Concepts and Events

coastal trade (p. 380)

inland system (p. 380)

chattel principle (p. 381)

benevolent masters (p. 382)

republican aristocracy (p. 386)

"positive good" argument (p. 386)

gang-labor system (p. 388)

slave society (p. 388)

Alamo (p. 391)

secret ballot (p. 393)

black Protestantism (p. 395)

task system (p. 397)

### Key People

Harriet Jacobs (p. 382)

James Henry Hammond (p. 384)

Stephen Austin (p. 391)

Antonio López de Santa Anna (p. 391)

Sam Houston (p. 391)

## REVIEW QUESTIONS    Answer these questions to demonstrate your understanding of the chapter's main ideas.

1. Why in 1860 did white southerners remain committed to the institution of slavery and its expansion?

2. Based on what you have learned in Part 4, compare and contrast society in the American South with that in the North. Was America, in fact, two distinct societies by 1860? If not, what bonds, beliefs, and cultural practices united Americans across regional boundaries? If so, what factors contributed to the development of separate regional identities?

3. **THEMATIC UNDERSTANDING** Review the events listed under "Identity" on the thematic timeline on page 283, and then discuss how the end of the Atlantic slave trade in 1807 and the subsequent rise of the domestic slave trade affected the identity of the African American population.

## MAKING CONNECTIONS    Recognize the larger developments and continuities within and across chapters by answering these questions.

1. **ACROSS TIME AND PLACE** After reviewing the relevant materials in Chapters 3, 8, and 12, explain how the plantation economy and the system of slavery changed between 1720 and 1860.

2. **VISUAL EVIDENCE** Chapter 12 contains a number of paintings or photographs of enslaved African Americans. In your judgment, do those images, either individually or as a group, capture the reality of slave life? Explain your position while evaluating the strengths and weaknesses of paintings and photographs as historical evidence.

## MORE TO EXPLORE    Start here to learn more about the events discussed in this chapter.

Edward Ball, *Slaves in the Family* (1998). Recounts Ball's ancestors' ownership of slaves, their illicit sexual unions, and the family's diverse racial identity.

Ira Berlin, *Generations of Captivity* (2003). Traces the history of slavery in the United States.

Charlene M. Boyer Lewis, *Ladies and Gentlemen on Display* (2001). Explores the lives of the planter class.

Stephanie McCurry, *Masters of Small Worlds* (1995). Evokes the patriarchal lives of yeomen families.

Adam Rothman, *Slave Country: American Expansion and the Origins of the Deep South* (2005). Analyzes the changing character of slavery and African American society.

For primary documents on the black Christian church, consult **docsouth.unc.edu/church/index .html**.

## TIMELINE    Ask yourself why this chapter begins and ends with these dates and then identify the links among related events.

| | |
|---|---|
| **1810s** | • Africans from Congo region influence black culture for decades<br>• Natural increase produces surplus of slaves in Old South<br>• Domestic slave trade expands, disrupting black family life |
| **1812** | • Louisiana becomes a state, and its sugar output increases |
| **1817** | • Mississippi becomes a state; Alabama follows (1819) |
| **1820s** | • Free black population increases in North and South<br>• Entrepreneurial planters in Cotton South turn to gang labor<br>• Southern Methodists and Baptists become socially conservative<br>• African Americans increasingly adopt Christian beliefs |
| **1830s** | • Gentry in Old South adopt paternalistic ideology and argue that slavery is a "positive good"<br>• Boom in cotton production<br>• Percentage of slave-owning white families falls<br>• Yeomen farm families retreat to hill country<br>• Lawyers become influential in southern politics |
| **1840s** | • Southern Whigs advocate economic diversification<br>• Gradual emancipation completed in North |
| **1850s** | • Cotton prices and production increase<br>• Slave prices rise<br>• Southern states subsidize railroads, but industry remains limited |

**KEY TURNING POINTS:** Using the five entries in the timeline for the 1830s, write an essay that describes the economy, society, and polity of the South in that decade and that analyzes the significance of the decade's developments in the evolution of the region between 1800 and 1860.

# Creating and Preserving a Continental Nation

## 1844–1877

Between 1844 and 1877, the United States became a continental nation by winning three wars and creating a stronger central government. This energetic process of national expansion and purposeful state building spanned three decades and three periods often treated as distinct: antebellum America, the Civil War, and Reconstruction. In fact, these decades constitute a single, distinct period of American political and constitutional development that produced a consolidated national republic.

This era of state building began in the 1840s as the United States expanded to the Pacific through a diplomatic deal with Great Britain and a war of conquest against Mexico. However, geographic expansion sharpened the conflict between free and slave states and led eventually to the secession of the South in 1861. The Union government defeated the secessionists in a bloody Civil War and reconstructed the Union under the ideals of the Republican Party. Freed from slavery, millions of African Americans fought for better pay and equal citizenship rights. Under pressure to assimilate, most Native Americans adapted selectively while maintaining tribal ties and traditional lifeways. Subsequently, the national government promoted Euro-American settlement of the West by conquering Indian peoples and confining them to reservations.

The story of these transforming events focuses on three sets of historical issues:

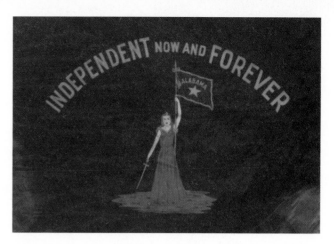

## Continental Empire and Cultural Conflict

A romantic spirit of geographic expansion grew during the 1840s, prompting southerners to demand the annexation of Texas and midwesterners to favor the acquisition of Oregon. Northeastern railroad entrepreneurs championed western settlement, as did merchants eager to trade across the Pacific. The quest for western lands sparked seizure of the Mexican provinces of New Mexico and California and purchase of Russian claims to Alaska. We analyze these events in Chapter 13.

This process of expansion and state building, combined with the arrival of millions of immigrants, created new systems of racial and ethnic conflict. In the East, Irish Catholics and German-speaking migrants organized politically to protect their churches, saloons, and cultural identity, prompting a sharp reaction among native-born Protestants. In the West, the U.S. government fought wars against Cheyennes, Sioux, and Comanches on the Great Plains as it sought to integrate the region into the national economy. In the conquered Mexican territories, newly arriving whites jostled uneasily with Hispanic residents and despised Chinese immigrants. In an era of rapid economic development, western disputes often centered on access to land, jobs, and natural resources. For these conflicts, see Chapters 13 and 16.

## Sectional Tensions, Political Divisions, and Civil War

The Mexican War prompted a decade-long debate over the expansion of slavery into the newly acquired lands. This bitter struggle led to the Compromise of 1850, a complex legislative agreement that won little support either in the North or in the South and divided the Whig Party. As southern Whigs became Democrats and northern Whigs turned into Republicans or Know-Nothings, the parties split along sectional lines. The Kansas-Nebraska Act of 1854 began a downward spiral of political conflict that ended in the election of Republican Abraham Lincoln in 1860 and the secession of thirteen southern states. Chapter 13 details this breakdown of the political system.

In the long Civil War that followed, the military forces of the North and South were at first evenly matched. However, the North's superior financial and industrial resources gradually gave it the advantage, as did Lincoln's proclamation of freedom for slaves in 1863. Emancipation undermined European support for the secessionists and added thousands of African Americans to the northern armies. Union forces swept across the South and ended the war, which left a legacy of half-won freedom for blacks and decades of bitter animosity between northern and southern whites. The Civil War is the focus of Chapter 14.

## National Power and Consolidation

The Civil War increased national authority. Three Republican-sponsored constitutional amendments limited the powers of the states and imposed definitions of citizenship—prohibiting slavery, mandating suffrage for black men, and forbidding state action that denied people equal protection under the law. The U.S. Army remained a significant force, enforcing Reconstruction in the South as late as 1877, while suppressing Indian uprisings and extending national control in the West.

The Civil War created a powerful American state, as the Union government mobilized millions of men and billions of dollars. It created a modern fiscal system, an elaborate network of national banks, and—for the first time in American history—a significant national bureaucracy. Inspired by Whig ideology, Republican-run Congresses intervened forcefully to integrate the national economy and promote industrialization, granting subsidies to railroad companies, protecting industries and workers through protective tariffs, and distributing western lands to farmers and cattlemen. In the 1850s and 1860s, U.S. officials also intervened aggressively in Japan and then built coaling stations that enabled U.S. steamships to carry products to Asia and bring Chinese workers to the United States. The nation's dynamic postwar economy had set the nation on a course toward global power. Chapters 15 and 16 discuss all of these events.

# Creating and Preserving a Continental Nation 1844–1877

## Thematic Understanding

This timeline arranges some of the important events of this period into themes. Consider the events listed under each of the five themes. Which set of events seems the most important? The least important? The theme of "Politics and Power" begins with a reference to sectional conflict and concludes with the section-driven Compromise of 1877. Based on other entries in this theme and your reading in Chapters 13, 14, and 15, explain how the nature of sectionalism and the power of the various sections changed between 1844 and 1877.  **>**

| | POLITICS & POWER | AMERICA IN THE WORLD | IDEAS, BELIEFS, & CULTURE | WORK, EXCHANGE, & TECHNOLOGY | IDENTITY |
|---|---|---|---|---|---|
| **1840** | • Mexican War and Wilmot Proviso (1846) increase sectional conflict<br><br>• Gold rush makes California eligible for statehood—free or slave? | • U.S. confronts Mexico and Britain: annexes Texas (1845), acquires Oregon (1846), fights Mexican War (1846–1848) extending U.S. borders to Pacific | • Ideology of Manifest Destiny prompts U.S. expansionism<br><br>• Free-Soil Party (1848) advocates white smallholder farm society<br><br>• Women seek legal rights at Seneca Falls (1848) | • Irish immigrants build northern canal system<br><br>• Some states default on canal bonds<br><br>• Walker Tariff (1846) lowers rates, increases foreign imports | • Whites migrate to Oregon and California<br><br>• Arrival of millions of Germans and Irish causes social conflicts<br><br>• Wars against Seminole peoples in Florida (1835–1842, 1855–1858) |
| **1850** | • Compromise of 1850<br><br>• Whig Party disintegrates; Know-Nothing Party attacks immigrants<br><br>• Kansas-Nebraska Act (1854) sparks creation of Republican Party | • President Pierce opens Japan to trade; seeks to expand American territory and slavery into Caribbean by diplomacy and filibustering actions | • Harriet Beecher Stowe's *Uncle Tom's Cabin* (1852) attacks slavery<br><br>• *Dred Scott* decision (1857) opens way to legalize slavery nationwide<br><br>• Southern secessionists agitate for independence | • Enslaved blacks expand cotton output in South<br><br>• White settlers expand farm society to trans-Mississippi west<br><br>• Entrepreneurs promote railroad building and manufacturing in North and Midwest | • Conflict of Hispanics and Anglos in the Southwest<br><br>• White diseases and brutality kill most California Indians<br><br>• Comanches and Sioux dominate Great Plains peoples and control trade in horses and buffalo hides |
| **1860** | • Eleven southern states secede from Union, sparking Civil War (1861–1865); the Union's triumph preserves a continental nation<br><br>• Fourteenth Amendment (1868) extends legal and political rights | • U.S. diplomacy and Union army victories in 1863 cause British government to stop sale of ironclad ships to the Confederacy<br><br>• Secretary of State Seward buys Alaska from Russia (1867)<br><br>• Burlingame Treaty (1868) protects missionaries in China and limits Chinese immigration | • Confederate States of America (1861–1865) vow to continue slavery<br><br>• Republicans seek to impose equal rights ideology on South<br><br>• Black families accept ideal of domesticity | • Republicans enact Whigs' economic policies: Homestead Act (1862), railroad aid, high tariffs, and national banking<br><br>• Women assume new tasks in war economies | • Emancipation Proclamation (1863) and Thirteenth Amendment (1865) free blacks from slavery<br><br>• Aided by Freedmen's Bureau, African Americans struggle for freedom, land, and education |
| **1870** | • Fifteenth Amendment (1870) extends vote to black men<br><br>• Compromise of 1877 ends Reconstruction | • Britain pays the U.S. $15.5 million for the depredations of the *Alabama* during the war<br><br>• Anti-Chinese riots in San Francisco in late 1870s prompt Chinese Exclusion Act (1882) | • Ku Klux Klan attacks Reconstruction governments<br><br>• Republicans embrace classical liberalism<br><br>• White elites challenge ideal of universal suffrage and deny women's suffrage | • Sharecropping spreads in South<br><br>• Ranchers create cattle empire on Great Plains<br><br>• Depression of 1873 halts railway expansion | • U.S. wars against Plains Indians (Cheyennes, Sioux, Apaches, and Nez Perce) open their lands to white miners, ranchers, and farmers<br><br>• Dawes Act (1887) seeks Indian assimilation |

# 13
## CHAPTER

# Expansion, War, and Sectional Crisis
# 1844–1860

The expansionist surge of the 1840s had deep roots. Since the nation's founding in 1776, visionaries conceived its future both as a republic and as an empire, and they predicted a glorious expansion across the continent. "It belongs of right to the United States to regulate the future destiny of North America," declared the *New-York Evening Post* in 1803. Politicians soon took up the refrain. "Our natural boundary is the Pacific Ocean," asserted Massachusetts congressman Francis Baylies in 1823. "The swelling tide of our population must and will roll on until that mighty ocean interposes its waters." However, the creation of a continental republic was far from inevitable. It would require a revolution in transportation—canals and railways—to access the nation's fertile core in the vast Mississippi River basin and a growing population and dynamic economy to exploit its riches. By the 1840s, all those prerequisites were in place.

Other obstacles remained. Well-armed Indian peoples controlled the Great Plains, Mexico held sovereignty over Texas and the lands west of the Rocky Mountains, and Great Britain laid claim to the Oregon Country. To extend the American republic would involve new Indian wars and possibly armed conflict with Great Britain and with Mexico (and perhaps France, its main creditor). An ardent imperialist, President James Polk willingly assumed those risks. "I would meet the war which either England or France . . . might wage and fight until the last man," he told Secretary of State James Buchanan in 1846.

Polk's aggressive expansionism sparked fighting abroad and conflict at home. A war with Mexico intended to be "brief, cheap, and bloodless" became "long, costly, and sanguinary," complained Senator Thomas Hart Benton of Missouri. Even Polk's great territorial acquisitions—New Mexico, California, the Oregon Country—proved double-edged by reigniting a bitter debate over slavery. Northerners vowed to prevent the expansion of bound labor into the newly acquired territories, prompting southerners to threaten secession from the Union. Rhetoric spiraled downward into violence, as white and black abolitionists attacked slave catchers in the North and secessionists harassed Union supporters in the South. When Massachusetts senator Charles Sumner accused his South Carolina colleague Andrew P. Butler of taking "the harlot slavery" as his mistress, a southern congressman beat Sumner unconscious with a walking cane. As this violence shook Washington in 1856, proslavery migrants fought armed New England abolitionists in the Kansas Territory. Passion had replaced compromise as the hallmark of American political life.

## IDENTIFY THE BIG IDEA
What were the causes of the Mexican War, and in what ways did it bring about a growing sectional crisis during the 1850s?

**John Gast, _American Progress_** In 1845, journalist John O'Sullivan coined the term _Manifest Destiny_ to describe Americans' suddenly urgent longing to extend the boundaries of the republic to the Pacific Ocean. More than a quarter century later, John Gast's _American Progress_ (1872) gave visual form to that aspiration in an allegorical painting that was widely distributed through color lithographs. The goddess Liberty floats westward, holding a "School Book" in one hand and telegraph lines trailing from the other as symbols of the advance of Anglo-American civilization across the continent. Library of Congress.

# Manifest Destiny: South and North

The upsurge in violence reflected a generational shift in culture and politics. The Missouri crisis of 1819–1822 (Chapter 8) had frightened the nation's leaders. For the next two decades, the professional politicians who ran the Second Party System avoided policies, such as the annexation of the slaveholding Republic of Texas, that would prompt regional strife. Then, during the 1840s, many citizens embraced an ideology of expansion and proclaimed a God-given duty to extend American republicanism to the Pacific Ocean. But whose republican institutions: the hierarchical slave system of the South, or the more egalitarian, reform-minded, capitalist-managed society of the North and Midwest? Or both? Ultimately, the failure to find a political solution to this question would rip the nation apart.

## The Push to the Pacific

As expansionists developed continental ambitions, the term **Manifest Destiny** captured those dreams. John L. O'Sullivan, editor of the *Democratic Review*, coined the phrase in 1845: "Our manifest destiny is to overspread the continent allotted by Providence for the free development of our yearly multiplying millions." Underlying the rhetoric of Manifest Destiny was a sense of Anglo-American cultural and racial superiority: the "inferior" peoples who lived in the Far West—Native Americans and Mexicans—would be subjected to American dominion, taught republicanism, and converted to Protestantism.

**Oregon** Land-hungry farmers of the Ohio River Valley had already cast their eyes toward the fertile lands of the Oregon Country, a region that stretched along the Pacific coast between the Mexican province of California and Russian settlements in Alaska. Since 1818, a British-American agreement had allowed settlement by people from both nations. The British-run Hudson's Bay Company developed a lucrative fur business north of the Columbia River, while Methodist missionaries and a few hundred American farmers settled to the south, in the Willamette Valley (Map 13.1).

In 1842, American interest in Oregon increased dramatically. The U.S. Navy published a glowing report of fine harbors in the Puget Sound, which New England merchants trading with China were already using. Simultaneously, a party of one hundred farmers journeyed along the Oregon Trail, which fur traders and explorers had blazed from Independence, Missouri, across the Great Plains and the Rocky Mountains (Map 13.2). Their letters from Oregon told of a mild climate and rich soil.

"Oregon fever" suddenly raged. A thousand men, women, and children—with a hundred wagons and

**MAP 13.1**

**Territorial Conflict in Oregon, 1819–1846**

As thousands of American settlers poured into the Oregon Country in the early 1840s, British authorities tried to keep them south of the Columbia River. However, the migrants—and fervent expansionists—asserted that Americans could settle anywhere in the territory, raising the prospect of armed conflict. In 1846, British and American diplomats resolved the dispute by dividing most of the region at the forty-ninth parallel while giving both nations access to fine harbors (Vancouver and Seattle) through the Strait of Juan de Fuca.

**Settling Oregon**

Americans quickly populated the Far West and re-created there the small-town life of the eastern states. As early as 1845, as this drawing by a British military officer shows, Oregon City boasted a steepled church, several large merchandise warehouses, and several dozen houses. On the riverbank opposite the town stand several Native Americans, who had a very different way of life and would be steadily pushed off the lands of their ancestors. Library of Congress.

five thousand oxen and cattle—gathered in Independence in April 1843. As the spring mud dried, they began their six-month trek, hoping to miss the winter snows. Another 5,000 settlers, mostly yeomen farm families from the southern border states (Missouri, Kentucky, and Tennessee), set out over the next two years. These pioneers overcame floods, dust storms, livestock deaths, and a few armed encounters with native peoples before reaching Oregon, a journey of 2,000 miles.

By 1860, about 250,000 Americans had braved the Oregon Trail, with 65,000 heading for Oregon, 185,000 to California, and others staying in Wyoming, Idaho, and Montana. More than 34,000 migrants died, mostly from disease and exposure; fewer than 500 deaths resulted from Indian attacks. The walking migrants wore paths 3 feet deep, and their wagons carved 5-foot ruts across sandstone formations in southern Wyoming—tracks that are visible today. Women found the trail especially difficult; in addition to their usual chores and the new work of driving wagons and animals, they lacked the support of female kin and the

security of their domestic space. About 2,500 women endured pregnancy or gave birth during the long journey, and some did not survive. "There was a woman died in this train yesterday," Jane Gould Tortillott noted in her diary. "She left six children, one of them only two days old."

The 10,000 migrants who made it to Oregon in the 1840s mostly settled in the Willamette Valley. Many families squatted on 640 acres and hoped Congress would legalize their claims so that they could sell surplus acreage to new migrants. The settlers quickly created a race- and gender-defined polity by restricting voting to a "free male descendant of a white man."

California   About 3,000 other early pioneers ended up in the Mexican province of California. They left the Oregon Trail along the Snake River, trudged down the California Trail, and mostly settled in the interior along the Sacramento River, where there were few Mexicans.

**IDENTIFY CAUSES**
Did the idea of Manifest Destiny actually cause events, such as the political support for territorial expansion, or simply justify actions taken for other reasons?

**MAP 13.2**

**The Great Plains: Settler Trails, Indian Raiders, and Traders**

By the 1850s, the Mormon, Oregon, and Santa Fe trails ran across "Indian Country," the semiarid, buffalo-filled Great Plains west of the 95th meridian, and then through the Rocky Mountains. Tens of thousands of Americans set out on these trails to found new communities in Utah, Oregon, New Mexico, and California. This mass migration exposed sedentary Indian peoples to American diseases, guns, and manufactures. However, raids by Comanches and Sioux affected their lives even more significantly, as did the Euro-American traders who provided a ready market for Indian horses and mules, dried meat, and buffalo skins.

A remote outpost of Spain's American empire, California had few nonnative residents until the 1770s, when Spanish authorities built a chain of forts and religious missions along the Pacific coast. When Mexico achieved independence in 1821, its government took over the Franciscan-run missions and freed the 20,000 Indians whom the monks had persuaded or coerced into working on them. Some mission Indians rejoined their tribes, but many intermarried with mestizos (Mexicans of mixed Spanish and Indian ancestry).

**William Henry Jackson, *California Crossing, South Platte River*, detail, 1867**
The South Platte River was wide (stretching from the foreground to the low bluff in the middle of the picture) but shallow, allowing relatively easy passage for the migrants' cattle and covered wagons. Wagon trains followed the course of the various branches of the Platte River for more than 300 miles across the Great Plains. During the late spring and early summer, wagons often stretched as far as the eye could see. National Park Service/Picture Research Consultants & Archives.

They worked on huge ranches — the 450 estates created by Mexican officials and bestowed primarily on their families and political allies. The owners of these vast properties (averaging 19,000 acres) mostly raised Spanish cattle, prized for their hides and tallow.

The ranches soon linked California to the American economy. New England merchants dispatched dozens of agents to buy leather for the booming Massachusetts boot and shoe industry and tallow to make soap and candles. Many agents married the daughters of the elite Mexican ranchers — the **Californios** — and adopted their manners, attitudes, and Catholic religion. A crucial exception was Thomas Oliver Larkin, a successful merchant in the coastal town of Monterey. Although Larkin worked closely with Mexican politicians and landowners, he remained strongly American in outlook.

Like Larkin, the American migrants in the Sacramento River Valley did not assimilate into Mexican society. Some hoped to emulate the Americans in Texas by colonizing the country and then seeking annexation. However, in the early 1840s, these settlers numbered only about 1,000, far outnumbered by the 7,000 Mexicans who lived along the coast.

## The Plains Indians

As the Pacific-bound wagon trains rumbled across Nebraska along the broad Platte River, the migrants encountered the unique ecology of the Great Plains. A vast sea of wild grasses stretched from Texas to Saskatchewan in Canada, and west from the Missouri River to the Rocky Mountains. Tall grasses flourished in the eastern regions of the future states of Kansas, Nebraska, and the Dakotas, where there was ample rainfall. To the west, in the semiarid region beyond the 100th meridian, the migrants found short grasses that sustained a rich wildlife dominated by buffalo and grazing antelopes. Nomadic buffalo-hunting Indian peoples roamed the western plains, while the eastern river valleys were home to semisedentary tribes and, since the 1830s, the Indian peoples whom Andrew Jackson had "removed" to the west. A line of military forts—stretching from Fort Jesup in Louisiana to Fort Snelling, then in the Wisconsin Territory—policed the boundary between white settlements and what Congress in 1834 designated as Permanent Indian Territory.

For centuries, the Indians who lived on the eastern edge of the plains, such as the Pawnees and the Mandans on the Upper Missouri River, subsisted primarily on corn and beans, supplemented by buffalo meat. They hunted buffalo on foot, driving them over cliffs or into canyons for the kill. To the south, the nomadic Apaches acquired horses from Spanish settlers in New Mexico and ranged widely across the plains. The Comanches, who migrated down the Arkansas River from the Rocky Mountains around 1750, developed both a horse-based culture and imperial ambitions. Skilled buffalo hunters and fierce warriors, the Comanches slowly pushed the Apaches to the southern edge of the plains. They also raided Spanish settlements in New Mexico, incorporating captured women and children into their society.

After 1800, the Comanches gradually built up a pastoral economy, raising horses and mules and selling them to northern Indian peoples and to Euro-American farmers in Missouri and Arkansas. Many Comanche families owned thirty to thirty-five horses or mules, far more than the five or six required for hunting buffalo and fighting neighboring peoples. The Comanches also exchanged goods with merchants and travelers along the Santa Fe Trail, which cut through their territory as it connected Missouri and New Mexico. By the early 1840s, goods worth nearly $1 million moved along the trail each year.

By the 1830s, the Kiowas, Cheyennes, and Arapahos had also adopted this horse culture and, allied with the Comanches, dominated the plains between the Arkansas and Red rivers. The new culture brought sharper social divisions. Some Kiowa men owned hundreds of horses and had several "chore wives" and captive children who worked for them. Poor men, who owned only a few horses, had difficulty finding marriage partners and often had to work for their wealthy kinsmen.

While European horses made Plains Indians wealthier and more mobile, European diseases and

**Comanches Meeting the Dragoons, 1830s**

In the 1830s, when artist George Catlin accompanied the dragoons of the U.S. Army into Indian Territory, the Comanches were masters of the southern plains. They hunted buffalo, raised horses and mules for sale, and used their skills as horsemen to dominate other Indian peoples and control the passage of Americans along the Santa Fe Trail. Smithsonian American Art Museum, Washington, DC/Art Resource, NY.

guns thinned their ranks. A devastating smallpox epidemic spread northward from New Spain in 1779–1781 and killed half of the Plains peoples. Twenty years later, another smallpox outbreak left dozens of deserted villages along the Missouri River. Smallpox struck the northern plains again from 1837 to 1840, killing half of the Assiniboines and Blackfeet and nearly a third of the Crows, Pawnees, and Cheyennes. "If I could see this thing, if I knew where it came from, I would go there and fight it," exclaimed a distressed Cheyenne warrior.

European weapons also altered the geography of native peoples. Around 1750, the Crees and Assiniboines, who lived on the far northern plains, acquired guns by trading wolf pelts and beaver skins to the British-run Hudson's Bay Company. Once armed, they drove the Blackfoot peoples westward into the Rocky Mountains and took control of the Saskatchewan and Upper Missouri River basins. When the Blackfeet obtained guns and horses around 1800, they emerged from the mountains and pushed the Shoshones and Crows to the south. Because horses could not easily find winter forage in the snow-filled plains north of the Platte River, Blackfoot families kept only five to ten horses and remained hunters rather than pastoralists.

The powerful Lakota Sioux, who acquired guns and ammunition from French, Spanish, and American traders along the Missouri River, also remained buffalo hunters. A nomadic war-prone people who lived in small groups, the Lakotas largely avoided major epidemics. They kept some sedentary peoples, such as the Arikaras, in subjection and raided others for their crops and horses. By the 1830s, the Lakotas were the dominant tribe on the central as well as the northern plains. "Those lands once belonged to the Kiowas and the Crows," boasted the Oglala Sioux chief Black Hawk, "but we whipped those nations out of them, and in this we did what the white men do when they want the lands of the Indians."

The Sioux's prosperity also came at the expense of the buffalo, which provided them with a diet rich in protein and with hides and robes to sell. The number of hides and robes shipped down the Missouri River each year by the American Fur Company and the Missouri Fur Company increased from 3,000 in the 1820s, to 45,000 in the 1830s, and to 90,000 annually after 1840. North of the Missouri, the story was much the same. The 24,000 Indians of that region — Blackfeet, Crees, and Assiniboines — annually killed about 160,000 buffalo. The women dried the meat to feed their people and to sell to white traders and soldiers. The women also undertook the arduous work of skinning and tanning the hides, which they fashioned into tepees, buffalo robes, and sleeping covers. Over time, Indian hunters increased the kill and traded surplus hides and robes — about 40,000 annually by the 1840s — for pots, knives, guns, and other Euro-American manufactures. As among the Kiowas, trade increased social divisions. "It is a fine sight," a traveler noted around 1850, "to see one of those big men among the Blackfeet, who has two or three lodges, five or six wives, twenty or thirty children, fifty to a hundred head of horses; for his trade amounts to upward of $2,000 per year."

Although the Blackfeet, Kiowas, and Lakotas contributed buffalo hides to the national economy, they did not fully grasp their market value as winter clothes, leather accessories, and industrial drive belts. Consequently, they could not demand the best price. Moreover, the increasing size of the kill diminished the buffalo herds. Between 1820 and 1870, the northern herd shrank from 5 million to less than 2 million. When the Assiniboines' cultural hero Inkton'mi had taught his people how to kill the buffalo, he told them, "The buffalo will live as long as your people. There will be no end of them until the end of time." Meant as a perpetual guarantee, by the 1860s Inkton'mi's words prefigured the end of time — the demise of traditional buffalo hunting and, perhaps, of the Assiniboines as well.

**TRACE CHANGE OVER TIME**
Why did some Great Plains peoples flourish between 1750 and 1860 while others did not?

## The Fateful Election of 1844

The election of 1844 changed the American government's policy toward the Great Plains, the Far West, and Texas. Since 1836, southern leaders had supported the annexation of Texas, but cautious party politicians, pressured by northerners who opposed the expansion of slavery, had rebuffed them (Chapter 12). Now rumors swirled that Great Britain was encouraging Texas to remain independent; wanted California as payment for the Mexican debts owed to British investors; and had designs on Spanish Cuba, which some slave owners wanted to add to the United States. To thwart such imagined schemes, southern expansionists demanded the immediate annexation of Texas.

At this crucial juncture, Oregon fever altered the political landscape in the North. In 1843, Americans in the Ohio River Valley and the Great Lakes states organized "Oregon conventions," and Democratic and Whig politicians alike called for American sovereignty over the entire Oregon Country, from Spanish California to Russian Alaska (which began at 54°40' north latitude). With northerners demanding Oregon,

President John Tyler, a proslavery zealot, called for the annexation of Texas. Disowned by the Whigs because he thwarted Henry Clay's nationalist economic program, Tyler hoped to win reelection in 1844 as a Democrat. To curry favor among northern expansionists, Tyler supported claims to all of Oregon.

In April 1844, Tyler and John C. Calhoun, his pro-slavery, expansionist-minded secretary of state, sent the Senate a treaty to bring Texas into the Union. However, the two major presidential hopefuls, Democrat Martin Van Buren and Whig Henry Clay, opposed Tyler's initiative. Fearful of raising the issue of slavery, they persuaded the Senate to reject the treaty.

**UNDERSTAND POINTS OF VIEW**
Why did party politicians initially oppose the annexation of Texas, and how did this view change during the election of 1844?

Nonetheless, expansion into Texas and Oregon became the central issue in the election of 1844. Most southern Democrats favored Texas annexation and refused to support Van Buren's candidacy. The party also passed over Tyler, whom they did not trust. Instead, the Democrats selected Governor James K. Polk of Tennessee, a slave owner and an avowed expansionist. Known as "Young Hickory" because he was a protégé of Andrew Jackson, Polk shared his mentor's iron will, boundless ambition, and determination to open up lands for American settlement. Accepting the false claim in the Democratic Party platform that both areas already belonged to the United States, Polk campaigned for the "Re-occupation of Oregon and the Re-annexation of Texas." He insisted that the United States defy British claims and occupy "the whole of the territory of Oregon" to the Alaskan border. **"Fifty-four forty or fight!"** became his jingoistic cry.

The Whigs nominated Henry Clay, who again advocated his American System of high tariffs, internal improvements, and national banking. Clay initially dodged the issue of Texas but, seeking southern votes, ultimately supported annexation. Northern Whigs who opposed the admission of a new slave state refused to vote for Clay and cast their ballots for James G. Birney of the Liberty Party (Chapter 11). Birney garnered less than 3 percent of the national vote but took enough Whig votes in New York to cost Clay that state — and the presidency.

Following Polk's narrow victory, congressional Democrats called for immediate Texas statehood. However, they lacked the two-thirds majority in the Senate needed to ratify a treaty of annexation. So the Democrats admitted Texas using a joint resolution of Congress, which required just a majority vote in each

house, and Texas became the twenty-eighth state in December 1845. Polk's strategy of linking Texas and Oregon had put him in the White House and Texas in the Union. Shortly, it would make the expansion of the South — and its system of slavery — the central topic of American politics.

# War, Expansion, and Slavery, 1846–1850

The acquisition of Texas whetted Polk's appetite for the Mexican lands between Texas and the Pacific Ocean. If necessary, he was ready to go to war for them. What he and many Democrats consciously ignored was the domestic crisis that a war of conquest to expand slavery would unleash.

## The War with Mexico, 1846–1848

Since gaining independence in 1821, Mexico had not prospered. Its civil wars and political instability produced a stagnant economy, a weak government, and modest tax revenues, which a bloated bureaucracy and debt payments to European bankers quickly devoured. Although the distant northern provinces of California and New Mexico remained undeveloped and sparsely settled, with a Spanish-speaking population of only 75,000 in 1840, Mexican officials vowed to preserve their nation's historic boundaries. When its breakaway province of Texas prepared to join the American Union, Mexico suspended diplomatic relations with the United States.

**Polk's Expansionist Program**   President Polk now moved quickly to acquire Mexico's other northern provinces. He hoped to foment a revolution in California that, like the 1836 rebellion in Texas, would lead to annexation. In October 1845, Secretary of State James Buchanan told merchant Thomas Oliver Larkin, now the U.S. consul for the Mexican province, to encourage influential Californios to seek independence and union with the United States. To add military muscle to this scheme, Polk ordered American naval commanders to seize San Francisco Bay and California's coastal towns in case of war with Mexico. The president also instructed the War Department to dispatch Captain John C. Frémont and an "exploring" party of soldiers into Mexican territory. By December 1845, Frémont's force had reached California's Sacramento River Valley.

With these preparations in place, Polk launched a secret diplomatic initiative: he sent Louisiana congressman John Slidell to Mexico, telling him to secure the Rio Grande boundary for Texas and to buy the provinces of California and New Mexico for $30 million. However, Mexican officials refused to meet with Slidell.

Events now moved quickly toward war. Polk ordered General Zachary Taylor and an American army of 2,000 soldiers to occupy disputed lands between the Nueces River (the historic southern boundary of Spanish Texas) and the Rio Grande, which the Republic of Texas had claimed as its border with Mexico. "We were sent to provoke a fight," recalled Ulysses S. Grant, then a young officer serving with Taylor, "but it was essential that Mexico should commence it." When the armies clashed near the Rio Grande in May 1846, Polk delivered the war message he had drafted long before. Taking liberties with the truth, the president declared that Mexico "has passed the boundary of the United States, has invaded our territory, and shed American blood upon the American soil." Ignoring pleas by some Whigs for a negotiated settlement, an overwhelming majority in Congress voted for war—a decision greeted with great popular acclaim. To avoid a simultaneous war with Britain, Polk retreated from his demand for "fifty-four forty or fight" and in June 1846 accepted British terms that divided the Oregon Country at the forty-ninth parallel.

**American Military Successes**    American forces in Texas quickly established their military superiority. Zachary Taylor's army crossed the Rio Grande; occupied the Mexican city of Matamoros; and, after a fierce six-day battle in September 1846, took the interior Mexican town of Monterrey. Two months later, a U.S. naval squadron in the Gulf of Mexico seized Tampico, Mexico's second most important port. By the end of 1846, the United States controlled much of northeastern Mexico (Map 13.3).

Fighting also broke out in California. In June 1846, naval commander John Sloat landed 250 marines in Monterey and declared that California "henceforward will be a portion of the United States." Simultaneously,

**MAP 13.3**

**The Mexican War, 1846–1848**

After moving west from Fort Leavenworth in present-day Kansas, American forces commanded by Captain John C. Frémont and General Stephen Kearny defeated Mexican armies in California in 1846 and early 1847. Simultaneously, U.S. troops under General Zachary Taylor and Colonel Alfred A. Doniphan won victories over General Santa Anna's forces south of the Rio Grande. In mid-1847, General Winfield Scott mounted a successful seaborne attack on Veracruz and Mexico City, ending the war.

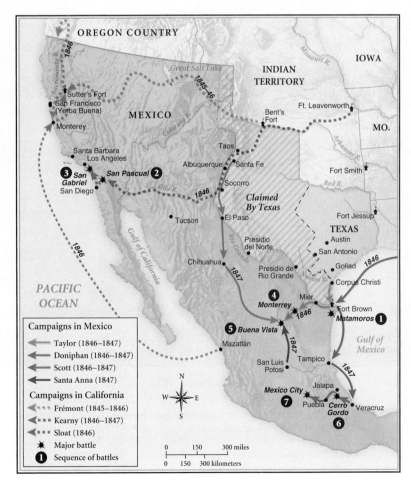

**COMPARE AND CONTRAST**
How was the American acquisition of California similar to, and different from, the American-led creation of the Texas Republic (discussed in Chapter 12)?

American settlers in the Sacramento River Valley staged a revolt and, supported by Frémont's force, captured the town of Sonoma, where they proclaimed the independence of the "Bear Flag Republic." To cement these victories, Polk ordered army units to capture Santa Fe in New Mexico and then march to southern California. Despite stiff Mexican resistance, American forces secured control of California early in 1847.

Polk expected these victories to end the war, but he underestimated the Mexicans' national pride and the determination of President Santa Anna. In February 1847 in the Battle of Buena Vista, Santa Anna nearly defeated Taylor's army in northeastern Mexico. With most Mexican troops deployed in the north, Polk approved General Winfield Scott's plan to capture the port of Veracruz and march 260 miles to Mexico City. An American army of 14,000 seized the Mexican capital in September 1847. That American victory cost Santa Anna his presidency, and a new Mexican government made a forced peace with the United States.

**Street Fighting in the Calle de Iturbide, 1846**
Monterrey, which had resisted Spanish troops during Mexico's war for independence (1820–1821), was captured by the Americans only after bloody house-to-house fighting in the Mexican War (1846–1848). Protected by thick walls and shuttered windows, Mexican defenders pour a withering fire on the dark-uniformed American troops and buckskin-clad frontier fighters. A large Catholic cathedral looms in the background, its foundations obscured by the smoke from the Mexicans' cannons. West Point Museum, United States Military Academy, West Point, NY.

## A Divisive Victory

Initially, the war with Mexico sparked an explosion of patriotic expansionism. The *Nashville Union* hailed it as a noble struggle to extend "the principles of free government." However, the war soon divided the nation (American Voices, p. 422). Some northern Whigs—among them Charles Francis Adams of Massachusetts (the son of John Quincy Adams) and Chancellor James Kent of New York—opposed the war on moral grounds, calling it "causeless & wicked & unjust." Adams, Kent, and other **conscience Whigs** accused Polk of waging a war of conquest to add new slave states and give slave-owning Democrats permanent control of the federal government. Swayed by such arguments, troops deserted in droves (creating the highest desertion rate of any American war), and antiwar activists denounced enlistees as "murderers and robbers." "The United States will conquer Mexico," Ralph Waldo Emerson had predicted as the war began, but "Mexico will poison us."

When voters repudiated Polk's war policy in the elections of 1846, the Whig Party took control of Congress. Whig leaders called for "No Territory"—a congressional pledge that the United States would not seek any land from the Mexican republic. "Away with this wretched cant about a 'manifest destiny,' a 'divine mission' . . . to civilize, and Christianize, and democratize our sister republics at the mouth of a cannon," declared New York senator William Duer.

**The Wilmot Proviso** Polk's expansionist policies also split the Democrats. As early as 1839, Ohio Democrat Thomas Morris had warned that "the power of slavery is aiming to govern the country, its Constitutions and laws." In 1846, David Wilmot, an antislavery Democratic congressman from Pennsylvania, took up that refrain and proposed the so-called **Wilmot Proviso**, a ban on slavery in any territories gained from the war. Whigs and antislavery Democrats in the House of Representatives quickly passed the bill, dividing Congress along sectional lines. "The madmen of the North . . . ," grumbled the *Richmond Enquirer*, "have, we fear, cast the die and numbered the days of this glorious Union." Fearing that outcome, a few proslavery northern senators joined their southern colleagues to kill the proviso.

Fervent Democratic expansionists now became even more aggressive. President Polk, Secretary of State Buchanan, and Senators Stephen A. Douglas of Illinois and Jefferson Davis of Mississippi called for the annexation of a huge swath of Mexican territory south of the Rio Grande. However, John C. Calhoun and other

southern whites feared this demand would extend the costly war and require the assimilation of many dark-skinned mestizos. They favored only the annexation of sparsely settled New Mexico and California. "Ours is a government of the white man," proclaimed Calhoun, which should never welcome "into the Union any but the Caucasian race." To unify the Democratic Party, Polk and Buchanan accepted Calhoun's policy. In 1848, Polk signed, and the Senate ratified, the Treaty of Guadalupe Hidalgo, in which the United States agreed to pay Mexico $15 million in return for more than one-third of its territory (Map 13.4).

Congress also created the Oregon Territory in 1848 and, two years later, passed the Oregon Donation Land Claim Act, which granted farm-sized plots of "free land" to settlers who took up residence before 1854. Soon, treaties with native peoples extinguished Indian titles to much of the new territory. With the settlement of Oregon and the acquisition of New Mexico and California, the American conquest of the Far West was far advanced.

**Free Soil** However, the political debate over expansion was far from over and dominated the election of 1848. The Senate's rejection of the Wilmot Proviso revived Thomas Morris's charge that leading southerners were part of a "Slave Power" conspiracy to dominate national life. To thwart any such plan, thousands of ordinary northerners, including farmer Abijah Beckwith of Herkimer County, New York, joined the **free-soil movement**. Slavery, Beckwith wrote in his diary, was an institution of "aristocratic men" and a danger to "the great mass of the people [because it] . . . threatens the general and equal distribution of our lands into convenient family farms."

The free-soilers quickly organized the Free-Soil Party in 1848. The new party abandoned the Garrisonians' and Liberty Party's emphasis on the sinfulness of slavery and the natural rights of African Americans. Instead, like Beckwith, it depicted slavery as a threat to republicanism and to the Jeffersonian ideal of a free-holder society, arguments that won broad support among aspiring white farmers. Hundreds of men and women in the Great Lakes states joined the free-soil organizations formed by the American and Foreign Anti-Slavery Society. So, too, did Frederick Douglass, the foremost black abolitionist, who attended the first Free-Soil Party convention in the summer of 1848 and endorsed its strategy. However, William Lloyd Garrison and other radical abolitionists condemned the Free-Soilers' stress on white freehold farming as racist "whitemanism."

## The Mexican War: Expansion and Slavery

Conflict with Mexico prompted debates over the Polk administration's aggressive efforts to acquire territory and spread slavery. Here, Polk's critics face off against the expansionists.

### John L. O'Sullivan, Editor
#### "Manifest Destiny," from *United States Magazine and Democratic Review*, July 1845

Texas is now ours . . . [Britain and France tried] to intrude themselves [into Texas affairs] . . . for the avowed object of thwarting our policy and hampering our power, limiting our greatness and checking the fulfillment of our manifest destiny to overspread the continent allotted by Providence for the free development of our yearly multiplying millions. . . .

The independence of Texas was complete and absolute. It was an independence, not only in fact, but of right. . . . What then can be more preposterous than all this clamor by Mexico and the Mexican interest, against Annexation, as a violation of any rights of hers . . . ?

Nor is there any just foundation for the charge that Annexation is a great pro-slavery measure — calculated to increase and perpetuate that institution. Slavery had nothing to do with it. . . . That it will tend to facilitate and hasten the disappearance of Slavery from all the northern tier of the present Slave States, cannot surely admit of serious question. The greater value in Texas of the slave labor now employed in those States, must soon produce the effect of draining off that labor southwardly. . . .

California will, probably, next fall away. . . . Already the advance guard of the irresistible army of Anglo-Saxon emigration has begun to pour down upon it, armed with the plough and the rifle, and marking its trail with schools and colleges, courts and representative halls, mills and meeting-houses. A population will soon be in actual occupation of California. . . . And they will have a right to independence — to self-government . . . a better and a truer right than the artificial title of sovereignty in Mexico, a thousand miles distant, inheriting from Spain a title good only against those who have none better.

Source: Sean Wilentz, ed., *Major Problems in the Early Republic, 1787–1848* (Lexington, MA: D. C. Heath, 1991), 525–528.

### James Buchanan, U.S. Secretary of State
#### Letter to John Slidell, Minister Plenipotentiary to Mexico, November 1845

In your negotiations with Mexico, the independence of Texas must be considered a settled fact, and is not to be called in question. . . .

It may, however, be contended on the part of Mexico, that the Nueces and not the Rio del Norte [Rio Grande], is the true western boundary of Texas. I need not furnish you arguments to controvert this position. . . . The jurisdiction of Texas has been extended beyond that river [the Nueces] and . . . representatives from the country between it and the Del Norte have participated in the deliberations both of her Congress and her Convention. . . .

The case is different in regard to New Mexico. Santa Fe, its capital, was settled by the Spaniards more than two centuries ago; and that province has been ever since in their possession and that of the Republic of Mexico. The Texans never have conquered or taken possession of it. . . . [However,] a great portion of New Mexico being on this side of the Rio Grande and included within the limits already claimed by Texas, it may hereafter, should it remain a Mexican province, become a subject of dispute. . . . It would seem to be equally the interest of both Powers, that New Mexico should belong to the United States. . . .

It is to be seriously apprehended that both Great Britain and France have designs upon California. . . . This Government . . . would vigorously interpose to prevent the latter from becoming either a British or a French Colony. . . . The possession of the Bay and harbor of San Francisco, is all important to the United States. . . . Money would be no object.

Source: Victoria Bissell Brown and Timothy J. Shannon, eds., *Going to the Source: The Bedford Reader in American History* (Boston: Bedford/St. Martin's, 2004), 1: 260–262.

### Charles Sumner, Conscience Whig and Future Republican Senator from Massachusetts

## Letter to Robert Winthrop, Whig Congressman from Massachusetts, October 25, 1846

If we regard Texas as a province of Mexico, its boundaries must be sought in the geography of that republic. If we regard it as an independent State, they must be determined by the extent of jurisdiction which the State was able to maintain. Now it seems clear that the river Nueces was always recognized by Mexico as the western boundary; and it is undisputed that the State of Texas, since its Declaration of Independence, never exercised any jurisdiction beyond the Nueces. . . .

In the month of January, 1846, the President of the United States directed the troops under General Taylor, called the Army of Occupation, to take possession of this region [west of the Nueces River]. Here was an act of aggression. As might have been expected, it produced collision. The Mexicans, aroused in self-defence, sought to repel the invaders. . . .

Here the question occurs, What was the duty of Congress in this emergency? Clearly to withhold all sanction to unjust war, — to aggression upon a neighboring Republic. . . . The American forces should have been directed to retreat, not from any human force, but from wrongdoing; and this would have been a true victory.

Alas! This was not the mood of Congress. With wicked speed a bill was introduced, furnishing large and unusual supplies of men and money. . . . This was adopted by a vote of 123 to 67; and the bill then leaped forth, fully armed, as a measure of open and active hostility against Mexico.

Source: Sean Wilentz, ed., *Major Problems in the Early Republic, 1787–1848* (Lexington, MA: D. C. Heath, 1991), 541.

### Walt Whitman, Poet and Editor of the *Brooklyn Eagle*

## Editorial, September 1, 1847

The question whether or no there shall be slavery in the new territories . . . is a question between the grand body of white workingmen, the millions of mechanics, farmers, and operatives of our country, with their interests on the one side — and the interests of the few thousand rich, "polished," and aristocratic owners of slaves at the South, on the other side.

Experience has proved . . . that a stalwart mass of respectable workingmen, cannot exist, much less flourish, in a thorough slave State. Let any one think for a moment what a different appearance New York, Pennsylvania, or Ohio, would present — how much less sturdy independence and family happiness there would be — were slaves the workmen there, instead of each man as a general thing being his own workman. . . .

Slavery is a good thing enough . . . to the rich — the one out of thousands; but it is destructive to the dignity and independence of all who work, and to labor itself. . . . All practice and theory . . . are strongly arrayed in favor of limiting slavery to where it already exists.

Source: Sean Wilentz, ed., *Major Problems in the Early Republic, 1787–1848* (Lexington, MA: D. C. Heath, 1991), 543.

---

### QUESTIONS FOR ANALYSIS

1. What arguments do Buchanan and Sumner make about the boundaries of Texas, the issue that sparked the fighting? Whose argument is more persuasive and why?

2. Do O'Sullivan's and Buchanan's assertions support or undercut the claim that the Mexican War was an aggressive act of imperialism?

3. Why does Whitman oppose the expansion of slavery? Given Whitman's views, who might have gotten his vote in the election of 1848? Why?

4. Two of the sources are newspaper editorials; two are letters written by or addressed to public officials. How does the nature of each of these sources influence its content?

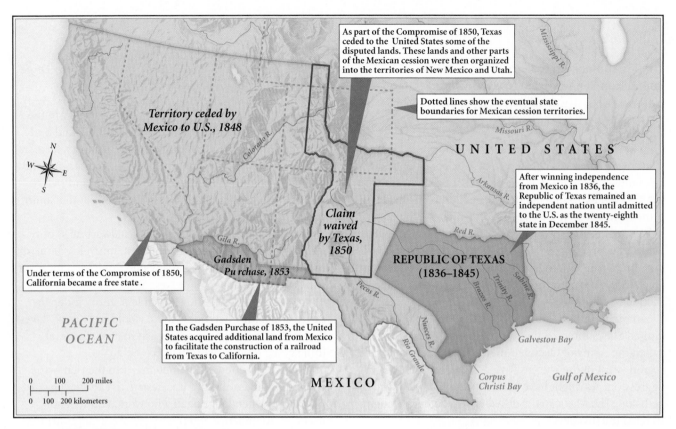

As part of the Compromise of 1850, Texas ceded to the United States some of the disputed lands. These lands and other parts of the Mexican cession were then organized into the territories of New Mexico and Utah.

Dotted lines show the eventual state boundaries for Mexican cession territories.

*Territory ceded by Mexico to U.S., 1848*

After winning independence from Mexico in 1836, the Republic of Texas remained an independent nation until admitted to the U.S. as the twenty-eighth state in December 1845.

*Claim waived by Texas, 1850*

Under terms of the Compromise of 1850, California became a free state.

*Gadsden Purchase, 1853*

**REPUBLIC OF TEXAS (1836–1845)**

**UNITED STATES**

In the Gadsden Purchase of 1853, the United States acquired additional land from Mexico to facilitate the construction of a railroad from Texas to California.

**PACIFIC OCEAN**

**MEXICO**

Galveston Bay

Corpus Christi Bay

Gulf of Mexico

0    100    200 miles
0    100    200 kilometers

**MAP 13.4**
**The Mexican Cession, 1848**

In the Treaty of Guadalupe Hidalgo (1848), Mexico ceded to the United States its vast northern territories—the present-day states of California, Nevada, Utah, Arizona, New Mexico, and half of Colorado. These new territories, President Polk boasted to Congress, "constitute of themselves a country large enough for a great empire, and the acquisition is second in importance only to that of Louisiana in 1803."

## The Election of 1848

The conflict over slavery took a toll on Polk and the Democratic Party. Scorned by Whigs and Free-Soilers and exhausted by his rigorous dawn-to-midnight work regime, Polk declined to run for a second term and died just three months after leaving office. In his place, the Democrats nominated Senator Lewis Cass of Michigan, an avid expansionist who had advocated buying Cuba, annexing Mexico's Yucatán Peninsula, and taking all of Oregon. To maintain party unity on the slavery issue, Cass promoted a new idea, **squatter sovereignty**. Under this plan, Congress would allow settlers in each territory to determine its status as free or slave.

Cass's doctrine of squatter sovereignty failed to persuade those northern Democrats who opposed any expansion of slavery. They joined the Free-Soil Party, as did former Democratic president Martin Van Buren, who became its candidate for president. To attract Whig votes, the Free-Soilers chose conscience Whig Charles Francis Adams for vice president.

The Whigs nominated General Zachary Taylor. Taylor was a Louisiana slave owner firmly committed to the defense of slavery in the South but not in the territories, a position that won him support in the North. Moreover, the general's military exploits had made him a popular hero, known affectionately among his troops as "Old Rough and Ready." In 1848, as in 1840 with the candidacy of William Henry Harrison, running a military hero worked for the Whigs. Taylor took 47 percent of the popular vote to Cass's 42 percent. However, Taylor won a majority in the electoral college (163 to 127) only because Van Buren and the Free-Soil ticket

**PLACE EVENTS IN CONTEXT**
What did conscience Whigs, David Wilmot, and free-soilers have in common, and why did they all rise to prominence between 1846 and 1848?

**"This Is the House That Polk Built"**

President James Polk's administration started off with a bang—a long-sought Democratic free-trade tariff, a compromise settlement of the Oregon boundary dispute with Great Britain, and a war to seize California and other Mexican provinces. This ambitious agenda promised fame for the president, but the cartoonist pictures Polk as a worried man, afraid that he has built a house of cards that might collapse at any time. © Bettmann/Corbis.

took enough votes in New York to deny Cass a victory there. Although their numbers were small, antislavery voters in New York had denied the presidency to Clay in 1844 and to Cass in 1848. The bitter debate over slavery had changed the dynamics of national politics.

## California Gold and Racial Warfare

Even before Taylor took office, events in sparsely settled California took center stage. In January 1848, workers building a milldam for John A. Sutter in the Sierra Nevada foothills came across flakes of gold. Sutter was a Swiss immigrant who came to California in 1839, became a Mexican citizen, and accumulated

land in the Sacramento River Valley. He tried to hide the discovery, but by mid-1848 Americans from Monterey and San Francisco were pouring into the foothills, along with hundreds of Indians and Californios and scores of Australians, Mexicans, and Chileans. The gold rush was on (America Compared, p. 426). By January 1849, sixty-one crowded ships had left New York and other northeastern ports to sail around Cape Horn to San Francisco; by May, twelve thousand wagons had crossed the Missouri River bound for the goldfields (Map 13.5). For Bernard Reid, the overland trip on the Pioneer Line was "a long dreadful dream," beset by cholera, scurvy, and near starvation. Still, by the end of 1849, more than 80,000 people, mostly men — the so-called **forty-niners** — had arrived in California.

**The Forty-Niners**    The forty-niners lived in crowded, chaotic towns and mining camps amid gamblers, saloon keepers, and prostitutes. They set up "claims clubs" to settle mining disputes and cobbled together a system of legal rules based on practice "back East." The American miners usually treated alien whites fairly but ruthlessly expelled Indians, Mexicans, and Chileans from the goldfields or confined them to marginal diggings. When substantial numbers of Chinese miners arrived in 1850, often in the employ of Chinese companies, whites called for laws to expel them from California.

The first miners to exploit a site often struck it rich. They scooped up the easily reached deposits, leaving small pickings for later arrivals. His "high hopes" wrecked, one latecomer saw himself and most other forty-niners as little better than "convicts condemned to exile and hard labor." They faced disease and death as well: "Diarrhea was so general during the fall and winter months" and so often fatal, a Sacramento doctor remarked, that it was called "the disease of California." Like many migrants, William Swain gave up the search for gold in 1850 and borrowed funds to return to his wife, infant daughter, and aged mother on a New York farm. "O William," his wife Sabrina had written, "I wish you had been content to stay at home, for there is no real home for me without you."

Thousands of disillusioned forty-niners were either too ashamed or too tired or too ambitious to go home. Some became wageworkers for companies that engaged in hydraulic or underground mining; others turned to farming. "Instead of going to the mines where fortune hangs upon the merest chance," a frustrated miner advised emigrants, "[you] should at once commence the cultivation of the soil."

# The Gold Rush: California and Australia

In 1849, hundreds of Australian men booked passage for San Francisco, hoping to make their fortune in the California goldfields. A mere two years later, thousands more Australian "diggers" flocked to the colony of Victoria in Australia itself, drawn by a gold strike that yielded one-third of the world's gold output during the 1850s.

In California and Victoria, miners lived mostly in canvas tents and flimsy wood shanties and found gold initially in stream beds. In both territories, the huge migration virtually wiped out the aboriginal peoples. Similarly, both rushes attracted about 40,000 Chinese miners, an influx that, in the race-conscious, English-speaking world of the nineteenth century, prompted riots and legislation in both regions to restrict Asian migrants. Finally, only a few California "forty-niners" or Australian "diggers" made a fortune, perhaps 5 of every 100.

There were differences as well. Upon a gold strike in California, the prospectors would stake their claims and collectively protect those claims—a rough system of democratic self-rule. In Victoria, the British crown owned much of the land and gold commissioners and police administered the diggings, selling licenses to dig for 30 shillings a month (about $200 in present-day U.S. dollars). Distressed by license fees and corrupt local officials, 10,000 miners at Ballarat voted to create a Reform League, which demanded abolition of fees and universal male suffrage. When authorities ignored their demands, 500 miners seized a rich mine at Eureka. In the ensuing struggle, British troops killed 22 miners, ending the armed uprising.

Despite these differences—as well as a significant disparity in the proportion of women—California and Victoria were both transformed by the nearly simultaneous discovery of gold. Within a few decades a mining boom vastly increased their wealth and boasted their populations, as the following chart indicates:

### TABLE 13.1

**Nonnative Population Increases from Gold Rush in United States and Australia**

| | California, United States | | | | Victoria, Australia | | |
|---|---|---|---|---|---|---|---|
| | Total | Women | Nonwhite | | Total | Women | Nonwhite |
| 1845 | 11,000 | | | | | | |
| 1850 | 93,000 | 7,000 7% | 1% | 1851 | 97,000 | 39,000 40% | 0% |
| 1860 | 380,000 | 120,000 31% | 15% | 1861 | 540,000 | 219,000 40% | 5% |
| 1870 | 560,000 | 211,000 37% | 11% | 1871 | 746,000 | 339,000 45% | 4% |

### QUESTIONS FOR ANALYSIS

1. How would you account for the relative numbers of women in Victoria and California and how those proportions changed over time? How might the percentage of women affect the character of the two societies?

2. Why were there no equivalents of the Ballarat Reform League and the Eureka Stockade in California, given that the two rushes were similar in so many ways and fostered similar anti-Chinese violence and legislation?

**Racial Warfare and Land Rights** Farming required arable land, and Mexican grantees and native peoples owned or claimed much of it. The American migrants brushed aside both groups, brutally eliminating the Indians and wearing down Mexican claimants with legal tactics and political pressure. The subjugation of the native peoples came first. When the gold rush began in 1848, there were about 150,000 Indians in California; by 1861, there were only 30,000. As elsewhere in the Americas, European diseases took the lives of thousands. In California, white settlers also undertook systematic campaigns of extermination,

**MAP 13.5**

**The California Gold Rush, 1849–1857**

Traveling from all parts of the world—South America, Europe, China, and Australia, as well as the eastern United States—tens of thousands of bonanza-seekers converged on the California gold-fields. Miners traveling by sea landed at San Francisco, which mushroomed into a substantial city; many other prospectors trekked overland to the goldfields on the California Trail. By the mid-1850s, the gold rush was over: almost as many people were sailing from San Francisco each year as were arriving to seek their fortune.

and local political leaders did little to stop them: "A war of extermination will continue to be waged . . . until the Indian race becomes extinct," predicted Governor Peter Burnett in 1851. Congress abetted these assaults. At the bidding of white Californians, it repudiated treaties that federal agents had negotiated with 119 tribes and that had provided the Indians with 7 million acres of land. Instead, in 1853, Congress authorized five reservations of only 25,000 acres each and refused to provide the Indians with military protection.

Consequently, some settlers simply murdered Indians to push them off nonreservation lands. The Yuki people, who lived in the Round Valley in northern California, were one target. As the *Petaluma Journal* reported in April 1857: "Within the past three weeks, from 300 to 400 bucks, squaws and children have been killed by whites." Other white Californians turned to slave trading: "Hundreds of Indians have been stolen and carried into the settlements and sold," the state's Indian Affairs superintendent reported in 1856. Labor-hungry farmers quickly put them to work. Indians were "all among us, around us, with no house and kitchen without them," recalled one farmer. Expelled from their lands and widely dispersed, many Indian peoples simply vanished as distinct communities. Those tribal communities that survived were a shadow of their former selves. In 1854, at least 5,000 Yukis lived in the Round Valley; a decade later, only 85 men and 215 women remained.

The Mexicans and Californios who held grants to thousands of acres were harder to dislodge. The Treaty of Guadalupe Hidalgo guaranteed that the property owned by Mexicans would be "inviolably respected." Although many of the 800 grants made by Spanish and Mexican authorities in California were either fraudulent or poorly documented, the Land Claims Commission created by Congress eventually upheld the validity of 75 percent of them. In the meantime, hundreds of Americans had set up farms on the sparsely settled grants. Having come of age in the antimonopoly Jacksonian era, these American squatters rejected the legitimacy of the Californios' claims to unoccupied and unimproved land and successfully pressured local land commissioners and judges to void or reduce the size of many grants. Indeed, the Americans' clamor for land was so intense and their numbers so large that many Californio claimants sold off their properties at bargain prices.

In northern California, farmers found that they could grow most eastern crops: corn and oats to feed work horses, pigs, and chickens; potatoes, beans, and

**EXPLAIN CONSEQUENCES**

What were the main changes caused by the huge increase in California's population and its composition between 1849 and 1870?

**A Californio Patriarch**

The descendant of a Spanish family that had lived—and prospered—in Mexico since the Spanish Conquest, Mariano Guadalupe Vallejo served in Mexican California as a military officer. In the 1830s and 1840s, he received land grants totaling 270,000 acres in the Sonoma Valley north of San Francisco. Vallejo, the father of seventeen children (eleven of whom survived childhood), presents himself in this photograph as a proud patriarch, surrounded by two daughters and three granddaughters. Although he favored the American conquest of 1846, Vallejo was imprisoned for a short period and subsequently suffered severe financial setbacks, losing most of his vast landholdings to squatters and rival claimants. University of California at Berkeley, Bancroft Library.

peas for the farm table; and refreshing grapes, apples, and peaches. Ranchers gradually replaced Spanish cattle with American breeds that yielded more milk and meat, which found a ready market as California's population shot up to 380,000 by 1860 and 560,000 by 1870. Most important, using the latest agricultural machinery and scores of hired workers, California farmers produced huge crops of wheat and barley, which San Francisco merchants exported to Europe at high prices. The gold rush turned into a wheat boom.

## 1850: Crisis and Compromise

The rapid settlement of California qualified it for admission to the Union. Hoping to avoid an extended debate over slavery, President Taylor advised the settlers to skip the territorial phase and immediately apply for statehood. In November 1849, Californians ratified a state constitution prohibiting slavery, and the president urged Congress to admit California as a free state.

**Constitutional Conflict**    California's bid for admission produced passionate debates in Congress and four distinct positions regarding the expansion of slavery. First, John C. Calhoun took his usual extreme stance. On the verge of death, Calhoun reiterated his deep resentment of the North's "long-continued agitation of the slavery question." To uphold southern honor (and political power), he proposed a constitutional amendment to create a dual presidency, permanently dividing executive power between the North and the South. Calhoun also advanced the radical argument that Congress had no constitutional authority to regulate slavery in the territories. Slaves were property, Calhoun insisted, and the Constitution restricted Congress's power to abrogate or limit property rights. That argument ran counter to a half century of practice: Congress had prohibited slavery in the Northwest Territory in 1787 and had extended that ban to most of the Louisiana Purchase in the Missouri Compromise of 1820. But Calhoun's assertion that **"slavery follows the flag"**— that planters could by right take their slave property into new territories—won support in the Deep South.

However, many southerners favored a second, more moderate proposal to extend the Missouri Compromise line to the Pacific Ocean. This plan won the backing of Pennsylvanian James Buchanan and other influential northern Democrats. It would guarantee slave owners access to some western territory, including a separate state in southern California.

A third alternative was squatter sovereignty— allowing settlers in a territory to decide the status of slavery. Lewis Cass had advanced this idea in 1848, and Democratic senator Stephen Douglas of Illinois now became its champion. Douglas called his plan "popular sovereignty" to link it to republican ideology, which placed ultimate power in the hands of the people (Chapter 5), and it had considerable appeal. Politicians hoped it would remove the explosive issue of slavery from Congress, and settlers welcomed the power it would give them. However, popular sovereignty was a slippery concept. Could residents accept or ban slavery when a territory was first organized? Or must they delay that decision until a territory had enough people to frame a constitution and apply for statehood? No one knew.

For their part, antislavery advocates refused to accept any plan for California or the territories that would allow slavery. Senator Salmon P. Chase of Ohio, elected by a Democratic–Free-Soil coalition, and Senator William H. Seward, a New York Whig, urged a fourth position: that federal legislation restrict slavery within its existing boundaries and eventually extinguish it completely. Condemning slavery as "morally unjust, politically unwise, and socially pernicious" and invoking "a higher law than the Constitution," Seward demanded bold action to protect freedom, "the common heritage of mankind."

**A Complex Compromise**   Standing on the brink of disaster, senior Whig and Democratic politicians worked desperately to preserve the Union. Aided by Millard Fillmore, who became president in 1850 after

Zachary Taylor's sudden death, Whig leaders Henry Clay and Daniel Webster and Democrat Stephen A. Douglas won the passage of five separate laws known collectively as the **Compromise of 1850**. To mollify the South, the compromise included a new Fugitive Slave Act giving federal support to slave catchers. To satisfy the North, the legislation admitted California as a free state, resolved a boundary dispute between New Mexico and Texas in favor of New Mexico, and abolished the slave trade (but not slavery) in the District of Columbia. Finally, the compromise organized the rest of the conquered Mexican lands into the territories of New Mexico and Utah and, invoking popular sovereignty, left the issue of slavery in the hands of their residents (Map 13.6).

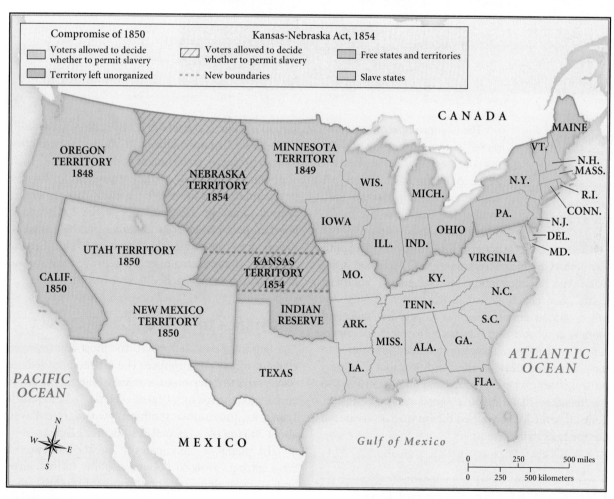

**MAP 13.6**

**The Compromise of 1850 and the Kansas-Nebraska Act of 1854**

The contest over the expansion of slavery involved vast territories. The Compromise of 1850 peacefully resolved the status of the Far West: California would be a free state, and settlers in the Utah and New Mexico territories would vote for or against slavery (the doctrine of popular sovereignty). However, the Kansas-Nebraska Act of 1854 voided the Missouri Compromise (1820) and instituted popular sovereignty in those territories. That decision sparked a bitter local war and revealed a fatal flaw in the doctrine.

**Resolving the Crisis of 1850**

By 1850, Whig Henry Clay had been in Congress for nearly four decades. Now in partnership with fellow Whig Daniel Webster and Democrat Stephen Douglas, Clay fashioned a complex—and controversial—compromise that preserved the Union. In this engraving, he addresses a crowded Senate chamber, with Webster sitting immediately to his left. Clay addresses his remarks to his prime antagonist, southern advocate John C. Calhoun, the man with the long white hair at the far right of the picture. Library of Congress.

**PLACE EVENTS IN CONTEXT**
How did the Compromise of 1850 resolve the various disputes over slavery, and who benefitted more from its terms?

The Compromise of 1850 preserved national unity by accepting once again the stipulation advanced by the South since 1787: no Union without slavery. Still, southerners feared for the future and threatened secession. Militant activists (or "fire-eaters") in South Carolina, Georgia, Mississippi, and Alabama organized special conventions to safeguard "southern rights." Georgia congressman Alexander H. Stephens called on convention delegates to prepare "men and money, arms and munitions, etc. to meet the emergency." A majority of delegates remained committed to the Union, but only on the condition that Congress protect slavery where it existed and grant statehood to any territory that ratified a proslavery constitution. Political wizardry had solved the immediate crisis, but not the underlying issues.

# The End of the Second Party System, 1850–1858

The Missouri Compromise had endured for a generation, and the architects of the Compromise of 1850 hoped their agreement would have an even longer life.

Religious leaders, conservative businessmen, and leading judges called upon citizens to support the compromise to preserve "government and civil society." Their hopes quickly faded. Demanding freedom for fugitive slaves and free soil in the West, antislavery northerners refused to accept the legitimacy of the compromise. For their part, proslavery southerners plotted to extend slavery into the West, the Caribbean, and Central America. The resulting disputes destroyed the Second Party System and deepened the crisis of the Union.

## Resistance to the Fugitive Slave Act

The Fugitive Slave Act proved the most controversial element of the compromise. The act required federal magistrates to determine the status of alleged runaways and denied them a jury trial or even the right to testify. Using its provisions, southern owners re-enslaved about 200 fugitives (as well as some free blacks).

The plight of the runaways and the presence of slave catchers aroused popular hostility in the North and Midwest. Ignoring the threat of substantial fines and prison sentences, free blacks and white abolitionists protected fugitives. In October 1850, Boston abolitionists helped two slaves escape from Georgia slave catchers. Rioters in Syracuse, New York, broke into a courthouse, freed a fugitive, and accused the U.S. marshal of kidnapping. Abandoning nonviolence,

Frederick Douglass declared, "The only way to make a Fugitive Slave Law a dead letter is to make half a dozen or more dead kidnappers." Precisely such a deadly result occurred in Christiana, Pennsylvania, in September 1851, when twenty African Americans exchanged gunfire with Maryland slave catchers, killing two of them. Federal authorities indicted thirty-six blacks and four whites for treason and other crimes, but a Pennsylvania jury acquitted one defendant, and the government dropped charges against the rest.

Harriet Beecher Stowe's novel *Uncle Tom's Cabin* (1852) boosted opposition to the Fugitive Slave Act. Conveying the moral principles of abolitionism in heartrending personal situations — using the now familiar literary trope of sentimental domesticity — Stowe's book quickly sold 310,000 copies in the United States and double that number in Britain, where it prompted an antislavery petition signed by 560,000 English women. As *Uncle Tom's Cabin* sparked an unprecedented discussion of race and slavery, state legislators in the North protested that the Fugitive Slave Act violated state sovereignty, and they passed **personal-liberty laws** that guaranteed to all residents, including alleged fugitives, the right to a jury trial. In 1857, the Wisconsin Supreme Court went further, ruling in *Ableman v. Booth* that the Fugitive Slave Act was unconstitutional because it violated the rights of Wisconsin's citizens. Taking a states' rights stance — traditionally a southern position — the Wisconsin court denied the authority of the federal judiciary to review its decision. In 1859, Chief Justice Roger B. Taney led a unanimous Supreme Court in affirming the supremacy of federal courts — a position that has withstood the test of time — and upholding the constitutionality of the Fugitive Slave Act. By then, as Frederick Douglass had hoped, popular opposition had made the law a "dead letter."

## The Whigs Disintegrate and New Parties Rise

The conflict over slavery split both major political parties along sectional lines. Hoping to unify their party, the Whigs ran another war hero, General Winfield Scott, as their presidential candidate in 1852. Among the Democrats, southerners demanded a candidate who embraced Calhoun's constitutional argument that all territories were open to slavery. However, northern and midwestern Democrats stood behind the three leading candidates — Lewis Cass of Michigan, Stephen Douglas of Illinois, and James Buchanan of Pennsylvania — who advocated popular sovereignty.

Ultimately, the party settled on Franklin Pierce of New Hampshire, a congenial man who was sympathetic to the South. As the Whig Party fragmented over slavery, Pierce swept to victory.

**IDENTIFY CAUSES**
Why did the Fugitive Slave Act fail?

**Proslavery Initiatives**  As president, Pierce pursued an expansionist foreign policy. To assist northern merchants, who wanted a commercial empire, he negotiated a trade-opening treaty with Japan. To mollify southern expansionists, who desired a plantation empire, he sought extensive Mexican lands south of the Rio Grande. Ultimately, Pierce settled for a smaller slice of land — the **Gadsden Purchase** of 1853, now part of Arizona and New Mexico — that opened the way for his negotiator, James Gadsden, to build a transcontinental rail line from New Orleans to Los Angeles.

Pierce's most controversial initiatives came in the Caribbean and Central America. Southern expansionists had long urged Cuban slave owners to declare independence from Spain and join the United States. To assist the expansionists and the American traders who still supplied enslaved Africans to Cuba, Pierce threatened war with Spain and covertly supported filibustering (private military) expeditions to Cuba. When Secretary of State William L. Marcy arranged in 1854 for American diplomats in Europe to compose the **Ostend Manifesto**, which urged Pierce to seize Cuba, northern Democrats denounced these aggressive initiatives and scuttled the planters' dreams of American expansion into the Caribbean.

**The Kansas-Nebraska Act**  The Caribbean was a sideshow. The main stage was the trans-Mississippi west, where a major controversy in 1854 destroyed the Whig Party and sent the Union spinning toward disaster. The Missouri Compromise prohibited new slave states in the Louisiana Purchase north of 36°30', so southern senators had long prevented the creation of new territories there. It remained Permanent Indian Territory. Now Senator Stephen A. Douglas of Illinois wanted to open it up, allowing a transcontinental railroad to link Chicago to California. Douglas proposed to extinguish Native American rights on the Great Plains and create a large free territory called Nebraska.

Southern politicians opposed Douglas's initiative. They hoped to extend slavery throughout the Louisiana Purchase and to have a southern city — New Orleans, Memphis, or St. Louis — as the eastern terminus of a transcontinental railroad. To win their support, Douglas amended his bill so that it explicitly repealed the Missouri Compromise and organized the region on the basis of popular sovereignty. He also agreed to the formation of two territories, Nebraska and Kansas, raising the prospect that settlers in the southern one, Kansas, would choose slavery. Knowing the revised bill would "raise a hell of a storm" in the North, Douglas argued that Kansas was not suited to plantation agriculture and would become a free state. After weeks of bitter debate, the Senate passed the **Kansas-Nebraska Act**. As 1,600 petitions opposing the bill flooded the House of Representatives, the measure barely squeaked through.

### The Republican and American Parties

The Kansas-Nebraska Act of 1854 was a disaster for the American political system. It finished off the Whig Party: "We went to bed one night old fashioned, conservative Union Whigs & and waked up stark mad abolitionists," cotton textile magnate Amos Lawrence lamented. And it crippled the Democracy, because "anti-Nebraska Democrats" denounced the act as "part of a great scheme for extending and perpetuating supremacy of the slave power." In 1854, they joined ex-Whigs, Free-Soilers, and abolitionists to form a new Republican Party.

The new party was a coalition of "strange, discordant and even hostile elements," one Republican observed. However, all its members opposed slavery, which, they argued, drove down the wages of free workers and degraded the dignity of manual labor. Like Thomas Jefferson, Republicans praised a society based on "the middling classes who own the soil and work it with their own hands." Abraham Lincoln, an ex-Whig from Illinois, conveyed the new party's vision of social mobility. "There is no permanent class of hired laborers among us," he declared, ignoring the growing social divisions in the industrializing North and Midwest. Lincoln and his fellow Republicans envisioned a society of independent farmers, artisans, and proprietors, and they celebrated middle-class values: domesticity and respectability, religious commitment, and capitalist enterprise.

The Republicans faced strong competition from the **American, or Know-Nothing, Party**, which had its origins in the anti-immigrant and anti-Catholic movements of the 1840s (Chapter 9). In 1850, these nativist societies banded together as the Order of the Star-Spangled Banner; the following year, they formed the American Party. When questioned, the party's secrecy-conscious members often replied, "I know nothing," hence the nickname. The American (or Know-Nothing) Party program was far from secret, however: party supporters wanted to mobilize native-born Protestants against the "alien menace" of Irish and German Catholics, prohibit further immigration, and institute literacy tests for voting. Northern members of the party had a strong antislavery outlook. In 1854, voters elected dozens of American Party candidates to the House of Representatives and gave the party control of the state governments of Massachusetts and Pennsylvania. The emergence of a Protestant-based nativist party to replace the Whigs became a real possibility.

### Bleeding Kansas

Meanwhile, thousands of settlers rushed into the Kansas Territory, putting Douglas's

**COMPARE AND CONTRAST**
What were the main policy objectives of the Republican and American parties?

### Armed Abolitionists in Kansas, 1859

The confrontation between North and South in Kansas took many forms. In the spring of 1859, Dr. John Doy (seated) slipped across the border into Missouri and tried to lead thirteen escaped slaves to freedom in Kansas, only to be captured and jailed in St. Joseph, Missouri. The serious-looking men standing behind Doy, well armed with guns and Bowie knives, attacked the jail and carried Doy back to Kansas. The photograph celebrated and memorialized their successful exploit. Kansas State Historical Society.

concept of popular sovereignty to the test. On the side of slavery, Missouri senator David R. Atchison encouraged residents of his state to cross temporarily into Kansas to vote in crucial elections there. Opposing Atchison was the abolitionist New England Emigrant Aid Society, which dispatched free-soilers to Kansas. In 1855, the Pierce administration accepted the legitimacy of a proslavery legislature in Lecompton, Kansas, which had been elected with aid from border-crossing Missourians. However, the majority of Kansas residents favored free soil and refused allegiance to the Lecompton government.

In 1856, both sides turned to violence, prompting Horace Greeley of the *New York Tribune* to label the territory **"Bleeding Kansas."** A proslavery force, seven hundred strong, looted and burned the free-soil town of Lawrence. The attack enraged John Brown, a fifty-six-year-old abolitionist from New York and Ohio, who commanded a free-state militia. Brown was a complex man with a record of failed businesses, but he had an intellectual and moral intensity that won the trust of influential people. Avenging the sack of Lawrence, Brown and his followers murdered five proslavery settlers at Pottawatomie. Abolitionists must "fight fire with fire" and "strike terror in the hearts of the proslavery people," Brown declared. The attack on Lawrence and the Pottawatomie killings started a guerrilla war in Kansas that took nearly two hundred lives.

## Buchanan's Failed Presidency

The violence in Kansas dominated the presidential election of 1856. The new Republican Party counted on anger over Bleeding Kansas to boost the party's fortunes. Its platform denounced the Kansas-Nebraska Act and demanded that the federal government prohibit slavery in all the territories. Republicans also called for federal subsidies for transcontinental railroads, reviving a Whig economic proposal popular among midwestern Democrats. For president, the Republicans nominated Colonel John C. Frémont, a free-soiler who had won fame in the conquest of Mexican California.

**The Election of 1856**  The American Party entered the election with equally high hopes, but like the Whigs and Democrats, it split along sectional lines over slavery. The southern faction of the American Party nominated former Whig president Millard Fillmore, while the northern contingent endorsed Frémont. During the campaign, the Republicans won the votes of many northern Know-Nothings by demanding legislation banning foreign immigrants and imposing high tariffs on foreign manufactures. As a Pennsylvania Republican put it, "Let our motto be, protection to everything American, against everything foreign." In New York, Republicans campaigned on a reform platform designed to unite "all of the Anti-Slavery, Anti-Popery and Anti-Whiskey" voters.

The Democrats reaffirmed their support for popular sovereignty and the Kansas-Nebraska Act, and they nominated James Buchanan of Pennsylvania. A tall, dignified, and experienced politician, Buchanan was staunchly prosouthern. He won the three-way race with 1.8 million popular votes (45.3 percent) and 174 electoral votes. Frémont polled 1.3 million popular votes (33.2 percent) and 114 electoral votes; Fillmore won 873,000 popular votes (21.5 percent) but captured only 8 electoral votes.

The dramatic restructuring of the political system was now apparent (Map 13.7). With the splintering of the American Party, the Republicans had replaced the Whigs as the second major party. However, Frémont had not won a single vote in the South; had he triumphed, a North Carolina newspaper warned, the result would have been "a separation of the states." The fate of the republic hinged on President Buchanan's ability to quiet the passions of the past decade and to hold the Democratic Party — the only national party — together.

**Dred Scott: Petitioner for Freedom**  Events — and his own values and weaknesses — conspired against Buchanan. Early in 1857, the Supreme Court decided the case of ***Dred Scott v. Sandford***, which raised the controversial issue of Congress's constitutional authority over slavery. Dred Scott was an enslaved African American who had lived for a time with his owner, an army surgeon, in the free state of Illinois and at Fort Snelling in the northern part of the Louisiana Purchase (then part of the Wisconsin Territory), where the Missouri Compromise (1820) prohibited slavery. Scott claimed that residence in a free state and a free territory had made him free. Buchanan opposed Scott's appeal and pressured the two justices from Pennsylvania to side with their southern colleagues. Seven of the nine justices declared that Scott was still a slave, but they disagreed on the legal rationale (Thinking Like a Historian, p. 434).

**PLACE EVENTS IN CONTEXT**
Why did northern Democratic presidents, such as Pierce and Buchanan, adopt prosouthern policies?

## Biography as History

Sometimes the life of one individual can exemplify an era, and Bridget "Biddy" Mason was such a person. Mason was born into slavery in Georgia in 1818, of mixed African American and Native American descent. In 1836, her owner gave Biddy, age eighteen, to his recently married cousins, Robert and Rebecca Smith, who owned a Mississippi plantation. Trained as a midwife, Biddy delivered all six of Rebecca's babies as well as working in the fields. Biddy herself gave birth to three daughters, probably fathered by Smith, as were at least two of her sister Hannah's eight children. In the mid-1840s, the Smiths converted to Mormonism and, in 1847, along with other Mississippi converts and their slaves, journeyed 1,700 miles to the Utah Territory.

1. **Joseph Smith's Plan to End Slavery, February 7, 1844.** *Like many Americans, members of the Church of Jesus Christ of Latter-day Saints struggled with the question of slavery. Running for president in 1844, its founder, Joseph Smith, decried the institution.*

Petition, also, ye goodly inhabitants of the slave States, your legislators to abolish slavery by the year 1850, or now. . . . Pray Congress to pay every man a reasonable price for his slaves out of the surplus revenue arising from the sale of public lands, and from the deduction of pay from the members of Congress. Break off the shackles from the poor black man, and hire him to labor like other human beings; for "an hour of virtuous liberty on earth is worth a whole eternity of bondage."

2. **Orson Hyde on slavery, the *Millennial Star*, February 15, 1851.** *Orson Hyde was an important Mormon missionary who, like most Mormons, refused to baptize slaves without their owner's permission.*

The laws of the land recognize slavery, we do not wish to oppose the laws of the country. . . . Our counsel to all our ministers in the North and South is, to avoid contention upon the subject, and to oppose no institution which the laws of the country authorize; but to labor to bring men into the Church and Kingdom of God, and teach them to do right, and honor their God in His creatures.

3. **Mormon apostle Amasa Mason Lyman and his wives.** *In 1851, at the behest of Brigham Young, five hundred Mormons—including the Robert Smiths and their slaves—moved to San Bernardino, California. They settled on land purchased from Antonio Maria Lugo, who held the 35,000 acres of the Rancho Bernardino under a Mexican grant, a claim protected by the Treaty of Guadalupe Hidalgo (1848) that ended the Mexican War. The settlement's leader was Amasa Mason Lyman, whom Biddy knew through the Smith family and whose middle name she eventually took for her surname.*

Source: George and Sadie Frey Family.

4. *Mason v. Smith*, 1856 (the Bridget "Biddy" Mason case). *Most Mormon migrants to California heeded Brigham Young's advice to free their slaves, as California was a free state. Robert Smith refused to do so and, in 1855, prepared to move to Texas. However, in 1856, members of the free black community assisted Biddy to file a habeas corpus petition and obtain freedom for herself and her extended family of thirteen women and children. In a later interview, Mason stated: "I feared this trip to Texas since I first heard of it."*

And it further appearing by satisfactory proof to the judge here, that all of the said persons of color are entitled to their freedom, and are free and cannot be held in slavery or involuntary servitude . . . And it further appearing to the satisfaction of the judge here that the said Robert Smith intended to and is about to remove from the State of California where slavery does not exist, to the State of Texas, where slavery of Negroes and persons of color does exist, and is established by the municipal laws, and intends to remove the said before-mentioned persons of color, to his own use without the free will and consent of all or any of the said persons of color, whereby their liberty will be greatly jeopardized, and there is good reason to apprehend and believe that they may be sold into slavery or involuntary servitude . . . and it further appearing that none of the said persons of color can read and write, and are almost entirely ignorant of the laws of the state of California as well as those of the State of Texas, and of their rights and that the said Robert Smith, from his past relations to them as members of his family does possess and exercise over them an undue influence in respect to the matter of their said removal insofar that they have been in duress and not in possession and exercise of their free will so as to give a binding consent to any engagement or arrangement with him.

5. **Photograph of Biddy Mason and the deed of her first land purchase, 1866.** *Once free, Biddy prospered as a midwife and an investor in Los Angeles real estate. When she died in 1891, Biddy had accumulated a fortune of $300,000 (about $7.6 million today). Despite her contact with Mormonism, Biddy Mason never joined the Mormon church. Instead, in 1872 she was a founding member of the first African Methodist Episcopal (AME) Church in Los Angeles. An active philanthropist of charitable causes, she funded a traveler's aid society and an elementary school for black children.*

Source: Los Angeles Public Library.

Sources: (1) *History of the Church of Jesus Christ of Latter-Day Saints*, Vol. VI (Salt Lake City, UT: Mormon Church, 1912), 205; (2) *The Latter-Day Saints' Millennial Star*, Vol. XIII (Liverpool: Franklin D. Richards, 1851), 63; (4) Golden State Insurance Company Records, UCLA, Dept. of Special Collections, Charles E. Young Research Library.

## ANALYZING THE EVIDENCE

1. Were Smith's and Hyde's positions on slavery and property rights (sources 1 and 2) similar or different?

2. How might the set of photographs of Amasa Mason Lyman and his wives (source 3) suggest that Mormon family life resembled Biddy's experience in growing up on a southern plantation? How might it mirror her own sexual experience, and that of her sister Hannah, as Robert Smith's slaves?

3. As a slave, Biddy did not have a surname. Why might have she taken Lyman's middle name as her surname when she became free in 1856?

4. How does the ruling in Biddy's case (source 4) by Judge Benjamin Ignatius Hayes, in a California state court, reflect the political and constitutional turmoil that westward expansion created with regard to slavery? How is this ruling similar to, and different from, the famous case brought by Dred Scott in Missouri and decided eventually by the U.S. Supreme Court in *Dred Scott v. Sandford* (1857)?

5. What do you think explains Biddy Mason's religious choices and charitable activities as described in the headnote to source 5?

## PUTTING IT ALL TOGETHER

List the main themes and arguments presented in Chapters 12 and 13. Then, write an essay that explores the ways in which Biddy Mason's experiences—plantation labor in Georgia and Mississippi, coerced miscegenation, exposure to the new religion of Mormonism, a trek by foot across a continent, legally won emancipation, and entrepreneurial success in formerly Mexican California—either exemplify or are inconsistent with those themes and arguments.

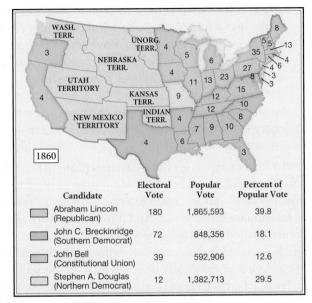

**MAP 13.7**

**Political Realignment, 1848 and 1860**

In the presidential election of 1848, both the Whig and Democratic candidates won electoral votes throughout the nation. Subsequently, the political conflict over slavery and the Compromise of 1850 destroyed the Whig Party in the South. As the only nationwide party, the Democrats won easily over the Whigs in 1852 and, with the opposition split between the Republican and American parties, triumphed in 1856 as well. However, a new region-based party system appeared by 1860 and persisted for the next seventy years—with Democrats dominant in the South and Republicans usually controlling the Northeast, Midwest, and Far West.

Chief Justice Roger B. Taney of Maryland, a slave owner himself, wrote the most influential opinion. He declared that Negroes, whether enslaved or free, could not be citizens of the United States and that Scott therefore had no right to sue in federal court. That argument was controversial, given that free blacks were citizens in many states and therefore had access to the federal courts. Taney then made two even more controversial claims. First, he endorsed John C. Calhoun's argument that the Fifth Amendment, which prohibited "taking" of property without due process of law, meant that Congress could not prevent southern citizens from moving their slave property into the territories and owning it there. Consequently, the chief justice concluded, the provisions of the Northwest Ordinance and the Missouri Compromise that prohibited slavery had never been constitutional. Second, Taney declared that Congress could not give to territorial governments any powers that it did not possess, such as the authority to prohibit slavery. Taney thereby endorsed Calhoun's interpretation of popular sovereignty: only when settlers wrote a constitution and requested statehood could they prohibit slavery.

In a single stroke, Taney had declared the Republican proposals to restrict the expansion of slavery through legislation to be unconstitutional. The Republicans could never accept the legitimacy of Taney's constitutional arguments, which indeed had significant flaws. Led by Senator Seward of New York, they accused the chief justice and President Buchanan of participating in the Slave Power conspiracy.

Buchanan then added fuel to the raging constitutional fire. Ignoring reports that antislavery residents held a clear majority in Kansas, he refused to allow a popular vote on the proslavery Lecompton constitution and in 1858 strongly urged Congress to admit Kansas as a slave state. Angered by Buchanan's machinations, Stephen Douglas, the most influential Democratic senator and architect of the Kansas-Nebraska Act, broke with the president and persuaded Congress to deny statehood to Kansas. (Kansas would enter the Union as a free state in 1861.) Still determined to aid the South, Buchanan resumed negotiations to buy Cuba in December 1858. By pursuing a proslavery agenda—first in *Dred Scott* and then in Kansas and Cuba—Buchanan widened the split in his party and the nation.

# Abraham Lincoln and the Republican Triumph, 1858–1860

As the Democratic Party split along sectional lines, the Republicans gained support in the North and Midwest. Abraham Lincoln of Illinois emerged as the only Republican leader whose policies and temperament might have saved the Union. However, few southerners trusted Lincoln, and his presidential candidacy revived secessionist agitation.

## Lincoln's Political Career

The middle-class world of storekeepers, lawyers, and entrepreneurs in the small towns of the Ohio River Valley shaped Lincoln's early career. He came from a hardscrabble yeoman farm family that was continually on the move — from Kentucky, where Lincoln was born in 1809, to Indiana, and then to Illinois. In 1831, Lincoln rejected his father's life as a subsistence farmer and became a store clerk in New Salem, Illinois. Socially ambitious, Lincoln won entry to the middle class by mastering its culture; he joined the New Salem Debating Society, read Shakespeare, and studied law.

Admitted to the bar in 1837, Lincoln moved to Springfield, the new state capital. There, he met Mary Todd, the cultured daughter of a Kentucky banker; they married in 1842. Her tastes were aristocratic; his were humble. She was volatile; he was easygoing but suffered bouts of depression that tried her patience and tested his character.

**An Ambitious Politician** Lincoln's ambition was "a little engine that knew no rest," a close associate remarked, and it propelled him into politics. An admirer of Henry Clay, Lincoln joined the Whig Party and won election to four terms in the Illinois legislature, where he promoted education, banks, canals, and railroads. He became a dexterous party politician, adept in the use of patronage and the passage of legislation.

In 1846, the rising lawyer-politician won election to a Congress that was bitterly divided over the Wilmot Proviso. Lincoln believed that human bondage was unjust but doubted that the federal government had the constitutional authority to tamper with slavery. With respect to the Mexican War, he took a middle ground by voting for military appropriations but also for the Wilmot Proviso's ban on slavery in any acquired territories. Lincoln also introduced legislation that

**Abraham Lincoln, 1859**
Lincoln was not a handsome man, and he photographed poorly. His campaign managers had this photo—and many others—retouched to soften Lincoln's features. However, no photograph, no matter how realistic, captured Lincoln's complex personality and wit or the intensity of his spirit and intellect. To grasp Lincoln, it is necessary to read his words. Chicago History Museum.

would require the gradual (and thus compensated) emancipation of slaves in the District of Columbia. To avoid future racial strife, he favored the colonization of freed blacks in Africa or South America. Both abolitionists and proslavery activists heaped scorn on Lincoln's middle-of-the-road policies, and he lost his bid for reelection. Dismayed by the rancor of ideological debate, he withdrew from politics and prospered as a lawyer by representing railroads and manufacturers.

Lincoln returned to the political fray because of the Kansas-Nebraska Act. Shocked by the act's repeal of the Missouri Compromise and Senator Douglas's advocacy of popular sovereignty, Lincoln reaffirmed his opposition to slavery in the territories. He now likened slavery to a cancer that had to be cut out if the nation's republican ideals and moral principles were to endure.

**The Lincoln-Douglas Debates** Abandoning the Whigs, Lincoln quickly emerged as the leading Republican in Illinois, and in 1858 he ran for the U.S. Senate seat held by Douglas. Lincoln pointed out that the proslavery Supreme Court might soon declare that the Constitution "does not permit a state to exclude slavery," just as it had decided in *Dred Scott* that "neither Congress nor the territorial legislature" could ban slavery in a territory. In that event, he warned, "we shall awake to the reality . . . that the Supreme Court has made Illinois a slave state." This prospect informed Lincoln's famous "House Divided" speech. Quoting the biblical adage "A house divided against itself cannot stand," he predicted that American society "cannot endure permanently half slave and half free. . . . It will become all one thing, or all the other."

The Senate race in Illinois attracted national interest because of Douglas's prominence and Lincoln's reputation as a formidable speaker. During a series of seven debates, Douglas declared his support for white supremacy: "This government was made by our fathers, by white men for the benefit of white men," he said, attacking Lincoln for supporting "negro equality." Lincoln parried Douglas's racist attacks by arguing that free blacks should have equal economic opportunities but not equal political rights. Taking the offensive, he asked how Douglas could accept the *Dred Scott* decision (which protected slave property in the territories) yet advocate popular sovereignty (which allowed settlers to exclude slavery). Douglas responded with the so-called **Freeport Doctrine**: that a territory's residents could exclude slavery by not adopting laws to protect it. That position pleased neither proslavery nor antislavery advocates. Nonetheless, when Democrats won a narrow majority in the state legislature, they reelected Douglas to the U.S. Senate.

> **UNDERSTAND POINTS OF VIEW**
>
> What was Lincoln's position on slavery and people of African descent during the 1840s and 1850s?

## The Union Under Siege

The debates with Douglas gave Lincoln a national reputation, and in the election of 1858 the Republican Party won control of the U.S. House of Representatives.

**The Rise of Radicalism**   Shaken by the Republicans' advance, southern Democrats divided again into moderates and fire-eaters. The moderates, who included Senator Jefferson Davis of Mississippi, strongly defended "southern rights" and demanded ironclad political or constitutional protections for slavery. The fire-eaters — men such as Robert Barnwell Rhett of South Carolina and William Lowndes Yancey of Alabama — repudiated the Union and actively promoted secession. Radical antislavery northerners likewise took a strong stance.

Senator Seward of New York declared that freedom and slavery were locked in "an irrepressible conflict," and ruthless abolitionist John Brown, who had perpetrated the Pottawatomie massacre, showed what that might mean. In October 1859, Brown led eighteen heavily armed black and white men in a raid on the federal arsenal at Harpers Ferry, Virginia. Brown hoped to arm slaves with the arsenal's weapons and mount a major rebellion to end slavery.

Republican leaders condemned Brown's unsuccessful raid, but Democrats called his plot "a natural, logical, inevitable result of the doctrines and teachings of the Republican party." When the state of Virginia sentenced Brown to be hanged, transcendentalist reformers Henry David Thoreau and Ralph Waldo Emerson (Chapter 11) proclaimed him a "saint awaiting his martyrdom." The slaveholding states looked to the future with terror. "The aim of the present black republican organization is the destruction of the social system of the Southern States," warned one newspaper. Once Republicans came to power, another cautioned, they "would create insurrection and servile war in the South — they would put the torch to our dwellings and the knife to our throats."

Nor could the South count any longer on the Democratic Party to protect its interests. At the party's convention in April 1860, northern Democrats rejected Jefferson Davis's proposal to protect slavery in the territories, and delegates from eight southern states quit the meeting. At a second Democratic convention, northern and midwestern delegates nominated Stephen Douglas for president; meeting separately, southern Democrats nominated the sitting vice president, John C. Breckinridge of Kentucky.

**The Election of 1860**   With the Democrats divided, the Republicans sensed victory. They courted white voters with a free-soil platform that opposed both slavery and racial equality: "Missouri for white men and white men for Missouri," declared that state's Republican platform. The national Republican convention chose Lincoln as its presidential candidate because he was more moderate on slavery than the best-known Republicans, Senators William Seward of New York and Salmon Chase of Ohio. Lincoln also conveyed a compelling egalitarian image that appealed to smallholding farmers, wage earners, and midwestern voters.

The Republican strategy worked. Although Lincoln received less than 1 percent of the popular vote in the South and only 40 percent of the national poll, he won every northern and western state except New Jersey, giving him 180 (of 303) electoral votes and an absolute

**THE NATIONAL GAME. THREE "OUTS" AND ONE "RUN".**
ABRAHAM WINNING THE BALL.

**Lincoln on Home Base**

Beginning in the 1820s, the language and imagery of sports penetrated politics, cutting across the lines of class and party. Wielding a long, bat-like rail labeled "EQUAL RIGHTS AND FREE TERRITORY," Abraham Lincoln holds a baseball and appears ready to score a victory in the election. His three opponents—from left to right, John Bell (the candidate of a new Constitutional Union Party), Stephen A. Douglas, and John C. Breckinridge—will soon be "out." Indeed, according to the pro-Lincoln cartoonist, they were about to be "skunk'd." As Douglas laments, their attempt to put a "short stop" to Lincoln's presidential ambitions had failed. Museum of American Political Life.

majority in the electoral college. Breckinridge took 72 electoral votes by sweeping the Deep South and picking up Delaware, Maryland, and North Carolina. Douglas won 30 percent of the popular ballot but secured only 51 electoral votes in Missouri and New Jersey. The Republicans had united voters in the Northeast, Midwest, and Pacific coast behind free soil.

A revolution was in the making. "Oh My God!!! This morning heard that Lincoln was elected," Keziah Brevard, a widowed South Carolina plantation mistress and owner of two hundred slaves, scribbled in her diary. "Lord save us." Slavery had permeated the

American federal republic so thoroughly that southerners saw it as a natural part of the constitutional order—an order that was now under siege. Fearful of a massive black uprising, Chief Justice Taney recalled "the horrors of St. Domingo [Haiti]." At the very least, warned John Townsend of South Carolina, a Republican administration in Washington would suppress "the inter-State slave trade" and thereby "cripple this vital Southern institution of slavery." To

**PLACE EVENTS IN CONTEXT**

What was the relationship between the collapse of the Second Party System and the Republican victory in the election of 1860?

many southerners, it seemed time to think carefully about Lincoln's 1858 statement that the Union must "become all one thing, or all the other."

 To see a longer excerpt of Keziah Brevard's diary, along with other primary sources from this period, see *Sources for America's History*.

## SUMMARY

In this chapter, we examined four related themes: the ideology of Manifest Destiny and the westward movement of Americans in the 1840s, the impact of American traders and settlers on the Indian peoples of the Great Plains and California, the causes and consequences of the Mexican War (1846–1848), and the disintegration of the Second Party System during the 1850s.

We saw that the determination of Presidents John Tyler and James Polk to add territory and slave states to the Union pushed the United States into the Mexican War and into a new debate over the expansion of slavery. To resolve the resulting crisis, Henry Clay, Daniel Webster, and Stephen Douglas devised the Compromise of 1850. Their efforts were in vain: antislavery northerners defied the Fugitive Slave Act, and expansionist-minded southerners sought new slave states in the Caribbean. Ideology (the pursuit of absolutes) replaced politics (the art of compromise) as the ruling principle of American political life.

The Second Party System rapidly disintegrated. The Whig Party vanished, and two issue-oriented parties, the nativist American Party and the antislavery Republican Party, competed for its members. As the Republicans gained strength, the Democratic Party splintered into sectional factions over Bleeding Kansas and other slavery-related issues. The stage was set for Lincoln's victory in the climactic election of 1860.

# CHAPTER REVIEW

 **MAKE IT STICK**   Go to **LearningCurve** to retain what you've read.

## TERMS TO KNOW   Identify and explain the significance of each term below.

### Key Concepts and Events

**Manifest Destiny** (p. 412)

**Californios** (p. 415)

**"Fifty-four forty or fight!"** (p. 418)

**conscience Whigs** (p. 421)

**Wilmot Proviso** (p. 421)

**free-soil movement** (p. 421)

**squatter sovereignty** (p. 424)

**forty-niners** (p. 425)

**"slavery follows the flag"** (p. 428)

**Compromise of 1850** (p. 429)

**personal-liberty laws** (p. 431)

**Gadsden Purchase** (p. 431)

**Ostend Manifesto** (p. 431)

**Kansas-Nebraska Act** (p. 432)

**American, or Know-Nothing, Party** (p. 432)

**"Bleeding Kansas"** (p. 433)

*Dred Scott v. Sandford* (p. 433)

**Freeport Doctrine** (p. 438)

### Key People

**James K. Polk** (p. 418)

**Frederick Douglass** (p. 421)

**Zachary Taylor** (p. 424)

**Lewis Cass** (p. 424)

**Stephen Douglas** (p. 431)

**Harriet Beecher Stowe** (p. 431)

**John Brown** (p. 433)

**Abraham Lincoln** (p. 437)

## REVIEW QUESTIONS   Answer these questions to demonstrate your understanding of the chapter's main ideas.

1. In what specific ways did the ideology of Manifest Destiny influence events during the 1840s and 1850s?

2. What were the main constitutional arguments presented during the debate over slavery in the territories? Which of those arguments influenced Chief Justice Taney's opinion in *Dred Scott*?

3. How did the Compromise of 1850, the Kansas-Nebraska Act, and the *Dred Scott* decision seek to address the issue of slavery, and what was the effect of each of them on sectional conflicts?

4. **THEMATIC UNDERSTANDING**   Some historians claim that the mistakes of a "blundering generation" of political leaders led, by 1860, to the imminent breakup of the Union. Using the events from "Politics and Power" on the thematic timeline on page 409, explain why you agree or disagree.

## MAKING CONNECTIONS   Recognize the larger developments and continuities within and across chapters by answering these questions.

1. **ACROSS TIME AND PLACE**   How were the American territorial acquisitions of the 1840s similar to, and/or different from, those of the Louisiana Purchase and the Paris Treaty of 1783 (discussed in Chapters 6 and 7)?

2. **VISUAL EVIDENCE**   In *American Progress* (p. 411), why does John Gast choose Liberty to lead the republic westward? How does he interpret the American experience, and what stories does he tell in the image's foreground, middle ground, and background? How does the evidence in the chapter challenge Gast's interpretation of westward expansion?

## MORE TO EXPLORE   Start here to learn more about the events discussed in this chapter.

Eric Foner, *Free Soil, Free Labor, Free Men* (1970). Still offers the best analysis of the ideology of the Republican Party.

Patricia Nelson Limerick, *The Legacy of Conquest* (1989). Highlights social conflicts in the West.

William A. Link, *Roots of Secession* (2003). A good state-focused study about the causes of secession.

Stephen Oates, *With Malice Toward None* (1977). A classic biography about Lincoln.

Leonard L. Richards, *The Slave Power: The Free North and Southern Domination, 1780–1860* (2000). Offers a broad cultural analysis.

The PBS documentary *The West* and its Web site (**pbs .org/weta/thewest**) offer a comprehensive history of the West, and the PBS Web site on the *U.S.-Mexican War: 1846–1848* (**pbs.org/usmexicanwar**) covers both American and Mexican perspectives of this pivotal event.

## TIMELINE
Ask yourself why this chapter begins and ends with these dates and then identify the links among related events.

| | |
|---|---|
| **1844** | • James Polk elected president |
| **1845** | • Texas admitted into Union |
| **1846** | • United States declares war on Mexico<br>• Treaty with Britain divides Oregon Country<br>• Wilmot Proviso approved by House but not by Senate |
| **1847** | • American troops capture Mexico City |
| **1848** | • Gold found in California<br>• Treaty of Guadalupe Hidalgo transfers Mexican lands to United States<br>• Free-Soil Party forms |
| **1850** | • President Taylor dies<br>• Millard Fillmore assumes presidency<br>• Compromise of 1850 preserves Union<br>• Northern abolitionists reject Fugitive Slave Act |
| **1851** | • American (Know-Nothing) Party forms |
| **1852** | • Harriet Beecher Stowe publishes *Uncle Tom's Cabin* |
| **1854** | • Ostend Manifesto urges seizure of Cuba<br>• Kansas-Nebraska Act tests policy of popular sovereignty<br>• Republican Party forms |
| **1856** | • Turmoil in Kansas undermines popular sovereignty<br>• James Buchanan elected president |
| **1857** | • *Dred Scott v. Sandford* allows slavery in U.S. territories |
| **1858** | • President Buchanan urges Congress to admit Kansas under the proslavery Lecompton constitution and seeks to buy and annex Cuba as a slave state<br>• Abraham Lincoln debates Stephen Douglas for U.S. Senate seat |
| **1859** | • John Brown raids federal arsenal at Harpers Ferry |
| **1860** | • Abraham Lincoln elected president in four-way contest |

**KEY TURNING POINT:** Three new political parties appeared in the six years from 1848 to 1854: Free-Soil, American (Know-Nothing), and Republican. What accounts for this upsurge in political activity, and what was its result?

# 14
## CHAPTER

# Two Societies at War
# 1861–1865

**IDENTIFY THE BIG IDEA**
How did the military and political goals of the war bring significant changes to social, economic, and cultural life?

"What a scene it was," Union soldier Elisha Hunt Rhodes wrote in his diary at Gettysburg in July 1863. "Oh the dead and the dying on this bloody field." Thousands of men had already died, and the slaughter would continue for two more years. "Why is it that 200,000 men of one blood and tongue . . . [are] seeking one another's lives?" asked Confederate lieutenant R. M. Collins as another gruesome battle ended. "We could settle our differences by compromising and all be at home in ten days." But there was no compromise. "God wills this contest, and wills that it shall not yet end," President Abraham Lincoln reflected. "The Almighty has His own purposes."

While the reasons for the war are complex, racial slavery played a primary role. To southern whites, the Republican victory in 1860 presented an immediate danger to the slave-owning republic that had existed since 1776. "[O]ur struggle is for inherited rights," declared one southern leader. Southerners did not believe Lincoln when he promised not "directly or indirectly, to interfere with the institution of slavery in the States where it exists." Soon, a southern senator warned, "cohorts of Federal office-holders, Abolitionists, may be sent into [our] midst" to encourage slave revolts and, even worse, racial mixture. By *racial mixture*, white southerners meant sexual relations between black men and white women, given that white masters had already fathered untold thousands of children by their enslaved black women. "Better, far better! [to] endure all horrors of civil war," insisted a Confederate recruit, "than to see the dusky sons of Ham leading the fair daughters of the South to the altar." To preserve black subordination and white supremacy, radical southerners chose the dangerous enterprise of secession.

Lincoln and the North would not let them go in peace. Living in a world still ruled by monarchies, northern leaders believed that the collapse of the American Union might forever destroy the possibility of democratic republican governments. "We cannot escape history," Lincoln eloquently declared. "We shall nobly save, or meanly lose, the last best hope of earth."

And so came the conflict. Called the War Between the States by southerners and the War of the Rebellion by northerners, the struggle finally resolved the great issues of the Union and slavery. The costs were terrible: more American lives lost than the combined total for all the nation's other wars, and a century-long legacy of bitterness between the triumphant North and the vanquished white South.

**Fields of Death**   Fought with mass armies and new weapons, the Civil War took a huge toll in human lives, as evidenced by this grisly photograph of a small section of the battlefield at Antietam, Maryland. The most costly single-day battle in American history, it left 22,700 dead, wounded, and missing Confederate and Union soldiers. After the equally bloody three-day battle at Shiloh, Tennessee, in April 1862, General Ulysses Grant surveyed a field "so covered with dead that it would have been possible to walk . . . in any direction, stepping on dead bodies, without a foot touching the ground." Library of Congress.

# Secession and Military Stalemate, 1861–1862

Following Lincoln's election in November 1860, secessionist fervor swept through the Deep South. Veteran party leaders in Washington still hoped to save the Union. In the four months between Lincoln's election and his inauguration on March 4, 1861, they sought a new compromise.

## The Secession Crisis

The Union collapsed first in South Carolina, the home of John C. Calhoun, nullification, and southern rights. Robert Barnwell Rhett and other fire-eaters had demanded secession since the Compromise of 1850, and their goal was now within reach. "Our enemies are about to take possession of the Government," warned one South Carolinian. Frightened by that prospect, a state convention voted unanimously on December 20, 1860, to dissolve "the union now subsisting between South Carolina and other States."

**The Lower South Secedes**    Fire-eaters elsewhere in the Deep South quickly called similar conventions and organized mobs to attack local Union supporters. In early January, white Mississippians joyously enacted a secession ordinance, and Florida, Alabama, Georgia, and Louisiana quickly followed. Texans soon joined them, ousting Unionist governor Sam Houston and ignoring his warning that "the North . . . will overwhelm the South" (Map 14.1). In February, the jubilant secessionists met in Montgomery, Alabama, to proclaim a new nation: the Confederate States of America. Adopting a provisional constitution, the delegates named Mississippian Jefferson Davis, a former U.S. senator and secretary of war, as the Confederacy's president and Georgia congressman Alexander Stephens as vice president.

Secessionist fervor was less intense in the four states of the Middle South (Virginia, North Carolina, Tennessee, and Arkansas), where there were fewer slaves. White opinion was especially divided in the four border slave states (Maryland, Delaware, Kentucky, and Missouri), where yeomen farmers held greater political power and, from bitter experience as well as the writings of journalist Hilton Helper, knew that all too often "the slaveholders . . . have hoodwinked you." Reflecting such sentiments, the legislatures of Virginia and Tennessee refused to join the secessionist movement and urged a compromise.

**Alabama Secession Flag**

In January 1861, a Secession Convention in Alabama voted to leave the Union and marked their decision for independence by designating this pennant—created by a group of Montgomery women—as their official flag. Like John Gast's *American Progress* (p. 411), the Goddess of Liberty forms the central image. Here she holds a sword and a flag with a single star, symbolizing Alabama's new status as an independent republic. Alabama Department of Archives and History.

Meanwhile, the Union government floundered. President Buchanan declared secession illegal but—in line with his states' rights outlook—claimed that the federal government lacked authority to restore the Union by force. Buchanan's timidity prompted South Carolina's new government to demand the surrender of Fort Sumter (a federal garrison in Charleston Harbor) and to cut off its supplies. The president again backed down, refusing to use the navy to supply the fort.

**The Crittenden Compromise**    Instead, the outgoing president urged Congress to find a compromise. The plan proposed by Senator John J. Crittenden of Kentucky received the most support. The **Crittenden Compromise** had two parts. The first, which Congress approved, called for a constitutional amendment to protect slavery from federal interference in any state where it already existed. Crittenden's second provision called for the westward extension of the Missouri Compromise line (36°30' north latitude) to the California border. The provision would ban slavery north of the line and allow bound labor to the south, including any territories "hereafter acquired," raising the prospect of expansion into Cuba or Central America. Congressional Republicans rejected Crittenden's second proposal on strict instructions from president-elect Lincoln. With good reason, Lincoln feared it

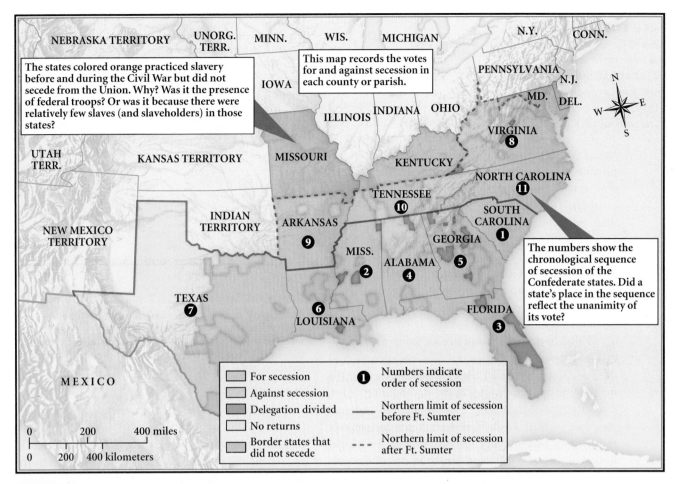

The states colored orange practiced slavery before and during the Civil War but did not secede from the Union. Why? Was it the presence of federal troops? Or was it because there were relatively few slaves (and slaveholders) in those states?

This map records the votes for and against secession in each county or parish.

The numbers show the chronological sequence of secession of the Confederate states. Did a state's place in the sequence reflect the unanimity of its vote?

| | For secession | ❶ | Numbers indicate order of secession |
| | Against secession | | |
| | Delegation divided | | Northern limit of secession before Ft. Sumter |
| | No returns | | |
| | Border states that did not secede | - - - | Northern limit of secession after Ft. Sumter |

0    200    400 miles
0    200    400 kilometers

**MAP 14.1**

**The Process of Secession, 1860–1861**

The states of the Lower South had the highest concentration of slaves, and they led the secessionist movement. After the attack on Fort Sumter in April 1861, the states of the Upper South joined the Confederacy. Yeomen farmers in Tennessee and the backcountry of Alabama, Georgia, and Virginia opposed secession but, except in the future state of West Virginia, initially rallied to the Confederate cause. Consequently, the South entered the Civil War with its white population relatively united.

would unleash new imperialist adventures. "I want Cuba," Senator Albert G. Brown of Mississippi had candidly stated in 1858. "I want Tamaulipas, Potosi, and one or two other Mexican States . . . for the planting or spreading of slavery." In 1787, 1821, and 1850, the North and South had resolved their differences over slavery. In 1861, there would be no compromise.

In his March 1861 inaugural address, Lincoln carefully outlined his positions. He promised to safeguard slavery where it existed but vowed to prevent its expansion. Equally important, the Republican president declared that the Union was "perpetual"; consequently, the secession of the Confederate states was illegal. Lincoln asserted his intention to "hold, occupy, and possess" federal property in the seceded states and "to

collect duties and imposts" there. If military force was necessary to preserve the Union, Lincoln—like Democrat Andrew Jackson during the nullification crisis—would use it. The choice was the South's: Return to the Union, or face war.

## The Upper South Chooses Sides

The South's decision came quickly. When Lincoln dispatched an unarmed ship to resupply Fort Sumter, Jefferson Davis and his associates in the Provisional Government of the Confederate States decided to seize the fort. The Confederate forces opened fire on April 12, with ardent fire-eater Edmund Ruffin supposedly firing the first cannon. Two days later, the Union

**PLACE EVENTS
IN CONTEXT**
How important was the
conflict at Fort Sumter, and
would the Confederacy—
or the Union—have gone
to war without it?

defenders capitulated. On April 15, Lincoln called 75,000 state militiamen into federal service for ninety days to put down an insurrection "too powerful to be suppressed by the ordinary course of judicial proceedings."

Northerners responded to Lincoln's call to arms with wild enthusiasm. Asked to provide thirteen regiments of volunteers, Republican governor William Dennison of Ohio sent twenty. Many northern Democrats also lent their support. "Every man must be for the United States or against it," Democratic leader Stephen Douglas declared. "There can be no neutrals in this war, only patriots—or traitors." How then could the Democratic Party function as a "loyal opposition," supporting the Union while challenging certain Republican policies? It would not be an easy task.

Whites in the Middle and Border South now had to choose between the Union and the Confederacy, and their decision was crucial. Those eight states accounted for two-thirds of the whites in the slaveholding states, three-fourths of their industrial production, and well over half of their food. They were home to many of the nation's best military leaders, including Colonel Robert E. Lee of Virginia, a career officer whom veteran General Winfield Scott recommended to Lincoln to lead the new Union army. Those states were also geographically strategic. Kentucky, with its 500-mile border on the Ohio River, was essential to the movement of troops and supplies. Maryland was vital to the Union's security because it bordered the nation's capital on three sides.

The weight of its history as a slave-owning society decided the outcome in Virginia. On April 17, 1861, a convention approved secession by a vote of 88 to 55, with the dissenters concentrated in the state's yeomen-dominated northwestern counties. Elsewhere, Virginia whites embraced the Confederate cause. "The North was the aggressor," declared Richmond lawyer William Poague as he enlisted. "The South resisted her invaders." Refusing General Scott's offer of the Union command, Robert E. Lee resigned from the U.S. Army. "Save in defense of my native state," Lee told Scott, "I never desire again to draw my sword." Arkansas, Tennessee, and North Carolina quickly joined Virginia in the Confederacy.

Lincoln moved aggressively to hold strategic areas where

**IDENTIFY CAUSES**
Per Figure 14.1, was slave
ownership in a state the
main cause of early secession? What other factors
drove the secession move-
ment?

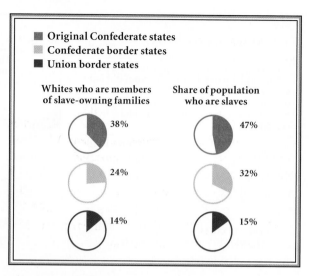

**FIGURE 14.1**
**Slavery and Secession**
As the pie charts indicate, slave labor dominated the economies of the Confederate states that initially seceded from the Union, but it was much less important in Confederate states further to the north that seceded later.

relatively few whites owned slaves (Figure 14.1). To secure the railway line connecting Washington to the Ohio River Valley, the president ordered General George B. McClellan to take control of northwestern Virginia. In October 1861, yeomen there voted overwhelmingly to create a breakaway territory, West Virginia. Unwilling to "act like madmen and cut our own throats merely to sustain . . . a most unwarrantable rebellion," West Virginia joined the Union in 1863. Unionists also carried the day in Delaware. In Maryland, where slavery was still entrenched, a pro-Confederate mob attacked Massachusetts troops traveling through Baltimore, causing the war's first combat deaths: four soldiers and twelve civilians. When Maryland secessionists destroyed railroad bridges and telegraph lines, Lincoln ordered Union troops to occupy the state and arrest Confederate sympathizers, including legislators. He released them only in November 1861, after Unionists had secured control of Maryland's government.

Lincoln was equally energetic in the Mississippi River Valley. To win control of Missouri (and the adjacent Missouri and Upper Mississippi rivers), Lincoln mobilized the state's German American militia, which strongly opposed slavery. In July, the German Americans defeated a force of Confederate sympathizers commanded by the state's governor. Despite continuing raids by Confederate guerrilla bands, which included the notorious outlaws Jesse and Frank James, the Union retained control of Missouri.

In Kentucky, where secessionist and Unionist sentiment was evenly balanced, Lincoln moved cautiously. He allowed Kentucky's thriving trade with the Confederacy to continue until August 1861, when Unionists took over the state government. When the Confederacy responded to the trade cutoff by invading Kentucky in September, Illinois volunteers commanded by Ulysses S. Grant drove them out. Mixing military force with political persuasion, Lincoln had kept four border states (Delaware, Maryland, Missouri, and Kentucky) and the northwestern portion of Virginia in the Union.

## Setting War Objectives and Devising Strategies

Speaking as provisional president of the Confederacy in April 1861, Jefferson Davis identified the Confederates' cause with that of the Patriots of 1776: like their grandfathers, he said, white southerners were fighting for the "sacred right of self-government." The Confederacy sought "no conquest, no aggrandizement . . . ; all we ask is to be let alone." Davis's renunciation of expansion was probably a calculated short-run policy; after all, the quest to extend slavery into Kansas and Cuba had sparked Lincoln's election. Still, this decision simplified the Confederacy's military strategy; it needed only to defend its boundaries to achieve independence. Ignoring strong antislavery sentiment among potential European allies, the Confederate constitution explicitly ruled out gradual emancipation or any other law "denying or impairing the right of property in negro slaves." Indeed, Confederate vice president Alexander Stephens insisted that his nation's "cornerstone rests upon the great truth that the Negro is not equal to the white man, that slavery— subordination to the superior race—is his natural or normal condition."

Lincoln responded to Davis in a speech to Congress on July 4, 1861. He portrayed secession as an attack on representative government, America's great contribution to world history. The issue, Lincoln declared, was "whether a constitutional republic" had the will and the means to "maintain its territorial integrity against a domestic foe." Determined to crush the rebellion, Lincoln rejected General Winfield Scott's strategy of peaceful persuasion through economic sanctions and a naval blockade. Instead, he insisted on an aggressive military campaign to restore the Union.

**Union Thrusts Toward Richmond**  Lincoln hoped that a quick strike against the Confederate capital of Richmond, Virginia, would end the rebellion. Many northerners were equally optimistic. "What a picnic," thought one New York volunteer, "to go down South for three months and clean up the whole business." So in July 1861, Lincoln ordered General Irvin McDowell's army of 30,000 men to attack General P. G. T. Beauregard's force of 20,000 troops at Manassas, a Virginia rail junction 30 miles southwest of Washington. McDowell launched a strong assault near Bull Run, but panic swept his troops when the Confederate soldiers counterattacked, shouting the hair-raising "rebel yell." "The peculiar corkscrew sensation that it sends down your backbone . . . can never be told," one Union veteran wrote. "You have to feel it." McDowell's troops— and the many civilians who had come to observe the battle—retreated in disarray to Washington.

The Confederate victory at Bull Run showed the strength of the rebellion. Lincoln replaced McDowell with General George McClellan and enlisted a million men to serve for three years in the new Army of the Potomac. A cautious military engineer, McClellan spent the winter of 1861–1862 training the recruits and launched a major offensive in March 1862. With great logistical skill, the Union general ferried 100,000 troops down the Potomac River to the Chesapeake Bay and landed them on the peninsula between the York and James rivers (Map 14.2). Ignoring Lincoln's advice to "strike a blow" quickly, McClellan advanced slowly toward Richmond, allowing the Confederates to mount a counterstrike. Thomas J. "Stonewall" Jackson marched a Confederate force rapidly northward through the Shenandoah Valley in western Virginia and threatened Washington. When Lincoln recalled 30,000 troops from McClellan's army to protect the Union capital, Jackson returned quickly to Richmond to bolster General Robert E. Lee's army. In late June, Lee launched a ferocious six-day attack that cost 20,000 casualties to the Union's 10,000. When McClellan failed to exploit the Confederates' losses, Lincoln ordered a withdrawal and Richmond remained secure.

**Lee Moves North: Antietam**  Hoping for victories that would humiliate Lincoln's government, Lee went on the offensive. Joining with Jackson in northern

> **COMPARE AND CONTRAST**
> In 1861 and 1862, what were the political and military strategies of the Confederate and Union leaders? Which side was the more successful and why?

**MAP 14.2**

**The Eastern Campaigns of 1862**

Many of the great battles of the Civil War took place in the 125 miles separating the Union capital, Washington, D.C., and the Confederate capital, Richmond, Virginia. During 1862, Confederate generals Thomas Jonathan "Stonewall" Jackson and Robert E. Lee won battles that defended the Confederate capital (3, 6, 8, and 13) and launched offensive strikes against Union forces guarding Washington (1, 4, 5, 7, 9, and 10). They also suffered a defeat—at Antietam (12), in Maryland—that was almost fatal to the Confederate cause. As was often the case in the Civil War, the victors in these battles were either too bloodied or too timid to exploit their advantage.

Virginia, he routed Union troops in the Second Battle of Bull Run (August 1862) and then struck north through western Maryland. There, he nearly met with disaster. When the Confederate commander divided his force, sending Jackson to capture Harpers Ferry in

West Virginia, a copy of Lee's orders fell into McClellan's hands. The Union general again failed to exploit his advantage, delaying an attack against Lee's depleted army, thereby allowing it to secure a strong defensive position west of Antietam Creek, near Sharpsburg,

Maryland. Outnumbered 87,000 to 50,000, Lee desperately fought off McClellan's attacks until Jackson's troops arrived and saved the Confederates from a major defeat. Appalled by the Union casualties, McClellan allowed Lee to retreat to Virginia.

The fighting at Antietam was savage. A Wisconsin officer described his men "loading and firing with demoniacal fury and shouting and laughing hysterically." A sunken road — nicknamed Bloody Lane — was filled with Confederate bodies two and three deep, and the advancing Union troops knelt on this "ghastly flooring" to shoot at the retreating Confederates. The battle at Antietam on September 17, 1862, remains the bloodiest single day in U.S. military history. Together,

the Confederate and Union dead numbered 4,800 and the wounded 18,500, of whom 3,000 soon died. (By comparison, there were 6,000 American casualties on D-Day, which began the invasion of Nazi-occupied France in World War II.)

In public, Lincoln claimed Antietam as a Union victory; privately, he criticized McClellan for not fighting Lee to the bitter end. A masterful organizer of men and supplies, McClellan refused to risk his troops, fearing that heavy casualties would undermine public support for the war. Lincoln worried more about the danger of a lengthy war. He dismissed McClellan and began a long search for an aggressive commanding general. His first choice, Ambrose E. Burnside, proved

BATTLE OF PEA RIDGE, ARK.

**The Battle of Pea Ridge, Arkansas, March 1862**
Pea Ridge was the biggest battle of the Civil War fought west of the Mississippi and was of considerable strategic significance. By routing one Confederate army and holding another to a draw, outnumbered Union forces maintained their control of Missouri for the duration of the war. The lithograph, published in Chicago in 1889, commemorates the Union units — from Illinois and other midwestern states — who fought at Pea Ridge. Here the Union troops, half of whom were German immigrants, face a charging column of Confederate cavalry and infantry from Texas and Missouri and their Native American allies. Each side had about 1,000 men killed or wounded, with another 200 taken prisoner. Library of Congress.

to be more daring but less competent than McClellan. In December, after heavy losses in futile attacks against well-entrenched Confederate forces at Fredericksburg, Virginia, Burnside resigned his command, and Lincoln replaced him with Joseph "Fighting Joe" Hooker. As 1862 ended, Confederates were optimistic: they had won a stalemate in the East.

**The War in the Mississippi Valley**    Meanwhile, Union commanders in the Upper South had been more successful (Map 14.3). Their goal was to control the Ohio, Mississippi, and Missouri rivers, dividing the Confederacy and reducing the mobility of its armies. Because Kentucky did not join the rebellion, the Union already dominated the Ohio River Valley. In February 1862, the Union army used an innovative tactic to take charge of the Tennessee and Mississippi rivers as well. General Ulysses S. Grant used riverboats clad with iron plates to capture Fort Donelson on the Cumberland River and Fort Henry on the Tennessee River. When Grant moved south toward Mississippi to seize critical railroad lines, Confederate troops led by Albert Sidney Johnston and P. G. T. Beauregard caught his army by surprise near a small log church at Shiloh, Tennessee. However, Grant relentlessly committed troops and forced a Confederate withdrawal. As the fighting at Shiloh ended on April 7, Grant surveyed a large field "so covered with dead that it would have been possible to walk over the clearing in any direction, stepping on dead bodies, without a foot touching the ground." The cost in lives was horrific, but Lincoln was resolute: "What I want . . . is generals who will fight battles and win victories."

Three weeks later, Union naval forces commanded by David G. Farragut struck the Confederacy from the Gulf of Mexico. They captured New Orleans, the South's financial center and largest city. The Union army also took control of fifteen hundred plantations and 50,000 slaves in the surrounding region, striking a strong blow against slavery. Workers on some plantations looted their owners' mansions; others refused to labor unless they were paid wages. "[Slavery there] is forever destroyed and worthless," declared one northern reporter. Union victories had significantly undermined Confederate strength in the Mississippi River Valley.

## Toward Total War

The military carnage in 1862 revealed that the war would be long and costly. Grant later remarked that, after Shiloh, he "gave up all idea of saving the Union except by complete conquest." Lincoln agreed. During the summer of 1862, he abandoned hope for a compromise peace that would restore the Union. Instead, he committed the nation to a **total war** that would mobilize all of society's resources — economic, political, and cultural — in support of the North's military effort and end slavery in the South. Aided by the Republican Party and a talented cabinet, Lincoln gradually organized an effective central government able to wage all-out war; and urged on by antislavery politicians and activists, he moved toward a controversial proclamation of emancipation. Jefferson Davis had less success at harnessing southern resources, because the eleven states of the Confederacy remained suspicious of centralized rule and southern yeomen grew increasingly skeptical of the war effort.

## Mobilizing Armies and Civilians

Initially, patriotic fervor filled both armies with eager young volunteers. All he heard was "War! War! War!" one Union recruit recalled. Even those of sober minds joined up. "I don't think a young man ever went over all the considerations more carefully than I did," reflected William Saxton of Cincinnatus, New York. "It might mean sickness, wounds, loss of limb, and even life itself. . . . But my country was in danger." The southern call for volunteers was even more successful, thanks to its strong military tradition and a culture that stressed duty and honor. "Would you, My Darling, . . . be willing to leave your Children under such a [despotic Union] government?" James B. Griffin of Edgefield, South Carolina, asked his wife. "No — I know you would sacrifice every comfort on earth, rather than submit to it." However, enlistments declined as potential recruits learned the realities of mass warfare: epidemic diseases in the camps and wholesale death on the battlefields. Both governments soon faced the need for conscription.

**The Military Draft**    The Confederacy acted first. In April 1862, following the bloodshed at Shiloh, the Confederate Congress imposed the first legally binding **draft (conscription)** in American history. New laws required existing soldiers to serve for the duration of the war and mandated three years of military service from all men between the ages of eighteen and thirty-five. In September 1862, after the heavy casualties at Antietam, the age limit jumped to forty-five. The South's draft had two loopholes, both controversial. First, it exempted one white man — the planter, a son, or an overseer — for each twenty slaves, allowing some

**MAP 14.3**

**The Western Campaigns, 1861–1862**

As the Civil War intensified in 1862, Union and Confederate military and naval forces sought control of the great valleys of the Ohio, Tennessee, and Mississippi rivers. From February through April 1862, Union armies moved south through western Tennessee (1–3 and 5). By the end of June, Union naval forces controlled the Mississippi River north of Memphis (4, 10, and 11) and from the Gulf of Mexico to Vicksburg (6, 7, 9, and 12). These military and naval victories gave the Union control of crucial transportation routes, kept Missouri in the Union, and carried the war to the borders of the states of the Lower South.

**Kansas Volunteers, 1862**
When they posed for this tintype photograph in 1862, these men from Company E, 8th Kansas Volunteer Infantry, had marched hundreds of miles through Kentucky and Tennessee in a largely fruitless pursuit of a Confederate army and wore the look of battle-hardened troops. Some of these volunteers appear to be in their thirties or forties, and perhaps were abolitionist veterans of the civil strife in Bloody Kansas during the 1850s. Kansas State Historical Society.

whites on large plantations to avoid military service. This provision, a Mississippi legislator warned Jefferson Davis, "has aroused a spirit of rebellion in some places." Second, draftees could hire substitutes. By the time the Confederate Congress closed this loophole in 1864, the price of a substitute had soared to $300 in gold, three times the annual wage of a skilled worker. Laborers and yeomen farmers angrily complained that it was "a rich man's war and a poor man's fight."

Consequently, some southerners refused to serve. Because the Confederate constitution vested sovereignty in the individual states, the government in Richmond could not compel military service. Independent-minded governors such as Joseph Brown of Georgia and Zebulon Vance of North Carolina simply ignored President Davis's first draft call in early 1862. Elsewhere, state judges issued writs of **habeas corpus** — legal instruments used to protect people from arbitrary arrest — and ordered the Confederate army to release reluctant draftees. However, the Confederate Congress overrode the judges' authority to free conscripted men, so the government was able to keep substantial armies in the field well into 1864.

The Union government acted more ruthlessly toward draft resisters and Confederate sympathizers. In Missouri and other border states, Union commanders levied special taxes on southern supporters. Lincoln went further, suspending habeas corpus and, over the course of the war, temporarily imprisoning about 15,000 southern sympathizers without trial. He also gave military courts jurisdiction over civilians who discouraged enlistments or resisted the draft, preventing acquittals by sympathetic local juries. However, most Union governments used incentives to lure recruits. To meet the local quotas set by the Militia Act of 1862, towns, counties, and states used cash bounties of as much as $600 (about $11,000 today) and signed up nearly 1 million men. The Union also allowed men to avoid military service by providing a substitute or paying a $300 fee.

When the Enrollment Act of 1863 finally initiated conscription, recent German and Irish immigrants often refused to serve. It was not their war, they said.

**PLACE EVENTS IN CONTEXT**
How did the Union and Confederacy mobilize their populations for war, and how effective were these methods?

Northern Democrats used the furor over conscription to bolster support for their party, which increasingly criticized Lincoln's policies. They accused Lincoln of drafting poor whites to liberate enslaved blacks, who would then flood the cities and take their jobs. Slavery was nearly "dead, [but] the negro is not, there is the misfortune," declared a Democratic newspaper in Cincinnati. In July 1863, the immigrants' hostility to conscription and blacks sparked riots in New York City. For five days, Irish and German workers ran rampant, burning draft offices, sacking the homes of influential Republicans, and attacking the police. The rioters lynched and mutilated a dozen African Americans, drove hundreds of black families from their homes, and burned down the Colored Orphan Asylum. To suppress the mobs, Lincoln rushed in Union troops who had just fought at Gettysburg; they killed more than a hundred rioters.

The Union government won much stronger support from native-born middle-class citizens. In 1861, prominent New Yorkers established the U.S. Sanitary Commission to provide the troops with clothing, food, and medical services. Seven thousand local auxiliaries assisted the commission's work. "I almost weep," reported a local agent, "when these plain rural people come to send their simple offerings to absent sons and brothers." The commission also recruited battlefield nurses and doctors for the Union Army Medical Bureau. Despite these efforts, dysentery, typhoid, and malaria spread through the camps, as did mumps and measles, viruses that were often deadly to rural recruits. Diseases and infections killed about 250,000 Union soldiers, nearly twice the 135,000 who died in combat. Still, thanks to the Sanitary Commission, Union troops had a far lower mortality rate than soldiers fighting in nineteenth-century European wars. Confederate

**The Business of Recruiting an Army**
Even before the antidraft riots in New York City in July 1863, Union governments used monetary bonuses to induce men to join the army, and the payments increased as the war continued. George Law's painting shows a New York recruiting post in 1864. To meet the state's quota of 30,000 men, the county and state governments offered volunteers bounties of $300 and $75 — on top of a U.S. government bounty of $302. The total — some $677 — was serious money at a time when the average worker earned $1.70 for a ten-hour day. Anne S. K. Brown Military Collection, Brown University Library.

**Hospital Nursing**

Working as nurses in battlefront hospitals, thousands of Union and Confederate women gained firsthand experience of the horrors of war. A sense of calm prevails in this behind-the-lines Union hospital in Nashville, Tennessee, as nurse Anne Belle tends to the needs of soldiers recovering from their wounds. Most Civil War nurses were volunteers with little medical training; they spent time cooking and cleaning for their patients as well as tending their injuries. U.S. Army Military History Institute.

troops were less fortunate, despite the efforts of thousands of women who volunteered as nurses, because the Confederate army's health system was poorly organized. Scurvy was a special problem for southern soldiers; lacking vitamin C in their diets, they suffered muscle ailments and had low resistance to camp diseases (Thinking Like a Historian, p. 458).

So much death created new industries and cultural rituals. Embalmers devised a zinc chloride fluid to preserve soldiers' bodies, allowing them to be shipped home for burial, an innovation that began modern funeral practices. Military cemeteries with hundreds of crosses in neat rows replaced the landscaped "rural cemeteries" in vogue in American cities before the Civil War. As thousands of mothers, wives, and sisters mourned the deaths of fallen soldiers, they faced changed lives. Confronting utter deprivation, working-class women grieved for the loss of a breadwinner. Middle-class wives often had financial resources but, having embraced the affectionate tenets of domesticity, mourned the death of a loved one by wearing black crape "mourning" dresses and other personal accessories of death. The destructive war, in concert with the emerging consumer culture and ethic of domesticity,

produced a new "cult of mourning" among the middle and upper classes.

**Women in Wartime**  As tens of thousands of wounded husbands and sons limped home, their wives and sisters helped them rebuild their lives. Another 200,000 women worked as volunteers in the Sanitary Commission and the Freedman's Aid Society, which collected supplies for liberated slaves.

The war also drew more women into the wage-earning workforce as nurses, clerks, and factory operatives. Dorothea Dix (Chapter 11) served as superintendent of female nurses and, by successfully combating the prejudice against women providing medical treatment to men, opened a new occupation to women. Thousands of educated Union women became government clerks, while southern women staffed the efficient Confederate postal service. In both societies, millions of women took over farm tasks; filled jobs in schools and offices; and worked in textile, shoe, and food-processing factories. A few even became spies, scouts, and (disguising themselves as men) soldiers. As Union nurse Clara Barton, who later founded the American Red Cross, recalled, "At the war's end, woman was at least fifty years in advance of the normal position which continued peace would have assigned her."

## Mobilizing Resources

Wars are usually won by the side that possesses greater resources. In that regard, the Union had a distinct advantage. With nearly two-thirds of the nation's population, two-thirds of the railroad mileage, and almost 90 percent of the industrial output, the North's economy was far superior to that of the South (Figure 14.2). Furthermore, many of its arms factories were equipped for mass production.

Still, the Confederate position was far from weak. Virginia, North Carolina, and Tennessee had substantial industrial capacity. Richmond, with its Tredegar Iron Works, was an important manufacturing center, and in 1861 it acquired the gun-making machinery from the U.S. armory at Harpers Ferry. The production at the Richmond armory, the purchase of Enfield rifles from Britain, and the capture of 100,000 Union guns enabled the Confederacy to provide every infantryman with a modern rifle-musket by 1863.

Moreover, with 9 million people, the Confederacy could mobilize enormous armies. Enslaved blacks, one-third of the population, became part of the war effort by producing food for the army and raw cotton for export. Confederate leaders counted on **King**

**FIGURE 14.2**

**Economies, North and South, 1860**

The military advantages of the North were even greater than this chart suggests. The population figures for the South include slaves, whom the Confederacy feared to arm. Also, the South's commodity output was primarily in farm goods rather than manufactures. Finally, southern factories were much smaller on average than those in the North.

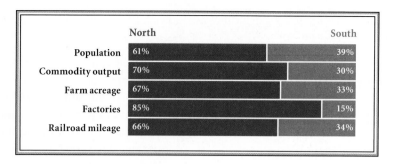

| | North | South |
|---|---|---|
| Population | 61% | 39% |
| Commodity output | 70% | 30% |
| Farm acreage | 67% | 33% |
| Factories | 85% | 15% |
| Railroad mileage | 66% | 34% |

Cotton—the leading American export and a crucial staple of the nineteenth-century economy—to purchase clothes, boots, blankets, and weapons from abroad. Leaders also saw cotton as a diplomatic weapon that would persuade Britain and France, which had large textile industries, to assist the Confederacy.

However, British manufacturers had stockpiled cotton and developed new sources in Egypt and India. Still, the South received some foreign support. Although Britain never recognized the Confederacy as an independent nation, it treated the rebel government as a belligerent power—with the right under international

**Richmond: Capital City and Industrial Center**

The Confederacy chose Richmond as its capital because of the historic importance of Virginia as the home of Washington, Jefferson, Madison, and Monroe. However, Richmond was also a major industrial center. Exploiting the city's location at the falls of the James River, the city's entrepreneurs had developed a wide range of industries: flour mills, tobacco factories, railroad and port facilities, and, most important, a substantial iron industry. In 1861, the Tredegar Iron Works employed nearly a thousand workers and, as the only facility in the South that could manufacture large machinery and heavy weapons, made a major contribution to the Confederate war effort. The Library of Virginia.

## Military Deaths — and Lives Saved — During the Civil War

The Civil War, like all wars before and since, encouraged innovation in both the destruction and the saving of human life. More than 620,000 soldiers — 360,000 on the Union side and 260,000 Confederates — died during the war, about 20 percent of those who served. However, thanks to advances in camp hygiene and battlefield treatment, the Union death rate was about 54–58 per 1,000 soldiers per year, less than half the level for British and French troops during the Crimean War of 1854–1855.

**1. Report by surgeon Charles S. Tipler, medical director of the Army of the Potomac, January 4, 1862.** *Most Civil War deaths came from disease. The major killers were bacterial intestinal diseases — typhoid fever, diarrhea, and dysentery — which spread because of unsanitary conditions in the camps.*

The aggregate strength of the forces from which I have received reports is 142,577. Of these, 47,836 have been under treatment in the field and general hospitals, 35,915 of whom have been returned to duty, and 281 have died; 9,281 remained under treatment at the end of the month; . . .

The diseases from which our men have suffered most have been continued remittent and typhoid fevers, measles, diarrhea, dysentery, and the various forms of catarrh [heavy discharge of mucus from the nose]. Of all the scourges incident to armies in the field I suppose that chronic diarrheas and dysenteries have always been the most prevalent and the most fatal. I am happy to say that in this army they are almost unknown. We have but 280 cases of chronic diarrhea and 69 of chronic dysentery reported in the month of November.

**2. Minie ball wounds: femur shot by Springfield 1862 rifle and Private George W. Lemon, 1867.**

Ninety percent of battle casualties were the victims of a new technology: musket-rifles that fired lethal soft-lead bullets called minie balls (after their inventor, Claude-Étienne Minié). The rifle-musket revolutionized military strategy by enormously strengthening defensive forces. Infantrymen could now kill reliably at 300 yards — triple the previous range of muskets. Initially, the new technology baffled commanders, who continued to use the tactics perfected during the heyday of the musket and bayonet charge, sending waves of infantrymen against enemy positions.

A minie ball strike to the abdomen, chest, or head was usually fatal, but injuries to the limbs gave some hope of survival, given advances in battlefield surgery. When

Private George W. Lemon suffered a minie ball wound to his femur similar to the one shown here (below), surgeons amputated his leg below the hip and, after the war, fitted him with a prosthetic leg.

Source: National Museum of Health & Medicine, Armed Forces Institute of Pathology.

Source: Courtesy National Library of Medicine.

**3. Kate Cumming, April 23, 1862, journal entry on treating a Confederate victim after the Battle of Shiloh.** *Union surgeons performed 29,980 battlefield amputations during the Civil War. Confederate records are less complete, but surgeons apparently undertook about 28,000 amputations. They quickly removed limbs too shattered to mend, which increased the chances of survival. According to one witness, "surgeons and their assistants, stripped to the waist and bespattered with blood, stood around, some holding the poor fellows while others, armed with long, bloody knives and saws, cut and sawed away with frightful rapidity, throwing the mangled limbs on a pile nearby as soon as removed." This journal entry from a young Confederate nurse in Corinth, Mississippi, describes the plight of one such victim after the Battle of Shiloh.*

A young man whom I have been attending is going to have his arm cut off. Poor fellow! I am doing all I can to cheer him. He says that he knows that he will die, as all who have had limbs amputated in this hospital have died. . . . He lived only a few hours after his amputation.

**4. William Williams Keen, MD, "Surgical Reminiscences of the Civil War," 1905.** *Although 73 percent of the Union amputees survived the war, infected wounds—deadly gangrene— took the lives of most soldiers who suffered certain gunshot injuries in this pre-antibiotic, pre-antiseptic era. Keen, who later became the first brain surgeon in the United States, served as a surgeon in the Union army.*

Not more than one incontestable example of recovery from a gunshot wound of the stomach and not a single incontestable case of wound of the small intestines are recorded during the entire war among the almost 250,000 wounded. . . .

Of 852 amputations of the shoulder-joint, 236 died, a mortality of 28.5 per cent. Of 66 cases of amputation of the hip-joint, 55, or 83.3 per cent died. Of 155 cases of trephining [cutting a hole in the skull to relieve pressure], 60 recovered and 95 died, a mortality of over 61 per cent. Of 374 ligations of the femoral artery, 93 recovered and 281 died, a mortality of over 75 per cent.

These figures afford a striking evidence of the dreadful mortality of military surgery in the days before antisepsis and first-aid packages. Happily such death-rates can never again be seen, at least in civilized warfare.

**5. John Tooker, MD, "Aspects of Medicine, Nursing, and the Civil War," 2007.** *The Union doctor Jonathan Letterman pioneered a new method of battlefield triage that was adopted by the entire army in 1864.*

Letterman had devised an efficient and, for the times, modern system of mass casualty management, beginning with first aid adjacent to the battlefield, removal of the wounded by an organized ambulance system to field hospitals for urgent and stabilizing treatment, such as wound closure and amputation, and then referral to general hospitals for longer term definitive management. This three-stage approach to casualty management, strengthened by effective and efficient transport, earned Letterman the title of "The Father of Battlefield Medicine."

---

Sources: (1) *The War of the Rebellion: A Compilation of the Official Records of the Union and Confederate Armies* (Washington, DC: Government Printing Office, 1889), Series 1, Vol. 5 (Part V), 111–112; (3) Kate Cumming, *A Journal of Hospital Life in the Confederate Army of Tennessee* (Louisville, KY: John P. Morton & Company, 1866), 19; (4) William Williams Keen, "Surgical Reminiscences of the Civil War," in *Addresses and Other Papers* (Philadelphia: W. B. Saunders, 1905), 433–434; (5) John Tooker, "Antietam: Aspects of Medicine, Nursing, and the Civil War," National Center for Biotechnology Information, U.S. National Library of Medicine, National Institutes of Health.

**ANALYZING THE EVIDENCE**

1. Based on Tipler's report (source 1), would you say the Union army was healthy or unhealthy? Ready for battle or not?

2. Consider sources 2–4. How do you think the reentry of tens of thousands of maimed veterans into civil society affected American culture?

3. What do sources 3–5 suggest about the successes and limitations of battlefield medicine during the Civil War?

4. Consider the Civil War in the context of the Industrial Revolution. What was the impact of factory production and technological advances on the number of weapons and their killing power? And how might the organizational innovations of the Industrial Revolution pertain to the conflict? In this regard, what do you make of the new method of battlefield triage pioneered by Union doctor Jonathan Letterman (source 5)?

**PUTTING IT ALL TOGETHER**

As a "total war" the Civil War involved the citizenry as well as the military, marshaling all of the two societies' resources and ingenuity. Using your understanding of these documents and the textbook, write an essay that discusses the relation of the war to technology, medicine, public finance, and the lives of women on the battle lines and the home front.

law to borrow money and purchase weapons. The odds, then, did not necessarily favor the Union, despite its superior resources.

### Republican Economic and Fiscal Policies

To mobilize northern resources, the Republican-dominated Congress enacted a neomercantilist program of government-assisted economic development that far surpassed Henry Clay's American System (Chapter 10). The Republicans imposed high tariffs (averaging nearly 40 percent) on various foreign goods, thereby encouraging domestic industries. To boost agricultural output, they offered "free land" to farmers. The Homestead Act of 1862 gave settlers the title to 160 acres of public land after five years of residence. To create an integrated national banking system (far more powerful than the First and Second Banks of the United States), Secretary of the Treasury Salmon P. Chase forced thousands of local banks to accept federal charters and regulations.

Finally, the Republican Congress implemented Clay's program for a nationally financed transportation system. Expansion to the Pacific, the California gold rush, and subsequent discoveries of gold, silver, copper, and other metals in Nevada, Montana, and other western lands had revived demands for such a network. Therefore, in 1862, Congress chartered the Union Pacific and Central Pacific companies to build a transcontinental railroad line and granted them lavish subsidies. This economic program won the allegiance of farmers, workers, and entrepreneurs and bolstered the Union's ability to fight a long war.

**TRACE CHANGE OVER TIME**
How did the economic policies of the Republican-controlled Congress redefine the character of the federal government?

New industries sprang up to provide the Union army — and its 1.5 million men — with guns, clothes, and food. Over the course of the war, soldiers consumed more than half a billion pounds of pork and other packed meats. To meet this demand, Chicago railroads built new lines to carry thousands of hogs and cattle to the city's stockyards and slaughterhouses. By 1862, Chicago had passed Cincinnati as the meatpacking capital of the nation, bringing prosperity to thousands of midwestern farmers and great wealth to Philip D. Armour and other meatpacking entrepreneurs.

Bankers and financiers likewise found themselves pulled into the war effort. The annual spending of the Union government shot up from $63 million in 1860 to more than $865 million in 1864. To raise that enormous sum, the Republicans created a modern system of public finance that secured funds in three ways. First, the government increased tariffs; placed high duties on alcohol and tobacco; and imposed direct taxes on business corporations, large inheritances, and the incomes of wealthy citizens. These levies paid about 20 percent of the cost. Second, interest-paying bonds issued by the U.S. Treasury financed another 65 percent. The National Banking Acts of 1863 and 1864 forced most banks to buy those bonds; and Philadelphia banker and Treasury Department agent Jay Cooke used newspaper ads and 2,500 subagents to persuade a million northern families to buy them.

The Union paid the remaining 15 percent by printing paper money. The Legal Tender Act of 1862 authorized $150 million in paper currency — soon known as **greenbacks** — and required the public to accept them as legal tender. Like the Continental currency of the Revolutionary era, greenbacks could not be exchanged for specie; however, the Treasury issued a limited amount of paper money, so it lost only a small part of its face value.

If a modern fiscal system was one result of the war, immense concentrations of capital in many industries — meatpacking, steel, coal, railroads, textiles, shoes — was another. The task of supplying the huge war machine, an observer noted, gave a few men "the command of millions of money." Such massed financial power threatened not only the prewar society of small producers but also the future of democratic self-government (America Compared, p. 461). Americans "are never again to see the republic in which we were born," lamented abolitionist and social reformer Wendell Phillips.

### The South Resorts to Coercion and Inflation

The economic demands on the South were equally great, but, true to its states' rights philosophy, the Confederacy initially left most matters to the state governments. However, as the realities of total war became clear, Jefferson Davis's administration took extraordinary measures. It built and operated shipyards, armories, foundries, and textile mills; commandeered food and scarce raw materials such as coal, iron, copper, and lead; requisitioned slaves to work on fortifications; and directly controlled foreign trade.

The Confederate Congress and ordinary southern citizens opposed many of Davis's initiatives, particularly those involving taxes. The Congress refused to tax cotton exports and slaves, the most valuable property held by wealthy planters, and the urban middle classes and yeomen farm families refused to pay more than their fair share. Consequently, the Confederacy covered less than 10 percent of its expenditures through

# War Debt: Britain and the United States, 1830–1900

Wars cost money, sometimes a lot of money, and nations often pay for them by issuing bonds and expanding the national debt. The British national debt grew enormously between 1750 and 1815 as it fought a great series of wars, all of which involved either its American colonies or the United States: the Great War for Empire (1754–1763), the War of American Independence (1776–1783), and the Wars of the French Revolution and Napoleon (1793–1815). Consequently, Britain's national debt peaked in 1815 at 260 percent of its gross domestic product (GDP). Even in 1830, after years of high taxation and economic growth, the debt amounted to 180 percent of British GDP.

By comparison, the United States in 1830 was virtually debt-free, as the policies of Jeffersonian Republicans reduced its debt from about 27 percent of GDP in 1790 to less than 5 percent. Ample tariff revenues and the frugal policies of Presidents Andrew Jackson and Martin Van Buren then cut the debt nearly to zero by the early 1840s. Even the war with Mexico barely raised the level of the debt, thanks to the return of prosperity and the growth of GDP between 1844 and 1857.

Then came the Civil War, which boosted the Union debt from $62 million in 1860 to $2.2 billion at the end of 1865, a 1,500 percent increase. (The Fourteenth Amendment, ratified in 1868, declared "illegal and void" all debts incurred by the Confederacy.) In relation to GDP, the U.S. national debt shot up to 27 percent, the same level as 1790, and then—thanks again to tariff revenue—decreased gradually to about 10 percent of GDP by 1900. By then, the British national debt had fallen to about 40 percent of its GDP, as the British—the world's strongest power—mostly avoided new wars and built a prosperous commercial and industrial economy. The cost of war, civil or international, may well be a high national debt.

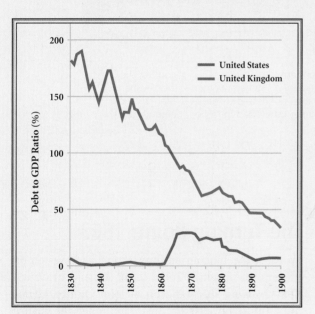

**FIGURE 14.3**
**United States and United Kingdom National Debt as a Percentage of Gross Domestic Product, 1830–1900**

## QUESTIONS FOR ANALYSIS

1. In 1864, President Lincoln lamented: "This war of ours, in its magnitude and in its duration, is one of the most terrible. It has produced a national debt and taxation unprecedented, at least in this country." Given the relative size of the Union debt in relation to that of Britain, were Lincoln's worries exaggerated?

2. In 2012, the national debt of the United States—now the world's premier economic and military power—was nearly 100 percent of GDP and, since 1940, has averaged about 60 percent of GDP. Given those facts, and the evidence in this chart, is it fair to conclude that one of the costs of global power is a high national debt?

taxation. The government paid another 30 percent by borrowing, but wealthy planters and foreign bankers grew increasingly fearful that the South would never redeem its bonds.

Consequently, the Confederacy paid 60 percent of its war costs by printing paper money. The flood of currency created a spectacular inflation: by 1865, prices had risen to ninety-two times their 1861 level. As food prices soared, riots erupted in more than a dozen southern cities and towns. In Richmond, several hundred women broke into bakeries, crying, "Our children are starving while the rich roll in

**A Southern Refugee Family**

As Union and Confederate armies swept back and forth across northern Virginia and other war zones, the civilian population feared for its property and personal security. Here, two southern women—their husbands presumably away at war—have hitched up their mules and piled their goods and children on a farm wagon in order to flee the fighting. Lucky refugees had relatives in safe areas; others had to rely on the goodwill of strangers. National Archives.

wealth." In Randolph County, Alabama, women confiscated grain from a government warehouse "to prevent starvation of themselves and their families." As inflation spiraled upward, southerners refused to accept paper money, whatever the consequences. When South Carolina storekeeper Jim Harris refused the depreciated currency presented by Confederate soldiers, they raided his storehouse and, he claimed, "robbed it of about five thousand dollars worth of goods." Army supply officers likewise seized goods from merchants and offered payment in worthless IOUs. Facing a public that feared strong government and high taxation, the Confederacy could sustain the war effort only by seizing its citizens' property—and by championing white supremacy: President Davis warned that a Union victory would destroy slavery "and reduce the whites to the degraded position of the African race."

# The Turning Point: 1863

By 1863, the Lincoln administration had created an efficient war machine and a set of strategic priorities. Henry Adams, the grandson of John Quincy Adams and a future novelist and historian, noted the change from his diplomatic post in London: "Little by little, one began to feel that, behind the chaos in Washington power was taking shape; that it was massed and guided as it had not been before." Slowly but surely, the tide of the struggle turned against the Confederacy.

## Emancipation

When the war began, antislavery Republicans demanded that abolition be a goal of the war. The fighting should continue, said a Massachusetts abolitionist, "until the Slave power is completely subjugated, and *emancipation made certain.*" Because slave-grown crops sustained the Confederacy, activists justified black emancipation on military grounds. As Frederick Douglass put it, "Arrest that hoe in the hands of the Negro, and you smite the rebellion in the very seat of its life."

**"Contrabands"**  As abolitionists pressed their case, African Americans exploited wartime chaos to seize freedom for themselves. When three slaves reached the camp of Union general Benjamin Butler in Virginia in May 1861, he labeled them "contraband of war" (enemy property that can be legitimately seized, according to international law) and refused to return them. Butler's term stuck, and soon thousands of **"contrabands"** were camping with Union armies. Near Fredericksburg, Virginia, an average of 200 blacks appeared every day, "with their packs on their backs and handkerchiefs tied over their heads — men, women, little children, and babies." This influx created a humanitarian crisis; abolitionist Harriet Jacobs reported that hundreds of refugees were "[p]acked together in the most miserable quarters," where many died from smallpox and dysentery. To provide legal status to the refugees — some 400,000 by the war's end — in August 1861 Congress passed the Confiscation Act, which authorized the seizure of all property, including slave property, used to support the rebellion.

With the Confiscation Act, **Radical Republicans** — the members of the party who had been bitterly opposed to the "Slave Power" since the mid-1850s — began to use wartime legislation to destroy slavery. Their leaders were treasury secretary Salmon Chase, Senator Charles Sumner of Massachusetts, and Representative Thaddeus Stevens of Pennsylvania. A long-time member of Congress, Stevens was a masterful politician, skilled at fashioning legislation that could win majority support. In April 1862, Stevens and the Radicals persuaded Congress to end slavery in the District of Columbia by providing compensation for owners; in June, Congress outlawed slavery in the federal territories (finally enacting the Wilmot Proviso of 1846); and in July, it passed a second Confiscation Act, which declared "forever free" the thousands of refugee slaves and all slaves captured by the Union army. Emancipation had become an instrument of war.

**The Emancipation Proclamation**  Initially, Lincoln rejected emancipation as a war aim, but faced with thousands of refugees and Radical Republican pressure, he moved cautiously toward that goal. The president

**Eastman Johnson, *A Ride for Freedom — The Fugitive Slaves,* c. 1862**

At the second battle of Manassas in September 1862, American genre painter Eastman Johnson (1824–1906) witnessed this "veritable incident" of an African American family fleeing slavery — and then painted it. A powerful, split-second image of the riders' silhouettes, Johnson's painting captures the father looking forward toward freedom, while the mother cradles a young child and looks back apprehensively for possible pursuers. By "freeing themselves," this family and thousands of blacks set the stage for Lincoln's Emancipation Proclamation. Brooklyn Museum of Art, New York, USA/The Bridgeman Art Library.

drafted a general proclamation of emancipation in July 1862, and he publicly linked black freedom with the preservation of the Union in August. "If I could save the Union without freeing any slave, I would do it," Lincoln told Horace Greeley of the *New York Tribune*, "and if I could save it by freeing all the slaves, I would do it."

Now he waited for a Union victory. Considering the Battle of Antietam "an indication of the Divine Will," Lincoln issued a preliminary proclamation of emancipation on September 22, 1862, basing its legal authority on his duty as commander in chief to suppress the rebellion. The proclamation legally abolished slavery in all states that remained out of the Union on January 1, 1863. The rebel states could preserve slavery by renouncing secession. None chose to do so.

The proclamation was politically astute. Lincoln conciliated slave owners in the Union-controlled border states, such as Maryland and Missouri, by leaving slavery intact in those states. It also permitted slavery to continue in areas occupied by Union armies: western and central Tennessee, western Virginia, and southern Louisiana. In Indian Territory, also under Union control, most mixed-blood Cherokee slave owners remained committed to the Confederacy and to bondage. They did not formally free their 4,000 slaves until July 1866, when a treaty with the U.S. government specified that their ex-slaves "shall have all the rights of native Cherokee."

**UNDERSTAND POINTS OF VIEW**
Some historians argue that slaves "freed themselves" by fleeing to Union armies, thereby forcing Lincoln to issue the Emancipation Proclamation. How persuasive is that argument?

Consequently, the **Emancipation Proclamation** did not immediately free a single slave. Yet, as abolitionist Wendell Phillips understood, Lincoln's proclamation had moved slavery to "the edge of Niagara," and would soon sweep it over the brink. Advancing Union troops became the agents of slavery's destruction. "I became free in 1863, in the summer, when the yankees come by and said I could go work for myself," recalled Jackson Daniel of Maysville, Alabama. As Lincoln now saw it, "the old South is to be destroyed and replaced by new propositions and ideas"—a system of free labor.

Hailed by reformers in Europe, emancipation was extraordinarily controversial in America. In the Confederacy, Jefferson Davis labeled it the "most execrable measure recorded in the history of guilty man"; in the North, white voters unleashed a racist backlash. During the elections of 1862, the Democrats denounced emancipation as unconstitutional, warned of slave uprisings, and predicted that freed blacks would take

white jobs. Every freed slave, suggested a nativist-minded New Yorker, should "shoulder an Irishman and leave the Continent." Such sentiments propelled Democrat Horatio Seymour into the governor's office in New York; if abolition was a war goal, Seymour argued, the South should not be conquered. In the November election, Democrats swept to victory in Pennsylvania, Ohio, and Illinois and gained thirty-four seats in Congress. However, Republicans still held a twenty-five-seat majority in the House and gained five seats in the Senate. Lincoln refused to retreat. Calling emancipation an "act of justice," he signed the final proclamation on New Year's Day 1863. "If my name ever goes into history," he said, "it was for this act."

 To see a longer excerpt of the Jefferson Davis document, along with other primary sources from this period, see *Sources for America's History*.

## Vicksburg and Gettysburg

The Emancipation Proclamation's fate would depend on Republican political success and Union military victories, neither of which looked likely. Democrats had made significant gains in 1862, and popular support was growing for a negotiated peace. Two brilliant victories in Virginia by General Robert E. Lee, whose army defeated Union forces at Fredericksburg (December 1862) and Chancellorsville (May 1863), further eroded northern support for the war.

**The Battle for the Mississippi**    At this critical juncture, General Grant mounted a major offensive to split the Confederacy in two. Grant drove south along the west bank of the Mississippi in Arkansas and then crossed the river near Vicksburg, Mississippi. There, he defeated two Confederate armies and laid siege to the city. After repelling Union assaults for six weeks, the exhausted and starving Vicksburg garrison surrendered on July 4, 1863. Five days later, Union forces took Port Hudson, Louisiana (near Baton Rouge), and seized control of the entire Mississippi River. Grant had taken 31,000 prisoners; cut off Louisiana, Arkansas, and Texas from the rest of the Confederacy; and prompted thousands of slaves to desert their plantations. Confederate troops responded by targeting refugees for re-enslavement and massacre. "The battlefield was sickening," a Confederate officer reported from Arkansas, "no orders, threats or commands could restrain the men from vengeance on the negroes, and they were piled in great heaps about the wagons, in the tangled brushwood, and upon the muddy and trampled road."

As Grant had advanced toward Vicksburg in May, Confederate leaders had argued over the best strategic response. President Davis and other politicians wanted to send an army to Tennessee to relieve the Union pressure along the Mississippi River. General Lee, buoyed by his recent victories, favored a new invasion of the North. That strategy, Lee suggested, would either draw Grant's forces to the east or give the Confederacy a major victory that would destroy the North's will to fight.

**Lee's Advance and Defeat**  Lee won out. In June 1863, he maneuvered his army north through Maryland into Pennsylvania. The Army of the Potomac moved along with him, positioning itself between Lee and Washington, D.C. On July 1, the two great armies met by accident at Gettysburg, Pennsylvania, in what became a decisive confrontation (Map 14.4). On the

first day of battle, Lee drove the Union's advance guard to the south of town. There, Union commander George G. Meade placed his troops in well-defended hilltop positions and called up reinforcements. By the morning of July 2, Meade had 90,000 troops to Lee's 75,000. Lee knew he was outnumbered but was intent on victory; he ordered assaults on Meade's flanks but failed to turn them.

On July 3, Lee decided on a dangerous frontal assault against the center of the Union line. After the heaviest artillery barrage of the war, Lee sent General George E. Pickett and his 14,000 men to take Cemetery Ridge. When Pickett's men charged across a mile of open terrain, they faced deadly fire from artillery and massed riflemen; thousands suffered death, wounds, or capture. As the three-day battle ended, the Confederates counted 28,000 casualties, one-third of the Army of Northern Virginia, while 23,000 of Meade's soldiers lay

**MAP 14.4**

**Lee Invades the North, 1863**

After Lee's victories at Chancellorsville (1) in May and Brandy Station (2) in June, the Confederate forces moved northward, constantly shadowed by the Union army. On July 1, the two armies met accidentally near Gettysburg, Pennsylvania. In the ensuing battle (3), the Union army, commanded by General George Meade, emerged victorious, primarily because it was much larger than the Confederate force and held well-fortified positions along Cemetery Ridge, which gave its units a major tactical advantage.

EXPLAIN
CONSEQUENCES
How did the battles at
Gettysburg and Vicksburg
significantly change the
tide of war?

killed or wounded. Shocked by the bloodletting, Meade allowed the Confederate units to escape. Lincoln was furious at Meade's caution, perceiving that "the war will be prolonged indefinitely."

Still, Gettysburg was a great Union victory and, together with the simultaneous triumph at Vicksburg, marked a major military, political, and diplomatic turning point. As southern citizens grew increasingly critical of their government, the Confederate elections of 1863 went sharply against the politicians who supported Jefferson Davis. Meanwhile, northern citizens rallied to the Union, and Republicans swept state elections in Pennsylvania, Ohio, and New York. In Europe, the victories boosted the leverage of American diplomats. Since 1862, the British-built ironclad cruiser the *Alabama* had sunk or captured more than a hundred Union merchant ships, and the Confederacy was about to accept delivery of two more ironclads. With a Union victory increasingly likely, the British government decided to impound the warships and, subsequently, to pay $15.5 million for the depredations of the *Alabama*. British workers and reformers had long condemned slavery and praised emancipation; moreover, because of poor grain harvests, Britain depended on imports of wheat and flour from the American Midwest. King Cotton diplomacy had failed and King Wheat stood triumphant. "Rest not your hopes in foreign nations," President Jefferson Davis advised his people. "This war is ours; we must fight it ourselves."

# The Union Victorious, 1864–1865

The Union victories of 1863 meant that the South could not win independence through a decisive military triumph. However, the Confederacy could still hope for a battlefield stalemate and a negotiated peace. To keep the Union in Republican hands, Lincoln faced the daunting task of conquering the South.

## Soldiers and Strategy

The promotion of aggressive generals and the enlistment of African American soldiers allowed the Union to prosecute the war vigorously. As early as 1861, free African Americans and fugitive slaves had volunteered, both to end slavery and, as Frederick Douglass put it, to win "the right to citizenship." Yet many northern whites refused to serve with blacks. "I am as much opposed to slavery as any of them," a New York soldier told his local newspaper, "but I am not willing to be put on a level with the negro and fight with them." Union generals also opposed the enlistment of African Americans, doubting they would make good soldiers. Nonetheless, free and contraband blacks formed volunteer regiments in New England, South Carolina, Louisiana, and Kansas.

**The Impact of Black Troops** The Emancipation Proclamation changed military policy and popular sentiment. The proclamation invited former slaves to serve in the Union army, and northern whites, having suffered thousands of casualties, now accepted that blacks should share in the fighting and dying. A heroic and costly attack by the 54th Massachusetts Infantry on Fort Wagner, South Carolina, in 1863 convinced Union officers of the value of black soldiers. By the spring of 1865, the Lincoln administration had recruited and armed nearly 200,000 African Americans. Without black soldiers, said Lincoln, "we would be compelled to abandon the war in three weeks."

Military service did not end racial discrimination. Black soldiers initially earned less than white soldiers ($10 a month versus $13) and died, mostly from disease, at higher rates than white soldiers. Nonetheless, African Americans continued to volunteer, seeking freedom and a new social order. "Hello, Massa," said one black soldier to his former master, who had been taken prisoner. "Bottom rail on top dis time." The worst fears of the secessionists had come true: through the disciplined agency of the Union army, African Americans had risen in a successful rebellion against slavery, just as six decades earlier enslaved Haitians had won emancipation in the army of Toussaint L'Ouverture (Chapter 7).

**Capable Generals Take Command** As African Americans bolstered the army's ranks, Lincoln finally found a ruthless commanding general. In March 1864, Lincoln placed General Ulysses S. Grant in charge of all Union armies; from then on, the president determined overall strategy and Grant implemented it. Lincoln favored a simultaneous advance against the major Confederate armies, a strategy Grant had long favored, in order to achieve a decisive victory before the election of 1864.

Grant knew how to fight a war that relied on industrial technology and targeted an entire society. At Vicksburg in July 1863, he had besieged the whole city

**Black Soldiers in the Union Army**

Determined to end racial slavery, tens of thousands of African Americans volunteered for service in the Union army in 1864 and 1865, boosting the northern war effort at a critical moment. These soldiers were members of the 107th Colored Infantry, stationed at Fort Corcoran near Washington, D.C. In January 1865, their regiment saw action in the daring capture of Fort Fisher, which protected Wilmington, North Carolina, the last Confederate port open to blockade runners. Library of Congress.

and forced its surrender. Then, in November, he had used railroads to rescue an endangered Union army near Chattanooga, Tennessee. Grant believed that the cautious tactics of previous Union commanders had prolonged the war. He was willing to accept heavy casualties, a stance that earned him a reputation as a butcher of enemy armies and his own men.

In May 1864, Grant ordered two major offensives. Personally taking charge of the 115,000-man Army of the Potomac, he set out to destroy Lee's force of 75,000 troops in Virginia. Grant instructed General William Tecumseh Sherman, who shared his harsh outlook, to invade Georgia and take Atlanta. "All that has gone before is mere skirmish," Sherman wrote as he prepared for battle. "The war now begins."

Grant advanced toward Richmond, hoping to force Lee to fight in open fields, where the Union's superior manpower and artillery would prevail. Remembering his tactical errors at Gettysburg, Lee remained in strong defensive positions and attacked only when he held an advantage. The Confederate general seized that opportunity twice in May 1864, winning costly victories at the battles of the Wilderness and Spotsylvania Court House. At Spotsylvania, the troops fought at point-blank range; an Iowa recruit recalled "lines of blue and grey [soldiers firing] into each other's faces; for an hour and a half." Despite heavy losses in these battles and then at Cold Harbor, Grant drove on (Map 14.5). His attacks severely eroded Lee's forces, which suffered 31,000 casualties, but Union losses were even higher: 55,000 killed or wounded.

**EXPLAIN CONSEQUENCES**

How did the Emancipation Proclamation and Grant's appointment as general in chief affect the course of the war?

**Stalemate**   The fighting took a heavy psychological toll. "Many a man has gone crazy since this campaign began from the terrible pressure on mind and body," observed a Union captain. As morale declined, soldiers deserted. In June 1864, Grant laid siege to Petersburg, an important railroad center near Richmond. As the siege continued, Union and Confederate soldiers built complex networks of trenches, tunnels, and artillery emplacements stretching for 40 miles along the eastern edge of Richmond and Petersburg, foreshadowing the devastating trench warfare in France in World War I. Invoking the intense imagery of the Bible, an officer described the continuous artillery barrages and sniping

**Grant Planning a Strategic Maneuver**

On May 21, 1864, the day this photograph was taken, Grant pulled his forces from Spotsylvania Court House, where a bitter two-week battle (May 8–21) resulted in 18,000 Union and 10,000 Confederate casualties. He moved his army to the southeast, seeking to outflank Lee's forces. Photographer Timothy H. O'Sullivan caught up to the Union army's high command at Massaponax Church, Virginia, and captured this image of Grant (to the left) leaning over a pew and reading a map held by General George H. Meade. As Grant plots the army's movement, his officers smoke their pipes and read reports of the war in newspapers that had just arrived from New York City. Intercepting Grant's forces, Lee took up fortified positions first at the North Anna River and then at Cold Harbor, where the Confederates scored their last major victory of the war (May 31–June 3). Library of Congress.

as "living night and day within the 'valley of the shadow of death.'" The stress was especially great for the outnumbered Confederate troops, who spent months in the muddy, hellish trenches without rotation to the rear.

As time passed, Lincoln and Grant felt pressures of their own. The enormous casualties and military stalemate threatened Lincoln with defeat in the November election. The Republican outlook worsened in July, when Jubal Early's cavalry raided and burned the Pennsylvania town of Chambersburg and threatened Washington. To punish farmers in the Shenandoah Valley who had aided the Confederate raiders, Grant ordered General Philip H. Sheridan to turn the region into "a barren waste." Sheridan's troops conducted a **scorched-earth campaign**, destroying grain, barns, and gristmills and any other resource useful to the Confederates. These tactics, like Early's raid, violated the military norms of the day, which treated civilians as noncombatants. Rising desperation and anger were changing the definition of conventional warfare.

## The Election of 1864 and Sherman's March

As the siege at Petersburg dragged on, Lincoln's hopes for reelection depended on General Sherman in Georgia. Sherman's army of 90,000 men had moved methodically toward Atlanta, a railway hub at the heart of the Confederacy. General Joseph E. Johnson's Confederate army of 60,000 stood in his way and, in June 1864, inflicted heavy casualties on Sherman's forces near Kennesaw Mountain, Georgia. By late July, the Union army stood on the northern outskirts of Atlanta, but the next month brought little gain. Like Grant, Sherman seemed bogged down in a hopeless campaign.

**The National Union Party Versus the Peace Democrats**    Meanwhile, the presidential campaign of 1864 was heating up. In June, the Republican Party's convention rebuffed attempts to prevent Lincoln's renomination. It endorsed the president's war strategy, demanded the Confederacy's unconditional surrender, and called for a constitutional amendment to abolish slavery. The delegates likewise embraced Lincoln's political strategy. To attract border-state and Democratic voters, the Republicans took a new name, the National Union Party, and chose Andrew Johnson, a Tennessee slave owner and Unionist Democrat, as Lincoln's running mate.

The Democratic Party met in August and nominated General George B. McClellan for president. Lincoln had twice removed McClellan from military commands: first for an excess of caution and then for

**MAP 14.5**

**The Closing Virginia Campaign, 1864–1865**

Beginning in May 1864, General Ulysses S. Grant launched an all-out campaign against Richmond, trying to lure General Robert E. Lee into open battle. Lee avoided a major test of strength. Instead, he retreated to defensive positions and inflicted heavy casualties on Union attackers at the Wilderness, Spotsylvania Court House, North Anna, and Cold Harbor (1–4). From June 1864 to April 1865, the two armies faced each other across defensive fortifications outside Richmond and Petersburg (5). Grant finally broke this ten-month siege by a flanking maneuver at Five Forks (6). Lee's surrender followed shortly.

his opposition to emancipation. Like McClellan, the Democratic delegates rejected emancipation and condemned Lincoln's repression of domestic dissent, particularly the suspension of habeas corpus and the use of military courts to prosecute civilians. However, they split into two camps over war policy. **War Democrats** vowed to continue fighting until the rebellion ended, while **Peace Democrats** called for a "cessation of hostilities" and a constitutional convention to negotiate a peace settlement. Although personally a War Democrat, McClellan promised if elected to recommend to Congress an immediate armistice and a peace convention. Hearing this news, Confederate vice president Alexander Stephens celebrated "the first ray of real light I have seen since the war began." He predicted that if Atlanta and Richmond held out, Lincoln would be defeated and McClellan would eventually accept an independent Confederacy.

**The Fall of Atlanta and Lincoln's Victory**   Stephens's hopes collapsed on September 2, 1864, as Atlanta fell to Sherman's army. In a stunning move, the Union general pulled his troops from the trenches, swept around the city, and destroyed its rail links to the south. Fearing that Sherman would encircle his army, Confederate general John B. Hood abandoned the city. "Atlanta is ours, and fairly won," Sherman telegraphed Lincoln, sparking hundred-gun salutes and wild Republican

celebration. "We are gaining strength," Lincoln warned Confederate leaders, "and may, if need be, maintain the contest indefinitely."

A deep pessimism settled over the Confederacy. Mary Chesnut, a plantation mistress and general's wife, wrote in her diary, "I felt as if all were dead within me, forever," and foresaw the end of the Confederacy: "We are going to be wiped off the earth." Recognizing the dramatically changed military situation, McClellan repudiated the Democratic peace platform. The National Union Party went on the offensive, attacking McClellan's inconsistency and labeling Peace Democrats as "copperheads" (poisonous snakes) who were hatching treasonous plots. "A man must go for the Union at all hazards," declared a Republican legislator in Pennsylvania, "if he would entitle himself to be considered a loyal man."

Lincoln won a clear-cut victory in November. The president received 55 percent of the popular vote and won 212 of 233 electoral votes. Republicans and National Unionists captured 145 of the 185 seats in the House of Representatives and increased their Senate majority to 42 of 52 seats. Many Republicans owed their victory to the votes of Union troops, who wanted to crush the rebellion and end slavery.

Legal emancipation was already under way at the edges of the South. In 1864, Maryland and Missouri amended their constitutions to end slavery, and the

**William Tecumseh Sherman**

A man of nervous energy, Sherman smoked cigars and talked continuously. When seated, he crossed and uncrossed his legs incessantly, and a journalist described his fingers as constantly "twitching his red whiskers—his coat buttons—playing a tattoo on the table—or running through his hair." On the battlefield Sherman was a decisive general who commanded the loyalty of his troops. A photographer captured this image of Sherman in 1865, following his devastating march through Georgia and the Carolinas. Library of Congress.

three Confederate states occupied by the Union army— Tennessee, Arkansas, and Louisiana—followed suit. Still, abolitionists worried that the Emancipation Proclamation, based legally on the president's wartime powers, would lose its force at the end of the war. Urged on by Lincoln and the National Equal Rights League, in January 1865 the Republican Congress approved the Thirteenth Amendment, ending slavery, and sent it to the states for ratification. Slavery was nearly dead.

### William Tecumseh Sherman: "Hard War" Warrior

Thanks to William Tecumseh Sherman, the Confederacy was nearly dead as well. As a young military officer stationed in the South, Sherman sympathized with the planter class and felt that slavery upheld social stability. However, Sherman believed in the Union. Secession meant "anarchy," he told his southern friends in early 1861: "If war comes . . . I must fight your

people whom I best love." Serving under Grant, Sherman distinguished himself at Shiloh and Vicksburg. Taking command of the Army of the Tennessee, he developed the philosophy and tactics of **"hard war."** "When one nation is at war with another, all the people of one are enemies of the other," Sherman declared. When Confederate guerrillas fired on a boat carrying Unionist civilians near Randolph, Tennessee, Sherman sent a regiment to destroy the town, asserting, "We are justified in treating all inhabitants as combatants."

After capturing Atlanta, Sherman advocated a bold strategy. Instead of pursuing the retreating Confederate army northward into Tennessee, he proposed to move south, live off the land, and "cut a swath through to the sea." To persuade Lincoln and Grant to approve his unconventional plan, Sherman argued that his march would be "a demonstration to the world, foreign and domestic, that we have a power [Jefferson] Davis cannot resist." The Union general lived up to his pledge. "We are not only fighting hostile armies," Sherman wrote, "but a hostile people, and must make old and young, rich and poor, feel the hard hand of war." He left Atlanta in flames, and during his 300-mile **March to the Sea** (Map 14.6) his army consumed or demolished everything in its path. A Union veteran wrote, "[We] destroyed all we could not eat, stole their niggers, burned their cotton & gins, spilled their sorghum, burned & twisted their R.Roads and raised Hell generally." Although Sherman's army usually did not harm noncombatants who kept to their peaceful business, the havoc so demoralized Confederate soldiers that many deserted their units and returned home (American Voices, p. 472). When Sherman reached Savannah in mid-December, the city's 10,000 defenders left without a fight.

Georgia's African Americans treated Sherman as a savior. "They flock to me, old and young," he wrote. "[T]hey pray and shout and mix up my name with Moses . . . as well as 'Abram Linkom,' the Great Messiah of 'Dis Jubilee.'" To provide for the hundreds of blacks now following his army, Sherman issued Special Field Order No. 15, which set aside 400,000 acres of prime rice-growing land for the exclusive use of freedmen. By June 1865, about 40,000 blacks were cultivating "Sherman lands." Many freedmen believed that the lands were to be theirs forever, belated payment for generations of unpaid labor: "All the land belongs to the Yankees now and they gwine divide it out among de coloured people."

 To see more of Sherman's writing, along with other primary sources from this period, see **Sources for America's History**.

In February 1865, Sherman invaded South Carolina to punish the instigators of nullification and secession. His troops ravaged the countryside as they cut a narrow swath across the state. After capturing South Carolina's capital, Columbia, they burned the business district, most churches, and the wealthiest residential neighborhoods. "This disappointment to me is extremely bitter," lamented Jefferson Davis. By March, Sherman had reached North Carolina, ready to link up with Grant and crush Lee's army.

**The Confederate Collapse**  Grant's war of attrition in Virginia had already exposed a weakness in the Confederacy: rising class resentment among poor whites. Angered by slave owners' exemptions from military service and fearing that the Confederacy was doomed, ordinary southern farmers now repudiated the draft. "All they want is to git you . . . to fight for

their infurnal negroes," grumbled an Alabama hill farmer. More and more soldiers fled their units. "I am now going to work instead of to the war," vowed David Harris, another backcountry yeoman. By 1865, at least 100,000 men had deserted from Confederate armies, prompting reluctant Confederate leaders to approve the enlistment of black soldiers and promising them freedom. However, the fighting ended too soon to reveal whether any slaves would have fought for the Confederacy.

The symbolic end of the war took place in Virginia. In April 1865, Grant finally gained control of the crucial railroad junction at Petersburg and forced Lee to abandon Richmond. As Lincoln visited the ruins of the Confederate capital, greeted by joyful

> **PLACE EVENTS IN CONTEXT**
> To what extent were Grant and Sherman's military strategy and tactics responsible for defeat of the Confederacy?

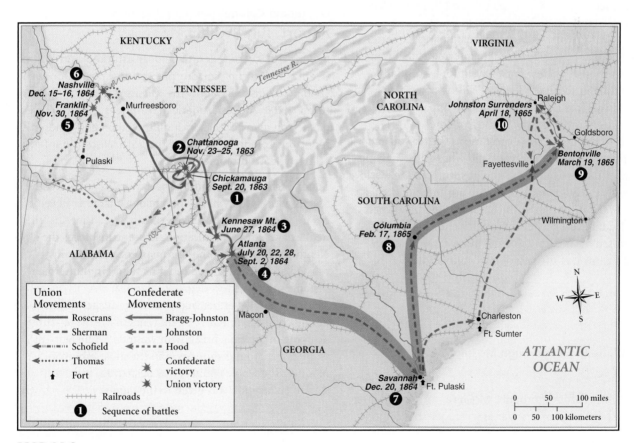

**MAP 14.6**
**Sherman's March Through the Confederacy, 1864–1865**
The Union victory in November 1863 at Chattanooga, Tennessee (2), was almost as critical as the victories in July at Gettysburg and Vicksburg, because it opened up a route of attack into the heart of the Confederacy. In mid-1864, General William Tecumseh Sherman advanced on the railway hub of Atlanta (3 and 4). After finally taking the city in September 1864, Sherman relied on other Union armies to stem General Hood's invasion of Tennessee (5 and 6) while he began his devastating March to the Sea. By December, he had reached Savannah (7); from there, he cut a swath through the Carolinas (8–10).

## Gender, Class, and Sexual Terror in the Invaded South

When the white men of the South marched off to war, they left behind their wives and children. Soon, Confederate women in the border states confronted an enemy army of occupation. Later, when Union armies invaded the Confederacy, southern women—both black and white—faced an even more dangerous army of conquest and destruction.

### Cornelia Peake McDonald
#### Journal

Cornelia Peake McDonald was the wife of an affluent lawyer in Winchester, Virginia, a town occupied by Union forces. She had nine children, born between 1848 and 1861.

[May 1863] 22nd . . . To day I received another intimation that my house would be wanted for a [Union] regimental hospital. I feel a sickening despair when I think of what will be my condition if they do take it. . . .

Major Butterworth . . . told me that he was a quarter master, and that he had been sent to inform me that I must give up the house, as they must have it for a hospital. . . . I lost no time in seeking [General] Milroy's presence. . . . "Gen. Milroy," said I. He looked around impatiently. "They have come to take my house from me." . . . [He replied,] "Why should you expect me to shelter you and your family, you who are a rebel, and whose husband and family are in arms against the best government the world ever saw?" . . . "But Gen. Milroy, you are commandant here . . . and you can suffer me to remain in mine, where at least I can have a shelter for my sick children." . . . At last he raised his head and looked in my face. "You can stay but I allow it at the risk of my commission."

Source: *A Woman's Civil War*, ed. Minrose C. Gwin (Madison: University of Wisconsin Press, 1992), 101, 150–153.

### Judith White Brockenbrough McGuire
#### Diary

Judith White Brockenbrough McGuire, of Alexandria, Virginia, spent most of the war as a refugee in Richmond.

June 11, 1865
These particulars . . . I have [heard] from our nephew, J. P. [in occupied central Virginia. He reports that] . . . the Northern officers seemed disposed to be courteous to the ladies, in the little intercourse which they had with them. General Ferrera, who commanded the negro troops, was humane, in having a coffin made for a young Confederate officer. . . . The surgeons, too, assisted in attending to the

Confederate wounded. An officer one morning sent for Mrs. N. [to return an item stolen by Union soldiers]. . . . She thanked him for his kindness. He seemed moved and said, "Mrs. N., I will do what I can for you, for I cannot be too thankful that my wife is not in an invaded country."

Source: Rod Gragg, *The Illustrated Confederate Reader* (New York: Harper & Row, 1989), 88–89.

### Lieutenant Colonel Samuel J. Nasmith
#### Report, July 1, 1863

In June 1863, Confederate raiders attacked and burned twenty Union-run cotton plantations near Goodrich's Landing, Louisiana, along the Mississippi River. They captured 1,200 African American refugees and took vengeance on many others, including women and children. A report by Colonel Nasmith of the 25th Wisconsin Infantry related the gruesome details.

Major Farnan, commanding the cavalry, reports that the scenes witnessed by him . . . were of a character never before witnessed in a civilized country. . . . They spared neither age, sex, nor condition. In some instances the Negroes were shut up in their quarters, and literally roasted alive. The charred remains found in numerous instances testified to a degree of fiendish atrocity such as has no parallel either in civilized or savage warfare. Young children, only five or six years of age, were found skulking in the cane break with wounds, while helpless women were found shot down in the most inhumane manner. The whole country was destroyed, and every sign of civilization was given to the flames.

Source: *The War of the Rebellion: A Compilation of the Official Records of the Union and Confederate Armies* (Washington, DC: Government Printing Office, 1889), Series 1, Vol. 24 (Part II), 517.

### Anna Maria Green
#### Diary

Twenty-year-old Anna Maria Green kept a diary as General William Tecumseh Sherman's army of 60,000 men approached Milledgeville, Georgia.

Saturday evening November 19th [1864] — Again we are in a state of excitement caused by the near approach to our town of the enemy. Last night they were two thousand strong at Monticello. . . . Minnie came in to call me to look at a fire in the west. My heart sank, and almost burst with grief as I beheld the horizon crimson and the desolation our hated foe was spreading. Great God! Deliver us, oh! Spare our city. . . .

Nov. 25th Friday evening . . . This morning the last of the vandals left our city and burned the bridge after them — leaving suffering and desolation behind them, and embittering every heart. The worst of their acts was committed to poor Mrs. Nichols — violence done, and atrocity committed that ought to make her husband an enemy unto death. Poor woman. I fear she has been driven crazy.

Source: Rod Gragg, *The Illustrated Confederate Reader* (New York: Harper & Row, 1989), 175–176.

## Unknown Woman
## Letter to Her Daughter

This letter was written by a woman in Columbia, South Carolina.

Columbia March 3, 1865
My dear Gracia

Doubtless your anxiety is very great to hear something about us after the great calamity that has befallen our town. We have lost everything, but thank God, our lives have been spared. Oh Gracia, what we have passed through no tongue can tell, it defies description! . . .

The first regiment sent into the city was what Sherman calls his "Tigers." Whenever he sends these men ahead, he intends to do his worst. . . . The first thing they did was break open the stores and distribute the goods right and left. They found liquor and all became heartily drunk. . . . When night came on, the soldiers . . . fired the houses. It was a fearful sight. . . .

We stayed all night in the street, protected by a Yankee Captain from Iowa who was very kind to us.

Source: Rod Gragg, *The Illustrated Confederate Reader* (New York: Harper & Row, 1989), 189–190.

## Daniel Heyward Trezevant
## Report

Daniel Heyward Trezevant, a doctor in Columbia, South Carolina, wrote a brief report after Sherman's departure.

The Yankees' gallantry, brutality and debauchery were afflicted on the negroes. . . . The case of Mr. Shane's old negro woman, who, after being subjected to the most brutal indecency from seven of the Yankees, was, at the proposition of one of them to "finish the old Bitch," put into a ditch and held under water until life was extinct. . . .

Mrs. T. B. C. was seized by one of the soldiers, an officer, and dragged by the hair and forced to the floor for the purpose of sensual enjoyment. She resisted as far as practical — held up her young infant as a plea for sparing her and succeeded, but they took her maid, and in her presence, threw her on the floor and had connection with her. . . . They pinioned Mrs. McCord and robbed her. They dragged Mrs. Gynn by the hair of her head about the house. Mrs. G. told me of a young lady about 16, Miss Kinsler, who . . . three officers brutally ravished and who became crazy.

Source: Rod Gragg, *The Illustrated Confederate Reader* (New York: Harper & Row, 1989), 192.

### QUESTIONS FOR ANALYSIS

1. How might class loyalties and shared cultural values have influenced General Milroy's decision to let Cornelia McDonald stay in her home? How do the actions of the "Yankee Captain from Iowa" compare with Milroy's?

2. Although none of these writers used the word *rape* (why not?), we can assume that Mrs. Nichols was raped, as were Miss Kinsler and the enslaved African American maid in Columbia. What about Mrs. T. B. C., Mrs. McCord, and Mrs. Gynn? How should we evaluate the credibility of these sources (and other, similar accounts written by whites) when they assert or imply that Union troops raped enslaved women and spared white women?

3. How should we compare the brutal actions of Confederate soldiers toward fugitive blacks and the treatment of southern women by Sherman's troops? Explain why they do — or do not — represent the same kind of wartime military misconduct.

ex-slaves, Grant cut off Lee's escape route to North Carolina. On April 9, almost four years to the day after the attack on Fort Sumter, Lee surrendered at Appomattox Court House, Virginia. In return for their promise not to fight again, Grant allowed the Confederate officers and men to go home. By late May, all of the secessionist armies and governments had simply melted away (Map 14.7).

The hard and bitter conflict was finally over. Northern armies had preserved the Union and destroyed slavery; many of the South's factories, railroads, and cities lay in ruins; and its farms and plantations had suffered years of neglect. Almost 260,000 Confederate soldiers had paid for secession with their lives. On the other side, more than 360,000 northerners had died for the Union, and thousands more had been maimed. Was it all worth the price? Delivering his second inaugural address in March 1865 — less than a month

before his assassination — Abraham Lincoln could justify the hideous carnage only by alluding to divine providence: "[S]o still it must be said 'the judgments of the Lord are true and righteous altogether.'"

What of the war's effects on society? A New York census taker suggested that the conflict had undermined "autocracy" and had an "equalizing effect." Slavery was gone from the South, he reflected, and in the North, "military men from the so called 'lower classes' now lead society, having been elevated by real merit and valor." However perceptive these remarks, they ignored the wartime emergence of a new financial aristocracy that would soon preside over what Mark Twain labeled the Gilded Age. Nor was the sectional struggle yet concluded. As the North began to reconstruct the South and the Union, it found those tasks to be almost as hard and bitter as the war itself.

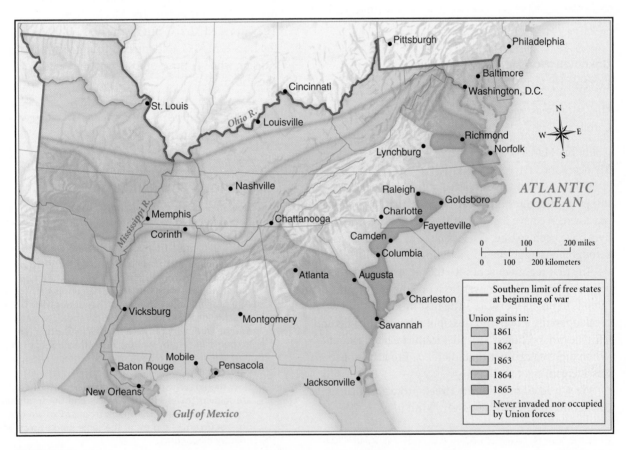

**MAP 14.7**

**The Conquest of the South, 1861–1865**

It took four years for the Union armies to defeat the Confederate forces. Until 1864, most of the South remained in Confederate hands; even at the end of the war, Union armies had never entered many parts of the rebellious states. Most of the Union's territorial gains came on the vast western front, where its control of strategic lines of communication (the Ohio and Mississippi rivers and major railroads) gave its forces a decisive advantage.

**An Uncounted Casualty of the War**

Many men who died in the war were husbands and fathers, leaving tens of thousands of widows—and even more children—to grieve over their loss. Dressed in mourning clothes, this unidentified, sad-faced young girl holds an image of her dead father, a cavalryman holding a sword and wearing a regulation dress hat. Library of Congress.

# SUMMARY

In this chapter, we surveyed the dramatic events of the Civil War. Looking at the South, we watched the fire-eaters declare secession, form a new Confederacy, and attack Fort Sumter. Subsequently, we saw its generals repulse Union attacks against Richmond and go on the offensive. However, as the war continued, the inherent weaknesses of the Confederacy came to the fore. Enslaved workers fled or refused to work, and yeomen farmers refused to fight for an institution that primarily benefitted wealthy planters.

Examining the North, we witnessed its military shortcomings. Its generals—McClellan and Meade—moved slowly to attack and did not pursue their weakened foes. However, the Union's significant advantages in industrial output, financial resources, and military manpower became manifest over time. Congress created efficient systems of banking and war finance, Lincoln found efficient and ruthless generals, and the emancipation and recruitment of African Americans provided an abundant supply of soldiers determined to end slavery.

We explored the impact of the war on civilians in both regions: the imposition of conscription and high taxes, the increased workload of farm women, and the constant food shortages and soaring prices. Above all else, there was the omnipresent fact of death—a tragedy that touched nearly every family, North and South.

# CHAPTER REVIEW

**MAKE IT STICK**   Go to **LearningCurve** to retain what you've read.

## TERMS TO KNOW   Identify and explain the significance of each term below.

### Key Concepts and Events

**Crittenden Compromise** (p. 446)
**total war** (p. 452)
**draft (conscription)** (p. 452)
**habeas corpus** (p. 454)
**King Cotton** (p. 456)
**greenbacks** (p. 460)
**"contrabands"** (p. 463)
**Radical Republicans** (p. 463)

**Emancipation Proclamation** (p. 464)
**scorched-earth campaign** (p. 468)
**War and Peace Democrats** (p. 469)
**"hard war"** (p. 470)
**March to the Sea** (p. 470)

### Key People

**Abraham Lincoln** (p. 444)
**Jefferson Davis** (p. 446)
**Robert E. Lee** (p. 448)
**George McClellan** (p. 449)
**Ulysses S. Grant** (p. 466)
**William T. Sherman** (p. 470)

## REVIEW QUESTIONS
Answer these questions to demonstrate your understanding of the chapter's main ideas.

1. Based on the evidence presented in this chapter, did Lee's surrender at Appomattox and Grant's magnanimity to the defeated forces save the nation from a drawn-out guerrilla war, as some historians have argued? Or, as other scholars have suggested, did the events at Appomattox undermine black emancipation by giving a high priority to the reconciliation of northern and southern whites?

2. In 1860, the institution of slavery was firmly entrenched in the United States; by 1865, it was dead. How did this happen? How and why did Union policy toward slavery and enslaved people change over the course of the war?

3. **THEMATIC UNDERSTANDING**   The thematic timeline for Part 5 (p. 409) lists six events or developments in the 1860s relating directly to the South's secession and the Civil War. Does that list capture the war's overwhelming importance to the history of nineteenth-century America? If not, is this deficiency inherent to timelines, or does it reflect a faulty construction of this specific timeline? How would you address this problem?

## MAKING CONNECTIONS
Recognize the larger developments and continuities within and across chapters by answering these questions.

1. **ACROSS TIME AND PLACE**   After reviewing the compromises over slavery at the Constitutional Convention (p. 206), in the Missouri Compromise (p. 269), and in the Compromise of 1850 (p. 429), write an essay analyzing why the opposing sides failed to compromise in 1861.

2. **VISUAL EVIDENCE**   The photographs of the Southern Refugee Family (p. 462) and Grant Planning a Strategic Maneuver (p. 468) remind us of a world in which people, goods, and soldiers moved either on foot or on horses and mules. How did this limited mobility affect civilians — slave and free — and military forces during the Civil War?

## MORE TO EXPLORE
Start here to learn more about the events discussed in this chapter.

Dora L. Costa and Matthew E. Kahn, *Heroes and Cowards: The Social Face of War* (2008). Demonstrates the role of friendship and community in soldiers' wartime behavior.

Drew Gilpin Faust, *This Republic of Suffering: Death and the American Civil War* (2008). Examines the cultural changes prompted by massive casualties.

William W. Freehling, *The South vs. the South* (2001). Explores anti-Confederate sentiment in the South.

Gary W. Gallagher, *The Confederate War* (1997). Views the fighting from the perspective of the secessionists.

Earl J. Hess, *The Union Soldier in Battle* (1997). Vividly describes the smell, sound, and feel of combat.

James M. McPherson, *The Battle Cry of Freedom* (1988). A fine narrative history of the Civil War.

## TIMELINE

Ask yourself why this chapter begins and ends with these dates and then identify the links among related events.

| | |
|---|---|
| **1860** | • Abraham Lincoln elected president (November 6)<br>• South Carolina secedes (December 20) |
| **1861** | • Lincoln inaugurated (March 4)<br>• Confederates fire on Fort Sumter (April 12)<br>• Virginia leaves Union (April 17)<br>• General Butler declares refugee slaves "contraband of war" (May)<br>• Confederates win Battle of Bull Run (July 21)<br>• First Confiscation Act (August) |
| **1862** | • Legal Tender Act authorizes greenbacks (February)<br>• Union triumphs at Shiloh (April 6–7)<br>• Confederacy introduces draft (April)<br>• Congress passes Homestead Act and Transcontinental Railroad Act (May, July)<br>• Union halts Confederates at Antietam (September 17)<br>• Preliminary emancipation proclamation (September 22) |
| **1863** | • Lincoln signs Emancipation Proclamation (January 1)<br>• Union wins battles at Gettysburg (July 1–3) and Vicksburg (July 4)<br>• Union initiates draft (March), sparking riots in New York City (July) |
| **1864** | • Ulysses S. Grant named Union commander (March)<br>• Grant advances on Richmond (May)<br>• William Tecumseh Sherman takes Atlanta (September 2)<br>• Lincoln reelected (November 8)<br>• Sherman marches through Georgia (November and December) |
| **1865** | • Congress approves Thirteenth Amendment (January 31)<br>• Robert E. Lee surrenders (April 9)<br>• Lincoln assassinated (April 14)<br>• Thirteenth Amendment ratified (December 6) |

**KEY TURNING POINTS:** The Emancipation Proclamations (1862/1863); Union victories at Gettysburg and Vicksburg (1863); and Sherman's taking of Atlanta (1864): historians have seen all of these events as important turning points. Assume that *one* of these events did not happen. What difference would it have made in the military and political struggle between the Union and the Confederacy?

# 15

## CHAPTER

# Reconstruction
# 1865–1877

On the last day of April 1866, black soldiers in Memphis, Tennessee, turned in their weapons as they mustered out of the Union army. The next day, whites who resented the soldiers' presence provoked a clash. At a street celebration where African Americans shouted "Hurrah for Abe Lincoln," a white policeman responded, "Your old father, Abe Lincoln, is dead and damned." The scuffle that followed precipitated three days of white violence and rape that left forty-eight African Americans dead and dozens more wounded. Mobs burned black homes and churches and destroyed all twelve of the city's black schools.

Unionists were appalled. They had won the Civil War, but where was the peace? Ex-Confederates murdered freedmen and flagrantly resisted federal control. After the Memphis attacks, Republicans in Congress proposed a new measure that would protect African Americans by defining and enforcing U.S. citizenship rights. Eventually this bill became the most significant law to emerge from Reconstruction, the Fourteenth Amendment to the Constitution.

Andrew Johnson, however—the Unionist Democrat who became president after Abraham Lincoln's assassination—refused to sign the bill. In May 1865, while Congress was adjourned, Johnson had implemented his own Reconstruction plan. It extended amnesty to all southerners who took a loyalty oath, except for a few high-ranking Confederates. It also allowed states to reenter the Union as soon as they revoked secession, abolished slavery, and relieved their new state governments of financial burdens by repudiating Confederate debts. A year later, at the time of the Memphis carnage, all ex-Confederate states had met Johnson's terms. The president rejected any further intervention.

Johnson's vetoes, combined with ongoing violence in the South, angered Unionist voters. In the political struggle that ensued, congressional Republicans seized the initiative from the president and enacted a sweeping program that became known as Radical Reconstruction. One of its key achievements would have been unthinkable a few years earlier: voting rights for African American men.

Black Southeners, though, had additional, urgent priorities. "We have toiled nearly all our lives as slaves [and] have made these lands what they are," a group of South Carolina petitioners declared. They pleaded for "some provision by which we as Freedmen can obtain a Homestead." Though northern Republicans and freedpeople agreed that black southerners must have physical safety and the right to vote, former slaves also wanted economic independence. Northerners sought, instead, to revive cash-crop plantations with wage labor. Reconstruction's eventual failure stemmed from the conflicting goals of lawmakers, freedpeople, and relentlessly hostile ex-Confederates.

## IDENTIFY THE BIG IDEA

What goals did Republican policymakers, ex-Confederates, and freedpeople pursue during Reconstruction? To what degree did each succeed?

**Celebrating the Fifteenth Amendment, 1870** This lithograph depicts a celebration in Baltimore on May 15, 1870. With perhaps 200,000 people attending, the grand parade and orations marked passage of the Fifteenth Amendment, which enfranchised men irrespective of "race, color, or previous condition of servitude." The heroes depicted at the top are Martin Delany, the first black man to become an officer in the U.S. Army; abolitionist Frederick Douglass, born in slavery on Maryland's eastern shore; and Mississippi senator Hiram Rhodes Revels. The images at the bottom carried the following captions: "Liberty Protects the Marriage Altar," "The Ballot Box is open to us," and "Our representative Sits in the National Legislature." Such lithographs, widely printed and sold, capture the pride, hope, and optimism of Reconstruction—but the optimism was not to last. Library of Congress.

# The Struggle for National Reconstruction

Congress clashed with President Johnson, in part, because the framers of the Constitution did not anticipate a civil war or provide for its aftermath. Had Confederate states legally left the Union when they seceded? If so, then their reentry required action by Congress. If not—if even during secession they had retained U.S. statehood—then restoring them might be an administrative matter, best left to the president. Lack of clarity on this fundamental question made for explosive politics.

## Presidential Approaches: From Lincoln to Johnson

As wartime president, Lincoln had offered a plan similar to Johnson's. It granted amnesty to most ex-Confederates and allowed each rebellious state to return to the Union as soon as 10 percent of its voters had taken a loyalty oath and the state had approved the Thirteenth Amendment, abolishing slavery. But even amid defeat, Confederate states rejected this **Ten Percent Plan**—an ominous sign for the

**COMPARE AND CONTRAST**
How did Lincoln and Johnson approach Reconstruction differently?

future. In July 1864, Congress proposed a tougher substitute, the **Wade-Davis Bill**, that required an oath of allegiance by a majority of each state's adult white men, new governments formed only by those who had never taken up arms against the Union, and permanent disenfranchisement of Confederate leaders. Lincoln defeated the Wade-Davis Bill with a pocket veto, leaving it unsigned when Congress adjourned. At the same time, he opened talks with key congressmen, aiming for a compromise.

We will never know what would have happened had Lincoln lived. His assassination in April 1865 plunged the nation into political uncertainty. As a special train bore the president's flag-draped coffin home to Illinois, thousands of Americans lined the railroad tracks in mourning. Furious and grief-stricken, many Unionists blamed all Confederates for the acts of southern sympathizer John Wilkes Booth and his accomplices in the murder. At the same time, Lincoln's death left the presidency in the hands of Andrew Johnson, a man utterly lacking in Lincoln's moral sense and political judgment.

Johnson was a self-styled "common man" from the hills of eastern Tennessee. Trained as a tailor, he built his political career on the support of farmers and laborers. Loyal to the Union, Johnson had refused to leave the U.S. Senate when Tennessee seceded. After federal forces captured Nashville in 1862, Lincoln appointed Johnson as Tennessee's military governor. In the election

**Memphis Riot, 1866**

Whites in postwar Memphis, as in much of the South, bitterly resented the presence in their city of former black soldiers mustered out of service with the U.S. Army. On April 30, 1866, when some black veterans—no longer protected by their uniforms—celebrated the end of their army service by drinking, violence broke out. For three days, whites burned black neighborhoods, churches, and schools, raped several African American women, and killed dozens of black residents. Two whites also died in the rioting, which hardened northern public opinion and prompted calls for stronger measures to put down ex-Confederate resistance. This tinted illustration is based on a lithograph that appeared in *Harper's Weekly. Harper's Weekly/* Picture Research Consultants & Archives.

of 1864, placing Lincoln and this War Democrat on the ticket together had seemed a smart move, designed to promote unity. But after Lincoln's death, Johnson's disagreement with Republicans, combined with his belligerent and contradictory actions, wreaked political havoc.

The new president and Congress confronted a set of problems that would have challenged even Lincoln. During the war, Unionists had insisted that rebel leaders were a small minority and most white southerners wanted to rejoin the Union. With even greater optimism, Republicans hoped the defeated South would accept postwar reforms. Ex-Confederates, however, contested that plan through both violence and political action. New southern state legislatures, created under Johnson's limited Reconstruction plan, moved to restore slavery in all but name. In 1865, they enacted **Black Codes**, designed to force former slaves back to plantation labor. Like similar laws passed in other places after slavery ended, the codes reflected plantation owners' economic interests (America Compared, p. 482). They imposed severe penalties on blacks who did not hold full-year labor contracts and also set up procedures for taking black children from their parents and apprenticing them to former slave masters.

Faced with these developments, Johnson gave all the wrong signals. He had long talked tough against southern planters. But in practice, Johnson allied himself with ex-Confederate leaders, forgiving them when they appealed for pardons. White southern leaders were delighted. "By this wise and noble statesmanship," wrote a Confederate legislator, "you have become the benefactor of the Southern people." Northerners and freedmen were disgusted. The president had left Reconstruction "to the tender mercies of the rebels," wrote one Republican. An angry Union veteran in Missouri called Johnson "a traitor to the loyal people of the Union." Emboldened by Johnson's indulgence, ex-Confederates began to filter back into the halls of power. When Georgians elected Alexander Stephens, former vice president of the Confederacy, to represent them in Congress, many outraged Republicans saw this as the last straw.

## Congress Versus the President

Under the Constitution, Congress is "the judge of the Elections, Returns and Qualifications of its own Members" (Article 1, Section 5). Using this power, Republican majorities in both houses had refused to admit southern delegations when Congress convened in December 1865, effectively blocking Johnson's program. Hoping to mollify Congress, some southern states dropped the most objectionable provisions from their Black Codes. But at the same time, antiblack violence erupted in various parts of the South.

Congressional Republicans concluded that the federal government had to intervene. Back in March 1865, Congress had established the **Freedmen's Bureau** to aid displaced blacks and other war refugees. In early 1866, Congress voted to extend the bureau, gave it direct funding for the first time, and authorized its agents to investigate southern abuses. Even more extraordinary was the **Civil Rights Act of 1866**, which declared formerly enslaved people to be citizens and granted them equal protection and rights of contract, with full access to the courts.

These bills provoked bitter conflict with Johnson, who vetoed them both. Johnson's racism, hitherto publicly muted, now blazed forth: "This is a country for white men, and by God, as long as I am president, it shall be a government for white men." Galvanized, Republicans in Congress gathered two-thirds majorities and overrode both vetoes, passing the Civil Rights Act in April 1866 and the Freedmen's Bureau law four months later. Their resolve was reinforced by continued upheaval in the South. In addition to the violence in Memphis, twenty-four black political leaders and their allies in Arkansas were murdered and their homes burned.

Anxious to protect freedpeople and reassert Republican power in the South, Congress took further measures to sustain civil rights. In what became the **Fourteenth Amendment** (1868), it declared that "all persons born or naturalized in the United States" were citizens. No state could abridge "the privileges or immunities of citizens of the United States"; deprive "any person of life, liberty, or property, without due process of law"; or deny anyone "equal protection." In a stunning increase of federal power, the Fourteenth Amendment declared that when people's essential rights were at stake, national citizenship henceforth took priority over citizenship in a state.

Johnson opposed ratification, but public opinion had swung against him. In the 1866 congressional elections, voters gave Republicans a 3-to-1 majority in Congress. Power shifted to the so-called Radical Republicans, who sought sweeping transformations in the defeated South. Radicals' leader in the Senate was Charles Sumner of Massachusetts, the fiery abolitionist who in 1856 had been nearly beaten to death by South Carolina congressman Preston

**PLACE EVENTS IN CONTEXT**
Under what circumstances did the Fourteenth Amendment win passage, and what problems did its authors seek to address?

## Labor Laws After Emancipation: Haiti and the United States

Many government officials agreed with former masters on the need to control rural workers. Often planters themselves or allied with the planter class, they believed that economic strength and public revenue depended on plantation export crops and that workers would not produce those without legal coercion.

This was true in the British Caribbean and also Haiti, which eventually, after a successful slave revolt ending in 1803, became an independent republic led by former slaves and, in particular, by propertied free men of color. In the passage below, a British observer describes a rural labor code adopted by Haiti's government in 1826. Despite the law, Haiti's large plantations did not revive; the island's economy, even more than that of the U.S. South, came to be dominated by small-scale, impoverished farmers.

---

The Code of Laws before us is one that could only have been framed by a legislature composed of proprietors of land, having at their command a considerable military power, of which they themselves were the leaders; for a population whom it was necessary to compel to labour. . . .

The choice of a master, altho' expressly reserved to the labourer, is greatly modified by the clauses which restrain the labourer from quitting the section of country to which he belongs; and from the absence of any clause compelling proprietors to engage him; so that the cultivator must consent to bind himself to whomsoever may be willing to engage him, or remain in prison, to be employed among convicts. . . .

The Code begins (Article 1) by declaring Agriculture to be the foundation of national prosperity; and then decrees (Article 3), That all persons, excepting soldiers, and civil servants of the State, professional persons, artizans, and domestic servants, shall cultivate the soil. The next clause (Article 4), forbids the inhabitants of the country quitting it to dwell in towns or villages; and every kind of wholesale or retail trade is forbidden (Article 7) to be exercised by persons dwelling in the country.

Further articles stipulate that any person dwelling in the country, not being the owner or occupier of land, and not having bound himself in the manner directed, . . . shall be considered a vagabond, be arrested, and taken before a Justice, who, after reading the Law to him, shall commit him to jail, until he consent to bind himself according to law.

. . . Those who are hired from a job-master [labor agent], . . . are entitled to receive half the produce, after deducting the expences of cultivation; [those who are bound to the proprietor directly], one-fourth of the gross produce of their labour. . . . Out of their miserable pittance, these Haitian labourers are to provide themselves and their children with almost every thing, and to lay by a provision for old age. . . .

These, with the regulations already detailed, clearly shew what is intended to be the condition of the labouring population of Haiti. I must not call it slavery; the word is objectionable; but few of the ingredients of slavery seem to be wanting.

### QUESTIONS FOR ANALYSIS

1. Compare this Haitian law with the Black Codes briefly adopted by ex-Confederate states, and with the share-cropping system that evolved in the United States during Reconstruction (p. 491). What did these labor systems—or proposed systems—have in common? How did they differ?

2. Why would the Haitian government, led by men of color, enact such laws? What considerations other than race might have shaped their views, and why?

---

Brooks. Radicals in the House followed Thaddeus Stevens of Pennsylvania, a passionate advocate of freedmen's political and economic rights. With such men at the fore, and with congressional Republicans now numerous and united enough to override Johnson's vetoes on many questions, Congress proceeded to remake Reconstruction.

## Radical Reconstruction

The **Reconstruction Act of 1867**, enacted in March, divided the conquered South into five military districts, each under the command of a U.S. general (Map 15.1). To reenter the Union, former Confederate states had to grant the vote to freedmen and deny it to

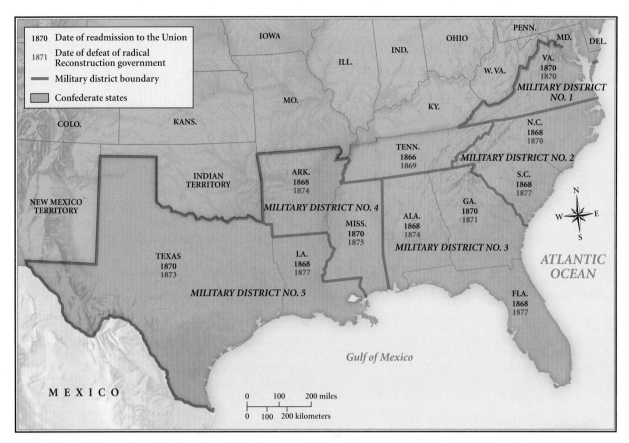

**MAP 15.1**

**Reconstruction**

The federal government organized the Confederate states into five military districts during Radical Reconstruction. For the states shown in this map, the first date indicates when that state was readmitted to the Union; the second date shows when Radical Republicans lost control of the state government. All the ex-Confederate states rejoined the Union between 1868 and 1870, but the periods of Radical government varied widely. Republicans lasted only a few months in Virginia; they held on until the end of Reconstruction in Louisiana, Florida, and South Carolina.

leading ex-Confederates. Each military commander was required to register all eligible adult males, black as well as white; supervise state constitutional conventions; and ensure that new constitutions guaranteed black suffrage. Congress would readmit a state to the Union once these conditions were met and the new state legislature ratified the Fourteenth Amendment. Johnson vetoed the Reconstruction Act, but Congress overrode his veto (Table 15.1).

**The Impeachment of Andrew Johnson**   In August 1867, Johnson fought back by "suspending" Secretary of War Edwin M. Stanton, a Radical, and replacing him with Union general Ulysses S. Grant, believing Grant would be a good soldier and follow orders. Johnson, however, had misjudged Grant, who publicly objected to the president's machinations. When the Senate overruled Stanton's suspension, Grant — now an open

enemy of Johnson — resigned so Stanton could resume his place as secretary of war. On February 21, 1868, Johnson formally dismissed Stanton. The feisty secretary of war responded by barricading himself in his office, precipitating a crisis.

Three days later, for the first time in U.S. history, legislators in the House of Representatives introduced articles of impeachment against the president, employing their constitutional power to charge high federal officials with "Treason, Bribery, or other high Crimes and Misdemeanors." The House serves, in effect, as the prosecutor in such cases, and the Senate serves as the court. The Republican majority brought eleven counts of misconduct against Johnson, most relating to infringement of the powers of Congress. After an eleven-week trial in the Senate, thirty-five senators voted for conviction — one vote short of the two-thirds majority required. Twelve Democrats and seven Republicans

## TABLE 15.1

### Primary Reconstruction Laws and Constitutional Amendments

| Law (Date of Congressional Passage) | Key Provisions |
|---|---|
| Thirteenth Amendment (December 1865*) | Prohibited slavery |
| Civil Rights Act of 1866 (April 1866) | Defined citizenship rights of freedmen<br>Authorized federal authorities to bring suit against those who violated those rights |
| Fourteenth Amendment (June 1866†) | Established national citizenship for persons born or naturalized in the United States<br>Prohibited the states from depriving citizens of their civil rights or equal protection under the law<br>Reduced state representation in House of Representatives by the percentage of adult male citizens denied the vote |
| Reconstruction Act of 1867 (March 1867) | Divided the South into five military districts, each under the command of a Union general<br>Established requirements for readmission of ex-Confederate states to the Union |
| Tenure of Office Act (March 1867) | Required Senate consent for removal of any federal official whose appointment had required Senate confirmation |
| Fifteenth Amendment (February 1869‡) | Forbade states to deny citizens the right to vote on the grounds of race, color, or "previous condition of servitude" |
| Ku Klux Klan Act (April 1871) | Authorized the president to use federal prosecutions and military force to suppress conspiracies to deprive citizens of the right to vote and enjoy the equal protection of the law |

*Ratified by three-fourths of all states in December 1865.
†Ratified by three-fourths of all states in July 1868.
‡Ratified by three-fourths of all states in March 1870.

voted for acquittal. The dissenting Republicans felt that removing a president for defying Congress was too damaging to the constitutional system of checks and balances. But despite the president's acquittal, Congress had shown its power. For the brief months remaining in his term, Johnson was largely irrelevant.

### Election of 1868 and the Fifteenth Amendment

The impeachment controversy made Grant, already the Union's greatest war hero, a Republican idol as well. He easily won the party's presidential nomination in 1868. Although he supported Radical Reconstruction, Grant also urged sectional reconciliation. His Democratic opponent, former New York governor Horatio Seymour, almost declined the nomination because he understood that Democrats could not yet overcome the stain of disloyalty. Grant won by an overwhelming margin, receiving 214 out of 294 electoral votes. Republicans retained two-thirds majorities in both houses of Congress.

In February 1869, following this smashing victory, Republicans produced the era's last constitutional amendment, the Fifteenth. It protected male citizens' right to vote irrespective of race, color, or "previous condition of servitude." Despite Radical Republicans' protests, the amendment left room for a poll tax (paid for the privilege of voting) and literacy requirements. Both were concessions to northern and western states that sought such provisions to keep immigrants and

**TRACE CHANGE OVER TIME**
How and why did federal Reconstruction policies evolve between 1865 and 1870?

### "We Accept the Situation"

This 1867 *Harper's Weekly* cartoon refers to the Military Reconstruction Act of 1867, which instructed ex-Confederate states to hold constitutional conventions and stipulated that the resulting constitutions must provide voting rights for black men. The two images here suggest white northerners' views of both ex-Confederates and emancipated slaves. How is each depicted? What does this suggest about the troubles that lay ahead for Reconstruction policy? The cartoonist was Thomas Nast (1840–1902), one of the most influential artists of his era. Nast first drew "Santa Claus" in his modern form, and it was he who began depicting the Democratic Party as a kicking donkey and Republicans as an elephant— suggesting (since elephants are supposed to have good memories) their long remembrance of the Civil War and emancipation. Library of Congress.

the "unworthy" poor from the polls. Congress required the four states remaining under federal control to ratify the measure as a condition for readmission to the Union. A year later, the **Fifteenth Amendment** became law.

Passage of the Fifteenth Amendment, despite its limitations, was an astonishing feat. Elsewhere in the Western Hemisphere, lawmakers had left emancipated slaves in a condition of semi-citizenship, with no voting rights. But, like almost all Americans, congressional Republicans had extraordinary faith in the power of the vote. Many African Americans agreed. "The colored people of these Southern states have cast their lot with the Government," declared a delegate to Arkansas's constitutional convention, "and with the great Republican Party. . . . The ballot is our only means of protection." In the election of 1870, hundreds of thousands of African Americans voted across the South, in an atmosphere of collective pride and celebration.

 To see a longer excerpt of the Arkansas delegate's document, along with other primary sources from this period, see *Sources for America's History*.

## Woman Suffrage Denied

Passage of the Fifteenth Amendment was a bittersweet victory for one group of Union loyalists: women. Some formerly enslaved women believed they would win voting rights along with their men, until northern allies

corrected that impression. National women's rights leaders, who had campaigned for the ballot since the Seneca Falls convention of 1848, hoped to secure voting rights for women and African American men at the same time. As Elizabeth Cady Stanton put it, women could "avail ourselves of the strong arm and the blue uniform of the black soldier to walk in by his side." The protected categories for voting in the Fifteenth Amendment could have read "race, color, *sex*, or previous condition of servitude." But that word proved impossible to obtain.

Enfranchising black men had clear benefits for the authors of Reconstruction. It punished ex-Confederates and ensured Republican support in the South. But women's partisan loyalties were not so clear, and a substantial majority of northern voters — all men, of course — opposed women's enfranchisement. Even Radicals feared that this "side issue" would overburden their program. Influential abolitionists such as Wendell Philips refused to campaign for women's suffrage, fearing it would detract from the focus on black men. Philips criticized women's leaders for being "selfish." "Do you believe," Stanton hotly replied, "the African race is entirely composed of males?"

By May 1869, the former allies were at an impasse. At a convention of the Equal Rights Association, black abolitionist and women's rights advocate Frederick Douglass pleaded for white women to consider the situation in the South and allow black male suffrage to take priority. "When women, because they are women, are hunted down, . . . dragged from their homes and

---

OUT IN THE COLD.

**"Out in the Cold"**

Though many women, including African American activists in the South, went to the polls in the early 1870s to test whether the new Fourteenth Amendment had given them the vote, federal courts subsequently rejected women's voting rights. Only Wyoming and Utah territories fully enfranchised women. At the same time, revised naturalization laws allowed immigrant men of African descent—though not of Asian descent—to become citizens. With its crude Irish, African, and Chinese racial caricatures, this 1884 cartoon from the humor magazine *The Judge* echoes the arguments of some white suffragists: though men of races stereotyped as inferior had been enfranchised, white women were not. The woman knocking on the door is also a caricature, with her harsh appearance and masculine hat. Library of Congress.

### UNDERSTAND POINTS OF VIEW

Abolitionists and women's suffrage advocates were generally close allies before 1865. What divisions emerged during Reconstruction and why?

hung upon lamp posts," Douglass said, "then they will have an urgency to obtain the ballot equal to our own." Some women's suffrage leaders joined Douglass in backing the Fifteenth Amendment without the word *sex*. But many, especially white women, rejected Douglass's plea. One African American woman remarked that they "all go for sex, letting race occupy a minor position." Embittered, Elizabeth Cady Stanton lashed out against "Patrick and Sambo and Hans and Ung Tung," maligning uneducated freedmen and immigrants who could vote while educated white women could not. Douglass's resolution in support of the Fifteenth Amendment failed, and the convention broke up.

At this searing moment, a rift opened in the women's movement. The majority, led by Lucy Stone, reconciled themselves to disappointment. Organized into the **American Woman Suffrage Association**, they remained loyal to the Republican Party in hopes that once Reconstruction had been settled, it would be women's turn. A group led by Elizabeth Cady Stanton and Susan B. Anthony struck out in a new direction. They saw that, once the Reconstruction Amendments had passed, women's suffrage was unlikely in the near future. Stanton declared that woman "must not put her trust in man." The new organization she headed,

the **National Woman Suffrage Association** (NWSA), focused exclusively on women's rights and took up the battle for a federal suffrage amendment.

In 1873, NWSA members decided to test the new constitutional amendments. Suffragists all over the United States, including some black women in the South, tried to register and vote. Most were turned away. In an ensuing lawsuit, suffrage advocate Virginia Minor of Missouri argued that the registrar who denied her a ballot had violated her rights under the Fourteenth Amendment. In *Minor v. Happersett* (1875), the Supreme Court dashed such hopes. It ruled that suffrage rights were not inherent in citizenship; women were citizens, but state legislatures could deny women the vote if they wished.

Despite these defeats, Radical Reconstruction had created the conditions for a nationwide women's rights movement. Some argued for suffrage as part of a broader expansion of democracy. Others, on the contrary, saw white women's votes as a possible counterweight to the votes of African American or Chinese men (while opponents pointed out that black and immigrant women would likely be enfranchised, too). When Wyoming Territory gave women full voting rights in 1869, its governor received telegrams of congratulation from around the world. Afterward, contrary to dire predictions, female voters in Wyoming did not appear to neglect their homes, abandon their children, or otherwise "unsex" themselves. Women's suffrage could no longer be dismissed as the absurd notion of a tiny minority. It had become a serious issue for national debate.

# The Meaning of Freedom

While political leaders wrangled in Washington, emancipated slaves acted on their own ideas about freedom (American Voices, p. 488). Emancipation meant many things: the end of punishment by the lash; the ability to move around; reunion of families; and opportunities to build schools and churches and to publish and read newspapers. Foremost among freedpeople's demands were voting rights and economic autonomy. Former Confederates opposed these goals. Most southern whites believed the proper place for blacks was as "servants and inferiors," as a Virginia planter testified to Congress. Mississippi's governor, elected under President Johnson's plan, vowed that "ours is and it shall ever be, a government of white men." Meanwhile, as Reconstruction unfolded, it became clear that on economic questions, southern blacks and northern Republican policymakers did not see eye to eye.

## The Quest for Land

During the Civil War, wherever Union forces had conquered portions of the South, rural black workers had formed associations that agreed on common goals and even practiced military drills. After the war, when resettlement became the responsibility of the Freedmen's Bureau, thousands of rural blacks hoped for land distributions. But Johnson's amnesty plan, which allowed pardoned Confederates to recover property seized during the war, blasted such hopes. In October 1865, for example, Johnson ordered General Oliver O. Howard, head of the Freedmen's Bureau, to restore plantations on South Carolina's Sea Islands to white property holders. Dispossessed blacks protested: "Why do you take away our lands? You take them from us who have always been true, always true to the Government! You give them to our all-time enemies! That is not right!" Former slaves resisted efforts to evict them. Led by black Union veterans, they fought pitched battles with former slaveholders and bands of ex-Confederate soldiers. But white landowners, sometimes aided by federal troops, generally prevailed.

## Freed Slaves and Northerners: Conflicting Goals

On questions of land and labor, freedmen in the South and Republicans in Washington seriously differed. The economic revolution of the antebellum period had transformed New England and the Mid-Atlantic states. Believing similar development could revolutionize the South, most congressional leaders sought to restore cotton as the country's leading export, and they envisioned former slaves as wageworkers on cash-crop plantations, not independent farmers. Only a handful of radicals, like Thaddeus Stevens, argued that freed slaves had earned a right to land grants, through what Lincoln had referred to as "four hundred years of unrequited toil." Stevens proposed that southern plantations be treated as "forfeited estates of the enemy" and broken up into small farms for former slaves. "Nothing will make men so industrious and moral," Stevens declared, "as to let them feel that they are above want and are the owners of the soil which they till."

Today, most historians of Reconstruction agree with Stevens: policymakers did not do enough to ensure freedpeople's economic security. Without land, former slaves were left poor and vulnerable. At the time, though, Stevens had few allies. A deep veneration for private property lay at the heart of his vision, but others interpreted the same principle differently: they defined ownership by legal title, not by labor invested. Though often accused of harshness toward the defeated Confederacy, most Republicans—even Radicals—could not imagine "giving" land to former slaves. The same congressmen, of course, had no difficulty giving away homesteads on the frontier that had been taken from Indians. But they were deeply reluctant to confiscate white-owned plantations.

Some southern Republican state governments did try, without much success, to use tax policy to break up large landholdings and get them into the hands of poorer whites and blacks. In 1869, South Carolina established a land commission to buy property and resell it on easy terms to the landless; about 14,000 black families acquired farms through the program. But such initiatives were the exception, not the rule. Over time, some rural blacks did succeed in becoming small-scale landowners, especially in Upper South states such as Virginia, North Carolina, and Tennessee. But it was an uphill fight, and policymakers provided little aid.

**Wage Labor and Sharecropping**   Without land, most freedpeople had few options but to work for former slave owners. Landowners wanted to retain the old gang-labor system, with wages replacing the food, clothing, and shelter that slaves had once received. Southern planters—who had recently scorned the North for the cruelties of wage labor—now embraced

# Freedom

Slavery meant one thing to slave masters, something altogether different to those enslaved. Emancipation exposed these radically different points of view.

## Henry William Ravenel
### Diary, March 8, 1865

Ravenel, from a (formerly) wealthy plantation family in South Carolina, wrote amid the Confederacy's collapse and the aftermath of defeat.

The breath of Emancipation has passed over the country, & we are now in that transition state between the new & the old systems — a state of chaos & disorder. Will the negro be materially benefitted by the change? Will the condition of the country in its productive resources, in material prosperity be improved? Will it be a benefit to the landed proprietors? These are questions which will have their solution in the future. They are in the hands of that Providence which over-ruleth all things for good. It was a strong conviction of my best judgment that the old relation of master & slave, had received the divine sanction & was the best condition in which the two races could live together for mutual benefit. There were many defects to be corrected & many abuses to be remedied. Among these defects I will enumerate the want of legislation to make the marriage contract binding — to prevent the separation of families, & to restrain the cupidity of cruel masters. Perhaps it is for neglecting these obligations that God has seen fit to dissolve that relation. I believe the negro must remain in this country & that his condition although a freed-man, must be to labour on the soil. Nothing but necessity will compel him to labour. Now the question is, will that necessity be so strong as to compel him to labour, which will be profitable to the landed proprietors. Will he make as much cotton, sugar, rice & tobacco for the world as he did previously? They will now have a choice *where* to labour. This will ensure good treatment & the best terms. The most humane, the most energetic & the most judicious managers have the best chances in the race for success. I expect to see a revolution in the ownership of landed estates. Those only can succeed who bring the best capacity for the business. Time will show.

Source: *The Civil War and Reconstruction: A Documentary Collection*, ed. William E. Gienapp (New York: W. W. Norton, 2001), 304–305.

## Edward Barnell Heyward
### Letter, January 22, 1866

In this letter to a friend in the North, the son of a South Carolina plantation owner made grim predictions for the future.

My dear Jim

Your letter of date July 1865, has just reached me and you will be relieved by my answers, to find that I am still alive, and extremely glad to hear from you. . . . I have served in the Army, my brother died in the Army, and every family has lost members. No one can know how reduced we are, particularly the refined & educated. . . .

My father had five plantations on the coast, and all the buildings were burnt, and the negroes, now left to themselves, are roaming in a starvation condition . . . like lost sheep, with no one to care for them.

They find the Yankee only a speculator, and they have no confidence in anyone. They very naturally, poor things, think that freedom means doing nothing, and this they are determined to do. They look to the government, to take care of them, and it will be many years, before this once productive country will be able to support itself. The former kind and just treatment of the slaves, and their docile and generous temper, make them now disposed to be [quiet] and obedient: but the determination of your Northern people to give them a place in the councils of the Country and make them the equal of the white man, will at last, bear its fruit, and we may *then* expect them, to rise against the whites, and in the end, be exterminated themselves.

I am now interested in a school for the negroes, who are around me, and will endeavor to do my duty, to them, as ever before, but I am afraid their best days are past. . . .

I feel now that I have *no country*, I *obey* like a subject, but I cannot love such a government. Perhaps the next letter, you get from me, will be from England. . . .

Source: Stanley I. Kutler, ed., *Looking for America: The People's History*, 2nd ed., 2 vols. (New York: W. W. Norton, 1979), 2: 4–6.

## Isabella Soustan
## Letter, July 10, 1865

Isabella Soustan, a freedwoman in Virginia, wrote to her former master not long after the Civil War ended.

I have the honor to appeal to you once more for assistance, Master. I am cramped hear nearly to death and no one ceares for me heare, and I want you if you please Sir, to Send for me. I dont care if I am free. I had rather live with you. I was as free while with you, as I wanted to be. Mas Man you know I was as well Satisfied with you as I wanted to be. . . . John is still hired out at the same and doing Well and well Satisfied only greaveing about home, he want to go home as bad as I do, if you ever Send for me I will Send for him immediately, and take him home to his kind Master. . . . Pleas to give my love to all of my friends, and especially to my young mistress don't forget to reserve a double portion for yourself. I Will close at present, hoping to bee at your Service Soon yes before yonder Sun Shal rise and set any more.

May I subscribe myself your Most affectionate humble friend and Servt.

Isabella A. Soustan

Source: Leon F. Litwack, *Been in the Storm So Long: The Aftermath of Slavery* (New York: Knopf, 1979), 332.

## Jourdon Anderson
## Letter, August 7, 1865

Anderson had escaped with his family from Tennessee and settled in Dayton, Ohio. He dictated this letter to a friend, and it later appeared in the *New York Tribune*. Folklorists have reported on ways that enslaved people found, even in bondage, for "puttin' down" masters. But only in freedom—and in a northern state—could Anderson's sarcasm be expressed so openly.

To My Old Master, Colonel P. H. Anderson, Big Spring, Tennessee.
Sir:

I got your letter, and was glad to find that you had not forgotten Jourdon. . . . I thought the Yankees would have hung you long before this, for harboring Rebs. . . .

I want to know particularly what the good chance is you propose to give me. I am doing tolerably well here. I get twenty-five dollars a month, with victuals and clothing; have a comfortable home for Mandy, — the folks here call her Mrs. Anderson, — and the children — Milly, Jane, and Grundy — go to school and are learning well. . . .

Mandy says she would be afraid to go back without some proof that you were disposed to treat us justly and kindly; and we have concluded to test your sincerity by asking you to send us our wages for the time we served you. This will make us forget and forgive old scores, and rely on your justice and friendship in the future. I served you faithfully for thirty-two years, and Mandy twenty years. At twenty-five dollars a month for me and two dollars a week for Mandy, our earnings would amount to eleven thousand six hundred and eighty dollars. Add to this the interest for the time our wages have been kept back, and deduct what you paid for our clothing, and three doctor's visits to me, and pulling a tooth for Mandy, and the balance will show what we are in justice entitled to. Please send the balance by Adams Express, in care of V. Winters, esq., Dayton, Ohio. If you do not pay us for faithful labors in the past we can have little faith in your promises in the future. . . .

In answering this letter, please state if there would be any safety for my Milly and Jane, who are now grown up, and both good-looking girls. . . . I would rather stay here and starve — and die, if it come to that — than have my girls brought to shame by the violence and wickedness of their young masters. You will also please state if there has been any schools opened for the colored children in your neighborhood. The great desire of my life now is to give my children an education, and have them form virtuous habits.

From your old servant,
Jourdon Anderson
P.S. Say howdy to George Carter, and thank him for taking the pistol from you when you were shooting at me.

Source: Leon F. Litwack, *Been in the Storm So Long: The Aftermath of Slavery* (New York: Knopf, 1979), 333–335.

---

### QUESTIONS FOR ANALYSIS

1. Compare Ravenel's and Heyward's attitudes toward freedmen and freedwomen. How did their views differ, and on what points did they agree?

2. What predictions did Ravenel and Heyward make about the South's postwar future? How might their expectations have shaped their own actions?

3. Soustan and Anderson both wrote to men who had formerly claimed them as property. How do you account for their different outlooks and approaches? What conditions of life does each mention? What inferences might be drawn from this about the varied postwar experiences of freedpeople?

**Sharecroppers in Georgia**

This photograph shows a Georgia sharecropping family in front of their cabin at cotton-harvesting time. The man in the buggy behind them is probably the landowner. What does this photograph reveal about the condition of sharecroppers? Is there evidence that they might have considered themselves to be doing fairly well—as well as evidence of limits on their success and independence? Note that cotton is growing all the way up to the house, suggesting that the family left little room for a garden or livestock. Through the relentless pressure of loans and debt, sharecropping forced southern farmers into a cash-crop monoculture. Brown Brothers.

wage work with apparent satisfaction. Maliciously comparing black workers to free-roaming pigs, landowners told them to "root, hog, or die." Former slaves found themselves with rock-bottom wages; it was a shock to find that emancipation and "free labor" did not prevent a hardworking family from nearly starving.

African American workers used a variety of tactics to fight back. As early as 1865, alarmed whites across the South reported that former slaves were holding mass meetings to agree on "plans and terms for labor." Such meetings continued through the Reconstruction years. Facing limited prospects at home, some workers left the fields and traveled long distances to seek better-paying jobs on the railroads or in turpentine and lumber camps. Others—from rice cultivators to laundry workers—organized strikes.

At the same time, struggles raged between employers and freedpeople over women's work. In slavery, African American women's bodies had been the sexual property of white men. Protecting black women from such abuse, as much as possible, was a crucial priority for freedpeople. When planters demanded that black women go back into the fields, African Americans resisted resolutely. "I seen on some plantations," one freedman recounted, "where the white men would . . . tell colored men that their wives and children could not live on their places unless they work in the fields. The colored men [answered that] whenever they wanted their wives to work they would tell them themselves."

There was a profound irony in this man's definition of freedom: it designated a wife's labor as her husband's property. Some black women asserted their independence and headed their own households, though this was often a matter of necessity rather than choice. For many freedpeople, the opportunity for a stable family life was one of the greatest achievements of emancipation. Many enthusiastically accepted the northern ideal of domesticity. Missionaries, teachers, and editors of black newspapers urged men to work diligently and support their families, and they told women (though many worked for wages) to devote themselves to motherhood and the home.

Even in rural areas, former slaves refused to work under conditions that recalled slavery. There would be no gang work, they vowed: no overseers, no whippings, no regulation of their private lives. Across the South, planters who needed labor were forced to yield to what one planter termed the "prejudices of the freedmen,

who desire to be masters of their own time." In a few areas, wage work became the norm — for example, on the giant sugar plantations of Louisiana financed by northern capital. But cotton planters lacked money to pay wages, and sometimes, in lieu of a wage, they offered a share of the crop. Freedmen, in turn, paid their rent in shares of the harvest.

Thus the Reconstruction years gave rise to a distinctive system of cotton agriculture known as **sharecropping**, in which freedmen worked as renters, exchanging their labor for the use of land, house, implements, and sometimes seed and fertilizer. Sharecroppers typically turned over half of their crops to the landlord (Map 15.2). In a credit-starved agricultural region that grew crops for a world economy, sharecropping was an effective strategy, enabling laborers and landowners to share risks and returns. But it was a very

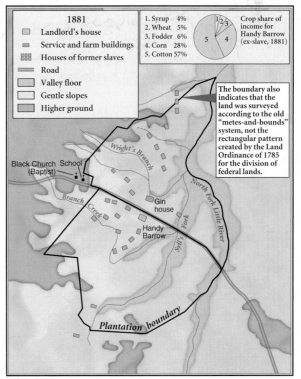

## MAP 15.2

### The Barrow Plantation, 1860 and 1881

This map is a modern redrawing of one that first appeared in the popular magazine *Scribner's Monthly* in April 1881, accompanying an article about the Barrow plantation. Comparing the 1860 map of this central Georgia plantation with the 1881 map reveals the impact of sharecropping on patterns of black residence. In 1860, the slave quarters were clustered near the planter's house. In contrast, by 1881 the sharecroppers were scattered across the plantation's 2,000 acres, having built cabins on the ridges between the low-lying streams. The surname *Barrow* was common among the sharecropping families, which means almost certainly that they had been slaves who, years after emancipation, still had not moved on. For sharecroppers, freedom meant not only their individual lots and cabins but also the school and church shown on the map.

unequal relationship. Starting out penniless, share-croppers had no way to make it through the first grow-ing season without borrowing for food and supplies.

Country storekeepers stepped in. Bankrolled by northern suppliers, they furnished sharecroppers with provisions and took as collateral a lien on the crop, effectively assuming ownership of croppers' shares and leaving them only what remained after debts had been paid. Crop-lien laws enforced lenders' ownership rights to the crop share. Once indebted at a store, share-croppers became easy targets for exorbitant prices, unfair interest rates, and crooked bookkeeping. As cot-ton prices declined in the 1870s, more and more share-croppers fell into permanent debt. If the merchant was also the landowner or conspired with the landowner, debt became a pretext for forced labor, or peonage.

Sharecropping arose in part because it was a good fit for cotton agriculture. Cotton, unlike sugarcane, could be raised efficiently by small farmers (provided they had the lash of indebtedness always on their backs). We can see this in the experience of other regions that became major pro-ducers in response to the global cotton shortage set off by the Civil War. In India, Egypt, Brazil, and West Africa, variants of the sharecropping system emerged. Everywhere international merchants and bankers, who put up cap-ital, insisted on passage of crop-lien laws. Indian and Egyptian villagers ended up, like their American coun-terparts, permanently under the thumb of furnishing merchants.

By 1890, three out of every four black farmers in the South were tenants or sharecroppers; among white farmers, the ratio was one in three. For freedmen, sharecropping was not the worst choice, in a world where former masters threatened to impose labor con-ditions that were close to slavery. But the costs were devastating. With farms leased on a year-to-year basis, neither tenant nor owner had much incentive to improve the property. The crop-lien system rested on expensive interest payments — money that might otherwise have gone into agricultural improvements or to meet human needs. And sharecropping committed the South inflexibly to cotton, a crop that generated the cash required by landlords and furnishing merchants. The result was a stagnant farm economy that blighted the South's future. As Republican governments tried to remake the region, they confronted not only wartime destruction but also the failure of their hopes that free

**IDENTIFY CAUSES**
Why did sharecropping emerge, and how did it affect freedpeople and the southern economy?

**Cotton Farmers, Marietta, Georgia, c. 1880**

Before the Civil War, the South had proudly called itself the "Cotton Kingdom." After the war, cotton was still king, but few southerners got rich on cot-ton profits. Instead, thousands of small-scale farmers, white and black, struggled with plunging crop prices, debt, and taxes on land to support an array of ambitious Reconstruction pro-grams. The farmers here have baled their cotton for market and pose with their wagons in Marietta's courthouse square. Courtesy Georgia Vanishing Archives Collection, cob262.

labor would create a modern, prosperous South, built in the image of the industrializing North. Instead, the South's rural economy remained mired in widespread poverty and based on an uneasy compromise between landowners and laborers.

## Republican Governments in the South

Between 1868 and 1871, all the former Confederate states met congressional stipulations and rejoined the Union. Protected by federal troops, Republican administrations in these states retained power for periods ranging from a few months in Virginia to nine years in South Carolina, Louisiana, and Florida. These governments remain some of the most misunderstood institutions in all U.S. history. Ex-Confederates never accepted their legitimacy. Many other whites agreed, focusing particularly on the role of African Americans who began to serve in public office. "It is strange, abnormal, and unfit," declared one British visitor to Louisiana, "that a *negro* Legislature should deal . . . with the gravest commercial and financial interests." During much of the twentieth century, historians echoed such critics, condemning Reconstruction leaders as ignorant and corrupt. These historians shared the racial prejudices of the British observer: Blacks were simply unfit to govern.

In fact, Reconstruction governments were ambitious. They were hated, in part, because they undertook impressive reforms in public education, family law, social services, commerce, and transportation. Like their northern allies, southern Republicans admired the economic and social transformations that had occurred in the North before the Civil War and worked energetically to import them.

The southern Republican Party included former Whigs, a few former Democrats, black and white newcomers from the North, and southern African Americans. From the start, its leaders faced the dilemma of racial prejudice. In the upcountry, white Unionists were eager to join the party but sometimes reluctant to work with black allies. In most areas, the Republicans also desperately needed African Americans, who constituted a majority of registered voters in Alabama, Florida, South Carolina, and Mississippi.

For a brief moment in the late 1860s, black and white Republicans joined forces through the **Union League**, a secret fraternal order. Formed in border states and northern cities during the Civil War, the league became a powerful political association that spread through the former Confederacy. Functioning as a grassroots wing of Radical Republicanism, it

pressured Congress to uphold justice for freedmen. After blacks won voting rights, the league organized meetings at churches and schoolhouses to instruct freedmen on political issues and voting procedures. League clubs held parades and military drills, giving a public face to the new political order.

The Freedmen's Bureau also supported grassroots Reconstruction efforts. Though some bureau officials sympathized with planters, most were dedicated, idealistic men who tried valiantly to reconcile opposing interests. Bureau men kept a sharp eye out for unfair labor contracts and often forced landowners to bargain with workers and tenants. They advised freedmen on economic matters; provided direct payments to desperate families, especially women and children; and helped establish schools. In cooperation with northern aid societies, the bureau played a key role in founding African American colleges and universities such as Fisk, Tougaloo, and the Hampton Institute. These institutions, in turn, focused on training teachers. By 1869, there were more than three thousand teachers instructing freedpeople in the South. More than half were themselves African Americans.

Ex-Confederates viewed the Union League, Freedmen's Bureau, and Republican Party as illegitimate forces in southern affairs, and they resented the political education of freedpeople. They referred to southern whites who supported Reconstruction as **scalawags**—an ancient Scots-Irish term for worthless animals—and denounced northern whites as **carpetbaggers**, self-seeking interlopers who carried all their property in cheap suitcases called carpetbags. Such labels glossed over the actual diversity of white Republicans. Many arrivals from the North, while motivated by personal profit, also brought capital and skills. Interspersed with ambitious schemers were reformers hoping to advance freedmen's rights. So-called scalawags were even more varied. Some southern Republicans were former slave owners; others were ex-Whigs or even ex-Democrats who hoped to attract northern capital. But most hailed from the backcountry and wanted to rid the South of its slaveholding aristocracy, believing slavery had victimized whites as well as blacks.

Southern Democrats' contempt for black politicians, whom they regarded as ignorant field hands, was just as misguided as their stereotypes about white Republicans. Many African American leaders in the South came from the ranks of antebellum free blacks. Others were skilled men like Robert Smalls of South Carolina, who as a slave had worked for wages that he turned over to his master. Smalls, a steamer pilot in

**Hiram R. Revels**

In 1870, Hiram Rhoades Revels (1827–1901) was elected to the U.S. Senate from Mississippi to fill Jefferson Davis's former seat. Revels was a free black from North Carolina who had moved to the North and attended Knox College in Illinois. During the Civil War he had recruited African Americans for the Union army and, as an ordained Methodist minister, served as chaplain of a black regiment in Mississippi, where he settled after the war. The Granger Collection, New York.

Charleston harbor, had become a war hero when he escaped with his family and other slaves and brought his ship to the Union navy. Buying property in Beaufort after the war, Smalls became a state legislator and later a congressman. Blanche K. Bruce, another former slave, had been tutored on a Virginia plantation by his white father; during the war, he escaped and established a school for freedmen in Missouri. In 1869, he moved to Mississippi and became, five years later, Mississippi's second black U.S. senator. Political leaders such as Smalls and Bruce were joined by northern blacks — including ministers, teachers, and Union veterans — who moved south to support Reconstruction.

During Radical Reconstruction, such men fanned out into plantation districts and recruited former slaves to participate in politics. Literacy helped freedman Thomas Allen, a Baptist minister and shoemaker, win election to the Georgia legislature. "The colored people came to me," Allen recalled, "and I gave them the best instructions I could. I took the *New York Tribune* and other papers, and in that way I found out a great deal, and I told them whatever I thought was right." Though never proportionate to their numbers in the population, blacks became officeholders across the South. In South Carolina, African Americans constituted a majority in the lower house of the legislature in 1868. Over the course of Reconstruction, twenty African Americans served in state administrations as governor, lieutenant governor, secretary of state, or lesser offices. More than six hundred became state legislators, and sixteen were congressmen.

Both white and black Republicans had big plans. Their southern Reconstruction governments eliminated property qualifications for the vote and abolished Black Codes. Their new state constitutions expanded the rights of married women, enabling them to own their own property and wages — "a wonderful reform," one white woman in Georgia wrote, for "the cause of Women's Rights." Like their counterparts in the North, southern Republicans also believed in using government to foster economic growth. Seeking to diversify the economy beyond cotton agriculture, they poured money into railroads and other projects.

In myriad ways, Republicans brought southern state and city governments up to date. They outlawed corporal punishments such as whipping and branding. They established hospitals and asylums for orphans and the disabled. South Carolina offered free public health services, while Alabama provided free legal representation for defendants who could not pay. Some municipal governments paved streets and installed streetlights. Petersburg, Virginia, established a board of health that offered free medical care during the smallpox epidemic of 1873. Nashville, Tennessee, created soup kitchens for the poor.

Most impressive of all were achievements in public education, where the South had lagged woefully. Republicans viewed education as the foundation of a true democratic order. By 1875, over half of black children were attending school in Mississippi, Florida, and South Carolina. African Americans of all ages rushed to the newly established schools, even when they had to pay tuition. They understood why slaveholders had criminalized slave literacy: the practice of freedom rested on the ability to read newspapers, labor contracts, history books, and the Bible. A school official in Virginia reported that freedpeople were "*crazy* to learn." One Louisiana man explained why he was sending his children to school, even though he needed their help in the field. It was "better than leaving them a fortune; because if you left them even five hundred dollars, some man having more education than they had would come along and cheat them out of it all."

**PLACE EVENTS IN CONTEXT**

What policies did southern Reconstruction legislators pursue, and what needs of the postwar South did they seek to serve?

Thousands of white children, particularly girls and the sons of poor farmers and laborers, also benefitted from new public education systems. Young white women's graduation from high school, an unheard-of occurrence before the Civil War, became a celebrated event in southern cities and towns.

Southern Reconstruction governments also had their flaws — flaws that would become more apparent as the 1870s unfolded. In the race for economic development, for example, state officials allowed private companies to hire out prisoners to labor in mines and other industries, in a notorious system known as **convict leasing**. Corruption was rife and conditions horrific. In 1866, Alabama's governor leased 200 state convicts to a railroad construction company for the grand total of $5. While they labored to build state-subsidized lines such as the Alabama and Chattanooga, prisoners were housed at night in open, rolling cages. Physical abuse was common and medical care nonexistent. At the start of 1869, Alabama counted 263 prisoners available for leasing; by the end of the year, a staggering 92 of them had died. While convict leasing expanded in later decades, it began during Reconstruction, supported by both Republicans and Democrats.

## Building Black Communities

In slavery days, African Americans had built networks of religious worship and mutual aid, but these operated largely in secret. After emancipation, southern blacks could engage in open community building. In doing so, they cooperated with northern missionaries and teachers, both black and white, who came to help in the great work of freedom. "Ignorant though they may be, on account of long years of oppression, they exhibit a desire to hear and to learn, that I never imagined," reported African American minister Reverend James Lynch, who traveled from Maryland to the Deep South. "Every word you say while preaching, they drink down and respond to, with an earnestness that sets your heart all on fire."

Independent churches quickly became central community institutions, as blacks across the South left white-dominated congregations, where they had sat in segregated balconies, and built churches of their own. These churches joined their counterparts in the North to become national denominations, including, most prominently, the National Baptist Convention and the African Methodist Episcopal Church. Black churches served not only as sites of worship but also as schools, social centers, and meeting halls. Ministers were often political spokesmen as well. As Charles H. Pearce, a black Methodist pastor in Florida, declared, "A man in this State cannot do his whole duty as a minister except he looks out for the political interests of his people." Religious leaders articulated the special destiny of freedpeople as the new "Children of Israel."

The flowering of black churches, schools, newspapers, and civic groups was one of the most enduring initiatives of the Reconstruction era. Dedicated teachers and charity leaders embarked on a project of "race uplift" that never ceased thereafter, while black

> **COMPARE AND CONTRAST**
> Compare the results of African Americans' community building with their struggles to obtain better working conditions. What links do you see between these efforts?

**Freedmen's School, Petersburg, Virginia, 1870s**

A Union veteran, returning to Virginia in the 1870s to photograph battlefields, captured this image of an African American teacher and her students at a freedmen's school. Note the difficult conditions in which they study: many are barefoot, and there are gaps in the walls and floor of the school building. Nonetheless, the students have a few books. Despite poverty and relentless hostility from many whites, freedpeople across the South were determined to get a basic education for themselves and their children. William L. Clements Library, University of Michigan.

**Fisk Jubilee Singers, 1873**
Fisk University in Nashville, Tennessee, was established in 1865 to provide higher education for African Americans from all across the South. When university funds ran short in 1871, the Jubilee Singers choral group was formed and began touring to raise money for the school. They performed African American spirituals and folksongs, such as "Swing Low, Sweet Chariot," arranged in ways that appealed to white audiences, making this music nationally popular for the first time. In 1872, the group performed for President Grant at the White House. Money raised by this acclaimed chorale saved Fisk from bankruptcy. Edmund Havel's portrait of the group was painted during their first European tour. Fisk University Art Galleries.

entrepreneurs were proud to build businesses that served their communities. The issue of desegregation — sharing public facilities with whites — was a trickier one. Though some black leaders pressed for desegregation, they were keenly aware of the backlash this was likely to provoke. Others made it clear that they preferred their children to attend all-black schools, especially if they encountered hostile or condescending white teachers and classmates. Many had pragmatic concerns. Asked whether she wanted her boys to attend an integrated school, one woman in New Orleans said no: "I don't want my children to be pounded by . . . white boys. I don't send them to school to fight, I send them to learn."

At the national level, congressmen wrestled with similar issues as they debated an ambitious civil rights bill championed by Radical Republican senator Charles Sumner. Sumner first introduced his bill in 1870, seeking to enforce, among other things, equal access to schools, public transportation, hotels, and churches. Despite a series of defeats and delays, the bill remained on Capitol Hill for five years. Opponents charged that shared public spaces would lead to race mixing and intermarriage. Some sympathetic Republicans feared a backlash, while others questioned whether, because of the First Amendment, the federal government had the right to regulate churches. On his deathbed in 1874, Sumner exhorted a visitor to remember the civil rights bill: "Don't let it fail." In the end, the Senate removed Sumner's provision for integrated churches, and the House removed the clause requiring integrated schools. But to honor the great Massachusetts abolitionist, Congress passed the **Civil Rights Act of 1875**. The law required "full and equal" access to jury service and to transportation and public accommodations, irrespective of race. It was the last such act for almost a hundred years — until the Civil Rights Act of 1964.

# The Undoing of Reconstruction

Sumner's death marked the waning of Radical Reconstruction. That movement had accomplished more than anyone dreamed a few years earlier. But a chasm had opened between the goals of freedmen, who wanted autonomy, and policymakers, whose first priorities were to reincorporate ex-Confederates into the nation and build a powerful national economy. Meanwhile, the North was flooded with one-sided, racist reports such as James M. Pike's influential book *The Prostrate State* (1873), which claimed South Carolina was in the grip of "black barbarism." Events of the 1870s deepened the northern public's disillusionment. Scandals rocked the Grant administration, and an economic depression curbed both private investment and public spending. At the same time, northern resolve was worn down by continued ex-Confederate resistance and violence. Only full-scale military intervention could reverse the situation in the South, and by the mid-1870s the North had no political willpower to renew the occupation.

## The Republicans Unravel

Republicans had banked on economic growth to underpin their ambitious program, but their hopes were dashed in 1873 by the sudden onset of a severe worldwide depression. In the United States, the initial panic was triggered by the bankruptcy of the Northern Pacific Railroad, backed by leading financier Jay Cooke. Cooke's supervision of Union finances during the Civil War had made him a national hero; his downfall was a shock, and since Cooke was so well connected in Washington, it raised suspicions that Republican financial manipulation had caused the depression. Officials in the Grant administration deepened public resentment toward their party when they rejected pleas to increase the money supply and provide relief from debt and unemployment.

The impact of the depression varied in different parts of the United States. Farmers suffered a terrible plight as crop prices plunged, while industrial workers faced layoffs and sharp wage reductions. Within a year, 50 percent of American iron manufacturing had stopped. By 1877, half the nation's railroad companies had filed for bankruptcy. Rail construction halted. With hundreds of thousands thrown out of work, people took to the road. Wandering "tramps," who camped by railroad tracks and knocked on doors to beg for work and food, terrified prosperous Americans.

In addition to discrediting Republicans, the depression directly undercut their policies, most dramatically in the South. The ex-Confederacy was still recovering from the ravages of war, and its new economic and social order remained fragile. The bold policies of southern Republicans—for education, public health, and grants to railroad builders—cost a great deal of money. Federal support, through programs like the Freedmen's Bureau, had begun to fade even before 1873. Republicans had banked on major infusions of northern and foreign investment capital; for the most part, these failed to materialize. Investors who had sunk money into Confederate bonds, only to have those repudiated, were especially wary. The South's economy grew more slowly than Republicans had hoped, and after 1873, growth screeched to a halt. State debts mounted rapidly, and as crushing interest on bonds fell due, public credit collapsed.

Not only had Republican officials failed to anticipate a severe depression; during the era of generous spending, considerable funds had also been wasted or had ended up in the pockets of corrupt officials. Two swindlers in North Carolina, one of them a former Union general, were found to have distributed more than $200,000 in bribes and loans to legislators to gain millions in state funds for rail construction. Instead of building railroads, they used the money to travel to Europe and speculate in stocks and bonds. Not only Republicans were on the take. "You are mistaken," wrote one southern Democrat to a northern friend, "if you suppose that all the evils . . . result from the carpetbaggers and negroes. The Democrats are leagued with them when anything is proposed that promises to pay." In South Carolina, when African American congressman Robert Smalls was convicted of taking a bribe, the Democratic governor pardoned him—in exchange for an agreement that federal officials would drop an investigation of Democratic election frauds.

One of the depression's most tragic results was the failure of the **Freedman's Savings and Trust Company.** This private bank, founded in 1865, had worked closely with the Freedmen's Bureau and Union army across the South. Former slaves associated it with the party of Lincoln, and thousands responded to northerners' call for thrift and savings by bringing their small deposits to the nearest branch. African American farmers, entrepreneurs, churches, and charitable groups opened accounts at the bank. But in the early 1870s, the bank's directors sank their money into risky loans and speculative investments. In June 1874, the bank failed.

Some Republicans believed that, because the bank had been so closely associated with the U.S. Army and federal agencies, Congress had a duty to step in. Even one southern Democrat argued that the government was "morally bound to see to it that not a dollar is lost." But in the end, Congress refused to compensate the 61,000 depositors. About half recovered small amounts — averaging $18.51 — but the others received nothing. The party of Reconstruction was losing its moral gloss.

### The Disillusioned Liberals

As a result of the depression and rising criticism of postwar activist government, a revolt emerged in the Republican Party. It was led by influential intellectuals, journalists, and businessmen who believed in **classical liberalism**: free trade, small government, low property taxes, and limitation of voting rights to men of education and property. Liberals responded to the massive increase in federal power, during the Civil War and Reconstruction, by urging a policy of *laissez faire*, in which government "let alone" business and the economy. In the postwar decades, *laissez faire* advocates never succeeded in ending federal policies such as the protective tariff and national banking system (Chapter 16), but their arguments helped roll back Reconstruction. Unable to block Grant's renomination for the presidency in 1872, the dissidents broke away and formed a new party under the name Liberal Republican. Their candidate was Horace Greeley, longtime publisher of the *New York Tribune* and veteran reformer and abolitionist. The Democrats, still in disarray, also nominated Greeley, notwithstanding his editorial diatribes against them. A poor campaigner, Greeley was assailed so severely that, as he said, "I hardly knew whether I was running for the Presidency or the penitentiary."

Grant won reelection overwhelmingly, capturing 56 percent of the popular vote and every electoral vote. Yet Liberal Republicans had shifted the terms of debate. The agenda they advanced — smaller government, restricted voting rights, and reconciliation with ex-Confederates — resonated with Democrats, who had long advocated limited government and were working to reclaim their status as a legitimate national party. Liberalism thus crossed party lines, uniting disillusioned conservative Republicans with Democrats who denounced government activism. E. L. Godkin of *The Nation* and other classical liberal editors played key roles in turning northern public opinion against Reconstruction. With unabashed elitism, Godkin and others claimed that freedmen were unfit to vote. They denounced universal suffrage, which "can only mean in plain English the government of ignorance and vice."

The second Grant administration gave liberals plenty of ammunition. The most notorious scandal involved **Crédit Mobilier**, a sham corporation set up by shareholders in the Union Pacific Railroad to secure government grants at an enormous profit. Organizers of the scheme protected it from investigation by providing gifts of Crédit Mobilier stock to powerful members of Congress. Another scandal involved the Whiskey Ring, a network of liquor distillers and treasury agents who defrauded the government of millions of dollars of excise taxes on whiskey. The ringleader was Grant's private secretary, Orville Babcock. Others went to prison, but Grant stood by Babcock, possibly perjuring himself to save his secretary from jail. The stench of scandal permeated the White House.

## Counterrevolution in the South

While northerners became preoccupied with scandals and the shock of economic depression, ex-Confederates seized power in the South. Most believed (as northern liberals had also begun to argue) that southern Reconstruction governments were illegitimate "regimes." Led by the planters, ex-Confederates staged a massive insurgency to take back the South.

When they could win at the ballot box, southern Democrats took that route. They got ex-Confederate voting rights restored and campaigned against "negro rule." But when force was necessary, southern Democrats used it. Present-day Americans, witnessing political violence in other countries, seldom remember that our own history includes the overthrow of elected governments by paramilitary groups. But this is exactly how Reconstruction ended in many parts of the South. Ex-Confederates terrorized Republicans, especially in districts with large proportions of black voters. Black political leaders were shot, hanged, beaten to death, and in one case even beheaded. Many Republicans, both black and white, went into hiding or fled for their lives. Southern Democrats called this violent process **"Redemption"** — a heroic name that still sticks today, even though this seizure of power was murderous and undemocratic.

No one looms larger in this bloody story than Nathan Bedford Forrest, a decorated Confederate general. Born in poverty in 1821, Forrest had risen to become a big-time slave trader and Mississippi planter. A fiery secessionist, Forrest had formed a Tennessee

**UNDERSTAND POINTS OF VIEW**
How did ex-Confederates, freedpeople, Republicans, and classical liberals view the end of Reconstruction?

Confederate cavalry regiment, fought bravely at the battle of Shiloh, and won fame as a daring raider. On April 12, 1864, his troops perpetrated one of the war's worst atrocities, the massacre at Fort Pillow, Tennessee, of black Union soldiers who were trying to surrender.

After the Civil War, Forrest's determination to uphold white supremacy altered the course of Reconstruction. William G. Brownlow, elected as Tennessee's Republican governor in 1865, was a tough man, a former prisoner of the Confederates who was not shy about calling his enemies to account. Ex-Confederates struck back with a campaign of terror, targeting especially Brownlow's black supporters. Amid the mayhem, ex-Confederates formed the first **Ku Klux Klan** group in late 1865 or early 1866. As it proliferated across the state, the Klan turned to Forrest, who had been trying, unsuccessfully, to rebuild his prewar fortune. Late in 1866, at a secret meeting in Nashville, Forrest donned the robes of Grand Wizard. His activities are mostly cloaked in mystery, but there is no mistake about his goals: the Klan would strike blows against the despised Republican government of Tennessee.

In many towns, the Klan became virtually identical to the Democratic Party. Klan members — including Forrest — dominated Tennessee's delegation to the Democratic national convention of 1868. At home, the Klan unleashed a murderous campaign of terror, and though Governor Brownlow responded resolutely, in the end Republicans cracked. The Klan and similar groups — organized under such names as the White League and Knights of the White Camelia — arose in other states. Vigilantes burned freedmen's schools, beat teachers, attacked Republican gatherings, and murdered political opponents. By 1870, Democrats had seized power in Georgia and North Carolina and were making headway across the South. Once they took power, they slashed property taxes and passed other laws favorable to landowners. They terminated Reconstruction programs and cut funding for schools, especially those teaching black students.

In responding to the Klan between 1869 and 1871, the federal government showed it could still exert power effectively in the South. Determined to end Klan violence, Congress held extensive hearings and in 1870 passed laws designed to protect freedmen's rights under the Fourteenth and Fifteenth Amendments. These so-called **Enforcement Laws** authorized federal prosecutions, military intervention, and martial law to suppress terrorist activity. Grant's administration made full use of these new powers. In South Carolina, where the Klan was deeply entrenched, U.S. troops occupied

**Ku Klux Klan Mask**
White supremacists of the 1870s organized under many names and wore many costumes, not simply (or often) the white cone-shaped hats that were made famous later, in the 1920s, when the Klan underwent a nationwide resurgence. Few masks from the 1870s have survived. The horns and fangs on this one, from North Carolina, suggest how Klan members sought to strike terror in their victims, while also hiding their own identities. North Carolina Museum of History.

nine counties, made hundreds of arrests, and drove as many as 2,000 Klansmen from the state.

This assault on the Klan, while raising the spirits of southern Republicans, revealed how dependent they were on Washington. "No such law could be enforced by state authority," one Mississippi Republican observed, "the local power being too weak." But northern Republicans were growing disillusioned with Reconstruction, while in the South, prosecuting Klansmen was an uphill battle against all-white juries and unsympathetic federal judges. After 1872, prosecutions dropped off. In the meantime, the Texas government fell to the Democrats in 1873 and Alabama and Arkansas in 1874.

## Reconstruction Rolled Back

As divided Republicans debated how to respond, voters in the congressional election of 1874 handed them one of the most stunning defeats of the nineteenth century. Responding especially to the severe depression that gripped the nation, they removed almost half of the party's 199 representatives in the House. Democrats, who had held 88 seats, now commanded an overwhelming majority of 182. "The election is not merely a victory but a revolution," exulted a Democratic newspaper in New York.

After 1874, with Democrats in control of the House, Republicans who tried to shore up their southern wing had limited options. Bowing to election results, the Grant administration began to reject southern Republicans' appeals for aid. Events in Mississippi showed the outcome. As state elections neared there in 1875, paramilitary groups such as the Red Shirts operated openly. Mississippi's Republican governor, Adelbert Ames, a Union veteran from Maine, appealed for U.S. troops, but Grant refused. "The whole public are tired out with these annual autumnal outbreaks in the South," complained a Grant official, who told southern Republicans that they were responsible for their own fate. Facing a rising tide of brutal murders, Governor Ames — realizing that only further bloodshed could result — urged his allies to give up the fight. Brandishing guns and stuffing ballot boxes, Democratic "Redeemers" swept the 1875 elections and took control of Mississippi. By 1876, Reconstruction was largely over. Republican governments, backed by token U.S. military units, remained in only three southern states: Louisiana, South Carolina, and Florida. Elsewhere, former Confederates and their allies took power.

### The Supreme Court Rejects Equal Rights

Though ex-Confederates seized power in southern states, new landmark constitutional amendments and federal laws remained in force. If the Supreme Court had left these intact, subsequent generations of civil rights advocates could have used the federal courts to combat racial discrimination and violence. Instead, the Court closed off this avenue for the pursuit of justice, just as it dashed the hopes of women's rights advocates.

As early as 1873, in a group of decisions known collectively as the *Slaughter-House Cases*, the Court began to undercut the power of the Fourteenth Amendment. In this case and a related ruling, *U.S. v. Cruikshank* (1876), the justices argued that the Fourteenth Amendment offered only a few, rather trivial federal protections to citizens (such as access to navigable waterways). In *Cruikshank* — a case that emerged from a gruesome killing of African American farmers by ex-Confederates in Colfax, Louisiana, followed by a Democratic political coup — the Court ruled that voting rights remained a state matter unless the state *itself* violated those rights. If former slaves' rights were violated by individuals or private groups (including the Klan), that lay beyond federal jurisdiction. The Fourteenth Amendment did not protect citizens from armed vigilantes, even when those vigilantes seized

political power. The Court thus gutted the Fourteenth Amendment. In the *Civil Rights Cases* (1883), the justices also struck down the Civil Rights Act of 1875, paving the way for later decisions that sanctioned segregation. The impact of these decisions endured well into the twentieth century.

### The Political Crisis of 1877

After the grim election results of 1874, Republicans faced a major battle in the presidential election of 1876. Abandoning Grant, they nominated Rutherford B. Hayes, a former Union general who was untainted by corruption and — even more important — hailed from the key swing state of Ohio. Hayes's Democratic opponent was New York governor Samuel J. Tilden, a Wall Street lawyer with a reform reputation. Tilden favored home rule for the South, but so, more discreetly, did Hayes. With enforcement on the wane, Reconstruction did not figure prominently in the campaign, and little was said about the states still led by Reconstruction governments: Florida, South Carolina, and Louisiana.

Once returns started coming in on election night, however, those states loomed large. Tilden led in the popular vote and seemed headed for victory until sleepless politicians at Republican headquarters realized that the electoral vote stood at 184 to 165, with the 20 votes from Florida, South Carolina, and Louisiana still uncertain. If Hayes took those votes, he would win by a margin of 1. Citing ample evidence of Democratic fraud and intimidation, Republican officials certified all three states for Hayes. "Redeemer" Democrats who had taken over the states' governments submitted their own electoral votes for Tilden. When Congress met in early 1877, it confronted two sets of electoral votes from those states.

The Constitution does not provide for such a contingency. All it says is that the president of the Senate (in 1877, a Republican) opens the electoral certificates before the House (Democratic) and the Senate (Republican) and "the Votes shall then be counted" (Article 2, Section 1). Suspense gripped the country. There was talk of inside deals or a new election — even a violent coup. Finally, Congress appointed an electoral commission to settle the question. The commission included seven Republicans, seven Democrats, and, as the deciding member, David Davis, a Supreme Court justice not known to have fixed party loyalties. Davis, however, disqualified himself by accepting an Illinois Senate seat. He was replaced by Republican justice Joseph P. Bradley, and by a vote of 8 to 7, on party lines, the commission awarded the election to Hayes.

In the House of Representatives, outraged Democrats vowed to stall the final count of electoral votes so

**"Grantism"**

President Grant was lampooned on both sides of the Atlantic for the problems of his scandal-ridden administration. The British magazine *Puck* shows Grant barely defying gravity to keep himself and his corrupt subordinates aloft and out of jail. To a great extent, however, the hero of the Union army remained personally popular at home and abroad. The British public welcomed Grant with admiration on his triumphant foreign tour in 1877. Library of Congress.

as to prevent Hayes's inauguration on March 4. But in the end, they went along — partly because Tilden himself urged that they do so. Hayes had publicly indicated his desire to offer substantial patronage to the South, including federal funds for education and internal improvements. He promised "a complete change of men and policy" — naively hoping, at the same time, that he could count on support from old-line southern Whigs and protect black voting rights. Hayes was inaugurated on schedule. He expressed hope in his inaugural address that the federal government could serve "the interests of both races carefully and equally." But,

setting aside the U.S. troops who were serving on border duty in Texas, only 3,000 Union soldiers remained in the South. As soon as the new president ordered them back to their barracks, the last Republican administrations in the South collapsed. Reconstruction had ended.

## Lasting Legacies

In the short run, the political events of 1877 had little impact on most southerners. Much of the work of "Redemption" had already been done. What mattered

## The South's "Lost Cause"

After Reconstruction ended, many white southerners celebrated the Confederacy as a heroic "Lost Cause." Through organizations such as the Sons of Confederate Veterans and United Daughters of the Confederacy, they profoundly influenced the nation's memories of slavery, the Civil War, and Reconstruction.

1. **Commemorative postcard of living Confederate flag, Robert E. Lee Monument, Richmond, Virginia, 1907.** *An estimated 150,000 people gathered in 1890 to dedicate this statue—ten times more than had attended earlier memorial events.*

Source: The Library of Virginia.

2. **From the United Daughters of the Confederacy Constitution, 1894.** *The United Daughters of the Confederacy (UDC), founded in 1894, grew in three years to 136 chapters and by the late 1910s counted a membership of 100,000.*

The objects of this association are historical, educational, memorial, benevolent, and social: To fulfill the duties of sacred charity to the survivors of the war and those dependent on them; to collect and preserve material for a truthful history of the war; to protect historic places of the Confederacy; to record the part taken by the Southern women . . . in patient endurance of hardship and patriotic devotion during the struggle; to perpetuate the memory of our Confederate heroes

and the glorious cause for which they fought; to cherish the ties of friendship among members of this Association; to endeavor to have used in all Southern schools only such histories as are just and true.

3. **McNeel Marble Co. advertisement in *Confederate Veteran* magazine, 1905.**

<u>To the Daughters of the Confederacy:</u> In regard to that Confederate monument which your Chapter has been talking about and planning for since you first got organized. Why not buy it NOW and have it erected before all the old veterans have answered the final roll call? Why wait and worry about raising funds? Our terms to U.D.C. Chapters are so liberal and our plans for raising funds

are so effective as to obviate the necessity of either waiting or worrying. During the last three or four years we have sold Confederate monuments to thirty-seven of your sister Chapters. . . . Our designs, our prices, our work, our business methods have pleased them, and we can please you. What your sister Chapters have done, you can do. . . . WRITE TO-DAY.

**4. Confederate veteran's letter, *Confederate Veteran* magazine, 1910.** *An anonymous Georgian who had served in Lee's army sent the following letter to the veterans' magazine after attending a reunion in Memphis.*

Reunion gatherings are supposed to be for the benefit of the old veterans; but will you show us where the privates, the men who stood the hardships and did the fighting, have any consideration when they get to the city that is expected to entertain them? . . . [In Memphis, I] stopped at the school building, where there were at least twenty-five or thirty old veterans lying on the ground, and had been there all night. All this while the officers were being banqueted, wined, dined, and quartered in the very best hotels; but the private must shift for himself, stand around on the street, or sit on the curbstone. He must march if he is able, but the officers ride in fine carriages. Pay more attention to the men of the ranks — men who did service! I always go prepared to pay my way; but I do not like to be ignored.

**5. Matthew Page Andrews, *The Women of the South in War Times*, 1923.** *Matthew Page Andrews's* The Women of the South in War Times, *approved by the UDC, was a popular textbook for decades in schools throughout the South.*

The Southern people of the "old regime" have been pictured as engaged primarily in a protracted struggle for the maintenance of negro slavery. . . . Fighting on behalf of slavery was as far from the minds of these Americans as going to war in order to free the slaves was from the purpose of Abraham Lincoln, whose sole object, frequently expressed by him, was to "preserve the Union." . . .

That, in the midst of war, there were almost no instances of arson, murder, or outrage committed by the negroes of the South is an everlasting tribute to the splendid character of the dominant race and their moral uplift of a weaker one. . . . When these negroes were landed on American shores, almost all were savages taken from the lowest forms of jungle life. It was largely the women of the South who trained these heathen people, molded their characters, and, in the second and third generations, lifted them up a thousand years in the scale of civilization.

**6. Susie King Taylor, *Reminiscences of My Life in Camp with the 33d United States Colored Troops, Late 1st S.C. Volunteers*, 1902.** *Susie King Taylor, born in slavery in Georgia in 1848, fled with her uncle during the Civil War and served as a nurse in the Union army.*

I read an article, which said the ex-Confederate Daughters had sent a petition to the managers of the local theatres in Tennessee to prohibit the performance of "Uncle Tom's Cabin," claiming it was exaggerated (that is, the treatment of the slaves), and would have a very bad effect on the children who might see the drama. I paused and thought back a few years of the heart-rending scenes I have witnessed. . . . I remember, as if it were yesterday, seeing droves of negroes going to be sold, and I often went to look at them, and I could hear the auctioneer very plainly from my house, auctioning these poor people off.

Do these Confederate Daughters ever send petitions to prohibit the atrocious lynchings and wholesale murdering and torture of the negro? Do you ever hear of them fearing this would have a bad effect on the children? Which of these two, the drama or the present state of affairs, makes a degrading impression upon the minds of our young generation? In my opinion it is not "Uncle Tom's Cabin." . . . It does not seem as if our land is yet civilized.

---

Sources: (2) *Minutes of the Seventh Annual Meeting of the United Daughters of the Confederacy* (Nashville, TN.: Press of Foster & Webb, Printers, 1901), 235; (3) *Confederate Veteran*, 1905; (4) *Confederate Veteran*, Vol. XVIII (Nashville, TN.: S. A. Cunningham, 1910); (5) Matthew Page Andrews, ed., *The Women of the South in War Times* (Baltimore: The Norman, Remington Co., 1923), 3–4, 9–10; (6) Susie King Taylor, *Reminiscences of My Life in Camp* (Boston: Published by the author, 1902), 65–66.

## ANALYZING THE EVIDENCE

1. What do sources 2 and 3 tell us about the work of local UDC chapters? What does the advertisement suggest about the economy of the postwar South?

2. What can you infer from these sources about the situation in the South after the Civil War? Why might women have played a particularly important role in memorial associations?

3. Compare and contrast sources 4 and 6. Who did "Lost Cause" associations serve, and how is this connected to issues of class and race?

4. How does source 5 depict slaves? Slaveholders? Is this an accurate account of the history of the South, and how does this compare to source 4? What do these different interpretations suggest about the legacy of "Redemption"?

## PUTTING IT ALL TOGETHER

"Lost Cause" advocates often stated that their work was not political. To what extent was this true, based on the evidence here? What do these documents suggest about the influence of the Lost Cause, and also the limitations and challenges it faced? What do they tell us about the legacies of Reconstruction more broadly?

was the long, slow decline of Radical Republican power and the corresponding rise of Democrats in the South and nationally. It was obvious that so-called Redeemers in the South had assumed power through violence. But many Americans—including prominent classical liberals who shaped public opinion—believed the Democrats had overthrown corrupt, illegitimate governments; thus the end justified the means. After 1874, those who deplored the results had little political traction. The only remaining question was how far Reconstruction would be rolled back.

The South never went back to the antebellum status quo. Sharecropping, for all its flaws and injustices, was not slavery. Freedmen and freedwomen managed to resist gang labor and work on their own terms. They also established their right to marry, read and write, worship as they pleased, and travel in search of a better life—rights that were not easily revoked. Across the South, black farmers overcame great odds to buy and work their own land. African American businessmen built thriving enterprises. Black churches and community groups sustained networks of mutual aid. Parents sacrificed to send their children to school, and a few proudly watched their sons and daughters graduate from college.

Reconstruction had also shaken, if not fully overturned, the legal and political framework that had made the United States a white man's country. This was a stunning achievement, and though hostile courts and political opponents undercut it, no one ever repealed the Thirteenth, Fourteenth, and Fifteenth Amendments. They remained in the Constitution, and the civil rights movement of the twentieth century would return and build on this framework (Chapter 26).

Still, in the final reckoning, Reconstruction failed. The majority of freedpeople remained in poverty, and by the late 1870s their political rights were also eroding. Vocal advocates of smaller government argued that Reconstruction had been a mistake; pressured by economic hardship, northern voters abandoned their southern Unionist allies. One of the enduring legacies of this process was the way later Americans remembered Reconstruction itself. After "Redemption," generations of schoolchildren were taught that ignorant, lazy blacks and corrupt whites had imposed illegitimate Reconstruction "regimes" on the South. White southerners won national support for their celebration of a heroic Confederacy (Thinking Like a Historian, p. 502).

One of the first historians to challenge these views was the great African American intellectual W. E. B. Du Bois. In *Black Reconstruction in America* (1935),

Du Bois meticulously documented the history of African American struggle, white vigilante violence, and national policy failure. If Reconstruction, he wrote, "had been conceived as a major national program . . . whose accomplishment at any price was well worth the effort, we should be living today in a different world." His words still ring true, but in 1935 historians ignored him. Not a single scholarly journal reviewed Du Bois's important book. Ex-Confederates had lost the war, but they won control over the nation's memory of Reconstruction.

Meanwhile, though their programs failed in the South, Republicans carried their nation-building project into the West, where their policies helped consolidate a continental empire. There, the federal power that had secured emancipation created the conditions for the United States to become an industrial power and a major leader on the world stage.

## SUMMARY

Postwar Republicans faced two tasks: restoring rebellious states to the Union and defining the role of emancipated slaves. After Lincoln's assassination, his successor, Andrew Johnson, hostile to Congress, unilaterally offered the South easy terms for reentering the Union. Exploiting this opportunity, southerners adopted oppressive Black Codes and put ex-Confederates back in power. Congress impeached Johnson and, though failing to convict him, seized the initiative and placed the South under military rule. In this second, or radical, phase of Reconstruction, Republican state governments tried to transform the South's economic and social institutions. Congress passed innovative civil rights acts and funded new agencies like the Freedmen's Bureau. The Fourteenth Amendment defined U.S. citizenship and asserted that states could no longer supersede it, and the Fifteenth Amendment gave voting rights to formerly enslaved men. Debate over this amendment precipitated a split among women's rights advocates, since women did not win inclusion.

Freedmen found that their goals conflicted with those of Republican leaders, who counted on cotton to fuel economic growth. Like southern landowners, national lawmakers envisioned former slaves as wageworkers, while freedmen wanted their own land. Sharecropping, which satisfied no one completely, emerged as a compromise suited to the needs of the cotton market and an impoverished, credit-starved region.

Nothing could reconcile ex-Confederates to Republican government, and they staged a violent counter-revolution in the name of white supremacy and "Redemption." Meanwhile, struck by a massive economic depression, northern voters handed Republicans a crushing defeat in the election of 1874. By 1876, Reconstruction was dead. Rutherford B. Hayes's narrow victory in the presidential election of that year resulted in withdrawal of the last Union troops from the South. A series of Supreme Court decisions also undermined the Fourteenth Amendment and civil rights laws, setting up legal parameters through which, over the long term, disenfranchisement and segregation would flourish.

# CHAPTER REVIEW

## MAKE IT STICK    Go to **LearningCurve** to retain what you've read.

## TERMS TO KNOW    Identify and explain the significance of each term below.

### Key Concepts and Events

**Ten Percent Plan** (p. 480)

**Wade-Davis Bill** (p. 480)

**Black Codes** (p. 481)

**Freedmen's Bureau** (p. 481)

**Civil Rights Act of 1866** (p. 481)

**Fourteenth Amendment** (p. 481)

**Reconstruction Act of 1867** (p. 482)

**Fifteenth Amendment** (p. 485)

**American Woman Suffrage Association** (p. 486)

**National Woman Suffrage Association** (p. 486)

*Minor v. Happersett* (p. 486)

**sharecropping** (p. 491)

**Union League** (p. 493)

**scalawags** (p. 493)

**carpetbaggers** (p. 493)

**convict leasing** (p. 495)

**Civil Rights Act of 1875** (p. 496)

**Freedman's Savings and Trust Company** (p. 497)

**classical liberalism** (p. 498)

*laissez faire* (p. 498)

**Crédit Mobilier** (p. 498)

**"Redemption"** (p. 498)

**Ku Klux Klan** (p. 499)

**Enforcement Laws** (p. 499)

*Slaughter-House Cases* (p. 500)

*U.S. v. Cruikshank* (p. 500)

*Civil Rights Cases* (p. 500)

### Key People

**Andrew Johnson** (p. 480)

**Charles Sumner** (p. 481)

**Thaddeus Stevens** (p. 482)

**Ulysses S. Grant** (p. 483)

**Elizabeth Cady Stanton** (p. 486)

**Robert Smalls** (p. 493)

**Blanche K. Bruce** (p. 494)

**Nathan Bedford Forrest** (p. 498)

## REVIEW QUESTIONS    Answer these questions to demonstrate your understanding of the chapter's main ideas.

1. How did U.S. presidents and Congress seek to reintegrate the Confederacy into the Union? What different approaches did they take, and what were the results?

2. Compare the goals of Radical Republicans, freedpeople, and ex-Confederates during Reconstruction. What conflicts ensued from their differing agendas?

3. Why did Reconstruction falter? To what extent was its failure the result of events in the South, the North, and Washington, D.C.?

4. Some of the language historians use to describe Reconstruction still reflects the point of view of ex-Confederates, who spoke of "Redemption." What other names might we use for that process? What difference (if any) would it make if scholars called it something else?

**5. THEMATIC UNDERSTANDING**    Look again at the events listed under "Politics and Power" and "Identity" on the thematic timeline on page 409. Some historians have argued that, during this era, the United States moved, politically and socially, from being a loose union of states to being a more unified and inclusive *nation*. To what extent do you agree? Use the events of Reconstruction as evidence in making your case.

## MAKING CONNECTIONS

Recognize the larger developments and continuities within and across chapters by answering these questions.

**1. ACROSS TIME AND PLACE**    Ex-Confederates were not the first Americans to engage in violent protest against what they saw as tyrannical government power. Imagine, for example, a conversation between a participant in Shays's Rebellion (Chapter 6) and a southern Democrat who participated in the overthrow of a Republican government in his state. How would each describe his grievances? Who would he name as enemies? Compare and contrast the tactics of these and other violent protests against government power in the United States. To what extent did these groups succeed?

**2. VISUAL EVIDENCE**    Return to the image at the start of this chapter (p. 479), which shows a celebration in Baltimore after ratification of the Fifteenth Amendment. Note the distinguished African American heroes depicted at the top and the three scenes at the bottom. In the complete version of this popular lithograph, additional images appear on the left and right: black Union soldiers in battle; an African American minister preaching at an independent black church; a teacher and her students in a freedpeople's school; an African American farmer in a wheat field; and a drawing of a proud black family on their farm with the caption "We till our own fields." If a freedperson and a former slave owner had seen this image in 1870, how might each have responded? Imagine that an African American family had placed the picture in their home in 1870. How might they have reflected differently, twenty years later, on its significance?

## MORE TO EXPLORE    Start here to learn more about the events discussed in this chapter.

American Social History Project, *Freedom's Unfinished Revolution* (1996). A wonderful collection of images and eyewitness accounts.

Philip Dray, *Capitol Men* (2008). A readable history of Reconstruction from the perspective of the first African American congressmen.

Faye E. Dudden, *Fighting Chance: The Struggle over Woman Suffrage and Black Suffrage in Reconstruction America* (2011). A thoughtful exploration of the split among radical reformers.

Eric Foner, *A Short History of Reconstruction* (1990). The best short overview of events in this decade, combining grassroots and political perspectives.

Steven Hahn, *A Nation Under Our Feet* (2003). Hahn's groundbreaking study of the rural South shows how African Americans' strategies during Reconstruction were built on earlier experiences during slavery and the Civil War.

Brooks D. Simpson, *The Reconstruction Presidents* (1998). A lively assessment of presidential politics from Lincoln through Hayes, full of entertaining quotations.

**TIMELINE**   Ask yourself why this chapter begins and ends with these dates and then identify the links among related events.

| | |
|---|---|
| **1864** | • Wade-Davis Bill passed by Congress but killed by Lincoln's pocket veto |
| **1865** | • Freedmen's Bureau established |
| | • Lincoln assassinated; Andrew Johnson succeeds him as president |
| | • Johnson implements restoration plan |
| | • Ex-Confederate states pass Black Codes to limit freedpeople's rights |
| **1866** | • Civil Rights Act passes over Johnson's veto |
| | • Major Republican gains in congressional elections |
| **1867** | • Reconstruction Act |
| **1868** | • Impeachment of Andrew Johnson |
| | • Fourteenth Amendment ratified |
| | • Ulysses S. Grant elected president |
| **1870** | • Ku Klux Klan at peak of power |
| | • Congress passes Enforcement Laws to suppress Klan |
| | • Fifteenth Amendment ratified |
| **1872** | • Grant reelected; Crédit Mobilier scandal emerges |
| **1873** | • Panic of 1873 ushers in severe economic depression |
| **1874** | • Sweeping Democratic gains in congressional elections |
| **1875** | • Whiskey Ring and other scandals undermine Grant administration |
| | • *Minor v. Happersett*: Supreme Court rules that Fourteenth Amendment does not extend voting rights to women |
| **1876** | • Supreme Court severely curtails Reconstruction in *U.S. v. Cruikshank* |
| **1877** | • Rutherford B. Hayes becomes president |
| | • Reconstruction officially ends |

**KEY TURNING POINTS:** Identify two crucial turning points in the course of Reconstruction. What caused those shifts in direction, and what were the results?

# 16

# Conquering a Continent
## 1854–1890

On May 10, 1869, Americans poured into the streets for a giant party. In big cities, the racket was incredible. Cannons boomed and train whistles shrilled. New York fired a hundred-gun salute at City Hall. Congregations sang anthems, while the less religious gathered in saloons to celebrate with whiskey. Philadelphia's joyful throngs reminded an observer of the day, four years earlier, when news had arrived of Lee's surrender. The festivities were prompted by a long-awaited telegraph message: executives of the Union Pacific and Central Pacific railroads had driven a golden spike at Promontory Point, Utah, linking up their lines. Unbroken track now stretched from the Atlantic to the Pacific. A journey across North America could be made in less than a week.

The first **transcontinental railroad** meant jobs and money. San Francisco residents got right to business: after firing a salute, they loaded Japanese tea on a train bound for St. Louis, marking California's first overland delivery to the East. In coming decades, trade and tourism fueled tremendous growth west of the Mississippi. San Francisco, which in 1860 had handled $7.4 million in imports, increased that figure to $49 million over thirty years. The new railroad would, as one speaker predicted in 1869, "populate our vast territory" and make America "the highway of nations."

The railroad was also a political triumph. Victorious in the Civil War, Republicans saw themselves as heirs to the American System envisioned by antebellum Whigs. They believed government intervention in the economy was the key to nation building. But unlike Whigs, whose plans had met stiff Democratic opposition, Republicans enjoyed a decade of unparalleled federal power. They used it vigorously: U.S. government spending per person, after skyrocketing in the Civil War, remained well above earlier levels. Republicans believed that national economic integration was the best guarantor of lasting peace. As a New York minister declared, the federally supported transcontinental railroad would "preserve the Union."

The minister was wrong on one point. He claimed the railroad was a peaceful achievement, in contrast to military battles that had brought "devastation, misery, and woe." In fact, creating a continental empire caused plenty of woe. Regions west of the Mississippi could only be incorporated if the United States subdued native peoples and established favorable conditions for international investors—often at great domestic cost. And while conquering the West helped make the United States into an industrial power, it also deepened America's rivalry with European empires and created new patterns of exploitation.

> **IDENTIFY THE BIG IDEA**
> How did U.S. policymakers seek to stimulate the economy and integrate the trans-Mississippi west into the nation, and how did this affect people living there?

**The Great West** In the wake of the Civil War, Americans looked westward. Republicans implemented an array of policies to foster economic development in the "Great West." Ranchers, farmers, and lumbermen cast hungry eyes on the remaining lands held by Native Americans. Steamboats and railroads, both visible in the background of this image, became celebrated as symbols of the expanding reach of U.S. economic might. This 1881 promotional poster illustrates the bountiful natural resources to be found out west, as well as the land available for ranching, farming, and commerce. The men in the lower left corner are surveying land for sale. Library of Congress.

# The Republican Vision

Reshaping the former Confederacy was only part of Republicans' plan for a reconstructed nation. They remembered the era after Andrew Jackson's destruction of the Second National Bank as one of economic chaos, when the United States had become vulnerable to international creditors and market fluctuations. Land speculation on the frontier had provoked extreme cycles of boom and bust. Failure to fund a transcontinental railroad had left different regions of the country disconnected. This, Republicans believed, had helped trigger the Civil War, and they were determined to set a new direction.

Even while the war raged, Congress made vigorous use of federal power, launching the transcontinental rail project and a new national banking system. Congress also raised the **protective tariff** on a range of manufactured goods, from textiles to steel, and on some agricultural products, like wool and sugar. At federal customhouses in each port, foreign manufacturers who brought merchandise into the United States had to pay import fees. These tariff revenues gave U.S. manufacturers, who did not pay the fees, a competitive advantage in America's vast domestic market.

**EXPLAIN CONSEQUENCES**

In what ways did Republicans use federal power on the world stage, and in what ways did they continue policies from the pre–Civil War era?

The economic depression that began in 1873 set limits on Republicans' economic ambitions, just as it hindered their Reconstruction plans in the South. But their policies continued to shape the economy. Though some historians argue that the late nineteenth century was an era of *laissez faire* or unrestrained capitalism, in which government sat passively by, the industrial United States was actually the product of a massive public-private partnership in which government played critical roles.

## The New Union and the World

The United States emerged from the Civil War with new leverage in its negotiation with European countries, especially Great Britain, whose navy dominated the seas. Britain, which had allowed Confederate raiding ships such as CSS *Alabama* to be built in its shipyards, submitted afterward to arbitration and paid the United States $15.5 million in damages. Flush with victory, many Americans expected more British and Spanish territories to drop into the Union's lap. Senator

Charles Sumner proposed, in fact, that Britain settle the *Alabama* claims by handing over Canada.

Such dreams were a logical extension of pre–Civil War conquests, especially in the Mexican War. With the coasts now linked by rail, merchants and manufacturers looked across the Pacific, hungry for trade with Asia. Americans had already established a dominant presence in Hawaii, where U.S. whalers and merchant ships stopped for food and repairs. With the advent of steam-powered vessels, both the U.S. Navy and private shippers wanted more refueling points in the Caribbean and Pacific.

Even before the Civil War, these commercial aims had prompted the U.S. government to force Japan to open trade. For centuries, since unpleasant encounters with Portuguese traders in the 1600s, Japanese leaders had adhered to a policy of strict isolation. Americans, who wanted coal stations in Japan, argued that trade would extend what one missionary called "commerce, knowledge, and Christianity, with their multiplied blessings." Whether or not Japan wanted these blessings was irrelevant. In 1854, Commodore Matthew Perry succeeded in getting Japanese officials to sign the **Treaty of Kanagawa**, allowing U.S. ships to refuel at two ports. By 1858, America and Japan had commenced trade, and a U.S. consul took up residence in Japan's capital, Edo (now known as Tokyo).

Union victory also increased U.S. economic influence in Latin America. While the United States was preoccupied with its internal war, France had deposed Mexico's government and installed an emperor. On May 5, 1867, Mexico overthrew the French invaders and executed Emperor Maximilian. But while Mexico regained independence, it lay open to the economic designs of its increasingly powerful northern neighbor.

A new model emerged for asserting U.S. power in Latin America and Asia: not by direct conquest, but through trade. The architect of this vision was William Seward, secretary of state from 1861 to 1869 under presidents Abraham Lincoln and Andrew Johnson. A New Yorker of grand ambition and ego, Seward believed, like many contemporaries, that Asia would become "the chief theatre of [world] events" and that commerce there was key to America's prosperity. He urged the Senate to purchase sites in both the Pacific and the Caribbean for naval bases and refueling stations. When Japan changed policy and tried to close its ports to foreigners, Seward dispatched U.S. naval vessels to join those of Britain, France, and the Netherlands in reopening trade by force. At the same time, Seward urged annexation of Hawaii. He also predicted that the

**An American Merchant Ship in Yokohama Harbor, 1861**

After the United States forcibly "opened" Japan to foreign trade in 1854, American and European ships and visitors became a familiar sight in the port of Yokohama. In these 1861 prints—two panels of a five-panel series—artist Hashimoto Sadahide meticulously details activity in Yokohama Harbor. On the left, goods are carried onto an American merchant ship; on the right, two women dressed in Western style watch the arrival of another boat. In the background, a steamship flies the Dutch flag; a rowboat heading to or from another (unseen) ship carries the flag of France. Library of Congress.

United States would one day claim the Philippines and build a Panama canal.

Seward's short-term achievements were modest. Exhausted by civil war, Americans had little enthusiasm for further military exploits. Seward achieved only two significant victories. In 1868, he secured congressional approval for the **Burlingame Treaty** with China, which guaranteed the rights of U.S. missionaries in China and set official terms for the emigration of Chinese laborers, some of whom were already clearing farmland and building railroads in the West. That same year, Seward negotiated the purchase of Alaska from Russia. After the Senate approved the deal, Seward waxed poetic:

> Our nation with united interests blest
> Not now content to poise, shall sway the rest;
> Abroad our empire shall no limits know,
> But like the sea in endless circles flow.

Many Americans scoffed at the purchase of Alaska, a frigid arctic tract that skeptics nicknamed "Seward's Icebox." But the secretary of state mapped out a path

his Republican successors would follow thirty years later in an aggressive bid for global power.

## Integrating the National Economy

Closer to home, Republicans focused on transportation infrastructure. Railroad development in the United States began well before the Civil War, with the first locomotives arriving from Britain in the early 1830s. Unlike canals or roads, railroads offered the promise of year-round, all-weather service. Locomotives could run in the dark and never needed to rest, except to take on coal and water. Steam engines crossed high mountains and rocky gorges where pack animals could find no fodder and canals could never reach. West of the Mississippi, railroads opened vast regions for farming, trade, and tourism. A transcontinental railroad executive was only half-joking when he said, "The West is purely a railroad enterprise."

Governments could choose to build and operate railroads themselves or promote construction by

**Building the Central Pacific Railroad**

In 1865, Chinese workers had labored to build the 1,100-foot-long, 90-foot-high trestle over the divide between the American and Bear rivers at Secret Town in the Sierra Nevada Mountains. In 1877, the Chinese workers shown in this photograph by Carleton Watkins were again at work on the site, burying the trestle to avoid replacement of the aging timbers, which had become a fire hazard. University of California at Berkeley, Bancroft Library.

private companies. Unlike most European countries, the United States chose the private approach. The federal government, however, provided essential loans, subsidies, and grants of public land. States and localities also lured railroads with offers of financial aid, mainly by buying railroad bonds. Without this aid, rail networks would have grown much more slowly and would probably have concentrated in urban regions. With it, railroads enjoyed an enormous—and reckless—boom. By 1900, virtually no corner of the country lacked rail service (Map 16.1). At the same time, U.S. railroads built across the border into Mexico (America Compared, p. 514).

Railroad companies transformed American capitalism. They adopted a legal form of organization, the corporation, that enabled them to raise private capital in prodigious amounts. In earlier decades, state legislatures had chartered corporations for specific public purposes, binding these creations to government goals and oversight. But over the course of the nineteenth

century, legislatures gradually began to allow any business to become a corporation by simply applying for a state charter. Among the first corporations to become large interstate enterprises, private railroads were much freer than earlier companies to do as they pleased. After the Civil War, they received lavish public aid with few strings attached. Their position was like that of American banks in late 2008 after the big federal bailout: even critics acknowledged that public aid to these giant companies was good for the economy, but they observed that it also lent government support to fabulous accumulations of private wealth.

**Tariffs and Economic Growth**    Along with the transformative power of railroads, Republicans' protective tariffs helped build other U.S. industries, including textiles and steel in the Northeast and Midwest and, through tariffs on imported sugar and wool, sugar beet farming and sheep ranching in the West. Tariffs also funded government itself. In an era when the United States did

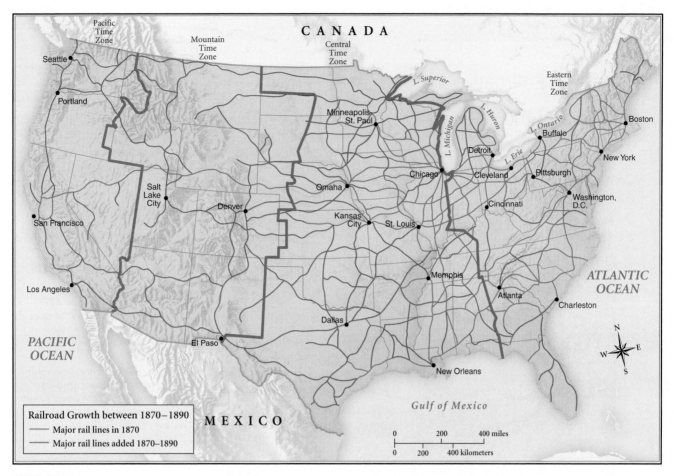

## MAP 16.1
### Expansion of the Railroad System, 1870–1890

In 1860, the nation had 30,000 miles of rail track; by 1890, it had 167,000 miles. The tremendous burst of construction during the last twenty years of that period essentially completed the nation's rail network, although there would be additional expansion for the next two decades. The main areas of growth were in the South and in lands west of the Mississippi. Time zones—introduced by the railroad companies in 1883—are marked by the gray lines.

not levy income taxes, tariffs provided the bulk of treasury revenue. The Civil War had left the Union with a staggering debt of $2.8 billion. Tariff income erased that debt and by the 1880s generated huge budget *surpluses*—a circumstance hard to imagine today.

As Reconstruction faltered, tariffs came under political fire. Democrats argued that tariffs taxed American consumers by denying them access to low-cost imported goods and forcing them to pay subsidies to U.S. manufacturers. Republicans claimed, conversely, that tariffs benefitted workers because they created jobs, blocked low-wage foreign competition, and safeguarded America from the kind of industrial poverty that had arisen in Europe. According to this argument, tariffs helped American men earn enough to support their families; wives could devote themselves to homemaking, and children could go to school, not the factory. For protectionist Republicans, high tariffs were akin to the abolition of slavery: they protected and uplifted the most vulnerable workers.

In these fierce debates, both sides were partly right. Protective tariffs did play a powerful role in economic growth. They helped transform the United States into a global industrial power. Eventually, though, even protectionist Republicans had to admit that Democrats had a point: tariffs had not prevented industrial poverty in the United States. Corporations accumulated massive benefits from tariffs but failed to pass them along to workers, who often toiled long hours for low wages. Furthermore, tariffs helped foster trusts, corporations that dominated whole sectors of the economy and wielded near-monopoly power. The rise of large private corporations and trusts generated enduring political problems.

## The Santa Fe Railroad in Mexico and the United States

This map, based on an 1885 traveler's guide published by the Atchison, Topeka, and Santa Fe Railroad, includes the company's U.S. lines and also those of its Mexican Central Railroad, an ATSF subsidiary that crossed the border and terminated at Guaymas and Mexico City, Mexico. The dots represent the many stops that the trains made along the routes between major cities. Most Mexican railroads in this era were built and operated by U.S. companies. As you analyze this map, consider how residents of the two countries may have experienced the railroad's arrival in different ways.

**MAP 16.2**
**The Santa Fe Railroad System, 1885**

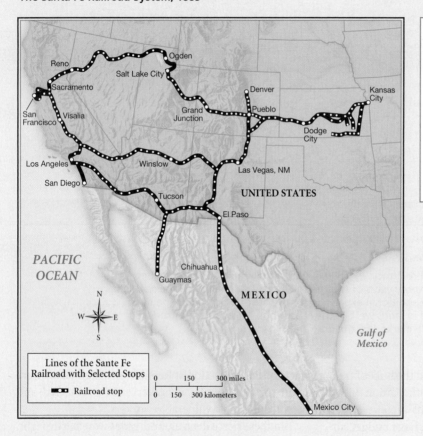

### QUESTIONS FOR ANALYSIS

1. In what directions could passengers and freight travel on ATSF lines in each country? What does this suggest about the objectives of railroad companies like this one?

2. Based on this evidence, how might Mexicans have experienced the arrival of railroads differently from residents of the western United States?

**The Role of Courts**   While fostering growth, most historians agree, Republicans did not give government enough regulatory power over the new corporations. State legislatures did pass hundreds of regulatory laws after the Civil War, but interstate companies challenged them in federal courts. In *Munn v. Illinois* (1877), the Supreme Court affirmed that states could regulate key businesses, such as railroads and grain elevators, that were "clothed in the public interest." However, the justices feared that too many state and local regulations would impede business and fragment the national marketplace. Starting in the 1870s, they interpreted the "due process" clause of the new Fourteenth Amendment — which dictated that no state could "deprive any person of life, liberty, or property, without due process of law" — as shielding corporations from excessive regulation. Ironically, the Court refused to use the same amendment to protect the rights of African Americans.

In the Southwest as well, federal courts promoted economic development at the expense of racial justice. Though the United States had taken control of New Mexico and Arizona after the Mexican War, much land remained afterward in the hands of Mexican farmers and ranchers. Many lived as *peónes*, under longstanding agreements with landowners who held large tracts originally granted by the Spanish crown. The post–Civil War years brought railroads and an influx of land-hungry Anglos. New Mexico's governor reported indignantly that Mexican shepherds were often "asked" to leave their ranges "by a cowboy or cattle herder with a brace of pistols at his belt and a Winchester in his hands."

Existing land claims were so complex that Congress eventually set up a special court to rule on land titles. Between 1891 and 1904, the court invalidated most traditional claims, including those of many New Mexico *ejidos*, or villages owned collectively by their communities. Mexican Americans lost about 64 percent of the contested lands. In addition, much land was sold or appropriated through legal machinations like those of a notorious cabal of politicians and lawyers known as the Santa Fe Ring. The result was displacement of thousands of Mexican American villagers and farmers. Some found work as railroad builders or mine workers; others, moving into the sparse high country of the Sierras and Rockies where cattle could not survive, developed sheep raising into a major enterprise.

**Silver and Gold**   In an era of nation building, U.S. and European policymakers sought new ways to rationalize markets. Industrializing nations, for example, tried to develop an international system of standard measurements and even a unified currency. Though these proposals failed as each nation succumbed to self-interest, governments did increasingly agree that, for "scientific" reasons, money should be based on gold, which was thought to have an intrinsic worth above other metals. Great Britain had long held to the **gold standard**, meaning that paper notes from the Bank of England could be backed by gold held in the bank's vaults. During the 1870s and 1880s, the United States, Germany, France, and other countries also converted to gold.

Beforehand, these nations had been on a bimetallic standard: they issued both gold and silver coins, with respective weights fixed at a relative value. The United States switched to the gold standard in part because treasury officials and financiers were watching developments out west. Geologists accurately predicted the discovery of immense silver deposits, such as Nevada's Comstock Lode, without comparable new gold strikes. A massive influx of silver would clearly upset the long-standing ratio. Thus, with a law that became infamous to later critics as the "**Crime of 1873**," Congress chose gold. It directed the U.S. Treasury to cease minting silver dollars and, over a six-year period, retire Civil War–era greenbacks (paper dollars) and replace them with notes from an expanded system of national banks. After this process was complete in 1879, the treasury exchanged these notes for gold on request. (Advocates of bimetallism did achieve one small victory: the Bland-Allison Act of 1878 required the U.S. Mint to coin a modest amount of silver.)

By adopting the gold standard, Republican policymakers sharply limited the nation's money supply, to the level of available gold. The amount of money circulating in the United States had been $30.35 per person in 1865; by 1880, it fell to only $19.36 per person. Today, few economists would sanction such a plan, especially for an economy growing at breakneck speed. They would recommend, instead, increasing money supplies to keep pace with development. But at the time, policymakers remembered rampant antebellum speculation and the hardships of inflation during the Civil War. The United States, as a developing country, also needed to attract investment capital from Britain, Belgium, and other European nations that were on the gold standard. Making it easy to exchange U.S. bonds and currency for gold encouraged European investors to send their money to the United States.

Republican policies fostered exuberant growth and a breathtakingly rapid integration of the economy. Railroads and telegraphs tied the nation together. U.S. manufacturers amassed staggering amounts of capital and built corporations of national and even global scope. With its immense, integrated marketplace of workers, consumers, raw materials, and finished products, the United States was poised to become a mighty industrial power.

> **IDENTIFY CAUSES**
> What federal policies contributed to the rise of America's industrial economy, and what were their results?

# Incorporating the West

Republicans wanted farms as well as factories. As early as 1860, popular lyrics hailed the advent of "Uncle Sam's Farm":

> A welcome, warm and hearty, do we give the sons of toil,
> To come west and settle and labor on Free Soil;
> We've room enough and land enough, they needn't feel
>     alarmed —
> Oh! Come to the land of Freedom and vote yourself
>     a farm.

The **Homestead Act** (1862) gave 160 acres of federal land to any applicant who occupied and improved the property. Republicans hoped the bill would help build up the interior West, which was inhabited by Indian peoples but remained "empty" on U.S. government survey maps.

Implementing this plan required innovative policies. The same year it passed the Homestead Act, Congress also created the federal Department of Agriculture and, through the **Morrill Act**, set aside 140 million federal acres that states could sell to raise money for public universities. The goal of these **land-grant colleges** was to broaden educational opportunities and foster technical and scientific expertise. After the Civil War, Congress also funded a series of geological surveys, dispatching U.S. Army officers, scientists, and photographers to chart unknown western terrain and catalog resources.

To a large extent, these policies succeeded in incorporating lands west of the Mississippi. The United States began to exploit its western empire for minerals, lumber, and other raw materials. But for ordinary Americans who went west, dreams often outran reality. Well-financed corporations, not individual prospectors, reaped most of the profits from western mines, while the Great Plains environment proved resistant to ranching and farming.

## Mining Empires

In the late 1850s, as easy pickings in the California gold rush diminished, prospectors scattered in hopes of finding riches elsewhere. They found gold at many sites, including Nevada, the Colorado Rockies, and South Dakota's Black Hills (Map 16.3). As news of each strike spread, remote areas turned overnight into mob scenes of prospectors, traders, prostitutes, and saloon keepers. At community meetings, white prospectors made their own laws, often using them as an instrument for excluding Mexicans, Chinese, and blacks.

The silver from Nevada's **Comstock Lode**, discovered in 1859, built the boomtown of Virginia City,

**Hydraulic Mining**

When surface veins of gold played out, miners turned to hydraulic mining, the modern form of which was invented in California in 1853. The technology was simple, using high-pressure streams of water to wash away hillsides of gold-bearing soil. Although building the reservoirs, piping systems, and sluices cost money, the profits from hydraulic mining helped transform western mining into big business. But, as this daguerreotype suggests, the large scale on which hydraulic mining was done wreaked large-scale havoc on the environment. Collection of Matthew Isenburg.

**MAP 16.3**

**Mining Frontiers, 1848–1890**

The Far West was America's gold country because of its geological history. Veins of gold and silver form when molten material from the earth's core is forced up into fissures caused by the tectonic movements that create mountain ranges, such as the ones that dominate the far western landscape. It was these veins, the product of mountain-forming activity many thousands of years earlier, that prospectors began to discover after 1848 and furiously exploit. Although widely dispersed across the Far West, the lodes that they found followed the mountain ranges bisecting the region and bypassing the great plateaus not shaped by the ancient tectonic activity.

which soon acquired fancy hotels, a Shakespearean theater, and even its own stock exchange. In 1870, a hundred saloons operated in Virginia City, brothels lined D Street, and men outnumbered women 2 to 1. In the 1880s, however, as the Comstock Lode played out, Virginia City suffered the fate of many mining camps: it became a ghost town. What remained was a ravaged landscape with mountains of debris, poisoned water sources, and surrounding lands stripped of timber.

In hopes of encouraging development of western resources, Congress passed the General Mining Act of 1872, which allowed those who discovered minerals on

federally owned land to work the claim and keep all the proceeds. (The law — including the $5-per-acre fee for filing a claim — remains in force today.) Americans idealized the notion of the lone, hardy mining prospector with his pan and his mule, but digging into deep veins of underground ore required big money. Consortiums of powerful investors, bringing engineers and advanced equipment, generally extracted the most wealth. This was the case for the New York trading firm Phelps Dodge, which invested in massive copper mines and smelting operations on both sides of the U.S.-Mexico border. The mines created jobs in new towns like Bisbee and Morenci, Arizona — but with dangerous conditions and low pay, especially for those who received the segregated "Mexican wage." Anglos, testified one Mexican mine worker, "occupied decorous residences . . . and had large amounts of money," while "the Mexican population and its economic condition offered a pathetic contrast." He protested this affront to "the most elemental principles of justice."

The rise of western mining created an insatiable market for timber and produce from the Pacific Northwest (Map 16.4). Seattle and Portland grew rapidly as

**MAP 16.4**

**Settlement of the Pacific Slope, 1860–1890**

In 1860, the economic development of the Pacific slope was remarkably uneven — fully under way in northern California and scarcely begun anywhere else. By 1890, a new pattern had begun to emerge, with the swift growth of southern California foreshadowed and the Pacific Northwest incorporated into the regional and national economy.

supply centers, especially during the great gold rushes of California (after 1849) and the Klondike in Canada's Yukon Territory (after 1897). Residents of Tacoma, Washington, claimed theirs was the "City of Destiny" when it became the Pacific terminus for the Northern Pacific, the nation's third transcontinental railroad, in 1887. But rival businessmen in Seattle succeeded in promoting their city as the gateway to Alaska and the Klondike. Seattle, a town with 1,000 residents in 1870, grew over the next forty years to a population of a quarter million.

## Cattlemen on the Plains

While boomtowns arose across the West, hunters began transforming the plains. As late as the Civil War years, great herds of bison still roamed this region. But overhunting and the introduction of European animal afflictions, like the bacterial disease brucellosis, were already decimating the herds. In the 1870s, hide hunters finished them off so thoroughly that at one point fewer than two hundred bison remained in U.S. territory. Hunters hidden downwind, under the right conditions, could kill four dozen at a time without moving from the spot. They took hides but left the meat to rot, an act of vast wastefulness that shocked native peoples.

Removal of the bison opened opportunities for cattle ranchers. South Texas provided an early model for their ambitious plans. By the end of the Civil War, about five million head of longhorn cattle grazed on Anglo ranches there. In 1865, the Missouri Pacific Railroad reached Sedalia, Missouri, far enough west to be accessible as Texas reentered the Union. A longhorn worth $3 in Texas might command $40 at Sedalia.

**Cowboys, Real and Mythic**

As early as the 1860s, popular dime novels such as this one (right) celebrated the alleged ruggedness, individual freedoms, and gun-slinging capabilities of western cowboys. (Note that this 1888 story, like most dime novels, was published in New York.) Generations of young Americans grew up on stories of frontier valor and "Cowboys versus Indians." In fact, cowboys like the ones depicted in the photograph were really wageworkers on horseback. An ethnically diverse group, including many blacks and Hispanics, they earned perhaps $25 a month, plus meals and a bed in the bunkhouse, in return for long hours of grueling, lonesome work. Library of Congress; Denver Public Library/Bridgeman Art Library.

**Advertisement for Silver Pine Healing Oil, c. 1880s**

Conquest of the Great Plains was made possible in part by the invention of barbed wire, which could cheaply enclose wide areas, even where trees and wood were scarce. Inventor Joseph Glidden received a patent in 1874 for the most familiar form of barbed wire. His wire proved durable, and Glidden invented machinery to mass-produce it—while his business associates skill-fully promoted the product to farmers in the West. By 1880, Glidden's company sold 80 million pounds of barbed wire a year. This image shows, however, that the new "thorny fence" also had a downside. Other businessmen profited by healing the injuries that barbed wire caused to valuable animals. Picture Research Consultants & Archives.

With this incentive, ranchers inaugurated the **Long Drive**, hiring cowboys to herd cattle hundreds of miles north to the new rail lines, which soon extended into Kansas. At Abilene and Dodge City, Kansas, ranchers sold their longhorns and trail-weary cowboys crowded into saloons. These cow towns captured the nation's imagination as symbols of the Wild West, but the reality was much less exciting. Cowboys, many of them African Americans and Latinos, were really farm-hands on horseback who worked long, harsh hours for low pay.

North of Texas, public grazing lands drew investors and adventurers eager for a taste of the West. By the early 1880s, as many as 7.5 million cattle were over-grazing the plains' native grasses. A cycle of good weather postponed disaster, which arrived in 1886: record blizzards and bitter cold. An awful scene of rot-ting carcasses greeted cowboys as they rode onto the range that spring. Further hit by a severe drought the following summer, the cattle boom collapsed.

Thanks to new strategies, however, cattle ranching survived and became part of the integrated national economy. As railroads reached Texas and ranchers there abandoned the Long Drive, the invention of barbed wire—which enabled ranchers and farmers to fence large areas cheaply and easily on the plains, where wood was scarce and expensive—made it easier for northern cattlemen to fence small areas and feed ani-mals on hay. Stockyards appeared beside the rapidly extending railroad tracks, and trains took these gath-ered cattle to giant slaughterhouses in cities like Chi-cago, which turned them into cheap beef for customers back east.

## Homesteaders

Republicans envisioned the Great Plains dotted with small farms, but farmers had to be persuaded that crops would grow there. Powerful interests worked hard to overcome the popular idea that the grassland was the Great American Desert. Railroads, eager to sell land the government had granted them, advertised aggressively. Land speculators, transatlantic steamship lines, and western states and territories joined the campaign.

Newcomers found the soil beneath the native prai-rie grasses deep and fertile. Steel plows enabled them to break through the tough roots, while barbed wire pro-vided cheap, effective fencing against roaming cattle. European immigrants brought strains of hard-kernel wheat that tolerated the extreme temperatures of the plains. As if to confirm promoters' optimism, a wet cycle occurred between 1878 and 1886, increasing rainfall in the arid regions east of the Rockies. Americans decided that **"rain follows the plow"**: settlement was increasing rainfall. Some attributed the rain to soil cultivation and tree planting, while others credited God. One Harvard professor proposed that

**Family on the L. W. Hall Farm, Buffalo County, Nebraska, 1903**
This family has moved from their original sod house into a new frame house. Perhaps they asked the photographer to include in his image the windmill, a key to their prosperity. Other photographs on this property, some taken in 1907, show thriving young trees and a woman proudly posed with her new hand-cranked washing machine. How might this family have responded to the argument, made in this textbook chapter and by some critics at the time, that farming was a failure on the arid Great Plains? What different story might they tell about their hardships and successes? Nebraska State Historical Society.

steel railroad tracks attracted moisture. Such optimists would soon learn their mistake.

The motivation for most settlers, American or immigrant, was to better themselves economically. Union veterans, who received favorable terms in staking homestead claims, played a major role in settling Kansas and other plains states. When severe depression hit northern Europe in the 1870s, Norwegians and Swedes joined German emigrants in large numbers. At the peak of "American fever" in 1882, more than 105,000 Scandinavians left for the United States. Swedish and Norwegian became the primary languages in parts of Minnesota and the Dakotas.

For some African Americans, the plains represented a promised land of freedom. In 1879, a group of black communities left Mississippi and Louisiana in a quest to escape poverty and white violence. Some 6,000 blacks departed together, most carrying little but the clothes on their backs and faith in God. They called themselves **Exodusters**, participants in a great exodus to Kansas. The 1880 census reported 40,000 blacks there, by far the largest African American concentration in the West aside from Texas, where the expanding cotton frontier attracted hundreds of thousands of black migrants.

For newcomers, taming the plains differed from pioneering in antebellum Iowa or Oregon. Dealers sold big new machines to help with plowing and harvesting.

Western wheat traveled by rail to giant grain elevators and traded immediately on world markets. Hoping frontier land values would appreciate rapidly, many farmers planned to profit from selling acres as much as (or more than) from their crops. In boom times, many rushed into debt to acquire more land and better equipment. All these enthusiasms — for cash crops, land speculation, borrowed money, and new technology — bore witness to the conviction that farming was, as one agricultural journal remarked, a business "like all other business."

**Women in the West**   Early miners, lumbermen, and cowboys were overwhelmingly male, but homesteading was a family affair. The success of a farm depended on the work of wives and children who tended the garden and animals, preserved food, and helped out at harvest time. Some women struck out on their own: a study of North Dakota found between 5 and 20 percent of homestead claims filed by single women, often working land adjacent to that of sisters, brothers, and parents. Family members thus supported one another in the difficult work of farming, while easing the loneliness many newcomers felt. Looking back with pride on her homesteading days, one Dakota woman said simply, "It was a place to stay and it was mine."

While promoting farms in the West, Republicans clashed with the distinctive religious group that had already settled Utah: Mormons, or members of the Church of Jesus Christ of Latter-day Saints (LDS). After suffering persecution in Missouri and Illinois, Mormons had moved west to Utah in the 1840s, attracting many working-class converts from England as well. Most Americans at the time were deeply hostile to Mormonism, especially the LDS practice of plural marriage — sanctioned by church founder Joseph Smith — through which some Mormon men married more than one wife.

Mormons had their own complex view of women's role, illustrated by the career of Mormon leader Emmeline Wells. Born in New Hampshire, Emmeline converted to Mormonism at age thirteen along with her mother and joined the exodus to Utah in 1848. After her first husband abandoned her when he left the church, Emmeline became the seventh wife of church elder Daniel Wells. In 1870, due in part to organized pressure from Wells and other Mormon women, the Utah legislature granted full voting rights to women, becoming the second U.S. territory to do so (after Wyoming, in 1869). The measure increased LDS control, since most Utah women were Mormons, while non-Mormons in mining camps were predominantly male. It also recognized the central role of women in Mormon life.

Amid the constitutional debates of Reconstruction, polygamy and women's voting rights became intertwined issues (American Voices, p. 522). Encouraged by other plural wives, Emmeline Wells began in 1877 to write for a Salt Lake City newspaper, the *Woman's Exponent*. She served as editor for forty years and led local women's rights groups. At first, Utah's legislature blocked Wells's candidacy in a local election, based on her sex. But when Utah won statehood in 1896, Wells had the pleasure of watching several women win seats in the new legislature, including Dr. Martha Hughes Cannon, a physician and Mormon plural wife who became the first American woman to serve in a state senate. Like their counterparts in other western states, Utah's women experienced a combination of severe frontier hardships and striking new opportunities.

**Environmental Challenges**   Homesteaders faced a host of challenges, particularly the natural environment of the Great Plains. Clouds of grasshoppers could descend and destroy a crop in a day; a prairie fire or hailstorm could do the job in an hour. In spring, homesteaders faced sudden, terrifying tornados, while their winter experiences in the 1870s added the word *blizzard* to America's vocabulary. On the plains, also, water and lumber were hard to find. Newly arrived families

often cut dugouts into hillsides and then, after a season or two, erected houses made of turf cut from the ground.

Over the long term, homesteaders discovered that the western grasslands did not receive enough rain to grow wheat and other grains. As the cycle of rainfall shifted from wet to dry, farmers as well as ranchers suffered. "A wind hot as an oven's fury . . . raged like a pestilence," reported one Nebraskan, leaving "farmers helpless, with no weapon against this terrible and inscrutable wrath of nature." By the late 1880s, some recently settled lands emptied as homesteaders fled in defeat — 50,000 from the Dakotas alone. It became obvious that farming in the arid West required methods other than those used east of the Mississippi.

Clearly, 160-acre homesteads were the wrong size for the West: farmers needed either small irrigated plots or immense tracts for dry farming, which involved deep planting to bring subsoil moisture to the roots and quick harrowing after rainfalls to slow evaporation. Dry farming developed most fully on huge corporate farms in the Red River Valley of North Dakota. But even family farms, the norm elsewhere, could not survive on less than 300 acres of grain. Crop prices were too low, and the climate too unpredictable, to allow farmers to get by on less.

In this struggle, settlers regarded themselves as nature's conquerors, striving, as one pioneer remarked, "to get the land subdued and the wilde nature out of it." Much about its "wilde nature" was hidden to the newcomers. They did not know that destroying biodiversity, which was what farming the plains really meant, opened pathways for exotic, destructive pests and weeds, and that removing native grasses left the soil vulnerable to erosion. By the turn of the twentieth century, about half the nation's cattle and sheep, one-third of its cereal crops, and nearly three-fifths of its wheat came from the Great Plains. But in the drier parts of the region, it was not a sustainable achievement. This renowned breadbasket was later revealed to be, in the words of one historian, "the largest, longest-run agricultural and environmental miscalculation in American history."

John Wesley Powell, a one-armed Union veteran, predicted the catastrophe from an early date. Powell, employed by the new U.S. Geological Survey, led a famous expedition in the West in which his team navigated the rapids of the Colorado River through the Grand Canyon in wooden boats. In his *Report on the*

**COMPARE AND CONTRAST**

Compare the development of mining, ranching, and farming in the West. How did their environmental consequences differ?

## Women's Rights in the West

In 1870, Utah's territorial legislature granted voting rights to women. The decision was a shock to advocates of women's suffrage in the East: they expected their first big victories would come in New England. Furthermore, Utah was overwhelmingly peopled by Mormons—members of the Church of Jesus Christ of Latter-day Saints (LDS). Critics saw Mormonism as a harshly patriarchal religion. They especially loathed the Mormon practice of "plural marriage," in which some Mormon men took more than one wife. Most easterners thought this practice was barbaric and demeaning to women. Over the next two decades, Republicans pressured Mormons to abolish plural marriage. They also disenfranchised Mormon women and required men to take an anti-polygamy oath; Congress refused to admit Utah as a state. Only after 1890, when the LDS church officially abolished plural marriage, was Utah statehood possible. In 1896, when Utah became a state, women's voting rights were finally reinstated.

### Fanny Stenhouse
### *Exposé of Polygamy: A Lady's Life Among the Mormons* (1872)

An Englishwoman who converted to the faith and moved to Utah, Stenhouse became disillusioned and published her book to criticize the practice of Mormon polygamy.

How little do the Mormon men of Utah know what it is, in the truest sense, to have a wife, though they have so many "wives," after their own fashion. Almost imperceptibly to the husband, and even the wife herself, a barrier rises between them the very day that he marries another woman. It matters not how much she believes in the doctrine of plural marriages, or how willing she may be to submit to it; the fact remains the same. The estrangement begins by her trying to hide from him all secret sorrow; for she feels that what has been can not be undone now, and she says, "I cannot change it; neither would I if I could, because it is the will of God, and I must bear it; besides, what good will it do to worry my husband with all my feelings?"

. . . A man may have a dozen wives; but from the whole of them combined he will not receive as much real love and devotion as he might from one alone, if he had made her feel that she had his undivided affection and confidence. How terribly these men deceive themselves! When peace, or rather quiet, reigns in their homes, they think that the spirit of God is there. But it is not so! It is a calm, not like the gentle silence of sleep, but as the horrible stillness of death—the death of the heart's best affections, and all that is worth calling love. All true love has fled, and indifference has taken its place. The very children feel it. What do they—what can they care about their fathers? They seldom see them.

Whatever, in the providence of God, may be the action of Congress toward Utah, if the word of a feeble woman can be listened to, let me respectfully ask the Honorable Senators and Representatives of the United States that, in the abolition of Polygamy, if such should be the decree of the nation, let no compromise be made where subtlety can bind the woman now living in Polygamy to remain in that condition.

Source: *Exposé of Polygamy: A Lady's Life Among the Mormons*, ed. Linda Wilcox DeSimone (Logan: Utah State University Press, 2008), 72–73, 155.

### Eliza Snow, Harriet Cook Young, Phoebe Woodruff
### A Defense of Plural Marriage

The vast majority of Mormon women defended their faith and the practice of plural marriage. The statements by Eliza Snow, Harriet Cook Young, and Phoebe Woodruff, below, were made at a public protest meeting in Salt Lake City in 1870. LDS women pointed proudly to their new suffrage rights as proof of their religion's just treatment of women. Why did Mormons, who dominated the Utah legislature, give women full voting rights? In part, they sought to protect their church by increasing Mormon voting power: most of the non-Mormons were single men who worked on ranches or in mining camps. But the LDS Church also celebrated women's central role in the family and community. Some women achieved prominence as midwives, teachers, and professionals.

*Eliza Snow:* Our enemies pretend that, in Utah, woman is held in a state of vassalage—that she does not act from choice, but by coercion—that we would even prefer life elsewhere, were it possible for us to make our escape. What nonsense! We all know that if we wished we could leave at any time — either go singly, or to rise en masse, and there is no power here that could, or would wish to, prevent us. I will now ask this assemblage of intelligent ladies, do you know of anyplace on the face of the earth, where woman has more liberty, and where she enjoys such high and glorious privileges as she does here, as a latter-day saint? No! The very idea of woman here in a state of slavery is a burlesque on good common sense.

*Harriet Cook Young:* Wherever monogamy reigns, adultery, prostitution and foeticide, directly or indirectly, are its concomitants. . . . The women of Utah comprehend this; and they see, in the principle of plurality of wives, the only safeguard against adultery, prostitution, and the reckless waste of pre-natal life, practiced throughout the land.

*Phoebe Woodruff:* God has revealed unto us the law of the patriarchal order of marriage, and commanded us to obey it. We are sealed to our husbands for time and eternity, that we may dwell with them and our children in the world to come; which guarantees unto us the greatest blessing for which we are created. If the rulers of the nation will so far depart from the spirit and letter of our glorious constitution as to deprive our prophets, apostles and elders of citizenship, and imprison them for obeying this law, let them grant this, our last request, to make their prisons large enough to hold their wives, for where they go we will go also.

Source: Edward W. Tullidge, *Women of Mormondom* (New York: Tullidge & Crandall, 1877), 390–391, 396, 400.

## Susan B. Anthony

## Letter to *The Revolution*, July 5, 1871

National women's suffrage leaders responded awkwardly to the Utah suffrage victory. Being associated with Mormons, they understood, damaged their fragile new movement in the eyes of most Americans. But they tried tentatively to forge alliances with Mormon women they viewed as progressive, as well as dissidents in the church. Suffrage leader Susan B. Anthony traveled to Salt Lake City in 1871 to try to forge alliances with Mormon women, especially dissidents such as Fanny Stenhouse. Anthony expressed strong disapproval of polygamy, but she also

tried to change the debate to focus on the vulnerability of all married women to exploitation by their husbands. Her report from Utah, published in her journal *The Revolution*, is below.

Woman's work in monogamy and polygamy is essentially one and the same — that of planting her feet on the solid ground of self-support; . . . there is and can be no salvation for womanhood but in the possession of power over her own subsistence.

The saddest feature here is that there really is nothing by which these women can earn an independent livelihood for themselves and children. No manufacturing establishments; no free schools to teach. Women here, as everywhere, must be able to live honestly and honorably without men, before it can be possible to save the masses of them from entering into polygamy or prostitution, legal or illegal. Whichever way I turn, whatever phase of social life presents itself, the same conclusion comes — independent bread alone can redeem woman from her sure subjection to man. . . .

Here is missionary ground. Not for "thus saith the Lord," divine rights, canting priests, or echoing priestesses of any sect whatsoever; but for great, god-like, humanitarian men and women, who "feel for them in bonds as bound with them," . . . a simple, loving, sisterly clasp of hands with these struggling women, and an earnest work with them. Not to modify nor ameliorate, but to ABOLISH the whole system of woman's subjection to man in both polygamy and monogamy.

Source: *The Revolution*, July 20, 1871.

### QUESTIONS FOR ANALYSIS

1. What arguments did the Mormon women make in defense of plural marriage? On what grounds did Stenhouse argue for its abolition?

2. Susan B. Anthony's letter was published in Boston. How might Mormon women have reacted to it? How might non-Mormon women have reacted to the statements by Snow, Young, and Woodruff?

3. Compare the experiences of plural marriage described by Stenhouse, on the one hand, and Snow, Young, and Woodruff, on the other. How do you account for these very different perspectives?

*Lands of the Arid Region of the United States* (1879), Powell told Congress bluntly that 160-acre homesteads would not work in dry regions. Impressed with the success of Mormon irrigation projects in Utah, Powell urged the United States to follow their model. He proposed that the government develop the West's water resources, building dams and canals and organizing landowners into local districts to operate them. Doubting that rugged individualism would succeed in the West, Powell proposed massive cooperation under government control.

After heated debate, Congress rejected Powell's plan. Critics accused him of playing into the hands of large ranching corporations; boosters were not yet willing to give up the dream of small homesteads. But Powell turned out to be right. Though environmental historians do not always agree with Powell's proposed solutions, they point to his *Report on Arid Lands* as a cogent critique of what went wrong on the Great Plains. Later,

**IDENTIFY CAUSES**
What factors led to the creation of the first national parks?

federal funding paid for dams and canals that supported intensive agriculture in many parts of the West.

## The First National Park

Powell was not the only one rethinking land use. The West's incorporation into the national marketplace occurred with such speed that some Americans began to fear rampant overdevelopment. Perhaps the federal government should not sell off all its public land, but instead hold and manage some of it. Amid the heady initiatives of Reconstruction, Congress began to preserve sites of unusual natural splendor. As early as 1864, Congress gave 10 square miles of the Yosemite Valley to California for "public use, resort, and recreation." (In 1890, Yosemite reverted to federal control.) In 1872, it set aside 2 million acres of Wyoming's Yellowstone Valley as the world's first national park: preserved as a public holding, it would serve as "a public park or pleasuring ground for the benefit and enjoyment of the people."

***The Yo-Hamite Falls,*** **1855**
This is one of the earliest artistic renderings of the Yosemite Valley, drawn, in fact, before the place came to be called Yosemite. The scale of the waterfall, which drops 2,300 feet to the valley below, is dramatized by artist Thomas A. Ayres's companions in the foreground. In this romantic lithograph, one can already see the grandeur of the West that Yosemite came to represent for Americans. University of California at Berkeley, Bancroft Library.

Railroad tourism, which developed side by side with other western industries, was an important motive for the creation of **Yellowstone National Park**. The Northern Pacific Railroad lobbied Congress vigorously to get the park established. Soon, luxury Pullman cars ushered visitors to Yellowstone's hotel, operated by the railroad itself. But creation of the park was fraught with complications. Since no one knew exactly what a "national park" was or how to operate it, the U.S. Army was dispatched to take charge; only in the early 1900s, when Congress established many more parks in the West, did consistent management policies emerge. In the meantime, soldiers spent much of their time arresting native peoples who sought to hunt on Yellowstone lands.

The creation of Yellowstone was an important step toward an ethic of respect for land and wildlife. So was the 1871 creation of a **U.S. Fisheries Commission**, which made recommendations to stem the decline in wild fish; by the 1930s, it merged with other federal wildlife bureaus to become the U.S. Fish and Wildlife Service. At the same time, eviction of Indians showed that defining small preserves of "uninhabited wilderness" was part of conquest itself. In 1877, for example, the federal government forcibly removed the Nez Perce tribe from their ancestral land in what is now Idaho, Washington, and Oregon. Under the leadership of young Chief Joseph, the Nez Perces tried to flee to Canada. After a journey of 1,100 miles, they were forced to surrender just short of the border. During their trek, five bands crossed Yellowstone; as a Nez Perce named Yellow Wolf recalled, they "knew that country well." For thirteen days, Nez Perce men raided the valley for supplies, waylaying several groups of tourists. The conflict made national headlines. Easterners, proud of their new "pleasuring ground," were startled to find that it remained a site of native resistance. Americans were not settling an empty West. They were *un*settling it by taking it from native peoples who already lived there.

## A Harvest of Blood: Native Peoples Dispossessed

Before the Civil War, when most Americans believed the prairie could not be farmed, Congress reserved the Great Plains for Indian peoples. But in the era of steel plows and railroads, policymakers suddenly had the power and desire to incorporate the whole region. The U.S. Army fought against the loosely federated Sioux — the major power on the northern grasslands — as well as other peoples who had agreed to live on reservations but found conditions so desperate that they fled (Map 16.5). These "reservation wars," caused largely by local violence and confused federal policies, were messy and bitter. Pointing to failed military campaigns, army atrocities, and egregious corruption in the Indian Bureau, reformers called for new policies that would destroy native people's traditional lifeways and "civilize" them — or, as one reformer put it, "kill the Indian and save the man."

**Killing the Bison**

This woodcut shows passengers shooting bison from a Kansas Pacific Railroad train—a small thrill added to the modern convenience of traveling west by rail. By the end of the 1870s, the plains bison shown here, which once numbered in the tens of millions and had been a large part of the Plains Indians' way of life, had been hunted almost to extinction. North Wind Picture Archives.

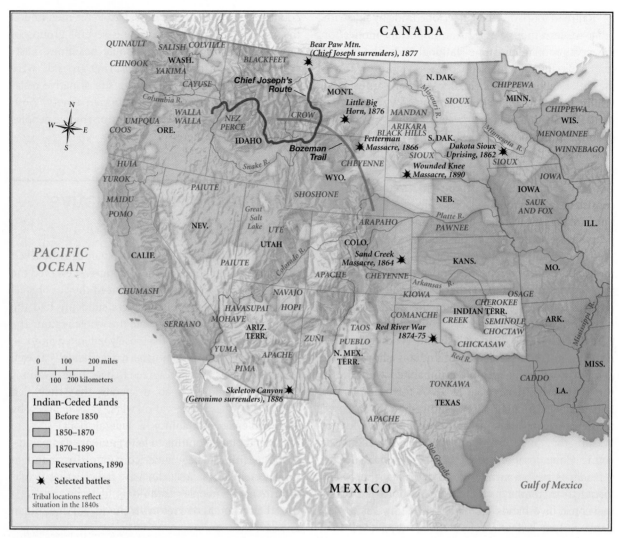

**MAP 16.5**

**Indian Country in the West, to 1890**

As settlement pushed onto the Great Plains after the Civil War, native peoples put up bitter resistance but ultimately to no avail. Over a period of decades, they ceded most of their lands to the federal government, and by 1890 they were confined to scattered reservations.

## The Civil War and Indians on the Plains

In August 1862, the attention of most Unionists and Confederates was riveted on General George McClellan's failing campaign in Virginia. But in Minnesota, the Dakota Sioux were increasingly frustrated. In 1858, the year Minnesota secured statehood, they had agreed to settle on a strip of land reserved by the government, in exchange for receiving regular payments and supplies. But Indian agents, contractors, and even Minnesota's territorial governor pocketed most of the funds. When the Dakotas protested that their children were starving, state officials dismissed their appeals. Corruption was so egregious that one

leading Minnesotan, Episcopal bishop Henry Whipple, wrote an urgent appeal to President James Buchanan. "A nation which sows robbery," he warned, "will reap a harvest of blood."

Whipple's prediction proved correct. During the summer of 1862, a decade of anger boiled over. In a surprise attack, Dakota fighters fanned out through the Minnesota countryside, killing immigrants and burning farms. They planned to sweep eastward to St. Paul but were stopped at Fort Ridgely. In the end, more than four hundred whites lay dead, including women and children from farms and small towns. Thousands fled; panicked officials telegraphed for aid, spreading hysteria from Wisconsin to Colorado.

**Enclosed Dakota Camp at Fort Snelling, Minnesota, 1862**

During the trial of Dakota warriors involved in the 1862 rebellion, and through the harsh Minnesota winter that followed, more than a thousand members of the tribe were imprisoned in an enormous enclosure on Pike Island, near St. Paul. A measles epidemic broke out in the crowded camp and dozens died, especially children. Though U.S. soldiers were often unfriendly toward their captives, local sentiment was even more hostile; troops regularly marched through the camp, in part to protect the Dakotas from vigilante violence. In 1863 all members of the tribe were forcibly removed from the state. In November 1862, photographer Benjamin Franklin Upton captured this image of Dakota tents in the Pike Island enclosure. Minnesota Historical Society.

Minnesotans' ferocious response to the uprising set the stage for further conflict. A hastily appointed military court, bent on revenge, sentenced 307 Dakotas to death, making it clear that rebellious Indians would be treated as criminals rather than warriors. President Abraham Lincoln reviewed the trial records and commuted most of the sentences but authorized the deaths of 38 Dakota men. They were hanged just after Christmas 1862 in the largest mass execution in U.S. history. Two months later, Congress canceled all treaties with the Dakotas, revoked their annuities, and expelled them from Minnesota. The scattered bands fled west to join nonreservation allies.

As the uprising showed, the Civil War created two dangerous conditions in the West, compounding the problems already caused by corruption. With the Union army fighting the Confederacy, western whites felt vulnerable to Indian attacks. They also discovered they could fight Indians with minimal federal oversight. In the wake of the Dakota uprising, worried Coloradans favored a military campaign against the Cheyennes — allies of the Sioux — even though the Cheyennes had shown little evidence of hostility. Colorado militia leader John M. Chivington, an aspiring politician, determined to quell public anxiety and make his career.

In May 1864, Cheyenne chief Black Kettle, fearing his band would be attacked, consulted with U.S. agents, who instructed him to settle along Sand Creek in eastern Colorado until a treaty could be signed. On November 29, 1864, Chivington's Colorado militia attacked the camp while most of the men were out hunting, slaughtering more than a hundred women and children. "I killed all I could," one officer testified later. "I think and earnestly believe the Indian to be an obstacle to civilization and should be exterminated." Captain Silas Soule, who served under Chivington but refused to give his men the order to fire, dissented. "It was hard to see little children on their knees," he wrote later, "having their brains beat out by men professing to be civilized." Chivington's men rode back for a celebration in Denver, where they hung Cheyenne scalps (and women's genitals) from the rafters of the Apollo Theater.

The northern plains exploded in conflict. Infuriated by the **Sand Creek massacre**, Cheyennes carried war pipes to the Arapahos and Sioux, who attacked and burned white settlements along the South Platte River. Ordered to subdue these peoples, the U.S. Army failed

**IDENTIFY CAUSES**
What factors led to warfare between whites and native peoples on the plains?

miserably: officers could not even locate the enemy, who traveled rapidly in small bands and knew the country well. A further shock occurred in December 1866 when 1,500 Sioux warriors executed a perfect ambush, luring Captain William Fetterman and 80 soldiers from a Wyoming fort and wiping them out. With the **Fetterman massacre**, the Sioux succeeded in closing the Bozeman Trail, a private road under army protection that had served as the main route into Montana.

General William Tecumseh Sherman, now commanding the army in the West, swore to defeat defiant Indians. But the Union hero met his match on the plains. Another year of fighting proved expensive and inconclusive. In 1868, the Sioux, led by the Oglala band under Chief Red Cloud, told a peace commission they would not sign any treaty unless the United States pledged to abandon all its forts along the Bozeman Trail. The commission agreed. Red Cloud had won.

In the wake of these events, eastern public opinion turned against the Indian wars, which seemed at best ineffective, at worst brutal. Congress held hearings on the slaughter at Sand Creek. Though Chivington, now a civilian, was never prosecuted, the massacre became an infamous example of western vigilantism. By the time Ulysses Grant entered the White House in 1869, the authors of Reconstruction in the South also began to seek solutions to what they called the "Indian problem."

## Grant's Peace Policy

Grant inherited an Indian policy in disarray. Federal incompetence was highlighted by yet another mass killing of friendly Indians in January 1870, this time on the Marias River in Montana, by an army detachment that shot and burned to death 173 Piegans (Blackfeet). Having run out of other options, Grant introduced a peace policy, based on recommendations from Christian advisors. He offered selected appointments to the reformers — including many former abolitionists — who had created such groups as the Indian Rights Association and the Women's National Indian Association.

Rejecting the virulent anti-Indian stance of many westerners, reformers argued that native peoples had the innate capacity to become equal with whites. They believed, however, that Indians could achieve this only if they embraced Christianity and white ways. Reformers thus aimed to destroy native languages, cultures, and religions. Despite humane intentions, their condescension was obvious. They ignored dissenters like Dr. Thomas Bland of the National Indian Defense

Association, who suggested that instead of an "Indian problem" there might be a "white problem" — refusal to permit Indians to follow their own lifeways. To most nineteenth-century Americans, such a notion was shocking and uncivilized. Increasingly dismissive of blacks' capacity for citizenship and hostile toward "heathen" Chinese immigrants, white Americans were even less willing to understand and respect Indian cultures. They believed that in the modern world, native peoples were fated for extinction (Thinking Like a Historian, p. 530).

**Indian Boarding Schools**   Reformers focused their greatest energy on educating the next generation. Realizing that acculturation — adoption of white ways — was difficult when children lived at home, agents and missionaries created off-reservation schools. Native families were exhorted, bullied, and bribed into sending their children to these schools, where, in addition to school lessons, boys learned farming skills and girls practiced housekeeping. "English only" was the rule; students were punished if they spoke their own languages. Mourning Dove, a Salish girl from what is now Washington State, remembered that her school "ran strictly. We never talked during meals without permission, given only on Sunday or special holidays. Otherwise there was silence — a terrible silent silence. I was used to the freedom of the forest, and it was hard to learn this strict discipline. I was punished many times before I learned." The Lakota boy Plenty Kill, who at boarding school received the new name Luther, remembered his loneliness and fear upon arrival: "The big boys would sing brave songs, and that would start the girls to crying. . . . The girls' quarters were about a hundred and fifty yards from ours, so we could hear them." After having his hair cut short, Plenty Kill felt a profound change in his identity. "None of us slept well that night," he recalled. "I felt that I was no more Indian, but would be an imitation of a white man."

 To see a longer excerpt of Mourning Dove's autobiography, along with other primary sources from this period, see *Sources for America's History*.

Even in the first flush of reform zeal, Grant's policies faced major hurdles. Most Indians had been pushed off traditional lands and assigned to barren ground that would have defeated the most enterprising farmer. Poverty and dislocation left Indians especially vulnerable to the ravages of infectious diseases like measles and scarlet fever. At the same time, Quaker, Presbyterian, and Methodist reformers fought turf

**Red Cloud's Bedroom, 1891**

Taken on the Pine Ridge Reservation in South Dakota by photographer C. G. Morledge, this photograph shows the bedroom of Red Cloud, a distinguished Oglala Lakota leader. Red Cloud had won a war against the U.S. Army just after the Civil War. He negotiated so tenaciously and shrewdly, afterward, with what he saw as meddlesome Indian agents, that his people nicknamed Pine Ridge "The Place Where Everything Is Disputed." Some of the contents of Red Cloud's bedroom may surprise you. How do you interpret the presence of five American flags? The visual images on the walls? What strategies and ways of life, blending old and new, does the photograph suggest? Compare it to Edward S. Curtis, "Little Plume and Yellow Kidney" (p. 533). In what ways did Morledge and Curtis craft different representations of Indian life? Denver Public Library/Bridgeman Art Library.

battles among themselves and with Catholic missionaries. Many traders and agents also continued to steal money and supplies from people they were supposed to protect. In the late 1870s, Rutherford B. Hayes's administration undertook more housecleaning at the Bureau of Indian Affairs, but corruption lingered.

From the Indians' point of view, reformers often became just another interest group in a crowded field of whites sending hopelessly mixed messages. The attitudes of individual army representatives, agents, and missionaries ranged from courageous and sympathetic to utterly ruthless. Many times, after chiefs thought they had reached a face-to-face agreement, they found it drastically altered by Congress or Washington bureaucrats. Nez Perce leader Joseph observed that "white people have too many chiefs. They do not understand each other. . . . I cannot understand why so many chiefs are allowed to talk so many different ways, and promise so many different things." A Kiowa chief agreed: "We make but few contracts, and them we remember well. The whites make so many they are liable to forget them. The white chief seems not to be able to govern his braves."

Native peoples were nonetheless forced to accommodate, as independent tribal governance and treaty making came to an end. Back in the 1830s, the U.S. Supreme Court had declared Indians no longer sovereign but rather "domestic dependent nations." On a practical basis, however, both the U.S. Senate and agents in the field continued to negotiate treaties as late as 1869. Two years later, the House of Representatives,

**UNDERSTAND POINTS OF VIEW**
How did post–Civil War reformers believe they were improving U.S. Indian policies, and in what ways did that prove to be true and untrue?

## Representing Indians

The documents below, designed for white audiences, all depict American Indians in the West.

---

1. **Buffalo Bill Cody's Wild West advertisement, 1899.** *Cody never called the Wild West a "show," placing tremendous emphasis on its allegedly authentic reenactments of events.*

Superstock.

2. **Lewis Henry Morgan, *Ancient Society*, 1877.** *Morgan, a leading American anthropologist, studied the Iroquois and other native peoples. In 1877 he published an influential theory of human development, ranking various peoples in their "progress" from the "lowest stage of savagery" through the pinnacle of "civilization"—northern Europeans.*

Some tribes and families have been left in geographical isolation to work out the problems of progress. . . . [Others] have been adulterated through external influence. Thus, while Africa was and is an ethnical chaos of savagery and barbarism, Australia and Polynesia were in savagery, pure and simple. . . . The Indian family of America, unlike any other existing family, exemplified the condition of mankind in three successive ethnical

### TABLE 16.1

**Status of Civilization (from Morgan, *Ancient Society*, 1877)**

| | |
|---|---|
| I. Lower Status of Savagery | From the Infancy of the Human Race to the commencement of the next Period. |
| II. Middle Status of Savagery | From the acquisition of a fish subsistence and a knowledge of the use of fire . . . |
| III. Upper Status of Savagery | From the Invention of the Bow and Arrow . . . |
| IV. Lower Status of Barbarism | From the Invention of the Art of Pottery . . . |
| V. Middle Status of Barbarism | From the Domestication of animals on the Eastern hemisphere, and in the Western from the cultivation of maize and plants by Irrigation . . . |
| VI. Upper Status of Barbarism | From the Invention of the process of Smelting Iron Ore, with the use of iron tools . . . |
| VII. Civilization | From the Invention of writing, to the present time. |

periods. . . . The far northern Indians and some of the coast tribes of North and South America were in the Upper Status of savagery; the partially Village Indians east of the Mississippi were in the Lower Status of barbarism, and the Village Indians of North and South America were in the Middle Status. . . .

Commencing, then, with the Australians and Polynesians, following with the American Indian tribes, and concluding with the Roman and Grecian, who afford the highest exemplifications respectively of the six great stages of human progress, the sum of their united experiences may be supposed fairly to represent that of the human family. . . . We are dealing substantially, with the ancient history and condition of our own remote ancestors.

3. **Touring Indian Country, 1888 and 1894.** *Hoping to lure eastern tourists, the Northern Pacific Railroad published an annual journal,* Wonderland, *describing the natural splendors and economic progress of the West, as seen from its rail lines.*

We are now in the far-famed Yellowstone Valley. . . . There are but few Indians now to be seen along the line of the railroad, and those are engaged in agricultural and industrial pursuits. The extinction of the buffalo has rendered the Indian much more amenable to the civilizing influences brought to bear upon him than he formerly was, and very fair crops of grain are being raised at some of the agencies. At the Devil's Lake agency, for example, 60,000 bushels of wheat have been raised by the [Sioux and Chippewa] Indians in a single season. . . .

[The Crows'] great reservation is probably the garden spot of Montana, and the throwing open of a large portion of it to [white] settlement, which cannot long be delayed, will assuredly give an immense impetus to the agricultural interests of the Territory. . . .

The Flatheads have probably 10,000 or more horses and 5,000 or 6,000 cattle. . . . As ranchers and farmers the Flatheads are a success. It would be a matter of surprise to some people who think that the only good Indian is a dead Indian, to see the way some of the women handle sewing machines.

---

Sources: (2) Lewis H. Morgan, *Ancient Society* (New York: Henry Holt and Company, 1878), 12–13, 16–18; (3) John Hyde, *Wonderland* (St. Paul, 1888), 21, and 1894, 27.

4. **Gertrude Käsebier, photograph of Joe Black Fox, 1898.** *One of the first women to become a professional photographer, Käsebier here depicts Joe Black Fox relaxing with a cigarette. Black Fox, an Oglala Sioux, toured with Buffalo Bill's Wild West in 1900.*

Photographic History Collection, National Museum of American History, Smithsonian Institution 69.236.22, 2004-57801

---

## ANALYZING THE EVIDENCE

1. Compare the depiction of the Plains Indians and Buffalo Bill Cody in source 1. How does source 4 differ from source 1? From Edward Curtis's "In a Piegan Lodge" (p. 533), in which all traces of modern life were erased? How might these depictions of "actual life" have shaped their audience's understanding of the West?

2. What bases did Morgan use for his rankings in source 2? How did he define the relationship between American Indians and whites (whom he refers to, in this passage, as "we")? Why did he suggest that Indians offered a unique opportunity for study?

3. Imagine that you were a wealthy, well-educated tourist preparing to travel west in 1900. Which of these documents would you most likely have encountered in advance? How might they have shaped your expectations and experiences?

4. These documents had different creators: an artist, a scholar, and two sets of entrepreneurs. What audiences did they have in mind? How do you think this affected their messages?

## PUTTING IT ALL TOGETHER

Many nineteenth-century commentators claimed that American Indians were "vanishing": that is, they could not adapt to modernity and would die out. This proved untrue, of course, but the idea circulated widely. Which of these sources lend support to the idea of the "vanishing Indian"? Which suggest counter-stories of survival and endurance? Using these sources and your knowledge of the period, analyze the myths and realities of Native American life in the late nineteenth century.

jealous of Senate privileges, passed a bill to abolish all treaty making with Indians. The Senate agreed, provided that existing treaties remained in force. It was one more step in a long, torturous erosion of native rights. Eventually, the U.S. Supreme Court ruled in **Lone Wolf v. Hitchcock** (1903) that Congress could make whatever Indian policies it chose, ignoring all existing treaties. That same year, in *Ex Parte Crow Dog*, the Court ruled that no Indian was a citizen unless Congress designated him so. Indians were henceforth wards of the government. These rulings remained in force until the New Deal of the 1930s.

**Breaking Up Tribal Lands**   Reformers' most sweeping effort to assimilate Indians was the **Dawes Severalty Act** (1887), the dream of Senator Henry L. Dawes of Massachusetts, a leader in the Indian Rights Association. Dawes saw the reservation system as an ugly relic of the past. Through severalty—division of tribal lands—he hoped to force Indians onto individual landholdings, partitioning reservations into homesteads, just like those of white farmers. Supporters of the plan believed that landownership would encourage Indians to assimilate. It would lead, as Dawes wrote, to "a personal sense of independence." Individual property, echoed another reformer, would make the Indian man "intelligently selfish, . . . with a *pocket that aches to be filled with dollars!*"

The Dawes Act was a disaster. It played into the hands of whites who coveted Indian land and who persuaded the government to sell them land that was not needed for individual allotments. In this and other ways, the Bureau of Indian Affairs (BIA) implemented the law carelessly, to the outrage of Dawes. In Indian Territory, a commission seized more than 15 million "surplus" acres from native tribes by 1894, opening the way for whites to convert the last federal territory set aside for native peoples into the state of Oklahoma. In addition to catastrophic losses of collectively held property, native peoples lost 66 percent of their individually allotted lands between the 1880s and the 1930s, through fraud, BIA mismanagement, and pressure to sell to whites.

## The End of Armed Resistance

As the nation consolidated control of the West in the 1870s, Americans hoped that Grant's peace policy was solving the "Indian problem." In the Southwest, such formidable peoples as the Kiowas and Comanches had been forced onto reservations. The Diné or Navajo nation, exiled under horrific conditions during the Civil War but permitted to reoccupy their traditional land, gave up further military resistance. An outbreak among California's Modoc people in 1873—again, humiliating to the army—was at last subdued. Only Sitting Bull, a leader of the powerful Lakota Sioux on the northern plains, openly refused to go to a reservation. When pressured by U.S. troops, he repeatedly crossed into Canada, where he told reporters that "the life of white men is slavery. . . . I have seen nothing that a white man has, houses or railways or clothing or food, that is as good as the right to move in open country and live in our own fashion."

In 1874, the Lakotas faced direct provocation. Lieutenant Colonel George Armstrong Custer, a brash self-promoter who had graduated last in his class at West Point, led an expedition into South Dakota's Black Hills and loudly proclaimed the discovery of gold. Amid the severe depression of the 1870s, prospectors rushed in. The United States, wavering on its 1868 treaty, pressured Sioux leaders to sell the Black Hills. The chiefs said no. Ignoring this answer, the government demanded in 1876 that all Sioux gather at the federal agencies. The policy backfired: not only did Sitting Bull refuse to report, but other Sioux, Cheyennes, and Arapahos slipped away from reservations to join him. Knowing they might face military attack, they agreed to live together for the summer in one great village numbering over seven thousand people. By June, they were camped on the Little Big Horn River in what is now southeastern Montana. Some of the young men wanted to organize raiding parties, but elders counseled against it. "We [are] within our treaty rights as hunters," they argued. "We must keep ourselves so."

The U.S. Army dispatched a thousand cavalry and infantrymen to drive the Indians back to the reservation. Despite warnings from experienced scouts—including Crow Indian allies—most officers thought the job would be easy. Their greatest fear was that the Indians would manage to slip away. But amid the nation's centennial celebration on the Fourth of July 1876, Americans received dreadful news. On June 26 and 27, Lieutenant Colonel Custer, leading the 7th Cavalry as part of a three-pronged effort to surround the Indians, had led 210 men in an ill-considered assault on Sitting Bull's camp. The Sioux and their allies had killed the attackers to the last man. "The Indians," one Oglala woman remembered, "acted just like they were driving buffalo to a good place where they could be easily slaughtered."

As retold by the press in sensational (and often fictionalized) accounts, the story of Custer's "last stand" quickly served to justify American conquest of Indian

**Little Plume and Yellow Kidney**

Photographer Edward S. Curtis took this photograph of the Piegan (Blackfeet) leader Little Plume and his son Yellow Kidney. Curtis's extensive collection of photographs of Native Americans remains a valuable resource for historians. However, Curtis altered his images to make his native subjects seem more "authentic": though Indians made widespread use of nonnative furniture, clothes, and other consumer goods (such as Singer sewing machines), Curtis removed those from the frame. He also retouched photographs to remove items such as belts and watches. Note the circular "shadow" here, against the lodge wall, near Little Plume's right arm: the original photograph included a clock. Library of Congress.

"savages." Long after Americans forgot the massacres of Cheyenne women and children at Sand Creek and of Piegan people on the Marias River, prints of the **Battle of Little Big Horn** hung in barrooms across the country. William F. "Buffalo Bill" Cody, in his traveling Wild West performances, enacted a revenge killing of a Cheyenne man named Yellow Hand in a tableau Cody called "first scalp for Custer." Notwithstanding that the tableau featured a white man scalping a Cheyenne, Cody depicted it as a triumph for civilization.

Little Big Horn proved to be the last military victory of Plains Indians against the U.S. Army. Pursued relentlessly after Custer's death and finding fewer and fewer bison to sustain them, Sioux parents watched their children starve through a bitter winter. Slowly, families trickled into the agencies and accommodated themselves to reservation life (Map 16.6). The next year,

the Nez Perces, fleeing for the Canadian border, also surrendered. The final holdouts fought in the Southwest with Chiricahua Apache leader Geronimo. Like many others, Geronimo had accepted reservation life but found conditions unendurable. Describing the desolate land the tribe had been allotted, one Apache said it had "nothing but cactus, rattlesnakes, heat, rocks, and insects. . . . Many, many of our people died of starvation." When Geronimo took up arms in protest, the army recruited other Apaches to track him and his band into the hills; in September 1886, he surrendered for the last time. The Chiricahua Apaches never returned to their homeland. The United States had completed its military conquest of the West.

**EXPLAIN CONSEQUENCES**

How did Grant's peace policy fail to consider the needs of Native Americans in the West, and what were its results?

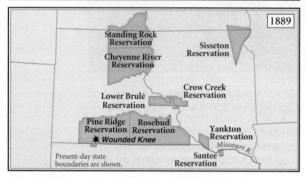

**MAP 16.6**

**The Sioux Reservations in South Dakota, 1868–1889**

In 1868, when they bent to the demand that they move onto the reservation, the Sioux thought they had gained secure rights to a substantial part of their ancestral hunting grounds. But harsh conditions on reservations led to continuing military conflicts. Land-hungry whites exerted continuous local pressure, and officials in Washington repeatedly changed the terms of Sioux land holdings—always eroding native claims.

## Strategies of Survival

Though the warpath closed, many native peoples continued secretly to practice traditional customs. Away from the disapproving eyes of agents and teachers, they passed on their languages, histories, and traditional arts and medicine to younger generations. Frustrated missionaries often concluded that little could be accomplished because bonds of kinship and

**TRACE CHANGE OVER TIME**

In what ways did the outlook of native peoples change in the era after armed resistance had ended?

custom were so strong. Parents also hated to relinquish their children to off-reservation boarding schools. Thus more and more Indian schools ended up on or near reservations; white teachers had to accept their pupils' continued participation in the rhythms of Indian community life.

Selectively, most native peoples adopted some white ways. Many parents urged their sons and daughters to study hard, learn English, and develop skills to help them succeed in the new world they confronted. Even Sitting Bull announced in 1885 that he wanted his children "to be educated like the white children are." Some Indian students grew up to be lawyers, doctors, and advocates for their people, including writers and artists who interpreted native experiences for national audiences. One of the most famous was a Santee Sioux boy named Ohiyesa, who became Dr. Charles Eastman. Posted to the Pine Ridge Reservation in South Dakota, Eastman practiced medicine side by side with traditional healers, whom he respected, and wrote popular books under his Sioux name. He remembered that when he left for boarding school, his father had said, "We have now entered upon this life, and there is no going back. . . . Remember, my boy, it is the same as if I sent you on your first war-path. I shall expect you to conquer."

Nothing exemplified this syncretism, or cultural blending, better than the **Ghost Dance movement** of the late 1880s and early 1890s, which fostered native peoples' hope that they could, through sacred dances, resurrect the bison and call a great storm to drive whites back across the Atlantic. The Ghost Dance drew on Christian elements as well as native ones. As the movement spread from reservation to reservation—Paiutes, Arapahos, Sioux—native peoples developed new forms of pan-Indian identity and cooperation.

White responses to the Ghost Dance showed continued misunderstanding and lethal exertion of authority. In 1890, when a group of Lakota Sioux Ghost Dancers left their South Dakota reservation, they were pursued by the U.S. Army, who feared that further spread of the religion would provoke war. On December 29, at **Wounded Knee**, the 7th Cavalry caught up with fleeing Lakotas and killed at least 150—perhaps as many as 300. Like other massacres, this one could have been avoided. The deaths at Wounded Knee stand as a final indictment of decades of relentless U.S. expansion, white ignorance and greed, chaotic and conflicting policies, and bloody mistakes.

## Western Myths and Realities

The post–Civil War frontier produced mythic figures who have played starring roles in America's national folklore ever since: "savage" Indians, brave pioneers, rugged cowboys, and gun-slinging sheriffs. Far from being invented by Hollywood in the twentieth century, these oversimplified characters emerged in the era when the nation incorporated the West. Pioneers helped develop the mythic ideal. As one Montana woman claimed, they had come west "at peril of their lives" and faced down "scalp dances" and other terrors; in the end, they "conquered the wilderness and transformed it into a land of peace and plenty." Some former cowboys, capitalizing on the popularity of dime novel Westerns, spiced up their memoirs for sale. Eastern readers were eager for stories like *The Life and Adventures of Nat Love* (1907), written by a Texas cowhand who had been born in slavery in Tennessee and who, as a rodeo star in the 1870s, had won the nickname "Deadwood Dick."

No myth-maker proved more influential than Buffalo Bill Cody. Unlike those who saw the West as free or empty, Bill understood that the United States had taken it by conquest. Ironically, his famous Wild West, which he insisted was not a "show" but an authentic representation of frontier experience, provided one of the few employment options for Plains Indians. To escape harsh reservation conditions, Sioux and Cheyenne men signed on with Bill and demonstrated their riding skills for cheering audiences across the United States and Europe, chasing buffalo and attacking U.S. soldiers and pioneer wagons in the arena. Buffalo Bill proved to be a good employer. Black Elk, a Sioux man who joined Cody's operation, recalled that Bill was generous and "had a strong heart." But Black Elk had a mixed reaction to the Wild West. "I liked the part of the show we made," he told an interviewer, "but not the part the Wasichus [white people] made." As he observed, the Wild West of the 1880s was at its heart a celebration of U.S. military conquest.

At this same moment of transition, a young historian named Frederick Jackson Turner reviewed recent census data and proclaimed the end of the frontier. Up to 1890, he wrote, a clear, westward-moving line had existed between "civilization and savagery." The frontier experience, Turner argued, shaped Americans' national character. It left them a heritage of "coarseness and strength, combined with acuteness and inquisitiveness," as well as "restless, nervous energy."

Today, historians reject Turner's depiction of Indian "savagery"—and his contradictory idea that white pioneers in the West claimed empty "free land." Many scholars have noted that frontier conquest was both violent and incomplete. The Dust Bowl of the 1930s, as well as more recent cycles of drought, have repeated late-nineteenth-century patterns of hardship and depopulation on the plains. During the 1950s and 1960s, also, uranium mining rushes in the West mimicked earlier patterns of boom and bust, leaving ghost towns in their wake. Turner himself acknowledged that the frontier had both good and evil elements. He noted that in the West, "frontier liberty was sometimes confused with absence of all effective government." But in 1893, when Turner first published "The Significance of the Frontier in American History," eager listeners heard only the positives. They saw pioneering in the West as evidence of American exceptionalism: of the nation's unique history and destiny. They claimed that "peaceful" American expansion was the opposite of European empires—ignoring the many military and economic similarities. Although politically the American West became a set of states rather than a colony, historians today emphasize the legacy of conquest that is central to its (and America's) history.

Less than two months after the massacre at Wounded Knee, General William T. Sherman died in New York. As the nation marked his passing with pomp and oratory, commentators noted that his career reflected a great era of conquest and consolidation of national power. Known primarily for his role in defeating the Confederacy, Sherman's first military exploits had been against Seminoles in Florida. Later, during the Mexican War (1846–1848), he had gone west with the U.S. Army to help claim California. After the Civil War, the general went west again, supervising the forced removal of Sioux and Cheyennes to reservations.

When Sherman graduated from West Point in 1840, the United States had counted twenty-six states, none of them west of Missouri. At his death in 1891, the nation boasted forty-four states, stretching to the Pacific coast. The United States now rivaled Britain and Germany as an industrial giant, and its dynamic economy was drawing immigrants from around the world. Over the span of Sherman's career, the United States had become a major player on the world stage. It had done so through the kind of fierce military conquest that Sherman made famous, as well as through bold expansions of federal authority to foster economic expansion. From the wars and policies of Sherman's lifetime, the children and grandchildren of Civil War heroes inherited a vast empire. In the coming decades, it would be up to them to decide how they would use the nation's new power.

# SUMMARY

Between 1861 and 1877, the United States completed its conquest of the continent. After the Civil War, expansion of railroads fostered integration of the national economy. Republican policymakers promoted this integration through protective tariffs, while federal court rulings facilitated economic growth and strengthened corporations. To attract foreign investment, Congress placed the nation on the gold standard. Federal officials also pursued a vigorous foreign policy, acquiring Alaska and asserting U.S. power indirectly through control of international trade in Latin America and Asia.

An important result of economic integration was incorporation of the Great Plains. Cattlemen built an industry linked to the integrated economy, in the process nearly driving the native bison to extinction. Homesteaders confronted harsh environmental conditions as they converted the grasslands for agriculture. Republicans championed homesteader families as representatives of domesticity, an ideal opposed to Mormon plural marriage in Utah. Homesteading accelerated the rapid, often violent, transformation of western environments. Perceiving this transformation, federal officials began setting aside natural preserves such as Yellowstone, often clashing with Native Americans who wished to hunt there.

Conflicts led to the dispossession of Native American lands. During the Civil War, whites clashed with the Sioux and their allies. Grant's peace policy sought to end this conflict by forcing Native Americans to acculturate to European-style practices. Indian armed resistance continued through the 1880s, ending with Geronimo's surrender in 1886. Thereafter, Native Americans survived by secretly continuing their traditions and selectively adopting white ways. Due in part to the determined military conquest of this period, the United States claimed a major role on the world stage. Frontier myths shaped Americans' view of themselves as rugged individualists with a unique national destiny.

# C H A P T E R   R E V I E W

 **MAKE IT STICK**   Go to **LearningCurve** to retain what you've read.

## TERMS TO KNOW   Identify and explain the significance of each term below.

### Key Concepts and Events

**transcontinental railroad** (p. 508)

**protective tariff** (p. 510)

**Treaty of Kanagawa** (p. 510)

**Burlingame Treaty** (p. 511)

*Munn v. Illinois* (p. 514)

**gold standard** (p. 515)

**Crime of 1873** (p. 515)

**Homestead Act** (p. 516)

**Morrill Act** (p. 516)

**land-grant colleges** (p. 516)

**Comstock Lode** (p. 516)

**Long Drive** (p. 519)

**"rain follows the plow"** (p. 519)

**Exodusters** (p. 520)

**Yellowstone National Park** (p. 525)

**U.S. Fisheries Commission** (p. 525)

**Sand Creek massacre** (p. 527)

**Fetterman massacre** (p. 528)

*Lone Wolf v. Hitchcock* (p. 532)

**Dawes Severalty Act** (p. 532)

**Battle of Little Big Horn** (p. 533)

**Ghost Dance movement** (p. 534)

**Wounded Knee** (p. 534)

### Key People

**William Seward** (p. 510)

**Emmeline Wells** (p. 521)

**John Wesley Powell** (p. 521)

**Chief Joseph** (p. 525)

**Sitting Bull** (p. 532)

**George Armstrong Custer** (p. 532)

**Geronimo** (p. 533)

**Ohiyesa (Dr. Charles Eastman)** (p. 534)

**Buffalo Bill Cody** (p. 535)

**Frederick Jackson Turner** (p. 535)

## REVIEW QUESTIONS
Answer these questions to demonstrate your understanding of the chapter's main ideas.

1. What national policies did Republicans pursue during the Civil War and Reconstruction to stimulate economic growth and consolidate a continental empire? What were the resulting achievements and costs?

2. How did the trans-Mississippi west develop economically in this era? What problems and conflicts resulted?

3. Why did U.S. policies toward Native Americans in this era result in so much violence? Why did armed struggle continue as late as 1890, despite the U.S. "peace policy" that was proclaimed in the 1870s?

4. **THEMATIC UNDERSTANDING**   Review the events listed under "Peopling" on the thematic timeline on page 409. Between the 1840s and the 1870s, what distinctive patterns of racial and ethnic conflict occurred along the northeastern seaboard and in the West? What were the results for immigrants in the Northeast, and for different ethnic and racial groups in the West?

## MAKING CONNECTIONS
Recognize the larger developments and continuities within and across chapters by answering these questions.

1. **ACROSS TIME AND PLACE**   During the Reconstruction years, Republican policymakers made sweeping policy decisions — especially having to do with land rights, voting rights, and education — that shaped the future of African Americans in the South and American Indians in the West. In an essay, compare U.S. policies toward the two groups. What assumptions and goals underlay each effort to incorporate racial minorities into the United States? To what extent did each effort succeed or fail, and why? How did the actions of powerful whites in each region shape the results?

2. **VISUAL EVIDENCE**   Review the images in this chapter. Find two that show how Americans of the era thought the landscapes of the West *ought* to look when settlement was complete. Identify at least three others that show what the natural and built environments of the West *really* looked like. What do you conclude from this comparison about the ambitions and limits of westward expansion?

## MORE TO EXPLORE
Start here to learn more about the events discussed in this chapter.

David Wallace Adams, *Education for Extinction* (1995). A powerful history of American Indian boarding schools.

*American Experience* (PBS), "Last Stand at Little Big Horn." A nuanced one-hour documentary about the famous battle.

Sarah Barringer Gordon, *The Mormon Question* (2002). An exploration of plural marriage debates in national politics.

Joy S. Kasson, *Buffalo Bill's Wild West* (2001). A wonderful study of Buffalo Bill's performances and their role in shaping mythologies of the West.

Patricia Nelson Limerick, *The Legacy of Conquest* (1987) and *Something in the Soil* (2000). Limerick's lively, accessible books are an excellent introduction to historians' recent rethinking of western history.

María Montoya, *Translating Property* (2002). Tells the story of the displacement of Mexican Americans (and their neighbors) in struggles over the Maxwell Land Grant in New Mexico and Colorado.

## TIMELINE

Ask yourself why this chapter begins and ends with these dates and then identify the links among related events.

| 1854 | • United States "opens" Japan to trade |
|------|------|
| 1859 | • Comstock silver lode discovered in Nevada |
| 1862 | • Homestead Act<br>• Dakota Sioux uprising in Minnesota<br>• Morrill Act funds public state universities |
| 1864 | • Sand Creek massacre of Cheyennes in Colorado<br>• Yosemite Valley reserved as public park |
| 1865 | • Long Drive of Texas longhorns begins |
| 1866 | • Fetterman massacre |
| 1868 | • Burlingame Treaty with China |
| 1869 | • Transcontinental railroad completed<br>• Wyoming women's suffrage |
| 1870 | • Utah women's suffrage |
| 1872 | • General Mining Act<br>• Yellowstone National Park created |
| 1873 | • United States begins move to gold standard |
| 1876 | • Battle of Little Big Horn |
| 1877 | • Nez Perces forcibly removed from ancestral homelands in Northwest<br>• *Munn v. Illinois* Supreme Court decision |
| 1879 | • Exoduster migration to Kansas<br>• John Wesley Powell presents *Report on the Lands of the Arid Region of the United States* |
| 1880s | • Rise of the Ghost Dance movement |
| 1885 | • Sitting Bull tours with Buffalo Bill's Wild West |
| 1886 | • Dry cycle begins on the plains<br>• Chiricahua Apache leader Geronimo surrenders |
| 1887 | • Dawes Severalty Act |
| 1890 | • Massacre of Sioux Ghost Dancers at Wounded Knee, South Dakota |

**KEY TURNING POINTS:** The military, political, and economic events of the Civil War years (1861–1865) are often treated as largely occurring in the Northeast and South — at places such as Shiloh, Gettysburg, and Washington, D.C. What impact did these developments have on the West, and what were their legacies?

# 6
## PART

# Industrializing America: Upheavals and Experiments
## 1877–1917

Touring the United States around 1900, a Hungarian Catholic abbot named Count Péter Vay visited the steel mills of Pittsburgh. "Fourteen-thousand tall chimneys . . . discharge their burning sparks and smoke incessantly," he reported. He was moved by the plight of fellow Hungarians, laboring "wherever the heat is most insupportable, the flames most scorching." One worker had just been killed in a foundry accident. Vay, attending the funeral, worried that immigration was "of no use except to help fill the moneybags of the insatiable millionaires."

Vay witnessed America's emergence as an industrial power — and the consequences of that transformation. In 1877, the United States was overwhelmingly rural and dependent on foreign capital. By 1917, its landscapes, population, and ways of life were forever altered. Industrialization brought millions of immigrants from around the globe and built immense cities whose governance and social relations offered unaccustomed rewards and challenges. It sharpened class divisions and led to the rise of national labor movements, while prompting Americans to redefine men's and women's roles. Industrialization also created pressure for political innovation. As ex-president Theodore Roosevelt declared in 1910, American citizens needed to "control the mighty commercial forces which they have called into being." Workers, farmers, and urban reformers sought to regulate corporations, fight poverty, and clean up politics and the environment. In their creative responses to the problems of the industrial age, such reformers gave their name to the Progressive Era.

## Corporations and Conflicts

In the post–Civil War decades, giant corporations developed national and even global networks of production, marketing, and finance. In many fields, vertical integration enabled corporate managers to control production from the harvesting of raw materials through the sale of finished products. Nationwide marketing networks developed through innovative use of railroads—and through ruthless competitive tactics such as predatory pricing.

Corporations' complex structures opened career opportunities for middle managers and salesmen. Women, filling new niches as telephone operators and department store clerks, also played an important role in the expanding service sector. At the same time, traditional craftsmen found themselves displaced as deskilled wage work steadily expanded. Factory workers and miners endured dangerous conditions, health hazards, low pay, and frequent bouts of unemployment.

The most dangerous, low-wage work was often allotted to African Americans and immigrants from Europe, Mexico, and Asia. Workers organized to protest these conditions. In addition to creating labor unions, they forged political alliances with farmers, who also found their livelihoods at risk in the changing global economy. Native-born workers and European immigrants successfully agitated for the legal exclusion of Chinese workers. These events are covered in Chapter 17.

## A Diverse, Urban Society

While the old values of thrift, piety, and domesticity never entirely faded, they faced challenges in the era of industrialization. Women asserted more independent roles in public life. The new model for men was an aggressive masculinity, embodied in the rise of sports. Widespread acceptance of Charles Darwin's theory of evolution prompted influential thinkers to justify economic inequality as a law of nature. In culture, the rise of literary realism and abstract art marked decisive innovations. Responding to these upheavals, people of religious faith reshaped their institutions. Some accepted modernity, while others called for a return to Christian "fundamentals." See Chapter 18 for these developments.

Great cities arose, becoming playgrounds for the new superrich while also housing millions of poor immigrants in tenements. At the same time, people of all classes in the vibrant cities enjoyed new pleasures, from amusement parks to vaudeville and movies. The fast-growing cities proved challenging to govern. To the frustration of middle-class reformers, many immigrant voters supported political machines like New York's Tammany Hall. By 1900, though, even some machine leaders admitted the need for reform, and big cities began to serve as seedbeds for progressive experiments. On these developments, see Chapters 18 and 19.

## Reform Initiatives

Political debates in this era centered on the scope of government power, as reformers called for regulation of corporations and other measures to blunt the impact of industrialization. After the 1880s, Republicans increasingly defended big business. Though Republican Theodore Roosevelt championed landmark legislation during his presidency (1901–1909), much reform energy passed to other parties. Democrats, who had long called for limited government, began to advocate stronger federal intervention to fight poverty and restrain big business. By the 1910s, during the presidency of Democrat Woodrow Wilson (1913–1921), the party enacted an impressive slate of laws. Meanwhile, the Populist, Socialist, and Progressive parties proposed more radical responses to industrialization and concentrated wealth. While none of these parties won national power, their ideas helped shape the course of reform.

Progressive Era reformers—a diverse group who were not at all united—sought to enhance democracy, rein in the power of corporations, uphold labor rights, protect the environment, and promote public health and safety. They faced formidable obstacles, especially from Supreme Court rulings. Nonetheless, by 1917, national, state, and local governments enacted a range of new laws, representing the early emergence of the modern state. Chapter 20 traces these events.

# Industrializing America: Upheavals and Experiments 1877–1917

## Thematic Understanding

This timeline arranges some of the important events of this period into themes. What was the relationship of the two severe economic depressions listed under "Work, Exchange, and Technology" to political reform? Did reform tend to come during or after periods of economic crisis? Why do you think this was the case? In what ways did Americans respond politically to the depression of the 1870s? What continuities and changes do you see in their responses to the next severe depression, in the 1890s?   **>**

| | WORK, EXCHANGE, AND TECHNOLOGY | PEOPLING | ENVIRONMENT AND GEOGRAPHY | POLITICS AND POWER | IDEAS, BELIEFS, AND CULTURE |
|---|---|---|---|---|---|
| **1870** | • Economic depression (1873–1879)<br>• First department store opens in Philadelphia (1874)<br>• Great Railroad Strike (1877)<br>• Deskilling of labor under mass production | • Hostility toward Chinese immigrants grows | • Successful containment of New York cholera outbreak spurs movement for public health (1866)<br>• First national park established at Yellowstone (1872)<br>• Appalachian Mountain Club founded (1876) | • Democrats make sweeping congressional gains (1874)<br>• Era of close party competition in national elections (1874–1894)<br>• Reconstruction ends (1877) | • Comstock Act bans circulation of most information about sex and birth control (1873)<br>• National League launches professional baseball (1876)<br>• Henry George, *Progress and Poverty* (1879) |
| **1880** | • First vertically integrated corporations<br>• Rockefeller establishes Standard Oil Trust<br>• Emergence of white-collar managerial work<br>• Women enter paid labor as office workers<br>• Knights of Labor grows rapidly (mid-1880s)<br>• American Federation of Labor founded (1886) | • Rapid industrialization draws immigrants from around the world; American cities grow rapidly<br>• Chinese Exclusion Act (1882–1943) | • Drought on the plains prompts calls for federal irrigation<br>• Hatch Act (1887) provides federal support for agricultural research and experiment stations<br>• Industrialization and urban growth cause rising pollution | • Pendleton Civil Service Act (1883)<br>• Peak influence of Woman's Christian Temperance Union (1880s)<br>• Interstate Commerce Act (1887)<br>• Hull House settlement founded (1889) | • Increasing numbers of students attend college<br>• Booker T. Washington founds Tuskegee Institute (1881)<br>• William Dean Howells calls for realism in literature (1881)<br>• Birth of American football<br>• Popularity of vaudeville (1880s–1890s) |
| **1890** | • Severe economic depression (1893–1897)<br>• Accelerated corporate mergers in key industries<br>• Birth of modern advertising | • Gorras Blancas confront wealthy Anglo interests in New Mexico<br>• Ellis Island opens (1892)<br>• Supreme Court upholds segregation of schools and public facilities in *Plessy v. Ferguson* (1896)<br>• Unemployed whites attack and drive Chinese farmworkers out of California | • Sierra Club founded (1892)<br>• "Bicycle craze" and rise of hiking and camping get more Americans outdoors | • Rise of People's Party (1890–1896)<br>• Sweeping Republican gains (1894)<br>• "Solid South" emerges; African American disenfranchisement in South (1890–1905)<br>• William McKinley defeats William Jennings Bryan (1896)<br>• National Consumers' League founded (1899) | • Chicago World's Fair (1893)<br>• Literary realism and naturalism gain recognition<br>• Popularity of ragtime music (1890s–1900s)<br>• Armory Show introduces modern art (1913)<br>• Rise of Social Gospel<br>• Joseph Pulitzer pioneers "yellow journalism" |
| **1900** | • U.S. Steel becomes nation's first billion-dollar corporation (1901)<br>• Women's Trade Union League founded (1903)<br>• International Workers of the World founded (1905)<br>• Marianna mine disaster (1907)<br>• *Muller v. Oregon* (1908) permits state regulation of women's working hours<br>• Triangle Shirtwaist fire (1911) | • Rising immigration from Eastern and Southern Europe<br>• Height of eugenics (1900s–1920s)<br>• Increasing numbers of blacks move to cities; responses include "race riots" by whites<br>• Japanese immigrants barred from becoming U.S. citizens (1906) | • Lacey Act (1900)<br>• Antiquities Act (1906) gives president authority to create and protect national monuments<br>• National Audubon Society forms (1901)<br>• Newlands Reclamation Act (1902)<br>• First national wildlife refuge created (1903)<br>• U.S. Forest Service created (1905)<br>• National Park Service created (1916) | • William McKinley assassinated; Theodore Roosevelt becomes president (1901)<br>• Niagara Movement calls for full voting rights and equal opportunities for blacks<br>• Women's suffrage movement grows | • Nickelodeons introduce commercial motion pictures<br>• Custom of unchaperoned "dating" arises<br>• Rise of the Negro Leagues<br>• Peak in overseas missionary activity<br>• Advent of literary and artistic modernism |

# 17

# Industrial America: Corporations and Conflicts 1877–1911

For millions of his contemporaries, Andrew Carnegie exemplified American success. Arriving from Scotland as a poor twelve-year-old in 1848, Carnegie found work as an errand boy for the Pennsylvania Railroad and rapidly scaled the managerial ladder. In 1865, he struck out on his own as an iron manufacturer, selling to friends in the railroad business. Encouraged by Republican tariffs to enter the steel industry, he soon built a massive steel mill outside Pittsburgh where a state-of-the-art Bessemer converter made steel refining dramatically more efficient. With Carnegie leading the way, steel became a major U.S. industry, reaching annual production of 10 million metric tons by 1900 — almost as much as the *combined* output of the world's other top producers, Germany (6.6 million tons) and Britain (4.8 million).

At first, skilled workers at Carnegie's mill in Homestead, Pennsylvania, earned good wages. They had a strong union, and Carnegie affirmed workers' right to organize. But Carnegie — confident that new machinery enabled him to replace many skilled laborers — eventually decided that collective bargaining was too expensive. In the summer of 1892, he withdrew to his estate in Scotland, leaving his partner Henry Clay Frick in command. A former coal magnate and veteran foe of labor, Frick was well qualified to do the dirty work. He announced that after July 1, members of the Amalgamated Association of Iron and Steel Workers would be locked out of the Homestead mill. If they wanted to return to work, they would have to abandon the union and sign new individual contracts. Frick fortified the mill and prepared to hire replacement workers. The battle was on.

At dawn on July 6, barges chugging up the Monongahela River brought dozens of private armed guards from the Pinkerton Detective Agency, hired by Carnegie to defend the plant. Locked-out workers opened fire, starting a gunfight that left seven workers and three Pinkertons dead. Frick appealed to Pennsylvania's governor, who sent the state militia to arrest labor leaders on charges of riot and murder. Most of the locked-out workers lost their jobs. The union was dead.

As the **Homestead lockout** showed, industrialization was a controversial and often bloody process. During the half century after the Civil War, more and more Americans worked not as independent farmers or artisans but as employees of large corporations. Conditions of work changed for people of all economic classes. Drawn by the dynamic economy, immigrants arrived from around the globe. These transformations provoked working people, including farmers as well as industrial workers, to organize and defend their interests.

## IDENTIFY THE BIG IDEA

**What new opportunities and risks did industrialization bring, and how did it reshape American society?**

**Marianna Mine Disaster** The bituminous mines of Marianna, Pennsylvania, and many other rich sites provided the coal that fueled American industrial growth. On November 28, 1908, an explosion in the mine killed 158 workers. Many were American-born; some were Irish, Welsh, Italian, and Polish immigrants. Here, a horse-drawn wagon carries bodies recovered from the mine. Such catastrophes laid bare the human cost of industrialization. Marianna was one among many: in the same decade, disasters at Scofield, Utah; Jacobs Creek, Pennsylvania; Monongah, West Virginia; and Cherry, Illinois, each killed over 200 men. Library of Congress.

# The Rise of Big Business

In the late 1800s, industrialization in Europe and the United States revolutionized the world economy. It brought large-scale commercial agriculture to many parts of the globe and prompted millions of migrants—both skilled workers and displaced peasants—to cross continents and oceans in search of jobs. Industrialization also created a production glut. The immense scale of agriculture and manufacturing caused a long era of deflation, when prices dropped worldwide (Figure 17.1).

Falling prices normally signal low demand for goods and services, and thus stagnation. In England, a mature industrial power, the late nineteenth century did bring economic decline. But in the United States, production expanded. Between 1877 and 1900, Americans' average real income increased from $388 to $573 per capita. In this sense, Andrew Carnegie was right when he argued that, even though industrialization increased the gap between rich and poor, everyone's standard of living rose. In his famous 1889 essay "Wealth"—later called "The Gospel of Wealth"—he observed that "the poor enjoy what the rich could not before afford. What were the luxuries have become the necessaries of life."

 To see a longer excerpt of "The Gospel of Wealth," along with other primary sources from this period, see *Sources for America's History*.

Technological and business efficiencies allowed American firms to grow, invest in new equipment, and earn profits even as prices for their products fell. Growth depended, in turn, on America's large and growing population, expansion into the West, and an integrated national marketplace. In many fields, large corporations became the dominant form of business.

## Innovators in Enterprise

As rail lines stretched westward between the 1850s and 1880s, operators faced a crisis. As one Erie Railroad executive noted, a superintendent on a 50-mile line could personally attend to every detail. But supervising a 500-mile line was impossible; trains ran late, communications failed, and trains crashed. Managers gradually invented systems to solve these problems. They distinguished top executives from those responsible for day-to-day operations. They departmentalized operations by function—purchasing, machinery, freight traffic, passenger traffic—and established clear lines of communication. They perfected cost accounting, which allowed an industrialist like Carnegie to track expenses and revenues carefully and thus follow his Scottish mother's advice: "Take care of the pennies, and the pounds will take care of themselves." This **management revolution** created the internal structure adopted by many large, complex corporations.

During these same years, the United States became an industrial power by tapping North America's vast natural resources, particularly in the West. Industries that had once depended on water power began to use prodigious amounts of coal. Steam engines replaced human and animal labor, and kerosene replaced whale oil and wood. By 1900, America's factories and urban homes were converting to electric power. With new management structures and dependency on fossil fuels (oil, coal, natural gas), corporations transformed both the economy and the country's natural and built environments.

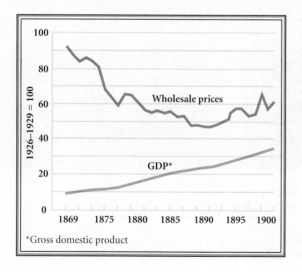

**FIGURE 17.1**

**Business Activity and Wholesale Prices, 1869–1900**

This graph shows the key feature of the performance of the late-nineteenth-century economy: while output was booming, wholesale prices were, on the whole, falling. Thus, while workers often struggled with falling wages—especially during decades of severe economic crisis—consumer products also became cheaper to buy.

**Production and Sales**   After Chicago's Union Stock Yards opened in 1865, middlemen shipped cows by rail from the Great Plains to Chicago and from there to eastern cities, where slaughter took place in local butchertowns. Such a system — a national livestock market with local processing — could have lasted, as it did in Europe. But Gustavus Swift, a shrewd Chicago cattle dealer, saw that local slaughterhouses lacked the scale to utilize waste by-products and cut labor costs. To improve productivity, Swift invented the assembly line, where each wageworker repeated the same slaughtering task over and over.

Swift also pioneered **vertical integration**, a model in which a company controlled all aspects of production from raw materials to finished goods. Once his engineers designed a cooling system, Swift invested in a fleet of refrigerator cars to keep beef fresh as he shipped it eastward, priced below what local butchers could afford. In cities that received his chilled meat, Swift built branch houses and fleets of delivery wagons. He also constructed factories to make fertilizer and chemicals from the by-products of slaughter, and he developed marketing strategies for those products as well. Other Chicago packers followed Swift's lead. By 1900, five firms, all vertically integrated, produced nearly 90 percent of the meat shipped in interstate commerce.

Big packers invented new sales tactics. For example, Swift & Company periodically slashed prices in certain markets to below production costs, driving independent distributors to the wall. With profits from its sales elsewhere, a large firm like Swift could survive temporary losses in one locality until competitors went under. Afterward, Swift could raise prices again. This technique, known as predatory pricing, helped give a few firms unprecedented market control.

**Standard Oil and the Rise of the Trusts**   No one used ruthless business tactics more skillfully than the king of petroleum, John D. Rockefeller. After inventors in the 1850s figured out how to extract kerosene — a clean-burning fuel for domestic heating and lighting — from crude oil, enormous oil deposits were discovered at Titusville, Pennsylvania. Just then, the Civil War severely disrupted whaling, forcing whale-oil customers to look for alternative lighting sources. Overnight, a forest of oil wells sprang up around Titusville. Connected to these Pennsylvania oil fields by rail in 1863, Cleveland, Ohio, became a refining

> **IDENTIFY CAUSES**
> Why did large corporations arise in the late nineteenth century, and how did leading industrialists consolidate their power?

**Swift & Co.'s Packing House, Chicago, c. 1906**

This photograph shows the processing system that enabled Swift and other large packers to save money through high volume and deskilled labor. The overhead pulley system shown in the upper right moved carcasses from place to place for completion of different tasks. Auto manufacturer Henry Ford, who won fame for his moving assembly line, claimed he got the idea after visiting a meat-packing plant such as this. Library of Congress.

center. John D. Rockefeller was then an up-and-coming Cleveland grain dealer. (He, like Carnegie and most other budding tycoons, hired a substitute to fight for him in the Civil War.) Rockefeller had strong nerves, a sharp eye for able partners, and a genius for finance. He went into the kerosene business and borrowed heavily to expand. Within a few years, his firm — Standard Oil of Ohio — was Cleveland's leading refiner.

Like Carnegie and Swift, Rockefeller succeeded through vertical integration: to control production and sales all the way from the oil well to the kerosene lamp, he took a big stake in the oil fields, added pipelines, and developed a vast distribution network. Rockefeller allied with railroad executives, who, like him, hated the oil market's boom-and-bust cycles. What they wanted was predictable, high-volume traffic, and they offered Rockefeller secret rebates that gave him a leg up on competitors.

Rockefeller also pioneered a strategy called **horizontal integration**. After driving competitors to the brink of failure through predatory pricing, he invited them to merge their local companies into his conglomerate. Most agreed, often because they had no choice. Through such mergers, Standard Oil wrested control of 95 percent of the nation's oil refining capacity by the 1880s. In 1882, Rockefeller's lawyers created a new legal form, the **trust**. It organized a small group of associates — the board of trustees — to hold stock from a group of combined firms, managing them as a single entity. Rockefeller soon invested in Mexican oil fields and competed in world markets against Russian and Middle Eastern producers.

Other companies followed Rockefeller's lead, creating trusts to produce such products as linseed oil, sugar, and salt. Many expanded sales and production overseas. As early as 1868, Singer Manufacturing Company established a factory in Scotland to produce sewing machines. By World War I, such brands as Ford and General Electric had become familiar around the world.

Distressed by the development of near monopolies, reformers began to denounce "the trusts," a term that in popular usage referred to any large corporation that seemed to wield excessive power. Some states outlawed trusts as a legal form. But in an effort to attract corporate headquarters to its state, New Jersey broke ranks in 1889, passing a law that permitted the creation of holding companies and other combinations. Delaware soon followed, providing another legal haven for consolidated corporations. A wave of mergers further concentrated corporate power during the depression of the 1890s, as weaker firms succumbed to powerful rivals.

By 1900, America's largest one hundred companies controlled a third of the nation's productive capacity. Purchasing several steel companies in 1901, including Carnegie Steel, J. P. Morgan created U.S. Steel, the nation's first billion-dollar corporation. Such familiar firms as DuPont and Eastman Kodak assumed dominant places in their respective industries.

**Assessing the Industrialists**   The work of men like Swift, Rockefeller, and Carnegie was controversial in their lifetimes and has been ever since. Opinions have tended to be harsh in eras of economic crisis, when the shortcomings of corporate America appear in stark relief. During the Great Depression of the 1930s, a historian coined the term *robber barons*, which is still used today. In periods of prosperity, both scholars and the public have tended to view early industrialists more favorably, calling them *industrial statesmen*.

Some historians have argued that industrialists benefitted the economy by replacing the chaos of market competition with a "visible hand" of planning and expert management. But one recent study of railroads asserts that the main skills of early tycoons (as well as those of today) were cultivating political "friends," defaulting on loans, and lying to the public. Whether we consider the industrialists heroes, villains, or something in between, it is clear that the corporate economy was not the creation of just a few individuals, however famous or influential. It was a systemic transformation of the economy.

**A National Consumer Culture**   As they integrated vertically and horizontally, corporations innovated in other ways. Companies such as Bell Telephone and Westinghouse set up research laboratories. Steelmakers invested in chemistry and materials science to make their products cheaper, better, and stronger. Mass markets brought an appealing array of goods to consumers who could afford them. Railroads whisked Florida oranges and other fresh produce to the shelves of grocery stores. Retailers such as F. W. Woolworth and the Great Atlantic and Pacific Tea Company (A&P) opened chains of stores that soon stretched nationwide.

The department store was pioneered in 1875 by John Wanamaker in Philadelphia. These megastores displaced small retail shops, tempting customers with large show windows and Christmas displays. Like industrialists, department store magnates developed economies of scale that enabled them to slash prices. An 1898 newspaper advertisement for Macy's Department Store urged shoppers to "read our books, cook in our saucepans, dine off our china, wear our silks, get

I want to see a Phonograph in every American Home

*Thomas A. Edison*

The New Edison

*Thomas A. Edison's*

Final Achievement

**Thomas Edison**

The wondrous inventions that emerged from Edison's laboratory in Menlo Park, New Jersey, ranged from the phonograph shown here to electric light bulbs, moving pictures, and Portland cement. Edison (1847–1931) became a national hero—and the holder of over one thousand patents. He was also a shrewd entrepreneur who artfully cultivated both publicity and investor support. In demonstrating electric lights, he chose first to illuminate the headquarters of the *New York Times* and the nearby offices of powerful financier J. P. Morgan. In this advertisement he makes a democratic appeal to all Americans—but only the affluent could afford a phonograph, which cost about $20. Dennis Nyhagen, The Digital Deli Online, www.digitaldeliftp.com.

under our blankets, smoke our cigars, drink our wines—Shop at Macy's—and Life will Cost You Less and Yield You More Than You Dreamed Possible."

While department stores became urban fixtures, Montgomery Ward and Sears built mail-order empires. Rural families from Vermont to California pored over the companies' annual catalogs, making wish lists of tools, clothes, furniture, and toys. Mail-order companies used money-back guarantees to coax wary customers to buy products they could not see or touch. "Don't be afraid to make a mistake," the Sears catalog counseled. "Tell us what you want, in your own way." By 1900, America counted more than twelve hundred mail-order companies.

The active shaping of consumer demand became, in itself, a new enterprise. Outdoors, advertisements appeared everywhere: in New York's Madison Square, the Heinz Company installed a 45-foot pickle made of green electric lights. Tourists had difficulty admiring Niagara Falls because billboards obscured the view. By 1900, companies were spending more than $90 million a year ($2.3 billion today) on print advertising, as the press itself became a mass-market industry. Rather than charging subscribers the cost of production, magazines began to cover their costs by selling ads. Cheap subscriptions built a mass readership, which in turn attracted more advertisers. In 1903, the *Ladies' Home Journal* became the first magazine with a million subscribers.

## The Corporate Workplace

Before the Civil War, most American boys had hoped to become farmers, small-business owners, or independent artisans. Afterward, more and more Americans—both male and female—began working for someone else. Because they wore white shirts with starched collars, those who held professional positions in corporations became known as white-collar workers, a term differentiating them from blue-collar employees, who labored with their hands. For a range of employees—managers and laborers, clerks and salespeople—the rise of corporate work had wide-ranging consequences.

**Managers and Salesmen**    As the managerial revolution unfolded, the headquarters of major corporations began to house departments handling specific activities such as purchasing and accounting. These departments were supervised by middle managers, something not seen before in American industry. Middle managers took on entirely new tasks, directing the flow of goods, labor, and information throughout the enterprise. They were key innovators, counterparts to the engineers in research laboratories who, in the same decades, worked to reduce costs and improve efficiency.

Corporations also needed a new kind of sales force. In post–Civil War America, the drummer, or traveling salesman, became a familiar sight on city streets and in remote country stores. Riding rail networks from town to town, drummers introduced merchants to new products, offered incentives, and suggested sales

> **EXPLAIN CONSEQUENCES**
> What opportunities did the rise of corporations offer to different types of "middle workers"—those who were neither top executives nor blue-collar laborers?

**The Salesman as Professional, 1906**

*Salesmanship* magazine featured this image in its June 1906 issue, depicting the traveling salesman as an energetic, well-dressed professional. The advertisement urges salesmen to join the United Commercial Travelers of America (UCTA), a fraternal organization founded by salesmen in 1888 (and still in existence today). UCTA offered its members the opportunity to purchase insurance and build business networks with fellow salesmen. Through such organizations, white-collar workers and managers (who were almost never unionized) banded together to pursue their common interests and express professional pride. *Salesmanship*, June 1906, Columbus Ohio.

displays. They built nationwide distribution networks for such popular consumer products as cigarettes and Coca-Cola. By the late 1880s, the leading manufacturer of cash registers produced a sales script for its employees' conversations with local merchants. "Take for granted that he will buy," the script directed. "Say to him, 'Now, Mr. Blank, what color shall I make it?' . . . Handing him your pen say, 'Just sign here where I have made the cross.'"

With such companies in the vanguard, sales became systematized. Managers set individual sales quotas and awarded prizes to top salesmen, while those who sold too little were singled out for remedial training or dismissal. Executives embraced the ideas of business psychologist Walter Dill Scott, who published *The Psychology of Advertising* in 1908. Scott's principles — which included selling to customers based on their presumed "instinct of escape" and "instinct of combat" — were soon taught at Harvard Business School. Others also promised that a "scientific attitude" would "attract attention" and "create desire."

### Women in the Corporate Office

Beneath the ranks of managers emerged a new class of female office workers. Before the Civil War, most clerks at small firms had been young men who expected to rise through the ranks. In a large corporation, secretarial work became a dead-end job, and employers began assigning it to women. By the turn of the twentieth century, 77 percent of all stenographers and typists were female; by 1920, women held half of all low-level office jobs.

For white working-class women, clerking and office work represented new opportunities. In an era before most families had access to day care, mothers most often earned money at home, where they could tend children while also taking in laundry, caring for boarders, or doing piecework (sewing or other assembly projects, paid on a per-item basis). Unmarried daughters could enter domestic service or factory work, but clerking and secretarial work were cleaner and better paid.

New technologies provide additional opportunities for women. The rise of the telephone, introduced by inventor Alexander Graham Bell in 1876, was a notable example. Originally intended for business use on local exchanges, telephones were eagerly adopted by residential customers. Thousands of young women found work as telephone operators. By 1900, more than four million women worked for wages. About a third worked in domestic service; another third in industry; the rest in office work, teaching, nursing, or sales. As new occupations arose, the percentage of wage-earning women in domestic service dropped dramatically, a trend that continued in the twentieth century.

## On the Shop Floor

Despite the managerial revolution at the top, skilled craft workers — almost all of them men — retained considerable autonomy in many industries. A coal miner, for example, was not an hourly wageworker but essentially an independent contractor, paid by the amount of coal he produced. He provided his own tools, worked at his own pace, and knocked off early

**Telephone Operators, 1888**

Like other women office workers, these switchboard operators enjoyed relatively high pay and comfortable working conditions—especially in the early years of the telephone industry, before operators' work routines speeded up. These young women worked for the Central Union Telephone Company in Canton, Ohio. Ohio Historical Society.

when he chose. The same was true for puddlers and rollers in iron works; molders in stove making; and machinists, glass blowers, and skilled workers in many other industries. Such workers abided by the stint, a self-imposed limit on how much they would produce each day. This informal system of restricting output infuriated efficiency-minded engineers, but to the workers it signified personal dignity, manly pride, and brotherhood with fellow employees. One shop in Lowell, Massachusetts, posted regulations requiring all employees to be at their posts by the time of the opening bell and to remain, with the shop door locked, until the closing bell. A machinist promptly packed his tools, declaring that he had not "been brought up under such a system of slavery."

Skilled workers—craftsmen, inside contractors, and foremen—enjoyed a high degree of autonomy. But those who paid helpers from their own pocket could also exploit them. Subcontracting arose, in part, to enable manufacturers to distance themselves from the consequences of shady labor practices. In Pittsburgh

steel mills, foremen were known as "pushers," notorious for driving their gangs mercilessly. On the other hand, industrial labor operated on a human scale, through personal relationships that could be close and enduring. Striking craft workers would commonly receive the support of helpers and laborers, and labor gangs would sometimes walk out on behalf of a popular foreman.

As industrialization advanced, however, workers increasingly lost the independence characteristic of craft work. The most important cause of this was the **deskilling** of labor under a new system of mechanized manufacturing that men like meat-packer Gustavus Swift had pioneered, and that automobile maker Henry Ford would soon call **mass production**. Everything from typewriters to automobiles came to be assembled from standardized parts, using machines that increasingly operated with little human oversight. A machinist protested

**TRACE CHANGE OVER TIME**
How did conditions change for industrial workers in the late nineteenth century, and why?

**Ironworkers—Noontime, 1880**

The ideal qualities of the nineteenth-century craft worker—dignity, brotherhood, manliness—shine through in this painting by Thomas P. Anschutz. *Ironworkers—Noontime* became a popular painting after it was reproduced as an engraving in *Harper's Weekly* in 1884. Fine Arts Museum of San Francisco.

in 1883 that the sewing machine industry was so "subdivided" that "one man may make just a particular part of a machine and may not know anything whatever about another part of the same machine." Such a worker, noted an observer, "cannot be master of a craft, but only master of a fragment." Employers, who originally favored automatic machinery because it increased output, quickly found that it also helped them control workers and cut labor costs. They could pay unskilled workers less and replace them easily.

By the early twentieth century, managers sought to further reduce costs through a program of industrial efficiency called **scientific management**. Its inventor, a metal-cutting expert named Frederick W. Taylor, recommended that employers eliminate all brain work from manual labor, hiring experts to develop rules for the shop floor. Workers must be required to "do what they are told promptly and without asking questions or making suggestions." In its most extreme form, scientific management called for engineers to time each task with a stopwatch; companies would pay workers more if they met the stopwatch standard. Taylor assumed

that workers would respond automatically to the lure of higher earnings. But scientific management was not, in practice, a great success. Implementing it proved to be expensive, and workers stubbornly resisted. Corporate managers, however, adopted bits and pieces of Taylor's system, and they enthusiastically agreed that decisions should lie with "management alone." Over time, in comparison with businesses in other countries, American corporations created a particularly wide gap between the roles of managers and those of the blue-collar workforce.

Blue-collar workers had little freedom to negotiate, and their working conditions deteriorated markedly as mass production took hold. At the same time, industrialization brought cheaper products that enabled many Americans to enjoy new consumer products—if they could avoid starvation. From executives down to unskilled workers, the hierarchy of corporate employment contributed to sharper distinctions among three economic classes: the wealthy elite; an emerging, self-defined "middle class"; and a struggling class of workers, who bore the brunt of the economy's new risks

**The Singer Sewing Machine**

The sewing machine was an American invention that swiftly found markets abroad. The Singer Manufacturing Company, the dominant firm by the time the Civil War began, exported sewing machines to markets as far-flung as Ireland, Russia, China, and India. The company also moved some manufacturing operations abroad, producing 200,000 machines annually at a Scottish plant that employed 6,000 workers. Singer's advertising rightly boasted of the international appeal of a product that the company dubbed "The Universal Sewing Machine." © Collection of the New-York Historical Society.

and included many Americans living in dire poverty. As it wrought these changes, industrialization prompted intense debate over inequality (Thinking Like a Historian, p. 554).

**Health Hazards and Pollution**   Industrialized labor also damaged workers' health. In 1884, a study of the Illinois Central Railroad showed that, over the previous decade, one in twenty of its workers had been killed or permanently disabled by an accident on the job. For brakemen — one of the most dangerous jobs — the rate was one in seven. Due to lack of regulatory laws and inspections, mining was 50 percent more dangerous in the United States than in Germany; between 1876 and 1925, an average of over 2,000 U.S. coal miners died each year from cave-ins and explosions. Silver, gold, and copper mines were not immune from such tragedies, but mining companies resisted demands for safety regulation.

Extractive industries and factories also damaged nearby environments and the people who lived there. In big cities, poor residents suffered from polluted air and the dumping of noxious by-products into the water supply. Mines like those in Leadville, Colorado, contaminated the land and water with mercury and lead.

Alabama convicts, forced to work in coal mines, faced brutal working conditions and fatal illnesses caused by the mines' contamination of local water. At the time, people were well aware of many of these dangers, but workers had an even more urgent priority: work. Pittsburgh's belching smokestacks meant coughing and lung damage, but they also meant running mills and paying jobs.

**Unskilled Labor and Discrimination**   As managers deskilled production, the ranks of factory workers came to include more and more women and children, who were almost always unskilled and low paid. Men often resented women's presence in factories, and male labor unions often worked to exclude women — especially wives, who they argued should remain in the home. Women vigorously defended their right to work. On hearing accusations that married women worked only to buy frivolous luxuries, one female worker in a Massachusetts shoe factory wrote a heated response to the local newspaper: "When the husband and father cannot provide for his wife and children, it is perfectly natural that the wife and mother should desire to work.... Don't blame married women if the land of the free has become a land of slavery and oppression."

## Poverty and Food

Amid rising industrial poverty, food emerged as a reference point. How much was too little, or too much? If some Americans were going hungry, how should others respond? The documents below show some contributions to these debates.

---

1. **Lewis W. Hine, "Mealtime, New York Tenement," 1910.** *Hine was an influential photographer and reformer. He took a famous series of photographs at Ellis Island, remarking that he hoped Americans would view new immigrants in the same way they thought of the Pilgrims. What does the photographer emphasize in the living conditions of this Italian immigrant family and their relationships with one another? Why do you think Hine photographed them at the table?*

George Eastman House.

2. **Louisa May Alcott, *Little Women*, 1869.** *Alcott's novel, popular for decades, exemplified the ideal of Christian charity. At the start of this scene, Mrs. March returns from a Christmas morning expedition.*

Merry Christmas, little daughters! . . . I want to say one word before we sit down [to breakfast]. Not far away from here lies a poor woman with a little newborn baby. Six children are huddled into one bed to keep from freezing, for they have no fire. There is nothing to eat. . . . My girls, will you give them your breakfasts as a Christmas present?

. . . For a minute no one spoke, only a minute, for Jo exclaimed impetuously, I'm so glad you came before we began!

May I go and help . . . ? asked Beth eagerly.

I shall take the cream and the muffins, added Amy. . . . Meg was already covering the buckwheats and piling the bread into one big plate.

I thought you'd do it, said Mrs. March, smiling.

. . . A poor, bare, miserable room it was, with broken windows, no fire, ragged bedclothes, a sick mother, wailing baby, and a group of pale, hungry children. . . . Mrs. March gave the mother tea and gruel [while] the girls meantime spread the table [and] set the children round the fire. . . .

That was a very happy breakfast, though they didn't get any of it. And when they went away, leaving comfort behind, I think there were not in all the city four merrier people than the hungry little girls who gave away their breakfasts and contented themselves with bread and milk on Christmas morning.

3. **Mary Hinman Abel, *Promoting Nutrition*, 1890.** *This excerpt is from a cookbook that won a prize from the American Public Health Association. The author had studied community cooking projects in Europe and worked to meet the needs of Boston's poor. How does she propose to feed people on 13 cents a day — her most basic menu? What assumptions does she make about her audience? In what ways was her cookbook, itself, a product of industrialization?*

**For family of six, average price 78 cents per day, or 13 cents per person.**

. . . I am going to consider myself as talking to the mother of a family who has six mouths to feed, and no more money than this to do it with. Perhaps this woman has never kept accurate accounts. . . . I have in mind the wife [who has] time to attend to the housework and children. If a woman helps earn, as in a factory, doing most of her housework after she comes home at night, she must certainly have more money than in the first case in order to accomplish the same result.

. . . The Proteid column is the one that you must look to most carefully because it is furnished at the most expense, and it is very important that it should not fall below the figures I have given [or] your family would be undernourished.

[Sample spring menu]
*Breakfast.* Milk Toast. Coffee.
*Dinner.* Stuffed Beef's Heart. Potatoes stewed with Milk. Dried Apple Pie. Bread and Cheese. Corn Coffee.
*Supper.* Noodle Soup (from Saturday). Boiled Herring. Bread. Tea.

| | |
|---|---|
| Proteids. (oz.) | 21.20 |
| Fats. (oz.) | 14.39 |
| Carbohydrates. (oz.) | 77.08 |
| Cost in Cents. | 76 |

4. **Werner Sombart, *Why Is There No Socialism in the United States?*, 1906.** *Sombart, a German sociologist, compared living conditions in Germany and the United States in order to answer the question above. What conclusion did he reach?*

The American worker eats almost three times as much meat, three times as much flour and four times as much sugar as his German counterpart. . . . The American worker is much closer to the better sections of the German middle class than to the German wage-labouring class. He does not merely eat, but dines. . . .

It is no wonder if, in such a situation, any dissatisfaction with the "existing social order" finds difficulty in establishing itself in the mind of the worker. . . . All Socialist utopias came to nothing on roast beef and apple pie.

5. **Helen Campbell, *Prisoners of Poverty*, 1887.** *A journalist, Campbell investigated the conditions of low-paid seamstresses in New York City who did piecework in their apartments. Like Abel (source 3), she tried to teach what she called "survival economics." Here, a woman responds to Campbell's suggestion that she cook beans for better nutrition.*

"Beans!" said one indignant soul. "What time have I to think of beans, or what money to buy coal to cook 'em? What you'd want if you sat over a machine fourteen hours a day would be tea like lye to put a back-bone in you. That's why we have tea always in the pot, and it don't make much odds what's with it. A slice of bread is about all. . . . We'd our tea an' bread an' a good bit of fried beef or pork, maybe, when my husband was alive an' at work. . . . It's the tea that keeps you up."

6. **Julian Street, Show and Extravagance, 1910.** *Street, a journalist, was invited to an elite home in Buffalo, New York, for a dinner that included cocktails, fine wines, caviar, a roast, Turkish coffee, and cigars.*

Before we left New York there was newspaper talk about some rich women who had organized a movement of protest against the ever-increasing American tendency toward show and extravagance. . . . Our hostess [in Buffalo] was the first to mention it, but several other ladies added details. . . .

"We don't intend to go to any foolish extremes," said one. . . . "We are only going to scale things down and eliminate waste. There is a lot of useless show in this country which only makes it hard for people who can't afford things. And even for those who can, it is wrong. . . . Take this little dinner we had tonight. . . . In future we are all going to give plain little dinners like this."

"*Plain?*" I gasped. . . . "But I didn't think it had begun yet! I thought this dinner was a kind of farewell feast — that it was —"

Our hostess looked grieved. The other ladies of the league gazed at me reproachfully. . . . "Didn't you notice?" asked my hostess. . . .

"Notice *what?*"

"That we didn't have champagne!"

Sources: (2) Louisa May Alcott, *Little Women*, Part 2, Chapter 2 at xroads.virginia.edu/~HYPER/ALCOTT/ch2.html; (3) Mary Hinman Abel, *Practical, Sanitary, and Economic Cooking Adapted to Persons of Moderate and Small Means* (American Public Health Association, 1890), 143–154; (4) Werner Sombart, *Why Is There No Socialism in the United States?*, trans. Patricia M. Hocking and C. T. Husbands (White Plains, NY: International Arts and Sciences Press, 1976), 97, 105–106; (5) Helen Campbell, *Prisoners of Poverty* (Cambridge, MA: University Press, 1887), 123–124; (6) Julian Street, *Abroad at Home* (New York: The Century Co., 1915), 37–39.

## ANALYZING THE EVIDENCE

1. These documents were created by journalists and reformers. What audiences did they seek to reach? Why do you think they all focused on food?

2. Imagine a conversation among these authors. How might we account for the differences in Sombart's and Campbell's findings? How might Hine, Abel, and Campbell respond to Alcott's vision of charitable Christian acts?

## PUTTING IT ALL TOGETHER

Using the documents above and your knowledge from this chapter, write a short essay explaining some challenges and opportunities faced by different Americans in the industrializing era — including those of the wealthy elite, the emerging middle class, skilled blue-collar men, and very poorest unskilled laborers. How did labor leaders and reformers seek to persuade prosperous Americans to concern themselves with workers' problems? To what dominant values did they appeal?

**Child Labor**

For many working-class families, children's wages—even though they were low—made up an essential part of the household income. These boys worked the night shift in a glass factory in Indiana. Lewis Hine, an investigative photographer for the National Child Labor Committee, took their picture at midnight, as part of a campaign to educate more prosperous Americans about the widespread employment of child labor and the harsh conditions in which many children worked. Library of Congress.

In 1900, one of every five children under the age of sixteen worked outside the home. Child labor was most widespread in the South, where a low-wage industrial sector emerged after Reconstruction (Map 17.1). Textile mills sprouted in the Carolinas and Georgia, recruiting workers from surrounding farms; whole families often worked in the mills. Many children also worked in Pennsylvania coal fields, where death and injury rates were high. State law permitted children as young as twelve to labor with a family member, but turn-of-the-century investigators estimated that about 10,000 additional boys, at even younger ages, were illegally employed in the mines.

Also at the bottom of the pay scale were most African Americans. Corporations and industrial manufacturers widely discriminated against them on the basis of race, and such prejudice was hardly limited to the South. After the Civil War, African American women who moved to northern cities were largely barred from office work and other new employment options; instead, they remained heavily concentrated in domestic service, with more than half employed as cooks or servants. African American men confronted similar exclusion. America's booming vertically integrated corporations turned black men away from all but the most menial jobs. In 1890, almost a third of black men worked in personal service. Employers in the North and West recruited, instead, a different kind of low-wage labor: newly arrived immigrants.

## Immigrants, East and West

Across the globe, industrialization set people in motion with the lure of jobs. Between the Civil War and World War I, over 25 million immigrants entered the United States. The American working class became truly global, including not only people of African and Western

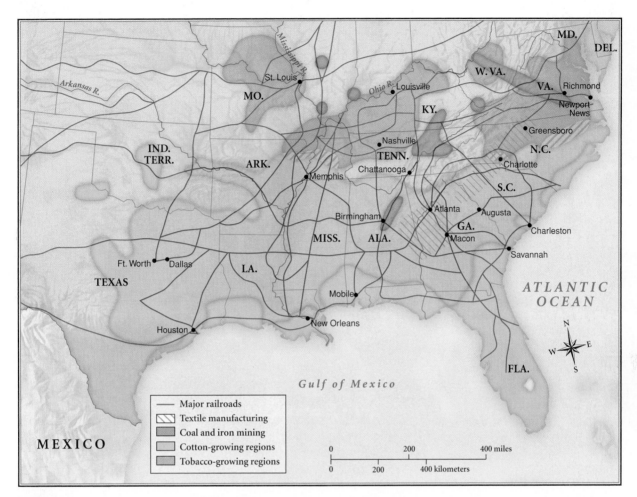

**MAP 17.1**

**The New South, 1900**

The economy of the Old South focused on raising staple crops, especially cotton and tobacco. In the New South, staple agriculture continued to dominate, but there was marked industrial development as well. Industrial regions evolved, producing textiles, coal, and iron. By 1900, the South's industrial pattern was well defined, though the region still served—like the West—as a major producer of raw materials for the industrial region that stretched from New England to Chicago.

European descent but also Southern and Eastern Europeans, Mexicans, and Asians. In 1900, census takers found that more than 75 percent of San Francisco and New York City residents had at least one parent who was foreign-born.

In the new industrial order, immigrants made an ideal labor supply. They took the worst jobs at low pay, and during economic downturns tens of thousands returned to their home countries, reducing the shock of unemployment in the United States. But many native-born Americans viewed immigrants with hostility, through the lens of racial, ethnic, and religious prejudices. They also feared that immigrants would take more coveted jobs and erode white men's wages.

For immigrants themselves, America could be disorienting, liberating, and disappointing.

## Newcomers from Europe

Mass migration from Western Europe had started in the 1840s, when more than one million Irish fled a terrible famine. In the following decades, as Europe's population grew rapidly and agriculture became commercialized, peasant economies suffered, first in Germany and Scandinavia, then across Austria-Hungary, Russia, Italy, and the Balkans. This upheaval displaced millions of rural people. Some went to Europe's mines and factories; others headed for South America and

**German Beer, Mexican Workers, c. 1900**

Immigrants from Germany owned and managed most of the breweries in the United States. But workers at the Maier and Zoblein Brewery in Los Angeles came from many nations, including Mexico. At that time, about 4,000 Mexicans lived in Los Angeles County (about 4 percent of the population); by 1930, 150,000 Mexican-born immigrants lived in Los Angeles, making up about 7 percent of the city's rapidly growing population. Los Angeles Public Library.

the United States (Map 17.2; America Compared, p. 560).

"America was known to foreigners," remembered one Jewish woman from Lithuania, "as the land where you'd get rich." But the reality was much harsher. Even in the age of steam, a transatlantic voyage was grueling. For ten to twenty days, passengers in steerage class crowded belowdecks, eating terrible food and struggling with seasickness. An investigator who traveled with immigrants from Naples asked, "How can a steerage passenger remember that he is a human being when he must first pick the worms from his food?" After 1892, European immigrants were routed through the enormous receiving station at New York's Ellis Island.

Some immigrants brought skills. Many Welshmen, for example, arrived in the United States as experienced tin-plate makers; Germans came as machinists and carpenters, Scandinavians as sailors. But industrialization required, most of all, increasing quantities of unskilled labor. As poor farmers from Italy, Greece, and Eastern Europe arrived in the United States, heavy, low-paid labor became their domain.

In an era of cheap railroad and steamship travel, many immigrants expected to work and save for a few years and then head home. More than 800,000 French

**UNDERSTAND POINTS OF VIEW**

What factors accounted for the different expectations and experiences of immigrants in this era?

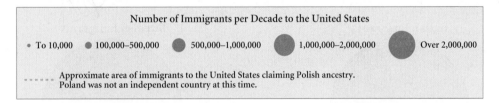

**MAP 17.2**
**Sources of European Immigration to the United States, 1871–1910**

Around 1900, Americans began to speak of the "new" immigration. They meant the large numbers of immigrants arriving from Eastern and Southern Europe—Poles, Slovaks and other Slavic peoples, Yiddish-speaking Jews, Italians—who overwhelmed the still substantial number of immigrants from the British Isles and Northern Europe.

Canadians moved to New England in search of textile jobs, many families with hopes of scraping together enough savings to return to Quebec and buy a farm. Thousands of men came alone, especially from Ireland, Italy, and Greece. Many single Irishwomen also immigrated. But some would-be sojourners ended up staying a lifetime, while immigrants who had expected to settle permanently found themselves forced to leave by an accident or sudden economic depression. One historian has estimated that a third of immigrants to the United States in this era returned to their home countries.

Along with Italians and Greeks, Eastern European Jews were among the most numerous arrivals. The first American Jews, who numbered around 50,000 in 1880, had been mostly of German-Jewish descent. In the next four decades, more than 3 million poverty-stricken Jews arrived from Russia, Ukraine, Poland, and other parts of Eastern Europe, transforming the Jewish presence in the United States. Like other immigrants, they sought economic opportunity, but they also came to escape religious repression (American Voices, p. 562).

Wherever they came from, immigrants took a considerable gamble in traveling to the United States. Some prospered quickly, especially if they came with education, money, or well-placed business contacts. Others, by toiling many years in harsh conditions, succeeded in securing a better life for their children or grandchildren. Still others met with catastrophe or early death. One Polish man who came with his parents in 1908 summed up his life over the next thirty years as "a mere struggle for bread." He added: "Sometimes I think life isn't worth a damn for a man

## Emigrants and Destinations, 1881–1915

The United States received more new residents than any other nation during the era of industrialization, but it was not the only place where emigrants (those departing) became immigrants (those arriving). The graph below shows six major destinations for emigrants from four European countries.

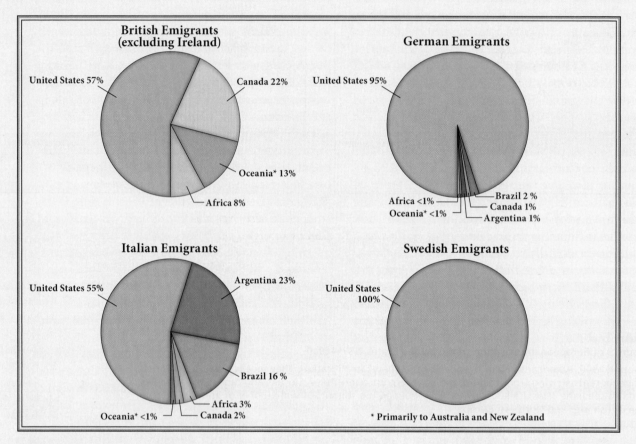

**FIGURE 17.2**
**Major Destinations for Emigrants, 1881–1915**

### QUESTIONS FOR ANALYSIS

1. What might account for the different emigration patterns shown here?
2. What choices and limitations might each group of emigrants have faced in choosing the country to which they emigrated? Do these figures suggest anything about the conditions various groups may have encountered in different countries, upon arrival?

like me. . . . Look at my wife and kids—undernourished, seldom have a square meal." But an Orthodox Russian Jewish woman told an interviewer that she "thanked God for America," where she had married, raised three children, and made a good life. She "liked everything about this country, especially its leniency toward the Jews."

## Asian Americans and Exclusion

Compared with Europeans, newcomers from Asia faced even harsher treatment. The first Chinese immigrants had arrived in the late 1840s during the California gold rush. After the Civil War, the Burlingame Treaty between the United States and China opened the way for increasing numbers to emigrate. Fleeing poverty and upheaval in southern China, they, like European immigrants, filled low-wage jobs in the American economy. The Chinese confronted threats and violence. "We kept indoors after dark for fear of being shot in the back," remembered one Chinese immigrant to California. During the depression of the 1870s, a rising tide of racism was especially extreme in the Pacific coast states, where the majority of Chinese immigrants lived. "The Chinese must go!" railed Dennis Kearney, leader of the California Workingmen's Party, who referred to Asians as "almond-eyed lepers." Incited by Kearney in July 1877, a mob burned San Francisco's Chinatown and beat up residents. In the 1885 Rock Springs massacre in Wyoming, white men burned the local Chinatown and murdered at least twenty-eight Chinese miners.

Despite such atrocities, some Chinese managed to build profitable businesses and farms. Many did so by filling the only niches native-born Americans left open to them: running restaurants and laundries. Facing intense political pressure, Congress in 1882 passed the **Chinese Exclusion Act**, specifically barring Chinese

laborers from entering the United States. Each decade thereafter, Congress renewed the law and tightened its provisions; it was not repealed until 1943. Exclusion barred almost all Chinese women, forcing husbands and wives to spend many years apart when men took jobs in the United States.

Asian immigrants made vigorous use of the courts to try to protect their rights. In a series of cases brought by Chinese and later Japanese immigrants, the U.S. Supreme Court ruled that all persons born in the United States had citizenship rights that could not be revoked, even if their parents had been born abroad. Nonetheless, well into the twentieth century, Chinese immigrants (as opposed to native-born Chinese Americans) could not apply for citizenship. Meanwhile, Japanese and a few Korean immigrants also began to arrive; by 1909, there were 40,000 Japanese immigrants working in agriculture, 10,000 on railroads, and 4,000 in canneries. In 1906, the U.S. attorney general ruled that Japanese and Koreans, like Chinese immigrants, were barred from citizenship.

The Chinese Exclusion Act created the legal foundations on which far-reaching exclusionary policies

**Chinese Workers in a Salmon Cannery, c. 1900**

Shut out of many fields of employment by racial discrimination, many Chinese immigrants founded their own restaurants, laundries, and other small businesses. Others, like these cannery workers in Astoria, Oregon, took on some of the most grueling and lowest-paid work in the American economy. Job segregation reinforced, in turn, racial prejudice. Visiting British author Rudyard Kipling, touring canneries along the Columbia River, described Chinese workers in the plants as "blood-besmeared yellow devils." These workers, refuting Kipling's slur, appear clean and respectable. Notice the man in an apron, on the left, who wears his traditional queue, or braided pigtail, tucked into his straw hat. Oregon Historical Society.

## Jewish Immigrants in the Industrial Economy

Following anti-Semitic violence in Russia during the 1880s, thousands of Jews fled to the United States. Almost a quarter million came between 1881 and 1890, the majority settling in New York City. These poverty-stricken newcomers posed problems for New York's assimilated Jews, most of whom were German- or American-born. Community support networks were quickly overwhelmed; New York's United Hebrew Charities almost went bankrupt. Jewish leaders watched with dismay the expansion of tenement wards. They worried that the presence of so many Eastern European "beggars," as one Reform rabbi put it, would heighten American anti-Semitism.

In 1901, New York's Jewish leaders founded an Industrial Removal Office (IRO) to help disperse Jewish newcomers. By 1922 the office sent over 79,000 Eastern European Jews to locations across the country. IRO correspondence provides a window on how newcomers sought to negotiate places in America's industrial economy. Note that most of the letters are translated from Yiddish. As one immigrant noted, inability to speak English could limit employment opportunities and cause "great distress."

### Alex Grubman
### Letter from Portland, Oregon, 1905

I write you how fortunate I am in being placed in one of the largest dry goods houses in Oregon by Hon. Sig Sichel. . . . He went personally with me until he procured the present position for me as inside salesman and to start at $60 a month. . . . [Many people here] wish me to thank the I.R.O. for helping them to success. . . . Mr. Lvov or Lvovsky, a tinsmith sent out direct 2 years ago has a stove and hardware store. M. Kaplan a tailor is earning $20–25.00 a week. Mr. Nathan Siegel who arrived only a few days ago is already employed as a clerk earning $10.00 for a start.

### Barnet Marlin
### Letter from Atlanta, Georgia, 1906

Dr. Wildauer secured a place for me to work, at wooden trunks. . . . I could not earn more than 60 cents a day and was working harder than a horse. . . . Atlanta does not pay to work, especially for a foreigner. . . . Several weeks passed by and at the end I was in debt. . . .

During that time I became acquainted with a Jewish policeman and he was the only one who took pity on me. . . . I told my friend the policeman that I had $15.00 (sent to me by my brother) and he advised me to go out peddling. He took me to a store and told the storekeeper to furnish me for over $30.00 worth of goods. He also acted as my reference and prepared me with everything. I went out peddling and gradually I earned enough money to pay all my debts; and so I kept on peddling. I earned enough money and bought a horse and wagon. I now convey goods from the city to the country and sell them there. I thank you very much for sending me to Atlanta.

### Raphael Gershoni
### Letter from Atlanta, Georgia, 1905

Why do you sent people to Atlanta? You give them eight days worth of food and then you let them starve in the street among Negroes. . . . I was given a job to work in a restaurant kitchen, to wait on Negroes, and to clean the Negroes' closets, for three dollars a week. . . . I was then given ten dollars for goods so that I might go around and peddle in Atlanta. But out of this ten dollars, I have to pay four dollars for lodging and three dollars a month for a place just to lay my head. . . . It is hopeless to work in Atlanta. The highest wage is 75 cents a day. And for what kind of work? . . . The competition is difficult here. Why should anyone hire a white greenhorn when they can get a black Negro, who is strong as iron. . . . Everyone says that the only choice here is to go out into the countryside and peddle. But one needs 40–50 dollars worth of goods. How do I get the money? . . . I would like to ask you to help me out. Help me crawl out of black Atlanta and go to Chicago. There I have friends and can make out better.

## Charles Zwirn
## Letter from La Crosse, Wisconsin, 1913

[Mr. Goldfish] took me into his house and gave me a very nice welcome. He then led me to the synagogue and introduced me to all the members. Mr. Goldfish is a Jew with a real Jewish heart. He is religiously inclined and the biggest businessman in the city. If any controversy arises, it is always settled by Mr. Goldfish. . . . [He] took me to a shop and they paid me $6 more than I earned in New York. When I wanted to thank him, he said that the only thing he expects of me is that I conduct myself properly and go on the right path so I can eventually succeed. This, he said, was the best reward I can give him. I did as he told me and saved a few hundred dollars. . . .

Another man sent here had been in the country two months. . . . He was sent to Mr. Goldfish, who found him a job sorting corks for $2 a day. . . . He then left. By the way, . . . would you be so kind as to send to me a boy to drive a milk wagon on Mr. Jacob's farm and an older man to work at junk? They must be honest and respectable people.

## Mary Rubin
## Letter from New Orleans, Louisiana, 1905

You have sent us out here to starve for hunger and live in the streets. . . . We have arrived in New Orleans about 12 o'clock in the night, and there was nobody to await us there, and we had to go around alnight and look for the address which you had given. . . . They put the nine of us all in one room, with out a bed or a pillow to sleep on. . . . Then they took Mr. Rubin and his wife up to the cigar factory and gave them both a job. Mrs. Rubin is getting about four ($4) a week and Mr. Rubin five ($5). Now we will ask you if a family man can make a living with that. And Mr. Rosenthal they told if he wants work he will have to look for it himself. . . . When he found work, they told him to bring his tools and come to work. He went to the office and asked for the tools; they told him that he can't have them.

. . . [The local Committee] sent mama to be a cook for $4 a month, which she had never done before, and if she wanted to be a cook in N.Y. she could have gotten 3 times that much or more, but it did not suit us to let our mother be a cook, and now we should have to do.

## Nathan Toplitzky
## Letter from Detroit, Michigan, 1908

I, Nathan Toplitzky, sent to the above city 5 months ago, wish to inform you that a great misfortune has happened to me. Your committee has placed me to work in a machine factory where I have earned $.75 a day, and being unskilled I have had 4 of my fingers torn from my right hand. I now remain a cripple throughout my life. For six weeks my sufferings were indescribable.

When the condition of my health improved a little, I called on the Committee and they advised me to go back to the old employer. I went back to him and he placed me to work at the same machine where the accident occurred. Having lost my fingers I was unable to operate the machine. . . . Kindly write to your Committee to find a position for me.

## S. Klein
## Letter from Cleveland, Ohio, 1905

In the past week something terrible has happened here. Two men sent here by the Removal Office committed suicide out of despair. One took poison and the other hanged himself. . . . That shows the deplorable condition of those who are sent here by the Removal Office. The Cleveland Removal Office is managed by an inexperienced young man who maintains his position merely through favoritism. . . . It was told to me that the one who hanged himself came to this agent and implored him with tears in his eyes to provide some kind of employment.

Source: Industrial Removal Office letters as they appear in Robert A. Rockaway, *Words of the Uprooted: Jewish Immigrants in Early 20th Century America* (Ithaca, NY: Cornell University Press, 1998). Used by permission of the American Jewish Historical Society.

### QUESTIONS FOR ANALYSIS

1. Based on the accounts above, what factors contributed to an immigrant's economic success or failure in a new location?
2. In at least ten places, the immigrants above report on wages—daily, weekly, or monthly. For comparison, make a rough conversion of all of these to weekly wages and list them. What do you conclude about compensation for professional, skilled, and unskilled work?
3. Using information from this chapter, as well as the documents above, explain why immigrants sent to the South might have faced more difficulties, on average, than those sent to other parts of the country.

**EXPLAIN CONSEQUENCES**

What were the long-term consequences of the Chinese Exclusion Act for U.S. immigration policy?

would be built in the 1920s and after (Chapter 22). To enforce the law, Congress and the courts gave sweeping new powers to immigration officials, transforming the Chinese into America's first illegal immigrants. Drawn, like others, by the promise of jobs in America's expanding economy, Chinese men stowed away on ships or walked across the borders. Disguising themselves as Mexicans — who at that time could freely enter the United States — some perished in the desert as they tried to reach California.

Huang Zunxian, a Chinese consul general who served in San Francisco in the early 1880s, became increasingly disillusioned as he tried to aid his immigrant countrymen. He expressed his bitterness in a poem:

> They have sealed all the gates tightly,
> Door after door with guards beating alarms. . . .
> Those who do not carry passports
> Are arrested as soon as they arrive.
> Anyone with a yellow-colored face
> Is beaten even if guiltless.
> . . . The American eagle strides the heavens soaring,
> With half of the globe clutched in his claw.
> Although the Chinese arrived later,
> Couldn't you leave them a little space?

Some would-be immigrants, known as paper sons, relied on Chinese residents in the United States, who generated documents falsely claiming the newcomers as American-born children. Paper sons memorized pages of information about their supposed relatives and hometowns. The San Francisco earthquake of 1906 helped their cause by destroying all the port's records. "That was a big chance for a lot of Chinese," remembered one immigrant. "They forged themselves certificates saying they could go back to China and bring back four or five sons, just like that!" Such persistence ensured that, despite the harsh policies of Chinese exclusion, the flow of Asian immigrants never fully ceased.

## Labor Gets Organized

In the American political system, labor has typically been weak. Industrial workers cluster in cities, near factories and jobs; compared with small towns and rural areas, urban areas have been underrepresented in bodies such as the U.S. Senate and the presidential electoral college, in which representation is calculated by state, rather than (or in addition to) individuals. This problem became acute in the era of industrialization, and it has lingered. Even today, the twenty-two U.S. senators elected from Alaska, Idaho, Iowa, Maine, Mississippi, Montana, New Mexico, North Dakota, Vermont, West Virginia, and Wyoming represent a smaller number of people, *combined*, than the two U.S. senators who represent heavily urban California.

Faced with this obstacle, labor advocates could adopt one of two strategies. First, they could try to make political alliances with sympathetic rural voters

**Anti-Chinese Racism**

This cartoon from the magazine *Puck*, drawn by James A. Wales during the 1880 presidential campaign, offers vivid evidence of the widespread and virulent American prejudice against Chinese immigrants. Republican candidate James Garfield, on the left, and Democratic candidate Winfield Scott Hancock, on the right, both nail up their party's "planks" in favor of restricting Chinese immigration. Asian immigrants were not permitted to apply for naturalization as U.S. citizens; they thus had no vote and no power in politics. Congress passed the Chinese Exclusion Act, with bipartisan support, soon after Garfield's victory. Library of Congress.

who shared their problems. Second, they could reject politics and create narrowly focused trade unions to negotiate directly with employers. In general, labor advocates emphasized the first strategy between the 1870s and the early 1890s, and the latter in the early twentieth century. Across this era, while industrialization made America increasingly rich and powerful, it also brought large-scale conflict between labor and capital.

## The Emergence of a Labor Movement

The problem of industrial labor entered Americans' consciousness dramatically with the **Great Railroad Strike of 1877**. Protesting steep wage cuts amid the depression that had begun in 1873, thousands of railroad workers walked off the job. Broader issues were at stake. "The officers of the road," reported strike leader Barney Donahue in upstate New York, "were bound to break the spirit of the men, and any or all organizations they belonged to." He believed railroad companies wanted to block workers from "all fellowship for mutual aid." The strike brought rail travel and commerce to a halt. Thousands of people poured into the streets of Buffalo, Pittsburgh, and Chicago to protest the economic injustice wrought by railroads — as well as fires caused by stray sparks from locomotives and injuries and deaths on train tracks in urban neighborhoods. When Pennsylvania's governor sent state militia to break the strike, Pittsburgh crowds reacted by burning railroad property and overturning locomotives. Similar clashes between police and protesters occurred in other cities across the country, from Galveston, Texas, to San Francisco.

The 1877 strike left more than fifty people dead and caused $40 million worth of damage, primarily to railroad property. "It seemed as if the whole social and political structure was on the very brink of ruin," wrote one journalist. For their role in the strike, many railroad workers were fired and blacklisted: railroad companies circulated their names on a "do not hire" list to prevent them from getting any work in the industry. In the aftermath of the strike, the U.S. government created the National Guard, intended not to protect Americans against foreign invasion but to enforce order at home.

Watching the upheavals of industrialization, some radical thinkers pointed out its impact on workers. Among the most influential was Henry George, whose book *Progress and Poverty* (1879) was a best-seller for decades after publication. George warned that Americans had been too optimistic about the impact of

railroads and manufacturing, which they hoped would — after an initial period of turmoil — bring prosperity to all. George believed the emerging industrial order meant permanent poverty. Industrialization, he wrote, was driving a wedge through society, lifting the fortunes of professionals and the middle class but pushing the working class down by forcing them into deskilled, dangerous, and low-paid labor. George's proposed solution, a federal "single tax" on landholdings, did not win widespread support, but his insightful diagnosis of the problem helped encourage radical movements for economic reform.

Many rural people believed they faced the same problems as industrial workers. In the new economy, they found themselves at the mercy of large corporations, from equipment dealers who sold them harvesters and plows to railroads and grain elevators that shipped and stored their products. Though farmers appeared to have more independence than corporate employees, many felt trapped in a web of middlemen who chipped away at their profits while international forces robbed them of decision-making power.

Farmers denounced not only corporations but also the previous two decades of government efforts to foster economic development — policies that now seemed wrongheaded. Farmers' advocates argued that high tariffs forced rural families to pay too much for basic necessities while failing to protect America's great export crops, cotton and wheat. At the same time, they charged, Republican financial policies benefitted banks, not borrowers. Farmers blamed railroad companies for taking government grants and subsidies to build but then charging unequal rates that privileged big manufacturers. From the farmers' point of view, public money had been used to build giant railroad companies that turned around and exploited ordinary people.

The most prominent rural protest group of the early postwar decades was the National Grange of the Patrons of Husbandry, founded in 1867. Like industrial workers, Grange farmers sought to counter the rising power of corporate middlemen through cooperation and mutual aid. Local Grange halls brought farm families together for recreation and conversation. The Grange set up its own banks, insurance companies, and grain elevators, and, in Iowa, even a farm implement factory. Many Grange members also advocated political action, building independent local parties that ran on anticorporate platforms.

During the 1870s depression, Grangers, labor advocates, and local workingmen's parties forged a national political movement, the **Greenback-Labor**

**Houston's Cotton Depot, c. 1909**
After the Civil War, cotton agriculture blossomed on the rich lands of east Texas, and Houston simultaneously blossomed as the region's commercial center. This tinted photograph from the 1890s reveals the tremendous volume of traffic that came through Houston, where Texas cotton was compacted in steam-powered cotton presses, loaded onto railcars, and shipped to cotton mills in the Southeast and Britain to be made into cloth.
University of Houston Libraries, Special Collections, George Fuerman Collection.

**COMPARE AND CONTRAST**

How did the methods used by railroad workers to protest their working conditions compare with the tactics employed by the Greenbackers, who also sought reform?

Party. In the South, Greenbackers protested the collapse of Reconstruction and urged that every man's vote be protected. Across the country, Greenbackers advocated laws to regulate corporations and enforce an eight-hour workday to reduce long, grueling work hours. They called for the federal government to print more greenback dollars and increase the amount of money in circulation; this, they argued, would stimulate the economy, create jobs, and help borrowers by allowing them to pay off debts in dollars that, over time, slowly decreased in value. Greenbackers, like many industrial labor leaders, subscribed to the ideal of **producerism**: they dismissed middlemen, bankers, lawyers, and investors as idlers who lived off the sweat of people who worked with their hands. As a Pittsburgh worker put it in an 1878 poem, it was not the money-handlers

or executives at the top but the "noble sons of Labor . . . / Who with bone, and brain, and fiber / Make the nation's wealth."

The Greenback movement radicalized thousands of farmers, miners, and industrial workers. In Alabama's coal-mining regions, black and white miners cooperated in the party. Texas boasted seventy African American Greenback clubs. In 1878, Greenback-Labor candidates won more than a million votes, and the party elected fifteen congressmen nationwide. In the Midwest, Greenback pressure helped trigger a wave of economic regulatory actions known as **Granger laws**. By the early 1880s, twenty-nine states had created railroad commissions to supervise railroad rates and policies; others appointed commissions to regulate insurance and utility companies. Such early regulatory efforts were not always effective, but they were crucial starting points for reform. While short-lived, the Greenback movement created the foundation for more sustained efforts to regulate big business.

## The Knights of Labor

The most important union of the late nineteenth century, the **Knights of Labor**, was founded in 1869 as a secret society of garment workers in Philadelphia. In 1878, as the Greenback movement reached its height, some Knights served as delegates to Greenback-Labor conventions. Like Grangers, Knights believed that ordinary people needed control over the enterprises in which they worked. They proposed to set up shops owned by employees, transforming America into what they called a cooperative commonwealth. In keeping with this broad-based vision, the order practiced open membership, irrespective of race, gender, or field of employment—though, like other labor groups, the Knights excluded Chinese immigrants.

The Knights had a strong political bent. They believed that only electoral action could bring about many of their goals, such as government regulation of corporations and laws that required employers to negotiate during strikes. Their 1878 platform denounced the "aggressiveness of great capitalists and corporations." "If we desire to enjoy the full blessings of life," the Knights warned, "a check [must] be placed upon unjust accumulation, and the power for evil of aggregated wealth." Among their demands were workplace safety laws, prohibition of child labor, a federal tax on the nation's highest incomes, public ownership of telegraphs and railroads, and government recognition of workers' right to organize. The Knights also advocated personal responsibility and self-discipline. Their leader, Terence Powderly, warned that the abuse of liquor robbed as many workers of their wages as did ruthless employers.

Growing rapidly in the 1880s, the Knights union was sprawling and decentralized. It included not only skilled craftsmen such as carpenters, ironworkers, and beer brewers but also textile workers in Rhode Island, domestic workers in Georgia, and tenant farmers in Arkansas. Knights organized workingmen's parties to advocate a host of reforms, ranging from an eight-hour workday to cheaper streetcar fares and better garbage collection in urban areas. One of their key innovations was hiring a full-time women's organizer, Leonora Barry. An Irish American widow who was forced into factory work after her husband's death, Barry became a labor advocate out of horror at the conditions she experienced on the job. To the discomfort of some male Knights, she investigated and exposed widespread evidence of sexual harassment on the job.

The Knights' growth in the 1880s showed the grassroots basis of labor activism. Powderly tried to avoid

**The Knights of Labor**

The caption on this union card—"By Industry we Thrive"—expresses the core principle of the Knights of Labor that everything of value is the product of honest labor. The two figures are ideal representations of that "producerist" belief—handsome workers, respectably attired, doing productive labor. A picture of the Grand Master Workman, Terence V. Powderly, hangs on the wall, benignly watching them. Picture Research Consultants & Archives.

strikes, which he saw as costly and risky. But the organization's greatest growth resulted from spontaneous, grassroots striking. In 1885, thousands of workers on the Southwest Railroad walked off the job to protest wage cuts; afterward, they telegraphed the Knights and asked to be admitted as members. The strike enhanced the Knights' reputation among workers and built membership to 750,000. By the following year, local assemblies had sprung up in every state and almost every county in the United States.

Just as the Knights reached this pinnacle of influence, an episode of violence brought them down. In 1886, a protest at the McCormick reaper works in

**IDENTIFY CAUSES**

What factors contributed to the rapid rise of the Knights of Labor? To its decline?

**Industrial Violence: A Dynamited Mine, 1894**

Strikes in the western mining regions pitted ruthless owners, bent on control of their property and work-force, against fiercely independent miners who knew how to use dynamite. Some of the bloodiest conflicts occurred in Colorado mining towns, where the Western Federation of Miners (WFM) had strong support and a series of Republican governors sent state militia to back the mine owners. Violence broke out repeatedly between the early 1890s and the 1910s. At Victor, Colorado, in May 1894, as dozens of armed sheriffs' deputies closed in on angry WFM members occupying the Strong Mine in protest, the miners blew up the mine's shaft house and boiler. Showered with debris, the deputies boarded the next train out of town. Because Colorado then had a Populist governor, Davis Waite, who sympathized with the miners and ordered the deputies to disband, this strike was one of the few in which owners and miners reached a peaceful settlement—a temporary victory for the union. Library of Congress.

Chicago led to a clash with police that left four strikers dead. (Three unions, including a Knights of Labor assembly, had struck, but the Knights had reached an agreement and returned to work. Only the machinists' union remained on strike when the incident occurred.) Chicago was a hotbed of **anarchism**, the revolutionary advocacy of a stateless society. Local anarchists, many of them German immigrants, called a protest meeting the next day, May 4, 1886, at **Haymarket Square**. When police tried to disperse the crowd, someone threw a bomb that killed several policemen. Officers responded with gunfire. In the trial that followed, eight anarchists were found guilty of murder and criminal conspiracy. All were convicted, not on any definitive evidence that one of them threw the bomb (the bomber's identity still remains unknown) but on the basis of their antigovernment speeches. Four of the eight were executed by hanging, one committed suicide in prison, and the others received long sentences.

The Haymarket violence profoundly damaged the American labor movement. Seizing on resulting anti-union hysteria, employers took the offensive. They broke strikes with mass arrests, tied up the Knights in expensive court proceedings, and forced workers to sign contracts pledging not to join labor organizations. The Knights of Labor never recovered. In the view of the press and many prosperous Americans, they were tainted by their alleged links with anarchism. Struggles between industrialists and workers had created bitter divides.

## Farmers and Workers: The Cooperative Alliance

In the aftermath of Haymarket, the Knights' cooperative vision did not entirely fade. A new rural movement, the **Farmers' Alliance**, arose to take up many of the issues that Grangers and Greenbackers had earlier sought to address. Founded in Texas during the depression of the 1870s, the Farmers' Alliance spread across the plains states and the South, becoming by the late 1880s the largest farmer-based movement in American history. A separate Colored Farmers' Alliance arose to represent rural African Americans. The harsh conditions farmers were enduring—including drought in the West and plunging global prices for corn, cotton, and wheat—intensified the movement's appeal. Traveling Alliance lecturers exhorted farmers to "stand as a great conservative body against . . . the growing corruption of wealth and power."

Like earlier movements, Alliance leaders pinned their initial hopes on cooperative stores and exchanges that would circumvent middlemen. Cooperatives gathered farmers' orders and bought in bulk at wholesale prices, passing the savings along. Alliance cooperatives achieved notable victories in the late 1880s. The Dakota Alliance, for example, offered members cheap hail insurance and low prices on machinery and farm supplies. The Texas Alliance established a huge cooperative enterprise to market cotton and provide farmers with cheap loans. When cotton prices fell further in 1891, however, the Texas exchange failed. Other cooperatives also suffered from chronic underfunding and lack of credit, and they faced hostility from merchants and lenders they tried to circumvent.

The Texas Farmers' Alliance thus proposed a federal price-support system for farm products, modeled on the national banks. Under this plan, the federal government would hold crops in public warehouses and issue loans on their value until they could be profitably sold. When Democrats—still wary of big-government schemes—declared the idea too radical, Alliances in Texas, Kansas, South Dakota, and elsewhere decided to create a new political party, the Populists (see Chapter 20). In this venture, the Alliance cooperated with the weakened Knights of Labor, seeking to use rural voters' substantial clout on behalf of urban workers who shared their vision.

By this time, farmer-labor coalitions had made a considerable impact on state politics. But state laws and commissions were proving ineffective against corporations of national and even global scope. It was difficult for Wisconsin, for instance, to enforce new laws against a railroad company whose lines might stretch from Chicago to Seattle and whose corporate headquarters might be in Minnesota. Militant farmers and labor advocates demanded federal action.

In 1887, responding to this pressure, Congress and President Grover Cleveland passed two landmark laws. The Hatch Act provided federal funding for agricultural research and education, meeting farmers' demands for government aid to agriculture. The **Interstate Commerce Act** counteracted a Supreme Court decision of the previous year, *Wabash v. Illinois* (1886), that had struck down states' authority to regulate railroads. The act created the Interstate Commerce Commission (ICC), charged with investigating interstate shipping, forcing railroads to make their rates public, and suing in court when necessary to make companies reduce "unjust or unreasonable" rates.

Though creation of the ICC was a direct response to farmer-labor demands, its final form represented a compromise. Radical leaders wanted Congress to establish a direct set of rules under which railroads must operate. If a railroad did not comply, any citizen could take the company to court; if the new rules triggered bankruptcy, the railroad could convert to public ownership. But getting such a plan through Congress proved impossible. Lawmakers more sympathetic to business called instead for an expert commission to oversee the railroad industry. In a pattern that repeated frequently over the next few decades, the commission model proved more acceptable to the majority of congressmen.

The ICC faced formidable challenges. Though the new law forbade railroads from reaching secret rate-setting agreements, evidence was difficult to gather and secret "pooling" continued. A hostile Supreme Court also undermined the commission's powers. In a series of sixteen decisions over the two decades after the ICC was created, the Court sided with railroads fifteen times. The justices delivered a particularly hard blow in 1897 when they ruled that the ICC had no power to interfere with shipping rates. Nonetheless, the ICC's existence was a major achievement. In the early twentieth century, Congress would strengthen the commission's powers, and the ICC would become one of the most powerful federal agencies charged with overseeing private business.

## Another Path: The American Federation of Labor

While the Knights of Labor exerted political pressure, other workers pursued a different strategy. In the 1870s, printers, ironworkers, bricklayers, and other skilled workers organized nationwide trade unions. These "brotherhoods" focused on the everyday needs of workers in skilled occupations. Trade unions sought

**PLACE EVENTS IN CONTEXT**
Why did farmers and industrial workers cooperate, and what political objectives did they achieve?

**Samuel Gompers, c. 1890s**

Samuel Gompers (1850–1924) was one of the founders of the American Federation of Labor, and its president for nearly forty years. A company detective took this photograph when the labor leader was visiting striking miners in West Virginia, an area where mine operators resisted unions with special fierceness. George Meany Memorial Archives.

the separate **American Federation of Labor** (AFL). The man who led them was Samuel Gompers, a Dutch-Jewish cigar maker whose family had emigrated to New York in 1863. Gompers headed the AFL for the next thirty years. He believed the Knights relied too much on electoral politics, where victories were likely to be limited, and he did not share their sweeping critique of capitalism. The AFL, made up of relatively skilled and well-paid workers, was less interested in challenging the corporate order than in winning a larger share of its rewards.

Having gone to work at age ten, Gompers always contended that what he missed at school he more than made up for in the shop, where cigar makers paid one of their members to read to them while they worked. As a young worker-intellectual, Gompers gravitated to New York's radical circles, where he participated in lively debates about which strategies workingmen should pursue. Partly out of these debates, and partly from his own experience in the Cigar Makers Union, Gompers hammered out a doctrine that he called pure-and-simple unionism. *Pure* referred to membership: strictly limited to workers, organized by craft and occupation, with no reliance on outside advisors or allies. *Simple* referred to goals: only those that immediately benefitted workers — better wages, hours, and working conditions. Pure-and-simple unionists distrusted politics. Their aim was collective bargaining with employers.

On one level, pure-and-simple unionism worked. The AFL was small at first, but by 1904 its membership rose to more than two million. In the early twentieth century, it became the nation's leading voice for workers, lasting far longer than movements like the Knights of Labor. The AFL's strategy — personified by Gompers — was well suited to an era when Congress and the courts were hostile to labor. By the 1910s, the political climate would become more responsive; at that later moment, Gompers would soften his antipolitical stance and join the battle for new labor laws (Chapter 20).

What Gompers gave up most crucially, in the meantime, was the inclusiveness of the Knights. By comparison, the AFL was far less welcoming to women and blacks; it included mostly skilled craftsmen. There was little room in the AFL for department-store clerks and other service workers, much less the farm tenants and domestic servants whom the Knights had organized. Despite the AFL's success among skilled craftsmen, the narrowness of its base was a problem that would come back to haunt the labor movement later on. Gompers, however, saw that corporate titans and their political allies held tremendous power, and he

a **closed shop** — with all jobs reserved for union members — that kept out lower-wage workers. Union rules specified terms of work, sometimes in minute detail. Many unions emphasized mutual aid. Because working on the railroads was a high-risk occupation, for example, brotherhoods of engineers, brakemen, and firemen pooled contributions into funds that provided accident and death benefits. Above all, trade unionism asserted craft workers' rights as active decision-makers in the workplace, not just cogs in a management-run machine.

In the early 1880s, many trade unionists joined the Knights of Labor coalition. But the aftermath of the Haymarket violence persuaded them to leave and create

**TRACE CHANGE OVER TIME**

How did the key institutions and goals of the labor movement change, and what gains and losses resulted from this shift?

advocated what he saw as the most practical defensive plan. In the meantime, the upheaval wrought by industrialization spread far beyond the workplace, transforming every aspect of American life.

# SUMMARY

The end of the Civil War ushered in the era of American big business. Exploiting the continent's vast resources, vertically integrated corporations emerged as the dominant business form, and giant companies built near monopolies in some sectors of the economy. Corporations devised new modes of production, distribution, and marketing, extending their reach through the department store, the mail-order catalog, and the new advertising industry. These developments laid the groundwork for mass consumer culture. They also offered emerging jobs in management, sales, and office work.

Rapid industrialization drew immigrants from around the world. Until the 1920s, most European and Latin American immigrants were welcome to enter the United States, though they often endured harsh conditions after they arrived. Asian immigrants, by contrast, faced severe discrimination. The Chinese Exclusion Act blocked all Chinese laborers from coming to the United States; it was later extended to other Asians, and it built the legal framework for broader forms of exclusion.

Nationwide movements for workers' rights arose in response to industrialization. During the 1870s and 1880s, coalitions of workers and farmers, notably the Knights of Labor and the Farmers' Alliance, sought political solutions to what they saw as large corporations' exploitation of working people. Pressure from such movements led to the first major attempts to regulate corporations, such as the federal Interstate Commerce Act. Radical protest movements were weakened, however, after public condemnation of anarchist violence in 1886 at Chicago's Haymarket Square. Meanwhile, trade unions such as the American Federation of Labor organized skilled workers and negotiated directly with employers, becoming the most popular form of labor organization in the early twentieth century.

# CHAPTER REVIEW

**MAKE IT STICK**   Go to **LearningCurve** to retain what you've read.

## TERMS TO KNOW   Identify and explain the significance of each term below.

### Key Concepts and Events

Homestead lockout (p. 544)

management revolution (p. 546)

vertical integration (p. 547)

horizontal integration (p. 548)

trust (p. 548)

deskilling (p. 551)

mass production (p. 551)

scientific management (p. 552)

Chinese Exclusion Act (p. 561)

Great Railroad Strike of 1877 (p. 565)

Greenback-Labor Party (p. 565)

producerism (p. 566)

Granger laws (p. 566)

Knights of Labor (p. 567)

anarchism (p. 568)

Haymarket Square (p. 568)

Farmers' Alliance (p. 568)

Interstate Commerce Act (p. 569)

closed shop (p. 570)

American Federation of Labor (p. 570)

### Key People

Andrew Carnegie (p. 544)

Gustavus Swift (p. 547)

John D. Rockefeller (p. 547)

Henry George (p. 565)

Terence Powderly (p. 567)

Leonora Barry (p. 567)

Samuel Gompers (p. 570)

## REVIEW QUESTIONS    Answer these questions to demonstrate your understanding of the chapter's main ideas.

1. How did the rise of big business in the United States transform the economy and affect the lives of working people?

2. How did patterns of immigration to the United States change between the 1840s and the 1910s? What roles did newly arrived immigrants play in the economy during the late nineteenth and early twentieth centuries?

3. Compare the accomplishments and limitations of American farmer-labor movements of the 1870s and 1880s, such as the Greenback-Labor Party and the Knights of Labor, with those of the American Federation of Labor. Why did the latter choose a different strategy?

4. This chapter explores the impact of industrialization from many points of view. Based on this information, do you think the term *industrial statesmen* or *robber barons* is more accurate as a description for Andrew Carnegie, John D. Rockefeller, and other early titans? Or would you prefer a different term? Explain why.

5. **THEMATIC UNDERSTANDING**    Review the events listed under "Politics and Power," "Peopling," and "Work, Exchange, and Technology" on the thematic timeline on page 543. Industrialization was an *economic* process, but it also transformed American society and politics. How?

## MAKING CONNECTIONS    Recognize the larger developments and continuities within and across chapters by answering these questions.

1. **ACROSS TIME AND PLACE**    Imagine a conversation in the 1890s between a young brother and sister in Chicago, who are working, respectively, in a meat-packing plant and as a telephone operator, and their grandmother, who as a young girl worked in a Lowell, Massachusetts, textile mill in the 1840s (Chapter 9) before the family moved west to take advantage of new opportunities. What similarities and differences might they see in their various experiences of work? What does this tell us about changes in workers' lives over these decades?

2. **VISUAL EVIDENCE**    Return to the chapter-opening photograph (p. 545), taken in the aftermath of a terrible mining accident in Pennsylvania. Imagine, first, that the young man in the middle of the picture, facing the camera, is the nephew of an Irish immigrant miner who was killed in the explosion. In the voice of this young man, write a letter to the editor of the local paper explaining what lessons Americans should take from the disaster.

Now imagine instead that the young man has enrolled in business school to become a manager; he is the son of a Scottish-born executive in the mining company, and Andrew Carnegie is his hero. In the voice of this young man, write a letter to the editor explaining what lessons Americans should take from the disaster.

## MORE TO EXPLORE    Start here to learn more about the events discussed in this chapter.

Roger Daniels, *Coming to America* (2002). A sweeping overview of immigration to the United States from colonial times to the 1980s.

Walter Friedman, *Birth of a Salesman* (2004). A lively treatment of the rise of salesmanship.

Erika Lee, *At America's Gates* (2003). One of several superb recent treatments of Chinese immigration and exclusion.

Harold Livesay, *Samuel Gompers and Organized Labor in America* (1978). A classic biography of the AFL's founder.

David Montgomery, *Citizen Worker* (1993). A brief exploration of workers' experiences with government, electoral politics, and the marketplace in the late nineteenth century.

Richard White, *Railroaded* (2011). A recent reassessment of big business and its impact, focusing on the railroad industry.

## TIMELINE   Ask yourself why this chapter begins and ends with these dates and then identify the links among related events.

| | |
|---|---|
| **1863** | • Cleveland, Ohio, becomes nation's petroleum refining center |
| **1865** | • Chicago's Union Stock Yard opens |
| **1867** | • National Grange of the Patrons of Husbandry founded |
| **1869** | • Knights of Labor founded |
| **1875** | • John Wanamaker opens nation's first department store in Philadelphia |
| **1876** | • Alexander Graham Bell invents the telephone |
| **1877** | • San Francisco mob attacks Chinatown<br>• Great Railroad Strike |
| **1878** | • Greenback-Labor Party elects 15 Congressmen. |
| **1879** | • Henry George publishes *Progress and Poverty* |
| **1882** | • John D. Rockefeller creates Standard Oil Trust<br>• Congress passes Chinese Exclusion Act |
| **1884** | • Knights of Labor at peak of membership |
| **1885** | • Rock Springs massacre of Chinese miners |
| **1886** | • Haymarket Square violence<br>• American Federation of Labor (AFL) founded |
| **1887** | • Hatch Act<br>• Interstate Commerce Act |
| **1889** | • New Jersey passes law enabling trusts to operate in the state |
| **1892** | • Homestead lockout |
| **1893** | • Severe depression hits; causes mass unemployment and wave of corporate mergers |
| **1900** | • America's one hundred largest companies control one-third of national productive capacity |
| **1901** | • J. P. Morgan creates U.S. Steel, America's first billion-dollar corporation |
| **1907** | • Marianna, Pennsylvania, mine disaster |
| **1908** | • Walter Dill publishes *The Psychology of Advertising* |

**KEY TURNING POINTS:** In the era of industrialization, what events prompted the rise of labor unions and other reform groups that called for stronger government responses to corporate power? Before 1900, what key events or turning points marked reformers' successes and failures?

# 18

**CHAPTER**

# The Victorians Make the Modern
# 1880–1917

When Philadelphia hosted the 1876 Centennial Exposition, Americans weren't sure what to expect from their first world's fair—including what foods exhibitors would offer. One cartoonist humorously proposed that Russians would serve castor oil, Arabs would bring camel's milk punch, and Germans would offer beer. Reflecting widespread racial prejudices, the cartoon showed Chinese men selling "hashed cat" and "rat pie." In reality, though, the 1876 Exposition offered only plain lunchrooms and, for the wealthiest visitors, expensive French fare.

By the early twentieth century, American food had undergone a revolution. Visitors to the St. Louis World's Fair in 1904 could try food from Scandinavia, India, and the Philippines. Across the United States, Chinese American restaurants flourished as a *chop suey* craze swept the nation. New Yorkers could sample Hungarian and Syrian cuisine; a San Francisco journalist enthusiastically reviewed local Mexican and Japanese restaurants. Even small-town diners could often find an Italian or German meal.

What had happened? Americans had certainly not lost all their prejudices: while plates of *chop suey* were being gobbled up, laws excluding Chinese immigrants remained firmly in place. Industrialization reshaped class identities, however, and promoted a creative consumer culture. In the great cities, amusement parks and vaudeville theaters catered to industrial workers (Chapter 19). Other institutions served middle-class customers who wanted novelty and variety at a reasonable price. A Victorian ethos of self-restraint and moral uplift gave way to expectations of leisure and fun. As African Americans and women claimed a right to public spaces—to shop, dine, and travel freely—they built powerful reform movements. At the same time, the new pressures faced by professional men led to aggressive calls for masculine fitness, exemplified by the rise of sports.

Stunning scientific discoveries—from dinosaur fossils to distant galaxies—also challenged long-held beliefs. Faced with electricity, medical vaccines, and other wonders, Americans celebrated technological solutions to human problems. But while science gained popularity, religion hardly faded. In fact, religious diversity grew, as immigrants brought new faiths and Protestants responded with innovations of their own. Americans found themselves living in a modern world—one in which their grandparents' beliefs and ways of life no longer seemed to apply. In a market-driven society that claimed to champion individual freedom, Americans took advantage of new ideas while expressing anxiety over the accompanying upheavals and risks.

**IDENTIFY THE BIG IDEA**

**How did the changes wrought by industrialization shape Americans' identities, beliefs, and culture?**

574

**Chicago Department Store Advertisement, 1893** In the same year that the Chicago World's Columbian Exhibition offered an array of dazzling experiences for visitors, the city's Siegel-Cooper Department Store did the same for consumers who could afford to shop in its halls. Note the many types of goods and services offered in its "Sixty-Five Complete Departments," from meat and groceries to medical and legal advice. What evidence, here, shows the types of customers the store sought to attract, inviting them to say, "I'll meet you at the Fountain"? How did the store encourage shoppers to linger?

Chicago History Museum.

## Commerce and Culture

As the United States industrialized, the terms *middle class* and *working class* came widely into use. Americans adopted these broad identities not only in the workplace but also in their leisure time. Professionals and corporate managers prospered; they and their families enjoyed rising income and an array of tempting ways to spend their dollars. Celebrating these new technological wonders, Americans hailed inventors as heroes. The most famous, Thomas Edison, operated an independent laboratory rather than working for a corporation. Edison, like many of the era's businessmen, was a shrewd entrepreneur who focused on commercial success. He and his colleagues helped introduce such lucrative products as the incandescent lightbulb and the phonograph, which came widely into use in American homes.

Even working-class Americans enjoyed cheaper products delivered by global trade and mass production, from bananas and cigarettes to colorful dime novels and magazines. Edison's moving pictures, for example, first found popularity among the urban working class (Chapter 19). Consumer culture *appeared*, at least, to be democratic: anyone should be able to eat at a restaurant or buy a rail ticket for the "ladies' car" — as long as she or he could pay. In practice, though, this was not the case, and consumer venues became sites of struggle over class inequality, race privilege, and proper male and female behavior.

### Consumer Spaces

America's public spaces — from election polls to saloons and circus shows — had long been boisterous and male-centered. A woman who ventured there

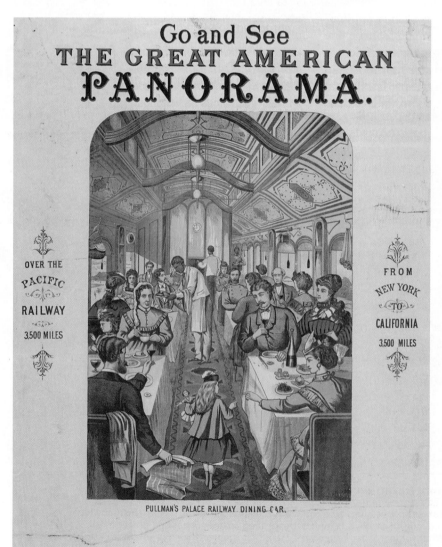

Go and See
THE GREAT AMERICAN
PANORAMA.

OVER THE
PACIFIC
RAILWAY
3,500 MILES

FROM
NEW YORK
TO
CALIFORNIA
3,500 MILES

PULLMAN'S PALACE RAILWAY DINING CAR.

**Pacific Railway Poster, c. 1900**
This color lithograph emphasized the family atmosphere of the railroad's Pullman Palace Dining Cars. Pullman, a Chicago-based manufacturer, became a household name by providing high-class sleeping and dining cars to the nation's railroads. Such advertisements invited prosperous Americans to make themselves "at home" in public, commercial spaces that were safe and comfortable for respectable women and children. Note that all the passengers are white, and the waiters black. Work as a railroad waiter or porter was one of the better-paid, more prestigious jobs available to African American men. Demands for segregated rail cars often focused on the alleged threat that black men might pose to white women — while, at the same time, such men and women regularly came in contact as railroad employees and passengers. Wisconsin Historical Society.

without a male chaperone risked damaging her reputation. But the rise of new businesses encouraged change. To attract an eager public, purveyors of consumer culture invited women and families, especially those of the middle class, to linger in department stores and enjoy new amusements.

No one promoted commercial domesticity more successfully than showman P. T. Barnum (1810–1891), who used the country's expanding rail network to develop his famous traveling circus. Barnum condemned earlier circus managers who had opened their tents to "the rowdy element." Proclaiming children as his key audience, he created family entertainment for diverse audiences (though in the South, black audiences sat in segregated seats or attended separate shows). He promised middle-class parents that his circus would teach children courage and promote the benefits of exercise. To encourage women's attendance, Barnum emphasized the respectability and refinement of his female performers.

Department stores also lured middle-class women by offering tearooms, children's play areas, umbrellas, and clerks to wrap and carry every purchase. Store credit plans enabled well-to-do women to shop without handling money in public. Such tactics succeeded so well that New York's department store district became known as Ladies' Mile. Boston department store magnate William Filene called the department store an "Adamless Eden."

These Edens were for the elite and middle class. Though bargain basements and neighborhood stores served working-class families, big department stores enlisted vagrancy laws and police to discourage the "wrong kind" from entering. Working-class women gained access primarily as clerks, cashiers, and cash girls, who at age twelve or younger served as internal store messengers, carrying orders and change for $1.50 a week. The department store was no Eden for these women, who worked long hours on their feet, often dealing with difficult customers. Nevertheless, many clerks claimed their own privileges as shoppers, making enthusiastic use of employee discounts and battling employers for the right to wear their fashionable purchases while they worked in the store.

In similar ways, class status was marked by the ways technology entered American homes. The rise of electricity, in particular, marked the gap between affluent urban consumers and rural and working-class families. In elite houses, domestic servants began to use — or find themselves replaced by — an array of new devices, from washing machines to vacuum cleaners. When Alexander Graham Bell invented the telephone in

1876, entrepreneurs introduced the device for business use, but it soon found eager residential customers. Telephones changed etiquette and social relations for middle-class suburban women — while providing their working-class counterparts with new employment options (Thinking Like a Historian, p. 578).

Railroads also reflected the emerging privileges of professional families. Finding prosperous Americans eager for excursions, railroad companies, like department stores, made things comfortable for middle-class women and children. Boston's South Terminal Station boasted of its modern amenities, including "everything that the traveler needs down to cradles in which the baby may be soothed." An 1882 tourist guide promised readers that they could live on the Pacific Railroad "with as much true enjoyment as the home drawing room." Rail cars manufactured by the famous Pullman Company of Chicago set a national standard for taste and elegance. Fitted with rich carpets, upholstery, and woodwork, Pullman cars embodied the growing prosperity of America's elite, influencing trends in home decor. Part of their appeal was the chance for people of modest means to emulate the rich. An experienced train conductor observed that the wives of grocers, not millionaires, were the ones most likely to "sweep . . . into a parlor car as if the very carpet ought to feel highly honored by their tread."

First-class "ladies' cars" soon became sites of struggle for racial equality. For three decades after the end of the Civil War, state laws and railroad regulations varied, and African Americans often succeeded in securing seats. One reformer noted, however, "There are few ordeals more nerve-wracking than the one which confronts a colored woman when she tries to secure a Pullman reservation in the South and even in some parts of the North." When they claimed first-class seats, black women often faced confrontations with conductors, resulting in numerous lawsuits in the 1870s and 1880s. Riding the Chesapeake & Ohio line in 1884, young African American journalist Ida B. Wells was told to leave. "I refused," she wrote later, "saying that the [nearest alternative] car was a smoker, and as I was in the ladies' car, I proposed to stay." Wells resisted, but the conductor and a baggage handler threw her bodily off the train. Returning home to Memphis, Wells sued and won in local courts, but Tennessee's supreme court reversed the ruling.

In 1896, the U.S. Supreme Court settled such issues decisively — but not justly. The case, ***Plessy v. Ferguson***,

**EXPLAIN CONSEQUENCES** How did new consumer practices, arising from industrialization, reshape Americans' gender, class, and race relationships?

## America Picks Up the Telephone

New consumer technologies often had different impacts on working-class and rural Americans than they did on the prosperous elite and the middle class. The documents below also suggest some of the ways that telephone use reflected new expectations about women's roles in the home, workplace, and society.

1. **"Hello Ma Baby" sheet music cover and lyrics, 1899.** *This popular music hit, this song was written in the voice of an African American man to his girl. The man's tuxedo is a bit disheveled; in 1899, most white Americans would have assumed he wore it for waiting tables or other service work. The woman wears a dressing gown—not how a respectable lady would want to appear. Nonetheless, the racial depiction here is more modern than those of old-fashioned minstrel shows. The song's chorus appears below. What changing expectations does it convey about courtship and dating?*

Courtesy of the E. Azalia Hackley Collection of Negro Music, Dance and Drama, Detroit Public Library.

Hello! ma Baby, Hello! ma honey, Hello! ma ragtime gal,
Send me a kiss by wire, Baby, my heart's on fire!
If you refuse me, honey, you'll lose me, then you'll be left alone;
Oh baby, telephone, and tell me I'm your own.

2. **"The Perfect Operator,"** *Saturday Evening Post,* **July 12, 1930.** *Katherine Schmitt opened the New York Operator's School in 1902. Looking back later, she described the qualities sought in operators. What does this document tell us about the values of the emerging corporate workplace?*

[The operator] must now be made as nearly as possible a paragon of perfection, a kind of human machine, the exponent of speed and courtesy; a creature spirited enough to move like chain lightning, and with perfect accuracy; docile enough to deny herself the sweet privilege of the last word. She must assume that the subscriber is always right, and even when she knows he is not, her only comeback must be: "Excuse it please," in the same smiling voice.

3. **"The Mischievous Telephone Girl Makes More Trouble,"** *Wheeling Register,* **West Virginia, October 26, 1884.** *Early operators had to speak to each caller and manually connect the call. Newspapers in the 1880s featured many stories like this one. Telephone companies predominantly hired young white native-born women as operators, or "hello girls." Many such employees came from the working class.*

The girl had been asleep a long time, when somebody called. Looking at the switch board, she observed that No. 1,111 was down, and leisurely raised the phone to her ear. . . . "Hello! . . . You bald headed old sinner! What do you want?"

"Dr. Highflyer. No. 2,222."

"Hello!"

"Hello, Highflyer! My wife is not very well to-night. She has a severe pain in the back of her neck, and complains of a sort of goneness in the abdomen. . . . What shall I do for her?"

Here the wicked telephone girl switched on a machinist who was telling the owner of a saw mill what he thought ailed his boiler and the answer . . . was as follows:

"I think she's covered with scales inside about an inch thick. Let her cool down during the night, and before she fires up in the morning, take a hammer and pound her

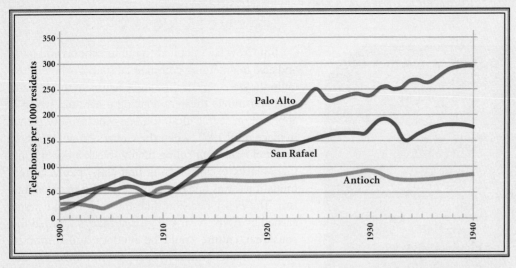

Based on Figure 9 from *A Social History of the Telephone to 1940*, by Claude S. Fischer (Berkeley: University of California Press, 1992). Copyright © 1992 by The Regents of the University of California. Used by permission of the University of California Press.

thoroughly all over, and then take a hose and hitch it on the fire plug and wash her out."

. . . The result is that No. 1,111 does not now speak to No. 2,222, and Dr. Highflyer has had the telephone taken out of his house.

**4. Estimated residential telephones in three California locations, 1900–1940 (top of page).** *Palo Alto was an affluent university town. Antioch was working-class. San Rafael had a mixed economy, including some industry; it served increasingly as a bedroom community for San Francisco professionals.*

**5. Telephone etiquette from "A Woman of Fashion,"** **1898.** *At the turn of the century, etiquette authorities began grudgingly to acknowledge the role of telephones in social life. Do you notice any contradictions in the advice below?*

Invitations by telephone, for anything other than informal engagements . . . are hopelessly vulgar. They should be the last resort. Invitations to bicycle or to play golf may be transmitted in this way, and the telephone is a blessing often in adjusting details, or making explanations; but for most social matters the use of the telephone is questionable, at best. Many women will stand with aching feet and irritated brow at a telephone for half an hour rather than write a note which would take four minutes. . . . Invitation by telephone is one of those modern innovations to which the conservative have never been accustomed, and which shocks elderly, conventional persons still. The convenience of the telephone for quickness and prompt response appeals, however, to so many persons, that it is hopeless and useless to inveigh against it. . . . If some one's note has been mislaid or forgotten, there is nothing simpler than to telephone to repair the error, and to explain. It is much speedier than sending a note. . . . There is no excuse for telephoning an invitation when time is not an object, or when the person invited is not an intimate friend.

**6. Bell Telephone advertisement, 1910.** *The text from this ad was accompanied by a picture of a young woman on the telephone with young men and women in a room behind her, dancing.*

*For Social Arrangements:* The informal invitation which comes over the phone is generally the most welcome. The Bell service makes it possible to arrange delightful social affairs at the last moment. . . .

*For Impromptu Invitations:* The easiest way to get up an informal party, quickly, is by telephone.

Sources: (2) Venus Green, *Race on the Line* (Durham, NC: Duke University Press, 2001), 67; (3) *Wheeling Register*, October 26, 1884; (5) *Etiquette for Americans* (New York: Herbert S. Stone & Co., 1898), 59, 70–71; (6) Claude S. Fischer, *America Calling* (Berkeley: University of California Press, 1992), 184.

## ANALYZING THE EVIDENCE

1. Consider the audience for each of these sources. Who was intended to read, view, or listen to it? What message does it convey?

2. Sources 2, 5, and 6 all give advice on how women should behave. Compare these pieces of advice. In what ways are they similar and different?

3. Based on these sources, which groups of Americans appear to have been affected by the arrival of telephones, and how?

## PUTTING IT ALL TOGETHER

Using evidence from these sources and your knowledge of the period, write an essay explaining how the telephone contributed to, and reflected, changes in American women's social and economic roles.

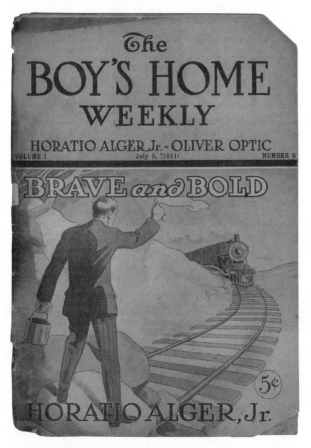

**Horatio Alger Jr.**

In dozens of popular boys' books published between 1867 and 1917, Horatio Alger Jr. assured young readers that if they were honest, worked hard, and cultivated good character, they could succeed in the new competitive economy. His heroes, such as the famous "Ragged Dick," often grew up in poverty on the streets of big cities. *Brave and Bold* (1874) told the story of a small-town boy forced to work in a factory; he is unfairly fired, but through persistence and courage he wins a good job and recovers an inheritance for his mother. Alger's books were republished often, as in this boys' magazine from 1911, and many remain in print today. Courtesy Stanford University Archives.

was brought by civil rights advocates on behalf of Homer Plessy, a New Orleans resident who was one-eighth black. Ordered to leave a first-class car and move to the "colored" car of a Louisiana train, Plessy refused and was arrested. The Court ruled that such segregation did not violate the Fourteenth Amendment as long as blacks had access to accommodations that were "separate but equal" to those of whites. "Separate but equal" was a myth: segregated facilities in the South were flagrantly inferior. Jim Crow segregation laws, named for a stereotyped black character who appeared in minstrel shows, clearly discriminated, but the Court allowed them to stand.

Jim Crow laws applied to public schools and parks and also to emerging commercial spaces—hotels, restaurants, streetcars, trains, and eventually sports stadiums and movie theaters. Placing a national stamp of approval on segregation, the *Plessy* decision remained in place until 1954, when the Court's *Brown v. Topeka Board of Education* ruling finally struck it down. Until then, blacks' exclusion from first-class "public accommodations" was one of the most painful marks of racism. The *Plessy* decision, like the rock-bottom wages earned by twelve-year-old girls at Macy's, showed that consumer culture could be modern and innovative without being politically progressive. Business and consumer culture were shaped by, and themselves shaped, racial and class injustices.

## Masculinity and the Rise of Sports

While industrialization spawned public domesticity—a consumer culture that courted affluent women and families—it also changed expectations for men in the workplace. Traditionally, the mark of a successful American man was economic independence: he was his own boss. Now, tens of thousands worked for other men in big companies—and in offices, rather than using their muscles. Would the professional American male, through his concentration on "brain work," become "weak, effeminate, [and] decaying," as one editor warned? How could well-to-do men assert their independence if work no longer required them to prove themselves physically? How could they develop toughness and strength? One answer was athletics.

**"Muscular Christianity"**   The **Young Men's Christian Association** (YMCA) was one of the earliest and most successful promoters of athletic fitness. Introduced in Boston in 1851, the group promoted muscular Christianity, combining evangelism with gyms and athletic facilities where men could make themselves "clean and strong." Focusing first on white-collar workers, the YMCA developed a substantial industrial program after 1900. Railroad managers and other corporate titans hoped YMCAs would foster a loyal and contented workforce, discouraging labor unrest. Business leaders also relied on sports to build physical and mental discipline and help men adjust their bodies to the demands of the industrial clock. Sports honed men's competitive spirit, they believed; employer-sponsored teams instilled teamwork and company pride.

Working-class men had their own ideas about sports and leisure, and YMCAs quickly became a site of negotiation. Could workers come to the "Y" to play billiards or cards? Could they smoke? At first, YMCA leaders said no, but to attract working-class men they had to make concessions. As a result, the "Y" became a place where middle-class and working-class customs blended—or existed in uneasy tension. At the same time, YMCA leaders innovated. Searching for winter activities in the 1890s, YMCA instructors invented the new indoor games of basketball and volleyball.

For elite Americans, meanwhile, country clubs flourished; both men and women could enjoy tennis, golf, and swimming facilities as well as social gatherings. By the turn of the century—perhaps because country club women were encroaching on their athletic turf—elite men took up even more aggressive physical sports, including boxing, weightlifting, and martial arts. As early as 1890, future president Theodore Roosevelt argued that such "virile" activities were essential to "maintain and defend this very civilization." "Most masterful nations," he claimed, "have shown a strong taste for manly sports." Roosevelt, son of a wealthy New York family, became one of the first American devotees of jujitsu. During his presidency (1901–1909), he designated a judo room in the White House and hired an expert Japanese instructor. Roosevelt also wrestled and boxed, urging other American men—especially among the elite—to increase their leadership fitness by pursuing the "strenuous life."

 To see a longer excerpt of Theodore Roosevelt's views on sports, along with other primary sources from this period, see *Sources for America's History*.

**America's Game**  Before the 1860s, the only distinctively American game was Native American lacrosse, and the most popular team sport among European Americans was cricket. After the Civil War, however, team sports became a fundamental part of American manhood, none more successfully than baseball. A derivative of cricket, the game's formal rules had begun to develop in New York in the 1840s and 1850s. Its popularity spread in military camps during the Civil War. Afterward, the idea that baseball "received its baptism in the bloody days of our Nation's direst danger," as one promoter put it, became part of the game's mythology.

Until the 1870s, most amateur players were clerks and white-collar workers who had leisure to play and the income to buy their own uniforms. Business frowned on baseball and other sports as a waste of time, especially for working-class men. But late-nineteenth-century employers came to see baseball, like other athletic pursuits, as a benefit for workers. It

provided fresh air and exercise, kept men out of saloons, and promoted discipline and teamwork. Players on company-sponsored teams, wearing uniforms emblazoned with their employers' names, began to compete on paid work time. Baseball thus set a pattern for how other American sports developed. Begun among independent craftsmen, it was taken up by elite men anxious to prove their strength and fitness. Well-to-do Americans then decided the sport could benefit the working class.

Big-time professional baseball arose with the launching of the National League in 1876. The league quickly built more than a dozen teams in large cities, from the Brooklyn Trolley Dodgers to the Cleveland Spiders. Team owners were, in their own right, profit-minded entrepreneurs who shaped the sport to please consumers. Wooden grandstands soon gave way to concrete and steel stadiums. By 1900, boys collected lithographed cards of their favorite players, and the baseball cap came into fashion. In 1903, the Boston Americans defeated the Pittsburgh Pirates in the first World Series. American men could now adopt a new consumer identity—not as athletes, but as fans.

**Rise of the Negro Leagues**  Baseball stadiums, like first-class rail cars, were sites of racial negotiation and conflict. In the 1880s and 1890s, major league managers hired a few African American players. As late as 1901, the Baltimore Orioles succeeded in signing Charlie Grant, a light-skinned black player from Cincinnati, by renaming him Charlie Tokohoma and claiming he was Cherokee. But as this subterfuge suggested, black players were increasingly barred. A Toledo team received a threatening note before one game in Richmond, Virginia: if their "negro catcher" played, he would be lynched. Toledo put a substitute on the field, and at the end of the season the club terminated the black player's contract.

Shut out of white leagues, players and fans turned to all-black professional teams, where black men could showcase athletic ability and race pride. Louisiana's top team, the New Orleans Pinchbacks, pointedly named themselves after the state's black Reconstruction governor. By the early 1900s, such teams organized into separate **Negro Leagues**. Though players suffered from erratic pay and rundown ball fields, the leagues thrived until the desegregation of baseball after World War II. In an era of stark discrimination, they celebrated black manhood and talent. "I liked the way their uniform fit, the way they wore their cap," wrote an admiring fan of

**TRACE CHANGE OVER TIME**
How and why did American sports evolve, and how did athletics soften or sharpen social divisions?

the Newark Eagles. "They showed a style in almost everything they did."

**American Football**   The most controversial sport of the industrializing era was football, which began at elite colleges during the 1880s. The great powerhouse was the Yale team, whose legendary coach Walter Camp went on to become a watch manufacturer. Between 1883 and 1891, under Camp's direction, Yale scored 4,660 points; its opponents scored 92. Drawing on the workplace model of scientific management, Camp emphasized drill and precision. He and other coaches argued that football offered perfect training for the competitive world of business. The game was violent: six players' deaths in the 1908 college season provoked a public outcry. Eventually, new rules protected quarterbacks and required coaches to remove injured players from the game. But such measures were adopted grudgingly, with supporters arguing that they ruined football's benefits in manly training.

Like baseball and the YMCA, football attracted sponsorship from business leaders hoping to divert workers from labor activism. The first professional teams emerged in western Pennsylvania's steel towns, soon after the defeat of the steelworkers' union. Carnegie Steel executives organized teams in Homestead and Braddock; the first league appeared during the anthracite coal strike of 1902. Other teams arose in the midwestern industrial heartland. The Indian-Acme Packing Company sponsored the Green Bay Packers; the future Chicago Bears, first known as the Decatur Staleys, were funded by a manufacturer of laundry starch. Like its baseball equivalent, professional football encouraged men to buy in as spectators and fans.

**Football Practice, Chilocco Indian School, 1911**

Football became widely popular, spreading from Ivy League schools and state universities to schools like this one, built on Cherokee land in Oklahoma. The uniforms of this team, typical of the day, show very limited padding and protection—a factor that contributed to high rates of injury and even death on the field. As they practiced in 1911, these Chilocco students had an inspiring model to look up to: in that year Jim Thorpe, a fellow Oklahoman and a member of the Sac and Fox tribe, was winning national fame by leading the all-Indian team at Pennsylvania's Carlisle School to victory against Harvard. Thorpe, one of the finest athletes of his generation, went on to win gold medals in the pentathlon and decathlon at the 1912 Olympics in Stockholm, Sweden. National Archives.

## The Great Outdoors

As the rise of sports suggests, elite and middle-class Americans began by the 1880s and 1890s to see Victorian culture as stuffy and claustrophobic. They revolted by heading outdoors. A craze for bicycling swept the country; in 1890, at the height of the mania, U.S. manufacturers sold an astonishing ten million bikes. Women were not far behind men in taking up athletics. By the 1890s, even elite women, long confined to corsets and heavy clothes that restricted their movement, donned lighter dresses and pursued archery and golf. Artist Charles Gibson became famous for his portraits of the Gibson Girl, an elite beauty depicted on the tennis court or swimming at the beach. The Gibson Girl personified the ideal of "New Women," more educated, athletic, and independent than their mothers.

Those with money and leisure time used railroad networks to get to the national parks of the West, which, as one senator put it, became a "breathing-place for the national lungs." People of more modest means began to take up camping. As early as 1904, California's Coronado Beach offered tent rentals for $3 a week. A decade later, campgrounds and cottages in many parts of the country catered to a working-class clientele. In an industrial society, the outdoors became associated with leisure and renewal rather than danger and hard work. One journalist, reflecting on urban life from the vantage point of a western vacation, wrote, "How stupid it all seems: the mad eagerness of money-making men, the sham pleasures of conventional society." In the wilderness, he wrote, "your blood clarifies; your brain becomes active. You get a new view of life."

As Americans searched for such renewal in remnants of unexploited land, the nation's first environmental movement arose. John Muir, who fell in love with the Yosemite Valley in 1869, became the most famous voice for wilderness. Raised in a stern Scots Presbyterian family on a Wisconsin farm, Muir knew much of the Bible by heart. He was a keen observer who developed a deeply spiritual relationship with the natural world. His contemporary Mary Austin, whose book *Land of Little Rain* (1905) celebrated the austere beauty of the California desert, called him "a devout man." In cooperation with his editor at *Century* magazine, Muir founded the **Sierra Club** in 1892. Like the earlier Appalachian Mountain Club, founded in Boston in 1876, the Sierra Club dedicated itself to preserving and enjoying America's great mountains.

Encouraged by such groups, national and state governments set aside more public lands for preservation and recreation. The United States substantially expanded its park system and, during Theodore Roosevelt's presidency, extended the reach of national forests. Starting in 1872 with the preservation of Yellowstone in Wyoming, Congress had begun to set aside land for national parks. In 1916, President Woodrow Wilson provided comprehensive oversight of these national parks, signing an act creating the **National Park Service** (Map 18.1). A year later, the system numbered thirteen parks — including Maine's Acadia, the first east of the Mississippi River.

Environmentalists also worked to protect wildlife. By the 1890s, several state Audubon Societies, named in honor of antebellum naturalist John James Audubon, banded together to advocate broader protections for wild birds, especially herons and egrets that were being slaughtered by the thousands for their plumes. They succeeded in winning the Lacey Act (1900), which established federal penalties for selling specified birds, animals, and plants. Soon afterward, state organizations joined together to form the **National Audubon Society**. Women played prominent roles in the movement, promoting boycotts of hats with plumage. In 1903, President Theodore Roosevelt created the first National Wildlife Refuge at Pelican Island, Florida.

Roosevelt also expanded preservation under the Antiquities Act (1906), which enabled the U.S. president, without congressional approval, to set aside "objects of historic and scientific interest" as national monuments. Two years later, Roosevelt used these powers to preserve 800,000 acres at Arizona's magnificent Grand Canyon. The act proved a mixed blessing for conservation. Monuments received weaker protection than national parks did; many fell under the authority of the U.S. Forest Service, which permitted logging and grazing. Business interests thus lobbied to have coveted lands designated as monuments rather than national parks so they could more easily exploit resources. Nonetheless, the creation of national monuments offered some protection, and many monuments (such as Alaska's Katmai) later obtained park status. The expanding network of parks and monuments became popular places to hike, camp, and contemplate natural beauty.

The great outdoors provided new opportunities for women with the means to travel. One writer, advising women to enjoy mountain hikes, hinted at liberating possibilities: "For those loving freedom and health," he recommended "short skirts, pantlets, stout shoes, tasty hat." And like other leisure venues, "wilderness" did not remain in the hands of elite men and women.

> **IDENTIFY CAUSES**
> What changes in American society precipitated the rise of national parks and monuments?

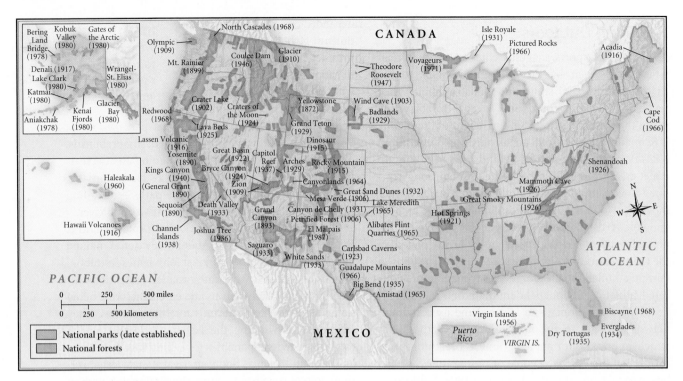

**MAP 18.1**

**National Parks and Forests, 1872–1980**

Yellowstone, the first national park in the United States, dates from 1872. In 1893, the federal government began to intervene to protect national forests. Without Theodore Roosevelt, however, the national forest program might have languished; during his presidency, he added 125 million acres to the forest system, plus six national parks in addition to several that had already been created during the 1890s. America's national forest and park systems remain one of the most visible and beloved legacies of federal policy innovation in the decades between the Civil War and World War I.

As early as the late 1880s, the lakes and hiking trails of the Catskill Mountains became so thronged with working-class tourists from nearby New York City, including many Jewish immigrants, that elite visitors began to segregate themselves into gated summer communities. They thus preserved the "seclusion and privacy" that they snobbishly claimed as the privilege of those who could demonstrate "mental and personal worth."

At the state level, meanwhile, new game laws triggered conflicts between elite conservationists and the poor. Shifting from year-round subsistence hunting to a limited, recreational hunting season brought hardship to poor rural families who depended on game for food. Regulation brought undeniable benefits: it suppressed such popular practices as songbird hunting and the use of dynamite to kill fish. Looking back on the era before game laws, one Alabama hunter remembered that "the slaughter was terrific." But while game laws prevented further extinctions like that of the passenger pigeon, which vanished around 1900, they made it harder for rural people to support themselves from the bounty of the land.

# Women, Men, and the Solitude of Self

Speaking to Congress in 1892, women's rights advocate Elizabeth Cady Stanton described what she called the "solitude of self." Stanton rejected the claim that women did not need equal rights because they enjoyed men's protection. "The talk of sheltering woman from the fierce storms of life is the sheerest mockery," she declared. "They beat on her from every point of the compass, just as they do on man, and with more fatal results, for he has been trained to protect himself."

Stanton's argument captured one of the dilemmas of industrialization: the marketplace of labor brought

**John Singer Sargent, *Mr. and Mrs. I. N. Phelps Stokes*, 1897**

This painting was a wedding gift to this wealthy young couple, both of whom inherited substantial fortunes. In what ways does the artist, a famous portraitist, represent Edith Minturn Stokes as a "New Woman" of the 1890s? What does he suggest about the relationship between husband and wife? How might we reconcile this with the painting's title, which identifies the central figure as "Mrs. I. N. Phelps Stokes," not as "Edith"? Mrs. Stokes was a noted beauty and active in an array of charitable causes. Here she wears a shirtwaist and skirt, more practical than the traditional heavy dresses and bustles of the previous decade. © The Metropolitan Museum of Art. Image source: Art Resource, NY.

both freedom and risk, and working-class women were particularly vulnerable. At the same time, middle-class women — expected to engage in selfless community service — often saw the impact of industrialization more clearly than fathers, brothers, and husbands did. In seeking to address alcoholism, poverty, and other social and economic ills, they gained a new sense of their own collective power. Women's protest and reform work thus helped lay the foundations for progressivism (Chapter 20) and modern women's rights.

## Changes in Family Life

The average American family, especially among the middle class, decreased in size during the industrial era. In 1800, white women who survived to menopause had borne an average of 7.0 children; by 1900, the average was 3.6. On farms and in many working-class families, youngsters counted as assets on the family balance sheet: they worked in fields or factories. But parents who had fewer sons and daughters could concentrate their resources, educating and preparing each child for success in the new economy. Among the professional classes, education became a necessity, while limiting family size became, more broadly, a key to upward mobility.

Several factors limited childbearing. Americans married at older ages, and many mothers tried to space pregnancies more widely — as their mothers and grandmothers had — by nursing children for several years, which suppressed fertility. By the late nineteenth century, as vulcanized rubber became available, couples also had access to a range of other contraceptive methods, such as condoms and diaphragms. With pressure for family limitation rising, these methods were widely used and apparently effective. But couples rarely wrote about them. Historians' evidence comes from the occasional frank diary and from the thriving success of the mail-order contraceptive industry, which advertised prominently and shipped products — wrapped in discreet brown paper packages — to customers nationwide.

Reluctance to talk about contraceptives was understandable, since information about them was stigmatized and, after 1873, illegal to distribute. During Reconstruction, Anthony Comstock, crusading secretary of the New York Society for the Suppression of Vice, secured a federal law banning "obscene materials" from the U.S. mail. The **Comstock Act** (1873) prohibited circulation of almost any information about sex and birth control. Comstock won support for the law, in part, by appealing to parents' fears that young people were receiving sexual information through the mail,

**Portrait of a Middle-Class American Family**

This photograph of the Hedlund family was taken on July 4, 1911, on the front porch of their home in St. Paul, Minnesota. Christian, Grace, and Anna Hedlund appear on the top row, Louis and George on the bottom. Families like this one — with three children — were becoming typical among the middle class, in contrast to larger families in earlier generations. This photo was taken by twenty-one-year-old Joseph Pavlicek, a recent immigrant from Eastern Europe who was boarding with the Hedlunds. Pavlicek bought fireworks for the children to celebrate the holiday. He remembered being so proud and grateful to be in America that his heart "was nearly bursting." Minnesota Historical Society.

**PLACE EVENTS IN CONTEXT**

In what ways did the Comstock Act reflect and contradict the realities of American life in the industrial era?

promoting the rise of "secret vice." Though critics charged Comstock with high-handed interference in private matters, others supported his work, fearful of the rising tide of pornography, sexual information, and contraceptives made available by industrialization. A committee of the New York legislature declared Comstock's crusade "wholly essential to the safety and decency of the community." It appears, however, that Comstock had little success in stopping the lucrative and popular trade in contraceptives.

## Education

In the industrial economy, the watchword for young people who hoped to secure good jobs was *education*. A high school diploma — now a gateway to a college

degree — was valuable for boys who hoped to enter professional or managerial work. Daughters attended in even larger numbers than their brothers (Table 18.1). Parents of the Civil War generation, who had witnessed the plight of war widows and orphans, encouraged girls to prepare themselves for teaching or office jobs, work before marriage, and gain skills they could fall back on, "just in case." By 1900, 71 percent of Americans between the ages of five and eighteen attended school. That figure rose further in the early twentieth century, as public officials adopted laws requiring school attendance.

Most high schools were coeducational, and almost every high school featured athletics. Recruited first as cheerleaders for boys' teams, girls soon established field hockey and other sports of their own. Boys and girls engaged in friendly — and sometimes not-so-friendly — rivalry in high school. In 1884, a high school newspaper in Concord, New Hampshire, published

| TABLE 18.1 | | | | |
| --- | --- | --- | --- | --- |
| **High School Graduates, 1870–1910** | | | | |
| Year | Number | Percent 17-Year-Olds | Male | Female |
| **1870** | 16,000 | 2.0 | 7,000 | 9,000 |
| **1890** | 44,000 | 3.0 | 19,000 | 25,000 |
| **1910** | 156,000 | 8.6 | 64,000 | 93,000 |

Source: *Historical Statistics of the United States*, 2 vols. (Washington, DC: U.S. Bureau of the Census, 1975), 1: 386.

this poem from a disgruntled boy who caricatured his female classmates:

> We know many tongues of living and dead,
> In science and fiction we're very well read,
> But we cannot cook meat and cannot make bread
> And we've wished many times that we were all dead.

A female student shot back a poem of her own, denouncing male students' smoking habit:

> But if boys will smoke cigarettes
> Although the smoke may choke them,
> One consolation still remains—
> *They kill the boys that smoke them.*

The rate of Americans attending college had long hovered around 2 percent; driven by public universities' expansion, the rate rose in the 1880s, reaching 8 percent by 1920. Much larger numbers attended a growing network of business and technical schools. "GET A PLACE IN THE WORLD," advertised one Minneapolis business college in 1907, "where your talents can be used to the best advantage." Typically, such schools offered both day and night classes in subjects such as bookkeeping, typewriting, and shorthand.

The needs of the new economy also shaped the curriculum at more traditional collegiate institutions. State universities emphasized technical training and fed the growing professional workforce with graduates trained in fields such as engineering. Many private colleges distanced themselves from such practical pursuits; their administrators argued that students who aimed to be leaders needed broad-based knowledge. But they modernized course offerings, emphasizing French and German, for example, rather than Latin and Greek. Harvard, led by dynamic president Charles W. Eliot from 1869 to 1909, pioneered the **liberal arts**. Students at the all-male college chose from a range of electives, as Eliot called for classes that developed each young man's "individual reality and creative power."

In the South, one of the most famous educational projects was Booker T. Washington's Tuskegee Institute, founded in 1881. Washington both taught and exemplified the goal of self-help; his autobiography, *Up from Slavery* (1901), became a best-seller. Because of the deep poverty in which most southern African Americans lived, Washington concluded that "book education" for most "would be almost a waste of time." He focused instead on industrial education. Students, he argued, would "be sure of knowing how to make a living after they had left us." Tuskegee sent female graduates into teaching and nursing; men more often entered the industrial trades or farmed by the latest scientific methods.

Washington gained national fame in 1895 with his **Atlanta Compromise** address, delivered at the Cotton States Exposition in Atlanta, Georgia. For the exposition's white organizers, the racial "compromise" was inviting Washington to speak at all. It was a move intended to show racial progress in the South. Washington, in turn, delivered an address that many interpreted as approving racial segregation. Stating that African Americans had, in slavery days, "proved our loyalty to you," he assured whites that "in our humble way, we shall stand by you . . . ready to lay down our lives, if need be, in defense of yours." The races could remain socially detached: "In all things that are purely social we can be as separate as the fingers, yet one as the hand in all things essential to mutual progress." Washington urged, however, that whites join him in working for "the highest intelligence and development of all."

Whites greeted this address with enthusiasm, and Washington became the most prominent black leader of his generation. His soothing rhetoric and style of leadership, based on avoiding confrontation and cultivating white patronage and

**TRACE CHANGE OVER TIME**
How did educational opportunities change after the Civil War, and for whom?

**Booker T. Washington**

In an age of severe racial oppression, Booker T. Washington emerged as the leading public voice of African Americans. He was remarkable both for his effectiveness in speaking to white Americans and for his deep understanding of the aspirations of blacks. Born a slave, Washington had plenty of firsthand experience with racism. But having befriended several whites in his youth, he also believed that African Americans could appeal to whites of good will—and maneuver around those who were hostile—in the struggle for equality. He hoped, most of all, that economic achievement would erase white prejudice. Brown Brothers.

institutions, including teacher-training colleges. For affluent families, private colleges offered an education equivalent to men's — for an equally high price. Vassar College started the trend when it opened in 1861; Smith, Wellesley, and others followed. Anxious doctors warned that these institutions were dangerous: intensive brain work would unsex young women and drain energy from their ovaries, leading them to bear weak children. But as thousands of women earned degrees and suffered no apparent harm, fears faded. Single-sex higher education for women spread from private to public institutions, especially in the South, where the Mississippi State College for Women (1885) led the way.

Coeducation was more prevalent in the Midwest and West, where many state universities opened their doors to female students after the Civil War. Women were also admitted to most African American colleges founded during Reconstruction. By 1910, 58 percent of America's colleges and universities were coeducational. While students at single-sex institutions forged strong bonds with one another, women also gained benefits from learning with men. When male students were friendly, they built comfortable working relationships; when men were hostile, women learned coping skills that served them well in later employment or reform work. One doctor who studied at the University of Iowa remembered later that he and his friends mercilessly harassed the first women who entered the medical school. But when the women showed they were good students, the men's attitudes changed to "wholesome respect."

Whether or not they got a college education, more and more women recognized, in the words of Elizabeth Cady Stanton, their "solitude of self." In the changing economy, they could not always count on fathers and husbands. Women who needed to support themselves could choose from dozens of guidebooks such as *What Girls Can Do* (1880) and *How to Make Money Although a Woman* (1895). The Association for the Advancement of Women, founded in 1873 by women's college graduates, defended women's higher education and argued that women's paid employment was a positive good.

Today, many economists argue that education and high-quality jobs for women are keys to reducing poverty in the developing world. In the United States, that process also led to broader gains in women's political rights. As women began to earn advanced degrees, work for wages and salaries, and live independently, it became harder to argue that women were "dependents" who did not need to vote.

private influence, was well suited to the difficult years after Reconstruction. Washington believed that money was color-blind, that whites would respect economic success. He represented the ideals of millions of African Americans who hoped education and hard work would erase white prejudice. That hope proved tragically overoptimistic. As the tide of disenfranchisement and segregation rolled in, Washington would come under fire from a younger generation of race leaders who argued that he accommodated too much to white racism.

In addition to African American education, women's higher education expanded notably. In the Northeast and South, women most often attended single-sex

**Class of 1896, Radcliffe College**

When Harvard University, long a bastion of male privilege, created an "Annex" for women's instruction in 1879, it was a sure sign of growing support for women's higher education. The Annex became Radcliffe College in 1894. Two years later, this graduating class of thirty posed for their portrait. Among them was Alice Sterling of Bridgeport, Connecticut, who went on to marry Harvard graduate Frank Cook and devote herself to Protestant foreign missions. On two trips around the world, Alice Sterling Cook visited all the women's colleges that missionaries had founded in India, China, and Japan. Cook's energetic public activities typified those of many women's college alumnae. Schlesinger Library, Radcliffe Institute for Advanced Study, Harvard University.

## From Domesticity to Women's Rights

As the United States confronted industrialization, middle-class women steadily expanded their place beyond the household, building reform movements and taking political action. Starting in the 1880s, women's clubs sprang up and began to study such problems as pollution, unsafe working conditions, and urban poverty. So many formed by 1890 that their leaders created a nationwide umbrella organization, the General Federation of Women's Clubs. Women justified such work through the ideal of **maternalism**, appealing to their special role as mothers. Maternalism was an intermediate step between domesticity and

modern arguments for women's equality. "Women's place is Home," declared the journalist Rheta Childe Dorr. But she added, "Home is the community. The city full of people is the Family. . . . Badly do the Home and Family need their mother."

**The Woman's Christian Temperance Union**   One maternalist goal was to curb alcohol abuse by prohibiting liquor sales. The **Woman's Christian Temperance Union** (WCTU), founded in 1874, spread rapidly after 1879, when charismatic Frances Willard became its leader. More than any other group of the late nineteenth century, the WCTU launched women into reform. Willard knew how to frame political demands

UNDERSTAND
POINTS OF VIEW
How did women use wide-
spread beliefs about their
"special role" to justify
political activism, and for
what goals?

in the language of feminine self-sacrifice. "Womanliness first," she advised her followers; "afterward, what you will." WCTU members vividly described the plight of abused wives and children when men suffered in the grip of alcoholism. Willard's motto was "Home Protection," and though it placed all the blame on alcohol rather than other factors, the WCTU became the first organization to identify and combat domestic violence.

The prohibitionist movement drew activists from many backgrounds. Middle-class city dwellers worried about the link between alcoholism and crime, especially in the growing immigrant wards. Rural citizens equated liquor with big-city sins such as prostitution and political corruption. Methodists, Baptists, Mormons, and members of other denominations condemned

drinking for religious reasons. Immigrants passionately disagreed, however: Germans and Irish Catholics enjoyed their Sunday beer and saw no harm in it. Saloons were a centerpiece of working-class leisure and community life, offering free lunches, public toilets, and a place to share neighborhood news. Thus, while some labor unions advocated voluntary temperance, attitudes toward prohibition divided along ethnic, religious, and class lines.

WCTU activism led some leaders to raise radical questions about the shape of industrial society. As she investigated alcohol abuse, Willard increasingly confronted poverty, hunger, unemployment, and other industrial problems. "Do Everything," she urged her members. Across the United States, WCTU chapters founded soup kitchens and free libraries. They introduced a German educational innovation, the kindergarten. They investigated prison conditions. Though she did not persuade most prohibitionists to follow her

THE TEMPERANCE CRUSADE—WHO WILL WIN?

**A Plea for Temperance, 1874**

The origins of the Woman's Christian Temperance Union lay in spontaneous prayer meetings held by women outside local saloons, where they appealed for men to stop drinking and liquor sellers to destroy their product. A string of such meetings in Ohio won national attention, as in this image from a popular magazine, the *Daily Graphic*. "Who Will Win?" asked the artist. The answers varied. A few saloon owners, struck with remorse over the damage caused by alcohol abuse, smashed their beer kegs and poured their liquor into the gutters. Far more refused, but in the 1880s, temperance women succeeded in organizing the largest grassroots movement of their day to build support for outlawing liquor sales. The Granger Collection, New York.

lead, Willard declared herself a Christian Socialist and urged more attention to workers' plight. She advocated laws establishing an eight-hour workday and abolishing child labor.

Willard also called for women's voting rights, lending powerful support to the independent suffrage movement that had emerged during Reconstruction. Controversially, the WCTU threw its energies behind the Prohibition Party, which exercised considerable clout during the 1880s. Women worked in the party as speakers, convention delegates, and even local candidates. Liquor was big business, and powerful interests mobilized to block antiliquor legislation. In many areas — particularly the cities — prohibition simply did not gain majority support. Willard retired to England, where she died in 1898, worn and discouraged by many defeats. But her legacy was powerful. Other groups took up the cause, eventually winning national prohibition after World War I.

Through its emphasis on human welfare, the WCTU encouraged women to join the national debate over poverty and inequality of wealth. Some became active in the People's Party of the 1890s, which welcomed women as organizers and stump speakers. Others led groups such as the National Congress of Mothers, founded in 1897, which promoted better child-rearing techniques in rural and working-class families. The WCTU had taught women how to lobby, raise money, and even run for office. Willard wrote that "perhaps the most significant outcome" of the movement was women's "knowledge of their own power."

**Women, Race, and Patriotism**   As in temperance work, women played central roles in patriotic movements and African American community activism. Members of the Daughters of the American Revolution (DAR), founded in 1890, celebrated the memory of Revolutionary War heroes. Equally influential was the United Daughters of the Confederacy (UDC), founded in 1894 to extol the South's "Lost Cause." The UDC's elite southern members shaped Americans' memory of the Civil War by constructing monuments, distributing Confederate flags, and promoting school textbooks that defended the Confederacy and condemned Reconstruction. The UDC's work helped build and maintain support for segregation and disenfranchisement (Chapter 15, Thinking Like a Historian, p. 502).

African American women did not sit idle in the face of this challenge. In 1896, they created the **National Association of Colored Women**. Through its local clubs, black women arranged for the care of orphans, founded homes for the elderly, advocated temperance,

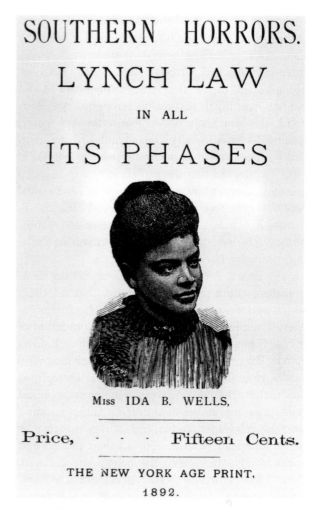

**Ida B. Wells**

In 1887, Ida Wells (Wells-Barnett after she married in 1895) was thrown bodily from a train in Tennessee for refusing to vacate her seat in a section reserved for whites, launching her into a lifelong crusade for racial justice. Her mission was to expose the evil of lynching in the South. This image is the title page of a pamphlet she published in 1892. Manuscripts, Archives and Rare Books Division, Schomburg Center for Research in Black Culture, New York Public Library, Astor, Lenox and Tilden Foundations.

and undertook public health campaigns. Such women shared with white women a determination to carry domesticity into the public sphere. Journalist Victoria Earle Matthews hailed the American home as "the foundation upon which nationality rests, the pride of the citizen, and the glory of the Republic." She and other African American women used the language of domesticity and respectability to justify their work.

One of the most radical voices was Ida B. Wells, who as a young Tennessee schoolteacher sued the Chesapeake & Ohio Railroad for denying her a seat in the ladies' car. In 1892, a white mob in Memphis invaded a grocery store owned by three of Wells's friends, angry that it competed with a nearby white-owned store. When the black store owners defended themselves, wounding several of their attackers, all three were lynched. Grieving their deaths, Wells left Memphis and urged other African Americans to join her in boycotting the city's white businesses. As a journalist, she launched a one-woman campaign against lynching. Wells's investigations demolished the myth that lynchers were reacting to the crime of interracial rape; she showed that the real cause was more often economic competition, a labor dispute, or a consensual relationship between a white woman and a black man. Settling in Chicago, Wells became a noted and accomplished reformer, but in an era of increasing racial injustice, few whites supported her cause.

The largest African American women's organization arose within the National Baptist Church (NBC), which by 1906 represented 2.4 million black churchgoers. Founded in 1900, the Women's Convention of the NBC funded night schools, health clinics, kindergartens, day care centers, and prison outreach programs. Adella Hunt Logan, born in Alabama, exemplified how such work could lead women to demand political rights. Educated at Atlanta University, Logan became a women's club leader, teacher, and suffrage advocate. "If white American women, with all their mutual and acquired advantage, need the ballot," she declared, "how much more do Black Americans, male and female, need the strong defense of a vote to help secure them their right to life, liberty, and the pursuit of happiness?"

**Women's Rights**   Though it had split into two rival organizations during Reconstruction, the movement for women's suffrage reunited in 1890 in the **National American Woman Suffrage Association** (NAWSA). Soon afterward, suffragists built on earlier victories in the West, winning full ballots for women in Colorado (1893), Idaho (1896), and Utah (1896, reestablished as Utah gained statehood). Afterward, movement leaders were discouraged by a decade of state-level defeats and Congress's refusal to consider a constitutional amendment. But suffrage again picked up momentum after 1911 (Map 18.2). By 1913, most women living west of the Mississippi River had the ballot. In other localities, women could vote in municipal elections, school elections, or liquor referenda.

The rising prominence of the women's suffrage movement had an ironic result: it prompted some women — and men — to organize against it, in groups such as the National Association Opposed to Woman Suffrage (1911). Antisuffragists argued that it was expensive to add so many voters to the rolls; wives' ballots would just "double their husbands' votes" or worse, cancel them out, subjecting men to "petticoat rule." Some antisuffragists also argued that voting would undermine women's special roles as disinterested reformers: no longer above the fray, they would be plunged into the "cesspool of politics." In short, women were "better citizens without the ballot." Such arguments helped delay passage of national women's suffrage until after World War I.

By the 1910s, some women moved beyond suffrage to take a public stance for what they called **feminism** — women's full political, economic, and social equality. A famous site of sexual rebellion was New York's Greenwich Village, where radical intellectuals, including many gays and lesbians, created a vibrant community. Among other political activities, women there founded the Heterodoxy Club (1912), open to any woman who pledged not to be "orthodox in her opinions." The club brought together intellectuals, journalists, and labor organizers. Almost all supported suffrage, but they had a more ambitious view of what was needed for women's liberation. "I wanted to belong to the human race, not to a ladies' aid society," wrote one divorced journalist who joined Heterodoxy. Feminists argued that women should not simply fulfill expectations of feminine self-sacrifice; they should work on their own behalf.

## Science and Faith

Amid rapid change, the United States remained a deeply religious nation. But new discoveries enhanced another kind of belief: faith in science. In the early nineteenth century, most Americans had believed the world was about six thousand years old. No one knew what lay beyond the solar system. By the 1910s, paleontologists were classifying the dinosaurs, astronomers had identified distant galaxies, and physicists could measure the speed of light. Many scientists and ordinary Americans accepted the theory of evolution.

Scientific discoveries received widespread publicity through a series of great world's fairs, most famously Chicago's 1893 World's Columbian Exposition, held (a year late) to celebrate Columbus's arrival in America in 1492. At the vast fairgrounds, visitors strolled through enormous buildings that displayed the latest inventions in industry, machinery, and transportation. They marveled over a moving sidewalk and, at dusk,

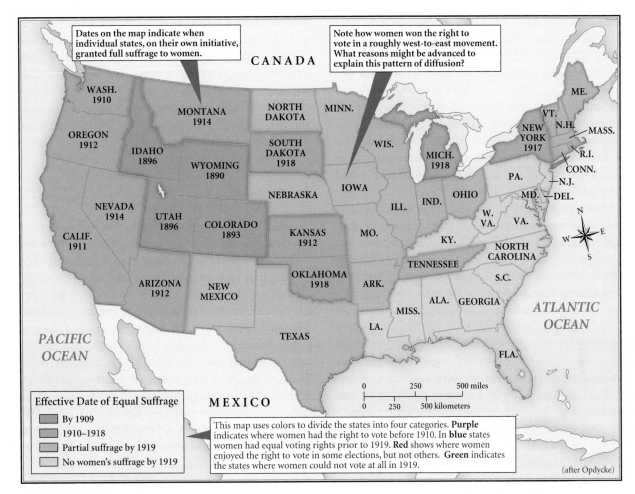

Dates on the map indicate when individual states, on their own initiative, granted full suffrage to women.

Note how women won the right to vote in a roughly west-to-east movement. What reasons might be advanced to explain this pattern of diffusion?

**Effective Date of Equal Suffrage**
- By 1909
- 1910–1918
- Partial suffrage by 1919
- No women's suffrage by 1919

This map uses colors to divide the states into four categories. **Purple** indicates where women had the right to vote before 1910. In **blue** states women had equal voting rights prior to 1919. **Red** shows where women enjoyed the right to vote in some elections, but not others. **Green** indicates the states where women could not vote at all in 1919.

(after Opdycke)

**MAP 18.2**
**Women's Suffrage, 1890–1919**

By 1909, after more than sixty years of agitation, only four lightly populated western states had granted women full voting rights. A number of other states offered partial suffrage, limited to voting for school boards and such issues as taxes and local referenda on whether or not to permit the sale of liquor licenses (the so-called local option). Between 1910 and 1918, as the effort shifted to the struggle for a constitutional amendment, eleven states joined the list granting full suffrage. The West remained the most progressive region in granting women's voting rights; the most stubborn resistance lay in the ex-Confederacy.

saw the fair buildings illuminated with strings of electric lights. One observer called the fair "a vast and wonderful university of the arts and sciences."

It is hardly surprising, amid these achievements, that "fact worship" became a central feature of intellectual life. Researchers in many fields argued that one could rely only on hard facts to understand the "laws of life." In their enthusiasm, some economists and sociologists rejected all social reform as sentimental. Fiction writers and artists kept a more humane emphasis, but they made use of similar methods—close observation and attention to real-life experience—to create works

of realism. Other Americans struggled to reconcile scientific discoveries with their religious faith.

## Darwinism and Its Critics

Evolution—the idea that species are not fixed, but ever changing—was not a simple idea on which all scientists agreed. In his immensely influential 1859 book, *On the Origin of Species*, British naturalist Charles Darwin argued that all creatures struggle to survive. When individual members of a species are born with random genetic mutations that better suit them for their environment — for example, camouflage coloring for a moth — these characteristics, since they are genetically transmissible, become dominant in future generations. Many scientists rejected this theory of **natural selection**. They followed a line of thinking laid out by French biologist Jean Baptiste Lamarck, who argued, unlike Darwin, that individual animals or plants could acquire transmittable traits within a single lifetime. A rhinoceros that fought fiercely, in Lamarck's view, could build up a stronger horn; its offspring would then be born with that trait.

Darwin himself disapproved of the word *evolution* (which does not appear in his book) because it implied upward progress. In his view, natural selection was blind: environments and species changed randomly. Others were less scrupulous about drawing sweeping conclusions from Darwin's work. In the 1870s, British philosopher Herbert Spencer spun out an elaborate theory of how human society advanced through "survival of the fittest." **Social Darwinism**, as Spencer's idea became (confusingly) known, found its American champion in William Graham Sumner, a sociology professor at Yale. Competition, said Sumner, was a law of nature, like gravity. Who were the fittest? "Millionaires," Sumner declared. Their success showed they were "naturally selected."

**PLACE EVENTS IN CONTEXT**
How did the ideas of scientists and social scientists reflect events they saw happening around them?

Even in the heyday of Social Darwinism, Sumner's views were controversial (American Voices, p. 596). Some thinkers objected to the application of biological findings to the realm of society and government. They pointed out that Darwin's theories applied to finches and tortoises, not human institutions. Social Darwinism, they argued, was simply an excuse for the worst excesses of industrialization. By the early twentieth century, intellectuals revolted against Sumner and his allies.

Meanwhile, though, the most dubious applications of evolutionary ideas were codified into new reproductive laws based on **eugenics**, a so-called science of human breeding. Eugenicists argued that mentally deficient people should be prevented from reproducing. They proposed sterilizing those deemed "unfit," especially residents of state asylums for the insane or mentally disabled. In early-twentieth-century America, almost half of the states enacted eugenics laws. By the time eugenics subsided in the 1930s, about twenty thousand people had been sterilized, with California and Virginia taking the lead. Women in Puerto Rico and other U.S. imperial possessions (Chapter 21) also suffered from eugenics policies. Advocates of eugenics had a broad impact. Because they associated mental unfitness with "lower races" — including people of African, Asian, and Native American descent — their arguments lent support to segregation and racial discrimination. By warning that immigrants from Eastern and Southern Europe would dilute white Americans' racial purity, eugenicists helped win passage of immigration restriction in the 1920s.

## Realism in the Arts

Inspired by the quest for facts, American authors rejected nineteenth-century romanticism and what they saw as its unfortunate product, sentimentality. Instead, they took up literary **realism**. In the 1880s, editor and novelist William Dean Howells called for writers "to picture the daily life in the most exact terms possible." By the 1890s, a younger generation of writers pursued this goal. Theodore Dreiser dismissed unrealistic novels that always had "a happy ending." In *Main-Travelled Roads* (1891), based on the struggles of his midwestern farm family, Hamlin Garland turned the same unsparing eye on the hardships of rural life. Stephen Crane's *Maggie: A Girl of the Streets* (1893), privately printed because no publisher would touch it, described the seduction, abandonment, and death of a slum girl.

Some authors believed realism did not go far enough to overturn sentimentalism. Jack London spent his teenage years as a factory worker, sailor, and tramp. In stories such as "The Law of Life" (1901), he dramatized what he saw as the harsh reality of an uncaring universe. American society, he said, was "a jungle wherein wild beasts eat and are eaten." Similarly, Stephen Crane tried to capture "a world full of fists." London and Crane helped create literary **naturalism**. They suggested that human beings were not so much rational shapers of their own destinies as blind victims of forces beyond their control — including their own subconscious impulses.

America's most famous writer, Samuel Langhorne Clemens, who took the pen name of Mark Twain, came to an equally bleak view. Though he achieved enormous success with such lighthearted books as *The Adventures of Tom Sawyer* (1876), Clemens courted controversy with *The Adventures of Huckleberry Finn* (1884), notable for its indictment of slavery and racism. In his novel *A Connecticut Yankee in King Arthur's Court* (1889), which ends with a bloody, technology-driven slaughter of Arthur's knights, Mark Twain became one of the bitterest critics of America's idea of

**John French Sloan, *A Woman's Work*, 1912**

The subject of this painting—a woman hanging out laundry behind a city apartment building—is typical of the subjects chosen by American artist John Sloan (1871–1951). Sloan and a group of his allies became famous as realists; critics derided them as the "Ash Can school" because they did not paint rural landscapes or other conventional subjects considered worthy of painting. Sloan, though, warned against seeing his paintings as simple representations of reality, even if he described his work as based on "a creative impulse derived out of a consciousness of life." " 'Looks like' is not the test of a good painting," he wrote: "Even the scientist is interested in effects only as phenomena from which to deduce order in life." Cleveland Museum of Art. Gift of Amelia Elizabeth White.

progress. Soon afterward, Clemens was devastated by the loss of his wife and two daughters, as well as by failed investments and bankruptcy. An outspoken critic of imperialism and foreign missions, Twain eventually denounced Christianity itself as a hypocritical delusion. Like his friend the industrialist Andrew Carnegie, Clemens "got rid of theology."

By the time Clemens died in 1910, realist and naturalist writers had laid the groundwork for **modernism**, which rejected traditional canons of literary taste. Questioning the whole idea of progress and order, modernists focused on the subconscious and "primitive" mind. Above all, they sought to overturn convention and tradition. Poet Ezra Pound exhorted, "Make it new!" Modernism became the first great literary and artistic movement of the twentieth century.

In the visual arts, new technologies influenced aesthetics. By 1900, some photographers argued that their "true" representations made painting obsolete. But painters invented their own forms of realism. Nebraska-born artist Robert Henri became fascinated with life in the great cities. "The backs of tenement houses are living documents," he declared, and he set out to put them on canvas. Henri and his followers, notably John Sloan and George Bellows, called themselves the New York Realists. Critics derided them as the Ash Can school because they chose subjects that were not conventionally beautiful.

In 1913, Realists participated in one of the most controversial events in American art history,

**EXPLAIN CONSEQUENCES**
What effect did technology and scientific ideas have on literature and the arts?

## Three Interpretations of Social Darwinism

The idea that human society advanced through "survival of the fittest" was a popular doctrine, referred to by historians as "Social Darwinism." Many Americans agreed with Harvard sociologist William Graham Sumner, who argued that the poor and weak were a "burden," a "dead-weight on the society in all its struggles." Such views prompted a range of responses, ranging from enthusiastic endorsement to uneasy accommodation to impassioned opposition.

### Theodore Dreiser
### *The Financier*

Theodore Dreiser (1871–1945) was an American literary naturalist. His novel *The Financier* (1912) traces the rise of Frank Cowperwood, a young man who, during the last years of the nineteenth century, becomes a powerful banker. Dreiser loosely based the character on the life of financier Charles Yerkes. In this excerpt, the narrator describes a transformative moment in Cowperwood's youth.

[Cowperwood] could not figure out how this thing he had come into — this life — was organized. How did all these people get into the world? What were they doing here? Who started things, anyhow? His mother told him the story of Adam and Eve, but he didn't believe it. . . .

One day he saw a squid and a lobster put in [a] tank, and in connection with them was witness to a tragedy which stayed with him all his life and cleared things up considerably intellectually. The lobster, it appeared from the talk of the idle bystanders, was offered no food, as the squid was considered his rightful prey. He lay at the bottom of the clear glass tank . . . apparently seeing nothing — you could not tell in which way his beady, black buttons of eyes were looking — but apparently they were never off the body of the squid. The latter, pale and waxy in texture, looking very much like pork fat or jade, moved about in torpedo fashion; but his movements were apparently never out of the eyes of his enemy, for by degrees small portions of his body began to disappear, snapped off by the relentless claws of his pursuer. . . .

[One day] only a portion of the squid remained. . . . In the corner of the tank sat the lobster, poised apparently for action. The boy stayed as long as he could, the bitter struggle fascinating him. Now, maybe, or in an hour or a day, the squid might die, slain by the lobster, and the lobster would eat him. He looked again at the greenish-copperish engine of destruction in the corner and wondered when this would be. . . .

He returned that night, and lo! the expected had happened. There was a little crowd around the tank.

The lobster was in the corner. Before him was the squid cut in two and partially devoured. . . .

The incident made a great impression on him. It answered in a rough way that riddle which had been annoying him so much in the past: "How is life organized?" Things lived on each other — that was it. Lobsters lived on squids and other things. What lived on lobsters? Men, of course! . . . And what lived on men? he asked himself. Was it other men? Wild animals lived on men. And there were Indians and cannibals. And some men were killed by storms and accidents. He wasn't so sure about men living on men; but men did kill each other. How about wars and street fights and mobs? . . .

Frank thought of this and of the life he was tossed into, for he was already pondering on what he should be in this world, and how he should get along. From seeing his father count money, he was sure that he would like banking; and Third Street, where his father's office was, seemed to him the cleanest, most fascinating street in the world.

Source: Theodore Dreiser, *The Financier* (New York: Harper and Brothers, 1912), 10–15.

### Lyman Abbott
### *The Evolution of Christianity*

Liberal Congregationalist Lyman Abbott (1835–1922) was a noted advocate of the Social Gospel. In *The Evolution of Christianity* (1892), Abbott sought to reconcile the theory of evolution with the development of Christianity.

The doctrine of evolution is not a doctrine of harmonious and uninterrupted progress. The most common, if not the most accurate formula of evolution is "struggle for existence, survival of the fittest." The doctrine of evolution assumes that there are forces in the world seemingly hostile to progress, that life is a perpetual battle and progress a perpetual victory.

The Christian evolutionist will then expect to find Christianity a warfare — in church, in society, in the individual. . . . He will remember that the divine life is resident in undivine humanity. He will not be surprised to find the waters of the stream disturbed; for he will reflect that the divine purity has come into a turbid stream, and that it can purify only by being itself indistinguishably combined with the impure. When he is told that modern Christianity is only a "civilized paganism," he will reply, "That is exactly what I supposed it to be; and it will continue to be a civilized paganism until civilization has entirely eliminated paganism." He will not be surprised to find pagan ceremonies in the ritual, ignorance and superstition in the church, and even errors and partialisms in the Bible. For he will remember that the divine life, which is bringing all life into harmony with itself, is a life resident in man. He will remember that the Bible does not claim to be the absolute Word of God; that, on the contrary . . . it claims to be the Word of God . . . as spoken to men, and understood and interpreted by men, which saw it in part as we still see it, and reflected it as from a mirror in enigmas.

He will remember that the Church is not yet the bride of Christ, but the plebeian daughter whom Christ is educating to be his bride. He will remember that Christianity is not the absolutely divine, but the divine in humanity, the divine force resident in man and transforming man into the likeness of the divine. Christianity is the light struggling with the darkness, life battling with death, the spiritual overcoming the animal. We judge Christianity as the scientist judges the embryo, as the gardener the bud, as the teacher the pupil, — not by what it is, but by what it promises to be.

Source: Lyman Abbott, *The Evolution of Christianity* (Boston: Houghton, Mifflin, 1892), 8–10.

## Lester Frank Ward
### Glimpses of the Cosmos

Lester Frank Ward (1841–1913) helped establish sociology in the United States. Following French philosopher Auguste Comte, he held that the social sciences should develop methods of improving society. In his autobiography *Glimpses of the Cosmos* (1913–1918), Ward rejected Social Darwinism.

How shall we distinguish this human, or anthropic, method from the method of nature? Simply by reversing all the definitions. Art is the antithesis of nature. If we call one the natural method, we must call the other the artificial method. If nature's process is rightly named natural selection, man's process is artificial selection. The survival of the fittest is simply the survival of the strong, which implies, and might as well be called, the destruction of the weak. And if nature progresses through the destruction of the weak, man progresses through the *protection* of the weak. . . .

. . . Man, through his intelligence, has labored successfully to resist the law of nature. His success is conclusively demonstrated by a comparison of his condition with that of other species of animals. No other cause can be assigned for his superiority. How can the naturalistic philosophers shut their eyes to such obvious facts? Yet, what is their attitude? They condemn all attempts to protect the weak, whether by private or public methods. They claim that it deteriorates the race by enabling the unfit to survive and transmit their inferiority. . . . Nothing is easier than to show that the unrestricted competition of nature does not secure the survival of the fittest possible, but only of the actually fittest, and in every attempt man makes to obtain something fitter than this actual fittest he succeeds, as witness improved breeds of animals and grafts of fruits. Now, the human method of protecting the weak deals in such way with men. It not only increases the number but improves the quality.

Source: Lester Frank Ward, *Glimpses of the Cosmos* (New York: Harper, 1913), 371, 374.

### QUESTIONS FOR ANALYSIS

1. By telling the squid and lobster story, what message was Dreiser conveying to readers, about men such as Cowperwood? If Abbott and Ward had read *The Financier*, how might they have responded? Why?

2. Historians sometimes claim that American thinkers of this era, endorsing Social Darwinism and "survival of the fittest," opposed social reform. How do Abbott and Ward complicate that view?

the Armory Show. Housed in an enormous National Guard building in New York, the exhibit introduced America to modern art. Some painters whose work appeared at the show were experimenting with cubism, characterized by abstract, geometric forms. Along with works by Henri, Sloan, and Bellows, organizers featured paintings by European rebels such as Pablo Picasso. America's academic art world was shocked. One critic called cubism "the total destruction of the art of painting." But as the exhibition went on to Boston and Chicago, more than 250,000 people crowded to see it.

A striking feature of both realism and modernism, as they developed, was that many leading writers and artists were men. In making their work strong and modern, they also strove to assert their masculinity. Paralleling Theodore Roosevelt's call for "manly sports," they denounced nineteenth-century culture as hopelessly feminized. Stephen Crane called for "virility" in literature. Jack London described himself as a "man's man, . . . lustfully roving and conquering." Artist Robert Henri banned small brushes as "too feminine." In their own ways, these writers and artists contributed to a broad movement to masculinize American culture.

## Religion: Diversity and Innovation

By the turn of the twentieth century, emerging scientific and cultural paradigms posed a significant challenge to religious faith. Some Americans argued that science and modernity would sweep away religion altogether. Contrary to such predictions, American religious practice remained vibrant. Protestants developed creative new responses to the challenges of industrialization, while millions of newcomers built institutions for worship and religious education.

**Immigrant Faiths**   Arriving in the United States in large numbers, Catholics and Jews wrestled with similar questions. To what degree should they adapt to Protestant-dominated American society? Should the education of clergy be changed? Should children attend

**Arthur B. Davies, *Dancers*, 1914–1915**
Artist Arthur Davies (1862–1928) was one of the primary organizers of New York's 1913 Armory Show, which introduced Americans to modernist art. An associate of John Sloan and other New York Realists, Davies experimented with an array of painting styles, as well as printmaking and tapestry making. This painting dates from a three-year period, just after the Armory Show, in which Davies experimented with Cubist techniques. *Dancers*, 1914–1915 (oil on canvas), Detroit Institute of Arts, USA/Gift of Ralph Harman Booth/The Bridgeman Art Library.

religious or public schools? What happened if they married outside the faith? Among Catholic leaders, Bishop John Ireland of Minnesota argued that "the principles of the Church are in harmony with the interests of the Republic." But traditionalists, led by Archbishop Michael A. Corrigan of New York, disagreed. They sought to insulate Catholics from the pluralistic American environment. Indeed, by 1920, almost two million children attended Catholic elementary schools nationwide, and Catholic dioceses operated fifteen hundred high schools. Catholics as well as Jews feared some of the same threats that distressed Protestants: industrial poverty and overwork kept working-class people away from worship services, while new consumer pleasures enticed many of them to go elsewhere.

Faithful immigrant Catholics were anxious to preserve familiar traditions from Europe, and they generally supported the Church's traditional wing. But they also wanted religious life to express their ethnic identities. Italians, Poles, and other new arrivals wanted separate parishes where they could celebrate their customs, speak their languages, and establish their own parochial schools. When they became numerous enough, they also demanded their own bishops. The Catholic hierarchy, dominated by Irishmen, felt the integrity of the Church was at stake. The demand for ethnic parishes implied local control of church property. With some strain, the Catholic Church managed to satisfy the diverse needs of the immigrant faithful. It met the demand for representation, for example, by appointing immigrant priests as auxiliary bishops within existing dioceses.

In the same decades, many prosperous native-born Jews embraced Reform Judaism, abandoning such religious practices as keeping a kosher kitchen and conducting services in Hebrew. This was not the way of Yiddish-speaking Jews from Eastern Europe, who arrived in large numbers after the 1880s. Generally much poorer and eager to preserve their own traditions, they founded Orthodox synagogues, often in vacant stores, and practiced Judaism as they had at home.

But in Eastern Europe, Judaism had been an entire way of life, one not easily replicated in a large American city. "The very clothes I wore and the very food I ate had a fatal effect on my religious habits," confessed the hero of Abraham Cahan's novel *The Rise of David Levinsky* (1917). "If you . . . attempt to bend your religion to the spirit of your surroundings, it breaks. It falls to pieces." Levinsky shaved off his beard and plunged into the Manhattan clothing business. Orthodox Judaism survived the transition to America, but like other immigrant religions, it had to renounce its claims to some of the faithful.

**Protestant Innovations**   One of the era's dramatic religious developments — facilitated by global steamship and telegraph lines — was the rise of Protestant foreign missions. From a modest start before the Civil War, this movement peaked around 1915, a year when American religious organizations sponsored more than nine thousand overseas missionaries, supported at home by armies of volunteers, including more than three million women. A majority of Protestant missionaries served in Asia, with smaller numbers posted to Africa and the Middle East. Most saw American-style domesticity as a central part of evangelism, and missionary societies sent married couples into the field. Many unmarried women also served overseas as missionary

**Christian Missions in Japan, 1909**

Through this colorful postcard, Protestant missionaries in Japan demonstrate their success in winning converts (at least a few) and their adaptation of missionary strategies to meet local needs and expectations. Here, outside their headquarters, they demonstrate "preaching by means of banners." The large characters on the vertical banner proclaim the "Association of Christian Gospel Evangelists." The horizontal banner is a Japanese translation of Matthew 11:28, "Come unto me, all ye who labor and are heavy laden, and I will give you rest."
© Bettmann/Corbis.

**IDENTIFY CAUSES**
How did America's religious life change in this era, and what prompted those changes?

teachers, doctors, and nurses, though almost never as ministers. "American woman," declared one Christian reformer, has "the exalted privilege of extending over the world those blessed influences, that are to renovate degraded man."

Protestant missionaries won converts, in part, by providing such modern services as medical care and women's education. Some missionaries developed deep bonds of respect with the people they served. Others showed considerable condescension toward the "poor heathen," who in turn bristled at their assumptions (America Compared, p. 601). One Presbyterian, who found Syrians uninterested in his gospel message, angrily denounced all Muslims as "corrupt and immoral." By imposing their views of "heathen races" and attacking those who refused to convert, Christian missionaries sometimes ended up justifying Western imperialism.

Chauvinism abroad reflected attitudes that also surfaced at home. Starting in Iowa in 1887, militant Protestants created a powerful political organization, the **American Protective Association** (APA), which for a brief period in the 1890s counted more than two million members. This virulently nativist group expressed outrage at the existence of separate Catholic schools while demanding, at the same time, that all public school teachers be Protestants. The APA called for a ban on Catholic officeholders, arguing that they were beholden to an "ecclesiastic power" that was "not created and controlled by American citizens." In its virulent anti-Catholicism and calls for restrictions on immigrants, the APA prefigured the revived Ku Klux Klan of the 1920s (Chapter 22).

The APA arose, in part, because Protestants found their dominance challenged. Millions of Americans, especially in the industrial working class, were now Catholics or Jews. Overall, in 1916, Protestants still constituted about 60 percent of Americans affiliated with a religious body. But they faced formidable rivals: the number of practicing Catholics in 1916—15.7 million—was greater than the number of Baptists, Methodists, and Presbyterians combined.

Some Protestants responded to the urban, immigrant challenge by evangelizing among the unchurched. They provided reading rooms, day nurseries, vocational classes, and other services. The goal of renewing religious faith through dedication to justice and social welfare became known as the **Social Gospel**. Its goals were epitomized by Charles Sheldon's novel *In His Steps* (1896), which told the story of a congregation

who resolved to live by Christ's precepts for one year. "If church members were all doing as Jesus would do," Sheldon asked, "could it remain true that armies of men would walk the streets for jobs, and hundreds of them curse the church, and thousands of them find in the saloon their best friend?"

The Salvation Army, which arrived from Great Britain in 1879, also spread a gospel message among the urban poor, offering assistance that ranged from soup kitchens to shelters for former prostitutes. When

**The Salvation Army on the Streets**

This theater poster for the popular play *On the Bowery* (1894), written by theater agent Robert Neilson Stephens, shows how many Americans perceived the Salvation Army. Here, Salvation Army workers in New York City offer the organization's newspaper, *War Cry*, to a man who brushes them off (rudely). The man is Steve Brodie, a celebrity who was recruited to portray himself onstage. A former East River lifesaving champion who became a saloon owner in New York's Bowery district, Brodie had won fame in 1886 by claiming to have jumped from the Brooklyn Bridge and survived. (It was later claimed that he faked the stunt, but "doing a Brodie" became popular slang for taking a big risk.) While many Americans admired the Salvation Army, others—particularly men of working-class origins, like Brodie— rejected its appeals. Library of Congress.

## Christianity in the United States and Japan

During the 1893 Chicago World's Columbian Exhibition, a Parliament of Religions brought together representatives of prominent faiths for discussion. English-speaking Protestants dominated the program, but several Asian representatives included Kinzo Hirai, a lay Buddhist from Japan. In his speech, Hirai reviewed Japan's experiences with the United States since Commodore Matthew C. Perry "opened" the country in 1853.

I do not understand why the Christian lands have ignored the rights and advantages of forty million souls of Japan for forty years. . . . One of the excuses offered by foreign nations is that our country is not yet civilized. Is it the principle of civilized law that the rights and profits of the so-called uncivilized, or the weaker, should be sacrificed? As I understand it, the spirit and necessity of law is to protect the rights and profits of the weaker against the aggression of the stronger. . . .

From the religious source, the claim is made that the Japanese are idolaters and heathen. . . . [A]dmitting for the sake of argument that we are idolaters and heathen, is it Christian morality to trample upon the rights and advantages of a non-Christian nation, coloring all their natural happiness with the dark stain of injustice? . . .

You send your missionaries to Japan and they advise us to be moral and believe Christianity. We like to be moral, we know that Christianity is good; and we are very thankful for this kindness. But at the same time our people are rather perplexed. . . . For when we think that the treaty stipulated in the time of feudalism, when we were yet in our youth, is still clung to by the powerful nations of Christendom; when we find that every year a good many western vessels of seal fishery are smuggled into our seas; when legal cases are always decided by the foreign authorities in Japan unfavorably to us; when some years ago a Japanese was not allowed to enter a university on the Pacific coast of America because of his being of a different race; when a few months ago the school board in San Francisco enacted a regulation that no Japanese should be allowed to enter the public school there; when last year the Japanese were driven out in wholesale from one of the territories of the United States; when our business men in San Francisco were compelled by some union not to employ Japanese assistants and laborers, but the Americans; when there are some in the same city who speak on the platform against those of us who are already here; when there are many who go in procession hoisting lanterns marked "Japs must go"; when the Japanese in the Hawaiian Islands were deprived of their suffrage; when we see some western people in Japan who erect before the entrance to their houses a special post upon which is the notice, "No Japanese is allowed to enter here" — just like a board upon which is written, "No dogs allowed"; when we are in such a situation, notwithstanding the kindness of the western nations from one point of view, who send their missionaries to us, that we unintelligent heathens are embarrassed and hesitate to swallow the sweet and warm liquid of the heaven of Christianity, will not be unreasonable.

Source: *The World's Parliament of Religions*, ed. John Henry Barrows (Chicago: Parliament Publishing Co., 1893), 444–450.

### ANALYZING THE EVIDENCE

1. What is Hirai's attitude toward American Christians?
2. Of what events is Hirai aware that are taking place in the United States? How does this shape his view of Christian missions in Japan?
3. How might American delegates to the Parliament, especially Protestant missionaries, have responded to Hirai?

all else failed, down-and-outers knew they could count on the Salvation Army, whose bell ringers became a familiar sight on city streets. The group borrowed up-to-date marketing techniques and used the latest business slang in urging its Christian soldiers to "hustle."

The Salvation Army succeeded, in part, because it managed to bridge an emerging divide between Social Gospel reformers and Protestants who were taking a different theological path. Disturbed by what they saw as rising secularism, conservative ministers and their allies held a series of Bible Conferences at Niagara Falls between 1876 and 1897. The resulting "Niagara Creed" reaffirmed the literal truth of the Bible and the certain damnation of those not born again in Christ. By the 1910s, a network of churches and Bible institutes had emerged from these conferences. They called their

**Billy Sunday with His Bible**
One of the most popular Protestant preachers of the early twentieth century, Billy Sunday (1862–1935) was a former professional baseball player with an imposing physique and dynamic preaching style. More willing than most of his predecessors to make direct political arguments, Sunday championed antiradicalism and prohibition—stances that foreshadowed the Protestant political crusades of the 1920s. Sunday's most famous sermon was his anti-liquor exhortation, "Get on the Water Wagon." Library of Congress.

movement **fundamentalism**, based on their belief in the fundamental truth of the Bible.

Fundamentalists and their allies made particularly effective use of revival meetings. Unlike Social Gospel advocates, revivalists said little about poverty or earthly justice, focusing not on the matters of the world, but on heavenly redemption. The pioneer modern evangelist was Dwight L. Moody, a former Chicago shoe salesman and YMCA official who won fame in the 1870s. Eternal life could be had for the asking, Moody promised. His listeners needed only "to come forward and take, TAKE!" Moody's successor, Billy Sunday, helped bring evangelism into the modern era. More often than his predecessors, Sunday took political stances based on his Protestant beliefs. Condemning the "booze traffic" was his greatest cause. Sunday also denounced unrestricted immigration and labor radicalism. "If I had my way with these ornery wild-eyed Socialists," he once threatened, "I would stand them up before a firing squad." Sunday supported some progressive reform causes; he opposed child labor, for example, and advocated voting rights for women. But in other ways, his views anticipated the nativism and antiradicalism that would dominate American politics after World War I.

Billy Sunday, like other noted men of his era, broke free of Victorian practices and asserted his leadership in a masculinized American culture. Not only was he a commanding presence on the stage, but before his conversion he had been a hard-drinking outfielder for the Chicago White Stockings. To advertise his revivals, Sunday often organized local men into baseball teams, then put on his own uniform and played for both sides. Through such feats and the fiery sermons that followed, Sunday offered a model of spiritual inspiration, manly strength, and political engagement. His revivals were thoroughly modern: marketed shrewdly, they provided mass entertainment and the chance to meet a pro baseball player. Like other cultural developments of the industrializing era, Billy Sunday's popularity showed how Americans often adjusted to modernity: they adapted older beliefs and values, enabling them to endure in new forms.

## SUMMARY

Industrialization and new consumer practices created foundations for modern American culture. While middle-class families sought to preserve the Victorian domestic ideal, a variety of factors transformed family life. Families had fewer children, and a substantial majority of young people achieved more education than their parents had obtained. Across class and gender lines, Americans enjoyed athletics and the outdoors, fostering the rise of environmentalism.

Among an array of women's reform movements, the Woman's Christian Temperance Union sought prohibition of liquor, but it also addressed issues such as domestic violence, poverty, and education. Members of women's clubs pursued a variety of social and economic reforms, while other women organized for race uplift and patriotic work. Gradually, the Victorian ideal of female moral superiority gave way to modern claims for women's equal rights.

New intellectual currents, including Darwinism, challenged Victorian certainties. In the arts, realist and naturalist writers rejected both romanticism and Vic–torian domesticity. Many Americans were shocked by the results, including Theodore Dreiser's scandalous novel *Sister Carrie*, Mark Twain's rejection of Christian faith, and the boldly modernist paintings displayed at New York's Armory Show. Science and modernism did not, however, displace religion. Newly arrived Catholics and Jews, as well as old-line Protestants, adapted their faith to the conditions of modern life. Foreign missions, in the meantime, spread the Christian gospel around the world, with mixed results for those receiving the message.

# CHAPTER REVIEW

**MAKE IT STICK**   Go to **LearningCurve** to retain what you've read.

## TERMS TO KNOW   Identify and explain the significance of each term below.

### Key Concepts and Events

*Plessy v. Ferguson* (p. 577)
**Young Men's Christian Association** (p. 580)
**Negro Leagues** (p. 581)
**Sierra Club** (p. 583)
**National Park Service** (p. 583)
**National Audubon Society** (p. 583)
**Comstock Act** (p. 585)
**liberal arts** (p. 587)
**Atlanta Compromise** (p. 587)
**maternalism** (p. 589)
**Woman's Christian Temperance Union** (p. 589)
**National Association of Colored Women** (p. 591)

**National American Woman Suffrage Association** (p. 592)
**feminism** (p. 592)
**natural selection** (p. 594)
**Social Darwinism** (p. 594)
**eugenics** (p. 594)
**realism** (p. 594)
**naturalism** (p. 594)
**modernism** (p. 595)
**American Protective Association** (p. 600)
**Social Gospel** (p. 600)
**fundamentalism** (p. 602)

### Key People

**Thomas Edison** (p. 576)
**John Muir** (p. 583)
**Booker T. Washington** (p. 587)
**Frances Willard** (p. 589)
**Ida B. Wells** (p. 591)
**Mark Twain (Samuel Langhorne Clemens)** (p. 594)
**Billy Sunday** (p. 602)

## REVIEW QUESTIONS   Answer these questions to demonstrate your understanding of the chapter's main ideas.

**1.** Why did athletics become popular in the late-nineteenth-century United States? In what ways did this trend represent broader changes in American society and culture?

**2.** What changes in women's private and public lives occurred in the decades after the Civil War, and how did these affect women from different backgrounds? Why do you think emphasis on the status of "ladies" became so insistent in this era?

3. Some historians argue that the changes brought by industrialization caused Americans to become a more secular people. To what extent do you agree or disagree, and why? Use evidence from this chapter to make your case.

4. What policy changes resulted, in part, from Americans' new zest for outdoor recreation? (You may also want to review Chapter 16, pp. 521 and 524–525 on John Wesley Powell, the creation of Yellowstone, and early wildlife conservation.)

5. **THEMATIC UNDERSTANDING**   On the Part 6 thematic timeline (p. 543), review developments in "Ideas, Beliefs, and Culture" and "Environment and Geography." How did industrialization change Americans' relationship to the outdoors — to natural environments? What connections do you see between those changes and other, broader shifts in American society and culture?

## MAKING CONNECTIONS

Recognize the larger developments and continuities within and across chapters by answering these questions.

1. **ACROSS TIME AND PLACE**   This chapter explains cultural transformation as largely the result of industrialization. That's true, but it's not the whole story: the Civil War also helped bring about change. Organizers of the WCTU, for example, were distressed by alcoholism among the industrial working class but also by the plight of veterans, some of whom anaesthetized their war wounds through heavy drinking. Review the material in Chapters 14 and 15, on the Civil War and its aftermath, and then write an essay in which you explain how changes in American society during the Civil War and Reconstruction laid the groundwork for new controversies in the areas of race relations, reform, science, and religious faith.

2. **VISUAL EVIDENCE**   This chapter contains several depictions of domestic spaces, and also of women in public. After studying these images, how would you describe the ideal roles that Americans of this era believed women should fulfill? Did the ideal differ, based on social and economic class? Compare these images to the photographs of women in this chapter. What differences do you see between the "ideal" depictions and the ways in which real women appeared in front of the camera?

## MORE TO EXPLORE   Start here to learn more about the events discussed in this chapter.

Patrick W. Carey, *The Roman Catholics in America* (1996). A major synthesis of American Catholic history.

Stephen Fox, *The American Conservation Movement* (1985). A history of the rise of environmentalism.

Glenda Gilmore, *Gender and Jim Crow* (1996). An influential account of African American women's activism in reform and politics.

Clifford Putney, *Muscular Christianity* (2001). A good introduction to the new ideas of masculinity that

emerged in this period, and their impact on religious faith.

Jonathan Sarna, *American Judaism* (2004). Provides an excellent account of the negotiations between Americanized Jews and new Eastern European immigrants in this era.

David Shi, *Facing Facts* (1994). Explores the impact of realism and scientific thinking on the arts and intellectual life.

**TIMELINE**   Ask yourself why this chapter begins and ends with these dates and then identify the links among related events.

| | |
|---|---|
| **1861** | • Vassar College founded for women |
| **1872** | • First national park established at Yellowstone |
| **1873** | • Association for the Advancement of Women founded<br>• Comstock Act |
| **1874** | • Woman's Christian Temperance Union founded |
| **1876** | • Baseball's National League founded<br>• Appalachian Mountain Club founded |
| **1879** | • Salvation Army established in the United States |
| **1881** | • Tuskegee Institute founded |
| **1885** | • Mississippi State College for Women founded |
| **1890** | • National American Woman Suffrage Association founded<br>• Daughters of the American Revolution founded |
| **1892** | • Elizabeth Cady Stanton delivers "solitude of self" speech to Congress<br>• John Muir founds Sierra Club |
| **1893** | • Chicago World's Columbian Exposition |
| **1894** | • United Daughters of the Confederacy founded |
| **1895** | • Booker T. Washington delivers Atlanta Compromise address |
| **1896** | • National Association of Colored Women founded<br>• Charles Sheldon publishes *In His Steps*<br>• *Plessy v. Ferguson* legalizes "separate but equal" doctrine |
| **1900** | • Lacey Act |
| **1903** | • First World Series<br>• First National Wildlife Refuge established |
| **1906** | • Antiquities Act |
| **1913** | • Armory Show of modern art held in New York City |
| **1916** | • National Park Service created |

**KEY TURNING POINT:** Some historians have argued that the 1890s was a crucial turning point in American culture — a decade when "modernity arrived." Based on events in this chapter, do you agree?

# 19
## CHAPTER

# "Civilization's Inferno": The Rise and Reform of Industrial Cities
## 1880–1917

Clarence Darrow, a successful lawyer from Ashtabula, Ohio, felt isolated and overwhelmed when he moved to Chicago in the 1880s. "There is no place so lonely to a young man as a great city," Darrow later wrote. "When I walked along the street I scanned every face I met to see if I could not perchance discover someone from Ohio." Instead, he saw a "sea of human units, each intent upon hurrying by." At one point, Darrow felt near despair. "If it had been possible I would have gone back to Ohio," he wrote, "but I didn't want to borrow the money, and I dreaded to confess defeat."

In the era of industrialization, more and more Americans had experiences like Darrow's. In 1860, the United States was rural: less than 20 percent of Americans lived in an urban area, defined by census takers as a place with more than 2,500 inhabitants. By 1910, more Americans lived in cities (42.1 million) than had lived in the entire nation on the eve of the Civil War (31.4 million). The country now had three of the world's ten largest cities (America Compared, p. 611). Though the Northeast remained by far the most urbanized region, the industrial Midwest was catching up. Seattle, San Francisco, and soon Los Angeles became hubs on the Pacific coast. Even the South boasted of thriving Atlanta and Birmingham. As journalist Frederic C. Howe declared in 1905, "Man has entered on an urban age."

The scale of industrial cities encouraged experiments that ranged from the amusement park to the art museum, the skyscraper to the subway. Yet the city's complexity also posed problems, some of them far worse than Clarence Darrow's loneliness. Brothels flourished, as did slums, pollution, disease, and corrupt political machines. Fast-talking hucksters enjoyed prime opportunities to fleece newcomers; homeless men slept in the shadows of the mansions of the superrich. One African American observer called the city "Civilization's Inferno." The locus of urgent problems, industrial cities became important sites of political innovation and reform.

**IDENTIFY THE BIG IDEA**

**How did the rise of large cities shape American society and politics?**

**George Bellows, *New York*** George Bellows, a member of the so-called Ash Can school of painters (Chapter 18), was fascinated by urban life. In this 1911 painting, he depicts Madison Square during a winter rush-hour, crowded with streetcars, horse-drawn wagons, and pedestrians. If you could enter the world of this painting, what might you hear, feel, and smell, as well as see? What does Bellows suggest about the excitement and challenges of life in the big city? Collection of Mr. and Mrs. Paul Mellon, National Gallery of Art, Washington, D.C.

# The New Metropolis

Mark Twain, arriving in New York in 1867, remarked, "You cannot accomplish anything in the way of business, you cannot even pay a friendly call without devoting a whole day to it. . . . [The] distances are too great." But new technologies allowed engineers and planners to reorganize urban geographies. Specialized districts began to include not only areas for finance, manufacturing, wholesaling, and warehousing but also immigrant wards, shopping districts, and business-oriented downtowns. It was an exciting and bewildering world.

## The Shape of the Industrial City

Before the Civil War, cities served the needs of commerce and finance, not industry. Early manufacturing sprang up mostly in the countryside, where mill owners could draw water power from streams, find plentiful fuel and raw materials, and recruit workers from farms and villages. The nation's largest cities were seaports; urban merchants bought and sold goods for distribution into the interior or to global markets.

As industrialization developed, though, cities became sites for manufacturing as well as finance and trade. Steam engines played a central role in this change. With them, mill operators no longer had to depend on less reliable water power. Steam power also vastly increased the scale of industry. A factory employing thousands of workers could instantly create a small city such as Aliquippa, Pennsylvania, which belonged body and soul to the Jones and Laughlin Steel Company. Older commercial cities also industrialized. Warehouse districts converted to small-scale manufacturing. Port cities that served as immigrant gateways offered abundant cheap labor, an essential element in the industrial economy.

**COMPARE AND CONTRAST**
How were America's industrial cities different from the typical city before 1860?

**Mass Transit**   New technologies helped residents and visitors negotiate the industrial city. Steam-driven cable cars appeared in the 1870s. By 1887, engineer Frank Sprague designed an electric trolley system for Richmond, Virginia. Electricity from a central generating plant was fed to trolleys through overhead power lines, which each trolley touched with a pole mounted on its roof. Trolleys soon became the primary mode of transportation in most American cities. Congestion and frequent accidents, however, led to demands that trolley lines be moved off streets. The "el" or elevated railroad, which began operation as early as 1871 in New York City, became a safer alternative. Other urban planners built down, not up. Boston opened a short underground line in 1897; by 1904, a subway running the length of Manhattan demonstrated the full potential of high-speed underground trains.

Even before the Civil War, the spread of railroads led to growth of outlying residential districts for the well-to-do. The high cost of transportation effectively segregated these wealthy districts. In the late nineteenth century, the trend accelerated. Businessmen and professionals built homes on large, beautifully landscaped lots in outlying towns such as Riverside, Illinois, and Tuxedo Park, New York. In such places, affluent wives and children enjoyed refuge from the pollution and perceived dangers of the city.

Los Angeles entrepreneur Henry Huntington, nephew of a wealthy Southern Pacific Railroad magnate, helped foster an emerging suburban ideal as he pitched the benefits of southern California sunshine. Huntington invested his family fortune in Los Angeles real estate and transportation. Along his trolley lines, he subdivided property into lots and built rows of bungalows, planting the tidy yards with lush trees and tropical fruits. Middle-class buyers flocked to purchase Huntington's houses. One exclaimed, "I have apparently found a Paradise on Earth." Anticipating twentieth-century Americans' love for affordable single-family homes near large cities, Huntington had begun to invent southern California sprawl.

**Skyscrapers**   By the 1880s, invention of steel girders, durable plate glass, and passenger elevators began to revolutionize urban building methods. Architects invented the skyscraper, a building supported by its steel skeleton. Its walls bore little weight, serving instead as curtains to enclose the structure. Although expensive to build, skyscrapers allowed downtown landowners to profit from small plots of land. By investing in a skyscraper, a landlord could collect rent for ten or even twenty floors of space. Large corporations commissioned these striking designs as symbols of business prowess.

The first skyscraper was William Le Baron Jenney's ten-story Home Insurance Building (1885) in Chicago. Though unremarkable in appearance—it looked just like other downtown buildings—Jenney's steel-girder construction inspired the creativity of American architects. A **Chicago school** sprang up, dedicated to the design of buildings whose form expressed, rather than masked, their structure and function. The presiding

**Woolworth Building, New York City**

Under construction in this photograph, taken between 1910 and 1913, the headquarters of the nationwide Woolworth's five-and-dime chain became a dominant feature of the New York skyline. Manhattan soon had more skyscrapers than any other city in the world. Library of Congress.

genius of this school was architect Louis Sullivan, whose "vertical aesthetic" of set-back windows and strong columns gave skyscrapers a "proud and soaring" presence and offered plentiful natural light for workers inside. Chicago pioneered skyscraper construction, but New York, with its unrelenting demand for prime downtown space, took the lead by the late 1890s. The fifty-five-story Woolworth Building, completed in 1913, marked the beginning of Manhattan's modern skyline.

**The Electric City**   One of the most dramatic urban amenities was electric light. Gaslight, produced from coal gas, had been used for residential light since the early nineteenth century, but gas lamps were too dim to brighten streets and public spaces. In the 1870s, as generating technology became commercially viable, electricity proved far better. Electric arc lamps, installed in Wanamaker's department store in Philadelphia in 1878, astonished viewers with their brilliant illumination. Electric streetlights soon replaced gaslights on city streets.

Before it had a significant effect on industry, electricity gave the city its modern tempo. It lifted elevators, illuminated department store windows, and above all, turned night into day. Electric streetlights made residents feel safer; as one magazine put it in 1912, "A light is as good as a policeman." Nightlife became less risky and more appealing. One journalist described Broadway in 1894: "All the shop fronts are lighted, and

the entrances to the theaters blaze out on the sidewalk." At the end of a long working day, city dwellers flocked to this free entertainment. Nothing, declared an observer, matched the "festive panorama" of Broadway "when the lights are on."

## Newcomers and Neighborhoods

Explosive population growth made cities a world of new arrivals, including many young women and men arriving from the countryside. Traditionally, rural daughters had provided essential labor for spinning and weaving cloth, but industrialization relocated those tasks from the household to the factory. Finding themselves without a useful household role, many farm daughters sought paid employment. In an age of declining rural prosperity, many sons also left the farm and—like immigrants arriving from other countries—set aside part of their pay to help the folks at home. Explaining why she moved to Chicago, an African American woman from Louisiana declared, "A child with any respect about herself or hisself wouldn't like to see their mother and father work so hard and earn nothing. I feel it my duty to help."

America's cities also became homes for millions of overseas immigrants. Most numerous in Boston were the Irish; in Minneapolis, Swedes; in other northern cities, Germans. Arriving in a great metropolis, immigrants confronted many difficulties. One Polish man,

**Lighting Up Minneapolis, 1883**
Like other American cities, Minneapolis at night had been lit by dim gaslight until the advent of Charles F. Brush's electric arc lamps. This photograph marks the opening day, February 28, 1883, of Minneapolis's new era: the first lighting of a 257-foot tower topped by a ring of electric arc lamps. The electric poles on the right, connecting the tower to a power station, would soon proliferate into a blizzard of poles and overhead wires, as Minneapolis became an electric city. © Minnesota Historical Society/CORBIS.

who had lost the address of his American cousins, felt utterly alone after disembarking at New York's main immigration facility, Ellis Island, which opened in 1892. Then he heard a kindly voice in Polish, offering to help. "From sheer joy," he recalled, "tears welled up in my eyes to hear my native tongue." Such experiences suggest why immigrants stuck together, relying on relatives and friends to get oriented and find jobs. A high degree of ethnic clustering resulted, even within a single factory. At the Jones and Laughlin steelworks

in Pittsburgh, for example, the carpentry shop was German, the hammer shop Polish, and the blooming mill Serbian. "My people . . . stick together," observed a son of Ukrainian immigrants. But he added, "We who are born in this country . . . feel this country is our home."

Patterns of settlement varied by ethnic group. Many Italians, recruited by *padroni*, or labor bosses, found work in northeastern and Mid-Atlantic cities. Their urban concentration was especially marked after the

# The World's Biggest Cities, 1800–2000

This table lists the ten largest cities in the world, by population in millions, at the start of the nineteenth, twentieth, and twenty-first centuries.

**TABLE 19.1**

### 1800

| City | Population |
| --- | --- |
| Beijing, China | 1.10 million |
| London, United Kingdom | 0.86 |
| Guangzhou, China | 0.80 |
| Istanbul, Turkey | 0.57 |
| Paris, France | 0.55 |
| Hangzhou, China | 0.50 |
| Edo (later Tokyo), Japan | 0.49 |
| Naples (later part of Italy) | 0.43 |
| Suzhou, China | 0.39 |
| Osaka, Japan | 0.38 |

### 1900

| City | Population |
| --- | --- |
| London, United Kingdom | 6.48 million |
| New York, United States | 4.24 |
| Paris, France | 3.33 |
| Berlin, Germany | 2.42 |
| Chicago, United States | 1.72 |
| Vienna, Austria | 1.66 |
| Tokyo, Japan | 1.50 |
| St. Petersburg, Russia | 1.44 |
| Philadelphia, United States | 1.42 |
| Manchester, United Kingdom | 1.26 |

### 2000

| City | Population |
| --- | --- |
| Tokyo, Japan | 34.45 million |
| Mexico City, Mexico | 18.02 |
| New York City/Newark, United States | 17.85 |
| São Paulo, Brazil | 17.10 |
| Mumbai (Bombay), India | 16.09 |
| Delhi, India | 15.73 |
| Shanghai, China | 13.22 |
| Calcutta, India | 13.06 |
| Buenos Aires, Argentina | 11.85 |
| Los Angeles, United States | 11.81 |

### QUESTIONS FOR ANALYSIS

1. In each year, how many of the world's ten largest cities were located in the United States? In what regions of the world were the other cities located? What does this tell us about the United States's role in the world at each of these historical moments?

2. The figures from 1900 and 2000 show, to a large degree, the effects of industrialization. What does the table suggest about its impact?

**The San Francisco Earthquake**

California's San Andreas Fault had caused earthquakes for centuries—but when a major metropolis arose nearby, it created new potential for catastrophe. The devastating earthquake of April 18, 1906, occurred at 5:12 A.M., when many residents were sleeping. This photograph of Sacramento Street shows the resulting devastation and fires. The quake probably killed over 2,000 people, though the exact number will never be known. A massive 296-mile rupture along the fault, felt as far away as Los Angeles, Oregon, and central Nevada, the earthquake refuted contemporary geological theories. It prompted researchers to open new lines of inquiry aimed at predicting tremors—and constructing urban buildings that could withstand them.
Universal History Archive / UIG / The Bridgeman Art Library.

1880s, as more and more laborers arrived from southern Italy. The attraction of America was obvious to one young man, who had grown up in a poor southern Italian farm family. "I had never gotten any wages of any kind before," he reported after settling with his uncle in New Jersey. "The work here was just as hard as that on the farm; but I didn't mind it much because I would receive what seemed to me like a lot." Amadeo Peter Giannini, who started off as a produce merchant in San Francisco, soon turned to banking. After the San Francisco earthquake in 1906, his Banca d'Italia was the first financial institution to reopen in the Bay area. Expanding steadily across the West, it eventually became Bank of America.

Like Giannini's bank, institutions of many kinds sprang up to serve ethnic urban communities. Throughout America, Italian speakers avidly read the newspaper *Il Progresso Italo-Americano*; Jews, the Yiddish-language *Jewish Daily Forward*, also published in New York. Bohemians gathered in singing societies,

while New York Jews patronized a lively Yiddish theater. By 1903, Italians in Chicago had sixty-six **mutual aid societies**, most composed of people from a particular province or town. These societies collected dues from members and paid support in case of death or disability on the job. Mutual benefit societies also functioned as fraternal clubs. "We are strangers in a strange country," explained one member of a Chinese *tong*, or mutual aid society, in Chicago. "We must have an organization (*tong*) to control our country fellows and develop our friendship."

Sharply defined ethnic neighborhoods such as San Francisco's Chinatown, Italian North Beach, and Jewish Hayes Valley grew up in every major city, driven by both discrimination and immigrants' desire to stick together (Map 19.1). In addition to patterns of ethnic and racial segregation, residential districts in almost all industrial cities divided along lines of economic class. Around Los Angeles's central plaza, Mexican neighborhoods diversified, incorporating Italians and Jews.

**MAP 19.1**

**The Lower East Side, New York City, 1900**

As this map shows, the Jewish immigrants dominating Manhattan's Lower East Side preferred to live in neighborhoods populated by those from their home regions of Eastern Europe. Their sense of a common identity made for a remarkable flowering of educational, cultural, and social institutions on the Jewish East Side. Ethnic neighborhoods became a feature of almost every American city.

Later, as the plaza became a site for business and tourism, immigrants were pushed into working-class neighborhoods like Belvedere and Boyle Heights, which sprang up to the east. Though ethnically diverse, East Los Angeles was resolutely working class; middle-class white neighborhoods grew up predominantly in West Los Angeles.

African Americans also sought urban opportunities. In 1900, almost 90 percent of American blacks still lived in the South, but increasing numbers had moved to cities such as Baton Rouge, Jacksonville, Montgomery, and Charleston, all of whose populations were more than 50 percent African American. Blacks also settled in northern cities, albeit not in the numbers that would arrive during the Great Migration of World War I. Though blacks constituted only 2 percent of New York City's population in 1910, they already numbered more than 90,000. These newcomers confronted conditions even worse than those for foreign-born immigrants. Relentlessly turned away from manufacturing jobs, most black men and

**PLACE EVENTS IN CONTEXT**

What opportunities did urban neighborhoods provide to immigrants and African Americans, and what problems did these newcomers face?

**The Cherry Family, 1906**

Wiley and Fannie Cherry migrated in 1893 from North Carolina to Chicago, settling in the small African American community that had established itself on the city's West Side. The Cherrys apparently prospered. By 1906, when this family portrait was taken, they had entered the black middle class. When migration intensified after 1900, longer-settled urban blacks like the Cherrys often became uncomfortable, and relations with needy rural newcomers were sometimes tense. Collection of Lorraine Heflin/Picture Research Consultants & Archives.

women took up work in the service sector, becoming porters, laundrywomen, and domestic servants.

Blacks faced another urban danger: the so-called **race riot**, an attack by white mobs triggered by street altercations or rumors of crime. One of the most virulent episodes occurred in Atlanta, Georgia, in 1906. The violence was fueled by a nasty political campaign that generated sensational false charges of "negro crime." Roaming bands of white men attacked black Atlantans, invading middle-class black neighborhoods and in one case lynching two barbers after seizing them in their shop. The rioters killed at least twenty-four blacks and wounded more than a hundred. The disease of hatred was not limited to the South. Race riots broke out in New York City's Tenderloin district (1900);

Evansville, Indiana (1903); and Springfield, Illinois (1908). By then, one journalist observed, "In every important Northern city, a distinct race-problem already exists which must, in a few years, assume serious proportions."

Whether they arrived from the South or from Europe, Mexico, or Asia, working-class city residents needed cheap housing near their jobs (Map 19.2). They faced grim choices. As urban land values climbed, speculators tore down houses that were vacated by middle-class families moving away from the industrial core. In their place, they erected five- or six-story **tenements**, buildings that housed twenty or more families in cramped, airless apartments (Figure 19.1). Tenements fostered rampant disease and horrific infant mortality.

**The Atlanta Race Riot—Seen from France**
The cover of this Paris newsmagazine depicts the Atlanta race riot of 1906. While the artist had almost certainly never visited Atlanta, his dramatic illustration shows that, from this early date, racial violence could be a source of embarrassment to the United States in its relations with other countries. Picture Research Consultants & Archives.

In New York's Eleventh Ward, an average of 986 persons occupied each acre. One investigator in Philadelphia described twenty-six people living in nine rooms of a tenement. "The bathroom at the rear of the house was used as a kitchen," she reported. "One privy compartment in the yard was the sole toilet accommodation for the five families living in the house." African Americans often suffered most. A study of Albany, Syracuse, and Troy, New York, noted, "The colored people are relegated to the least healthful buildings."

Denouncing these conditions, reformers called for model tenements financed by public-spirited citizens willing to accept a limited return on their investment. When private philanthropy failed to make a dent, cities turned to housing codes. The most advanced was New York's Tenement House Law of 1901, which required interior courts, indoor toilets, and fire safeguards for new structures. The law, however, had no effect on the 44,000 tenements that already existed in Manhattan and the Bronx. Reformers were thwarted by the economic facts of urban development. Industrial workers could not afford transportation and had to live near their jobs; commercial development pushed up land values. Only high-density, cheaply built housing earned landlords a significant profit.

## City Cultures

Despite their dangers and problems, industrial cities could be exciting places to live. In the nineteenth century, white middle-class Protestants had set the cultural standard; immigrants and the poor were expected to follow cues from their betters, seeking "uplift" and respectability. But in the cities, new mass-based entertainments emerged among the working classes, especially youth. These entertainments spread from the working class to the middle class—much to the distress of many middle-class parents. At the same time, cities became stimulating centers for intellectual life.

**Urban Amusements**   One enticing attraction was **vaudeville theater**, which arose in the 1880s and 1890s. Vaudeville customers could walk in anytime and watch a continuous sequence of musical acts, skits, magic shows, and other entertainment. First popular among the working class, vaudeville quickly broadened its appeal to include middle-class audiences. By the early 1900s, vaudeville faced competition from early movie theaters, or nickelodeons, which offered short films for a nickel entry fee. With distaste, one reporter described a typical movie audience as "mothers of bawling infants" and "newsboys, bootblacks, and smudgy urchins." By the 1910s, even working girls who refrained from less respectable amusements might indulge in a movie once or twice a week.

More spectacular were the great amusement parks that appeared around 1900, most famously at New York's Coney Island. These parks had their origins in world's fairs, whose paid entertainment areas had offered giant Ferris wheels and camel rides through "a street in Cairo." Entrepreneurs found that such attractions were big business. Between 1895 and 1904, they installed them at several rival amusement parks near Coney Island's popular beaches. The parks offered New Yorkers a

**COMPARE AND CONTRAST**
How did working-class and elite city residents differ in how they spent their money and leisure time?

The residential areas of the city tended to spread out along elevated (light-rail) railroad lines and streetcar tracks. These new forms of mass transit enabled people living in distant neighborhoods to reach the central business district and other places of employment.

Note that the number of square miles within Chicago's city limits increased more than 300 percent between 1865 and 1902.

Note that some areas of the old city were not used for either residence or industry. Most of these were large regional parks or undeveloped land.

City limits, 1902

*Lake Michigan*

Central Business District

Horsecar lines, 1865

City limits, 1865

*Lake Calumet*

0    1    2    3 miles

■ Central Business District
■ Industrial area
■ Residential area
■ Parks and undeveloped land
•••• Elevated lines, 1902
— Streetcar lines, 1902

**MAP 19.2**

**The Expansion of Chicago, 1865–1902**

In 1865, Chicagoans depended on horsecar lines to get around town. By 1900, the city limits had expanded enormously and so had the streetcar service, which was by then electrified. Elevated trains eased the congestion on downtown streets. Ongoing extension of the streetcar lines, some beyond the city limits, ensured that suburban development would continue as well.

Air Shaft (Toilets)

Parlor | Kitchen | Bed Room | Bed Room | Bed Room | Kitchen | Parlor

Public    Hall

Parlor | Kitchen | Bed Room | Bed Room | Bed Room | Kitchen | Parlor

Air Shaft

50'0"

10'

Fire Escape

**FIGURE 19.1**

**Floor Plan of a Dumbbell Tenement**

In a contest for a design that met an 1879 requirement for every room to have a window, the dumbbell tenement won. The interior indentation, which created an airshaft between adjoining buildings, gave the tenement its "dumbbell" shape. But what was touted as a model tenement demonstrated instead the futility of trying to reconcile maximum land usage with decent housing. Each floor contained four apartments of three or four rooms, the largest only 10 by 11 feet. The two toilets in the hall became filthy or broke down under daily use by forty or more people. The narrow airshaft provided almost no light for the interior rooms and served mainly as a dumping ground for garbage. So deplorable were these tenements that they became the stimulus for the next wave of New York housing reform.

**Amusement Park, Long Beach, California**
The origins of the roller coaster go back to a Switchback Railway installed at New York's Coney Island in 1884, featuring gentle dips and curves. By 1900, when the Jack Rabbit Race was constructed at Long Beach, California, the goal was to create the biggest possible thrill. Angelenos journeyed by trolley to Long Beach to take a dip in the ocean as well as to ride the new roller coaster—and the airplane ride in the foreground. © Curt Teich Postcard Archives, Lake County Museum.

chance to come by ferry, escape the hot city, and enjoy roller coasters, lagoon plunges, and "hootchy-kootchy" dance shows. Among the amazed observers was Cuban revolutionary José Martí, working as a journalist in the United States. "What facilities for every pleasure!" Martí wrote. "What absolute absence of any outward sadness or poverty! . . . The theater, the photographers' booth, the bathhouses!" He concluded that Coney Island epitomized America's commercial society, driven not by "love or glory" but by "a desire for gain." Similar parks grew up around the United States. By the summer of 1903, Philadelphia's Willow Grove counted three million visitors annually; so did two amusement parks outside Los Angeles.

**Ragtime and City Blues**   Music also became a booming urban entertainment. By the 1890s, Tin Pan Alley, the nickname for New York City's song-publishing district, produced such national hit tunes as "A Bicycle Built for Two" and "My Wild Irish Rose." The most famous sold more than a million copies of sheet music, as well as audio recordings for the newly invented phonograph. To find out what would sell, publishers had musicians play at New York's working-class beer gardens and dance halls. One publishing agent, who visited "sixty joints a week" to test new songs, declared that "the best songs came from the gutter."

African American musicians brought a syncopated beat that began, by the 1890s, to work its way into mainstream hits like "A Hot Time in the Old Town Tonight." Black performers became stars in their own right with the rise of **ragtime**. This music, apparently named for its ragged rhythm, combined a steady beat in the bass (played with the left hand on the piano) with syncopated, off-beat rhythms in the treble (played with the right). Ragtime became wildly popular among audiences of all classes and races who heard in its infectious rhythms something exciting—a decisive break with Victorian hymns and parlor songs.

For the master of the genre, composer Scott Joplin, ragtime was serious music. Joplin, the son of former slaves, grew up along the Texas-Arkansas border and took piano lessons as a boy from a German teacher. He and other traveling performers introduced ragtime to national audiences at the Chicago World's Fair in 1893. Seeking to elevate African American music and secure a broad national audience, Joplin warned pianists, "It is never right to play 'Ragtime' fast." But his instructions were widely ignored. Young Americans embraced ragtime.

They also embraced each other, as ragtime ushered in an urban dance craze. By 1910, New York alone had more than five hundred dance halls. In Kansas City, shocked guardians of morality counted 16,500 dancers on the floor on a Saturday night; Chicago had 86,000. Some young Polish and Slovak women chose restaurant jobs rather than domestic service so they would have free time to visit dance halls "several nights a week." New dances like the Bunny Hug and Grizzly Bear were overtly sexual: they called for close body contact and plenty of hip movement. In fact, many of these dances originated in brothels. Despite widespread denunciation, dance mania quickly spread from the urban working classes to rural and middle-class youth.

By the 1910s, black music was achieving a central place in American popular culture. African American trumpet player and bandleader W. C. Handy, born in Alabama, electrified national audiences by performing music drawn from the cotton fields of the Mississippi Delta. Made famous when it reached the big city, this music became known as the **blues**. Blues music spoke of hard work and heartbreak, as in Handy's popular hit "St. Louis Blues" (1914):

> Got de St. Louis Blues jes blue as I can be,
> Dat man got a heart lak a rock cast in the sea,
> Or else he wouldn't gone so far from me.

Blues spoke to the emotional lives of young urbanites who were far from home, experiencing dislocation, loneliness, and bitter disappointment along with the thrills of city life. Like Coney Island and other leisure activities, ragtime and blues helped forge new collective experiences in a world of strangers.

Ragtime and blues spread quickly and had a profound influence on twentieth-century American culture. By the time Handy published "St. Louis Blues," composer Irving Berlin, a Russian Jewish immigrant, was introducing altered ragtime pieces into musical theater — which eventually transferred to radio and film. Lyrics often featured sexual innuendo, as in the title of Berlin's hit song "If You Don't Want My Peaches (You'd Better Stop Shaking My Tree)." The popularity of such music marked the arrival of modern youth culture. Its enduring features included "crossover" music that originated in the black working class and a commercial music industry that brazenly appropriated African American musical styles.

### Sex and the City

In the city, many young people found parental oversight weaker than it had been before. Amusement parks and dance halls helped foster the new custom of dating, which like other cultural innovations emerged first among the working class. Gradually, it became acceptable for a young man to escort a young woman out on the town for commercial entertainments rather than spending time at home under a chaperone's watchful eye. Dating opened a new world of pleasure, sexual adventure, and danger. Young women headed to dance halls alone to meet men; the term *gold digger* came into use to describe a woman who wanted a man's money more than the man himself.

But young women, not men, proved most vulnerable in the system of dating. Having less money to spend because they earned half or less of men's wages, working-class girls relied on the "treat." Some tried to maintain strict standards of respectability, keenly aware that their prospects for marriage depended on a virtuous reputation. Others became so-called charity girls, eager for a good time. Such young women, one investigator reported, "offer themselves to strangers, not for money, but for presents, attention and pleasure." For some women, sexual favors were a matter of practical necessity. "If I did not have a man," declared one waitress, "I could not get along on my wages." In the anonymous city, there was not always a clear line between working-class treats and casual prostitution.

Dating and casual sex were hallmarks of an urban world in which large numbers of residents were young and single. The 1900 census found that more than 20 percent of women in Detroit, Philadelphia, and Boston lived as boarders and lodgers, not in family units; the percentage topped 30 percent in St. Paul and Minneapolis. Single men also found social opportunities in the city. One historian has called the late nineteenth century the Age of the Bachelor, a time when being an unattached male lost its social stigma. With boardinghouses, restaurants, and abundant personal services, the city afforded bachelors all the comforts of home and, on top of that, an array of men's clubs, saloons, and sporting events.

Many industrial cities developed robust gay subcultures. New York's gay underground, for example, included an array of drinking and meeting places, as well as clubs and drag balls. Middle-class men, both straight and gay, frequented such venues for entertainment or to find companionship. One medical student remembered being taken to a ball at which he was startled to find five hundred gay and lesbian couples waltzing to "a good band." By the 1910s, the word *queer* had come into use as slang for *homosexual*. Though harassment was frequent and moral reformers like Anthony Comstock issued regular denunciations of sexual "degeneracy," arrests were few. Gay sex shows and saloons were lucrative for those who ran them (and for police, who took bribes to look the other way, just as they did for brothels). The exuberant gay urban subculture offered a dramatic challenge to Victorian ideals.

### High Culture

For elites, the rise of great cities offered an opportunity to build museums, libraries, and other cultural institutions that could flourish only in major metropolitan centers. Millionaires patronized the arts partly to advance themselves socially but also out of a sense of civic duty and national pride. As early as the 1870s, symphony orchestras emerged in Boston and New York. Composers and conductors soon joined Europe in new experiments. The Metropolitan Opera, founded in 1883 by wealthy businessmen, drew enthusiastic crowds to hear the innovative work of Richard Wagner. In 1907, the Met shocked audiences by presenting Richard Strauss's sexually scandalous opera *Salome*.

Art museums and natural history museums also became prominent new institutions in this era. The nation's first major art museum, the Corcoran Gallery of Art, opened in Washington, D.C., in 1869, while New York's Metropolitan Museum of Art settled into its permanent home in 1880. In the same decades, public libraries grew from modest collections into major urban institutions. The greatest library benefactor was steel magnate Andrew Carnegie, who announced in 1881 that he would build a library in any town or city that was prepared to maintain it. By 1907, Carnegie had spent more than $32.7 million to establish over a thousand libraries throughout the United States.

**Urban Journalism**    Patrons of Carnegie's libraries could read, in addition to books, an increasing array of mass-market newspapers. Joseph Pulitzer, owner of the *St. Louis Post-Dispatch* and *New York World*, led the way in building his sales base with sensational investigations, human-interest stories, and targeted sections covering sports and high society. By the 1890s, Pulitzer faced a challenge from William Randolph Hearst (Thinking Like a Historian, p. 620). The arrival of Sunday color comics featuring the "Yellow Kid" gave such publications the name *yellow journalism*, a derogatory term for mass-market newspapers. Hearst's and Pulitzer's sensational coverage was often irresponsible. In the late 1890s, for example, their papers helped whip up frenzied pressure for the United States to declare war against Spain (Chapter 21). But Hearst and Pulitzer also exposed scandals and injustices. They believed their papers should challenge the powerful by speaking to and for ordinary Americans.

Along with Hearst's and Pulitzer's stunt reporters, other urban journalists also worked to promote reform. New magazines such as *McClure's* introduced national audiences to reporters such as Ida Tarbell, who exposed the machinations of John D. Rockefeller, and David Graham Phillips, whose "Treason of the Senate," published in *Cosmopolitan* in 1906, documented the deference of U.S. senators — especially Republicans — to wealthy corporate interests. Theodore Roosevelt dismissed such writers as **muckrakers** who focused too much on the negative side of American life. The term stuck, but muckrakers' influence was profound. They inspired thousands of readers to get involved in reform movements and tackle the problems caused by industrialization.

# Governing the Great City

One of the most famous muckrakers was Lincoln Steffens, whose book *The Shame of the Cities* (1904), first published serially in *McClure's* magazine, denounced the corruption afflicting America's urban governments. Steffens used dramatic language to expose "swindling" politicians. He claimed, for example, that the mayor of Minneapolis had turned his city over to "outlaws." In St. Louis, "bribery was a joke," while Pittsburgh's Democratic Party operated a private company that handled most of the city's street-paving projects — at a hefty profit. Historians now believe that Steffens and other middle-class crusaders took a rather extreme view of urban politics; the reality was more complex. But charges of corruption could hardly be denied. As industrial cities grew with breathtaking speed, they posed a serious problem of governance.

## Urban Machines

In the United States, cities relied largely on private developers to build streetcar lines and provide urgently needed water, gas, and electricity. This preference for business solutions gave birth to what one urban historian calls the "private city" — an urban environment shaped by individuals and profit-seeking businesses. Private enterprise, Americans believed, spurred great innovations — trolley cars, electric lighting, skyscrapers — and drove urban real estate development. Investment opportunities looked so tempting, in fact, that new cities sprang up almost overnight from the ruins of a catastrophic Chicago fire in 1871 and a major San Francisco earthquake in 1906. Real estate interests were often instrumental in encouraging streetcar lines to build outward from the central districts.

When contractors sought city business, or saloonkeepers needed licenses, they turned to **political machines**: local party bureaucracies that kept an unshakable grip on both elected and appointed public offices. A machine like New York's infamous Tammany Society — known by the name of its meeting place, Tammany Hall — consisted of layers of political functionaries. At the bottom were precinct captains who knew every city neighborhood and block; above them were ward bosses and, at the top, powerful citywide leaders, who had usually started at the bottom and worked their way up. Machines dispensed jobs and patronage, arranged for urban services, and devoted their energies to staying in office, which they did, year after year, on the strength of their political clout and popularity among urban voters.

For constituents, political machines acted as a rough-and-ready social service agency, providing jobs for the jobless or a helping hand for a bereaved family. Tammany ward boss George Washington Plunkitt, for example, reported that he arranged housing for

## Making Mass Media: Newspaper Empires

Among the businesses that served urban consumers were mass-market newspapers. Joseph Pulitzer's *New York World* led the way in the 1880s; a decade later Pulitzer had a powerful rival in the *New York Journal*, owned by William Randolph Hearst.

1. **R. F. Outcault's "The Yellow Kid" comic,** *The World,* **August 9, 1896.** *Pulitzer and Hearst introduced Sunday color comics, including "The Yellow Kid" (shown here on a bicycle). Working-class readers instantly recognized the "kid," slang that then referred to working-class immigrant children. The Kid, like other boys of his age, wore skirts; tenement toddlers' heads were shaved to discourage lice.*

*The World,* Sunday, August 9, 1896.

2. **Editorial,** *Wheeling Register,* **April 6, 1885.** *A West Virginia newspaper commented on a campaign by the* New York World *to complete the Statue of Liberty. Parts of the statue, donated by France, were languishing in New York City parks.*

The *New York World* is a liberty-loving journal. It has taken the responsibility of being foster mother to that much abused piece of bronze called the "BARTHOLDI statue." It begins to look as if the *World* may nurse it to a successful termination by raising funds enough through public contributions to complete the pedestal upon which it is to stand. Success to the enterprise.

3. **"HOMELESS, HOPELESS! Nellie Bly in a Night Haunt of the City's Wretchedest of Women,"** *New York World,* **February 9, 1896.** *Pulitzer and Hearst hired many "stunt reporters." The most famous was Elizabeth Jane Cochrane, who took her pen name, Nellie Bly, from a popular song. In 1892, sponsored by the* World, *Bly beat the record in Jules Verne's famous novel Around the World in Eighty Days, circumnavigating the world in seventy-two days. She filed many investigative pieces such as this one.*

An old woman stood with her back against the side of a building. Over her head was a ragged shawl that had once been red. Around her knees hung a limp and shapeless calico skirt. The rain and sleet were falling steadily and lay thick and slushy upon the streets.

I shivered as I stopped to watch. . . . If the old woman felt the cold she gave no sign. She stood motionless, peeping around the corner. Her eyes were fixed upon the door of the Oak Street Station-House.

Just then three small boys, unmindful of the weather, came trudging down the street . . . industriously gathering every white spot that showed upon the pavement to add to the black snowballs they held in their wet red hands.

Turning the corner suddenly they came upon the old woman. For a second they paused and looked at her and she glared at them. It reminded me of the way dogs behave when they turn a corner and espy a cat. . . . The old woman started on a frantic hobble across the street, the boys after her. Their black snowballs landed squarely and soakingly against her bent back. . . . The old woman shouted things as she ran, things that do not sound well and are never by any chance reproduced in print, but they seemed to increase the delight of the fiendish boys. . . . She could hobble she made for the station-house and the boys pursued her, pelting her.

4. **Lewis Wickes Hine, newsboys selling at a Hartford, Connecticut saloon, 9:30 P.M., March 1909.** *In addition to subscriptions and sales at newsstands, newspapers sold bundles of one hundred papers to boys and girls, who resold as many as they could. Photographer Lewis Hine's caption, included below, suggests one strategy for selling papers. Hine, working for the National Child Labor Committee, took many such images.*

Library of Congress.

A common case of "team work." The smaller boy . . . goes into one of the saloons and sells his "last" papers. Then comes out and his brother gives him more. Joseph said, "Drunks are me best customers. . . . Dey buy me out so I kin go home." He sells every afternoon and night. Extra late Saturday. At it again at 6 A.M.

5. **Newsboys strike coverage, *New York Herald-Tribune*, July 25, 1899.** *As sales plummeted after the War of 1898, Pulitzer and other newspaper titans raised the cost of a newspaper bundle, for children who resold them, from 50 to 60 cents. Newsboys struck. They failed to get the 50-cent price reinstated, but the* World *and other companies agreed to buy back unsold papers, which they had not done before. Kid Blink, the strike leader, was blind in one eye.*

The newsboys' strike gathered new strength last night in a monster mass meeting held at New Irving Hall. . . . "Kid" Blink, who has been made Grand Master Workman of the union, led the procession. . . . The unbiased spectator last evening could not fail to be impressed with the resolute, manly fight the little fellows are making. . . .

SPEECH OF "KID" BLINK

. . . Dis is de time when we'se got to stick togedder like glue! But der's one ting I want ter say before I goes any furder. I don't believe in getting' no feller's papers frum him and tearin' 'em up. I know I done it. (Cries of "You bet you did!") But I'm sorry fer it. No! der ain't nuttin in dat. We know wot we wants and we'll git it. . . . Dem 10 cents is as good ter us as to de millionaires — maybe better. . . . We'll strike and restrike till we get it. . . . We'll stick togedder like plaster, won't we, boys?

The boys answered that they would.

6. **Circulation statistics for the *New York World* from *N. W. Ayer and Son's American Newspaper Annual and Directory*, 1910.**

| Edition | Political affiliation | No. of Pages | Circulation |
| --- | --- | --- | --- |
| Morning | Democratic | 16 | 361,412 |
| Evening | Independent | 12–16 | 410,259 |
| Sunday | Democratic | 56–72 | 459,663 |

Sources: (2) *Wheeling Register*, April 6, 1885; (3) *New York World*, February 9, 1896; (5) *New York Herald-Tribune*, July 25, 1899; (6) *N. W. Ayer and Son's American Newspaper Annual and Directory* (Philadelphia: N. W. Ayer and Son, 1910), 623.

### ANALYZING THE EVIDENCE

1. Based on these sources, why do you think "yellow journalism" was popular and profitable? What audiences did it serve, and how?

2. Consider the tone and point of view of sources 1, 3, and 5. What do they suggest about American attitudes toward the urban poor?

3. What do these sources say about how Pulitzer and Hearst viewed their role as publishers? How might we compare their newspaper empires to other corporations of the industrial era (Chapter 17)?

### PUTTING IT ALL TOGETHER

Write a brief essay in which you explain the ways in which the rise of mass-market newspapers might have contributed to and helped to publicize calls for progressive reform.

families after their apartments burned, "fix[ing] them up until they get things runnin' again." Plunkitt was an Irishman, and so were most Tammany Hall leaders. But by the 1890s, Plunkitt's Fifteenth District was filling up with Italians and Russian Jews. On a given day (as recorded in his diary), he might attend an Italian funeral in the afternoon and a Jewish wedding in the evening. Wherever he went, he brought gifts, listened to his constituents' troubles, and offered a helping hand.

The favors dispensed by men like Plunkitt came via a system of boss control that was, as Lincoln Steffens charged, corrupt. Though rural, state, and national politics were hardly immune to such problems, cities offered flagrant opportunities for bribes and kickbacks. The level of corruption, as Plunkitt observed, was greater in cities, "accordin' to the opportunities." When politicians made contracts for city services, some of the money ended up in their pockets. In the 1860s, William Marcy Tweed, known as Boss Tweed, had made Tammany Hall a byword for corruption, until he was brought down in 1871 by flagrant overpricing of contracts for a lavish city courthouse. Thereafter, machine corruption became more surreptitious. Plunkitt declared that he had no need for outright bribes. He favored what he called "honest graft"—the profits that came to savvy insiders who knew where and when to buy land. Plunkitt made most of his money building wharves on Manhattan's waterfront.

Middle-class reformers condemned immigrants for supporting machines. But urban immigrants believed that few middle-class Americans cared about the plight of poor city folk like themselves. Machines were hardly perfect, but immigrants could rely on them for jobs, emergency aid, and the only public services they could hope to obtain. Astute commentators saw that bosses dominated city government because they provided what was needed, with no condescending moral judgments. As reformer Jane Addams put it, the ward boss was a "stalking survival of village kindness." Voters knew he was corrupt, but on election day they might say, "Ah, well, he has a big Irish heart. He is good to the widow and the fatherless," or, "he knows the poor." Addams concluded that middle-class reformers would only make headway if they set aside their prejudices, learned to "stand by and for and with the people," and did a better job of it than the machine bosses did.

To see a longer excerpt of the Jane Addams essay, along with other primary sources from this period, see *Sources for America's History*.

Machine-style governments achieved some notable successes. They arranged (at a profit) for companies to operate streetcars, bring clean water and gaslight, and remove garbage. Nowhere in the world were there more massive public projects—aqueducts, sewage systems, bridges, and spacious parks—than in the great cities of the United States. The nature of this achievement can be grasped by comparing Chicago, Illinois, with Berlin, the capital of Germany, in 1900. At that time, Chicago's waterworks pumped 500 million gallons of water a day, providing 139 gallons per resident; Berliners made do with 18 gallons each. Flush toilets, a rarity in Berlin, could be found in 60 percent of Chicago homes. Chicago lit its streets with electricity, while Berlin still relied mostly on gaslight. Chicago had twice as many parks as the German capital, and it had just completed an ambitious sanitation project that reversed the course of the Chicago River, carrying sewage into Lake Michigan, away from city residents.

These achievements were remarkable, because American municipal governments labored under severe political constraints. Judges did grant cities some authority: in 1897, for example, New York's state supreme court ruled that New York City was entirely within its rights to operate a municipally owned subway. Use of private land was also subject to whatever regulations a city might impose. But, starting with an 1868 ruling in Iowa, the American legal system largely classified the city as a "corporate entity" subject to state control. In contrast to state governments, cities had only a limited police power, which they could use, for example, to stop crime but not to pass more ambitious measures for public welfare. States, not cities, held most taxation power and received most public revenues. Machines and their private allies flourished, in part, because cities were starved for legitimate cash.

Thus money talked; powerful economic interests warped city government. Working-class residents—even those loyal to their local machines—knew that the newest electric lights and best trolley lines served affluent neighborhoods, where citizens had the most clout. Hilda Satt, a Polish immigrant who moved into a poor Chicago neighborhood in 1893, recalled garbage-strewn streets and filthy backyard privies. "The streets were paved with wooden blocks," she later wrote, "and after a heavy rainfall the blocks would become loose and float about in the street." She remembered that on one such occasion, local pranksters posted a sign

**EXPLAIN CONSEQUENCES**

Why, given that everyone agreed machines were corrupt, did urban voters support them?

**City Garbage**
"How to get rid of the garbage?" was a question that bedeviled every American city. The difficulties of keeping up are all too clear in this ground-level photograph by the great urban investigator Jacob Riis, looking down Tammany Street in New York City around 1890. Museum of the City of New York.

saying, "The Mayor and the Aldermen are Invited to Swim Here." As cities expanded, the limitations of political machines became increasingly clear.

## The Limits of Machine Government

The scale of urban problems became dramatically evident in the depression of the 1890s, when unemployment reached a staggering 25 percent in some cities. Homelessness and hunger were rampant; newspapers nationwide reported on cases of starvation, desperation, and suicide. To make matters worse, most cities had abolished the early-nineteenth-century system of outdoor relief, which provided public support for the indigent. Fearing the system promoted laziness among the poor, middle-class reformers had insisted on private, not public, charity. Even cities that continued to provide outdoor relief in the 1890s were overwhelmed by the magnitude of the crisis. Flooded with "tramps," police stations were forced to end the long-standing practice of allowing homeless individuals to sleep inside.

Faced with this crisis, many urban voters proved none too loyal to the machines when better alternatives arose. Cleveland, Ohio, for example, experienced eighty-three labor strikes between 1893 and 1898. Workers' frustration centered on corrupt businesses with close ties to municipal officials. The city's Central Labor Union, dissatisfied with Democrats' failure to address its concerns, worked with middle-class allies to build a thriving local branch of the People's Party (Chapter 20). Their demands for stronger government measures, especially to curb corporate power, culminated in citywide protests in 1899 during a strike against the hated streetcar company. That year, more than eight thousand workers participated in the city's annual Labor Day parade. As they passed the mayor's reviewing stand, the bands fell silent and the unions furled their flags in a solemn protest against the mayor's failure to support their cause.

To recapture support from working-class Clevelanders, Democrats made a dramatic change in 1901, nominating Tom Johnson for mayor. Johnson, a reform-minded businessman, advocated municipal ownership of utilities and a tax system in which "monopoly and privilege" bore the main burdens. (Johnson once thanked Cleveland's city appraisers for raising taxes on his own mansion.) Johnson's comfortable victory transformed Democrats into Cleveland's leading reform party. While the new mayor did not fulfill the whole agenda of the Central Labor Union and its allies, he became an advocate of publicly owned utilities, and one of the nation's most famous and innovative reformers.

Like Johnson, other mayors began to oust machines and launch ambitious programs of reform. Some modeled their municipal governments on those of Glasgow, Scotland; Düsseldorf, Germany; and other European cities on the cutting edge of innovation. In Boston, Mayor Josiah Quincy built public baths, gyms, swimming pools, and playgrounds and provided free public concerts. Like other mayors, he battled streetcar companies to bring down fares. The scope of such projects varied. In 1912, San Francisco managed to open one small municipally owned streetcar line to compete with private companies. Milwaukee, Wisconsin, on the other hand, elected socialists who experimented with a sweeping array of measures, including publicly subsidized medical care and housing.

Republican Hazen Pingree, mayor of Detroit from 1890 to 1897, was a particularly noted reformer who worked for better streets and public transportation. During the depression, Pingree opened a network of vacant city-owned lots as community vegetable gardens. Though some people ridiculed "Pingree's Potato Patches," the gardens helped feed thousands of Detroit's working people during the harsh depression years. By 1901, a coalition of reformers who campaigned against New York's Tammany Hall began to borrow ideas from Pingree and other mayors. In the wealthier wards of New York, they promised to reduce crime and save taxpayer dollars. In working-class neighborhoods, they vowed to provide affordable housing and municipal ownership of gas and electricity. They defeated Tammany's candidates, and though they did not fulfill all of their promises, they did provide more funding for overcrowded public schools.

Reformers also experimented with new ways of organizing municipal government itself. After a devastating hurricane in 1900 killed an estimated six thousand people in Galveston, Texas, and destroyed much of the city, rebuilders adopted a commission system that became a nationwide model for efficient government. Leaders of the **National Municipal League** advised cities to elect small councils and hire professional city managers who would direct operations like a corporate executive. The league had difficulty persuading politicians to adopt its business-oriented model; it won its greatest victories in young, small cities like Phoenix, Arizona, where the professional classes held political power. Other cities chose, instead, to enhance democratic participation. As part of the Oregon System, which called for direct voting on key political questions, Portland voters participated in 129 municipal referendum votes between 1905 and 1913.

# Crucibles of Progressive Reform

The challenges posed by urban life presented rich opportunities for experimentation and reform. As happened in Cleveland with Tom Johnson's election as mayor, working-class radicals and middle-class reformers often mounted simultaneous challenges to political machines, and these combined pressures led to dramatic change. Many reformers pointed to the plight of the urban poor, especially children. Thus it is not surprising that **progressivism**, an overlapping set of movements to combat the ills of industrialization (Chapter 20), had important roots in the city. In the slums and tenements of the metropolis, reformers invented new forms of civic participation that shaped the course of national politics.

**PLACE EVENTS IN CONTEXT**
How did reformers try to address the limits of machine government? To what extent did they succeed?

# Fighting Dirt and Vice

As early as the 1870s and 1880s, news reporters drew attention to corrupt city governments, the abuse of power by large corporations, and threats to public health. Researcher Helen Campbell reported on tenement conditions in such exposés as *Prisoners of Poverty* (1887). Making innovative use of the invention of flash photography, Danish-born journalist Jacob Riis included photographs of tenement interiors in his famous 1890 book, *How the Other Half Lives*. Riis had a profound influence on Theodore Roosevelt when the future president served as New York City's police commissioner. Roosevelt asked Riis to lead him on tours around the tenements, to help him better understand the problems of poverty, disease, and crime.

**Cleaning Up Urban Environments**   One of the most urgent problems of the big city was disease. In the late nineteenth century, scientists in Europe came to understand the role of germs and bacteria. Though researchers could not yet cure epidemic diseases, they could recommend effective measures for prevention. Following up on New York City's victory against cholera in 1866 — when government officials instituted an effective quarantine and prevented large numbers of deaths — city and state officials began to champion more public health projects. With a major clean-water initiative for its industrial cities in the late nineteenth century, Massachusetts demonstrated that it could largely eliminate typhoid fever. After a horrific yellow fever epidemic in 1878 that killed perhaps 12 percent of its population, Memphis, Tennessee, invested in state-of-the-art sewage and drainage. Though the new system did not eliminate yellow fever, it unexpectedly cut death rates from typhoid and cholera, as well as infant deaths from water-borne disease. Other cities followed suit. By 1913, a nationwide survey of 198 cities found that they were spending an average of $1.28 per resident for sanitation and other health measures.

**IDENTIFY CAUSES**
What prompted the rise of urban environmental and antiprostitution campaigns?

**A Hint to Boards of Health**

In 1884, *Frank Leslie's Illustrated Newspaper* urged municipal and state boards of health to work harder to protect urban children. When this cartoon appeared, New Yorkers were reading shocking reports of milk dealers who diluted milk with borax and other chemicals. Note the range of health threats that the cartoonist identifies. Rutherford B. Hayes Presidential Center.

A HINT TO BOARDS OF HEALTH.—HOW OUR CITIES INVITE THE CHOLERA.

The public health movement became one of the era's most visible and influential reforms. In cities, the impact of pollution was obvious. Children played on piles of garbage, breathed toxic air, and consumed poisoned food, milk, and water. Infant mortality rates were shocking: in the early 1900s, a baby born to a Slavic woman in an American city had a 1 in 3 chance of dying in infancy. Outraged, reformers mobilized to demand safe water and better garbage collection. Hygiene reformers taught hand-washing and other techniques to fight the spread of tuberculosis.

Americans worked in other ways to make industrial cities healthier and more beautiful to live in. Many municipalities adopted smoke-abatement laws, though they had limited success with enforcement until the post–World War I adoption of natural gas, which burned cleaner than coal. Recreation also received attention. Even before the Civil War, urban planners had established sanctuaries like New York's Central Park, where city people could stroll, rest, and contemplate natural landscapes. By the turn of the twentieth century, the **"City Beautiful" movement** arose to advocate more and better urban park spaces. Though most parks still featured flower gardens and tree-lined paths, they also made room for skating rinks, tennis courts, baseball fields, and swimming pools. Many included play areas with swing sets and seesaws, promoted by the National Playground Association as a way to keep urban children safe and healthy.

**Closing Red Light Districts**  Distressed by the commercialization of sex, reformers also launched a campaign against urban prostitution. They warned, in dramatic language, of the threat of white slavery, alleging (in spite of considerable evidence to the contrary) that large numbers of young white women were being kidnapped and forced into prostitution. In *The City's Perils* (1910), author Leona Prall Groetzinger wrote

**"FRIENDS" MEETING EMIGRANT GIRL AT THE DOCK**
"The girl was met at New York by two 'friends' who took her in charge. These 'friends' were two of the most brutal of all the white slave traders who are in the traffic."
—U. S. Dist. Attorney Edwin W. Sims
Foreign girls are more helplessly at the mercy of white slave hunters than girls at home. Every year thousands of girls arriving in America from Italy, Sweden, Germany, etc., are never heard of again.

**The Crusade Against "White Slavery"**
With the growth of large cities, prostitution was a major cause of concern in the Progressive Era. Though the number of sex workers per capita in the United States was probably declining by 1900, the presence of red light districts was obvious; thousands of young women (as well as a smaller number of young men) were exploited in the sex trade. This image appeared in *The Great War on White Slavery*, published by the American Purity Foundation in 1911. It illustrates how immigrant women could be ensnared in the sex trade by alleged "friends" who offered them work. Reformers' denunciations of "white slavery" show an overt racial bias: while antiprostitution campaigners reported on the exploitation of Asian and African American women, the victimization of white women received the greatest emphasis and most effectively grabbed the attention of prosperous, middle-class Americans. From *The Great War on White Slavery*, by Clifford G. Roe, 1911. Courtesy Vassar College Special Collections.

that young women arrived from the countryside "burning with high hope and filled with great resolve, but the remorseless city takes them, grinds them, crushes them, and at last deposits them in unknown graves."

Practical investigators found a more complex reality: women entered prostitution as a result of many factors, including low-wage jobs, economic desperation, abandonment, and often sexual and domestic abuse. Women who bore a child out of wedlock were often shunned by their families and forced into prostitution. Some working women and even housewives undertook casual prostitution to make ends meet. For decades, female reformers had tried to "rescue" such women and retrain them for more respectable employments, such as sewing. Results were, at best, mixed. Efforts to curb demand—that is, to focus on arresting and punishing men who employed prostitutes—proved unpopular with voters.

Nonetheless, with public concern mounting over "white slavery" and the payoffs machine bosses exacted from brothel keepers, many cities appointed vice commissions in the early twentieth century. A wave of brothel closings crested between 1909 and 1912, as police shut down red light districts in cities nationwide. Meanwhile, Congress passed the Mann Act (1910) to prohibit the transportation of prostitutes across state lines.

The crusade against prostitution accomplished its main goal, closing brothels, but in the long term it worsened the conditions under which many prostitutes worked. Though conditions in some brothels were horrific, sex workers who catered to wealthy clients made high wages and were relatively protected by madams, many of whom set strict rules for clients and provided medical care for their workers. In the wake of brothel closings, such women lost control of the prostitution business. Instead, almost all sex workers became "streetwalkers" or "call girls," more vulnerable to violence and often earning lower wages than they had before the antiprostitution crusade began.

## The Movement for Social Settlements

Some urban reformers focused their energies on building a creative new institution, the **social settlement**. These community welfare centers investigated the plight of the urban poor, raised funds to address urgent needs, and helped neighborhood residents advocate on their own behalf. At the movement's peak in the early twentieth century, dozens of social settlements operated across the United States. The most famous, and one of the first, was **Hull House** on Chicago's West Side, founded in 1889 by Jane Addams and her companion Ellen Gates Starr. Their dilapidated mansion, flanked

**Hull House Playground, Chicago, 1906**

When this postcard was made, the City of Chicago's Small Parks Commission had just taken over management of the playground from settlement workers at Hull House, who had created it. In a pattern repeated in many cities, social settlements introduced new institutions and ideas—such as safe places for urban children to play—and inspired municipal authorities to assume responsibility and control. Picture Research Consultants & Archives.

**TRACE CHANGE OVER TIME**

What were the origins of social settlements, and how did they develop over time?

by saloons in a neighborhood of Italian and Eastern European immigrants, served as a spark plug for community improvement and political reform.

The idea for Hull House came partly from Toynbee Hall, a London settlement that Addams and Starr had visited while touring Europe. Social settlements also drew inspiration from U.S. urban missions of the 1870s and 1880s. Some of these, like the Hampton Institute, had aided former slaves during Reconstruction; others, like Grace Baptist in Philadelphia, arose in northern cities. To meet the needs of urban residents, missions offered employment counseling, medical clinics, day care centers, and sometimes athletic facilities in cooperation with the Young Men's Christian Association (YMCA).

Jane Addams, a daughter of the middle class, first expected Hull House to offer art classes and other cultural programs for the poor. But Addams's views quickly changed as she got to know her new neighbors and struggled to keep Hull House open during the depression of the 1890s. Addams's views were also influenced by conversations with fellow Hull House resident Florence Kelley, who had studied in Europe and returned a committed socialist. Dr. Alice Hamilton, who opened a pediatric clinic at Hull House, wrote that Addams came to see her settlement as "a bridge between the classes. . . . She always held that this bridge was as much of a help to the well-to-do as to the poor." Settlements offered idealistic young people "a place where they could live as neighbors and give as much as they could of what they had."

Addams and her colleagues believed that working-class Americans already *knew* what they needed. What they lacked were resources to fulfill those needs, as well as a political voice. These, settlement workers tried to provide. Hull House was typical in offering a bathhouse, playground, kindergarten, and day care center. Some settlements opened libraries and gymnasiums; others operated penny savings banks and cooperative kitchens where tired mothers could purchase a meal at the end of the day. (Addams humbly closed the Hull House kitchen when she found that her bland New England cooking had little appeal for Italians; her coworker, Dr. Alice Hamilton, soon investigated the health benefits of garlic.) At the Henry Street Settlement in New York, Lillian Wald organized visiting nurses to improve health in tenement wards. Addams, meanwhile, encouraged local women to inspect the neighborhood and bring back a list of dangers to health and safety. Together, they prepared a complaint to city

council. The women, Addams wrote, had shown "civic enterprise and moral conviction" in carrying out the project themselves.

Social settlements took many forms. Some attached themselves to preexisting missions and African American colleges. Others were founded by energetic college graduates. Catholics ran St. Elizabeth Center in St. Louis; Jews, the Boston Hebrew Industrial School. Whatever their origins, social settlements were, in Addams's words, "an experimental effort to aid in the solution of the social and industrial problems which are engendered by the modern condition of life in a great city."

Settlements served as a springboard for many other projects. Settlement workers often fought city hall to get better schools and lobbied state legislatures for new workplace safety laws. At Hull House, Hamilton investigated lead poisoning and other health threats at local factories. Her colleague Julia Lathrop investigated the plight of teenagers caught in the criminal justice system. She drafted a proposal for separate juvenile courts and persuaded Chicago to adopt it. Pressuring the city to experiment with better rehabilitation strategies for juveniles convicted of crime, Lathrop created a model for juvenile court systems across the United States.

Another example of settlements' long-term impact was the work of Margaret Sanger, a nurse who moved to New York City in 1911 and volunteered with a Lower East Side settlement. Horrified by women's suffering from constant pregnancies — and remembering her devout Catholic mother, who had died young after bearing eleven children — Sanger launched a crusade for what she called birth control. Her newspaper column, "What Every Girl Should Know," soon garnered an indictment for violating obscenity laws. The publicity that resulted helped Sanger launch a national birth control movement.

Settlements were thus a crucial proving ground for many progressive experiments, as well as for the emerging profession of social work, which transformed the provision of public welfare. Social workers rejected the older model of private Christian charity, dispensed by well-meaning middle-class volunteers to those in need. Instead, social workers defined themselves as professional caseworkers who served as advocates of social justice. Like many reformers of the era, they allied themselves with the new social sciences, such as sociology and economics, and undertook statistical surveys and other systematic methods for gathering facts. Social work proved to be an excellent opportunity for educated women who sought professional careers. By 1920, women made up 62 percent of U.S. social workers.

## Cities and National Politics

Despite reform efforts, the problems wrought by industrialization continued to cause suffering in urban workplaces and environments. In 1906, journalist Upton Sinclair exposed some of the most extreme forms of labor exploitation in his novel *The Jungle*, which described appalling conditions in Chicago meatpacking plants. What caught the nation's attention was not Sinclair's account of workers' plight, but his descriptions of rotten meat and filthy packing conditions. With constituents up in arms, Congress passed the **Pure Food and Drug Act** (1906) and created the federal Food and Drug Administration to oversee compliance with the new law.

The impact of *The Jungle* showed how urban reformers could affect national politics. Even more significant was the work of Josephine Shaw Lowell, a Civil War widow from a prominent family. After years of struggling to aid poverty-stricken individuals in New York City, Lowell concluded that charity was not enough. In 1890, she helped found the New York Consumers' League to improve wages and working conditions for female store clerks. The league encouraged shoppers to patronize only stores where wages and working conditions were known to be fair. By 1899, the organization had become the **National Consumers' League** (NCL). At its head stood the outspoken and skillful Florence Kelley, a Hull House worker and former chief factory inspector of Illinois. Kelley believed that only government oversight could protect exploited workers. Under her crusading leadership, the NCL became one of the most powerful progressive organizations advocating worker protection laws.

Many labor organizations also began in a single city and then grew to national stature. One famous example was the **Women's Trade Union League**, founded in New York in 1903. Financed by wealthy women who supported its work, the league trained working-class leaders like Rose Schneiderman, who organized unions among garment workers. Although often frustrated by the patronizing attitude of elite sponsors, trade-union women joined together in the broader struggle for women's rights. When New York State held referenda on women's suffrage in 1915 and 1917, strong support came from Jewish and Italian precincts where unionized garment workers lived. Working-class voters hoped, in turn, that enfranchised women would use their ballots to help industrial workers.

Residents of industrial cities, then, sought allies in state and national politics. The need for broader action was made clear in New York City by a shocking event

***The Jungle***
This poster advertises a 1914 silent film based on Sinclair's reform novel, which tells the story of Lithuanian immigrants struggling to get by amid the dangerous work, starvation wages, and abysmal living conditions of Chicago's meatpacking district. The film launched the film careers of actors George Nash and Gail Kane, who played the hero, Jurgis Rutkus, and his wife, Ona. Sinclair himself appeared at the start of the film, explaining how he conducted research for his story. Socialist clubs often screened the film, which ended—like the book—with a ringing call for workers to organize and create a "cooperative commonwealth" to take control of their conditions of life and work. Courtesy Lilly Library, Indiana University, Bloomington, IN.

on March 25, 1911. On that Saturday afternoon, just before quitting time, a fire broke out at the **Triangle Shirtwaist** Company. It quickly spread through the three floors the company occupied at the top of a ten-story building. Panicked workers discovered that, despite fire safety laws, employers had locked the emergency doors to prevent theft. Dozens of Triangle workers, mostly young immigrant women, were trapped in the flames. Many leaped to their deaths; the rest never reached the windows. The average age of the 146 people who died was just nineteen (American Voices, p. 630).

## "These Dead Bodies Were the Answer": The Triangle Fire

Entire books have been written about the catastrophic 1911 fire at the Triangle Shirtwaist Company in New York City. The following excerpts are from documents by four contemporaries who in various ways played a part in the Triangle tragedy and its aftermath. Note the different audiences that these speakers and authors were addressing and the lessons that each one draws from this horrific event.

### William G. Shepherd, Reporter

William G. Shepherd's eyewitness account appeared in newspapers across the country. Working for the United Press, Shepherd phoned the story to his editor as he watched the unfolding tragedy.

I was walking through Washington Square when a puff of smoke issuing from a factory building caught my eye. I reached the building before the alarm was turned in. I saw every feature of the tragedy visible from outside the building. I learned a new sound — a more horrible sound than description can picture. It was the thud of a speeding, living body on a stone sidewalk. . . .

I looked up — saw that there were scores of girls at the windows. The flames from the floor below were beating in their faces. Somehow I knew that they, too, must come down, and something within me — something I didn't know was there — steeled me.

I even watched one girl falling. Waving her arms, trying to keep her body upright until the very instant she struck the sidewalk, she was trying to balance herself. Then came the thud — then a silent, unmoving pile of clothing and twisted, broken limbs. . . .

On the sidewalk lay heaps of broken bodies. A policeman later went about with tags, which he fastened with wire to the wrists of the dead girls, numbering each with a lead pencil, and I saw him fasten tag no. 54 to the wrist of a girl who wore an engagement ring. . . .

The floods of water from the firemen's hose that ran into the gutter were actually stained red with blood. I looked upon the heap of dead bodies and I remembered these girls were the shirtwaist makers. I remembered their great strike of last year in which these same girls had demanded more sanitary conditions and more safety precautions in the shops. These dead bodies were the answer.

### Stephen S. Wise, Rabbi

A week after the fire, on April 2, 1911, a memorial meeting was held at the Metropolitan Opera House. One of the speakers, Rabbi Stephen S. Wise, a prominent figure in New York reform circles, made the following remarks.

This was not an inevitable disaster which man could neither foresee nor control. We might have foreseen it, and some of us did; we might have controlled it, but we chose not to do so. . . . It is not a question of enforcement of law nor of inadequacy of law. We have the wrong kind of laws and the wrong kind of enforcement. Before insisting upon inspection and enforcement, let us lift up the industrial standards so as to make conditions worth inspecting, and, if inspected, certain to afford security to workers. . . . And when we go before the legislature of the state, and demand increased appropriations in order to ensure the possibility of a sufficient number of inspectors, we will not forever be put off with the answer: We have no money.

The lesson of the hour is that while property is good, life is better; that while possessions are valuable, life is priceless. The meaning of the hour is that the life of the lowliest worker in the nation is sacred and inviolable, and, if that sacred human right be violated, we shall stand adjudged and condemned before the tribunal of God and history.

### Rose Schneiderman, Trade Unionist

Rose Schneiderman also spoke at the Metropolitan Opera House meeting. At age thirteen, she had gone to work in a garment factory like Triangle Shirtwaist's and, under the tutelage of the Women's Trade Union League, had become a labor organizer. The strike she mentions in her speech was popularly known as the Uprising of the 30,000, a nearly spontaneous walkout in 1909 that launched the union movement in the women's garment trades.

I would be a traitor to these poor burned bodies if I came here to talk good fellowship. We have tried you good people of the public and we have found you wanting. The old Inquisition had its rack and its thumbscrews and its instruments of torture with iron teeth. We know what these things are today; the iron teeth are our necessities, the thumbscrews are the high-powered and swift machinery close to which we must work, and the rack is here in the firetrap structures that will destroy us the minute they catch on fire.

This is not the first time girls have been burned alive in the city. . . . Every year thousands of us are maimed. The life of men and women is so cheap and property is so sacred. There are so many of us for one job it matters little if 146 of us are burned to death.

We have tried you citizens; we are trying you now, and you have a couple of dollars for the sorrowing mothers, brothers, and sisters by way of a charity gift. But every time the workers come out in the only way they know to protest against conditions which are unbearable the strong hand of the law is allowed to press down heavily upon us . . . [and] beats us back, when we rise, into the conditions that make life unbearable.

I can't talk fellowship to you who are gathered here. Too much blood has been spilled. I know from my experience it is up to the working people to save themselves. The only way they can save themselves is by a strong working-class movement.

## Max D. Steuer, Lawyer

After finding physical evidence of the locked door that had blocked escape from the fire, New York's district attorney brought manslaughter charges against the Triangle proprietors, Max Blanck and Isaac Harris, who hired in their defense the best, highest-priced trial attorney in town, Max D. Steuer. In this talk, delivered some time later to a rapt audience of lawyers, Steuer described how he undermined the testimony of the key witness for the prosecution by suggesting that she had been coached to recite her answer. The trial judge instructed the jury that they could only convict Blanck and Harris if it was *certain* they had known the emergency exits were locked; as Steuer notes, the jury voted to acquit.

There are many times, many times when a witness has given evidence very hurtful to your cause and you say, "No questions," and dismiss him or her in the hope that the jury will dismiss the evidence too. [*Laughter.*] But can you do that when the jury is weeping, and the little girl witness is weeping too? [*Laughter.*] . . . There is one [rule] that commands what not to do. Do not attack the witness. Suavely, politely, genially, toy with the story.

In the instant case, about half an hour was consumed by the examiner [Steuer]. . . . Very little progress was made; but the tears had stopped. And then [the witness] was asked, "Now, Rose, in your own words, and in your own way will you tell the jury everything you did, everything you said, and everything you saw from the moment you first saw flames."

The question was put in precisely the same words that the District Attorney had put it, and little Rose started her answer with exactly the same word that she had started it to the District Attorney . . . and the only change in her recital was that Rose left out one word. And then Rose was asked, "Didn't you leave out a word that you put in when you answered it before?" . . . So Rose started to repeat to herself the answer [*laughter*], and as she came to the missing word she said, "Oh, yes!" and supplied it; and thereupon the examiner went on to an entirely different subject. . . . [W]hen again he [asked her to repeat her story] . . . Rose started with the same word and finished with the same word, her recital being identical with her first reply to the same question.

The jurymen were not weeping. Rose had not hurt the case, and the defendants were acquitted; there was not a word of reflection at any time during that trial upon poor little Rose.

Source: Excerpt from *Out of the Sweatshop: The Struggle of Industrial Democracy* by Leon Stein, copyright © 1977 by Leon Stein. Used by permission of Quadrangle Books, an imprint of Random House LLC. All rights reserved. Any third party use of this material, outside of this publication, is prohibited. Interested parties must apply directly to Random House LLC for permission.

### QUESTIONS FOR ANALYSIS

1. The hardest task of the historian is to conjure up the reality of the past—to say, "This is what it was really like." That's where eyewitness evidence like the reporter Shepherd's comes in. What is there in his account that you could only obtain from an eyewitness?

2. Both Rabbi Wise and Rose Schneiderman were incensed at the Triangle carnage, yet their speeches are quite different. In what ways? What conclusions do you draw about the different motivations and arguments that led to reform?

3. Max Steuer and Rose Schneiderman came from remarkably similar backgrounds. They were roughly the same age, grew up in poverty on the Lower East Side, and started out as child workers in the garment factories. The differences in their adult lives speak to the varieties of immigrant experience in America. Does anything in their statements help to account for their differing life paths? What might have happened if Rose Schneiderman, rather than "little Rose," had faced Max Steuer on the witness stand?

**EXPLAIN CONSEQUENCES**
How did urban reform movements impact state and national politics?

Shocked by this horrific event, New Yorkers responded with an outpouring of anger and grief that crossed ethnic, class, and religious boundaries. Many remembered that, only a year earlier, shirtwaist workers had walked off the job to protest abysmal safety and working conditions — and that the owners of Triangle, among other employers, had broken the strike. Facing demands for action, New York State appointed a factory commission that developed a remarkable program of labor reform: fifty-six laws dealing with such issues as fire hazards, unsafe machines, and wages and working hours for women and children. The chairman and vice chairman of the commission were Robert F. Wagner and Alfred E. Smith, both Tammany Hall politicians then serving in the state legislature. They established the commission, participated fully in its work, and marshaled party regulars to pass the proposals into law — all with the approval of Tammany. The labor code that resulted was the most advanced in the United States.

Tammany's response to the Triangle fire showed that it was acknowledging its need for help. The social and economic problems of the industrial city had outgrown the power of party machines; only stronger state and national laws could bar industrial firetraps, alleviate sweatshop conditions, and improve slums. Politicians like Wagner and Smith saw that Tammany had to change or die. The fire had unforeseen further consequences. Frances Perkins, a Columbia University student who witnessed the horror of Triangle workers leaping from the windows to their deaths, decided she would devote her efforts to the cause of labor. Already active in women's reform organizations, Perkins went to Chicago, where she volunteered for several years at Hull House. In 1929, she became New York State's first commissioner of labor; four years later, during the New Deal (Chapter 23), Franklin D. Roosevelt appointed her as U.S. secretary of labor — the first woman to hold a cabinet post.

The political aftermath of the Triangle fire demonstrated how challenges posed by industrial cities pushed politics in new directions, transforming urban government and initiating broader movements for reform. The nation's political and cultural standards had long been set by native-born, Protestant, middle-class Americans. By 1900, the people who thronged to the great cities helped build America into a global industrial power — and in the process, created an electorate that was far more ethnically, racially, and religiously diverse.

In the era of industrialization, some rural and native-born commentators warned that immigrants were "inferior breeds" who would "mongrelize" American culture. But urban political leaders defended cultural pluralism, expressing appreciation — even admiration — for immigrants, including Catholics and Jews, who sought a better life in the United States. At the same time, urban reformers worked to improve conditions of life for the diverse residents of American cities. Cities, then, and the innovative solutions proposed by urban leaders, held a central place in America's consciousness as the nation took on the task of progressive reform.

## SUMMARY

After 1865, American cities grew at an unprecedented rate, and urban populations swelled with workers from rural areas and abroad. To move burgeoning populations around the city, cities pioneered innovative forms of mass transit. Skyscrapers came to mark urban skylines, and new electric lighting systems encouraged nightlife. Neighborhoods divided along class and ethnic lines, with the working class inhabiting crowded, shoddily built tenements. Immigrants developed new ethnic cultures in their neighborhoods, while racism followed African American migrants from the country to the city. At the same time, new forms of popular urban culture bridged class and ethnic lines, challenging traditional sexual norms and gender roles. Popular journalism rose to prominence and helped build rising sympathy for reform.

Industrial cities confronted a variety of new political challenges. Despite notable achievements, established machine governments could not address urban problems through traditional means. Forward-looking politicians took the initiative and implemented a range of political, labor, and social reforms. Urban reformers also launched campaigns to address public health, morals, and welfare. They did so through a variety of innovative institutions, most notably social settlements, which brought affluent Americans into working-class neighborhoods to learn, cooperate, and advocate on behalf of their neighbors. Such projects began to increase Americans' acceptance of urban diversity and their confidence in government's ability to solve the problems of industrialization.

# CHAPTER REVIEW

**MAKE IT STICK**   Go to **LearningCurve** to retain what you've read.

## TERMS TO KNOW   Identify and explain the significance of each term below.

### Key Concepts and Events

Chicago school (p. 608)

mutual aid society (p. 612)

race riot (p. 614)

tenement (p. 614)

vaudeville (p. 615)

ragtime (p. 617)

blues (p. 618)

yellow journalism (p. 619)

muckrakers (p. 619)

political machine (p. 619)

National Municipal League
  (p. 624)

progressivism (p. 624)

"City Beautiful" movement
  (p. 626)

social settlement (p. 627)

Hull House (p. 627)

Pure Food and Drug Act (p. 629)

National Consumers' League
  (p. 629)

Women's Trade Union League
  (p. 629)

Triangle Shirtwaist Fire (p. 629)

### Key People

Scott Joplin (p. 617)

Tom Johnson (p. 624)

Jacob Riis (p. 625)

Jane Addams (p. 627)

Margaret Sanger (p. 628)

Upton Sinclair (p. 629)

Florence Kelley (p. 629)

## REVIEW QUESTIONS   Answer these questions to demonstrate your understanding of the chapter's main ideas.

1. What were the major features of industrial cities that arose in the United States in the late nineteenth and early twentieth centuries? What institutions and innovations helped make urban life distinctive?

2. What were the limitations and achievements of urban governments run by political machines?

3. Why did so many reform initiatives of the early twentieth century emerge in large cities? What were some of those initiatives, and what was their political impact?

4. **THEMATIC UNDERSTANDING** Using the thematic timeline on page 543, consider some of the ways in which mass migrations of people — both from other countries and from places within the United States — shaped industrial cities. How did this influence American society, culture, and national identity?

## MAKING CONNECTIONS

Recognize the larger developments and continuities within and across chapters by answering these questions.

1. **ACROSS TIME AND PLACE**   In Chapter 17 we explored the activities of agrarian reformers and labor unions who protested the impact of industrialization on their lives. In Chapters 18 and 19 we considered the work of middle-class and urban reformers who sought to address some of the same conditions. Chronologically, their work overlapped: note, for example, that Jane Addams founded Hull House in 1889, just as the Farmers' Alliance was reaching a peak of activism and workers had organized the Knights of Labor and American Federation of Labor. Imagine a conversation among the following individuals: a rural man or woman active in the Farmers' Alliance; a skilled workman who joined the American Federation of Labor; an urban antiprostitution reformer; and a middle-class volunteer who worked in a settlement house. How would each have described the problems caused by industrialization? What remedies would each suggest? On what points would they have disagreed? Can you imagine any issues on which they might have worked together? What does this suggest about the opportunities and limits of alliance building, in the late 1800s and early 1900s, across class and geographic lines?

2. **VISUAL EVIDENCE**   Imagine that you have just arrived in a big American city in the early 1900s. Look carefully at all the images in this chapter and group them under two categories: (1) problems and dangers you might have encountered as a new urban resident; (2) sights and opportunities that might have been appealing and exciting to you as a newcomer. On balance, do you think you would have wanted to stay, or turn around and head back home? Why? What factors might have shaped your decision?

## MORE TO EXPLORE

Start here to learn more about the events discussed in this chapter.

Jane Addams, *Twenty Years at Hull House* (1910). An inspiring must-read by a great American reformer.

George Chauncey, *Gay New York* (1994). A groundbreaking study of the rise of urban gay subcultures.

Kathy Peiss, *Cheap Amusements* (1986). Explores urban working-class dating and the world of young working-class women.

Harold Platt, *The Electric City* (1991). A study of how electricity shaped the urban industrial society and economy.

Ruth Rosen, *The Lost Sisterhood* (1982). A poignant account of Progressive Era antiprostitution campaigns and their tragic impact on sex workers.

David Von Drehle, *Triangle: The Fire That Changed America* (2003). The most recent account of the fire and its consequences.

TIMELINE   Ask yourself why this chapter begins and ends with these dates
and then identify the links among related events.

| | |
|---|---|
| **1866** | • New York City contains cholera epidemic |
| **1869** | • Corcoran Gallery of Art opens in Washington, D.C. |
| **1871** | • First elevated railroad begins operation in New York |
| **1878** | • Yellow fever epidemic in Memphis, Tennessee |
| **1883** | • Metropolitan Opera opens in New York |
| **1885** | • First skyscraper completed in Chicago |
| **1887** | • First electric trolley system built in Richmond, Virginia |
| **1889** | • Jane Addams and Ellen Gates Starr found Hull House in Chicago |
| **1890** | • Jacob Riis's *How the Other Half Lives* |
| **1892** | • New York's Ellis Island opens |
| **1893** | • Ragtime introduced to national audiences at Chicago World's Fair |
| **1897** | • First subway line opened in Boston |
| **1899** | • Central Labor Union protests in Cleveland<br>• National Consumers' League founded |
| **1901** | • New York passes Tenement House Law<br>• "City Beautiful" plan developed for Washington, D.C. |
| **1903** | • Women's Trade Union League founded |
| **1904** | • Subway running the length of Manhattan completed |
| **1906** | • Upton Sinclair's *The Jungle* published<br>• Food and Drug Administration established<br>• Atlanta race riot |
| **1910** | • Mann Act prohibits transportation of prostitutes across state lines |
| **1911** | • Triangle Shirtwaist Company fire in New York |
| **1913** | • Fifty-five-story Woolworth Building completed in New York |

**KEY TURNING POINTS:** On the timeline above, what tipping points can you identify when Americans began to propose political solutions for urban industrial problems? What issues did they emphasize?

# Whose Government? Politics, Populists, and Progressives 1880–1917

W e are living in a grand and wonderful time," declared Kansas political organizer Mary E. Lease in 1891. "Men, women and children are in commotion, discussing the mighty problems of the day." This "movement among the masses," she said, was based on the words of Jesus: "Whatsoever ye would that men should do unto you, do ye even so unto them." Between the 1880s and the 1910s, thousands of reformers like Lease confronted the problems of industrialization. Lease herself stumped not only for the People's Party, which sought more government regulation of the economy, but also for the Knights of Labor and Woman's Christian Temperance Union (WCTU), as well as for women's suffrage and public health.

Between the end of Reconstruction and the start of World War I, political reformers focused on four main goals: cleaning up politics, limiting the power of big business, reducing poverty, and promoting social justice. Historians call this period of agitation and innovation the Progressive Era. In the 1880s and 1890s, labor unions and farm groups took the lead in critiquing the industrial order and demanding change. But over time, more and more middle-class and elite Americans took up the call, earning the name *progressives*. On the whole, they proposed more limited measures than farmer-labor advocates did, but since they had more political clout, they often had greater success in winning new laws. Thus both radicals and progressives played important roles in advancing reform.

No single group defined the Progressive Era. On the contrary, reformers took opposite views on such questions as immigration, racial justice, women's rights, and imperialism. Leaders such as Theodore Roosevelt and Woodrow Wilson, initially hostile to the sweeping critiques of capitalism offered by radicals, gradually adopted bolder ideas. Dramatic political changes influenced the direction of reform. Close party competition in the 1880s gave way to Republican control between 1894 and 1910, followed by a period of Democratic leadership during Wilson's presidency (1913–1919). Progressives gave the era its name, not because they acted as a unified force, but because they engaged in diverse, energetic movements to improve America.

**IDENTIFY THE BIG IDEA**
In the Progressive Era, how and why did reformers seek to address the problems of industrial America? To what extent did they succeed?

**Coxey's Army on the March, 1894** During the severe depression of the 1890s, Ohio businessman Jacob Coxey organized unemployed men for a peaceful march to the U.S. Capitol to plead for an emergency jobs program. They called themselves the Commonweal of Christ but won the nickname "Coxey's Army." Though it failed to win sympathy from Congress, the army's march on Washington—one of the nation's first—inspired similar groups to set out from many cities. Here, Coxey's group nears Washington, D.C. The man on horseback is Carl Browne, one of the group's leaders and a flamboyant publicist. As the marchers entered Washington, Coxey's seventeen-year-old daughter Mamie, dressed as the "Goddess of Peace," led the procession on a white Arabian horse. Library of Congress.

# Reform Visions, 1880–1892

In the 1880s, radical farmers' groups and the Knights of Labor provided a powerful challenge to industrialization (Chapter 17). At the same time, groups such as the WCTU (Chapter 18) and urban settlements (Chapter 19) laid the groundwork for progressivism, especially among women. Though they had different goals, these groups confronted similar dilemmas upon entering politics. Should they work through existing political parties? Create new ones? Or generate pressure from the outside? Reformers tried all these strategies.

## Electoral Politics After Reconstruction

The end of Reconstruction ushered in a period of fierce partisan conflict. Republicans and Democrats traded control of the Senate three times between 1880 and 1894, and the House majority five times. Causes of this tight competition included northerners' disillusionment with Republican policies and the resurgence of southern Democrats, who regained a strong base in Congress. Dizzying population growth also changed the size and shape of the House of Representatives. In 1875, it counted 243 seats; two decades later, that had risen to 356. Between 1889 and 1896, entry of seven new western states—Montana, North and South Dakota, Washington, Idaho, Wyoming, and Utah—contributed to political instability.

**IDENTIFY CAUSES**
What factors led to close party competition in the 1880s?

Heated competition and the legacies of the Civil War drew Americans into politics. Union veterans donned their uniforms to march in Republican parades, while ex-Confederate Democrats did the same in the South. When politicians appealed to war loyalties, critics ridiculed them for **"waving the bloody shirt"**: whipping up old animosities that ought to be set aside. For those who had fought or lost beloved family members in the conflict, however—as well as those struggling over African American rights in the South—war issues remained crucial. Many voters also had strong views on economic policies, especially Republicans' high protective tariffs. Proportionately more voters turned out in presidential elections from 1876 to 1892 than at any other time in American history.

The presidents of this era had limited room to maneuver in a period of narrow victories, when the opposing party often held one or both houses of Congress. Republicans Rutherford B. Hayes and Benjamin Harrison both won the electoral college but lost the popular vote. In 1884, Democrat Grover Cleveland won only 29,214 more votes than his opponent, James Blaine, while almost half a million voters rejected both major candidates (Map 20.1). With key states decided by razor-thin margins, both Republicans and Democrats engaged in vote buying and other forms of fraud. The fierce struggle for advantage also prompted innovations in political campaigning (Thinking Like a Historian, p. 640).

Some historians have characterized this period as a **Gilded Age**, when politics was corrupt and stagnant and elections centered on "meaningless hoopla." The term *Gilded Age*, borrowed from the title of an 1873 novel cowritten by Mark Twain, suggested that America had achieved a glittery outer coating of prosperity and lofty rhetoric, but underneath suffered from moral decay. Economically, the term *Gilded Age* seems apt: as we have seen in previous chapters, a handful of men made spectacular fortunes, and their "Gilded" triumphs belied a rising crisis of poverty, pollution, and erosion of workers' rights. But political leaders were not blind to these problems, and the political scene was hardly idle or indifferent. Rather, Americans bitterly disagreed about what to do. Nonetheless, as early as the 1880s, Congress passed important new federal measures to clean up corruption and rein in corporate power. That decade deserves to be considered an early stage in the emerging Progressive Era.

**New Initiatives**   One of the first reforms resulted from tragedy. On July 2, 1881, only four months after entering the White House, James Garfield was shot at a train station in Washington, D.C. ("Assassination," he had told a friend, "can no more be guarded against than death by lightning, and it is best not to worry about either.") After lingering for several agonizing months, Garfield died. Most historians now believe the assassin, Charles Guiteau, suffered from mental illness. But reformers then blamed the spoils system, arguing that Guiteau had murdered Garfield out of disappointment in the scramble for patronage, the granting of government jobs to party loyalists.

In the wake of Garfield's death, Congress passed the **Pendleton Act** (1883), establishing a nonpartisan Civil Service Commission to fill federal jobs by examination. Initially, civil service applied to only 10 percent of such jobs, but the act laid the groundwork for a sweeping transformation of public employment. By the 1910s, Congress extended the act to cover most federal positions; cities and states across the country enacted similar laws.

## MAP 20.1

### The Presidential Elections of 1880, 1884, and 1888

The anatomy of hard-fought, narrowly won presidential campaigns is evident in this trio of electoral maps. First, note the equal division of the popular vote between Republicans and Democrats. Second, note the persistent pattern of electoral votes, as states overwhelmingly went to the same party in all three elections. Here, we can identify who determined the outcomes—"swing" states, such as New York and Indiana, whose vote shifted every four years and always in favor of the winning candidate.

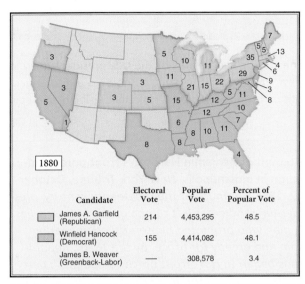

| Candidate | Electoral Vote | Popular Vote | Percent of Popular Vote |
|---|---|---|---|
| James A. Garfield (Republican) | 214 | 4,453,295 | 48.5 |
| Winfield Hancock (Democrat) | 155 | 4,414,082 | 48.1 |
| James B. Weaver (Greenback-Labor) | — | 308,578 | 3.4 |

1880

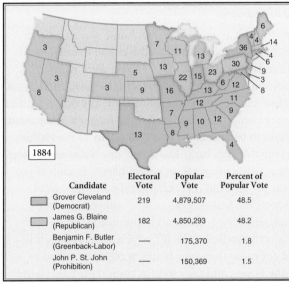

| Candidate | Electoral Vote | Popular Vote | Percent of Popular Vote |
|---|---|---|---|
| Grover Cleveland (Democrat) | 219 | 4,879,507 | 48.5 |
| James G. Blaine (Republican) | 182 | 4,850,293 | 48.2 |
| Benjamin F. Butler (Greenback-Labor) | — | 175,370 | 1.8 |
| John P. St. John (Prohibition) | — | 150,369 | 1.5 |

1884

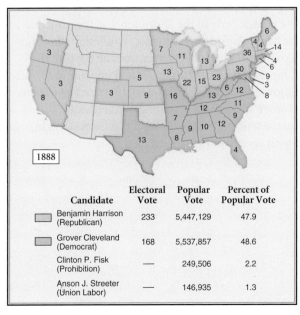

| Candidate | Electoral Vote | Popular Vote | Percent of Popular Vote |
|---|---|---|---|
| Benjamin Harrison (Republican) | 233 | 5,447,129 | 47.9 |
| Grover Cleveland (Democrat) | 168 | 5,537,857 | 48.6 |
| Clinton P. Fisk (Prohibition) | — | 249,506 | 2.2 |
| Anson J. Streeter (Union Labor) | — | 146,935 | 1.3 |

1888

Civil service laws had their downside. In the race for government jobs, they tilted the balance toward middle-class applicants who could perform well on tests. "Firemen now must know equations," complained a critic, "and be up on Euclid too." But the laws put talented professionals in office and discouraged politicians from appointing unqualified party hacks. The civil service also brought stability and consistency to government, since officials did not lose their jobs every time their party lost power. In the long run, civil service laws markedly reduced corruption.

Leaders of the civil service movement included many classical liberals (Chapter 15): former Republicans who became disillusioned with Reconstruction and advocated smaller, more professionalized government. Many had opposed President Ulysses S. Grant's reelection in 1872. In 1884, they again left the Republican Party because they could not stomach its scandal-tainted candidate, James Blaine. Liberal Republicans—ridiculed by their enemies as **Mugwumps** (fence-sitters who had their "mugs" on one side and their "wumps" on the other)—helped elect Democrat Grover Cleveland. They believed he shared their vision of smaller government.

As president, Cleveland showed that he largely did share their views. He vetoed, for example, thousands of bills providing pensions for individual Union veterans. But in 1887, responding to pressure from farmer-labor advocates in the Democratic Party who demanded action to limit corporate power, he signed the Interstate Commerce Act (Chapter 17). At the same time, municipal and state-level initiatives were showing how expanded government could help solve industrial problems. In the 1870s and early 1880s, many states created Bureaus of Labor Statistics to investigate workplace safety and unemployment. Some appointed commissions to oversee key industries, from banking to dairy farming. By later standards, such commissions were underfunded, but even when they lacked legal

## Making Modern Presidents

Between 1880 and 1917, the stature and powers of the U.S. president grew in relation to those of Congress. Presidential campaign techniques also changed. The sources below shed light on candidates' increasing public visibility and new uses of campaign funds.

**1. Household sewing machine company advertisement, 1880s.** *President Grover Cleveland, a bachelor, married young Frances Folsom in a quiet White House ceremony in June 1886. The bride, a college graduate who was twenty-six years younger than her husband, proved wildly popular. The Clevelands never authorized political or commercial use of the First Lady's image. Nonetheless, over their objections, young women organized "Frankie Cleveland Clubs" to march in Democratic parades, while companies such as this one capitalized on her popularity in advertising.*

Picture Research Consultants & Archives.

**2. Account of Benjamin Harrison's front porch campaign in Indianapolis,** *New York Tribune,* **October 12, 1888.** *For much of the nineteenth century, presidential candidates left campaigning to their allies. A man who promoted himself risked appearing vain and greedy for office. By the 1880s, Republicans began to run "front porch campaigns": party leaders arranged for delegations to visit the candidate at home.*

This morning General Harrison's home was surrounded by visitors, who had arrived in the city in the night and on the early morning trains. . . . There were many relic-hunters among the early visitors and they swarmed about the house, taking, without protest from any one, whatever they were pleased to seize. There is no longer a fence about the house to be converted into relics, and so the visitors are taking the trees now. The shrubbery has almost disappeared. . . . The informal reception began as soon as the General got up from [breakfast] and continued until afternoon. The first delegation was composed of representatives of the Cincinnati Republican Clubs. . . . A delegation from Belleville, Ill., which . . . had patiently waited for more than four hours, were next invited to enter the house, and they were accorded the usual handshaking reception. . . .

The parade early in the afternoon was the principal feature of the day's demonstration. Two hundred or more clubs participated and they came from all parts of the State, representing various classes and interests. . . . There were mounted men and men on foot, women in wagons and women in uniform marching, brass bands. . . .

On the balcony beside General Harrison stood his wife, with several of her lady friends.

3. **Henry George on money in politics, *Wheeling Register*, September 19, 1896.** *Reformer Henry George was among many who warned of the influence of corporate contributions, solicited brilliantly in 1896 by William McKinley's campaign manager, Mark Hanna. Short of funds, Democratic candidate William Jennings Bryan undertook exhausting nationwide speaking tours.*

There is no question which of the great parties represents the house of Have and which the house of Want. . . . Democrat[s] are cramped for want of funds. . . . On the other hand there is practically "no end of money" at the disposal of the McKinley committees. . . .

As for the banks, the great railroad companies and insurance companies, who, even in ordinary times find it to their interest to help financially one, and frequently both, sides . . . , their purse strings are unloosed more freely than ever before, but only in one direction.

The danger to a republican form of government of a money interest in politics is so clear that it needs not to be dwelt upon. . . . The steady tendency of American legislation, national and state, has not merely been to create great special interests, but in the very effort to control them for the benefit of the public, to concern them directly in politics.

4. **Theodore Roosevelt on the campaign trail, 1904.** *Having watched Bryan's electrifying tours, Theodore Roosevelt became the first winning candidate to adopt the practice. In 1904, after a summer front porch campaign, he undertook a thirty-day speaking tour of the West. To cover as much ground as possible, Roosevelt often spoke from the last car of his train.*

Library of Congress.

5. **"Expenses of the Campaign," *Springfield Daily Republican*, September 22, 1900.**

It is estimated that it costs $25,000,000 to elect a president of the United States. The annual allowance which the British Parliament makes to Queen Victoria is $1,925,000 . . . indicat[ing] that it is much cheaper to maintain a queen permanently than it is to elect a president. . . .

More than half of the money spent by both national and state committees goes for campaign orators. During the next three months it is estimated that the Republican national committee will have 3000 "spellbinders" traveling out of the Chicago headquarters and 2500 who will report to the New York office. . . .

The next largest item on the campaign bill is that for printing. . . . Each of the national committees will spend at least $500,000 in this way. Before the campaign is over it is estimated that both the Republican and Democratic committees will send out 100,000,000 separate documents. . . .

One more important branch of the work is the two house-to-house canvasses of the voters. . . . Hundreds of men are employed in each state, and the work of tabulating and classifying the results is by no means small. . . .

Some novel campaign methods will be adopted by both the great parties during the campaign just opening. The Republicans, it is stated, have decided to use phonographs. . . . Some eloquent party man . . . will deliver a speech before a phonographic record, from which any desired number of copies may be made . . . and sent far out into the rural districts, where it would be impossible for the more popular and important orators to go. . . .

Democrats, on the other hand, will pin their faith to stereopticons [an early slide projector].

Sources: (2) *New York Tribune*, October 12, 1888; (3) *Wheeling Register*, September 19, 1896; (5) *Springfield Daily Republican*, September 22, 1900.

## ANALYZING THE EVIDENCE

1. What did a presidential candidate need in the 1880s to run an effective campaign? Two decades later, what had changed, and what had not?

2. Based on these documents, what developments both inside and outside of politics seem to have influenced changing campaign strategies?

## PUTTING IT ALL TOGETHER

Historians have traced the rise of an "imperial presidency" in the late 1890s and early 1900s. How might new campaign techniques have reflected, and perhaps contributed to, this rise? To what extent was it a Republican invention?

**"Political Purity," *Puck*, 1884**

This Democratic cartoon suggests the disillusionment with Republicans that emerged among many voters in the 1880s. Here, the party chooses a dress, bustle, and plume to celebrate Republicans' achievements in prior decades: the Union war record, Emancipation, and "high moral ideals." Her undergarments tell a different story: they are marked with scandals of the Grant era (Chapter 15), while the economic interests of tariff supporters ("protection") are depicted as her corset. The hats in the upper right corner show Republicans' attempts to appeal to various constituencies: temperance advocates and German immigrants, workingmen and business leaders. Whitelaw Reid, staunchly Republican editor of the *New York Tribune*, appears as the party's handmaiden. *Puck*, August 20, 1884.

power, energetic commissioners could serve as public advocates, exposing unsafe practices and generating pressure for further laws.

**Republican Activism**   In 1888, after a decade of divided government, Republicans gained control of both Congress and the White House. They pursued an ambitious agenda they believed would meet the needs of a modernizing nation. In 1890, Congress extended pensions to all Union veterans and yielded to growing public outrage over trusts by passing a law to regulate interstate corporations. Though it proved difficult to enforce and was soon weakened by the Supreme Court, the **Sherman Antitrust Act** (1890) was the first federal attempt to forbid any "combination, in the form of trust or otherwise, or conspiracy, in restraint of trade."

President Benjamin Harrison also sought to protect black voting rights in the South. Warned during his campaign that the issue was politically risky, Harrison vowed that he would not "purchase the presidency by a compact of silence upon this question." He found allies in Congress. Massachusetts representative Henry Cabot Lodge drafted the Federal Elections Bill of 1890, or **Lodge Bill**, proposing that whenever one hundred citizens in any district appealed for intervention, a bipartisan federal board could investigate and seat the rightful winner.

Despite cries of outrage from southern Democrats, who warned that it meant "Negro supremacy," the House passed the measure. But it met resistance in the Senate. Northern classical liberals, who wanted the "best men" to govern through professional expertise, thought it provided too much democracy, while machine bosses feared the threat of federal interference in the cities. Unexpectedly, many western Republicans also opposed the bill — and with the entry of ten new states since 1863, the West had gained enormous clout. Senator William Stewart of Nevada, who had southern family ties, claimed that federal oversight of elections would bring "monarchy or revolution." He and his allies killed the bill by a single vote.

The defeat was a devastating blow to those seeking to defend black voting rights. In the verdict of one furious Republican leader who supported Lodge's proposal, the episode marked the demise of the party of emancipation. "Think of it," he fumed. "Nevada, barely a respectable *county*, furnished two senators to betray the Republican Party and the rights of citizenship."

Other Republican initiatives also proved unpopular — at the polls as well as in Congress. In the Midwest, swing voters reacted against local Republican campaigns to prohibit liquor sales and end state funding for Catholic schools. Blaming high consumer prices on protective tariffs, other voters rejected Republican economic policies. In a major shift in the 1890 election, Democrats captured the House of Representatives. Two years later, by the largest margin in twenty years, voters reelected Democrat Grover Cleveland to the presidency for a nonconsecutive second term. Republican congressmen abandoned any further attempt to enforce fair elections in the South.

## The Populist Program

As Democrats took power in Washington, they faced rising pressure from rural voters in the South and West who had organized the Farmers' Alliance. Savvy politicians responded quickly. Iowa Democrats, for example,

**Riding to a Populist Rally, Dickinson County, Kansas, 1890s**

Farm families in wagons carry their banners to a local meeting of the People's Party. Men, women, and children often traveled together to campaign events, which included not only stump speeches but also picnics, glee club music, and other family entertainments. Kansas State Historical Society.

took up some of the farmers' demands, forestalling creation of a separate farmer-labor party in that state. But other politicians listened to Alliance pleas and did nothing. It was a response they came to regret.

Republicans utterly dominated Kansas, a state chock-full of Union veterans and railroad boosters. But politicians there treated the Kansas Farmers' Alliance with contempt. In 1890, the Kansas Alliance joined with the Knights of Labor to create a People's Party. They then stunned the nation by capturing four-fifths of the lower house of the Kansas legislature and most of the state's congressional seats. The victory electrified labor and agrarian radicals nationwide. In July 1892, delegates from these groups met at Omaha, Nebraska, and formally created the national People's Party.

Nominating former Union general and Greenback-Labor leader James B. Weaver for president, the Populists, as they became known, captured a million votes in November and carried four western states (Map 20.2).

In recognizing an "irrepressible conflict between capital and labor," Populists split from the mainstream parties, calling for stronger government to protect ordinary Americans. "We believe," declared their **Omaha Platform** (1892), "that the power of government — in other words, of the people — should be expanded as rapidly and as far as the good sense of an intelligent people and the teachings of experience shall justify, to

**UNDERSTAND POINTS OF VIEW**

How did the political goals of Populists differ in this period from those of Democrats and Republicans?

**MAP 20.2**

**The Heyday of Western Populism, 1892**

This map shows the percentage of the popular vote won by James B. Weaver, the People's Party candidate, in the presidential election of 1892. Except in California and Montana, the Populists won broad support across the West and genuinely threatened the established parties in that region.

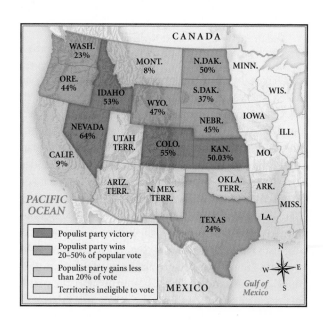

CANADA

WASH. 23%
MONT. 8%
N.DAK. 50%
MINN.
ORE. 44%
IDAHO 53%
S.DAK. 37%
WIS.
WYO. 47%
NEBR. 45%
IOWA
NEVADA 64%
UTAH TERR.
COLO. 55%
KAN. 50.03%
MO.
ILL.
CALIF. 9%
ARIZ. TERR.
N. MEX. TERR.
OKLA. TERR.
ARK.
PACIFIC OCEAN
TEXAS 24%
LA.
MISS.

Populist party victory
Populist party wins 20–50% of popular vote
Populist party gains less than 20% of vote
Territories ineligible to vote

MEXICO
Gulf of Mexico

the end that oppression, injustice and poverty should eventually cease." Populists called for public ownership of railroad and telegraph systems, protection of land from monopoly and foreign ownership, a federal income tax on the rich, and a looser monetary policy to help borrowers. Some Populist allies went further to make their point: in New Mexico, the Gorras Blancas, a vigilante group of small-scale Mexican American farmers, protested exploitative railroads and "land grabbers" by intimidating railroad workers and cutting fences on large Anglo farms.

 To see a longer excerpt of the Omaha Platform, along with other primary sources from this period, see *Sources for America's History*.

Populist leaders represented a grassroots uprising of ordinary farmers, and some won colorful nicknames. After a devastating debate triumph, James H. Davis of Texas became known as "Cyclone." Mary E. Lease was derided as "Yellin' Mary Ellen"; her fellow Kansan Jerry Simpson was called "Sockless Jerry" after he ridiculed a wealthy opponent for wearing "fine silk hosiery," boasting that he himself wore no socks at all. The national press, based in northeastern cities, ridiculed such "hayseed politicians," but farmers insisted on being taken seriously. In the run-up to one election, a Populist writer encouraged party members to sing these lyrics to the tune of an old gospel hymn:

> I once was a tool of oppression,
>     As green as a sucker could be
> And monopolies banded together
>     To beat a poor hayseed like me. . . .
>
> But now I've roused up a little,
>     And their greed and corruption I see,
> And the ticket we vote next November
>     Will be made up of hayseeds like me.

Driven by farmers' votes, the People's Party had mixed success in attracting other constituencies. Its labor planks won support among Alabama steelworkers and Rocky Mountain miners, but not among many other industrial workers, who stuck with the major parties. Prohibitionist and women's suffrage leaders attended Populist conventions, hoping their issues would be taken up, but they were disappointed. The legacies of the Civil War also hampered the party. Southern Democrats warned that Populists were really Radical Republicans in disguise, while northeastern Republicans claimed the southern "Pops" were ex-Confederates plotting another round of treason. Amid these heated debates, the political system suddenly confronted an economic crisis.

# The Political Earthquakes of the 1890s

In 1893, a severe economic depression hit the United States. Though it was a global shock, and the agriculture sector had already lagged for years, Republicans blamed Grover Cleveland, who had just reentered the White House. "On every hand can be seen evidences of Democratic times," declared one Republican. "The deserted farm, the silent factory."

Apparently receptive to such appeals, voters outside the South abandoned the Democrats in 1894 and 1896. Republicans, promising prosperity, gained control of the White House and both chambers of Congress for the next fifteen years. This development created both opportunities and challenges for progressive reformers. A different pattern emerged in the South: Democrats deployed fraud, violence, and race-based appeals for white solidarity to defeat the Populist revolt.

## Depression and Reaction

When Cleveland took the oath of office in March 1893, hard times were prompting European investors to pull money out of the United States; farm foreclosures and railroad bankruptcies signaled economic trouble. A few weeks later, a Pennsylvania railroad went bankrupt, followed by several other companies. Investors panicked; the stock market crashed. By July, major banks had drained their reserves and "suspended," unable to give depositors access to their money. By year's end, five hundred banks and thousands of other businesses had gone under. "Boston," one man remembered, "grew suddenly old, haggard, and thin." The unemployment rate in industrial cities soared above 20 percent.

For Americans who had lived through the terrible 1870s, conditions looked grimly familiar. Even fresher in the public mind were recent labor uprisings, including the 1886 Haymarket violence and the 1892 showdown at Homestead—followed, during the depression's first year, by a massive Pennsylvania coal strike and a Pullman railroad boycott that ended with bloody clashes between angry crowds and the U.S. Army. Prosperous Americans, fearful of Populism, were even more terrified that workers would embrace socialism or Marxism. Reminding Americans of upheavals such as the Paris Commune of 1871 and its bloody aftermath, conservative commentators of the 1890s launched America's first "Red Scare"—a precursor to similar episodes of hysteria in the 1920s (Chapter 22) and 1950s (Chapter 25).

In the summer of 1894, a further protest jolted affluent Americans. Radical businessman Jacob Coxey of Ohio proposed that the U.S. government hire the unemployed to fix America's roads. In 1894, he organized hundreds of jobless men—nicknamed Coxey's Army—to march peacefully to Washington and appeal for the program. Though public employment of the kind Coxey proposed would become central to the New Deal in the 1930s, many Americans in the 1890s viewed Coxey as a dangerous extremist. Public alarm grew when more protesters, inspired by Coxey, started out from Los Angeles, Seattle, and other cities. As they marched east, these men found warm support and offers of aid in Populist-leaning cities and towns. In other places, police and property owners drove marchers away at gunpoint. Coxey was stunned by what happened when he reached Capitol Hill: he was jailed for trespassing on the grass. Some of his men, arrested for vagrancy, ended up in Maryland chain gangs. The rest went home hungry.

As this response suggested, President Grover Cleveland's administration was increasingly out of step with rural and working-class demands. Any president would have been hard-pressed to cope with the depression, but Cleveland made a particularly bad hash of it. He steadfastly resisted pressure to loosen the money supply by expanding federal coinage to include silver as well as gold. Advocates of this **free silver** policy ("free" because, under this plan, the U.S. Mint would not charge a fee for minting silver coins) believed the policy would encourage borrowing and stimulate industry. But Cleveland clung to the gold standard; however dire things became, he believed, the money supply must remain tied to the nation's reserves of gold.

Even collapsing prices and a hemorrhage of gold to Europe did not budge the president. With gold reserves dwindling in 1895, he made a secret arrangement with a syndicate of bankers led by John Pierpont Morgan to arrange gold purchases to replenish the treasury. Morgan helped maintain America's gold supply—preserving the gold standard—and turned a tidy profit by earning interest on the bonds he provided. Cleveland's deal, once discovered, enraged fellow Democrats. South Carolina governor Ben Tillman vowed to go to Washington and "poke old Grover with a pitchfork," earning the nickname "Pitchfork Ben."

As the 1894 midterm elections loomed, Democratic candidates tried to distance themselves from the president. But on election day, large numbers of voters chose Republicans, who promised to support business, put down social unrest, and bring back prosperity. Western voters turned many Populists out of office. In the next congressional session, Republicans controlled the House by a margin of 245 to 105. The election began sixteen years of Republican national dominance.

## Democrats and the "Solid South"

In the South, the only region where Democrats gained strength in the 1890s, the People's Party lost ground for distinctive reasons. After the end of Reconstruction, African Americans in most states had continued to vote in significant numbers. As long as Democrats competed for (and sometimes bought) black votes, the possibility remained that other parties could win them away. Populists proposed new measures to help farmers and wage earners—an appealing message for poverty-stricken people of both races. Some white Populists went out of their way to build cross-racial ties. "The accident of color can make no difference in the interest of farmers, croppers, and laborers," argued Georgia Populist Tom Watson. "You are kept apart that you may be separately fleeced of your earnings."

Such appeals threatened the foundations of southern politics. Democrats struck back, calling themselves the "white man's party" and denouncing Populists for advocating "Negro rule." From Georgia to Texas, many poor white farmers, tenants, and wage earners ignored such appeals and continued to support the Populists in large numbers. Democrats found they could put down the Populist threat only through fraud and violence. Afterward, Pitchfork Ben Tillman of South Carolina openly bragged that he and other southern whites had "done our level best" to block "every last" black vote. "We stuffed ballot boxes," he said in 1900. "We shot them. We are not ashamed of it." "We had to do it," a Georgia Democrat later argued. "Those damned Populists would have ruined the country."

Having suppressed the political revolt, Democrats looked for new ways to enforce white supremacy. In 1890, a constitutional convention in Mississippi had adopted a key innovation: an "understanding clause" that required would-be voters to interpret parts of the state constitution, with local Democratic officials deciding who met the standard. After the Populist uprising, such measures spread to other southern states. Louisiana's grandfather clause, which denied the ballot to any man whose grandfather had been unable to vote in slavery days, was struck down by the U.S. Supreme Court. But in *Williams v. Mississippi* (1898), the Court allowed poll taxes and literacy tests to stand.

**EXPLAIN CONSEQUENCES**
How did different groups of Americans react to the economic depression of the 1890s, and what happened as a result?

**TRACE CHANGE OVER TIME**

How did politics change in the South between the 1880s and the 1910s?

By 1908, every southern state had adopted such measures.

The impact of disenfranchisement can hardly be overstated (Map 20.3). Across the South, voter turnout plunged, from above 70 percent to 34 percent or even lower. Not only blacks but also many poor whites ceased to vote. Since Democrats faced virtually no opposition, action shifted to the "white primaries," where Democratic candidates competed for nominations. Some former Populists joined the Democrats in openly advocating white supremacy. The racial climate hardened. Segregation laws proliferated. Lynchings of African Americans increasingly occurred in broad daylight, with crowds of thousands gathered to watch.

The convict lease system, which had begun to take hold during Reconstruction, also expanded. Blacks received harsh sentences for crimes such as "vagrancy," often when they were traveling to find work or if they could not produce a current employment contract. By the 1890s, Alabama depended on convict leasing for 6 percent of its total revenue. Prisoners were overwhelmingly black: a 1908 report showed that almost 90 percent of Georgia's leased convicts were black; out of a white population of 1.4 million, only 322 were in prison. Calling attention to the torture and deaths of prisoners, as well as the damaging economic effect of their unpaid labor, reformers, labor unions, and Populists protested the situation strenuously. But "reforms" simply replaced convict leasing with the chain gang, in which prisoners worked directly for the state on roadbuilding and other projects, under equally cruel conditions. All these developments depended on a political **Solid South** in which Democrats exercised almost complete control.

The impact of the 1890s counterrevolution was dramatically illustrated in Grimes County, a cotton-growing area in east Texas where blacks comprised more than half of the population. African American voters kept the local Republican Party going after Reconstruction and regularly sent black representatives to the Texas legislature. Many local white Populists dismissed Democrats' taunts of "negro supremacy," and a Populist-Republican coalition swept the county elections in 1896 and 1898. But after their 1898 defeat, Democrats in Grimes County organized a secret brotherhood and forcibly prevented blacks from voting in town elections, shooting two in cold blood. The Populist sheriff proved unable to bring the murderers to justice. Reconstituted in 1900 as the White Man's Party, Democrats carried Grimes County by an overwhelming margin. Gunmen then laid siege to the Populist sheriff's office, killed his brother and a friend, and drove the wounded sheriff out of the county. The White Man's Party ruled Grimes County for the next fifty years.

## New National Realities

While their southern racial policies were abhorrent, the national Democrats simultaneously amazed the country in 1896 by embracing parts of the Populists' radical farmer-labor program. They nominated for

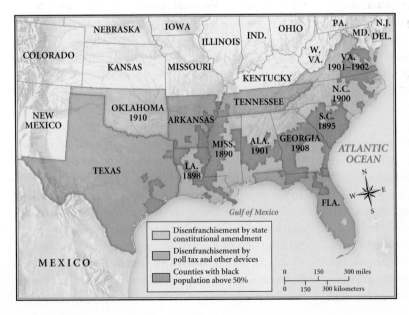

**MAP 20.3**

**Disenfranchisement in the New South**

In the midst of the Populist challenge to Democratic one-party rule in the South, a movement to deprive blacks of the right to vote spread from Mississippi across the South. By 1910, every state in the region except Tennessee, Arkansas, Texas, and Florida had made constitutional changes designed to prevent blacks from voting, and these four states accomplished much the same result through poll taxes and other exclusionary methods. For the next half century, the political process in the South would be for whites only.

**Lynching in Texas**

Lynchings peaked between 1890 and 1910; while most common in the South, they occurred in almost every state, from Oregon to Minnesota to New York. After many lynchings—such as this one in the town of Center, Texas, in 1920—crowds posed to have their pictures taken. Commercial photographers often, as in this case, produced photographic postcards to sell as souvenirs. What do we make of these gruesome rituals? Who is in the crowd, and who is not? What do we learn from the fact that this group of white men, some of whom may have been responsible for the lynching, felt comfortable having their photographs recorded with the body? The victim in this photograph, a young man named Lige Daniels, was seized from the local jail by a mob that broke down the prison door to kidnap and kill him. The inscription on the back of the postcard includes information about the killing, along with the instructions "Give this to Bud From Aunt Myrtle." Private Collection.

president a young Nebraska congressman, free-silver advocate William Jennings Bryan, who passionately defended farmers and attacked the gold standard. "Burn down your cities and leave our farms," Bryan declared in his famous convention speech, "and your cities will spring up again as if by magic; but destroy our farms and the grass will grow in the streets of every city in the country." He ended with a vow: "You shall not crucify mankind on a cross of gold." Cheering delegates endorsed a platform calling for free silver and a federal income tax on the wealthy that would replace tariffs as a source of revenue. Democrats, long defenders of limited government, were moving toward a more activist stance.

Populists, reeling from recent defeats, endorsed Bryan in the campaign, but their power was waning. Populist leader Tom Watson, who wanted a separate program, more radical than Bryan's, observed that Democrats in 1896 had cast the Populists as "Jonah

while they play whale." The People's Party never recovered from its electoral losses in 1894 and from Democrats' ruthless opposition in the South. By 1900, rural voters pursued reform elsewhere, particularly through the new Bryan wing of the Democratic Party.

Meanwhile, horrified Republicans denounced Bryan's platform as anarchistic. Their nominee, the Ohio congressman and tariff advocate William McKinley, chose a brilliant campaign manager, Ohio coal and shipping magnate Marcus Hanna, who orchestrated an unprecedented corporate fund-raising campaign. Under his guidance, the party backed away from moral issues such as prohibition of liquor and reached out to new immigrants. Though the popular vote was closer, McKinley won big: 271 electoral votes to Bryan's 176 (Map 20.4).

Nationwide, as in the South, the realignment of the 1890s prompted new measures to exclude voters. Influenced by classical liberals' denunciations of "unfit

**William Jennings Bryan**

This 1896 campaign poster emphasizes the youth of the thirty-six-year-old Nebraska Democrat and includes portraits of his wife Mary and their three young children. The full text of his famous "Cross of Gold" speech appears flanked by silver coins and overlaid with "16 to 1," representing the Chicago platform's proposal to mint U.S. silver coins at a 16-to-1 ratio with gold, increasing the money supply to stimulate the economy and aid borrowers. At the bottom stand a farmer and industrial workingman—primary bases of Democratic support. Many farmers and workers voted for McKinley, however, especially in the industrial heartland of the Northeast and Midwest. Though Bryan secured the electoral votes of the South and a substantial majority of western states, McKinley won the election. Library of Congress.

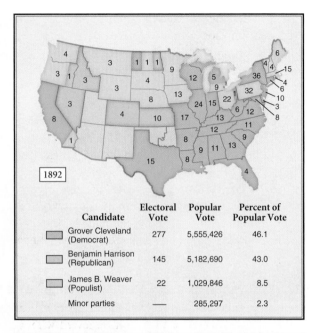

| Candidate | Electoral Vote | Popular Vote | Percent of Popular Vote |
|---|---|---|---|
| Grover Cleveland (Democrat) | 277 | 5,555,426 | 46.1 |
| Benjamin Harrison (Republican) | 145 | 5,182,690 | 43.0 |
| James B. Weaver (Populist) | 22 | 1,029,846 | 8.5 |
| Minor parties | — | 285,297 | 2.3 |

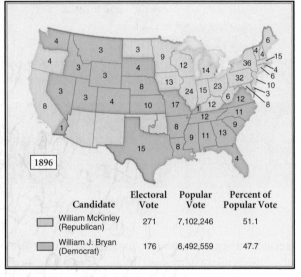

| Candidate | Electoral Vote | Popular Vote | Percent of Popular Vote |
|---|---|---|---|
| William McKinley (Republican) | 271 | 7,102,246 | 51.1 |
| William J. Bryan (Democrat) | 176 | 6,492,559 | 47.7 |

**MAP 20.4**

**The Presidential Elections of 1892 and 1896**

In the 1890s, the age of political stalemate came to an end. Students should compare the 1892 map with Map 20.1 (p. 639) and note especially Cleveland's breakthrough in the normally Republican states of the Upper Midwest. In 1896, the pendulum swung in the opposite direction, with McKinley's consolidation of Republican control over the Northeast and Midwest far overbalancing the Democratic advances in the thinly populated western states. The 1896 election marked the beginning of sixteen years of Republican dominance in national politics.

voters," many northern states imposed literacy tests and restrictions on immigrant voting. Leaders of both major parties, determined to prevent future Populist-style threats, made it more difficult for new parties to get candidates listed on the ballot. In the wake of such laws, voter turnout declined, and the electorate narrowed in ways that favored the native-born and wealthy.

Antidemocratic restrictions on voting helped, paradoxically, to foster certain democratic innovations.

Having excluded or reduced the number of poor, African American, and immigrant voters, elite and middle-class reformers felt more comfortable increasing the power of the voters who remained. Both major parties increasingly turned to the direct primary, asking voters (in most states, registered party members) rather than party leaders to choose nominees. Another measure that enhanced democratic participation was the Seventeenth Amendment to the Constitution (1913), requiring that U.S. senators be chosen not by state legislatures, but by popular vote. Though many states had adopted the practice well before 1913, southern states had resisted, since Democrats feared that it might give more power to their political opponents. After disenfranchisement, such objections faded and the measure passed. Thus disenfranchisement enhanced the power of remaining voters in multiple, complicated ways.

At the same time, the Supreme Court proved hostile to many proposed reforms. In 1895, for example, it struck down a recently adopted federal income tax on the wealthy. The Court ruled that unless this tax was calculated on a per-state basis, rather than by the wealth of individuals, it could not be levied without a constitutional amendment. It took progressives nineteen years to achieve that goal.

Labor organizations also suffered in the new political regime, as federal courts invalidated many regulatory laws passed to protect workers. As early as 1882, in the case of *In re Jacobs*, the New York State Court of Appeals struck down a public-health law that prohibited cigar manufacturing in tenements, arguing that such regulation exceeded the state's police powers. In **Lochner v. New York** (1905), the U.S. Supreme Court told New York State it could not limit bakers' workday to ten hours because that violated bakers' rights to make contracts. Judges found support for such rulings in the due process clause of the Fourteenth Amendment, which prohibited states from depriving "any person of life, liberty, or property, without due process of law." Though the clause had been intended to protect former slaves, courts used it to shield contract rights, with judges arguing that they were protecting workers'

> **PLACE EVENTS IN CONTEXT**
> What developments caused the percentage of Americans who voted to plunge after 1900, and what role did courts play in antidemocratic developments?

**The U.S. Supreme Court, 1894**

During the 1890s, the Supreme Court struck down a number of pieces of progressive legislation, including a progressive federal income tax that had been signed into law by Congress and the president. In the Knight Sugar Case (*United States v. E. C. Knight Co.*), the Court ruled that the federal government had limited power over interstate commerce when a company did most of its manufacturing in a single state. In another 1894 decision, *In re Debs*, manufacturers were allowed free use of injunctions to shut down strikes. Two years later, in *Plessy v. Ferguson*, the Court gave national sanction to racial segregation. In the front row, from left to right, are justices Horace Gray, Stephen J. Field, Chief Justice Melville W. Fuller, John Marshall Harlan I, and David J. Brewer. Standing in the back row, left to right, are justices Howell Jackson, Henry B. Brown, George Shiras, and Edward Douglas White. C. M. Bell, Collection of the Supreme Court of the United States.

freedom *from* government regulation. Interpreted in this way, the Fourteenth Amendment was a major obstacle to regulation of private business.

Farmer and labor advocates, along with urban progressives who called for more government regulation, disagreed with such rulings. They believed judges, not state legislators, were overreaching. While courts treated employers and employees as equal parties, critics dismissed this as a legal fiction. "Modern industry has reduced 'freedom of contract' to a paper privilege," declared one labor advocate, "a mere figure of rhetoric." Supreme Court justice Oliver Wendell Holmes Jr., dissenting in the *Lochner* decision, agreed. If the choice was between working and starving, he observed, how could bakers "choose" their hours of work? Holmes's view, known as legal realism, eventually won judicial favor, but only after years of progressive and labor activism.

# Reform Reshaped, 1901–1912

William McKinley, a powerful presence in the White House, was no reformer. His victory was widely understood as a triumph for business and especially for industrial titans who had contributed heavily to his campaign. But the depression of the 1890s, by subjecting millions to severe hardship, had dramatically illustrated the problems of industrialization. At the same time, the success of McKinley's campaign managers — who spent more than $3.5 million, versus Bryan's $300,000 — raised unsettling questions about corporate power. Once the crisis of the 1890s passed, many middle-class Americans proved ready to embrace progressive ideas. The rise of such ideas was aided by historical chance, when a shocking assassination put a reformer in the White House.

## Theodore Roosevelt as President

On September 14, 1901, only six months after William McKinley won his second face-off against Democrat William Jennings Bryan, the president was shot as he attended the Pan-American Exposition in Buffalo, New York. He died eight days later. The murderer, Leon Czolgosz, was influenced by anarchists who had carried out recent assassinations in Europe. Though Czolgosz was American-born, many feared that McKinley's violent death was another warning of the threat posed by radical immigrants. As the nation mourned its third murdered president in less than four decades, Vice President Theodore Roosevelt was sworn into office.

Roosevelt, from a prominent family, had chosen an unconventional path. After graduating from Harvard, he plunged into politics, winning a seat as a Republican New York assemblyman. Disillusioned by his party's resistance to reform, he left politics in the mid-1880s and moved to a North Dakota ranch. But his cattle herd was wiped out in the blizzards of 1887. He returned east, winning appointments as a U.S. Civil Service commissioner, head of the New York City Police Commission, and McKinley's assistant secretary of the navy. An energetic presence in all these jobs, Roosevelt gained broad knowledge of the problems America faced at the municipal, state, and federal levels.

After serving in the War of 1898 (Chapter 21), Roosevelt was elected as New York's governor. In this job, he pushed through civil service reform and a tax on corporations. Seeking to neutralize this progressive and rather unpredictable political star, Republican bosses chose Roosevelt as McKinley's running mate in 1900, hoping the vice-presidency would be a political dead end. Instead, they suddenly found Roosevelt in the White House. The new president, who called for vigorous reform, represented a major shift for the Republicans.

**Antitrust Legislation**   Roosevelt blended reform with the needs of private enterprise, but on occasion he challenged corporations in new ways. During a bitter 1902 coal strike, for example, he threatened to nationalize the big coal companies if their owners refused to negotiate with the miners' union. The owners hastily came to the table. Roosevelt also sought better enforcement of the Interstate Commerce Act and Sherman Antitrust Act. He pushed through the Elkins Act (1903), which prohibited discriminatory railway rates that favored powerful customers. That same year, he created the Bureau of Corporations, empowered to investigate business practices and bolster the Justice Department's capacity to mount antitrust suits. The department had already filed such a suit against the Northern Securities Company, arguing that this combination of northwestern railroads had created a monopoly in violation of the Sherman Antitrust Act. In a landmark decision in 1904, the Supreme Court ordered Northern Securities dissolved.

That year, calling for every American to get what he called a Square Deal, Roosevelt handily defeated Democratic candidate Alton B. Parker. Now president in his own right, Roosevelt stepped up his attack on trusts. He regarded large-scale enterprise as the natural tendency of modern industry, but he hoped to

**Reining in Big Business**

This 1904 cartoon from *Puck* shows Theodore Roosevelt as a tiny figure with a sword marked "public service," taking on railroad developer Jay Gould, financier John Pierpont Morgan, and other Wall Street titans. The figure at the top right is oil magnate John D. Rockefeller. In its reference to the folktale "Jack the Giant Killer," the cartoon suggests how difficult it will be for the president to limit the power of globally connected bankers and financiers. Library of Congress.

**UNDERSTAND POINTS OF VIEW**
To what degree, and in what ways, were Roosevelt's policies progressive?

to his successor, William Howard Taft. In its *Standard Oil* decision (1911), the Supreme Court agreed with Taft's Justice Department that John D. Rockefeller's massive oil monopoly should be broken up into several competing companies. After this ruling, Taft's attorney general undertook antitrust actions against other giant companies.

**Environmental Conservation**   Roosevelt was an ardent outdoorsman and hunter. It was after the president went bear hunting in Mississippi in 1902, in fact, that a Russian Jewish immigrant couple in New York began to sell stuffed "Teddy's bears," which became an American childhood tradition. After John Muir gave Roosevelt a tour of Yosemite Valley, the president described the transcendent experience of camping in the open air under the giant sequoias. "The majestic trunks, beautiful in color and in symmetry," he wrote, "rose round us like the pillars of a mightier cathedral than ever was conceived."

Roosevelt translated his love of nature into environmental action. By the end of his presidency, he had issued fifty-one executive orders creating wildlife refuges and signed a number of bills advocated by environmentalists. He also oversaw creation of three national parks, including Colorado's Mesa Verde, the first to "protect the works of man": American Indian archaeological sites. Also notable was his vigorous use of the Antiquities Act, through which he set aside such beautiful sites as Arizona's Grand Canyon and Washington's Mt. Olympus.

Some of Roosevelt's conservation policies, however, had a probusiness bent. He increased the amount of land held in federal forest reserves and turned their management over to the new, independent U.S. Forest Service, created in 1905. But his forestry chief, Gifford Pinchot, insisted on fire suppression to maximize logging potential. In addition, Roosevelt lent support to the **Newlands Reclamation Act** (1902), which had much in common with earlier Republican policies to promote economic development in the West. Under the act, the federal government sold public lands to raise money for irrigation projects that expanded agriculture on arid lands. The law, interestingly, fulfilled one of the demands of the unemployed men who had marched with Coxey's Army.

**Roosevelt's Legacies**   Like the environmental laws enacted during his presidency, Theodore Roosevelt was full of contradictions. An unabashed believer in

identify and punish "malefactors of great wealth" who abused their power. After much wrangling in Congress, Roosevelt won a major victory with the passage of the Hepburn Act (1906), which enabled the Interstate Commerce Commission to set shipping rates.

At the time Roosevelt acted, trusts had partially protected themselves with the help of two friendly states, New Jersey and Delaware, whose legislatures had loosened regulations and invited trusts to incorporate under their new state laws. With its Northern Securities ruling, however, the Supreme Court began to recognize federal authority to dissolve the most egregious monopolies. Roosevelt left a powerful legacy what he called "Anglo-Saxon" superiority, Roosevelt nonetheless incurred the wrath of white supremacists by inviting Booker T. Washington to dine at the White House. Roosevelt called for elite "best men" to enter politics, but he also defended the dignity of labor.

In 1908, Roosevelt chose to retire, bequeathing the Republican nomination to talented administrator William Howard Taft. Taft portrayed himself as Roosevelt's man, though he maintained a closer relationship than his predecessor with probusiness Republicans in Congress. In 1908, Taft faced off against Democrat William Jennings Bryan, who, eloquent as ever, attacked Republicans as the party of "plutocrats": men who used their wealth to buy political influence. Bryan outdid Taft in urging tougher antitrust and prolabor legislation, but Taft won comfortably.

In the wake of Taft's victory, however, rising pressure for reform began to divide Republicans. Conservatives dug in, while militant progressives within the party thought Roosevelt and his successor had not gone far enough. Reconciling these conflicting forces was a daunting task. For Taft, it spelled disaster. Through various incidents, he found himself on the opposite side of progressive Republicans, who began to call themselves "Insurgents" and to plot their own path.

## Diverse Progressive Goals

The revolt of Republican Insurgents signaled the strength of grassroots demands for change. No one described these emerging goals more eloquently than Jane Addams, who famously declared in *Democracy and Social Ethics* (1902), "The cure for the ills of Democracy is more Democracy." It was a poignant statement, given the sharply antidemocratic direction American politics had taken since the 1890s. What, now, should more democracy look like? Various groups of progressives — women, antipoverty reformers, African American advocates — often disagreed about priorities and goals. Some, frustrated by events in the United States, traveled abroad to study inspiring experiments in other nations, hoping to bring ideas home (America Compared, p. 653).

States also served as seedbeds of change. Theodore Roosevelt dubbed Wisconsin a "laboratory of democracy" under energetic Republican governor Robert La Follette (1901–1905). La Follette promoted what he called the **Wisconsin Idea** — greater government intervention in the economy, with reliance on experts, particularly progressive economists, for policy recommendations. Like Addams, La Follette combined respect for expertise with commitment to "more Democracy."

He won battles to restrict lobbying and to give Wisconsin citizens the right of **recall** — voting to remove unpopular politicians from office — and **referendum** — voting directly on a proposed law, rather than leaving it in the hands of legislators. Continuing his career in the U.S. Senate, La Follette, like Roosevelt, advocated increasingly aggressive measures to protect workers and rein in corporate power.

**Protecting the Poor**   The urban settlement movement called attention to poverty in America's industrial cities. In the emerging social sciences, experts argued that unemployment and crowded slums were not caused by laziness and ignorance, as elite Americans had long believed. Instead, as journalist Robert Hunter wrote in his landmark study, *Poverty* (1904), such problems resulted from "miserable and unjust social conditions." Charity work was at best a limited solution. "How vain to waste our energies on single cases of relief," declared one reformer, "when *society* should aim at removing the prolific sources of all the woe."

By the early twentieth century, reformers placed particular emphasis on labor conditions for women and children. The **National Child Labor Committee**, created in 1907, hired photographer Lewis Hine to record brutal conditions in mines and mills where children worked. (See Hine's photograph on p. 621.) Impressed by the committee's investigations, Theodore Roosevelt sponsored the first White House Conference on Dependent Children in 1909, bringing national attention to child welfare issues. In 1912, momentum from the conference resulted in creation of the Children's Bureau in the U.S. Labor Department.

Those seeking to protect working-class women scored a major triumph in 1908 with the Supreme Court's decision in **Muller v. Oregon**, which upheld an Oregon law limiting women's workday to ten hours. Given the Court's ruling three years earlier in *Lochner v. New York*, it was a stunning victory. To win the case, the National Consumers' League (NCL) recruited Louis Brandeis, a son of Jewish immigrants who was widely known as "the people's lawyer" for his eagerness to take on vested interests. Brandeis's legal brief in the *Muller* case devoted only two pages to the constitutional issue of state police powers. Instead, Brandeis rested his arguments on data gathered by the NCL describing the toll that long work hours took on women's health. The "Brandeis brief" cleared the way for use of social science research in court decisions. Sanctioning a more expansive role for state governments, the *Muller* decision encouraged women's organizations to lobby for further reforms. Their achievements included

## A Progressive Reports from New Zealand

Henry Demarest Lloyd, a reform journalist discouraged by populism's defeat in the United States, toured New Zealand in 1899. Lloyd wanted to study New Zealand's sudden burst of reform legislation stemming from a great industrial strike in 1890 and, in its wake, a Labor Party election victory that precipitated dramatic change.

Lloyd was one of many reformers who looked overseas for progressive ideas. The urban settlement movement in the United States was inspired by British examples. Municipal, state, and federal officials borrowed innovative policies from other parts of the industrializing world—from scientific forest management to workmen's compensation laws.

New Zealand democracy is the talk of the world to-day. It has made itself the policeman and partner of industry to an extent unknown elsewhere. It is the "experiment station" of advanced legislation. . . .

Instead of escaping from the evils of the social order by going to a new country, the Englishmen who settled New Zealand found that they had brought all its problems with them. . . . The best acres were in the hands of monopolists. . . . The little farmer, forced by unjust and deliberately contrived laws to pay his own and his rich neighbor's taxes, had to sell out his little homestead to that neighbor for what he could get. The workingman, able to get neither land nor work, had to become a tramp. . . . The blood of the people was the vintage of the rich.

Here is the record of ten years [of progressive legislation]: . . . The rich man, because rich, is made to pay more. . . .

By compulsory arbitration the public gets for the guidance of public opinion all the facts as to disputes between labor and capital, [and] puts an end to strikes and lockouts. . . . For the unemployed the nation makes itself a labor bureau. It brings them and the employers together. It reorganizes its public works and land system so as to give land to the landless and work to the workless. . . . The state itself insures the working people against accident.

. . . The nation's railroads are used to redistribute unemployed labour, to rebuild industry shattered by calamity, to stimulate production by special rates to and from farms and factories, to give health and education to the school and factory population and the people generally by cheap excursions.

. . . Women are enfranchised. . . . On election day one can see the baby-carriage standing in front of the polls while the father and mother go in and vote—against each other if they choose.

Last of all, pensions are given to the aged poor.

. . . We are exhorted to take "one step at a time" [but] this theory does not fit the New Zealand evolution. . . . It was not merely a change in parties; it was a change in principles and institutions that amounted to nothing less than a social right-about-face. It was a New Zealand revolution, one which without destruction passed at once to the tasks of construction.

Source: Henry Demarest Lloyd, *Newest England* (New York: Doubleday, 1901), 1, 364–374.

### QUESTIONS FOR ANALYSIS

1. What reforms had New Zealand enacted, according to Lloyd, and what problems did they solve?
2. New Zealand had a population of one million in 1890, mostly British immigrants and their descendants, with a smaller number of native Maori. Why might reform have been easier to achieve there than in the United States?

the first law providing public assistance for single mothers with dependent children (Illinois, 1911) and the first minimum wage law for women (Massachusetts, 1912).

*Muller* had drawbacks, however. Though men as well as women suffered from long work hours, the *Muller* case did not protect men. Brandeis's brief treated all women as potential mothers, focusing on the state's interest in protecting future children. Brandeis and his allies hoped this would open the door to broader regulation of working hours. The Supreme Court, however, seized on motherhood as the key issue, asserting that the female worker, because of her maternal function, was "in a class by herself, and legislation for her protection may be sustained, even when like legislation is not

**Robert M. La Follette**

La Follette was transformed into a political reformer when, in 1891, a Wisconsin Republican boss attempted to bribe him to influence a judge in a railway case. As he described it in his autobiography, "Out of this awful ordeal came understanding; and out of understanding came resolution. I determined that the power of this corrupt influence . . . should be broken." This photograph captures him at the top of his form, expounding his progressive vision to a rapt audience of Wisconsin citizens at an impromptu street gathering. Library of Congress.

necessary for men." This conclusion dismayed labor advocates and divided female reformers for decades afterward.

Male workers did benefit, however, from new workmen's compensation measures. Between 1910 and 1917, all the industrial states enacted insurance laws covering on-the-job accidents, so workers' families would not starve if a breadwinner was injured or killed. Some states also experimented with so-called mothers' pensions, providing state assistance after a breadwinner's desertion or death. Mothers, however, were subjected to home visits to determine whether they "deserved" government aid; injured workmen were not judged on this basis, a pattern of gender discrimination that reflected the broader impulse to protect women, while also treating them differently from men. Mothers' pensions reached relatively small numbers of women, but they laid foundations for the national program Aid to Families with Dependent Children, an important component of the Social Security Act of 1935.

While federalism gave the states considerable freedom to innovate, it hampered national reforms. In some states, for example, opponents of child labor won laws barring young children from factory work and strictly regulating hours and conditions for older children's labor. In the South, however, and in coal-mining states like Pennsylvania, companies fiercely resisted such laws — as did many working-class parents who relied on children's income to keep the family fed. A proposed U.S. constitutional amendment to abolish child labor never won ratification; only four states passed it. Tens of thousands of children continued to work in low-wage jobs, especially in the South. The same decentralized power that permitted innovation in Wisconsin hampered the creation of national minimum standards for pay and job safety.

**The Birth of Modern Civil Rights**   Reeling from disenfranchisement and the sanction of racial segregation in *Plessy v. Ferguson* (1896), African American leaders faced distinctive challenges. Given the obvious deterioration of African American rights, a new generation of black leaders proposed bolder approaches than those popularized earlier by Booker T. Washington. Harvard-educated sociologist W. E. B. Du Bois called

**W. E. B. Du Bois**

W. E. B. Du Bois was born in western Massachusetts in 1868, the son of a barber and a domestic worker. He received an excellent local education and went on to earn his BA and PhD at Harvard, as well as to study with cutting-edge social scientists in Germany. By 1900, Du Bois had become a national civil rights leader and America's leading black intellectual. Famous for his sociological and historical studies, including *The Souls of Black Folk* (1903), Du Bois helped found the National Association for the Advancement of Colored People (NAACP) and edited the organization's journal, *The Crisis*. Between 1900 and 1945, he helped organize Pan-African conferences in locations around the world. Toward the end of his life, Du Bois pursued this Pan-African ideal by moving to Ghana, the first modern African nation formed after the end of European colonialism. He died there in 1963. Special Collections and Archives, W. E. B. Du Bois Library, University of Massachusetts Amherst.

for a **talented tenth** of educated blacks to develop new strategies. "The policy of compromise has failed," declared William Monroe Trotter, pugnacious editor of the *Boston Guardian*. "The policy of resistance and aggression deserves a trial."

In 1905, Du Bois and Trotter called a meeting at Niagara Falls — on the Canadian side, because no hotel on the U.S. side would admit blacks. The resulting Niagara Principles called for full voting rights; an end to segregation; equal treatment in the justice system; and equal opportunity in education, jobs, health care,

and military service. These principles, based on African American pride and an uncompromising demand for full equality, guided the civil rights movement throughout the twentieth century.

In 1908, a bloody race riot broke out in Springfield, Illinois. Appalled by the white mob's violence in the hometown of Abraham Lincoln, New York settlement worker Mary White Ovington called together a group of sympathetic progressives to formulate a response. Their meeting led in 1909 to creation of the **National Association for the Advancement of Colored People (NAACP)**. Most leaders of the Niagara Movement soon joined; W. E. B. Du Bois became editor of the NAACP journal, *The Crisis*. The fledgling group found allies in many African American women's clubs and churches. It also cooperated with the National Urban League (1911), a union of agencies that assisted black migrants in the North. Over the coming decades, these groups grew into a powerful force for racial justice.

**The Problem of Labor**   Leaders of the nation's dominant union, the American Federation of Labor, were slow to ally with progressives. They had long believed workers should improve their situation through strikes and direct negotiation with employers, not through politics. But by the 1910s, as progressive reformers came forward with solutions, labor leaders in state after state began to join the cause.

The nation also confronted a daring wave of radical labor militancy. In 1905, the Western Federation of Miners (WFM), led by fiery leaders such as William "Big Bill" Haywood, helped create a new movement, the **Industrial Workers of the World** (IWW). The Wobblies, as they were called, fervently supported the Marxist class struggle. As syndicalists, they believed that by resisting in the workplace and ultimately launching a general strike, workers could overthrow capitalism. A new society would emerge, run directly by workers. At its height, around 1916, the IWW had about 100,000 members. Though divided by internal conflicts, the group helped spark a number of local protests during the 1910s, including strikes of rail car builders in Pennsylvania, textile operatives in Massachusetts, rubber workers in Ohio, and miners in Minnesota.

Meanwhile, after midnight on October 1, 1910, an explosion ripped through the *Los Angeles Times* headquarters, killing twenty employees and wrecking the building. It turned out that John J. McNamara, a high official

**COMPARE AND CONTRAST**

How did various grassroots reformers define "progressivism," and how did their views differ from Theodore Roosevelt's version of "progressivism"?

**The Ludlow Massacre, 1914**

Like his drawings of Triangle Shirtwaist fire victims in New York, this cover illustration for the popular socialist magazine *The Masses* demonstrates John Sloan's outrage at social injustice in progressive America. The drawing memorializes a tragic episode during a coal miners' strike at Ludlow, Colorado—the asphyxiation of women and children when vigilantes torched the tent city of evicted miners—and the aftermath, an armed revolt by enraged miners. *The Masses*, June 1914.

of the American Federation of Labor's Bridge and Structural Iron Workers Union, had planned the bombing against the fiercely antiunion *Times*. McNamara's brother and another union member had carried out the attack. The bombing created a sensation, as did the terrible Triangle Shirtwaist fire (Chapter 19) and the IWW's high-profile strikes. What should be done? As the election of 1912 approached, labor issues moved high on the nation's agenda.

## The Election of 1912

Retirement did not sit comfortably with Theodore Roosevelt. Returning from a yearlong safari in Africa in 1910 and finding Taft wrangling with the Insurgents, Roosevelt itched to jump in. In a speech in Osawatomie, Kansas, in August 1910, he called for a **New Nationalism**. In modern America, he argued, private property had to be controlled "to whatever degree the public

welfare may require it." He proposed a federal child labor law, more recognition of labor rights, and a national minimum wage for women. Pressed by friends like Jane Addams, Roosevelt also endorsed women's suffrage. Most radical was his attack on the legal system. Insisting that courts blocked reform, Roosevelt proposed sharp curbs on their powers (American Voices, p. 658).

Early in 1912, Roosevelt announced himself as a Republican candidate for president. A battle within the party ensued. Roosevelt won most states that held primary elections, but Taft controlled party caucuses elsewhere. Dominated by regulars, the Republican convention chose Taft. Roosevelt then led his followers into what became known as the Progressive Party, offering his New Nationalism directly to the people. Though Jane Addams harbored private doubts (especially about Roosevelt's mania for battleships), she seconded his nomination, calling the Progressive Party

**The Republicans Resist Roosevelt, August 7, 1912**

This cartoon appeared in the political humor journal *Puck*, six weeks after the Republican convention nominated Taft and two days after the new Progressive Party nominated Theodore Roosevelt. The baptismal choir consists of men such as Gifford Pinchot, who helped Roosevelt form the new party. The G.O.P. elephant refuses to be baptized in "Teddyism," though Preacher Roosevelt insists, "Salvation is Free." President William Howard Taft, dressed in brown with a hat, pulls on the elephant's tail. Library of Congress.

SALVATION IS FREE, BUT IT DOESN'T APPEAL TO HIM.
THIRD-PARTY CHOIR.—"And sinners bath'd beneath that flood lose all their guilty stains."

"the American exponent of a world-wide movement for juster social conditions." In a nod to Roosevelt's combative stance, party followers called themselves "Bull Mooses."

Roosevelt was not the only rebel on the ballot: the major parties also faced a challenge from charismatic socialist Eugene V. Debs. In the 1890s, Debs had founded the American Railway Union (ARU), a broad-based group that included both skilled and unskilled workers. In 1894, amid the upheavals of depression and popular protest, the ARU had boycotted luxury Pullman sleeping cars, in support of a strike by workers at the Pullman Company. Railroad managers, claiming the strike obstructed the U.S. mail, persuaded Grover Cleveland's administration to intervene against the union. The strike failed, and Debs served time in prison along with other ARU leaders. The experience radicalized him, and in 1901 he launched the Socialist Party of America. Debs translated socialism into an American idiom, emphasizing the democratic process as a means to defeat capitalism. By the early 1910s, his party had secured a minor but persistent role in politics. Both the Progressive and Socialist parties drew strength from the West, a region with vigorous urban reform movements and a legacy of farmer-labor activism.

Watching the rise of the Progressives and Socialists, Democrats were keen to build on dramatic gains they had made in the 1910 midterm election. Among their younger leaders was Virginia-born Woodrow Wilson, who as New Jersey's governor had compiled an impressive reform record, including passage of a direct primary, workers' compensation, and utility regulation. In 1912, he won the Democrats' nomination. Wilson possessed, to a fault, the moral certainty that characterized many elite progressives. He had much in common with Roosevelt. "The old time of individual competition is probably gone by," he admitted, agreeing for more federal measures to restrict big business. But his goals were less sweeping than Roosevelt's, and only gradually did he hammer out a reform program, calling it the New Freedom. "If America is not to have free enterprise," Wilson warned, "then she can have freedom of no sort whatever." He claimed Roosevelt's program represented collectivism, whereas the New Freedom would preserve political and economic liberty.

With four candidates in the field—Taft, Roosevelt, Wilson, and Debs—the 1912 campaign generated intense excitement. Democrats continued to have an enormous blind spot: their opposition to African American rights. But Republicans, despite plentiful opportunities, had also conspicuously failed to end segregation or pass antilynching laws. Though African American leaders had high hopes for the Progressive Party, they were crushed when the new party refused to seat southern black delegates or take a stand for racial equality. W. E. B. Du Bois considered voting for Debs, calling the Socialists the only party "which openly recognized Negro manhood." But he ultimately endorsed Wilson. Across the North, in a startling shift, thousands of African American men and women worked and voted for Wilson, hoping Democrats' reform

**COMPARE AND CONTRAST**

Why did the election of 1912 feature four candidates, and how did their platforms differ?

## Theodore Roosevelt: From Anti-Populist to New Nationalist

Theodore Roosevelt published the first piece below in a leading journal in 1897. At the time he was serving as police commissioner of New York City. The second document is a famous speech he delivered in 1910, when he had retired from the presidency but was planning a bid for the 1912 Republican nomination.

### "How Not to Help Our Poorer Brother," 1897

In the 1890s Roosevelt, a rising Republican star, forcefully denounced populism and other radical movements. The comments below were part of an exchange with Populists' 1896 vice-presidential nominee, Tom Watson of Georgia.

There are plenty of ugly things about wealth and its possessors in the present age, and I suppose there have been in all ages. There are many rich people who so utterly lack patriotism, or show such sordid and selfish traits of character, . . . that all right-minded men must look upon them with angry contempt; but, on the whole, the thrifty are apt to be better citizens than the thriftless; and the worst capitalist cannot harm laboring men as they are harmed by demagogues. . . .

The first lesson to teach the poor man is that, as a whole, the wealth of the community is distinctly beneficial to him; that he is better off in the long run because other men are well off, and that the surest way to destroy what measure of prosperity he may have is to paralyze industry and the well-being of those men who have achieved success.

. . . It may become necessary to interfere even more than we have done with the right of private contract, and to shackle cunning as we have shackled force. All I insist upon is that we must be sure of our ground before trying to get any legislation, and that we must not expect too much from this legislation. . . . The worst foe of the poor man is the labor leader, whether philanthropist or politician, who tried to teach him that he is a victim of conspiracy and injustice, when in reality he is merely working out his fate with blood and sweat as the immense majority of men who are worthy of the name always have done and always will have to do. . . .

Something can be done by good laws; more can be done by honest administration of the laws; but most of all can be done by frowning resolutely upon the preachers of vague discontent; and by upholding the true doctrine of self-reliance, self-help, and self-mastery. This doctrine sets forth many things. Among them is that, though a man can occasionally be helped when he stumbles, yet that it is useless to try to carry him when he will not or cannot walk; and worse than useless to try to bring down the work and reward of the thrifty and intelligent to the level of the capacity of the weak, the shiftless, and the idle. . . .

If an American is to amount to anything he must rely upon himself, and not upon the State. . . . It is both foolish and wicked to teach the average man who is not well off that some wrong or injustice has been done him, and that he should hope for redress elsewhere than in his own industry, honesty and intelligence.

### New Nationalism Speech, August 31, 1910

Roosevelt delivered this speech to a gathering of Union veterans at Osawatomie, Kansas, a site associated with abolitionist John Brown (Chapter 13). Why do you think Roosevelt chose this occasion and audience?

Of that [Civil War] generation of men to whom we owe so much, the man to whom we owe most is, of course, Lincoln. Part of our debt to him is because he forecast our present struggle and saw the way out. He said:

. . . "Labor is prior to, and independent of, capital. Capital is only the fruit of labor, and could never have existed if labor had not first existed. Labor is the superior of capital, and deserves much the higher consideration."

If that remark was original with me, I should be even more strongly denounced as a Communist agitator than I shall be anyhow. It is Lincoln's. I am only quoting it; and that is one side; that is the side the capitalist should hear. Now, let the working man hear his side.

"Capital has its rights, which are as worthy of protection as any other rights. . . . Nor should this lead to a war upon the owners of property. Property is the fruit of labor; property is desirable."

. . . It seems to me that, in these words, Lincoln took substantially the attitude that we ought to take; he showed the proper sense of proportion in his relative estimates of capital and labor, of human rights and property rights. One of the chief factors in progress is the destruction of special privilege. The essence of any struggle for healthy liberty has always been, and must always be, to take from some one man or class of men the right to enjoy power, or wealth, or position, or immunity, which has not been earned by service to his or their fellows. That is what you fought for in the Civil War, and that is what we strive for now.

. . . Practical equality of opportunity for all citizens, when we achieve it, will have two great results. First, every man will have a fair chance to make of himself all that in him lies; to reach the highest point to which his capacities, unassisted by special privilege of his own and unhampered by the special privilege of others, can carry him, and to get for himself and his family substantially what he has earned. Second, equality of opportunity means that the commonwealth will get from every citizen the highest service of which he is capable.

. . . When I say that I am for the square deal, I mean not merely that I stand for fair play under the present rules of the game, but that I stand for having those rules changed so as to work for a more substantial equality of opportunity and of reward for equally good service. . . . This means that our government, national and State, must be freed from the sinister influence or control of special interests. Exactly as the special interests of cotton and slavery threatened our political integrity before the Civil War, so now the great special business interests too often control and corrupt the men and methods of government for their own profit. We must drive the special interests out of politics. . . .

The Constitution guarantees protections to property, and we must make that promise good. But it does not give the right of suffrage to any corporation. The true friend of property, the true conservative, is he who insists that property shall be the servant and not the master of the commonwealth. . . . The citizens of the United States must effectively control the mighty commercial forces which they have themselves called into being.

There can be no effective control of corporations while their political activity remains. To put an end to it will be neither a short nor an easy task, but it can be done. . . .

We are face to face with new conceptions of the relations of property to human welfare, chiefly because certain advocates of the rights of property as against the rights of men have been pushing their claims too far. The man who wrongly holds that every human right is secondary to his profit must now give way to the advocate of human welfare. . . .

No man can be a good citizen unless he has a wage more than sufficient to cover the bare cost of living, and hours of labor short enough so that after his day's work is done he will have time and energy to bear his share in the management of the community. . . . We keep countless men from being good citizens by the conditions of life with which we surround them. We need comprehensive workmen's compensation acts [and] laws to regulate child labor and work for women. . . .

The New Nationalism puts the national need before sectional or personal advantage. It is impatient of the utter confusion that results from local legislatures attempting to treat national issues as local issues, [and] the impotence which makes it possible for local selfishness or for legal cunning, hired by wealthy special interests, to bring national activities to a deadlock. This New Nationalism regards the executive power as the steward of the public welfare. It demands of the judiciary that it shall be interested primarily in human welfare rather than in property. . . .

The object of government is the welfare of the people. The material progress and prosperity of a nation are desirable chiefly so far as they lead to the moral and material welfare of all good citizens.

Sources: Article from *Review of Reviews*, January 1897; speech from theodore-roosevelt.com/trspeeches.html.

---

### QUESTIONS FOR ANALYSIS

1. In what ways did Roosevelt's views change between 1897 and 1910? What factors might have contributed to the change? Can you identify aspects of Roosevelt's thinking that remained the same?

2. How might the jobs Roosevelt held or sought, in 1897 and in 1910, have influenced his ideas?

3. If you were asked, after reading these documents, what Roosevelt stood for, how would you respond?

energy would benefit Americans across racial lines. The change helped lay the foundations for Democrats' New Deal coalition of the 1930s.

Despite the intense campaign, Republicans' division between Taft and Roosevelt made the result fairly easy to predict. Wilson won, though he received only 42 percent of the popular vote and almost certainly would have lost if Roosevelt had not been in the race (Map 20.5). In comparison with Roosevelt and Debs, Wilson appeared to be a rather old-fashioned choice. But with labor protests cresting and progressives gaining support, Wilson faced intense pressure to act.

# Wilson and the New Freedom, 1913–1917

In his inaugural address, Wilson acknowledged that industrialization had precipitated a crisis. "There can be no equality of opportunity," he said, "if men and women and children be not shielded . . . from the consequences of great industrial and social processes which they cannot alter, control, or singly cope with." Wilson was a Democrat, and labor interests and farmers — some previously radicalized in the People's Party — were important components of his base. In the South, many of those voters also upheld strong support for white supremacy. Despite many northern African Americans' support for Wilson, his administration did little for those constituents. But he undertook bold economic reforms.

## Economic Reforms

In an era of rising corporate power, many Democrats believed workers needed stronger government to intervene on their behalf, and they began to transform themselves into a modern, state-building party. The Wilson administration achieved a series of landmark measures — at least as significant as those enacted during earlier administrations, and perhaps more so (Table 20.1). The most enduring was the federal progressive income tax. "Progressive," by this definition, referred to the fact that it was not a flat tax but rose progressively toward the top of the income scale. The tax, passed in the 1890s but rejected by the Supreme Court, was reenacted as the Sixteenth Amendment to the Constitution, ratified by the states in February 1913. The next year, Congress used the new power to enact an income tax of 1 to 7 percent on Americans with annual incomes of $4,000 or more. At a time when white

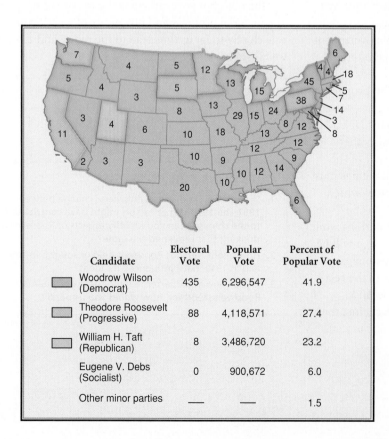

| Candidate | Electoral Vote | Popular Vote | Percent of Popular Vote |
|---|---|---|---|
| Woodrow Wilson (Democrat) | 435 | 6,296,547 | 41.9 |
| Theodore Roosevelt (Progressive) | 88 | 4,118,571 | 27.4 |
| William H. Taft (Republican) | 8 | 3,486,720 | 23.2 |
| Eugene V. Debs (Socialist) | 0 | 900,672 | 6.0 |
| Other minor parties | — | — | 1.5 |

**MAP 20.5**
**The Presidential Election of 1912**

The 1912 election reveals why the two-party system is so strongly rooted in American politics — especially in presidential elections. The Democrats, though a minority party, won an electoral landslide because the Republicans divided their vote between Roosevelt and Taft. This result indicates what is at stake when major parties splinter. The Socialist Party candidate, Eugene V. Debs, despite a record vote of 900,000, received no electoral votes.

THE FINISHING TOUCH
*Drawn by E. W. Kemble*

**"The Finishing Touch," November 2, 1912**

Three days before the election, *Harper's Weekly*, which endorsed Woodrow Wilson, suggested in this cartoon some of the reasons why he would win. Roosevelt supported protective tariffs, while Wilson called for tariff reform; Democrats also claimed that Roosevelt's antitrust proposals were not sufficiently aggressive and that in 1904 he had taken a large campaign contribution from Standard Oil. Such controversies showed the nation's accelerating momentum for reform. The man in the middle is Wilson's campaign manager, William McAdoo. *Harper's Weekly*, November 2, 1912, p. 26.

male wageworkers might expect to make $800 per year, the tax affected less than 5 percent of households.

Three years later, Congress followed this with an inheritance tax. These measures created an entirely new way to fund the federal government, replacing Republicans' high tariff as the chief source of revenue. Over subsequent decades, especially between the 1930s and the 1970s, the income tax system markedly reduced America's extremes of wealth and poverty.

Wilson also reorganized the financial system to address the absence of a central bank. At the time, the main function of national central banks was to back up commercial banks in case they could not meet their obligations. In the United States, the great private banks of New York (such as J. P. Morgan's) assumed this role; if they weakened, the entire system could collapse. This had nearly happened in 1907, when the Knickerbocker Trust Company failed, precipitating a panic. The **Federal Reserve Act** (1913) gave the nation

a banking system more resistant to such crises. It created twelve district reserve banks funded and controlled by their member banks, with a central Federal Reserve Board to impose regulation. The Federal Reserve could issue currency — paper money based on assets held in the system — and set the interest rate that district reserve banks charged to their members. It thereby regulated the flow of credit to the general public. The act strengthened the banking system and, to a modest degree, discouraged risky speculation on Wall Street.

Wilson and the Democratic Congress turned next to the trusts. In doing so, Wilson relied heavily on Louis D. Brandeis, the celebrated people's lawyer. Brandeis denied that monopolies were efficient. On the contrary, he believed the best source of

**TRACE CHANGE OVER TIME**

To what degree did reforms of the Wilson era fulfill goals that various agrarian-labor advocates and progressives had sought?

**TABLE 20.1**

| Major Federal Progressive Measures, 1883–1921 |
| --- |
| **Before 1900** |
| Pendleton Civil Service Act (1883) |
| Hatch Act (1887; Chapter 17) |
| Interstate Commerce Act (1887; Chapter 17) |
| Sherman Antitrust Act (1890) |
| Federal income tax (1894; struck down by Supreme Court, 1895) |
| **During Theodore Roosevelt's Presidency, 1901–1909** |
| Newlands Reclamation Act for federal irrigation (1902) |
| Elkins Act (1903) |
| First National Wildlife Refuge (1903; Chapter 18) |
| Bureau of Corporations created to aid Justice Department antitrust work (1903) |
| National Forest Service created (1905) |
| Antiquities Act (1906; Chapter 18) |
| Pure Food and Drug Act (1906; Chapter 19) |
| Hepburn Act (1906) |
| First White House Conference on Dependent Children (1909) |
| **During William Howard Taft's Presidency, 1909–1913** |
| Mann Act preventing interstate prostitution (1910; Chapter 19) |
| Children's Bureau created in the U.S. Labor Department (1912) |
| U.S. Commission on Industrial Relations appointed (1912) |
| **During Woodrow Wilson's Presidency, 1913–1920** |
| Sixteenth Amendment to the Constitution; federal income tax (1913) |
| Seventeenth Amendment to the Constitution; direct election of U.S. senators (1913) |
| Federal Reserve Act (1913) |
| Clayton Antitrust Act (1914) |
| Seamen's Act (1915) |
| Workmen's Compensation Act (1916) |
| Adamson Eight-Hour Act (1916) |
| National Park Service created (1916; Chapter 18) |
| Eighteenth Amendment to the Constitution; prohibition of liquor (1919; Chapter 22) |
| Nineteenth Amendment to the Constitution; women's suffrage (1920; Chapter 21) |

efficiency was vigorous competition in a free market. The trick was to prevent trusts from unfairly using their power to curb such competition. In the **Clayton Antitrust Act** (1914), which amended the Sherman Act, the definition of illegal practices was left flexible, subject to the test of whether an action "substantially lessen[ed] competition." The new Federal Trade Commission received broad powers to decide what was fair, investigating companies and issuing "cease and desist" orders against anticompetitive practices.

Labor issues, meanwhile, received attention from a blue-ribbon U.S. Commission on Industrial Relations, appointed near the end of Taft's presidency and charged with investigating the conditions of labor. In its 1913 report, the commission summed up the impact of industrialization on low-skilled workers. Many earned $10 or less a week and endured regular episodes of unemployment; some faced long-term poverty and hardship. Workers held "an almost universal conviction" that they were "denied justice." The commission concluded that a major cause of industrial violence was the ruthless antiunionism of American employers. In its key recommendation, the report called for federal laws protecting workers' right to organize and engage in collective bargaining. Though such laws were, in 1915, too radical to win passage, the commission helped set a new national agenda that would come to fruition in the 1930s.

Guided by the commission's revelations, President Wilson warmed up to labor. In 1915 and 1916, he championed a host of bills to benefit American workers. They included the Adamson Act, which established an eight-hour day for railroad workers; the Seamen's Act, which eliminated age-old abuses of merchant sailors; and a workmen's compensation law for federal employees. Wilson, despite initial modest goals, presided over a major expansion of federal authority, perhaps the most significant since Reconstruction. The continued growth of U.S. government offices during Wilson's term reflected a reality that transcended party lines: corporations had grown in size and power, and Americans increasingly wanted federal authority to grow, too.

Wilson's reforms did not extend to the African Americans who had supported him in 1912. In fact, the president rolled back certain Republican policies, such as selected appointments of black postmasters. "I tried to help elect Wilson," W. E. B. Du Bois reflected gloomily, but "under Wilson came the worst attempt at Jim Crow legislation and discrimination in civil service that we had experienced since the Civil War." Wilson famously praised the film *Birth of a Nation* (1915), which depicted the Reconstruction-era Ku Klux Klan in heroic terms. In this way, Democratic control of the White House helped set the tone for the Klan's return in the 1920s.

## Progressive Legacies

In the industrial era, millions of Americans decided that their political system needed to adjust to new conditions. Whatever their specific goals — and whether they were rural, working-class, or middle-class — reformers faced fierce opposition from powerful business interests. When they managed to win key

regulatory laws, they often found these struck down by hostile courts and were forced to try again by different means. Thus the Progressive Era in the United States should be understood partly by its limitations. Elitism and racial prejudice, embodied in new voting restrictions, limited working-class power at the polls; African Americans, their plight ignored by most white reformers, faced segregation and violence. Divided power in a federalist system blocked passage of uniform national policies on such key issues as child labor. Key social welfare programs that became popular in Europe during these decades, including national health insurance and old-age pensions, scarcely made it onto the American agenda until the 1930s.

An international perspective suggests several reasons for American resistance to such programs. Business interests in the United States were exceptionally successful and powerful, flush with recent expansion. At the time, also, voters in countries with older, more native-born populations tended to support government regulation and welfare spending to a greater extent than their counterparts in countries with younger populations and large numbers of immigrants. Younger voters, understandably, seem to have been less concerned than older voters about health insurance and old-age security. Divisions in the American working class also played a role. Black, immigrant, and native-born white laborers often viewed one another as enemies or strangers rather than as members of a single class with common interests. This helps explain why the Socialist Party drew, at peak, less than 6 percent of the U.S. vote at a time when its counterparts in Finland, Germany, and France drew 40 percent or more. Lack of pressure from a strong, self-conscious workingmen's party contributed to more limited results in the United States.

But it would be wrong to underestimate progressive achievements. Over several decades, in this period, more and more prosperous Americans began to support stronger economic regulations. Even the most cautious, elite progressives recognized that the United States had entered a new era. Multinational corporations overshadowed small businesses; in vast cities, old support systems based on village and kinship melted away. Outdated political institutions — from the spoils system to urban machines — would no longer do. Walter Lippmann, founding editor of the progressive magazine *New Republic*, observed in 1914 that Americans had "no precedents to guide us, no wisdom

**PLACE EVENTS IN CONTEXT**
What factors explain the limits of progressive reform in the United States?

that wasn't made for a simpler age." Progressives created new wisdom. By 1917, they had drawn blueprints for a modern American state, one whose powers more suited the needs of an industrial era.

## SUMMARY

The Progressive Era emerged from the political turmoil of the 1880s and 1890s. In the 1880s, despite the limits imposed by close elections, federal and state governments managed to achieve important administrative and economic reforms. After 1888, Republican leaders undertook more sweeping efforts, including the Sherman Antitrust Act, but failed in a quest to protect black voting rights. In the South and West, the People's Party called for much stronger government intervention in the economy, but its radical program drew bitter Republican and Democratic resistance.

The depression of the 1890s brought a wave of reaction. Labor unrest threw the nation into crisis,

and Cleveland's intransigence over the gold standard cost the Democrats dearly in the 1894 and 1896 elections. While Republicans took over the federal government, southern Democrats restricted voting rights in the Solid South. Federal courts struck down regulatory laws and supported southern racial discrimination.

After McKinley's assassination, Roosevelt launched a program that balanced reform and private enterprise. At both the federal and state levels, progressive reformers made extensive use of elite expertise. At the grassroots, black reformers battled racial discrimination; women reformers worked on issues ranging from public health to women's working conditions; and labor activists tried to address the problems that fueled persistent labor unrest. The election of 1912 split the Republicans, giving victory to Woodrow Wilson, who launched a Democratic program of economic and labor reform. Despite the limits of the Progressive Era, the reforms of this period laid the foundation for a modern American state.

# CHAPTER REVIEW

**MAKE IT STICK**   Go to **LearningCurve** to retain what you've read.

## TERMS TO KNOW   Identify and explain the significance of each term below.

### Key Concepts and Events

"waving the bloody shirt" (p. 638)
Gilded Age (p. 638)
Pendleton Act (p. 638)
Mugwumps (p. 639)
Sherman Antitrust Act (p. 642)
Lodge Bill (p. 642)
Omaha Platform (p. 643)
free silver (p. 645)
*Williams v. Mississippi* (p. 645)
Solid South (p. 646)
*Lochner v. New York* (p. 649)
Newlands Reclamation Act (p. 651)
Wisconsin Idea (p. 652)

recall (p. 652)
referendum (p. 652)
National Child Labor Committee (p. 652)
*Muller v. Oregon* (p. 652)
talented tenth (p. 655)
National Association for the Advancement of Colored People (NAACP) (p. 655)
Industrial Workers of the World (p. 655)
New Nationalism (p. 656)
Federal Reserve Act (p. 662)
Clayton Antitrust Act (p. 662)

### Key People

Mary E. Lease (p. 636)
William Jennings Bryan (p. 647)
Theodore Roosevelt (p. 650)
Robert La Follette (p. 652)
Louis Brandeis (p. 652)
W. E. B. Du Bois (p. 654)
Eugene V. Debs (p. 657)

## REVIEW QUESTIONS   Answer these questions to demonstrate your understanding of the chapter's main ideas.

1. Reformers in the Progressive Era came from different backgrounds and represented several distinct interests. What were some of those backgrounds and interests? How did their goals differ?

2. How did the economic crisis of the 1890s shape American politics?

3. Compare the reform legislation passed during Theodore Roosevelt's presidency with that of Wilson's term. How were these goals and achievements shaped by the broader agenda of the party that held power (Republicans, in Roosevelt's case, and Democrats, in Wilson's)?

4. **THEMATIC UNDERSTANDING**   Look at the events on the thematic timeline on page 543. Historians often call the decades from the 1880s to the 1910s the Progressive Era. Given the limitations and new problems that emerged during this time, as well as the achievements of progressive policymaking, do you think the name is warranted? What other names might we suggest for this era?

## MAKING CONNECTIONS

Recognize the larger developments and continuities within and across chapters by answering these questions.

1. **ACROSS TIME AND PLACE** Returning to Chapter 17, review the strategies and goals of the labor and agrarian organizations that flourished in the 1880s. The People's Party embodied many of those ideas. Imagine that you are a journalist interviewing a former People's Party leader in 1917. To what extent might he or she have said that progressives had, after 1900, fulfilled the agrarian-labor agenda? To what extent might he or she criticize progressives for failing to achieve important reforms? What do you conclude from this about the similarities and differences of populism and progressivism?

2. **VISUAL EVIDENCE** Study the cartoons that appear on pages 642, 651, and 660. One depicts a woman's dressing room; two depict combat among men. What do these cartoons tell us about the ways that ideals of masculinity and femininity were deployed in political campaigns? How might you use these cartoons to explain the challenges that women faced in winning suffrage during the Progressive Era? (For a counterpoint, you may also want to examine John Sloan's drawing about the Ludlow Massacre, on p. 656, and compare its depiction of masculine violence to the other three cartoons.)

## MORE TO EXPLORE    Start here to learn more about the events discussed in this chapter.

Charles Calhoun, *Conceiving a New Republic* (2006). An excellent account of post-Reconstruction politics, emphasizing issues of race and Republicans' dilemma in the South.

John Milton Cooper, *The Warrior and the Priest* (1983). A provocative dual biography of Theodore Roosevelt and Woodrow Wilson.

Maureen Flanagan, *America Reformed* (2007). A readable introduction and guide to further sources on progressive movements.

Michael Kazin, *A Godly Hero* (2006). This biography of William Jennings Bryan is a good starting point on the era's Democrats and their charismatic leader.

Robert C. McMath, *American Populism* (1993). A lively history of the Farmers' Alliance and People's Party.

Nancy Woloch, ed., *Muller v. Oregon* (1996). An excellent analysis and collection of primary documents on this critical legal decision.

## TIMELINE

Ask yourself why this chapter begins and ends with these dates and then identify the links among related events.

| | |
|---|---|
| **1881** | • President James Garfield assassinated |
| **1883** | • Pendleton Act establishes the Civil Service Commission |
| **1890** | • Sherman Antitrust Act<br>• People's Party created in Kansas |
| **1893** | • Economic depression begins |
| **1894** | • Coxey's Army marches on Washington, D.C. |
| **1895** | • John Pierpont Morgan arranges gold purchases to rescue U.S. Treasury |
| **1896** | • William McKinley wins presidency<br>• *Plessy v. Ferguson* establishes "separate but equal" doctrine |
| **1898** | • *Williams v. Mississippi* allows poll taxes and literacy tests for voters |
| **1899** | • National Consumers' League founded |
| **1901** | • Eugene Debs founds the Socialist Party of America<br>• McKinley assassinated; Theodore Roosevelt assumes presidency |
| **1902** | • Newlands Reclamation Act |
| **1903** | • Elkins Act |
| **1904** | • Robert Hunter publishes *Poverty* |
| **1905** | • Industrial Workers of the World founded<br>• Niagara Principles articulated |
| **1906** | • Hepburn Act |
| **1908** | • *Muller v. Oregon* limits women's work hours |
| **1909** | • NAACP created |
| **1912** | • Four-way election gives presidency to Woodrow Wilson |
| **1913** | • Sixteenth Amendment<br>• Seventeenth Amendment<br>• Federal Reserve Act |
| **1914** | • Clayton Antitrust Act |

**KEY TURNING POINTS:** In the timeline above, identify key actions taken by Congress and the Progressive Era presidents, and those enacted by the Supreme Court. What role did each branch of government play in the Progressive Era, and how did those roles change over time?

# Domestic and Global Challenges
## 1890–1945

In a famous speech he made in 1918, amid the horrors of World War I, President Woodrow Wilson outlined his Fourteen Points for international peace. Americans, he argued, must help make the world "fit and safe to live in." "We cannot be separated in interest or divided in purpose," Wilson declared. Fifteen years later, President Franklin Delano Roosevelt made a similar call for solidarity during the Great Depression. "We face the arduous days that lie before us," he said, "in the warm courage of national unity." Soon, even more grit and determination were needed, as Americans faced another looming world war.

In these years, America's political leaders met major challenges at home and abroad with bold responses. The exception to this pattern was the 1920s, a decade of limited government under Republican presidents who deferred to business interests and to Americans' isolationist, consumer-oriented mood. During the crises of World War I, the Great Depression, and World War II, however, American voters called for — and got — what Roosevelt called "action and action now."

Wilson's proposals met with failure at the end of World War I, but Roosevelt won immense popularity for his measures to combat the depression, which helped millions of Americans survive unemployment and hardship. FDR, however, had limited success in ending the depression until World War II reignited the American economy. The United States emerged from the war with unprecedented global power, and the federal government with a broad mandate for sustaining the new welfare state. Part 7 addresses these transformations.

## America's Rise to World Power

The United States became a major international power after the 1890s, first in the Western Hemisphere and by the 1940s across the world, renewing debates at home about America's global role. After defeating Spain in the War of 1898, the United States claimed overseas colonies and asserted control over the Caribbean basin. Though President Wilson attempted to maintain neutrality at the start of World War I, trade ties and old alliances drew America into the conflict on the Allied side. Wilson sought to influence the peace, but Allied leaders ignored his proposals and the Senate rejected the Treaty of Versailles. By war's end, the United States's position on the world stage remained uncertain.

The 1920s was an era of dollar diplomacy and U.S. business expansion abroad. In the 1930s, faced with isolationist sentiment at home and the rise of fascist powers in Europe and Japan, the Roosevelt administration steered a middle course. In the late 1930s, it began to send aid to its traditional ally Great Britain without committing U.S. forces, keeping the nation out of the brewing wars in Europe and the Pacific. When the United States entered World War II in 1941, it did so as part of an alliance with both England and the Soviet Union against Germany and Japan (and their ally Italy). The United States emerged from the war as the dominant global power. These events are covered in Chapters 21, 22, and 24.

## Modernity and Its Discontents

World War I had a powerful domestic impact in the United States. The Great Migration brought African Americans northward, and Mexicans across the U.S. border, to take up wartime jobs. A full-blown modern consumer culture also emerged by the 1920s as radio, cars, and Hollywood movies transformed leisure pastimes. While many Americans embraced consumer culture, others expressed deep fear and antagonism toward a new modern sensibility, especially secularism and sexual freedoms. Repressive impulses also came from above; during World War I, the federal government introduced new laws to police dissent, and the country took a sharp right turn. A Red Scare, rollback of labor and immigrant rights, and rising nativism marked the political scene. A resurgent nationwide Klan arose to target Catholics and Jews as well as African Americans. Many cultural conflicts emerged: the teaching of evolution in the schools angered religious fundamentalists, while "wets" and "drys" debated the prohibition of liquor.

Later events showed that racism took many forms: the U.S. government deported hundreds of thousands of people of Mexican descent during the Great Depression, including American citizens, and temporarily imprisoned Japanese Americans in a mass relocation policy during World War II. These, too, represented battles over what a diverse, modern nation would look like. We explore these conflicts in Chapters 21, 22, and 24.

## Creation of the Welfare State

In comparison with their progressive predecessors (Chapters 19 and 20), Republican policymakers of the 1920s believed in hands-off government. Their policies likely helped trigger the Great Depression and deepened its impact after it arrived. Starting in 1932, Americans voted for change: President Franklin Roosevelt's New Deal programs, 1933–1937, expanded federal responsibility for the welfare of ordinary citizens, sweeping away the *laissez faire* individualism of the previous decade. Though the New Deal faced considerable challenges on the political right—especially from business and corporate leaders and a hostile Supreme Court—the popularity of its programs, such as Social Security, established a broad consensus that the United States needed a modern welfare state to regulate the economy and provide a basic safety net for the nation's citizens. For an exploration of the New Deal, see Chapter 23.

Wartime measures went even further, as the government mobilized the entire economy and tens of millions of citizens to fight the Axis powers. The welfare state became a "warfare state," and Congress gave the president broad powers to fight the war abroad and reorganize the economy at home. Under the government-directed wartime economy, business boomed and productivity grew, but other policies, such as the internment of Japanese immigrants and Japanese Americans, violated fragile civil liberties, leaving a mixed legacy. On America's roles in World War II, see Chapter 24.

# Domestic and Global Challenges 1890–1945

## Thematic Understanding

This timeline arranges some of the important events of this period into themes. Consider the entries under "America in the World," "Politics and Power," "Identity," and "Ideas, Beliefs, and Culture." What connections do you see between events on the world stage and developments within the United States? What impact did World War I, the Great Depression, and World War II appear to have on American politics, society, and culture?  **>**

| | AMERICA IN THE WORLD | POLITICS AND POWER | IDENTITY | IDEAS, BELIEFS, AND CULTURE | WORK, EXCHANGE, AND TECHNOLOGY |
|---|---|---|---|---|---|
| **1890** | • Congress funds construction of modern battleships<br>• U.S.-backed planters overthrow Hawaii's queen (1892)<br>• U.S. wins War of 1898 against Spain; claims Hawaii, Puerto Rico, Guam, and Philippines | • Republicans sweep congressional elections as Americans respond to severe depression (1894)<br>• Republican William McKinley elected president (1896) | • "American exceptionalism" and rise of imperialism<br>• Alfred Mahan, *The Influence of Sea Power upon History* (1890) | • "Remember the *Maine*" campaign fuels surge in nationalism | • Depression of 1890s increases pressure for U.S. to secure foreign markets |
| **1900** | • U.S. war against Philippine revolutionaries<br>• Roosevelt Corollary to Monroe Doctrine (1904) | • William McKinley reelected on pro-imperialist platform (1900)<br>• William McKinley assassinated; Theodore Roosevelt becomes president (1901) | • *Insular Cases* establish noncitizenship status for new territories (1901)<br>• California, Washington, and Hawaii limit rights for Asian immigrants | • Rise of modernism | • Root-Takahira Agreement affirms free oceanic commerce (1908) |
| **1910** | • Wilson intervenes in Mexico (1914)<br>• Panama Canal opened (1914)<br>• United States enters WWI (1917)<br>• War ends; Wilson seeks to influence peace treaty negotiations (1918) | • Woodrow Wilson elected president (1912)<br>• Red Scare (1919)<br>• Woodrow Wilson issues Fourteen Points (1919)<br>• U.S. Senate rejects Treaty of Versailles (1919, 1920) | • New Ku Klux Klan founded (1915)<br>• Post-WWI race riots<br>• Wartime pressure for "100% loyalty"; dissent suppressed | • Moviemaking industry moves to southern California<br>• *Birth of a Nation* glorifies the Reconstruction-era Klan (1915)<br>• Radio Corporation of America created (1919) | • Great Migration brings African Americans to northern cities, Mexicans north to United States<br>• Assembly-line production begins |
| **1920** | • Heyday of "dollar diplomacy"<br>• U.S. occupation of Haiti and other Caribbean and Central American nations | • Nineteenth Amendment grants women's suffrage (1920)<br>• Prohibition (1920–1933)<br>• Teapot Dome scandal (1923)<br>• Republican "associated state," probusiness policies (1920–1932) | • National Origins Act limits immigration (1924) | • Rise of Hollywood<br>• Harlem Renaissance<br>• Popularity of jazz music<br>• Scopes "monkey trial" (1925) | • Economic prosperity (1922–1929)<br>• Labor gains rolled back<br>• Era of welfare capitalism<br>• Rise of automobile loans and consumer credit |
| **1930** | • Rise of European fascist powers<br>• Japan invades China (1937) | • Franklin Roosevelt elected president (1932)<br>• First New Deal (1933)<br>• Second New Deal (1935)<br>• Roosevelt attempts to reform Supreme Court (1937) | • Bonus Army (1932)<br>• Indian Reorganization Act (1934)<br>• Social Security created (1935) | • Documentary impulse in arts<br>• WPA assists artists<br>• Federal Writers' Project | • Great Depression (1929–1941)<br>• Rise of CIO and organized labor |
| **1940** | • United States enters WWII (1941)<br>• Atomic bombing of Japan and end of WWII (1945)<br>• United Nations founded (1945) | • Roosevelt elected to fourth term (1944)<br>• Roosevelt dies (1945)<br>• Harry Truman becomes president (1945) | • Internment of Japanese Americans<br>• Segregation in armed services until 1948 | • Film industry aids war effort | • War spending ends depression<br>• Rationing curbs consumer spending<br>• Married women take war jobs |

# 21

CHAPTER

# An Emerging World Power
# 1890–1918

Accepting the Democratic presidential nomination in 1900, William Jennings Bryan delivered a famous speech denouncing U.S. military occupations overseas. "God Himself," Bryan declared, "placed in every human heart the love of liberty. . . . He never made a race of people so low in the scale of civilization or intelligence that it would welcome a foreign master." At the time, Republican president William McKinley was leading an ambitious and popular plan of overseas expansion. The United States had asserted control over the Caribbean, claimed Hawaii, and sought to annex the Philippines. Bryan failed to convince a majority of voters that imperialism—the exercise of military, political, and economic power overseas—was the wrong direction. He lost the election by a landslide.

By the 1910s, however, American enthusiasm for overseas involvement cooled. Despite efforts to stay neutral, the United States got caught up in the global catastrophe of World War I, which killed 8 million combatants, including over 50,000 U.S. soldiers. By the war's end, European powers' grip on their colonial empires was weakening. The United States also ceased acquiring overseas territories and pursued a different path. It did so in part because the war brought dramatic changes at home, leaving Americans a postwar legacy of economic upheaval and political disillusionment.

President Woodrow Wilson, who in 1913 appointed Bryan as his secretary of state, tried to steer a middle course between revolutionary socialism and European-style imperialism. In Wilson's phrase, America would "make the world safe for democracy" while unapologetically working to advance U.S. economic interests. The U.S. Senate, however, rejected the 1919 Treaty of Versailles and with it Wilson's vision, leaving the nation's foreign policy in doubt. Should the United States try to promote democracy abroad? If so, how? To what degree should the federal government seek to promote American business interests? Under what conditions was overseas military action justified? When, on the contrary, did it impinge on others' sovereignty, endanger U.S. soldiers, and invite disaster? Today's debates over foreign policy still center to a large degree on questions that Americans debated in the era of McKinley, Bryan, and Wilson, when the nation first asserted itself as a major world power.

## IDENTIFY THE BIG IDEA

As the United States became a major power on the world stage, what ideas and interests did policymakers seek to promote in international affairs?

**American Soldiers on a French Battlefield, 1918** As the United States asserted its power on the world stage, American soldiers found themselves fighting on foreign battlefields. This 1918 photograph shows a few of the 1 million U.S. soldiers who joined French and British troops fighting on the brutal Western Front to defeat Germany in the Great War. Over 26,000 American soldiers lost their lives on the battlefield during World War I, and 95,000 were wounded. Library of Congress.

# From Expansion to Imperialism

Historians used to describe turn-of-the-twentieth-century U.S. imperialism as something new and unprecedented. Now they stress continuities between foreign policy in this era and the nation's earlier, relentless expansion across North America. Wars against native peoples had occurred almost continuously since the country's founding; in the 1840s, the United States had annexed a third of Mexico. The United States never administered a large colonial empire, as did European powers like Spain, England, and Germany, partly because it had a plentiful supply of natural resources in the American West. But policymakers undertook a determined quest for global markets. Events in the 1890s opened opportunities to pursue this goal in new ways.

## Foundations of Empire

American empire builders around 1900 fulfilled a vision laid out earlier by William Seward, secretary of state under presidents Abraham Lincoln and Andrew Johnson, who saw access to global markets as the key to power (Chapter 16). Seward's ideas had won only limited support at the time, but the severe economic depression of the 1890s brought Republicans into power and Seward's ideas back into vogue. Confronting high unemployment and mass protests, policymakers feared American workers would embrace socialism or Marxism. The alternative, they believed, was to create jobs and prosperity at home by selling U.S. products in overseas markets.

Intellectual trends also favored imperialism. As early as 1885, in his popular book *Our Country*, Congregationalist minister Josiah Strong urged Protestants to proselytize overseas. He predicted that the American "Anglo-Saxon race," which represented "the largest liberty, the purest Christianity, the highest civilization," would "spread itself over the earth." Such arguments were grounded in **American exceptionalism**, the idea that the United States had a unique destiny to foster democracy and civilization.

As Strong's exhortation suggested, imperialists also drew on popular racial theories, which claimed that people of "Anglo-Saxon" descent—English and often German—were superior to all others. "Anglo-Saxon" rule over foreign people of color made sense in an era when, at home, most American Indians and Asian immigrants were denied citizenship and most southern blacks were disenfranchised. Imperialists argued that "free land" on the western frontier was dwindling, and thus new outlets needed to be found for American energy and enterprise. Responding to critics of U.S. occupation of the Philippines, Theodore Roosevelt scoffed: if Filipinos should control their own islands, he declared, then America was "morally bound to return Arizona to the Apaches."

Imperialists also justified their views through racialized Social Darwinism (Chapter 18). Josiah Strong, for example, predicted that with the globe fully occupied, a "competition of races" would ensue, with victory based on "survival of the fittest." Fear of ruthless competition drove the United States, like European nations, to invest in the latest weapons. Policymakers saw that European powers were amassing steel-plated battleships and carving up Africa and Asia among themselves. In his book *The Influence of Sea Power upon History* (1890), U.S. naval officer Alfred Mahan urged the United States to enter the fray, observing that naval power had been essential to past empires. As early as 1886, Congress ordered construction of two steel-hulled battleships, the USS *Texas* and USS *Maine*; in 1890, it appropriated funds for three more, a program that expanded over the next two decades.

During Grover Cleveland's second term (1893–1897), his secretary of state, Richard Olney, turned to direct confrontation. He warned Europe to stay away from Latin America, which he saw as the United States's rightful sphere of influence. Without consulting the nation of Venezuela, Olney suddenly demanded in 1895 that Britain resolve a long-standing border dispute between Venezuela and Britain's neighboring colony, British Guiana. Invoking the Monroe Doctrine, which stated that the Western Hemisphere was off-limits to further European colonization, Olney warned that the United States would brook no challenge to its interests. Startled, Britain agreed to arbitrate. U.S. power was on the rise.

## The War of 1898

Events in the Caribbean presented the United States with far greater opportunities. In 1895, Cuban patriots mounted a major guerrilla war against Spain, which had lost most of its other New World territories. The Spanish commander responded by rounding up Cuban civilians into concentration camps, where as many as 200,000 died of starvation, exposure,

**TRACE CHANGE OVER TIME**
How did imperialism in the 1890s reflect both continuities and changes from earlier eras?

or dysentery. In the United States, "yellow journalists" such as William Randolph Hearst turned their plight into a cause célèbre. Hearst's coverage of Spanish atrocities fed a surge of nationalism, especially among those who feared that industrialization was causing American men to lose physical strength and valor. The government should not pass up this opportunity, said Indiana senator Albert Beveridge, to "manufacture manhood." Congress called for Cuban independence.

President Cleveland had no interest in supporting the Cuban rebellion but worried over Spain's failure to end it. The war disrupted trade and damaged American-owned sugar plantations on the island. Moreover, an unstable Cuba was incompatible with U.S. strategic interests, including a proposed canal whose Caribbean approaches had to be safeguarded. Taking office in 1897, President William McKinley took a tough stance. In September, a U.S. diplomat informed Spain that it must ensure an "early and certain peace" or the United States would step in. At first, this hard line seemed to work: Spain's conservative regime fell, and a liberal government, taking office in October 1897, offered Cuba limited self-rule. But Spanish loyalists in Havana rioted against this proposal, while Cuban rebels held out for full independence.

In February 1898, Hearst's *New York Journal* published a private letter in which a Spanish minister to the United States belittled McKinley. The minister, Dupuy de Lôme, resigned, but exposure of the de Lôme letter intensified Americans' indignation toward Spain. The next week brought shocking news: the U.S. battle cruiser *Maine* had exploded and sunk in Havana harbor, with 260 seamen lost. "Whole Country Thrills with the War Fever," proclaimed the *New York Journal*. **"Remember the *Maine*"** became a national chant. Popular passions were now a major factor in the march toward war.

McKinley assumed the sinking of the *Maine* had been accidental. Improbably, though, a naval board of inquiry blamed an underwater mine, fueling public outrage. (Later investigators disagreed: the more likely cause was a faulty ship design that placed explosive munitions too close to coal bunkers, which were prone to fire.) No evidence linked Spain to the purported mine, but if a mine sank the *Maine*, then Spain was responsible for not protecting the ship.

Business leaders became impatient, believing war was preferable to an unending Cuban crisis. On March 27, McKinley cabled an ultimatum to Madrid: an immediate ceasefire in Cuba for six months and, with the United States mediating, peace negotiations with the rebels. Spain, while desperate to avoid war, balked at the added demand that mediation must result

in Cuban independence. On April 11, McKinley asked Congress for authority to intervene in Cuba "in the name of civilization, [and] in behalf of endangered American interests."

Historians long referred to the ensuing fight as the Spanish-American War, but because that name ignores the central role of Cuban revolutionaries, many historians now call the three-way conflict the War of 1898. Though Americans widely admired Cubans' aspirations for freedom, the McKinley administration defeated a congressional attempt to recognize the rebel government. In response, Senator Henry M. Teller of Colorado added an amendment to the war bill, disclaiming any intention by the United States to occupy Cuba. The **Teller Amendment** reassured Americans that their country would uphold democracy abroad as well as at home. McKinley's expectations differed. He wrote privately, "We must keep all we get; when the war is over we must keep what we want."

On April 24, 1898, Spain declared war on the United States. The news provoked full-blown war fever. Across the country, young men enlisted for the fight. Theodore Roosevelt, serving in the War Department, resigned to become lieutenant colonel of a cavalry regiment. Recruits poured into makeshift bases around Tampa, Florida, where confusion reigned. Rifles failed to arrive; food was bad, sanitation worse. No provision had been made for getting troops to Cuba, so the government hastily collected a fleet of yachts and commercial boats. Fortunately, the regular army was a disciplined, professional force; its 28,000 seasoned troops provided a nucleus for 200,000 volunteers. The navy was in better shape: Spain had nothing to match America's seven battleships and armored cruisers. The Spanish admiral bitterly predicted that his fleet would "like Don Quixote go out to fight windmills and come back with a broken head."

The first, decisive military engagement took place in the Pacific. This was the handiwork of Theodore Roosevelt, who, in his government post, had gotten the intrepid Commodore George Dewey appointed commander of the Pacific fleet. In the event of war, Dewey had instructions to sail immediately for the Spanish-owned Philippines. When war was declared, Roosevelt confronted his surprised superior and pressured him into validating Dewey's instructions. On May 1, 1898, American ships cornered the Spanish fleet in Manila Bay and destroyed it. Manila, the Philippine capital, fell on August 13. "We must on no account let the [Philippines] go," declared Senator Henry Cabot Lodge. McKinley agreed. The United States now had a major foothold in the western Pacific.

**Hawaii's Queen**

Hawaiian queen Liliuokalani (1838–1917) was the great-granddaughter of Keaweaheulu, founder of the Kamehameha dynasty that had ruled the islands since the late 1700s. Liliuokalani assumed the throne after her brother's death in 1891. As an outspoken critic, however, of treaties ceding power to U.S. economic interests, she was deposed three years later by a cabal of sugar planters who established a republic. When secret plans to revolt and restore the monarchy were discovered, the queen was imprisoned for a year in Iolani Palace. She lived the remainder of her life in Hawaii but never regained power. Fluent in English and influenced from childhood by Congregational missionaries, she used this background to advocate for her people; in her book *Hawaii's Story by Hawaii's Queen* (1898), she appealed for justice from fellow Christians. George Bacon Collection, Hawaii State Archives.

**IDENTIFY CAUSES**
Why did the United States go to war against Spain in 1898, and what led to U.S. victory?

Dewey's victory directed policymakers' attention to Hawaii. Nominally independent, these islands had long been subject to U.S. influence, including a horde of resident American sugarcane planters. An 1876 treaty between the United States and the island's monarch gave Hawaiian sugar free access to the American market, without tariff payments, and Hawaii pledged to sign no such agreement with any other power. When this treaty was renewed in 1887, Hawaii also granted a long-coveted lease for a U.S. naval base at Pearl Harbor. Four years later, succeeding her brother as Hawaii's monarch, Queen Liliuokalani made known her frustration with these treaties. In response, an Annexation Club of U.S.-backed planters organized secretly and in 1892, with the help of U.S. Marines, overthrew the queen and then negotiated a treaty of annexation. Grover Cleveland, however, rejected it when he entered office, declaring that it would violate America's "unbroken tradition" against acquiring territory overseas.

Dewey's victory in Manila delivered what the planters wanted: Hawaii acquired strategic value as a halfway station to the Philippines. In July 1898, Congress voted for annexation, over the protests of Hawaii's deposed queen. "Oh, honest Americans," she pleaded, "as Christians hear me for my down-trodden people! Their form of government is as dear to them as yours is precious to you. Quite as warmly as you love your country, so they love theirs." But to the great powers, Hawaii was not a country. One congressman dismissed Hawaii's monarchy as "absurd, grotesque, tottering"; the "Aryan race," he declared, would "rescue" the islands from it.

 To see a longer excerpt from Queen Liliuokalani's appeal, along with other primary sources from this period, see *Sources for America's History*.

Further U.S. annexations took on their own logic. The navy pressed for another coaling base in the central Pacific; that meant Guam, a Spanish island in the Marianas. A strategic base was needed in the Caribbean; that meant Puerto Rico. By early summer, before U.S. troops had fired a shot in Cuba, McKinley's broader war aims were crystallizing.

In Cuba, Spanish forces were depleted by the long guerrilla war. Though poorly trained and equipped, American forces had the advantages of a demoralized foe and knowledgeable Cuban allies. The main battle occurred on July 1 at San Juan Hill, near Santiago, where the Spanish fleet was anchored. Roosevelt's Rough Riders took the lead, but four African American regiments bore the brunt of the fighting. Observers credited much of the victory to the "superb gallantry" of these soldiers. Spanish troops retreated to a well-fortified second line, but U.S. forces were spared the test of a second assault. On July 3, the Spanish fleet in Santiago harbor tried a desperate run through the American blockade and was destroyed. Days later, Spanish forces surrendered. American combat casualties had been few; most U.S. soldiers' deaths had resulted from malaria and yellow fever.

**The Battle of San Juan Hill**

On July 1, 1898, the key battle for Cuba took place on heights overlooking Santiago. African American troops bore the brunt of the fighting. Although generally overlooked, black soldiers' role in the San Juan battle is done justice in this contemporary lithograph, without the demeaning stereotypes by which blacks were normally depicted in an age of intensifying racism. Note, however, that as in the Civil War, blacks enlisted as foot soldiers; their officers were white. Library of Congress.

## Spoils of War

The United States and Spain quickly signed a preliminary peace agreement in which Spain agreed to liberate Cuba and cede Puerto Rico and Guam to the United States. But what would happen to the Philippines, an immense archipelago that lay more than 5,000 miles from California? Initially, the United States aimed to keep only Manila, because of its fine harbor. Manila was not defensible, however, without the whole island of Luzon, on which it sat. After deliberating, McKinley found a justification for annexing all of the Philippines. He decided that "we could not leave [the Filipinos] to themselves — they were unfit for self-rule."

This declaration provoked heated debate. Under the Constitution, as Republican senator George F. Hoar argued, "no power is given to the Federal Government to acquire territory to be held and governed permanently as colonies" or "to conquer alien people and hold them in subjugation." Leading citizens and peace advocates, including Jane Addams and Mark Twain, enlisted in the anti-imperialist cause. Steel king Andrew Carnegie offered $20 million to purchase Philippine independence. Labor leader Samuel Gompers warned union members about the threat of competition from low-wage Filipino immigrants. Anti-imperialists, however, were a diverse lot. Some argued that Filipinos were perfectly capable of self-rule; others warned about the dangers of annexing eight million Filipinos of an "inferior race." "No matter whether they are fit to govern themselves or not," declared a Missouri congressman, "they are not fit to govern us."

Beginning in late 1898, anti-imperialist leagues sprang up around the country, but they never sparked a mass movement. On the contrary, McKinley's "splendid little war" proved immensely popular. Confronted with that reality, Democrats waffled. Their standard-bearer, William Jennings Bryan, decided not to stake Democrats' future on opposition to a policy that he believed to be irreversible. He threw his party into turmoil by declaring last-minute support for McKinley's proposed treaty. Having met military defeat, Spanish representatives had little choice. In the Treaty of Paris, Spain ceded the Philippines to the United States for $20 million.

**EXPLAIN CONSEQUENCES**

What were the long-term results of the U.S. victory over Spain, in Hawaii and in former Spanish possessions?

Annexation was not as simple as U.S. policymakers had expected. On February 4, 1899, two days before the Senate ratified the treaty, fighting broke out between American and Filipino patrols on the edge of Manila. Confronted by annexation, rebel leader Emilio Aguinaldo asserted his nation's independence and turned his guns on occupying American forces. Though Aguinaldo found it difficult to organize a mass-based resistance movement, the ensuing conflict between Filipino nationalists and U.S. troops far exceeded in length and ferocity the war just concluded with Spain. Fighting tenacious guerrillas, the U.S. Army resorted to the same tactics Spain had employed in Cuba: burning crops and villages and rounding up civilians. Atrocities became commonplace on both sides. In three years of warfare, 4,200 Americans and an estimated 200,000 Filipinos died; many of the latter were dislocated civilians, particularly children, who succumbed to malnutrition and disease.

McKinley's convincing victory over William Jennings Bryan in 1900 suggested popular satisfaction with America's overseas adventures, even in the face of dogged Filipino resistance to U.S. rule. The fighting ended in 1902, and William Howard Taft, appointed as governor-general of the Philippines, sought to make the territory a model of roadbuilding and sanitary engineering. Yet misgivings lingered as Americans confronted the brutality of the war. Philosopher William James noted that the United States had destroyed "these islanders by the thousands, their villages and cities. . . . Could there be any more damning indictment of that whole bloated ideal termed 'modern civilization'?" (American Voices, p. 680).

Constitutional issues also remained unresolved. The treaty, while guaranteeing freedom of religion to inhabitants of ceded Spanish territories, withheld any promise of citizenship. It was up to Congress to decide Filipinos' "civil rights and political status." In 1901, the Supreme Court upheld this provision in a set of decisions known as the **Insular Cases**. The Constitution, declared the Court, did not automatically extend citizenship to people in acquired territories; Congress could decide. Puerto Rico, Guam, and the Philippines were thus marked as colonies, not future states.

The next year, as a condition for withdrawing from Cuba, the United States forced the newly independent island to accept a proviso in its constitution called the **Platt Amendment** (1902). This blocked Cuba from making a treaty with any country except the United States and gave the United States the right to intervene in Cuban affairs if it saw fit. Cuba also granted the United States a lease on Guantánamo Bay (still in effect), where the U.S. Navy built a large base. Cubans' hard-fought independence was limited; so was that of Filipinos. Eventually, the Jones Act of 1916 committed the United States to Philippine independence but set no date. (The Philippines at last achieved independence in 1946.) Though the war's carnage had rubbed off some of the moralizing gloss, America's global aspirations remained intact.

# A Power Among Powers

No one appreciated America's emerging influence more than the man who, after William McKinley's assassination, became president in 1901. Theodore Roosevelt was an avid student of world affairs who called on "the civilized and orderly powers to insist on the proper policing of the world." He meant, in part, directing the affairs of "backward peoples." For Roosevelt, imperialism went hand in hand with domestic progressivism (Chapter 20). He argued that a strong federal government, asserting itself both at home and abroad, would enhance economic stability and political order. Overseas, Roosevelt sought to arbitrate disputes and maintain a global balance of power, but he also asserted U.S. interests.

## The Open Door in Asia

U.S. officials and business leaders had a burning interest in East Asian markets, but they were entering a crowded field (Map 21.1). In the late 1890s, following Japan's victory in the Sino-Japanese War of 1894–1895, Japan, Russia, Germany, France, and Britain divided

**MAP 21.1**

**The Great Powers in East Asia, 1898–1910**

European powers established dominance over China by way of "treaty ports," where the powers based their naval forces, and through "spheres of influence" that extended from the ports into the hinterland. This map reveals why the United States had a weak hand: it lacked a presence on this colonized terrain. An uprising of Chinese nationalists in 1900 gave the United States a chance to insert itself on the Chinese mainland by sending an American expeditionary force. American diplomats made the most of the opportunity to defend U.S. commercial interests in China. As noted in the key, all place names in this map are those in use in 1910: Modern *Beijing*, for example, is shown as *Peking*.

coastal China into spheres of influence. Fearful of being shut out, U.S. Secretary of State John Hay sent these powers a note in 1899, claiming the right of equal trade access—an "**open door**"—for all nations seeking to do business in China. The United States lacked leverage in Asia, and Hay's note elicited only noncommittal responses. But he chose to interpret this as acceptance of his position.

When a secret society of Chinese nationalists, known outside China as "Boxers" because of their pugnacious political stance, rebelled against foreign occupation in 1900, the United States sent 5,000 troops to join a multinational campaign to break the nationalists' siege of European offices in Beijing. Hay took this opportunity to assert a second open door principle: China must be preserved as a "territorial and administrative entity." As long as the legal fiction of an independent China survived, Americans could claim equal access to its market.

European and American plans were, however, unsettled by Japan's emergence as East Asia's dominant power. A decade after its victory over China, Japan responded to Russian bids for control of both Korea

and Manchuria, in northern China, by attacking the tzar's fleet at Russia's leased Chinese port. In a series of brilliant victories, the Japanese smashed the Russian forces. Westerners were shocked: for the first time, a European power had been defeated by a non-Western nation. Conveying both admiration and alarm, American cartoonists sketched Japan as a martial artist knocking down the Russian giant. Roosevelt mediated a settlement to the war in 1905, receiving for his efforts the first Nobel Peace Prize awarded to an American.

Though he was contemptuous of other Asians, Roosevelt respected the Japanese, whom he called "a wonderful and civilized people." More important, he understood Japan's rising military might and aligned himself with the mighty. The United States approved Japan's "protectorate" over Korea in 1905 and, six years later, its seizure of full control. With Japan asserting harsh authority over Manchuria, energetic Chinese diplomat Yüan Shih-k'ai tried to encourage the United States to intervene. But

**COMPARE AND CONTRAST**

What factors constrained and guided U.S. actions in Asia and in Latin America?

## Debating the Philippines

As President McKinley privately acknowledged in writing—"when the war is over we must keep what we want"—seizing the Philippines was an act of national self-interest. Of the alternatives, it was the one that seemed best calculated to serve America's strategic aims in Asia. But McKinley's geopolitical decision had unintended consequences. For one, it provoked a bloody insurrection. For another, it challenged the United States's democratic principles. As these consequences hit home, a divided Senate set up a special committee and held closed hearings. Congressional testimony is a source much prized by historians. Though some of it is prepared, once questioning begins, testimony becomes unscripted and can be especially revealing. The following documents are taken from the 1902 testimony before the Senate Committee on the Philippines.

### Ideals

General Arthur MacArthur (1845–1912) was in on the action in the Philippines almost from the start. He commanded one of the first units to arrive there in 1898 and in 1900 was reassigned as the islands' military governor and general commander of the troops. His standing as a military man—holder of the Congressional Medal of Honor from the Civil War—was matched later by his more famous son, Douglas MacArthur, who fought in the Pacific during World War II. Here the elder MacArthur explains in prepared testimony his vision of America's mission to the Philippines.

At the time I returned to Manila [May 1900] to assume the supreme command it seemed to me that . . . our occupation of the island was simply one of the necessary consequences in logical sequence of our great prosperity, and to doubt the wisdom of [occupation] was simply to doubt the stability of our own institutions and in effect to declare that a self-governing nation was incapable of successfully resisting strains arising naturally from its own productive energy. It seemed to me that our conception of right, justice, freedom, and personal liberty was the precious fruit of centuries of strife . . . [and that] we must regard ourselves simply as the custodians of imperishable ideas held in trust for the general benefit of mankind. In other words, I felt that we had attained a moral and intellectual height from which we were bound to proclaim to all as the occasion arose the true message of humanity as embodied in the principles of our own institutions. . . .

All other governments that have gone to the East have simply planted trading establishments; they have not materially affected the conditions of the people. . . . There is not a single establishment, in my judgment, in Asia to-day that would survive five years if the original power which planted it was withdrawn therefrom.

The contrasting idea with our idea is this: In planting our ideas we plant something that can not be destroyed. To my mind the archipelago is a fertile soil upon which to plant republicanism. . . . We are planting the best traditions, the best characteristics of Americanism in such a way that they can never be removed from that soil. That in itself seems to me a most inspiring thought. It encouraged me during all my efforts in those lands, even when conditions seemed most disappointing, when the people themselves, not appreciating precisely what the remote consequences of our efforts were going to be, mistrusted us; but that fact was always before me — that going deep down into that fertile soil were the indispensable ideas of Americanism.

### Skepticism

At this point, the general was interrupted by Colorado senator Thomas Patterson, a Populist-Democrat and a vocal anti-imperialist.

Sen. Patterson: Do you mean that imperishable idea of which you speak is the right of self-government?

Gen. MacArthur: Precisely so; self-government regulated by law as I understand it in this Republic.

Sen. Patterson: Of course you do not mean self-government regulated by some foreign and superior power?

Gen. MacArthur: Well, that is a matter of evolution, Senator. We are putting these institutions there so they will evolve themselves just as here and everywhere else where freedom has flourished. . . .

Sen. Patterson [after the General concluded his statement]: Do I understand your claim of right and duty to retain the Philippine Islands is based upon the proposition that they have come to us upon the basis of our morals, honorable dealing, and unassailable international integrity?

Gen. MacArthur: That proposition is not questioned by anybody in the world, excepting a few people in the United States. . . . We will be benefited, and the Filipino people will be benefited, and that is what I meant by the original proposition —

Sen. Patterson: Do you mean the Filipino people that are left alive?

Gen. MacArthur: I mean the Filipino people. . . .

Sen. Patterson: You mean those left alive after they have been subjugated?

Gen. MacArthur: I do not admit that there has been any unusual destruction of life in the Philippine Islands. The destruction is simply the incident of war, and of course it embraces only a very small percentage of the total population.

. . . I doubt if any war — either international or civil, any war on earth — has been conducted with as much humanity, with as much careful consideration, with as much self-restraint, as have been the American operations in the Philippine Archipelago. . . .

## Realities

Brigadier General Robert P. Hughes, a military district commander, testified as follows.

Q: In burning towns, what would you do? Would the entire town be destroyed by fire or would only the offending portions of the town be burned?

Gen. Hughes: I do not know that we ever had a case of burning what you would call a town in this country, but probably a barrio or a sitio; probably half a dozen houses, native shacks, where the insurrectos would go in and be concealed, and if they caught a detachment passing they would kill some of them.

Q: What did I understand you to say would be the consequences of that?

Gen. Hughes: They usually burned the village.

Q: All of the houses in the village?

Gen. Hughes: Yes, every one of them.

Q: What would become of the inhabitants?

Gen. Hughes: That was their lookout.

Q: If these shacks were of no consequence what was the utility of their destruction?

Gen. Hughes: The destruction was as a punishment. They permitted these people to come in there and conceal themselves. . . .

Q: The punishment in that case would fall, not upon the men, who could go elsewhere, but mainly upon the women and little children.

Gen. Hughes: The women and children are part of the family, and where you wish to inflict a punishment you

can punish the man probably worse in that way than in any other.

Q: But is that within the ordinary rules of civilized warfare? . . .

Gen. Hughes: These people are not civilized.

## Cruelties

Daniel J. Evans, Twelfth Infantry, describes the "water cure."

Q: The committee would like to hear . . . whether you were the witness to any cruelties inflicted upon the natives of the Philippine Islands; and if so, under what circumstances.

Evans: The case I had reference to was where they gave the water cure to a native in the Ilicano Province at Ilocos Norte . . . about the month of August 1900. There were two native scouts with the American forces. They went out and brought in a couple of insurgents. . . . They tried to get from this insurgent . . . where the rest of the insurgents were at that time. . . . The first thing one of the Americans — I mean one of the scouts for the Americans — grabbed one of the men by the head and jerked his head back, and then they took a tomato can and poured water down his throat until he could hold no more. . . . Then they forced a gag into his mouth; they stood him up . . . against a post and fastened him so that he could not move. Then one man, an American soldier, who was over six feet tall, and who was very strong, too, struck this native in the pit of the stomach as hard as he could. . . . They kept that operation up for quite a time, and finally I thought the fellow was about to die, but I don't believe he was as bad as that, because finally he told them he would tell, and from that day on he was taken away, and I saw no more of him.

Source: From *American Imperialism and the Philippine Insurrection*, edited by Henry F. Graff (Boston: Little, Brown, 1969). Reprinted by permission of the author.

### QUESTIONS FOR ANALYSIS

1. The text of this chapter offers the U.S. reasons for holding on to the Philippines. In what ways does General MacArthur's testimony confirm, add to, or contradict the text account?

2. The chapter text also describes the anti-imperialist movement. What does Senator Patterson's cross-examination of General MacArthur reveal about the anti-imperialists' beliefs?

3. Does the clash of ideas in these excerpts remain relevant to our own time? How does it compare to what you might read or hear about in a news source today?

Roosevelt reviewed America's weak position in the Pacific and declined. He conceded that Japan had "a paramount interest in what surrounds the Yellow Sea." In 1908, the United States and Japan signed the **Root-Takahira Agreement**, confirming principles of free oceanic commerce and recognizing Japan's authority over Manchuria.

William Howard Taft entered the White House in 1909 convinced that the United States had been short-changed in Asia. He pressed for a larger role for American investors, especially in Chinese railroad construction. Eager to promote U.S. business interests abroad, he hoped that infusions of American capital would offset Japanese power. When the Chinese Revolution of 1911 toppled the Manchu dynasty, Taft supported the victorious Nationalists, who wanted to modernize their country and liberate it from Japanese domination. The United States had entangled itself in China and entered a long-term rivalry with Japan for power in the Pacific, a competition that would culminate thirty years later in World War II.

## The United States and Latin America

Roosevelt famously argued that the United States should "speak softly and carry a big stick." By "big stick," he meant naval power, and rapid access to two oceans required a canal. European powers conceded the United States's "paramount interest" in the Caribbean. Freed by Britain's surrender of canal-building rights in the Hay-Pauncefote Treaty (1901), Roosevelt persuaded Congress to authorize $10 million, plus future payments of $250,000 per year, to purchase from Colombia a six-mile strip of land across Panama, a Colombian province.

Furious when Colombia rejected this proposal, Roosevelt contemplated outright seizure of Panama but settled on a more roundabout solution. Panamanians, long separated from Colombia by remote jungle, chafed under Colombian rule. The United States lent covert assistance to an independence movement, triggering a bloodless revolution. On November 6, 1903, the United States recognized the new nation of Panama; two weeks later, it obtained a perpetually renewable lease on a canal zone. Roosevelt never regretted the venture, though in 1922 the United States paid Colombia $25 million as a kind of conscience money.

To build the canal, the U.S. Army Corps of Engineers hired 60,000 laborers, who came from many countries to clear vast swamps, excavate 240 million cubic yards of earth, and construct a series of immense locks. The project, a major engineering feat, took eight years and cost thousands of lives among the workers who built it. Opened in 1914, the **Panama Canal** gave

### Panama Canal Workers, 1910

The 51-mile-long Panama Canal includes seven sets of locks that can raise and lower fifty large ships in a twenty-four-hour period. Building the canal took eight years and required over 50,000 workers, including immigrants from Spain and Italy and many West Indians such as these men, who accomplished some of the worst-paid, most dangerous labor. Workers endured the horrors of rockslides, explosions, and a yellow fever epidemic that almost halted the project. But American observers hailed the canal as a triumph of modern science and engineering—especially in medical efforts to eradicate the yellow fever and malaria that had stymied earlier canal-building efforts. Theodore Roosevelt insisted on making a personal visit in November 1906. "He made the men that were building there feel like they were special people," recalled the descendant of one canal worker. "Give them pride of what they were doing for the United States." Library of Congress.

the United States a commanding position in the Western Hemisphere.

Meanwhile, arguing that instability invited European intervention, Roosevelt announced in 1904 that the United States would police all of the Caribbean (Map 21.2). This so-called **Roosevelt Corollary** to the Monroe Doctrine actually turned that doctrine upside down: instead of guaranteeing that the United States would protect its neighbors from Europe and help preserve their independence, it asserted the United States's unrestricted right to regulate Caribbean affairs. The Roosevelt Corollary was not a treaty but a unilateral declaration sanctioned only by America's military and economic might. Citing it, the United States intervened regularly in Caribbean and Central American nations over the next three decades.

Entering office in 1913, Democratic president Woodrow Wilson criticized his predecessors' foreign policy. He pledged that the United States would "never again seek one additional foot of territory by conquest." This stance appealed to anti-imperialists in the Democratic base, including longtime supporters of William Jennings Bryan. But the new president soon showed that, when American interests called for it, his actions were not so different from those of Roosevelt and Taft.

Since the 1870s, Mexican dictator Porfirio Díaz had created a friendly climate for American companies that purchased Mexican plantations, mines, and oil fields. By the early 1900s, however, Díaz feared the extraordinary power of these foreign interests and began to nationalize — reclaim — key resources. American investors who faced the loss of Mexican holdings began to back Francisco Madero, an advocate of constitutional government who was friendly to U.S. interests. In 1911, Madero forced Díaz to resign and proclaimed himself president. Thousands of poor Mexicans took this opportunity to mobilize rural armies and demand more radical change. Madero's position was weak, and several strongmen sought to overthrow him; in 1913, he was deposed and murdered by a leading general. Immediately, several other military men vied for control.

Wilson, fearing that the unrest threatened U.S. interests, decided to intervene in the emerging Mexican Revolution. On the pretext of a minor insult to the navy, he ordered U.S. occupation of the port of Veracruz on April 21, 1914, at the cost of 19 American and 126 Mexican lives. Though the intervention helped Venustiano Carranza, the revolutionary leader whom Wilson most favored, Carranza protested it as illegitimate meddling in Mexican affairs. Carranza's forces, after nearly engaging the Americans themselves, entered Mexico City in triumph a few months later. Though Wilson had supported this outcome, his interference caused lasting mistrust.

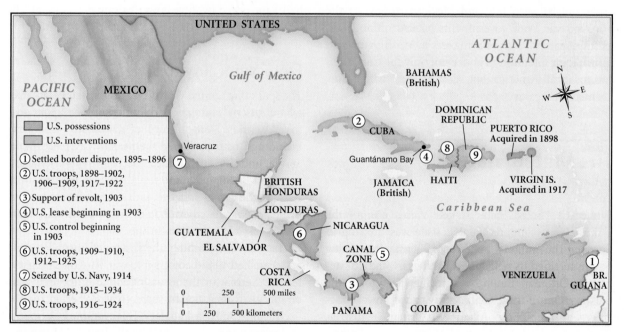

**MAP 21.2**

**Policeman of the Caribbean**

After the War of 1898, the United States vigorously asserted its interest in the affairs of its neighbors to the south. As the record of interventions shows, the United States truly became the "policeman" of the Caribbean and Central America.

**Pancho Villa, 1914**

This photograph captures Mexican general Pancho Villa at the height of his power, at the head of Venustiano Carranza's northern army in 1914. The next year, he broke with Carranza and, among other desperate tactics, began to attack Americans. Though he had been much admired in the United States, Villa instantly became America's foremost enemy. He evaded General John J. Pershing's punitive expedition of 1916, however, demonstrating the difficulties even modern armies could have against a guerrilla foe who knows his home terrain and can melt away into a sympathetic population. Brown Brothers.

Carranza's victory did not subdue revolutionary activity in Mexico. In 1916, General Francisco "Pancho" Villa — a thug to his enemies, but a heroic Robin Hood to many poor Mexicans — crossed the U.S.-Mexico border, killing sixteen American civilians and raiding the town of Columbus, New Mexico. Wilson sent 11,000 troops to pursue Villa, a force that soon resembled an army of occupation in northern Mexico. Mexican public opinion demanded withdrawal as armed clashes broke out between U.S. and Mexican troops. At the brink of war, both governments backed off and U.S. forces departed. But policymakers in Washington had shown their intention to police not only the Caribbean and Central America but also Mexico when they deemed it necessary.

# The United States in World War I

While the United States staked claims around the globe, a war of unprecedented scale was brewing in Europe. The military buildup of Germany, a rising power, terrified its neighbors. To the east, the disintegrating Ottoman Empire was losing its grip on the Balkans. Out of these conflicts, two rival power blocs emerged: the Triple Alliance (Germany, Austria-Hungary, and Italy) and Triple Entente (Britain, France, and Russia). Within each alliance, national governments pursued their own interests but were bound to one another by both public and secret treaties.

Americans had no obvious stake in these developments. In 1905, when Germany suddenly challenged French control of Morocco, Theodore Roosevelt arranged an international conference to defuse the crisis. Germany got a few concessions, but France — with British backing — retained Morocco. Accomplished in the same year that Roosevelt brokered peace between Russia and Japan, the conference seemed another diplomatic triumph. One U.S. official boasted that America had kept peace by "the power of our detachment." It was not to last.

## From Neutrality to War

The spark that ignited World War I came in the Balkans, where Austria-Hungary and Russia competed for control. Austria's 1908 seizure of Ottoman provinces, including Bosnia, angered the nearby Slavic nation of Serbia and its ally, Russia. Serbian revolutionaries recruited Bosnian Slavs to resist Austrian rule. In June 1914, in the city of Sarajevo, university student Gavrilo Princip assassinated Archduke Franz Ferdinand, heir to the Austro-Hungarian throne.

Like dominos falling, the system of European alliances pushed all the powers into war. Austria-Hungary blamed Serbia for the assassination and declared war on July 28. Russia, tied by secret treaty to Serbia, mobilized against Austria-Hungary. This prompted Germany to declare war on Russia and its ally France. As a preparation for attacking France, Germany launched a brutal invasion of the neutral country of Belgium, which caused Great Britain to declare war on Germany.

Within a week, most of Europe was at war, with the major Allies — Great Britain, France, and Russia — confronting the Central Powers of Germany and Austria-Hungary. Two military zones emerged. On the Western Front, Germany battled the British and French; on the Eastern Front, Germany and Austria-Hungary fought Russia. Because most of the warring nations held colonial empires, the conflict soon spread to the Middle East, Africa, and Asia.

The so-called Great War wreaked terrible devastation. New technology, some of it devised in the United States, made warfare deadlier than ever before. Every soldier carried a long-range, high-velocity rifle that could hit a target at 1,000 yards — a vast technical advancement over the 300-yard range of rifles used in the U.S. Civil War. The machine gun was even more deadly. Its American-born inventor, Hiram Maxim, had moved to Britain in the 1880s to follow a friend's advice: "If you want to make your fortune, invent something which will allow those fool Europeans to kill each other more quickly." New technologies helped soldiers in defensive positions; once advancing Germans ran into French fortifications, they stalled. Across a swath of Belgium and northeastern France, millions of soldiers on both sides hunkered down in fortified trenches. During 1916, repeatedly trying to break through French lines at Verdun, Germans suffered 450,000 casualties. The French fared even worse, with 550,000 dead or wounded. It was all to no avail. From 1914 to 1918, the Western Front barely moved.

At the war's outbreak, President Wilson called on Americans to be "neutral in fact as well as in name." If the United States remained out of the conflict, Wilson reasoned, he could influence the postwar settlement, much as Theodore Roosevelt had done after previous conflicts. Even if Wilson had wished to, it would have been nearly impossible in 1914 to unite Americans behind the Allies. Many Irish immigrants viewed Britain as an enemy — based on its continued occupation of Ireland — while millions of German Americans maintained ties to their homeland. Progressive-minded Republicans, such as Senator Robert La Follette of Wisconsin, vehemently opposed taking sides in a European fight, as did socialists, who condemned the war as a conflict among greedy capitalist empires. Two giants of American industry, Andrew Carnegie and Henry Ford, opposed the war. In December 1915, Ford sent a hundred men and women to Europe on a "peace ship" to urge an end to the war. "It would be folly," declared the *New York Sun*, "for the country to sacrifice itself to . . . the clash of ancient hatreds which is urging the Old World to destruction."

**Flying Aces**

As millions of men suffered and died in the trenches during the Great War, a few hundred pilots did battle in the sky. America's best-known ace pilot was Eddie Rickenbacker (right) of the 94th Aero Pursuit Squadron — a pilot who was credited with shooting down twenty-six enemy aircraft. The 94th was known as the hat-in-the-ring squadron, after the American custom by which a combatant threw his hat into the ring as an invitation to fight. Note the hat insignia on the plane. © Bettmann/Corbis.

**The Struggle to Remain Neutral**   The United States, wishing to trade with all the warring nations, might have remained neutral if Britain had not held commanding power at sea. In September 1914, the British imposed a naval blockade on the Central Powers to cut off vital supplies of food and military equipment. Though the Wilson administration protested this infringement of the rights of neutral carriers, commerce with the Allies more than made up for the economic loss. Trade with Britain and France grew fourfold over the next two years, to $3.2 billion in 1916;

by 1917, U.S. banks had lent the Allies $2.5 billion. In contrast, American trade and loans to Germany stood then at a mere $56 million. This imbalance undercut U.S. neutrality. If Germany won and Britain and France defaulted on their debts, American companies would suffer catastrophic losses.

To challenge the British navy, Germany launched a devastating new weapon, the U-boat (short for *Unterseeboot*, "undersea boat," or submarine). In April 1915, Germany issued a warning that all ships flying flags of Britain or its allies were liable to destruction. A few weeks later, a U-boat torpedoed the British luxury liner *Lusitania* off the coast of Ireland, killing 1,198 people, including 128 Americans. The attack on the passenger ship (which was later revealed to have been carrying munitions) incensed Americans. The following year, in an agreement known as the Sussex pledge, Germany agreed not to target passenger liners or merchant ships unless an inspection showed the latter carried weapons. But the *Lusitania* sinking prompted Wilson to reconsider his options. After quietly trying to mediate in Europe but finding neither side interested in peace, he endorsed a $1 billion U.S. military buildup.

American public opinion still ran strongly against entering the war, a fact that shaped the election of 1916. Republicans rejected the belligerently prowar Theodore Roosevelt in favor of Supreme Court justice Charles Evans Hughes, a progressive former governor of New York. Democrats renominated Wilson, who campaigned on his domestic record and as the president who "kept us out of war." Wilson eked out a narrow victory; winning California by a mere 4,000 votes, he secured a slim majority in the electoral college.

**America Enters the War**   Despite Wilson's campaign slogan, events pushed him toward war. In February 1917, Germany resumed unrestricted submarine warfare, a decision dictated by the impasse on the Western Front. In response, Wilson broke off diplomatic relations with Germany. A few weeks later, newspapers published an intercepted dispatch from German foreign secretary Arthur Zimmermann to his minister in Mexico. The **Zimmermann telegram** urged Mexico to join the Central Powers, promising that if the United States entered the war, Germany would help Mexico recover "the lost territory of Texas, New Mexico, and Arizona." With Pancho Villa's border raids still fresh in Americans' minds,

**IDENTIFY CAUSES**
What factors led the United States to enter World War I, despite the desire of so many Americans, including the president, to stay out of the war?

this threat jolted public opinion. Meanwhile, German U-boats attacked U.S. ships without warning, sinking three on March 18 alone.

On April 2, 1917, Wilson asked Congress for a declaration of war. He argued that Germany had trampled on American rights and imperiled U.S. trade and citizens' lives. "We desire no conquest," Wilson declared, "no material compensation for the sacrifices we shall freely make." Reflecting his progressive idealism, Wilson promised that American involvement would make the world "safe for democracy." On April 6, the United States declared war on Germany. Reflecting the nation's divided views, the vote was far from unanimous. Six senators and fifty members of the House voted against entry, including Representative Jeannette Rankin of Montana, the first woman elected to Congress. "You can no more win a war than you can win an earthquake," Rankin said. "I want to stand by my country, but I cannot vote for war."

## "Over There"

To Americans, Europe seemed a great distance away. Many assumed the United States would simply provide munitions and economic aid. "Good Lord," exclaimed one U.S. senator to a Wilson administration official, "you're not going to send soldiers over there, are you?" But when General John J. Pershing asked how the United States could best support the Allies, the French commander put it bluntly: "Men, men, and more men." Amid war fever, thousands of young men prepared to go "over there," in the words of George M. Cohan's popular song: "Make your Daddy glad to have had such a lad. / Tell your sweetheart not to pine, / To be proud her boy's in line."

**Americans Join the War**   In 1917, the U.S. Army numbered fewer than 200,000 soldiers; needing more men, Congress instituted a military draft in May 1917. In contrast to the Civil War, when resistance was common, conscription went smoothly, partly because local, civilian-run draft boards played a central role in the new system. Still, draft registration demonstrated government's increasing power over ordinary citizens. On a single day—June 5, 1917—more than 9.5 million men between the ages of twenty-one and thirty registered at local voting precincts for possible military service.

President Wilson chose General Pershing to head the American Expeditionary Force (AEF), which had to be trained, outfitted, and carried across the submarine-plagued Atlantic. This required safer shipping. When

**Safe Sex, Vintage 1919**

To teach young American men how to avoid venereal diseases, the War Department used posters, pep talks, and films. There were no effective treatments for venereal infections until 1928, when Alexander Fleming discovered penicillin, and so the army urged soldiers to refrain from visiting prostitutes or to use condoms. *Fit to Win* starred handsome Ray McKee, who had already appeared in eighty films, and was directed by E. H. Griffith, who would go on to direct sixty Hollywood films between 1920 and 1946. Social Welfare History Archives Center, University of Minnesota/Picture Research Consultants & Archives.

the United States entered the war, German U-boats were sinking 900,000 tons of Allied ships each month. By sending merchant and troop ships in armed convoys, the U.S. Navy cut that monthly rate to 400,000 tons by the end of 1917. With trench warfare grinding on, Allied commanders pleaded for American soldiers to fill their depleted units, but Pershing waited until the AEF reached full strength. As late as May 1918, the brunt of the fighting fell to the French and British.

The Allies' burden increased when the Eastern Front collapsed following the Bolshevik (Communist) Revolution in Russia in November 1917. To consolidate power at home, the new Bolshevik government, led by Vladimir Lenin, sought peace with the Central Powers. In a 1918 treaty, Russia surrendered its claims over vast parts of its territories in exchange for peace. Released from war against Germany, the Bolsheviks turned their attention to a civil war at home. Terrified by communism, Japan and several Allied countries, including the United States, later sent troops to fight the Bolsheviks and aid forces loyal to the deposed tsar. But after a four-year civil war, Lenin's forces established full control over Russia and reclaimed Ukraine and other former possessions.

Peace with Russia freed Germany to launch a major offensive on the Western Front. By May 1918, German troops had advanced to within 50 miles of Paris. Pershing at last committed about 60,000 U.S. soldiers to support the French defense. With American soldiers engaged in massive numbers, Allied forces brought the Germans to a halt in July; by September, they forced a retreat. Pershing then pitted more than one million

American soldiers against an outnumbered and exhausted German army in the Argonne forest. By early November, this attack broke German defenses at a crucial rail hub, Sedan. The cost was high: 26,000 Americans killed and 95,000 wounded (Map 21.3). But the flood of U.S. troops and supplies determined the outcome. Recognizing inevitable defeat and facing popular uprisings at home, Germany signed an armistice on November 11, 1918. The Great War was over.

**The American Fighting Force**   By the end of World War I, almost 4 million American men — popularly known as "doughboys" — wore U.S. uniforms, as did several thousand female nurses. The recruits reflected America's heterogeneity: one-fifth had been born outside the United States, and soldiers spoke forty-nine different languages. Though ethnic diversity worried some observers, most predicted that military service would promote Americanization.

Over 400,000 African American men enlisted, accounting for 13 percent of the armed forces. Their wartime experiences were often grim: serving in segregated units, they were given the most menial tasks. Racial discrimination hampered military efficiency and provoked violence at several camps. The worst incident occurred in August 1917, when, after suffering a string of racial attacks, black members of the 24th Infantry's Third Battalion rioted in Houston, killing 15 white civilians and police officers. The army tried 118

**EXPLAIN CONSEQUENCES**
How did U.S. military entry into World War I affect the course of the war?

**MAP 21.3**

**U.S. Participation on the Western Front, 1918**

When American troops reached the European front in significant numbers in 1918, the Allies and Central Powers had been fighting a deadly war of attrition for almost four years. The influx of American troops and supplies helped break the stalemate. Successful offensive maneuvers by the American Expeditionary Force included those at Belleau Wood and Château-Thierry and the Meuse-Argonne campaign.

of the soldiers in military courts for mutiny and riot, hanged 19, and sentenced 63 to life in prison.

Unlike African Americans, American Indians served in integrated combat units. Racial stereotypes about Native Americans' prowess as warriors enhanced their military reputations, but it also prompted officers to assign them hazardous duties as scouts and snipers. About 13,000, or 25 percent, of the adult male American Indian population served during the war; roughly 5 percent died, compared to 2 percent for the military as a whole.

Most American soldiers escaped the horrors of sustained trench warfare. Still, during the brief period of U.S. participation, over 50,000 servicemen died in action; another 63,000 died from disease, mainly the devastating influenza pandemic that began early in 1918 and, over the next two years, killed 50 million people worldwide. The nation's military deaths, though substantial, were only a tenth as many as the 500,000 American civilians who died of this terrible epidemic — not to mention the staggering losses of Europeans in the war (America Compared, p. 689).

## War on the Home Front

In the United States, opponents of the war were a minority. Helping the Allies triggered an economic boom that benefitted farmers and working people.

Many progressives also supported the war, hoping Wilson's ideals and wartime patriotism would renew Americans' attention to reform. But the war bitterly disappointed them. Rather than enhancing democracy, it chilled the political climate as government agencies tried to enforce "100 percent loyalty."

**Mobilizing the Economy** American businesses made big bucks from World War I. As grain, weapons, and manufactured goods flowed to Britain and France, the United States became a creditor nation. Moreover, as the war drained British financial reserves, U.S. banks provided capital for investments around the globe.

Government powers expanded during wartime, with new federal agencies overseeing almost every part of the economy. The **War Industries Board** (WIB), established in July 1917, directed military production. After a fumbling start that showed the limits of voluntarism, the Wilson administration reorganized the board and placed Bernard Baruch, a Wall Street financier and superb administrator, at its head. Under his direction, the WIB allocated scarce resources among industries, ordered factories to convert to war production, set prices, and standardized procedures. Though he could compel compliance, Baruch preferred to win voluntary cooperation. A man of immense charm, he usually succeeded — helped by the lucrative military contracts at his disposal. Despite higher taxes, corporate

## The Human Cost of World War I

The United States played a crucial role in financing World War I. In its war-related expenditures, totaling $22.6 billion, the United States ranked fourth among all nations that participated, ranking behind only Germany ($37.7 billion), Britain ($35.3 billion), and France ($24.3 billion). In human terms, however, the U.S. role was different. Note that the figures below for military casualties are rough estimates. Civilian casualties are even more uncertain: the exact number of Russians, Italians, Romanians, Serbians, and others who died will never be known.

**TABLE 21.1**

### World War I Casualties

| Country | Total Population | Military Killed or Missing | Total Civilian Deaths |
|---|---|---|---|
| Germany | 67,000,000 | 2,037,000 | 700,000 |
| Russia | 167,000,000 | 1,800,000 | 2,000,000 |
| France | 39,000,000 | 1,385,300 | 40,000 |
| Austria-Hungary | 49,900,000 | 1,016,200 | unknown |
| United Kingdom | 46,400,000 | 702,410 | 1,386 |
| Italy | 35,000,000 | 462,400 | unknown |
| Turkey | 21,300,000 | 236,000 | 2,000,000* |
| Romania | 7,510,000 | 219,800 | 265,000–500,000 |
| Serbia | 5,000,000 | 127,500 | 600,000 |
| Bulgaria | 5,500,000 | 77,450 | 275,000 |
| India | 316,000,000 | 62,060 | negligible |
| Canada | 7,400,000 | 58,990 | negligible |
| Australia | 4,872,000 | 53,560 | negligible |
| United States | 92,000,000 | 51,822 | negligible |

*Mostly Armenians

### QUESTIONS FOR ANALYSIS

1. What does this data suggest about the comparative role of the United States in World War I? The experience of its soldiers? The war's impact on civilians in each nation?

2. Which other countries made contributions similar to that of the United States, and why?

profits soared, as military production sustained a boom that continued until 1920.

Some federal agencies took dramatic measures. The **National War Labor Board** (NWLB), formed in April 1918, established an eight-hour day for war workers with time-and-a-half pay for overtime, and it endorsed equal pay for women. In return for a no-strike pledge, the NWLB also supported workers' right to organize — a major achievement for the labor movement. The Fuel

Administration, meanwhile, introduced daylight saving time to conserve coal and oil. In December 1917, the Railroad Administration seized control of the nation's hodgepodge of private railroads, seeking to facilitate rapid movement of troops and equipment — an experiment that had, at best, mixed results.

Perhaps the most successful wartime agency was the Food Administration, created in August 1917 and led by engineer Herbert Hoover. With the slogan "Food

**Fighting the Flu**

Influenza traversed the globe in 1918–1919, becoming a pandemic that killed as many as 50 million people. According to recent research, the flu began as a virus native to wild birds and then mutated into a form that passed easily from one human to another. In the United States, one-fifth of the population was infected and more than 500,000 civilians died — ten times the number of American soldiers who died in combat during World War I. The flu virus spread with frightening speed, and the epidemic strained the resources of a U.S. public health system already fully mobilized for the war effort. In October 1918 alone, 200,000 Americans died. This photo shows doctors, army officers, and reporters who donned surgical masks and gowns before touring hospitals that treated influenza patients. © Bettmann/Corbis.

will win the war," Hoover convinced farmers to nearly double their acreage of grain. This increase allowed a threefold rise in food exports to Europe. Among citizens, the Food Administration mobilized a "spirit of self-denial" rather than mandatory rationing. Female volunteers went from door to door to persuade housekeepers to observe "Wheatless" Mondays and "Porkless" Thursdays. Hoover, a Republican, emerged from the war as one of the nation's most admired public figures.

**Promoting National Unity**   Suppressing wartime dissent became a near obsession for President Wilson. In April 1917, Wilson formed the **Committee on Public**

**Information** (CPI), a government propaganda agency headed by journalist George Creel. Professing lofty goals — educating citizens about democracy, assimilating immigrants, and ending the isolation of rural life — the committee set out to mold Americans into "one white-hot mass" of war patriotism. The CPI touched the lives of nearly all civilians. It distributed seventy-five million pieces of literature and enlisted thousands of volunteers — **Four-Minute Men** — to deliver short prowar speeches at movie theaters.

The CPI also pressured immigrant groups to become "One Hundred Percent Americans." German Americans bore the brunt of this campaign (Thinking Like a Historian, p. 692). With posters exhorting

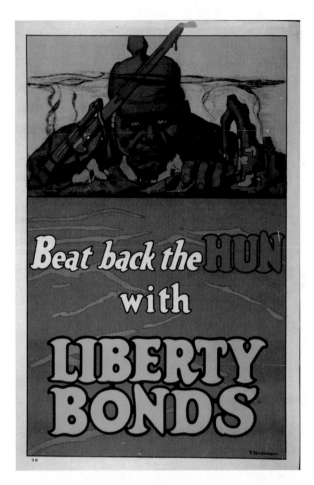

**Selling Liberty Bonds: Two Appeals**

Once the United States entered the Great War, government officials sought to enlist all Americans in the battle against the Central Powers. They carefully crafted patriotic advertising campaigns that urged Americans to buy bonds, conserve food, enlist in the military, and support the war effort in many other ways. One of these posters appeals to recent immigrants, reminding them of their debt to American Liberty. The other shows the overtly anti-German prejudices of many war appeals: it depicts the "Hun," a slur for a German soldier, with bloody hands and bayonet. Library of Congress.

citizens to root out German spies, a spirit of conformity pervaded the home front. A quasi-vigilante group, the American Protective League, mobilized about 250,000 "agents," furnished them with badges issued by the Justice Department, and trained them to spy on neighbors and coworkers. In 1918, members of the league led violent raids against draft evaders and peace activists. Government propaganda helped rouse a nativist hysteria that lingered into the 1920s.

Congress also passed new laws to curb dissent. Among them was the **Sedition Act of 1918**, which prohibited any words or behavior that might "incite, provoke, or encourage resistance to the United States, or promote the cause of its enemies." Because this and an earlier Espionage Act (1917) defined treason loosely, they led to the conviction of more than a thousand

people. The Justice Department prosecuted members of the Industrial Workers of the World, whose opposition to militarism threatened to disrupt war production of lumber and copper. When a Quaker pacifist teacher in New York City refused to teach a prowar curriculum, she was fired. Socialist Party leader Eugene V. Debs was sentenced to ten years in jail for the crime of arguing that wealthy capitalists had started the conflict and were forcing workers to fight.

Federal courts mostly supported the acts. In *Schenck v. United States* (1919), the Supreme Court upheld the conviction of a socialist who was jailed for circulating pamphlets that urged army draftees to resist induction. The justices followed this with a similar decision in *Abrams v. United States* (1919), ruling that authorities could prosecute speech they believed to

## German Americans in World War I

Before 1917, Americans expressed diverse opinions about the war in Europe. After the United States joined the Allies, however, German Americans' loyalty became suspect. German immigrant men who were not U.S. citizens were required to register as "alien enemies," and government propaganda fueled fear of alleged German spies. In April 1918 in Collinsville, Illinois, a German-born socialist named Robert Prager—who had sought U.S. citizenship and tried to enlist in the navy—was lynched by drunken miners. The documents below shed light on German Americans' wartime experiences.

1. **Advertisement,** *Fatherland,* **1915.** *This ad appeared in a political journal for German Americans. The translation of the songs offered on this recording are "Germany, Germany Above All" and "Precious Homeland."*

Patriotic German Music on Columbia Double-Disc Records

E2039      Deutschland, Deutschland über alles. . . .

10 in. — 75¢      Teure Heimat. . . .

COLUMBIA GRAMOPHONE COMPANY . . . DEALERS EVERYWHERE.

2. **C. J. Hexamer, speech, Milwaukee, 1915.** *This address by a German American community leader was widely cited during a 1918 investigation by the Senate Judiciary Committee.*

Whoever casts his Germanism from him like an old glove, is not worthy to be spit upon. . . . We have long suffered the preachment that "you Germans must allow yourselves to be assimilated, you must merge more in the American people;" but no one will ever find us prepared to step down to a lesser culture. No, we have made it our aim to elevate the others to us. . . . Be strong, and German. Remember, you German pioneers, that we are giving to this people the best the earth affords, the benefits of Germanic *kultur.*

3. **Sign in a Chicago park, 1917.**

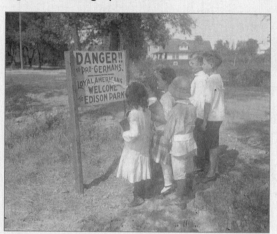

Chicago History Museum.

4. **"Lager Uber Alles" cartoon, 1918.** *This cartoon was part of an Ohio Anti-Saloon League referendum campaign to prohibit liquor sales. Ohio voters had rejected such a measure in 1915 and 1917, but in 1918 a majority voted for prohibition. Many U.S. breweries, such as Anheuser-Busch and Pabst, were owned by German Americans. "Hun" was an epithet for Germans; "Lager (Beer) Uber Alles" refers to the German national anthem cited in source 1.*

Courtesy of The Ohio State University Department of History.

5. **James W. Gerard, radio address, 1917.** *Gerard was U.S. ambassador to Great Britain.*

The great majority of American citizens of German descent have, in this great crisis in our history, shown themselves splendidly loyal to our flag. Everyone has a right to sympathize with any warring nation. But now that we are in the war there are only two sides, and the time has come when every citizen must declare himself American — or traitor!

. . . The Foreign Minister of Germany once said to me ". . . we have in your country 500,000 German reservists who will rise in arms against your government if you dare to make a move against Germany." Well, I told him that that might be so, but that we had 500,001 lampposts in this country, and that that was where the reservists would be hanging the day after they tried to rise. And if there are any German-Americans here who are so ungrateful for all the benefits they have received that they are still for the Kaiser, there is only one thing to do with them. And that is to hog-tie them, give them back the wooden shoes and the rags they landed in, and ship them back. . . . There is no animal that bites and kicks and squeals . . . equal to a fat German-American, if you commenced to tie him up and told him that he was on his way back to the Kaiser.

6. **Actions by New York *liederkranz* reported in *New Orleans Times-Picayune*, May 16, 1918.** *Lieder-kranz, or singing societies, played a vital role in German immigrant communities. Before World War I the city of Wheeling, West Virginia, counted eleven such societies, with names like Harmonie, Germania, and Mozart. By 1918 most liederkranz had vanished. New York City's was one of the few that did not.*

Members of the [New York] Liederkranz, an organiza-tion founded seventy-one years ago by Germans . . . met tonight and placed on record their unqualified Ameri-canism.

. . . They declared English the official language of the organization, and for the first time in years the sound of an enemy tongue will not be heard in the club's halls. Likewise they reiterated their offer to turn the buildings over to the government as a hospital if it were necessary.

7. **Lola Gamble Clyde, 1976 interview on life in Idaho during World War I.** *In the 1970s, historians inter-viewed residents of rural Latah County, Idaho, about their experiences in World War I. Frank*

*Brocke, a farmer, recalled that neighbors on their joint telephone line would slam down the phone when his mother or sister spoke German. "We had to be so careful," he said.*

I remember when they smashed out store windows at Uniontown that said [sauer]kraut. . . . Nobody would eat kraut. Throw the Kraut out, they were Germans. . . . Even the great Williamson store, he went in and gathered up everything that was made in Germany, and had a big bon-fire out in the middle of the street, you know. Although he had many good German friends all over the county that had helped make him rich. . . . And if it was a German name — we'll just change our name. . . . There were some [German American] boys that got draft deferments. . . . Some of them said that their fathers were sick and dying, and their father had so much land they had to stay home and farm it for them. . . . [Local men] tarred and feath-ered some of them. Some of them as old men dying still resented and remembered.

Sources: (1) Frederick C. Luebke, *Bonds of Loyalty: German Americans and World War I* (Dekalb: Northern Illinois University Press, 1974), 109; (2) *Hearings Before the Subcommittee on the Judiciary, United States Senate, 65th Congress, Second Session* (Washington, DC: Government Printing Office, 1918), 300; (5) Gerard speech, transcript and recording, at Library of Congress American Memory: memory.loc.gov /ammem/nfhtml/nforSpeakers01.html; (6) *New Orleans Times-Picayune*, May 16, 1918; (7) Oral histories of Idaho residents at GMU History Matters, historymatters.gmu .edu/d/2/. Excerpt courtesy of Latah County Historical Society.

## ANALYZING THE EVIDENCE

1. How did conditions change for German Americans between 1915 and 1918?
2. According to these sources, what aspects of German American culture did other Americans find threatening? What forms did anti-German hostility take?
3. Compare the sources that offer a German American per-spective (sources 1, 2, 6, and 7) to those that represent a threat to German Americans' way of life (3, 4, 5). How did German Americans respond to growing anti-German sentiment in this period?

## PUTTING IT ALL TOGETHER

World War I heightened anxieties about who was a "true" American. What groups were singled out in particular and why? What continuities do you see between these fears over "hyphenated" identities and controversies in earlier eras of U.S. history? Today?

**The Labor Agent in the South**

This evocative painting from 1940 is part of the famous Great Migration series by African American painter Jacob Lawrence. It shows how many African American workers found a route to opportunity: northern manufacturers, facing severe wartime labor shortages, sent agents to the South to recruit workers. Agents often arranged loans to pay for train fare and other travel expenses; once laborers were settled and employed in the North, they repaid the loans from their wages. Here, a line of men waits for the agent to record their names in his open ledger. The bare tree in the background suggests the barrenness of economic prospects for impoverished rural blacks in the South; it also hints at the threat of lynching and racial violence. Digital Image © The Museum of Modern Art/Licensed by SCALA/Art Resource, NY.

pose "a clear and present danger to the safety of the country." In an important dissent, however, Justices Oliver Wendell Holmes, Jr. and Louis Brandeis objected to the *Abrams* decision. Holmes's probing questions about the definition of "clear and present danger" helped launch twentieth-century legal battles over free speech and civil liberties.

**Great Migrations**    World War I created tremendous economic opportunities at home. Jobs in war industries drew thousands of people to the cities. With so many men in uniform, jobs in heavy industry opened for the first time to African Americans, accelerating the pace of black migration from South to North. During World War I, more than 400,000 African Americans moved to such cities as St. Louis, Chicago, New York, and Detroit, in what became known as the **Great Migration**. The rewards were great, and taking war jobs could be a source of patriotic pride. "If it hadn't been for the negro," a Carnegie Steel manager later recalled, "we could hardly have carried on our operations."

Blacks in the North encountered discrimination in jobs, housing, and education. But in the first flush of opportunity, most celebrated their escape from the repressive racism and poverty of the South. "It is a matter of a dollar with me and I feel that God made the path and I am walking therein," one woman reported to her sister back home. "Tell your husband work is plentiful here." "I just begin to feel like a man," wrote another migrant to a friend in Mississippi. "My children are going to the same school with the whites. . . . Will vote the next election and there isn't any 'yes sir' and 'no sir' — it's all yes and no and Sam and Bill."

Wartime labor shortages prompted Mexican Americans in the Southwest to leave farmwork for urban industrial jobs. Continued political instability in Mexico, combined with increased demand for farmworkers in the United States, also encouraged more Mexicans to move across the border. Between 1917 and 1920, at least 100,000 Mexicans entered the United States; despite discrimination, large numbers stayed. If asked why, many might have echoed the words of an African American man who left New Orleans for Chicago: they were going "north for a better chance." The same was true for Puerto Ricans such as Jésus Colón, who also confronted racism. "I came to New York to poor pay, long hours, terrible working conditions, discrimination even in the slums and in the poor paying factories," Colón recalled, "where the bosses very dexterously pitted Italians against Puerto Ricans and Puerto Ricans against American Negroes and Jews."

Women were the largest group to take advantage of wartime job opportunities. About 1 million women joined the paid labor force for the first time, while another 8 million gave up low-wage service jobs for higher-paying industrial work. Americans soon got used to the sight of female streetcar conductors, train engineers, and defense workers. Though most people expected these jobs to return to men in peacetime, the

**Women Riveters at the Puget Sound Navy Yard, 1919**

With men at the front, women took many new jobs during World War I—as mail carriers, police officers, and farm laborers who joined the Women's Land Army. African American women, generally limited by white prejudice to jobs in domestic service and agriculture, found that the war opened up new opportunities and better wages in industry. When the war ended, women usually lost jobs deemed to be men's work. In 1919, however, these women were still hard at work in the Puget Sound Navy Yard, near Seattle. What clues indicate their attitudes toward their work, and toward one another? National Archives.

war created a new comfort level with women's employment outside the home—and with women's suffrage.

**Women's Voting Rights**   The National American Woman Suffrage Association (NAWSA) threw the support of its 2 million members wholeheartedly into the war effort. Its president, Carrie Chapman Catt, declared that women had to prove their patriotism to win the ballot. NAWSA members in thousands of communities promoted food conservation and distributed emergency relief through organizations such as the Red Cross.

Alice Paul and the **National Woman's Party** (NWP) took a more confrontational approach. Paul was a Quaker who had worked in the settlement movement and earned a PhD in political science. Finding as a NAWSA lobbyist that congressmen dismissed her, Paul founded the NWP in 1916. Inspired by militant British suffragists, the group began in July 1917 to picket the White House. Standing silently with their banners, Paul and other NWP activists faced arrest for obstructing traffic and were sentenced to seven months in jail. They protested by going on a hunger strike, which prison authorities met with forced feeding. Public shock at the women's treatment drew attention to the suffrage cause.

Impressed by NAWSA's patriotism and worried by the NWP's militancy, the antisuffrage Wilson reversed his position. In January 1918, he urged support for woman suffrage as a "war measure." The constitutional amendment quickly passed the House of Representatives; it took eighteen months to get through the Senate and another year to win ratification by the states. On August 26, 1920, when Tennessee voted for ratification, the Nineteenth

**EXPLAIN CONSEQUENCES**

What were the different effects of African Americans', Mexican Americans', and women's civilian mobilization during World War I?

**Wagon Decorated for the Labor Day Parade, San Diego, California, 1910**

As the woman suffrage movement grew stronger in the years before and during World War I, working-class women played increasingly prominent and visible roles in its leadership. This Labor Day parade float, created by the Women's Union Label League of San Diego, showed that activists championed equal pay for women in the workplace as well as women's voting rights. "Union Label Leagues" urged middle-class shoppers to purchase only clothing with a union label, certifying that the item had been manufactured under safe conditions and the workers who made it had received a fair wage. San Diego Historical Society, Title Insurance Trust Collection.

Amendment became law. The state thus joined Texas as one of two ex-Confederate states to ratify it. In most parts of the South, the measure meant that *white* women began to vote: in this Jim Crow era, African American women's voting rights remained restricted along with men's.

In explaining suffragists' victory, historians have debated the relative effectiveness of Catt's patriotic strategy and Paul's militant protests. Both played a role in persuading Wilson and Congress to act, but neither might have worked without the extraordinary impact of the Great War. Across the globe, before 1914, the only places where women had full suffrage were New Zealand, Australia, Finland, and Norway. After World War I, many nations moved to enfranchise women. The new Soviet Union acted first, in 1917, with Great Britain and Canada following in 1918; by 1920, the measure had passed in Germany, Austria, Poland, Czechoslovakia, and Hungary as well as the United States. (Major exceptions were France and Italy, where women did not gain voting rights until after World War II, and Switzerland, which held out until 1971.) Thus, while World War I introduced modern horrors on the battlefield — machine guns and poison gas — it brought some positive results at home: economic opportunity and women's political participation.

## Catastrophe at Versailles

The idealistic Wilson argued that no victor should be declared after World War I: only "peace among equals" could last. Having won at an incredible price, Britain and France showed zero interest in such a plan. But the devastation wrought by the war created popular pressure for a just and enduring outcome. Wilson scored a diplomatic victory at the peace conference, held at Versailles, near Paris, in 1919, when the Allies chose to base the talks on his **Fourteen Points**, a blueprint for

PEACE AND FUTURE CANNON FODDER

The Tiger: "*Curious! I seem to hear a child weeping!*"

**"Peace and Future Cannon Fodder"**

This scathing cartoon, published in 1920, was drawn by Australian-born artist Will Dyson and published in a British magazine. It shows the "Big Four" power brokers at Versailles—from left to right, Vittorio Orlando of Italy, David Lloyd George of Britain, Georges Clemenceau of France, and Woodrow Wilson of the United States. Clemenceau, who was nicknamed "The Tiger," turns his head and comments on the crying child. Even at the time, astute observers such as Dyson argued that the treaty might have horrific consequences, particularly in the brutal conditions it imposed on Germany. Dyson sketched "1940 Class" over the head of the child. The young children of 1920 grew up to inherit the consequences of the Versailles treaty, which contributed to the rise of fascism, Nazism, and World War II. *British Daily Herald,* May 13, 1919.

collective military action. Wilson hoped the League would "end all wars." But his ideals had marked limits, and in negotiations he confronted harsh realities.

## The Fate of Wilson's Ideas

The peace conference included ten thousand representatives from around the globe, but leaders of France, Britain, and the United States dominated the proceedings. When the Japanese delegation proposed a declaration for equal treatment of all races, the Allies rejected it. Similarly, the Allies ignored a global Pan-African Congress, organized by W. E. B. Du Bois and other black leaders; they snubbed Arab representatives who had been military allies during the war. Even Italy's prime minister—included among the influential "Big Four," because in 1915 Italy had switched to the Allied side—withdrew from the conference, aggrieved at the way British and French leaders marginalized him. The Allies excluded two key players: Russia, because they distrusted its communist leaders, and Germany, because they planned to dictate terms to their defeated foe. For Wilson's "peace among equals," it was a terrible start.

Prime Minister David Lloyd George of Britain and Premier Georges Clemenceau of France imposed harsh punishments on Germany. Unbeknownst to others at the time, they had already made secret agreements to divide up Germany's African colonies and take them as spoils of war. At Versailles, they also forced the defeated nation to pay $33 billion in reparations and surrender coal supplies, merchant ships, valuable patents, and even territory along the French border. These terms caused keen resentment and economic hardship in Germany, and over the following two decades they helped lead to World War II.

Given these conditions, it is remarkable that Wilson influenced the **Treaty of Versailles** as much as he did. He intervened repeatedly to soften conditions imposed on Germany. In accordance with the Fourteen Points, he worked with the other Allies to fashion nine new nations, stretching from the Baltic to the Mediterranean (Map 21.4). These were intended as a buffer to protect Western Europe from communist Russia; the plan also embodied Wilson's principle of self-determination for European states. Elsewhere in the world, the Allies dismantled their enemies' empires but did not create independent nations, keeping colonized people subordinate to European power. France, for example, refused to give up its long-standing occupation of Indochina; Clemenceau's snub of future Vietnamese leader Ho Chi Minh, who sought representation at Versailles, had

peace that he had presented a year earlier in a speech to Congress.

Wilson's Points embodied an important strand in progressivism. They called for open diplomacy; "absolute freedom of navigation upon the seas"; arms reduction; removal of trade barriers; and national self-determination for peoples in the Austro-Hungarian, Russian, and German empires. Essential to Wilson's vision was the creation of an international regulatory body, eventually called the **League of Nations**, that would guarantee each country's "independence and territorial integrity." The League would mediate disputes, supervise arms reduction, and—according to its crucial Article X—curb aggressor nations through

**EXPLAIN CONSEQUENCES**

In what ways did the Treaty of Versailles embody—or fail to embody—Wilson's Fourteen Points?

grave long-term consequences for both France and the United States.

The establishment of a British mandate in Palestine (now Israel) also proved crucial. During the war, British foreign secretary Sir Arthur Balfour had stated that his country would work to establish there a "national home for the Jewish people," with the condition that "nothing shall be done which may prejudice the civil and religious rights of existing non-Jewish communities in Palestine." Under the British mandate, thousands of Jews moved to Palestine and purchased land, in some cases evicting Palestinian tenants. As early as 1920, riots erupted between Jews and Palestinians—a situation that, even before World War II, escalated beyond British control.

The Versailles treaty thus created conditions for horrific future bloodshed, and it must be judged one of history's great catastrophes. Balfour astutely described Clemenceau, Lloyd George, and Wilson as "all-powerful, all-ignorant men, sitting there and carving up continents." Wilson, however, remained optimistic as he returned home, even though his health was beginning to fail. The president hoped the new League of Nations, authorized by the treaty, would moderate the settlement and secure peaceful resolutions of other disputes. For this to occur, U.S. participation was crucial.

## Congress Rejects the Treaty

The outlook for U.S. ratification was not promising. Though major opinion makers and religious denominations supported the treaty, openly hostile Republicans

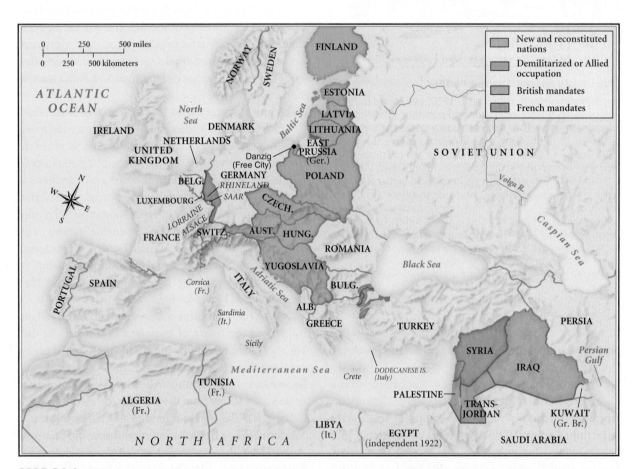

**MAP 21.4**

**Europe and the Middle East After World War I**

World War I and its aftermath dramatically altered the landscape of Europe and the Middle East. In central Europe, the collapse of the German, Russian, and Austro-Hungarian empires brought the reconstitution of Poland and the creation of a string of new states based on the principle of national (ethnic) self-determination. The demise of the Ottoman Empire resulted in the appearance of the quasi-independent territories, or "mandates," of Iraq, Syria, Lebanon, and Palestine. The League of Nations stipulated that their affairs would be supervised by one of the Allied powers.

held a majority in the Senate. One group, called the "irreconcilables," consisted of western progressive Republicans such as Hiram Johnson of California and Robert La Follette of Wisconsin, who opposed U.S. involvement in European affairs. Another group, led by Senator Henry Cabot Lodge of Massachusetts, worried that Article X — the provision for collective security — would prevent the United States from pursuing an independent foreign policy. Was the nation, Lodge asked, "willing to have the youth of America ordered to war" by an international body? Wilson refused to accept any amendments, especially to placate Lodge, a hated rival. "I shall consent to nothing," the president told the French ambassador. "The Senate must take its medicine."

To mobilize support, Wilson embarked on an exhausting speaking tour. His impassioned defense of the League of Nations brought audiences to tears, but the strain proved too much for the president. While visiting Colorado in September 1919, Wilson collapsed. A week later, back in Washington, he suffered a stroke that left one side of his body paralyzed. Wilson still urged Democratic senators to reject all Republican amendments. When the treaty came up for a vote in November 1919, it failed to win the required two-thirds majority. A second attempt, in March 1920, fell seven votes short.

The treaty was dead, and so was Wilson's leadership. The president never fully recovered from his stroke. During the last eighteen months of his administration, the government drifted as Wilson's physician, his wife, and various cabinet heads secretly took charge. The United States never ratified the Versailles treaty or joined the League of Nations. In turn, the League was weak. When Wilson died in 1924, his dream of a just and peaceful international order lay in ruins.

The impact of World War I can hardly be overstated. Despite bids for power by Britain and France, Europe's hold on its colonial empires never recovered. The United States, now a major world power, appeared to turn its back on the world when it rejected the Versailles treaty. But in laying claim to Hawaii and the Philippines, asserting power in Latin America, and intervening in Asia, the United States had entangled itself deeply in global politics. By 1918, the nation had gained too much diplomatic clout — and was too dependent on overseas trade — for isolation to be a realistic long-term option.

On the home front, the effects of World War I were no less dramatic. Wartime jobs and prosperity ushered in an era of exuberant consumerism, while the achievements of women's voting rights seemed to presage a new progressive era. But as peace returned, it became clear that the war had not advanced reform. Rather than embracing government activism, Americans of the 1920s proved eager to relinquish it.

## SUMMARY

Between 1877 and 1918, the United States rose as a major economic and military power. Justifications for overseas expansion emphasized access to global markets, the importance of sea power, and the need to police international misconduct and trade. These justifications shaped U.S. policy toward European powers in Latin America, and victory in the War of 1898 enabled the United States to take control of former Spanish colonies in the Caribbean and Pacific. Victory, however, also led to bloody conflict in the Philippines as the United States struggled to suppress Filipino resistance to American rule.

After 1899, the United States aggressively asserted its interests in Asia and Latin America. In China, the United States used the so-called Boxer Rebellion to make good its claim to an "open door" to Chinese markets. Later, President Theodore Roosevelt strengthened relations with Japan, and his successor, William Howard Taft, supported U.S. business interests in China. In the Caribbean, the United States constructed the Panama Canal and regularly exercised the right, claimed under the Roosevelt Corollary, to intervene in the affairs of states in the region. President Woodrow Wilson publicly disparaged the imperialism of his predecessors but repeatedly used the U.S. military to "police" Mexico.

At the outbreak of World War I, the United States asserted neutrality, but its economic ties to the Allies rapidly undercut that claim. In 1917, German submarine attacks drew the United States into the war on the side of Britain and France. Involvement in the war profoundly transformed the economy, politics, and society of the nation, resulting in an economic boom, mass migrations of workers to industrial centers, and the achievement of national voting rights. At the Paris Peace Conference, Wilson attempted to implement his Fourteen Points. However, the designs of the Allies in Europe undermined the Treaty of Versailles, while Republican resistance at home prevented ratification of the treaty. Although Wilson's dream of a just international order failed, the United States had taken its place as a major world power.

# CHAPTER REVIEW

 **MAKE IT STICK**    Go to **LearningCurve** to retain what you've read.

**TERMS TO KNOW**    Identify and explain the significance of each term below.

## Key Concepts and Events

American exceptionalism (p. 674)
"Remember the *Maine*" (p. 675)
Teller Amendment (p. 675)
*Insular Cases* (p. 678)
Platt Amendment (p. 678)
open door policy (p. 679)
Root-Takahira Agreement
  (p. 682)
Panama Canal (p. 682)
Roosevelt Corollary (p. 683)
Zimmermann telegram (p. 686)
War Industries Board (p. 688)

National War Labor Board
  (p. 689)
Committee on Public Informa-
  tion (p. 690)
Four-Minute Men (p. 690)
Sedition Act of 1918 (p. 691)
Great Migration (p. 694)
National Woman's Party (p. 695)
Fourteen Points (p. 696)
League of Nations (p. 697)
Treaty of Versailles (p. 697)

## Key People

Theodore Roosevelt (p. 674)
Alfred Mahan (p. 674)
Queen Liliuokalani (p. 676)
Emilio Aguinaldo (p. 678)
Porfirio Díaz (p. 683)
Woodrow Wilson (p. 683)
Herbert Hoover (p. 689)
Alice Paul (p. 695)

**REVIEW QUESTIONS**    Answer these questions to demonstrate your understanding of the chapter's main ideas.

1. What factors prompted the United States to claim overseas territories in the 1890s and early 1900s?

2. What role did the United States play in World War I? On balance, do you think U.S. entry into the war was justified? Why or why not?

3. How did World War I shape America on the home front, economically and politically?

4. **THEMATIC UNDERSTANDING**    Review the events listed under "America in the World" on the thematic timeline on page 671. By the end of World War I, what influence did the United States exercise in the Caribbean, Latin America, the Pacific, and China, and in European affairs? How, and to what extent, had its power in each region expanded over the previous four decades? Compare and contrast the role of the United States to the roles of other powers in each region.

## MAKING CONNECTIONS

Recognize the larger developments and continuities within and across chapters by answering these questions.

1. **ACROSS TIME AND PLACE**   Read again the documents from "Representing Indians" in Chapter 16 (Thinking Like a Historian, p. 530). In what ways might ideas about Native Americans have informed attitudes toward Hawaiians, Filipinos, and other people of color overseas? How might this explain which peoples Woodrow Wilson included and excluded in his ideal of "national self-determination"? Write a short essay in which you explain how Americans' policies and attitudes toward native peoples within North America shaped U.S. foreign policy between 1898 and 1918. You may also wish to review relevant information in Chapters 15 and 20 and consider how attitudes toward African Americans shaped white Americans' racial assumptions in this era.

2. **VISUAL EVIDENCE**   Review the images on pages 673, 685, and 695. What do they tell us about how the 1910s, especially the experiences of World War I, changed gender expectations for men and women? At the start of the war, would you rather have been a young man or a young woman? Why? How did new opportunities vary according to a young person's race and ethnicity? (The posters on pp. 687 and 691 may also be useful in considering this question.)

## MORE TO EXPLORE   Start here to learn more about the events discussed in this chapter.

Jean H. Baker, *Votes for Women* (2002). A collection of essays on the achievement of women's suffrage.

Frank Freidel, *Over There* (1990). A collection of American soldiers' firsthand accounts of their experiences in World War I.

*The Great War and the Shaping of the 20th Century*. An excellent PBS documentary with accompanying documents at **pbs.org/greatwar/index.html**.

Julie Greene, *The Canal Builders* (2009). The story of the Panama Canal through the viewpoint of the diverse workers who constructed it.

James R. Grossman, *Land of Hope* (1999). A sweeping study of the Great Migration.

Walter LaFeber, *The American Search for Opportunity, 1865–1913* (1993). An excellent, up-to-date synthesis of foreign policy in this era.

## TIMELINE

Ask yourself why this chapter begins and ends with these dates and then identify the links among related events.

| 1886 | • U.S. begins building modern battleships |
|---|---|
| 1892 | • U.S.-backed planters overthrow Hawaii's Queen Liliuokalani |
| 1895 | • United States arbitrates border dispute between Britain and Venezuela<br>• Guerrilla war against Spanish rule begins in Cuba |
| 1898 | • War between United States and Spain<br>• United States annexes Hawaii, Puerto Rico, and Guam |
| 1899–1902 | • U.S.-Philippine War, ending in U.S. occupation of Philippines<br>• United States pursues open door policy in China |
| 1900 | • United States helps suppress nationalist rebellion in China ("Boxer Rebellion") |
| 1901 | • Hay-Pauncefote Treaty |
| 1902 | • Platt Amendment gives U.S. exclusive role in Cuba |
| 1903 | • U.S. recognizes Panama's independence from Colombia |
| 1905 | • Russo-Japanese War; Roosevelt mediates peace |
| 1908 | • Root-Takahira Agreement |
| 1914 | • Panama Canal opens<br>• U.S. military action in Veracruz, Mexico<br>• World War I begins in Europe |
| 1916 | • Jones Act commits United States to future Philippine independence |
| 1917 | • United States declares war on Germany and its allies, creates new agencies to mobilize economy and promote national unity<br>• Espionage Act |
| 1918 | • Sedition Act<br>• World War I ends<br>• Beginning of two-year influenza pandemic that kills 50 million people worldwide |
| 1919 | • *Schenck v. United States* and *Abrams v. United States*<br>• Wilson promotes Fourteen Points at Paris Peace Conference<br>• Senate rejects the Treaty of Versailles |
| 1920 | • Nineteenth Amendment grants women suffrage |

**KEY TURNING POINTS:** On the timeline above, identify at least five events that demonstrated the rising global power of the United States. Compare their consequences. If you had been an observer in London or Tokyo, how might you have interpreted the United States's actions in each case?

# 22 CHAPTER

# Cultural Conflict, Bubble, and Bust 1919–1932

Rising to fame in *The Sheik* (1922), Rudolph Valentino became a controversial Hollywood star. Calling him "dark, darling, and delightful," female fans mobbed his appearances. In Chicago, Mexican American boys slicked back their hair and called each other "sheik." But some Anglo men said they loathed Valentino. One reviewer claimed the star had stolen his style from female "vamps" and ridiculed him for wearing a bracelet (a gift from his wife). The *Chicago Tribune* blamed Valentino for the rise of "effeminate men," shown by the popularity of "floppy pants and slave bracelets." Outraged, Valentino challenged the journalist to a fight—and defeated the writer's stand-in.

Valentino, an Italian immigrant, upset racial and ethnic boundaries. Nicknamed the Latin Lover, he played among other roles a Spanish bullfighter and the son of a maharajah. When a reporter called his character in *The Sheik* a "savage," Valentino retorted, "People are not savages because they have dark skins. The Arab civilization is one of the oldest in the world."

But to many American-born Protestants, movies were morally dangerous—"vile and atrocious," one women's group declared. The appeal of "dark" stars like Valentino and his predecessor, Japanese American actor Sessue Hayakawa, was part of the problem. Hollywood became a focal point for political conflict as the nation took a sharp right turn. A year before *The Sheik* appeared, the Reverend Wilbur Crafts published a widely reprinted article warning of "Jewish Supremacy in Film." He accused "Hebrew" Hollywood executives of "gross immorality" and claimed they were racially incapable of understanding "the prevailing standards of the American people." These were not fringe views. Crafts's editorial first appeared in a newspaper owned by prominent auto-maker Henry Ford.

Critics, though, failed to slow Hollywood's success. Faced with threats of regulation, movie-makers did what other big businesses did in the 1920s: they used their clout to block government intervention. At the same time, they expanded into world markets; when Valentino visited Paris, he was swarmed by thousands of French fans. *The Sheik* highlighted America's business success and its political and cultural divides. Young urban audiences, including women "flappers," were eager to challenge older sexual and religious mores. Rural Protestants saw American values going down the drain. In Washington, meanwhile, Republican leaders abandoned two decades of reform and deferred to business. Americans wanted prosperity, not progressivism—until the consequences arrived in the shock of the Great Depression.

**IDENTIFY THE BIG IDEA**

What conflicts in culture and politics arose in the 1920s, and how did economic developments in that decade help cause the Great Depression?

**Celebrating the Fourth of July, 1926** This *Life* magazine cover celebrates two famous symbols of the 1920s: jazz music and the "flapper," in her droopy tights and scandalously short skirt, who loves to dance to its rhythms. The flags at the top record the latest slang expressions, including "so's your old man" and "step on it" ("it" being the accelerator of an automobile, in a decade when cars were America's hottest commodity). The bottom of the picture also added a note of protest: while July 4, 1926, marked the 150th anniversary of the Declaration of Independence, *Life* says that Americans have had only "one hundred and forty-three years of liberty" —followed by "seven years of Prohibition."

Picture Research Consultants & Archives.

# Conflicted Legacies of World War I

"The World War has accentuated all our differences," a journalist observed in 1919. "It has not created those differences, but it has revealed and emphasized them." In the war's immediate aftermath, thousands of strikes revealed continuing labor tensions. Violent riots exposed white resistance to the rising expectations of African Americans, while an obsessive hunt for "foreign" radicals — like angry denunciations of Hollywood's Latin Lover — showed that ethnic pluralism would not win easy acceptance.

## Racial Strife

African Americans emerged from World War I determined to achieve citizenship rights. Millions had loyally supported the war effort; 350,000 had served in uniform. At the same time, the Great Migration drew hundreds of thousands from the South to northern industrial cities, where they secured good wartime jobs and found they could vote and use their new economic clout to build community institutions and work for racial justice. The black man, one observer wrote, "realized that he was part and parcel of the great army of democracy. . . . With this realization came the consciousness of pride in himself as a man, and an American citizen."

These developments sparked white violence. In the South, the number of lynchings rose from 48 in 1917 to 78 in 1919, including several murders of returning black soldiers in their military uniforms. In 1921, after a brutal lynching in the railroad town of Rosewood, Florida, black residents armed for self-defense; mobs of furious whites responded by torching houses and hunting down African Americans. Police and state authorities refused to intervene. The town of Rosewood vanished from the map.

In northern and midwestern cities, the arrival of southern migrants deepened existing racial tensions. Blacks competed with whites — including recent immigrants — for scarce housing and jobs. Unionized white workers resented blacks who served as strikebreakers. Racism turned such conflicts into violent confrontations. Attacks on African Americans broke out in more than twenty-five cities. One of the deadliest riots

### Chicago Race Riot

When racial violence exploded in Chicago during the summer of 1919, *Chicago Evening Post* photographer Jun Fujita was on the scene to capture it. As one of the few Japanese immigrants in Chicago at the time, Fujita was probably no stranger to racism, and it took personal courage to put himself in the midst of the escalating violence. When the riot finally ended, thirty-eight people were dead and more than five hundred were injured. Chicago Historical Society/Photo by Jun Fujita.

occurred in 1917 in East St. Louis, Illinois, where nine whites and more than forty blacks died. Chicago endured five days of rioting in July 1919. By September, the national death toll from racial violence reached 120.

The oil boomtown of Tulsa, Oklahoma, was the site of a horrific incident in June 1921. Sensational, false reports of an alleged rape helped incite white mobs who resented growing black prosperity. Anger focused on the 8,000 residents of Tulsa's prosperous Greenwood district, locally known as "the black Wall Street." The mob—helped by National Guardsmen, who arrested blacks who resisted—burned thirty-five blocks of Greenwood and killed several dozen people. The city's leading paper acknowledged that "semi-organized bands of white men systematically applied the torch, while others shot on sight men of color." It took a decade for black residents to rebuild Greenwood.

## Erosion of Labor Rights

African Americans were not the only ones who faced challenges to their hard-won gains. The war effort, overseen by a Democratic administration sympathetic to labor, had temporarily increased the size and power of labor unions. The National War Labor Board had instituted a series of prolabor measures, including recognition of workers' right to organize. Membership in the American Federation of Labor (AFL) grew by a third during World War I, reaching more than 3 million by war's end, and continued to climb afterward. Workers' expectations also rose as the war economy brought higher pay and better working conditions.

But when workers tried to maintain these standards after the war, employers cut wages and rooted out unions, prompting massive confrontations. In 1919, more than four million wage laborers—one in every five—went on strike, a proportion never since equaled. A walkout of shipyard workers in Seattle sparked a general strike that shut down the city. Another strike disrupted the steel industry, as 350,000 workers demanded union recognition and an end to twelve-hour shifts. Elbert H. Gary, head of United States Steel Corporation, refused to negotiate; he hired Mexican and African American replacements and broke the strike. Meanwhile, business leaders in rising industries, such as automobile manufacturing, resisted unions, creating more and more nonunionized jobs.

Public employees fared no better. Late in 1919, Boston's police force demanded a union and went on strike to get it. Massachusetts governor Calvin Coolidge won national fame by declaring, "There is no right to strike against the public safety by anybody, anywhere,

**Fear of "Bolshevism," 1919**

This cartoon from the *Post Dispatch* in Cleveland, Ohio, reflects nationwide panic over the general strike by 110 unions that paralyzed Seattle in February 1919. Opponents of radical labor unrest had a deeper fear: the Bolshevik Revolution in Russia, resulting in creation of the USSR, had brought into existence the world's first enduring communist state. By crushing unions in Seattle with a club of "Law and Order," this image suggests that Uncle Sam could beat back the global communist threat. This aspect of the 1919 Red Scare prefigured, at an early date, the anxieties of the Cold War era. Ohio Historical Society.

anytime." Coolidge fired the entire police force; the strike failed. A majority of the public supported the governor. Republicans rewarded Coolidge by nominating him for the vice-presidency in 1920.

Antilabor decisions by the Supreme Court were an additional key factor in unions' decline. In *Coronado Coal Company v. United Mine Workers* (1925), the Court ruled that a striking union could be penalized for illegal restraint of trade. The Court also struck down federal legislation regulating child labor; in *Adkins v. Children's Hospital* (1923), it voided a minimum wage for women

**PLACE EVENTS IN CONTEXT**

What factors contributed to antiblack violence, labor defeats, and the Red Scare, and what connections might we draw among these events?

workers in the District of Columbia, reversing many of the gains that had been achieved through the ground-breaking decision in *Muller v. Oregon* (Chapter 20). Such decisions, along with aggressive antiunion campaigns, caused membership in labor unions to fall from 5.1 million in 1920 to 3.6 million in 1929 — just 10 percent of the nonagricultural workforce.

In place of unions, the 1920s marked the heyday of **welfare capitalism**, a system of labor relations that stressed management's responsibility for employees' well-being. Automaker Henry Ford, among others, pioneered this system before World War I, famously paying $5 a day. Ford also offered a profit-sharing plan to employees who met the standards of its Social Department, which investigated to ensure that workers' private lives met the company's moral standards. At a time when government unemployment compensation and Social Security did not exist, General Electric and U.S. Steel provided health insurance and old-age pensions. Other employers, like Chicago's Western Electric Company, built athletic facilities and selectively offered paid vacations. Employers hoped this would build a loyal workforce and head off labor unrest. But such plans covered only about 5 percent of the industrial workforce. Facing new financial pressures in the 1920s, even Henry Ford cut back his $5 day. In the tangible benefits it offered workers, welfare capitalism had serious limitations.

## The Red Scare

Many well-off Americans sided with management in the upheavals of the postwar years. They blamed workers for the rapidly rising cost of living, which jumped nearly 80 percent between 1917 and 1919. The socialist views of some recent immigrants frightened native-born citizens; communism terrified them. When in 1919 the Soviet Union's new Bolshevik leaders founded the Third International, intended to foster revolutions abroad, some Americans began to fear that dangerous radicals were hiding everywhere. Wartime hatred of Germans was replaced by hostility toward Bolsheviks (labeled "Reds," after the color of communist flags). Ironically, American communists remained few in number and had little political influence. Of the 50 million adults in the United States in 1920, no more than 70,000 belonged to either the fledgling U.S. Communist Party or the Communist Labor Party.

In April 1919, alert postal workers discovered and defused thirty-four mail bombs addressed to government officials. In June, a bomb detonated outside the Washington town house of recently appointed attorney

*The Passion of Sacco and Vanzetti*, **by Ben Shahn, 1931–1932**

Ben Shahn (1898–1969) came to the United States from Lithuania as a child and achieved fame as a social realist painter and photographer. Shahn used his art to advance his belief in social justice. In this painting, Sacco and Vanzetti lie dead and pale, hovered over by three distinguished Massachusetts citizens. These grim-faced men — holding lilies, a symbol of death — are Harvard University president A. Lawrence Lowell and the two other members of a commission appointed by the governor in 1927 to review the case. The commission concluded that the men were guilty, a finding that led to their execution. Judge Webster Thayer, who presided at the original trial in 1921, stands in the window in the background. *The Passion of Sacco and Vanzetti* by Ben Shahn (1931–1932) Art © Estate of Ben Shahn/Licensed by VAGA, New York, NY. Photo © Geoffrey Clements.

general A. Mitchell Palmer. Palmer escaped unharmed, but he used the incident to fan public fears, precipitating a hysterical **Red Scare**. With President Woodrow Wilson incapacitated by stroke, Palmer had a free hand. He set up an antiradicalism division in the Justice Department and appointed his assistant J. Edgar Hoover to direct it; shortly afterward, it became the Federal Bureau of Investigation (FBI). In November 1919, Palmer's agents stormed the headquarters of radical organizations. The dragnet captured thousands of aliens who had committed no crimes but who held anarchist or revolutionary beliefs. Lacking the protection of U.S. citizenship, many were deported without indictment or trial.

The **Palmer raids** peaked on a notorious night in January 1920, when federal agents invaded homes and meeting halls, arrested six thousand citizens and aliens, and denied the prisoners access to legal counsel. Then Palmer, who had presidential ambitions, overreached. He predicted that on May 1 a radical conspiracy would attempt to overthrow the U.S. government. State militia and police went on twenty-four-hour alert to guard against the alleged threat, but not a single incident occurred. As the summer of 1920 passed without major strikes or renewed bombings, the Red Scare began to abate.

Like other postwar legacies, however, antiradicalism had broad, long-lasting effects. In May 1920, at the height of the Red Scare, police arrested Nicola Sacco, a shoemaker, and Bartolomeo Vanzetti, a fish peddler, for the murder of two men during a robbery of a shoe company in South Braintree, Massachusetts. Sacco and Vanzetti were Italian aliens and self-proclaimed anarchists who had evaded the draft. Convicted of the murders, Sacco and Vanzetti sat in jail for six years while supporters appealed their verdicts. In 1927, Judge Webster Thayer denied a motion for a new trial and sentenced them to death. Scholars still debate their guilt or innocence. But the case was clearly biased by prosecutors' emphasis on their ties to radical groups. The execution of Sacco and Vanzetti was one of the ugly scars left by the ethnic and political hostilities of the Great War.

## Politics in the 1920s

As the plight of labor suggested, the 1920s were a tough decade for progressives who had gained ground before World War I. After a few early reform victories, including achievement of national women's suffrage, the dominant motif of the 1920s was limited government. Native-born white Protestants rallied against what they saw as big-city values and advocated such goals as immigration restriction. A series of Republican presidents placed responsibility for the nation's well-being in the hands of business. President Calvin Coolidge declared, "The man who builds a factory builds a temple. The man who works there worships there." The same theme prevailed in continued U.S. interventions in Latin America and elsewhere: American business needs were the top priority.

## Women in Politics

At the start of the 1920s, many progressives hoped the attainment of women's voting rights would offer new leverage to tackle poverty. They created organizations like the Women's Joint Congressional Committee, a Washington-based advocacy group. The committee's greatest accomplishment was the first federally funded health-care legislation, the **Sheppard-Towner Federal Maternity and Infancy Act** (1921). Sheppard-Towner provided federal funds for medical clinics, prenatal education programs, and visiting nurses. Though opponents warned that the act would lead to socialized medicine, Sheppard-Towner improved health care for the poor and significantly lowered infant mortality rates. It also marked the first time that Congress designated federal funds for the states to encourage them to administer a social welfare program.

In 1923, Alice Paul, founder of the National Woman's Party, also persuaded congressional allies to consider an Equal Rights Amendment (ERA) to the U.S. Constitution. It stated simply, "men and women shall have equal rights throughout the United States." Advocates were hopeful; Wisconsin had passed a similar law two years earlier, and it helped women fight gender discrimination. But opponents pointed out that the ERA would threaten recent labor laws that protected women from workplace abuses. Such laws recognized women's vulnerable place in a heavily sex-segregated labor market. Would a theoretical statement of "equality" help poor and working women more than existing protections did? This question divided women's rights advocates. Introduced repeatedly in Congress over the next five decades but rarely making it out of committee, the ERA was debated again and again until the bitter ratification struggle of the 1970s (Chapter 29).

Horrified at the suffering caused by World War I, some women joined a growing international peace movement. While diplomats conducted negotiations at Versailles, women peace advocates from around the

> **EXPLAIN CONSEQUENCES**
> Before World War I, women didn't have full voting rights, but they had considerable success as reformers. After the war they *could* vote, but their proposals met defeat. How might we account for this apparent contradiction?

**The League of Women Voters**

The League of Women Voters was the brainchild of Carrie Chapman Catt, president of the National American Woman Suffrage Association. Formed in 1920, as the Nineteenth Amendment was about to give women the vote, the league undertook to educate Americans in responsible citizenship and to win enactment of legislation favorable to women. The league helped secure passage of the Sheppard-Towner Act of 1921, which provided federal aid for maternal and child-care programs. In the 1930s, members campaigned for the enactment of Social Security and other social welfare legislation. The Library of Virginia

world convened in Zurich and called on all nations to use their resources to end hunger and promote human welfare. Treaty negotiators ignored them, but the women organized for sustained activism. In 1919, they created the **Women's International League for Peace and Freedom** (WILPF), whose leading American members included Jane Addams. Members of the league denounced imperialism, stressed the human suffering caused by militarism, and proposed social justice measures.

Such women faced serious opposition. The WILPF came under fierce attack during the Red Scare because it included socialist women in its ranks. And though women proved to be effective lobbyists, they had difficulty gaining access to positions inside the Republican and Democratic parties. Finding that women did not vote as a bloc, politicians in both parties began to take their votes for granted. New reforms failed to gain support, and others were rolled back. Many congressmen, for example, had supported the Sheppard-Towner Act because they feared the voting power of women, but Congress ended the program in the late 1920s.

## Republicans and Business

With President Wilson ailing in 1920, Democrats nominated Ohio governor James M. Cox for president, on a platform calling for U.S. participation in the League of Nations and continuation of Wilson's progressivism. Republicans, led by their probusiness wing, tapped genial Ohio senator Warren G. Harding. In a dig at Wilson's idealism, Harding promised "not nostrums but normalcy." On election day, he won in a landslide, beginning an era of Republican dominance that lasted until 1932.

Harding's most energetic appointee was Secretary of Commerce Herbert Hoover, well known as head of the wartime Food Administration. Under Hoover's direction, the Commerce Department helped create two thousand trade associations representing companies in almost every major industry. Government officials worked closely with the associations, providing statistical research, suggesting industry-wide standards, and promoting stable prices and wages. Hoover hoped that through voluntary business cooperation with government—an **associated state**—he could achieve what progressives had sought through governmental regulation. This meant, of course, giving corporate leaders greater policymaking power.

More sinister links between government and corporate interests were soon revealed. When President Harding died suddenly of a heart attack in August 1923, evidence was just emerging that parts of his administration were riddled with corruption. The worst scandal concerned secret leasing of government oil reserves in **Teapot Dome**, Wyoming, and Elk Hills, California, to private companies. Secretary of the Interior Albert Fall was eventually convicted of taking $300,000 in bribes and became the first cabinet officer in U.S. history to serve a prison sentence.

Vice President Calvin Coolidge became president upon Harding's death. He maintained Republican dominance while offering, with his austere Yankee morality, a contrast to his predecessor's cronyism. Campaigning for election in his own right in 1924, Coolidge called for limited government and tax cuts for business. Rural and urban Democrats, deeply divided over such issues as prohibition and immigration restriction, deadlocked at their national convention; after 102 ballots, delegates finally nominated John W. Davis, a Wall Street lawyer. Coolidge easily defeated Davis and staved off a challenge from Senator Robert M. La Follette of Wisconsin, who tried to resuscitate the Progressive Party. The 1924 Progressive platform called for stronger government regulation at home and international efforts to reduce weapons production and prevent war. "Free men of every generation," it declared, "must combat the renewed efforts of organized force and greed." In the end, Coolidge received 15.7 million votes to Davis's 8.4 million and La Follette's 4.9 million.

 To see a longer excerpt of the Progressive Party platform, along with other primary sources from this period, see *Sources for America's History*.

For the most part, Republicans dropped progressive initiatives of the prewar years. The Federal Trade Commission failed to enforce antitrust laws. The Supreme Court, now headed by former Republican president William Howard Taft, refused to break up the mammoth U.S. Steel Corporation, despite evidence of its near-monopoly status. With the agricultural sector facing hardship, Congress sought to aid farmers with the McNary-Haugen bills of 1927 and 1928, which proposed a system of federal price supports for major crops. But President Coolidge opposed the bills as "special-interest legislation" and vetoed them both. While some state and municipal leaders continued to pursue ambitious agendas, they were shut out of federal power.

## Dollar Diplomacy

Political campaigns emphasized domestic issues in the 1920s, but while the United States refused to join the League of Nations, the federal government remained deeply engaged in foreign affairs. Republican presidents worked to advance U.S. business interests, especially by encouraging private banks to make foreign loans — part of the broader government-business alliance in Republicans' associated state. Policymakers hoped loans would stimulate growth and increase demand for U.S. products in developing markets. Bankers, though, wanted government guarantees of repayment in countries they perceived as weak or unstable.

Officials provided such assurance. In 1922, for example, when American banks offered an immense loan to Bolivia (at a hefty profit), State Department officials pressured the South American nation to accept it. Diplomats also forced Bolivia to agree to financial oversight by a commission under the banks' control. A similar arrangement was reached with El Salvador's government in 1923. In other cases, the United States intervened militarily, often to force repayment of debt. To implement such policies, the U.S. Marines occupied Nicaragua almost continuously from 1912 to 1933, the Dominican Republic from 1916 to 1924, and Haiti from 1915 to 1934.

In these lengthy military deployments, Americans came to think of the occupied countries as essentially U.S. possessions, much like Puerto Rico and the Philippines. Sensational memoirs by marines who had served in Haiti popularized the island as the "American Africa." White Americans became fascinated by *vodou* (voodoo) and other Haitian religious customs, reinforcing their view of Haitians as dangerous savages or childlike people who needed U.S. guidance and supervision. One commander testified that his troops saw themselves as "trustees of a huge estate that belonged to minors. . . . The Haitians were our wards."

At home, critics denounced loan guarantees and military interventions as **dollar diplomacy**. The term was coined in 1924 by Samuel Guy Inman, a Disciples of Christ missionary who toured U.S.-occupied Haiti and the Dominican Republic. "The United States," Inman declared, "cannot go on destroying with impunity the sovereignty of other peoples, however weak." African American leaders also denounced the Haitian occupation. On behalf of the Women's International League for Peace and Freedom and the International Council of Women of the Darker Races, a delegation conducted a fact-finding tour of Haiti in 1926. Their report exposed, among other things, the sexual exploitation of Haitian women by U.S. soldiers.

By the late 1920s, dollar diplomacy was on the defensive, in keeping with a broader disgust over international affairs. At the same time, political leaders became frustrated with their poor results. Dollar diplomacy usually managed to get loans repaid, securing bankers' profits. But the loans

**COMPARE AND CONTRAST**
What choices did Americans face in the elections of 1920 and 1924, and what directions did they choose?

**PLACE EVENTS IN CONTEXT**
What were the economic goals of U.S. foreign policymakers in the 1920s?

often ended up in the pockets of local elites; U.S. policies failed to build broad-based prosperity overseas. Military intervention had even worse results. In Haiti, for example, the marines crushed peasant protests and helped the Haitian elite consolidate power. U.S. occupation thus helped create the conditions for harsh dictatorships that Haitians endured through the rest of the twentieth century.

## Culture Wars

By 1929, ninety-three U.S. cities had populations of more than 100,000. New York City's population exceeded 7 million; Los Angeles's had exploded to 1.2 million. The lives and beliefs of urban Americans often differed dramatically from those in small towns and farming areas. Native-born rural Protestants, faced with a dire perceived threat, rallied in the 1920s to protect what they saw as American values.

**Prohibition** Rural and native-born Protestants started the decade with the achievement of a longtime goal: national **prohibition** of liquor (Chapter 18). Wartime anti-German prejudice was a major spur. Since breweries like Pabst and Anheuser-Busch were owned by German Americans, many citizens decided it was unpatriotic to drink beer. Mobilizing the economy for war, Congress also limited brewers' and

distillers' use of barley and other scarce grains, causing consumption to decline. The decades-long prohibition campaign culminated with Congress's passage of the Eighteenth Amendment in 1917. Ratified over the next two years by nearly every state and taking effect in January 1920, the amendment prohibited "manufacture, sale, or transportation of intoxicating liquors" anywhere in the United States.

Defenders hailed prohibition as a victory for health, morals, and Christian values. In urban areas, though, thousands flagrantly ignored the law. Patrons flocked to urban speakeasies, or illegal drinking sites, which flourished in almost every Chicago neighborhood; one raid on a South Side speakeasy yielded 200,000 gallons of alcohol. Profits from the secret clubs enriched notorious gangsters such as Chicago's Al Capone and New York's Jack Diamond.

In California, Arizona, and Texas, tens of thousands of Americans streamed "south of the border." Mexico regulated liquor but kept it legal (along with gambling, drugs, and prostitution), leading to the rise of booming vice towns such as Tijuana and Mexicali, places that had been virtually uninhabited before 1900. U.S. nightclub owners in these cities included such prominent figures as African American boxer Jack Johnson. By 1928, the American investors who built a $10 million resort, racetrack, and casino in Tijuana became known as border barons. Prohibitionists were

**Wine in the Gutters, Brooklyn**

This photograph captures America's cultural conflicts over prohibition. When the law went into effect, federal agents seized and destroyed supplies of alcohol, often dumping it in the streets. Here, working-class children in Brooklyn race to scoop it up in buckets before it drains away. In tenement neighborhoods, children eager to earn a nickel often toted buckets of beer, wine, and homemade liquor for their parents or neighbors. How might a rural temperance advocate have responded to this photograph? How about a working-class man in Chicago, Atlanta, Seattle, or New York? Picture Research Consultants & Archives.

outraged by Americans' circumventions of the law. Religious leaders on both sides of the border denounced illegal drinking — but profits were staggering. The difficulties of enforcing prohibition contributed to its repeal in 1933 (Chapter 23).

### Evolution in the Schools

At the state and local levels, controversy erupted as fundamentalist Protestants sought to mandate school curricula based on the biblical account of creation. In 1925, Tennessee's legislature outlawed the teaching of "any theory that denies the story of the Divine creation of man as taught in the Bible, [and teaches] instead that man has descended from a lower order of animals." The **American Civil Liberties Union** (ACLU), formed during the Red Scare to protect free speech rights, challenged the law's constitutionality. The ACLU intervened in the trial of John T. Scopes, a high school biology teacher who taught the theory of evolution to his class and faced a jail sentence for doing so. The case attracted national attention because Clarence Darrow, a famous criminal lawyer, defended Scopes, while William Jennings Bryan, the three-time Democratic presidential candidate, spoke for the prosecution.

Journalists dubbed the **Scopes trial** "the monkey trial." This label referred both to Darwin's argument that human beings and other primates share a common ancestor and to the circus atmosphere at the trial, which was broadcast live over a Chicago radio station. (Proving that urbanites had their own prejudices, acerbic critic H. L. Mencken dismissed antievolutionists as "gaping primates of the upland valleys," implying that they had not evolved.) The jury took only eight minutes to deliver its verdict: guilty. Though the Tennessee Supreme Court later overturned Scopes's conviction, the law remained on the books for more than thirty years.

### Nativism

Some native-born Protestants pointed to immigration as the primary cause of what they saw as America's moral decline. A nation of 105 million people had added more than 23 million immigrants over the previous four decades; the newcomers included many Catholics and Jews from Southern and Eastern Europe, whom one Maryland congressman referred to as "indigestible lumps" in the "national stomach." Such attitudes recalled hostility toward Irish and Germans in the 1840s and 1850s. In this case, they fueled a momentous shift in immigration policy. "America must be kept American," President Coolidge declared in 1924. Congress had banned Chinese immigration in 1882, and Theodore Roosevelt had

negotiated a so-called gentleman's agreement that limited Japanese immigration in 1907. Now nativists charged that there were also too many European arrivals, some of whom undermined Protestantism and imported anarchism, socialism, and other radical doctrines. Responding to this pressure, Congress passed emergency immigration restrictions in 1921 and a permanent measure three years later. The **National Origins Act** (1924) used backdated census data to establish a baseline: in the future, annual immigration from each country could not exceed 2 percent of that nationality's percentage of the U.S. population as it had stood in 1890. Since only small numbers of Italians, Greeks, Poles, Russians, and other Southern and Eastern European immigrants had arrived before 1890, the law drastically limited immigration from those places. In 1929, Congress imposed even more restrictive quotas, setting a cap of 150,000 immigrants per year from Europe and continuing to ban most immigrants from Asia.

The new laws, however, permitted unrestricted immigration from the Western Hemisphere. As a result, Latin Americans arrived in increasing numbers, finding jobs in the West that had gone to other immigrants before exclusion. More than 1 million Mexicans entered the United States between 1900 and 1930, including many during World War I. Nativists lobbied Congress to cut this flow; so did labor leaders, who argued that impoverished migrants lowered wages for other American workers. But Congress heeded the pleas of employers, especially farmers in Texas and California, who wanted cheap labor. Only the Great Depression cut off migration from Mexico.

Other anti-immigrant measures emerged at the state level. In 1913, by an overwhelming majority, California's legislature had passed a law declaring that "aliens ineligible to citizenship" could not own "real property." The aim was to discourage Asians, especially Japanese immigrants, from owning land, though some had lived in the state for decades and built up prosperous farms. In the wake of World War I, California tightened these laws, making it increasingly difficult for Asian families to establish themselves. California, Washington, and Hawaii also severely restricted any school that taught Japanese language, history, or culture. Denied both citizenship and land rights, Japanese Americans would be in a vulnerable position at the outbreak of World War II, when anti-Japanese hysteria swept the United States.

**TRACE CHANGE OVER TIME**
How did debates over alcohol use, the teaching of evolution, immigration, anti-Semitism, and racism evolve in the 1920s?

**The U.S. Border Patrol, Laredo, Texas, 1926**

In 1926, San Antonio photographer Eugene O. Goldbeck took this photograph of U.S. Border Patrol officers in Laredo. Since 1917, Mexicans, like other immigrants, had been subject to a head tax and literacy test. The U.S. government had not enforced these provisions, however, because of pressure from southwestern employers eager for cheap Mexican labor. Following passage of the National Origins Act in 1924, the United States established the Border Patrol. Its increasing efforts to police the border slowed the casual movement of Mexican workers in and out of the United States. Why do you think the Border Patrol posed in this way for Goldbeck's picture? Notice that some of the officers depicted here were dressed as civilians. What might this signify? Harry Ransom Center, University of Texas at Austin.

**The National Klan**   The 1920s brought a nation-wide resurgence of the **Ku Klux Klan** (KKK), the white supremacist group formed in the post–Civil War South. Soon after the premiere of *Birth of a Nation* (1915), a popular film glorifying the Reconstruction-era Klan, a group of southerners gathered on Georgia's Stone Mountain to revive the group. With its blunt motto, "Native, white, Protestant supremacy," the Klan recruited supporters across the country (Thinking Like a Historian, p. 716). KKK members did not limit their harassment to blacks but targeted immigrants, Catholics, and Jews as well, with physical intimidation, arson, and economic boycotts.

At the height of its power, the Klan wielded serious political clout and counted more than three million members, including many women. The Klan's main-stream appeal was illustrated by President Woodrow Wilson's public praise for *Birth of a Nation*. Though the Klan declined nationally after 1925, robbed of a potent issue by passage of the anti-immigration bill, it remained strong in the South, and pockets of KKK activity persisted in all parts of the country (Map 22.1). Klan activism lent a menacing cast to political issues. Some local Klansmen, for example, cooperated with

members of the Anti-Saloon League to enforce prohibition laws through threats and violent attacks.

The rise of the Klan was part of an ugly trend that began before World War I and extended into the 1930s. In 1915, for example, rising anti-Semitism was marked by the lynching of Leo Frank, a Jewish factory supervisor in Marietta, Georgia, who was wrongly accused of the rape and murder of a thirteen-year-old girl. The rise of the national Klan helped prepare the way for white supremacist movements of the 1930s, such as the Los Angeles–based Silver Legion, a fringe paramilitary group aligned with Hitler's Nazis. Far more influential were major figures such as industrialist Henry Ford, whose *Dearborn Independent* railed against immigrants and warned that members of "the proud Gentile race" must arm themselves against a Jewish conspiracy aimed at world domination. Challenged by critics, Ford issued an apology in 1927 and admitted that his allegations had been based on "gross forgeries." But with his paper's editorials widely circulated by the Klan and other groups, considerable long-term damage had been done.

**The Election of 1928**   Conflicts over race, religion, and ethnicity created the climate for a stormy

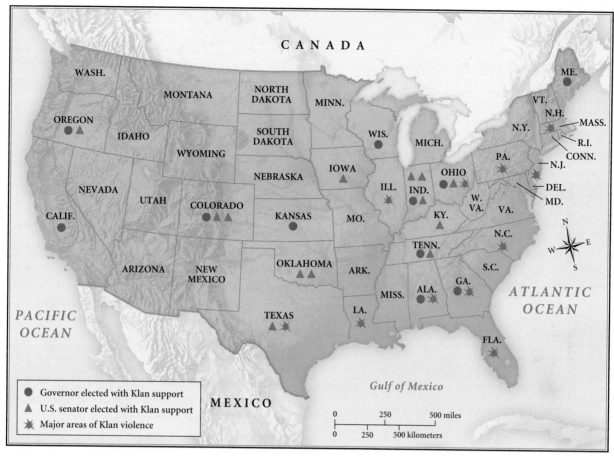

**MAP 22.1**

**Ku Klux Klan Politics and Violence in the 1920s**

Unlike the Reconstruction-era Klan, the Klan of the 1920s was geographically dispersed and had substantial strength in the West and Midwest as well as in the South. Although the Klan is often thought of as a rural movement, some of the strongest "klaverns" were in Chicago, Los Angeles, Atlanta, Detroit, and other large cities. The organization's members operated as vigilantes in areas where they were strong; elsewhere, their aggressive tactics triggered riots between Klansmen and their ethnic and religious targets.

presidential election in 1928. Democrats had traditionally drawn strength from white voters in the South and immigrants in the North: groups that divided over prohibition, immigration restriction, and the Klan. By 1928, the northern urban wing gained firm control. Democrats nominated Governor Al Smith of New York, the first presidential candidate to reflect the aspirations of the urban working class. A grandson of Irish peasants, Smith had risen through New York City's Democratic machine to become a dynamic reformer. But he offended many small-town and rural Americans with his heavy New York accent and brown derby hat, which highlighted his ethnic working-class origins. Middle-class reformers questioned his ties to Tammany Hall; temperance advocates opposed him as a "wet." But the governor's greatest handicap was his religion.

Although Smith insisted that his Catholic beliefs would not affect his duties as president, many Protestants opposed him. "No Governor can kiss the papal ring and get within gunshot of the White House," vowed one Methodist bishop.

Smith proved no match for the Republican nominee, Secretary of Commerce Herbert Hoover, who embodied the technological promise of the modern age. Women who had mobilized for Hoover's conservation campaigns during World War I enlisted as Hoover Hostesses, inviting friends to their homes to hear the candidate's radio speeches. Riding on eight years of Republican prosperity, Hoover promised that individualism and voluntary cooperation would banish poverty. He won overwhelmingly, with 444 electoral votes to Smith's 87 (Map 22.2). Because many

## Who Joined the Ku Klux Klan?

Asked why a person would join the Klan, you might cite racism and religious bigotry. But the story is complicated: many whites with strong prejudices did not join the Klan in the 1920s, while others did. Why?

**1. Klan wedding in Washington, D.C., 1925.**

Source: Getty Images

**2. Poem read at a meeting of KKK Grand Dragons, North Carolina, 1923.**

God Give Us Men! The Invisible Empire demands
    strong
Minds, great hearts, true faith and ready hands . . .
Men who possess opinions and a will;
Men who have honor; men who will not lie;
Men who can stand before a demagogue and damn
    his treacherous flattering without winking! . . .
Men of dependable character; men of sterling worth;
Then wrongs will be redressed, and right will rule the
    earth.

**3. "95% of Bootleggers Jews," editorial, *Dearborn Independent*, Michigan, 1922.**

Violation and evasion of the Prohibition laws has had a deep Jewish complexion from the very beginning. . . . This does not mean, of course, that every bootlegger is a Jew. Unless you live in Chicago, New York or other large cities, an actual meeting with the Jew in this minor capacity will not be frequent. The Jew is the possessor of the wholesale stocks; . . . But notwithstanding all this carefulness, the bulk of the arrests made in the United States have been among Jews. . . . The maintenance of *the idea of drink* in the minds of the people is due to Jewish

propaganda. . . . *The idea of drink* will be maintained by means of the Jewish stage, Jewish jazz, and the Jewish comics, until somebody comes down hard upon it.

**4. Report on a Klan gathering in Birmingham, Alabama, 1923.**

Edgewood Park was crowded by noon. Klansmen and their wives and families enjoyed a great barbecue, went swimming, dancing, and picnicking. There were airplane stunts during the day with band concerts thrown in for good measure. At night there was a wonderful display of fireworks following the initiation and the address of the Imperial Wizard.

**5. Klansmen in Buffalo, New York, 1924.** *Data based on historical research into a Klan membership list of almost 2,000 men in the Buffalo area.*

### TABLE 22.1

### Klansmen in Buffalo, New York, 1924

| Occupational Group | Percentage of KKK Members | Percentage of Total Native White Male Workers in Buffalo |
|---|---|---|
| Professional (predominantly clergy, doctors, engineers, pharmacists) | 6.1 | 4.7 |
| Business (small businessmen, managers, inspectors, accountants) | 18.5 | 10.4 |
| Low nonmanual (salesmen, clerks, foremen) | 27.7 | 22.6 |
| Skilled (machinists, electricians, railroad engineers, construction trades) | 30.6 | 25.3 |
| Semiskilled and service (factory and rail workers, deliverymen, policemen, repairmen) | 16.4 | 30.2 |
| Unskilled (laborers, gardeners) | 0.5 | 14.5 |

6. **Interviews conducted in the 1980s with Indiana Klanswomen about Klan life in the 1920s.** *Seeking truthful accounts, the interviewer allowed the women to remain anonymous.*

*Anonymous*

For [the Klan] to say, we want to get rid of the niggers, we want to get rid of the Catholics, it didn't mean a thing to us. . . . I can remember quite well the stories that you hear sitting on the porch. . . . They'd talk about religion, and they'd talk about Catholics. . . . The Catholics were considered horrible people. . . .

*Anonymous*

Kelly had a grocery store. Well, it hurt their business terribly because people wouldn't go in there, because the Klan would tell you not to. . . . If you had a empty house . . . , why you were told not to rent it to a Catholic.

Some Klan leader said that the Pope was coming to take over the country, and he said he might be on the next train that went through North Manchester. You know, just trying to make it specific. So, about a thousand people went out to the train station and stopped the train. It only had . . . one passenger on it. They took him off, and he finally convinced them that he wasn't the Pope. He was a carpet salesman. And so they put him on the next train and he went on to Chicago.

7. **Editorial by National Imperial Wizard Hiram Wesley Evans in the KKK periodical** *Dawn: A Journal for True American Patriots*, **November 10, 1923.**

Humanity has become a commodity. For mercenary motives, our importers of it want the most inferior grade. Industry desires cheap labor. Therefore, we have had this recent flood of 5 and 10-cent citizenship. Take any map which shows the concentration of the South and Eastern European type of immigrant and you will see [that] wherever manufacturing and mining and lumbering predominate, there the hordes of unskilled labor have overwhelmingly been assembled. . . .

The present and recent flood of inferior foreigners has vastly increased our illiteracy, vitally lowered the health level and visibly menaced America by inheritable mental and moral deficiencies. . . . [Farms are] the only legitimate and justifiable excuse for cheap labor, yet that class is moving irresistibly cityward to swell the slums and multiply immorality. For example, throughout the south the colored race . . . is migrating to the North — not to its rural districts, but to its industrial centers.

8. **"Program for America," in the KKK newspaper** *American Standard*, **April 15, 1925.**

• Laws to require the reading of the Holy Bible in every American public school.

• Recognition of the fact . . . that Romanism is working here to undermine Americanism. . . . Since Roman Catholics give first allegiance to an alien political potentate, the pope . . . their claim to citizenship, to the ballot, and to public office in this Protestant country is illegitimate, and must be forbidden by law. . . .

• A law to destroy the alien influence of the foreign language press [by] requiring that the English language be used exclusively.

• . . . Recognition of the tendency toward moral disintegration, resulting from the activities . . . of the anti-Christian Jews, in our theaters, our motion pictures, and in American business circles; the discontinuance of these anti-Christian activities, and the exclusion of Jews of this character from America.

• The return of the Negroes to their homeland of Africa, under the protection and with the help of the United States Government.

• Strict adherence to the Constitution of the United States, including the Prohibition Amendment, by every citizen.

Sources: (2) Kelly J. Baker, *Gospel According to the Klan* (Lawrence: University Press of Kansas, 2011), 119; (3) *Dearborn Independent* editorial reprinted in *Aspects of Jewish Power in the United States* (Dearborn, MI: Dearborn Publishing, 1922), 34–40; (4) Rory McVeigh, *The Rise of the Ku Klux Klan* (Minneapolis: University of Minnesota Press, 2009), 150; (5) Shawn Lay, *Hooded Knights on the Niagara* (New York: New York University Press, 1995), chapter 4 (esp. 87); (6) Kathleen M. Blee, *Women in the Klan* (Berkeley and Los Angeles: University of California Press, 1991), 78–79, 149–151; (7) McVeigh, 64–65; (8) *American Standard*, April 15, 1925, 172.

## ANALYZING THE EVIDENCE

1. Based on the documents above, identify factors that made the KKK appealing to some Americans in the 1920s.

2. Which groups in source 5 were over- and underrepresented in the Klan? The same historian found that at least 34 percent of local Klan members were German American. Review the Thinking Like a Historian feature in Chapter 21, page 692. Why might Germans have been especially likely to join the Klan in this period?

3. What are the advantages and limitations of source 6?

4. Imagine that Republican president Calvin Coolidge had set up a federal agency to discourage KKK activity (an action he did NOT take). He put you in charge of the effort and gave you a generous budget. How would you have spent the funds? Explain why you believe your strategy might have been effective.

## PUTTING IT ALL TOGETHER

Using your knowledge of Chapter 22, and drawing on evidence from the documents above, write a brief essay explaining how the rise of the KKK in the 1920s reflected larger patterns in American society and politics.

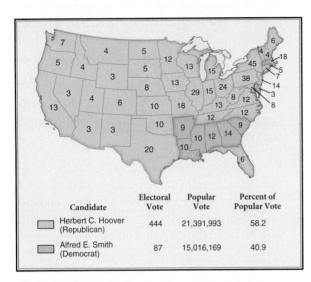

| Candidate | Electoral Vote | Popular Vote | Percent of Popular Vote |
|---|---|---|---|
| Herbert C. Hoover (Republican) | 444 | 21,391,993 | 58.2 |
| Alfred E. Smith (Democrat) | 87 | 15,016,169 | 40.9 |

**MAP 22.2**

**The Presidential Election of 1928**

Historians still debate the extent to which 1928 was a critical election—an election that produced a significant realignment in voting behavior. Although Republican Herbert Hoover swept the popular and the electoral votes, Democrat Alfred E. Smith won majorities not only in the South, his party's traditional stronghold, but also in Rhode Island, Massachusetts, and (although it is not evident on this map) all of the large cities of the North and Midwest. In subsequent elections, the Democrats won even more votes among African Americans and European ethnic groups and, until 1980, were the nation's dominant political party.

southern Protestants refused to vote for a Catholic, Hoover carried five ex-Confederate states, breaking the Democratic "Solid South" for the first time since Reconstruction. Smith, though, carried industrialized Massachusetts and Rhode Island as well as the nation's twelve largest cities, suggesting that urban voters were moving into the Democrats' camp.

## Intellectual Modernism

The horrors of World War I prompted many intellectuals to question long-standing assumptions about civilization, progress, and the alleged superiority of Western cultures over so-called primitive ways of life. In the United States, these questions contributed to struggles between modernity and tradition, reflected not only in politics but also in art and literature. Some of these intellectual movements had their roots in the devastation of Europe; others—such as the Harlem Renaissance—emerged from social upheavals the Great War had wrought at home.

## Harlem in Vogue

The Great Migration tripled New York's black population in the decade after 1910. Harlem stood as "the symbol of liberty and the Promised Land to Negroes everywhere," as one minister put it. Talented African Americans flocked to the district, where they created bold new art forms and asserted ties to Africa.

**Black Writers and Artists**  Poet Langston Hughes captured the upbeat spirit of the **Harlem Renaissance** when he asserted, "I am a Negro—and beautiful." Other writers and artists also championed race pride. Claude McKay and Jean Toomer represented in fiction what philosopher Alain Locke called, in an influential 1925 book, *The New Negro*. Painter Jacob Lawrence, who had grown up in crowded tenement districts of the urban North, used bold shapes and vivid colors to portray the daily life, aspirations, and suppressed anger of African Americans.

No one embodied the energy and optimism of the Harlem Renaissance more than Zora Neale Hurston. Born in the prosperous black community of Eatonville, Florida, Hurston had been surrounded as a child by examples of achievement, though she struggled later with poverty and isolation. In contrast to some other black thinkers, Hurston believed African American culture could be understood without heavy emphasis on the impact of white oppression. After enrolling at Barnard College and studying with anthropologist Franz Boas, Hurston traveled through the South and the Caribbean for a decade, documenting folklore, songs, and religious beliefs. She incorporated this material into her short stories and novels, celebrating the humor and spiritual strength of ordinary black men and women. Like other work of the Harlem Renaissance, Hurston's stories and novels sought to articulate what it meant, as black intellectual W. E. B. Du Bois wrote, "to be both a Negro and an American."

**Jazz**  To millions of Americans, the most famous product of the Harlem Renaissance was **jazz**. Though the origins of the word are unclear, many historians believe it was a slang term for sex—an etymology that makes sense, given the music's early association with urban vice districts. As a musical form, jazz coalesced in New Orleans and other parts of the South before World War I. Borrowing from blues, ragtime, and other popular forms, jazz musicians developed an ensemble style in which performers, keeping a rapid ragtime beat, improvised around a basic melodic line. The majority of early jazz musicians were black, but white

**Archibald Motley, *Blues*, 1929**

Painter Archibald Motley (1891–1981) was born in New Orleans but arrived in Chicago as a small child, when his family—like thousands of other African Americans—moved north in search of opportunity. Motley was able to study at the Art Institute of Chicago and by the 1920s also showed his work in New York City. Many of his paintings depicted life in the predominantly African American neighborhood on Chicago's South Side that was widely known as the Black Belt. This piece, *Blues*, was painted when Motley was living in Paris. It shows the powerful impact jazz had on European listeners. Art Institute of Chicago.

performers, some of whom had more formal training, injected elements of European concert music.

In the 1920s, as jazz spread nationwide, musicians developed its signature mode, the improvised solo. The key figure in this development was trumpeter Louis Armstrong. A native of New Orleans, Armstrong learned his craft playing in the saloons and brothels of the city's vice district. Like tens of thousands of other African Americans he moved north, settling in Chicago in 1922. Armstrong showed an inexhaustible capacity for melodic invention, and his dazzling solos inspired other musicians. By the late 1920s, soloists became the celebrities of jazz, thrilling audiences with their improvisational skill.

As jazz spread, it followed the routes of the Great Migration from the South to northern and midwestern cities, where it met consumers primed to receive it. Most cities had plentiful dance halls where jazz could be featured. Radio also helped popularize jazz, with the emerging record industry marketing the latest tunes. As white listeners flocked to ballrooms and clubs to hear Duke Ellington and other stars, Harlem became the hub of this commercially lucrative jazz. Those who hailed "primitive" black music rarely suspended their racial condescension: visiting a mixed-race club became known as "slumming."

The recording industry soon developed race records specifically aimed at urban working-class blacks. The breakthrough came in 1920, when Otto

K. E. Heinemann, a producer who sold immigrant records in Yiddish, Swedish, and other languages, recorded singer Mamie Smith performing "Crazy Blues." This smash hit prompted big recording labels like Columbia and Paramount to copy Heinemann's approach. Yet, while its marketing reflected the segregation of American society, jazz brought black music to the center stage of American culture. It became the era's signature music, so much so that novelist F. Scott Fitzgerald dubbed the 1920s the "Jazz Age."

**Marcus Garvey and the UNIA**   Harlem's creative energy generated broad political aspirations. The Harlem-based **Universal Negro Improvement Association** (UNIA), led by charismatic Jamaican-born Marcus Garvey, arose in the 1920s to mobilize African American workers and champion black separatism. Garvey urged followers to move to Africa, arguing that people of African descent would never be treated justly in white-run countries.

The UNIA soon claimed four million followers, including many recent migrants to northern cities. It published a newspaper, *Negro World*, and solicited funds for the Black Star steamship company, which Garvey created as an enterprise that would foster trade with the West Indies and carry

**EXPLAIN CONSEQUENCES**
How did the Great Migration lead to flourishing African American culture, politics, and intellectual life, and what form did these activities take?

**Augusta Fells Savage, African American Sculptor**
Born in Florida in 1892, Augusta Fells Savage arrived in New York in 1921 to study and remained to take part in the Harlem Renaissance. Widowed at a young age and struggling to support her parents and young daughter, Savage faced both racism and poverty. Much of her work has been lost because she sculpted in clay and could not afford to cast in bronze. Savage began to speak out for racial justice after she was denied, on the basis of her race, a fellowship to study in Paris. In 1923, she married a close associate of UNIA leader Marcus Garvey. Augusta Savage with her sculpture *Realization*, c. 1938/Andrew Herman, photographer. Federal Art Project, Photographic Division collection, Archives of American Art/Smithsonian Institution.

that had sought representation at the Versailles treaty table, protests against U.S. occupation of Haiti, and modernist experiments in literature and the arts. One African American historian wrote in 1927, "The grandiose schemes of Marcus Garvey gave to the race a consciousness such as it had never possessed before. The dream of a united Africa, not less than a trip to France, challenged the imagination."

## Critiquing American Life

Paralleling the defiant creativity of Harlem, other artists and intellectuals of the 1920s raised voices of dissent. Some had endured firsthand the shock of World War I, an experience so searing that American writer Gertrude Stein dubbed those who survived it the **Lost Generation**. Novelist John Dos Passos railed at the obscenity of "Mr. Wilson's war" in *The Three Soldiers* (1921). Ernest Hemingway's novel *A Farewell to Arms* (1929) portrayed war's futility and dehumanizing consequences.

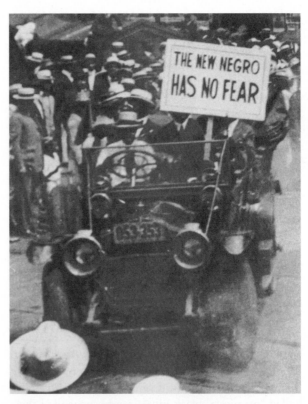

**UNIA Parade in Harlem, Early 1920s**
This photo, taken at 138th Street in Harlem, shows the collective pride fostered by Marcus Garvey's Universal Negro Improvement Association. What types of people do you see in the crowd? How are they dressed? Note the slogan carried by a rider in the automobile: "The New Negro Has No Fear." Schomburg Center for Research in Black Culture, New York Public Library.

American blacks to Africa. But the UNIA declined as quickly as it had risen. In 1925, Garvey was imprisoned for mail fraud because of his solicitations for the Black Star Line. President Coolidge commuted his sentence but ordered his deportation to Jamaica. Without Garvey's leadership, the movement collapsed.

However, the UNIA left a legacy of activism, especially among the working class. Garvey and his followers represented an emerging **pan-Africanism**. They argued that people of African descent, in all parts of the world, had a common destiny and should cooperate in political action. Several developments contributed to this ideal: black men's military service in Europe during World War I, the Pan-African Congress

**UNDERSTAND POINTS OF VIEW**
What criticisms of mainstream culture did modernist American writers offer in the 1920s?

Other writers also explored the dark side of the human psyche. In such dramas as *Desire Under the Elms* (1924), playwright Eugene O'Neill depicted characters driven by raw, ungovernable sexual impulses. O'Neill first made his mark with *The Emperor Jones* (1920), a popular Broadway drama about a black dictator driven from power by his people. Appealing to Americans' fascination with Haiti, the play offered an ambiguous message: its black protagonist was played not by the customary white actors made up in blackface, but by African Americans who won acclaim for their performances. W. E. B. Du Bois called it "a splendid tragedy." But others were dissatisfied with the play's primitivism; one actor who played Emperor Jones altered the script to omit offensive racial epithets. The white crowds who made *The Emperor Jones* a hit, like those who flocked to Harlem's jazz clubs, indulged a problematic fascination with "primitive" sexuality.

In a decade of conflict between traditional and modern worldviews, many writers exposed what they saw as the hypocrisy of small-town and rural life (American Voices, p. 722.) The most savage critic of conformity was Sinclair Lewis, whose novel *Babbitt* (1922) depicted the disillusionment of an ordinary small-town salesman. *Babbitt* was widely denounced as un-American; *Elmer Gantry* (1927), a satire about a greedy evangelical minister on the make, provoked even greater outrage. But critics found Lewis's work superb, and in 1930 he became the first American to win the Nobel Prize for literature. Even more famous was F. Scott Fitzgerald's *The Great Gatsby* (1925), which offered a scathing indictment of Americans' mindless pursuit of pleasure and material wealth.

# From Boom to Bust

Spurred by rapid expansion during the war, American business thrived in the 1920s. Corporations expanded more and more into overseas markets, while at home a national consumer culture emphasized leisure and fun. But some sectors of the economy, notably agriculture, never recovered from a sharp recession in the wake of World War I. Meanwhile, close observers worried over the rapid economic growth and easy credit that fueled the Roaring Twenties. Their fears proved well founded: the "Roar" ended in the Great Depression.

## The Postwar Economy

Immediately after World War I, the United States experienced a series of economic shocks. They began with rampant inflation, as prices jumped by one-third in 1919 alone. Then came a two-year recession that raised unemployment to 10 percent. Finally, the economy began to grow smoothly, and more Americans began to benefit. Between 1922 and 1929, national per capita income rose an impressive 24 percent.

Large-scale corporations continued to replace small business in many sectors of the economy. By 1929, through successive waves of consolidation, the two hundred largest businesses had come to control almost half of the country's nonbanking corporate wealth. The greatest number of mergers occurred in rising industries such as chemicals (with DuPont in the lead) and electrical appliances (General Electric). At the same time, mergers between Wall Street banks enhanced New York City's position as the financial center of the nation and increasingly the world. Aided by Washington's dollar diplomats, U.S. companies exercised growing global power. Seeking cheaper livestock, giant American meat-packers opened plants in Argentina; the United Fruit Company developed plantations in Costa Rica, Honduras, and Guatemala; General Electric set up production facilities in Latin America, Asia, and Australia.

Despite the boom, the U.S. economy had areas of significant weakness throughout the 1920s. Agriculture, which still employed one-fourth of all American workers, never fully recovered from the postwar recession. Once Europe's economy revived, its farmers flooded world markets with grain and other farm products, causing agricultural prices to fall. Other industries, including coal and textiles, languished for similar reasons. As a consequence, many rural Americans shared little of the decade's prosperity. The bottom 40 percent of American families earned an average annual income of only $725 (about $9,100 today). Many, especially rural tenants and sharecroppers, languished in poverty and malnutrition.

## Consumer Culture

In middle-class homes, Americans of the 1920s sat down to a breakfast of Kellogg's corn flakes before getting into Ford Model Ts to work or shop at Safeway. On weekends, they might head to the local theater to see the newest Charlie Chaplin film. By 1929, electric refrigerators and vacuum cleaners came into use in affluent homes; 40 percent of American households owned a radio. The advertising industry reached new levels of ambition and sophistication, entering what one historian calls the era of the "aggressive hard sell." The 1920s gave birth, for example, to fashion modeling and style consulting. "Sell them their dreams," one radio announcer urged advertisers in 1923. "People

## Urban Writers Describe Small-Town America

In the early twentieth century, the United States was becoming an urban society. By 1920, life outside the metropolis seemed sufficiently remarkable to warrant sociological investigation—or at least, city people thought so. Presented here are three views of rural and small-town America, all published during the 1920s. Though cities had become the wellspring of American intellectual life, urban writers juxtaposed their own experiences with those of people they thought of as living in "Middletown, U.S.A."

### Sinclair Lewis
### *Main Street*

In his novel *Main Street* (1920), Sinclair Lewis portrayed the fictional midwestern town of Gopher Prairie. In the excerpts below, Lewis's narrator describes the reactions of young, urban Carol Kennicott, wife of the town's new doctor, and Bea Sorenson, a Swedish American farm girl.

When Carol had walked for thirty-two minutes she had completely covered the town, east and west, north and south; and she stood at the corner of Main Street and Washington Avenue and despaired.

Main Street with its two-story brick shops, its story-and-a-half wooden residences, its muddy expanse from concrete walk to walk, its huddle of Fords and lumber-wagons, was too small to absorb her. The broad, straight, unenticing gashes of the streets let in the grasping prairie on every side. She realized the vastness and the emptiness of the land. The skeleton iron windmill on the farm a few blocks away, at the north end of Main Street, was like the ribs of a dead cow. She thought of the coming of the Northern winter, when the unprotected houses would crouch together in terror of storms galloping out of that wild waste. They were so small and weak, the little brown houses. They were shelters for sparrows. . . .

She wanted to run, fleeing from the encroaching prairie, demanding the security of a great city. Her dreams of creating a beautiful town were ludicrous. Oozing out from every drab wall, she felt a forbidding spirit which she could never conquer.

She trailed down the street on one side, back on the other, glancing into the cross streets. It was a private Seeing Main Street tour. She was within ten minutes beholding not only the heart of a place called Gopher Prairie, but ten thousand towns from Albany to San Diego.

Dyer's Drug Store, a corner building of regular and unreal blocks of artificial stone. Inside the store, a greasy marble soda-fountain with an electric lamp of red and green and curdled-yellow mosaic shade. Pawed-over heaps of toothbrushes and combs and packages of shaving-soap. Shelves of soap-cartons, teething-rings, garden-seeds, and patent medicines in yellow packages — nostrums for consumption, for "women's diseases" — notorious mixtures of opium and alcohol, in the very shop to which her husband sent patients for the filling of prescriptions.

The train which brought Carol to Gopher Prairie also brought Miss Bea Sorenson.

Miss Bea was a stalwart, corn-colored, laughing young woman, and she was bored by farm-work. She desired the excitements of city-life, and the way to enjoy city-life was, she had decided, to "go get a yob as a hired girl in Gopher Prairie." . . .

Bea had never before been in a town larger than Scandia Crossing, which has sixty-seven inhabitants.

As she marched up the street she was meditating that it didn't hardly seem like it was possible there could be so many folks all in one place at the same time. My! It would take years to get acquainted with them all. And swell people, too! A fine big gentleman in a new pink shirt with a diamond, and not no washed-out blue denim working-shirt. A lovely lady in a longery dress (but it must be an awful hard dress to wash). And the stores! . . . A drug store with a soda fountain that was just huge, awful long, and all lovely marble . . . and the soda spouts, they were silver, and they came right out of the bottom of the lamp-stand! Behind the fountain there were glass shelves, and bottles of new kinds of soft drinks, that nobody ever heard of. Suppose a fella took you *there*!

### Anzia Yezierska
### *Bread Givers*

A child of Jewish immigrants from Eastern Europe, Anzia Yezierska grew up on the Lower East Side of New York City. In her autobiographical novel *Bread Givers* (1925), Yezierska described her arrival in the Ohio town where she attended college.

Before this, New York was all of America to me. But now I came to a town of quiet streets, shaded with green trees. No crowds, no tenements. No hurrying noise to beat the race of the hours. Only a leisured quietness whispered in the air: Peace. . . .

Each house had its own green grass in front, its own free space all around, and it faced the street with the calm security of being owned for generations, and not rented by the month from a landlord. In the early twilight, it was like a picture out of fairyland to see people sitting on their porches, lazily swinging in their hammocks, or watering their own growing flowers.

So these are the real Americans, I thought, thrilled by the lean, straight bearing of the passers-by. They had none of that terrible fight for bread and rent that I always saw in the New York people's eyes. . . . All the young people I had ever seen were shut up in factories. But here were young girls and young men enjoying life, free from the worry for a living. . . . The spick-and-span cleanliness of these people! It smelled from them, the soap and the bathing. Their fingernails so white and pink. . . . What a feast of happenings each day of college was to those other students. Societies, dances, letters from home, packages of food, midnight spreads and even birthday parties. I never knew that there were people glad enough of life to celebrate the day they were born.

Source: From *Bread Givers* by Anzia Yezierska. Copyright © 1970 by Louise Levitas Henriksen. Reprinted by permission of Persea Books, Inc., New York. All rights reserved.

### Robert S. Lynd and Helen Merrell Lynd
## *Middletown*

In 1929, sociologists Robert S. Lynd and Helen Merrell Lynd published *Middletown*, a study of life in a small midwestern city. Middletown was not a single community but a composite of several communities studied by the Lynds.

The first real automobile appeared in Middletown in 1900. . . . At the close of 1923 there were 6,221 passenger cars in the city, one for every 6.1 persons, or roughly two for every three families. . . . As, at the turn of the century, business class people began to feel apologetic if they did not have a telephone, so ownership of an automobile has now reached the point of being an accepted essential of normal living. . . .

According to an officer of a Middletown automobile financing company, 75 to 90 percent of the cars purchased locally are bought on time payment, and a working man earning $35.00 a week frequently plans to use one week's pay each month as payment for his car. The automobile has apparently unsettled the habit of careful saving for some families. . . . "I'll go without food before I'll see us give up the car," said one woman emphatically. . . .

Many families feel that an automobile is justified as an agency holding the family group together. . . . [But] the fact that 348 boys and 382 girls in the three upper years of the high school placed "use of the automobile" fifth and fourth respectively in a list of twelve possible sources of disagreement between them and their parents suggests that this may be an increasing decentralizing agent. . . .

If the automobile touches the rest of Middletown's living at many points, it has revolutionized its leisure . . . making leisure-time enjoyment a regularly expected part of every day and week rather than an occasional event. . . . The frequency of movie attendance of high school boys and girls is about equal, business class families tend to go more often than do working class families, and children of both groups attend more often without their parents than do all the individuals or combinations of family members put together. . . . It is probable that time formerly spent in lodges, saloons, and unions is now being spent in part at the movies, at least occasionally with other members of the family. Like the automobile and radio, the movies [break] up leisure time into an individual, family, or small group affair.

Source: Excerpt from *Middletown: A Study in American Culture*, by Robert S. Lynd and Helen M. Lynd. Copyright © 1929 by Harcourt, Inc. and renewed 1957 by Robert S. and Helen M. Lynd. Reprinted by permission of Houghton Mifflin Harcourt Publishing Company. All rights reserved.

---

### QUESTIONS FOR ANALYSIS

1. What attitudes toward the small town and big city does *Main Street* represent? Why do you think Lewis includes views as different as Carol's and Bea's?

2. How does the urban experience of Yezierska's narrator shape her reaction to life in an Ohio town? How might small-town residents have reacted to her description of them as "the real Americans"? How might Lewis have responded to Yezierska's description?

3. How do the two novelists (Lewis and Yezierska) differ from the sociologists (the Lynds) in the issues they emphasize, and in their tone and point of view? What features of small-town life does each text emphasize?

### Bananas
#### . . . a good mixer
#### with every fruit that grows

Oranges, apples, grapefruit, pineapples, pears, melons, grapes—all these and many others—blend perfectly with bananas. The distinctive flavor of the banana, when added to a fruit cup, a fruit salad, or any fruit combination, brings out the flavor of the other fruits and makes them taste better.

"Ripe bananas are good for little children."

"EAT plenty of fresh fruits" is now an accepted principle of diet—and the mere sight of mellow, luscious bananas is an invitation to serve many delicious and nourishing fruit combinations.

*All year round from the tropics* . . . Easter, Fourth of July, Thanksgiving, Christmas—every season, every day—bananas are available. Thanks to the nearness and all-year-round productiveness of the tropics, they always can be had at your grocery or fruit store.

Children crave the temptingly flavored banana instinctively. And it is well that they do, for bananas are one of the most important energy-producing foods. Doctors and dietitians consider the banana not only one of the most *valuable* foods, but also one of the most *easily digested* . . . as beneficial for grown-ups as for children.

Serve bananas with other fruits, with cereals, with milk or cream . . . or serve them plain. But always be sure they are fully ripe (generously flecked with brown spots). If they are not at the proper stage of ripeness when you buy them, let them ripen at room temperature. Never place them in the ice-box.

### UNIFRUIT BANANAS
*A United Fruit Company Product*
Imported and Distributed by Fruit Dispatch Company
17 Battery Place, New York, N. Y.

**American Companies Abroad**
United Fruit was one of the many American companies that found opportunities for investment in South America in the 1920s and that introduced tropical foods to the United States. The company used elaborate and informative color advertisements to sell its products. Bananas were sufficiently exotic that the ads explained to consumers how to tell when bananas were ripe and how to store them ("Never place them in the ice-box"). John W. Hartman Center/Duke University Special Collections Library.

don't buy things to have things. . . . They buy hope—hope of what your merchandise will do for them."

In practice, participation in consumer culture was as contested as the era's politics. It was no accident that white mobs in the Tulsa race riot plundered radios and phonograph players from prosperous African American homes: the message was that whites deserved such items and blacks did not. But neither prosperity nor poverty was limited by race. Surrounded by exhortations to indulge in luxuries, millions of working-class Americans barely squeaked by, with wives and mothers often working to pay for basic necessities. In times of crisis, some families sold their furniture, starting with pianos and phonographs and continuing, if necessary, to dining tables and beds. In the Los Angeles suburb of South Gate, white working-class men secured jobs in the steel and automobile industries, but prices were high and families often found it difficult to make ends meet. *Self-help* was the watchword as families bartered with neighbors and used their yards to raise vegetables, rabbits, and chickens.

The lure of consumer culture created friction. Wives resented husbands who spent all their discretionary cash at the ballpark. Generational conflicts emerged, especially when wage-earning children challenged the expectation that their pay should go "all to mother." In St. Louis, a Czech-born woman was exasperated when her son and daughter stopped contributing to rent and food and pooled their wages to buy a car. In Los Angeles, one fifteen-year-old girl spent her summer earning $2 a day at a local factory. Planning to enroll in business school, she spent $75 on dressy shoes and "a black coat with a red fox collar." Her brother reported that "Mom is angry at her for 'squandering' so much money."

Many poor and affluent families shared one thing in common: they stretched their incomes, small or large, through new forms of borrowing such as auto loans and installment plans. "Buy now, pay later," said the ads, and millions did. Anyone, no matter how rich, could get into debt, but **consumer credit** was particularly perilous for those living on the economic margins. In Chicago, one Lithuanian man described his neighbor's situation: "She ain't got no money. Sure she buys on credit, clothes for the children and everything." Such borrowing turned out to be a factor in the bust of 1929.

### The Automobile

No possession proved more popular than the automobile, a showpiece of modern consumer capitalism that revolutionized American life. Car sales played a major role in the decade's economic boom: in one year, 1929, Americans spent $2.58 billion on automobiles. By the end of the decade, they owned 23 million cars—about 80 percent of the world's automobiles—or an average of one for every six people.

The auto industry's exuberant expansion rippled through the economy, with both positive and negative results. It stimulated steel, petroleum, chemical, rubber, and glass production and, directly or indirectly, created 3.7 million jobs. Highway construction became a billion-dollar-a-year enterprise, financed by federal subsidies and state gasoline taxes. Car ownership spurred urban sprawl and, in 1924, the first suburban shopping center: Country Club Plaza outside Kansas City, Missouri. But cars were expensive, and most Americans bought them on credit. This created risks not only for buyers but for the whole economy. Borrowers who could not pay off car loans lost their entire investment in the vehicle; if they defaulted, banks were left holding unpaid loans. Amid the boom of the 1920s, however, few worried about this result.

Cars changed the way Americans spent their leisure time, as proud drivers took their machines on the road. An infrastructure of gas stations, motels, and drive-in restaurants soon catered to drivers. Railroad travel faltered. The American Automobile Association, founded in 1902, estimated that by 1929 almost a third of the population took vacations by car. As early as 1923, Colorado had 247 autocamps. "I had a few days after I got my wheat cut," reported one Kansas farmer, "so I just loaded my family . . . and lit out." An elite Californian complained that automobile travel was no

**PLACE EVENTS IN CONTEXT**
How did the radio, automobile, and Hollywood movies exemplify the opportunities and the risks of 1920s consumer culture?

**Automobiles at Jacksonville Beach, Florida, 1923**
The automobile transformed Americans' leisure pursuits. As proud car owners took to the road in ever-larger numbers, the "vacation" became a summer staple. Auto travel created a booming business in gas stations, roadside motels, campgrounds, and sightseeing destinations. A Florida vacation—once reserved for wealthy northeasterners who had traveled to Miami's exclusive hotels by first-class rail car—became an attainable luxury for middle-class and even some working-class families. © Curt Teich Postcard Archives, Lake County Museum.

**Charlie Chaplin and Jackie Coogan**

Charlie Chaplin (left) and Jackie Coogan starred together in *The Kid* (1921), a silent comedy that also included sentimental and dramatic moments, promising viewers "a smile . . . and perhaps a tear." Chaplin, born in London in 1889, moved to the United States in 1912 and over the next two decades reigned as one of Hollywood's most famous silent film stars. In 1919, he joined with D. W. Griffith, Mary Pickford, and other American directors and stars to create the independent studio United Artists. *The Kid* made the Los Angeles–born Coogan—discovered by Chaplin on the vaudeville stage—into America's first child star. Library of Congress.

longer "aristocratic." "The clerks and their wives and sweethearts," observed a reporter, "driving through the Wisconsin lake country, camping at Niagara, scattering tin cans and pop bottles over the Rockies, made those places taboo for bankers."

**Hollywood**    Movies formed a second centerpiece of consumer culture. In the 1910s, the moviemaking industry had begun moving to southern California to take advantage of cheap land, sunshine, and varied scenery within easy reach. The large studios — United Artists, Paramount, and Metro-Goldwyn-Mayer — were run mainly by Eastern European Jewish immigrants like Adolph Zukor, who arrived from Hungary in the 1880s. Starting with fur sales, Zukor and a partner then set up five-cent theaters in Manhattan. "I spent a good

deal of time watching the faces of the audience," Zukor recalled. "With a little experience I could see, hear, and 'feel' the reaction to each melodrama and comedy." Founding Paramount Pictures, Zukor signed emerging stars and produced successful feature-length films.

By 1920, **Hollywood** reigned as the world's movie capital, producing nearly 90 percent of all films. Large, ornate movie palaces attracted both middle-class and working-class audiences. Idols such as Rudolph Valentino, Mary Pickford, and Douglas Fairbanks set national trends in style. Thousands of young women followed the lead of actress Clara Bow, Hollywood's famous **flapper**, who flaunted her boyish figure. Decked out in knee-length skirts, flappers shocked the older generation by smoking and wearing makeup.

Flappers represented only a tiny minority of women, but thanks to the movies and advertising, they became influential symbols of women's sexual and social emancipation. In cities, young immigrant women eagerly bought makeup and the latest flapper fashions and went dancing to jazz. Jazz stars helped popularize the style among working-class African Americans. Mexican American teenagers joined the trend, though they usually found themselves under the watchful eyes of *la dueña*, the chaperone.

Politicians quickly grasped the publicity value of American radio and film to foreign relations. In 1919, with government support, General Electric spearheaded the creation of Radio Corporation of America (RCA) to expand U.S. presence in foreign radio markets. RCA — which had a federal appointee on its board of directors — emerged as a major provider of radio transmission in Latin America and East Asia. Meanwhile, by 1925, American films made up 95 percent of the movies screened in Britain, 80 percent in Latin America, and 70 percent in France (America Compared, p. 727). The United States was experimenting with what historians call **soft power** — the exercise of popular cultural influence — as radio and film exports celebrated the American Dream.

## The Coming of the Great Depression

By 1927, strains on the economy began to show. Consumer lending had become the tenth-largest business in the country, topping $7 billion that year. Increasing numbers of Americans bought into the stock market, often with unrealistic expectations. One Yale professor proclaimed that stocks had reached a "permanently high plateau." Corporate profits were so high that some companies, fully invested in their own operations, plowed excess earnings into the stock

# AMERICA COMPARED

## Hollywood in Europe

European film studios struggled after World War I to reach audiences who had fallen in love with American movies. Working-class Europeans, in particular, preferred Hollywood's offerings to the films produced in Europe. In this 1928 article from a cinematography journal, German expressionist filmmaker Erich Pommer suggested new strategies for expanding an audience for European films. Expressionists, influenced by romanticism and modernism, explored dark themes such as spiritual crisis and insanity. (A famous example of expressionist painting is Edvard Munch's *The Scream*.) Pommer worked for American studios and later fled to the United States after the rise of Hitler.

The towering importance of the American motion picture on the world's markets cannot be safely explained by the unlimited financial resources at the disposal of the American producers. . . . Its main reason is the mentality of the American picture, which, notwithstanding all attacks and claims to the contrary, apparently comes nearest to the taste of international cinema audiences.

. . . The specific and unique element of the American film is the fact of its being absolutely uncomplicated. Being what is called "naïve" it knows no problems. . . .

*Universal Appeal.* It is really preferable to have a picture too light rather than too heavy, because in the latter case there is a danger that the public will not understand the story. This is the worst thing that can happen with a picture. . . .

*Spectacular Appeal.* The international appeal of a picture has its foundation in a story. It is totally independent of the capital invested and of the splendor and luxury used in its production. The fact that in most cases the supers and monumental pictures have proved to be such international successes, does not disprove this claim.

Such productions always have a simple story of universal appeal, because it is simply impossible to use spiritual thoughts and impressions of the soul in a picture deluxe. The splendour in such production is not merely created for decoration — it is its outstanding purpose. . . . But splendour means show, and a show is always and everywhere easy to understand. . . .

Source: Excerpt from "The International Picture: A Lesson on Simplicity" by Erich Pommer from *"Film Europe" and "Film America": Cinema, Commerce and Cultural Exchange 1920–1939*, edited by Andrew Higson and Richard Maltby, 1999, ISBN: 978-0-85989-546-0. Used by permission of Exeter University Press.

### QUESTIONS FOR ANALYSIS

1. How does Pommer characterize the attraction of popular American films for European audiences? What does he mean when he calls those films "naïve"?
2. How does Pommer propose to produce German films that will compete with Hollywood? What constraints and challenges did he face?

---

market. Other market players compounded risk by purchasing on margin. An investor might, for example, spend $20 of his own money and borrow $80 to buy a $100 share of stock, expecting to pay back the loan as the stock rose quickly in value. This worked as long as the economy grew and the stock market climbed. But those conditions did not last.

Yet when the stock market fell, in a series of plunges between October 25 and November 13, 1929, few onlookers understood the magnitude of the crisis. Cyclical downturns had been a familiar part of the industrializing economy since the panic of the 1830s; they tended to follow periods of rapid growth and speculation. A sharp recent recession, in 1921, had not

triggered disaster. The market rose again in late 1929 and early 1930, and while a great deal of money had been lost, most Americans hoped the aftermath of the crash would be brief. In fact, the nation had entered the Great Depression. Over the next four years, industrial production fell 37 percent. Construction plunged 78 percent. Prices for crops and other raw materials, already low, fell by half. By 1932, unemployment had reached a staggering 24 percent (Figure 22.1).

A precipitous drop in consumer spending deepened the crisis. Facing hard times and unemployment, Americans cut back dramatically, creating a

### IDENTIFY CAUSES
What domestic and global factors helped cause the Great Depression?

727

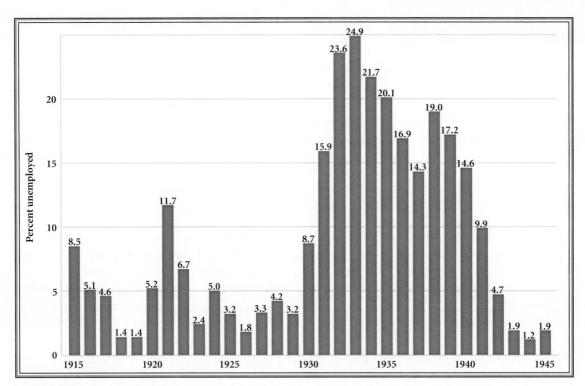

**FIGURE 22.1**

**Unemployment, 1915–1945**

During the 1920s, business prosperity and low rates of immigration resulted in historically low unemployment levels. The Great Depression threw millions of people out of work; by 1933, one in four American workers was unemployed, and the rate remained high until 1941, when the nation mobilized for World War II.

vicious cycle of falling demand and forfeited loans. In late 1930, several major banks went under, victims of overextended credit and reckless management. The following year, as industrial production slowed, a much larger wave of bank failures occurred, causing an even greater shock. Since the government did not insure bank deposits, accounts in failed banks simply vanished. Some people who had had steady jobs and comfortable savings found themselves broke and out of work.

Not all Americans were devastated by the depression; the middle class did not disappear and the rich lived in accustomed luxury. But incomes plummeted even among workers who kept their jobs. Salt Lake City went bankrupt in 1931. Barter systems developed, as barbers traded haircuts for onions and potatoes and laborers worked for payment in eggs or pork. "We do not dare to use even a little soap," reported one jobless Oregonian, "when it will pay for an extra egg, a few more carrots for our children." "I would be only too glad to dig ditches to keep my family from going hungry," wrote a North Carolina man.

Where did desperate people turn for aid? Their first hope lay in private charity, especially churches and synagogues. But by the winter of 1931, these institutions were overwhelmed, unable to keep pace with the extraordinary need. Only eight states provided even minimal unemployment insurance. There was no public support for the elderly, statistically among the poorest citizens. Few Americans had any retirement savings, and many who had saved watched their accounts erased by failing banks.

Even those who were not wiped out had to adapt to depression conditions. Couples delayed marriage and reduced the number of children they conceived. As a result, the marriage rate fell to a historical low, and by 1933 the birthrate dropped from 97 births per 1,000 women to 75. Often the responsibility for birth control fell to women. It was "one of the worst problems of women whose husbands were out of work," a Californian told a reporter. Campaigns against hiring married women were common, on the theory that available jobs should go to male breadwinners. Three-quarters of the nation's school districts banned married women

**Minnesota Potato Farmers**

The prosperity and consumer pleasures of the 1920s hardly extended to all Americans. This Minnesota family had horses, not a tractor; many of the women's clothes were probably made by hand. Rural and working-class Americans, who often struggled in the 1920s, found conditions even harsher after 1929. On the other hand, farmers had resources to fall back on that city folks did not: they could grow their own food, and they had long experience in "making do." Minnesota Historical Society.

from working as teachers — ignoring the fact that many husbands were less able to earn than ever before. Despite restrictions, female employment increased, as women expanded their financial contributions to their families in hard times.

The depression crossed regional boundaries, though its severity varied from place to place. Bank failures clustered heavily in the Midwest and plains, while areas dependent on timber, mining, and other extractive industries suffered catastrophic declines. Although southern states endured less unemployment because of their smaller manufacturing base, farm wages plunged. In many parts of the country, unemployment rates among black men stood at double that of white men; joblessness among African American women was triple that of white women.

By 1932, comprehending the magnitude of the crisis, Americans went to the ballot box and decisively rejected the probusiness, antiregulatory policies of the 1920s. A few years earlier, with business booming, politics had been so placid that people chuckled when President Coolidge disappeared on extended fishing trips. Now, Americans wanted bold action in Washington. Faced with the cataclysm of the Great Depression, Americans would transform their government and create a modern welfare state.

# SUMMARY

Although involvement in World War I strengthened the United States economically and diplomatically, it left the nation profoundly unsettled. Racial tensions exploded after the war as African Americans pursued new opportunities and asserted their rights. Meanwhile, labor unrest grew as employers cut wages and sought to break unions. Labor's power declined sharply in the war's aftermath, while anxieties over radicalism and immigration prompted a nationwide Red Scare.

The politics of the 1920s brought a backlash against prewar progressivism. The agenda of women reformers met very limited success. Republican administrations pursued probusiness "normalcy" at home and "dollar diplomacy" abroad. Prohibition and the Scopes trial demonstrated the influence religion could exert on public policy, while rising nativism fueled a resurgent Ku Klux Klan and led to sweeping new restrictions on immigration.

Postwar alienation found artistic expression in new forms of modernism, which denounced the dehumanizing effects of war and criticized American materialism and hypocrisy. Spreading throughout the nation from New Orleans, jazz appealed to elite and popular audiences alike. Black artists and intellectuals of the Harlem Renaissance, including many inspired by pan-African ideas, explored the complexities of African American life.

Business thrived and a booming consumer culture, exemplified by the radio, the automobile, and Hollywood films, created new forms of leisure, influencing daily life and challenging older sexual norms. However, the risky speculation and easy credit of the 1920s undermined the foundations of the economy. After the 1929 crash, these factors, along with a range of interconnected global conditions, plunged the United States into the Great Depression.

# C H A P T E R   R E V I E W

 **MAKE IT STICK**   Go to **LearningCurve** to retain what you've read.

## TERMS TO KNOW   Identify and explain the significance of each term below.

### Key Concepts and Events

*Adkins v. Children's Hospital* (p. 707)

welfare capitalism (p. 708)

Red Scare (p. 708)

Palmer raids (p. 709)

Sheppard-Towner Federal Maternity and Infancy Act (p. 709)

Women's International League for Peace and Freedom (p. 710)

associated state (p. 710)

Teapot Dome (p. 710)

dollar diplomacy (p. 711)

prohibition (p. 712)

American Civil Liberties Union (p. 713)

Scopes trial (p. 713)

National Origins Act (p. 713)

Ku Klux Klan (p. 714)

Harlem Renaissance (p. 718)

jazz (p. 718)

Universal Negro Improvement Association (p. 719)

pan-Africanism (p. 720)

Lost Generation (p. 720)

consumer credit (p. 725)

Hollywood (p. 726)

flapper (p. 726)

soft power (p. 726)

### Key People

A. Mitchell Palmer (p. 708)

Nicola Sacco and Bartolomeo Vanzetti (p. 709)

Henry Ford (p. 714)

Leo Frank (p. 714)

Zora Neale Hurston (p. 718)

Louis Armstrong (p. 719)

Marcus Garvey (p. 719)

Adolph Zukor (p. 726)

## REVIEW QUESTIONS   Answer these questions to demonstrate your understanding of the chapter's main ideas.

1. What was the Republican vision of "normalcy," and how did the Harding and Coolidge administrations seek to realize it?

2. Along what lines did Americans find themselves divided in the 1920s? How were those conflicts expressed in politics? In culture and intellectual life?

**3.** What factors contributed to the economic boom of the 1920s and the crash that followed?

**4. THEMATIC UNDERSTANDING**  Between 1917 and 1945, the "Roaring Twenties" were the only years when the United States did not face a major economic or international crisis. Review the categories of "America in the World," "Politics and Power," and "Identity" on the thematic timeline on page 671. In what ways do they suggest that the prosperous 1920s were a politically distinctive era? What continuities do you see in politics and foreign policy?

## MAKING CONNECTIONS

Recognize the larger developments and continuities within and across chapters by answering these questions.

**1. ACROSS TIME AND PLACE**  The Ku Klux Klan of the Reconstruction era (Chapter 15) emerged in a specific political and social context; while the Klan of the 1920s built on its predecessor, its goals and scope were different. Using material from Chapters 15 and 22, imagine that you are investigating a series of Klan meetings in each era (1870s and 1920s). Where would you conduct your investigation? How might you explain, to the public, the Klan's membership and activities? How would you compare the two Klans?

**2. VISUAL EVIDENCE**  This chapter includes two depictions of people dancing to jazz: the *Life* magazine cover that opens the chapter (p. 705) and *Blues* (p. 719) by Archibald John Motley Jr., an African American painter of the Harlem Renaissance. Look at these pictures carefully. Who do you think were the intended audiences for each? What evidence could you point to in support of that conclusion? What messages do you think the *Life* artist and Motley wanted to convey?

## MORE TO EXPLORE   Start here to learn more about the events discussed in this chapter.

Lynn Dumenil, *The Modern Temper* (1995). A readable overview of events in the 1920s.

David Levering Lewis, *When Harlem Was in Vogue* (1979). A wonderful account of politics, arts, and culture in the vibrant "Negro capital of the world."

Daniel Okrent, *Last Call: The Rise and Fall of Prohibition* (2010). A lively recent history of the movement to ban liquor.

Martha L. Olney, *Buy Now, Pay Later* (1991). Explores the rise and impact of consumer credit.

Mary A. Renda, *Taking Haiti* (2001). A compelling exploration of U.S. occupation of Haiti and its impact on Haiti and especially the United States.

The PBS series *American Experience* has produced an excellent documentary on the Scopes trial; information and documents are available at **pbs.org/wgbh/amex/monkeytrial/**. For a broad view of the 1929 crash and its impact, see **pbs.org/wgbh/amex/crash**.

## TIMELINE

Ask yourself why this chapter begins and ends with these dates and then identify the links among related events.

| 1915 | • New Ku Klux Klan founded<br>• United States occupies Haiti |
|---|---|
| 1916 | • United States occupies Dominican Republic |
| 1917 | • Race riot in East St. Louis, Illinois |
| 1919 | • Race riot in Chicago<br>• Boston police strike<br>• Palmer raids<br>• Women's International League for Peace and Freedom founded |
| 1920 | • Height of Red Scare<br>• Eighteenth Amendment (prohibition) takes effect<br>• Warren Harding wins presidency<br>• Eugene O'Neill's *The Emperor Jones* |
| 1921 | • Race riots in Rosewood, Florida, and Tulsa, Oklahoma<br>• Sheppard-Towner Federal Maternity and Infancy Act |
| 1923 | • *Adkins v. Children's Hospital*<br>• President Harding dies<br>• Calvin Coolidge assumes presidency<br>• Teapot Dome scandal<br>• Equal Rights Amendment first introduced in Congress |
| 1924 | • National Origins Act<br>• Coolidge wins presidential election against Democrats and La Follette's Progressive Party<br>• First suburban shopping center opens outside Kansas City, Missouri |
| 1925 | • *Coronado Coal Company v. United Mine Workers*<br>• Scopes "monkey trial"<br>• Alain Locke's *The New Negro*<br>• F. Scott Fitzgerald's *The Great Gatsby* |
| 1927 | • Sacco and Vanzetti executed |
| 1928 | • Herbert Hoover wins presidency |
| 1929 | • Stock market crashes precipitate Great Depression |

**KEY TURNING POINTS:** American politics underwent two shifts in the period covered in this chapter: one in the aftermath of World War I, and another in 1932. What caused each turning point? What factors in American Society, economics, and culture help explain each moment of political change?

# 23
## CHAPTER

# Managing the Great Depression, Forging the New Deal
## 1929–1939

I n his inaugural address in March 1933, President Franklin Delano Roosevelt did not hide the country's precarious condition. "A host of unemployed citizens face the grim problem of existence," he said, "and an equally great number toil with little return. Only a foolish optimist can deny the dark realities of the moment." Roosevelt, his demeanor sincere and purposeful, saw both despair and determination as he looked out over the country. "This nation asks for action, and action now." From Congress he would request "broad Executive power to wage a war against the emergency, as great as the power that would be given to me if we were in fact invaded by a foreign foe." With these words, Roosevelt launched a program of federal activism—which he called the New Deal—that would change the nature of American government.

The New Deal represented a new form of liberalism, a fresh interpretation of the ideology of individual rights that had long shaped the character of American society and politics. Classical nineteenth-century liberals believed that, to protect those rights, government should be small and relatively weak. However, the "regulatory" liberals of the early twentieth century had safeguarded individual freedom and opportunity by strengthening state and federal control over large businesses and monopolies. New Deal activists went much further: their social-welfare liberalism expanded individual rights to include economic security. Beginning in the 1930s and continuing through the 1960s, they increased the responsibility of the national government for the welfare of ordinary citizens. Their efforts did not go unchallenged. Conservative critics of the New Deal charged that its "big government" programs were paternalistic and dangerous, undermining individual responsibility and constraining personal freedom. This division between the advocates and the critics of the New Deal shaped American politics for the next half century.

## IDENTIFY THE BIG IDEA
What new roles did the American government take on during the New Deal, and how did these roles shape the economy and society?

 To see a longer excerpt of Roosevelt's inaugural address, along with other primary sources from this period, see *Sources for America's History*.

Before Roosevelt was elected president, between the onset of the depression in 1929 and November 1932, the "dark realities of the moment" wore down American society. Rising unemployment, shuttered businesses, failing banks, and home foreclosures tore at the nation's social fabric. As crisis piled upon crisis and the federal government's initiatives under President Hoover proved ineffectual, Americans had to reconsider more than the role of government in economic life: they had to rethink many of the principles of individualism and free enterprise that had guided so much of the nation's history.

**The New Deal** This Federal Arts Project poster from 1936 captured the spirit of the New Deal under President Franklin Roosevelt. Roosevelt and other "New Dealers" hoped to get people working again during the depths of the Great Depression, raise their spirits, and help rebuild the national infrastructure.
Library of Congress.

# Early Responses to the Depression, 1929–1932

The American economy collapsed between 1929 and 1932. U.S. gross domestic product fell almost by half, from $103.1 billion to $58 billion. Consumption dropped by 18 percent, construction by 78 percent, and private investment by 88 percent. Nearly 9,000 banks closed their doors, and 100,000 businesses failed. Corporate profits fell from $10 billion to $1 billion. Unemployment rose to 25 percent. Fifteen million people were out of work by 1933, and many who had jobs took wage cuts. "Hoover made a souphound outa me!" sang jobless harvest hands in the Southwest.

The depression respected no national boundaries. Germany had preceded the United States into economic contraction in 1928, and its economy, burdened by heavy World War I reparations payments, was brought to its knees by 1929. France, Britain, Argentina, Brazil, Poland, and Canada were hard hit as well (America Compared, p. 737). The legacies of World War I made recovery difficult in two respects. First, Britain's central bank was in no position to resume its traditional role in managing the international financial system. Second, the war disrupted the international gold standard. The United States and most European nations had tied the value of their currencies to the price of gold, and the amount of gold held in reserves, since the late nineteenth century. This system had worked fairly well for a few decades, but it was vulnerable during economic downturns, when large financiers withdrew their investments and demanded gold payments. The gold standard rendered the international monetary system inflexible at a moment that required great flexibility in global finance.

## Enter Herbert Hoover

President Herbert Hoover and Congress responded to the downturn by drawing on two powerful American traditions. The first was the belief that economic outcomes were the product of individual character. People's fate was in their own hands, and success went to those who deserved it. The second tradition held that through voluntary action, the business community could right itself and recover from economic downturns without relying on government assistance. Following these principles, Hoover asked Americans to tighten their belts and work hard. After the stock market crash, he cut federal taxes in an attempt to boost private spending and corporate investment. "Any lack of confidence in the economic future or the strength of business in the United States is foolish," Hoover assured the country in late 1929. Treasury secretary Andrew Mellon suggested that the downturn would help Americans "work harder" and "live a more moral life."

While many factors caused the Great Depression, Hoover's adherence to the gold standard was a major reason for its length and severity in the United States. Faced with economic catastrophe, both Britain and Germany abandoned the gold standard in 1931; when they did so, their economies recovered modestly. But the Hoover administration feared that such a move would weaken the value of the dollar. In reality, an inflexible money supply discouraged investment and therefore prevented growth. The Roosevelt administration would ultimately remove the United States from the burdens of the gold standard in 1933. By that time, however, the crisis had achieved catastrophic dimensions. Billions had been lost in business and bank failures, and the economy had stalled completely.

Along with their adherence to the gold standard, the Hoover administration and many congressional Republicans believed in another piece of economic orthodoxy that had protected American manufacturing in good economic times but that proved damaging during the downturn: high tariffs (taxes on imported goods designed to encourage American manufacturing). In 1930, Republicans enacted the **Smoot-Hawley Tariff**. Despite receiving a letter from more than a thousand economists urging him to veto it, Hoover approved the legislation. What served American interests in earlier eras now confounded them. Smoot-Hawley triggered retaliatory tariffs in other countries, which further hindered global trade and led to greater economic contraction throughout the industrialized world.

The president recognized that individual initiative, voluntarism, and high tariffs might not be enough, given the depth of the crisis, so he proposed government action as well. He called on state and local governments to provide jobs by investing in public projects. And in 1931, he secured an unprecedented increase of $700 million in federal spending for public works. Hoover's most innovative program was the Reconstruction Finance Corporation (RFC), which provided federal loans to railroads, banks, and other businesses. But the RFC lent money too cautiously, and by the end of 1932, after a year in operation, it had loaned out only 20 percent of its $1.5 billion in funds.

**PLACE EVENTS IN CONTEXT**
What economic principles guided President Hoover and Congress in their response to the Great Depression?

# AMERICA COMPARED

## The Great Depression in England and the United States

In a 1954 book, Denis Brogan, a professor at Cambridge University in England, looked back at the descent into the Great Depression between 1929 and 1932 and explained the significance of Franklin Roosevelt's election from an English perspective. The second selection is from an oral history conducted in the 1970s with an ordinary resident of London, who recalled life in the 1930s.

### Denis W. Brogan, "From England"

No event . . . has so colored the European view of the United States as "the Depression." The first news of the crash of 1929 was not ill received. There was not only a marked feeling of *Schadenfreude* at the snub that destiny had given to the overconfident masters of the new world, but also a widespread belief that the extravagant gambling of the New York market was one of the chief causes of our ills. . . . But as the extent, depth, and duration of the American depression began to be appreciated, as its impact on all the world, especially on the dangerously unstable political and economic status quo of Germany and Austria, became more evident, as the old wound of unemployment was made to bleed more deeply in Britain, the tendency to blame the United States became overwhelming. Gone were the illusions about the "secret of high wages." If ever found, it had now been lost.

American politics was seen as not only sterile but positively immoral and dangerous. . . . American business and its political arm, the Republican Party, had been tried in the balance and found wanting. And it is safe to say that the election of F. D. Roosevelt was welcomed in every country of Europe as good news almost overshadowing the nomination of Adolf Hitler as Chancellor of the German Reich.

### Gladys Gibson, a Resident of London in the 1930s

Most of the unemployed were genuinely seeking work. A heavy snowfall was a blessing, when men with broken boots earned a little money by sweeping the streets. The Boroughs [a form of local administration in London] took on unemployed, in strict rotation, for thirteen weeks of unskilled work. It sometimes put a man back in benefit and took him off the hated dole. The situation began to change after Munich, when more men found work. Salvation came with the War, when the despised unemployed became valued workers or serving helpers.

Source: Joseph, Franz M., *As Others See Us.* © 1959 Princeton University Press, 1987 renewed PUP. Reprinted by permission of Princeton University Press.

Nigel Gray, *The Worst of Times: An Oral History of the Great Depression in Britain* (Totowa, NJ: Barnes & Noble Books, 1985), 54.

---

### QUESTIONS FOR ANALYSIS

1. Why would Brogan call the United States "overconfident masters of the new world"? What are his criticisms of U.S. economic policy?
2. How does the testimony of Gladys Gibson about the "hated dole" compare with what you have learned about attitudes in the United States in these years?

---

Like most federal initiatives under Hoover, the RFC was not nearly aggressive enough given the severity of the depression. With federal officials fearing budget deficits and reluctant to interfere with the private market, caution was the order of the day.

Few chief executives could have survived the downward economic spiral of 1929–1932, but Hoover's reluctance to break with the philosophy of limited government and his insistence that recovery was always just around the corner contributed to his unpopularity.

By 1932, Americans perceived Hoover as insensitive to the depth of the country's economic suffering. The nation had come a long way since the depressions of the 1870s and 1890s, when no one except the most radical figures, such as Jacob Coxey, called for direct federal aid to the unemployed (Chapter 20). Compared with previous chief executives — and in contrast to his popular image as a "do-nothing" president — Hoover had responded to the national emergency with unprecedented government action. But the nation's needs

737

**Hooverville**

The depression cast hundreds of thousands of Americans out of their homes. Most found shelter with relatives, but those with little choice had to make do as they could. Encampments such as this one south of downtown Seattle, Washington—places where the homeless crafted makeshift lodging out of whatever materials were at hand—became known as Hoovervilles. The name reflected Americans' attitudes toward President Hoover, whose popularity plummeted as the depression deepened. University of Washington Libraries, Special Collections, UW2129.

were even more unprecedented, and Hoover's programs failed to meet them (Map 23.1).

## Rising Discontent

As the depression deepened, the American vocabulary now included the terms *Hoovervilles* (shantytowns where people lived in packing crates) and *Hoover blankets* (newspapers). Bankrupt farmers banded together to resist the bank agents and sheriffs who tried to evict them from their land. To protest low prices for their goods, in the spring of 1932 thousands of midwestern farmers joined the Farmers' Holiday Association, which cut off supplies to urban areas by barricading roads and dumping milk, vegetables, and other food-stuffs onto the roadways. Agricultural prices were so low that the Farmers' Holiday Association favored a government-supported farm program.

In the industrial sector, layoffs and wage cuts led to violent strikes. When coal miners in Harlan County, Kentucky, went on strike over a 10 percent wage cut in 1931, the mine owners called in the state's National Guard, which crushed the union. A 1932 confrontation between workers and security forces at the Ford Motor Company's giant River Rouge factory outside Detroit left five workers dead and fifty with serious injuries. A photographer had his camera shot from his hands, and fifteen policemen were clubbed or stoned. Whether on farms or in factories, those who produced the nation's food and goods had begun to push for a more aggressive response to the nation's economic troubles.

Veterans staged the most publicized—and most tragic—protest. In the summer of 1932, the **Bonus Army**, a determined group of 15,000 unemployed World War I veterans, hitchhiked to Washington to demand

**MAP 23.1**

**The Great Depression: Families on Relief**

Although the Great Depression was a nationwide crisis, some regions were hit harder than others. Economic hardship was widespread in the agricultural-based southern and Appalachian states of the Northeast and Midwest. As the depression worsened in 1931 and 1932, local and state governments, as well as charitable organizations, could not keep up with the demand for relief. After Franklin D. Roosevelt assumed the presidency in 1933, the national government began a massive program of aid through the Federal Emergency Relief Administration (FERA).

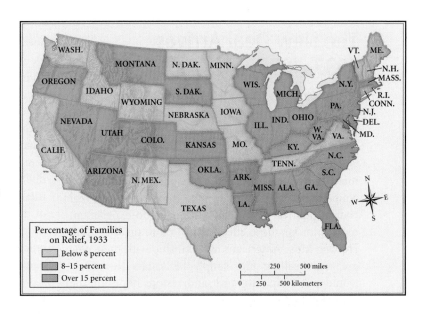

Percentage of Families on Relief, 1933
- Below 8 percent
- 8–15 percent
- Over 15 percent

immediate payment of pension awards that were due to be paid in 1945. "We were heroes in 1917, but we're bums now," one veteran complained bitterly. While their leaders unsuccessfully lobbied Congress, the Bonus Army set up camps near the Capitol building. Hoover called out regular army troops under the command of General Douglas MacArthur, who forcefully evicted the marchers and burned their main encampment to the ground. When newsreel footage showing the U.S. Army attacking and injuring veterans reached movie theaters across the nation, Hoover's popularity plunged. In another measure of how the country had changed since the 1890s, what Americans had applauded when done to Coxey in 1894 was condemned in 1932.

## The 1932 Election

Despite rising discontent, the national mood was mixed as the 1932 election approached. Many Americans had internalized the ideal of the self-made man and blamed themselves for their economic hardships. Despair, not anger, characterized their mood. Others, out of work for a year or more, perhaps homeless, felt the deeper stirrings of frustration and rage. Regardless of their circumstances, most Americans believed that something altogether new had to be tried — whatever that might be. The Republicans, reluctant to dump an incumbent president, unenthusiastically renominated Hoover. The Democrats turned to New York governor Franklin Delano Roosevelt, whose state had initiated innovative relief and unemployment programs.

Roosevelt, born into a wealthy New York family, was a distant cousin to former president Theodore

Roosevelt, whose career he emulated. After attending Harvard College and Columbia University, Franklin Roosevelt served as assistant secretary of the navy during World War I (as Theodore Roosevelt had done before the War of 1898). Then, in 1921, a crippling attack of polio left both of his legs permanently paralyzed. Supported by his wife, Eleanor, he slowly returned to public life and campaigned successfully for the governorship of New York in 1928 and again in 1930. Running for the presidency in 1932, Roosevelt pledged vigorous action but gave no indication what that action might be, arguing simply that "the country needs and, unless I mistake its temper, the country demands bold, persistent experimentation." He won easily, receiving 22.8 million votes to Hoover's 15.7 million.

Elected in November, Roosevelt would not begin his presidency until March 1933. (The Twentieth Amendment, ratified in 1933, set subsequent inaugurations for January 20.) Meanwhile, Americans suffered through the worst winter of the depression. Unemployment continued to climb, and in three major industrial cities in Ohio, it shot to staggering levels: 50 percent in Cleveland, 60 percent in Akron, and 80 percent in Toledo. Private charities and public relief agencies reached only a fraction of the needy. The nation's banking system was so close to collapse that many state governors closed banks temporarily to avoid further withdrawals. Several states were approaching bankruptcy, their tax revenues too low to pay for basic services. By March 1933, the nation had hit rock bottom.

**UNDERSTAND POINTS OF VIEW**
What did the depression look like when seen from the vantage of ordinary Americans?

# The New Deal Arrives, 1933–1935

The ideological differences between Herbert Hoover and Franklin Roosevelt were not vast. Both leaders wished to maintain the nation's economic institutions and social values, to save capitalism while easing its worst downturns. Both believed in a balanced government budget and extolled the values of hard work, cooperation, and sacrifice. But Roosevelt's personal charm, political savvy, and willingness to experiment made him far more effective and more popular than Hoover. Most Americans felt a kinship with their new president, calling him simply FDR. His New Deal would put people to work and restore hope for the nation's future.

## Roosevelt and the First Hundred Days

A wealthy patrician, Roosevelt was an unlikely figure to inspire millions of ordinary Americans. But his close rapport with the American people was critical to his political success. More than 450,000 letters poured into the White House in the week after his inauguration. The president's masterful use of the new medium of radio, especially his evening radio addresses to the American public known as **fireside chats**, made him an intimate presence in people's lives. Thousands of citizens felt a personal relationship with FDR, saying, "He gave me a job" or "He saved my home" (American Voices, p. 742).

Citing the national economic emergency, Roosevelt further expanded the presidential powers that Theodore Roosevelt and Woodrow Wilson had increased previously. To draft legislation and policy, he relied heavily on financier Bernard Baruch and a "Brains Trust" of professors from Columbia, Harvard, and other leading universities. Roosevelt also turned to his talented cabinet, which included Harold L. Ickes, secretary of the interior; Frances Perkins at the Labor Department; Henry A. Wallace at Agriculture; and Henry Morgenthau Jr., secretary of the treasury. These intellectuals and administrators attracted hundreds of highly qualified recruits to Washington. Inspired by New Deal idealism, many of them would devote their lives to public service and the principles of social-welfare liberalism.

**EXPLAIN CONSEQUENCES**

What specific new roles did the American government take up as a result of the legislation passed during the first hundred days?

Roosevelt could have done little, however, without a sympathetic Congress. The 1932 election had swept Democratic majorities into both the House and Senate, giving the new president the lawmaking allies he needed. The first months of FDR's administration produced a whirlwind of activity on Capitol Hill. In a legendary session, known as the **Hundred Days**, Congress enacted fifteen major bills that focused primarily on four problems: banking failures, agricultural overproduction, the business slump, and soaring unemployment. Derided by some as an "alphabet soup" because of their many abbreviations (CCC, WPA, AAA, etc.), the new policies and agencies were more than bureaucracies: they represented the emergence of a new American state.

**Banking Reform**   The weak banking system hobbled the entire economy, curtailing consumer spending and business investment. Widespread bank failures had reduced the savings of nearly nine million families, and panicked account holders raced to withdraw their funds. On March 5, 1933, the day after his inauguration, FDR declared a national "bank holiday"—closing all the banks—and called Congress into special session. Four days later, Congress passed the Emergency Banking Act, which permitted banks to reopen if a Treasury Department inspection showed that they had sufficient cash reserves.

In his first Sunday night fireside chat, to a radio audience of sixty million, the president reassured citizens that their money was safe. When the banks reopened on March 13, calm prevailed and deposits exceeded withdrawals, restoring stability to the nation's basic financial institutions. "Capitalism was saved in eight days," quipped Roosevelt's advisor Raymond Moley. Four thousand banks had collapsed in the months prior to Roosevelt's inauguration; only sixty-one closed their doors in all of 1934 (Table 23.1). A second banking law, the **Glass-Steagall Act**, further restored public confidence by creating the Federal Deposit Insurance Corporation (FDIC), which insured deposits up to $2,500 (and now insures them up to $250,000). The act also prohibited banks from making risky, unsecured investments with the deposits of ordinary people. And in a profoundly important economic and symbolic gesture, Roosevelt removed the U.S. Treasury from the gold standard in June 1933, which allowed the Federal Reserve to lower interest rates; since 1931, it had been raising rates, which had only deepened the downturn. Saving the banks and leaving the gold standard led to a mild and, it would turn out, brief recovery.

## TABLE 23.1

### American Banks and Bank Failures, 1920–1940

| Year | Total Number of Banks | Total Assets ($ billion) | Bank Failures |
|------|----------------------|--------------------------|---------------|
| 1920 | 30,909 | 53.1 | 168 |
| 1929 | 25,568 | 72.3 | 659 |
| 1931 | 22,242 | 70.1 | 2,294 |
| 1933 | 14,771 | 51.4 | 4,004 |
| 1934 | 15,913 | 55.9 | 61 |
| 1940 | 15,076 | 79.7 | 48 |

SOURCE: *Historical Statistics of the United States: Colonial Times to 1970* (Washington, DC: U.S. Government Printing Office, 1975), 1019, 1038–1039.

**Agriculture and Manufacturing**   Roosevelt and the New Deal Congress next turned to agriculture and manufacturing. In those sectors, a seeming paradox was evident: the depression led to overproduction in agriculture and underproduction in manufacturing. Reversing both problematic trends was critical. The **Agricultural Adjustment Act** (AAA) began direct governmental regulation of the farm economy for the first time. To solve the problem of overproduction, which lowered prices, the AAA provided cash subsidies to farmers who cut production of seven major commodities: wheat, cotton, corn, hogs, rice, tobacco, and dairy products. Policymakers hoped that farm prices would rise as production fell.

By dumping cash in farmers' hands, the AAA briefly stabilized the farm economy. But the act's benefits were not evenly distributed. Subsidies went primarily to the owners of large and medium-sized farms, who often cut production by reducing the amount of land they rented to tenants and sharecroppers. In Mississippi, one plantation owner received $26,000 from the federal government, while thousands of black sharecroppers living in the same county received only a few dollars in relief payments.

In manufacturing, the New Deal attacked declining production with the National Industrial Recovery Act. A new government agency, the **National Recovery Administration** (NRA), set up separate self-governing private associations in six hundred industries. Each industry — ranging from large corporations producing coal, cotton textiles, and steel to small businesses making pet food and costume jewelry — regulated itself by agreeing on prices and production quotas. Because large companies usually ran these associations, the NRA solidified their power at the expense of smaller enterprises and consumer interests.

The AAA and the NRA were designed to rescue the nation's productive industries and stabilize the economy. The measures had positive effects in some regions, but most historians agree that, overall, they did little to end the depression.

**Unemployment Relief**   The Roosevelt administration next addressed the massive unemployment problem. By 1933, local governments and private charities had exhausted their resources and were looking to Washington for assistance. Although Roosevelt wanted to avoid a budget deficit, he asked Congress to provide relief for millions of unemployed Americans. In May, Congress established the Federal Emergency Relief Administration (FERA). Directed by Harry Hopkins, a hard-driving social worker from New York, the FERA provided federal funds for state relief programs.

Roosevelt and Hopkins had strong reservations about the "dole," the nickname for government welfare payments. As Hopkins put it, "I don't think anybody can go year after year, month after month, accepting relief without affecting his character." To support the traditional values of individualism, the New Deal put people to work. Early in 1933, Congress established the **Public Works Administration** (PWA), a construction program, and several months later, Roosevelt created the Civil Works Administration (CWA) and named Hopkins its head. Within thirty days, Hopkins had put 2.6 million men and women to work; at its peak in 1934, the CWA provided jobs for 4 million Americans repairing bridges, building highways, and constructing public buildings. A stopgap measure to get the country through the winter of 1933–1934, the CWA lapsed in the spring, when Republican opposition compelled New Dealers to abandon it. A longer-term program, the **Civilian Conservation Corps** (CCC), mobilized

## Ordinary People Respond to the New Deal

Franklin Roosevelt's fireside chats and his relief programs prompted thousands of ordinary Americans to write directly to the president and his wife, Eleanor. Taken together, their letters offer a vivid portrait of depression-era America that includes popular support for, and opposition to, the New Deal.

**Mrs. M. H. A.**

Mrs. M. H. A. worked in the County Court House in Eureka, California.

June 14, 1934
Dear Mrs. Roosevelt:
I know you are overburdened with requests for help and if my plea cannot be recognized, I'll understand it is because you have so many others, all of them worthy. . . .

My husband and I are a young couple of very simple, almost poor families. We married eight years ago on the proverbial shoe-string but with a wealth of love. . . . We managed to build our home and furnish it comfortably. . . . Then came the depression. My work has continued and my salary alone has just been sufficient to make our monthly payments on the house and keep our bills paid. . . . But with the exception of two and one-half months work with the U.S. Coast and Geodetic Survey under the C.W.A. [Civil Works Administration], my husband has not had work since August, 1932.

My salary could continue to keep us going, but I am to have a baby. . . . I can get a leave of absence from my job for a year. But can't you, won't you do something so my husband can have a job, at least during that year? . . .

As I said before, if it were only ourselves, or if there were something we could do about it, we would never ask for help.

We have always stood on our own feet and been proud and happy. But you are a mother and you'll understand this crisis.

Very sincerely yours,
Mrs. M. H. A.

**Unsigned Letter**

This unsigned letter came from a factory worker in Paris, Texas.

November 23, 1936
Dear President,
[N]ow that we have had a land Slide [in the election of 1936] and done just what was best for our country . . .

I do believe you Will Strain a point to help the ones who helped you mostly & that is the Working Class of People I am not smart or I would be in a different line of work & better up in ever way yet I will know you are the one & only President that ever helped a Working Class of People. . . .

I am a White Man American age, 47 married wife 2children in high School am a Finishing room foreman I mean a Working foreman & am in a furniture Factory here in Paris Texas where thaire is 175 to 200 Working & when the NRA [National Recovery Administration] came in I was Proud to See my fellow workmen Rec 30 Per hour in Place of 8 cents to 20 cents Per hour. . . .

I can't see for my life President why a man must toil &work his life out in Such factories 10 long hours ever day except Sunday for a small sum of 15 cents to 35 cents per hour & pay the high cost of honest & deason living expences. . . .

please see if something can be done to help this one Class of Working People the factories are a man killer not venelated or kept up just a bunch of Republickins Grafters 90/100 of them Please help us some way I Pray to God for relief. I am a Christian . . . and a truthful man & have not told you wrong & am for you to the end.

[not signed]

**R. A.**

R. A. was sixty-nine years old and an architect and builder in Lincoln, Nebraska.

May 19/34
Dear Mrs Roosevelt:
In the Presidents inaugral address delivered from the capitol steps the afternoon of his inauguration he made mention of The Forgotten Man, and I with thousands of others am wondering if the folk who was borned here in America some 60 or 70 years a go are this Forgotten Man, the President had in mind, if we are this Forgotten Man then we are still Forgotten.

We who have tried to be diligent in our support of this most wonderful nation of ours boath social and other wise, we in our younger days tried to do our duty without complaining. . . .

And now a great calamity has come upon us and seemingly no cause of our own it has swept away what little savings we had accumulated and we are left in a condition that is imposible for us to correct, for two very prominent reasons if no more.

First we have grown to what is termed Old Age, this befalls every man.

Second, . . . we are confronted on every hand with the young generation, taking our places, this of corse is what we have looked forward to in training our children. But with the extra ordinary crisese which left us helpless and placed us in the position that our fathers did not have to contend with. . . .

We have been honorable citizens all along our journey, calamity and old age has forced its self upon us please do not send us to the Poor Farm but instead allow us the small pension of $40.00 per month. . . .

Mrs. Roosevelt I am asking a personal favor of you as it seems to be the only means through which I may be able to reach the President, some evening very soon, as you and Mr. Roosevelt are having dinner together privately will you ask him to read this. And we American citizens will ever remember your kindness.

Yours very truly.

R. A.

## M. A.

M. A. was a woman who held a low-level salaried position in a corporation.

Jan. 18, 1937
[Dear Mrs. Roosevelt:]
I . . . was simply astounded to think that anyone could be nitwit enough to wish to be included in the so called social security act if they could possibly avoid it. Call it by any name you wish it, in my opinion, (and that of many people I know) [it] is nothing but downright stealing. . . .

I am not an "economic royalist," just an ordinary white collar worker at $1600 per [year — about $23,600 in 2009]. Please show this to the president and ask him to remember the wishes of the forgotten man, that is, the one who dared to vote against him. We expect to be tramped on but we do wish the stepping would be a little less hard.

Security at the price of freedom is never desired by intelligent people.

M. A.

## M. A. H.

M. A. H. was a widow who ran a small farm in Columbus, Indiana.

December 14, 1937
Mrs. Roosevelt:
I suppose from your point of view the work relief, old age pensions, slum clearance and all the rest seems like a perfect remedy for all the ills of this country, but I would like for you to see the results, as the other half see them.

We have always had a shiftless, never-do-well class of people whose one and only aim in life is to live without work. I have been rubbing elbows with this class for nearly sixty years and have tried to help some of the most promising and have seen others try to help them, but it can't be done. We cannot help those who will not try to help themselves and if they do try a square deal is all they need, . . . let each one paddle their own canoe, or sink. . . .

I live alone on a farm and have not raised any crops for the last two years as there was no help to be had. I am feeding the stock and have been cutting the wood to keep my home fires burning. There are several reliefers around here now who have been kicked off relief but they refuse to work unless they can get relief hours and wages, but they are so worthless no one can afford to hire them. . . . They are just a fair sample of the class of people on whom so much of our hard earned tax-money is being squandered and on whom so much sympathy is being wasted. . . .

You people who have plenty of this worlds goods and whose money comes easy have no idea of the heart-breaking toil and self-denial which is the lot of the working people who are trying to make an honest living, and then to have to shoulder all these unjust burdens seems like the last straw. . . . No one should have the right to vote theirself a living at the expense of the tax payers. . . .

M. A. H.

Sources (in order): Robert S. McElvaine, *Down & Out in the Great Depression* (Chapel Hill: University of North Carolina Press, 1983), 54–55; Gerald Markowitz and David Rosner, eds., *"Slaves of the Depression": Worker's Letters About Life on the Job* (Ithaca, NY: Cornell University Press, 1987), 21; Robert S. McElvaine, *Down & Out in the Great Depression* (Chapel Hill: University of North Carolina Press, 1983), 97, 147, 143.

### QUESTIONS FOR ANALYSIS

1. How do you explain the personal, almost intimate, tone of these letters to the Roosevelts?
2. How have specific New Deal programs helped or hurt the authors of these letters?
3. What are the basic values of the authors? Do the values of those who support the New Deal differ from the values of those who oppose it?

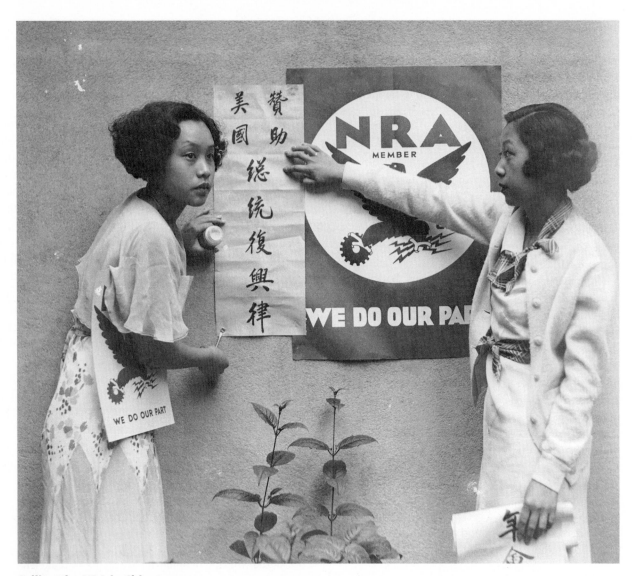

**Selling the NRA in Chinatown**
To mobilize support for its program, the National Recovery Administration (NRA) distributed millions of posters to businesses and families, urging them to display its symbol, the Blue Eagle, in shops, factories, and homes. Here Constance King and Mae Chinn of the Chinese YMCA affix a poster (and a Chinese translation) to a shop in San Francisco that is complying with the NRA codes. © Bettmann/Corbis.

250,000 young men to do reforestation and conservation work. Over the course of the 1930s, the "CCC boys" built thousands of bridges, roads, trails, and other structures in state and national parks, bolstering the national infrastructure (Map 23.2).

**Housing Crisis**  Millions of Americans also faced the devastating prospect of losing their homes. The economic expansion of the 1920s had produced the largest inflationary housing bubble in American history to that point, a scenario in which home prices rose wildly, fueled by excessive borrowing. In the early 1930s, as

home prices collapsed and banks closed, home owners were dragged down with them. More than half a million Americans lost their homes between 1930 and 1932, and in cities such as Cleveland and Indianapolis, half of all home mortgage holders faced possible foreclosure. In response, Congress created the Home Owners Loan Corporation (HOLC) to refinance home mortgages. In just two years, the HOLC helped more than a million Americans retain their homes. The Federal Housing Act of 1934 would extend this program under a new agency, the **Federal Housing Administration** (FHA). Together, the HOLC, the FHA,

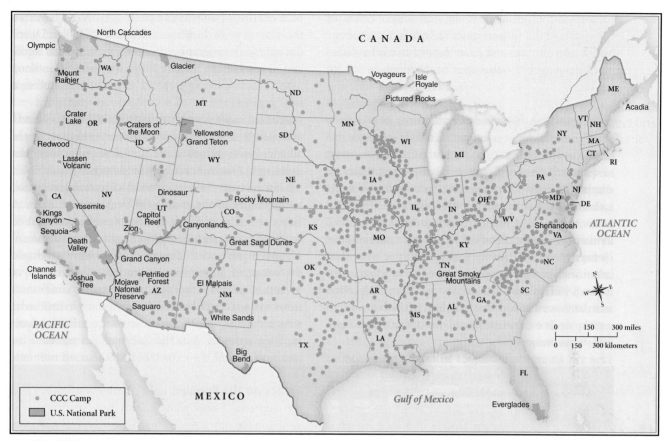

**MAP 23.2**

**Civilian Conservation Corps Camps**

The Civilian Conservation Corps (CCC) gave hope to unemployed young men during the Great Depression. The first camp opened in Big Meadows, Virginia, in July 1933, and by the end of the decade CCC camps had appeared across the length of the country, located in rural, mountainous, and forested regions alike. Young men constructed bridges and roads, built hiking trails, erected public campgrounds, and performed other improvements. By the early 1940s, the CCC had planted three billion trees, among its many other contributions to the national infrastructure.

and the subsequent Housing Act of 1937 permanently changed the mortgage system and set the foundation for the broad expansion of home ownership in the post–World War II decades (Chapter 25).

When an exhausted Congress recessed in June 1933, at the end of the Hundred Days, it had enacted Roosevelt's agenda: banking reform, recovery programs for agriculture and industry, public works, and unemployment relief. Few presidents had won the passage of so many measures in so short a time. The new federal agencies were far from perfect and had their critics on both the radical left and the conservative right. But the vigorous actions taken by Roosevelt and Congress had halted the downward economic spiral of the Hoover years, stabilized the financial sector, and sent a message of hope from the nation's political leaders. For all that,

however, the New Deal did not break the grip of the depression.

## The New Deal Under Attack

As New Dealers waited anxiously for the economy to revive, Roosevelt turned his attention to the reform of Wall Street, where reckless speculation and overleveraged buying of stocks had helped trigger the financial panic of 1929. In 1934, Congress established the **Securities and Exchange Commission** (SEC) to regulate the stock market. The commission had broad powers to determine how stocks and bonds were sold to the public, to set rules for margin (credit) transactions, and to prevent stock sales by those with inside information about corporate plans. The Banking Act of 1935 authorized the president to appoint a new Board of Governors of the Federal Reserve System, placing control of interest rates and other money-market policies in a federal agency rather than in the hands of private bankers.

### Critics on the Right

Such measures exposed the New Deal to attack from economic conservatives — also known as the political right. A man of wealth, Roosevelt saw himself as the savior of American capitalism, declaring simply, "To preserve we had to reform." Many bankers and business executives disagreed. To them, FDR became "That Man," a traitor to his class. In 1934, Republican business leaders joined with conservative Democrats in the **Liberty League** to fight what they called the "reckless spending" and "socialist" reforms of the New Deal. Herbert Hoover condemned the NRA as a "state-controlled or state-directed social or economic system." That, declared the former president, was "tyranny, not liberalism."

The **National Association of Manufacturers** (NAM) was even more important than the Liberty League in opposing the New Deal, as the NAM's influence stretched far into the post–World War II decades. Sparked by a new generation of business leaders who believed that a publicity campaign was needed to "serve the purposes of business salvation," the NAM produced radio programs, motion pictures, billboards, and direct mail in the late 1930s. In response to what many conservatives perceived as Roosevelt's antibusiness policies, the NAM promoted free enterprise and unfettered capitalism. After World War II, the NAM emerged as a staunch critic of liberalism and forged alliances with influential conservative politicians such as Barry Goldwater and Ronald Reagan.

For its part, the Supreme Court repudiated several cornerstones of the early New Deal. In May 1935, in *Schechter v. United States*, the Court unanimously ruled the National Industrial Recovery Act unconstitutional because it delegated Congress's lawmaking power to the executive branch and extended federal authority to intrastate (in contrast to interstate) commerce. Roosevelt protested but watched helplessly as the Court struck down more New Deal legislation: the Agricultural Adjustment Act, the Railroad Retirement Act, and a debt-relief law known as the Frazier-Lemke Act.

### Critics on the Populist Left

If business leaders and the Supreme Court thought that the New Deal had gone too far, other Americans believed it had not gone far enough. Among these were public figures who, in the tradition of American populism, sought to place government on the side of ordinary citizens against

---

**COMPARE AND CONTRAST**

How did critics on the right and left represent different kinds of challenges to Roosevelt and the New Deal?

---

**Father Coughlin**

One of the foremost critics of the New Deal was the "Radio Priest," Father Charles E. Coughlin. Coughlin believed that Roosevelt and the Democratic Party had not gone far enough in their efforts to ensure the social welfare of all citizens. For instance, he and his organization, the National Union for Social Justice, urged Roosevelt to nationalize the banks. Coughlin, whose radio audience reached 30 million at the height of his popularity, was one of the most recognizable religious leaders in the country. Unfortunately, his remarks in the early 1930s were often laced with anti-Semitism (anti-Jewish sentiment). © Bettmann/Corbis.

corporations and the wealthy. Francis Townsend, a doctor from Long Beach, California, spoke for the nation's elderly, most of whom had no pensions and feared poverty. In 1933, Townsend proposed the Old Age Revolving Pension Plan, which would give $200 a month (about $3,300 today) to citizens over the age of sixty. To receive payments, the elderly would have to retire and open their positions to younger workers. Townsend Clubs sprang up across the country in support of the **Townsend Plan**, mobilizing mass support for old-age pensions.

The most direct political threat to Roosevelt came from Louisiana senator Huey Long. As the Democratic governor of Louisiana from 1928 to 1932, the flamboyant Long had achieved stunning popularity. He increased taxes on corporations, lowered the utility bills of consumers, and built new highways, hospitals, and schools. To push through these measures, Long seized almost dictatorial control of the state government. Now a U.S. senator, Long broke with the New Deal in 1934 and, like Townsend, established a national movement. According to his Share Our Wealth Society, inequalities in the distribution of wealth prohibited millions of ordinary families from buying goods, which kept factories humming. Long's society advocated a tax of 100 percent on all income over $1 million and on all inheritances over $5 million. He hoped that this populist program would carry him into the White House.

That prospect encouraged conservatives, who hoped that a split between New Dealers and populist reformers might return the Republican Party, and its ideology of limited government and free enterprise, to political power. In fact, Roosevelt feared that Townsend and Long, along with the popular "radio priest," Father Charles Coughlin, might join forces to form a third party. He had to respond or risk the political unity of the country's liberal forces (Map 23.3).

# The Second New Deal and the Redefining of Liberalism, 1935–1938

As attacks on the New Deal increased, Roosevelt and his advisors moved politically to the left. Historians have labeled this shift in policy the Second New Deal. Roosevelt now openly criticized the "money classes," proudly stating, "We have earned the hatred of entrenched greed." He also decisively countered the rising popularity of Townsend, Coughlin, and Long by

adopting parts of their programs. The administration's Revenue Act of 1935 proposed a substantial tax increase on corporate profits and higher income and estate taxes on the wealthy. When conservatives attacked this legislation as an attempt to "soak the rich," Congress moderated its taxation rates. But FDR was satisfied. He had met the Share Our Wealth Society's proposal with a tax plan of his own.

## The Welfare State Comes into Being

The Revenue Act symbolized the administration's new outlook. Unlike the First New Deal, which focused on economic recovery, the Second New Deal emphasized social justice and the creation of a safety net: the use of the federal government to assist working people and to provide economic security for the old, the disabled, and the unemployed. The resulting **welfare state** — a term applied to industrial democracies that adopted various government-guaranteed social-welfare programs — fundamentally changed American society.

> **COMPARE AND CONTRAST**
> How did the Second New Deal differ from the first?

**The Wagner Act and Social Security**   The first beneficiary of Roosevelt's Second New Deal was the labor movement. Section 7(a) of the National Industrial Recovery Act (NIRA) had given workers the right to organize unions, producing a dramatic growth in rank-and-file militancy and leading to a strike wave in 1934. When the Supreme Court voided the NIRA in 1935, labor unions called for new legislation that would allow workers to organize and bargain collectively with employers. Named for its sponsor, Senator Robert F. Wagner of New York, the **Wagner Act** (1935) upheld the right of industrial workers to join unions. The act outlawed many practices that employers had used to suppress unions, such as firing workers for organizing activities. It also established the National Labor Relations Board (NLRB), a federal agency with the authority to protect workers from employer coercion and to guarantee collective bargaining.

A second initiative, the **Social Security Act** of 1935, had an equally widespread impact. Other industrialized societies, such as Germany and Britain, had created national old-age pension systems at the turn of the century, but American reformers had failed to secure a similar program in the United States. The Townsend and Long movements now pressed Roosevelt to act, giving political muscle to pension proponents within the administration. Children's welfare advocates,

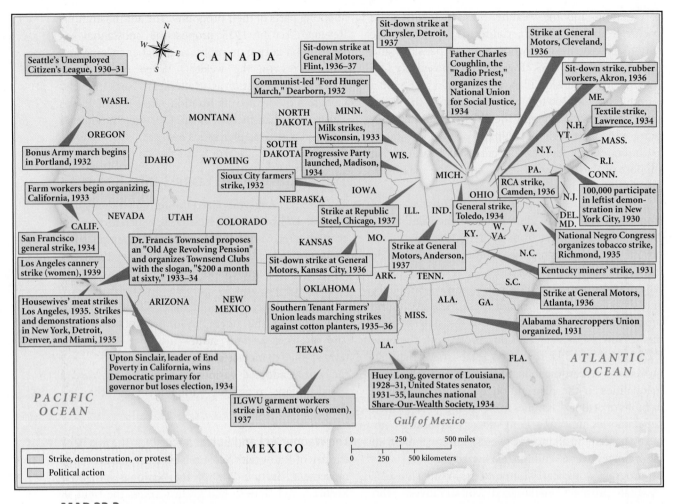

Seattle's Unemployed Citizen's League, 1930–31

Sit-down strike at Chrysler, Detroit, 1937

Sit-down strike at General Motors, Flint, 1936–37

Strike at General Motors, Cleveland, 1936

Father Charles Coughlin, the "Radio Priest," organizes the National Union for Social Justice, 1934

Communist-led "Ford Hunger March," Dearborn, 1932

Sit-down strike, rubber workers, Akron, 1936

Textile strike, Lawrence, 1934

Milk strikes, Wisconsin, 1933

Bonus Army march begins in Portland, 1932

Progressive Party launched, Madison, 1934

Sioux City farmers' strike, 1932

Farm workers begin organizing, California, 1933

RCA strike, Camden, 1936

100,000 participate in leftist demonstration in New York City, 1930

San Francisco general strike, 1934

Dr. Francis Townsend proposes an "Old Age Revolving Pension" and organizes Townsend Clubs with the slogan, "$200 a month at sixty," 1933–34

General strike, Toledo, 1934

National Negro Congress organizes tobacco strike, Richmond, 1935

Strike at Republic Steel, Chicago, 1937

Los Angeles cannery strike (women), 1939

Strike at General Motors, Anderson, 1937

Sit-down strike at General Motors, Kansas City, 1936

Kentucky miners' strike, 1931

Housewives' meat strikes Los Angeles, 1935. Strikes and demonstrations also in New York, Detroit, Denver, and Miami, 1935

Strike at General Motors, Atlanta, 1936

Southern Tenant Farmers' Union leads marching strikes against cotton planters, 1935–36

Alabama Sharecroppers Union organized, 1931

Upton Sinclair, leader of End Poverty in California, wins Democratic primary for governor but loses election, 1934

Huey Long, governor of Louisiana, 1928–31, United States senator, 1931–35, launches national Share-Our-Wealth Society, 1934

ILGWU garment workers strike in San Antonio (women), 1937

Strike, demonstration, or protest
Political action

**MAP 23.3**

**Popular Protest in the Great Depression, 1933–1939**

The depression forced Americans to look closely at their society, and many of them did not like what they saw. Some citizens expressed their discontent through popular movements, and this map suggests the geography of discontent. The industrial Midwest witnessed union movements, strikes, and Radio Priest Charles Coughlin's demands for social reform. Simultaneously, farmers' movements—tenants in the South, smallholders in the agricultural Midwest—engaged in strikes and dumping campaigns and rallied behind the ideas of progressives in Wisconsin and Huey Long in the South. Protests took diverse forms in California, which was home to strikes by farmworkers, women, and—in San Francisco—all wageworkers. The West was also the seedbed of two important reform proposals: Upton Sinclair's End Poverty in California (EPIC) movement and Francis Townsend's Old Age Revolving Pension clubs.

concerned about the fate of fatherless families, also pressured the president. The resulting Social Security Act had three main provisions: old-age pensions for workers; a joint federal-state system of compensation for unemployed workers; and a program of payments to widowed mothers and the blind, deaf, and disabled. Roosevelt, however, limited the reach of the legislation. Knowing that compulsory pension and unemployment legislation alone would be controversial, he dropped a provision for national health insurance, fearing it would doom the entire bill.

The Social Security Act was a milestone in the creation of an American welfare state. Never before had the federal government assumed such responsibility for the well-being of so many citizens. Social Security, as old-age pensions were known, became one of the most popular government programs in American history. On the other hand, the assistance program for widows and children known as Aid to Dependent Children (ADC) became one of its most controversial measures. ADC covered only 700,000 youngsters in 1939; by 1994, its successor, Aid to

**United Auto Workers Strike**

Trade unions were among the most active and vocal organizations of the 1930s. Organized labor led a number of major strikes between 1934 and 1936 in various industries. None was more important to the future of trade unions than the sit-down strikes at major automobile plants, including General Motors and Chevrolet in Flint, Michigan, in 1936 and 1937. These strikes, in which workers stopped the assembly lines but refused to leave the factories, compelled GM to recognize the United Auto Workers (UAW), which became one of the strongest trade unions in American history. © Bettmann/Corbis.

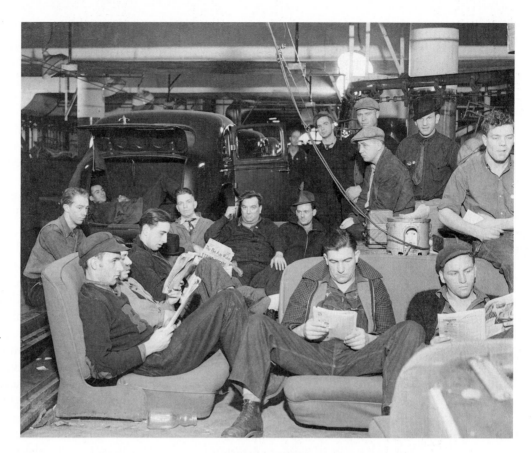

Families with Dependent Children (AFDC), enrolled 14.1 million Americans. A minor program during the New Deal, AFDC grew enormously in the 1960s and remained an often maligned cornerstone of the welfare state until it was eliminated under President Clinton in 1996.

**New Deal Liberalism**   The Second New Deal created what historians call New Deal liberalism. **Classical liberalism** held individual liberty to be the foundation of a democratic society, and the word *liberal* had traditionally denoted support for free-market policies and weak government. Roosevelt and his advisors, along with intellectuals such as British economist John Maynard Keynes, disagreed. They countered that, to preserve individual liberty, government must assist the needy and guarantee the basic welfare of citizens. This liberal welfare state was opposed by inheritors of the nineteenth-century ideology of *laissez-faire* capitalism, who gradually became known as conservatives. These two visions of liberty and government — with liberals on one side and conservatives on the other — would shape American politics for the next half century.

## From Reform to Stalemate

Roosevelt's first term had seen an extraordinary expansion of the federal state. The great burst of government action between 1933 and 1935 was unequaled in the nation's history (though Congress and President Lyndon Johnson nearly matched it in 1965–1966; see Chapter 28). Roosevelt's second term, however, was characterized by a series of political entanglements and economic bad news that stifled further reform.

**The 1936 Election**   FDR was never enthusiastic about public relief programs. But with the election of 1936 on the horizon and 10 million Americans still out of work, he won funding for the **Works Progress Administration** (WPA). Under the energetic direction of Harry Hopkins, the WPA employed 8.5 million Americans between 1935, when it was established, and 1943. The agency's workers constructed or repaired 651,087 miles of road, 124,087 bridges, 125,110 public buildings, 8,192 parks, and 853 airports. But although the WPA was an extravagant operation by 1930s standards, it reached only about one-third of the nation's unemployed.

As the 1936 election approached, new voters joined the Democratic Party. Many had personally benefitted from New Deal programs such as the WPA or knew people who had (Table 23.2). One was Jack Reagan, a down-on-his-luck shoe salesman (and the father of future president Ronald Reagan), who took a job as a federal relief administrator in Dixon, Illinois, and became a strong supporter of the New Deal. In

addition to voters such as Reagan, Roosevelt could count on a powerful coalition of organized labor, midwestern farmers, white ethnic groups, northern African Americans, and middle-class families concerned about unemployment and old-age security. He also commanded the support of intellectuals and progressive Republicans. With difficulty, the Democrats held on to the votes of their white southern constituency as well.

Republicans recognized that the New Deal was too popular to oppose directly, so they chose as their candidate the progressive governor of Kansas, Alfred M. Landon. Landon accepted the legitimacy of many New Deal programs but criticized their inefficiency and expense. He also pointed to authoritarian regimes in Italy and Germany and hinted that FDR harbored similar dictatorial ambitions. These charges fell on deaf ears. Roosevelt's victory in 1936 was one of the most lopsided in American history. The assassination of Huey Long by a Louisiana political rival in September 1935 had eliminated the threat of a serious third-party challenge. Roosevelt received 60 percent of the popular vote and carried every state except Maine and Vermont. Organized labor, in particular, mobilized on behalf of FDR, donating money, canvassing door to door, and registering hundreds of thousands of new voters. The *New Republic*, a liberal publication, boasted that "it was the greatest revolution in our political history."

"I see one-third of a nation ill-housed, ill-clad, ill-nourished," the president declared in his second inaugural address in January 1937. But any hopes that FDR had for expanding the liberal welfare state were quickly dashed. Within a year, staunch opposition to Roosevelt's initiatives arose in Congress, and a sharp recession undermined confidence in his economic leadership.

**Court Battle and Economic Recession**   Roosevelt's first setback in 1937 came when he surprised the nation by asking for fundamental changes to the Supreme Court. In 1935, the Court had struck down a series of New Deal measures by the narrow margin of 5 to 4. With the Wagner Act, the Tennessee Valley Authority, and Social Security all slated to come before the Court, the future of the New Deal rested in the hands of a few elderly, conservative-minded judges. To diminish their influence, the president proposed adding a new justice to the Court for every member over the age of seventy, a scheme that would have brought six new judges to the bench at the time the legislation was proposed. Roosevelt's opponents protested that he was trying to "pack" the Court. After a bitter, months-long debate, Congress rejected this blatant attempt to alter the judiciary to the president's advantage.

| TABLE 23.2 | |
|---|---|
| **Major New Deal Legislation** | |
| **Agriculture** | |
| 1933 | Agricultural Adjustment Act (AAA) |
| 1935 | Resettlement Administration (RA) |
|  | Rural Electrification Administration |
| 1937 | Farm Security Administration (FSA) |
| 1938 | Agricultural Adjustment Act of 1938 |
| **Finance and Industry** | |
| 1933 | Emergency Banking Act |
|  | Glass-Steagall Act (created the FDIC) |
|  | National Industrial Recovery Act (NIRA) |
| 1934 | Securities and Exchange Commission (SEC) |
| 1935 | Banking Act of 1935 |
|  | Revenue Act (wealth tax) |
| **Conservation and the Environment** | |
| 1933 | Tennessee Valley Authority (TVA) |
|  | Civilian Conservation Corps (CCC) |
|  | Soil Conservation and Domestic Allotment Act |
| **Labor and Social Welfare** | |
| 1933 | Section 7(a) of NIRA |
| 1935 | National Labor Relations Act (Wagner Act) |
|  | National Labor Relations Board (NLRB) |
|  | Social Security Act |
| 1937 | National Housing Act |
| 1938 | Fair Labor Standards Act (FLSA) |
| **Relief and Reconstruction** | |
| 1933 | Federal Emergency Relief Administration (FERA) |
|  | Civil Works Administration (CWA) |
|  | Public Works Administration (PWA) |
| 1935 | Works Progress Administration (WPA) |
|  | National Youth Administration (NYA) |

If Roosevelt lost the battle, he went on to win the war. Swayed in part by the president's overwhelming electoral victory in the 1936 election, the Court upheld the Wagner and Social Security Acts. Moreover, a series of timely resignations allowed Roosevelt to reshape the Supreme Court after all. His new appointees—who included the liberal-leaning and generally pro–New Deal Hugo Black, Felix Frankfurter, and William O. Douglas—viewed the Constitution as a "living document" that had to be interpreted in the light of present conditions.

The so-called **Roosevelt recession** of 1937–1938 dealt another blow to the president. From 1933 to 1937, gross domestic product had grown at a yearly rate of about 10 percent, bringing industrial output back to 1929 levels. Unemployment had declined from 25 percent to 14 percent. "The emergency has passed," declared Senator James F. Byrnes of South Carolina. Acting on this assumption, Roosevelt slashed the federal budget. Following the president's lead, Congress cut the WPA's funding in half, causing layoffs of about 1.5 million workers, and the Federal Reserve, fearing inflation, raised interest rates. These measures halted recovery. The stock market responded by dropping sharply, and unemployment jumped to 19 percent. Quickly reversing course, Roosevelt began once again to spend his way out of the recession by boosting funding for the WPA and resuming public works projects.

Although improvised, this spending program accorded with the theories of John Maynard Keynes, a visionary British economist. Keynes transformed economic thinking in capitalist societies in the 1920s by arguing that government intervention could smooth out the highs and lows of the business cycle through deficit spending and the manipulation of interest rates, which determined the money supply. This view was sharply criticized by Republicans and conservative Democrats in the 1930s, who disliked government intervention in the economy. But **Keynesian economics** gradually won wider acceptance as World War II defense spending finally ended the Great Depression.

A reformer rather than a revolutionary, Roosevelt had preserved capitalism and liberal individualism—even as he transformed them in significant ways. At the same time, conservatives had reclaimed a measure of power in Congress, and those who believed the New Deal had created an intrusive federal bureaucracy kept reform in check after 1937. Throughout Roosevelt's second term, a conservative coalition of southern Democrats, rural Republicans, and industrial interests in both parties worked to block or impede social legislation. By 1939, the era of change was over.

# The New Deal's Impact on Society

Whatever its limits, the New Deal had a tremendous impact. Its ideology of social-welfare liberalism fundamentally altered Americans' relationship to their government and provided assistance to a wide range of ordinary people: the unemployed, the elderly, workers, and the poor. In doing so, New Dealers created a sizable federal bureaucracy: the number of civilian federal employees increased by 80 percent between 1929 and 1940, reaching a total of 1 million. The expenditures—and deficits—of the federal government grew at an even faster rate. In 1930, the Hoover administration spent $3.1 billion and had a surplus of almost $1 billion; in 1939, New Dealers expended $9.4 billion and ran a deficit of nearly $3 billion (still small by later standards). But the New Deal represented more than figures on a balance sheet. Across the country, the new era in government inspired democratic visions among ordinary citizens (Thinking Like a Historian, p. 752).

## A People's Democracy

In 1939, writer John La Touche and musician Earl Robinson produced "Ballad for Americans." A patriotic song, it called for uniting "everybody who's nobody . . . Irish, Negro, Jewish, Italian, French, and English, Spanish, Russian, Chinese, Polish, Scotch, Hungarian, Litvak, Swedish, Finnish, Canadian, Greek, and Turk, and Czech and double Czech American." The song captured the democratic aspirations that the New Deal had awakened. Millions of ordinary people believed that the nation could, and should, become more egalitarian. Influenced by the liberal spirit of the New Deal, Americans from all walks of life seized the opportunity to push for change in the nation's social and political institutions.

**Organized Labor**   Demoralized and shrinking during the 1920s, labor unions increased their numbers and clout during the New Deal, thanks to the Wagner Act. "The era of privilege and predatory individuals is over," labor leader John L. Lewis declared. By the end of the decade, the number of unionized workers had tripled to 23 percent of the nonagricultural workforce. A new union movement, led by the Congress of Industrial Organizations (CIO), promoted "industrial unionism"—organizing all the workers in an industry, from skilled machinists to unskilled janitors, into a single union. The American Federation of Labor (AFL),

## The New Deal and Public Works

More than half a dozen New Deal programs were devoted to building up the physical and cultural infrastructure of the country. The former included roads, bridges, dams, trails, and national parks. The latter included artwork, murals, plays, and other forms of literary expression. Examine the following documents and use them collectively to analyze the New Deal's relationship to infrastructure, art, culture, and politics.

**1. Harold L. Ickes, secretary of the interior, *The New Democracy*, 1934.**

Our Government is no longer a laissez-faire Government, exercising traditional and more or less impersonal powers. There exists in Washington a sense of responsibility for the health, safety, and well-being of the people. . . . I believe that we are at the dawn of a day when the average man, woman, and child in the United States will have an opportunity for a happier and richer life. And it is just and desirable that this should be so. . . . We are not here merely to endure a purgatorial existence in anticipation of a beatific eternity after the grave closes on us. We are here with hopes and aspirations and legitimate desires that we are entitled to have satisfied to at least a reasonable degree. Nor will such a social program as we are discussing cause a strain on our economic system.

**2. Herbert Johnson cartoon, *Saturday Evening Post*, 1935.**

**3. Federal Writers' Project interview with a WPA draftsman, Newburyport, Massachusetts, June 25, 1939.**

One reason people here don't like the WPA is because they don't understand it's not all bums and drunks and aliens! Nobody ever explains to them that they'd never have had the new High School they're so [. . .] proud of if it hadn't been for the WPA. They don't stop to figure that new brick sidewalks wouldn't be there, the shade trees wouldn't be all dressed up to look at along High Street and all around town, if it weren't for WPA projects. To most in this town, and I guess it's not much different in this, than any other New England place, WPA's just a racket, set up to give a bunch of loafers and drunks steady pay to indulge in their vices! They don't stop to consider that on WPA are men and women who have traveled places and seen things, been educated and found their jobs folded up and nothing to replace them with.

The Granger Collection, New York.

4. **Ben Shahn, WPA mural, 1938.** *This is part of a three-panel mural commissioned by the Works Progress Administration (WPA) and painted at a public school in Roosevelt, New Jersey, by the well-known artist Ben Shahn.*

Courtesy of Roosevelt Arts Project/Picture Research Consultants & Archives

5. **David E. Lilienthal, *TVA: Democracy on the March*, 1944.** *Written by the former chairman of the Tennessee Valley Authority.*

I believe men may learn to work in harmony with the forces of nature, neither despoiling what God has given nor helpless to put them to use. I believe in the great potentialities for well-being of the machine and technology and science; and though they do hold a real threat of enslavement and frustration for the human spirit, I believe those dangers can be averted. I believe that through the practice of democracy the world of technology holds out the greatest opportunity in all history for the development of the individual, according to his own talents, aspirations, and willingness to carry the responsibilities of a free man. . . .

Such are the things that have happened in the Tennessee Valley. Here men and science and organizational skills applied to the resources of waters, land, forests, and minerals have yielded great benefits for the people. And it is just such fruits of technology and resources that people all over the world will, more and more, demand for themselves. That people believe these things can be theirs — this it is that constitutes the real revolution of our time, the dominant political fact of the generation that lies ahead.

Sources: (1) Harold L. Ickes, *The New Democracy* (New York: W. W. Norton & Company Inc., 1934), 60–61; (3) Federal Writers' Project Life Histories, Library of Congress, lcweb2.loc.gov/ammem/wpaintro/wpahome.html; (5) David E. Lilienthal, *TVA: Democracy on the March* (New York: Harper & Row Publishers, 1944), xxii, 3.

## ANALYZING THE EVIDENCE

1. What sorts of reasons do the authors of sources 1 and 5 give for supporting New Deal programs? What does the "good life" look like in their view, and how is it connected to the New Deal?

2. What do sources 2 and 3 suggest about possible opposition to New Deal programs? What sorts of public burdens do New Deal opponents envision?

3. Consider source 4. What can we learn from a mural about the spirit of the New Deal? Identity specific elements of the mural and think about what they might signify about the society the muralist envisioned. What kind of faith in the federal government does the mural reveal?

## PUTTING IT ALL TOGETHER

Using evidence from the sources in this feature, alongside material from the chapter and from your knowledge of the period, write an essay in which you analyze Americans' attitudes toward New Deal public works projects. If they were positive or optimistic, what was the basis of their optimism? If they were critical, what was the basis of their criticism? From these sources, can you identify a governing spirit of New Deal reform?

representing the other major group of unions, favored organizing workers on a craft-by-craft basis. Both federations dramatically increased their membership in the second half of the 1930s.

Labor's new vitality translated into political action and a long-lasting alliance with the Democratic Party. The CIO helped fund Democratic campaigns in 1936, and its political action committee became a major Democratic contributor during the 1940s. These successes were real but limited. The labor movement did not become the dominant force in the United States that it was in Europe, and unions never enrolled a majority of American wageworkers. Antiunion employer groups such as the National Association of Manufacturers and the Chamber of Commerce remained powerful forces in American business life. After a decade of gains, organized labor remained an important, but secondary, force in American industry.

**Women and the New Deal**  Because policymakers saw the depression primarily as a crisis of male breadwinners, the New Deal did not directly challenge gender inequities. New Deal measures generally enhanced women's welfare, but few addressed their specific needs and concerns. However, the Roosevelt administration did welcome women into the higher ranks of government. Frances Perkins, the first woman named to a cabinet post, served as secretary of labor throughout Roosevelt's presidency. While relatively few, female appointees often worked to open up other opportunities in government for talented women.

The most prominent woman in American politics was the president's wife, Eleanor Roosevelt. In the 1920s, she had worked to expand positions for women in political parties, labor unions, and education. A tireless advocate for women's rights, during her years in the White House Mrs. Roosevelt emerged as an independent public figure and the most influential First Lady in the nation's history. Descending into coal mines to view working conditions, meeting with African Americans seeking antilynching laws, and talking to people on breadlines, she became the conscience of the New Deal, pushing her husband to do more for the disadvantaged. "I sometimes acted as a spur," Mrs. Roosevelt later reflected, "even though the spurring was not always wanted or welcome."

Without the intervention of Eleanor Roosevelt, Frances Perkins, and other prominent women, New Deal policymakers would have largely ignored the needs of women. A fourth of the National Recovery Act's employment rules set a lower minimum wage for women than for men performing the same jobs, and only 7 percent of the workers hired by the Civil Works Administration were female. The Civilian Conservation Corps excluded women entirely. Women fared better under the Works Progress Administration; at its peak, 405,000 women were on the payroll. Most Americans agreed with such policies. When Gallup pollsters in 1936 asked people whether wives should work outside the home when their husbands had jobs, 82 percent said no. Such sentiment reflected a persistent belief in women's secondary status in American economic life.

**African Americans Under the New Deal**  Across the nation, but especially in the South, African Americans held the lowest-paying jobs and faced harsh social and political discrimination. Though FDR did not fundamentally change this fact, he was the most popular president among African Americans since Abraham Lincoln. African Americans held 18 percent of WPA jobs, although they constituted 10 percent of the population. The Resettlement Administration, established in 1935 to help small farmers and tenants buy land, actively protected the rights of black tenant

**Roosevelts Visit Camp Tara**

Franklin Roosevelt was a wealthy patrician, but one of his great political skills was the ability to connect with ordinary Americans. His wife, Eleanor, shared a similar gift, perhaps to an even greater degree. In an era when staged photographs had become an important part of a politician's image-making, Roosevelt made certain to appear frequently in settings in which he mingled with the public. Here, he and Eleanor visit a vocational training camp for jobless women in 1934; FDR is seated on the far left while Eleanor greets two women standing beside the car. AP/Wide World Photos.

**COMPARE AND CONTRAST**
What aspects of the New Deal inspired ordinary Americans? What stymied their ambitions?

farmers. Black involvement in the New Deal, however, could not undo centuries of racial subordination, nor could it change the overwhelming power of southern whites in the Democratic Party.

Nevertheless, black Americans received significant benefits from New Deal relief programs and believed that the White House cared about their plight, which caused a momentous shift in their political allegiance. Since the Civil War, black voters had staunchly supported the Republican Party, the party of Abraham Lincoln, known as the Great Emancipator. Even in the depression year of 1932, they overwhelmingly supported Republican candidates. But in 1936, as part of the tidal wave of national support for FDR, northern African Americans gave Roosevelt 71 percent of their votes and have remained solidly Democratic ever since.

African Americans supported the New Deal partly because the Roosevelt administration appointed a number of black people to federal office, and an informal "black cabinet" of prominent African American intellectuals advised New Deal agencies. Among the most important appointees was Mary McLeod Bethune. Born in 1875 in South Carolina to former slaves, Bethune founded Bethune-Cookman College and served during the 1920s as president of the National Association of Colored Women. She joined the New Deal in 1935, confiding to a friend that she "believed in the democratic and humane program" of FDR. Americans, Bethune observed, had to become "accustomed to seeing Negroes in high places." Bethune had access to the White House and pushed continually for New Deal programs to help African Americans.

But the New Deal was limited in its approach to race. Roosevelt did not go further in support of black rights, because of both his own racial blinders and his need for the votes of the white southern Democrats in Congress — including powerful southern senators, many of whom held influential committee posts in Congress. Most New Deal programs reflected prevailing racial attitudes. Roosevelt and other New Dealers had to trim their proposals of measures that would substantially benefit African Americans. Civilian Conservation Corps camps segregated blacks, and most NRA rules did not protect black workers from discrimination. Both Social Security and the Wagner Act explicitly excluded the domestic and agricultural jobs held by most African Americans in the 1930s. Roosevelt also refused to support legislation making lynching a federal crime, which was one of the most pressing demands of African Americans in the 1930s. Between 1882 and 1930, more than 2,500 African Americans were lynched by white mobs in the southern

states, which means that statistically, one man, woman, or child was murdered every week for fifty years. But despite pleas from black leaders, and from Mrs. Roosevelt herself, FDR feared that southern white Democrats would block his other reforms in retaliation for such legislation.

If lynching embodied southern lawlessness, southern law was not much better. In an infamous 1931 case in Scottsboro, Alabama, nine young black men were accused of rape by two white women hitching a ride on a freight train. The women's stories contained many inconsistencies, but within weeks a white jury had convicted all nine defendants; eight received the death sentence. After the U.S. Supreme Court overturned the sentences because the defendants had been denied adequate legal counsel, five of the men were again convicted and sentenced to long prison terms. Across the country, the Scottsboro Boys, as they were known, inspired solidarity within African American communities. Among whites, the Communist Party took the lead in publicizing the case — and was one of the only white organizations to do so — helping to support the Scottsboro Defense Committee, which raised money for legal efforts on the defendants' behalf.

In southern agriculture, where many sharecroppers were black while landowners and government administrators were white, the Agricultural Adjustment Act hurt rather than helped the poorest African Americans. White landowners collected government subsidy checks but refused to distribute payments to their sharecroppers. Such practices forced 200,000 black families off the land. Some black farmers tried to protect themselves by joining the Southern Tenant Farmers Union (STFU), a biracial organization founded in 1934. "The same chain that holds you holds my people, too," an elderly black farmer reminded his white neighbors. But landowners had such economic power and such support from local sheriffs that the STFU could do little.

A generation of African American leaders came of age inspired by the New Deal's democratic promise. But it remained just a promise. From the outset, New Dealers wrestled with potentially fatal racial politics. Franklin Roosevelt and the Democratic Party depended heavily on white voters in the South, who were determined to maintain racial segregation and white supremacy. But many Democrats in the North and West — centers of New Deal liberalism — would come to oppose racial discrimination. This meant, ironically, that the nation's most liberal political forces and some of its most conservative political forces existed side by side in the same political party. Another thirty years

**Scottsboro Defendants**
The 1931 trial in Scottsboro, Alabama, of nine black youths accused of raping two white women became a symbol of the injustices African Americans faced in the South's legal system. Denied access to an attorney, the defendants were found guilty after a three-day trial, and eight were sentenced to death. When the U.S. Supreme Court overturned their convictions in 1932, the International Labor Defense Organization hired noted criminal attorney Samuel Leibowitz to argue the case. Leibowitz eventually won the acquittal of four defendants and jail sentences for the rest. This 1933 photograph, taken in a Decatur jail, shows Leibowitz conferring with Haywood Patterson, in front of the other eight defendants. Brown Brothers.

would pass before black Americans would gain an opportunity to reform U.S. racial laws and practices.

**Indian Policy**   New Deal reformers seized the opportunity to implement their vision for the future of Native Americans, with mixed results. Indian peoples had long been one of the nation's most disadvantaged and powerless groups. In 1934, the average individual Indian income was only $48 per year, and the Native American unemployment rate was three times the national average. The plight of Native Americans won the attention of the progressive commissioner of the Bureau of Indian Affairs (BIA), John Collier, an intellectual and critic of past BIA practices. Collier understood what Native Americans had long known: that the government's decades-long policy of forced assimilation, prohibition of Indian religions, and confiscation of Indian lands had left most tribes poor, isolated, and without basic self-determination.

Collier helped to write and push through Congress the **Indian Reorganization Act** of 1934, sometimes called the Indian New Deal. On the positive side, the law reversed the Dawes Act of 1887 (Chapter 16) by promoting Indian self-government through formal constitutions and democratically elected tribal councils. A majority of Indian peoples — some 181 tribes — accepted the reorganization policy, but 77 declined to participate, primarily because they preferred the traditional way of making decisions by consensus rather than by majority vote. Through the new law, Indians won a greater degree of religious freedom, and tribal governments regained their status as semisovereign dependent nations. When the latter policy was upheld by the courts, Indian people gained a measure of leverage that would have major implications for native rights in the second half of the twentieth century.

Like so many other federal Indian policies, however, the "Indian New Deal" was a mixed blessing. For some peoples, the act imposed a model of self-government that proved incompatible with tribal traditions and languages. The Papagos of southern Arizona, for instance, had no words for *budget* or

**Indian New Deal**

Commissioner of Indian Affairs John Collier poses with chiefs of the Blackfoot Indian tribe in 1934. Collier helped reform the way the U.S. federal government treated Native Americans. As part of what many called the Indian New Deal, Collier lobbied Congress to pass the Indian Reorganization Act. The act gave Indian tribes greater control over their own affairs and ended many of the most atrocious federal practices, such as forcing Indian children into white-run boarding schools and dividing up and selling reservation land. The legislation's long-term results were mixed, but it signaled the beginning of greater autonomy for Indian tribes across the country. © Bettmann/Corbis.

*representative*, and they made no linguistic distinctions among *law*, *rule*, *charter*, and *constitution*. In another case, the nation's largest tribe, the Navajos, rejected the BIA's new policy, largely because the government was simultaneously reducing Navajo livestock to protect the Boulder Dam project. In theory, the new policy gave Indians a much greater degree of self-determination. In practice, however, although some tribes did benefit, the BIA and Congress continued to interfere in internal Indian affairs and retained financial control over reservation governments.

**Struggles in the West**   By the 1920s, agriculture in California had become a big business — intensive, diversified, and export-oriented. Large-scale corporate-owned farms produced specialty crops — lettuce, tomatoes, peaches, grapes, and cotton — whose staggered harvests allowed the use of transient laborers. Thousands of workers, immigrants from Mexico and Asia and white migrants from the midwestern states,

trooped from farm to farm and from crop to crop during the long picking season. Some migrants settled in the rapidly growing cities along the West Coast, especially the sprawling metropolis of Los Angeles. Under both Hoover and FDR, the federal government promoted the "repatriation" of Mexican citizens — their deportation to Mexico. Between 1929 and 1937, approximately half a million people of Mexican descent were deported. But historians estimate that more than 60 percent of these were legal U.S. citizens, making the government's actions constitutionally questionable.

Despite the deportations, many Mexican Americans benefitted from the New Deal and generally held Roosevelt and the Democratic Party in high regard. People of Mexican descent, like other Americans, took jobs with the WPA and the CCC, or received relief in the worst years of the depression. The National Youth Administration (NYA), which employed young people from families on relief and sponsored a variety of school programs, was especially important in

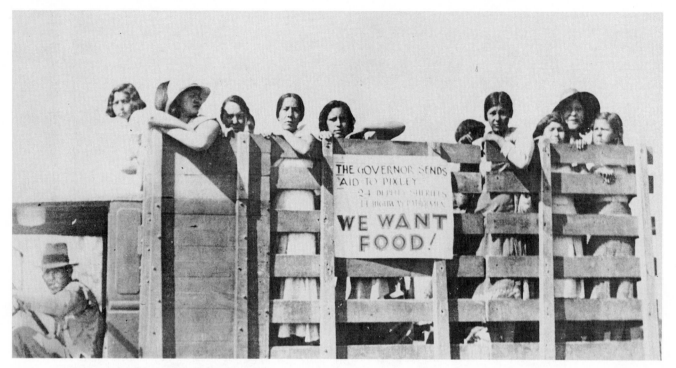

THE GOVERNOR SENDS
AID TO PIXLEY
24 DEPUTY SHERIFFS
11 HIGHWAY PATROLMEN

WE WANT
FOOD!

**Mexican American Farm Workers**

Among the most hard-pressed workers during the Great Depression were those who labored in the nation's agricultural field, orchards, and processing plants. Agriculture was a big-time corporate business by the 1930s, and in California and other parts of the Southwest it employed hundreds of thousands of poor Mexican Americans and Mexican immigrants. Seizing on the spirit of social protest sweeping the country in the early 1930s, many of these workers went on strike for better wages and working conditions. Here, women from Mexican American communities are heading to the cotton fields near Corcoran, California, to urge workers to join a major strike of cotton pickers. Though the workers in Corcoran won some wage improvements in this 1933 strike, the fierce battle between employers and workers in American agriculture was far from over and continues to this day. Library of Congress.

southwestern cities. In California, the Mexican American Movement (MAM), a youth-focused organization, received assistance from liberal New Dealers. New Deal programs did not fundamentally improve the migrant farm labor system under which so many people of Mexican descent labored, but Mexicans joined the New Deal coalition in large numbers because of the Democrats' commitment to ordinary Americans. "Franklin D. Roosevelt's name was the spark that started thousands of Spanish-speaking persons to the polls," noted one Los Angeles activist.

Men and women of Asian descent — mostly from China, Japan, and the Philippines — formed a small minority of the American population but were a significant presence in some western cities. Immigrants from Japan and China had long faced discrimination. A 1913 California law prohibited them from owning land. Japanese farmers, who specialized in fruit and vegetable crops, circumvented this restriction by putting land titles in the names of their American-born children. As the depression cut farm prices and racial

discrimination excluded young Japanese Americans from nonfarm jobs, about 20 percent of the immigrants returned to Japan.

Chinese Americans were less prosperous than their Japanese counterparts. Only 3 percent of Chinese Americans worked in professional and technical positions, and discrimination barred them from most industrial jobs. In San Francisco, the majority of Chinese worked in small businesses: restaurants, laundries, and firms that imported textiles and ceramics. During the depression, they turned for assistance to Chinese social organizations such as *huiguan* (district associations) and to the city government; in 1931, about one-sixth of San Francisco's Chinese population was receiving public aid. But few Chinese benefitted from the New Deal. Until the repeal of the Exclusion Act in 1943, Chinese immigrants were classified as "aliens ineligible for citizenship" and therefore were excluded from most federal programs.

Because Filipino immigrants came from a U.S. territory, they were not affected by the ban on Asian immigration enacted in 1924. During the 1920s, their numbers swelled to about 50,000, many of whom worked as laborers on large corporate-owned farms. As the depression cut wages, Filipino immigration slowed to a trickle, and it was virtually cut off by the Tydings-McDuffie Act of 1934. The act granted independence to the Philippines (which since 1898 had been an American colony), classified all Filipinos in the United States as aliens, and restricted immigration from the Philippines to fifty people per year.

## Reshaping the Environment

Attention to natural resources was a dominant theme of the New Deal, and the shaping of the landscape was among its most visible legacies. Franklin Roosevelt and Interior Secretary Harold Ickes saw themselves as conservationists in the tradition of FDR's cousin, Theodore Roosevelt. In an era before environmentalism, FDR practiced what he called the "gospel of conservation." The president cared primarily about making the land—and other natural resources, such as trees and water—better serve human needs. National policy stressed scientific land management and ecological balance. Preserving wildlife and wilderness was of secondary importance. Under Roosevelt, the federal government both responded to environmental crises and

reshaped the use of natural resources, especially water, in the United States.

**The Dust Bowl**  Among the most hard-pressed citizens during the depression were farmers fleeing the "**dust bowl**" of the Great Plains. Between 1930 and 1941, a severe drought afflicted the semiarid states of Oklahoma, Texas, New Mexico, Colorado, Arkansas, and Kansas. Farmers in these areas had stripped the land of its native vegetation, which destroyed the delicate ecology of the plains. To grow wheat and other crops, they had pushed agriculture beyond the natural limits of the soil, making their land vulnerable, in times of drought, to wind erosion of the topsoil (Map 23.4). When the winds came, huge clouds of thick dust rolled over the land, turning the day into night. This ecological disaster prompted a mass exodus. At least 350,000 "Okies" (so called whether or not they were from Oklahoma) loaded their belongings into cars and trucks and headed to California. John Steinbeck's novel *The Grapes of Wrath* (1939) immortalized them, and New Deal photographer Dorothea Lange's haunting images of California migrant camps made them the public face of the depression's human toll.

> **IDENTIFY CAUSES**
> Why did the natural environment receive so much attention under New Deal programs, and with what result?

## MAP 23.4
### The Dust Bowl and Federal Building Projects in the West, 1930–1941

A U.S. Weather Bureau scientist called the drought of the 1930s "the worst in the climatological history of the country." Conditions were especially severe in the southern plains, where farming on marginal land threatened the environment even before the drought struck. As farm families migrated west on U.S. Route 66, the federal government began a series of massive building projects that provided flood control, irrigation, electric power, and transportation facilities to residents of the states of the Far West.

**The Human Face of the Great Depression**

*Migrant Mother* by Dorothea Lange is one of the most famous documentary photographs of the 1930s. On assignment for the Resettlement Administration, Lange spent only ten minutes in a pea-pickers' camp in Nipomo, California. There she captured this image (though not the name) of the woman whose despair and resignation she so powerfully recorded. In the 1970s the woman was identified as Florence Thompson, a native Cherokee from Oklahoma, who disagreed with Lange's recollections of the circumstances of the taking of the photograph. Thompson and her family had left Nipomo, however, by the time the publication of this image sparked a large relief effort directed at the camp's migrant workers. Library of Congress.

Roosevelt and Ickes believed that poor land practices made for poor people. Under their direction, government agencies tackled the dust bowl's human causes. Agents from the newly created Soil Conservation Service, for instance, taught farmers to prevent soil erosion by tilling hillsides along the contours of the land. They also encouraged (and sometimes paid) farmers to take certain commercial crops out of production and plant soil-preserving grasses instead. One of the U.S. Forest Service's most widely publicized programs was the Shelterbelts, the planting of 220 million trees running north along the 99th meridian from Abilene, Texas, to the Canadian border. Planted as a windbreak, the trees also prevented soil erosion. A variety of government agencies, from the CCC to the U.S. Department of Agriculture, lent their expertise to establishing sound farming practices in the plains.

**Tennessee Valley Authority** The most extensive New Deal environmental undertaking was the **Tennessee Valley Authority** (TVA), which Roosevelt saw as the first step in modernizing the South. Funded by Congress in 1933, the TVA integrated flood control, reforestation, electricity generation, and agricultural and industrial development. The dams and their hydroelectric plants provided cheap electric power for homes and factories as well as ample recreational opportunities for the valley's residents. The massive project won praise around the world (Map 23.5).

The TVA was an integral part of the Roosevelt administration's effort to keep farmers on the land by enhancing the quality of rural life. The **Rural Electrification Administration** (REA), established in 1935, was also central to that goal. Fewer than one-tenth of the nation's 6.8 million farms had electricity. The REA addressed this problem by promoting nonprofit farm cooperatives that offered loans to farmers to install power lines. By 1940, 40 percent of the nation's farms had electricity; a decade later, 90 percent did. Electricity brought relief from the drudgery and isolation of farm life. Electric irons, vacuum cleaners, and washing machines eased women's burdens, and radios brightened the lives of the entire family. Along with the automobile and the movies, electricity broke down the barriers between urban and rural life.

**Grand Coulee** As the nation's least populated but fastest-growing region, the West benefitted enormously from the New Deal's attention to the environment. With the largest number of state and federal parks in the country, the West gained countless trails, bridges, cabins, and other recreational facilities, laying the groundwork for the post–World War II expansion of western tourism. On the Colorado River, Boulder Dam (later renamed Hoover Dam) was completed in 1935 with Public Works Administration funds; the dam generated power for the region's growing cities such as Las Vegas, Los Angeles, and Phoenix.

The largest project in the West, however, took shape in an obscure corner of Washington State, where the PWA and the Bureau of Reclamation built the Grand Coulee Dam on the Columbia River. When it was completed in 1941, Grand Coulee was the largest electricity-producing structure in the world, and its 150-mile lake provided irrigation for the state's major crops: apples, cherries, pears, potatoes, and wheat. Inspired by the dam and the modernizing spirit of the

**MAP 23.5**

**The Tennessee Valley Authority, 1933–1952**

The Tennessee Valley Authority was one of the New Deal's most far-reaching environmental projects. Between 1933 and 1952, the TVA built twenty dams and improved five others, taming the flood-prone Tennessee River and its main tributaries. The cheap hydro-electric power generated by the dams brought electricity to industries as well as hundreds of thousands of area residents, and artificial lakes provided extensive recreational facilities. Widely praised at the time, the TVA came under attack in the 1970s for its practice of strip mining and the pollution caused by its power plants and chemical factories.

New Deal, folk singer Woody Guthrie wrote a song about the Columbia. "Your power is turning our darkness to dawn," he sang, "so roll on, Columbia, roll on!"

New Deal projects that enhanced people's enjoyment of the natural environment can be seen today throughout the country. CCC and WPA workers built the famous Blue Ridge Parkway, which connects the Shenandoah National Park in Virginia with the Great Smoky Mountains National Park in North Carolina. In the West, government workers built the San Francisco Zoo, Berkeley's Tilden Park, and the canals of San Antonio. The Civilian Conservation Corps helped to complete the East Coast's Appalachian Trail and the West Coast's Pacific Crest Trail through the Sierra Nevada. In state parks across the country, cabins, shelters, picnic areas, lodges, and observation towers stand as monuments to the New Deal ethos of recreation coexisting with nature.

## The New Deal and the Arts

In response to the Great Depression, many American writers and artists redefined their relationship to society. Never had there been a decade, critic Malcolm Cowley suggested in 1939, "when literary events followed so closely on the flying coat-tails of social events." New Deal administrators encouraged artists to create projects that would be of interest to the entire community, not just the cultured elite. Encouraged by the popular New Deal slogan "Art for the millions," artists painted murals in hundreds of public buildings. The WPA's Federal Art Project gave work to many young artists who would become the twentieth century's

leading painters, muralists, and sculptors. Jackson Pollock, Alice Neel, Willem de Kooning, and Louise Nevelson all received support. The Federal Music Project and Federal Writers' Project (FWP) employed 15,000 musicians and 5,000 writers, respectively. Among the latter were Saul Bellow, Ralph Ellison, and John Cheever, who became great American writers. The FWP also collected oral histories, including two thousand narratives by former slaves. The black folklorist and novelist Zora Neale Hurston finished three novels while in the Florida FWP, among them *Their Eyes Were Watching God* (1937). Richard Wright won the 1938 *Story* magazine prize for the best tale by a WPA writer and went on to complete *Native Son* (1940), a searing novel about white racism. Similarly, the Federal Theatre Project (FTP) nurtured such talented directors, actors, and playwrights as Orson Welles, John Huston, and Arthur Miller.

## The Legacies of the New Deal

The New Deal addressed the Great Depression by restoring hope and promising security. FDR and Congress created a powerful social-welfare state that took unprecedented responsibility for the well-being of American citizens. During the 1930s, millions of people began to pay taxes directly to the Social Security Administration, and more than one-third of the population received direct government assistance from federal programs, including old-age pensions, unemployment compensation, farm loans, relief work, and mortgage guarantees. New legislation regulated the stock market, reformed the Federal Reserve System,

**Grand Coulee Dam**

This extraordinary photo from a *Life* magazine essay shows workers hitching a ride on a 13-ton conduit as it is lowered into place on the Grand Coulee Dam in Washington State. Dozens of dams were constructed across the country under the auspices of various New Deal programs, but none were more majestic than two in the West: Boulder Dam (renamed Hoover Dam in 1947) and Grand Coulee. Built to harness the awesome power of the Columbia River as it rushed to the Pacific, Grand Coulee would ultimately provide electric power to Seattle, Portland, and other West Coast cities and new irrigation waters for Washington's apple and cherry orchards, among many other crops. Library of Congress.

and subjected business corporations to federal regulation. The New Deal's pattern of government involvement in social life would persist for the rest of the twentieth century. In the 1960s, Lyndon Johnson and the "Great Society" Congress dramatically expanded social-welfare programs, most of which remained intact in the wake of the "Reagan Revolution" of the 1980s.

Like all other major social transformations, the New Deal was criticized both by those who thought it did too much and by those who believed it did too little. Conservatives, who prioritized limited government and individual freedom, pointed out that the New Deal state intruded deeply into the personal and financial lives of citizens and the affairs of business. Conversely, advocates of social-welfare liberalism complained that the New Deal's safety net had too many holes: no national health-care system, welfare programs that excluded domestic workers and farm laborers, and state governments that often

**EXPLAIN CONSEQUENCES**
What was the New Deal's long-term legacy?

limited the benefits distributed under New Deal programs.

Whatever the merits of its critics, the New Deal unquestionably transformed the American political landscape. From 1896 to 1932, the Republican Party had commanded the votes of a majority of Americans. That changed as Franklin Roosevelt's magnetic personality and innovative programs brought millions of voters into the Democratic fold. Democratic recruits included first- and second-generation immigrants from southern and central Europe — Italians, Poles, Slovaks, and Jews — as well as African American migrants to northern cities. Organized labor aligned itself with a Democratic administration that had recognized unions as a legitimate force in modern industrial life. The elderly and the unemployed, assisted by the Social Security Act, likewise supported FDR. This New Deal coalition of ethnic groups, city dwellers, organized labor, African Americans, and a cross section of the middle class formed the nucleus of the northern Democratic Party and supported additional liberal reforms in the decades to come.

# SUMMARY

We have seen how Franklin Delano Roosevelt's First New Deal focused on stimulating recovery, providing relief to the unemployed, and regulating banks and other financial institutions. The Second New Deal was different. Influenced by the persistence of the depression and the growing popularity of Huey Long's Share Our Wealth proposals, Roosevelt promoted social-welfare legislation that provided Americans with economic security.

We also explored the impact of the New Deal on various groups of citizens, especially African Americans, women, and unionized workers. Our survey paid particular attention to the lives of the Mexicans, Asians, and Okies who worked in the farms and factories of California. Because of New Deal assistance, the mem-

bers of those groups gravitated toward the Democratic Party. The party's coalition of ethnic workers, African Americans, farmers, parts of the middle classes, and white southerners gave FDR and other Democrats a landslide victory in 1936.

Finally, we examined the accomplishments of the New Deal. In 1933, New Deal programs resolved the banking crisis while preserving capitalist institutions. Subsequently, these programs expanded the federal government and, through the Social Security system, farm subsidy programs, and public works projects, launched federal policies that were important to nearly every American. Great dams and electricity projects sponsored by the Tennessee Valley Authority, the Works Progress Administration in the West, and the Rural Electrification Administration permanently improved the quality of life for the nation's citizens.

# C H A P T E R   R E V I E W

**MAKE IT STICK**   Go to **LearningCurve** to retain what you've read.

## TERMS TO KNOW   Identify and explain the significance of each term below.

### Key Concepts and Events

**Smoot-Hawley Tariff** (p. 736)

**Bonus Army** (p. 738)

**fireside chats** (p. 740)

**Hundred Days** (p. 740)

**Glass-Steagall Act** (p. 740)

**Agricultural Adjustment Act** (p. 741)

**National Recovery Administration** (p. 741)

**Public Works Administration** (p. 741)

**Civilian Conservation Corps** (p. 741)

**Federal Housing Administration** (p. 744)

**Securities and Exchange Commission** (p. 745)

**Liberty League** (p. 746)

**National Association of Manufacturers** (p. 746)

**Townsend Plan** (p. 747)

**welfare state** (p. 747)

**Wagner Act** (p. 747)

**Social Security Act** (p. 747)

**classical liberalism** (p. 749)

**Works Progress Administration** (p. 749)

**Roosevelt recession** (p. 751)

**Keynesian economics** (p. 751)

**Indian Reorganization Act** (p. 756)

**dust bowl** (p. 759)

**Tennessee Valley Authority** (p. 760)

**Rural Electrification Administration** (p. 760)

### Key People

**Herbert Hoover** (p. 736)

**Franklin Delano Roosevelt** (p. 739)

**Father Charles Coughlin** (p. 747)

**Huey Long** (p. 747)

**Frances Perkins** (p. 754)

**Eleanor Roosevelt** (p. 754)

**Mary McLeod Bethune** (p. 755)

**John Collier** (p. 756)

## REVIEW QUESTIONS
Answer these questions to demonstrate your understanding of the chapter's main ideas.

1. Some historians have seen the New Deal as a natural evolution of progressive reforms from earlier in the century. Others have argued that it represented a revolution in social values and government institutions. Do you view the New Deal as an extension of progressivism, or a radical break with the past? Provide evidence for your argument.

2. How did the lives of women, workers, and racial and ethnic minority groups change during the Great Depression? What role did the New Deal play in helping those groups of Americans?

3. **THEMATIC UNDERSTANDING** Review the events listed under "Politics and Power," "Identity," and "Ideas, Beliefs, and Culture" on the thematic timeline on page 671. In what ways did the New Deal coalition and the emergence of the welfare state change the character of American politics? Why did Republicans oppose the Democratic initiatives, and how did these public debates shape visions of American national identity?

## MAKING CONNECTIONS
Recognize the larger developments and continuities within and across chapters by answering these questions.

1. **ACROSS TIME AND PLACE** People often view the New Deal as a set of government programs and policies enacted by President Roosevelt and Congress. In this version, change comes from above. Yet there is also evidence that ordinary Americans played an important role in inspiring and championing aspects of the New Deal. Find several specific examples of this, and think about the possible connections between the struggles, protests, and actions of ordinary people and the programs of the New Deal.

2. **VISUAL EVIDENCE** Consider two images: the famous Dorothea Lange photograph of Florence Thompson on page 760 and the photograph of workers building the Grand Coulee Dam on page 762. Why is the first image more frequently associated with the Great Depression than the second? How would it change our understanding of the era if we made the second photograph the iconic representation of the depression?

## MORE TO EXPLORE
Start here to learn more about the events discussed in this chapter.

Kristen Downey, *The Woman Behind the New Deal: The Life of Frances Perkins, FDR's Secretary of Labor and His Moral Conscience* (2009). Discusses women and the New Deal years as seen through the life and career of an important reformer.

Ira Katznelson, *Fear Itself: The New Deal and the Origins of Our Times* (2013). A powerful explanation of the New Deal's racial politics.

Robert S. McElvaine, *The Great Depression* (1984) and *Down & Out in the Great Depression* (1983). The first is an excellent overview of the depression and the New Deal; the second contains letters written by ordinary people.

James F. Simon, *FDR and Chief Justice Hughes: The President, the Supreme Court, and the Epic Battle over the New Deal* (2012). Shows the legal controversies surrounding FDR's expansion of the state.

John Steinbeck, *The Grapes of Wrath* (1939); Josephine Herbst, *Pity Is Not Enough* (1933); and Richard Wright, *Native Son* (1940). Classic depression-era novels.

For extensive collections of 1930s materials, see the "New Deal Network" at **newdeal.feri.org**; government-commissioned art at **archives.gov /exhibits/new_deal_for_the_arts**; and the slave narratives collected by the Federal Writers' Project at **memory.loc.gov/ammem/snhtml**.

## TIMELINE

Ask yourself why this chapter begins and ends with these dates and then identify the links among related events.

| | |
|---|---|
| **1930** | • Smoot-Hawley Tariff |
| **1931–1937** | • Scottsboro case: trials and appeals |
| **1932** | • Bonus Army marches on Washington, D.C.<br>• Franklin Delano Roosevelt elected president |
| **1933** | • FDR's inaugural address and first fireside chats<br>• Emergency Banking Act begins the Hundred Days<br>• FDR takes U.S. off the gold standard<br>• Civilian Conservation Corps (CCC) created<br>• Agricultural Adjustment Act (AAA)<br>• National Industrial Recovery Act (NIRA)<br>• Tennessee Valley Authority (TVA) established<br>• Townsend Clubs promote Old Age Revolving Pension Plan |
| **1934** | • Securities and Exchange Commission (SEC) created<br>• Southern Tenant Farmers Union (STFU) founded<br>• Indian Reorganization Act<br>• Senator Huey Long promotes Share Our Wealth Society<br>• Father Charles Coughlin founds National Union for Social Justice |
| **1935** | • Supreme Court voids NIRA in *Schechter v. United States*<br>• National Labor Relations (Wagner) Act<br>• Social Security Act creates old-age pension system<br>• Works Progress Administration (WPA) created<br>• Rural Electrification Administration (REA) established<br>• Supreme Court voids Agricultural Adjustment Act<br>• Congress of Industrial Organizations (CIO) formed |
| **1936** | • Landslide reelection of FDR marks peak of New Deal power |
| **1937** | • FDR's Supreme Court plan fails |
| **1937–1938** | • "Roosevelt recession" raises unemployment |

**KEY TURNING POINTS:** Identify two critical turning points between 1934 and 1937, when the New Deal faced specific challenges.

# The World at War
# 1937–1945

The Second World War was the defining international event of the twentieth century. Battles raged across six of the world's seven continents and all of its oceans. It killed more than 50 million people and wounded hundreds of millions more. When it was over, the industrial economies and much of the infrastructure of Europe and East Asia lay in ruins. Waged with both technologically advanced weapons and massive armies, the war involved every industrialized power in Europe, North America, and Asia, as well as dozens of other nations, many of them colonies of the industrialized countries.

The military conflict began on two continents: in Asia with Japan's 1937 invasion of China across the Sea of Japan, and in Europe with the 1939 blitzkrieg (lightning war) conducted by Germany in Poland. It ended in 1945 after American planes dropped two atomic bombs, the product of stunning yet ominous scientific breakthroughs, on the Japanese cities of Hiroshima and Nagasaki. In between these demonstrations of technological prowess and devastating power, huge armies confronted and destroyed one another in the fields of France, the forests and steppes of Russia, the river valleys of China, the volcanic islands of the Pacific, and the deserts of North Africa.

"Armed defense of democratic existence is now being gallantly waged in four continents," President Franklin Delano Roosevelt told the nation in January 1941. After remaining neutral for several years, the United States would commit to that "armed defense." Both FDR and British prime minister Winston Churchill came to see the war as a defense of democratic values from the threat posed by German, Italian, and Japanese fascism. For them, the brutal conflict was the "good war." When the grim reality of the Jewish Holocaust came to light, U.S. participation in the war seemed even more just. But as much as it represented a struggle between democracy and fascism, it was also inescapably a war to maintain British, French, and Dutch control of colonies in Africa, India, the Middle East, and Southeast Asia. By 1945, democracy in the industrialized world had been preserved, and a new Euro-American alliance had taken hold; the future of the vast European colonial empires, however, remained unresolved.

On the U.S. domestic front, World War II ended the Great Depression, hastened profound social changes, and expanded the scope and authority of the federal government. Racial politics and gender roles shifted under the weight of wartime migration and labor shortages. The pace of urbanization increased as millions of Americans uprooted themselves and moved hundreds or thousands of miles to join the military or to take a war job. A stronger, more robust federal government, the product of a long, hard-fought war, would remain in place to fight an even longer, more expensive, and potentially more dangerous Cold War in the ensuing years. These developments, which accelerated transformations already under way, would have repercussions far into the postwar decades.

**IDENTIFY THE BIG IDEA**
How did World War II transform the United States domestically and change its relationship with the world?

**Black Mechanics in Tuskegee, Alabama** World War II was a "total war," fought on seven continents by hundreds of millions of people and massive national armies. Though a late arrival to the conflict, the United States played a critical role in defeating the Axis powers. Here, African American soldiers in Tuskegee, Alabama, make engine adjustments for a training flight. Jeff Ethell Color Archives.

# The Road to War

The Great Depression disrupted economic life around the world and brought the collapse of traditional political institutions. In response, an antidemocratic movement known as **fascism**, which had originated in Italy during the 1920s, developed in Germany, Spain, and Japan. By the mid-1930s, these nations had instituted authoritarian, militaristic governments led by powerful dictators: Benito Mussolini in Italy, Adolf Hitler in Nazi Germany, Francisco Franco in Spain, and, after 1940, Hideki Tojo in Japan. As early as 1936, President Roosevelt warned that other peoples had "sold their heritage of freedom" and urged Americans to work for "the survival of democracy" both at home and abroad. Constrained by strong isolationist sentiment, by 1940 FDR was cautiously leading the nation toward war against the fascist powers.

## The Rise of Fascism

World War II had its roots in the settlement of World War I. Germany struggled under the harsh terms of the Treaty of Versailles, and Japan and Italy had their desire for overseas empires thwarted by the treaty makers. Faced with the expansive ambitions and deep resentments of those countries, the League of Nations, the collective security system established at Versailles, proved unable to maintain the existing international order.

Fascism, as instituted in Germany by Hitler, combined a centralized, authoritarian state, a doctrine of Aryan racial supremacy, and intense nationalism in a call for the spiritual reawakening of the German people. Fascist leaders worldwide disparaged parliamentary government, independent labor movements, and individual rights. They opposed both the economic collectivism of the Soviet Union — where, in theory, the state managed the economy to ensure social equality — and the competitive capitalist economies of the United States and Western Europe. Fascist movements arose around the world in the 1930s but managed to achieve power in only a handful of countries. Those countries were at the center of global war making in the 1930s.

**Japan and Italy**    The first challenge came from Japan. To become an industrial power, Japan required raw materials and overseas markets. Like the Western European powers and the United States before it, Japan embraced an expansionary foreign policy in pursuit of colonial possessions and overseas influence. In 1931, its troops occupied Manchuria, an industrialized province in northern China, and in 1937 the Japanese launched a full-scale invasion of China. In both instances, the League of Nations condemned Japan's actions but did nothing to stop them.

Japan's defiance of the League encouraged a fascist leader half a world away: Italy's Benito Mussolini, who had come to power in 1922. Il Duce (The Leader), as Mussolini was known, had long denounced the Versailles treaty, which denied Italy's colonial claims in Africa and the Middle East after World War I. As in Japan, the Italian fascists desired overseas colonies for raw materials, markets, and national prestige. In 1935, Mussolini invaded Ethiopia, one of the few remaining independent countries in Africa. Ethiopian emperor Haile Selassie appealed to the League of Nations, but the League's verbal condemnation and limited sanctions, its only real leverage, did not stop Italy from taking control of Ethiopia in 1936.

**Hitler's Germany**    Germany, however, posed the gravest threat to the existing world order. Huge World War I reparation payments, economic depression, fear of communism, labor unrest, and rising unemployment fueled the ascent of Adolf Hitler and his **National Socialist (Nazi) Party**. When Hitler became chancellor of Germany in 1933, the Reichstag (the German legislature) granted him dictatorial powers to deal with the economic crisis. Hitler promptly outlawed other political parties, arrested many of his political rivals, and declared himself führer (leader). Under Nazi control, the Reichstag invested all legislative power in Hitler's hands.

Hitler's goal was nothing short of European domination and world power, as he had made clear in his 1925 book *Mein Kampf* (*My Struggle*). The book outlined his plans to overturn the territorial settlements of the Versailles treaty, unite Germans living throughout central Europe in a great German fatherland, and annex large areas of Eastern Europe. The "inferior races" who lived in these regions — Jews, Gypsies, and Slavs — would be removed or subordinated to the German "master race." These territories would provide Germany with what Hitler called "lebensraum" — a new region of settlement and farming and a source of natural resources. A virulent anti-Semite, Hitler had long blamed Jews for Germany's problems. Once in power, he began a sustained and brutal persecution of Jews, which expanded into a campaign of extermination in the early 1940s.

In 1935, Hitler began to rearm Germany, in violation of the Versailles treaty. No one stopped him. In

**IDENTIFY CAUSES**
What motivated Japanese, Italian, and German expansionism?

**Adolf Hitler**

Adolf Hitler salutes German troops during a parade at the Nazi Party's annual congress at Nuremberg. German fascism reveled in great public spectacles, such as the famous Nuremberg rallies held every year between the early 1920s and the late 1930s. Hitler used these mass rallies, at which tens and sometimes hundreds of thousands of soldiers and civilians gathered, to build wide support for his policies of aggressive militarism abroad and suppression of Jews and other minorities at home. Getty Images.

1936, he sent troops into the Rhineland, a demilitarized zone under the terms of Versailles. Again, France and Britain took no action. Later that year, Hitler and Mussolini formed the **Rome-Berlin Axis**, a political and military alliance between the two fascist nations. Also in 1936, Germany signed a pact to create a military alliance with Japan against the Soviet Union. With these alliances in place, and with France and Great Britain reluctant to oppose him, Hitler had seized the military advantage in Europe by 1937.

## War Approaches

As Hitler pushed his initiatives in Europe, which was mired in economic depression as deeply as the United States, the Roosevelt administration faced widespread isolationist sentiment at home. In part, this desire to avoid European entanglements reflected disillusion with American participation in World War I. In 1934, Gerald P. Nye, a progressive Republican senator from North Dakota, launched an investigation into the profits of munitions makers during that war. Nye's committee alleged that arms manufacturers (popularly labeled "merchants of death") had maneuvered President Wilson into World War I.

Although Nye's committee failed to prove its charge against weapon makers, its factual findings prompted an isolationist-minded Congress to pass a series of acts to prevent the nation from being drawn into another overseas war. The **Neutrality Act of 1935** imposed an embargo on selling arms to warring countries and declared that Americans traveling on the ships of belligerent nations did so at their own risk. In 1936, Congress banned loans to belligerents, and in 1937 it imposed a "cash-and-carry" requirement: if a warring country wanted to purchase nonmilitary goods from the United States, it had to pay cash and carry them in its own ships, keeping the United States out of potentially dangerous naval warfare.

Americans for the most part had little enthusiasm for war, and a wide variety of groups and individuals espoused isolationism. Many isolationists looked to Republican Ohio senator Robert Taft, who distrusted both Roosevelt and European nations with equal conviction, or to the aviator hero Charles A. Lindbergh, who delivered impassioned speeches against intervention in Europe. Some isolationists, such as the conservative National Legion of Mothers of America, combined anticommunism, Christian morality, and even anti-Semitism. Isolationists were primarily

**Charles Lindbergh Cartoon**

Charles Lindbergh, the first person to fly solo nonstop across the Atlantic Ocean, was an American hero in the 1930s. In 1941, he had become the public face of the America First Committee, which was determined the keep the United States from entering the wars raging in Europe and Asia. In this political cartoon from October 1941, Lindbergh is shown standing on a soapbox labeled "Fascism," looking up at the figure of "Democracy." The implication is that Lindbergh had been fooled by German propaganda into taking its side. Less than two months after the cartoon appeared, Japan attacked Pearl Harbor, and isolationist sentiment all but disappeared in the United States. Library of Congress.

conservatives, but a contingent of progressives (or liberals) opposed America's involvement in the war on pacifist or moral grounds. Whatever their philosophies, ardent isolationists forced Roosevelt to approach the brewing war cautiously.

**The Popular Front**   Other Americans responded to the rise of European fascism by advocating U.S. intervention. Some of the most prominent Americans pushing for greater involvement in Europe, even if it meant war, were affiliated with the **Popular Front.** Fearful of German and Japanese aggression, the Soviet Union instructed Communists in Western Europe and the United States to join with liberals in a broad coalition opposing fascism. This Popular Front supported various international causes—backing the Loyalists in their fight against fascist leader Francisco Franco in the Spanish Civil War (1936–1939), for example, even

as the United States, France, and Britain remained neutral.

In the United States, the Popular Front drew from a wide range of social groups. The American Communist Party, which had increased its membership to 100,000 as the depression revealed flaws in the capitalist system, led the way. African American civil rights activists, trade unionists, left-wing writers and intellectuals, and even a few New Deal administrators also joined the coalition. In time, however, many supporters in the United States grew uneasy with the Popular Front because of the rigidity of Communists and the brutal political repression in the Soviet Union under Joseph Stalin. Nevertheless, Popular Front activists were among a small but vocal group of Americans encouraging Roosevelt to take a stronger stand against European fascism.

**The Failure of Appeasement**   Encouraged by the weak worldwide response to the invasions of China, Ethiopia, and the Rhineland, and emboldened by British and French neutrality during the Spanish Civil War, Hitler grew more aggressive in 1938. He sent troops to annex German-speaking Austria while making clear his intention to seize part of Czechoslovakia. Because Czechoslovakia had an alliance with France, war seemed imminent. But at the **Munich Conference** in September 1938, Britain and France capitulated, agreeing to let Germany annex the Sudetenland—a German-speaking border area of Czechoslovakia—in return for Hitler's pledge to seek no more territory. The agreement, declared British prime minister Neville Chamberlain, guaranteed "peace for our time." Hitler drew a different conclusion, telling his generals: "Our enemies are small fry. I saw them in Munich."

Within six months, Hitler's forces had overrun the rest of Czechoslovakia and were threatening to march into Poland. Realizing that their policy of appeasement—capitulating to Hitler's demands—had been disastrous, Britain and France warned Hitler that further aggression meant war. Then, in August 1939, Hitler and Stalin shocked the world by signing a mutual nonaggression pact. For Hitler, this pact was crucial, as it meant that Germany would not have to wage a two-front war against Britain and France in the west and the Soviet Union in the east. On September 1, 1939, Hitler launched a blitzkrieg against Poland. Two days later, Britain and France declared war on Germany. World War II had officially begun.

Two days after the European war started, the United States declared its neutrality. But President Roosevelt made no secret of his sympathies. When war broke out in 1914, Woodrow Wilson had told Americans to be neutral "in thought as well as in action." FDR, by contrast, now said: "This nation will remain a neutral nation, but I cannot ask that every American remain neutral in thought as well." The overwhelming majority of Americans — some 84 percent, according to a poll in 1939 — supported Britain and France rather than Germany, but most wanted America to avoid another European war.

At first, the need for U.S. intervention seemed remote. After Germany conquered Poland in September 1939, calm settled over Europe. Then, on April 9, 1940, German forces invaded Denmark and Norway. In May, the Netherlands, Belgium, and Luxembourg fell to the swift German army. The final shock came in mid-June, when France too surrendered. Britain now stood alone against Hitler's plans for domination of Europe.

**Isolationism and Internationalism**  What *Time* magazine would later call America's "thousand-step road to war" had already begun. After a bitter battle in Congress in 1939, Roosevelt won a change in the neutrality laws to allow the Allies to buy arms as well as nonmilitary goods on a cash-and-carry basis. Interventionists, led by journalist William Allen White and his **Committee to Defend America by Aiding the Allies**, became increasingly vocal in 1940 as war escalated in Europe. (Interventionists were also known as "internationalists," since they believed in engaging with, rather than withdrawing from, international developments.) In response, isolationists formed the **America First Committee** (AFC), with well-respected figures such as Lindbergh and Senator Nye urging the nation to stay out of the war. The AFC held rallies across the United States, and its posters, brochures, and broadsides warning against American involvement in Europe suffused many parts of the country, especially the Midwest.

Because of the America Firsters' efforts, Roosevelt proceeded cautiously in 1940 as he moved the United States closer to involvement. The president did not want war, but he believed that most Americans "greatly underestimate the serious implications to our own future," as he confided to White. In May, Roosevelt created the National Defense Advisory Commission and brought two prominent Republicans, Henry Stimson and Frank Knox, into his cabinet as secretaries of war and the navy, respectively. During the summer, the president traded fifty World War I destroyers to Great Britain in exchange for the right to build military bases on British possessions in the Atlantic, circumventing neutrality laws by using an executive order to complete the deal. In October 1940, a bipartisan vote in Congress approved a large increase in defense spending and instituted the first peacetime draft in American history. "We must be the great arsenal of democracy," FDR declared.

As the war in Europe and the Pacific expanded, the United States was preparing for the 1940 presidential election. The crisis had convinced Roosevelt to seek an unprecedented third term. The Republicans nominated Wendell Willkie of Indiana, a former Democrat who supported many New Deal policies. The two parties' platforms differed only slightly. Both pledged aid to the Allies, and both candidates promised not to "send an American boy into the shambles of a European war," as Willkie put it. Willkie's spirited campaign resulted in a closer election than that of 1932 or 1936; nonetheless, Roosevelt won 55 percent of the popular vote.

Having been reelected, Roosevelt now undertook to persuade Congress to increase aid to Britain, whose survival he viewed as key to American security. In January 1941, he delivered one of the most important speeches of his career. Defining "four essential human freedoms" — freedom of speech, freedom of religion, freedom from want, and freedom from fear — Roosevelt cast the war as a noble defense of democratic societies. He then linked the fate of democracy in Western Europe with the new welfare state at home. Sounding a decidedly New Deal note, Roosevelt pledged to end "special privileges for the few" and to preserve "civil liberties for all." Like President Wilson's speech championing national self-determination at the close of World War I, Roosevelt's **"Four Freedoms"** speech outlined a liberal international order with appeal well beyond its intended European and American audiences.

> **PLACE EVENTS IN CONTEXT**
> How did Roosevelt use the Four Freedoms speech and the Atlantic Charter to define the war for Americans?

 To see a longer excerpt of the "Four Freedoms" speech, along with other primary sources from this period, see *Sources for America's History*.

Two months later, in March 1941, with Britain no longer able to pay cash for arms, Roosevelt persuaded Congress to pass the **Lend-Lease Act**. The legislation authorized the president to "lease, lend, or otherwise dispose of" arms and equipment to Britain or any other country whose defense was considered vital to the security of the United States. When Hitler abandoned his nonaggression pact with Stalin and invaded the

Soviet Union in June 1941, the United States extended lend-lease to the Soviets. The implementation of lend-lease marked the unofficial entrance of the United States into the European war.

Roosevelt underlined his support for the Allied cause by meeting in August 1941 with British prime minister Winston Churchill (who had succeeded Chamberlain in 1940). Their joint press release, which became known as the **Atlantic Charter**, provided the ideological foundation of the Western cause. Drawing from Wilson's Fourteen Points and Roosevelt's Four Freedoms, the charter called for economic cooperation, national self-determination, and guarantees of political stability after the war to ensure "that all men in all the lands may live out their lives in freedom from fear and want." It would become the basis for a new American-led transatlantic alliance after the war's conclusion. Its promise of national self-determination,

however, set up potential conflict in Asia and Africa, where European powers would be reluctant to abandon their imperial holdings.

In the fall of 1941, the reality of U.S. involvement in the war drew closer. By September, Nazi U-boats and the American navy were exchanging fire in the Atlantic. With isolationists still a potent force, Roosevelt hesitated to declare war and insisted that the United States would defend itself only against a direct attack. But behind the scenes, the president openly discussed American involvement with close advisors and considered war inevitable.

## The Attack on Pearl Harbor

The crucial provocation came not from Germany but from Japan. After Japan invaded China in 1937, Roosevelt had denounced "the present reign of terror

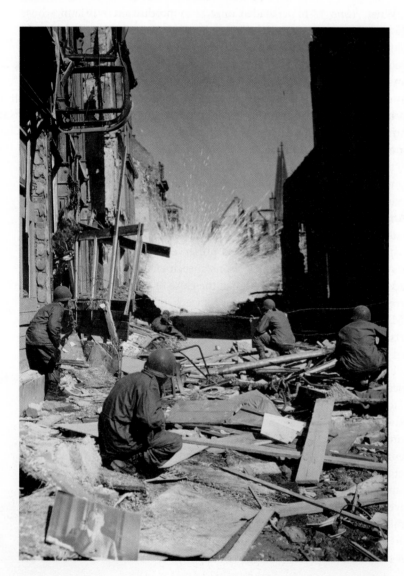

**One City (and Island) at a Time**

By late 1944, the victory of the United States and its allies was nearly certain, but Japanese and German troops continued to fight with great courage and determination. Many European cities and every Pacific island had to be taken foot by foot. Here, American troops from the 325th Regiment of the 82nd Airborne Division advance slowly through the rubble-filled street of a German city in early 1945. Jeff Ethell Color Archives.

and international lawlessness" and suggested that aggressors be "quarantined" by peaceful nations. Despite such rhetoric, the United States refused to intervene later that year when Japanese troops sacked the city of Nanjing, massacred 300,000 Chinese residents, and raped thousands of women.

FDR and other American officials prioritized events in Europe over those in East Asia, and without a counterweight, Japan's military and imperial ambitions expanded. In 1940, General Hideki Tojo became war minister. After concluding a formal military alliance with Germany and Italy that year, Tojo dispatched Japanese troops to occupy the northern part of the French colony of Indochina (present-day Vietnam, Cambodia, and Laos). Tojo's goal, supported by Emperor Hirohito, was to create a "Greater East Asia Co-Prosperity Sphere" under Japan's control stretching from the Korean Peninsula south to Indonesia. Like Germany and Italy, Japan sought to match the overseas empires of Britain, France, Holland, and the United States.

The United States responded to the stationing of Japanese troops in Indochina by restricting trade with Japan. Roosevelt hoped that these economic sanctions would deter Japanese aggression. But in July 1941, Japanese troops staged a full-scale invasion of Indochina. Roosevelt then froze Japanese assets in the United States and stopped all trade with Japan, including vital oil shipments that accounted for almost 80 percent of Japanese consumption.

In October 1941, General Tojo became prime minister and accelerated secret preparations for war against the United States. By November, American military intelligence knew that Japan was planning an attack but did not know where it would occur. Early on Sunday morning, December 7, 1941, Japanese bombers attacked **Pearl Harbor** in Hawaii, killing more than 2,400 Americans. They destroyed or heavily damaged eight battleships, three cruisers, three destroyers, and almost two hundred airplanes.

Although the assault was devastating, it united the American people. Calling December 7 "a date which will live in infamy," President Roosevelt asked Congress for a declaration of war against Japan. The Senate voted unanimously for war, and the House concurred by a vote of 388 to 1. The lone dissenter was Jeannette Rankin of Montana, a committed pacifist — she also voted against entry into World War I — and the first female member of Congress. Three days later, Germany and Italy declared war on the United States, which in turn declared war on the Axis powers. The long shadows of two wars, one in Europe and one in Asia, had at long last converged over the United States.

# Organizing for Victory

The task of fighting on a global scale dramatically increased the power of the federal government. Shifting from civilian to military production, raising an army, and assembling the necessary workforce required a massive expansion in government authority. When Congress passed the **War Powers Act** in December 1941, it gave President Roosevelt unprecedented control over all aspects of the war effort. This act marked the beginning of what some historians call the imperial presidency: the far-reaching use (and sometimes abuse) of executive authority during the latter part of the twentieth century.

## Financing the War

Defense mobilization, not the New Deal efforts of the 1930s, ended the Great Depression. Between 1940 and 1945, the annual gross national product doubled, and after-tax profits of American businesses nearly doubled (America Compared, p. 774). Federal spending on war production powered this advance. By late 1943, two-thirds of the economy was directly involved in the war effort (Figure 24.1). The government paid for these

**FIGURE 24.1**

**Government Military and Civilian Spending as a Percentage of GDP, 1920–1980**

Government military spending was about 3 percent of the gross domestic product (GDP) in the 1920s and 1930s, but it ballooned to more than 25 percent during World War II, to 13 percent during the Korean War, and to nearly 10 percent during the Vietnam War. Federal government spending for civilian purposes doubled during the New Deal and has remained at about 17 to 20 percent of GDP ever since.

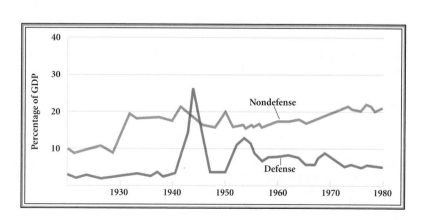

## The Scales of War: Losses and Gains During World War II

World War II saw an extraordinary loss of life. Worldwide, at least 50 million people perished between 1939 and 1945 from war-related causes. The majority of those who died were civilians, though many millions of soldiers perished in battle as well. For most countries, we have reasonable estimates rather than precise figures. The chart below compares the United States with other major combatants and nations caught in this global struggle.

On the other side of the scale, the war fueled tremendous economic growth, at least in the United States, which was spared the physical devastation of Europe and East Asia. Military production for World War II lifted the United States out of the Great Depression. Gross domestic product (GDP) nearly doubled between 1938 and 1945. Economic production in other combatant nations, as shown in the second figure, grew little if at all.

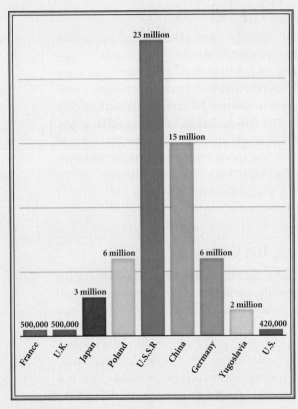

**FIGURE 24.2**
**World War II Military and Civilian Deaths, 1939–1945**

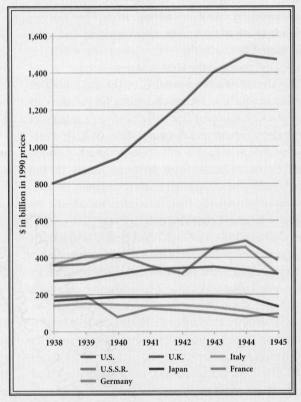

**FIGURE 24.3**
**Gross Domestic Product Rates Worldwide, 1938–1945**

Source: GDP data adapted From Mark Harrison, "The Economics of World War II: Six Great Powers" in *International Comparison* (1998), 11. Copyright © 1998 Cambridge University Press. Reprinted by permission of Cambridge University Press.

### QUESTIONS FOR ANALYSIS

1. Why did the United States experience so many fewer deaths than other nations? Why were there so many deaths in Eastern Europe and the Soviet Union?

2. Note the relative position of U.S. GDP to other industrial nations in 1938 and in 1945. How were some of the key domestic changes discussed in the chapter, such as rural-urban migration, racial conflict, and women's employment, linked to this economic growth?

3. How might you use these comparisons to add to your understanding of key wartime developments, such as the Holocaust, Stalin's demand for a second front, or the entry of the United States into the war?

military expenditures by raising taxes and borrowing money. The **Revenue Act** of 1942 expanded the number of people paying income taxes from 3.9 million to 42.6 million. Taxes on personal incomes and business profits paid half the cost of the war. The government borrowed the rest, both from wealthy Americans and from ordinary citizens, who invested in long-term treasury bonds known as war bonds.

Financing and coordinating the war effort required far-reaching cooperation between government and private business. The number of civilians employed by the government increased almost fourfold, to 3.8 million—a far higher rate of growth than that during the New Deal. The powerful War Production Board (WPB) awarded defense contracts, allocated scarce resources—such as rubber, copper, and oil—for military uses, and persuaded businesses to convert to military production. For example, it encouraged Ford and General Motors to build tanks rather than cars by granting generous tax advantages for re-equipping existing factories and building new ones. In other instances, the board approved "cost-plus" contracts, which guaranteed corporations a profit, and allowed them to keep new steel mills, factories, and shipyards after the war. Such government subsidies of defense

industries would intensify during the Cold War and continue to this day.

To secure maximum production, the WPB preferred to deal with major enterprises rather than with small businesses. The nation's fifty-six largest corporations received three-fourths of the war contracts; the top ten received one-third. The best-known contractor was Henry J. Kaiser. Already highly successful from building roads in California and the Hoover and Grand Coulee dams, Kaiser went from government construction work to navy shipbuilding. At his shipyard in Richmond, California, he revolutionized ship construction by applying Henry Ford's techniques of mass production. To meet wartime production schedules, Kaiser broke the work process down into small, specialized tasks that newly trained workers could do easily. Soon, each of his work crews was building a "Liberty Ship," a large vessel to carry cargo and troops to the war zone, every two weeks. The press dubbed him the Miracle Man.

Central to Kaiser's success were his close ties to federal agencies. The government financed the great

## TRACE CHANGE OVER TIME

How did the war affect the relationship between private corporations and the federal government?

### Shipyards in Wartime

The shipyard workers shown here are laying the keel of the *Joseph N. Teal*, a 10,500-ton "Liberty" freighter bound for the war in the Pacific in 1942. Amidst scaffolding, tools, and wires, these workers at Henry J. Kaiser's shipyard in Portland, Oregon, constructed the entire ship in just ten days after the keel was laid, to shatter all previous shipbuilding records. Kaiser was the king of shipbuilding on the West Coast, with massive yards in Portland and the San Francisco Bay area. In all, Kaiser's workers built nearly 1,500 ships in three years, one-quarter of the total constructed during the war. © Bettmann/Corbis.

dams that he built during the depression, and the Reconstruction Finance Corporation lent him $300 million to build shipyards and manufacturing plants during the war. Working together in this way, American business and government turned out a prodigious supply of military hardware: 86,000 tanks; 296,000 airplanes; 15 million rifles and machine guns; 64,000 landing craft; and 6,500 cargo ships and naval vessels. The American way of war, wrote the Scottish historian D. W. Brogan in 1944, was "mechanized like the American farm and kitchen." America's productive industrial economy, as much as or more than its troops, proved the decisive factor in winning World War II.

The system of allotting contracts, along with the suspension of antitrust prosecutions during the war, created giant corporate enterprises. By 1945, the largest one hundred American companies produced 70 percent of the nation's industrial output. These corporations would form the core of what became known as the nation's "military-industrial complex" during the Cold War (Chapter 25).

## Mobilizing the American Fighting Force

The expanding federal bureaucracy also had a human face. To fight the war, the government mobilized tens of millions of soldiers, civilians, and workers—coordinated on a scale unprecedented in U.S. history. During World War II, the armed forces of the United States enlisted more than fifteen million men and women. In no other military conflict have so many American citizens served in the armed services. They came from every region and economic station: black sharecroppers from Alabama; white farmers from the Midwest; the sons and daughters of European, Mexican, and Caribbean immigrants; native men from Navajo and Choctaw reservations and other tribal communities; women from every state in the nation; even Hollywood celebrities. From urban, rural, and suburban areas, from working-class and middle-class backgrounds—they all served in the military.

In contrast to its otherwise democratic character, the American army segregated the nearly one million African Americans in uniform. The National Association for the Advancement of Colored People (NAACP) and other civil rights groups reprimanded the government, saying, "A Jim Crow army cannot fight for a free world," but the military continued to separate African Americans and assign them menial duties. The poet Langston Hughes observed the irony: "We are elevator boys, janitors, red caps, maids—a race in uniform." The military uniform, Hughes implied, was not assigned to African Americans so readily. Native Americans and Mexican Americans, on the other hand, were never officially segregated; they rubbed elbows with the sons of European immigrants and native-born soldiers from all regions of the country.

Among the most instrumental soldiers were the Native American "**code talkers**." In the Pacific theater, native Navajo speakers communicated orders to fleet commanders. Japanese intelligence could not decipher the code because it was based on the Navajo language, which fewer than fifty non-Navajos in the world understood. At the battle of Iwo Jima, for instance—one of the war's fiercest—Navajo code talkers, working around the clock, sent and received more than eight hundred messages without error. In the European theater, army commanders used Comanche, Choctaw, and Cherokee speakers to thwart the Nazis and exchange crucial military commands on the battlefield. No Axis nation ever broke these Native American codes.

Approximately 350,000 American women enlisted in the military. About 140,000 served in the Women's Army Corps (WAC), and 100,000 served in the navy's Women Accepted for Volunteer Emergency Service (WAVES). One-third of the nation's registered nurses, almost 75,000 overall, volunteered for military duty. In addition, about 1,000 Women's Airforce Service Pilots (WASPs) ferried planes and supplies in noncombat areas. The armed forces limited the duties assigned to women, however. Female officers could not command men, and WACs and WAVES were barred from combat duty, although nurses of both sexes served close to the front lines, risking capture or death. Most of the jobs that women did in the military—clerical work, communications, and health care—resembled women's jobs in civilian life.

Historians still debate how to characterize the World War II American military. As an army of "citizen-soldiers," it represented a wide stratum of society. Military service gave a generation of men a noble purpose, following a decade of economic depression. And its ethic of patriotism further advanced the children of immigrants into mainstream American life. Yet the military embodied the tensions and contradictions of American society as well. The draft revealed appalling levels of health, fitness, and education among millions of Americans, spurring reformers to call for improved literacy and nutrition. Women's integration into the military was marked by deep anxieties about their potentially negative effects on male soldiers as well as the threat to "womanhood" posed by service. The American army was like the nation itself.

United in wartime purpose, the military reflected the strengths and weaknesses of a diverse, fractious society.

## Workers and the War Effort

As millions of working-age citizens joined the military, the nation faced a critical labor shortage. Consequently, many women and African Americans joined the industrial workforce, taking jobs unavailable to them before the conflict. Unions, benefitting from the demand for labor, negotiated higher wages and improved conditions for America's workers. By 1943, with the economy operating at full capacity, the breadlines and double-digit unemployment of the 1930s were a memory.

**Rosie the Riveter**   Government officials and corporate recruiters urged women to take jobs in defense industries, creating a new image of working women. "Longing won't bring him back sooner . . . GET A WAR JOB!" one poster urged, while artist Norman Rockwell's famous "Rosie the Riveter" illustration beckoned to women from the cover of the *Saturday Evening Post*. The government directed its publicity at housewives, but many working women gladly abandoned low-paying "women's jobs" as domestic servants or secretaries for higher-paying work in the defense industry. Suddenly, the nation's factories were full of women working as airplane riveters, ship welders, and drill-press

operators (American Voices, p. 778). Women made up 36 percent of the labor force in 1945, compared with 24 percent at the beginning of the war. War work did not free women from traditional expectations and limitations, however. Women often faced sexual harassment on the job and usually received lower wages than men did. In shipyards, women with the most seniority and responsibility earned $6.95 a day, whereas the top men made as much as $22.

Wartime work was thus bittersweet for women, because it combined new opportunities with old constraints. The majority labored in low-wage service jobs. Child care was often unavailable, despite the largest government-sponsored child-care program in history. When the men returned from war, Rosie the Riveter was usually out of a job. Government propaganda now encouraged women back into the home—where, it was implied, their true calling lay in raising families and standing behind the returning soldiers. But many married women refused, or could not afford, to put on aprons and stay home. Women's participation in the paid labor force rebounded by the late 1940s and continued to rise over the rest of the twentieth century, bringing major changes in family life (Chapter 26).

**Wartime Civil Rights**   Among African Americans, a new militancy prevailed during the war. Pointing to parallels between anti-Semitism in Germany and racial

**Rosie the Riveter**

Women workers install fixtures and assemblies to a tail fuselage section of a B-17 bomber at the Douglas Aircraft Company plant in Long Beach, California. To entice women to become war workers, the War Manpower Commission created the image of "Rosie the Riveter," later immortalized in posters and by a Norman Rockwell illustration on the cover of the *Saturday Evening Post*. A popular 1942 song celebrating Rosie went: "Rosie's got a boyfriend, Charlie / Charlie, he's a marine / Rosie is protecting Charlie / Working overtime on the riveting machine." Even as women joined the industrial workforce in huge numbers (half a million in the aircraft industry alone), they were understood as fulfilling a nurturing, protective role. Library of Congress.

## Women in the Wartime Workplace

During World War II, millions of men served in the armed forces and millions of women worked in war-related industries. A generation later, some of these women workers recounted their wartime experiences to historians in oral interviews.

### Evelyn Gotzion
### Becoming a Union Activist

Evelyn Gotzion went to work at Rayovac, a battery company in Madison, Wisconsin, in 1935; she retired in 1978. While at Rayovac, Gotzion and her working husband raised three children.

I had all kinds of jobs. [During the war] we had one line, a big line, where you'd work ten hours and you'd stand in one spot or sit in one spot. It got terrible, all day long. So I suggested to my foreman, the general foreman, that we take turns of learning everybody's job and switching every half hour. Well, they [the management] didn't like it, but we were on the side, every once in a while, learning each other's job and learning how to do it, so eventually most all of us got so we could do all the jobs, [of] which there were probably fifteen or twenty on the line. We could do every job so we could go up and down the line and rotate. And then they found out that that was really a pretty good thing to do because it made the people happier. . . .

One day I was the steward, and they wouldn't listen to me. They cut our rates, so I shut off the line, and the boss came up and he said, "What are you doing?" I said, "Well, I have asked everybody that I know why we have gotten a cut in pay and why we're doing exactly the same amount of work as we did." . . . So, anyhow, we wrote up a big grievance and they all signed it and then I called the president of the union and then we had a meeting. . . . At that point the president decided that I should be added to the bargaining committee so that I would go in and argue our case, because I could do it better than any of the rest of them because I knew what it was. . . . We finally got it straightened out, and we got our back pay, too. From then on I was on the bargaining committee all the years that I worked at Rayovac.

Source: *Women Remember the War, 1941–1945*, edited by Michael E. Stevens and Ellen D. Goldlust (State Historical Society of Wisconsin Press, 1993). Reprinted with permission of the Wisconsin Historical Society.

### Donna Jean Harvey
### Wartime Challenges and New Experiences

During the war Harvey raised her first child while working as a riveter and radio installer at a plant in Cheyenne, Wyoming.

I graduated from Cheyenne High School in 1940. I married Lewis Early Harvey in January 1941. He was drafted when the war broke out and was sent to the Aleutian Islands, and from there he transferred to the Paratroopers. In October I gave birth to my first son, Lewis Early Jr.

Labor force was critical at that time so I went to United Modification Plant and learned how to rivet, do installations of various kinds and etc. When the "new" radar system was implemented, I asked to be put on that crew. The F.B.I. investigated me and found me to be worthy and I proceeded to install radar along with my riveting duties, while waiting for the next shipment of planes to come in. . . . I was awarded the Army-Navy E Award and was presented with a pin. I've always been very proud of that!!! I certainly got educated in more ways than I ever expected, being a very young girl. But looking back I wouldn't trade my experiences for anything.

My feeling about the war in most instances was a conglomerate of mixed emotions. I had lived a fairly sheltered life, but I listened and learned and managed to survive, but I must admit, it left a scar on my memory that can never be erased.

I was living in one of my parent's apartments during the war and since they were both retired, they baby-sat my young son. My mother decided after a while that she too would like to do something in some little way to help. So she applied for maintenance and between my father and the girl next door, I managed to have a baby-sitter available at all times. The government was asking for rubber donations so my mother and I gave them our rubber girdles!! We liked to think that our girdles helped win the war!!!

My life took on a totally new perspective the longer I worked there. I saw many tragic accidents, none of which I care to talk about which haunt me to this day.

I couldn't do much socializing as I had a small infant at home to care for when off work and besides I was really pooped. Those midnight shifts were "killers." I hope I never have to do that again!! I tried to write weekly letters to my husband in between my other duties. . . .

Our community gathered together and collected scrap metals and such to help in the war effort and thanks to a good neighbor, who was growing a victory garden; we managed to get gifts of potatoes and lettuce etc. The government issued coupon books that allowed us two bananas a week, one pound of sugar and so many gallons of gas. We traded back and forth depending on our individual needs. I had a 1934 Ford and fortunately, it wasn't a gas eater and it managed to get me where I was going when I needed it. . . .

There were no unions there at that time and no baby sitting service provided. The single people formed a club and they entertained themselves after work but I was a married person with a child and so I didn't participate in any of their activities. . . .

After the war was over, most people went back to their previous jobs. I opened a beauty salon and when my husband returned home from the service he got a job with the Frontier Refinery.

Source: National Park Service, *Rosie the Riveter: Women Working During World War II*, nps. gov/pwro/collection/website/donna.htm.

### Fanny Christina (Tina) Hill
## War Work: Social and Racial Mobility

After migrating to California from Texas and working as a domestic servant, Tina Hill, an African American, got a wartime job at North American Aircraft. After time off for a pregnancy in 1945, Hill worked there until 1980.

Most of the men was gone, and . . . most of the women was in my bracket, five or six years younger or older. I was twenty-four. There was a black girl that hired in with me. I went to work the next day, sixty cents an hour. . . . I could see where they made a difference in placing you in certain jobs. They had fifteen or twenty departments, but all the Negroes went to Department 17 because there was

nothing but shooting and bucking rivets. You stood on one side of the panel and your partner stood on this side and he would shoot the rivets with a gun and you'd buck them with the bar. That was about the size of it. I just didn't like it . . . went over to the union and they told me what to do. I went back inside and they sent me to another department where you did bench work and I liked that much better. . . .

Some weeks I brought home twenty-six dollars . . . then it gradually went up to thirty dollars [about $420 in 2010]. . . . Whatever you make you're supposed to save some. I was also getting that fifty dollars a month from my husband and that was just saved right away. I was planning on buying a home and a car. . . . My husband came back [from the war, and] . . . looked for a job in the cleaning and pressing place, which was just plentiful. . . . That's why he didn't bother to go out to North American. But what we both weren't thinking about was that they [North American] have better benefits because they did have an insurance plan and a union to back you up. Later he did come to work there, in 1951 or 1952. . . .

When North American called me back [after I left to have a baby,] was I a happy soul! . . . It made me live better. It really did. We always say that Lincoln took the bale off of the Negroes. I think there is a statue up there in Washington, D.C., where he's lifting something off the Negro. Well, my sister always said — that's why you can't interview her because she's so radical — "Hitler was the one that got us out of the white folks' kitchen."

Source: *Rosie the Riveter Revisited*, by Sherna B. Gluck (Boston: G.K. Hall & Co., 1987). Used by permission of Susan Berger Gluck.

---

### ANALYZING THE EVIDENCE

1. How did the war change the lives of these women?
2. Consider how the themes of identity and work, technology, and economic change, connect to the lives of these two women. How was their experience of the wartime industrial workplace tied to their class and gender identities? How did labor unions affect their conditions of employment?
3. These interviews occurred long after the events they describe. How might that long interval have affected the women's accounts of those years?

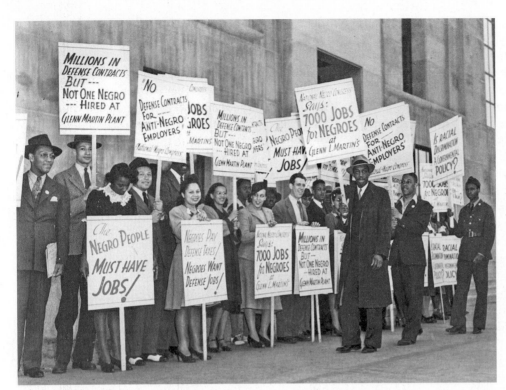

**Wartime Civil Rights**
Fighting fascism abroad while battling racism at home was the approach taken by black communities across the country during World War II. Securing democracy in Europe and Asia while not enjoying it in the United States did not seem just. Jobs were plentiful as the wartime economy hummed along at a fevered pitch. But when employers and unions kept Jim Crow hiring policies in place, African Americans did not hesitate to protest. Here picketers rally for defense jobs outside the Glenn Martin Plant in Omaha, Nebraska, in the early 1940s. Schomburg Center for Research in Black Culture, New York Public Library/Art Resource, NY.

discrimination in the United States, black leaders waged the Double V campaign: calling for victory over Nazism abroad and racism at home. "This is a war for freedom. Whose freedom?" the renowned black leader W. E. B. Du Bois asked. If it meant "the freedom of Negroes in the Southern United States," Du Bois answered, "my gun is on my shoulder."

Even before Pearl Harbor, black labor activism was on the rise. In 1940, only 240 of the nation's 100,000 aircraft workers were black, and most of them were janitors. African American leaders demanded that the government require defense contractors to hire more black workers. When Washington took no action, A. Philip Randolph, head of the Brotherhood of Sleeping Car Porters, the largest black labor union in the country, announced plans for a march on Washington in the summer of 1941.

Roosevelt was not a strong supporter of African American equality, but he wanted to avoid public protest and a disruption of the nation's war preparations. So the president made a deal: he issued **Executive Order 8802**, and in June 1941 Randolph canceled the march. The order prohibited "discrimination in the employment of workers in defense industries or government because of race,

creed, color, or national origin" and established the Fair Employment Practices Commission (FEPC). Mary McLeod Bethune called the wartime FEPC "a refreshing shower in a thirsty land." This federal commitment to black employment rights was unprecedented but limited: it did not affect segregation in the armed forces, and the FEPC could not enforce compliance with its orders.

Nevertheless, wartime developments laid the groundwork for the civil rights revolution of the 1960s. The NAACP grew ninefold, to 450,000 members, by 1945. In Chicago, James Farmer helped to found the Congress of Racial Equality (CORE) in 1942, a group that would become known nationwide in the 1960s for its direct action protests such as sit-ins. The FEPC inspired black organizing against employment discrimination in hundreds of cities and workplaces. Behind this combination of government action and black militancy, the civil rights movement would advance on multiple fronts in the postwar years.

Mexican Americans, too, challenged long-standing practices of discrimination and exclusion. Throughout much of the Southwest, it was still common for signs to read "No Mexicans Allowed," and Mexican American workers were confined to menial, low-paying jobs. Several organizations, including the League of United Latin American Citizens (LULAC) and the Congress of Spanish Speaking Peoples, pressed the government

**UNDERSTAND POINTS OF VIEW**
How does the slogan "A Jim Crow army cannot fight for a free world" connect the war abroad with the civil rights struggle at home?

and private employers to end anti-Mexican discrimination. Mexican American workers themselves, often in Congress of Industrial Organizations (CIO) unions such as the Cannery Workers and Shipyard Workers, also led efforts to enforce the FEPC's equal employment mandate.

Exploitation persisted, however. To meet wartime labor demands, the U.S. government brought tens of thousands of Mexican contract laborers into the United States under the Bracero Program. Paid little and treated poorly, the braceros (who took their name from the Spanish *brazo*, "arm") highlighted the oppressive conditions of farm labor in the United States. After the war, the federal government continued to participate in labor exploitation, bringing hundreds of thousands of Mexicans into the country to perform low-wage agricultural work. Future Mexican American civil rights leaders Dolores Huerta and Cesar Chavez began to fight this labor system in the 1940s.

**Organized Labor**   During the war, unions solidified their position as the most powerful national voice for American workers and extended gains made during the New Deal. By 1945, almost 15 million workers belonged to a union, up from 9 million in 1939. Representatives of the major unions made a no-strike pledge for the duration of the war, and Roosevelt rewarded them by creating the National War Labor Board (NWLB), composed of representatives of labor, management, and the public. The NWLB established wages, hours, and working conditions and had the authority to seize manufacturing plants that did not comply. The Board's "maintenance of membership" policy, which encouraged workers in major defense industries to join unions, also helped organized labor grow.

Despite these arrangements, unions endured government constraints and faced a sometimes hostile Congress. Frustrated with limits on wage increases and the no-strike pledge, in 1943 more than half a million United Mine Workers went out on strike, demanding a higher wage increase than that recommended by the NWLB. Congress responded by passing (over Roosevelt's veto) the Smith-Connally Labor Act of 1943, which allowed the president to prohibit strikes in defense industries and forbade political contributions by unions. Congressional hostility would continue to hamper the union movement in the postwar years. Although organized labor would emerge from World War II more powerful than at any time in U.S. history, its business and corporate opponents, too, would emerge from the war with new strength.

## Politics in Wartime

In his 1944 State of the Union address, FDR called for a second Bill of Rights, one that would guarantee all Americans access to education and jobs, adequate food and clothing, and decent housing and medical care. Like his Four Freedoms speech, this was a call to extend the New Deal by broadening the rights to individual security and welfare guaranteed by the government. The answer to his call, however, would have to wait for the war's conclusion. Congress created new government benefits only for military veterans, known as GIs (short for "government issue"). The **Servicemen's Readjustment Act (1944)**, an extraordinarily influential program popularly known as the "GI Bill of Rights," provided education, job training, medical care, pensions, and mortgage loans for men and women who had served in the armed forces (Chapter 26).

The president's call for social legislation sought to reinvigorate the New Deal political coalition. In the election of 1944, Roosevelt again headed the Democratic ticket. But party leaders, aware of FDR's health problems and fearing that Vice President Henry Wallace's outspoken support for labor and civil rights would alienate moderate voters, dropped him from the ticket. In his place, they chose Senator Harry S. Truman of Missouri, a straight-talking, no-nonsense politician with little national experience. The Republicans nominated Governor Thomas E. Dewey of New York. Dewey, who accepted the general principles of welfare-state liberalism domestically and favored internationalism in foreign affairs, attracted some of Roosevelt's supporters. But a majority of voters preferred political continuity, and Roosevelt was reelected with 53.5 percent of the nationwide vote. The Democratic coalition retained its hold on government power, and the era of Republican political dominance (1896–1932) slipped further into the past.

## Life on the Home Front

The United States escaped the physical devastation that ravaged Europe and East Asia, but the war profoundly changed the country. Americans welcomed wartime prosperity but shuddered when they saw a Western Union boy on his bicycle, fearing that he carried a War Department telegram reporting the death of someone's son, husband, or father. Citizens also grumbled about annoying wartime regulations and rationing but accepted that their lives would be different "for the duration."

**A Family Effort**

After migrating from the Midwest to Portland, Oregon, fifteen members of the family of John R. Brauckmiller (sixth from left) found jobs at Henry Kaiser's Swan Island shipyard. From 1943 to 1945, the shipyard turned out 152 T-2 Tankers, mostly for use by the U.S. Navy to carry fuel oil. A local newspaper pronounced the Brauckmillers as "the shipbuildingest family in America," and because of the importance of shipbuilding to the war effort, *Life* magazine featured the family in its issue of August 16, 1943. Ralph Vincent, *The Journal*, Portland, Oregon/Picture Research Consultants & Archives.

## "For the Duration"

Spurred by both government propaganda and a desire to serve the war cause, people on the home front took on wartime responsibilities. They worked on civilian defense committees, recycled old newspapers and scrap material, and served on local rationing and draft boards. About twenty million backyard "victory gardens" produced 40 percent of the nation's vegetables. Various federal agencies encouraged these efforts, especially the Office of War Information (OWI), which disseminated news and promoted patriotism. The OWI urged advertising agencies to link their clients' products to the war effort, arguing that patriotic ads would not only sell goods but also "invigorate, instruct and inspire" citizens (Thinking Like a Historian, p. 784).

Popular culture, especially the movies, reinforced connections between the home front and the war effort. Hollywood producers, directors, and actors offered their talents to the War Department. Director Frank Capra created a documentary series titled *Why We Fight* to explain war aims to conscripted soldiers. Movie stars such as John Wayne and Spencer Tracy portrayed heroic American fighting men in numerous films, such as *Guadalcanal Diary* (1943) and *Thirty Seconds over Tokyo* (1945). In this pretelevision era, newsreels accompanying the feature films kept the public up-to-date on the war, as did on-the-spot radio broadcasts by Edward R. Murrow and Mary Marvin Breckenridge, the first female radio correspondent for CBS.

For many Americans, the major inconvenience during the war years was the shortage of consumer goods. Beginning in 1942, federal agencies subjected almost everything Americans ate, wore, or used to rationing or regulation. The first major scarcity was rubber. The Japanese conquest of Malaysia and Dutch Indonesia cut off 97 percent of America's imports of that essential raw material. To conserve rubber for the war effort, the government rationed tires, so many of the nation's 30 million car owners put their cars in storage. As more people walked, they wore out their shoes. In 1944, shoes were rationed to two pairs per person a year. By 1943, the government was rationing meat, butter, sugar, and other foods. Most citizens cooperated with the complicated rationing and coupon system, but at least one-quarter of the population bought items on the black market, especially meat, gasoline, cigarettes, and nylon stockings.

## Migration and the Wartime City

The war determined where people lived. When men entered the armed services, their families often followed them to training bases or points of debarkation. Civilians moved to take high-paying defense jobs. About 15 million Americans changed residences during the war years, half of them moving to another state. One of them was Peggy Terry, who grew up in Paducah, Kentucky; worked in a shell-loading plant in nearby Viola; and then moved to a defense plant in Michigan. There, she recalled, "I met all those wonderful Polacks [Polish Americans]. They were the first people I'd ever known that were any different from me. A whole new world just opened up."

As the center of defense production for the Pacific war, California experienced the largest share of wartime migration. The state welcomed nearly three million new residents and grew by 53 percent during the war. "The Second Gold Rush Hits the West," announced the *San Francisco Chronicle* in 1943. One-tenth of all federal dollars flowed into California, and the state's factories turned out one-sixth of all war materials. People went where the defense jobs were: to Los Angeles, San Diego, and cities around San Francisco Bay. Some towns grew practically overnight; within two years of the opening of the Kaiser Corporation shipyard in Richmond, California, the town's population had quadrupled. Other industrial states — notably New York, Illinois, Michigan, and Ohio — also attracted

both federal dollars and migrants on a large scale.

The growth of war industries accelerated patterns of rural-urban migration. Cities grew dramatically, as factories, shipyards, and other defense work drew millions of citizens from small towns and rural areas. This new mobility, coupled with people's distance from their hometowns, loosened the authority of traditional institutions and made wartime cities vibrant and exciting. Around-the-clock work shifts kept people on the streets night and day, and bars, jazz clubs, dance halls, and movie theaters proliferated, fed by the ready cash of war workers.

**EXPLAIN CONSEQUENCES**
What effects did wartime migration have on the United States?

**Racial Conflict**   Migration and more fluid social boundaries meant that people of different races and ethnicities mixed in the booming cities. Over one million African Americans left the rural South for California, Illinois, Michigan, Ohio, and Pennsylvania — a continuation of the Great Migration earlier in the century (Chapter 21). As blacks and whites competed for jobs and housing, racial conflicts broke out in more than a hundred cities in 1943. Detroit saw the worst violence. In June 1943, a riot incited by southern-born whites and Polish Americans against African Americans left thirty-four people dead and hundreds injured.

Racial conflict struck the West as well. In Los Angeles, male Hispanic teenagers formed *pachuco* (youth) gangs. Many dressed in "**zoot suits**" — broad-brimmed felt hats, thigh-length jackets with wide lapels and padded shoulders, pegged trousers, and clunky shoes. Pachucas (young women) favored long coats, huarache sandals, and pompadour hairdos. Other working-class teenagers in Los Angeles and elsewhere took up the zoot-suit style to underline their rejection of middle-class values. To many adults, the zoot suit symbolized juvenile delinquency. Rumors circulating in Los Angeles in June 1943 that a pachuco gang had beaten an Anglo (white) sailor set off a four-day riot in which hundreds of Anglo servicemen roamed through Mexican American neighborhoods and attacked zoot-suiters, taking special pleasure in slashing their pegged pants. In a stinging display of bias, Los Angeles police officers arrested only Mexican American youth, and the City Council passed an ordinance outlawing the wearing of the zoot suit.

**Gay and Lesbian Communities**   Wartime migration to urban centers created new opportunities for gay men and women to establish communities. Religious

## Mobilizing the Home Front

The U.S. Office of War Information (OWI) promoted everything from food rationing to car-pooling during World War II, and the U.S. Treasury encouraged millions of Americans to buy war bonds. More than 20 million victory gardens were planted by ordinary Americans. By 1944 they were producing more than 40 percent of all vegetables grown in the United States. Through these and other measures, those on the home front were encouraged to see themselves as part of the war effort.

**1. U.S. government advertisement from the *Minneapolis Star Journal*, 1943.**

John W. Hartman Center for Sales, Advertising and Marketing History, Duke University.

**2. Copy from War Advertising Council/U.S. Treasury Department advertisement, 1943.**

Farmer: "Well, there's something we *really* want now — *more than anything else* . . . and I guess everybody does. It's VICTORY IN THIS WAR! We had started saving for a new milking machine and a deep-well pump that we will be needing in a few years. . . . We're still going to have that milking machine and that pump — and a lot of other new improvements after the war. When our son comes home from the fighting front, he'll help us pick them out. And we'll have the cash to pay for them. With the money we are saving now in War Bonds. And we are going to hang on to as many War Bonds as possible to take care of us after our boy takes over on the farm. For after ten years, we get four dollars back for every three we have invested."

**3. Poster from the U.S. Office of Price Administration, 1943.**

United States Office of Price Administration/Northwestern University Library.

**4. 4-H Club exhibiting victory garden posters, c. 1943.**

"4-H club boys and girls" ID: 0016623, Special Collections Research Center, North Carolina State University Libraries, Raleigh, North Carolina.

**5. Oral histories about life during the war.**

*Tessie Hickam Wilson, a young woman from Oklahoma.*

It was a hard time, but we felt like we were doing our part, and all the people we knew were doing their part. We had rationing. Sugar, coffee, gasoline and meat were some of the items that were hard to come by. We had ration books every so often, and we had to use them sparingly. We bought savings bonds to help in the war effort.

We also had radios and record players, and when we could afford it, we went to the movies. And even though there were hard times, we did what we could in the war effort, and I will always be glad I was part of it.

*Virginia J. Bondra, a student and clothing worker from Ohio.*

The only newsreel footage we saw was in the theaters when we went to a movie. And we used to bring scrap metal or cans, and we'd get in the movies free. They needed scrap metal and they — the USA needed scrap fat. My mother used to scrap fat, you know, in a can. She'd save it, and we'd bring it to a certain place. Sugar was rationed. Each member of the family would get one pound of sugar a week. And I always had time to bake because we had sugar. . . .

Different things were rationed. We couldn't buy nylons because it was needed . . . for parachutes. So we'd — we'd — my older sisters would paint their legs with a certain makeup that came out in place of nylons. . . . It was makeup for legs.

They painted a eyebrow pencil line down the back of their leg so it would look like real nylons. And we would write V-mail. I had brother — brothers-in-law in the service. We — we'd write V-mail to them. It was called V-mail. Victory mail. . . . We couldn't put their address on because they were moved around a lot and we didn't want the enemy to know. There were a lot of secrets. They would say "zip your lip was the" — was the word of the days then. "Zip your lip" because we didn't want the enemy to get information.

---

Sources: (2) Digital Collections, Duke University Libraries; (4) National Park Service, *Rosie the Riveter: Women Working During World War II*, and the Library of Congress Veterans History Project.

## ANALYZING THE EVIDENCE

1. Examine sources 1, 2, and 3. Who created these sources, and what does this suggest about the context and purpose of these documents? Can you tell from their content who the intended audience was?

2. Study the photograph (source 4). Who is depicted, and how were they posed? What does this suggest about the victory garden program as well as war efforts on the home front more broadly?

3. How do the oral histories in source 5 add to your understanding of home front involvement in the war effort? Does their testimony force you to question the other documents in any way, and if so, how?

## PUTTING IT ALL TOGETHER

Analyze some of the ways the U.S. government encouraged ordinary citizens to participate in the war effort, and evaluate the objectives and results of these efforts.

**Zoot-Suit Youth in Los Angeles**
During a four-day riot in June 1943, servicemen in Los Angeles attacked young Latino men wearing distinctive zoot suits, which were widely viewed as emblems of gang membership and a delinquent youth culture. The police response was to arrest scores of zoot-suiters. Here, a group of handcuffed young Latino men is about to board a Los Angeles County sheriff's bus to make a court appearance. Note the wide-legged pants that taper at the ankle, a hallmark of the zoot suit. The so-called zoot-suit riot was evidence of cracks in wartime unity on the home front. Library of Congress.

morality and social conventions against gays and lesbians kept the majority of them silent and their sexuality hidden. During the war, however, cities such as New York, San Francisco, Los Angeles, Chicago, and even Kansas City, Buffalo, and Dallas developed vibrant gay neighborhoods, sustained in part by a sudden influx of migrants and the relatively open wartime atmosphere. These communities became centers of the gay rights movement of the 1960s and 1970s (Chapter 29).

**New Urban Communities**
Folk singer Pete Seeger performs at the opening of the Washington, D.C., labor canteen in 1944, sponsored by the Congress of Industrial Organizations (CIO). Wartime migration brought people from across the country to centers of industry and military operations. Migration opened new possibilities for urban communities. African American neighborhoods grew dramatically; urban populations grew younger and more mobile; and gay and lesbian communities began to flourish and become more visible. The Granger Collection, New York.

The military tried to screen out homosexuals but had limited success. Once in the services, homosexuals found opportunities to participate in a gay culture often more extensive than that in civilian life. In the last twenty years, historians have documented thriving communities of gay and lesbian soldiers in the World War II military. Some "came out under fire," as one historian put it, but most kept their sexuality hidden from authorities, because army officers, doctors, and psychiatrists treated homosexuality as a psychological disorder that was grounds for dishonorable discharge.

## Japanese Removal

Unlike World War I, which evoked widespread harassment of German Americans, World War II produced relatively little condemnation of European Americans. Federal officials held about 5,000 potentially dangerous German and Italian aliens during the war. Despite the presence of small but vocal groups of Nazi sympathizers and Mussolini supporters, German American and Italian American communities were largely left in peace during the war. The relocation and temporary imprisonment of Japanese immigrants and Japanese American citizens was a glaring exception to this otherwise tolerant policy. Immediately after the attack on Pearl Harbor, the West Coast remained calm. Then, as residents began to fear spies, sabotage, and further attacks, California's long history of racial animosity toward Asian immigrants surfaced. Local politicians and newspapers whipped up hysteria against Japanese Americans, who numbered only about 112,000, had no political power, and lived primarily in small enclaves in the Pacific coast states.

Early in 1942, President Roosevelt responded to anti-Japanese fears by issuing **Executive Order 9066**, which authorized the War Department to force Japanese Americans from their West Coast homes and hold them in relocation camps for the rest of the war. Although there was no disloyal or seditious activity among the evacuees, few public leaders opposed the plan. "A Jap's a Jap," snapped General John DeWitt, the officer charged with defense of the West Coast. "It makes no difference whether he is an American citizen or not."

The relocation plan shocked Japanese Americans, more than two-thirds of whom were Nisei; that is, their parents were immigrants, but they were native-born American citizens. Army officials gave families only a few days to dispose of their property. Businesses that had taken a lifetime to build were liquidated overnight. The War Relocation Authority moved the prisoners to hastily built camps in desolate areas in California, Arizona, Utah, Colorado, Wyoming, Idaho, and Arkansas (Map 24.1). Ironically, the Japanese Americans who made up one-third of the population of Hawaii, and presumably posed a greater threat because of their numbers and proximity to Japan, were not imprisoned. They provided much of the unskilled labor in the island territory, and the Hawaiian economy could not have functioned without them.

Cracks soon appeared in the relocation policy. An agricultural labor shortage led the government to furlough seasonal farmworkers from the camps as early as 1942. About 4,300 students were allowed to attend colleges outside the West Coast military zone. Other

> **IDENTIFY CAUSES**
>
> Why were Japanese Americans treated differently than German and Italian Americans during the war?

**MAP 24.1**

**Japanese Relocation Camps**

In 1942, the government ordered 112,000 Japanese Americans living on the West Coast into internment camps in the nation's interior because of their supposed threat to public safety. Some of the camps were as far away as Arkansas. The federal government rescinded the mass evacuation order in December 1944, but 44,000 people still remained in the camps when the war ended in August 1945.

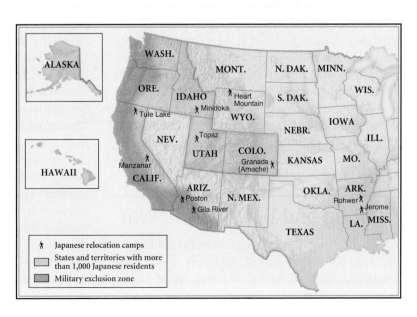

Legend:
- Japanese relocation camps
- States and territories with more than 1,000 Japanese residents
- Military exclusion zone

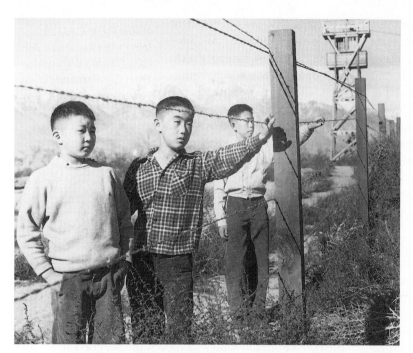

**Behind Barbed Wire**

As part of the forced relocation of 112,000 Japanese Americans, Los Angeles photographer Toyo Miyatake and his family were sent to Manzanar, a camp in the California desert east of the Sierra Nevada. Miyatake secretly began shooting photographs of the camp with a handmade camera. Eventually, Miyatake received permission from the authorities to document life in the camp—its births, weddings, deaths, and high school graduations. To communicate the injustice of internment, he also took staged photographs, such as this image of three young boys behind barbed wire with a watchtower in the distance. For Miyatake, the image gave new meaning to the phrase "prisoners of war." Toyo Miyatake.

internees were permitted to join the armed services. The 442nd Regimental Combat Team, a unit composed almost entirely of Nisei volunteers, served with distinction in Europe.

Gordon Hirabayashi was among the Nisei who actively resisted incarceration. A student at the University of Washington, Hirabayashi was a religious pacifist who had registered with his draft board as a conscientious objector. He refused to report for evacuation and turned himself in to the FBI. "I wanted to uphold the principles of the Constitution," Hirabayashi later stated, "and the curfew and evacuation orders which singled out a group on the basis of ethnicity violated them." Tried and convicted in 1942, he appealed his case to the Supreme Court in *Hirabayashi v. United States* (1943). In that case and in *Korematsu v. United States* (1944), the Court allowed the removal of Japanese Americans from the West Coast on the basis of "military necessity" but avoided ruling on the constitutionality of the incarceration program. The Court's decision underscored the fragility of civil liberties in wartime. Congress issued a public apology in 1988 and awarded $20,000 to each of the eighty thousand surviving Japanese Americans who had once been internees.

# Fighting and Winning the War

World War II was a war for control of the world. Had the Axis powers triumphed, Germany would have dominated, either directly or indirectly, all of Europe

and much of Africa and the Middle East; Japan would have controlled most of East and Southeast Asia. To prevent this outcome, which would have crippled democracy in Europe and restricted American power to the Western Hemisphere, the Roosevelt administration took the United States to war. The combination of American intervention, the perseverance of Britain, and the profound civilian and military sacrifices of the Soviet Union decided the outcome of the conflict and shaped the character of the postwar world.

## Wartime Aims and Tensions

Great Britain, the United States, and the Soviet Union were the key actors in the Allied coalition. China, France, and other nations played crucial but smaller roles. The leaders who became known as the Big Three—President Franklin Roosevelt, Prime Minister Winston Churchill of Great Britain, and Premier Joseph Stalin of the Soviet Union—set military strategy. However, Stalin was not a party to the Atlantic Charter, which Churchill and Roosevelt had signed in August 1941, and disagreed fundamentally with some of its precepts, such as a capitalist-run international trading system. The Allies also disagreed about military strategy and timing. The Big Three made defeating Germany (rather than Japan) the top military priority, but they differed over how best to do it. In 1941, a massive German force had invaded the Soviet Union and reached the outskirts of Leningrad, Moscow, and Stalingrad before being halted in early 1942 by hard-pressed Russian troops. To relieve pressure on the Soviet army, Stalin wanted the British and Americans to open a second front with a major invasion of Germany through France.

Roosevelt informally assured Stalin that the Allies would comply in 1942, but Churchill opposed an early invasion, and American war production was not yet sufficient to support it. For eighteen months, Stalin's pleas went unanswered, and the Soviet Union bore the brunt of the fighting; in the 1943 Battle of Kursk alone, the Soviet army suffered 860,000 casualties, several times what the Allies would suffer for the first two months of the European campaign after D-Day. Then, at a conference of the Big Three in Tehran, Iran, in November 1943, Churchill and Roosevelt agreed to open a second front in France within six months in return for Stalin's promise to join the fight against Japan. Both sides adhered to this agreement, but the long delay angered Stalin, who became increasingly suspicious of American and British intentions.

## The War in Europe

Throughout 1942, the Allies suffered one defeat after another. German armies pushed deep into Soviet territory, advancing through the wheat farms of the Ukraine and the rich oil region of the Caucasus. Simultaneously, German forces began an offensive in North Africa aimed at seizing the Suez Canal. In the Atlantic, U-boats devastated American convoys carrying oil and other vital supplies to Britain and the Soviet Union.

Over the winter of 1942–1943, however, the tide began to turn in favor of the Allies. In the epic Battle of Stalingrad, Soviet forces not only halted the German advance but also allowed the Russian army to push westward (Map 24.2). By early 1944, Stalin's troops had driven the German army out of the Soviet Union. Meanwhile, as Churchill's temporary substitute

**UNDERSTAND POINTS OF VIEW**
How did the Allies disagree over military strategy?

**Hitting the Beach at Normandy**
These U.S. soldiers were among the 156,000 Allied troops who stormed the beaches of Normandy on D-Day, June 6, 1944: on that day alone, more than 10,000 were killed or wounded. Within a month, 1 million Allied troops had come ashore. Most Americans learned of the invasion at 3:30 A.M. Eastern Time, when Edward R. Murrow, the well-known radio journalist whose reports from war-torn London had gripped the nation in 1940, read General Eisenhower's statement to the troops. "The eyes of the world are upon you," Eisenhower told the men as they prepared to invade the European mainland. Library of Congress.

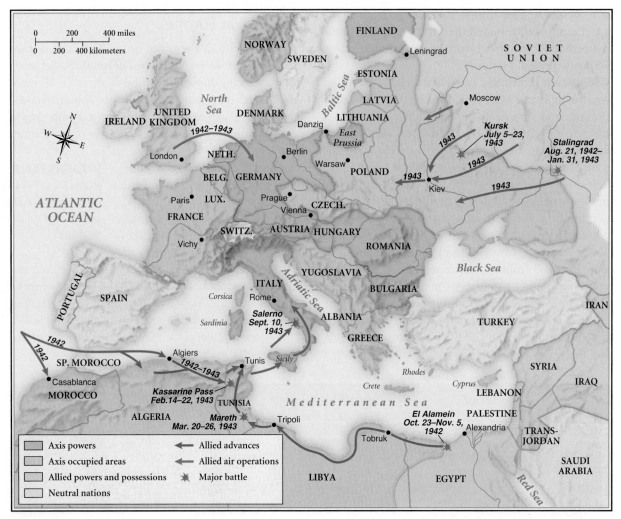

**MAP 24.2**

**World War II in Europe, 1941–1943**

Hitler's Germany reached its greatest extent in 1942, by which time Nazi forces had occupied Norway, France, North Africa, central Europe, and much of western Russia. The tide of battle turned in late 1942 when the German advance stalled at Leningrad and Stalingrad. By early 1943, the Soviet army had launched a massive counterattack at Stalingrad, and Allied forces had driven the Germans from North Africa and launched an invasion of Sicily and the Italian mainland.

for a second front in France, the Allies launched a major counteroffensive in North Africa. Between November 1942 and May 1943, Allied troops under the leadership of General Dwight D. Eisenhower and General George S. Patton defeated the German Afrika Korps, led by General Erwin Rommel.

From Africa, the Allied command followed Churchill's strategy of attacking the Axis through its "soft underbelly": Sicily and the Italian peninsula. Faced with an Allied invasion, the Italian king ousted Mussolini's fascist regime in July 1943. But German troops, who far outmatched the Allies in skill and organization, took control of Italy and strenuously resisted

the Allied invasion. American and British divisions took Rome only in June 1944 and were still fighting German forces in northern Italy when the European war ended in May 1945 (Map 24.3). Churchill's southern strategy proved a time-consuming and costly mistake.

**D-Day**   The long-promised invasion of France came on **D-Day**, June 6, 1944. That morning, the largest armada ever assembled moved across the English Channel under the command of General Eisenhower. When American, British, and Canadian soldiers hit the beaches of Normandy, they suffered terrible casualties but secured a beachhead. Over the next few days, more

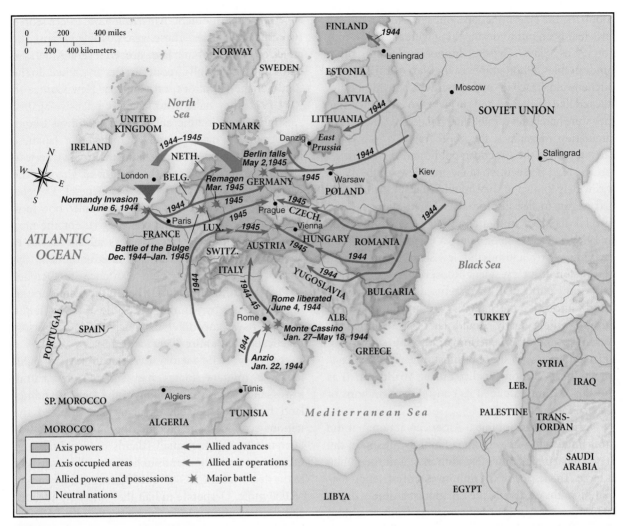

**MAP 24.3**

**World War II in Europe, 1944–1945**

By the end of 1943, the Russian army had nearly pushed the Germans out of the Soviet Union, and by June 1944, when the British and Americans finally invaded France, the Russians had liberated eastern Poland and most of southeastern Europe. By the end of 1944, British and American forces were ready to invade Germany from the west, and the Russians were poised to do the same from the east. Germany surrendered on May 7, 1945.

than 1.5 million soldiers and thousands of tons of military supplies and equipment flowed into France. Much to the Allies' advantage, they never faced more than one-third of Hitler's Wehrmacht (armed forces), because the Soviet Union continued to hold down the Germans on the eastern front. In August, Allied troops liberated Paris; by September, they had driven the Germans out of most of France and Belgium. Meanwhile, long-range Allied bombers attacked German cities such as Hamburg and Dresden as well as military and industrial targets. The air campaign killed some 305,000 civilians and soldiers and injured another 780,000 — a grisly reminder of the war's human brutality.

The Germans were not yet ready to give up, however. In December 1944, they mounted a final offensive in Belgium, the so-called Battle of the Bulge, before being pushed back across the Rhine River into Germany. American and British troops drove toward Berlin from the west, while Soviet troops advanced east through Poland. On April 30, 1945, as Russian troops massed outside Berlin, Hitler committed suicide; on May 7, Germany formally surrendered.

**The Holocaust**   When Allied troops advanced into Poland and Germany in the spring of 1945, they came face-to-face with Hitler's "final solution" for the Jewish population of Germany and the German-occupied countries: the extermination camps in which 6 million Jews had been put to death, along with another 6 million Poles, Slavs, Gypsies, homosexuals, and other "undesirables." Photographs of the Nazi death camps at Buchenwald, Dachau, and Auschwitz showed bodies stacked like cordwood and survivors so emaciated that they were barely alive. Published in *Life* and other mass-circulation magazines, the photographs of the **Holocaust** horrified the American public and the world.

The Nazi persecution of German Jews in the 1930s was widely known in the United States. But when Jews had begun to flee Europe, the United States refused to relax its strict immigration laws to take them in. In 1939, when the SS *St. Louis*, a German ocean liner carrying nearly a thousand Jewish refugees, sought permission from President Roosevelt to dock at an American port, FDR had refused. Its passengers' futures uncertain, the *St. Louis* was forced to return to Europe, where many would later be deported to Auschwitz and other extermination camps. American officials, along with those of most other nations, continued this exclusionist policy during World War II as the Nazi regime extended its control over millions of Eastern European Jews.

Various factors inhibited American action, but the most important was widespread anti-Semitism: in the State Department, Christian churches, and the public at large. The legacy of the immigration restriction legislation of the 1920s and the isolationist attitudes of the 1930s also discouraged policymakers from assuming responsibility for the fate of the refugees. Taking a narrow view of the national interest, the State Department allowed only 21,000 Jewish refugees to enter the United States during the war. But the War Refugee Board, which President Roosevelt established in 1944 at the behest of Secretary of the Treasury Henry Morgenthau, helped move 200,000 European Jews to safe havens in other countries.

## The War in the Pacific

Winning the war against Japan was every bit as arduous as waging the campaign against Germany. After crippling the American battle fleet at Pearl Harbor, the Japanese quickly expanded into the South Pacific, with seaborne invasions of Hong Kong, Wake Island, and Guam. Japanese forces then advanced into Southeast Asia, conquering the Solomon Islands, Burma, and Malaya and threatening Australia and India. By May 1942, they had forced the surrender of U.S. forces in the Philippine Islands and, in the Bataan "death march," caused the deaths of 10,000 American prisoners of war.

At that dire moment, American naval forces scored two crucial victories. These were possible because the attack on Pearl Harbor had destroyed several American battleships but left all aircraft carriers unscathed. In the Battle of the Coral Sea, off southern New Guinea in May 1942, they halted the Japanese offensive against Australia. Then, in June, at the Battle of Midway Island, the American navy severely damaged the Japanese fleet. In both battles, planes launched from American aircraft carriers provided the margin of victory. The U.S. military command, led by General Douglas MacArthur and Admiral Chester W. Nimitz, now took the offensive in the Pacific (Map 24.4). For the next eighteen months, American forces advanced slowly toward Japan, taking one island after another in the face of determined Japanese resistance. In October 1944, MacArthur and Nimitz began the reconquest of the Philippines by winning the Battle of Leyte Gulf, a massive naval encounter in which the Japanese lost practically their entire fleet (Map 24.5).

By early 1945, victory over Japan was in sight. Japanese military forces had suffered devastating losses, and American bombing of the Japanese homeland had killed 330,000 civilians and crippled the nation's economy. The bloodletting on both sides was horrendous. On the small islands of Iwo Jima and Okinawa, tens of thousands of Japanese soldiers fought to the death, killing 13,000 U.S. Marines and wounding 46,000 more. Desperate to halt the American advance and short on ammunition, Japanese pilots flew suicidal kamikaze missions, crashing their bomb-laden planes into American ships.

Among the grim realities of war in the Pacific was the conflict's racial overtones. The attack on Pearl Harbor reawakened the long tradition of anti-Asian sentiment in the United States. In the eyes of many Americans, the Japanese were "yellow monkeys," an inferior race whose humanity deserved minimal respect. Racism was evident among the Japanese as well. Their brutal attacks on China (including the rape of Nanjing), their forcing of Korean "comfort women" to have sex with Japanese soldiers, and their treatment of American prisoners in the Philippines flowed from their own sense of racial superiority. Anti-Japanese attitudes in the United States would subside in the 1950s as the island nation became a trusted ally. But racism would again play a major role in the U.S. war in Vietnam in the 1960s.

As the American navy advanced on Japan in the late winter of 1945, President Roosevelt returned to the United States from the Yalta Conference, a major meeting of the Big Three at Yalta, a resort town on the Black

**MAP 24.4**

**World War II in the Pacific, 1941–1942**

After the attacks on Pearl Harbor in December 1941, the Japanese rapidly extended their domination in the Pacific. The Japanese flag soon flew as far east as the Marshall and Gilbert islands and as far south as the Solomon Islands and parts of New Guinea. Japan also controlled the Philippines, much of Southeast Asia, and parts of China, including Hong Kong. By mid-1942, American naval victories at the Coral Sea and Midway stopped further Japanese expansion.

Sea (Chapter 25). The sixty-three-year-old president was a sick man, visibly exhausted by his 14,000-mile trip and suffering from heart failure and high blood pressure. On April 12, 1945, during a short visit to his vacation home in Warm Springs, Georgia, Roosevelt suffered a cerebral hemorrhage and died.

## The Atomic Bomb and the End of the War

When Harry Truman assumed the presidency, he learned for the first time about the top-secret **Manhattan Project**, which was on the verge of testing a new weapon: the atomic bomb. Working at the University of Chicago in December 1942, Enrico Fermi and Leo

Szilard, refugees from fascist Italy and Nazi Germany, produced the first controlled atomic chain reaction using highly processed uranium. With the aid of German-born refugee Albert Einstein, the greatest theorist of modern physics and a scholar at Princeton, they persuaded Franklin Roosevelt to develop an atomic weapon, warning that German scientists were also working on such nuclear reactions.

The Manhattan Project cost $2 billion, employed 120,000 people, and involved the construction of thirty-seven installations in nineteen states — with all of its activity hidden from Congress, the American people, and even Vice President Truman. Directed by General Leslie Graves and scientist J. Robert Oppenheimer, the nation's top physicists assembled the

**MAP 24.5**

**World War II in the Pacific, 1943–1945**

Allied forces retook the islands of the central Pacific in 1943 and 1944 and ousted the Japanese from the Philippines early in 1945. Carrier-launched planes had started bombing Japan itself in 1942, but the capture of these islands gave U.S. bombers more bases from which to strike Japanese targets. As the Soviet army invaded Japanese-occupied Manchuria in August 1945, U.S. planes took off from one of the newly captured Mariana Islands to drop the atomic bombs on Hiroshima and Nagasaki. The Japanese offered to surrender on August 10.

first bomb in Los Alamos, New Mexico, and successfully tested it on July 16, 1945. Overwhelmed by its frightening power, as he witnessed the first mushroom cloud, Oppenheimer recalled the words from the Bhagavad Gita, one of the great texts of Hindu scripture: "I am become Death, the Destroyer of Worlds."

Three weeks later, President Truman ordered the dropping of atomic bombs on two Japanese cities: Hiroshima on August 6 and Nagasaki on August 9. Truman's rationale for this order—and the implications of his decision—have long been the subject of scholarly and popular debate. The

**IDENTIFY CAUSES**

What factors influenced Truman's decision to use atomic weapons against Japan?

principal reason was straightforward: Truman and his American advisors, including Secretary of War Henry Stimson and Army Chief of Staff General George Marshall, believed that Japan's military leaders would never surrender unless their country faced national ruin. Moreover, at the Potsdam Conference on the outskirts of Berlin in July 1945, the Allies had agreed that only the "unconditional surrender" of Japan was acceptable—the same terms under which Germany and Italy had been defeated. To win such a surrender, an invasion of Japan itself seemed necessary. Stimson and Marshall told Truman that such an invasion would produce between half a million and a million Allied casualties.

**The Big Three at Yalta**
With victory in Europe at hand, Roosevelt journeyed in February 1945 to Yalta, on the Black Sea, and met for what would be the final time with Churchill and Stalin. The leaders discussed the important and controversial issues of the treatment of Germany, the status of Poland, the creation of the United Nations, and Russian entry into the war against Japan. The Yalta agreements mirrored a new balance of power and set the stage for the Cold War. Franklin D. Roosevelt Library.

Before giving the order to drop the atomic bomb, Truman considered other options. His military advisors rejected the most obvious alternative: a nonlethal demonstration of the bomb's awesome power, perhaps on a remote Pacific island. If the demonstration failed — not out of the question, as the bomb had been tested only once — it would embolden Japan further. A detailed advance warning designed to scare Japan into surrender was also rejected. Given Japan's tenacious fighting in the Pacific, the Americans believed that only massive devastation or a successful invasion would lead Japan's military leadership to surrender. After all, the deaths of more than 100,000 Japanese civilians in the U.S. firebombing of Tokyo and other cities in the spring of 1945 had brought Japan no closer to surrender.

In any event, the atomic bombs achieved the immediate goal. The deaths of 100,000 people at Hiroshima and 60,000 at Nagasaki prompted the Japanese government to surrender unconditionally on August 10 and to sign a formal agreement on September 2, 1945. Fascism had been defeated, thanks to a fragile alliance between the capitalist nations of the West and the communist government of the Soviet Union. The coming of peace would strain and then destroy the victorious coalition. Even as the global war came to an end, the early signs of the coming Cold War were apparent, as were the stirrings of independence in the European colonies.

## The Toll of the War

After the battle of Iwo Jima, one of the fiercest and bloodiest of the Pacific war, a rabbi chaplain in the Marine Corps delivered the eulogy for the fallen. "This shall not be in vain," he said, surveying a battlefield that

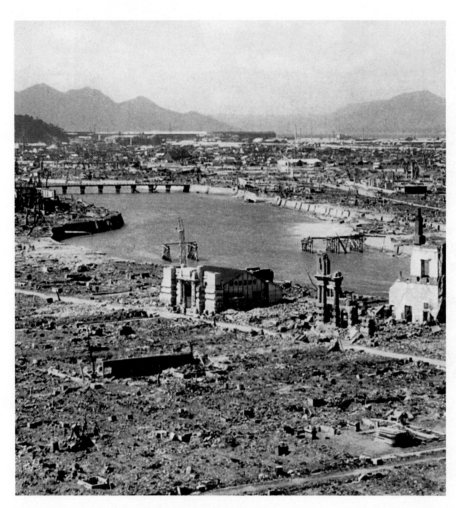

**Hiroshima, March 1946**
Though the atomic bomb had been dropped on the port city of Hiroshima six months previous to this photo being taken, the devastation is still apparent. The U.S. Army report on the bombing described the immediate effects of the blast: "At 8:15 A.M., the bomb exploded with a blinding flash in the sky, and a great rush of air and a loud rumble of noise extended for many miles around the city; the first blast was soon followed by the sounds of falling buildings and of growing fires, and a great cloud of dust and smoke began to cast a pall of darkness over the city." The only buildings not leveled were those with concrete reinforcement, meant to withstand earthquakes. The human toll of this weapon was unprecedented: of the estimated population of 350,000, 100,000 were likely killed by the explosion, and many tens of thousands more died slowly of the effects of radiation poisoning. U.S. Air Force.

witnessed the deaths of nearly 30,000 American and Japanese soldiers. Speaking of American losses, he said, "from the suffering and sorrow of those who mourn this, will come — we promise — the birth of a new freedom for the sons of man everywhere." The toll of "suffering and sorrow" from World War II was enormous. Worldwide, more than 50 million soldiers and civilians were killed, nearly 2.5 percent of the globe's population. The Holocaust took the lives of 6 million European Jews, 2.6 million from Poland alone. Nearly 100 million additional soldiers and civilians were wounded, and 30 million people across the globe were rendered homeless. It was one of the most wrenching, disruptive, and terrible wars in human history.

Alongside the human toll stood profound economic and political transformations. Hundreds of cities in Europe and Asia had been bombed. Some of them, like Dresden, Warsaw, Hamburg, and Hiroshima, had been simply obliterated. Much of the industrial infrastructure of Germany and Japan, two of the world's most important industrial economies before the war, lay in ruins. Moreover, despite emerging as one of the

victors, Britain was no longer a global power. The independence movement in India was only the most obvious sign of its waning influence. Indeed, throughout the colonized world in Asia and Africa, people had taken the Atlantic Charter, and FDR's insistence that this was a war for *democracy*, seriously. For them, resumption of European imperialism was unacceptable, and the war represented a step toward national self-determination.

In the United States, too, the toll of war was great. More than 400,000 lives were lost, and nearly 300,000 American soldiers were wounded. Yet millions returned home, and in the coming decades veterans would play a central role in national life. Incredibly, in 1950 World War II veterans made up one-third of all American men over the age of nineteen. Only the Civil War involved a comparable commitment of military service from a generation. Americans paid dearly for that commitment — though not, it must be noted, as dearly as other peoples in Europe and Asia — and the legacies of the war shaped families, politics, and foreign policy for the remainder of the century.

## SUMMARY

The rise of fascism in Germany, Italy, and Japan led to the outbreak of World War II. Initially, the American public opposed U.S. intervention. But by 1940, President Roosevelt was mobilizing support for the military and preparing the country for war. The Japanese attack on Pearl Harbor in December 1941 brought the nation fully into the conflict. War mobilization dramatically expanded the federal government and led to substantial economic growth. It also boosted geographical and social mobility as women, rural whites, and southern blacks found employment in new defense plants across the country. Government rules assisted both the labor movement and the African American campaign for civil rights. However, religious and racial animosity caused the exclusion of Jewish refugees and the internment of 112,000 Japanese Americans.

By 1942, Germany and Japan seemed to be winning the war. But in 1943, the Allies took the offensive — with advances by the Soviet army in Europe and the American navy in the Pacific — and by the end of 1944, Allied victory was all but certain. Germany finally surrendered in May 1945, and Japan surrendered in August, after the atomic bombing of the Japanese cities Hiroshima and Nagasaki. The United States emerged from the war with an undamaged homeland, sole possession of the atomic bomb, and a set of unresolved diplomatic disputes with the Soviet Union that would soon lead to the four-decade-long Cold War. Federal laws and practices established during the war — the universal income tax, a huge military establishment, and multibillion-dollar budgets, to name but a few — became part of American life. So, too, did the active participation of the United States in international politics and alliances, an engagement intensified by the unresolved issues of the wartime alliance with the Soviet Union and the postwar fate of colonized nations.

# CHAPTER REVIEW

**MAKE IT STICK**   Go to **LearningCurve** to retain what you've read.

## TERMS TO KNOW   Identify and explain the significance of each term below.

### Key Concepts and Events

fascism (p. 768)

National Socialist (Nazi) Party (p. 768)

Rome-Berlin Axis (p. 769)

Neutrality Act of 1935 (p. 769)

Popular Front (p. 770)

Munich Conference (p. 770)

Committee to Defend America By Aiding the Allies (p. 771)

America First Committee (p. 771)

Four Freedoms (p. 771)

Lend-Lease Act (p. 771)

Atlantic Charter (p. 772)

Pearl Harbor (p. 773)

War Powers Act (p. 773)

Revenue Act (p. 775)

code talkers (p. 776)

Executive Order 8802 (p. 780)

Servicemen's Readjustment Act (1944) (p. 781)

zoot suits (p. 783)

Executive Order 9066 (p. 787)

D-Day (p. 790)

Holocaust (p. 792)

Manhattan Project (p. 793)

### Key People

Benito Mussolini (p. 768)

Adolf Hitler (p. 768)

Hideki Tojo (p. 773)

Charles A. Lindbergh (p. 769)

Winston Churchill (p. 772)

Harry S. Truman (p. 781)

Gordon Hirabayashi (p. 788)

Dwight D. Eisenhower (p. 790)

**REVIEW QUESTIONS** Answer these questions to demonstrate your understanding of the chapter's main ideas.

1. World War II has popularly been called the "good war." Do you agree with this assessment? Why do you think it earned that nickname?

2. Overall, what effects—positive or negative—did World War II have on social change in the United States, particularly among women and minority groups?

3. How did World War II affect the federal government's regulating of the economy and its taxing power?

4. **THEMATIC UNDERSTANDING** Review the events listed under "America in the World" on the thematic timeline on page 671. How did World War II change the relationship between the United States and the rest of the world in the first half of the twentieth century?

**MAKING CONNECTIONS** Recognize the larger developments and continuities within and across chapters by answering these questions.

1. **ACROSS TIME AND PLACE** For the United States, the period between World War I (1914–1918) and World War II (1937–1945) was a prolonged series of conflicts and crises, both domestically and internationally. What connections can be drawn between World War I, the Great Depression, and World War II? Did this "long" conflict draw the United States and Europe closer together or drive them further apart? How did American attitudes toward involvement in European affairs change over this period?

2. **VISUAL EVIDENCE** Compare the photographs of soldiers and those contributing to the war effort. How do these images help us understand a major event like World War II from different perspectives? How would their proximity to battle affect people's experience of war?

**MORE TO EXPLORE** Start here to learn more about the events discussed in this chapter.

Ronald A. Goldberg, *America in the Forties* (2012). An engaging account of the home front during World War II.

David Kennedy, *Freedom from Fear: The American People in Depression and War, 1929–1945* (1999). A fascinating exploration of both the domestic and military experience of World War II.

Elizabeth Mullener, *War Stories: Remembering World War II* (2002). Fifty-three personal stories of war.

Emily Yellin, *Our Mothers' War: American Women at Home and at the Front During World War II* (2004). The war seen from the point of view of women.

For documents and images related to the war, see "A People at War" and "Powers of Persuasion: Poster Art from World War II" (**archives.gov/exhibits/exhibits-list.html**); "Women Come to the Front: Journalists, Photographers, and Broadcasters During World War II" (**lcweb.loc.gov/exhibits/wcf/wcf0001.html**); "The Japanese American Legacy Project" (**densho.org/densho.asp**); and "Ansel Adams's Photographs of Japanese-American Internment at Manzanar" (**memory.loc.gov/ammem/aamhtml**).

"The Enola Gay Controversy: How Do We Remember a War That We Won?" at **lehigh.edu/~ineng/enola**. Lehigh University professor Edward J. Gallagher's site on the decision to drop the atomic bomb.

**TIMELINE**   Ask yourself why this chapter begins and ends with these dates and then identify the links among related events.

| | |
|---|---|
| **1933** | • Adolf Hitler becomes chancellor of Germany |
| **1935** | • Italy invades Ethiopia |
| **1935–1937** | • U.S. Neutrality Acts |
| **1936** | • Germany reoccupies Rhineland demilitarized zone<br>• Rome-Berlin Axis established |
| **1937** | • Japan invades China |
| **1938** | • Munich conference |
| **1939** | • German-Soviet nonaggression pact<br>• Germany invades Poland<br>• Britain and France declare war on Germany |
| **1940** | • Germany, Italy, and Japan form alliance |
| **1941** | • Germany invades Soviet Union<br>• Lend-Lease Act and Atlantic Charter established<br>• Japanese attack Pearl Harbor (December 7) |
| **1942** | • Executive Order 9066 leads to Japanese internment camps<br>• Battles of Coral Sea and Midway halt Japanese advance |
| **1942–1945** | • Rationing of scarce goods |
| **1943** | • Race riots in Detroit and Los Angeles |
| **1944** | • D-Day: Allied landing in France (June 6) |
| **1945** | • Yalta Conference (February)<br>• Germany surrenders (May 7)<br>• United Nations founded<br>• Potsdam Conference (July–August)<br>• United States drops atomic bombs on Hiroshima and Nagasaki (August 6 and 9)<br>• Japan surrenders (August 10) |

**KEY TURNING POINTS:** On the timeline, identify the key turning points for the Allies in the European and Pacific campaigns.

# PART 8

## The Modern State and the Age of Liberalism

### 1945–1980

Between 1945 and 1980, the United States became the world's leading economic and military power. That development defines these decades as a distinct period of American history. Internationally, a prolonged period of tension and conflict known as the Cold War drew the United States into an engagement in world affairs unprecedented in the nation's history. Domestically, three decades of sustained economic growth, whose benefits were widely, though imperfectly, distributed, expanded the middle class and brought into being a mass consumer society. These international and domestic developments were intertwined with the predominance of liberalism in American politics and public policy. One might think of an "age of liberalism" in this era, encompassing the social-welfare liberalism that was a legacy of the New Deal and the rights liberalism of the 1960s, both of which fell under the larger umbrella of Cold War liberalism.

Global leadership abroad and economic prosperity at home were conditioned on further expansions in government power. How that power was used proved controversial. Immediately following World War II, a national security state emerged to investigate so-called subversives in the United States and, through the clandestine Central Intelligence Agency (CIA), to destabilize foreign governments abroad. Meanwhile, American troops went to war in Korea and Vietnam. At home, African Americans, women, the poor, and other social groups called for greater equality in American life and sought new laws and government initiatives to make that equality a reality. Here, in brief, are the three key dimensions of this convulsive, turbulent era.

## Global Leadership and the Cold War

When the United States officially joined the combatants of World War II, it entered into an alliance with England and the Soviet Union. That alliance proved impossible to sustain after 1945, as the United States and the Soviet Union became competitors to shape postwar Europe, East Asia, and the developing world. The resulting Cold War lasted four decades, during which the United States extended its political and military reach onto every continent. Under the presidency of Harry S. Truman, American officials developed the policy of containment—a combination of economic, diplomatic, and military actions to limit the expansion of communism—that subsequent presidents embraced and expanded.

Diplomatic and military intervention abroad was a hallmark of the Cold War. Most American interventions took place in developing countries, in recently independent, decolonized nations, and in countries where nationalist movements pressed for independence. In the name of preventing the spread of communism, the United States intervened directly or indirectly in China, Iran, Guatemala, Cuba, Indonesia, and the Dominican Republic, among many other nations, and fought major wars in Korea and Vietnam. This new global role for the United States inspired support but also spurred detractors. The latter eventually included the antiwar movement during the war in Vietnam. Chapter 25 focuses on the Cold War, and Vietnam is addressed in Chapter 28.

## The Age of Liberalism

In response to the Great Depression, President Franklin Roosevelt's New Deal expanded federal responsibility for the social welfare of ordinary citizens, sweeping away much of the *laissez-faire* individualism of earlier eras (see Chapter 23). Legislators from both parties embraced liberal ideas about the role of government and undertook such measures as the GI Bill, subsidies for suburban home ownership, and investment in infrastructure and education. Poverty, however, affected nearly one-third of Americans in the 1960s, and racial discrimination denied millions of nonwhites full citizenship. Lack of opportunity became a driving force in the civil rights movement and in the Great Society under President Lyndon Johnson.

Inspired by African American civil rights, other social movements sought equality based on gender, sexuality, ethnicity, and other identities. If "New Deal liberalism" had focused on social welfare, this "rights liberalism" focused on protecting people from discrimination and ensuring equal citizenship. These struggles resulted in new laws, such as the Civil Rights Act of 1964, and transformative Supreme Court decisions. Conservative opponents, however, mobilized in the 1960s against what they saw as the excesses of liberal activism. The resulting conflict began to reshape politics in the 1970s and laid the groundwork for a new conservative resurgence. These developments are discussed in Chapters 27 and 28.

## Mass Consumption and the Middle Class

More than ever, the postwar American economy was driven by mass consumption and the accompanying process of suburbanization. Rising wages, increasing access to higher education, and the availability of suburban home ownership raised living standards and allowed more Americans than ever to afford consumer goods. Suburbanization transformed the nation's cities, and the Sunbelt led the nation in population growth. But the new prosperity had mixed results. Cities declined and new racial and ethnic ghettos formed. Suburbanization and mass consumption raised concerns that the nation's rivers, streams, air, and open land were being damaged, and an environmental movement arose in response. And prosperity itself proved short-lived. By the 1970s, deindustrialization had eroded much of the nation's once prosperous industrial base.

A defining characteristic of the postwar decades was the growth of the American middle class. That growth was predicated on numerous demographic changes. Home ownership increased, as did college enrollments. Women worked more outside the home and spurred a new feminism. Children enjoyed more purchasing power, and a "teen culture" arose on television, in popular music, and in film. The family became politicized, too, and by the late 1970s, liberals and conservatives were divided over how best to address the nation's family life. All these developments are discussed in Chapters 25 and 29.

# The Modern State and the Age of Liberalism 1945–1980

## Thematic Understanding

This timeline arranges some of the important events of this period into themes. Consider the entries under "America in the World" and "Politics and Power" across all four decades. What connections were there between international developments and domestic politics in this era of the Cold War?  **>**

| | AMERICA IN THE WORLD | POLITICS AND POWER | IDENTITY | ENVIRONMENT AND GEOGRPAHY | WORK, EXCHANGE, AND TECHNOLOGY |
|---|---|---|---|---|---|
| **1940** | • Truman Doctrine<br>• Israel created (1947)<br>• Marshall Plan (1948)<br>• Containment strategy emerges<br>• NATO created; West Germany created (1949) | • GI Bill (1944)<br>• Loyalty-Security Program<br>• Taft-Hartley Act (1947)<br>• Truman reelected (1948)<br>• Truman's Fair Deal (1949) | • *To Secure These Rights* (1947)<br>• Desegregation of armed services (1948)<br>• *Shelley v. Kraemer* (1948) | • Continued South-North migration of African Americans<br>• First Levittown opens (1947)<br>• FHA and VA subsidize suburbanization | • Bretton Woods system established: World Bank, International Monetary Fund<br>• Baby boom establishes new consumer generation |
| **1950** | • Permanent mobilization as a result of NSC-68<br>• Korean War (1950–1953)<br>• Geneva Accords regarding Vietnam (1954) | • Cold War liberalism<br>• McCarthyism and Red Scare<br>• Eisenhower's presidency (1953–1961) | • *Brown v. Board of Education* (1954)<br>• Montgomery Bus Boycott (1955)<br>• Little Rock — Central High School desegregation battle<br>• Southern Christian Leadership Conference founded (1957) | • Disneyland opens (1955)<br>• National Highway Act (1956)<br>• Growth of suburbia and Sunbelt<br>• Atomic bomb testing in Nevada and Pacific Ocean | • Treaty of Detroit (1950)<br>• Military-industrial complex begins to rise<br>• National Defense Education Act (1958) spurs development of technology |
| **1960** | • Cuban missile crisis (1962)<br>• Gulf of Tonkin Resolution (1964)<br>• Johnson sends ground troops to Vietnam; war escalates (1965)<br>• Tet offensive (1968); peace talks begin | • John F. Kennedy's New Frontier<br>• John F. Kennedy assassinated (1963)<br>• Lyndon B. Johnson's landslide victory (1964)<br>• War on Poverty; Great Society<br>• Riots at Democratic National Convention (1968) | • Greensboro sit-ins<br>• *The Feminine Mystique* (1963)<br>• Civil Rights and Voting Rights Acts (1964–1965)<br>• National Organization for Women founded (1966)<br>• Alcatraz occupation (1969)<br>• Black Power<br>• Student and antiwar activism | • Great Society environmental initiatives<br>• Urban riots (1964–1968)<br>• Kerner Commission Report (1968) | • Economic boom<br>• Government spending on Vietnam and Great Society<br>• Medicare and Medicaid created (1965) |
| **1970** | • Nixon invades Cambodia (1971)<br>• Paris Accords end Vietnam War (1973)<br>• Camp David Accords between Egypt and Israel (1978)<br>• Iranian Revolution (1979) and hostage crisis (1979–1981) | • Richard Nixon's landslide victory (1972)<br>• Watergate scandal; Nixon resigns (1974)<br>• Jimmy Carter elected president (1976)<br>• Moral Majority founded (1979) | • Equal Rights Amendment (1972)<br>• *Roe v. Wade* (1973)<br>• *Bakke v. University of California* (1978)<br>• Harvey Milk assassinated (1978) | • First Earth Day (1970)<br>• Environmental Protection Agency established (1970)<br>• Endangered Species Act (1973)<br>• Three Mile Island accident (1979) | • Energy crisis (1973)<br>• Inflation surges, while economy stagnates (stagflation)<br>• Deindustrialization<br>• Tax revolt in California (1978) |

# 25
## CHAPTER

# Cold War America
# 1945–1963

In the autumn of 1950, a little-known California congressman running for the Senate named Richard M. Nixon stood before reporters in Los Angeles. His opponent, Helen Gahagan Douglas, was a Hollywood actress and a New Deal Democrat. Nixon told the gathered reporters that Douglas had cast "Communist-leaning" votes and that she was "pink right down to her underwear." Gahagan's voting record was not much different from Nixon's. But tarring her with communism made her seem un-American, and Nixon defeated the "pink lady" with nearly 60 percent of the vote.

A few months earlier, U.S. tanks, planes, and artillery supplies had arrived in French Indochina. A French colony since the nineteenth century, Indochina (present-day Vietnam, Laos, and Cambodia) was home to an independence movement led by Ho Chi Minh and supported by the Soviet Union and China. In the summer of 1950, President Harry S. Truman authorized $15 million worth of military supplies to aid France, which was fighting Ho's army to keep possession of its Indochinese empire. "Neither national independence nor democratic evolution exists in any area dominated by Soviet imperialism," Secretary of State Dean Acheson warned ominously as he announced U.S. support for French imperialism.

Connecting these coincidental historical moments, one domestic and the other international, was a decades-old force in American life that gained renewed strength after World War II: anticommunism. The events in Los Angeles and Vietnam, however different on the surface, were part of the global geopolitical struggle between the democratic United States and the communist, authoritarian Soviet Union known as the Cold War. Beginning in Europe as World War II ended and extending to Asia, Latin America, the Middle East, and Africa by the mid-1950s, the Cold War reshaped international relations and dominated global politics for more than forty years.

In the United States, the Cold War fostered suspicion of "subversives" in government, education, and the media. The arms race that developed between the two superpowers prompted Congress to boost military expenditures. The resulting military-industrial complex enhanced the power of the corporations that built planes, munitions, and electronic devices. In politics, the Cold War stifled liberal initiatives as the New Deal coalition tried to advance its domestic agenda in the shadow of anticommunism. In these ways, the line between the international and the domestic blurred—and that blurred line was another enduring legacy of the Cold War.

## IDENTIFY THE BIG IDEA

In the first two decades of the Cold War, how did competition on the international stage and a climate of fear at home affect politics, society, and culture in the United States?

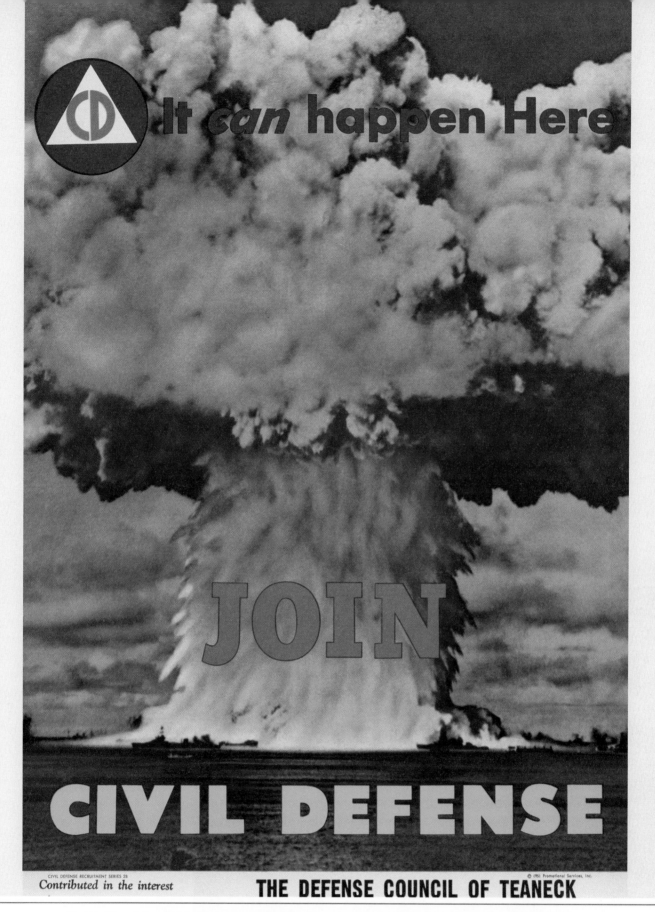

**The Perils of the Cold War**   Americans, like much of the world, lived under the threat of nuclear warfare during the tense years of the Cold War between the United States and the Soviet Union. This 1951 civil defense poster, with the message "It *can* happen Here," suggests that Americans should be prepared for such a dire outcome. © Bettmann/Corbis.

# Containment and a Divided Global Order

The Cold War began on the heels of World War II and ended in 1991 with the dissolution of the Soviet Union. While it lasted, this conflict raised two critical questions at the center of global history: What conditions, and whose interests, would determine the balance of power in Europe and Asia? And how would the developing nations (the European colonies in Asia, the Middle East, and Africa) gain their independence and take their places on the world stage? Cold War rivalry framed the possible answers to both questions as it drew the United States into a prolonged engagement with world affairs, unprecedented in the nation's history, that continues to the present day.

## Origins of the Cold War

World War II set the basic conditions for the Cold War. With Germany and Japan defeated and Britain and France weakened by years of war, only two geopolitical powers remained standing in 1945. Even had nothing divided them, the United States and the Soviet Union would have jostled each other as they moved to fill the postwar power vacuum. But, of course, the two countries were divided — by geography, history, ideology, and strategic interest. Little united them other than their commitment to defeating the Axis powers. President Franklin Roosevelt understood that maintaining the U.S.-Soviet alliance was essential for postwar global stability. But he also believed that permanent peace and long-term U.S. interests depended on the Wilsonian principles of collective security, self-determination, and free trade (Chapter 21).

**Yalta**   At the **Yalta Conference** of February 1945, Wilsonian principles yielded to U.S.-Soviet power realities. As Allied forces neared victory in Europe and advanced toward Japan in the Pacific, Roosevelt, Churchill, and Stalin met in Yalta, a resort in southern Ukraine on the Black Sea. Roosevelt focused on maintaining Allied unity and securing Stalin's commitment to enter the war against Japan. But the fates of the nations of Eastern Europe divided the Big Three. Stalin insisted that Russian national security required pro-Soviet governments in Eastern Europe. Roosevelt pressed for an agreement, the "Declaration on Liberated Europe," that guaranteed self-determination and democratic elections in Poland and neighboring countries, such as Romania and Hungary. However, given the

**East Meets West**

With an "East Meets West" placard providing inspiration, Private Frank B. Huff of Virginia (on the left) and a Russian soldier shake hands. Huff was one of the first four Americans to contact the Russians when the two armies met at the River Elbe (seen in the background of this photo) in eastern Germany, on April 25, 1945. The good will in evidence in the spring of 1945, as Americans and Russians alike celebrated the defeat of Nazi Germany, would within two short years be replaced by Cold War suspicion and hostility. © Bettmann/Corbis.

presence of Soviet troops in those nations, FDR had to accept a pledge from Stalin to hold "free and unfettered elections" at a future time. The three leaders also formalized their commitment to divide Germany into four administrative zones, each controlled by one of the four Allied powers, and to similarly partition the capital city, Berlin, which was located in the middle of the Soviet zone.

At Yalta, the Big Three also agreed to establish an international body to replace the discredited League of Nations. Based on plans drawn up at the 1944 Dumbarton Oaks conference in Washington, D.C., the new organization, to be known as the **United Nations**, would have both a General Assembly, in which all nations would be represented, and a Security Council composed of the five major Allied powers — the United States, Britain, France, China, and the Soviet Union — and seven other nations elected on a rotating basis. The Big Three determined that the five permanent members of the Security Council should have veto power over decisions of the General Assembly. They announced that the United Nations would convene for the first time in San Francisco on April 25, 1945.

**Potsdam**   Following the Yalta Conference, developments over the ensuing year further hardened relations between the Soviets on one side and the Americans and British on the other. At the **Potsdam Conference** outside Berlin in July 1945, Harry Truman replaced the deceased Roosevelt. Inexperienced in world affairs and thrown into enormously complicated negotiations, Truman's instinct was to stand up to Stalin. "Unless Russia is faced with an iron fist and strong language," he said, "another war is in the making." But Truman was in no position to realign events in Eastern Europe, where Soviet-imposed governments in Poland, Hungary, and Romania were backed by the Red Army and could not be eliminated by Truman's bluster. In Poland and Romania, in particular, Stalin was determined to establish communist governments, punish wartime Nazi collaborators, and win boundary concessions that augmented Soviet territory (the Soviet leader sought eastern Polish lands for the Soviet Union and sought to make far northeastern Germany part of Poland).

Yalta and Potsdam thus set the stage for communist rule to descend over Eastern Europe. The elections called for at Yalta eventually took place in Finland, Hungary, Bulgaria, and Czechoslovakia, with varying degrees of democratic openness. Nevertheless, Stalin got the client regimes he desired in those countries and would soon exert near-complete control over their governments. Stalin's unwillingness to honor

self-determination for nations in Eastern Europe was, from the American point of view, the precipitating event of the Cold War.

Germany represented the biggest challenge of all. American officials at Potsdam believed that a revived German economy was essential to ensuring the prosperity of democratic regimes throughout Western Europe — and to keeping ordinary Germans from turning again to Nazism. In contrast, Stalin hoped merely to extract reparations from Germany in the form of industrial machines and goods. In exchange for recognizing the new German-Polish border, Truman and Secretary of State James Byrnes convinced the Soviet leader to accept German reparations only from the Soviet zone, which lay in the far eastern, and largely rural, portion of Germany and promised little wealth or German industry to plunder. As they had done for Europe as a whole, the Yalta and Potsdam agreements paved the way for the division of Germany into East and West (Map 25.1).

Yalta and Potsdam had demonstrated that in private negotiations the United States and the Soviet Union had starkly different objectives. Subsequent public utterances only intensified those differences. In February 1946, Stalin delivered a speech in which he insisted that, according to Marxist-Leninist principles, "the unevenness of development of the capitalist countries" was likely to produce "violent disturbance" and even another war. He seemed to blame any future war on the capitalist West. Churchill responded in kind a month later. While visiting Truman in Missouri to be honored for his wartime leadership, Churchill accused Stalin of raising an "iron curtain" around Eastern Europe and allowing "police government" to rule its people. He went further, claiming that "a fraternal association of English-speaking peoples," and not Russians, ought to set the terms of the postwar world.

> **UNDERSTAND POINTS OF VIEW**
> How did American and Soviet viewpoints differ over the postwar fate of Europe?

The cities and fields of Europe had barely ceased to run with the blood of World War II before they were menaced again by the tense standoff between the Soviet Union and the United States. With Stalin intent on establishing client states in Eastern Europe and the United States equally intent on reviving Germany and ensuring collective security throughout Europe, the points of agreement were few and far between. Among the Allies, anxiety about a Nazi victory in World War II had been quickly replaced by fear of a potentially more cataclysmic war with the Soviet Union.

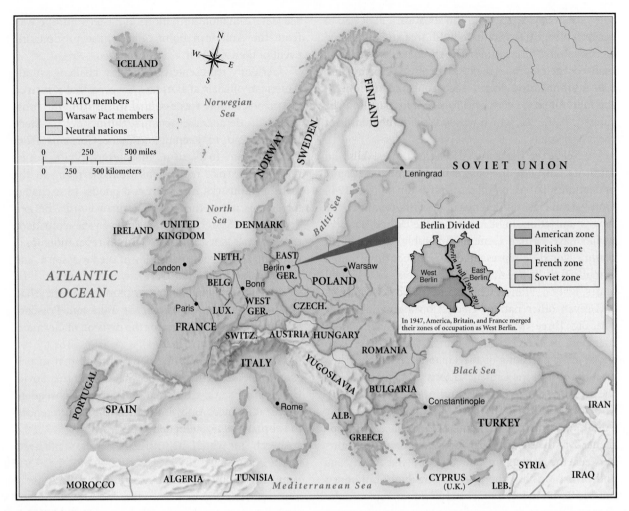

**MAP 25.1**
**Cold War in Europe, 1955**

This map vividly shows the Cold War division of Europe. The NATO countries (colored green) are allies of the United States; the Warsaw Pact countries (in purple) are allied to the USSR. At that point, West Germany had just been admitted to NATO, completing Europe's stabilization into two rival camps. But Berlin remained divided, and one can see from its location deep in East Germany why the former capital was always a flash point in Cold War controversies.

## The Containment Strategy

In the late 1940s, American officials developed a clear strategy toward the Soviet Union that would become known as **containment**. Convinced that the USSR was methodically expanding its reach, the United States would counter by limiting Stalin's influence to Eastern Europe while reconstituting democratic governments in Western Europe. In 1946–1947, three specific issues worried Truman and his advisors. First, the Soviet Union was pressing Iran for access to oil and Turkey for access to the Mediterranean. Second, a civil war was roiling in Greece, between monarchists backed by England and insurgents supported by the Greek and

Yugoslavian Communist parties. Third, as European nations suffered through terrible privation in 1946 and 1947, Communist parties gained strength, particularly in France and Italy. All three developments, as seen from the United States, threatened to expand the influence of the Soviet Union outside of Eastern Europe.

**Toward an Uneasy Peace** In this anxious context, the strategy of containment emerged in a series of incremental steps between 1946 and 1949. In February 1946, American diplomat George F. Kennan first proposed the idea in an 8,000-word cable — a confidential message to the U.S. State Department — from his post at the U.S. embassy in Moscow. Kennan argued that the

Soviet Union was an "Oriental despotism" and that communism was merely the "fig leaf" justifying Soviet aggression. A year after writing this cable (dubbed the Long Telegram), he published an influential *Foreign Affairs* article, arguing that the West's only recourse was to meet the Soviets "with unalterable counter-force at every point where they show signs of encroaching upon the interests of a peaceful and stable world." Kennan called for "long-term, patient but firm and vigilant containment of Russian expansive tendencies." *Containment*, the key word, came to define America's evolving strategic stance toward the Soviet Union.

 To see a longer excerpt of the Long Telegram, along with other primary sources from this period, see *Sources for America's History*.

Kennan believed that the Soviet system was inherently unstable and would eventually collapse. Containment would work, he reasoned, as long as the United States and its allies opposed Soviet expansion in all parts of the world. Kennan's attentive readers included Stalin himself, who quickly obtained a copy of the classified Long Telegram. The Soviet leader saw the United States as an imperialist aggressor determined to replace Great Britain as the world's dominant capitalist power. Just as Kennan thought that the Soviet system was despotic and unsustainable, Stalin believed that the West suffered from its own fatal weaknesses. Neither side completely understood or trusted the other, and each projected its worst fears onto the other.

In fact, Britain's influence in the world was declining. Exhausted by the war, facing enormous budget deficits and a collapsing economy at home, and confronted with a determined independence movement in India led by Mohandas Gandhi and growing nationalist movements throughout its empire, Britain was waning as a global power. "The reins of world leadership are fast slipping from Britain's competent but now very weak hands," read a U.S. State Department report. "These reins will be picked up either by the United States or by Russia." The United States was wedded to the notion—dating to the Wilson administration—that communism and capitalism were incompatible on the world stage. With Britain faltering, American officials saw little choice but to fill its shoes.

It did not take long for the reality of Britain's decline to resonate across the Atlantic. In February 1947, London informed Truman that it could no longer afford to support the anticommunists in the Greek civil war. Truman worried that a communist victory in Greece would lead to Soviet domination of the eastern Mediterranean and embolden Communist parties in France and Italy. In response, the president announced what became known as the **Truman Doctrine.** In a speech on March 12, he asserted an American responsibility "to support free peoples who are resisting attempted subjugation by armed minorities or by outside pressures." To that end, Truman proposed large-scale assistance for Greece and Turkey (then involved in a dispute with the Soviet Union over the Dardanelles, a strait connecting the Aegean Sea and the Sea of Marmara). "If we falter in our leadership, we may endanger the peace of the world," Truman declared (Thinking Like a Historian, p. 810). Despite the open-endedness of this military commitment, Congress quickly approved Truman's request for $300 million in aid to Greece and $100 million for Turkey.

Soviet expansionism was part of a larger story. Europe was sliding into economic chaos. Already devastated by the war, in 1947 the continent suffered the worst winter in memory. People were starving, credit was nonexistent, wages were stagnant, and the consumer market had collapsed. For both humanitarian and practical reasons, Truman's advisors believed something had to be done. A global depression might ensue if the European economy, the largest foreign market for American goods, did not recover. Worse, unemployed and dispirited Western Europeans might fill the ranks of the Communist Party, threatening political stability and the legitimacy of the United States. Secretary of State George C. Marshall came up with a remarkable proposal: a massive infusion of American capital to rebuild the European economy. Speaking at the Harvard University commencement in June 1947, Marshall urged the nations of Europe to work out a comprehensive recovery program based on U.S. aid.

This pledge of financial assistance required congressional approval, but the plan ran into opposition in Washington. Republicans castigated the **Marshall Plan** as a huge "international WPA." But in the midst of the congressional stalemate, on February 25, 1948, Stalin supported a communist-led coup in Czechoslovakia. Congress rallied and voted overwhelmingly in 1948 to approve the Marshall Plan. Over the next four years, the United States contributed nearly $13 billion to a highly successful recovery effort that benefitted both Western Europe and the United States. European industrial production increased by 64 percent, and the appeal of Communist parties waned in the West. Markets for American goods grew stronger

**PLACE EVENTS IN CONTEXT**
Why did the United States enact the Marshall Plan, and how did the program illustrate America's new role in the world?

## The Global Cold War

Until 1950, the U.S. policy of containment was confined to economic measures, such as financial assistance to Greece and Turkey and the Marshall Plan, and focused on Europe. That changed between 1950 and 1954. In those years, containment became militarized, and its scope was expanded to include Asia and Latin America. What had begun as a limited policy to contain Soviet influence in war-torn Europe had by the mid-1950s become a global campaign against communism and social revolution.

1. **President Harry S. Truman, address before joint session of Congress, March 12, 1947.** *Known as the Truman Doctrine, this speech outlined Truman's plan to give large-scale assistance to Greece and Turkey as part of a broader anticommunist policy.*

To ensure the peaceful development of nations, free from coercion, the United States has taken a leading part in establishing the United Nations. The United Nations is designed to make possible lasting freedom and independence for all its members. We shall not realize our objectives, however, unless we are willing to help free peoples to maintain their free institutions and their national integrity against aggressive movements that seek to impose upon them totalitarian regimes. . . .

At the present moment in world history nearly every nation must choose between alternative ways of life. The choice is too often not a free one.

One way of life is based upon the will of the majority, and is distinguished by free institutions, representative government, free elections, guarantees of individual liberty, freedom of speech and religion, and freedom from political oppression.

The second way of life is based upon the will of a minority forcibly imposed upon the majority. It relies upon terror and oppression, a controlled press and radio; fixed elections, and the suppression of personal freedoms.

I believe that it must be the policy of the United States to support free peoples who are resisting attempted subjugation by armed minorities or by outside pressures.

I believe that we must assist free peoples to work out their own destinies in their own way.

I believe that our help should be primarily through economic and financial aid which is essential to economic stability and orderly political processes.

2. **Syngman Rhee, president of South Korea, criticizing U.S. policy in 1950.** *The Korean War, 1950–1953, represented the militarization of the Truman Doctrine.*

A few days ago one American friend said that if the U.S. gave weapons to South Korea, she feared that South Korea would invade North Korea. This is a useless worry of some Americans, who do not know South Korea. Our present war is not a Cold War, but a real shooting war. Our troops will take all possible counter-measures. . . . In South Korea the U.S. has one foot in South Korea and one foot outside so that in case of an unfavorable situation it could pull out of the country. I daresay that if the U.S. wants to aid our country, it should not be only lip-service.

3. **Secretary of State Dean Acheson's testimony before the Senate Armed Forces and Foreign Relations Committee, 1951.**

The attack on Korea was . . . a challenge to the whole system of collective security, not only in the Far East, but everywhere in the world. It was a threat to all nations newly arrived at independence. . . .

This was a test which would decide whether our collective security system would survive or would crumble. It would determine whether other nations would be intimidated by this show of force. . . .

As a people we condemn aggression of any kind. We reject appeasement of any kind. If we stood with our arms folded while Korea was swallowed up, it would have meant abandoning our principles, and it would have meant the defeat of the collective security system on which our own safety ultimately depends.

4. **Shigeru Yoshida, prime minister of Japan, speech before the Japanese Diet (parliament), July 14, 1950.**

It is heartening . . . that America and so many members of the United Nations have gone to the rescue of an invaded country regardless of the heavy sacrifices involved. In case a war breaks out on an extensive scale how would Japan's security be preserved [since we are disarmed]? . . . This has been hotly discussed. However, the measures taken by the United Nations have done much to stabilize our people's minds.

5. **John Foster Dulles, secretary of state (1953–1959), June 30, 1954, radio and television address to the American people.** *In 1951, Jacobo Arbenz was elected president of Guatemala. Arbenz pursued reform policies that threatened large landholders, including the United Fruit Company. In 1954, the United States CIA engineered a coup that overthrew Arbenz and replaced him with Carlos Castillo Armas, a colonel in the Guatemalan military.*

Tonight I should like to speak with you about Guatemala. It is the scene of dramatic events. They expose the evil purpose of the Kremlin to destroy the inter-American system, and they test the ability of the American States to maintain the peaceful integrity of the hemisphere.

For several years international communism has been probing here and there for nesting places in the Americas. It finally chose Guatemala as a spot which it could turn into an official base from which to breed subversion which would extend to other American Republics.

This intrusion of Soviet despotism was, of course, a direct challenge to our Monroe Doctrine, the first and most fundamental of our foreign policies.

6. **Guillermo Toriello, Guatemalan foreign minister, speech to delegates at the Tenth Inter-American Conference of the Organization of American States in Caracas, Venezuela, March 5, 1954.**

What is the real and effective reason for describing our government as communist? From what sources comes the accusation that we threaten continental solidarity and security? Why do they [United States] wish to intervene in Guatemala?

The answers are simple and evident. The plan of national liberation being carried out with firmness by my government has necessarily affected the privileges of the foreign enterprises that are impeding the progress and the economic development of the country. . . . With construction of publically owned ports and docks, we are putting an end to the monopoly of the United Fruit Company. . . .

They wanted to find a ready expedient to maintain the economic dependence of the American Republics and suppress the legitimate desires of their peoples, cataloguing as "communism" every manifestation of nationalism or economic independence, any desire for social progress, any intellectual curiosity, and any interest in progressive and liberal reforms.

7. **Herblock cartoon from the *Washington Post*, February 11, 1962.** *Many Latin American countries were beset by a wide gap between a small wealthy elite and the mass of ordinary, much poorer citizens. American officials worried that this made social revolution an attractive alternative for those at the bottom.*

A 1962 Herblock Cartoon, by The Herb Block Foundation.

Sources: (1) The Avalon Project at avalon.law.yale.edu; (2) Reinhard Drifte, "Japan's Involvement in the Korean War," in *The Korean War in History*, ed. James Cotton and Ian Neary (Atlantic Highlands, NJ: Humanities Press International, 1989), 43; (3) Glenn D. Paige, *The Korean Decision* (New York: The Free Press, 1968), 175–176; (4) Drifte, 122; (5) Jonathan L. Fried et al., eds., *Guatemala in Rebellion: Unfinished History* (New York: Grove Press, 1983), 78; (6) Stephen C. Schlesinger and Stephen Kinzer, *Bitter Fruit: The Untold Story of the American Coup in Guatemala* (Garden City, NY: Doubleday, 1982), 143–144.

### ANALYZING THE EVIDENCE

1. In source 1, Truman presents the choice facing the world in stark terms: totalitarianism or democracy. Why would he frame matters in this way in 1947? How did Truman anticipate the militarization of American foreign policy?

2. Analyze the audience, purpose, and point of view presented in the documents dealing with the war in Korea (sources 2–4). What does Acheson mean by "collective security"? Why is Yoshida thankful for the UN intervention? What can you infer about U.S. involvement in world affairs during the postwar period based on these documents?

3. In document 6, how does Toriello characterize accusations that the elected Guatemalan government is communist? What are his accusations of the United States?

4. How does source 7 express one of the obstacles to democracy in developing nations?

### PUTTING IT ALL TOGETHER

Using these documents, and based on what you have learned in class and in this chapter, write an essay in which you analyze the goals of American foreign policy during the early years of the Cold War.

**The Marshall Plan**

Officials from the United States and Britain watch as the first shipment of Caribbean sugar provided under the Marshall Plan arrives in England, lowered from the decks of the *Royal Victoria*. Passed by Congress in 1948, the Marshall Plan (known officially as the European Recovery Program) committed the United States to spend $17 billion over a four-year period to assist the war-ravaged nations of Western Europe. Marshall Plan funds helped the struggling British, French, and especially German economies, but they also benefitted the United States itself: the plan required European nations who participated to purchase most of their goods from American companies. Keystone/Getty Images.

and fostered economic interdependence between Europe and the United States. Notably, however, the Marshall Plan intensified Cold War tensions. U.S. officials invited the Soviets to participate but insisted on certain restrictions that would virtually guarantee Stalin's refusal. When Stalin refused, ordering Soviet client states to do so as well, the onus of dividing Europe appeared to fall on the Soviet leader and deprived his threadbare partners of assistance they sorely needed.

**East and West in the New Europe**  The flash point for a hot war remained Germany, the most important industrial economy and the key strategic landmass in Europe. When no agreement could be reached to unify

the four zones of occupation into a single state, the Western allies consolidated their three zones in 1947. They then prepared to establish an independent federal German republic. Marshall Plan funds would jumpstart economic recovery. Some of those funds were slated for West Berlin, in hopes of making the city a capitalist showplace 100 miles deep inside the Soviet zone.

Stung by the West's intention to create a German republic, in June 1948 Stalin blockaded all traffic to West Berlin. Instead of yielding, as Stalin had expected, Truman and the British were resolute. "We are going to stay, period," Truman said plainly. Over the next year, American and British pilots, who had been dropping bombs on Berlin only four years earlier, improvised the Berlin Airlift, which flew 2.5 million tons of food and fuel into the Western zones of the city—nearly a ton for each resident. Military officials reported to Truman that General Lucius D. Clay, the American commander in Berlin, was nervous and on edge, "drawn as tight as a steel spring." But after a prolonged stalemate, Stalin backed down: on May 12, 1949, he lifted the blockade. Until the Cuban missile crisis in 1962, the Berlin crisis was the closest the two sides came to actual war, and West Berlin became a symbol of resistance to communism.

The crisis in Berlin persuaded Western European nations to forge a collective security pact with the United States. In April 1949, for the first time since the end of the American Revolution, the United States entered into a peacetime military alliance, the **North Atlantic Treaty Organization (NATO)**. Under the NATO pact, twelve nations—Belgium, Canada, Denmark, France, Great Britain, Iceland, Italy, Luxembourg, the Netherlands, Norway, Portugal, and the United States—agreed that "an armed attack against one or more of them in Europe or North America shall be considered an attack against them all." In May 1949, those nations also agreed to the creation of the Federal Republic of Germany (West Germany), which eventually joined NATO in 1955. In response, the Soviet Union established the German Democratic Republic (East Germany); the Council for Mutual Economic Assistance (COMECON); and, in 1955, the **Warsaw Pact**, a military alliance for Eastern Europe that included Albania, Bulgaria, Czechoslovakia, East Germany, Hungary, Poland, Romania, and the Soviet Union. In these parallel steps, the two superpowers had institutionalized the Cold War through a massive division of the continent.

By the early 1950s, West and East were the stark markers of the new Europe. As Churchill had observed

**The Berlin Airlift**

For 321 days U.S. planes like this one flew missions to bring food and other supplies to Berlin after the Soviet Union had blocked all surface routes into the former German capital. The blockade was finally lifted on May 12, 1949, after the Soviets conceded that it had been a failure. AP Images.

in 1946, the line dividing the two stretched "from Stettin in the Baltic to Trieste in the Adriatic," cutting off tens of millions of Eastern Europeans from the rest of the continent. Stalin's tactics had often been ruthless, but they were not without reason. The Soviet Union acted out of the sort of self-interest that had long defined powerful nations — ensuring a defensive perimeter of allies, seeking access to raw materials, and pressing the advantage that victory in war allowed.

**NSC-68**   Atomic developments, too, played a critical role in the emergence of the Cold War. As the sole nuclear power at the end of World War II, the United States entertained the possibility of international control of nuclear technology but did not wish to lose its advantage over the Soviet Union. When the American Bernard Baruch proposed United Nations oversight of atomic energy in 1946, for instance, the plan assured the United States of near-total control of the technology, which further increased Cold War tensions. America's brief tenure as sole nuclear power ended in September 1949, however, when the Soviet Union detonated an atomic bomb. Truman then turned to the U.S. National Security Council (NSC), established by the National Security Act of 1947, for a strategic reassessment.

In April 1950, the NSC delivered its report, known as **NSC-68**. Bristling with alarmist rhetoric, the document marked a decisive turning point in the U.S. approach to the Cold War. The report's authors described the Soviet Union not as a typical great power but as one with a "fanatic faith" that seeks to "impose its absolute authority." Going beyond even the stern language used by George Kennan, NSC-68 cast Soviet ambitions as nothing short of "the domination of the Eurasian landmass."

To prevent that outcome, the report proposed "a bold and massive program of rebuilding the West's defensive potential to surpass that of the Soviet world" (America Compared, p. 814). This included the development of a hydrogen bomb, a thermonuclear device that would be a thousand times more destructive than the atomic bombs dropped on Japan, as well as dramatic increases in conventional military forces. Critically, NSC-68 called for Americans to pay higher taxes to support the new military program and to accept whatever sacrifices were necessary to achieve national unity of purpose against the Soviet enemy. Many historians see the report as having "militarized" the American approach to the Cold War, which had to that point relied largely on economic measures such as aid to Greece and the Marshall Plan. Truman was reluctant to commit to a major defense buildup, fearing that it would overburden the national budget. But shortly after NSC-68 was completed, events in Asia led him to reverse course.

## Containment in Asia

As with Germany, American officials believed that restoring Japan's economy, while limiting its military influence, would ensure prosperity and contain communism in East Asia. After dismantling Japan's military, American occupation forces under General Douglas MacArthur drafted a democratic constitution and

## Arming for the Cold War

To fight the Cold War, the United States and the Soviet Union increased overall military spending and assembled massive arsenals of nuclear weapons.

### TABLE 25.1

**Worldwide Nuclear Stockpiles, 1945–1975**

| Country | 1945 | 1955 | 1965 | 1975 |
|---|---|---|---|---|
| United States | 2 | 3,057 | 32,135 | 27,235 |
| USSR | 0 | 200 | 6,129 | 19,443 |
| United Kingdom | 0 | 10 | 310 | 350 |
| France | 0 | 0 | 32 | 188 |
| China | 0 | 0 | 5 | 185 |
| Israel | 0 | 0 | 0 | 20* |

*Estimated

SOURCES: Adapted from *Bulletin of the Atomic Scientists*, National Resources Defense Council, and *Nuclear Weapons and Nonproliferation* (2007).

**QUESTIONS FOR ANALYSIS**

1. Do you see evidence of the effects of NSC-68 in this table? What kinds of changes did NSC-68 bring about?
2. In what ways does the data in this table suggest the emergence of two "superpowers" after World War II?

paved the way for the restoration of Japanese sovereignty in 1951. Considering the scorched-earth war that had just ended, this was a remarkable achievement, thanks partly to the imperious MacArthur but mainly to the Japanese, who embraced peace and accepted U.S. military protection. However, events on the mainland of Asia proved much more difficult for the United States to shape to its advantage.

**Civil War in China**   A civil war had been raging in China since the 1930s as Communist forces led by Mao Zedong (Mao Tse-tung) fought Nationalist forces under Jiang Jieshi (Chiang Kai-shek). Fearing a Communist victory, between 1945 and 1949 the United States provided $2 billion to Jiang's army. Pressing Truman to "save" China, conservative Republican Ohio senator Robert A. Taft predicted that "the Far East is ultimately even more important to our future peace than is Europe." By 1949, Mao's forces held the advantage. Truman reasoned that to save Jiang, the United States would have to intervene militarily. Unwilling to do so, he cut off aid and left the Nationalists to their fate. The People's Republic of China was formally established under Mao on October 1, 1949, and the remnants of Jiang's forces fled to Taiwan.

Both Stalin and Truman expected Mao to take an independent line, as the Communist leader Tito had just done in Yugoslavia. Mao, however, aligned himself with the Soviet Union, partly out of fear that the United States would re-arm the Nationalists and invade the mainland. As attitudes hardened, many Americans viewed Mao's success as a defeat for the United States. The pro-Nationalist "China lobby" accused Truman's State Department of being responsible for the "loss" of China. Sensitive to these charges, the Truman administration refused to recognize "Red China" and blocked China's admission to the United Nations. But the United States pointedly declined to guarantee Taiwan's independence, and in fact accepted the outcome on the

**COMPARE AND CONTRAST**

How did U.S. containment strategy in Asia compare to containment in Europe?

## Communist China

People in Beijing raise their clenched fists in a welcoming salute for Chinese Communist forces entering the city after the Nationalists surrendered on January 31, 1949. The center portrait behind them is of General Mao Zedong, the leader of the Communist Party of China. Mao's victory in the civil war (1946–1950) meant that from East Germany to the Pacific Ocean, much of the Eurasian landmass (including Eastern Europe, the Soviet Union, and China) was ruled by Communist governments. AP Images.

mainland. (Since 1982, however, the United States has recognized Taiwanese sovereignty.)

## The Korean War

The United States took a stronger stance in Korea. The United States and the Soviet Union had agreed at the close of World War II to occupy the Korean peninsula jointly, temporarily dividing the former Japanese colony at the 38th parallel. As tensions rose in Europe, the 38th parallel hardened into a permanent demarcation line. The Soviets supported a Communist government, led by Kim Il Sung, in North Korea; the United States backed a right-wing Nationalist, Syngman Rhee, in South Korea. The two sides had waged low-level war since 1945, and

## The Korean War

As a result of President Truman's 1948 Executive Order 9981, for the first time in the nation's history all troops in the Korean War served in racially integrated combat units. This photo taken during the Battle of Ch'ongch'on in 1950 shows a sergeant and his men of the 2nd Infantry Division. National Archives.

both leaders were spoiling for a more definitive fight. However, neither Kim nor Rhee could launch an all-out offensive without the backing of his sponsor. Washington repeatedly said no, and so did Moscow. But Kim continued to press Stalin to permit him to reunify the nation. Convinced by the North Koreans that victory would be swift, the Soviet leader finally relented in the late spring of 1950.

On June 25, 1950, the North Koreans launched a surprise attack across the 38th parallel (Map 25.2). Truman immediately asked the UN Security Council to authorize a "police action" against the invaders. The Soviet Union was boycotting the Security Council to protest China's exclusion from the United Nations and could not veto Truman's request. With the Security Council's approval of a "peacekeeping force," Truman ordered U.S. troops to Korea. The rapidly assembled UN army in Korea was overwhelmingly American, with General Douglas MacArthur in command. At first, the North Koreans held a distinct advantage, but MacArthur's surprise amphibious attack at Inchon gave the UN forces control of Seoul, the South Korean

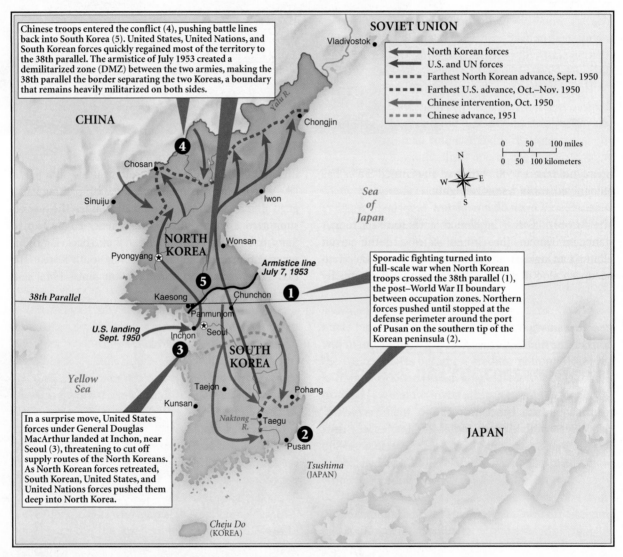

**MAP 25.2**

**The Korean War, 1950–1953**

The Korean War, which the United Nations officially deemed a "police action," lasted three years and cost the lives of more than 36,000 U.S. troops. South and North Korean deaths were estimated at more than 900,000. Although hostilities ceased in 1953, the South Korean Military (with U.S. military assistance) and the North Korean Army continue to face each other across the demilitarized zone, more than fifty years later.

capital, and almost all the territory up to the 38th parallel.

The impetuous MacArthur then ordered his troops across the 38th parallel and led them all the way to the Chinese border at the Yalu River. It was a major blunder, certain to draw China into the war. Sure enough, a massive Chinese counterattack forced MacArthur's forces into headlong retreat back down the Korean peninsula. Then stalemate set in. With weak public support for the war in the United States, Truman and his advisors decided to work for a negotiated peace. MacArthur disagreed and denounced the Korean stalemate, declaring, "There is no substitute for victory." On April 11, 1951, Truman relieved MacArthur of his command. Truman's decision was highly unpopular, especially among conservative Republicans, but he had likely saved the nation from years of costly warfare with China.

Notwithstanding MacArthur's dismissal, the war dragged on for more than two years. An armistice in July 1953, pushed by the newly elected president, Dwight D. Eisenhower, left Korea divided at the original demarcation line. North Korea remained firmly allied with the Soviet Union; South Korea signed a mutual defense treaty with the United States. It had been the first major proxy battle of the Cold War, in which the Soviet Union and United States took sides in a civil conflict. It would not be the last.

The Korean War had far-reaching consequences. Truman's decision to commit troops without congressional approval set a precedent for future undeclared wars. His refusal to unleash atomic bombs, even when American forces were reeling under a massive Chinese attack, set ground rules for Cold War conflict. The war also expanded American involvement in Asia, transforming containment into a truly global policy — and significantly boosting Japan's struggling postwar economy. Finally, the Korean War ended Truman's resistance to a major military buildup. Defense expenditures grew from $13 billion in 1950, roughly one-third of the federal budget, to $50 billion in 1953, nearly two-thirds of the budget (Map 25.3). American

**MAP 25.3**

**The Military-Industrial Complex**

Defense spending gave a big boost to the Cold War economy, but, as the upper map suggests, the benefits were by no means equally distributed. The big winners were the Middle Atlantic states, the industrialized Upper Midwest, Washington State (with its aircraft and nuclear plants), and California. The epicenter of California's military-industrial complex was Los Angeles, which, as is evident in the lower map, was studded with military facilities and major defense contractors like Douglas Aircraft, Lockheed, and General Dynamics. There was work aplenty for engineers and rocket scientists.

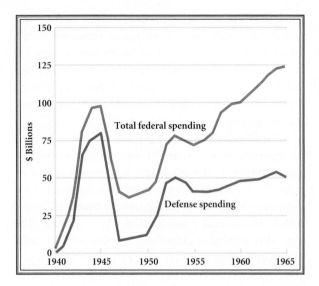

**FIGURE 25.1**
**National Defense Spending, 1940–1965**
In 1950, the U.S. defense budget was $13 billion, less than a third of total federal outlays. In 1961, U.S. defense spending reached $47 billion, fully half of the federal budget and almost 10 percent of the gross domestic product.

foreign policy had become more global, more militarized, and more expensive (Figure 25.1). Even in times of peace, the United States now functioned in a state of permanent military mobilization.

**The Munich Analogy**   Behind much of U.S. foreign policy in the first two decades of the Cold War lay the memory of appeasement (Chapter 24). The generation of politicians and officials who designed the containment strategy had come of age in the shadow of Munich, the conference in 1938 at which the Western democracies had appeased Hitler by offering him part of Czechoslovakia, paving the road to World War II. Applying the lessons of Munich, American presidents believed that "appeasing" Stalin (and subsequent Soviet rulers Nikita Khrushchev and Leonid Brezhnev) would have the same result: wider war. Thus in Germany, Greece, and Korea, and later in Iran, Guatemala, and Vietnam, the United States staunchly resisted the Soviets — or what it perceived as Soviet influence. The Munich analogy strengthened the U.S. position in a number of strategic conflicts, particularly over the fate of Germany. But it also drew Americans into armed conflicts — and convinced them to support repressive, right-wing regimes — that compromised, as much as supported, stated American principles.

# Cold War Liberalism

Harry Truman cast himself in the mold of his predecessor, Franklin Roosevelt, and hoped to seize the possibilities afforded by victory in World War II to expand the New Deal at home. But the crises in

postwar Europe and Asia, combined with the spectacular rise of anticommunism in the United States, forced him to take a different path. In the end, Truman went down in history not as a New Dealer, but as a Cold Warrior. The Cold War consensus that he ultimately embraced — the notion that resisting communism at home and abroad represented America's most important postwar objective — shaped the nation's life and politics for decades to come.

## Truman and the End of Reform

Truman and the Democratic Party of the late 1940s and early 1950s forged what historians call **Cold War liberalism**. They preserved the core programs of the New Deal welfare state, developed the containment policy to oppose Soviet influence throughout the world, and fought so-called subversives at home. But there would be no second act for the New Deal. The Democrats adopted this combination of moderate liberal policies and anticommunism — Cold War liberalism — partly by choice and partly out of necessity. A few high-level espionage scandals and the Communist victories in Eastern Europe and China reenergized the Republican Party, which forced Truman and the Democrats to retreat to what historian Arthur Schlesinger called the "vital center" of American politics. However, Americans on both the progressive left and the conservative right remained dissatisfied with this development. Cold War liberalism was a practical centrist policy for a turbulent era. But it would not last.

Organized labor remained a key force in the Democratic Party and played a central role in championing

Cold War liberalism. Stronger than ever, union membership swelled to more than 14 million by 1945. Determined to make up for their wartime sacrifices, unionized workers made aggressive demands and mounted major strikes in the automobile, steel, and coal industries after the war. Republicans responded. They gained control of the House in a sweeping repudiation of Democrats in 1946 and promptly passed — over Truman's veto — the **Taft-Hartley Act** (1947), an overhaul of the 1935 National Labor Relations Act.

Taft-Hartley crafted changes in procedures and language that, over time, weakened the right of workers to organize and engage in collective bargaining. Unions especially disliked Section 14b, which allowed states to pass "right-to-work" laws prohibiting the union shop. Additionally, the law forced unions to purge communists, who had been among the most successful labor organizers in the 1930s, from their ranks. Taft-Hartley effectively "contained" the labor movement. Trade unions would continue to support the Democratic Party, but the labor movement would not move into the largely non-union South and would not extend into the many American industries that remained unorganized.

**The 1948 Election**   Democrats would have dumped Truman in 1948 had they found a better candidate. But the party fell into disarray. The left wing split off and formed the Progressive Party, nominating Henry A. Wallace, an avid New Dealer whom Truman had fired as secretary of commerce in 1946 because Wallace opposed America's actions in the Cold War. A right-wing challenge came from the South. When northern liberals such as Mayor Hubert H. Humphrey of Minneapolis pushed through a strong civil rights platform at the Democratic convention, the southern delegations bolted and, calling themselves Dixiecrats, nominated for president South Carolina governor Strom Thurmond, an ardent supporter of racial segregation. The Republicans meanwhile renominated Thomas E. Dewey, the politically moderate governor of New York who had run a strong campaign against FDR in 1944.

Truman surprised everyone. He launched a strenuous cross-country speaking tour and hammered away at the Republicans for opposing progressive legislation and, in general, for running a "do-nothing" Congress. By combining these issues with attacks on the Soviet menace abroad, Truman began to salvage his troubled campaign. At his rallies, enthusiastic listeners shouted, "Give 'em hell, Harry!" Truman won, receiving 49.6 percent of the vote to Dewey's 45.1 percent (Map 25.4).

> **PLACE EVENTS IN CONTEXT**
> How was the Democratic Party divided in 1948, and what were its primary constituencies?

**Truman Triumphant**

In one of the most famous photographs in U.S. political history, Harry S. Truman gloats over an erroneous headline in the November 3 *Chicago Daily Tribune*. Pollsters had predicted an easy victory for Thomas E. Dewey. Their primitive techniques, however, missed the dramatic surge in support for Truman during the last days of the campaign.
© Bettmann/Corbis.

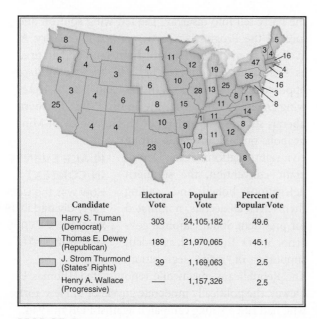

| Candidate | Electoral Vote | Popular Vote | Percent of Popular Vote |
|---|---|---|---|
| Harry S. Truman (Democrat) | 303 | 24,105,182 | 49.6 |
| Thomas E. Dewey (Republican) | 189 | 21,970,065 | 45.1 |
| J. Strom Thurmond (States' Rights) | 39 | 1,169,063 | 2.5 |
| Henry A. Wallace (Progressive) | — | 1,157,326 | 2.5 |

**MAP 25.4**

**The Presidential Election of 1948**

Truman's electoral strategy in 1948 was to concentrate his campaign in areas where the Democrats had their greatest strength. In an election with a low turnout, Truman held on to enough support from Roosevelt's New Deal coalition of blacks, union members, and farmers to defeat Dewey by more than 2 million votes.

This remarkable election foreshadowed coming political turmoil. Truman occupied the center of FDR's sprawling New Deal coalition. On his left were progressives, civil rights advocates, and anti–Cold War peace activists. On his right were segregationist southerners, who opposed civil rights and were allied with Republicans on many economic and foreign policy issues. In 1948, Truman performed a delicate balancing act, largely retaining the support of Jewish and Catholic voters in the big cities, black voters in the North, and organized labor voters across the country. But Thurmond's strong showing—he carried four states in the Deep South—demonstrated the fragile nature of the Democratic coalition and prefigured the revolt of the party's southern wing in the 1960s. As he tried to manage contending forces in his own party, Truman faced mounting pressure from Republicans to denounce radicals at home and to take a tough stand against the Soviet Union.

**The Fair Deal**   Despite having to perform a balancing act, Truman and progressive Democrats forged ahead. In 1949, reaching ambitiously to extend the New Deal, Truman proposed the **Fair Deal**: national health insurance, aid to education, a housing program, expansion of Social Security, a higher minimum wage, and a new agricultural program. In its attention to civil rights, the Fair Deal also reflected the growing role of African Americans in the Democratic Party. Congress, however, remained a huge stumbling block, and the Fair Deal fared poorly. The same conservative coalition that had blocked Roosevelt's initiatives in his second term continued the fight against Truman's. Cold War pressure shaped political arguments about domestic social programs, while the nation's growing paranoia over internal subversion weakened support for bold extensions of the welfare state. Truman's proposal for national health insurance, for instance, was a popular idea, with strong backing from organized labor. But it was denounced as "socialized medicine" by the American Medical Association and the insurance industry. In the end, the Fair Deal's only significant breakthrough, other than improvements to the minimum wage and Social Security, was the National Housing Act of 1949, which authorized the construction of 810,000 low-income units.

## Red Scare: The Hunt for Communists

Cold War liberalism was premised on the grave domestic threat posed, many believed, by Communists and Communist sympathizers. Was there any significant Soviet penetration of the American government? Records opened after the 1991 disintegration of the Soviet Union indicate that there was, although it was largely confined to the 1930s. Among American suppliers of information to Moscow were FDR's assistant secretary of the treasury, Harry Dexter White; FDR's administrative aide Laughlin Currie; a strategically placed midlevel group in the State Department; and several hundred more, some identified only by code name, working in a range of government departments and agencies.

How are we to explain this? Many of these enlistees in the Soviet cause had been bright young New Dealers in the mid-1930s, when the Soviet-backed Popular Front suggested that the lines separating liberalism, progressivism, and communism were permeable (Chapter 24). At that time, the United States was not at war and never expected to be. And when war did come, the Soviet Union was an American ally. For critics of the informants, however, there remained the time between the Nazi-Soviet Pact and the German invasion of the Soviet Union, a nearly two-year period during which cooperation with the Soviet Union could be seen in a less positive light. Moreover, passing secrets to another country, even a wartime ally, was simply indefensible to many Americans. The lines between U.S. and Soviet interests blurred for some; for others, they remained clear and definite.

After World War II, however, most suppliers of information to the Soviets apparently ceased spying. For one thing, the professional apparatus of Soviet spying in the United States was dismantled or disrupted by American counterintelligence work. For another, most of the well-connected amateur spies moved on to other careers. Historians have thus developed a healthy skepticism that there was much Soviet espionage in the United States after 1947, but this was not how many Americans saw it at the time. Legitimate suspicions and real fears, along with political opportunism, combined to fuel the national Red Scare, which was longer and more far-reaching than the one that followed World War I (Chapter 22).

**Loyalty-Security Program**    To insulate his administration against charges of Communist infiltration, Truman issued Executive Order 9835 on March 21, 1947, which created the **Loyalty-Security Program**. The order permitted officials to investigate any employee of the federal government (some 2.5 million people) for "subversive" activities. Representing a profound centralization of power, the order sent shock waves through every federal agency. Truman intended the order to apply principally to actions designed to harm the United States (sabotage, treason, etc.), but it was broad enough to allow anyone to be accused of subversion for the slightest reason—for marching in a Communist-led demonstration in the 1930s, for instance, or signing a petition calling for public housing. Along with suspected political subversives, more than a thousand gay men and lesbians were dismissed from federal employment in the 1950s, victims of an obsessive search for anyone deemed "unfit" for government work.

Following Truman's lead, many state and local governments, universities, political organizations, churches, and businesses undertook their own antisubversion campaigns, which often included loyalty oaths. In the labor movement, charges of Communist domination led to the expulsion of a number of unions by the Congress of Industrial Organizations (CIO) in 1949. Civil rights organizations such as the National Association for the Advancement of Colored People (NAACP) and the National Urban League also expelled Communists and "fellow travelers," or Communist sympathizers. Thus the Red Scare spread from the federal government to the farthest reaches of American organizational, economic, and cultural life.

**HUAC**    The Truman administration had legitimized the vague and malleable concept of "disloyalty." Others proved willing to stretch the concept even further, beginning with the **House Un-American Activities Committee** (HUAC), which Congressman Martin Dies of Texas and other conservatives had launched in 1938. After the war, HUAC helped spark the Red Scare by holding widely publicized hearings in 1947 on alleged Communist infiltration in the movie industry. A group of writers and directors dubbed the Hollywood Ten went to jail for contempt of Congress after they refused to testify about their past associations. Hundreds of other actors, directors, and writers whose names had been mentioned in the HUAC investigation were unable to get work, victims of an unacknowledged but very real blacklist honored by industry executives.

Other HUAC investigations had greater legitimacy. One that intensified the anticommunist crusade in 1948 involved Alger Hiss, a former New Dealer and State Department official who had accompanied Franklin Roosevelt to Yalta. A former Communist, Whitaker Chambers, claimed that Hiss was a member of a secret Communist cell operating in the government and had passed him classified documents in the 1930s. Hiss denied the allegations, but California Republican congressman Richard Nixon doggedly pursued the case against him. In early 1950, Hiss was found guilty not of spying but of lying to Congress about his Communist affiliations and was sentenced to five years in federal prison. Many Americans doubted at the time that Hiss was a spy. But the Venona transcripts in the 1990s corroborated a great deal of Chambers's testimony, and though no definitive proof has emerged, many historians now recognize the strong circumstantial evidence against Hiss.

> **IDENTIFY CAUSES**
> What factors led to the postwar Red Scare, and what were its ramifications for civil liberties in the United States?

**McCarthyism**    The meteoric career of Senator Joseph McCarthy of Wisconsin marked first the apex and then the finale of the Red Scare. In February 1950, McCarthy delivered a bombshell during a speech in Wheeling, West Virginia: "I have here in my hand a list of 205 . . . a list of names that were made known to the Secretary of State as being members of the Communist Party and who nevertheless are still working and shaping policy in the State Department." McCarthy later reduced his numbers, gave different figures in different speeches, and never released any names or proof. But he had gained the attention he sought (American Voices, p. 822).

## Hunting Communists and Liberals

The onset of the Cold War created an opportunity for some conservatives to use anticommunism as a weapon to attack the Truman administration. In Senator Joseph McCarthy's case, the charge was that the U.S. government was harboring Soviet spies. There was also a broader, more amorphous attack on people accused not of spying but of having communist sympathies; such "fellow travelers" were considered "security risks" and thus unsuitable for government positions. The basis of suspicion for this targeted group was generally membership in organizations that supported policies that either overlapped with or seemed similar to policies supported by the Communist Party.

### Senator Joseph McCarthy
### Speech Delivered in Wheeling, West Virginia, February 9, 1950

Though Senator McCarthy was actually late getting on board the anticommunist rocket ship, this was the speech that launched him into orbit. No one else ever saw the piece of paper he waved about during this speech with the names of 57 spies in the State Department. Over time, the numbers he cited fluctuated (in early versions of this speech he claimed to have a list of 205 names) and never materialized into a single indictment for espionage. Still, McCarthy had an extraordinary talent for whipping up anticommunist hysteria. His downfall came in 1954, when the U.S. Senate formally censured him for his conduct; three years later, he died of alcoholism at the age of forty-eight.

Today we are engaged in a final, all-out battle between communistic atheism and Christianity. The modern champions of communism have selected this as the time. And, ladies and gentlemen, the chips are down — they are truly down. . . .

The reason why we find ourselves in a position of impotency is not because our only powerful potential enemy has sent men to invade our shores, but rather because of the traitorous actions of those who have been treated so well by this Nation. It has not been the less fortunate or members of minority groups who have been selling this Nation out, but rather those who have had all the benefits that the wealthiest nation on earth has had to offer — the finest homes, the finest college education, and the finest jobs in Government we can give. . . .

I have in my hand 57 cases of individuals who would appear to be either card carrying members or certainly loyal to the Communist Party, but who nevertheless are still helping to shape our foreign policy.

### Fulton Lewis Jr.
### Radio Address, January 13, 1949

The groundwork for McCarthy's anticommunist crusade was laid by the House Un-American Activities Committee (HUAC), which had been formed in 1938 by conservative southern Democrats seeking to investigate alleged communist influence around the country. One of its early targets had been Dr. Frank P. Graham, the distinguished president of the University of North Carolina. A committed southern liberal, Graham was a leading figure in the Southern Conference on Human Welfare, the most prominent southern organization supporting the New Deal, free speech, organized labor, and greater rights for southern blacks—causes that some in the South saw as pathways for communist subversion. After the war, HUAC stepped up its activities and kept a close eye on Graham. Among Graham's duties was to serve as the head of the Oak Ridge Institute of Nuclear Studies, a consortium of fourteen southern universities designed to undertake joint research with the federal government's atomic energy facility at Oak Ridge, Tennessee. To enable him to carry on his duties, the Atomic Energy Commission (AEC) granted Graham a security clearance, overriding the negative recommendation of the AEC's Security Advisory Board. That was the occasion for the following statement by Fulton Lewis Jr., a conservative radio commentator with a nationwide following.

About Dr. Frank P. Graham, president of the University of North Carolina, and the action of the Atomic Energy Commission giving him complete clearance for all atomic secrets despite the fact that the security officer of the commission flatly rejected him. . . .

President Truman was asked to comment on the matter today at his press and radio conference, and his reply was that he has complete confidence in Dr. Graham.

. . . The defenders of Dr. Graham today offered the apology that during the time he joined the various subversive and Communist front organizations [like the Southern Conference for Human Welfare] — organizations so listed by the Attorney General of the United States — this country was a co-belligerent with Soviet Russia, and numerous people joined such groups and causes. That argument is going to sound very thin to most American citizens, because the overwhelming majority of us would have no part of any Communist or Communist front connections at any time.

### Frank Porter Graham
## Telegram to Fulton Lewis Jr., January 13, 1949

One can imagine Graham's shock at hearing himself pilloried on national radio. (He had not even been aware of the AEC's investigation of him.) The following is from his response to Lewis.

In view of your questions and implications I hope you will use my statement to provide for my answers. . . . I have always been opposed to Communism and all totalitarian dictatorships. I opposed both Nazi and Communist aggression against Czechoslovakia and the earlier Russian aggression against Finland and later Communist aggression against other countries. . . .

During the period of my active participation, the overwhelming number of members of the Southern Conference were to my knowledge anti-Communists. There were several isolationist stands of the Conference with which I disagreed. The stands which I supported as the main business of the Conference were such as the following: Federal aid to the states for schools; abolition of freight rate discrimination against Southern commerce, agriculture, and industry; anti–poll tax bill; anti-lynching bill; equal right of qualified Negroes to vote in both primaries and general elections; the unhampered lawful right of labor to organize and bargain collectively in our region; . . . minimum wages and social security in the Southern and American tradition. . . .

I have been called a Communist by some sincere people. I have been called a spokesman of American capitalism by Communists and repeatedly called a tool of imperialism by the radio from Moscow. I shall simply continue to oppose Ku Kluxism, imperialism, fascism, and Communism whether in America . . . or behind the "iron curtain."

### House Un-American Activities Committee
## Report on Frank Graham, February 4, 1949

Because of the controversy, HUAC released a report on Graham.

A check of the files, records and publications of the Committee on Un-American Activities has revealed the following information: Letterheads dated September 22, 1939, January 17, 1940, and May 26, 1940, as well as the "Daily Worker" of March 18, 1939, . . . reveal that Frank P. Graham was a member of the American Committee for Democracy and Intellectual Freedom. . . . In Report 2277, dated June 25, 1942, the Special Committee on Un-American Activities found that "the line of the American Committee for Democracy and Intellectual Freedom has fluctuated in complete harmony with the line of the Communist Party." The organization was again cited by the Special Committee . . . as a Communist front "which defended Communist teachers." . . .

A letterhead of February 7, 1946, a letterhead of June 4, 1947 . . . and an announcement of the Third Meeting, April 19–21, 1942, at Nashville, Tennessee, reveal that Frank P. Graham was honorary President of the Southern Conference for Human Welfare. . . .

In a report on the Southern Conference for Human Welfare, dated June 16, 1947, the Committee on Un-American Activities found "the most conclusive proof of Communist domination of the Southern Conference for Human Welfare is to be found in the organization's strict and unvarying conformance to the line of the Communist Party in the field of foreign policy. It is also a clear indication of the fact that the real purpose of the organization was not 'human welfare' in the South, but rather to serve as a convenient vehicle in support of the current Communist Party line."

Source: # 1819 Frank Porter Graham Papers. Courtesy of the Southern Historical Collection, Wilson Library, The University of North Carolina at Chapel Hill.

### QUESTIONS FOR ANALYSIS

1. On what grounds did Fulton Lewis Jr. and HUAC assert that Frank Graham was a security risk? Did they charge that he was a Communist? Is there any evidence in these documents that Graham might have been a security risk?
2. How did Graham defend himself? Are you persuaded by his argument?
3. Compare McCarthy's famous speech at Wheeling, West Virginia, and the suspicions voiced against Graham by Lewis and HUAC a year earlier. What similarities do you see?

For the next four years, from his position as chair of the Senate Permanent Subcommittee on Investigations, McCarthy waged a virulent smear campaign. Critics who disagreed with him exposed themselves to charges of being "soft" on communism. Truman called McCarthy's charges "slander, lies, [and] character assassination" but could do nothing to curb him. Republicans, for their part, refrained from publicly challenging their most outspoken senator and, on the whole, were content to reap the political benefits. McCarthy's charges almost always targeted Democrats.

Despite McCarthy's failure to identify a single Communist in government, several national developments gave his charges credibility with the public. The dramatic 1951 espionage trial of Julius and Ethel Rosenberg, followed around the world, fueled McCarthy's allegations. Convicted of passing atomic secrets to the Soviet Union, the Rosenbergs were executed in 1953. As in the Hiss case, documents released decades later provided some evidence of Julius Rosenberg's guilt, though not Ethel's. Their execution nevertheless remains controversial — in part because some felt that anti-Semitism played a role in their sentencing. Also fueling McCarthy's charges were a series of trials of American Communists between 1949 and 1955 for violation of the 1940 Smith Act, which prohibited Americans from advocating the violent overthrow of the government. Though civil libertarians and two Supreme Court justices vigorously objected, dozens of Communist Party members were convicted. McCarthy was not involved in either the Rosenberg trial or the Smith Act convictions, but these sensational events gave his wild charges some credence.

In early 1954, McCarthy overreached by launching an investigation into subversive activities in the U.S. Army. When lengthy hearings — the first of their kind

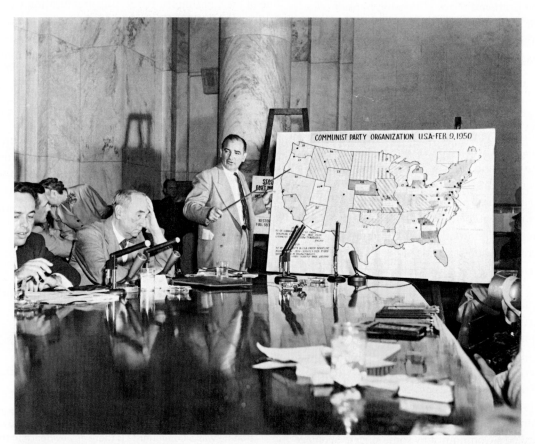

**The Army-McCarthy Hearings**

These 1954 hearings contributed to the downfall of Senator Joseph McCarthy by exposing his reckless accusations and bullying tactics to the huge television audience that tuned in each day. Some of the most heated exchanges took place between McCarthy (center) and Joseph Welch (seated, left), the lawyer representing the army. When the gentlemanly Welch finally asked, "Have you no sense of decency sir, at long last? Have you left no sense of decency?" he fatally punctured McCarthy's armor. The audience broke into applause because someone had finally had the courage to stand up to the senator from Wisconsin. © Bettmann/Corbis.

broadcast on the new medium of television—brought McCarthy's tactics into the nation's living rooms, support for him plummeted. In December 1954, the Senate voted 67 to 22 to censure McCarthy for unbecoming conduct. He died from an alcohol-related illness three years later at the age of forty-eight, his name forever attached to a period of political repression of which he was only the most flagrant manifestation.

## The Politics of Cold War Liberalism

As election day 1952 approached, the nation was embroiled in the tense Cold War with the Soviet Union and fighting a "hot" war in Korea. Though Americans gave the Republicans victory, radical change was not in the offing. The new president, Dwight D. Eisenhower, set the tone for what his supporters called modern Republicanism, an updated GOP approach that aimed at moderating, not dismantling, the New Deal state. Eisenhower and his supporters were more successors of FDR than of Herbert Hoover. Foreign policy revealed a similar continuity. Like their predecessors, Republicans saw the world in Cold War polarities.

Republicans rallied around Eisenhower, the popular former commander of Allied forces in Europe, but divisions in the party persisted. More conservative party activists preferred Robert A. Taft of Ohio, the Republican leader in the Senate who was a vehement opponent of the New Deal. A close friend of business, he particularly detested labor unions. Though an ardent anticommunist, the isolationist-minded Taft criticized Truman's aggressive containment policy and opposed U.S. participation in NATO. Taft ran for president three times, and though he was never the Republican nominee, he won the loyalty of conservative Americans who saw the welfare state as a waste and international affairs as dangerous foreign entanglements.

In contrast, moderate Republicans looked to Eisenhower and even to more liberal-minded leaders like Nelson Rockefeller, who supported international initiatives such as the Marshall Plan and NATO and were willing to tolerate labor unions and the welfare state. Eisenhower was a man without a political past. Believing that democracy required the military to stand aside, he had never voted. Rockefeller, the scion of one of the richest families in America, was a Cold War internationalist. He served in a variety of capacities under Eisenhower, including as an advisor on foreign affairs. Having made his political name, Rockefeller was elected the governor of New York in 1959 and became the de facto leader of the liberal wing of the Republican Party.

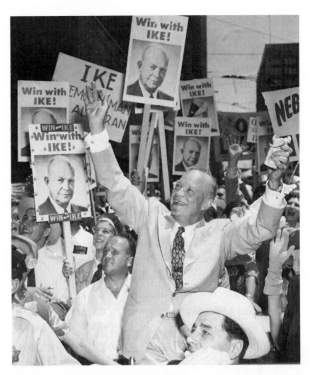

**Dwight Eisenhower**

In this photo taken during the 1952 presidential campaign, Dwight D. Eisenhower acknowledges cheers from supporters in Chicago. "Ike," as he was universally known, had been a popular five-star general in World War II (also serving as Supreme Allied Commander in the European theater) and turned to politics in the early 1950s as a member of the Republican Party. However, Eisenhower was a centrist who did little to disrupt the liberal social policies that Democrats had pursued since the 1930s.
© Bettmann/Corbis.

For eight years, between 1952 and 1960, Eisenhower steered a precarious course from the middle of the party, with conservative Taft Republicans on one side and liberal Rockefeller Republicans on the other. His popularity temporarily kept the two sides at bay, though more ardent conservatives considered him a closet New Dealer. "Ike," as he was widely known, proved willing to work with the mostly Democratic-controlled Congresses of those years. Eisenhower signed bills increasing federal outlays for veterans' benefits, housing, highway construction (Chapter 26), and Social Security, and he increased the minimum wage from 75 cents an hour to $1. Like Truman, Eisenhower accepted some government responsibility for the economic security of individuals, part of a broad consensus in American politics in these years.

**UNDERSTAND POINTS OF VIEW**

What were the components of Cold War liberalism, and why did the Democratic Party embrace them?

**America Under Eisenhower** The global power realities that had called forth containment guided Eisenhower's foreign policy. New developments, however, altered the tone of the Cold War. Stalin's death in March 1953 precipitated an intraparty struggle in the Soviet Union that lasted until 1956, when Nikita Khrushchev emerged as Stalin's successor. Khrushchev soon startled communists around the world by denouncing Stalin and detailing his crimes and blunders. He also surprised many Americans by calling for "peaceful coexistence" with the West and by dealing more flexibly with dissent in the Communist world. But the new Soviet leader had his limits, and when Hungarians rose up in 1956 to demand independence from Moscow, Khrushchev crushed the incipient revolution.

With no end to the Cold War in sight, Eisenhower focused on limiting the cost of containment. The president hoped to economize by relying on a nuclear arsenal and deemphasizing expensive conventional forces. Under this **"New Look"** defense policy, the Eisenhower administration stepped up production of the hydrogen bomb and developed long-range bombing capabilities. The Soviets, however, matched the United States weapon for weapon. By 1958, both nations had intercontinental ballistic missiles. When an American nuclear submarine launched an atomic-tipped Polaris missile in 1960, Soviet engineers raced to produce an equivalent weapon. This arms race was another critical feature of the Cold War. American officials believed the best deterrent to Soviet aggression was the threat of an all-out nuclear response by the United States, which was dubbed "massive retaliation" by Secretary of State Dulles.

 To see a longer excerpt of the Dulles document, along with other primary sources from this period, see *Sources for America's History*.

Although confident in the international arena, Eisenhower started out as a novice in domestic affairs. Doing his best to set a less confrontational tone after the rancorous Truman years, he was reluctant to speak out against Joe McCarthy, and he was not a leader on civil rights. Democrats meanwhile maintained a strong presence in Congress but proved weak in presidential elections in the 1950s. In the two presidential contests of the decade, 1952 and 1956, Eisenhower defeated the admired but politically ineffectual liberal Adlai Stevenson. In the 1952 election, Stevenson was hampered by the unpopularity of the Truman administration. The deadlocked Korean War and a series of scandals that Republicans dubbed "the mess in

Washington" combined to give the war-hero general an easy victory. In 1956, Ike won an even more impressive victory over Stevenson, an eloquent and sophisticated spokesman for liberalism but no match for Eisenhower's popularity with the public.

During Eisenhower's presidency, new political forces on both the right and the left had begun to stir. But they had not yet fully transformed the party system itself. Particularly at the national level, Democrats and Republicans seemed in broad agreement about the realities of the Cold War and the demands of a modern, industrial economy and welfare state. Indeed, respected commentators in the 1950s declared "the end of ideology" and wondered if the great political clashes that had wracked the 1930s were gone forever. Below the apparent calm of national party politics, however, lay profound differences among Americans over the direction of the nation. Those differences were most pronounced regarding the civil rights of African Americans. But a host of other issues had begun to emerge as controversial subjects that would soon starkly divide the country and, in the 1960s, bring an end to the brief and fragile Cold War consensus.

# Containment in the Postcolonial World

As the Cold War took shape, the world scene was changing at a furious pace. New nations were emerging across Asia, Africa, and the Middle East, created in the wake of powerful anticolonial movements whose origins dated to before World War II. Between 1947 and 1962, the British, French, Dutch, and Belgian empires all but disintegrated in a momentous collapse of European global reach. FDR had favored the idea of national self-determination, often to the fury of his British and French allies. He expected emerging democracies to be new partners in an American-led, free-market world system. But colonial revolts produced many independent- or socialist-minded regimes in the so-called Third World, as well. *Third World* was a term that came into usage after World War II to describe developing or ex-colonial nations in Asia, Africa, Latin America, and the Middle East that were not aligned with the Western capitalist countries led by the United States or the socialist states of Eastern Europe led by the Soviet Union. The Truman and Eisenhower administrations often treated Third World countries as pawns of the Soviet Union to be opposed at all costs.

## The Cold War and Colonial Independence

Insisting that all nations had to choose sides, the United States drew as many countries as possible into collective security agreements, with the NATO alliance in Europe as a model. Secretary of State John Foster Dulles orchestrated the creation of the Southeast Asia Treaty Organization (SEATO), which in 1954 linked the United States and its major European allies with Australia, New Zealand, Pakistan, the Philippines, and Thailand. An extensive system of defense alliances eventually tied the United States to more than forty other countries (Map 25.5). The United States also sponsored a strategically valuable defensive alliance between Iraq and Iran, on the southern flank of the Soviet Union.

Despite American rhetoric, the United States was often concerned less about democracy than about stability. The Truman and Eisenhower administrations tended to support governments, no matter how repressive, that were overtly anticommunist. Some of America's staunchest allies — the Philippines, South Korea, Iran, Cuba, South Vietnam, and Nicaragua — were governed by dictatorships or right-wing regimes that lacked broad-based support. Moreover, Eisenhower's

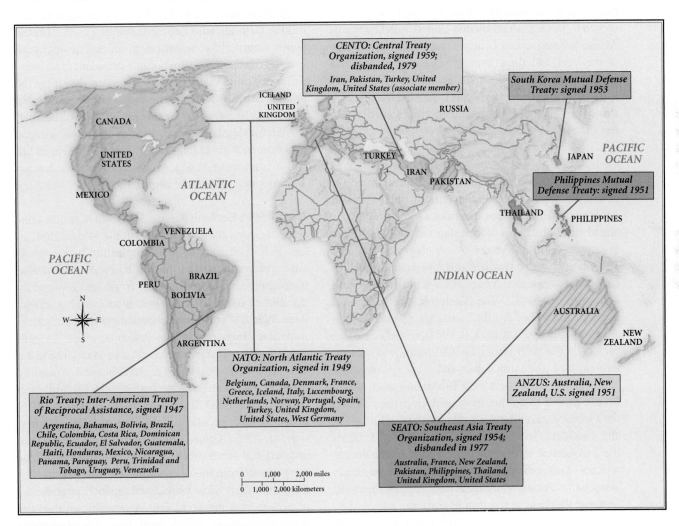

**MAP 25.5**

**American Global Defense Treaties in the Cold War Era**

The advent of the Cold War led to a major shift in American foreign policy—the signing of mutual defense treaties. Dating back to George Washington's call "to steer clear of permanent alliances with any portion of the foreign world," the United States had avoided treaty obligations that entailed the defense of other nations. As late as 1919, the U.S. Senate had rejected the principle of "collective security," the centerpiece of the League of Nations established by the Treaty of Versailles that ended World War I. But after World War II, in response to fears of Soviet global expansion, the United States entered defense alliances with much of the non-Communist world.

secretary of state Dulles often resorted to covert operations against governments that, in his opinion, were too closely aligned with the Soviets.

For these covert tasks, Dulles used the newly created (1947) Central Intelligence Agency (CIA), run by his brother, Allen Dulles. When Iran's democratically elected nationalist premier, Mohammad Mossadegh, seized British oil properties in 1953, CIA agents helped depose him and installed the young Mohammad Reza Pahlavi as shah of Iran. Iranian resentment of the coup, followed by twenty-five years of U.S. support for the shah, eventually led to the 1979 Iranian Revolution (Chapter 30). In 1954, the CIA also engineered a coup in Guatemala against the democratically elected president, Jacobo Arbenz Guzmán, who had seized land owned by the American-owned United Fruit Company. Arbenz offered to pay United Fruit the declared value of the land, but the company rejected the offer and turned to the U.S. government. Eisenhower specifically approved those CIA efforts and expanded the agency's mandate from gathering intelligence to intervening in the affairs of sovereign states.

**Vietnam**   But when covert operations and coups failed or proved impractical, the American approach to emerging nations could entangle the United States in deeper, more intractable conflicts. One example was already unfolding on a distant stage, in a small country unknown to most Americans: Vietnam. In August 1945, at the close of World War II, the Japanese occupiers of Vietnam surrendered to China in the north and Britain in the south. The Vietminh, the nationalist movement that had led the resistance against the Japanese (and the French, prior to 1940), seized control in the north. But their leader, Ho Chi Minh, was a Communist, and this single fact outweighed American and British commitment to self-determination. When France moved to restore its control over the country, the United States and Britain sided with their European ally. President Truman rejected Ho's plea to support the Vietnamese struggle for nationhood, and France rejected Ho's offer of a negotiated independence. Shortly after France returned, in late 1946, the Vietminh resumed their war of national liberation.

Eisenhower picked up where Truman left off. If the French failed, Eisenhower argued, all non-Communist governments in the region would fall like dominoes. This so-called **domino theory** — which represented an extension of the containment

doctrine — guided U.S. policy in Southeast Asia for the next twenty years. The United States eventually provided most of the financing for the French war, but money was not enough to defeat the determined Vietminh, who were fighting for the liberation of their country. After a fifty-six-day siege in early 1954, the French were defeated at the huge fortress of Dien Bien Phu. The result was the 1954 Geneva Accords, which partitioned Vietnam temporarily at the 17th parallel and called for elections within two years to unify the strife-torn nation.

The United States rejected the Geneva Accords and set about undermining them. With the help of the CIA, a pro-American government took power in South Vietnam in June 1954. Ngo Dinh Diem, an anticommunist Catholic who had been residing in the United States, returned to Vietnam as premier. The next year, in a rigged election, Diem became president of an independent South Vietnam. Facing certain defeat by the popular Ho Chi Minh, Diem called off the scheduled reunification elections. As the last French soldiers left in March 1956, the Eisenhower administration propped up Diem with an average of $200 million a year in aid and a contingent of 675 American military advisors. This support was just the beginning.

**The Middle East**   If Vietnam was still of minor concern, the same could not be said of the Middle East, an area rich in oil and political complexity. The most volatile area was Palestine, populated by Arabs but also historically the ancient land of Israel and coveted by the Zionist movement as a Jewish national homeland. After World War II, many survivors of the Nazi extermination camps resettled in Palestine, which was still controlled by Britain under a World War I mandate. On November 29, 1947, the UN General Assembly voted to partition Palestine between Jewish and Arab sectors. When the British mandate ended in 1948, Zionist leaders proclaimed the state of Israel. A coalition of Arab nations known as the Arab League invaded, but Israel survived. Many Palestinians fled or were driven from their homes during the fighting. The Arab defeat left these people permanently stranded in refugee camps. President Truman recognized the new state immediately, which won him crucial support from Jewish voters in the 1948 election but alienated the Arab world.

Southeast of Palestine, Egypt began to assert its presence in the region. Having gained independence from Britain several decades earlier, Egypt remained a monarchy until 1952, when Gamal Abdel Nasser led a military coup that established a constitutional republic.

**IDENTIFY CAUSES**
How did the Cold War between the United States and the Soviet Union affect disparate regions such as the Middle East and Southeast Asia?

**The Suez Crisis, 1956**

In this photograph, Egyptian president Gamal Abdel Nasser is greeted ecstatically by Cairo crowds after he nationalized the Suez Canal. Nasser's gamble paid off. Thanks to American intervention, military action by Britain, France, and Israel failed, and Nasser emerged as the triumphant voice of Arab nationalism across the Middle East. The popular emotions he unleashed against the West survived his death in 1970 and are more potent today than ever, although now expressed more through Islamic fundamentalism than Nasser's brand of secular nationalism. Getty Images.

Caught between the Soviet Union and the United States, Nasser sought an independent route: a pan-Arab socialism designed to end the Middle East's colonial relationship with the West. When negotiations with the United States over Nasser's plan to build a massive hydroelectric dam on the Nile broke down in 1956, he nationalized the Suez Canal, which was the lifeline for Western Europe's oil. Britain and France, in alliance with Israel, attacked Egypt and seized the canal. Concerned that the invasion would encourage Egypt to turn to the Soviets for help, Eisenhower urged France and Britain to pull back. He applied additional pressure through the UN General Assembly, which called for a truce and troop withdrawal. When the Western nations backed down, however, Egypt reclaimed the Suez Canal and built the Aswan Dam on the Nile with Soviet support. Eisenhower had likely avoided a larger war, but the West lost a potential ally in Nasser.

In early 1957, concerned about Soviet influence in the Middle East, the president announced the **Eisenhower Doctrine**, which stated that American forces would assist any nation in the region that required aid "against overt armed aggression from any nation controlled by International Communism." Invoking the doctrine later that year, Eisenhower helped King Hussein of Jordan put down a Nasser-backed revolt and propped up a pro-American government in

Lebanon. The Eisenhower Doctrine was further evidence that the United States had extended the global reach of containment, in this instance accentuated by the strategic need to protect the West's access to steady supplies of oil.

## John F. Kennedy and the Cold War

Charisma, style, and personality— these, more than platforms and issues, defined a new brand of politics in the early 1960s. This was John F. Kennedy's natural environment. Kennedy, a Harvard alumnus, World War II hero, and senator from Massachusetts, had inherited his love of politics from his grandfathers—colorful, and often ruthless, Irish Catholic politicians in Boston. Ambitious and deeply aware of style, the forty-three-year-old Kennedy made use of his many advantages to become, as novelist Norman Mailer put it, "our leading man." His one disadvantage— that he was Catholic in a country that had never elected a Catholic president— he masterfully neutralized. And thanks to both media advisors and his youthful attractiveness, Kennedy projected a superb television image.

At heart, however, Kennedy was a Cold Warrior who had

**COMPARE AND CONTRAST**

How was Kennedy's approach to the Cold War similar to and different from Eisenhower's and Truman's?

**The Kennedy Magnetism**

John F. Kennedy, the 1960 Democratic candidate for president, used his youth and personality (and those of his equally personable and stylish wife) to attract voters. Here the Massachusetts senator draws an enthusiastic crowd on a campaign stop in Elgin, Illinois. AP Images.

come of age in the shadow of Munich, Yalta, and McCarthyism. He projected an air of idealism, but his years in the Senate (1953–1960) had proved him to be a conventional Cold War politician. Once elected president, Kennedy would shape the nation's foreign policy by drawing both on his ingenuity and on old-style Cold War power politics.

### The Election of 1960 and the New Frontier

Kennedy's Republican opponent in the 1960 presidential election, Eisenhower's vice president, Richard Nixon, was a seasoned politician and Cold Warrior himself. The great innovation of the 1960 campaign was a series of four nationally televised debates. Nixon, less photogenic than Kennedy, looked sallow and unshaven under the intense studio lights. Voters who heard the first debate on the radio concluded that Nixon had won, but those who viewed it on television favored Kennedy. Despite the edge Kennedy enjoyed in the debates, he won only the narrowest of electoral victories, receiving 49.7 percent of the popular vote to Nixon's 49.5 percent. Kennedy attracted Catholics, African Americans, and the labor vote; his vice-presidential running mate, Texas senator Lyndon Baines Johnson, helped bring in southern Democrats. Yet only 120,000 votes separated the two candidates, and a shift of a few thousand votes in key states would have reversed the outcome.

Kennedy brought to Washington a cadre of young, ambitious newcomers, including Robert McNamara, a renowned systems analyst and former head of Ford Motor Company, as secretary of defense. A host of trusted advisors and academics flocked to Washington to join the New Frontier — Kennedy's term for the challenges the country faced. Included on the team as attorney general was Kennedy's younger brother Robert, who had made a name as a hard-hitting investigator of organized crime. Relying on an old American trope, Kennedy's New Frontier suggested masculine toughness and adventurism and encouraged Americans to again think of themselves as exploring uncharted terrain. That terrain proved treacherous, however, as the new administration immediately faced a crisis.

**Crises in Cuba and Berlin** In January 1961, the Soviet Union announced that it intended to support "wars of national liberation" wherever in the world they occurred. Kennedy took Soviet premier Nikita Khrushchev's words as a challenge, especially as they applied to Cuba, where in 1959 Fidel Castro had overthrown the right-wing dictator Fulgencio Batista and declared a revolution. Determined to keep Cuba out of the Soviet orbit, Kennedy followed through on Eisenhower administration plans to dispatch Cuban exiles to foment an anti-Castro uprising. The invaders, trained by the Central Intelligence Agency, were ill-prepared for their task. On landing at Cuba's **Bay of Pigs** on April 17, 1961, the force of 1,400 was crushed by Castro's troops. Kennedy prudently rejected CIA pleas for a U.S. air strike. Accepting defeat, Kennedy went before the American people and took full responsibility for the fiasco (Map 25.6).

Already strained by the Bay of Pigs incident, U.S.-Soviet relations deteriorated further in June 1961 when Khrushchev stopped movement between Communist-controlled East Berlin and the city's Western sector. Kennedy responded by dispatching 40,000 more troops to Europe. In mid-August, to stop the exodus of East Germans, the Communist regime began constructing the Berlin Wall, policed by border guards under shoot-to-kill orders. Until the 12-foot-high concrete barrier came down in 1989, it served as the supreme symbol of the Cold War.

A perilous Cold War confrontation came next, in October 1962. In a somber televised address on October 22, Kennedy revealed that U.S. reconnaissance

planes had spotted Soviet-built bases for intermediate-range ballistic missiles in Cuba. Some of those weapons had already been installed, and more were on the way. Kennedy announced that the United States would impose a "quarantine on all offensive military equipment" on its way to Cuba. As the world held its breath waiting to see if the conflict would escalate into war, on October 25, ships carrying Soviet missiles turned back. After a week of tense negotiations, both sides made concessions: Kennedy pledged not to invade Cuba, and Khrushchev promised to dismantle the missile bases. Kennedy also secretly ordered U.S. missiles to be removed from Turkey, at Khrushchev's insistence. The risk of nuclear war, greater during the **Cuban missile crisis** than at any other time in the Cold War, prompted a slight thaw in U.S.-Soviet relations. As National

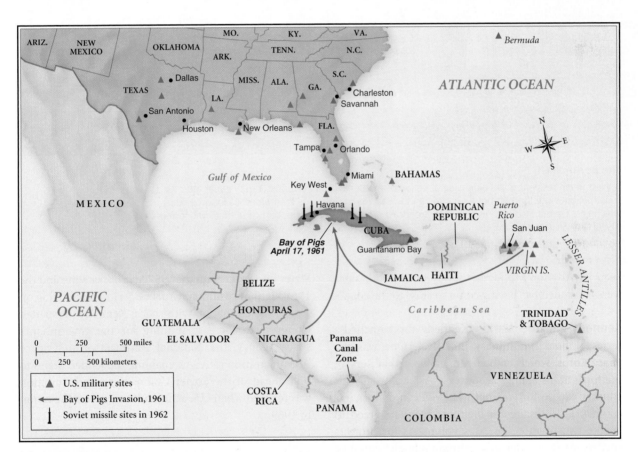

## MAP 25.6
### The United States and Cuba, 1961–1962

Fidel Castro's 1959 Communist takeover of Cuba brought Cold War tensions to the Caribbean. In 1961, the United States tried unsuccessfully to overthrow Castro's regime by sponsoring the Bay of Pigs invasion of Cuban exiles launched from Nicaragua and other points in the Caribbean. In 1962, the United States confronted the Soviet Union over Soviet construction of nuclear missile sites in Cuba. After President Kennedy ordered a naval blockade of the island, the Soviets backed down from the tense standoff and removed the missiles. Despite the 1991 dissolution of the Soviet Union and the official end of the Cold War, the United States continues to view Cuba, governed in 2012 by Raúl Castro, Fidel's brother, as an enemy nation.

**The Berlin Wall**
A West Berlin resident walks alongside a section of the Berlin Wall in August 1962, a year after its construction. Note the two border guards on the East Berlin side, plus the numerous loudspeakers, which East German Communists used to broadcast propaganda over the barricade that divided the city. © Bettmann/Corbis.

Security Advisor McGeorge Bundy put it, both sides were chastened by "having come so close to the edge."

**Kennedy and the World**   Kennedy also launched a series of bold nonmilitary initiatives. One was the **Peace Corps**, which embodied a call to public service put forth in his inaugural address ("Ask not what your country can do for you, but what you can do for your country"). Thousands of men and women agreed to devote two or more years as volunteers for projects such as teaching English to Filipino schoolchildren or helping African villagers obtain clean water. Exhibiting the idealism of the early 1960s, the Peace Corps was also a low-cost Cold War weapon intended to show the developing world that there was an alternative to communism. Kennedy championed space exploration, as well. In a 1962 speech, he proposed that the nation commit itself to landing a man on the moon within the decade. The Soviets had already beaten the United

States into space with the 1957 *Sputnik* satellite and the 1961 flight of cosmonaut Yuri Gagarin. Capitalizing on America's fascination with space, Kennedy persuaded Congress to increase funding for the government's space agency, the National Aeronautics and Space Administration (NASA), enabling the United States to pull ahead of the Soviet Union. Kennedy's ambition was realized when U.S. astronauts arrived on the moon in 1969.

## Making a Commitment in Vietnam

Despite slight improvements, U.S.-Soviet relations stayed tense and containment remained the cornerstone of U.S. policy. When Kennedy became president, he inherited Eisenhower's commitment in Vietnam. Kennedy saw Vietnam in Cold War terms, but rather than practicing brinksmanship — threatening nuclear war to stop communism — Kennedy sought what at

**The Cuban Missile Crisis**
During the 1962 Cuban missile crisis, President Kennedy meets with U.S. Army officials. Over two tense weeks, the world watched as the United States and the Soviet Union went to the brink of war when it became known that Soviet military officials had begun to construct nuclear weapons bases in Cuba, a mere 90 miles from the southern tip of Florida. Kennedy's threat to intercept Soviet missile shipments with American naval vessels forced the Cold War adversary to back down. © Corbis.

the time seemed a more intelligent and realistic approach. In 1961, he increased military aid to the South Vietnamese and expanded the role of U.S. Special Forces ("Green Berets"), who would train the South Vietnamese army in unconventional, small-group warfare tactics.

South Vietnam's corrupt and repressive Diem regime, propped up by Eisenhower since 1954, was losing ground in spite of American aid. By 1961, Diem's opponents, with backing from North Vietnam, had formed a revolutionary movement known as the National Liberation Front (NLF). NLF guerrilla forces — the Vietcong — found allies among peasants alienated by Diem's "strategic hamlet" program, which had uprooted entire villages and moved villagers into barbed-wire compounds. Furthermore, Buddhists charged Diem, a Catholic, with religious persecution. Starting in May 1963, militant Buddhists staged dramatic demonstrations, including self-immolations recorded by reporters covering the activities of the 16,000 U.S. military personnel then in Vietnam.

These self-immolations, shown on television to an uneasy global audience, powerfully illustrated the dilemmas of American policy in Vietnam. To ensure a stable southern government and prevent victory for Ho Chi Minh and the North, the United States had to support Diem's authoritarian regime. But the regime's political repression of its opponents made Diem more unpopular. He was assassinated on November 3, 1963. Whether one supported U.S. involvement in Vietnam or not, the elemental paradox remained unchanged: in its efforts to win, the United States brought defeat ever closer.

## SUMMARY

The Cold War began as a conflict between the United States and the Soviet Union over Eastern Europe and the fate of post–World War II Germany. Early in the conflict, the United States adopted a strategy of containment, which quickly expanded to Asia after China became a communist state under Mao Zedong. The first effect of that expansion was the Korean War, after which, under Dwight D. Eisenhower, containment of communism became America's guiding principle across the developing world — often called the Third World. Cold War tensions relaxed in the late 1950s but erupted again under John F. Kennedy with the Cuban missile crisis, the building of the Berlin Wall, and major increases in American military assistance to South Vietnam. Cold War imperatives between 1945 and the early 1960s meant a major military buildup, a massive nuclear arms race, and unprecedented entanglements across the globe.

On the domestic front, Harry S. Truman started out with high hopes for an expanded New Deal, only to be confounded by resistance from Congress and the competing demands of the Cold War. The greatest Cold War–inspired development was a climate of fear over internal subversion by Communists that gave rise to McCarthyism. Truman's successor, Eisenhower, brought the Republicans back into power. Although personally conservative, Eisenhower actually proved a New Dealer in disguise. When Eisenhower left office and Kennedy became president, it seemed that a "liberal consensus" prevailed, with old-fashioned, *laissez-faire* conservatism mostly marginalized in American political life.

# CHAPTER REVIEW

 **MAKE IT STICK**    Go to **LearningCurve** to retain what you've read.

## TERMS TO KNOW    Identify and explain the significance of each term below.

### Key Concepts and Events

Yalta Conference (p. 806)
United Nations (p. 807)
Potsdam Conference (p. 807)
containment (p. 808)
Truman Doctrine (p. 809)
Marshall Plan (p. 809)
North Atlantic Treaty
  Organization (NATO) (p. 812)
Warsaw Pact (p. 812)
NSC-68 (p. 813)
Cold War liberalism (p. 818)
Taft-Hartley Act (p. 819)

Fair Deal (p. 820)
Loyalty-Security Program
  (p. 821)
House Un-American Activities
  Committee (HUAC) (p. 821)
"New Look" (p. 826)
domino theory (p. 828)
Eisenhower Doctrine (p. 829)
Bay of Pigs (p. 830)
Cuban missile crisis (p. 831)
Peace Corps (p. 832)

### Key People

Joseph Stalin (p. 806)
George F. Kennan (p. 808)
Joseph McCarthy (p. 821)
Nikita Khrushchev (p. 826)
John F. Kennedy (p. 829)
Fidel Castro (p. 830)
Ho Chi Minh (p. 833)

## REVIEW QUESTIONS    Answer these questions to demonstrate your understanding of the chapter's main ideas.

1. What factors led to the Cold War?

2. What was the domestic impact of the anticommunist crusade of the late 1940s and 1950s?

3. Why did the United States become involved in Vietnam?

4. **THEMATIC UNDERSTANDING** Review the events listed under "Politics and Power" and "Identity" on the thematic timelines on pages 671 and 803. Radicalism played a significant role in American history between 1890 and 1945. What radical politics took root in the United States during this time, and how did the government, the business community, and different social groups respond to that radicalism?

## MAKING CONNECTIONS

Recognize the larger developments and continuities within and across chapters by answering these questions.

1. **ACROSS TIME AND PLACE** How was America's Cold War foreign policy an extension of principles and policies from earlier eras, and in what ways was it a break with those traditions? Was the Cold War inevitable? Why or why not?

2. **VISUAL EVIDENCE** Look at the map of the military-industrial complex (Map 25.3) on page 817 and the map of population changes (Chapter 26, Map 26.2) on page 862. Where were the majority of military weapons manufactured? What were the connections between weapons and geography? How did those connections affect population distribution in the United States and within individual metropolitan areas?

## MORE TO EXPLORE

Start here to learn more about the events discussed in this chapter.

John Lewis Gaddis, *The Cold War: A New History* (2005), and Walter LaFeber, *America, Russia, and the Cold War, 1945–2006*, 10th ed. (2008). Excellent overviews of the Cold War from distinct perspectives.

John Earl Haynes and Harvey Klehr, *Venona: Decoding Soviet Espionage in America* (1999). A thoughtful analysis of Soviet espionage.

W. J. Rorabaugh, *Kennedy and the Promise of the Sixties* (2002). A good starting point for Kennedy's presidency.

Ellen Schrecker, *Many Are the Crimes: McCarthyism in America* (1998). An excellent, detailed account of the McCarthy period.

The Center for the Study of the Pacific Northwest's site, "The Cold War and Red Scare in Washington State," at **washington.edu/uwired/outreach/cspn /Website/Classroom Materials/Curriculum Packets /Cold War & Red Scare/Cold War and Red Scare .html**, provides detailed information on how the Red Scare operated in one state.

The Woodrow Wilson International Center has established the Cold War International History Project at **wilsoncenter.org/cwihp**.

## TIMELINE

Ask yourself why this chapter begins and ends with these dates and then identify the links among related events.

| | |
|---|---|
| **1945** | • End of World War II; Yalta and Potsdam conferences |
| | • Senate approves U.S. participation in United Nations |
| **1946** | • George F. Kennan outlines containment policy |
| | • U.S. sides with French in war between French and Vietminh over control of Vietnam |
| **1947** | • Truman Doctrine |
| | • House Un-American Activities Committee (HUAC) investigates film industry |
| **1948** | • Communist coup in Czechoslovakia |
| | • Marshall Plan aids economic recovery in Europe |
| | • State of Israel created |
| | • Stalin blockades West Berlin; Berlin Airlift begins |
| **1949** | • North Atlantic Treaty Organization (NATO) founded |
| | • Soviet Union detonates atomic bomb |
| | • Mao Zedong establishes People's Republic of China |
| **1950–1953** | • Korean War |
| **1950** | • NSC-68 leads to nuclear buildup |
| | • Joseph McCarthy announces "list" of Communists in government |
| **1952** | • Dwight D. Eisenhower elected president |
| **1954** | • Army-McCarthy hearings on army subversion |
| | • Geneva Accords partition Vietnam |
| **1956** | • Nikita Khrushchev emerges as Stalin's successor |
| | • Suez Canal crisis |
| **1960** | • John F. Kennedy elected president |
| **1961** | • Kennedy orders the first contingent of Special Forces ("Green Berets") to Vietnam |
| **1963** | • Diem assassinated in South Vietnam |

**KEY TURNING POINTS:** What turning points and crises defined American containment policy between 1946 and 1953? Explain your answer with evidence from the timeline and chapter.

# 26
## CHAPTER

# Triumph of the Middle Class
# 1945–1963

At the height of the Cold War, in 1959, U.S. vice president Richard Nixon debated Soviet premier Nikita Khrushchev on the merits of Pepsi-Cola, TV dinners, and electric ovens. Face-to-face at the opening of an American exhibition in Moscow, Nixon and Khrushchev strolled through a model American home, assembled to demonstrate the consumer products available to the typical citizen of the United States. Nixon explained to Khrushchev that although the Soviet Union may have had superior rockets, the United States was ahead in other areas, such as color television.

This was Cold War politics by other means—a symbolic contest over which country's standard of living was higher. What was so striking about the so-called **kitchen debate** was Nixon's insistence, to a disbelieving Khrushchev, that a modern home filled with shiny new toasters, televisions, and other consumer products was accessible to the average American worker. "Any steelworker could buy this house," Nixon told the Soviet leader. The kitchen debate settled little in the geopolitical rivalry between the United States and the Soviet Union. But it speaks to us across the decades because it reveals how Americans had come to see themselves by the late 1950s: as home owners and consumers, as a people for whom the middle-class American Dream was a commercial aspiration.

The real story of the postwar period was the growing number of Americans who embraced that aspiration. In the two decades following the end of World War II, a new middle class was born in the United States. *Fortune* magazine estimated that in the 1950s, the middle class—which *Fortune* defined as families with more than $5,000 in annual earnings after taxes (about $40,000 today)—was increasing at the rate of 1.1 million people per year. Riding a wave of rising incomes, American dominance in the global economy, and Cold War federal spending, the postwar middle class enjoyed the highest standard of living in the world.

However, the success of the middle class could not hide deeper troubles. This was an era of neither universal conformity nor diminishing social strife. Jim Crow laws, contradictions in women's lives, a rebellious youth culture, and changing sexual mores were only the most obvious sources of social tension. Suburban growth came at the expense of cities, hastening urban decay and exacerbating racial segregation. Nor was prosperity ever as widespread as the Moscow exhibit implied. The suburban lifestyle was beyond the reach of the working poor, the elderly, immigrants, Mexican Americans, and most African Americans—indeed, the majority of the country.

**IDENTIFY THE BIG IDEA**

Why did consumer culture become such a fixture of American life in the postwar decades, and how did it affect politics and society?

**The Middle-Class Family Ideal**   A family eats breakfast at a campground in Zion National Park, Utah. Americans embraced a middle-class, nuclear family ideal in the postwar decades. Photo by Justin Locke/ National Geographic/Getty Images.

# Postwar Prosperity and the Affluent Society

The United States enjoyed enormous economic advantages at the close of World War II. While the Europeans and Japanese were still clearing the war's rubble, America stood poised to enter a postwar boom. As the only major industrial nation not devastated by war, the United States held an unprecedented global position. The American economy also benefitted from an expanding internal market and heavy investment in research and development. Two additional developments stood out: First, for the first time in the nation's history, employers generally accepted collective bargaining, which for workers translated into rising wages, expanding benefits, and an increasing rate of home ownership. Second, the federal government's outlays for military and domestic programs gave a huge boost to the economy.

## Economy: From Recovery to Dominance

U.S. corporations, banks, and manufacturers so dominated the global economy that the postwar period has been called the Pax Americana (a Latin term meaning "American Peace" and harking back to the Pax Romana of the first and second centuries A.D.). *Life* magazine publisher Henry Luce was so confident in the nation's growing power that during World War II he had predicted the dawning of the "American century." The preponderance of American economic power in the postwar decades, however, was not simply an artifact of the world war — it was not an inevitable development. Several key elements came together, internationally and at home, to propel three decades of unprecedented economic growth.

**The Bretton Woods System**   American global supremacy rested partly on the economic institutions created at an international conference in **Bretton Woods**, New Hampshire, in July 1944. The first of those institutions was the **World Bank**, created to provide loans for the reconstruction of war-torn Europe as well as for the development of former colonized nations — the so-called Third World or developing world. A second institution, the **International Monetary Fund (IMF)**, was set up to stabilize currencies and provide a predictable monetary environment for trade, with the U.S. dollar serving as the benchmark. The World Bank and the IMF formed the cornerstones of the Bretton Woods system, which guided the global economy after the war.

The Bretton Woods system was joined in 1947 by the first General Agreement on Tariffs and Trade (GATT), which established an international framework for overseeing trade rules and practices. Together, the Bretton Woods system and GATT served America's conception of an open-market global economy and complemented the nation's ambitious diplomatic aims in the Cold War. The chief idea of the Bretton Woods system was to make American capital available, on cheap terms, to nations that adopted free-trade capitalist economies. Critics charged, rightly, that Bretton Woods and GATT favored the United States at the

**The Kitchen Debate**

At the American National Exhibition in Moscow in 1959, the United States put on display the technological wonders of American home life. When Vice President Richard Nixon visited, he and Soviet premier Nikita Khrushchev got into a heated debate over the relative merits of their rival systems, with the up-to-date American kitchen as a case in point. This photograph shows the debate in progress. Khrushchev is the bald man pointing his finger at Nixon. To Nixon's left stands Leonid Brezhnev, who would be Khrushchev's successor. Getty Images.

expense of recently independent countries, because the United States could dictate lending terms and stood to benefit as nations purchased more American goods. But the system provided needed economic stability.

### The Military-Industrial Complex

A second engine of postwar prosperity was defense spending. In his final address to the nation in 1961, President Dwight D. Eisenhower spoke about the power of what he called the **military-industrial complex**, which by then employed 3.5 million Americans. Even though his administration had fostered this defense establishment, Eisenhower feared its implications: "We must guard against the acquisition of unwarranted influence, whether sought or unsought, by the military-industrial complex," he said. This complex had its roots in the business-government partnerships of World War II. After 1945, though the country was nominally at peace, the economy and the government operated in a state of perpetual readiness for war.

Based at the sprawling Pentagon in Arlington, Virginia, the Defense Department evolved into a massive bureaucracy. In the name of national security, defense-related industries entered into long-term relationships with the Pentagon. Some companies did so much business with the government that they in effect became private divisions of the Defense Department. Over 60 percent of the income of Boeing, General Dynamics, and Raytheon, for instance, came from military contracts, and the percentages were even higher for Lockheed and Republic Aviation. In previous peacetime years, military spending had constituted only 1 percent of gross domestic product (GDP); now it represented 10 percent. Economic growth was increasingly dependent on a robust defense sector.

**IDENTIFY CAUSES**
What primary factors led to the growth of the American economy after World War II?

**The Military-Industrial Complex**

Often, technology developed for military purposes, such as the complex design of jet airplanes, was easily transferred to the consumer market. The Boeing Aircraft Company—their Seattle plant is pictured here in the mid-1950s—became one of the leading commercial airplane manufacturers in the world in the 1960s, boosted in part by tax dollar–financed military contracts. Major American corporations—such as Boeing, McDonnell Douglas, General Electric, General Dynamics, and dozens of others—benefitted enormously from military contracts from the Department of Defense in the years after World War II. © Bettmann/Corbis.

As permanent mobilization took hold, science, industry, and government became intertwined. Cold War competition for military supremacy spawned both an arms race and a space race as the United States and the Soviet Union each sought to develop more explosive bombs and more powerful rockets. Federal spending underwrote 90 percent of the cost of research for aviation and space, 65 percent for electricity and electronics, 42 percent for scientific instruments, and even 24 percent for automobiles. With the government footing the bill, corporations lost little time in transforming new technology into useful products. Backed by the Pentagon, for instance, IBM and Sperry Rand pressed ahead with research on integrated circuits, which later spawned the computer revolution.

When the Soviet Union launched the world's first satellite, **Sputnik**, in 1957, the startled United States went into high gear to catch up in the Cold War space competition. Alarmed that the United States was falling behind in science and technology, Eisenhower persuaded Congress to appropriate additional money for college scholarships and university research. The **National Defense Education Act** of 1958 funneled millions of dollars into American universities, helping institutions such as the University of California at Berkeley, Stanford University, the Massachusetts Institute of Technology, and the University of Michigan become the leading research centers in the world.

**Corporate Power**   Despite its massive size, the military-corporate partnership was only one part of the nation's economy. For over half a century, the consolidation of economic power into large corporate firms had characterized American capitalism. In the postwar decades, that tendency accelerated. By 1970, the top four U.S. automakers produced 91 percent of all motor vehicles sold in the country; the top four firms in tires produced 72 percent; those in cigarettes, 84 percent; and those in detergents, 70 percent. Eric Johnston, former president of the American Chamber of Commerce, declared that "we have entered a period of accelerating bigness in all aspects of American life." Expansion into foreign markets also spurred corporate growth. During the 1950s, U.S. exports nearly doubled, giving the nation a trade surplus of close to $5 billion in 1960. By the 1970s, such firms as Coca-Cola, Gillette, IBM, and Mobil made more than half their profits abroad.

To staff their bureaucracies, the postwar corporate giants required a huge white-collar army. A new generation of corporate chieftains emerged, operating in a complex environment that demanded long-range forecasting. Companies turned to the universities, which

grew explosively after 1945. Postwar corporate culture inspired numerous critics, who argued that the obedience demanded of white-collar workers was stifling creativity and blighting lives. In *The Lonely Crowd* (1950), the sociologist David Riesman mourned a lost masculinity and contrasted the independent businessmen and professionals of earlier years with the managerial class of the postwar world. The sociologist William Whyte painted a somber picture of "organization men" who left the home "spiritually as well as physically to take the vows of organization life." Andrew Hacker, in *The Corporation Take-Over* (1964), warned that a small handful of such organization men "can draw up an investment program calling for the expenditure of several billions of dollars" and thereby "determine the quality of life for substantial segments of society."

Many of these "investment programs" relied on mechanization, or automation—another important factor in the postwar boom. From 1947 to 1975, worker productivity more than doubled across the whole of the economy. American factories replaced manpower with machines, substituting cheap fossil energy for human muscle. As industries mechanized, they could turn out products more efficiently and at lower cost. Mechanization did not come without social costs, however. Over the course of the postwar decades, millions of high-wage manufacturing jobs were lost as machines replaced workers, affecting entire cities and regions. Corporate leaders approved, but workers and their union representatives were less enthusiastic. "How are you going to sell cars to all of these machines?" wondered Walter Reuther, president of the United Auto Workers (UAW).

**The Economic Record**   The American economy produced an extraordinary postwar record. Annual GDP jumped from $213 billion in 1945 to more than $500 billion in 1960; by 1970, it exceeded $1 trillion (Figure 26.1). This sustained economic growth meant a 25 percent rise in real income for ordinary Americans between 1946 and 1959. Even better, the new prosperity featured low inflation. After a burst of high prices in the immediate postwar period, inflation slowed to 2 to 3 percent annually, and it stayed low until the escalation of the Vietnam War in the mid-1960s. Feeling secure about the future, Americans were eager to spend and rightly felt that they were better off than ever before. In 1940, 43 percent of American families owned their homes; by 1960, 62 percent did. In that period, moreover, income inequality dropped sharply. The share of total income going to the top tenth—the

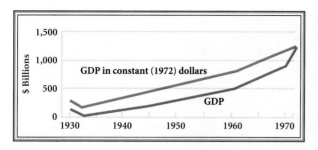

**FIGURE 26.1**

**Gross Domestic Product, 1930–1972**

After a sharp dip during the Great Depression, the GDP rose steadily in both real and constant dollars in the postwar period.

richest Americans — declined by nearly one-third from the 45 percent it had been in 1940. American society had become not only more prosperous but also more egalitarian.

However, the picture was not as rosy at the bottom, where tenacious poverty accompanied the economic boom. In *The Affluent Society* (1958), which analyzed the nation's successful, "affluent" middle class, economist John Kenneth Galbraith argued that the poor were only an "afterthought" in the minds of economists and politicians, who largely celebrated the new growth. As Galbraith noted, one in thirteen families at the time earned less than $1,000 a year (about $7,500 in today's dollars). Four years later, in *The Other America* (1962), the left-wing social critic Michael Harrington chronicled "the economic underworld of American life," and a U.S. government study, echoing a well-known sentence from Franklin Roosevelt's second inaugural address ("I see one-third of a nation ill-housed, ill-clad, ill-nourished"), declared "one-third of the nation" to be poorly paid, poorly educated, and poorly housed. It appeared that in economic terms, as the top and the middle converged, the bottom remained far behind.

## A Nation of Consumers

The most breathtaking development in the postwar American economy was the dramatic expansion of the domestic consumer market. The sheer quantity of consumer goods available to the average person was without precedent. In some respects, the postwar decades seemed like the 1920s all over again, with an abundance of new gadgets and appliances, a craze for automobiles, and new types of mass media. Yet there was a significant difference: in the 1950s, consumption became associated with citizenship. Buying things, once a sign of personal indulgence, now meant participating

fully in American society and, moreover, fulfilling a social responsibility. What the suburban family consumed, asserted *Life* magazine in a photo essay, would help to ensure "full employment and improved living standards for the rest of the nation."

**The GI Bill**   The new ethic of consumption appealed to the postwar middle class, the driving force behind the expanding domestic market. Middle-class status was more accessible than ever before because of the Servicemen's Readjustment Act of 1944, popularly known as the GI Bill. In the immediate postwar years, more than half of all U.S. college students were veterans attending class on the government's dime. By the middle of the 1950s, 2.2 million veterans had attended college and another 5.6 million had attended trade school with government financing. Before the GI Bill, commented one veteran, "I looked upon college education as likely as my owning a Rolls-Royce with a chauffeur."

Government financing of education helped make the U.S. workforce the best educated in the world in the 1950s and 1960s. American colleges, universities, and trade schools grew by leaps and bounds to accommodate the flood of students — and expanded again when the children of those students, the baby boomers, reached college age in the 1960s. At Rutgers University, enrollment went from 7,000 before the war to 16,000 in 1947; at the University of Minnesota, from 15,000 to more than 27,000. The GI Bill trained nearly half a million engineers; 200,000 doctors, dentists, and nurses; and 150,000 scientists (among many other professions). Better education meant higher earning power, and higher earning power translated into the consumer spending that drove the postwar economy. One observer of the GI Bill was so impressed with its achievements that he declared it responsible for "the most important educational and social transformation in American history."

The GI Bill stimulated the economy and expanded the middle class in another way: by increasing home ownership. Between the end of World War II and 1966, one of every five single-family homes built in the United States was financed through a GI Bill mortgage — 2.5 million new homes in all. In cities and suburbs across the country, the **Veterans Administration** (VA), which helped former soldiers purchase new homes with no down payment, sparked a building boom that created jobs in the construction industry and fueled consumer spending in home appliances and automobiles. Education and home ownership were more than personal triumphs for the families of World

**College on the GI Bill**

In 1947—the year this photo was taken of a crowded lecture hall at the University of Iowa—more than 6,000 of this university's 10,000 students (60 percent) were veterans whose education was financed by the GI Bill. Across the country, American universities were bursting at the seams from the massive enrollment of World War II veterans. Government financing of college education for these vets made the U.S. workforce one of the best educated in the world in the 1950s and 1960s. Margaret Bourke-White/Time Life Pictures/Getty Images.

War II veterans (and Korean and Vietnam War veterans, after a new GI Bill was passed in 1952). They were concrete financial *assets* that helped lift more Americans than ever before into a mass-consumption-oriented middle class.

**Trade Unions** Organized labor also expanded the ranks of the middle class. For the first time ever, trade unions and **collective bargaining** became major factors in the nation's economic life. In the past, organized labor had been confined to a narrow band of craft trades and a few industries, primarily coal mining, railroading, and the building and metal trades. The power balance shifted during the Great Depression, and by the time the dust settled after World War II, labor unions overwhelmingly represented America's industrial workforce (Figure 26.2). By the beginning of the 1950s, the nation's major industries, including auto, steel, clothing, chemicals, and virtually all consumer product manufacturing, were operating with union contracts.

That outcome did not arrive without a fight. Unions staged major strikes in nearly all American industries in 1945 and 1946, and employers fought back. Head of the UAW Walter Reuther and CIO president Philip Murray declared that employers could afford a 30 percent wage increase, which would fuel postwar consumption. When employers, led by the giant General

Motors, balked at that demand, the two sides seemed set for a long struggle. Between 1947 and 1950, however, a broad "labor-management accord" gradually

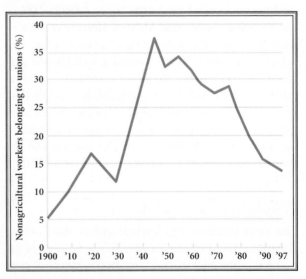

**FIGURE 26.2**
**Labor Union Strength, 1900–1997**

Labor unions reached their peak strength immediately after World War II, when they represented close to 40 percent of the nonfarm workforce. Although there was some decline after the mid-1950s, unions still represented nearly 30 percent in 1973. Thereafter, their decline was precipitous.
AFL-CIO Information Bureau, Washington, DC.

emerged across most industries. This was not industrial peace, because the country still experienced many strikes, but a general acceptance of collective bargaining as the method for setting the terms of employment. The result was rising real income. The average worker with three dependents gained 18 percent in spendable real income in the 1950s.

In addition, unions delivered greater leisure (more paid holidays and longer vacations) and, in a startling departure, a social safety net. In postwar Europe, America's allies were constructing welfare states. But having lost the bruising battle in Washington for national health care during Truman's presidency, American unions turned to the bargaining table. By the end of the 1950s, union contracts commonly provided pension plans and company-paid health insurance. Collective bargaining, the process of trade unions and employers negotiating workplace contracts, had become, in effect, the American alternative to the European welfare state and, as Reuther boasted, the passport into the middle class.

The labor-management accord, though impressive, was never as durable or universal as it seemed. Vulnerabilities lurked. For one thing, the sheltered domestic markets — the essential condition for generous contracts — were quite fragile. In certain industries, the lead firms were already losing market share. Second, generally overlooked were the many unorganized workers with no middle-class passport — those consigned to unorganized industries, casual labor, or low-wage jobs in the service sector. A final vulnerability was the most basic: the abiding antiunionism of American employers. At heart, managers regarded the labor-management accord as a negotiated truce, not a permanent peace. The postwar labor-management accord turned out to be a transitory event, not a permanent condition of American economic life.

**Houses, Cars, and Children**  Increased educational levels, growing home ownership, and higher wages all enabled more Americans than ever before to become members of what one historian has called a "consumer republic." But what did they buy? The postwar emphasis on nuclear families and suburbs provides the answer. In the emerging suburban nation, three elements came together to create patterns of consumption that would endure for decades: houses, cars, and children.

A feature in a 1949 issue of *McCall's*, a magazine targeting middle-class women, illustrates the connections. "I now have three working centers," a typical housewife explains. "The baby center, a baking center and a cleaning center." Accompanying illustrations reveal the interior of the brand-new house, stocked with the latest consumer products: accessories for the baby's room; a new stove, oven, and refrigerator; and a washer and dryer, along with cleaning products and other household goods. The article does not mention automobiles, but the photo of the house's exterior makes the point clear: father drives home from work in a new car.

Consumption for the home, including automobiles, drove the postwar American economy as much as, or more than, the military-industrial complex did. If we think like advertisers and manufacturers, we can see why. Between 1945 and 1970, more than 25 million new houses were built in the United States. Each required its own supply of new appliances, from refrigerators to lawn mowers. In 1955 alone, Americans purchased 4 million new refrigerators, and between 1940 and 1951 the sale of power mowers increased from 35,000 per year to more than 1 million. Moreover, as American industry discovered planned obsolescence — the encouragement of consumers to replace appliances and cars every few years — the home became a site of perpetual consumer desire.

Children also encouraged consumption. The baby boomers born between World War II and the late 1950s have consistently, throughout every phase of their lives, been the darlings of American advertising and consumption. When they were infants, companies focused on developing new baby products, from disposable diapers to instant formula. When they were toddlers and young children, new television programs, board games, fast food, TV dinners, and thousands of different kinds of toys came to market to supply the rambunctious youth. When they were teenagers, rock music, Hollywood films, and a constantly marketed "teen culture" — with its appropriate clothing, music, hairstyles, and other accessories — bombarded them. Remarkably, in 1956, middle-class American teenagers on average had a weekly income of more than $10, close to the weekly disposable income of an entire family a generation earlier.

> **EXPLAIN CONSEQUENCES**
> How did the tastes and values of the postwar middle class affect the country?

**Television**  The emergence of commercial television in the United States was swift and overwhelming. In the realm of technology, only the automobile and the personal computer were its equal in transforming everyday life in the twentieth century. In 1947, there were 7,000 TV sets in American homes. A year later, the CBS and NBC radio networks began offering regular

**Teenagers**

These teenage girls and boys are being restrained by police outside an Elvis Presley concert in Florida in 1956. Elvis, who was instrumental in popularizing rock 'n' roll music among white middle-class teenagers in the mid-1950s, was one example of a broader phenomenon: the creation of the "teenager" as a distinct demographic, cultural category and, perhaps most significantly, consumer group. Beginning in the 1950s, middle-class teenagers had money to spend, and advertisers and other entrepreneurs—such as the music executives who marketed Elvis or the Hollywood executives who invented the "teen film"—sought ways to win their allegiance and their dollars. Photo by Charles Trainor/Time Life Pictures/ Getty Images.

programming, and by 1950 Americans owned 7.3 million sets. Ten years later, 87 percent of American homes had at least one television set. Having conquered the home, television would soon become the principal mediator between the consumer and the marketplace.

Television advertisers mastered the art of manufacturing consumer desire. TV stations, like radio stations before them, depended entirely on advertising for profits. The first television executives understood that as long as they sold viewers to advertisers they would stay on the air. Early corporate-sponsored shows (such as *General Electric Theater* and *U.S. Steel Hour*) and simple product jingles (such as "No matter what the time or place, let's keep up with that happy pace. 7-Up your thirst away!") gave way by the early 1960s to slick advertising campaigns that used popular music, movie stars, sports figures, and stimulating graphics to captivate viewers.

By creating powerful visual narratives of comfort and plenty, television revolutionized advertising and changed forever the ways products were sold to American, and global, consumers. On *Queen for a Day*, a show popular in the mid-1950s, women competed to see who could tell the most heartrending story of tragedy and loss. The winner was lavished with household products: refrigerators, toasters, ovens, and the like. In a groundbreaking advertisement for Anacin aspirin, a tiny hammer pounded inside the skull of a headache sufferer. Almost overnight, sales of Anacin increased by 50 percent.

By the late 1950s, what Americans saw on television, both in the omnipresent commercials and in the programming, was an overwhelmingly white, Anglo-Saxon, Protestant world of nuclear families, suburban homes, and middle-class life. A typical show was *Father Knows Best*, starring Robert Young and Jane Wyatt. Father left home each morning wearing a suit and carrying a briefcase. Mother was a full-time housewife and stereotypical female, prone to bad driving and tears. *Leave It to Beaver*, another immensely popular series about suburban family life, embodied similar late-fifties themes. Earlier in the decade, however, television featured grittier realities. *The Honeymooners*, starring Jackie Gleason as a Brooklyn bus driver, and

### Advertising in the TV Age

Aggressive advertising of new products such as the color television helped fuel the surge in consumer spending during the 1950s. Marketing experts emphasized television's role in promoting family togetherness, while interior designers offered decorating tips that placed the television at the focal point of living rooms and the increasingly popular "family rooms." In this 1951 magazine advertisement, the family is watching a variety program starring singer Dinah Shore, who was the television spokeswoman for Chevrolet cars. Every American probably could hum the tune of the little song she sang in praise of the Chevy. Courtesy of Motorola Museum © 1951 Motorola, Inc./Picture Research Consultants & Archives.

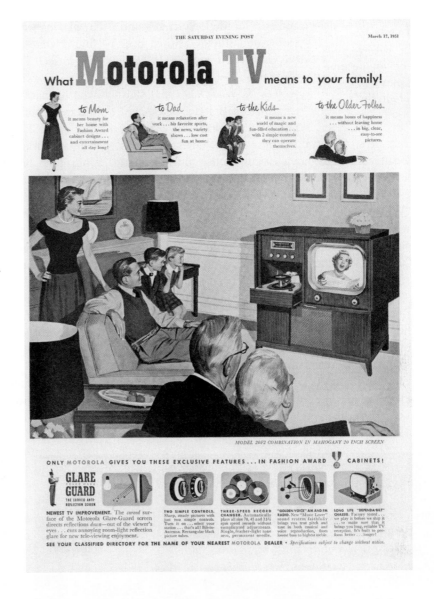

*The Life of Riley*, a situation comedy featuring a California aircraft worker, treated working-class lives. Two other early-fifties television series, *Beulah*, starring Ethel Waters and then Louise Beavers as an African American maid, and the comedic *Amos 'n' Andy*, were the only shows featuring black actors in major roles. Television was never a showcase for the breadth of American society, but in the second half of the 1950s broadcasting lost much of its ethnic, racial, and class diversity and became a vehicle for the transmission of a narrow range of middle-class tastes and values.

## Youth Culture

One of the most striking developments in American life in the postwar decades was the emergence of the **teenager** as a cultural phenomenon. In 1956, only partly in jest, the CBS radio commentator Eric Sevareid questioned "whether the teenagers will take over the United States lock, stock, living room, and garage." Sevareid was grumbling about American youth culture, a phenomenon first noticed in the 1920s and with its roots in the lengthening years of education, the role of peer groups, and the consumer tastes of young people. Market research revealed a distinct teen market to be exploited. *Newsweek* noted with awe in 1951 that the aggregate of the weekly spending money of teenagers was enough to buy 190 million candy bars, 130 million soft drinks, and 230 million sticks of gum. Increasingly, advertisers targeted the young, both to capture their spending money and to exploit their influence on family purchases.

Hollywood movies played a large role in fostering a teenage culture. Young people made up the largest

**UNDERSTAND POINTS OF VIEW**

How did rebellion become an integral part of consumer culture in the postwar period?

audience for motion pictures, and Hollywood studios learned over the course of the 1950s to cater to them. The success of films such as *The Wild One* (1953), starring Marlon Brando; *Blackboard Jungle* (1955), with Sidney Poitier; and *Rebel Without a Cause* (1955), starring James Dean, convinced movie executives that films directed at teenagers were worthy investments. "What are you rebelling against?" Brando is asked in *The Wild One*. "Whattaya got?" he replies. By the early 1960s, Hollywood had retooled its business model, shifting emphasis away from adults and families to teenagers. The "teenpic" soon included multiple genres: horror, rock 'n' roll, dangerous youth, and beach party, among others.

**Rock 'n' Roll**   What really defined the youth culture, however, was its music. Rejecting the romantic ballads of the 1940s, teenagers discovered rock 'n' roll, which originated in African American rhythm and blues. The Cleveland disc jockey Alan Freed took the lead in introducing white America to the black-created sound

by playing what were called "race" records. "If I could find a white man who had the Negro sound and the Negro feel, I could make a billion dollars," a record company owner is quoted as saying. The performer who fit that bill was Elvis Presley, who rocketed into instant celebrity in 1956 with his hit records "Hound Dog" and "Heartbreak Hotel," covers of songs originally recorded by black artists such as Big Mama Thornton. Between 1953 and 1959, record sales increased from $213 million to $603 million, with rock 'n' roll as the driving force.

Many unhappy adults saw in rock 'n' roll music an invitation to interracial dating, rebellion, and a more flagrant sexuality. The media featured hundreds of stories on problem teens, and denunciations of the new music poured forth from many corners. Such condemnation only deflected off the new youth culture or, if anything, increased its popularity. Both Hollywood and the music industry had learned that youth rebellion sold tickets.

**Cultural Dissenters**   Youth rebellion was only one aspect of a broader discontent with the sometimes

**Motown**

Mary Wilson, Diana Ross, and Florence Ballard (from left to right) were the founding members of the Motown singing group the Supremes (shown here in concert in 1964), which produced twelve number-one singles. Motown, a record label owned by African American entrepreneur Berry Gordy, specialized in so-called cross-over acts: black singers who sold records to white audiences. In the era of Jim Crow, Motown represented a small but noteworthy step toward a less racially segregated American culture. Photo by RB/Redferns/Getty Images.

saccharine consumer culture of the 1950s. Many artists, writers, and jazz musicians embarked on powerful new experimental projects in a remarkable flowering of intensely personal, introspective art forms. Black musicians developed a hard-driving improvisational style known as bebop. Whether the "hot" bebop of saxophonist Charlie Parker or the more subdued "cool" sound of the influential trumpeter Miles Davis, postwar jazz was cerebral, intimate, and individualistic. As such, it stood in stark contrast to the commercialized, dance-oriented "swing" bands of the 1930s and 1940s.

Black jazz musicians found eager fans not only in the African American community but also among young white **Beats**, a group of writers and poets centered in New York and San Francisco who disdained middle-class materialism. In his poem "Howl" (1956), which became a manifesto of the Beat generation, Allen Ginsberg lamented: "I saw the best minds of my generation destroyed by madness, starving hysterical naked, dragging themselves through the negro streets at dawn looking for an angry fix." In works such as Jack Kerouac's novel *On the Road* (1957), the Beats glorified spontaneity, sexual adventurism, drug use, and spirituality. The Beats were apolitical, but their cultural rebellion would, in the 1960s, inspire a new generation of young rebels disenchanted with both the political and cultural status quo.

## Religion and the Middle Class

In an age of anxiety about nuclear annihilation and the spread of "godless communism," Americans yearned for a reaffirmation of faith. Church membership jumped from 49 percent of the population in 1940 to 70 percent in 1960. People flocked to the evangelical Protestant denominations, beneficiaries of a remarkable new crop of preachers. Most eloquent was the young Reverend Billy Graham, who made brilliant use of television, radio, and advertising. His massive 1949 revival in Los Angeles and his 1957 crusade at Madison Square Garden in New York, attended or viewed by hundreds of thousands of Americans, established Graham as the nation's leading evangelical.

Rather than clashing with the new middle-class ethic of consumption, the religious reawakening was designed to mesh with it. Preachers such as Graham and the California-based Robert Schuller told Americans that so long as they lived moral lives, they deserved the material blessings of modern life. No one was more influential in this regard than the minister and author Norman Vincent Peale, whose best-selling book *The Power of Positive Thinking* (1952) embodied the therapeutic use of religion as an antidote to life's trials and tribulations. Peale taught that with faith in God and "positive thinking," anyone could overcome obstacles and become a success. Graham, Schuller, Peale, and other 1950s evangelicals laid the foundation for the rise of the televangelists, who created popular television ministries in the 1970s.

The postwar purveyors of religious faith cast Americans as a righteous people opposed to communist atheism. When Julius and Ethel Rosenberg were sentenced to death in 1953, the judge criticized them for "devoting themselves to the Russian ideology of denial of God." Cold War imperatives drew Catholics, Protestants, and Jews into an influential ecumenical movement that downplayed doctrinal differences. The phrase "under God" was inserted into the Pledge of Allegiance in 1954, and U.S. coins carried the words

**Billy Graham**
Charismatic and inspiring, Billy Graham wore down shoe leather to bring Christian conversion to hundreds of thousands of Americans in the 1940s and 1950s, preaching to large crowds such as this one in Columbia, South Carolina. He also migrated onto the radio and television airwaves, using technology to reach even wider audiences. Graham used the Cold War to sharpen his message, telling Americans that "godless communism" was an inferior system, but that democracy in America required belief in God and a constant struggle against "sin." Photo by John Dominis/Time Life Pictures/Getty Images.

"In God We Trust" after 1956. These religious initiatives struck a distinctly moderate tone, however, in comparison with the politicized evangelism that emerged in the 1960s and 1970s (Chapter 29).

# The American Family in the Era of Containment

Marriage, family structure, and gender roles had been undergoing significant changes since the turn of the twentieth century (Chapter 18). Beginning in the nineteenth century, middle-class Americans increasingly saw marriage as "companionate," that is, based on romantic love and a lifetime of shared friendship. *Companionate* did not mean *equal*. In the mid-twentieth century, family life remained governed by notions of paternalism, in which men provided economic support and controlled the family's financial resources, while women cared for children and occupied a secondary position in public life.

The resurgent postwar American middle class was preoccupied with the virtues of paternalism. Everyone from professional psychologists to television advertisers and every organization from schools to the popular press celebrated nuclear families. Children were prized, and women's caregiving roles were valorized. This view of family life, and especially its emphasis on female "domesticity," was bolstered by Cold War politics. Americans who deviated from prevailing gender and familial norms were not only viewed with scorn but were also sometimes thought to be subversive and politically dangerous. The word *containment* could apply to the home as easily as to foreign policy. The family had become politicized by the Cold War.

The model of domesticity so highly esteemed in postwar middle-class morality hid deeper, longer-term changes in the way marriage, gender roles, women's work, and even sex were understood. To comprehend the postwar decades, we have to keep in mind both the value placed on domesticity and the tumultuous changes surging beneath its prescriptions.

## The Baby Boom

A popular 1945 song was called "Gotta Make Up for Lost Time," and Americans did just that. Two things were noteworthy about the families they formed after World War II: First, marriages were remarkably stable. Not until the mid-1960s did the divorce rate begin to rise sharply. Second, married couples were intent on

having babies. Everyone expected to have several children—it was part of adulthood, almost a citizen's responsibility. After a century and a half of decline, the birthrate shot up. More babies were born in the six years between 1948 and 1953 than in the previous thirty years (Figure 26.3).

One of the reasons for this **baby boom** was that people were having children at the same time. A second was a drop in the average marriage age—down to twenty-two for men and twenty for women. Younger parents meant a bumper crop of children. Women who came of age in the 1930s averaged 2.4 children; their counterparts in the 1950s averaged 3.2 children. Such a dramatic turnaround reflected couples' decisions during the Great Depression to limit childbearing and couples' contrasting decisions in the postwar years to have more children. The baby boom peaked in 1957 and remained at a high level until the early 1960s. Far from "normal," all of these developments were anomalies, temporary reversals of long-standing demographic trends. From the perspective of the whole of the twentieth century, the 1950s and early 1960s stand out as exceptions to declining birthrates, rising divorce rates, and the steadily rising marriage age.

The passage of time revealed the ever-widening impact of the baby boom. When baby boomers competed for jobs during the 1970s, the labor market became tight. When career-oriented baby boomers belatedly began having children in the 1980s, the birthrate jumped. And in our own time, as baby boomers

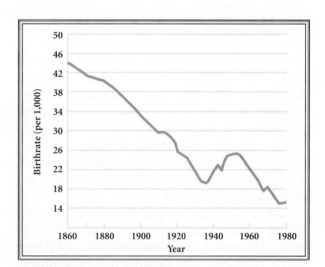

**FIGURE 26.3**

**The American Birthrate, 1860–1980**

When birthrates are viewed over more than a century, the postwar baby boom is clearly only a temporary reversal of the long-term downward trend in the American birthrate.

begin retiring, huge funding problems threaten to engulf Social Security and Medicare. The intimate decisions of so many couples after World War II continued to shape American life well into the twenty-first century.

### Improving Health and Education

Baby boom children benefitted from a host of important advances in public health and medical practice in the postwar years. Formerly serious illnesses became merely routine after the introduction of such "miracle drugs" as penicillin (introduced in 1943), streptomycin (1945), and cortisone (1946). When Dr. Jonas Salk perfected a polio vaccine in 1954, he became a national hero. The free distribution of Salk's vaccine in the nation's schools, followed in 1961 by Dr. Albert Sabin's oral polio vaccine, demonstrated the potential of government-sponsored public health programs.

The baby boom also gave the nation's educational system a boost. Postwar middle-class parents, America's first college-educated generation, placed a high value on education. Suburban parents approved 90 percent of school bond issues during the 1950s. By 1970, school expenditures accounted for 7.2 percent of the gross national product, double the 1950 level. In the 1960s, the baby boom generation swelled college enrollments. State university systems grew in tandem: the pioneering University of California, University of Wisconsin, and State University of New York systems added dozens of new campuses and offered students in their states a low-cost college education.

### Dr. Benjamin Spock

To keep baby boom children healthy and happy, middle-class parents increasingly relied on the advice of experts. Dr. Benjamin Spock's *Common Sense Book of Baby and Child Care* sold 1 million copies every year after its publication in 1946. Spock urged mothers to abandon the rigid feeding and baby-care schedules of an earlier generation. New mothers found Spock's commonsense approach liberating. "Your little paperback is still in my cupboard, with loose pages, rather worn from use because I brought up two babies using it as my 'Bible,'" a California housewife wrote to Spock.

Despite his commonsense approach to child rearing, Spock was part of a generation of psychological experts whose advice often failed to reassure women. If mothers were too protective, Spock and others argued, they might hamper their children's preparation for adult life. On the other hand, mothers who wanted to work outside the home felt guilty because Spock recommended that they be constantly available for their children. As American mothers aimed for the perfection demanded of them seemingly at every turn, many began to question these mixed messages. Some of them would be inspired by the resurgence of feminism in the 1960s.

**PLACE EVENTS IN CONTEXT**
Why was there an increase in births in the decades after World War II, and what were some of the effects of this baby boom?

## Women, Work, and Family

Two powerful forces shaped women's relationships to work and family life in the postwar decades. One was the middle-class domestic ideal, in which women were expected to raise children, attend to other duties in the home, and devote themselves to their husbands' happiness. So powerful was this ideal that in 1957 the *Ladies' Home Journal* entitled an article, "Is College Education Wasted on Women?" The second force was the job market. Most working-class women had to earn a paycheck to help their family. And despite their education, middle-class women found that jobs in the professions and business were dominated by men and often closed to them. For both groups, the market offered mostly "women's jobs" — in teaching, nursing, and other areas of the growing service sector — and little room for advancement (American Voices, p. 852).

The idea that a woman's place was in the home was, of course, not new. The postwar obsession with femininity and motherhood bore a remarkable similarity to the nineteenth century's notion of domesticity. The updated version drew on new elements of twentieth-century science and culture. Psychologists equated motherhood with "normal" female identity and suggested that career-minded mothers needed therapy. "A mother who runs out on her children to work — except in cases of absolute necessity — betrays a deep dissatisfaction with motherhood or with her marriage," wrote one leading psychiatrist. Television shows and movies depicted career women as social misfits. The postwar consumer culture also emphasized women's domestic role as purchasing agents for home and family. "Can a woman ever feel right cooking on a dirty range?" asked one advertisement.

The postwar domestic ideal held that women's principal economic contribution came through consumption — women shopped for the family. In reality, their contributions increasingly took them outside their homes and into the workforce. In 1954, married women made up half of all women workers. Six years later, the 1960 census reported a stunning fact: the number of mothers who worked had increased four times, and over one-third of these women had children

## Coming of Age in the Postwar Years

At the dawn of the postwar era, Americans faced new opportunities and new anxieties. Many former soldiers attended college and purchased new homes on the GI Bill, which forever changed their lives. Women faced new pressures to realize the ideal role of housewife and mother. On the horizon, both in reality and in the American imagination, lurked communism, which Americans feared but little understood. And racial segregation continued to shape the ordinary lives of Americans. Recorded here are several different reactions to these postwar tensions, distinct experiences of coming of age in the 1940s and 1950s.

### Art Buchwald
### Studying on the GI Bill

Art Buchwald was one of the best-known humorists in American journalism. But in 1946, he was an ordinary ex-serviceman using the GI Bill to go to college.

It was time to face up to whether I was serious about attending school. My decision was to go down to the University of Southern California and find out what I should study at night to get into the place. There were at least 4,000 ex-GIs waiting to register. I stood in line with them. Hours later, I arrived at the counter and said, "I would like to . . ." The clerk said, "Fill this out."

Having been accepted as a full-time student under the G.I. Bill, I was entitled to seventy-five dollars a month plus tuition, books, and supplies. Meanwhile, I found a boardinghouse a few blocks from campus, run by a cheery woman who was like a mother to her thirteen boarders. . . . At the time, just after the Second World War had ended, an undeclared class war was going on at USC. The G.I.s returning home had little use for the fraternity men, since most of the frat boys were not only much younger, but considered very immature.

The G.I.s were intent on getting their educations and starting new lives.

Source: From *Leaving Home: A Memoir*, by Art Buchwald (New York: G. P. Putnam's Sons, 1993). Used by permission of Joel Buchwald.

### Betty Friedan
### Living the Feminine Mystique

Like Buchwald, Betty Friedan would one day become famous as a writer—author of one of the most widely read books of the 1960s, *The Feminine Mystique*. In the late 1940s, Friedan was not yet a feminist, but she was deeply engaged in the politics of the era.

And then the boys our age had come back from the war. I was bumped from my job on a small labor news service by a returning veteran, and it wasn't so easy to find another job I really liked. I filled out the applications for *Time-Life* researcher, which I'd always scorned before. All the girls I knew had jobs like that, but it was official policy that no matter how good, researchers, who were women, could never become writers or editors. They could write the whole article, but the men they were working with would always get the by-line as writer. I was certainly not a feminist then — none of us were a bit interested in women's rights. But I could never bring myself to take that kind of job.

After the war, I had been very political, very involved, consciously radical. Not about women, for heaven's sake! If you were a radical in 1949, you were concerned about the Negroes, and the working class, and World War III, and the Un-American Activities Committee and McCarthy and loyalty oaths, and Communist splits and schisms, Russia, China and the UN, but you certainly didn't think about being a woman, politically.

Source: From *"It Changed My Life": Writings on the Women's Movement*, by Betty Friedan (Cambridge, MA: Harvard University Press, 1976). Copyright © 1963 by Betty Friedan. Reprinted by permission of Curtis Brown, Ltd.

### Susan Allen Toth
### Learning About Communism

Toth is a writer who grew up in Ames, Iowa, surrounded by cornfields. She writes here about her experience learning just how anxious people could become in the 1950s when the issue of communism was raised.

Of course, we all knew there was Communism. As early as sixth grade our teacher warned us about its dangers. I listened carefully to Mr. Casper describe what Communists wanted, which sounded terrible. World domination. Enslavement. Destruction of our way of life. I hung around school one afternoon hoping to catch Mr. Casper, whom I secretly adored, to ask him why Communism was so bad. He stayed in another teacher's room so late I finally scrawled my question on our blackboard: "Dear Mr. Casper, why is Communism so bad . . . Sue Allen" and went home. Next morning the message was still there. Like a warning from heaven it had galvanized Mr. Casper. He began class with a stern lecture, repeating everything he had said about dangerous Russians and painting a vivid picture of how we would all suffer if the Russians took over the city government in Ames. We certainly wouldn't be able to attend a school like this, he said, where free expression of opinion was allowed. At recess that day one of the boys asked me if I was a "dirty Commie": two of my best friends shied away from me on the playground; I saw Mr. Casper talking low to another teacher and pointing at me. I cried all the way home from school and resolved never to commit myself publicly with a question like that again.

Source: From Susan Allen Toth, "Boyfriend" from *Blooming: A Small-Town Girlhood*. Reprinted by permission of Molly Friedrich on behalf of the author.

## Melba Patillo Beals
## Encountering Segregation

Melba Patillo Beals was one of the "Little Rock Nine," the high school students who desegregated Central High School in Little Rock, Arkansas, in 1957. Here she recounts an experience documenting what it was like to come of age as a black southerner under Jim Crow.

An experience I endured on a December morning would forever affect any decision I made to go "potty" in a public place. We were Christmas shopping when I felt the twinge of emergency. I convinced Mother and Grandmother that I knew the way to restroom by myself. I was moving as fast as I could when suddenly I knew I wasn't going to make it all the way down those stairs and across the warehouse walkway to the "Colored Ladies" toilet. So I pushed open the door marked "White Ladies" and, taking a deep breath, I crossed the threshold. It was just as bright and pretty as I had imagined it to be. . . . Across the room, other white ladies sat on a couch reading the newspaper. Suddenly realizing I was there, two of them looked at me in astonishment. Unless I was the maid, they said, I was in the wrong place. While they shouted at me to "get out," my throbbing bladder consumed my attention as I frantically headed for the unoccupied stall. They kept shouting "Good lord, do something." I was doing something by that time, seated comfortably on the toilet, listening to the hysteria building outside my locked stall. One woman even knelt down to peep beneath the door to make certain that I didn't put my bottom on the toilet seat. She ordered me not to pee.

Source: Reprinted with permission of Atria Publishing Group, a Division of Simon & Schuster, Inc. *Warriors Don't Cry: A Searing Memoir of the Battle to Integrate Little Rock* by Melba Patillo Beals. Copyright © 1994, 1995 by Melba Beals. All rights reserved.

## David Beers
## California Suburbia

David Beers grew up in the suburbs of California, in what would eventually become known as Silicon Valley. In his memoir, he recalls the ritual of buying a house.

"We never looked at a used house," my father remembers of those days in the early 1960s when he and my mother went shopping for a home of their own in the Valley of Heart's Delight. "A used house did not interest us." Instead, they roved in search of balloons and bunting and the many billboards advertising *Low Interest! No Money Down!* to military veterans like my father. They would follow the signs to the model homes standing in empty fields and tour the empty floor plans and leave with notes carefully made about square footage and closet space. "We shopped for a new house," my father says, "the way you shopped for a car." . . . We were blithe conquerors, my tribe. When we chose a new homeland, invaded a place, settled it, and made it over in our image, we did so with a smiling sense of our own inevitability. . . . We were drawn to the promise of a blank page inviting *our* design upon it.

Source: David Beers, *Blue Sky Dream: A Memoir of America's Fall from Grace* (New York: Harcourt, Brace, & Company, 1996), 31, 39.

### QUESTIONS FOR ANALYSIS

1. What do you think Buchwald meant by "an undeclared class war"? Why would the influx of GI Bill veterans into colleges create conflict?

2. Why do you think Friedan "didn't think about being a woman, politically" in the 1940s and 1950s? Why do you think she was "bumped from" her job by a "returning veteran"?

3. What does Toth's experience as a young student suggest about American anxieties during the Cold War? Why would her question cause embarrassment and ridicule?

4. What does Beals's experience suggest about the indignities faced by young people on the front lines of challenging racial segregation? Does it help explain why youth were so important in breaking racial barriers?

5. What do you think Beers means by "our tribe"? What was the "blank page"?

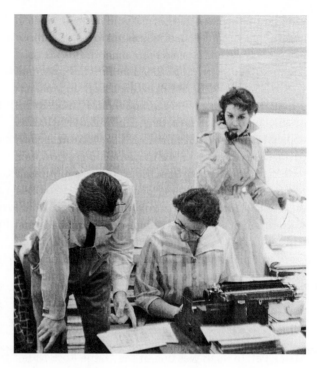

**Mom at Home and at Work**

Middle-class women's lives grew increasingly complicated in the postwar decades. They may have dreamed of a suburban home with a brand-new kitchen, like the one shown in this 1955 photograph (left), but laboring all day over children, dirty dishes, and a hot stove proved dissatisfying to many. Betty Friedan called the confinement of women's identities to motherhood the "feminine mystique," but did the working woman have it much better? Hardly. Most women in the 1950s and 1960s were confined to low-level secretarial work (right), waitressing, and other service-sector work—or, worse, factory or domestic labor. By the end of the 1960s, women had begun to crack the "glass ceiling" and enter the professions in larger numbers. But regardless of their occupation, the majority of working women performed the "double day": a full day at work and a full day at home. Such were the expectations and double bind women faced. Elliott Erwitt/Magnum Photos./Inge Morath © The Inge Morath Foundation/Magnum Photos.

between the ages of six and seventeen. In that same year, 30 percent of wives worked, and by 1970, it was 40 percent. For working-class women, in particular, the economic needs of their families demanded that they work outside the home.

Despite rising employment rates, occupational segmentation still haunted women. Until 1964, the classified sections of newspapers separated employment ads into "Help Wanted Male" and "Help Wanted Female." More than 80 percent of all employed women did stereotypical women's work as salesclerks, health-care technicians, waitresses, stewardesses, domestic servants, receptionists, telephone operators, and secretaries. In 1960, only 3 percent of lawyers and 6 percent of physicians were women; on the flip side, 97 percent of nurses and 85 percent of librarians were women. Along with women's jobs went

**TRACE CHANGE OVER TIME**

What transformations in women's economic role took place in the 1950s and 1960s?

women's pay, which averaged 60 percent of men's pay in 1963.

Contrary to stereotype, however, women's paid work was not merely supplementary. It helped lift families into the middle class. Even in the prosperous 1950s, many men found that their wages could not pay for what middle-class life demanded: cars, houses, vacations, and college education for the children. Many families needed more than one wage earner just to get by. Among married women, the highest rates of labor-force participation in the 1950s were found in families at the lower end of the middle class. Over the course of the postwar decades, from 1945 to 1965, more and more women, including married women, from all class backgrounds, entered the paid workforce.

How could American society steadfastly uphold the domestic ideal when so many wives and mothers were out of the house and at work? In many ways, the contradiction was hidden by the women themselves. Fearing public disapproval, women would explain their work in family-oriented terms—as a way to save money for the children's college education, for instance. Moreover, when women took jobs outside the home, they still bore full responsibility for child care and household management, contributing to the "double day" of paid work and family work. As one overburdened woman noted, she now had "two full-time jobs instead of just one—underpaid clerical worker and unpaid housekeeper." Finally, the pressures of the Cold War made strong nuclear families with breadwinning fathers and domesticated mothers symbols of a healthy nation. Americans wanted to believe this even if it did not perfectly describe the reality of their lives.

## Challenging Middle-Class Morality

In many ways, the two decades between 1945 and 1965 were a period of cultural conservatism that reflected the values of domesticity. At the dawn of the 1960s, going steady as a prelude to marriage was the fad in high school. College women had curfews and needed permission to see a male visitor. Americans married young; more than half of those who married in 1963 were under the age of twenty-one. After the birth control pill came on the market in 1960, few doctors prescribed it to unmarried women, and even married women did not enjoy unfettered access to contraception until the Supreme Court ruled it a "privacy" right in the 1965 decision *Griswold v. Connecticut*.

**Alfred Kinsey**   Yet beneath the surface of middle-class morality, Americans were less repressed than confused. They struggled to reconcile new freedoms with older moral traditions. This was especially true with regard to sex. Two controversial studies by an unassuming Indiana University zoologist named Alfred Kinsey forced questions about sexuality into the open. Kinsey and his research team published *Sexual Behavior in the Human Male* in 1948 and followed it up in 1953 with *Sexual Behavior in the Human Female*—an 842-page book that sold 270,000 copies in the first month after its publication. Taking a scientific, rather than moralistic, approach, Kinsey, who became known as "the sex doctor," documented the full range of sexual experiences of thousands of Americans. He broke numerous taboos, discussing such topics as homosexuality and marital infidelity in the detached language of science.

Both studies confirmed that a sexual revolution, although a largely hidden one, had already begun to transform American society by the early 1950s. Kinsey estimated that 85 percent of men had had sex prior to marriage and that more than 25 percent of married women had had sex outside of marriage by the age of forty. These were shocking public admissions in the late 1940s and early 1950s, and "hotter than the Kinsey

> **EXPLAIN CONSEQUENCES**
> What were the contradictions in postwar domesticity and middle-class morality?

**The Kinsey Reports**
Like the woman on the cover of this lighthearted 1953 book of photographs, many Americans reacted with surprise when Alfred Kinsey revealed the country's sexual habits. In his 1948 book about men and his 1953 book about women, Kinsey wrote about American sexual practices in the detached language of science. But it still made for salacious reading. Evangelical minister Billy Graham (p. 849) warned: "It is impossible to estimate the damage this book will do to the already deteriorated morals of America." Picture Research Consultants & Archives.

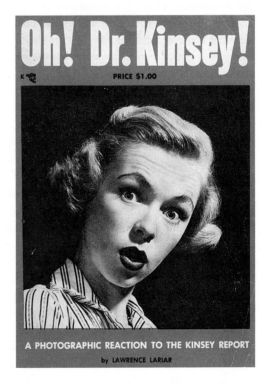

report" became a national figure of speech. Kinsey was criticized by statisticians—because his samples were not randomly selected—and condemned even more fervently by religious leaders, who charged him with encouraging promiscuity and adultery. But his research opened a national conversation with profound implications for the future. Even if Kinsey's numbers were off, he helped Americans learn to talk more openly about sex.

### The Homophile Movement

Among the most controversial of Kinsey's claims was that homosexuality was far more prevalent than most Americans believed. Although the American Psychiatric Association would officially define homosexuality as a mental illness in 1952, Kinsey's research found that 37 percent of men had engaged in some form of homosexual activity by early adulthood, as had 13 percent of women. Even more important, Kinsey claimed that 10 percent of American men were *exclusively* homosexual. These claims came as little surprise, but great encouragement, to a group of gay and lesbian activists who called themselves "homophiles." Organized primarily in the Mattachine Society (the first gay rights organization in the country, founded in 1951) and the Daughters of Bilitis (a lesbian organization founded in 1955), homophiles were a small but determined collection of activists who sought equal rights for gays and lesbians. "The lesbian is a woman endowed with all the attributes of any other woman," wrote the pioneer lesbian activist Del Martin in 1956. "The salvation of the lesbian lies in her acceptance of herself without guilt or anxiety."

Building on the urban gay and lesbian communities that had coalesced during World War II, homophiles sought to change American attitudes about same-sex love. They faced daunting obstacles, since same-sex sexual relations were illegal in every state and scorned, or feared, by most Americans. To combat prejudice and change the laws, homophile organizations cultivated a respectable, middle-class image. Members were encouraged to avoid bars and nightclubs, to dress in conservative shirts and ties (for men) and modest skirts and blouses (for women), and to seek out professional psychologists who would attest to their "normalcy." Only in the 1960s did homophiles begin to talk about the "homophile vote" and their "rights as citizens," laying the groundwork for the gay rights movement of the 1970s.

### Media and Morality

The homophile movement remained unknown to most Americans. But other challenges to traditional morality received national media attention, and the media themselves became a controversial source of these challenges. Concerned that excessive crime, violence, and sex in comic books were encouraging juvenile delinquency, the U.S. Senate held nationally televised hearings in 1954. The Senate's final report, written largely by the Tennessee Democrat Estes Kefauver, complained of the "scantily clad women" and "penchant for violent death" common in comic books aimed at teenagers. Kefauver's report forced the comics industry to tame its wildest practices but did little to slow the growing frankness about both sex and violence in the nation's printed media and films.

 To see a longer excerpt from the Senate hearing on juvenile delinquency, along with other primary sources from this period, see *Sources for America's History*.

A magazine entrepreneur from Chicago named Hugh Hefner played a leading role in that growing frankness. Hefner founded *Playboy* magazine in 1953, in which he created a countermorality to domesticity: a fictional world populated by "hip" bachelor men and sexually available women. Hefner's imagined bachelors condemned marriage and lived in sophisticated apartments filled with the latest stereo equipment and other consumer products. While domesticated fathers bought lawn mowers and patio furniture, Hefner's magazine encouraged men to spend money on clothing and jazz albums for themselves, and for the "scantily clad women" that filled its pages. Hefner and his numerous imitators became powerful purveyors of sex in the media. But Hefner was the exception that proved the rule: marriage, not swinging bachelorhood, remained the destination for the vast majority of men. Millions of men read *Playboy*, but few adopted its fantasy lifestyle.

# A Suburban Nation

Prosperity—how much an economy produces, how much people earn—is more easily measured than is quality of life. During the 1950s, however, the American definition of the good life emerged with exceptional distinctness: a high value on consumption, a devotion to family and domesticity, and preference for suburban living. In this section, we consider the third dimension of that definition: suburbanization. What drove the nation to abandon its cities for the suburbs, and what social and political consequences did this shift have?

## The Postwar Housing Boom

Migration to the suburbs had been going on for a hundred years, but never before on the scale that the country experienced after World War II. Within a decade, farmland on the outskirts of cities filled up with tract housing and shopping malls. Entire counties that had once been rural—such as San Mateo, south of San Francisco, or Passaic and Bergen in New Jersey, west of Manhattan—went suburban. By 1960, one-third of Americans lived in suburbs. Home construction, having ground to a halt during the Great Depression, surged after the war. One-fourth of the country's entire housing stock in 1960 had not even existed a decade earlier.

**William J. Levitt and the FHA** Two unique postwar developments remade the national housing market and gave it a distinctly suburban shape. First, an innovative Long Island building contractor, William J. Levitt, revolutionized suburban housing by applying mass-production techniques and turning out new homes at a dizzying speed. Levitt's basic four-room house, complete with kitchen appliances, was priced at $7,990 when homes in the first Levittown went on sale in 1947 (about $76,000 today). Levitt did not need to advertise; word of mouth brought buyers flocking to his developments (all called Levittown) in New York, Pennsylvania, and New Jersey. Dozens of other developers were soon snapping up cheap farmland and building subdivisions around the country.

Even at $7,990, Levitt's homes would have been beyond the means of most young families had the traditional home-financing standard—a down payment of half the full price and ten years to pay off the balance—still prevailed. That is where the second postwar development came in. The Federal Housing Administration (FHA) and the Veterans Administration (VA)—that is, the federal government—brought the home mortgage market within the reach of a broader range of Americans than ever before. After the war, the FHA insured thirty-year mortgages with as little as 5 percent down and interest at 2 or 3 percent. The VA was even more generous, requiring only a token $1 down for qualified ex-GIs. FHA and VA mortgages best explain why, after hovering around 45 percent for the previous half century, home ownership jumped to 60 percent by 1960.

What purchasers of suburban houses got, in addition to a good deal, were homogeneous communities. The developments contained few elderly people or unmarried adults. Even the trees were young. Levitt's company enforced regulations about maintaining lawns and not hanging out laundry on the weekends. Then there was the matter of race. Levitt's houses came with restrictive covenants prohibiting occupancy "by members of other than the Caucasian Race." (Restrictive covenants often applied to Jews and, in California,

Asian Americans as well.) Levittowns were hardly alone. Suburban developments from coast to coast exhibited the same age, class, and racial homogeneity (Thinking Like a Historian, p. 858).

In ***Shelley v. Kraemer*** (1948), the Supreme Court outlawed restrictive covenants, but racial discrimination in housing changed little. The practice persisted long after *Shelley*, because the FHA and VA continued the policy of redlining: refusing mortgages to African Americans and members of other minority groups seeking to buy in white neighborhoods. Indeed, no federal law—or even Court decisions like *Shelley*—actually prohibited racial discrimination in housing until Congress passed the Fair Housing Act in 1968.

> **PLACE EVENTS IN CONTEXT**
> Place postwar suburbanization in the context of the growing size and influence of the federal government. How did the national government encourage suburbanization?

**Interstate Highways** Without automobiles, suburban growth on such a massive scale would have been impossible. Planners laid out subdivisions on the assumption that everybody would drive. And they did—to get to work, to take the children to Little League, to shop. With gas plentiful and cheap (15 cents a gallon), no one cared about the fuel efficiency of their V-8 engines or seemed to mind the elaborate tail fins and chrome that weighed down their cars. In 1945, Americans owned twenty-five million cars; by 1965, just two decades later, the number had tripled to seventy-five million (America Compared, p. 860). American oil consumption followed course, tripling as well between 1949 and 1972.

More cars required more highways, and the federal government obliged. In 1956, in a move that drastically altered America's landscape and driving habits, the **National Interstate and Defense Highways Act** authorized $26 billion over a ten-year period for the construction of a nationally integrated highway system—42,500 miles (Map 26.1). Cast as a Cold War necessity because broad highways made evacuating crowded cities easier in the event of a nuclear attack, the law changed American cities forever. An enormous public works program surpassing anything undertaken during the New Deal, and enthusiastically endorsed by the Republican president, Dwight Eisenhower, federal highways made possible the massive suburbanization of the nation in the 1960s. Interstate highways rerouted traffic away from small towns, bypassed well-traveled main roads such as the cross-country Route 66, and cut wide swaths through old neighborhoods in the cities.

## The Suburban Landscape of Cold War America

Between the end of World War II and the 1980s, Americans built and moved into suburban homes in an unprecedented wave of construction and migration that changed the nation forever. New home loan rules, and government backing under the Federal Housing Administration and Veterans Administration, made new suburban houses cheaper and brought home ownership within reach of a larger number of Americans than ever before. Commentators cheered these developments as a boon to ordinary citizens, but by the 1960s a generation of urban critics, led by journalist Jane Jacobs, had begun to find fault with the nation's suburban obsession. The following documents provide the historian with evidence of how these new suburban communities arose and how they began to transform American culture.

**1.** **"Peacetime Cornucopia,"** *The New Yorker*, **October 6, 1945.**

© Constanin Alajalov/New Yorker/Conde Nast Publications.

**2.** *Life* **magazine, "A** *Life* **Round Table on Housing," January 31, 1949.**

The most aggressive member of *Life's* Round Table, whether as builder or debater, was William J. Levitt, president of Levitt and Sons, Inc. of Manhasset, NY. He feels that he has started a revolution, the essence of which is size. Builders in his estimation are a poor and puny lot, too small to put pressure on materials manufacturers or the local czars of the building codes or the bankers or labor. A builder ought to be a manufacturer, he said, and to this end must be big. He himself is a nonunion operator.

The Levitt prescription for cheaper houses may be summarized as follows: 1) take infinite pains with infinite details; 2) be aggressive; 3) be big enough to throw your weight around; 4) buy at wholesale; and 5) build houses in concentrated developments where mass-production methods can be used on the site.

**3.** **Site plan sketch for Park Forest, Illinois, 1946.**

The Park Forest Historical Society.

## 4. William H. Whyte Jr., *The Organization Man*, 1956. *Whyte, a prominent journalist, wrote about the decline of individualism and the rise of a national class of interchangeable white-collar workers.*

And is this not the whole drift of our society? We are not interchangeable in the sense of being people without differences, but in the externals of existence we are united by a culture increasingly national. And this is part of the momentum of mobility. The more people move about, the more similar American environments become, and the more similar they become, the easier it is to move about.

More and more, the young couples who move do so only physically. With each transfer the décor, the architecture, the faces, and the names may change; the people, the conversation, and the values do not — and sometimes the décor and architecture don't either. . . .

Suburban residents like to maintain that their suburbia not only looks classless but is classless. That is, they are apt to add on second thought, there are no extremes, and if the place isn't exactly without class, it is at least a one-class society — identified as the middle or upper middle, according to the inclination of the residents. "We are all," they say, "in the same boat."

## 5. Jane Jacobs, *The Death and Life of Great American Cities*, 1961. *A classic celebration of vibrant urban neighborhoods by a New York writer and architectural critic.*

Although it is hard to believe, while looking at dull gray areas, or at housing projects or at civic centers, the fact is that big cities are natural generators of diversity and prolific incubators of new enterprises and ideas of all kinds. . . .

This is because city populations are large enough to support wide ranges of variety and choice in these things. And again we find that bigness has all the advantages in smaller settlements. Towns and suburbs, for instance, are natural homes for huge supermarkets and for little else in the way of groceries, for standard movie houses or drive-ins and for little else in the way of theater. There are simply not enough people to support further variety, although there may be people (too few of them) who would draw upon it were it there. Cities, however, are the natural homes of supermarkets and standard movie houses plus delicatessens, Viennese bakeries, foreign groceries, art movies, and so on. . . .

The diversity, of whatever kind, that is generated by cities rests on the fact that in cities so many people are so close together, and among them contain so many different tastes, skills, needs, supplies, and bees in their bonnets.

## 6. Herbert J. Gans, *The Levittowners*, 1967. *One of the first sociological studies of the new postwar suburbs and their residents.*

The strengths and weakness of Levittown are those of many American communities, and the Levittowners closely resemble other young middle class Americans. They are not America, for they are not a numerical majority of the population, but they represent the major constituency of the latest and more powerful economic and political institutions in American society — the favored customers and voters whom these seek to attract and satisfy. . . .

Although they are citizens of a national polity and their lives are shaped by national economic, social, and political forces, Levittowners deceive themselves into thinking that the community, or rather the home, is the single most important unit of their lives. . . .

In viewing their homes as the center of life, Levittowners are still using a societal model that fit the rural America of self-sufficient farmers and the feudal Europe of self-isolating extended families.

Sources: (2) *Life*, January 31, 1949, 74; (4) William H. Whyte Jr., *The Organization Man* (New York: Simon and Schuster, 1956), 276, 299; (5) Jane Jacobs, *The Death and Life of Great American Cities* (Westminster, MD: Vintage, 1992), 145–147; (6) Herbert J. Gans, *The Levittowners* (New York: Columbia University Press, 1982), 417–418.

### ANALYZING THE EVIDENCE

1. Compare sources 1, 4, and 6. How do they reinforce or contradict one another?
2. In source 4, what does Whyte mean by "classless"? Why would suburbanites wish to think of their communities as not beset by class inequality? Were they right in this point of view?
3. Do you see evidence in source 2 of the ways the postwar housing market was transformed? How does Levitt's vision of the home-building industry relate to other kinds of American industries?
4. In source 5, what advantages does Jacobs see in large cities over suburbs? Can you interpret source 3 from the perspective that Jacobs outlines in source 5?

### PUTTING IT ALL TOGETHER

Write an essay in which you use the knowledge you've gained from this chapter and the documents provided above to explore postwar suburbanization. What did it mean to the American economy? To ordinary Americans? What flaws did its critics see?

## Hanoch Bartov:
## Everyone Has a Car

One of Israel's foremost writers and journalists, Hanoch Bartov spent two years in the United States working as a correspondent for the newspaper *Lamerchav*. As a newcomer to Los Angeles in the early 1960s, he was both fascinated and appalled by Americans' love affair with the automobile.

Our immediate decision to buy a car sprang from healthy instincts. Only later did I learn from bitter experience that in California, death was preferable to living without one. Neither the views from the plane nor the weird excursion that first evening hinted at what I would go through that first week.

Very simple — the nearest supermarket was about half a kilometer south of our apartment, the regional primary school two kilometers east, and my son's kindergarten even farther away. A trip to the post office — an undertaking, to the bank — an ordeal, to work — an impossibility. . . .

There are no tramways. No one thought of a subway. Railroads — not now and not in the future. Why? Because everyone has a car. A man invited me to his house, saying, "We are neighbors, within ten minutes of each other." After walking for an hour and a half I realized what he meant — "ten minute drive within the speed limit." Simply put, he never thought I might interpret his remark to refer to the walking distance. The moment a baby sees the light of day in Los Angeles, a car is registered in his name in Detroit. . . .

At first perhaps people relished the freedom and independence a car provided. You get in, sit down, and grab the steering wheel, your mobility exceeding that of any other generation. No wonder people refuse to live down-town, where they can hear their neighbors, smell their cooking, and suffer frayed nerves as trains pass by bedroom windows. Instead, they get a piece of the desert, far from town, at half price, drag a water hose, grow grass, flowers, and trees, and build their dream house.

The result? A widely scattered city, its houses far apart, its streets stretched in all directions. Olympic Boulevard from west to east, forty kilometers. Sepulveda Boulevard, from Long Beach in the south to the edge of the desert, forty kilometers. Altogether covering 1,200 square kilometers. As of now.

Source: "Measures of Affluence" by Hanoch Bartov (1963) in Chapter 16 from *The Outer World*, edited by Oscar Handlin and Lilian Handlin (Cambridge, MA: Harvard University Press, 1997). © 1997. Reprinted by permission of Oscar and Lillian Handlin.

### QUESTIONS FOR ANALYSIS

1. From Bartov's observations, what are the pluses and minuses of America's car culture? In what ways was the automobile changing American society?
2. Why did Bartov find that owning a car was necessary, especially in southern California?
3. How would suburbanization have contributed to the construction of new highways in the United States? How would highway construction have facilitated suburbanization?

**Fast Food and Shopping Malls**  Americans did not simply fill their new suburban homes with the latest appliances and gadgets; they also pioneered entirely new forms of consumption. Through World War II, downtowns had remained the center of retail sales and restaurant dining with their grand department stores, elegant eateries, and low-cost diners. As suburbanites abandoned big-city centers in the 1950s, ambitious entrepreneurs invented two new commercial forms that would profoundly shape the rest of the century: the shopping mall and the fast-food restaurant.

By the late 1950s, the suburban shopping center had become as much a part of the American landscape as the Levittowns and their imitators. A major developer of shopping malls in the Northeast called them "crystallization points for suburbia's community life." He romanticized the new structures as "today's village green," where "the fountain in the mall has replaced the downtown department clock as the gathering place for young and old alike." Romanticism aside, suburban shopping centers worked perfectly in the world of suburban consumption; they brought "the market to the people instead of people to the market," commented the *New York Times*. In 1939, the suburban share of total metropolitan retail trade in the United States was a paltry 4 percent. By 1961, it was an astonishing 60 percent in the nation's ten largest metropolitan regions.

No one was more influential in creating suburban patterns of consumption than a Chicago-born son of Czech immigrants named Ray Kroc. A former jazz

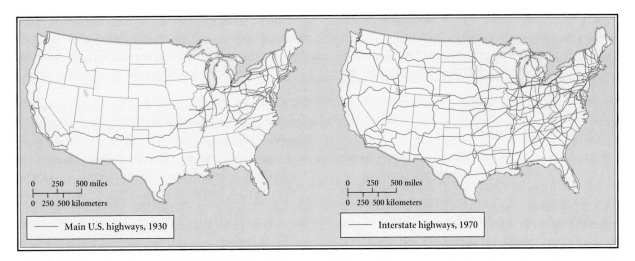

**MAP 26.1**

**Connecting the Nation: The Interstate Highway System, 1930 and 1970**

The 1956 National Interstate and Defense Highways Act paved the way for an extensive network of federal highways throughout the nation. The act not only pleased American drivers and enhanced their love affair with the automobile but also benefitted the petroleum, construction, trucking, real estate, and tourist industries. The new highway system promoted the nation's economic integration, facilitated the growth of suburbs, and contributed to the erosion of America's distinct regional identities.

musician and traveling salesman, Kroc found his calling in 1954 when he acquired a single franchise of the little-known McDonald's Restaurant, based in San Bernardino, California. In 1956, Kroc invested in twelve more franchises and by 1958 owned seventy-nine. Three years later, Kroc bought the company from the McDonald brothers and proceeded to turn it into the largest chain of restaurants in the world. Based on inexpensive, quickly served hamburgers that hungry families could eat in the restaurant, in their cars, or at home, Kroc's vision transformed the way Americans consumed food. "Drive-in" or "fast" food became a

**Fast Food, 1949**

The sign atop this suburban Los Angeles restaurant says it all. Suburbanization laid the foundation for a unique postwar phenomenon that would forever change American life: the rise of fast food. Cheap, convenient, and "fast," the food served in the new restaurants, modeled after the industry's pioneer, McDonald's, was not necessarily nutritious, but its chief advantage was portability. Loomis Dean/Time Life Pictures/Getty Images.

staple of the American diet in the subsequent decades. By the year 2000, fast food was a $100 billion industry, and more children recognized Ronald McDonald, the clown in McDonald's television commercials, than Santa Claus.

## Rise of the Sunbelt

Suburban living, although a nationwide phenomenon, was most at home in the **Sunbelt** (the southern and southwestern states), where taxes were low, the climate was mild, and open space allowed for sprawling subdivisions (Map 26.2). Florida added 3.5 million people, many of them retired, between 1940 and 1970. Texas profited from expanding petrochemical and defense industries. Most dramatic was California's growth, spurred especially by the state's booming defense-related aircraft and electronics industries. By 1970,

California contained one-tenth of the nation's population and surpassed New York as the most populous state. At the end of the century, California's economy was among the top ten largest in the world—among nations.

A distinctive feature of Sunbelt suburbanization was its close relationship to the military-industrial complex. Building on World War II expansion, military bases proliferated in the South and Southwest in the postwar decades, especially in Florida, Texas, and California. In some instances, entire metropolitan regions—such as San Diego County, California, and the Houston area in Texas—expanded in tandem with nearby military outposts. Moreover, the aerospace, defense, and electronics industries were based largely in Sunbelt metropolitan regions. With government contracts fueling the economy and military bases providing thousands of jobs, Sunbelt politicians had every

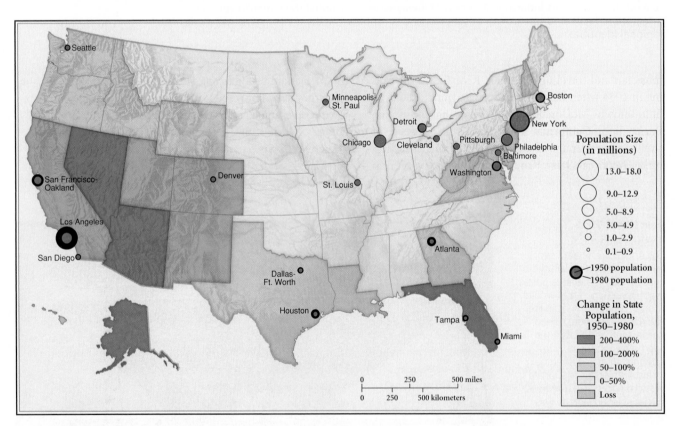

**MAP 26.2**

**Shifting Population Patterns, 1950–1980**

This map shows the two major, somewhat overlapping, patterns of population movement between 1950 and 1980. Most striking is the rapid growth of the Sunbelt states. All the states experiencing increases of over 100 percent in that period are in the Southwest, plus Florida. The second pattern involves the growth of metropolitan areas, defined as a central city or urban area and its suburbs. The central cities were themselves mostly not growing, however. The metropolitan growth shown in this map was accounted for by the expanding suburbs. And because Sunbelt growth was primarily suburban growth, that's where we see the most rapid metropolitan growth, with Los Angeles the clear leader.

incentive to support vigorous defense spending by the federal government.

Sunbelt suburbanization was best exemplified by Orange County, California. Southwest of Los Angeles, Orange County was until the 1940s mostly just that — a land of oranges, groves of them. But during World War II, boosters attracted new bases and training facilities for the marines, navy, and air force (at the time the army air corps). Cold War militarization and the Korean War kept those bases humming, and Hughes Aircraft, Ford Aeronautics, and other defense-related manufacturers built new plants in the sunny, sprawling groves. So did subdivision developers, who built so many new homes that the population of the county jumped from 130,760 in 1940 to 703,925 in 1960. Casting his eye on all this development in the early 1950s, an entrepreneurial filmmaker and cartoonist named Walt Disney chose Anaheim in Orange County as the place for a massive new amusement park. Disneyland was to the new generation of suburbanites what Coney Island had been to an earlier generation of urbanites.

## Two Societies: Urban and Suburban

While middle-class whites flocked to the suburbs, an opposite stream of working-class migrants, many of them southern African Americans, moved into the cities. In the 1950s, the nation's twelve largest cities lost 3.6 million whites while gaining 4.5 million nonwhites. These urban newcomers inherited a declining economy and a decaying infrastructure. To those enjoying prosperity, the "other America," as the social critic Michael Harrington called it, remained largely invisible. In 1968, however, a report by the National Advisory Commission on Civil Disorders (informally known as the **Kerner Commission** and formed by the president to investigate the causes of the 1967 urban riots), delivered to President Lyndon Johnson, warned that "our nation is moving toward two societies, one black, one white, separate and unequal."

American cities had long been the home of poverty, slum housing, and the hardships and cultural dislocations brought on by immigration from overseas or migration from rural areas. But postwar American cities, especially those in the industrial Northeast and Midwest, experienced these problems with new intensity. By the 1950s, the manufacturing sector was contracting, and mechanization was eliminating thousands upon thousands of unskilled and semiskilled jobs, the kind traditionally taken up by new urban residents. The disappearing jobs were the ones "in which [African Americans] are disproportionately

concentrated," noted the civil rights activist Bayard Rustin.

**The Urban Crisis**   The intensification of poverty, the deterioration of older housing stock, and the persistence of racial segregation produced what many at the time called the urban crisis. Unwelcome in the shiny new suburbs built by men such as William J. Levitt, African Americans found low-paying jobs in the city and lived in aging, slumlike apartment buildings. Despite a thriving black middle class — indeed, larger than ever before — for those without resources, upward mobility remained elusive. Racism in institutional forms frustrated African Americans at every turn: housing restrictions, increasingly segregated schools, and an urban infrastructure that stood underfunded and decaying as whites left for the suburbs.

Housing and job discrimination were compounded by the frenzy of urban renewal that hit black neighborhoods in the 1950s and early 1960s. Seeking to revitalize declining city centers, politicians and real estate developers proposed razing blighted neighborhoods to make way for modern construction projects that would appeal to the fleeing middle class. In Boston, almost one-third of the old city — including the historic West End, a long-established Italian neighborhood — was demolished to make way for a new highway, high-rise housing, and government and commercial buildings. In San Francisco, some 4,000 residents of the Western Addition, a predominantly black neighborhood, lost out to an urban renewal program that built luxury housing, a shopping center, and an express boulevard. Between 1949 and 1967, urban renewal nationwide demolished almost 400,000 buildings and displaced 1.4 million people.

> **COMPARE AND CONTRAST**
> In what sense was the United States becoming, in the language of the Kerner Commission report, "two societies"?

The urban experts believed they knew what to do with the dislocated: relocate them to federally funded housing projects, an outgrowth of New Deal housing policy, now much expanded. However well intended, these grim projects too often took the form of cheap high-rises that isolated their inhabitants from surrounding neighborhoods. The impact was felt especially strongly among African Americans, who often found that public housing increased racial segregation and concentrated the poor. The Robert Taylor Homes in Chicago, with twenty-eight buildings of sixteen stories each, housed 20,000 residents, almost all of them black. Despite the planners' wish to build

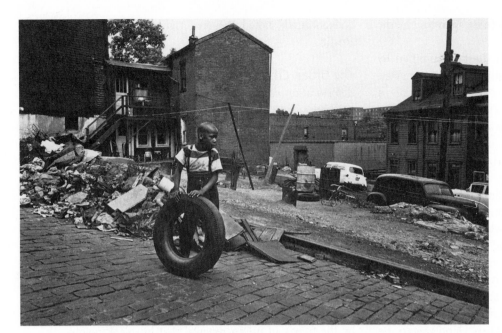

**Urban Crisis**

This Pittsburgh neighborhood, photographed in 1955, typified what many came to call the "urban crisis" of the 1950s and 1960s. As suburbanization drew middle-class residents, investment, and jobs away from the core of older cities, those cities began to rot from the inside. Urban neglect left many working-class neighborhoods, increasingly occupied by the nation's poor, with few jobs, little industry, and dilapidated housing. W. Eugene Smith/Black Star/Stockphoto.com.

decent affordable apartments, the huge complex became a notorious breeding ground for crime and hopelessness.

**Urban Immigrants**   Despite the evident urban crisis, cities continued to attract immigrants from abroad. Since the passage of the National Origins Act of 1924 (Chapter 22), U.S. immigration policy had aimed mainly at keeping foreigners out. But World War II and the Cold War began slowly to change American policy. The Displaced Persons Act of 1948 permitted the entry of approximately 415,000 Europeans, many of them Jewish refugees. In a gesture to an important war ally, the Chinese Exclusion Act was repealed in 1943. More far-reaching was the 1952 McCarran-Walter Act, which ended the exclusion of Japanese, Koreans, and Southeast Asians.

After the national-origins quota system went into effect in 1924, Mexico replaced Eastern and Southern Europe as the nation's labor reservoir. During World War II, the federal government introduced the Bracero Program to ease wartime labor shortages (Chapter 24) and then revived it in 1951, during the Korean War. The federal government's ability to force workers to return to Mexico, however, was strictly limited. The Mexican immigrant population continued to grow, and by the time the Bracero Program ended in 1964, many of that group—an estimated 350,000—had settled permanently in the United States. Braceros were joined by other Mexicans from small towns and villages, who immigrated to the United States to escape poverty or to earn money to return home and purchase land for farming.

As generations of immigrants had before them, Mexicans gravitated to major cities. Mostly, they settled in Los Angeles, Long Beach, San Jose, El Paso, and other southwestern cities. But many also went north, augmenting well-established Mexican American communities in Chicago, Detroit, Kansas City, and Denver. Although still important to American agriculture, Mexican Americans were employed in substantial numbers as industrial and service workers by 1960.

Another major group of Spanish-speaking migrants came from Puerto Rico. American citizens since 1917, Puerto Ricans enjoyed an unrestricted right to move to the mainland United States. Migration increased dramatically after World War II, when mechanization of the island's sugarcane agriculture left many Puerto Ricans jobless. Airlines began to offer cheap direct flights between San Juan and New York City. With the fare at about $50 (two weeks' wages), Puerto Ricans became America's first immigrants to arrive en masse by air. Most Puerto Ricans went to New York, where they settled first in East ("Spanish") Harlem and then scattered in neighborhoods across the city's five boroughs. This massive migration, which increased the Puerto Rican population to 613,000 by 1960, transformed the ethnic composition of the city. More Puerto Ricans now lived in New York City than in San Juan.

Cuban refugees constituted the third-largest group of Spanish-speaking immigrants. In the six years after Fidel Castro's seizure of power in 1959 (Chapter 25), an estimated 180,000 people fled Cuba for the United States. The Cuban refugee community grew so quickly that it turned Miami into a cosmopolitan, bilingual city almost overnight. Unlike other urban migrants, Miami's Cubans quickly prospered, in large part because they had arrived with money and middle-class skills.

Spanish-speaking immigrants — whether Mexican, Puerto Rican, or Cuban — created huge barrios in major American cities, where bilingualism flourished, the Catholic Church shaped religious life, and families sought to join the economic mainstream. Though distinct from one another, these Spanish-speaking communities remained largely segregated from white, or Anglo, neighborhoods and suburbs as well as from African American districts.

## SUMMARY

We have explored how, at the same time it became mired in the Cold War, the United States entered an unparalleled era of prosperity in which a new middle class came into being. Indeed, the Cold War was one of the engines of prosperity. The postwar economy was marked by the dominance of big corporations and defense spending.

After years of depression and war-induced insecurity, Americans turned inward toward religion, home, and family. Postwar couples married young, had several children, and — if they were white and middle class — raised their children in a climate of suburban comfort and consumerism. The profamily orientation of the 1950s celebrated traditional gender roles, even though millions of women entered the workforce in those years. Not everyone, however, shared in the postwar prosperity. Postwar cities increasingly became places of last resort for the nation's poor. Black migrants, unlike earlier immigrants, encountered an urban economy that had little use for them. Without opportunity, and faced with pervasive racism, many of them were on their way to becoming an American underclass, even as sparkling new suburbs emerged outside cities to house the new middle class. Many of the smoldering contradictions of the postwar period — Cold War anxiety in the midst of suburban domesticity, tensions in women's lives, economic and racial inequality — helped spur the protest movements of the 1960s.

# CHAPTER REVIEW

**MAKE IT STICK**   Go to **LearningCurve** to retain what you've read.

## TERMS TO KNOW   Identify and explain the significance of each term below.

### Key Concepts and Events

kitchen debate (p. 838)

**Bretton Woods** (p. 840)

**World Bank** (p. 840)

**International Monetary Fund (IMF)** (p. 840)

**military-industrial complex** (p. 841)

*Sputnik* (p. 842)

**National Defense Education Act** (p. 842)

*The Affluent Society* (p. 843)

*The Other America* (p. 843)

**Veterans Administration** (p. 843)

**collective bargaining** (p. 844)

**teenager** (p. 847)

**Beats** (p. 849)

**baby boom** (p. 850)

*Shelley v. Kraemer* (p. 857)

**National Interstate and Defense Highways Act** (p. 857)

**Sunbelt** (p. 862)

**Kerner Commission** (p. 863)

### Key People

**Dwight D. Eisenhower** (p. 841)

**Miles Davis** (p. 849)

**Allen Ginsberg** (p. 849)

**Jack Kerouac** (p. 849)

**Billy Graham** (p. 849)

**Dr. Benjamin Spock** (p. 851)

**William J. Levitt** (p. 857)

## REVIEW QUESTIONS   Answer these questions to demonstrate your understanding of the chapter's main ideas.

1. What factors led to the economic prosperity of the postwar era?

2. Why did the suburbs become so significant for Americans in the 1950s? How was suburban life related to middle-class consumption?

3. Who were the people left out of the postwar boom? How do you account for their exclusion?

4. **THEMATIC UNDERSTANDING**   Review the events listed under "America in the World" and "Work, Exchange, and Technology" for the period 1930–1945 on the thematic timeline on page 671 and for 1945–1960 on page 803. Explain how the United States began the 1930s in deep depression with unemployment near 25 percent and ended the 1950s with an expanded middle class and a consumption-driven economy.

## MAKING CONNECTIONS   Recognize the larger developments and continuities within and across chapters by answering these questions.

1. **ACROSS TIME AND PLACE**   Think back to earlier chapters that discussed gender roles, marriage, and American family life in the late nineteenth and early twentieth centuries (Chapters 18, 19, 22, 24). How had the American family changed by the 1950s? What aspects of family life remained similar across many decades? For example, how did the working-class immigrant family of the 1890s differ from the middle-class family of the 1950s?

2. **VISUAL EVIDENCE**   Examine the Motorola TV advertisement featured on page 847. What different types of appeals does this advertisement make, and what do they suggest about family and gender roles in this period? How many distinct themes from the chapter can you explain using this image?

## MORE TO EXPLORE   Start here to learn more about the events discussed in this chapter.

Lizabeth Cohen, *A Consumers' Republic: The Politics of Mass Consumption in Postwar America* (2003). An important interpretation of the United States as a consumer society.

James Gilbert, *Men in the Middle: Searching for Masculinity in the 1950s* (2005). An engaging account of cultural figures from the 1950s, including Billy Graham and John Wayne.

David Halberstam, *The Fifties* (1993). An engaging and accessible introduction to postwar American society.

Karal Ann Marling, *As Seen on TV* (1996). An insightful explanation of the impact of television.

Elaine Tyler May, *Homeward Bound* (1988). The classic introduction to postwar family life.

Thomas J. Sugrue, *The Origins of the Urban Crisis: Race and Inequality in Postwar Detroit* (1996). The best account of the urban crisis.

## TIMELINE
Ask yourself why this chapter begins and ends with these dates and then identify the links among related events.

| 1944 | • Bretton Woods economic conference<br>• World Bank and International Monetary Fund (IMF) founded<br>• GI Bill (Servicemen's Readjustment Act) |
|------|---|
| 1946 | • First edition of Dr. Spock's *Common Sense Book of Baby and Child Care* |
| 1947 | • First Levittown built |
| 1948 | • Beginning of network television<br>• *Shelley v. Kraemer*<br>• Alfred Kinsey's *Sexual Behavior in the Human Male* published |
| 1949 | • Billy Graham revival in Los Angeles |
| 1951 | • Bracero Program revived<br>• Mattachine Society founded |
| 1952 | • McCarran-Walter Act |
| 1953 | • Kinsey's *Sexual Behavior of the Human Female* published |
| 1954 | • Ray Kroc buys the first McDonald's franchise |
| 1955 | • Daughters of Bilitis founded |
| 1956 | • National Interstate and Defense Highways Act<br>• Elvis Presley's breakthrough records<br>• Allen Ginsberg's poem "Howl" published |
| 1957 | • Peak of postwar baby boom |
| 1961 | • Eisenhower warns nation against military-industrial complex |
| 1965 | • *Griswold v. Connecticut* |

**KEY TURNING POINTS:** What were the major turning points in the creation of postwar suburbia?

# 27
## CHAPTER

# Walking into Freedom Land: The Civil Rights Movement
# 1941–1973

In June 1945, as World War II was ending, Democratic senator James O. Eastland of Mississippi stood on the floor of the U.S. Senate and brashly told his colleagues that "the Negro race is an inferior race." Raising his arms, his tie askew from vigorous gesturing, Eastland ridiculed black troops. "The Negro soldier was an utter and dismal failure in combat," he said.

Eastland's assertions were untrue. Black soldiers had served honorably; many won medals for bravery in combat. All-black units, such as the 761st "Black Panther" Tank Battalion and the famous Tuskegee Airmen, were widely praised by military commanders. But segregationists like Eastland were a nearly unassailable force in Congress, able to block civil rights legislation and shape national opinion.

In the 1940s, two generations after W. E. B. Du Bois famously wrote that "the problem of the twentieth century is the problem of the color line," few white Americans believed wholeheartedly in racial equality. Racial segregation remained entrenched across the country. Much of the Deep South, like Eastland's Mississippi, was a "closed society": black people had no political rights and lived on the margins of white society, impoverished and exploited. Northern cities proved more hospitable to African Americans, but schools, neighborhoods, and many businesses remained segregated and unequal in the North as well.

Across the nation, however, winds of change were gathering. Between World War II and the 1970s, slowly at first, and then with greater urgency in the 1960s, the civil rights movement swept aside systematic racial segregation. It could not sweep away racial inequality completely, but the movement constituted a "second Reconstruction" in which African American activism reshaped the nation's laws and practices. Civil rights was the paradigmatic social movement of the twentieth century. Its model of nonviolent protest and its calls for self-determination inspired the New Left, feminism, the Chicano movement, the gay rights movement, the American Indian movement, and many others.

The black-led civil rights movement, joined at key moments by Latinos, Asian Americans, and Native Americans, redefined *liberalism*. In the 1930s, New Deal liberalism had established a welfare state to protect citizens from economic hardship. The civil rights movement forged a new **rights liberalism**: the notion that individuals require state protection from discrimination. This version of liberalism focused on identities—such as race or sex—rather than general social welfare, and as such would prove to be both a necessary expansion of the nation's ideals and a divisive force that produced political backlash. Indeed, the quest for racial justice would contribute to a crisis of liberalism itself.

### IDENTIFY THE BIG IDEA
How did the civil rights movement evolve over time, and how did competing ideas and political alliances affect its growth and that of other social movements?

**The March from Selma to Montgomery, 1965** Leading a throng of 25,000 marchers, Martin Luther King Jr. holds the hand of his wife, Coretta Scott King, as they enter downtown Montgomery, Alabama, at the end of the Selma to Montgomery march. Bob Adelman/Magnum Photos, Inc.

# The Emerging Civil Rights Struggle, 1941–1957

As it took shape during World War II and the early Cold War, the battle against racial injustice proceeded along two tracks: at the grass roots and in governing institutions — federal courts, state legislatures, and ultimately the U.S. Congress. Labor unions, churches, and protest organizations such as the Congress of Racial Equality (CORE) inspired hundreds of thousands of ordinary citizens to join the movement. But grassroots struggle was not African Americans' only weapon. They also had the Bill of Rights and the Reconstruction amendments to the Constitution. Civil rights lived in those documents — especially in the Fourteenth Amendment, which guaranteed equal protection under the law to all U.S. citizens, and in the Fifteenth, which guaranteed the right to vote regardless of "race, color, or previous condition of servitude" — but had been ignored or violated for nearly a century. The task was to restore the Constitution's legal force. Neither track — grassroots or legal/legislative — was entirely independent of the other. Together, they were the foundation of the fight for racial equality in the post-war decades.

## Life Under Jim Crow

Racial segregation and economic exploitation defined the lives of the majority of African Americans in the postwar decades. Numbering 15 million in 1950, African Americans were approximately 10 percent of the U.S. population. In the South, however, they constituted between 30 and 50 percent of the population of several states, such as South Carolina and Mississippi. Segregation, commonly known as **Jim Crow** (Chapter 18), prevailed in every aspect of life in the southern states, where two-thirds of all African Americans lived in 1950. African Americans could not eat in restaurants patronized by whites or use the same waiting rooms at bus stations. All forms of public transportation were rigidly segregated by custom or by law. Public parks and libraries were segregated. Even drinking fountains were labeled "White" and "Colored."

This system of segregation underlay economic and political structures that further marginalized and disempowered black citizens. Virtually no African

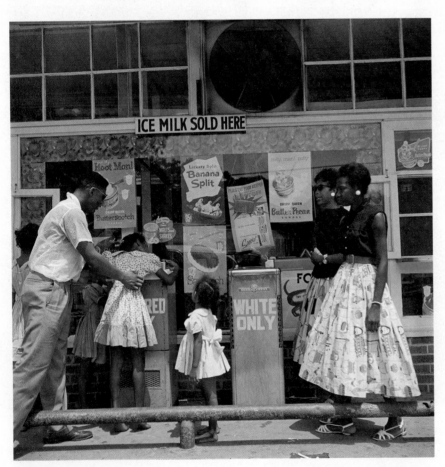

**Segregation in Mobile, 1956**

As the law of the land in most southern states, racial segregation (known as Jim Crow) required the complete separation of blacks and whites in most public spaces. The "white only" drinking fountain shown in this 1956 photograph in Mobile, Alabama, was typical. Everything from waiting areas to libraries, public parks, schools, restrooms, and even cola vending machines was subject to strict racial segregation. Gordon Parks, courtesy of the Gordon Parks Foundation.

American could work for city or state government, and the best jobs in the private sector were reserved for whites. Black workers labored "in the back," cleaning, cooking, stocking shelves, and loading trucks for the lowest wages. Rural African Americans labored in a sharecropping system that kept them stuck in poverty, often prevented them from obtaining an education, and offered virtually no avenue of escape. Politically, less than 20 percent of eligible black voters were allowed to vote, the result of poll taxes, literacy tests, intimidation, fraud, and the "white primary" (elections in which only whites could vote). This near-total disenfranchisement gave whites power disproportionate to their numbers — black people were one-third of the residents of Mississippi, South Carolina, and Georgia but had virtually no political voice in those states.

In the North, racial segregation in everyday life was less acute but equally tangible. Northern segregation took the form of a spatial system in which whites increasingly lived in suburbs or on the outskirts of cities, while African Americans were concentrated in declining downtown neighborhoods. The result was what many called ghettos: all-black districts characterized by high rents, low wages, and inadequate city services. Employment discrimination and lack of adequate training left many African Americans without any means of support. Few jobs other than the most menial were open to African Americans; journalists, accountants, engineers, and other highly educated men from all-black colleges and universities often labored as railroad porters or cooks because jobs commensurate with their skills remained for whites only. These conditions produced a self-perpetuating cycle that kept far too many black citizens trapped on the social margins.

To be certain, African Americans found greater freedom in the North and West than in the South. They could vote, participate in politics, and, at least after the early 1960s, enjoy equal access to public accommodations. But we err in thinking that racial segregation was only a southern problem or that poverty and racial discrimination were not also deeply entrenched in the North and West. In northern cities such as Detroit, Chicago, and Philadelphia, for instance, white home owners in the 1950s used various tactics — from police harassment to thrown bricks, burning crosses, bombs, and mob violence — to keep African Americans from living near them. Moreover, as we saw in Chapter 26, Federal Housing Administration (FHA) and bank redlining excluded African American home buyers from the all-white suburbs emerging around major cities. Racial segregation was a national, not regional, problem.

## Origins of the Civil Rights Movement

Since racial discrimination had been part of American life for hundreds of years, why did the civil rights movement arise when it did? After all, the National Association for the Advancement of Colored People (NAACP), founded in 1909, had begun challenging racial segregation in a series of court cases in the 1930s. And other organizations, such as Marcus Garvey's United Negro Improvement Association in the 1920s, had attracted significant popular support. These precedents were important, but several factors came together in the middle of the twentieth century to make a broad movement possible.

An important influence was World War II. "The Jewish people and the Negro people both know the meaning of Nordic supremacy," wrote the African American poet Langston Hughes in 1945. In the war against fascism, the Allies sought to discredit racist Nazi ideology. Committed to fighting racism abroad, Americans increasingly condemned racism at home. The Cold War placed added pressure on U.S. officials. "More and more we are learning how closely our democracy is under observation," President Harry S. Truman commented in 1947. To inspire other nations in the global standoff with the Soviet Union, Truman explained, "we must correct the remaining imperfections in our practice of democracy."

Among the most consequential factors was the growth of the urban black middle class. Historically small, the black middle class experienced robust growth after World War II. Its ranks produced most of the civil rights leaders: ministers, teachers, trade unionists, attorneys, and other professionals. Churches, for centuries a sanctuary for black Americans, were especially important. Moreover, in the 1960s African American college students — part of the largest expansion of college enrollment in U.S. history — joined the movement, adding new energy and fresh ideas (Table 27.1). With access to education, media, and institutions, this new middle class had more resources than ever before. Less dependent on white patronage, and therefore less vulnerable to white retaliation, middle-class African Americans were in a position to lead a movement for change.

> **IDENTIFY CAUSES**
> How did the growth of the black middle class assist the civil rights movement?

Still other influences assisted the movement. White labor leaders were generally more equality-minded than the rank and file, but the United Auto Workers, the United Steelworkers, and the Communications Workers of America, among many other trade unions,

| TABLE 27.1 | |
| --- | --- |
| **African American College Enrollment** | |
| Year | Number of African Americans Enrolled (rounded to nearest thousand) |
| 1940 | 60,000 |
| 1950 | 110,000 |
| 1960 | 185,000 |
| 1970 | 430,000 |
| 1980 | 1.4 million |
| 1990 | 3.6 million |

were reliable allies at the national level. The new medium of television, too, played a crucial role. When television networks covered early desegregation struggles, such as the 1957 integration of Little Rock High School, Americans across the country saw the violence of white supremacy firsthand. None of these factors alone was decisive. None ensured an easy path. The civil rights movement faced enormous resistance and required dauntless courage and sacrifice from thousands upon thousands of activists for more than three decades. Ultimately, however, the movement changed the nation for the better and improved the lives of millions of Americans.

## World War II: The Beginnings

During the war fought "to make the world safe for democracy," the United States was far from ready to extend full equality to its own black citizens. Black workers faced discrimination in wartime employment, and the more than one million black troops who served in World War II were placed in segregated units commanded by whites. Both at home and abroad, World War II "immeasurably magnified the Negro's awareness of the disparity between the American profession

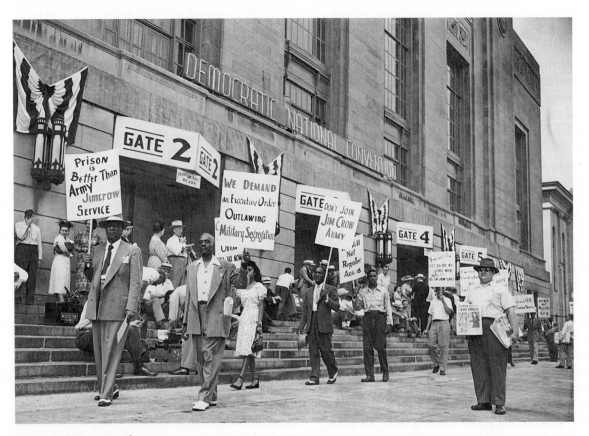

**Postwar Desegregation**
Picketers outside the July 1948 Democratic National Convention demand that the party include equal rights and anti–Jim Crow planks in its official platform and desegregate the armed services. Leading the pickets is A. Philip Randolph, president of the Brotherhood of Sleeping Car Porters. Randolph headed the March on Washington Movement that pressured President Roosevelt to desegregate defense employment during World War II, and he led the committee that convinced President Truman to desegregate the armed forces in 1948. © Bettmann/Corbis.

and practice of democracy," NAACP president Walter White observed.

**Executive Order 8802**   On the home front, activists pushed two strategies. First, A. Philip Randolph, whose **Brotherhood of Sleeping Car Porters** was the most prominent black trade union, called for a march on Washington in early 1941. Randolph planned to bring 100,000 protesters to the nation's capital if African Americans were not given equal opportunity in war jobs — then just beginning to expand with President Franklin Roosevelt's pledge to supply the Allies with materiel. To avoid a divisive protest, FDR issued Executive Order 8802 in June of that year, prohibiting racial discrimination in defense industries, and Randolph agreed to cancel the march. The resulting Fair Employment Practices Commission (FEPC) had few enforcement powers, but it set an important precedent: federal action. Randolph's efforts showed that white leaders and institutions could be swayed by concerted African American action. It would be a critical lesson for the movement.

**The Double V Campaign**   A second strategy jumped from the pages of the *Pittsburgh Courier*, one of the foremost African American newspapers of the era. It was the brainchild of an ordinary cafeteria worker from Kansas. In a 1942 letter to the editor, James G. Thompson urged that "colored Americans adopt the double VV for a double victory" — victory over fascism abroad and victory over racism at home. Edgar Rouzeau, editor of the paper's New York office, agreed: "Black America must fight two wars and win in both." Instantly dubbed the Double V Campaign, Thompson's notion, with Rouzeau's backing, spread like wildfire through black communities across the country. African Americans would demonstrate their loyalty and citizenship by fighting the Axis powers. But they would also demand, peacefully but emphatically, the defeat of racism at home. "The suffering and privation may be great," Rouzeau told his readers, "but the rewards loom even greater."

The Double V efforts met considerable resistance. In war industries, factories periodically shut down in Chicago, Baltimore, Philadelphia, and other cities because of "hate strikes": the refusal of white workers to labor alongside black workers. Detroit was especially tense. Referring to the potential for racial strife, *Life* magazine reported in 1942 that "Detroit is Dynamite. . . . It can either blow up Hitler or blow up America." In 1943, it nearly did the latter. On a hot summer day, whites from the city's ethnic neighborhoods

**Wartime Workers**
During World War II, hundreds of thousands of black migrants left the South, bound for large cities in the North and West. There, they found jobs such as the welding work done by these African American women at the Landers, Frary, and Clark plant in New Britain, Connecticut. Fighting employment discrimination during the war represented one of the earliest phases in the long struggle against racial segregation in the United States. Library of Congress.

taunted and beat African Americans in a local park. Three days of rioting ensued in which thirty-four people were killed, twenty-five of them black. Federal troops were called in to restore order.

Despite and because of such incidents, a generation was spurred into action during the war years. In New York City, employment discrimination on the city's transit lines prompted one of the first bus boycotts in the nation's history, led in 1941 by Harlem minister Adam Clayton Powell Jr. In Chicago, James Farmer and three other members of the Fellowship of Reconciliation (FOR), a nonviolent peace organization, founded the **Congress of Racial Equality (CORE)** in 1942. FOR and CORE adopted the philosophy of nonviolent direct action espoused by Mahatma Gandhi of India. Another FOR member in New York, Bayard Rustin, was equally instrumental in promoting direct action; he led one of

**EXPLAIN CONSEQUENCES**
Why did World War II play such a critical role in the civil rights movement?

the earliest challenges to southern segregation, the 1947 Journey of Reconciliation. Meanwhile, after the war, hundreds of thousands of African American veterans used the GI Bill to go to college, trade school, or graduate school, placing themselves in a position to push against segregation. At the war's end, Powell affirmed that "the black man . . . is ready to throw himself into the struggle to make the dream of America become flesh and blood, bread and butter."

## Cold War Civil Rights

Demands for justice persisted in the early years of the Cold War. African American efforts were propelled by symbolic victories—as when Jackie Robinson broke through the color line in major league baseball by joining the Brooklyn Dodgers in 1947—but the growing black vote in northern cities proved more decisive. During World War II, more than a million African Americans migrated to northern and western cities, where they joined the Democratic Party of Franklin Roosevelt and the New Deal (Map 27.1). This newfound political leverage awakened northern liberals, many of whom became allies of civil rights advocates. Ultimately, the Cold War produced mixed results, as the nation's commitment to anticommunism opened some avenues for civil rights while closing others.

**Civil Rights and the New Deal Coalition**    African American leaders were uncertain what to expect from President Truman, inheritor of the New Deal coalition but not opposed to using racist language himself.

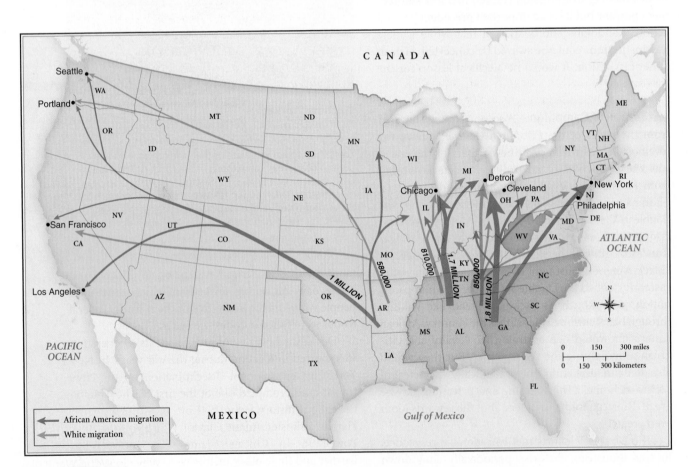

**MAP 27.1**

**Internal Migrations**

The migration of African Americans from the South to other regions of the country produced one of the most remarkable demographic shifts of the mid-twentieth century. Between World War I—which marked the start of the Great Migration—and the 1970s, more than 6 million African Americans left the South. Where they settled in the North and West, they helped change the politics of entire cities and even states. Seeking black votes, which had become a key to victory in major cities, liberal Democrats and Republicans alike in New York, Illinois, California, and Pennsylvania, for instance, increasingly made civil rights part of their platform. In this way, migration advanced the political cause of black equality.

Though he did not immediately support social equality for African Americans, Truman supported civil rights because he believed in equality before the law. Moreover, he understood the growing importance of the small but often decisive black vote in key northern states such as New York, Illinois, Pennsylvania, and Michigan. Civil rights activists Randolph and Powell — along with vocal white liberals such as Hubert Humphrey, the mayor of Minneapolis, and members of Americans for Democratic Action (ADA), a liberal organization — pressed Truman to act.

With no support for civil rights in Congress, Truman turned to executive action. In 1946, he appointed the Presidential Committee on Civil Rights, whose 1947 report, **"To Secure These Rights,"** called for robust federal action to ensure equality for African Americans. With the report fresh in his mind, in 1948 Truman issued an executive order desegregating employment in federal agencies and, under pressure from Randolph's Committee Against Jim Crow in Military Service, desegregated the armed forces. Truman then sent a message to Congress asking that all of the report's recommendations — including the abolition of poll taxes and the restoration of the Fair Employment Practices Commission — be made into law. It was the most aggressive, and politically bold, call for racial equality by the leader of a major political party since Reconstruction.

Truman's boldness was too much for southern Democrats. Under the leadership of Strom Thurmond, governor of South Carolina, white Democrats from the South formed the **States' Rights Democratic Party**, known popularly as the Dixiecrats, for the 1948 election (Chapter 25). This brought into focus an internal struggle developing within the Democratic Party and its still-formidable New Deal coalition. Would the civil rights aims of the party's liberal wing alienate southern white Democrats, as well as many suburban whites in the North? It was the first hint of the discord that would eventually divide the Democratic Party in the 1960s.

**Race and Anticommunism**   The Cold War shaped civil rights in both positive and negative terms. In a time of growing fear of communist expansionism, Truman worried about America's image in the world. He reminded Americans that when whites and blacks "fail to live together in peace," that failure hurt "the cause of democracy itself in the whole world." Indeed, the Soviet Union used American racism as a means of discrediting the United States abroad. "We cannot escape the fact that our civil rights record has been an issue in world politics," the Committee on Civil Rights wrote. International tensions between the United States and the Soviet Union thus appeared to strengthen the hand of civil rights leaders, because America needed to demonstrate to the rest of the world that its race relations were improving (America Compared, p. 876).

However, the Cold War strengthened one hand while weakening the other. McCarthyism and the hunt for subversives at home held the civil rights movement back. Civil rights opponents charged that racial integration was "communistic," and the NAACP was banned in many southern states as an "anti-American" organization. Black Americans who spoke favorably of the Soviet Union, such as the actor and singer Paul Robeson, or had been "fellow travelers" in the 1930s, such as the pacifist Bayard Rustin, were persecuted. Robeson, whose career was destroyed by such accusations, told House Un-American Activities Committee (HUAC) interrogators, "My father was a slave, and my people died to build this country, and I am going to . . . have a part of it just like you." The fate of people like Robeson showed that the Cold War could work *against* the civil rights cause just as easily as for it.

> **UNDERSTAND POINTS OF VIEW**
> How did the Cold War work in the favor of civil rights? How did it work against the movement?

## Mexican Americans and Japanese Americans

African Americans were the most prominent, but not the only, group in American society to organize against racial injustice in the 1940s. In the Southwest, from Texas to California, Mexican immigrants and Mexican Americans endured a "caste" system not unlike the Jim Crow system in the South. In Texas, for instance, poll taxes kept most Mexican American citizens from voting. Decades of discrimination by employers in agriculture and manufacturing — made possible by the constant supply of cheap labor from across the border — suppressed wages and kept the majority of Mexican Americans barely above poverty. Many lived in *colonias* or barrios, neighborhoods separated from Anglos and often lacking sidewalks, reliable electricity and water, and public services.

Developments within the Mexican American community set the stage for fresh challenges to these conditions in the 1940s. Labor activism in the 1930s and 1940s, especially in Congress of Industrial Organizations (CIO) unions with large numbers of Mexican Americans, improved wages and working conditions in some industries and produced a new generation of

# Freedom in the United
# States and Africa

## Hailou Wolde-Giorghis

Hailou Wolde-Giorghis was an Ethiopian student who visited the United States at the invitation of the State Department in the early 1960s.

"Negroes are dirty," say the whites, but in nearly all restaurants I saw Negro waiters and cooks. "They're lazy": I noticed that it is the Negro who does the hardest manual work. They are said to be uncultivated and are therefore denied access to culture. As George Bernard Shaw said, "The haughty American nation makes the Negro shine its shoes, and then demonstrates his physical and mental inferiority by the fact that he is a shoe-cleaner." . . .

What is known as integration in the South is the ability of a Negro to enter a shop and buy a record, or the fact that, of ten thousand students enrolled in a university, two of them are Negroes. "A miracle!" they cry. Real integration, however, does not exist, not even in the North, and by real integration I mean interracial communication, complete equality in the strict sense of the word. Still another example drawn from the South: the manager of a television studio told me in frigid terms that he would not hire Negroes; there would be a scandal and all his sponsors would protest.

Source: Hailou Wolde-Giorghis, "My Encounters with Racism in the United States," in *Views of America*, ed. Alan F. Westin et al. (New York: Harcourt, Brace, and World, 1966), 228–231.

## Martin Luther King Jr.

Here, the American civil rights leader celebrates the independence of the African nation of Ghana in 1957.

And it's a beautiful thing, isn't it that . . . [Ghana] is now free and is free without rising up with arms and ammunition. It is free through nonviolent means. Because of that the British Empire will not have the bitterness for Ghana that she has for China, so to speak. Because of that when the British Empire leaves Ghana she leaves with a different attitude than she would have left with if she had been driven out by armies. We've got to revolt in such a way

that after revolt is over we can live with people as their brothers and sisters.

Source: Martin Luther King Jr., "The Birth of a New Nation," *Liberation* 28 (April 1957).

## Kwame Nkrumah

Kwame Nkrumah was the first president of the independent nation of Ghana. In the 1930s and 1940s, Nkrumah studied in the United States, earning degrees at Lincoln University and the University of Pennsylvania.

The "wind of change" has become a raging hurricane, sweeping away the old colonialist Africa. The year 1960 was Africa's year. In that year alone, seventeen African States emerged as proud and independent sovereign nations. Now the ultimate freedom of the whole of Africa can no more be in doubt.

For centuries, Europeans dominated the African continent. The white man arrogated to himself the right to rule and to be obeyed by the non-white. . . .

All this makes a sad story, but now we must be prepared to bury the past with its unpleasant memories and look to the future. All we ask of the former colonial powers is their goodwill and cooperation to remedy past mistakes and injustices and to grant independence to the colonies in Africa.

Source: Kwame Nkrumah, *I Speak of Freedom: A Statement of African Ideology* (New York: Praeger, 1961), ix.

### QUESTIONS FOR ANALYSIS

1. Wolde-Giorghis is especially critical of southern "integration." As an African, what kind of perspective would he bring to this question?
2. What values and goals do King and Nkrumah seem to share? How were their circumstances and goals different?
3. Compare the circumstances of African Americans in the United States and Africans in nations colonized by Europeans. What were the similarities and differences?

**Bracero Worker Card**

In the Southwest, Mexican immigrants and many Mexican Americans encountered a caste system not unlike Jim Crow segregation. Most of the hardest, lowest-paying work in states such as Texas, Arizona, and California was performed by people of Mexican descent. Under a government program, braceros, or migrant Mexican workers, were allowed into the United States for a limited time to harvest a variety of fruit and vegetable crops. A worker card issued to one such bracero is pictured here. National Museum of American History, Smithsonian Institution, Behring Center.

leaders. More than 400,000 Mexican Americans also served in World War II. Having fought for their country, many returned to the United States determined to challenge their second-class citizenship. Additionally, a new Mexican American middle class began to take shape in major cities such as Los Angeles, San Antonio, El Paso, and Chicago, which, like the African American middle class, gave leaders and resources to the cause.

In Texas and California, Mexican Americans created new civil rights organizations in the postwar years. In Corpus Christi, Texas, World War II veterans founded the **American GI Forum** in 1948 to protest the poor treatment of Mexican American soldiers and veterans. Activists in Los Angeles created the Community Service Organization (CSO) the same year.

Both groups arose to address specific local injustices (such as the segregation of military cemeteries), but they quickly broadened their scope to encompass political and economic justice for the larger community. Among the first young activists to work for the CSO were Cesar Chavez and Dolores Huerta, who would later found the United Farm Workers (UFW) and inspire the Chicano movement of the 1960s.

Activists also pushed for legal change. In 1947, five Mexican American fathers in California sued a local school district for placing their children in separate "Mexican" schools. The case, *Mendez v. Westminster School District*, never made it to the U.S. Supreme Court. But the Ninth Circuit Court ruled such segregation unconstitutional, laying the legal groundwork for broader challenges to racial inequality. Among those filing briefs in the case was the NAACP's Thurgood Marshall, who was then developing the legal strategy to strike at racial segregation in the South. In another significant legal victory, the Supreme Court ruled in 1954—just two weeks before the landmark *Brown v. Board of Education* decision—that Mexican Americans constituted a "distinct class" that could claim protection from discrimination.

Also on the West Coast, Japanese Americans accelerated their legal challenge to discrimination. Undeterred by rulings in the *Hirabayashi* (1943) and *Korematsu* (1944) cases upholding wartime imprisonment (Chapter 24), the Japanese American Citizens League (JACL) filed lawsuits in the late 1940s to regain property lost during the war. The JACL also challenged the constitutionality of California's Alien Land Law, which prohibited Japanese immigrants from owning land, and successfully lobbied Congress to enable those same immigrants to become citizens—a right they were denied for fifty years. These efforts by Mexican and Japanese Americans enlarged the sphere of civil rights and laid the foundation for a broader notion of racial equality in the postwar years.

## Fighting for Equality Before the Law

With civil rights legislation blocked in Congress by southern Democrats throughout the 1950s, activists looked in two different directions for a breakthrough: to northern state legislatures and to the federal courts. School segregation remained a stubborn problem in northern states, but the biggest obstacle to black

**COMPARE AND CONTRAST**
How were the circumstances facing Mexican and Japanese Americans similar to those facing African Americans? How were they different?

progress there was persistent job and housing discrimination. The states with the largest African American populations, and hence the largest share of black Democratic Party voters, became testing grounds for state legislation to end such discriminatory practices.

Winning antidiscrimination legislation depended on coalition politics. African American activists forged alliances with trade unions and liberal organizations such as the American Friends Service Committee (a Quaker group), among many others. Progress was slow and often occurred only after long periods of unglamorous struggle to win votes in state capitals such as Albany, New York; Springfield, Illinois; and Lansing, Michigan. The first fair employment laws had come in New York and New Jersey in 1945. A decade passed, however, before other states with significant black populations passed similar legislation. Antidiscrimination laws in housing were even more difficult to pass, with most progress not coming until the 1960s. These legislative campaigns in northern states received little national attention, but they were instrumental in laying the groundwork for legal equality outside the South.

**Thurgood Marshall**    Because the vast majority of southern African Americans were prohibited from voting, state legislatures there were closed to the kind of organized political pressure possible in the North. Thus activists also looked to federal courts for leverage. In the late 1930s, NAACP lawyers Thurgood Marshall, Charles Hamilton Houston, and William Hastie had begun preparing the legal ground in a series of cases challenging racial discrimination. The key was prodding the U.S. Supreme Court to use the Fourteenth Amendment's "equal protection" clause to overturn its 1896 ruling in *Plessy v. Ferguson*, which upheld racial segregation under the "separate but equal" doctrine.

Marshall was the great-grandson of slaves. Of modest origins, his parents instilled in him a faith in law and the Constitution. After his 1930 graduation from Lincoln University, a prestigious African American institution near Philadelphia, Marshall applied to the University of Maryland Law School. Denied admission because the school did not accept black applicants, he enrolled at all-black Howard University. There Marshall met Houston, a law school dean, and the two forged a friendship and intellectual partnership that would change the face of American legal history. Marshall, with Houston's and Hastie's critical strategic input, would argue most of the NAACP's landmark cases. In the late 1960s,

President Johnson appointed Marshall to the Supreme Court—the first African American to have that honor.

Marshall, Houston, Hastie, and six other attorneys filed suit after suit, deliberately selecting each one from dozens of possibilities. The strategy was slow and time-consuming, but progress came. In 1936, Marshall and Hamilton won a state case that forced the University of Maryland Law School to admit qualified African Americans—a ruling of obvious significance to Marshall. Eight years later, in *Smith v. Allwright* (1944), Marshall convinced the U.S. Supreme Court that all-white primaries were unconstitutional. In 1950, with Marshall once again arguing the case, the Supreme Court ruled in *McLaurin v. Oklahoma* that universities could not segregate black students from others on campus. None of these cases produced swift changes in the daily lives of most African Americans, but they confirmed that civil rights attorneys were on the right track.

**Brown v. Board of Education**    The NAACP's legal strategy achieved its ultimate validation in a case involving Linda Brown, a black pupil in Topeka, Kansas, who had been forced to attend a distant segregated school rather than the nearby white elementary school. In **Brown v. Board of Education of Topeka** (1954), Marshall argued that such segregation was unconstitutional because it denied Linda Brown the "equal protection of the laws" guaranteed by the Fourteenth Amendment (Map 27.2). In a unanimous decision on May 17, 1954, the Supreme Court agreed, overturning the "separate but equal" doctrine at last. Writing for the Court, the new chief justice, Earl Warren, wrote: "We conclude that in the field of public education the doctrine of 'separate but equal' has no place. Separate educational facilities are inherently unequal." In an implementing 1955 decision known as *Brown II*, the Court declared simply that integration should proceed "with all deliberate speed."

In the South, however, Virginia senator Harry F. Byrd issued a call for "massive resistance." Calling May 17 "Black Monday," the Mississippi segregationist Tom P. Brady invoked the language of the Cold War to discredit the decision, assailing the "totalitarian government" that had rendered the decision in the name of "socialism and communism." That year, half a million southerners joined White Citizens' Councils dedicated to blocking school integration. Some whites revived the old tactics of violence and intimidation, swelling the ranks of the Ku Klux Klan to levels not seen since the 1920s. The "Southern Manifesto," signed in 1956 by 101 members of Congress, denounced the

**TRACE CHANGE OVER TIME**
How did the NAACP go about developing a legal strategy to attack racial segregation?

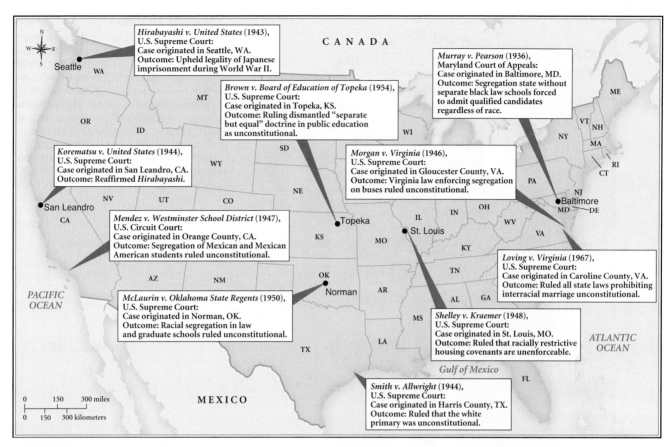

**MAP 27.2**

**Desegregation Court Cases**

Desegregation court battles were not limited to the South. Note the important California cases regarding Mexican Americans and Japanese Americans. Two seminal decisions, the 1948 housing decision in *Shelley v. Kraemer* and the 1954 school decision in *Brown v. Board of Education*, originated in Missouri and Kansas, respectively. This map helps show that racial segregation and discrimination were a national, not simply a southern, problem.

*Brown* decision as "a clear abuse of judicial power" and encouraged local officials to defy it. The white South had declared all-out war on *Brown*.

Enforcement of the Supreme Court's decision was complicated further by Dwight Eisenhower's presence in the White House — the president was no champion of civil rights. Eisenhower accepted the *Brown* decision as the law of the land, but he thought it a mistake. Ike was especially unhappy about the prospect of committing federal power to enforce the decision. A crisis in Little Rock, Arkansas, finally forced his hand. In September 1957, when nine black students attempted to enroll at the all-white Central High School, Governor Orval Faubus called out the National Guard to bar them. Angry white mobs appeared daily to taunt the students, chanting "Go back to the jungle." As the vicious scenes played out on television night after night, Eisenhower finally acted. He sent 1,000 federal troops to Little Rock and nationalized the Arkansas National Guard, ordering them to protect the black students. Eisenhower thus became the first president since Reconstruction to use federal troops to enforce the rights of African Americans. But Little Rock also showed that southern officials had more loyalty to local custom than to the law — a repeated problem in the post-*Brown* era.

# Forging a Protest Movement, 1955–1965

Declaring racial segregation integral to the South's "habits, traditions, and way of life," the Southern Manifesto signaled that many whites would not accept African American equality readily. As Americans had

**The Legal Strategy**

On the steps of the Supreme Court, on the day in 1954 that *Brown v. Board of Education of Topeka* was decided, are the architects of the NAACP legal strategy in the *Brown* case and dozens of others. Together (from left to right), George E. C. Hayes, Thurgood Marshall, and James M. Nabrit pursued cases that undermined the constitutional foundation of racial segregation. Their efforts were not enough to destroy Jim Crow, however—that would take marches, protests, and sacrifices from ordinary citizens. AP Images.

witnessed in Little Rock, the unwillingness of local officials to enforce *Brown* could render the decision invalid in practice. If legal victories would not be enough, citizens themselves, black and white, would have to take to the streets and demand justice. Following the *Brown* decision, they did just that, forging a protest movement unique in the history of the United States.

## Nonviolent Direct Action

*Brown* had been the law of the land for barely a year when a single act of violence struck at the heart of black America. A fourteen-year-old African American from the South Side of Chicago, Emmett Till, was visiting relatives in Mississippi in the summer of 1955. Seen talking to a white woman in a grocery store, Till was tortured and murdered under cover of night. His mutilated body was found at the bottom of a river, tied with barbed wire to a heavy steel cotton gin fan. Photos of

Till's body in *Jet* magazine brought national attention to the heinous crime.

Two white men were arrested for Till's murder. During the trial, followed closely in African American communities across the country, the lone witness to Till's kidnapping—his uncle, Mose Wright—identified both killers. Feeling "the blood boil in hundreds of white people as they sat glaring in the courtroom," Wright said, "it was the first time in my life I had the courage to accuse a white man of a crime." Despite Wright's eyewitness testimony, the all-white jury found the defendants innocent. This miscarriage of justice—later, the killers even admitted their guilt in a *Look* magazine article—galvanized an entire generation of African Americans; no one who lived through the Till case ever forgot it.

**Montgomery Bus Boycott**    In the wake of the Till case, civil rights advocates needed some good news.

**School Desegregation in Little Rock, Arkansas**
Less well known than the crisis at Little Rock's Central High School the same year, the circumstances at North Little Rock were nonetheless strikingly similar: white resistance to the enrollment of a handful of black students. In this photograph, white students block the doors of North Little Rock High School, preventing six African American students from entering on September 9, 1957. This photograph is noteworthy because it shows a striking new feature of southern racial politics: the presence of film and television cameras that broadcast these images to the nation and the world. AP Images.

They received it three months later, as southern black leaders embraced an old tactic put to new ends: nonviolent protest. On December 1, 1955, Rosa Parks, a civil rights activist in Montgomery, Alabama, refused to give up her seat on a bus to a white man. She was arrested and charged with violating a local segregation ordinance. Parks's act was not the spur-of-the-moment decision that it seemed: a woman of sterling reputation and a longtime NAACP member, she had been contemplating such an act for some time. Middle-aged and unassuming, Rosa Parks fit the bill perfectly for the NAACP's challenge against segregated buses.

Once the die was cast, the black community turned for leadership to the Reverend Martin Luther King Jr., the recently appointed pastor of Montgomery's Dexter Street Baptist Church. The son of a prominent Atlanta minister, King embraced the teachings of Mahatma Gandhi. Working closely, but behind the scenes, with Bayard Rustin, King studied nonviolent philosophy, which Rustin and others in the Fellowship of

Reconciliation had first used in the 1940s. After Rosa Parks's arrest, King endorsed a plan proposed by a local black women's organization to boycott Montgomery's bus system. The **Montgomery Bus Boycott** was inspired by similar boycotts that had taken place in Harlem in 1941 and Baton Rouge, Louisiana, in 1953.

For the next 381 days, Montgomery's African Americans formed car pools or walked to work. "Darling, it's empty!" Coretta Scott King exclaimed to her husband as a bus normally filled with black riders rolled by their living room window on the first day of the boycott. The transit company neared bankruptcy, and downtown stores complained about the loss of business. But only after the Supreme Court ruled in November 1956 that bus segregation was unconstitutional did the city of Montgomery finally comply. "My feets is tired, but my soul is rested," said one woman boycotter.

The Montgomery Bus Boycott catapulted King to national prominence. In 1957, along with the Reverend

Ralph Abernathy and dozens of black ministers from across the South, he founded the Atlanta-based **Southern Christian Leadership Conference (SCLC)**. The black church, long the center of African American social and cultural life, now lent its moral and organizational strength to the civil rights movement. Black church-women were a tower of strength, transferring the skills they had honed during years of church work to the fight for civil rights. The SCLC quickly joined the NAACP at the leading edge of the movement for racial justice.

**Greensboro Sit-Ins**   The battle for civil rights entered a new phase in Greensboro, North Carolina, on February 1, 1960, when four black college students took seats at the whites-only lunch counter at the local Woolworth's five-and-dime store. This simple act was entirely the brainchild of the four students, who had discussed it in their dorm rooms over several preceding nights. A New York–based spokesman for Woolworth's said the chain would "abide by local custom," which meant refusing to serve African Americans at the lunch counter. The students were determined to "sit in" until they were served. For three weeks, hundreds of students inspired by the original foursome took turns sitting at the counters, quietly eating, doing homework, or reading. Taunted by groups of whites, pelted with food and other debris, the black students — often occupying more than sixty of the sixty-six seats — held strong. Although many were arrested, the tactic worked: the Woolworth's lunch counter was desegregated, and sit-ins quickly spread to other southern cities (American Voices, p. 884).

**Ella Baker and SNCC**   Inspired by the developments in Greensboro and elsewhere, Ella Baker, an administrator with the SCLC, helped organize the **Student Nonviolent Coordinating Committee** (**SNCC**, pronounced "Snick") in 1960 to facilitate student sit-ins. Rolling like a great wave across the Upper South, from North Carolina into Virginia, Maryland, and Tennessee, by the end of the year students had launched sit-ins in 126 cities. More than 50,000 people participated, and 3,600 were jailed. The sit-ins drew African American college students into the movement in significant numbers for the first time. Northern students formed solidarity committees and raised money for bail. SNCC quickly emerged as the most important student protest organization in the country and inspired a generation of students on college campuses across the nation.

Baker took a special interest in these students, because she found them receptive to her notion of

**Ella Baker**

Born in Virginia and educated at Shaw University in Raleigh, North Carolina, Ella Baker was one of the foremost theorists of grassroots, participatory democracy in the United States. Active all her life in the black freedom movement, in 1960 Baker cofounded the Student Nonviolent Coordinating Committee (SNCC). Her advocacy of leadership by ordinary, nonelite people often led her to disagree with the top-down movement strategy of Martin Luther King Jr. and other ministers of the Southern Christian Leadership Conference (SCLC). AP Images.

participatory democracy. The granddaughter of slaves, Baker had moved to Harlem in the 1930s, where she worked for New Deal agencies and then the NAACP. She believed in nurturing leaders from the grass roots, encouraging ordinary people to stand up for their rights rather than to depend on charismatic figureheads. "My theory is, strong people don't need strong leaders," she once said. Nonetheless, Baker nurtured a generation of young activists in SNCC, including Stokely Carmichael, Anne Moody, John Lewis, and Diane Nash, who went on to become some of the most important civil rights leaders in the United States.

**Freedom Rides**   Emboldened by SNCC's sit-in tactics, in 1961 the Congress of Racial Equality (CORE) organized a series of what were called Freedom Rides on interstate bus lines throughout the South. The aim was to call attention to blatant violations of recent Supreme Court rulings against segregation in interstate commerce. The activists who signed on — mostly young, both black and white — knew that they were taking their lives in their hands. They found courage in song, as civil rights activists had begun to do across the country, with lyrics such as "I'm taking a ride on the Greyhound bus line. . . . Hallelujah, I'm traveling down freedom's main line!"

Courage they needed. Club-wielding Klansmen attacked the buses when they stopped in small towns. Outside Anniston, Alabama, one bus was firebombed; the Freedom Riders escaped only moments before it exploded. Some riders were then brutally beaten. Freedom Riders and news reporters were also viciously attacked by Klansmen in Birmingham and Montgomery. Despite the violence, state authorities refused to intervene. "I cannot guarantee protection for this bunch of rabble rousers," declared Governor John Patterson of Alabama.

Once again, local officials' refusal to enforce the law left the fate of the Freedom Riders in Washington's hands. The new president, John F. Kennedy, was cautious about civil rights. Despite a campaign commitment, he failed to deliver on a civil rights bill. Elected by a thin margin, Kennedy believed that he could ill afford to lose the support of powerful southern senators. But civil rights was unlike other domestic issues. Its fate was going to be decided not in the halls of Congress, but on the streets of southern cities. Although President Kennedy discouraged the Freedom Rides, beatings shown on the nightly news forced Attorney General Robert Kennedy to dispatch federal marshals. Civil rights activists thus learned the value of nonviolent protest that provoked violent white resistance.

The victories so far had been limited, but the groundwork had been laid for a civil rights offensive that would transform the nation. The NAACP's legal strategy had been followed closely by the emergence of a major protest movement. And now civil rights leaders focused their attention on Congress.

## Legislating Civil Rights, 1963–1965

The first civil rights law in the nation's history came in 1866 just after the Civil War. Its provisions were long ignored (Chapter 15). A second law was passed during Reconstruction in 1875, but it was declared unconstitutional by the Supreme Court. For nearly ninety years, new civil rights legislation was blocked or filibustered by southern Democrats in Congress. Only a weak, largely symbolic act was passed in 1957 during the Eisenhower administration. But by the early 1960s, with legal precedents in their favor and nonviolent protest awakening the nation, civil rights leaders believed the time had come for a serious civil rights bill. The challenge was getting one through a still-reluctant Congress.

**TRACE CHANGE OVER TIME**
What lessons did activists learn from the evolution of the civil rights movement between 1957 and 1961?

**The Battle for Birmingham**   The road to such a bill began when Martin Luther King Jr. called for demonstrations in "the most segregated city in the United States": Birmingham, Alabama. King and the SCLC needed a concrete victory in Birmingham to validate their strategy of nonviolent protest. In May 1963, thousands of black marchers tried to picket Birmingham's department stores. Eugene "Bull" Connor, the city's public safety commissioner, ordered the city's police troops to meet the marchers with violent force: snarling dogs, electric cattle prods, and high-pressure fire hoses. Television cameras captured the scene for the evening news.

While serving a jail sentence for leading the march, King, scribbling in pencil on any paper he could find, composed one of the classic documents of nonviolent direct action: "Letter from Birmingham Jail." "Why direct action?" King asked. "There is a type of constructive, nonviolent tension that is necessary for growth." The civil rights movement sought, he continued, "to create such a crisis and establish such a creative tension." Grounding his actions in equal parts Christian brotherhood and democratic liberalism, King argued that Americans confronted a moral choice: they could "preserve the evil system of segregation" or take the side of "those great wells of democracy . . . the Constitution and the Declaration of Independence."

Outraged by the brutality in Birmingham and embarrassed by King's imprisonment for leading a nonviolent march, President Kennedy decided that it was time to act. On June 11, 1963, after newly elected Alabama governor George Wallace barred two black students from the state university, Kennedy denounced racism on national television and promised a new civil rights bill. Many black leaders felt Kennedy's action was long overdue, but they nonetheless hailed this "Second Emancipation Proclamation." That night, Medgar Evers, president of the Mississippi chapter of the NAACP, was shot in the back in his driveway in

## Challenging White Supremacy

Among the many challenges historians face is figuring out the processes by which long-oppressed ordinary people finally rise up and demand justice. During the 1950s, a liberating process was quietly under way among southern blacks, bursting forth dramatically in the Montgomery Bus Boycott of 1955 and then, by the end of the decade, emerging across the South. Here are excerpts of the testimony of two individuals who stepped forward and took the lead in those struggles.

### Franklin McCain
### Desegregating Lunch Counters

Franklin McCain was one of the four African American students at North Carolina A&T College in Greensboro, North Carolina, who sat down at the Woolworth's lunch counter on February 1, 1960, setting off a wave of student sit-ins that rocked the South and helped initiate a national civil rights movement. In the following interview, McCain describes how he and his friends took that momentous step.

The planning process was on a Sunday night, I remember it quite well. I think it was Joseph who said, "It's time that we take some action now. We've been getting together, and we've been, up to this point, still like most people we've talked about for the past few weeks or so — that is, people who talk a lot but, in fact, make very little action." After selecting the technique, then we said, "Let's go down and just ask for service." It certainly wasn't titled a "sit-in" or "sit-down" at that time. "Let's just go down to Woolworth's tomorrow and ask for service, and the tactic is going to be simply this: we'll just stay there."

. . . Once getting there . . . we did make purchases of school supplies and took the patience and time to get receipts for our purchases, and Joseph and myself went over to the counter and asked to be served coffee and doughnuts. As anticipated, the reply was, "I'm sorry, we don't serve you here." And of course we said, "We just beg to disagree with you. We've in fact already been served." . . . The attendant or waitress was a little bit dumbfounded, just didn't know what to say under circumstances like that. . . .

At that point there was a policeman who had walked in off the street, who was pacing the aisle . . . behind us, where we were seated, with his club in his hand, just sort of knocking it in his hand, and just looking mean and red and a little bit upset and a little bit disgusted. And you had the feeling that he didn't know what the hell to do. . . . Usually his defense is offense, and we've provoked him, yes, but we haven't provoked outwardly enough for

him to resort to violence. And I think this is just killing him; you can see it all over him.

If it's possible to know what it means to have your soul cleansed — I felt pretty clean at that time. I probably felt better on that day than I've ever felt in my life. Seems like a lot of feelings of guilt or what-have-you suddenly left me, and I felt as though I had gained my manhood. . . . Not Franklin McCain only as an individual, but I felt as though the manhood of a number of other black persons had been restored and had gotten some respect from just that one day.

The movement started out as a movement of nonviolence and a Christian movement. . . . It was a movement that was seeking justice more than anything else and not a movement to start a war. . . .We knew that probably the most powerful and potent weapon that people have literally no defense for is love, kindness. That is, whip the enemy with something that he doesn't understand. . . . The individual who had probably the most influence on us was Gandhi. . . . Yes, Martin Luther King's name was well-known when the sit-in movement was in effect, but . . . no, he was not the individual we had upmost in mind when we started the sit-in movement.

Source: *My Soul Is Rested* by Howell Raines, copyright 1977 Howell Raines. Used by permission of G. P. Putnam's Sons, a division of Penguin Group (USA) Inc. and Russell & Volkening as agents for the author.

### John McFerren
### Demanding the Right to Vote

In this interview, given about ten years after the events he describes, John McFerren tells of the battle he undertook in 1959 to gain the vote for the blacks of Fayette County, Tennessee. By the time of the interview, McFerren had risen in life and become a grocery-store owner and property holder, thanks, he says, to the economic boycott imposed on him by angry whites. Unlike Greensboro, the struggle in Fayette County never made national headlines. It was just one of many local struggles that signaled the beginning of a new day in the South.

My name is John McFerren. I'm forty-six years old. I'm a Negro was born and raised in West Tennessee, the county of Fayette, District 1. My foreparents was brought here from North Carolina five years before the Civil War . . . because the rumor got out among the slaveholders that West Tennessee was still goin to be a slaveholdin state. And my people was brought over here and sold. And after the Civil War my people settled in West Tennessee. That's why Fayette and Haywood counties have a great number of Negroes.

Back in 1957 and '58 there was a Negro man accused of killin a deputy sheriff. This was Burton Dodson. He was brought back after he'd been gone twenty years. J. F. Estes was the lawyer defendin him. Myself and him both was in the army together. And the stimulation from the trial got me interested in the way justice was bein used. The only way to bring justice would be through the ballot box.

In 1959 we got out a charter called the Fayette County Civic and Welfare League. Fourteen of us started out in that charter. We tried to support a white liberal candidate that was named L. T. Redfearn in the sheriff election and the local Democrat party refused to let Negroes vote.

We brought a suit against the Democrat party and I went to Washington for a civil-rights hearing. Myself and Estes and Harpman Jameson made the trip. It took us twenty-two hours steady drivin. . . . I was lookin all up — lotsa big, tall buildins. I had never seen old, tall buildins like that before. After talkin to [John Doar] we come on back to the Justice Department building and we sat out in the hall while he had a meetin inside the attorney general's office. And when they come out they told us they was gonna indict the landowners who kept us from voting. . . .

Just after that, in 1960, in January, we organized a thousand Negroes to line up at the courthouse to register to vote. We started pourin in with big numbers — in this county it was 72 percent Negroes — when we started to register to vote to change the situation.

In the followin . . . October and November they started puttin our people offa the land. Once you registered you had to move. Once you registered they took your job. Then after they done that, in November, we had three hundred people forced to live in tents on Shepard Towles's land. And when we started puttin em in tents,

then that's when the White Citizens Council and the Ku Klux Klan started shootin in the tents to run us out.

Tent City was parta an economic squeeze. The local merchants run me outa the stores and said I went to Washington and caused this mess to start. . . . They had a blacklist . . . And they had the list sent around to all merchants. Once you registered you couldn't buy for credit or cash. But the best thing in the world was when they run me outa them stores. It started me thinkin for myself. . . .

The southern white has a slogan: "Keep em niggers happy and keep em singin in the schools." And the biggest mistake of the past is that the Negro has not been taught economics and the value of a dollar. . . . Back at one time we had a teacher . . . from Mississippi — and he pulled up and left the county because he was teachin the Negroes to buy land, and own land, and work it for hisself, and the county Board of Education didn't want that taught in the county.

And they told him, "Keep em niggers singin and keep em happy and don't teach em nothin." . . . You cannot be free when you're beggin the man for bread. But when you've got the dollar in your pocket and then got the vote in your pocket, that's the only way to be free. . . . And I have been successful and made good progress because I could see the only way I could survive is to stay independent.

. . . The Negro is no longer goin back. He's goin forward.

Source: From *Looking for America*, second edition, 2 volumes, edited by Stanley I. Kutler (New York: Norton, 1979). Reprinted with permission of Stanley Kutler.

### QUESTIONS FOR ANALYSIS

1. McCain took a stand on segregated lunch counters. McFerren took a stand on the right to vote. How did these targets represent two different goals of the civil rights movement?

2. McCain speaks of the sense of "manhood" he felt as he sat at that Woolworth's counter. What does his personal feeling suggest about the civil rights movement as a whole?

3. Almost certainly, McCain and McFerren never met. Suppose they had. What would they have had in common? Would what they had in common have been more important than what separated them?

4. McCain speaks knowingly of the figures and ideas that influenced him. Why do you suppose McFerren is silent about such matters?

**The Battle of Birmingham**
One of the hardest-fought desegregation struggles of the early 1960s took place in April and May 1963 in Birmingham, Alabama. In response to the daily rallies and peaceful protests, authorities cracked down, arresting hundreds. They also employed tactics such as those shown here, turning fire hoses on young, nonviolent student demonstrators and using police dogs to intimidate peaceful marchers. These protests, led by Martin Luther King Jr. and broadcast on television news, prompted President Kennedy to introduce a civil rights bill in Congress in June 1963. © Bob Adelman/Corbis.

Jackson by a white supremacist. Evers's martyrdom became a spur to further action (Map 27.3).

**The March on Washington and the Civil Rights Act**  To marshal support for Kennedy's bill, civil rights leaders adopted a tactic that A. Philip Randolph had first advanced in 1941: a massive demonstration in Washington. Under the leadership of Randolph and Bayard Rustin, thousands of volunteers across the country coordinated car pools, "freedom buses," and "freedom trains," and on August 28, 1963, delivered a quarter of a million people to the Lincoln Memorial for the officially named **March on Washington** for Jobs and Freedom (Thinking Like a Historian, p. 888).

Although other people did the planning, Martin Luther King Jr. was the public face of the march. It was King's dramatic "I Have a Dream" speech, beginning with his admonition that too many black people lived "on a lonely island of poverty" and ending with the exclamation from a traditional black spiritual—"Free

at last! Free at last! Thank God almighty, we are free at last!"—that captured the nation's imagination. The sight of 250,000 blacks and whites marching solemnly together marked the high point of the civil rights movement and confirmed King's position as the leading spokesperson for the cause.

To have any chance of getting the civil rights bill through Congress, King, Randolph, and Rustin knew they had to sustain this broad coalition of blacks and whites. They could afford to alienate no one. Reflecting a younger, more militant set of activists, however, SNCC member John Lewis had prepared a more provocative speech for that afternoon. Lewis wrote, "The time will come when we will not confine our marching to Washington. We will march through the South, through the Heart of Dixie, the way Sherman did." Signaling a growing restlessness among black youth, Lewis warned: "We shall fragment the South into a thousand pieces and put them back together again in the image of democracy." Fearing the speech would

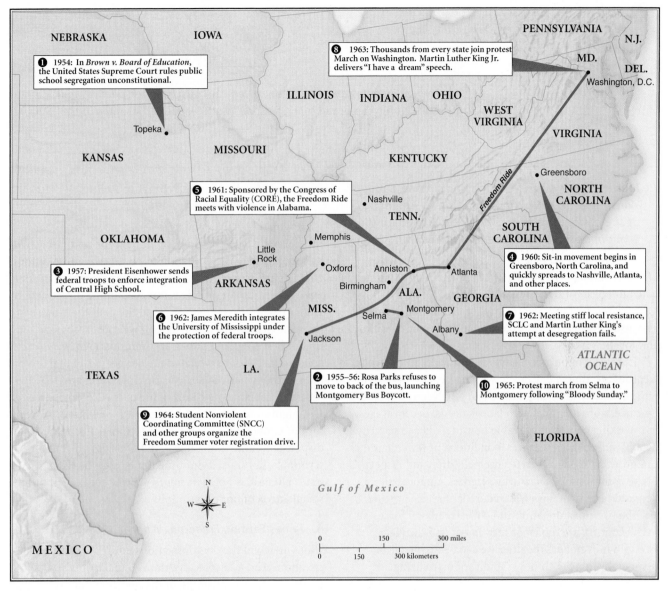

**1** 1954: In *Brown v. Board of Education*, the United States Supreme Court rules public school segregation unconstitutional.

**8** 1963: Thousands from every state join protest March on Washington. Martin Luther King Jr. delivers "I have a dream" speech.

**5** 1961: Sponsored by the Congress of Racial Equality (CORE), the Freedom Ride meets with violence in Alabama.

**4** 1960: Sit-in movement begins in Greensboro, North Carolina, and quickly spreads to Nashville, Atlanta, and other places.

**3** 1957: President Eisenhower sends federal troops to enforce integration of Central High School.

**6** 1962: James Meredith integrates the University of Mississippi under the protection of federal troops.

**7** 1962: Meeting stiff local resistance, SCLC and Martin Luther King's attempt at desegregation fails.

**2** 1955–56: Rosa Parks refuses to move to back of the bus, launching Montgomery Bus Boycott.

**10** 1965: Protest march from Selma to Montgomery following "Bloody Sunday."

**9** 1964: Student Nonviolent Coordinating Committee (SNCC) and other groups organize the Freedom Summer voter registration drive.

## MAP 27.3

### The Civil Rights Struggle, 1954–1965

In the postwar battle for black civil rights, the first major victory was the NAACP litigation of *Brown v. Board of Education*, which declared public school segregation unconstitutional. As indicated on this map, the struggle then quickly spread, raising other issues and seeding new organizations. Other organizations quickly joined the battle and shifted the focus away from the courts to mass action and organization. The year 1965 marked the high point, when violence against the Selma, Alabama, marchers spurred the passage of the Voting Rights Act.

alienate white supporters, Rustin and others implored Lewis to tone down his rhetoric. With only minutes to spare before he stepped up to the podium, Lewis agreed. He delivered a more conciliatory speech, but his conflict with march organizers signaled an emerging rift in the movement.

Although the March on Washington galvanized public opinion, it changed few congressional votes. Southern senators continued to block Kennedy's legislation. Georgia senator Richard Russell, a leader of the opposition, refused to support any bill that would "bring about social equality and intermingling and amalgamation of the races." Then, suddenly, tragedies piled up, one on another. In September, white supremacists bombed a Baptist church in Birmingham, killing four black girls in Sunday school. Less than two months later, Kennedy himself lay dead, the victim of assassination.

## Civil Rights and Black Power: Strategy and Ideology

The documents collected below reveal the range of perspectives and ideas at work within the broad civil rights, or "black freedom," struggle in the 1960s.

1. **Martin Luther King Jr., "If the Negro Wins, Labor Wins" speech, 1962.** *King, speaking to a meeting of the nation's trade union leaders, explained the economic objectives of the black freedom struggle.*

If we do not advance, the crushing burden of centuries of neglect and economic deprivation will destroy our will, our spirits and our hopes. In this way labor's historic tradition of moving forward to create vital people as consumers and citizens has become our own tradition, and for the same reasons.

This unity of purpose is not an historical coincidence. Negroes are almost entirely a working people. There are pitifully few Negro millionaires and few Negro employers. Our needs are identical with labor's needs: decent wages, fair working conditions, livable housing, old age security, health and welfare measures, conditions in which families can grow, have education for their children and respect in the community. That is why Negroes support labor's demands and fight laws which curb labor. . . .

The two most dynamic and cohesive liberal forces in the country are the labor movement and the Negro freedom movement. Together we can be architects of democracy in a South now rapidly industrializing.

2. **Police in Birmingham, Alabama, use trained German shepherds against peaceful African American protesters, 1963.**

Bill Hudson / AP Images.

3. **Bayard Rustin, "From Protest to Politics," *Commentary*, February 1965.**

. . . it would be hard to quarrel with the assertion that the elaborate legal structure of segregation and discrimination, particularly in relation to public accommodations, has virtually collapsed. On the other hand, without making light of the human sacrifices involved in the direct-action tactics (sit-ins, freedom rides, and the rest) that were so instrumental to this achievement, we must recognize that in desegregating public accommodations, we affected institutions which are relatively peripheral both to the American socio-economic order and to the fundamental conditions of life of the Negro people. In a highly-industrialized, 20th-century civilization, we hit Jim Crow precisely where it was most anachronistic, dispensable, and vulnerable — in hotels, lunch counters, terminals, libraries, swimming pools, and the like. . . . At issue, after all, is not civil rights, strictly speaking, but social and economic conditions.

4. **James Farmer, *Freedom, When?*, 1965.**

"But when will the demonstrations end?" The perpetual question. And a serious question. Actually, it is several questions, for the meaning of the question differs, depending upon who asks it.

Coming from those whose dominant consideration is peace — public peace and peace of mind — the question means: "When are you going to stop tempting violence and rioting?" Some put it more strongly: "When are you going to stop sponsoring violence?" Assumed is the necessary connection between demonstration and violence. . . .

"Isn't the patience of the white majority wearing thin? Why nourish the displeasure of 90 percent of the population with provocative demonstrations? Remember, you need allies." And the assumptions of these Cassandras of the backlash is that freedom and equality are, in the last analysis, wholly gifts in the white man's power to bestow. . . .

What the public must realize is that in a demonstration more things are happening, at more levels of human activity, than meets the eye. Demonstrations in the last few years have provided literally millions of Negroes with their first taste of self-determination and political self-expression.

**5. Stokely Carmichael and Charles Hamilton, *Black Power: The Politics of Liberation in America*, 1967.**

Black people must redefine themselves, and only they can do that. Throughout this country, vast segments of the black communities are beginning to recognize the need to assert their own definitions, to reclaim their history, their culture; to create their own sense of community and togetherness. There is a growing resentment of the word "Negro," for example, because this term is the invention of our oppressor; it is his image of us that he describes. . . .

The concept of Black Power rests on a fundamental premise: Before a group can enter the open society, it must first close ranks. By this we mean that group solidarity is necessary before a group can operate effectively from a bargaining position of strength in a pluralistic society.

**6. Black Power salute at the 1968 Olympics in Mexico City.** *Tommie Smith and John Carolos (right) won gold and bronze medals in the 200 meters. The silver medalist, Australian Peter Norman (left), is wearing an Olympic Project for Human Rights badge to show his support.*

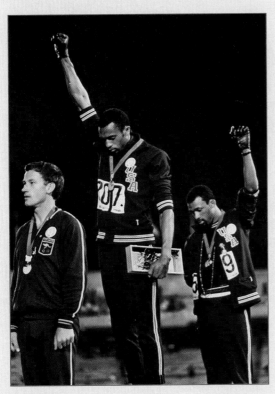

AP images.

Sources: (1) "If the Negro Wins, Labor Wins," by Martin Luther King delivered February 12, 1962. Reprinted by arrangement with the Heirs to the Estate of Martin Luther King Jr., c/o Writers House as agent for the proprietor, New York, NY. Copyright © 1962 Martin Luther King Jr. Copyright renewed 1991 Coretta Scott King; (3) *Commentary*, February 1965; (4) James Farmer, *Freedom, When?* (New York: Random House, 1965), 25–27, 42–47; (5) Stokely Carmichael and Charles V. Hamilton, *Black Power: The Politics of Liberation* (New York: Vintage, 1992, orig. 1967), 37, 44.

### ANALYZING THE EVIDENCE

1. Compare sources 1 and 3. What does Rustin mean when he says that ending segregation in public accommodations has not affected the "fundamental conditions" of African American life? How does King's point in document 1 address such issues?

2. Examine the two photographs. What do they reveal about different kinds of protest? About different perspectives among African Americans?

3. What does "self-determination" mean for Farmer and Carmichael and Hamilton?

### PUTTING IT ALL TOGETHER

Compose an essay in which you use the documents above, in addition to your reading of the chapter, to explore and explain different approaches to African American rights in the 1960s. In particular, think about how all of the documents come from a single movement, yet each expresses a distinct viewpoint and a distinct way of conceiving what "the struggle" is about. How do these approaches compare to the tactics of earlier struggles for civil rights?

**COMPARE AND CONTRAST**
In what ways did white resistance hinder the civil rights movement? In what ways did it help?

On assuming the presidency, Lyndon Johnson made passing the civil rights bill a priority. A southerner and former Senate majority leader, Johnson was renowned for his fierce persuasive style and tough political bargaining. Using equal parts moral leverage, the memory of the slain JFK, and his own brand of hardball politics, Johnson overcame the filibuster. In June 1964, Congress approved the most far-reaching civil rights law since Reconstruction. The keystone of the **Civil Rights Act of 1964**, Title VII, outlawed discrimination in employment on the basis of race, religion, national origin, and sex. Another section guaranteed equal access to public accommodations and schools. The law granted new enforcement powers to the U.S. attorney general and established the Equal Employment Opportunity Commission to implement the prohibition against job discrimination.

**Freedom Summer**   The Civil Rights Act was a law with real teeth, but it left untouched the obstacles to black voting rights. So protesters went back into the streets. In 1964, in what came to be known as Freedom Summer, black organizations mounted a major campaign in Mississippi. The effort drew several thousand volunteers from across the country, including nearly one thousand white college students from the North. Led by the charismatic SNCC activist Robert Moses, the four major civil rights organizations (SNCC, CORE, NAACP, and SCLC) spread out across the state. They established freedom schools for black children and conducted a major voter registration drive. Yet so determined was the opposition that only about twelve hundred black voters were registered that summer, at a cost of four murdered civil rights workers and thirty-seven black churches bombed or burned.

The murders strengthened the resolve of the **Mississippi Freedom Democratic Party** (MFDP), which had been founded during Freedom Summer. Banned

**Women in the Movement**

Though often overshadowed by men in the public spotlight, women were crucial to the black freedom movement. Here, protesting at the 1964 Democratic National Convention in Atlantic City, are (left to right) Fannie Lou Hamer, Eleanor Holmes, and Ella Baker. The men are (left to right) Emory Harris, Stokely Carmichael, and Sam Block. Hamer had been a sharecropper before she became a leader under Baker's tutelage, and Holmes was a Yale University–trained lawyer who went on to become the first female chair of the federal Equal Employment Opportunity Commission. © 1976 George Ballis/Take Stock/The Image Works.

from the "whites only" Mississippi Democratic Party, MFDP leaders were determined to attend the 1964 Democratic National Convention in Atlantic City, New Jersey, as the legitimate representatives of their state. Inspired by Fannie Lou Hamer, a former sharecropper turned civil rights activist, the MFDP challenged the most powerful figures in the Democratic Party, including Lyndon Johnson, the Democrats' presidential nominee. "Is this America?" Hamer asked party officials when she demanded that the MFDP, and not the all-white Mississippi delegation, be recognized by the convention. Democratic leaders, however, seated the white Mississippi delegation and refused to recognize the MFDP. Demoralized and convinced that the Democratic Party would not change, Moses told television reporters: "I will have nothing to do with the political system any longer."

### Selma and the Voting Rights Act
Martin Luther King Jr. and the SCLC did not share Moses's skepticism. They believed that another confrontation with southern injustice could provoke further congressional action. In March 1965, James Bevel of the SCLC called for a march from Selma, Alabama, to the state capital, Montgomery, to protest the murder of a voting-rights activist. As soon as the six hundred marchers left Selma, crossing over the Edmund Pettus Bridge, mounted state troopers attacked them with tear gas and clubs. The scene was shown on national television that night, and the day became known as Bloody Sunday. Calling the episode "an American tragedy," President Johnson went back to Congress.

The **Voting Rights Act of 1965**, which was signed by President Johnson on August 6, outlawed the literacy tests and other devices that prevented African Americans from registering to vote, and authorized the attorney general to send federal examiners to register voters in any county where registration was less than 50 percent. Together with the Twenty-fourth Amendment (1964), which outlawed the poll tax in federal elections, the Voting Rights Act enabled millions of African Americans to vote for the first time since the Reconstruction era.

In the South, the results were stunning. In 1960, only 20 percent of black citizens had been registered to vote; by 1971, registration reached 62 percent (Map 27.4). Moreover, across the nation the number of black elected officials began to climb, quadrupling from 1,400 to 4,900 between 1970 and 1980 and doubling again by the early 1990s. Most of those elected held local offices—from sheriff to county commissioner—but nonetheless embodied a shift in political representation nearly unimaginable a generation earlier. As Hartman Turnbow, a Mississippi farmer who risked his life to register in 1964, later declared, "It won't never go back where it was."

Something else would never go back either: the liberal New Deal coalition. By the second half of the 1960s, the liberal wing of the Democratic Party had won its battle with the conservative, segregationist wing. Democrats had embraced the civil rights movement and made African American equality a cornerstone of a new "rights" liberalism. But over the next generation, between the 1960s and the 1980s, southern whites and many conservative northern whites would respond by switching to the Republican Party. Strom Thurmond, the segregationist senator from South Carolina, symbolically led the revolt by renouncing the

**MAP 27.4**

**Black Voter Registration in the South, 1964 and 1975**

After passage of the Voting Rights Act of 1965, black registration in the South increased dramatically. The bars on the map show the number of African Americans registered in 1964, before the act was passed, and in 1975, after it had been in effect for ten years. States in the Deep South, such as Mississippi, Alabama, and Georgia, had the biggest increases.

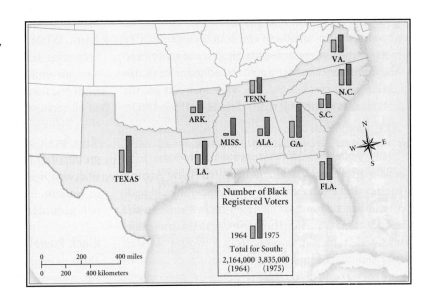

Democrats and becoming a Republican in 1964. The New Deal coalition — which had joined working-class whites, northern African Americans, urban professionals, and white southern segregationists together in a fragile political alliance since the 1930s — was beginning to crumble.

# Beyond Civil Rights, 1966–1973

Activists had long known that Supreme Court decisions and new laws do not automatically produce changes in society. But in the mid-1960s, civil rights advocates confronted a more profound issue: perhaps even protests were not enough. In 1965, Bayard Rustin wrote of the need to move "from protest to politics" in order to build institutional black power. Some black leaders, such as the young SNCC activists Stokely Carmichael, Frances Beal, and John Lewis, grew frustrated with the slow pace of reform and the stubborn resistance of whites. Still others believed that addressing black poverty and economic disadvantage remained the most important objective. Neither new laws nor long marches appeared capable of meeting these varied and complex challenges.

The conviction that civil rights alone were incapable of guaranteeing equality took hold in many minority communities in this period. African Americans were joined by Mexican Americans, Puerto Ricans, and American Indians. They came at the problem of inequality from different perspectives, but each group asked a similar question: As crucial as legal equality was, how much did it matter if most people of color remained in or close to poverty, if white society still regarded nonwhites as inferior, and if the major social and political institutions in the country were run by whites? Black leaders and representatives of other nonwhite communities increasingly asked themselves this question as they searched for ways to build on the achievements of the civil rights decade of 1954–1965.

## Black Nationalism

Seeking answers to these questions led many African Americans to embrace **black nationalism**. The philosophy of black nationalism signified many things in the 1960s. It could mean anything from pride in one's community to total separatism, from building African American–owned businesses to wearing dashikis in honor of African traditions. Historically, nationalism had emphasized the differences between blacks and whites as well as black people's power (and right) to shape their own destiny. In the late nineteenth century, nationalists founded the Back to Africa movement, and in the 1920s the nationalist Marcus Garvey inspired African Americans to take pride in their racial heritage (Chapter 22).

In the early 1960s, the leading exponent of black nationalism was the **Nation of Islam**, which fused a rejection of Christianity with a strong philosophy of self-improvement. Black Muslims, as they were known, adhered to a strict code of personal behavior; men were recognizable by their dark suits, white shirts, and ties, women by their long dresses and head coverings. Black Muslims preached an apocalyptic brand of Islam, anticipating the day when Allah would banish the white "devils" and give the black nation justice. Although its full converts numbered only about ten thousand, the Nation of Islam had a wide popular following among African Americans in northern cities.

**Malcolm X**    The most charismatic Black Muslim was Malcolm X (the *X* stood for his African family name, lost under slavery). A spellbinding speaker, Malcolm X preached a philosophy of militant separatism, although he advocated violence only for self-defense. Hostile to mainstream civil rights organizations, he caustically referred to the 1963 March on Washington as the "Farce on Washington." Malcolm X said plainly, "I believe in the brotherhood of man, all men, but I don't believe in brotherhood with anybody who doesn't want brotherhood with me." Malcolm X had little interest in changing the minds of hostile whites. Strengthening the black community, he believed, represented a surer path to freedom and equality.

In 1964, after a power struggle with founder Elijah Muhammad, Malcolm X broke with the Nation of Islam. While he remained a black nationalist, he moderated his antiwhite views and began to talk of a class struggle uniting poor whites and blacks. Following an inspiring trip to the Middle East, where he saw Muslims of all races worshipping together, Malcolm X formed the Organization of Afro-American Unity to promote black pride and to work with traditional civil rights groups. But he got no further. On February 21, 1965, Malcolm X was assassinated while delivering a speech in Harlem. Three Black Muslims were later convicted of his murder.

**Black Power**    A more secular brand of black nationalism emerged in 1966 when SNCC and CORE activists, following the lead of Stokely Carmichael, began to

**Malcolm X**

Until his murder in 1965, Malcolm X was the leading proponent of black nationalism in the United States. A brilliant and dynamic orator, Malcolm had been a minister in the Nation of Islam for nearly thirteen years, until he broke with the Nation in 1964. His emphasis on black pride and self-help and his unrelenting criticism of white supremacy made him one of the freedom movement's most inspirational figures, both in life and well after his death. ©Topham/The Image Works.

call for black self-reliance under the banner of Black Power. Advocates of Black Power asked fundamental questions: If alliances with whites were necessary to achieve racial justice, as King believed they were, did that make African Americans dependent on the good intentions of whites? If so, could black people trust those good intentions in the long run? Increasingly, those inclined toward Black Power believed that African Americans should build economic and political power in their own communities. Such power would translate into a less dependent relationship with white America. "For once," Carmichael wrote, "black people are going to use the words they want to use — not the words whites want to hear."

Spurred by the Black Power slogan, African American activists turned their attention to the poverty and social injustice faced by so many black people. President Johnson had declared the War on Poverty, and black organizers joined, setting up day care centers, running community job training programs, and working to improve housing and health care in urban neighborhoods. In major cities such as Philadelphia, New York, Chicago, and Pittsburgh, activists sought to

open jobs in police and fire departments and in construction and transportation to black workers, who had been excluded from these occupations for decades. Others worked to end police harassment — a major problem in urban black communities — and to help black entrepreneurs to receive small-business loans. CORE leader Floyd McKissick explained, "Black Power is not Black Supremacy; it is a united Black Voice reflecting racial pride."

> **UNDERSTAND POINTS OF VIEW**
>
> Why were Black Power and black nationalism compelling to many African Americans?

The attention to racial pride led some African Americans to reject white society and to pursue more authentic cultural forms. In addition to focusing on economic disadvantage, Black Power emphasized black pride and self-determination. Those subscribing to these beliefs wore African clothing, chose natural hairstyles, and celebrated black history, art, and literature. The Black Arts movement thrived, and musical tastes shifted from the crossover sounds of Motown to the soul music of Philadelphia, Memphis, and Chicago.

**Black Panther Party**    One of the most radical nationalist groups was the **Black Panther Party**, founded in Oakland, California, in 1966 by two college students, Huey Newton and Bobby Seale. A militant organization dedicated to protecting African Americans from police violence, the Panthers took their cue from the slain Malcolm X. They vehemently opposed the Vietnam War and declared their affinity for Third World revolutionary movements and armed struggle (Map 27.5). In their manifesto, "What We Want, What We Believe," the Panthers outlined their Ten Point Program for black liberation.

The Panthers' organization spread to other cities in the late 1960s, where members undertook a wide range of community-organizing projects. Their free breakfast program for children and their testing program for sickle-cell anemia, an inherited disease with a high incidence among African Americans, were especially popular. However, the Panthers' radicalism and belief in armed self-defense resulted in violent clashes with police. Newton was charged with murdering a police

officer, several Panthers were killed by police, and dozens went to prison. Moreover, under its domestic counterintelligence program, the Federal Bureau of Investigation (FBI) had begun disrupting party activities.

**Young Lords**    Among those inspired by the Black Panthers were Puerto Ricans in New York. Their vehicle was the **Young Lords Organization** (YLO), later renamed the Young Lords Party. Like the Black Panthers, YLO activists sought self-determination for Puerto Ricans, both those in the United States and those on the island in the Caribbean. In practical terms, the YLO focused on improving neighborhood conditions: city garbage collection was notoriously poor in East Harlem, where most Puerto Ricans lived, and slumlords had allowed the housing to become squalid. Women in the YLO were especially active, protesting sterilization campaigns against Puerto Rican women and fighting to improve access to health care. As was true of so many nationalist groups, immediate victories for the YLO were few, but their dedicated community

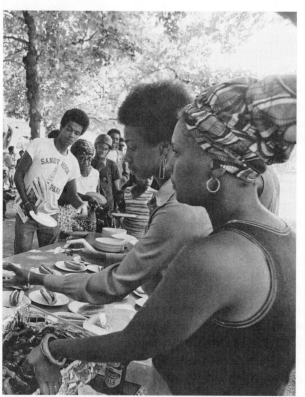

**The Black Panther Party**

One of the most radical organizations of the 1960s, the Black Panther Party was founded in 1966 by Bobby Seale and Huey Newton (shown together in the photograph on the left) in Oakland, California. Its members carried weapons, advocated socialism, and fought police brutality in black communities, but they also ran into their own trouble with the law. Nevertheless, the party had great success in reaching ordinary people, often with programs targeted at the poor. On the right, party members distribute free hot dogs to the public in New Haven, Connecticut, in 1969. LEFT: Bruno Barbey/Magnum Photos. RIGHT: Photo by David Fenton/Getty Images.

**MAP 27.5**
**Decolonization and the Third World, 1943–1990**

In the decades after World War II, African nations threw off the yoke of European colonialism. Some new nations, such as Ghana, the former British colony of Gold Coast, achieved independence rather peacefully. Others, such as Algeria and Mozambique, did so only after bloody anticolonial wars. American civil rights activists watched African decolonization with great enthusiasm, seeing the two struggles as linked. "Sure we identified with the blacks in Africa," civil rights leader John Lewis said. "Here were black people, talking of freedom and liberation and independence thousands of miles away." In 1960 alone, the year that student sit-ins swept across the American South, more than a dozen African nations gained independence.

organizing produced a generation of leaders (many of whom later went into politics) and awakened community consciousness.

**The New Urban Politics**   Black Power also inspired African Americans to work within the political system. By the mid-1960s, black residents neared 50 percent of the population in several major American cities — such as Atlanta, Cleveland, Detroit, and Washington, D.C. Black Power in these cities was not abstract; it counted in real votes. Residents of Gary, Indiana, and Cleveland, Ohio, elected the first black mayors of large cities in 1967. Richard Hatcher in Gary and Carl Stokes in Cleveland helped forge a new urban politics in the United States. Their campaign teams registered thousands of black voters and made alliances with enough whites to create a working majority. Many saw Stokes's victory, in particular, as heralding a new day. As one of Stokes's campaign staffers said: "If Carl Stokes could run for mayor in the eighth largest city in America, then maybe who knows. We could be senators. We could be anything we wanted."

Having met with some political success, black leaders gathered in Gary for the 1972 National Black Political Convention. In a meeting that brought together radicals, liberals, and centrists, debate centered on whether to form a third political party. Hatcher recalled that many in attendance believed that "there was going to be a black third party." In the end, however, delegates decided to "give the Democratic Party one more chance." Instead of creating a third party, the convention issued the National Black Political Agenda, which included calls for community control of schools in black neighborhoods, national health insurance, and the elimination of the death penalty.

Democrats failed to enact the National Black Political Agenda, but African Americans were increasingly integrated into American political institutions. By the end of the century, black elected officials had become commonplace in major American cities. There were forty-seven African American big-city mayors by the 1990s, and blacks had led most of the nation's most prominent cities: Atlanta, Chicago, Detroit, Los Angeles, New York, Philadelphia, and Washington, D.C.

These politicians had translated black power not into a wholesale rejection of white society but into a revitalized liberalism that would remain an indelible feature of urban politics for the rest of the century.

## Poverty and Urban Violence

Black Power was not, fundamentally, a violent political ideology. But violence did play a decisive role in the politics of black liberation in the mid-1960s. Too many Americans, white and black, had little knowledge or understanding of the rage that existed just below the surface in many poor northern black neighborhoods. That rage boiled over in a wave of riots that struck the nation's cities in mid-decade. The first "long hot summer" began in July 1964 in New York City when police shot a black criminal suspect in Harlem. Angry youths looted and rioted there for a week. Over the next four years, the volatile issue of police brutality set off riots in dozens of cities.

In August 1965, the arrest of a young black motorist in the Watts section of Los Angeles sparked six days of rioting that left thirty-four people dead. "There is a different type of Negro emerging," one riot participant told investigators. "They are not going to wait for the evolutionary process for their rights to be a man." The riots of 1967, however, were the most serious, engulfing twenty-two cities in July and August. Forty-three people were killed in Detroit alone, nearly all of them black, and $50 million worth of property was destroyed. President Johnson called in the National Guard and U.S. Army troops, many of them having just returned from Vietnam, to restore order.

Johnson, who believed that the Civil Rights Act and the Voting Rights Act had immeasurably helped African Americans, was stunned by the rioting. Despondent at the news from Watts, "he refused to look at the cables from Los Angeles," recalled one aide. Virtually all black leaders condemned the rioting, though they understood its origins in poverty and deprivation. At a meeting in Watts, Martin Luther King Jr. admitted that he had "failed to take the civil rights movement to the masses of the people," such as those in the Los Angeles ghetto. His appearance appeased few. "We don't need your dreams; we need jobs!" one heckler shouted at King.

Following the gut-wrenching riots in Detroit and Newark in 1967, Johnson appointed a presidential commission, headed by Illinois governor Otto Kerner, to investigate the causes of the violence. Released in 1968, the Kerner Commission Report was a searing look at race in America, the most honest and forthright government document about race since the Presidential Committee on Civil Rights' 1947 report "To Secure These Rights." "Our nation is moving toward two societies," the Kerner Commission Report concluded, "one black, one white — separate and unequal." The report did not excuse the brick-throwing, firebombing, and looting of the previous summers, but it placed the riots in sociological context. Shut out of white-dominated society, impoverished African Americans felt they had no stake in the social order.

Stirred by turmoil in the cities, and seeing the limitations of his civil rights achievements, Martin Luther King Jr. began to expand his vision beyond civil rights to confront the deep-seated problems of poverty and racism in America as a whole. He criticized President Johnson and Congress for prioritizing the war in Vietnam over the fight against poverty at home, and he planned a massive movement called the Poor People's Campaign to fight economic injustice. To advance that cause, he went to Memphis, Tennessee, to support a strike by predominantly black sanitation workers. There, on April 4, 1968, he was assassinated by escaped white convict James Earl Ray. King's death set off a further round of urban rioting, with major violence breaking out in more than a hundred cities.

Tragically, King was murdered before achieving the transformations he sought: an end to racial injustice and a solution to poverty. The civil rights movement had helped set in motion permanent, indeed revolutionary, changes in American race relations. Jim Crow segregation ended, federal legislation ensured black Americans' most basic civil rights, and the white monopoly on political power in the South was broken. However, by 1968, the fight over civil rights had also divided the nation. The Democratic Party was splitting, and a new conservatism was gaining strength. Many whites felt that the issue of civil rights was receiving too much attention, to the detriment of other national concerns. The riots of 1965, 1967, and 1968 further alienated many whites, who blamed the violence on the inability of Democratic officials to maintain law and order.

## Rise of the Chicano Movement

Mexican Americans had something of a counterpart to Martin Luther King: Cesar Chavez. In Chavez's case, however, economic struggle in community organizations and the labor movement had shaped his approach to mobilizing society's disadvantaged. He and Dolores Huerta had worked for the Community Service Organization (CSO), a California group founded in the 1950s to promote Mexican political participation and civil rights. Leaving that organization in 1962, Chavez concentrated on the agricultural region around Delano,

California. With Huerta, he organized the **United Farm Workers (UFW)**, a union for migrant workers.

Huerta was a brilliant organizer, but the deeply spiritual and ascetic Chavez embodied the moral force behind what was popularly called La Causa. A 1965 grape pickers' strike led the UFW to call a nationwide boycott of table grapes, bringing Chavez huge publicity and backing from the AFL-CIO. In a bid for attention to the struggle, Chavez staged a hunger strike in 1968, which ended dramatically after twenty-eight days with Senator Robert F. Kennedy at his side to break the fast. Victory came in 1970 when California grape growers signed contracts recognizing the UFW.

Mexican Americans shared some civil rights concerns with African Americans—especially access to jobs—but they also had unique concerns: the status of the Spanish language in schools, for instance, and immigration policy. Mexican Americans had been politically active since the 1940s, aiming to surmount factors that obstructed their political involvement: poverty, language barriers, and discrimination. Their efforts began to pay off in the 1960s, when the Mexican American Political Association (MAPA) mobilized support for John F. Kennedy and worked successfully with other organizations to elect Mexican American candidates such as Edward Roybal of California and Henry González of Texas to Congress. Two other organizations, the Mexican American Legal Defense Fund (MALDF) and the Southwest Voter Registration and Education Project, carried the fight against discrimination to Washington, D.C., and mobilized Mexican Americans into an increasingly powerful voting bloc.

Younger Mexican Americans grew impatient with civil rights groups such as MAPA and MALDF, however. The barrios of Los Angeles and other western cities produced the militant Brown Berets, modeled on the Black Panthers (who wore black berets). Rejecting their elders' assimilationist approach (that is, a belief in adapting to Anglo society), fifteen hundred Mexican American students met in Denver in 1969 to hammer out a new political and cultural agenda. They proclaimed a new term, *Chicano* (and its feminine form, *Chicana*), to replace *Mexican American*, and later organized a political party, La Raza Unida (The United Race), to promote Chicano interests. Young Chicana feminists formed a number of organizations, including Las Hijas (The Daughters), which organized women both on college campuses and in the barrios. In California and many southwestern states, students staged demonstrations to press for bilingual education, the hiring of more Chicano teachers, and the creation of Chicano studies programs. By the 1970s, dozens of such programs were offered at universities throughout the region.

**COMPARE AND CONTRAST**
What did the Chicano and American Indian movements have in common with the black freedom movement?

## The American Indian Movement

American Indians, inspired by the Black Power and Chicano movements, organized to address their unique circumstances. Numbering nearly 800,000 in the 1960s, native people were exceedingly diverse—divided by

**Cesar Chavez**

Influenced equally by the Catholic Church and Mahatma Gandhi, Cesar Chavez was one of the leading Mexican American civil rights and social justice activists of the 1960s. With Dolores Huerta, he cofounded the United Farm Workers (UFW), a union of primarily Mexican American agricultural laborers in California. Here he speaks at a rally in support of the grape boycott, an attempt by the UFW to force the nation's grape growers—and, by extension, the larger agriculture industry—to improve wages and working conditions and to bargain in good faith with the union. © Jason Laure/The Image Works.

language, tribal history, region, and degree of integration into American life. As a group, they shared a staggering unemployment rate — ten times the national average — and were the worst off in housing, disease rates, and access to education. Native people also had an often troubling relationship with the federal government. In the 1960s, the prevailing spirit of protest swept through Indian communities. Young militants challenged their elders in the National Congress of American Indians. Beginning in 1960, the National Indian Youth Council (NIYC), under the slogan "For a Greater Indian America," promoted the ideal of Native Americans as a single ethnic group. The effort to both unite Indians and celebrate individual tribal culture proved a difficult balancing act.

The NIYC had substantial influence within tribal communities, but two other organizations, the militant Indians of All Tribes (IAT) and the **American Indian Movement (AIM)**, attracted more attention in the larger society. These groups embraced the concept of Red Power, and beginning in 1968 they staged escalating protests to draw attention to Indian concerns, especially the concerns of urban Indians, many of whom had been encouraged, or forced, to leave reservations by the federal government in earlier decades. In 1969, members of the IAT occupied the deserted federal penitentiary on

Alcatraz Island in San Francisco Bay and proclaimed: "We will purchase said Alcatraz Island for twenty-four dollars in glass beads and red cloth, a precedent set by the white man's purchase of a similar island [Manhattan] about 300 years ago." In 1972, AIM members joined the Trail of Broken Treaties, a march sponsored by a number of Indian groups. When AIM activists seized the headquarters of the hated Bureau of Indian Affairs in Washington, D.C., and ransacked the building, older tribal leaders denounced them.

 To see a longer excerpt of the "Proclamation To the Great White Father and All His People," along with other primary sources from this period, see *Sources for America's History*.

However, AIM managed to focus national media attention on Native American issues with a siege at Wounded Knee, South Dakota, in February 1973. The site of the infamous 1890 massacre of the Sioux, Wounded Knee was situated on the Pine Ridge Reservation, where young AIM activists had cultivated ties to sympathetic elders. For more than two months, AIM members occupied a small collection of buildings, surrounded by a cordon of FBI agents and U.S. marshals. Several gun battles left two dead, and the siege was finally brought to a negotiated end. Although upsetting

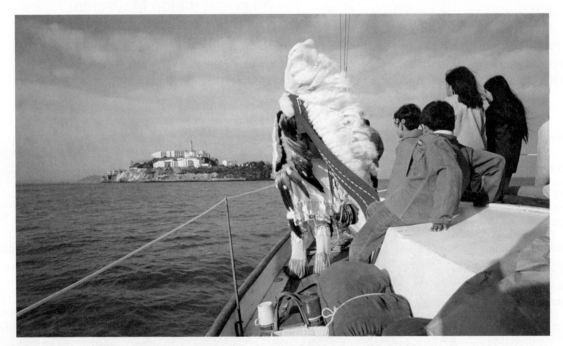

**Native American Activism**

In November 1969, a group of Native Americans, united under the name *Indians of All Tribes*, occupied Alcatraz Island in San Francisco Bay. They claimed the land under a nineteenth-century treaty, but their larger objective was to force the federal government — which owned the island — to address the long-standing grievances of native peoples, including widespread poverty on reservations. Shown here is the view along the gunwale of the boat carrying Tim Williams, a chief of the Klamath River Hurek tribe in full ceremonial regalia, to the island. Ralph Crane/Time Life Pictures/Getty Images.

to many white onlookers and Indian elders alike, AIM protests attracted widespread mainstream media coverage and spurred government action on tribal issues.

# SUMMARY

African Americans and others who fought for civil rights from World War II through the early 1970s sought equal rights and economic opportunity. That quest was also inspired by various forms of nationalism that called for self-determination for minority groups. For most of the first half of the twentieth century, African Americans faced a harsh Jim Crow system in the South and a segregated, though more open, society in the North. Segregation was maintained by a widespread belief in black inferiority and by a southern political system that denied African Americans the vote. In the Southwest and West, Mexican Americans, Native Americans, and Americans of Asian descent faced discriminatory laws and social practices that marginalized them.

The civil rights movement attacked racial inequality in three ways. First, the movement sought equality under the law for all Americans, regardless of race. This required patient work through the judicial system and the more arduous task of winning congressional legislation, such as the Civil Rights Act of 1964 and the Voting Rights Act of 1965. Second, grassroots activists, using nonviolent protest, pushed all levels of government (from city to federal) to abide by Supreme Court decisions (such as *Brown v. Board of Education*) and civil rights laws. Third, the movement worked to open economic opportunity for minority populations. This was embodied in the 1963 March on Washington for Jobs and Freedom. Ultimately, the civil rights movement successfully established the principle of legal equality, but it faced more difficult problems in fighting poverty and creating widespread economic opportunity.

The limitations of the civil rights model led black activists—along with Mexican Americans, Native Americans, and others—to adopt a more nationalist stance after 1966. Nationalism stressed the creation of political and economic power in communities of color, the celebration of racial heritage, and the rejection of white cultural standards.

# C H A P T E R   R E V I E W

**MAKE IT STICK**    Go to **LearningCurve** to retain what you've read.

## TERMS TO KNOW    Identify and explain the significance of each term below.

### Key Concepts and Events

rights liberalism (p. 868)

Congress of Racial Equality (CORE) (p. 870)

Jim Crow (p. 870)

Brotherhood of Sleeping Car Porters (p. 873)

"To Secure These Rights" (p. 875)

States' Rights Democratic Party (p. 875)

American GI Forum (p. 877)

*Brown v. Board of Education of Topeka* (p. 878)

Montgomery Bus Boycott (p. 881)

Southern Christian Leadership Conference (SCLC) (p. 882)

Student Nonviolent Coordinating Committee (SNCC) (p. 882)

March on Washington (p. 886)

Civil Rights Act of 1964 (p. 890)

Mississippi Freedom Democratic Party (p. 890)

Voting Rights Act of 1965 (p. 891)

black nationalism (p. 892)

Nation of Islam (p. 892)

Black Panther Party (p. 894)

Young Lords Organization (p. 894)

United Farm Workers (UFW) (p. 897)

American Indian Movement (AIM) (p. 898)

### Key People

A. Philip Randolph (p. 873)

James Farmer (p. 873)

Cesar Chavez (p. 877)

Dolores Huerta (p. 877)

Thurgood Marshall (p. 877)

Rosa Parks (p. 881)

Martin Luther King Jr. (p. 881)

Malcolm X (p. 892)

Stokely Carmichael (p. 892)

## REVIEW QUESTIONS
Answer these questions to demonstrate your understanding of the chapter's main ideas.

**1.** Why did the civil rights movement begin when it did?

**2.** How would you explain the rise of the protest movement after 1955? How did nonviolent tactics help the movement?

**3.** How did the civil rights movement create a crisis in liberalism and in the Democratic Party?

**4.** How did the civil rights movement and other activist groups cause changes to government and society?

**5. THEMATIC UNDERSTANDING** One of the most significant themes of the period from 1945 to the 1980s is the growth of the power of the federal government. (See "Politics and Power" and "Identity" on the thematic timeline on p. 803.) In what ways is the civil rights movement also part of that story?

## MAKING CONNECTIONS
Recognize the larger developments and continuities within and across chapters by answering these questions.

**1. ACROSS TIME AND PLACE** Why is the decade of the 1960s often referred to as the "second Reconstruction"? Think broadly about the century between the end of the Civil War in 1865 and the passage of the Voting Rights Act of 1965. What are the key turning points in African American history in that long period?

**2. VISUAL EVIDENCE** Examine the photograph of a confrontation at North Little Rock High School on page 881. How does this photograph reveal the role that the media played in the civil rights struggle? Can you find similar evidence in other photographs from this chapter?

## MORE TO EXPLORE
Start here to learn more about the events discussed in this chapter.

Peniel Joseph, *Waiting 'til the Midnight Hour: A Narrative History of Black Power in America* (2006). An important history of Black Power.

Ian F. Haney López, *Racism on Trial: The Chicano Fight for Justice* (2003). An exceptional case study of the Chicano movement in Los Angeles.

Charles Payne, *I've Got the Light of Freedom: The Organizing Tradition and the Mississippi Freedom Struggle* (1995). A detailed case study that provides a local view of movement activism.

Barbara Ransby, *Ella Baker and the Black Freedom Movement* (2003). A powerful biography of a key activist.

Thomas J. Sugrue, *Sweet Land of Liberty: The Forgotten Struggle for Civil Rights in the North* (2008). A significant, readable overview of the civil rights movement.

The Civil Rights in Mississippi Digital Archive, at **digilib.usm.edu/crmda.php**, offers 150 oral histories relating to Mississippi.

## TIMELINE

Ask yourself why this chapter begins and ends with these dates and then identify the links among related events.

| | |
|---|---|
| **1941** | • A. Philip Randolph proposes march on Washington<br>• Roosevelt issues Executive Order 8802 |
| **1942** | • Double V Campaign launched<br>• Congress of Racial Equality (CORE) founded |
| **1947** | • "To Secure These Rights" published<br>• Jackie Robinson integrates major league baseball<br>• *Mendez v. Westminster School District* |
| **1948** | • States' Rights Democratic Party (Dixiecrats) founded |
| **1954** | • *Brown v. Board of Education of Topeka* |
| **1955** | • Emmett Till murdered (August)<br>• Montgomery Bus Boycott (December) |
| **1956** | • Southern Manifesto issued against *Brown* ruling |
| **1957** | • Integration of Little Rock High School<br>• Southern Christian Leadership Conference (SCLC) founded |
| **1960** | • Greensboro, North Carolina, sit-ins (February)<br>• Student Nonviolent Coordinating Committee (SNCC) founded |
| **1961** | • Freedom Rides (May) |
| **1963** | • Demonstrations in Birmingham, Alabama<br>• March on Washington for Jobs and Freedom |
| **1964** | • Civil Rights Act passed by Congress<br>• Freedom Summer |
| **1965** | • Voting Rights Act passed by Congress<br>• Malcolm X assassinated (February 21)<br>• Riot in Watts neighborhood of Los Angeles (August) |
| **1966** | • Black Panther Party founded |
| **1967** | • Riots in Detroit and Newark |
| **1968** | • Martin Luther King Jr. assassinated (April 4) |
| **1969** | • Young Lords founded<br>• Occupation of Alcatraz |
| **1972** | • National Black Political Convention<br>• "Trail of Broken Treaties" protest |

**KEY TURNING POINTS:** The history of the civil rights movement is more than a list of significant events. Pick two or three events from this timeline and explain how their timing and the broader historical context contributed to the precise role each played in the movement as a whole.

# 28
## CHAPTER

# Uncivil Wars: Liberal Crisis and Conservative Rebirth
# 1961–1972

The civil rights movement stirred American liberals and pushed them to initiate bold new government policies to advance racial equality. That progressive spirit inspired an even broader reform agenda that came to include women's rights, new social programs for the poor and the aged, job training, environmental laws, and other educational and social benefits for the middle class. All told, Congress passed more liberal legislation between 1964 and 1972 than in any period since the 1930s. The great bulk of it came during the 1965–1966 legislative session, one of the most active in American history. Liberalism was at high tide.

It did not stay there long. Liberals quickly came under assault from two directions. First, young activists became frustrated with slow progress on civil rights and rebelled against the Vietnam War. At the 1968 Democratic National Convention in Chicago, police teargassed and clubbed antiwar demonstrators, who chanted (as the TV cameras rolled), "The whole world is watching!" Some of them had been among the young idealists inspired by Kennedy's inaugural address and the civil rights movement. Now they rejected everything that Cold War liberalism stood for. Inside the convention hall, the proceedings were chaotic, the atmosphere poisonous, the delegates bitterly divided over Vietnam.

A second assault on liberalism came from conservatives, who found their footing after being marginalized during the 1950s. Conservatives opposed the dramatic expansion of the federal government under President Lyndon B. Johnson and disdained the "permissive society" they believed liberalism had unleashed. Advocating law and order, belittling welfare, and resisting key civil rights reforms, conservatives leaped back to political life in the late sixties. Their champion was Barry Goldwater, a Republican senator from Arizona, who warned that "a government big enough to give you everything you want is also big enough to take away everything you have."

The clashing of left, right, and center made the decade between the inauguration of President John F. Kennedy in 1961 and the 1972 landslide reelection of Richard Nixon one of the most contentious, complicated, and explosive eras in American history. There were thousands of marches and demonstrations; massive new federal programs aimed at achieving civil rights, ending poverty, and extending the welfare state; and new voices among women, African Americans, and Latinos demanding to be heard. With heated, vitriolic rhetoric on all sides, these developments overlapped with political assassinations and violence both overseas and at home. In this chapter, we undertake to explain how the rekindling of liberal reform under the twin auspices of the civil rights movement and the leadership of President Johnson gave way to a profound liberal crisis and the resurgence of conservatism.

## IDENTIFY THE BIG IDEA

What were liberalism's social and political achievements in the 1960s, and how did debates over liberal values contribute to conflict at home and reflect tension abroad?

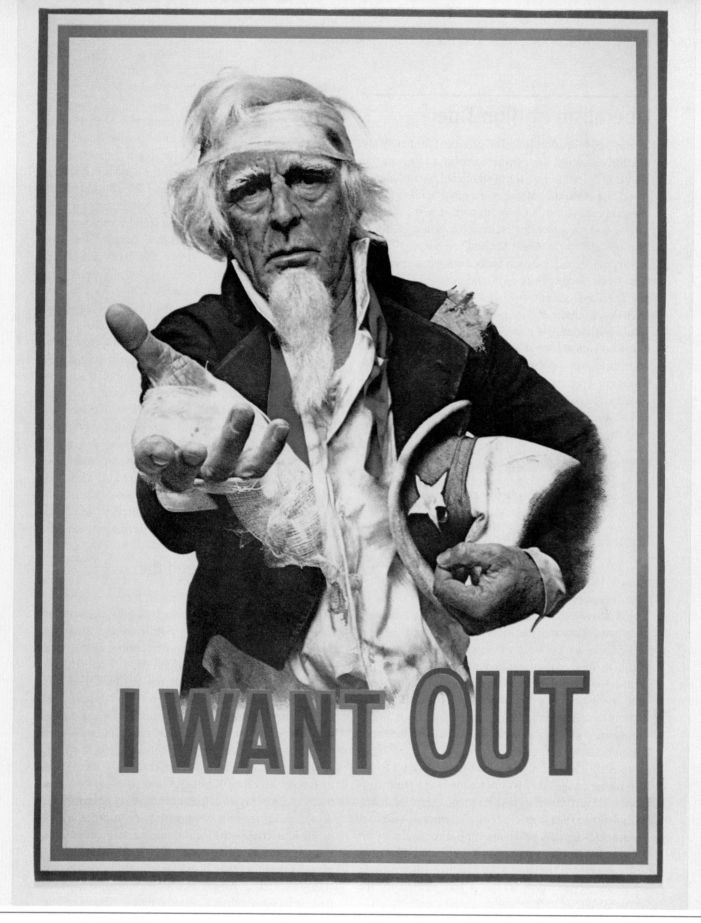

**"I Want Out"** Protest movements of all kinds shook the foundations of American society and national politics in the 1960s. No issue was more controversial and divisive than the war in Vietnam. Private Collection/ Peter Newark American Pictures/The Bridgeman Art Library.

# Liberalism at High Tide

In May 1964, Lyndon Johnson, president for barely six months, delivered the commencement address at the University of Michigan. Johnson offered his audience a grand and inspirational vision of a new liberal age. "We have the opportunity to move not only toward the rich society and the powerful society," Johnson continued, "but upward to the **Great Society**." As the sun-baked graduates listened, Johnson spelled out what he meant: "The Great Society rests on abundance and liberty for all. It demands an end to poverty and racial injustice." Even this, Johnson declared, was just the beginning. He would push to renew American education, rebuild the cities, and restore the natural environment. Ambitious — even audacious — Johnson's vision was a New Deal for a new era. From that day forward, the president would harness his considerable political skills to make that vision a reality. A tragic irony, however, was that he held the presidency at all.

 To see a longer excerpt of Johnson's commencement address, along with other primary sources from this period, see *Sources for America's History*.

## John F. Kennedy's Promise

In 1961, three years before Johnson's Great Society speech, John F. Kennedy declared at his inauguration: "Let the word go forth from this time and place, to friend and foe alike, that the torch has been passed to a new generation of Americans." He challenged his fellow citizens to "ask what you can do for your country," a call to service that inspired many Americans. The British journalist Henry Fairley called Kennedy's activism "the politics of expectation." Over time, the expectations Kennedy embodied, combined with his ability to inspire a younger generation, laid the groundwork for an era of liberal reform.

Kennedy's legislative record did not live up to his promising image. This was not entirely his fault; congressional partisanship and resistance stymied many presidents in the twentieth century. Kennedy's domestic advisors devised bold plans for health insurance for the aged, a new antipoverty program, and a tax cut. After enormous pressure from Martin Luther King Jr. and other civil rights leaders — and pushed by the demonstrations in Birmingham, Alabama, in 1963 — they added a civil rights bill. None of these initiatives went anywhere in the Senate, where powerful conservative interests practiced an old legislative art: delay,

delay, delay. All Kennedy's bills were at a virtual standstill when tragedy struck.

On November 22, 1963, Kennedy was in Dallas, Texas, on a political trip. As he and his wife, Jacqueline, rode in an open car past the Texas School Book Depository, he was shot through the head and neck by a sniper. He died within the hour. (The accused killer, twenty-four-year-old Lee Harvey Oswald, was himself killed while in custody a few days later by an assassin, a Dallas nightclub owner named Jack Ruby.) Before Air Force One left Dallas to take the president's body back to Washington, a grim-faced Lyndon Johnson was sworn in as Kennedy's successor.

Kennedy's youthful image, the trauma of his assassination, and the nation's sense of loss contributed to a powerful Kennedy mystique. His canonization after death capped what had been an extraordinarily stage-managed presidency. An admiring country saw in Jack and Jackie Kennedy an ideal American marriage (though JFK was, in fact, an obsessive womanizer); in Kennedy the epitome of robust good health (though he was actually afflicted by Addison's disease); and in the Kennedy White House a glamorous world of high fashion and celebrity. No other presidency ever matched the Kennedy aura, but every president after him embraced the idea that image mattered as much as reality in conducting a politically effective presidency.

## Lyndon B. Johnson and the Great Society

In many ways, Lyndon Johnson was the opposite of Kennedy. A seasoned Texas politician and longtime Senate leader, Johnson was most at home in the back rooms of power. He was a rough-edged character who had scrambled his way up, with few scruples, to wealth and political eminence. But he never forgot his modest, hill-country origins or lost his sympathy for the downtrodden. Johnson lacked Kennedy's style, but he rose to the political challenge after Kennedy's assassination, applying his astonishing energy and negotiating skills to revive several of Kennedy's stalled programs, and many more of his own, in the ambitious Great Society.

On assuming the presidency, Johnson promptly pushed for civil rights legislation as a memorial to his slain predecessor (Chapter 27). His motives were complex. As a southerner who had previously opposed civil rights for African Americans, Johnson wished to prove that he was more than a regional figure — he would be the president of all the people. He also wanted to make a mark on history, telling Martin Luther King Jr. and other civil rights leaders to lace up their sneakers

## The Great Society

President Lyndon Johnson toured poverty-stricken regions of the country in 1964. Here he visits with Tom Fletcher, a father of eight children in Martin County, Kentucky. Johnson envisioned a dramatic expansion of liberal social programs, both to assist the needy and to strengthen the middle class, that he called the Great Society. © Bettmann/Corbis.

because he would move so fast on civil rights they would be running to catch up. Politically, the choice was risky. Johnson would please the Democratic Party's liberal wing, but because most northern African Americans already voted Democratic, the party would gain few additional votes. Moreover, southern white Democrats would likely revolt, dividing the party at a time when Johnson's legislative agenda most required unanimity. But Johnson pushed ahead, and the 1964 Civil Rights Act stands, in part, as a testament to the president's political risk-taking.

More than civil rights, what drove Johnson hardest was his determination to "end poverty in our time." The president called it a national disgrace that in the midst of plenty, one-fifth of all Americans — hidden from most people's sight in Appalachia, urban ghettos, migrant labor camps, and Indian reservations — lived in poverty. But, Johnson declared, "for the first time in our history, it is possible to conquer poverty."

The **Economic Opportunity Act** of 1964, which created a series of programs to reach these Americans, was the president's answer — what he called the War on Poverty. This legislation included several different initiatives. Head Start provided free nursery schools to prepare disadvantaged preschoolers for kindergarten. The Job Corps and Upward Bound provided young people with training and employment. Volunteers in Service to America (VISTA), modeled on the Peace Corps, offered technical assistance to the urban and rural poor. An array of regional development programs

focused on spurring economic growth in impoverished areas. On balance, the 1964 legislation provided services to the poor rather than jobs, leading some critics to charge the War on Poverty with doing too little.

### The 1964 Election

With the Civil Rights Act passed and his War on Poverty initiatives off the ground, Johnson turned his attention to the upcoming presidential election. Not content to govern in Kennedy's shadow, he wanted a national mandate of his own. Privately, Johnson cast himself less like Kennedy than as the heir of Franklin Roosevelt and the expansive liberalism of the 1930s. Johnson had come to Congress for the first time in 1937 and had long admired FDR's political skills. He reminded his advisors never to forget "the meek and the humble and the lowly," because "President Roosevelt never did."

In the 1964 election, Johnson faced Republican Barry Goldwater of Arizona. An archconservative, Goldwater ran on an anticommunist, antigovernment platform, offering "a choice, not an echo" — meaning he represented a genuinely conservative alternative to liberalism rather than the echo of liberalism offered by the moderate wing of the Republican Party (Chapter 25). Goldwater campaigned against the Civil Rights Act of 1964 and promised a more vigorous Cold War foreign policy. Among those supporting him was former actor Ronald Reagan, whose speech on behalf of Goldwater at the Republican convention, called "A

Time for Choosing," made him a rising star in the party.

But Goldwater's strident foreign policy alienated voters. "Extremism in the defense of liberty is no vice," he told Republicans at the convention. Moreover, there remained strong national sentiment for Kennedy. Telling Americans that he was running to fulfill Kennedy's legacy, Johnson and his running mate, Hubert H. Humphrey of Minnesota, won in a landslide (Map 28.1). In the long run, Goldwater's candidacy marked the beginning of a grassroots conservative revolt that would eventually transform the Republican Party. In the short run, however, Johnson's sweeping victory gave him a popular mandate and, equally important, congressional majorities that rivaled FDR's in 1935 — just what he needed to push the Great Society forward (Table 28.1).

**Great Society Initiatives** One of Johnson's first successes was breaking a congressional deadlock on education and health care. Passed in April 1965, the Elementary and Secondary Education Act authorized $1 billion in federal funds for teacher training and other educational programs. Standing in his old Texas schoolhouse, Johnson, a former teacher, said: "I believe no law I have signed or will ever sign means more to the future of America." Six months later, Johnson signed the Higher Education Act, providing federal scholarships for college students. Johnson also had the votes he needed to achieve some form of national health insurance. That year, he also won passage of two new programs: **Medicare**, a health plan for the elderly funded by a surcharge on Social Security payroll taxes, and **Medicaid**, a health plan for the poor paid for by general tax revenues and administered by the states.

The Great Society's agenda included environmental reform as well: an expanded national park system, improvement of the nation's air and water, protection for endangered species, stronger land-use planning, and highway beautification. Hardly pausing for breath, Johnson oversaw the creation of the Department of Housing and Urban Development (HUD); won funding for hundreds of thousands of units of public housing; made new investments in urban rapid transit such as the new Washington, D.C., Metro and the Bay Area Rapid Transit (BART) system in San Francisco; ushered new child safety and consumer protection laws through Congress; and helped create the National Endowment for the Arts and the National Endowment for the Humanities to support the work of artists, writers, and scholars.

It even became possible, at this moment of reform zeal, to tackle the nation's discriminatory immigration policy. The Immigration Act of 1965 abandoned the quota system that favored northern Europeans, replacing it with numerical limits that did not discriminate among nations. To promote family reunification, the law also stipulated that close relatives of legal residents in the United States could be admitted outside the numerical limits, an exception that especially benefitted Asian and Latin American immigrants. Since 1965, as a result, immigrants from those regions have become increasingly visible in American society (Chapter 31).

**Assessing the Great Society** The Great Society enjoyed mixed results. The proportion of Americans living below the poverty line dropped from 20 percent to 13 percent between 1963 and 1968 (Figure 28.1). Medicare and Medicaid, the most enduring of the Great Society programs, helped millions of elderly and poor citizens afford necessary health care. Further, as millions of African Americans moved into the middle

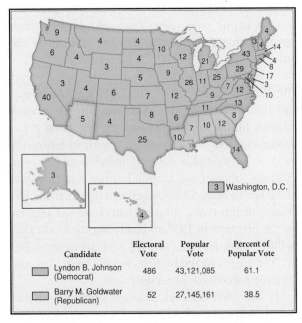

| Candidate | Electoral Vote | Popular Vote | Percent of Popular Vote |
|---|---|---|---|
| Lyndon B. Johnson (Democrat) | 486 | 43,121,085 | 61.1 |
| Barry M. Goldwater (Republican) | 52 | 27,145,161 | 38.5 |

**MAP 28.1**

**The Presidential Election of 1964**

This map reveals how one-sided was the victory of Lyndon Johnson over Barry Goldwater in 1964. Except for Arizona, his home state, Goldwater won only five states in the Deep South — not of much immediate consolation to him, but a sure indicator that the South was cutting its historic ties to the Democratic Party. Moreover, although soundly rejected in 1964, Goldwater's far right critique of "big government" laid the foundation for a Republican resurgence in the 1980s.

**TABLE 28.1**

**Major Great Society Legislation**

| | | |
|---|---|---|
| | **Civil Rights** | |
| 1964 | Twenty-fourth Amendment | Outlawed poll tax in federal elections |
| | Civil Rights Act | Banned discrimination in employment and public accommodations on the basis of race, religion, sex, or national origin |
| 1965 | Voting Rights Act | Outlawed literacy tests for voting; provided federal supervision of registration in historically low-registration areas |
| | **Social Welfare** | |
| 1964 | Economic Opportunity Act | Created Office of Economic Opportunity (OEO) to administer War on Poverty programs such as Head Start, Job Corps, and Volunteers in Service to America (VISTA) |
| 1965 | Medical Care Act | Provided medical care for the poor (Medicaid) and the elderly (Medicare) |
| 1966 | Minimum Wage Act | Raised hourly minimum wage from $1.25 to $1.40 and expanded coverage to new groups |
| | **Education** | |
| 1965 | Elementary and Secondary Education Act | Granted federal aid for education of poor children |
| | National Endowment for the Arts and Humanities | Provided federal funding and support for artists and scholars |
| | Higher Education Act | Provided federal scholarships for postsecondary education |
| | **Housing and Urban Development** | |
| 1964 | Urban Mass Transportation Act | Provided federal aid to urban mass transit |
| | Omnibus Housing Act | Provided federal funds for public housing and rent subsidies for low-income families |
| 1965 | Housing and Urban Development Act | Created Department of Housing and Urban Development (HUD) |
| 1966 | Metropolitan Area Redevelopment and Demonstration Cities Acts | Designated 150 "model cities" for combined programs of public housing, social services, and job training |
| | **Environment** | |
| 1964 | Wilderness Preservation Act | Designated 9.1 million acres of federal lands as "wilderness areas," barring future roads, buildings, or commercial use |
| 1965 | Air and Water Quality Acts | Set tougher air quality standards; required states to enforce water quality standards for interstate waters |
| | **Miscellaneous** | |
| 1964 | Tax Reduction Act | Reduced personal and corporate income tax rates |
| 1965 | Immigration Act | Abandoned national quotas of 1924 law, allowing more non-European immigration |
| | Appalachian Regional and Development Act | Provided federal funding for roads, health clinics, and other public works projects in economically depressed regions |

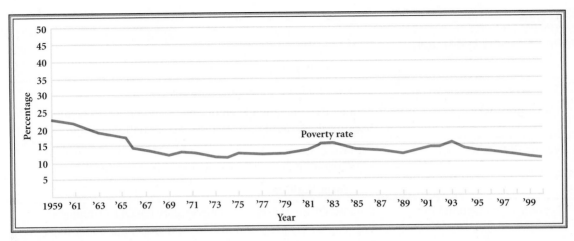

**FIGURE 28.1**

**Americans in Poverty, 1959–2000**

Between 1959 and 1973 the poverty rate among American families dropped by more than half—from 23 percent to 11 percent. There was, however, sharp disagreement about the reasons for that notable decline. Liberals credited the War on Poverty, while conservatives favored the high-performing economy, with the significant poverty dip of 1965–1966 caused by military spending, not Johnson's domestic programs.

**PLACE EVENTS IN CONTEXT**

What new roles did the federal government assume under Great Society initiatives, and how did they extend the New Deal tradition?

class, the black poverty rate fell by half. Liberals believed they were on the right track.

Conservatives, however, gave more credit for these changes to the decade's booming economy than to government programs. Indeed, conservative critics accused Johnson and other liberals of believing that every social problem could be solved with a government program. In the final analysis, the Great Society dramatically improved the financial situation of the elderly, reached millions of children, and increased the racial diversity of American society and workplaces. However, entrenched poverty remained, racial segregation in the largest cities worsened, and the national distribution of wealth remained highly skewed. In relative terms, the bottom 20 percent remained as far behind as ever. In these arenas, the Great Society made little progress.

## Rebirth of the Women's Movement

The new era of liberal reform reawakened the American women's movement. Inspired by the civil rights movement and legislative advances under the Great Society, but frustrated by the lack of attention both gave to women, feminists entered the political fray and demanded not simply inclusion, but a rethinking of national priorities.

**Labor Feminists**    The women's movement had not languished entirely in the postwar years. Feminist concerns were kept alive in the 1950s and early 1960s by working women, who campaigned for such things as maternity leave and equal pay for equal work. One historian has called these women "labor feminists," because they belonged to unions and fought for equality and dignity in the workplace. "It became apparent to me why so many employers could legally discriminate against women — because it was written right into the law," said one female labor activist. Trade union women were especially critical in pushing for, and winning, congressional passage of the 1963 **Equal Pay Act**, which established the principle of equal pay for equal work.

Labor feminists were responding to the times. More women — including married women (40 percent by 1970) and mothers with young children (30 percent by 1970) — were working outside the home than ever before. But they faced a labor market that undervalued their contributions. Moreover, most working women faced the "double day": they were expected to earn a paycheck and then return home to domestic labor. One woman put the problem succinctly: "The working mother has no 'wife' to care for her children."

**Betty Friedan and the National Organization for Women**    When Betty Friedan's indictment of suburban domesticity, *The Feminine Mystique*, appeared in 1963, it targeted a different audience: college-educated, middle-class women who found themselves not working for wages but rather stifled by their domestic routine. Tens of thousands of women read Friedan's book and thought, "She's talking about me." *The Feminine Mystique* became a runaway best-seller. Friedan persuaded middle-class women that they needed more than the convenience foods, improved diapers, and better laundry detergents that magazines and television urged them to buy. To live rich and fulfilling lives, they needed education and work outside the home.

Paradoxically, the domesticity described in *The Feminine Mystique* was already crumbling. After the postwar baby boom, women were again having fewer children, aided now by the birth control pill, first marketed in 1960. And as states liberalized divorce laws, more women were divorcing. Educational levels were also rising: by 1970, women made up 42 percent of the college population. All of these changes undermined traditional gender roles and enabled many women to embrace *The Feminine Mystique*'s liberating prescriptions.

Government action also made a difference. In 1961, Kennedy appointed the **Presidential Commission on the Status of Women**, which issued a 1963 report documenting job and educational discrimination. A bigger breakthrough came when Congress added the word *sex* to the categories protected against discrimination in the Civil Rights Act of 1964. Women suddenly had a powerful legal tool for fighting sex discrimination.

To force compliance with the new act, Friedan and others, including many labor feminists from around the country, founded the **National Organization for Women (NOW)** in 1966. Modeled on the NAACP, NOW intended to be a civil rights organization for women, with the aim of bringing "women into full participation in . . . American society now, exercising all the privileges and responsibilities thereof in truly equal partnership with men." Under Friedan's leadership, membership grew to fifteen thousand by 1971, and NOW became, like the NAACP, a powerful voice for equal rights.

One of the ironies of the 1960s was the enormous strain that all of this liberal activism placed on the New Deal coalition. Faced with often competing demands from the civil rights movement, feminists, the poor, labor unions, conservative southern Democrats, the suburban middle class, and urban political machines, the old Rooseveltian coalition had begun to fray. Johnson hoped that the New Deal coalition was strong enough to negotiate competing demands among its own constituents while simultaneously resisting conservative attacks. In 1965, that still seemed possible. It would not remain so for long.

> **IDENTIFY CAUSES**
> What factors accounted for the resurgence of feminism in the 1960s?

**National Organization for Women**

Kathryn F. Clarenbach (left) and Betty Friedan (right) announced a "Bill of Rights for Women in 1968" to be presented to candidates in that election year. Clarenbach was the first chairwoman of the National Organization for Women (NOW) and Friedan the organization's first president. NOW became a fixture of the women's movement and the leading liberal voice for women's legal and social equality. © Bettmann/Corbis.

# The Vietnam War Begins

As the accelerating rights revolution placed strain on the Democratic coalition, the war in Vietnam divided the country. In a CBS interview before his death, Kennedy remarked that it was up to the South Vietnamese whether "their war" would be won or lost. But the young president had already placed the United States on a course that would make retreat difficult. Like other presidents, Kennedy believed that giving up in Vietnam would weaken America's "credibility." Withdrawal "would be a great mistake," he said.

It is impossible to know how JFK would have managed Vietnam had he lived. What is known is that in the fall of 1963, Kennedy had lost patience with Ngo Dinh Diem, the dictatorial head of South Vietnam whom the United States had supported since 1955. The president let it be known in Saigon that the United States would support a military coup. Kennedy's hope was that if Diem, reviled throughout the South because of his brutal repression of political opponents, could be replaced by a popular general or other military figure, a stable government would emerge—one strong enough to repel the South Vietnam National Liberation Front (NLF), or Vietcong. But when Diem was overthrown on November 1, the South Vietnamese generals went further than Kennedy's team had anticipated and assassinated both Diem and his brother. This made the coup look less like an organic uprising and more like an American plot.

South Vietnam fell into a period of chaos marked by several coups and defined by the increasing ungovernability of both the cities and countryside. Kennedy himself was assassinated in late November and would not live to see the grim results of Diem's murder: American engagement in a long and costly civil conflict in the name of fighting communism.

## Escalation Under Johnson

Just as Kennedy had inherited Vietnam from Eisenhower, so Lyndon Johnson inherited Vietnam from Kennedy. Johnson's inheritance was more burdensome, however, for by now only massive American intervention could prevent the collapse of South Vietnam (Map 28.2). Johnson, like Kennedy, was a subscriber to the Cold War tenets of global containment.

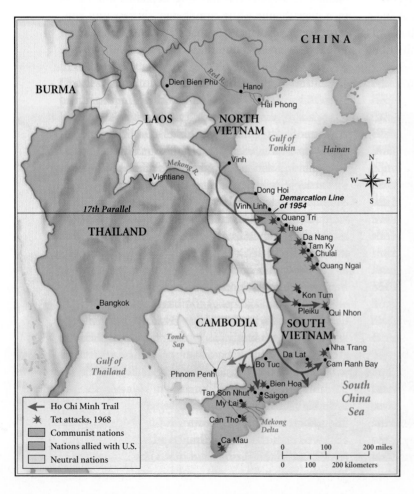

**MAP 28.2**

**The Vietnam War, 1968**

The Vietnam War was a guerrilla war, fought in skirmishes rather than set-piece battles. Despite repeated airstrikes, the United States was never able to halt the flow of North Vietnamese troops and supplies down the Ho Chi Minh Trail, which wound through Laos and Cambodia. In January 1968, Vietcong forces launched the Tet offensive, a surprise attack on cities and provincial centers across South Vietnam. Although the attackers were pushed back with heavy losses, the Tet offensive revealed the futility of American efforts to suppress the Vietcong guerrillas and marked a turning point in the war.

"I am not going to lose Vietnam," he vowed on taking office. "I am not going to be the President who saw Southeast Asia go the way China went" (Chapter 25).

**Gulf of Tonkin**   It did not take long for Johnson to place his stamp on the war. During the summer of 1964, the president got reports that North Vietnamese torpedo boats had fired on the U.S. destroyer *Maddox* in the Gulf of Tonkin. In the first attack, on August 2, the damage inflicted was limited to a single bullet hole; a second attack, on August 4, later proved to be only misread radar sightings. To Johnson, it didn't matter if the attack was real or imagined; the president believed a wider war was inevitable and issued a call to arms, sending his national approval rating from 42 to 72 percent. In the entire Congress, only two senators voted against his request for authorization to "take all necessary measures to repel any armed attack against the forces of the United States and to prevent further aggression." The **Gulf of Tonkin Resolution**, as it became known, gave Johnson the freedom to conduct operations in Vietnam as he saw fit.

Despite his congressional mandate, Johnson was initially cautious about revealing his plans to the American people. "I had no choice but to keep my foreign policy in the wings . . . ," Johnson later said. "I knew that the day it exploded into a major debate on the war, that day would be the beginning of the end of the Great Society." So he ran in 1964 on the pledge that there would be no escalation — no American boys fighting Vietnam's fight. Privately, he doubted the pledge could be kept.

**The New American Presence**   With the 1964 election safely behind him, Johnson began an American takeover of the war in Vietnam (American Voices, p. 912). The escalation, beginning in the early months of 1965, took two forms: deployment of American ground troops and the intensification of bombing against North Vietnam.

On March 8, 1965, the first marines waded ashore at Da Nang. By 1966, more than 380,000 American soldiers were stationed in Vietnam; by 1967, 485,000; and by 1968, 536,000 (Figure 28.2). The escalating demands of General William Westmoreland, the commander of U.S. forces, and Robert McNamara, the secretary of defense, pushed Johnson to Americanize the ground war in an attempt to stabilize South Vietnam. "I can't run and pull a Chamberlain at Munich," Johnson privately told a reporter in early March 1965, referring to the British prime minister who had appeased Hitler in 1938.

Meanwhile, Johnson authorized **Operation Rolling Thunder**, a massive bombing campaign against North Vietnam in 1965. Over the entire course of the war, the United States dropped twice as many tons of bombs on Vietnam as the Allies had dropped in both Europe and the Pacific during the whole of World War II. To McNamara's surprise, the bombing had little effect on the Vietcong's ability to wage war in the South. The North Vietnamese quickly rebuilt roads and bridges and moved munitions plants underground. Instead of destroying the morale of the North Vietnamese, Operation Rolling Thunder hardened their will to fight. The massive commitment of troops and air power devastated Vietnam's countryside, however. After one harsh but not unusual engagement, a commanding officer reported that "it became necessary to destroy

> **UNDERSTAND POINTS OF VIEW**
>
> In what larger context did President Johnson view the Vietnam conflict, and why was he determined to support South Vietnam?

**FIGURE 28.2**

**U.S. Troops in Vietnam, 1960–1973**

This figure graphically tracks America's involvement in Vietnam. After Lyndon Johnson decided on escalation in 1964, troop levels jumped from 23,300 to a peak of 543,000 personnel in 1968. Under Richard Nixon's Vietnamization program, beginning in the summer of 1969, levels drastically declined; the last U.S. military forces left South Vietnam on March 29, 1973.

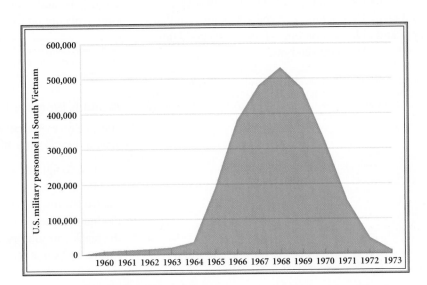

## The Toll of War

The Vietnam War produced a rich and graphic literature: novels, journalists' reports, interviews, and personal letters. These brief selections suggest the war's profound impact on those Americans who experienced it firsthand.

### Donald Whitfield

Donald L. Whitfield was a draftee from Alabama who was interviewed some years after the war.

I'm gonna be honest with you. I had heard some about Vietnam in 1968, but I was a poor fellow and I didn't keep up with it. I was working at a Standard Oil station making eight dollars a day. I pumped gas and tinkered a little with cars. I had a girl I saw every now and then, but I still spent most of my time with a car. When I got my letter from the draft lady, I appealed it on the reason it was just me and my sister at home. We were a poor family and they needed me at home, but it did no good.

My company did a lot of patrolling. We got the roughest damn deal. Shit, I thought I was going to get killed every night. I was terrified the whole time. We didn't have no trouble with the blacks. I saw movies that said we done the blacks wrong, but it wasn't like that where I was. Let's put it like this: they make pretty good soldiers, but they're not what we are. White Americans, can't nobody whip our ass. We're the baddest son of a bitches on the face of this earth. You can take a hundred Russians and twenty-five Americans, and we'll whip their ass. . . .

I fly the Rebel flag because this is the South, Bubba. The American flag represents the whole fifty states. That flag represents the southern part. I'm a Confederate, I'm a Southerner. . . .

I feel cheated about Vietnam, I sure do. Political restrictions — we won every goddamned battle we was in, but didn't win the whole goddamn little country. . . . Before I die, the Democratic-controlled Congress of this country — and I blame it on 'em — they gonna goddamn apologize to the Vietnam veterans.

Source: From "Donald L. Whitfield" in *Landing Zones: Southern Veterans Remember Vietnam*, by James R. Wilson, pp. 202–211. Copyright 1990, Duke University Press. All rights reserved. Republished by permission of the copyright holder, www.dukepress.edu.

### George Olsen

George Olsen served in Vietnam from August 1969 to March 1970, when he was killed in action. He wrote this letter to a close female friend.

31 Aug '69
Dear Red,
Last Monday I went on my first hunter-killer operation. . . . The frightening thing about it all is that it is so very easy to kill in war. There's no remorse, no theatrical "washing of the hands" to get rid of nonexistent blood, not even any regrets. When it happens, you are more afraid than you've ever been in your life — my hands shook so much I had trouble reloading. . . . You're scared, really scared, and there's no thinking about it. You kill because that little SOB is doing his best to kill you and you desperately want to live, to go home, to get drunk or walk down the street on a date again. And suddenly the grenades aren't going off any more, the weapons stop and, unbelievably fast it seems, it's all over. . . .

I have truly come to envy the honest pacifist who honestly believes that no killing is permissible and can, with a clear conscience, stay home and not take part in these conflicts. I wish I could do the same, but I can't see letting another take my place and my risks over here. . . . The only reason pacifists such as the Amish can even live in an orderly society is because someone — be they police or soldiers — is taking risks to keep the wolves away. . . . I guess that's why I'm over here, why I fought so hard to come here, and why, even though I'm scared most of the time, I'm content to be here.

Source: From *Dear America: Letters Home from Vietnam*, edited by Bernard Edelman for the New York Vietnam Veterans Memorial Commission, published by W.W. Norton & Company, 1985.

### Arthur E. Woodley Jr.

Special Forces Ranger Arthur E. Woodley Jr. gave this interview a decade after his return.

You had to fight to survive where I grew up. Lower east Baltimore. . . . It was a mixed-up neighborhood of Puerto Ricans, Indians, Italians, and blacks. Being that I'm lightskinned, curly hair, I wasn't readily accepted in the black community. I was more accepted by Puerto Ricans and some rednecks. They didn't ask what my race classification was. I went with them to white movies, white restaurants, and so forth. But after I got older, I came to the realization that I was what I am and came to deal with my black peers. . . .

I figured I was just what my country needed. A black patriot who could do any physical job they could come up with. Six feet, one hundred and ninety pounds, and healthy. . . .

I didn't ask no questions about the war. I thought communism was spreading, and as an American citizen, it was my part to do as much as I could to defeat the Communist from coming here. Whatever America states is correct was the tradition that I was brought up in. And I thought the only way I could possibly make it out of the ghetto was to be the best soldier I possibly could. . . .

Then came the second week of February of '69. . . . We recon this area, and we came across this fella, a white guy, who was staked to the ground. His arms and legs tied down to stakes. . . . He had numerous scars on his face where he might have been beaten and mutilated. And he had been peeled from his upper part of chest to down to his waist.

Skinned. Like they slit your skin with a knife. And they take a pair of pliers or a instrument similar, and they just peel the skin off your body and expose it to the elements. . . .

And he start to cryin', beggin' to die.

He said, "I can't go back like this. I can't live like this. I'm dying. You can't leave me here like this dying." . . .

It took me somewhere close to 20 minutes to get my mind together. Not because I was squeamish about killing someone, because I had at that time numerous body counts. Killing someone wasn't the issue. It was killing another American citizen, another GI. . . . We buried him. We buried him. Very deep. Then I cried. . . .

When we first started going into the fields, I would not wear a finger, ear, or mutilate another person's body. Until I had the misfortune to come upon those American soldiers who were castrated. Then it got to be a game between the Communists and ourselves to see how many fingers and ears that we could capture from each other. After a kill we would cut his finger or ear off as a trophy, stuff our unit patch in his mouth, and let him die.

With 89 days left in country, I came out of the field. What I now felt was emptiness. . . . I started seeing the atrocities that we caused each other as human beings. I came to the realization that I was committing crimes against humanity and myself. That I really didn't believe in these things I was doin'. I changed.

Source: Wallace Terry, *Bloods: An Oral History of the Vietnam War by Black Veterans* (New York: Ballantine, 1984), 243–263.

## Gayle Smith

Gayle Smith was a nurse in a surgical unit in Vietnam in 1970–1971 and gave this interview a few years later.

I objected to the war and I got the idea into my head of going there to bring people back. I started thinking about it in 1966 and knew that I would eventually go when I felt I was prepared enough. . . .

Boy, I remember how they came in all torn up. It was incredible. The first time a medevac came in, I got right into it. I didn't have a lot of feeling at that time. It was later on that I began to have a lot of feeling about it, after I'd seen it over and over and over again. . . . I turned that pain into anger and hatred and placed it onto the Vietnamese. . . . I did not consider the Vietnamese to be people. They were human, but they weren't people. They weren't like us, so it was okay to kill them. It was okay to hate them. . . .

I would have dreams about putting a .45 to someone's head and see it blow away over and over again. And for a long time I swore that if the Vietnamese ever came to this country I'd kill them.

It was in a Vietnam veterans group that I realized that all my hatred for the Vietnamese and my wanting to kill them was really a reflection of all the pain that I had felt for seeing all those young men die and hurt. . . . I would stand there and look at them and think to myself, "You've just lost your leg for no reason at all." Or "You're going to die and it's for nothing." For nothing. I would never, never say that to them, but they knew it.

Source: Albert Santoli, ed., *Everything We Had* (New York: Random House, 1981), 141–148.

### QUESTIONS FOR ANALYSIS

1. Why did these four young people end up in Vietnam? How are their reasons for going to war similar and different?
2. How would you describe their experiences there?
3. What are their attitudes about the war, and how were they changed by it? What do their reflections suggest about Vietnam's impact on American society?

the town in order to save it"—a statement that came to symbolize the terrible logic of the war.

The Johnson administration gambled that American superiority in personnel and weaponry would ultimately triumph. This strategy was inextricably tied to political considerations. For domestic reasons, policymakers searched for an elusive middle ground between all-out invasion of North Vietnam, which included the possibility of war with China, and disengagement. "In effect, we are fighting a war of attrition," said General Westmoreland. "The only alternative is a war of annihilation."

## Public Opinion and the War

Johnson gradually grew more confident that his Vietnam policy had the support of the American people. Both Democrats and Republicans approved Johnson's escalation in Vietnam, and so did public opinion polls in 1965 and 1966. But then opinion began to shift (Thinking Like a Historian, p. 916).

Every night, Americans saw the carnage of war on their television screens, including images of dead and wounded Americans. One such incident occurred in the first months of fighting in 1965. Television reporter Morley Safer witnessed a marine unit burning the village of Cam Ne to the ground. "Today's operation is the frustration of Vietnam in miniature," Safer explained. America can "win a military victory here, but to a Vietnamese peasant whose home is [destroyed] it will take more than presidential promises to convince him that we are on his side."

With such firsthand knowledge of the war, journalists began to write about a "credibility gap." The Johnson administration, they charged, was concealing bad news about the war's progress. In February 1966, television coverage of hearings by the Senate Foreign Relations Committee (chaired by J. William Fulbright, an outspoken critic of the war) raised further questions about the administration's policy. Johnson complained to his staff in 1966 that "our people can't stand firm in the face of heavy losses, and they can bring down the government." Economic problems put Johnson even more on the defensive. The Vietnam War cost taxpayers $27 billion in 1967, pushing the federal deficit from $9.8 billion to $23 billion. By then, military spending had set in motion the inflationary spiral that would plague the U.S. economy throughout the 1970s.

Out of these troubling developments, an antiwar movement began to crystallize. Its core, in addition to long-standing pacifist groups, comprised a new generation of peace activists such as SANE (the National Committee for a Sane Nuclear Policy), which in the 1950s had protested atmospheric nuclear testing. After the escalation in 1965, the activist groups were joined by students, clergy, civil rights advocates, and even Dr. Benjamin Spock, whose book on child care had helped raise many of the younger activists. Despite their diversity, these opponents of the war shared a skepticism about U.S. policy in Vietnam. They charged variously that intervention was antithetical to American ideals; that an independent, anticommunist South Vietnam was unattainable; and that no American objective justified the suffering that was being inflicted on the Vietnamese people.

## Rise of the Student Movement

College students, many of them inspired by the civil rights movement, had begun to organize and agitate for social change. In Ann Arbor, Michigan, they founded **Students for a Democratic Society (SDS)** in 1960. Two years later, forty students from Big Ten and Ivy League universities held the first national SDS convention in Port Huron, Michigan. Tom Hayden penned a manifesto, the **Port Huron Statement**, expressing students' disillusionment with the nation's consumer culture and the gulf between rich and poor. "We are people of this generation," Hayden wrote, "bred in at least modest comfort, housed now in universities, looking uncomfortably to the world we inherit." These students rejected Cold War foreign policy, including the war in Vietnam.

**The New Left**   The founders of SDS referred to their movement as the **New Left** to distinguish themselves from the Old Left—communists and socialists of the 1930s and 1940s. As New Left influence spread, it hit major university towns first—places such as Madison, Wisconsin, and Berkeley, California. One of the first major demonstrations erupted in the fall of 1964 at the University of California at Berkeley after administrators banned student political activity on university grounds. In protest, student organizations formed the Free Speech Movement and organized a sit-in at the administration building. Some students had just returned from Freedom Summer in Mississippi, radicalized by their experience. Mario Savio spoke for many when he compared the conflict in Berkeley to the civil rights struggle in the South: "The same rights are at stake in both places—the right to participate as citizens in a democratic society and to struggle against the same enemy." Emboldened by the Berkeley movement, students across the nation were soon protesting their

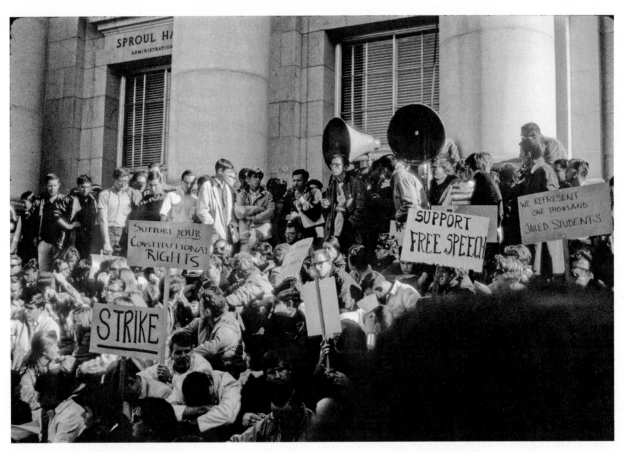

**Free Speech at Berkeley, 1964**
Students at the University of California's Berkeley campus protested the administration's decision to ban political activity in the school plaza. Free speech demonstrators, many of them active in the civil rights movement, relied on the tactics and arguments that they learned during that struggle. Dr. Jim Jumblatt, Free Speech Movement Archive.

universities' academic policies and then, more passionately, the Vietnam War.

One spur to student protest was the military's Selective Service System, which in 1967 abolished automatic student deferments. To avoid the draft, some young men enlisted in the National Guard or applied for conscientious objector status; others avoided the draft by leaving the country, most often for Canada or Sweden. In public demonstrations, opponents of the war burned their draft cards, picketed induction centers, and on a few occasions broke into Selective Service offices and destroyed records. Antiwar demonstrators numbered in the tens or, at most, hundreds of thousands — a small fraction of American youth — but they were vocal, visible, and determined.

Students were on the front lines as the campaign against the war escalated. The 1967 Mobilization to End the War brought 100,000 protesters into the streets of San Francisco, while more than a quarter million followed Martin Luther King Jr. from Central Park to the United Nations in New York. Another 100,000 marched on the Pentagon. President Johnson absorbed the blows and counterpunched — "The enemy's hope for victory . . . is in our division, our weariness, our uncertainty," he proclaimed — but it had become clear that Johnson's war, as many began calling it, was no longer uniting the country.

**Young Americans for Freedom**   The New Left was not the only political force on college campuses. Conservative students were less noisy but more numerous. For them, the 1960s was not about protesting the war, staging student strikes, and idolizing Black Power. Inspired by the group **Young Americans for Freedom (YAF)**, conservative students asserted their faith in "God-given free will" and their fear that the federal government "accumulates power which tends

> **COMPARE AND CONTRAST**
> Contrast the political views of the SDS, the YAF, and the counterculture. How would you explain the differences?

## Debating the War in Vietnam

The war in Vietnam divided Americans and ultimately divided world opinion. A product of the Cold War policy of containment, the war led many to question the application of that policy to Southeast Asia. Yet every American president from Truman to Nixon believed that opposing the unification of Vietnam under communist rule was essential. Historians continue to research, and debate, what led to the war and what effects the war had on both Vietnam and the United States. The following documents help us to consider different views of the war.

### 1. President Dwight Eisenhower's "Domino Theory" speech, April 7, 1954.

Finally, you have broader considerations that might follow what you would call the "falling domino" principle. You have a row of dominoes set up, you knock over the first one, and what will happen to the last one is the certainty that it will go over very quickly. So you could have a beginning of a disintegration that would have the most profound influences. . . .

But when we come to the possible sequence of events, the loss of Indochina, of Burma, of Thailand, of the Peninsula, and Indonesia following, now you begin to talk about areas that not only multiply the disadvantages that you would suffer through loss of materials, sources of materials, but now you're talking about millions and millions and millions of people.

### 2. Manifesto of the South Vietnam National Front for Liberation (NLF), 1968.

Over the past hundred years the Vietnamese people repeatedly rose up to fight against foreign aggression for the independence and freedom of their fatherland. In 1945, the people throughout the country surged up in an armed uprising, overthrew the Japanese and French domination, and seized power. . . .

However, the American imperialists, who had in the past helped the French colonialists to massacre our people, have now replaced the French in enslaving the southern part of our country through a disguised colonial regime. They have been using their stooge — the Ngo Dinh Diem administration — in their downright repression and exploitation of our compatriots, in their maneuvers to permanently divide our country and to turn its southern part into a base in preparation for war in Southeast Asia.

### 3. President Lyndon Johnson, Johns Hopkins University speech, April 7, 1965.

Over this war — and all Asia — is another reality: the deepening shadow of Communist China. The rulers in Hanoi are urged on by Peiping [Peking]. This is a regime which has destroyed freedom in Tibet, which has attacked India, and has been condemned by the United Nations for aggression in Korea. It is helping the forces of violence in almost every continent. The contest in Viet-Nam is part of a wider pattern of aggressive purposes.

### 4. James Fallows, "What Did You Do in the Class War, Daddy?" *Washington Monthly*, October 1975. *The journalist Fallows highlighted the economic unfairness of the Vietnam-era draft.*

The children of the bright, good parents were spared the more immediate sort of suffering that our inferiors were undergoing. And because of that, when our parents were opposed to the war, they were opposed in a bloodless, theoretical fashion, as they might be opposed to political corruption or racism in South Africa. As long as the little gold stars [sent to parents whose son was killed in war] kept going to homes in Chelsea [a working-class part of Boston] and the backwoods of West Virginia, the mothers of Beverly Hills and Chevy Chase and Great Neck and Belmont [all affluent suburbs] were not on the telephone to their congressman screaming, "*You killed my boy.*" . . . It is clear by now that if the men of Harvard had wanted to do the very most they could to help shorten the war, they should have been drafted or imprisoned en masse.

**5. Students for a Democratic Society, Call for a March on Washington to End the War, 1965.**

The current war in Vietnam is being waged on behalf of a succession of unpopular South Vietnamese dictatorships, not in behalf of freedom. No American-supported South Vietnamese regime in the past few years has gained the support of its people, for the simple reason that the people overwhelmingly want peace, self-determination, and the opportunity for development. American prosecution of the war has deprived them of all three.

 The war is fundamentally a *civil* war. . . .

 It is a *losing* war. . . .

 It is a *self-defeating* war. . . .

 It is a *dangerous* war. . . .

 It is a war never declared by Congress. . . .

 It is a hideously *immoral* war.

**6. Richard Nixon, address to the nation on the Vietnam War, November 3, 1969.**

. . . President Eisenhower sent economic aid and military equipment to assist the people of South Vietnam in their efforts to prevent a Communist takeover. Seven years ago, President Kennedy sent 16,000 military personnel to Vietnam as combat advisors. Four years ago, President Johnson sent American combat forces to South Vietnam. . . .

 For these reasons, I reject the recommendation that I should end the war by immediately withdrawing all our forces. I choose instead to change American policy on both the negotiating front and the battlefront. . . .

**7. Evacuation of Vietnamese civilians in a burning village, c. 1965.**

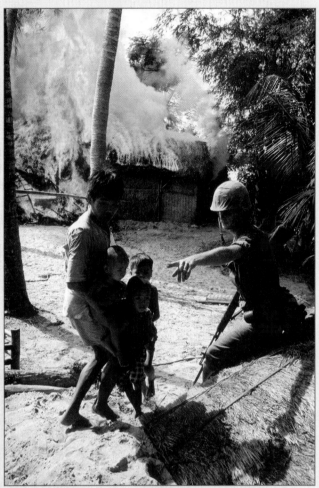

Source: Photo by Dominique BERETTY/Gamma-Rapho via Getty Images.

Sources: (1) George Katsiaficas, ed., *Vietnam Documents: American and Vietnamese Views of the War* (Armonk, NY: M. E. Sharpe, Inc., 1992), pp. 120–121. Used by permission of the author; (2) Katsiaficas, 43–44; (3) John Clark Pratt, *Vietnam Voices: Perspectives on the War Years, 1941–1982* (New York: Penguin Books, 1984), 201; (4) *The Washington Monthly*, October 1975, 5–19; (5) Katsiaficas, 120–121; (6) Katsiaficas, 147.

## ANALYZING THE EVIDENCE

1. Three of the sources (1, 3, and 6) feature remarks by U.S. presidents. What common feature do they share? Are there differences among the comments? Source 2 is also an attempt by a political figure to persuade. How should historians evaluate such documents?

2. In source 4, which Americans does the author believe have sacrificed the most in fighting the war in Vietnam?

3. Compare sources 2 and 5. What is the intended audience of each? What common features do they share?

4. Journalists and electronic media (photography and television) played an important role in the war. How would images, such as that in source 7, shape opinion about the war both in the United States and globally?

## PUTTING IT ALL TOGETHER

Using the knowledge you have gained from this chapter, analyze the documents above to construct an essay in which you explore the Vietnam War's causes and effects, both domestic and international. Choose at least one domestic and one international theme and use the documents to providence evidence for your conclusions.

to diminish order and liberty." The YAF, the largest student political organization in the country, defended free enterprise and supported the war in Vietnam. Its founding principles were outlined in "The **Sharon Statement**," drafted (in Sharon, Connecticut) two years before the Port Huron Statement, and inspired young conservatives, many of whom would play important roles in the Reagan administration in the 1980s.

**The Counterculture**   While the New Left organized against the political and economic system and the YAF defended it, many other young Americans embarked on a general revolt against authority and middle-class respectability. The "hippie" — identified by ragged blue jeans or army fatigues, tie-dyed T-shirts, beads, and long unkempt hair — symbolized the new **counterculture**. With roots in the 1950s Beat culture of New York's Greenwich Village and San Francisco's North Beach, the 1960s counterculture initially turned to folk

music for its inspiration. Pete Seeger set the tone for the era's idealism with songs such as the 1961 antiwar ballad "Where Have All the Flowers Gone?" In 1963, the year of the civil rights demonstrations in Birmingham and President Kennedy's assassination, Bob Dylan's "Blowin' in the Wind" reflected the impatience of people whose faith in America was wearing thin. Joan Baez emerged alongside Dylan and pioneered a folk sound that inspired a generation of female musicians.

By the mid-1960s, other winds of change in popular music came from the Beatles, four working-class Brits whose awe-inspiring music — by turns lyrical and driving — spawned a commercial and cultural phenomenon known as Beatlemania. American youths' embrace of the Beatles — as well as even more rebellious bands such as the Rolling Stones, the Who, and the Doors — deepened the generational divide between young people and their elders. So did the recreational

**The Counterculture**
The three-day outdoor Woodstock concert in August 1969 was a defining moment in the rise of the counterculture. The event attracted 400,000 young people, like those pictured here, to Bethel, New York, for a weekend of music, drugs, and sex. The counterculture was distinct from the New Left and was less a political movement than a shifting set of cultural styles, attitudes, and practices. It rejected conformity of all kinds and placed rebellion and contrariness among its highest values. Another concept held dear by the counterculture was, simply, "love." In an era of military violence abroad and police violence at home, many in the counterculture hoped that "peace and love" would prevail instead. Bill Eppridge/Time Life Pictures/Getty Images.

use of drugs — especially marijuana and the hallucinogen popularly known as LSD or acid — which was celebrated in popular music in the second half of the 1960s.

For a brief time, adherents of the counterculture believed that a new age was dawning. In 1967, the "world's first Human Be-In" drew 20,000 people to Golden Gate Park in San Francisco. That summer — called the Summer of Love — San Francisco's Haight-Ashbury, New York's East Village, Chicago's Uptown neighborhoods, and the Sunset Strip in Los Angeles swelled with young dropouts, drifters, and teenage runaways whom the media dubbed "flower children." Although most young people had little interest in all-out revolt, media coverage made it seem as though all of American youth was rejecting the nation's social and cultural norms.

# Days of Rage, 1968–1972

By 1968, a sense of crisis gripped the country. Riots in the cities, campus unrest, and a nose-thumbing counterculture escalated into a general youth rebellion that seemed on the verge of tearing America apart. Calling 1968 "the watershed year for a generation," SDS founder Tom Hayden wrote that it "started with legendary events, then raised hopes, only to end by immersing innocence in tragedy." It was perhaps the most shocking year in all the postwar decades. Violent clashes both in Vietnam and back home in the United States combined with political assassinations to produce a palpable sense of despair and hopelessness (America Compared, p. 920).

## War Abroad, Tragedy at Home

President Johnson had gambled in 1965 on a quick victory in Vietnam, before the political cost of escalation came due. But there was no quick victory. North Vietnamese and Vietcong forces fought on, the South Vietnamese government repeatedly collapsed, and American casualties mounted. By early 1968, the death rate of U.S. troops had reached several hundred a week. Johnson and his generals kept insisting that there was "light at the end of the tunnel." Facts on the ground showed otherwise.

**The Tet Offensive**   On January 30, 1968, the Vietcong unleashed a massive, well-coordinated assault in South Vietnam. Timed to coincide with Tet, the Vietnamese new year, the offensive struck thirty-six provincial capitals and five of the six major cities, including Saigon, where the Vietcong nearly overran the U.S. embassy. In strictly military terms, the Tet offensive was a failure, with very heavy Vietcong losses. But psychologically, the effect was devastating. Television brought into American homes shocking live images: the American embassy under siege and the Saigon police chief placing a pistol to the head of a Vietcong suspect and executing him.

The **Tet offensive** made a mockery of official pronouncements that the United States was winning the war. How could an enemy on the run manage such a large-scale, complex, and coordinated attack? Just before Tet, a Gallup poll found that 56 percent of Americans considered themselves "hawks" (supporters of the war), while only 28 percent identified with the "doves" (war opponents). Three months later, doves outnumbered hawks 42 to 41 percent. Without embracing the peace movement, many Americans simply concluded that the war was unwinnable.

The Tet offensive undermined Johnson and discredited his war policies. When the 1968 presidential primary season got under way in March, antiwar senators Eugene McCarthy of Minnesota and Robert Kennedy of New York, JFK's brother, challenged Johnson for the Democratic nomination. Discouraged, perhaps even physically exhausted, on March 31 Johnson stunned the nation by announcing that he would not seek reelection.

**Political Assassinations**   Americans had barely adjusted to the news that a sitting president would not stand for reelection when, on April 4, James Earl Ray shot and killed Martin Luther King Jr. in Memphis. Riots erupted in more than a hundred cities. The worst of them, in Baltimore, Chicago, and Washington, D.C., left dozens dead and hundreds of millions of dollars in property damaged or destroyed. The violence on the streets of Saigon had found an eerie parallel on the streets of the United States.

One city that did not erupt was Indianapolis. There, Robert Kennedy, in town campaigning in the Indiana primary, gave a quiet, somber speech to the black community on the night of King's assassination. Americans could continue to move toward "greater polarization," Kennedy said, "black people amongst blacks, white amongst whites," or "we can replace that violence . . . with an effort to understand, compassion and love." Kennedy sympathized with African

**TRACE CHANGE OVER TIME**
What changed between 1965 and 1968, and how did these developments affect national political life?

## The Global Protests of 1968

Nineteen sixty-eight was a year of youthful protest, political unrest, and violence across the globe. The year of massive antiwar protests at the Democratic National Convention in Chicago as well as the assassinations of Martin Luther King Jr. and Robert Kennedy saw equal or greater turmoil around the world. Half of Italy's universities were occupied; a massive student strike in France turned into a violent confrontation with police; prodemocracy students in Mexico City led huge protests that drew police gunfire; and protests and street battles with police took place in Prague, Berlin, Tokyo, Rome, and London.

### René Bourrigaud, French Student

My most vivid memory of May '68? The new-found ability for everyone to speak — to speak of anything with anyone. In that month of talking during May you learnt more than in the whole of your five years of studying.

Source: Ronald Fraser, *1968: A Student Generation in Revolt* (New York: Pantheon Books, 1988), 9.

### The "Two Thousand Words" Manifesto, June 27, 1968, Prague, Czechoslovakia

Throughout the spring and summer of 1968, the government of Czechoslovakia, under new communist leadership, pursued reforms pushed by students and other protesters. In August, the Soviet Union invaded and put an end to the new openness.

This spring a great opportunity was given to us once again, as it was at the end of the war [World War II]. Again we have the chance to take into our own hands our common cause, which for working purposes we will call socialism, and give it a form more appropriate to our once-good reputation and to the fairly good opinion we used to have of ourselves.

Source: Jaromír Navrátil, *The Prague Spring 1968: A National Security Archive Documents Reader* (Budapest: Central European University Press, 1998), 181.

### Interview with Participants in 1968 Protests in Mexico City

During the summer of 1968, hundreds of thousands of students protested against Mexico's authoritarian national government and brutal police repression.

*Sergio Aguayo*: It was, in a symbolic way, the clash of a new Mexico and an old Mexico.

*Antonio Azuela*: You have a middle class with eyes closed and a group of students saying, this was not a democracy. And this is not working.

*Marcela Fernandez de Violante*: And so we were together hundred and hundreds and hundreds. We had these big, big meetings at the campus crowded, crowded. And people singing, Que Vivan los Estudiantes . . . ta-ri-ra-ra-ra-ra.

*Marcela Fernandez de Violante*: We were very young, very naive. But for the first time, you had this notion that this country was going to be changed by the power of our convictions.

*Miguel Breseda*: You would get in a bus and give a speech and inform the people. Because newspaper wouldn't publish anything. And people would give you money, they would congratulate you and they would say, "We are with you young people. . . ."

Source: Produced by Radio Diaries (radiodiaries.org) and originally broadcast on NPR's *All Things Considered*. To hear the entire documentary, visit radiodiaries.org. Used by permission of Radio Diaries.

### QUESTIONS FOR ANALYSIS

1. Why did free speech figure so prominently in the protests of the 1960s?
2. What do all of these activists seem to be struggling for, or against? How do their struggles seem similar to — or different from — those occurring simultaneously in the United States?

Americans' outrage at whites, but he begged them not to strike back in retribution. Impromptu and heartfelt, Kennedy's speech was a plea to follow King's nonviolent example, even as the nation descended into greater violence.

But two months later, having emerged as the front-runner for the Democratic presidential nomination, Kennedy, too, would be gone. On June 5, as he was celebrating his victory in the California primary over Eugene McCarthy, Kennedy was shot dead by a young

**Robert Kennedy**

After the assassination of Martin Luther King Jr. and with President Johnson out of the presidential race, Robert Kennedy emerged in 1968 as the leading liberal figure in the nation. A critic of the Vietnam War, a strong supporter of civil rights, and committed to fighting poverty, Kennedy (the brother of the late President John Kennedy) ran a progressive campaign for president. In this photograph he is shown shaking hands with supporters in Detroit in May 1968. However, less than three weeks after this picture was taken, Kennedy, too, was dead, the victim of yet another assassination. Andrew Sacks/Getty Images.

Palestinian named Sirhan Sirhan. Amid the national mourning for yet another political murder, one newspaper columnist declared that "the country does not work anymore." *Newsweek* asked, "Has violence become a way of life?" Kennedy's assassination was a calamity for the Democratic Party because only he had seemed able to surmount the party's fissures over Vietnam. In the space of eight weeks, American liberals had lost two of their most important national figures, King and Kennedy. A third, Johnson, was unpopular and politically damaged. Without these unifying leaders, the crisis of liberalism had become unmanageable.

## The Antiwar Movement and the 1968 Election

Before their deaths, Martin Luther King Jr. and Robert Kennedy had spoken eloquently against the Vietnam War. To antiwar activists, however, bold speeches and marches had not produced the desired effect. "We are no longer interested in merely protesting the war," declared one. "We are out to stop it." They sought nothing short of an immediate American withdrawal. Their anger at Johnson and the Democratic Party — fueled by news of the Tet offensive, the murders of King and Kennedy, and the general youth rebellion — had radicalized the movement.

**Democratic Convention**   In August, at the **1968 Democratic National Convention** in Chicago, the political divisions generated by the war consumed the party. Thousands of protesters descended on the city. The most visible group, led by Jerry Rubin and Abbie Hoffman, a remarkable pair of troublemakers, claimed to represent the Youth International Party. To mock those inside the convention hall, these "Yippies" nominated a pig, Pigasus, for president. The Yippies' stunts were geared toward maximum media exposure. But a far larger and more serious group of activists had come to Chicago to demonstrate against the war as well — and they staged what many came to call the Siege of Chicago.

Democratic mayor Richard J. Daley ordered the police to break up the demonstrations. Several nights of skirmishes between protesters and police culminated on the evening of the nominations. In what an official report later described as a "police riot," police officers attacked protesters with tear gas and clubs. As the nominating speeches proceeded, television networks broadcast scenes of the riot, cementing a popular impression of the Democrats as the party of disorder. "They are going to be spending the next four years picking up the pieces," one Republican said gleefully. Inside the hall, the party dispiritedly nominated Hubert H. Humphrey, Johnson's vice president. The delegates approved a middle-of-the-road platform that endorsed continued fighting in Vietnam while urging a diplomatic solution to the conflict.

**Richard Nixon**    On the Republican side, Richard Nixon had engineered a remarkable political comeback. After losing the presidential campaign in 1960 and the California gubernatorial race in 1962, he won the Republican presidential nomination in 1968. Sensing Democratic weakness, Nixon and his advisors believed there were two groups of voters ready to switch sides: northern working-class voters and southern whites.

Tired of the antiwar movement, the counterculture, and urban riots, northern blue-collar voters, especially Catholics, had drifted away from the Democratic Party. Growing up in the Great Depression, these families were admirers of FDR and perhaps even had his picture on their living-room wall. But times had changed over three decades. To show how much they had changed, the social scientists Ben J. Wattenberg and Richard Scammon profiled blue-collar workers in their study *The Real Majority* (1970). Wattenberg and Scammon asked their readers to consider people such as a forty-seven-year-old machinist's wife from Dayton, Ohio: "[She] is afraid to walk the streets alone at night. . . . She has a mixed view about blacks and civil rights." Moreover, they wrote, "she is deeply distressed that her son is going to a community junior college where LSD was found on campus." Such northern blue-collar

**UNDERSTAND POINTS OF VIEW**

Why might a Democratic supporter of FDR in the 1940s have decided to vote for Republican Richard Nixon in 1968?

families were once reliable Democratic voters, but their political loyalties were increasingly up for grabs—a fact Republicans knew well.

**George Wallace**    Working-class anxieties over student protests and urban riots were first exploited by the controversial governor of Alabama, George C. Wallace. Running in 1968 as a third-party presidential candidate, Wallace traded on his fame as a segregationist governor. He had tried to stop the federal government from desegregating the University of Alabama in 1963, and he was equally obstructive during the Selma crisis of 1965. Appealing to whites in both the North and the South, Wallace called for "law and order" and claimed that mothers on public assistance were, thanks to Johnson's Great Society, "breeding children as a cash crop."

Wallace's hope was that by carrying the South, he could deny a major candidate an electoral majority and force the election into the House of Representatives. That strategy failed, as Wallace finished with just 13.5 percent of the popular vote. But he had defined hot-button issues—liberal elitism, welfare policies, and law and order—that became hallmarks for the next generation of mainstream conservatives.

**Nixon's Strategy**    Nixon offered a subtler version of Wallace's populism in a two-pronged approach to the campaign. He adopted what his advisors called the "southern strategy," which aimed at attracting southern white voters still smarting over the civil rights gains by

**George Wallace**

George Wallace had become famous as the segregationist governor who stood "in the schoolhouse door" to prevent black students from enrolling at the University of Alabama in 1963 (though after being confronted by federal marshals, he stepped aside). In 1968, he campaigned for the Democratic presidential nomination on a populist "law and order" platform that appealed to many blue-collar voters concerned about antiwar protests, urban riots, and the rise of the counterculture. In this 1968 photograph, Wallace greets supporters on the campaign trail. Lee Balterman/Time Life Pictures/Getty Images.

African Americans. Nixon won over the key southerner, Democrat-turned-Republican senator Strom Thurmond of South Carolina, the 1948 Dixiecrat presidential nominee. Nixon informed Thurmond that while formally he had to support civil rights, his administration would go easy on enforcement. He also campaigned against the antiwar movement, urban riots, and protests, calling for a strict adherence to "law and order." He pledged to represent the "quiet voice" of the "great majority of Americans, the forgotten Americans, the nonshouters, the nondemonstrators." Here Nixon was speaking not just to the South, but to the many millions of suburban voters across the country who worried that social disorder had gripped the nation.

These strategies—southern and suburban—worked. Nixon received 43.4 percent of the vote to Humphrey's 42.7 percent, defeating him by a scant 500,000 votes out of the 73 million that were cast (Map 28.3). But the numerical closeness of the race could not disguise the devastating blow to the Democrats. Humphrey received almost 12 million fewer votes than Johnson had in 1964. The white South largely abandoned the Democratic Party, an exodus that would accelerate in the 1970s. In the North, Nixon and Wallace made significant inroads among traditionally Democratic voters. New Deal Democrats lost the unity of purpose that had served them for thirty years. A nation exhausted by months of turmoil and violence had chosen a new direction. Nixon's victory in 1968 foreshadowed—and helped propel—a national electoral realignment in the coming decade.

## The Nationalist Turn

Vietnam and the increasingly radical youth rebellion intersected with the turn toward racial and ethnic nationalism by young African American and Chicano activists. As we saw in Chapter 27, the Black Power and Chicano movements broke with the liberal "rights" politics of an older generation of leaders. These new activists expressed fury at the poverty and white racism that were beyond the reach of civil rights laws; they also saw Vietnam as an unjust war against other people of color.

In this spirit, the **Chicano Moratorium Committee** organized demonstrations against the war. Chanting "Viva la Raza, Afuera Vietnam" ("Long live the Chicano people, Get out of Vietnam"), 20,000 Mexican Americans marched in Los Angeles in August 1970. At another rally, Cesar Chavez said: "For the poor it is a terrible irony that they should rise out of their misery to do battle against other poor people." He and other

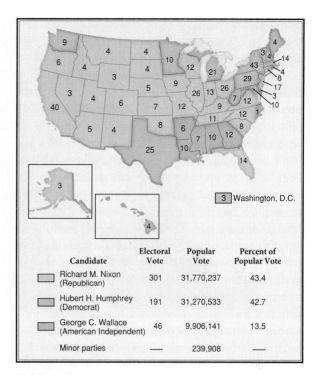

| Candidate | Electoral Vote | Popular Vote | Percent of Popular Vote |
|---|---|---|---|
| Richard M. Nixon (Republican) | 301 | 31,770,237 | 43.4 |
| Hubert H. Humphrey (Democrat) | 191 | 31,270,533 | 42.7 |
| George C. Wallace (American Independent) | 46 | 9,906,141 | 13.5 |
| Minor parties | — | 239,908 | |

**MAP 28.3**
**The Presidential Election of 1968**

With Lyndon B. Johnson's surprise withdrawal and the assassination of the party's most charismatic contender, Robert Kennedy, the Democrats faced the election of 1968 in disarray. Governor George Wallace of Alabama, who left the Democrats to run as a third-party candidate, campaigned on the backlash against the civil rights movement. As late as mid-September Wallace held the support of 21 percent of the voters. But in November he received only 13.5 percent of the vote, winning five southern states. Republican Richard M. Nixon, who like Wallace emphasized "law and order" in his campaign, defeated Hubert H. Humphrey with only 43.4 percent of the popular vote, but it was now clear, given that Wallace's southern support would otherwise have gone to Nixon, that the South had shifted decisively to the Republican side.

Mexican American activists charged that the draft was biased against the poor—like most wars in history, Vietnam was, in the words of one retired army colonel, "a poor boy's fight."

Among African Americans, the Black Panther Party and the National Black Antiwar Antidraft League spoke out against the war. "Black Americans are considered to be the world's biggest fools," Eldridge Cleaver of the Black Panther Party wrote in his typically acerbic style, "to go to another country to fight for something they don't have for themselves." Muhammad Ali, the most famous boxer in the world, refused his army induction. Sentenced to prison, Ali was eventually acquitted on appeal. But his action cost him his heavyweight

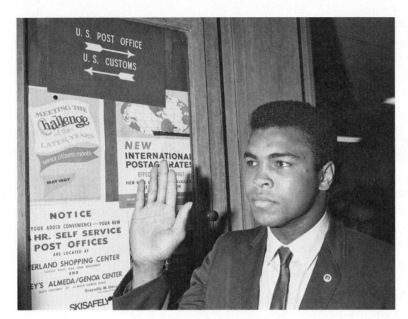

**Muhammad Ali Refuses Army Induction**
On April 28, 1967, heavyweight champion boxer Muhammad Ali refused to be drafted into the U.S. Army, claiming that the war in Vietnam was immoral and that as a member of the Nation of Islam he was a conscientious objector. In this photograph, Ali stands outside the U.S. Army induction center in Houston, Texas. Ali's refusal, which was applauded by the antiwar movement, led to a five-year prison sentence. Though that conviction was overturned in 1971 after numerous appeals, Ali's stand against the war cost him his heavyweight boxing title. © Bettmann/Corbis.

title, and for years he was not allowed to box professionally in the United States.

## Women's Liberation

Among women, 1968 also marked a break with the past. The late 1960s spawned a new brand of feminism: **women's liberation**. These feminists were primarily younger, college-educated women fresh from the New Left, antiwar, and civil rights movements. Those movements' male leaders, they discovered, considered women little more than pretty helpers who typed memos and fetched coffee. Women who tried to raise feminist issues at civil rights and antiwar events were shouted off the platform with jeers such as "Move on, little girl, we have more important issues to talk about here than women's liberation."

Fed up with second-class status, and well versed in the tactics of organization and protest, women radicals broke away and organized on their own. Unlike the National Organization for Women (NOW), the women's liberation movement was loosely structured, comprising an alliance of collectives in New York, San Francisco, Boston, and other big cities and college towns. "Women's lib," as it was dubbed by a skeptical media, went public in 1968 at the Miss America pageant. Demonstrators carried posters of women's bodies labeled as slabs of beef—implying that society treated them as meat. Mirroring the identity politics of Black

**COMPARE AND CONTRAST**
How did women's liberation after 1968 differ from the women's movement of the early 1960s?

Power activists and the self-dramatization of the counterculture, women's liberation sought an end to the denigration and exploitation of women. "Sisterhood is powerful!" read one women's liberationist manifesto. The national Women's Strike for Equality in August 1970 brought hundreds of thousands of women into the streets of the nation's cities for marches and demonstrations.

By that year, new terms such as *sexism* and *male chauvinism* had become part of the national vocabulary. As converts flooded in, the two branches of the women's movement began to converge. Radical women realized that key feminist goals—child care, equal pay, and reproduction rights—could best be achieved in the political arena. At the same time, more traditional activists, exemplified by Betty Friedan, developed a broader view of women's oppression. They came to understand that women required more than equal opportunity: the culture that regarded women as nothing more than sexual objects and helpmates to men had to change as well. Although still largely white and middle class, feminists began to think of themselves as part of a broad social crusade.

"Sisterhood" did not unite all women, however. Rather than joining white-led women's liberation organizations, African American and Latina women continued to work within the larger framework of the civil rights movement. New groups such as the Combahee River Collective and the National Black Feminist Organization arose to speak for the concerns of African American women. They criticized sexism but were reluctant to break completely with black men and the

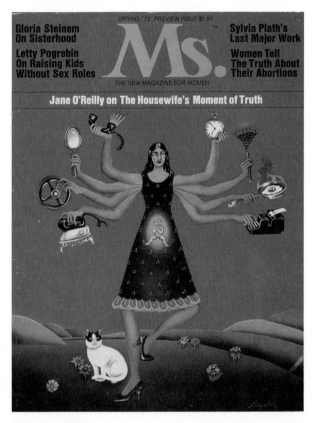

**Ms. Magazine**

Cofounded by the feminist Gloria Steinem, *Ms.* magazine made its initial appearance in 1972. Steinem and her cofounders believed that American women needed an explicitly feminist magazine distinct from the slew of available female-focused "lifestyle" magazines, such as *McCall's* and *Redbook. Ms.* would take on crucial, but neglected, issues relevant to women: reproductive rights, child care, employment and educational equality, sexual harassment, and marriage and relations between men and women. Inspired by women's liberation, *Ms.* has remained an important forum for feminist opinion and debate down to the present. Reprinted by permission of *Ms.* magazine, © 1972.

struggle for racial equality. Chicana feminists came from Catholic backgrounds in which motherhood and family were held in high regard. "We want to walk hand in hand with the Chicano brothers, with our children, our *viejitos* [elders], our Familia de la Raza," one Chicana feminist wrote. Black and Chicana feminists embraced the larger movement for women's rights but carried on their own struggles to address specific needs in their communities.

One of the most important contributions of women's liberation was to raise awareness about what feminist Kate Millett called sexual politics. Liberationists argued that unless women had control over their own bodies, they could not freely shape their destinies. They campaigned for reproductive rights, especially

access to abortion, and railed against a culture that blamed women in cases of sexual assault and turned a blind eye to sexual harassment in the workplace.

Meanwhile, women's opportunities expanded dramatically in higher education. Dozens of formerly all-male bastions such as Yale, Princeton, and the U.S. military academies admitted women undergraduates for the first time. Colleges started women's studies programs, which eventually numbered in the hundreds, and the proportion of women attending graduate and professional schools rose markedly. With the adoption of **Title IX** in 1972, Congress broadened the 1964 Civil Rights Act to include educational institutions, prohibiting colleges and universities that received federal funds from discriminating on the basis of sex. By requiring comparable funding for sports programs, Title IX made women's athletics a real presence on college campuses.

Women also became increasingly visible in public life. Congresswomen Bella Abzug and Shirley Chisholm joined Betty Friedan and Gloria Steinem, the founder of *Ms.* magazine, to create the National Women's Political Caucus in 1971. Abzug and Chisholm, both from New York, joined Congresswomen Patsy Mink from Hawaii and Martha Griffiths from Michigan to sponsor equal rights legislation. Congress authorized childcare tax deductions for working parents in 1972 and in 1974 passed the Equal Credit Opportunity Act, which enabled married women to get credit, including credit cards and mortgages, in their own names.

Antiwar activists, black and Chicano nationalists, and women's liberationists had each challenged the Cold War liberalism of the Democratic Party. In doing so, they helped build on the "rights liberalism" forged first by the African American–led civil rights movement. But they also created rifts among competing parts of the former liberal consensus. Many Catholics, for instance, opposed abortion rights and other freedoms sought by women's liberationists. Still other Democrats, many of them blue-collar trade unionists, believed that antiwar protesters were unpatriotic and that supporting one's government in time of war was a citizen's duty. The antiwar movement and the evolving rights liberalism of the sixties had made the old Democratic coalition increasingly unworkable.

## Stonewall and Gay Liberation

The liberationist impulse transformed the gay rights movement as well. Homophile activists in the 1960s (Chapter 26) had pursued rights by protesting, but they adopted the respectable dress and behavior they knew

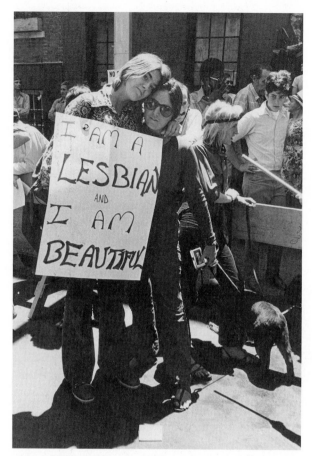

**A Lesbian and Gay Rights Protest in Greenwich Village, New York City, 1970**

Building on the momentum of the Black Power and women's liberation movements of the late 1960s, a gay liberation movement had emerged by the early 1970s. Its history was longer than most Americans recognized, dating to the homophile movement of the 1950s, but the struggle for gay and lesbian rights and freedoms gained new adherents after the Stonewall riots of 1969. Under the banner of "coming out," lesbian and gay Americans refused to accept second-class citizenship. Rue des Archives/The Granger Collection, NYC.

rights. A gay newspaper in New York bore the title *Come Out!*

The new gay liberation found multiple expressions in major cities across the country, but a defining event occurred in New York's Greenwich Village. Police had raided gay bars for decades, making arrests, publicizing the names of patrons, and harassing customers simply for being gay. When a local gay bar called the **Stonewall Inn** was raided by police in the summer of 1969, however, its patrons rioted for two days, burning the bar and battling with police in the narrow streets of the Village. Decades of police repression had taken their toll. Few commentators excused the violence, and the Stonewall riots were not repeated, but activists celebrated them as a symbolic demand for full citizenship. The gay liberation movement grew quickly after Stonewall. Local gay and lesbian organizations proliferated, and activists began pushing for nondiscrimination ordinances and consensual sex laws at the state level. By 1975, the National Gay Task Force and other national organizations lobbied Congress, served as media watchdogs, and advanced suits in the courts. Despite all the activity, progress was slow; in most arenas of American life, gays and lesbians did not enjoy the same legal protections and rights as other Americans.

# Richard Nixon and the Politics of the Silent Majority

Vietnam abroad and the antiwar movement and the counterculture at home tore at the fabric of the Democratic coalition and proved too difficult for Lyndon Johnson to navigate. Richard Nixon, in contrast, showed himself adept at taking advantage of the nation's unrest through carefully timed speeches and displays of moral outrage. A centrist by nature and temperament, Nixon was not part of the conservative Goldwater wing of the Republican Party. Though he was an ardent anticommunist like Goldwater, Nixon also shared some of Eisenhower's traits, including a basic acceptance of government's role in economic matters. Nixon is thus most profitably viewed as a transitional figure, a national politician who formed a bridge between the liberal postwar era and the much more conservative decades that followed the 1970s.

In late 1969, following a massive antiwar rally in Washington, President Nixon gave a televised speech in which he referred to his supporters as the **silent majority**. It was classic Nixonian rhetoric. In a single phrase, he summed up a generational and cultural

straight society demanded. Meanwhile, the vast majority of gay men and lesbians remained "in the closet." So many were closeted because homosexuality was considered immoral and was even illegal in the vast majority of states — sodomy statutes outlawed same-sex relations, and police used other morals laws to harass and arrest gay men and lesbians. In the late 1960s, however, inspired by the Black Power and women's movements, gay activists increasingly demanded immediate and unconditional recognition of their

**EXPLAIN CONSEQUENCES**

How did the antiwar movement, women's liberation, and gay liberation break with an earlier liberal politics?

struggle, placing himself on the side of ordinary Americans against the rabble-rousers and troublemakers. It was an oversimplification, but the label *silent majority* stuck, and Nixon had defined a political phenomenon. For the remainder of his presidency, Nixon cultivated the impression that he was the defender of a reasonable middle ground under assault from the radical left.

## Nixon in Vietnam

On the war in Vietnam, Nixon picked up where Johnson had left off. Cold War assumptions continued to dictate presidential policy. Abandoning Vietnam, Nixon insisted, would damage America's "credibility" and make the country seem "a pitiful, helpless giant." Nixon wanted peace, but only "peace with honor." The North Vietnamese were not about to oblige him. The only outcome acceptable to them was a unified Vietnam under their control.

**Vietnamization and Cambodia**   To neutralize criticism at home, Nixon began delegating the ground

fighting to the South Vietnamese. Under this new policy of **Vietnamization**, American troop levels dropped from 543,000 in 1968 to 334,000 in 1971 to barely 24,000 by early 1973. American casualties dropped correspondingly. But the killing in Vietnam continued. As Ellsworth Bunker, the U.S. ambassador to Vietnam, noted cynically, it was just a matter of changing "the color of the bodies."

Far from abating, however, the antiwar movement intensified. In November 1969, half a million demonstrators staged a huge protest in Washington called the Vietnam Moratorium. On April 30, 1970, as part of a secret bombing campaign against Vietcong supply lines, American troops destroyed enemy bases in neutral Cambodia. When news of the invasion of Cambodia came out, American campuses exploded in outrage—and, for the first time, students died. On May 4, 1970, at Kent State University in Ohio, panicky National Guardsmen fired into an antiwar rally, wounding eleven students

> **COMPARE AND CONTRAST**
> How was President Nixon's Vietnam policy different from President Johnson's?

**Richard Nixon**
Richard Nixon completed one of the more remarkable political rehabilitations in modern times. He had lost the 1960 presidential election and the 1962 California gubernatorial election. But he came back strong in 1968 to ride—and help direct—a growing wave of reaction among conservative Americans against Great Society liberalism, the antiwar movement, civil rights, and the counterculture. In this photograph, President Nixon greets supporters in June 1969, just a few months after his inauguration. © Wally McNamee/Corbis.

**Prowar Rally**
Under a sea of American flags, construction workers in New York City march in support of the Vietnam War. Wearing hard hats, tens of thousands of marchers jammed Broadway for four blocks opposite City Hall, and the overflow crammed the side streets. Working-class patriotism became a main source of support for Nixon's war. Paul Fusco/Magnum Photos, Inc.

and killing four. Less than two weeks later, at Jackson State College in Mississippi, Guardsmen stormed a dormitory, killing two black students. More than 450 colleges closed in protest. Across the country, the spring semester was essentially canceled.

**My Lai Massacre**   Meanwhile, one of the worst atrocities of the war had become public. In 1968, U.S. Army troops had executed nearly five hundred people in the South Vietnamese village of **My Lai**, including a large number of women and children. The massacre was known only within the military until 1969, when journalist Seymour Hersh broke the story and photos of the massacre appeared in *Life* magazine, discrediting the United States around the world. Americans, *Time* observed, "must stand in the larger dock of guilt and human conscience." Although high-ranking officers participated in the My Lai massacre and its cover-up,

only one soldier, a low-ranking second lieutenant named William Calley, was convicted.

Believing that Calley had been made a fall guy for official U.S. policies that inevitably brought death to innocent civilians, a group called Vietnam Veterans Against the War publicized other atrocities committed by U.S. troops. In a controversial protest in 1971, they returned their combat medals at demonstrations outside the U.S. Capitol, literally hurling them onto the Capitol steps. "Here's my merit badge for murder," one vet said. Supporters of the war called these veterans cowardly and un-American, but their heartfelt antiwar protest exposed the deep personal torment that Vietnam had caused many soldiers.

**Détente**   As protests continued at home, Nixon pursued two strategies to achieve his declared "peace with honor," one diplomatic and the other brutal. First, he sought **détente** (a lessening of tensions) with the Soviet Union and a new openness with China. In a series of meetings between 1970 and 1972, Nixon and Soviet premier Leonid Brezhnev resolved tensions over Cuba and Berlin and signed the first Strategic Arms Limitation Treaty (SALT I), the latter a symbolic step toward ending the Cold War arms race. Heavily influenced by his national security advisor, the Harvard professor Henry Kissinger, Nixon believed that he could break the Cold War impasse that had kept the United States from productive dialogue with the Soviet Union.

Then, in 1972, Nixon visited China, becoming the first sitting U.S. president to do so. In a televised week-long trip, the president pledged better relations with China and declared that the two nations — one capitalist, the other communist — could peacefully coexist. This was the man who had risen to prominence in the 1950s by railing against the Democrats for "losing" China and by hounding communists and fellow travelers. Indeed, the president's impeccable anticommunist credentials gave him the political cover to travel to Beijing. He remarked genially to Mao: "Those on the right can do what those on the left only talk about." Praised for his efforts to lessen Cold War tensions, Nixon also had tactical objectives in mind. He hoped that by befriending both the Soviet Union and China, he could play one against the other and strike a better deal over Vietnam at the ongoing peace talks in Paris. His second strategy, however, would prove less praiseworthy and cost more lives.

**Exit America**   In April 1972, in an attempt to strengthen his negotiating position, Nixon ordered B-52 bombing raids against North Vietnam. A month later, he approved the mining of North Vietnamese ports, something Johnson had never dared to do. The North Vietnamese were not isolated, however: supplies from China and the Soviet Union continued, and the Vietcong fought on.

With the 1972 presidential election approaching, Nixon sent Kissinger back to the Paris peace talks, which had been initiated under Johnson. In a key concession, Kissinger accepted the presence of North Vietnamese troops in South Vietnam. North Vietnam then agreed to an interim arrangement whereby the South Vietnamese government in Saigon would stay in power while a special commission arranged a final settlement. With Kissinger's announcement that "peace is at hand," Nixon got the election lift he wanted, but the agreement was then sabotaged by General Nguyen Van Thieu, the South Vietnamese president. So Nixon,

in one final spasm of bloodletting, unleashed the two-week "Christmas bombing," the most intense of the entire war. On January 27, 1973, the two sides signed the Paris Peace Accords.

Nixon hoped that with massive U.S. aid, the Thieu regime might survive. But Congress was in revolt. It refused appropriations for bombing Cambodia after August 15, 1973, and gradually cut back aid to South Vietnam. In March 1975, North Vietnamese forces launched a final offensive, and on April 30, Vietnam was reunited. Saigon, the South Vietnamese capital, was renamed Ho Chi Minh City, after the founding father of the communist regime.

The collapse of South Vietnam in 1975 produced a powerful, and tragic, historical irony: an outcome little different from what would likely have resulted from the unification vote in 1954 (Chapter 25). In other words, America's most disastrous military adventure of the twentieth century barely altered the geopolitical realities in Southeast Asia. The Hanoi regime called itself communist but never intended to be a satellite of any country, least of all China, Vietnam's ancient enemy.

Many paid a steep price for the Vietnam War. America's Vietnamese friends lost jobs and property, spent years in "reeducation" camps, or had to flee the country. Millions of Vietnamese had died in a decade of war, which included some of the most intensive aerial bombing of the twentieth century. In bordering Cambodia, the maniacal Khmer Rouge, followers of Cambodia's ruling Communist Party, took power and murdered 1.7 million people in bloody purges. And in the United States, more than 58,000 Americans had sacrificed their lives, and 300,000 had been wounded. On top of the war's $150 billion price tag, slow-to-heal internal wounds divided the country, and Americans increasingly lost confidence in their political leaders.

## The Silent Majority Speaks Out

Nixon placed himself on the side of what he called "the nonshouters, the nondemonstrators." But moderate and conservative Americans increasingly spoke out. They were not in the mood to simply remain silent. During Nixon's first presidential term, those opposed to the direction liberalism had taken since the early 1960s focused their discontent on what they believed were the excesses of the "rights revolution" — the enormous changes in American law and society initiated by the civil rights movement and advanced by feminists and others thereafter.

**The Fall of Saigon**
After the 1973 U.S. withdrawal from Vietnam, the South Vietnamese government lasted another two years. In March 1975, the North Vietnamese forces launched a final offensive; by April, they had surrounded the capital, Saigon. As seen here, many Vietnamese, some of them associated with the fallen South Vietnamese regime, sought sanctuary at the U.S. embassy compound. Thousands of Vietnamese and Americans were evacuated before the last helicopter left the embassy on April 30. Nik Wheeler/Sipa/AP/Wide World Photos.

**Law and Order and the Supreme Court**    The rights revolution found an ally in an unexpected place: the U.S. Supreme Court. The decision that stood as a landmark in the civil rights movement, *Brown v. Board of Education* (1954), triggered a larger judicial revolution. Following *Brown*, the Court increasingly agreed to hear human rights and civil liberties cases — as opposed to its previous focus on property-related suits. Surprisingly, this shift was led by the man whom President Dwight Eisenhower had appointed chief justice in 1953: Earl Warren. A popular Republican governor of California, Warren surprised many, including Eisenhower himself, with his robust advocacy of civil rights and civil liberties. The **Warren Court** lasted from 1954 until 1969 and established some of the most far-reaching liberal jurisprudence in U.S. history.

Right-wing activists fiercely opposed the Warren Court, which they accused of "legislating from the bench" and contributing to social breakdown. They pointed, for instance, to the Court's rulings that people who are arrested have a constitutional right to counsel (1963, 1964) and, in *Miranda v. Arizona* (1966), that arrestees have to be informed by police of their right to remain silent. Compounding conservatives' frustration was a series of decisions that liberalized restrictions on pornography. Trying to walk the fine line between censorship and obscenity, the Court ruled in *Roth v. United States* (1957) that obscene material had to be "utterly without redeeming social importance" to be banned. The "social importance" test, however, proved nearly impossible to define and left wide latitude for pornography to flourish.

That measure was finally abandoned in 1972, when the Court ruled in *Miller v. California* that "contemporary community standards" were the rightful measure of obscenity. But *Miller*, too, had little effect on the pornographic magazines, films, and peep shows proliferating in the 1970s. Conservatives found these decisions especially distasteful, since the Court had also ruled that religious ritual of any kind in public schools — including prayers and Bible reading — violated the constitutional separation of church and state. To many religious Americans, the Court had taken the side of immorality over Christian values.

Supreme Court critics blamed rising crime rates and social breakdown on the Warren Court's liberal judicial record. Every category of crime was up in the 1970s, but especially disconcerting was the doubling of the murder rate since the 1950s and the 76 percent increase in burglary and theft between 1967 and 1976. Sensational crimes had always grabbed headlines, but now "crime" itself preoccupied politicians, the media, and the public. However, no one could establish a direct causal link between increases in crime and Supreme Court decisions, given a myriad of other social factors, including drugs, income inequality, enhanced statistical record-keeping, and the proliferation of guns. But when many Americans looked at their cities in the 1970s, they saw pornographic theaters, X-rated bookstores, and rising crime rates. Where, they wondered, was law and order?

**Busing**   Another major civil rights objective — desegregating schools — produced even more controversy and fireworks. For fifteen years, southern states, by a variety of stratagems, had fended off court directives that they desegregate "with all deliberate speed." In 1968, only about one-third of all black children in the South attended schools with whites. At that point, the federal courts got serious and, in a series of stiff decisions, ordered an end to "dual school systems."

Where schools remained highly segregated, the courts increasingly endorsed the strategy of busing students to achieve integration. Plans differed across the country. In some states, black children rode buses from their neighborhoods to attend previously all-white schools. In others, white children were bused to black or Latino neighborhoods. In an important 1971 decision, the Supreme Court upheld a countywide busing plan for Charlotte-Mecklenburg, a North Carolina school district. Despite local opposition, desegregation proceeded, and many cities in the South followed suit. By the mid-1970s, 86 percent of southern black children were attending school with whites. (In recent years, this trend has reversed.)

In the North, where segregated schooling was also a fact of life — arising from suburban residential patterns — busing orders proved less effective. Detroit dramatized the problem. To integrate Detroit schools would have required merging city and suburban school districts. A lower court ordered just such a merger in 1971, but in *Milliken v. Bradley* (1974), the Supreme Court reversed the ruling, requiring busing plans to remain within the boundaries of a single school district. Without including the largely white suburbs in busing efforts, however, achieving racial balance in Detroit, and other major northern cities, was all but impossible. Postwar suburbanization had produced in the North what law had mandated in the South: entrenched racial segregation of schools.

As the 1972 election approached, President Nixon took advantage of rising discontent over "law and order" and busing. He was the political beneficiary of a growing reaction against liberalism that had begun to take hold between 1968 and the early 1970s.

## The 1972 Election

Political realignments have been infrequent in American history. One occurred between 1932 and 1936, when many Republicans, despairing over the Great Depression, had switched sides and voted for FDR. The

**An Antibusing Confrontation in Boston**
Where busing was implemented, it often faced stiff resistance. Many white communities resented judges dictating which children would attend which neighborhood school. In working-class Irish South Boston, mobs attacked African American students bused in from Roxbury in 1974. A police presence was required to keep South Boston High School open. When lawyer and civil rights activist Ted Landsmark tried to enter Boston's city hall during a 1976 antibusing demonstration, he was assaulted. Stanley Forman's Pulitzer Prize–winning photo for the Boston *Herald-American* — titled *The Soiling of Old Glory* — shows Joseph Rakes lunging at Landsmark with an American flag. Busing also had the perverse effect of speeding up "white flight" to city suburbs. Pulitzer Prize, 1977, www.stanleyformanphotos.com.

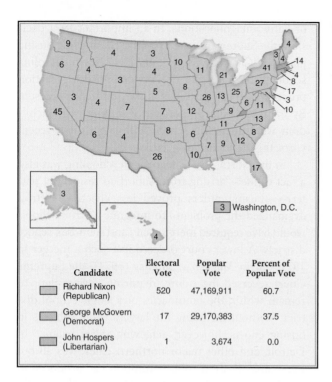

**MAP 28.4**
**The Presidential Election of 1972**

In one of the most lopsided presidential elections of the twentieth century, Republican Richard Nixon defeated Democrat George McGovern in a landslide in 1972. It was a reversal of the 1964 election, just eight years before, in which Republican Barry Goldwater had been defeated by a similar margin. Nixon hoped that his victory signaled what Kevin Phillips called "the emerging Republican majority," but the president's missteps and criminal actions in the Watergate scandal would soon bring an end to his tenure in office.

| Candidate | Electoral Vote | Popular Vote | Percent of Popular Vote |
|---|---|---|---|
| Richard Nixon (Republican) | 520 | 47,169,911 | 60.7 |
| George McGovern (Democrat) | 17 | 29,170,383 | 37.5 |
| John Hospers (Libertarian) | 1 | 3,674 | 0.0 |

3 | Washington, D.C.

years between 1968 and 1972 were another such pivotal moment. This time, Democrats were the ones who abandoned their party.

After the 1968 elections, the Democrats fell into disarray. Bent on sweeping away the party's old guard, reformers took over, adopting new rules that granted women, African Americans, and young people delegate seats "in reasonable relation to their presence in the population." In the past, an alliance of urban machines, labor unions, and white ethnic groups — the heart of the New Deal coalition — dominated the nominating process. But at the 1972 convention, few of the party faithful qualified as delegates under the changed rules. The crowning insult came when the convention rejected the credentials of Chicago mayor Richard Daley and his delegation, seating instead an Illinois delegation led by Jesse Jackson, a firebrand young black minister and former aide to Martin Luther King Jr.

Capturing the party was one thing; beating the Republicans was quite another. These party reforms opened the door for George McGovern, a liberal South Dakota senator and favorite of the antiwar and women's movements, to capture the nomination. But McGovern took a number of missteps, including failing to mollify key party backers such as the AFL-CIO, which, for the first time in memory, refused to endorse the Democratic ticket. A weak campaigner, McGovern was also no match for Nixon, who pulled out all the stops. Using the advantages of incumbency, Nixon gave the economy a well-timed lift and proclaimed (prematurely) a cease-fire in Vietnam. Nixon's appeal to the "silent majority" — people who "care about a strong United States, about patriotism, about moral and spiritual values" — was by now well honed.

Nixon won in a landslide, receiving nearly 61 percent of the popular vote and carrying every state except Massachusetts and the District of Columbia (Map 28.4). The returns revealed how fractured traditional Democratic voting blocs had become. McGovern received only 38 percent of the big-city Catholic vote and lost 42 percent of self-identified Democrats overall. The 1972 election marked a pivotal moment in the country's shift to the right. Yet observers legitimately wondered whether the 1972 election results proved the popularity of conservatism or merely showed that the country had grown weary of liberalism and the changes it had wrought in national life.

## SUMMARY

In this chapter, we saw that the combined pressures of the Vietnam War and racial and cultural conflict fractured and split the New Deal coalition. Following John Kennedy's assassination in 1963, Lyndon Johnson advanced the most ambitious liberal reform program since the New Deal, securing not only civil rights legislation but also many programs in education, medical care, transportation, environmental protection, and, above all, his War on Poverty. But the Great Society fell short of its promise as Johnson escalated American involvement in Vietnam.

The war bitterly divided Americans. Galvanized by the carnage of war and the draft, the antiwar movement spread rapidly among young people, and the spirit of rebellion spilled beyond the war. The New Left took the lead among college students, while the more apolitical counterculture preached liberation through sex, drugs, music, and personal transformation. Women's liberationists broke from the New Left and raised new concerns about society's sexism. Conservative students rallied in support of the war and on behalf of conservative principles, but they were often drowned out by the more vocal and demonstrative liberals and radicals.

In 1968, the nation was rocked by the assassinations of Martin Luther King Jr. and Robert F. Kennedy, as well as by a wave of urban riots, fueling a growing popular desire for law and order. Adding to the national disquiet was the Democratic National Convention that summer, divided by the Vietnam War and besieged by street riots outside. The stage was set for a new wave of conservatism to take hold of the country, and a resurgence of the Republican Party under Richard Nixon between 1968 and 1972. President Nixon ended the war in Vietnam, but only after five more years and many more casualties.

# CHAPTER REVIEW

**MAKE IT STICK**   Go to **LearningCurve** to retain what you've read.

## TERMS TO KNOW   Identify and explain the significance of each term below.

### Key Concepts and Events

Great Society (p. 904)

Economic Opportunity Act (p. 905)

Medicare (p. 906)

Medicaid (p. 906)

Equal Pay Act (p. 908)

*The Feminine Mystique* (p. 908)

Presidential Commission on the Status of Women (p. 909)

National Organization for Women (NOW) (p. 909)

Gulf of Tonkin Resolution (p. 911)

Operation Rolling Thunder (p. 911)

Students for a Democratic Society (SDS) (p. 914)

Port Huron Statement (p. 914)

New Left (p. 914)

Young Americans for Freedom (YAF) (p. 915)

Sharon Statement (p. 918)

counterculture (p. 918)

Tet offensive (p. 919)

1968 Democratic National Convention (p. 921)

Chicano Moratorium Committee (p. 923)

women's liberation (p. 924)

Title IX (p. 925)

Stonewall Inn (p. 926)

silent majority (p. 926)

Vietnamization (p. 927)

My Lai (p. 928)

détente (p. 929)

Warren Court (p. 930)

### Key People

Lyndon B. Johnson (p. 904)

Barry Goldwater (p. 905)

Betty Friedan (p. 908)

Ngo Dinh Diem (p. 910)

Robert Kennedy (p. 919)

Richard M. Nixon (p. 922)

George C. Wallace (p. 922)

Henry Kissinger (p. 929)

## REVIEW QUESTIONS
Answer these questions to demonstrate your understanding of the chapter's main ideas.

1. How do you explain the liberal resurgence in the first half of the 1960s?

2. What were the main elements of Johnson's Great Society?

3. How did the debates over civil liberties, particularly with respect to Supreme Court decisions under Chief Justice Earl Warren, influence political life in the 1960s and 1970s?

4. In what ways was the Vietnam War part of the Cold War? How did the antiwar movement represent a break with Cold War assumptions?

5. **THEMATIC UNDERSTANDING**   Look at the events listed under "America in the World" on the thematic timeline on page 803. American global leadership is a major theme of Part 8. How did the global role of the United States shift in the 1960s?

## MAKING CONNECTIONS
Recognize the larger developments and continuities within and across chapters by answering these questions.

1. **ACROSS TIME AND PLACE**   In what ways was the Great Society an extension of the New Deal? In what ways was it different? What factors made the period between 1932 and 1972 a "liberal" era in American politics? What events and developments would you use to explain your answer?

2. **VISUAL EVIDENCE**   Compare the photographs of the prowar rally (p. 928) and the counterculture (p. 918). Why did clothing and appearance become so important to many social movements in the 1960s — the women's movement, the Black Power movement, the antiwar movement, and others? How are these visual images historical evidence?

## MORE TO EXPLORE
Start here to learn more about the events discussed in this chapter.

Robert Dallek, *Flawed Giant: Lyndon Johnson and His Times, 1961–1973* (1998). An engaging biography of Johnson and an account of his era.

Maurice Isserman and Michael Kazin, *America Divided: The Civil War of the 1960s* (1999). A vivid account of dissent in the 1960s.

G. Calvin Mackenzie and Robert Weisbrot, *The Liberal Hour: Washington and the Politics of Change in the 1960s* (2008). A thoughtful account of the Great Society.

Ruth Rosen, *The World Split Open* (2000). An accessible exploration of the women's movement and feminism.

Bruce Schulman, *The Seventies: The Great Shift in American Culture, Society, and Politics* (2001). A thoughtful explanation of Nixon and political realignment.

Marilyn Young, *The Vietnam Wars, 1945–1990* (1991). An excellent history of the decades-long conflict in Vietnam.

**TIMELINE**   Ask yourself why this chapter begins and ends with these dates and then identify the links among related events.

| | |
|---|---|
| **1963** | • John F. Kennedy assassinated; Lyndon B. Johnson assumes presidency |
| **1964** | • Civil Rights Act |
| | • Economic Opportunity Act inaugurates War on Poverty |
| | • Free Speech Movement at Berkeley |
| | • Gulf of Tonkin Resolution |
| **1965** | • Immigration Act abolishes national quota system |
| | • Medicare and Medicaid programs established |
| | • Operation Rolling Thunder escalates bombing campaign (March) |
| | • First U.S. combat troops arrive in Vietnam |
| **1967** | • Hippie counterculture's "Summer of Love" |
| | • 100,000 march in antiwar protest in Washington, D.C. (October) |
| **1968** | • Tet offensive begins (January) |
| | • Martin Luther King Jr. and Robert F. Kennedy assassinated |
| | • Women's liberation protest at Miss America pageant |
| | • Riot at Democratic National Convention in Chicago (August) |
| | • Richard Nixon elected president |
| **1969** | • Stonewall riots (June) |
| **1970** | • National Women's Strike for Equality |
| **1971** | • *Swan v. Charlotte-Mecklenburg* approves countywide busing |
| **1972** | • Nixon visits China (February) |
| | • Nixon wins a second term (November 7) |
| **1973** | • Paris Peace Accords end Vietnam War |
| **1974** | • *Milliken v. Bradley* limits busing to school district boundaries |
| **1975** | • Vietnam reunified under Communist rule |

**KEY TURNING POINTS:** Which specific developments from this timeline made the years 1964, 1965, and 1968 turning points in politics, foreign policy, and culture and why?

# The Search for Order
# in an Era of Limits
# 1973–1980

Early in 1971, a new fictional character appeared on national television. Archie Bunker was a gruff blue-collar worker who berated his wife and bemoaned his daughter's marriage to a bearded hippie. Prone to bigoted and insensitive remarks, Archie and his wife Edith sang "Those Were the Days" at the opening of each episode of *All in the Family*, a half-hour comedy. The song celebrated a bygone era, when "girls were girls and men were men." Disdainful of the liberal social movements of the 1960s, Archie professed a conservative, hardscrabble view of the world.

Archie Bunker became a folk hero to many conservative Americans in the 1970s; he said what they felt. But his significance went beyond his politics. *All in the Family* gave voice to a national search for order. His feminist daughter, liberal son-in-law, and black neighbors brought that changing world into Archie's modest home in Queens, New York. Not all Americans were as resistant to change as Archie. Most were ordinary, middle-of-the-road people confronting the aftermath of the tumultuous late 1960s and early 1970s. The liberalism of those years challenged Americans to think in new ways about race, gender roles, sexual morality, and the family. Vietnam and the Watergate scandal had compounded matters by producing a crisis of political authority. An "old order" had seemingly collapsed. But what would take its place was not yet clear.

Alongside cultural dislocation and political alienation, the country confronted economic setbacks. In 1973, inflation began to climb at a pace unprecedented in the post–World War II decades, and economic growth slowed. An energy crisis, aggravated by U.S. foreign policy in the Middle East, produced fuel shortages. Foreign competition in manufacturing brought less expensive, and often more reliable, goods into the U.S. market from nations such as Japan and West Germany. As a result, more American plants closed. The great economic ride enjoyed by the United States since World War II was over.

What distinguishes the period between the energy crisis (1973) and the election of Ronald Reagan to the presidency (1980) is the collective national search for order in the midst of economic crisis, political realignment, and rapid social change. Virtually all the verities and touchstones of the postwar decades—Cold War liberalism, rising living standards, and the nuclear family—had come under question, and most agreed on the urgency to act. For some, this search demanded new forms of liberal experimentation. For others, it led instead to the conservatism of the emerging New Right.

**IDENTIFY THE BIG IDEA**

How did the legacy of social changes—such as shifting gender roles, civil rights, and challenges to the family—in the 1960s continue to reverberate in the 1970s, leading to both new opportunities and political disagreement?

**Shifting Gender Roles**   As American society underwent dramatic changes in the 1970s, women seized new opportunities and expanded their role in national life. Donna Wright, shown here on break from her work at the Blue Ribbon Mine, was the only woman working at the mine in 1979. Photo by Kit Miniciler/The Denver Post via Getty Images.

# An Era of Limits

The economic downturn of the early 1970s was the deepest slump since the Great Depression. Every major economic indicator — employment, productivity, growth — turned negative, and by 1973 the economy was in a tailspin. Inflation, brought on in part by military spending in Vietnam, proved especially difficult to control. When a Middle East embargo cut oil supplies in 1973, prices climbed even more. Unemployment remained high and productivity growth low until 1982. Overall, the 1970s represented the worst economic decade of the postwar period — what California governor Jerry Brown called an "era of limits." In this time of distress, Americans were forced to consider other limits to the growth and expansion that had long been markers of national progress. The environmental movement brought attention to the toxic effects of modern industrial capitalism on the natural world. As the urban crisis grew worse, several major cities verged on bankruptcy. Finally, political limits were reached as well: None of the presidents of the 1970s could reverse the nation's economic slide, though each spent years trying.

## Energy Crisis

Modern economies run on oil. If the oil supply is drastically reduced, woe follows. Something like that happened to the United States in the 1970s. Once the world's leading oil producer, the United States had become heavily dependent on inexpensive imported oil, mostly from the Persian Gulf (Figure 29.1). American and European oil companies had discovered and developed the Middle Eastern fields early in the twentieth century, when much of the region was ruled by the British and French empires. When Middle Eastern states threw off the remnants of European colonialism, they demanded concessions for access to the fields. Foreign companies still extracted the oil, but now they did so under profit-sharing agreements with the Persian Gulf states. In 1960, these nations and other oil-rich developing countries formed a cartel (a business association formed to control prices), the **Organization of Petroleum Exporting Countries (OPEC)**.

Conflict between Israel and the neighboring Arab states of Egypt, Syria, and Jordan prompted OPEC to take political sides between 1967 and 1973. Following Israel's victory in the 1967 Six-Day War, Israeli-Arab tensions in the region grew closer to boiling over with each passing year. In the 1973 Yom Kippur War, Egypt and Syria invaded Israel to regain territory lost in the 1967 conflict. Israel prevailed, but only after being resupplied by an emergency American airlift. In response to U.S. support for Israel, the Arab states in OPEC declared an oil embargo in October 1973. Gas prices in the United States quickly jumped by 40 percent and heating oil prices by 30 percent. Demand outpaced supply, and Americans found themselves parked for

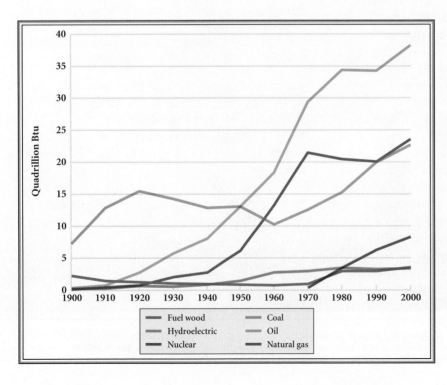

**FIGURE 29.1**

**U.S. Energy Consumption, 1900–2000**

Coal was the nation's primary source of energy until the 1950s, when it was surpassed by oil and natural gas. The revival of coal consumption after 1960 stemmed from new open-pit mining in the West that provided cheaper fuel for power plants. The decline in oil consumption in 1980 reflects the nation's response to the oil crisis of the 1970s, including, most notably, fuel-efficient automobiles. Nuclear energy became an important new fuel source, but after 1990 its contribution leveled off as a result of the safety concerns triggered by the Three Mile Island incident.

hours in mile-long lines at gasoline stations for much of the winter of 1973–1974. Oil had become a political weapon, and the West's vulnerability stood revealed.

The United States scrambled to meet its energy needs in the face of the oil shortage. Just two months after the OPEC embargo began, Congress imposed a national speed limit of 55 miles per hour to conserve fuel. Americans began to buy smaller, more fuel-efficient cars such as Volkswagens, Toyotas, and Datsuns (later Nissans) — while sales of Detroit-made cars (now nicknamed "gas guzzlers") slumped. With one of every six jobs in the country generated directly or indirectly by the auto industry, the effects rippled across the economy. Compounding the distress was the raging inflation set off by the oil shortage; prices of basic necessities, such as bread, milk, and canned goods, rose by nearly 20 percent in 1974 alone. "THINGS WILL GET WORSE," one newspaper headline warned, "BEFORE THEY GET WORSE."

## Environmentalism

The **energy crisis** drove home the realization that the earth's resources are not limitless. Such a notion was also at the heart of the era's revival of **environmentalism**. The environmental movement was an offshoot of sixties activism, but it had numerous historical precedents: the preservationist, conservationist, and wilderness movements of the late nineteenth century; the conservationist ethos of the New Deal; and anxiety about nuclear weapons and overpopulation in the 1940s. Three of the nation's leading environmental organizations — the Sierra Club, the Wilderness Society, and the Natural Resources Council — were founded in 1892, 1935, and 1942, respectively. Environmental activists in the 1970s extended the movement's historical roots through renewed efforts to ensure a healthy environment and access to unspoiled nature (Thinking Like a Historian, p. 940).

The movement had received a hefty boost back in 1962 when biologist Rachel Carson published *Silent Spring*, a stunning analysis of the pesticide DDT's toxic impact on the human and natural food chains. A succession of galvanizing developments followed in the late 1960s. The Sierra Club successfully fought two dams in 1966 that would have flooded the Grand Canyon. And in 1969, three major events spurred the movement: an offshore drilling rig spilled millions of gallons of oil off the coast of Santa Barbara; the Cuyahoga River near Cleveland burst into flames because of the accumulation of flammable chemicals on its surface; and Friends of the Everglades opposed an airport that threatened

**Earth Day, 1970**
No single event better encapsulated the growing environmental awareness of Americans than the nationwide celebration of the first Earth Day on April 22, 1970. In this photograph, college students in California release a balloon as part of that day's activities. Julian Wasser/ Time & Life Pictures/Getty Images.

plants and wildlife in Florida. With these events serving as catalysts, environmentalism became a certifiable mass movement on the first **Earth Day**, April 22, 1970, when 20 million citizens gathered in communities across the country to express their support for a cleaner, healthier planet.

**Environmental Protection Agency**   Earlier that year, on the heels of the Santa Barbara oil spill, Congress passed the National Environmental Policy Act, which created the **Environmental Protection Agency (EPA)**. A bipartisan bill with broad support, including that of President Nixon, the law required developers to file environmental impact statements assessing the effect of their projects on ecosystems. A

**IDENTIFY CAUSES**
What major factors led to the birth of the environmental movement in the 1970s?

## The Environmental Movement: Reimagining the Human-Earth Relationship

The 1970s witnessed the emergence of the environmental movement in the United States. Environmentalism took a variety of forms and initially was embraced by politicians across the political spectrum, including Republican president Richard Nixon, who signed the National Environmental Policy Act in 1970. Yet environmentalism also proved to be politically divisive. The following documents provide a range of perspectives on an important social and political movement discussed in this chapter.

### 1. Rachel Carson, *Silent Spring*, 1962.

For the first time in the history of the world, every human being is now subjected to contact with dangerous chemicals, from the moment of conception until death. In the less than two decades of their use, synthetic pesticides have been so thoroughly distributed throughout the animate and inanimate world that they occur virtually everywhere. They have been recovered from most of the major river systems and even from streams of groundwater flowing unseen through the earth.

### 2. Ralph Nader, foreword to *Ecotactics: The Sierra Club Handbook for Environmental Activists*, 1970.
*In the Sierra Club's guide to environmental activism, environmental and consumer rights activist Nader discusses "environmental violence."*

Pollution is violence and environmental pollution is environmental violence. It is a violence that has different impacts, styles and time factors than the more primitive kinds of violence such as crime in the streets. Yet in the size of the population exposed and the seriousness of the harm done, environmental violence far exceeds that of street crime. . . .

To deal with a system of oppression and suppression, which characterizes the environmental violence in this country, the first priority is to deprive the polluters of their unfounded legitimacy.

### 3. President Richard Nixon, State of the Union Address, January 22, 1970.

I shall propose to this Congress a $10 billion nationwide clean waters program to put modern municipal waste treatment plants in every place in America where they are needed to make our waters clean again, and do it now. . . .

As our cities and suburbs relentlessly expand [. . .] priceless open spaces needed for recreation areas accessible to their people are swallowed up — often forever. Unless we preserve these spaces while they are available,

we will have none to preserve. Therefore, I shall propose new financing methods for purchasing open space and parklands now, before they are lost to us.

The automobile is our worst polluter of the air. Adequate control requires further advances in engine design and fuel composition. We shall intensify our research, set increasingly strict standards, and strengthen enforcement procedures — and we shall do it now.

We can no longer afford to consider air and water common property, free to be abused by anyone without regard to the consequences. Instead, we should begin now to treat them as scarce resources, which we are no more free to contaminate than we are free to throw garbage into our neighbor's yard.

### 4. "Earthrise" over the moon's surface, December 24, 1968. *Photo taken by* Apollo 8 *crewmember Bill Anders, as the* Apollo *spacecraft orbited the moon.*

NASA.

**5. Paul Ehrlich, *The Population Bomb*, 1969.** *A best-selling book that warned of a coming global overpopulation straining the world's resources.*

Nothing could be more misleading to our children than our present affluent society. They will inherit a totally different world, a world in which the standards, politics, and economics of the 1960s are dead. As the most powerful nation in the world today, and its largest consumer, the United States cannot stand isolated. We are today involved in the events leading to famine; tomorrow we may be destroyed by its consequences.

Our position requires that we take immediate action at home and promote effective action world-wide. We must have population control at home, hopefully through a system of incentives and penalties, but by compulsion if voluntary methods fail. We must use our political power to push other countries into programs which combine agricultural development and population control. And while this is being done we must take action to reverse the deterioration of our environment before population pressure permanently ruins our planet.

**6. President Ronald Reagan, speech at the Republican National Convention, July 17, 1980.**

Make no mistake. We will not permit the safety of our people or our environmental heritage to be jeopardized, but we are going to reaffirm that the economic prosperity of our people is a fundamental part of our environment.

Our problems are both acute and chronic, yet all we hear from those in positions of leadership are the same tired proposals for more government tinkering, more meddling, and more control—all of which led us to this state in the first place.

**7. "Waste Produced by a Typical Family in a Year."**

© Martyn Goddard/Corbis.

Sources: (1) Rachel Carson, *Silent Spring* (New York: Mariner Books, 2002), 15; (2) John G. Mitchell and Constance L. Hastings, eds., *Ecotactics: The Sierra Club Handbook for Environmental Activists* (New York: Trident Press, 1970), 13–15; (3 & 6) Gerhard Peters and John T. Woolley, *The American Presidency Project*, presidency.ucsb.edu; (5) Louis Warren, ed., *American Environmental History* (Malden, MA: Blackwell Publishing, 2003), 296.

## ANALYZING THE EVIDENCE

1. Compare sources 1, 2, 3, 5, and 7. What are the different ways the environmental threat was understood and characterized? What kinds of solutions were proposed?

2. Source 4 is one of the first ever photographs of the earth taken from space. How would this visual perspective encourage viewers to think of the earth's resources as finite?

3. How does source 6 help us understand the opposition that developed to environmentalism? Why did some Americans oppose the environmental movement?

## PUTTING IT ALL TOGETHER

Using what you have learned about the environmental movement in this chapter and the documents above, construct an essay in which you make a historical argument about the origins of the movement, the issues that it raised, and the opposition that developed. How did the movement shape politics in the 1970s?

spate of new laws followed: the Clean Air Act (1970), the Occupational Health and Safety Act (1970), the Water Pollution Control Act (1972), and the Endangered Species Act (1973).

The Democratic majority in Congress and the Republican president generally found common ground on these issues, and *Time* magazine wondered if the environment was "the gut issue that can unify a polarized nation." Despite the broad popularity of the movement, however, *Time*'s prediction was not borne out. Corporations opposed environmental regulations, as did many of their workers, who believed that tightened standards threatened their jobs. "IF YOU'RE HUNGRY AND OUT OF WORK, EAT AN ENVIRONMENTALIST," read one labor union bumper sticker. By the 1980s, environmentalism starkly divided Americans, with proponents of unfettered economic growth on one side and environmental activists preaching limits on the other.

**Nuclear Power**   An early foreshadowing of those divisions came in the brewing controversy over nuclear power. Electricity from the atom — what could be better? That was how Americans had greeted the arrival of power-generating nuclear technology in the 1950s. By 1974, U.S. utility companies were operating forty-two nuclear power plants, with a hundred more planned. Given the oil crisis, nuclear energy might have seemed a godsend; unlike coal- or oil-driven plants, nuclear operations produced no air pollutants.

Environmentalists, however, publicized the dangers of nuclear power plants: a reactor meltdown would be catastrophic, and so, in slow motion, would the dumping of the radioactive waste, which would generate toxic levels of radioactivity for hundreds of years. These fears seemed to be confirmed in March 1979, when the reactor core at the **Three Mile Island** nuclear plant near Harrisburg, Pennsylvania, came close to meltdown. More than 100,000 people fled their homes. A prompt shutdown saved the plant, but the near catastrophe enabled environmentalists to win the battle over nuclear energy. After the incident at Three Mile Island, no new nuclear plants were authorized, though a handful with existing authorization were built in the 1980s. Today, nuclear reactors account for 20 percent of all U.S. power generation — substantially less than several European nations, but still fourth in the world.

## Economic Transformation

In addition to the energy crisis, the economy was beset by a host of longer-term problems. Government spending on the Vietnam War and the Great Society made for a growing federal deficit and spiraling inflation. In the industrial sector, the country faced more robust competition from West Germany and Japan. America's share of world trade dropped from 32 percent in 1955 to 18 percent in 1970 and was headed downward. As a result, in a blow to national pride, nine Western European countries had surpassed the United States in per capita gross domestic product (GDP) by 1980.

Many of these economic woes highlighted a broader, multigenerational transformation in the United States: from an industrial-manufacturing economy to a postindustrial-service one. That transformation, which continues to this day, meant that the United States began to produce fewer automobiles, appliances, and televisions and more financial services, health-care services, and management consulting services — not to mention many millions of low-paying jobs in the restaurant, retail, and tourist industries.

In the 1970s, the U.S. economy was hit simultaneously by unemployment, stagnant consumer demand, and inflation — a combination called **stagflation** — which contradicted a basic principle taught by economists: prices were not supposed to rise in a stagnant economy (Figure 29.2). For ordinary Americans, stagflation meant a noticeable decline in purchasing power, as discretionary income per worker dropped 18 percent between 1973 and 1982. None of the three presidents of the decade — Richard Nixon, Gerald Ford, and Jimmy Carter — had much luck tackling stagflation. Nixon's New Economic Policy was perhaps the most radical attempt. Nixon imposed temporary price and wage controls in 1971 in an effort to curb inflation. Then he took an even bolder step: removing the United States from the gold standard, which allowed the dollar to float in international currency markets and effectively ended the Bretton Woods monetary system established after World War II.

The underlying weaknesses in the U.S. economy remained, however. Ford, too, had little success. His Whip Inflation Now (WIN) campaign urged Americans to cut food waste and do more with less, a noble but deeply unpopular idea among the American public. Carter's policies, considered in a subsequent section of this chapter, were similarly ineffective. The fruitless search for a new economic order was a hallmark of 1970s politics.

**Deindustrialization**   America's economic woes struck hardest at the industrial sector, which suddenly — shockingly — began to be dismantled. Worst hit was the steel industry, which for seventy-five years had been the economy's crown jewel. Unscathed by World

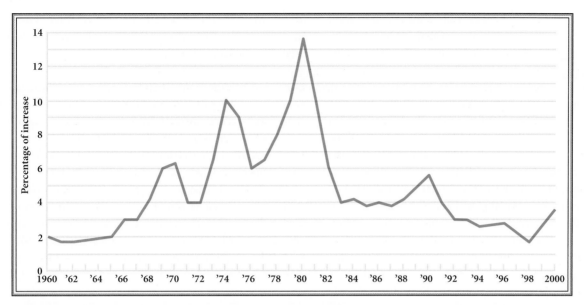

**FIGURE 29.2**

**The Inflation Rate, 1960–2000**

The impact of the oil crisis of 1973 on the inflation rate appears all too graphically in this figure. The dip in 1974 reflects the sharp recession that began that year, after which the inflation rate zoomed up to a staggering 14 percent in 1980. The return to normal levels after 1980 stemmed from very harsh measures by the Federal Reserve Board, which, while they succeeded, came at the cost of a painful slowdown in the economy.

War II, U.S. steel producers had enjoyed an open, hugely profitable market. But lack of serious competition left them without incentives to replace outdated plants and equipment. When West Germany and Japan rebuilt their steel industries, these facilities incorporated the latest technology. Foreign steel flooded into the United States during the 1970s, and the American industry was simply overwhelmed. Formerly titanic steel companies began a massive dismantling; virtually the entire Pittsburgh region, once a national hub of steel production, lost its heavy industry in a single generation. By the mid-1980s, downsizing, automation, and investment in new technologies made the American steel industry competitive again — but it was

**Deindustrialization**

Increasing economic competition from overseas created hard times for American industry in the 1970s and 1980s. Many of the nation's once-proud core industries, such as steel, declined precipitously in these decades. This photo shows a steel mill in Pittsburgh, Pennsylvania, being demolished in 1982. Once the center of American steel production, Pittsburgh suffered hard times in the 1970s and 1980s. The result of such closures was the creation of the so-called Rust Belt in the Northeast and Midwest (Map 29.1). Lynn Johnson/National Geographic/Getty Images.

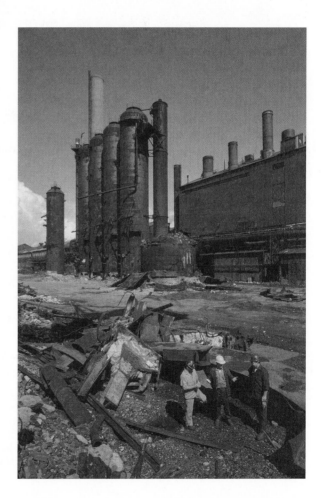

**PLACE EVENTS IN CONTEXT**
What major developments shaped the American economy in the 1970s and contributed to its transformation?

a shadow of its former self, and it continues to struggle to this day.

The steel industry was the prime example of what became known as **deindustrialization**. The country was in the throes of an economic transformation that left it largely stripped of its industrial base. Steel was hardly alone. A swath of the Northeast and Midwest, the country's manufacturing heartland, became the nation's **Rust Belt** (Map 29.1), strewn with abandoned plants and distressed communities. The automobile, tire, textile, and other consumer durable industries (appliances, electronics, furniture, and the like) all started shrinking in the

1970s. In 1980, *Business Week* bemoaned "plant closings across the continent" and called for the "*reindustrialization of America*."

**Organized Labor in Decline** Deindustrialization threw many tens of thousands of blue-collar workers out of well-paid union jobs. One study followed 4,100 steelworkers left jobless by the 1977 shutdown of the Campbell Works of the Youngstown Sheet & Tube Co. Two years later, 35 percent had retired early at half pay; 10 percent had moved; 15 percent were still jobless, with unemployment benefits long gone; and 40 percent had found local work, but mostly in low-paying, service-sector jobs. In another instance, between 1978 and 1981, eight Los Angeles companies — including

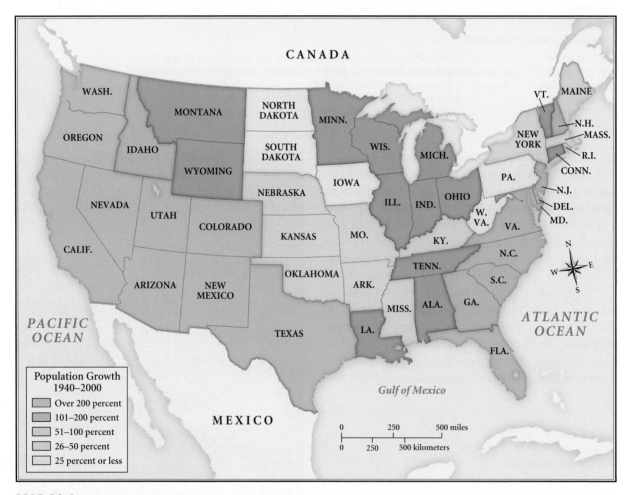

**MAP 29.1**

**From Rust Belt to Sunbelt, 1940–2000**

One of the most significant developments of the post–World War II era was the growth of the Sunbelt. Sparked by federal spending for military bases, the defense industry, and the space program, states of the South and Southwest experienced an economic boom in the 1950s. This growth was further enhanced in the 1970s, as the heavily industrialized regions of the Northeast and Midwest declined and migrants from what was quickly dubbed the Rust Belt headed to the South and West in search of jobs.

such giants as Ford, Uniroyal, and U.S. Steel — closed factories employing 18,000 workers. These Ohio and California workers, like hundreds of thousands of their counterparts across the nation, had fallen from their perch in the middle class (America Compared, p. 946).

Deindustrialization dealt an especially harsh blow to the labor movement, which had facilitated the postwar expansion of that middle class. In the early 1970s, as inflation hit, the number of strikes surged; 2.4 million workers participated in work stoppages in 1970 alone. However, industry argued that it could no longer afford union demands, and labor's bargaining power produced fewer and fewer concrete results. In these hard years, the much-vaunted labor-management accord of the 1950s, which raised profits and wages by passing costs on to consumers, went bust. Instead of seeking higher wages, unions now mainly fought to save jobs. Union membership went into steep decline, and by the mid-1980s organized labor represented less than 18 percent of American workers, the lowest level since the 1920s. The impact on liberal politics was huge. With labor's decline, a main buttress of the New Deal coalition was coming undone.

## Urban Crisis and Suburban Revolt

The economic downturn pushed already struggling American cities to the brink of fiscal collapse. Middle-class flight to the suburbs continued apace, and the "urban crisis" of the 1960s spilled into the "era of limits." Facing huge price inflation and mounting piles of debt — to finance social services for the poor and to replace disappearing tax revenue — nearly every major American city struggled to pay its bills in the 1970s. Surrounded by prosperous postwar suburbs, central cities seemingly could not catch a break.

New York, the nation's financial capital and its largest city, fared the worst. Its annual budget was in the billions, larger than that of most states. Unable to borrow on the tightening international bond market, New York neared collapse in the summer of 1975; bankruptcy was a real possibility. When Mayor Abraham Beame appealed to the federal government for assistance, President Ford refused. "Ford to City: Drop Dead" read the headline in the *New York Daily News*. Fresh appeals ultimately produced a solution: the federal government would lend New York money, and banks would declare a three-year moratorium on municipal debt. The arrangement saved the city from defaulting, but the mayor was forced to cut city services, freeze wages, and lay off workers. One pessimistic observer declared that "the banks have been saved, and the city has been condemned."

Cities faced declining fortunes in these years for many reasons, but one key was the continued loss of

> **COMPARE AND CONTRAST**
> How did cities and suburbs experience the "era of limits" differently, and why?

**"Ford to City: Drop Dead"**

In the summer of 1975, New York City nearly went bankrupt. When Mayor Abraham Beame appealed to President Gerald Ford for assistance, these newspaper headlines captured the chief executive's response. Though it was ultimately saved from financial ruin, the city's brush with insolvency symbolized the larger problems facing the nation: economic stagnation, high inflation, and unemployment. Hard times had seemingly spared no one. AP Images.

## Economic Malaise in the Seventies

Most major economic indicators in the United States turned downward in the 1970s, as the long postwar expansion ground to an unmistakable halt. The figures below offer evidence of how developments in the United States compared with other industrialized countries.

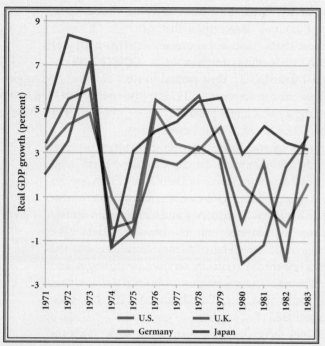

**FIGURE 29.3**
**Falling Gross Domestic Product**

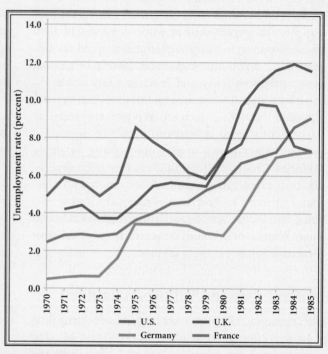

**FIGURE 29.4**
**Rising Unemployment**

### QUESTIONS FOR ANALYSIS

1. In what ways do these figures demonstrate an integrated global economy?

2. What does the GDP graph indicate about how global economic integration affected the U.S. economy? Notice that Japan's GDP growth remained strong in the late 1970s and early 1980s. With what historical development within the U.S. does that correspond?

residents and businesses to nearby suburbs. In the 1970s alone, 13 million people (6 percent of the total U.S. population) moved to the suburbs. New suburban shopping centers opened weekly across the country, and other businesses—such as banks, insurance companies, and technology firms—increasingly sought suburban locations. More and more, people lived *and* worked in suburbs. In the San Francisco Bay area, 75 percent of all daily commutes were suburb-to-suburb, and 78 percent of New York's suburban

residents worked in nearby suburbs. The 1950s "organization man," commuting downtown from his suburban home, had been replaced by the engineer, teacher, nurse, student, and carpenter who lived in one suburb and worked in another.

Beyond city limits, suburbanization and the economic crisis combined powerfully in what became known as the **tax revolt**, a dramatic reversal of the postwar spirit of generous public investment. The premier example was California. Inflation pushed real

946

estate values upward, and property taxes skyrocketed. Hardest hit were suburban property owners, along with retirees and others on fixed incomes, who suddenly faced unaffordable tax bills. Into this dire situation stepped Howard Jarvis, a conservative anti–New Dealer and a genius at mobilizing grassroots discontent. In 1978, Jarvis proposed **Proposition 13**, an initiative that would roll back property taxes, cap future increases for present owners, and require that all tax measures have a two-thirds majority in the legislature. Despite opposition by virtually the entire state leadership, including politicians from both parties, Californians voted overwhelmingly for Jarvis's measure.

Proposition 13 hobbled public spending in the nation's most populous state. Per capita funding of California public schools, once the envy of the nation, plunged from the top tier to the bottom, where it was second only to Mississippi. Moreover, Proposition 13's complicated formula benefitted middle-class and wealthy home owners at the expense of less-well-off citizens, especially those who depended heavily on public services. Businesses, too, came out ahead, because commercial property got the same protection as residential property. More broadly, Proposition 13 inspired tax revolts across the country and helped conservatives define an enduring issue: low taxes.

In addition to public investment, another cardinal marker of New Deal and Great Society liberalism had been a remarkable decline in income inequality. In the 1970s, that trend reversed, and the wealthiest Americans, those among the top 10 percent, began to pull ahead again. As corporations restructured to boost profits during the 1970s slump, they increasingly laid off high-wage workers, paid the remaining workers less, and relocated overseas. Thus upper-class Americans benefitted, while blue-collar families who had been lifted into the middle class during the postwar boom increasingly lost out. An unmistakable trend was apparent by the end of the 1970s. The U.S. labor market was dividing in two: a vast, low-wage market at the bottom and a much narrower high-wage market at the top, with the middle squeezed smaller and smaller.

# Politics in Flux, 1973–1980

A search for order characterized national politics in the 1970s as well. It began with a scandal. Misbehavior is endemic to politics. Yet what became known as the Watergate affair — or simply **Watergate** — implicated President Richard Nixon in illegal behavior severe enough to bring down his presidency. Liberals benefitted from Nixon's fall in the short term, but their long-term retreat continued. Politics remained in flux because while liberals were on the defensive, conservatives had not yet put forth a clear alternative.

## Watergate and the Fall of a President

On June 17, 1972, something strange happened at Washington's Watergate office/apartment/hotel complex. Early that morning, five men carrying wiretapping equipment were apprehended there attempting to break into the headquarters of the Democratic National Committee (DNC). Queried by the press, a White House spokesman dismissed the episode as "a third-rate burglary attempt." Pressed further, Nixon himself denied any White House involvement in "this very bizarre incident." In fact, the two masterminds of the break-in, G. Gordon Liddy and E. Howard Hunt, were former FBI and CIA agents currently working for Nixon's Committee to Re-elect the President (CREEP).

The Watergate burglary was no isolated incident. It was part of a broad pattern of abuse of power by a White House obsessed with its enemies. Liddy and Hunt were on the White House payroll, part of a clandestine squad hired to stop leaks to the press. But they were soon arranging illegal wiretaps at DNC headquarters, part of a campaign of "dirty tricks" against the Democrats. Nixon's siege mentality best explains his fatal misstep. He could have dissociated himself from the break-in by firing his guilty aides or even just by letting justice take its course. But it was election time, and Nixon did not trust his political future to such a strategy. Instead, he arranged hush money for the burglars and instructed the CIA to stop an FBI investigation into the affair. This was obstruction of justice, a criminal offense.

Nixon kept the lid on until after the election, but in early 1973, one of the Watergate burglars began to talk. In the meantime, two reporters at the *Washington Post*, Carl Bernstein and Bob Woodward, uncovered CREEP's links to key White House aides. In May 1973, a Senate investigating committee began holding nationally televised hearings, at which administration officials implicated Nixon in the illegal cover-up. The president kept investigators at bay for a year, but in June 1974, the House Judiciary Committee began to consider articles of impeachment. Certain of being convicted by the Senate, Nixon became, on August 9, 1974, the first U.S. president to resign his office. The next day, Vice President Gerald Ford was sworn in as president. Ford, the Republican minority leader in the House of Representatives, had replaced Vice President Spiro Agnew, who had himself resigned in 1973 for accepting kickbacks while governor of Maryland. A month after he took office, Ford stunned the nation by granting Nixon a "full, free, and absolute" pardon.

Congress pushed back, passing a raft of laws against the abuses of the Nixon administration: the **War Powers Act** (1973), which reined in the president's ability to deploy U.S. forces without congressional approval; amendments strengthening the **Freedom of Information Act** (1974), which gave citizens access to federal records; the **Ethics in Government Act** (1978); and the Foreign Intelligence Surveillance Act (1978), which prohibited domestic wiretapping without a warrant.

Popular disdain for politicians, evident in declining voter turnout, deepened with Nixon's resignation in 1974. "Don't vote," read one bumper sticker in 1976. "It only encourages them." Watergate not only damaged short-term Republican prospects but also shifted the party's balance to the right. Despite mastering the populist appeal to the "silent majority," the moderate Nixon was never beloved by conservatives. His relaxation of tensions with the Soviet Union and his visit to communist China, in particular, won him no friends on the right. His disgraceful exit benefitted the more conservative Republicans, who proceeded to reshape the party in their image.

**Watergate Babies**    As for the Democrats, Watergate granted them a reprieve, a second chance at recapturing their eroding base. Backed by a public deeply disenchanted with politicians, especially scandal-tainted Republicans, congressional Democrats had an opportunity to repair the party's image. Ford's pardon of Nixon saved the nation a prolonged and agonizing trial, which was Ford's rationale, but it was decidedly unpopular among the public. Pollster Louis Harris remarked that should a politician "defend that pardon in any part of this country, North or South, [he] is almost literally going to have his head handed to him." Democratic candidates in the 1974 midterm elections made Watergate and Ford's pardon their top issues. It worked. Seventy-five new Democratic members of the House came to Washington in 1975, many of them under the age of forty-five, and the press dubbed them Watergate babies.

Young and reform-minded, the Watergate babies solidified huge Democratic majorities in both houses of Congress and quickly set to work. They eliminated the House Un-American Activities Committee (HUAC), which had investigated alleged Communists in the 1940s and 1950s and antiwar activists in the 1960s. In the Senate, Democrats reduced the number of votes needed to end a filibuster from 67 to 60 — a move intended to weaken the power of the minority to block legislation. In both houses, Democrats dismantled the existing committee structure, which had entrenched power in the hands of a few elite committee chairs. And in 1978, the Ethics in Government Act forced political candidates to disclose financial contributions and limited the lobbying activities of former elected officials. Overall, the Watergate babies helped to decentralize power in Washington and bring greater transparency to American government.

In one of the great ironies of American political history, however, the post-Watergate reforms made government *less* efficient and *more* susceptible to special interests — the opposite of what had been intended. Under the new committee structure, smaller subcommittees proliferated, and the size of the congressional staff doubled to more than 20,000. A diffuse power structure actually gave lobbyists more places to exert influence. As the power of committee chairs weakened, influence shifted to party leaders, such as the Speaker of the House and the Senate majority leader. With little incentive to compromise, the parties grew more rigid, and bipartisanship became rare. Finally, filibustering, a seldom-used tactic largely employed by anti–civil rights southerners, increased in frequency. The Congress that we have come to know today — with its partisan rancor, its army of lobbyists, and its slow-moving response to public needs — came into being in the 1970s.

**Political Realignment**    Despite Democratic gains in 1974, the electoral realignment that had begun with Richard Nixon's presidential victories in 1968 and 1972 continued. As liberalism proved unable to stop runaway inflation or speed up economic growth, conservatism gained greater traction with the public. The postwar liberal economic formula — sometimes known as the Keynesian consensus — consisted of microadjustments to the money supply coupled with federal spending. When that formula failed to restart the economy in the mid-1970s, conservatives in Congress used this opening to articulate alternatives, especially economic deregulation and tax cuts.

On a grander scale, deindustrialization in the Northeast and Midwest and continued population growth in the Sunbelt was changing the political geography of the country. Power was shifting, incrementally but perceptibly, toward the West and South (Table 29.1). As states with strong trade unions at the center of the postwar

**EXPLAIN CONSEQUENCES**
What changed and what remained the same in American politics as a result of the Watergate scandal?

## TABLE 29.1

### Political Realignment: Congressional Seats

| State | Apportionment | |
|---|---|---|
|  | 1940 | 1990 |
| **Rust Belt** | | |
| Massachusetts | 14 | 10 |
| Connecticut | 6 | 6 |
| New York | 45 | 31 |
| New Jersey | 14 | 13 |
| Pennsylvania | 33 | 21 |
| Ohio | 23 | 19 |
| Illinois | 26 | 20 |
| Indiana | 11 | 10 |
| Michigan | 17 | 16 |
| Wisconsin | 10 | 9 |
| **Total** | **199** | **155** |
| **Sunbelt** | | |
| California | 23 | 52 |
| Arizona | 2 | 6 |
| Nevada | 1 | 2 |
| Colorado | 4 | 6 |
| New Mexico | 2 | 3 |
| Texas | 21 | 30 |
| Georgia | 10 | 11 |
| North Carolina | 12 | 12 |
| Virginia | 9 | 11 |
| Florida | 6 | 23 |
| **Total** | **90** | **156** |

In the fifty years between 1940 and 1990, the Rust Belt states lost political clout, while the Sunbelt states gained it — measured here in congressional seats (which are apportioned based on population). Sunbelt states gained 66 seats, with the Rust Belt losing 44. This shifting political geography helped undermine the liberal coalition, which was strongest in industrial states with large labor unions, and paved the way for the rise of the conservative coalition, which was strongest in southern and Bible Belt states, as well as California. Source: Office of the Clerk of the House, clerk.house.gov/art_history/house_history/congApp/bystate.html.

liberal political coalition — such as New York, Illinois, and Michigan — lost industry, jobs, and people, states with traditions of libertarian conservatism — such as

California, Arizona, Florida, and Texas — gained greater political clout. The full impact of this shifting political geography would not be felt until the 1980s and 1990s, but its effects had become apparent by the mid-1970s.

## Jimmy Carter: The Outsider as President

"Jimmy who?" was how journalists first responded when James Earl Carter, who had been a naval officer, a peanut farmer, and the governor of Georgia, emerged from the pack to win the Democratic presidential nomination in 1976. When Carter told his mother that he intended to run for president, she had asked, "President of what?" Trading on Watergate and his down-home image, Carter pledged to restore morality to the White House. "I will never lie to you," he promised voters. Carter played up his credentials as a Washington outsider, although he selected Senator Walter F. Mondale of Minnesota as his running mate, to ensure his ties to traditional Democratic voting blocs. Ford still might have prevailed, but his pardon of Nixon likely cost him enough votes in key states to swing the election to the Democratic candidate. Carter won with 50 percent of the popular vote to Ford's 48 percent.

For a time, Carter got some mileage as an outsider — the common man who walked to the White House after the inauguration and delivered fireside chats in a cardigan sweater. The fact that he was a born-again Christian also played well. But Carter's inexperience began to show. He responded to feminists, an important Democratic constituency, by establishing a new women's commission in his administration. But later he dismissed the commission's concerns and became embroiled in a public fight with prominent women's advocates. Most consequentially, his outsider strategy made for chilly relations with congressional leaders. Disdainful of the Democratic establishment, Carter relied heavily on inexperienced advisors from Georgia. And as a detail-oriented micromanager, he exhausted himself over the fine points of policy better left to his aides.

On the domestic front, Carter's big challenge was managing the economy. The problems that he faced defied easy solution. Most confounding was stagflation. If the government focused on inflation — forcing prices down by raising interest rates — unemployment became worse. If the government tried to stimulate employment, inflation became worse. None of the levers of government economic policy seemed to work. At heart, Carter was an economic conservative. He

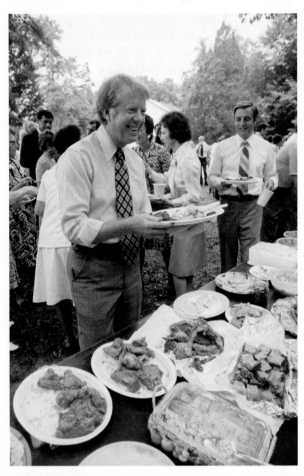

**Jimmy Carter**

President Jimmy Carter is seen here at a family picnic in his hometown of Plains, Georgia, just after he received the Democratic nomination for president in 1976. Carter was content to portray himself as a political outsider, an ordinary American who could restore trust to Washington after the Watergate scandal. A thoughtful man and a born-again Christian, Carter nonetheless proved unable to solve the complex economic problems, especially high inflation, and international challenges of the late 1970s. © Owen Franken/Corbis.

Carter lectured Americans about the nation's "crisis of the spirit." He called energy conservation "the moral equivalent of war"—or, in the media's shorthand, "MEOW," which aptly captured the nation's assessment of Carter's sermonizing. By then, his approval rating had fallen below 30 percent. And it was no wonder, given an inflation rate over 11 percent, failing industries, and long lines at the pumps. It seemed the worst of all possible economic worlds, and the first-term president could not help but worry about the political costs to him and his party.

 To see a longer excerpt of Carter's TV address, along with other primary sources from this period, see *Sources for America's History*.

# Reform and Reaction in the 1970s

Having lived through a decade of profound social and political upheaval—the Vietnam War, protests, riots, Watergate, recession—many Americans were exhausted and cynical by the mid-1970s. But while some retreated to private concerns, others took reform in new directions. Civil rights battles continued, the women's movement achieved some of its most far-reaching aims, and gay rights blossomed. These movements pushed the "rights revolution" of the 1960s deeper into American life. Others, however, pushed back. Social conservatives responded by forming their own organizations and resisting the emergence of what they saw as a permissive society.

## Civil Rights in a New Era

When Congress banned job discrimination in the 1964 Civil Rights Act, the law required only that employers hire without regard to "race, color, religion, sex, or national origin." But after centuries of slavery and decades of segregation, would nondiscrimination bring African Americans into the economic mainstream? Many liberals thought not. They believed that government, universities, and private employers needed to take positive steps to open their doors to a wider, more diverse range of Americans—including other minority groups and women.

Among the most significant efforts to address the legacy of exclusion was **affirmative action**—procedures designed to take into account the disadvantaged position of minority groups after centuries

toyed with the idea of an "industrial policy" to bail out the ailing manufacturing sector, but he moved instead in a free-market direction by lifting the New Deal–era regulation of the airline, trucking, and railroad industries. **Deregulation** stimulated competition and cut prices, but it also drove firms out of business and hurt unionized workers.

The president's efforts failed to reignite economic growth. Then, the Iranian Revolution curtailed oil supplies, and gas prices jumped again. In a major TV address,

**UNDERSTAND POINTS OF VIEW**

What kind of president did Jimmy Carter hope to be, and how successful was he at implementing his agenda?

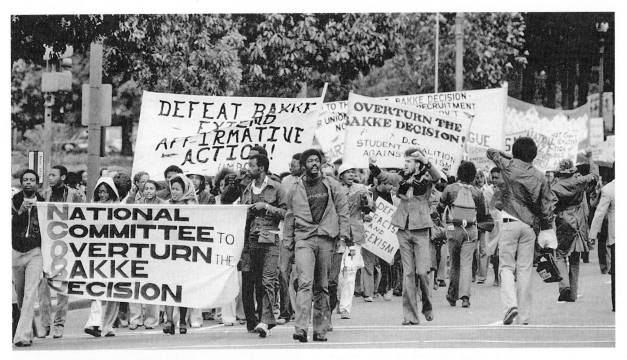

**March for Affirmative Action**

Following the Supreme Court's 1978 Bakke decision, Americans grew even more divided over the policy of affirmative action. For many people, such as African Americans and Latinos, affirmative action promised that groups who faced historical discrimination would have equal opportunity in jobs and education. For many whites, affirmative action looked like "reverse discrimination," and they fought its implementation. AP/Wide World Photos.

of discrimination. First advanced by the Kennedy administration in 1961, affirmative action received a boost under President Lyndon Johnson, whose Labor Department fashioned a series of plans in the late 1960s to encourage government contractors to recruit underrepresented racial minorities. Women were added under the last of these plans, when pressure from the women's movement highlighted the problem of sex discrimination. By the early 1970s, affirmative action had been refined by court rulings that identified acceptable procedures: hiring and enrollment goals, special recruitment and training programs, and set-asides (specially reserved slots) for both racial minority groups and women.

Affirmative action, however, did not please many whites, who felt that the deck was being stacked against them. Much of the dissent came from conservative groups that had opposed civil rights all along. They charged affirmative action advocates with "reverse discrimination." Legal challenges abounded, as employees, students, and university applicants went to court to object to these new procedures. Some liberal groups sought a middle position. In a widely publicized 1972 letter, Jewish organizations, seared by the memory of

quotas that once kept Jewish students out of elite colleges, came out against all racial quotas but nonetheless endorsed "rectifying the imbalances resulting from past discrimination."

A major shift in affirmative action policy came in 1978. Allan Bakke, a white man, sued the University of California at Davis Medical School for rejecting him in favor of less-qualified minority-group candidates. Headlines across the country sparked anti–affirmative action protest marches on college campuses and vigorous discussion on television and radio and in the White House. Ultimately, the Supreme Court rejected the medical school's quota system, which set aside 16 of 100 places for "disadvantaged" students. The Court ordered Bakke admitted but indicated that a more flexible affirmative action plan, in which race could be considered along with other factors, would still pass constitutional muster. *Bakke v. University of California* thus upheld affirmative action but, by rejecting a quota system, also called it into question. Future court rulings and state referenda, in the 1990s and 2000s, would further limit

**TRACE CHANGE OVER TIME**

How did affirmative action evolve between 1961 and 1978?

the scope of affirmative action. In particular, California voters passed Proposition 209 in 1996, prohibiting public institutions from using affirmative action to increase diversity in employment and education.

## The Women's Movement and Gay Rights

Unlike the civil rights movement, whose signal achievements came in the 1960s, the women's and gay rights movements flourished in the 1970s. With three influential wings — radical, liberal, and "Third World" — the women's movement inspired both grassroots activism and legislative action across the nation. For their part, gay activists had further to go: they needed to convince Americans that same-sex relationships were natural and that gay men and lesbians deserved the same protection of the law as all other citizens. Neither movement achieved all of its aims in this era, but each laid a strong foundation for the future.

**EXPLAIN CONSEQUENCES**
How did the idea of civil rights expand during the 1970s?

**Women's Activism**   In the first half of the 1970s, the women's liberation movement reached its historic peak. Taking a dizzying array of forms — from lobbying legislatures to marching in the streets and establishing all-female collectives — women's liberation produced activism on the scale of the earlier black-led civil rights movement. Women's centers, as well as women-run child-care facilities, began to spring up in cities and towns. A feminist art and poetry movement flourished. Women challenged the admissions policies of all-male colleges and universities — opening such prestigious universities as Yale and Columbia and nearly bringing an end to male-only institutions of higher education. Female scholars began to transform higher education: by studying women's history, by increasing the number of women on college and university faculties, and by founding women's studies programs.

Much of women's liberation activism focused on the female body. Inspired by the Boston collective that first published *Our Bodies, Ourselves* — a groundbreaking book on women's health — the women's health movement founded dozens of medical clinics, encouraged women to become physicians, and educated millions of women about their bodies. To reform antiabortion laws, activists pushed for remedies in more than thirty state legislatures. Women's liberationists founded the antirape movement, established rape crisis centers around the nation, and lobbied state legislatures and

Congress to reform rape laws. Many of these endeavors and movements began as shoestring operations in living rooms and kitchens: *Our Bodies, Ourselves* was first published as a 35-cent mimeographed booklet, and the antirape movement began in small consciousness-raising groups that met in churches and community centers. By the end of the decade, however, all of these causes had national organizations and touched the lives of millions of American women.

**Equal Rights Amendment**   Buoyed by this flourishing of activism, the women's movement renewed the fight for an **Equal Rights Amendment (ERA)** to the Constitution. First introduced in 1923, the ERA stated, in its entirety, "Equality of rights under the law shall not be denied or abridged by the United States or any State on the basis of sex." Vocal congressional women, such as Patsy Mink (Democrat, Hawaii), Bella Abzug

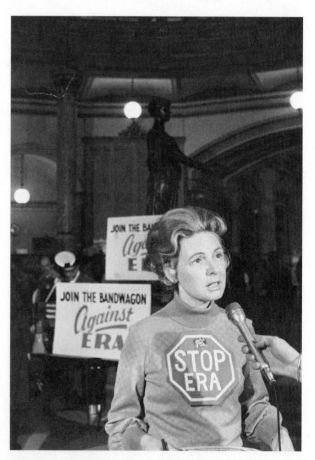

**Phyllis Schlafly**
Phyllis Schlafly, leader of the organization STOP ERA, talks with reporters during a rally at the Illinois State Capitol on March 4, 1975, at a time when the state legislature was considering whether to ratify the Equal Rights Amendment. Schlafly described herself as a housewife and called her strenuous political career a hobby. © Bettmann/Corbis.

(Democrat, New York), and Shirley Chisholm (Democrat, New York), found enthusiastic male allies — among both Democrats and Republicans — and Congress adopted the amendment in 1972. Within just two years, thirty-four of the necessary thirty-eight states had ratified it, and the ERA appeared headed for adoption. But then, progress abruptly halted (Map 29.2).

Credit for putting the brakes on ERA ratification goes chiefly to a remarkable woman: Phyllis Schlafly, a lawyer long active in conservative causes. Despite her own flourishing career, Schlafly advocated traditional roles for women. The ERA, she proclaimed, would create an unnatural "unisex society," with women drafted into the army and forced to use single-sex toilets. Abortion, she alleged, could never be prohibited by law. Led by Schlafly's organization, **STOP ERA** (founded in 1972), thousands of women mobilized, showing up at statehouses with home-baked bread and apple pies. As labels on baked goods at one anti-ERA rally

expressed it: "My heart and hand went into this dough / For the sake of the family please vote no." It was a message that resonated widely, especially among those troubled by the rapid pace of social change (American Voices, p. 954). The ERA never was ratified, despite a congressional extension of the deadline to June 30, 1982.

*Roe v. Wade*   In addition to the ERA, the women's movement had identified another major goal: winning reproductive rights. Activists pursued two tracks: legislative and judicial. In the early 1960s, abortion was illegal in virtually every state. A decade later, thanks to intensive lobbying by women's organizations, liberal ministers, and physicians, a handful of states, such as New York, Hawaii, California, and Colorado, adopted laws making legal abortions easier to obtain. But progress after that was slow, and women's advocates turned to the courts. There was reason to be optimistic. The

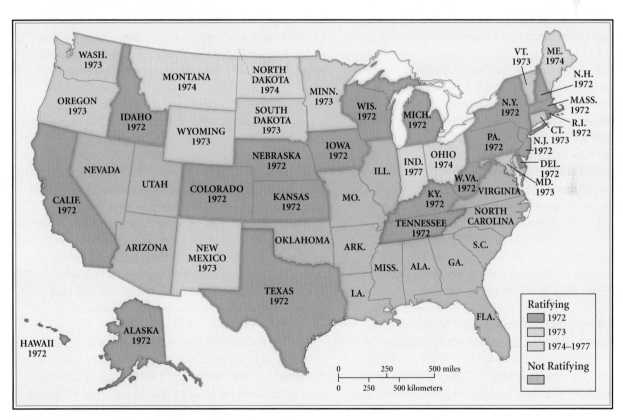

**MAP 29.2**

**States Ratifying the Equal Rights Amendment, 1972–1977**

The ratifying process for the Equal Rights Amendment (ERA) went smoothly in 1972 and 1973 but then stalled. The turning point came in 1976, when ERA advocates lobbied extensively, particularly in Florida, North Carolina, and Illinois, but failed to sway the conservative legislatures in those states. After Indiana ratified in 1977, the amendment still lacked three votes toward the three-fourths majority needed for adoption. Efforts to revive the ERA in the 1980s were unsuccessful, and it became a dead issue.

## Debating the Equal Rights Amendment

Fifty years after its introduction, the Equal Rights Amendment ("Equality of rights under the law shall not be denied or abridged by the United States or by any State on account of sex") finally met congressional approval in 1972 and was sent to the states for ratification. The amendment set off a furious debate, especially in the South and Midwest, and fell short of ratification. Following are four of the voices in that debate.

### Phyllis Schlafly

Lawyer and political activist Phyllis Schlafly was the most prominent opponent of the ERA. Her organization, STOP ERA, campaigned against the amendment in critical states and helped to halt ratification.

Women's magazines, the women's pages of newspapers, and television and radio talk shows have been filled for months with a strident advocacy of the "rights" of women to be treated on an equal basis with men in all walks of life. But what about the rights of the woman who doesn't want to compete on an equal basis with men? Does she have the right to be treated as a woman — by her family, by society, and by the law? . . .

The laws of every one of our 50 states now guarantee the right to be a woman — protected and provided for in her career as a woman, wife, and mother. The proposed Equal Rights Amendment will wipe out all our laws which — through rights, benefits, and exemptions — guarantee this right to be a woman. . . . Is this what American women want? Is this what American men want?

The laws of every one of the 50 states now require the husband to support his wife and children — and to provide a home for them to live in. In other words, the law protects a woman's right to be a full-time wife and mother, her right not to take a job outside the home, her right to care for her own baby in her own home while being financially supported by her husband. . . .

There are two very different types of women lobbying for the Equal Rights Amendment. One group is the women's liberationists. Their motive is totally radical. They hate men, marriage, and children. They are out to destroy morality and the family. . . . There is another type of woman supporting the Equal Rights Amendment from the most sincere motives. It is easy to see why the business and professional women are supporting the Equal Rights Amendment — many of them have felt the keen edge of discrimination in their employment.

Source: From *The Phyllis Schlafly Report*, November 1972. Reprinted by permission.

### Jerry Falwell

Jerry Falwell was a fundamentalist Baptist preacher in Virginia, a television evangelist, and the founder of the political lobbying organization known as the Moral Majority.

I believe that at the foundation of the women's liberation movement there is a minority core of women who were once bored with life, whose real problems are spiritual problems. Many women have never accepted their God-given roles. . . . God Almighty created men and women biologically different and with differing needs and roles. He made men and women to complement each other and to love each other. . . . Women who work should be respected and accorded dignity and equal rewards for equal work. But this is not what the present feminist movement and equal rights movement are all about.

The Equal Rights Amendment is a delusion. I believe that women deserve more than equal rights. And, in families and in nations where the Bible is believed, Christian women are honored above men. Only in places where the Bible is believed and practiced do women receive more than equal rights. Men and women have differing strengths. The Equal Rights Amendment can never do for women what needs to be done for them. Women need to know Jesus Christ as their Lord and Savior and be under His Lordship. They need a man who knows Jesus Christ as his Lord and Savior, and they need to be part of a home where their husband is a godly leader and where there is a Christian family. . . .

ERA is not merely a political issue, but a moral issue as well. A definite violation of holy Scripture, ERA defies the mandate that "the husband is the head of the wife, even as Christ is the head of the church" (Ep. 5:23). In 1 Peter 3:7 we read that husbands are to give their wives honor as unto the weaker vessel, that they are both heirs together of the grace of life. Because a woman is weaker does not mean that she is less important.

Source: Excerpt from *Listen America!* by Jerry Falwell, copyright © 1980 by Jerry Falwell. Used by permission of Doubleday, an imprint of the Knopf Doubleday Publishing Group, a division of Random House LLC. All rights reserved. Any third party use of this material, outside of this publication, is prohibited. Interested parties must apply directly to Random House LLC for permission.

## Elizabeth Duncan Koontz

Elizabeth Duncan Koontz was a distinguished educator and the first black woman to head the National Education Association and the U.S. Women's Bureau. At the time she made this statement at state legislative hearings on the ERA in 1977, she was assistant state superintendent for public instruction in North Carolina.

A short time ago I had the misfortune to break my foot. . . . The pain . . . did not hurt me as much as when I went into the emergency room and the young woman upon asking me my name, the nature of my ailment, then asked me for my husband's social security number and his hospitalization number. I asked her what did that have to do with my emergency.

And she said, "We have to be sure of who is going to pay your bill." I said, "Suppose I'm not married, then." And she said, "Then give me your father's name." I did not go through that twenty years ago when I was denied the use of that emergency room because of my color.

I went through that because there is an underlying assumption that all women in our society are protected, dependent, cared for by somebody who's got a social security number and hospitalization insurance. Never once did she assume I might be a woman who might be caring for my husband, instead of him by me, because of some illness. She did not take into account the fact that one out of almost eight women heading families in poverty today [is] in the same condition as men in families and poverty. . . .

My greater concern is that so many women today . . . oppose the passage of the ERA very sincerely and . . . tell you without batting an eye, "I don't want to see women treated that way." And I speak up, "What way is that?" . . . Women themselves have been a bit misguided. We have mistaken present practice for law, and women have . . . assumed too many times that their present condition cannot change. The rate of divorce, the rate of desertion, the rate of separation, and the death rate of male supporters is enough for us to say: "Let us remove all legal barriers to women and girls making their choices — this state cannot afford it."

Source: William A. Link and Marjorie Spruill Wheeler, eds., *The South in the History of the Nation* (Boston: Bedford/St. Martin's, 1999), 295–296.

## Caroline Bird

Caroline Bird was the lead author of *What Women Want*, a report produced by women's rights advocates following the 1977 National Women's Conference, held in Houston, Texas.

The Declaration of Independence, signed in 1776, stated that "all Men are created equal" and that governments derive their powers "from the Consent of the Governed." Women were not included in either concept. The original American Constitution of 1787 was founded on English common law, which did not recognize women as citizens or as individuals with legal rights. A woman was expected to obey her husband or nearest male kin, and if she was married her person and her property were owned by her husband. . . .

It has been argued that the ERA is not necessary because the Fourteenth Amendment, passed after the Civil War, guarantees that no state shall deny to "any person within its jurisdiction the equal protection of the laws." . . .

Aside from the fact that women have been subjected to varying, inconsistent, and often unfavorable decisions under the Fourteenth Amendment, the Equal Rights Amendment is a more immediate and effective remedy to sex discrimination in Federal and State laws than case-by-case interpretation under the Fourteenth Amendment could ever be.

Source: Caroline Bird, *What Women Want* (New York: Simon & Schuster, 1978), 120–121.

---

### QUESTIONS FOR ANALYSIS

1. Schlafly and Koontz have different notions of what it means to be a woman. Explain what these differences are and how they inform the authors' distinct views of the ERA.

2. Why does Schlafly believe that women will be harmed by the ERA?

3. Schlafly and Falwell argue that women need the protection and support of men. Are they right? How would Koontz likely respond?

4. How do each of the four authors define women's roles and responsibilities in society?

Supreme Court had first addressed reproductive rights in a 1965 case, *Griswold v. Connecticut*. *Griswold* struck down an 1879 state law prohibiting the possession of contraception as a violation of married couples' constitutional "right of privacy." Following the logic articulated in *Griswold*, the Court gradually expanded the right of privacy in a series of cases in the late 1960s and early 1970s.

Those cases culminated in **Roe v. Wade** (1973). In that landmark decision, the justices nullified a Texas law that prohibited abortion under any circumstances, even when the woman's health was at risk, and laid out a new national standard: Abortions performed during the first trimester were protected by the right of privacy. At the time and afterward, some legal authorities questioned whether the Constitution recognized any such privacy right and criticized the Court's seemingly arbitrary first-trimester timeline. Nevertheless, the Supreme Court chose to move forward, transforming a traditionally state-regulated policy into a national, constitutionally protected right.

For the women's movement, *Roe v. Wade* represented a triumph. For evangelical and fundamentalist Christians, Catholics, and conservatives generally, it was a bitter pill. In their view, abortion was, unequivocally, the taking of a human life. These Americans, represented by groups such as the National Right to Life Committee, did not believe that something they regarded as immoral and sinful could be the basis for women's equality. Women's advocates responded that illegal abortions—common prior to *Roe*—were often unsafe procedures, which resulted in physical harm to women and even death. *Roe* polarized what was already a sharply divided public and mobilized conservatives to seek a Supreme Court reversal or, short of that, to pursue legislation that would strictly limit the conditions under which abortions could be performed. In 1976, they convinced Congress to deny Medicaid funds for abortions, an opening round in a campaign against *Roe v. Wade* that continues today.

**Harvey Milk**    The gay rights movement had achieved notable victories as well. These, too, proved controversial. More than a dozen cities had passed gay rights ordinances by the mid-1970s, protecting gay men and lesbians from employment and housing discrimination. One such ordinance in Dade County (Miami), Florida, sparked a protest led by Anita Bryant, a conservative Baptist and a television celebrity. Her "Save Our Children" campaign in 1977, which garnered national media attention, resulted in the repeal of the ordinance and symbolized the emergence of a conservative religious movement opposed to gay rights.

Across the country from Miami, developments in San Francisco looked promising for gay rights advocates, then turned tragic. No one embodied the combination of gay liberation and hard-nosed politics better than a San Francisco camera-shop owner named

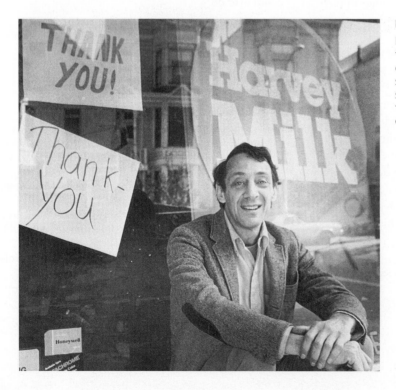

**Harvey Milk**

In November 1977, Harvey Milk became the first openly gay man to be elected to public office in the United States, when he won a seat on the San Francisco Board of Supervisors. Shockingly, almost exactly a year from the day of his election, Milk was assassinated. © Bettmann/Corbis.

Harvey Milk. A closeted businessman in New York until he was forty, Milk arrived in San Francisco in 1972 and threw himself into city politics. Fiercely independent, he ran as an openly gay candidate for city supervisor (city council) twice and the state assembly once, both times unsuccessfully.

By mobilizing the "gay vote" into a powerful bloc, Milk finally won a supervisor seat in 1977. He was not the first openly gay elected official in the country — Kathy Kozachenko of Michigan and Elaine Noble of Massachusetts share that distinction — but he became a national symbol of emerging gay political power. Tragically, after he helped to win passage of a gay rights ordinance in San Francisco, he was assassinated in 1978 — along with the city's mayor, George Moscone — by a disgruntled former supervisor named Dan White. When White was convicted of manslaughter rather than murder, five thousand gays and lesbians in San Francisco marched on city hall.

### After the Warren Court

In response to what conservatives considered the liberal judicial revolution under the Warren Court, President Nixon came into the presidency promising to appoint "strict constructionists" (conservative-minded justices) to the bench. In three short years, between 1969 and 1972, he was able to appoint four new justices to the Supreme Court, including the new chief justice, Warren Burger. Surprisingly, despite the conservative credentials of its new members, the Burger Court refused to scale back the liberal precedents set under Warren. Most prominently, in *Roe v. Wade* the Burger Court extended the "right of privacy" developed under Warren to include women's access to abortion. As we saw above, few Supreme Court decisions in the twentieth century have disappointed conservatives more.

In a variety of cases, the Burger Court either confirmed previous liberal rulings or chose a centrist course. In 1972, for instance, the Court deepened its intervention in criminal procedure by striking down all existing capital punishment laws, in *Furman v. Georgia*. In response, Los Angeles police chief Ed Davis accused the Court of establishing a "legal oligarchy" that had ignored the "perspective of the average citizen." He and other conservatives vowed a nationwide campaign to bring back the death penalty — which was in fact shortly restored, in *Gregg v. Georgia* (1976). Other decisions advanced women's rights. In 1976, the Court ruled that arbitrary distinctions based on sex in the workplace and other arenas were unconstitutional, and in 1986 that sexual harassment violated the Civil Rights Act. These rulings helped women break employment barriers in the subsequent decades.

In all of their rulings on privacy rights, however, the Burger Court was reluctant to move ahead of public attitudes toward homosexuality. Gay men and lesbians still had no legal recourse if state laws prohibited same-sex relations. In a controversial 1986 case, *Bowers v. Hardwick*, the Supreme Court upheld a Georgia sodomy statute that criminalized same-sex sexual acts. The majority opinion held that homosexuality was contrary to "ordered liberty" and that extending sexual privacy to gays and lesbians "would be to cast aside millennia of moral teaching." Not until 2003 (*Lawrence v. Texas*) would the Court overturn that decision, recognizing for all Americans the right to sexual privacy.

## The American Family on Trial

In 1973, the Public Broadcasting System (PBS) aired a twelve-part television series that followed the life of a real American family. Producers wanted the show, called simply *An American Family*, to document how a middle-class white family coped with the stresses of a changing society. They did not anticipate that the family would dissolve in front of their cameras. Tensions and arguments raged, and in the final episode, Bill, the husband and father (who had had numerous extramarital affairs), moved out. By the time the show aired, the couple was divorced and Pat, the former wife, had become a single working mother with five children.

*An American Family* captured a traumatic moment in the twentieth-century history of the family. Between 1965 and 1985, the divorce rate doubled, and children born in the 1970s had a 40 percent chance of spending part of their youth in a single-parent household. As wages stagnated and inflation pushed prices up, more and more families depended on two incomes for survival. Furthermore, the women's movement and the counterculture had called into question traditional sex roles — father as provider and mother as homemaker — and middle-class baby boomers rebelled against what they saw as the puritanical sexual values of their parents' generation. In the midst of such rapid change, where did the family stand?

### Working Families in the Age of Deindustrialization

One of the most striking developments of the 1970s and 1980s was the relative stagnation of wages. After World War II, hourly wages had grown steadily ahead of inflation, giving workers more buying power with each passing decade. By 1973, that trend had stopped in its tracks. The decline of organized labor, the loss of manufacturing jobs, and runaway inflation all played a role in the reversal. Hardest hit were blue-collar and pink-collar workers and those without college degrees.

**Women Enter the Workforce**    Millions of wives and mothers had worked for wages for decades. But many Americans still believed in the "family wage": a bread-winner income, earned by men, sufficient to support a family. After 1973, fewer and fewer Americans had access to that luxury. Between 1973 and the early 1990s, every major income group except the top 10 percent saw their real earnings (accounting for inflation) either remain the same or decline. Over this period, the typical worker saw a 10 percent drop in real wages. To keep their families from falling behind, women streamed into the workforce. Between 1950 and 1994, the proportion of women ages 25 to 54 working for pay increased from 37 to 75 percent. Much of that increase occurred in the 1970s.

**PLACE EVENTS IN CONTEXT**

Why did the struggles of working families become more prominent in the 1970s, and what social and economic concerns did those families have?

Americans were fast becoming dependent on the two-income household (Figure 29.5).

The numbers tell two different stories of American life in these decades. On the one hand, the trends unmistakably show that women, especially in blue-collar and pink-collar families, *had* to work for wages to sustain their family's standard of living: to buy a car, pay for college, afford medical bills, support an aging parent, or simply pay the rent. Moreover, the number of single women raising children nearly doubled between 1965 and 1990. Women's paid labor was making up for the declining earning power or the absence of men in American households. On the other hand, women's real income overall grew during the same period. This increase reflected the opening of professional and skilled jobs to educated baby-boomer women. As older barriers began to fall, women poured into law and medicine, business and government, and, though more slowly, the sciences and engineering. Beneficiaries of feminism, these women pursued careers of which their mothers had only dreamed.

**Workers in the National Spotlight**    For a brief period in the 1970s, the trials of working men and women made a distinct imprint on national culture.

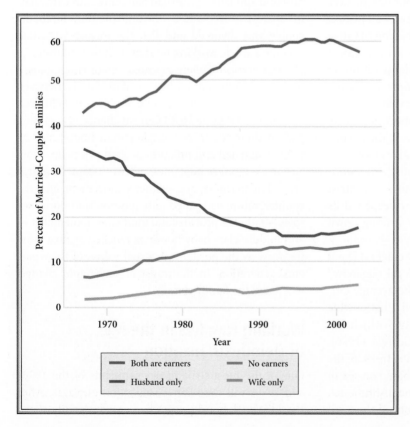

**FIGURE 29.5**

**The Increase in Two-Worker Families**

In 1968, about 43 percent of married couples sent both the husband and the wife into the workforce; thirty years later, 60 percent were two-earner families. The percentage of families in which the wife alone worked increased from 3 to 5 percent during these years, while those with no earners (welfare recipients and, increasingly, retired couples) rose from 8 to 13 percent. Because these figures do not include unmarried persons and most illegal immigrants, they do not give a complete picture of the American workplace. But there is no doubt that women now play a major role in the workforce.

## Blue-Collar Blues

Unemployment in the 1970s affected blue-collar workers most, with many factories closing and new construction at a standstill. In many cities, joblessness among construction workers stood between 20 and 30 percent. In this 1976 photo, an unemployed carpenter in Cleveland, Ohio, files for unemployment insurance. The "blue-collar blues" caused by long unemployment lines, high inflation, and difficult economic times hit American workers hard in the late 1970s. © 1976 Settle/The New York Times Company. Reprinted with Permission.

Reporters wrote of the "blue-collar blues" associated with plant closings and the hard-fought strikes of the decade. A 1972 strike at the Lordstown, Ohio, General Motors plant captivated the nation. Holding out not for higher wages but for better working conditions—the plant had the most complex assembly line in the nation—Lordstown strikers spoke out against what they saw as an inhumane industrial system. Across the nation, the number of union-led strikes surged, even as the number of Americans in the labor movement continued to decline. In Lordstown and most other sites of strikes and industrial conflict, workers won a measure of public attention but typically gained little economic ground.

When Americans turned on their televisions in the mid-1970s, the most popular shows reflected the "blue-collar blues" of struggling families. *All in the Family* was joined by *The Waltons*, set during the Great Depression. *Good Times*, *Welcome Back, Kotter*, and *Sanford and Son* dealt with poverty in the inner city. *The Jeffersons* featured an upwardly mobile black couple. *Laverne and Shirley* focused on young working women

## Good Times

The popular 1970s sitcom *Good Times* examined how the "blue-collar blues" affected a working-class black family struggling to make ends meet in tough economic times. The show's theme song spoke of "temporary layoffs . . . easy credit ripoffs . . . scratchin' and surviving." Its actors, many of them classically trained, brought a realistic portrait of working-class African American life to television. © Bettmann/Corbis.

in the 1950s and *One Day at a Time* on working women in the 1970s making do after divorce. The most-watched television series of the decade, 1977's eight-part *Roots*, explored the history of slavery and the survival of African American culture and family roots despite the oppressive labor system. Not since the 1930s had American culture paid such close attention to working-class life.

The decade also saw the rise of musicians such as Bruce Springsteen, Johnny Paycheck, and John Cougar (Mellencamp), who became stars by turning the hardscrabble lives of people in small towns and working-class communities into rock anthems that filled arenas. Springsteen wrote songs about characters who "sweat it out in the streets of a runaway American dream," and, to the delight of his audience, Paycheck famously sang, "Take this job and shove it!" Meanwhile, on the streets of Harlem and the South Bronx in New York, young working-class African American men experimenting with dance and musical forms invented break dancing and rap music — styles that expressed both the hardship and the creativity of working-class black life in the deindustrialized American city.

## Navigating the Sexual Revolution

The economic downturn was not the only force that placed stress on American families in this era. Another such force was what many came to call the "sexual revolution." Hardly revolutionary, sexual attitudes in the 1970s were, in many ways, a logical evolution of developments in the first half of the twentieth century. Beginning in the 1910s, Americans increasingly viewed sex as a component of personal happiness, distinct from reproduction. Attitudes toward sex grew even more lenient in the postwar decades, a fact reflected in the Kinsey studies of the 1940s and 1950s. By the 1960s, sex before marriage had grown more socially acceptable — an especially profound change for women — and frank discussions of sex in the media and popular culture had grown more common.

In that decade, three developments dramatically accelerated this process: the introduction of the birth control pill, the rise of the baby-boomer-led counterculture, and the influence of feminism. First made available in the United States in 1960, the birth control pill gave women an unprecedented degree of control over reproduction. By 1965, more than 6 million American women were taking advantage of this pharmaceutical advance.

**EXPLAIN CONSEQUENCES**
What were three major consequences of the sexual revolution of the 1960s and 1970s?

Rapid shifts in attitude accompanied the technological breakthrough. Middle-class baby boomers embraced a sexual ethic of greater freedom and, in many cases, a more casual approach to sex outside marriage. "I just feel I am expressing myself the way I feel at that moment in the most natural way," a female California college student, explaining her sex life, told a reporter in 1966. The rebellious counterculture encouraged this attitudinal shift by associating a puritanical view of sex with their parents' generation.

Finally, women's rights activists reacted to the new emphasis on sexual freedom in at least two distinct ways. Many feminists felt that the sexual revolution was by and for men: the emphasis on casual sex seemed to perpetuate male privilege — the old double standard; sexual harassment was all too common in the workplace; and the proliferation of pornography continued to commercialize women as sex objects. On the other hand, they remained optimistic that the new sexual ethic could free women from those older moral constraints. They called for a revolution in sexual *values*, not simply behavior, that would end exploitation and grant women the freedom to explore their sexuality on equal terms with men.

**Sex and Popular Culture**    In the 1970s, popular culture was suffused with discussions of the sexual revolution. Mass-market books with titles such as *Everything You Always Wanted to Know About Sex*, *Human Sexual Response*, and *The Sensuous Man* shot up the best-seller list. William Masters and Virginia Johnson became the most famous sex researchers since Alfred Kinsey by studying couples in the act of lovemaking. In 1972, English physician Alex Comfort published *The Joy of Sex*, a guidebook for couples that became one of the most popular books of the decade. Comfort made certain to distinguish his writing from pornographic exploitation. "Sex is the one place where we today can learn to treat people as people," he wrote.

Hollywood took advantage of the new sexual ethic by making films with explicit erotic content that pushed the boundaries of middle-class taste. Films such as *Midnight Cowboy* (1969), *Carnal Knowledge* (1971), and *Shampoo* (1974), the latter starring Hollywood's leading ladies' man, Warren Beatty, led the way. Throughout the decade, and into the 1980s, the Motion Picture Association of America (MPAA) scrambled to keep its guide for parents — the system of rating pictures G, PG, R, and X (and, after 1984, PG-13) — in tune with Hollywood's advancing sexual revolution.

On television, the popularity of social problem shows, such as *All in the Family*, and the fear of losing

**Midnight Cowboy**

In the mid-1970s, the movie industry embraced the "sexual revolution" and pushed the boundaries of middle-class taste. Movies such as *Midnight Cowboy* (1975)—starring Dustin Hoffman and Jon Voight—were part of a larger shift in American culture in which frank sexual discussions and the portrayal of sexual situations in various media grew more acceptable. John Springer Collection/Corbis.

advertising revenue moderated the portrayal of sex in the early 1970s. However, in the second half of the decade networks both exploited and criticized the new sexual ethic. In frivolous, lighthearted shows such as the popular *Charlie's Angels*, *Three's Company*, and *The Love Boat*, heterosexual couples explored the often confusing, and usually comical, landscape of sexual morality. At the same time, between 1974 and 1981, the major networks produced more than a dozen made-for-TV movies about children in sexual danger—a sensationalized warning to parents of the potential threats to children posed by a less strict sexual morality.

**Middle-Class Marriage**   Many Americans worried that the sexual revolution threatened marriage itself. The notion of marriage as romantic companionship had defined middle-class norms since the late nineteenth century. It was also quite common throughout most of the twentieth century for Americans to see sexual satisfaction as a healthy part of the marriage bond.

But what defined a healthy marriage in an age of rising divorce rates, changing sexual values, and feminist critiques of the nuclear family? Only a small minority of Americans rejected marriage outright; most continued to create monogamous relationships codified in marriage. But many came to believe that they needed help as marriage came under a variety of economic and psychological stresses.

A therapeutic industry arose in response. Churches and secular groups alike established marriage seminars and counseling services to assist couples in sustaining a healthy marriage. A popular form of 1960s psychotherapy, the "encounter group," was adapted to marriage counseling: couples met in large groups to explore new methods of communicating. One of the most successful of these organizations, Marriage Encounter, was founded by the Catholic Church. It expanded into Protestant and Jewish communities in the 1970s and became one of the nation's largest counseling organizations. Such groups embodied another long-term shift in how middle-class Americans understood marriage. Spurred by both feminism and psychotherapeutic models that stressed self-improvement, Americans increasingly defined marriage not simply by companionship and sexual fidelity but also by the deeply felt emotional connection between two people.

## Religion in the 1970s: The Fourth Great Awakening

For three centuries, American society has been punctuated by intense periods of religious revival—what historians have called Great Awakenings (Chapters 4 and 8). These periods have seen a rise in church membership, the appearance of charismatic religious leaders, and the increasing influence of religion, usually of the evangelical variety, on society and politics. One such awakening, the fourth in U.S. history, took shape in the 1970s and 1980s. It had many elements, but one of its central features was a growing concern with the family.

In the 1950s and 1960s, many mainstream Protestants had embraced the reform spirit of the age. Some of the most visible Protestant leaders were social activists who condemned racism and opposed the Vietnam War. Organizations such as the National Council of Churches—along with many progressive Catholics and Jews—joined with Martin Luther King Jr. and other African American ministers in the long battle for civil rights. Many mainline Protestant churches, among them the Episcopal, Methodist, and Congregationalist denominations, practiced a version of the "Social Gospel," the reform-minded Christianity of the early twentieth century.

### Evangelical Resurgence

Meanwhile, **evangelicalism** survived at the grass roots. Evangelical Protestant churches emphasized an intimate, personal salvation (being "born again"); focused on a literal interpretation of the Bible; and regarded the death and resurrection of Jesus as the central message of Christianity. These tenets distinguished evangelicals from mainline Protestants as well as from Catholics and Jews, and they flourished in a handful of evangelical colleges, Bible schools, and seminaries in the postwar decades.

No one did more to keep the evangelical fire burning than Billy Graham. A graduate of the evangelical Wheaton College in Illinois, Graham cofounded Youth for Christ in 1945 and then toured the United States and Europe preaching the gospel. Following a stunning 1949 tent revival in Los Angeles that lasted eight weeks, Graham shot to national fame. His success in Los Angeles led to a popular radio program, but

**EXPLAIN CONSEQUENCES**
How did evangelical Christianity influence American society in the 1970s?

**Televangelism**

Television minister ("televangelist") and conservative political activist Pat Robertson, shown here in the control room of his *700 Club* TV show, was a leading figure in the resurgence of evangelical Christianity in the 1970s and 1980s. Reaching millions of viewers through their television ministries, men such as Robertson built huge churches and large popular followings. © Wally McNamee/CORBIS he continued to travel relentlessly, conducting old-fashioned revival meetings he called crusades. A massive sixteen-week 1957 crusade held in New York City's Madison Square Garden made Graham, along with the conservative Catholic priest Fulton Sheen, one of the nation's most visible religious leaders.

Graham and other evangelicals in the 1950s and 1960s laid the groundwork for the Fourth Great Awakening. But it was a startling combination of events in the late 1960s and early 1970s that sparked the evangelical revival. First, rising divorce rates, social unrest, and challenges to prevailing values led people to seek the stability of faith. Second, many Americans regarded feminism, the counterculture, sexual freedom, homosexuality, pornography, and legalized abortion not as distinct issues, but as a collective sign of moral decay in society. To seek answers and find order, more and more people turned to evangelical ministries, especially Southern Baptist, Pentecostal, and Assemblies of God churches.

Numbers tell part of the story. As mainline churches lost about 15 percent of their membership between 1970 and 1985, evangelical church membership soared. The Southern Baptist Convention, the largest Protestant denomination, grew by 23 percent, while the Assemblies of God grew by an astounding 300 percent. *Newsweek* magazine declared 1976 "The Year of the Evangelical," and that November the nation made Jimmy Carter the nation's first evangelical president. In a national Gallup poll, 34 percent of Americans answered yes when asked, "Would you describe yourself as a 'born again' or evangelical Christian?"

Much of this astonishing growth came from the creative use of television. Graham had pounded the pavement and worn out shoe leather to reach his converts. But a new generation of preachers brought religious conversion directly into Americans' living rooms through television. These so-called televangelists built huge media empires through small donations from millions of avid viewers — not to mention advertising. Jerry Falwell's *Old Time Gospel Hour*, Pat Robertson's *700 Club*, and Jim and Tammy Bakker's *PTL (Praise the Lord) Club* were the leading pioneers in this televised race for American souls, but another half dozen — including Oral Roberts and Jimmy Swaggart — followed them onto the airwaves. Together, they made the 1970s and 1980s the era of Christian broadcasting.

### Religion and the Family
Of primary concern to evangelical Christians was the family. Drawing on selected Bible passages, evangelicals believed that the nuclear family, and not the individual, represented the fundamental unit of society. The family itself was organized along paternalist lines: father was breadwinner and disciplinarian; mother was nurturer and supporter. "Motherhood is the highest form of femininity," the evangelical author Beverly LaHaye wrote in an influential book on Christian women. Another popular Christian author declared, "A church, a family, a nation is only as strong as its men."

Evangelicals spread their message about the Christian family through more than the pulpit and television. They founded publishing houses, wrote books, established foundations, and offered seminars. Helen B. Andelin, for instance, a California housewife, produced a homemade book called *Fascinating Womanhood* that eventually sold more than 2 million copies. She used the book as the basis for her classes, which by the early 1970s had been attended by 400,000 women and boasted 11,000 trained teachers. *Fascinating Womanhood* led evangelical women in the opposite direction of feminism. Whereas the latter encouraged women to be independent and to seek equality with men, Andelin taught that "submissiveness will bring a strange but righteous power over your man." Andelin was but one of dozens of evangelical authors and educators who encouraged women to defer to men.

Evangelical Christians held that strict gender roles in the family would ward off the influences of an immoral society. Christian activists were especially concerned with sex education in public schools, the proliferation of pornography, legalized abortion, and the rising divorce rate. For them, the answer was to strengthen what they called "traditional" family structures. By the early 1980s, Christians could choose from among hundreds of evangelical books, take classes on how to save a marriage or how to be a Christian parent, attend evangelical churches and Bible study courses, watch evangelical ministers on television, and donate to foundations that promoted "Christian values" in state legislatures and the U.S. Congress.

Wherever one looked in the 1970s and early 1980s, American families were under strain. Nearly everyone agreed that the waves of social liberalism and economic transformation that swept over the nation in the 1960s and 1970s had destabilized society and, especially, family relationships. But Americans did not agree about how to *re*stabilize families. Indeed, different approaches to the family would further divide the country in the 1980s and 1990s, as the New Right would increasingly make "family values" a political issue.

**"Family Values"**
During the 1980 presidential campaign, the Reverend Jerry Falwell, pictured here with Phyllis Schlafly, supported Ronald Reagan and the Republican Party with "I Love America" rallies around the country. Falwell, head of the Moral Majority, helped to bring a new focus on "family values" to American politics in the late 1970s. This was a conservative version of the emphasis on male-breadwinner nuclear families that had long been characteristic of American values. AP/Wide World Photos.

## SUMMARY

For much of the 1970s, Americans struggled with economic problems, including inflation, energy shortages, income stagnation, and deindustrialization. These challenges highlighted the limits of postwar prosperity and forced Americans to consider lowering their economic expectations. A movement for environmental protection, widely supported, led to new laws and an awareness of nature's limits, and the energy crisis highlighted the nation's dependence on resources from abroad, especially oil.

In the midst of this gloomy economic climate, Americans also sought political and cultural resolutions to the upheavals of the 1960s. In politics, the Watergate scandal led to a brief period of political reform. Meanwhile, the battle for civil rights entered a second stage, expanding to encompass women's rights, gay rights, and the rights of alleged criminals and prisoners and, in the realm of racial justice, focusing on the problem of producing concrete results rather than legislation. Many liberals cheered these developments, but another effect was to strengthen a new, more conservative social mood that began to challenge liberal values in politics and society more generally. Finally, we considered the multiple challenges faced by the American family in the 1970s and how a perception that the family was in trouble helped to spur an evangelical religious revival that would shape American society for decades to come.

# CHAPTER REVIEW

**MAKE IT STICK**    Go to **LearningCurve** to retain what you've read.

## TERMS TO KNOW    Identify and explain the significance of each term below.

### Key Concepts and Events

Organization of Petroleum
   Exporting Countries (OPEC)
   (p. 938)
energy crisis (p. 939)
environmentalism (p. 939)
*Silent Spring* (p. 939)
Earth Day (p. 939)
Environmental Protection
   Agency (EPA) (p. 939)
Three Mile Island (p. 942)
stagflation (p. 942)
deindustrialization (p. 944)
Rust Belt (p. 944)
tax revolt (p. 946)
Proposition 13 (p. 947)

Watergate (p. 947)
War Powers Act (p. 948)
Freedom of Information Act
   (p. 948)
Ethics in Government Act
   (p. 948)
deregulation (p. 950)
affirmative action (p. 950)
*Bakke v. University of California*
   (p. 951)
Equal Rights Amendment (ERA)
   (p. 952)
STOP ERA (p. 953)
*Roe v. Wade* (p. 956)
evangelicalism (p. 962)

### Key People

Rachel Carson (p. 939)
Gerald Ford (p. 947)
Howard Jarvis (p. 947)
Jimmy Carter (p. 949)
Phyllis Schlafly (p. 953)
Harvey Milk (p. 956)
Billy Graham (p. 962)

## REVIEW QUESTIONS    Answer these questions to demonstrate your understanding of the chapter's main ideas.

1. Why did the U.S. economy struggle in the 1970s? How was the period after 1973 different from 1945–1972?

2. How was the "rights liberalism" of this era different from the "welfare liberalism" of the 1930s and 1940s?

3. How was the American family of the 1970s different from that of the 1950s? Without romanticizing either period, how would you account for the differences?

4. **THEMATIC UNDERSTANDING**    Examine the category "Work, Exchange, and Technology" on the thematic timeline on page 803. How did economic developments in the 1970s reverse the course the national economy had been on since World War II? More broadly, can you identify events in each of the timeline categories that made the 1970s a decade of important historical transition?

## MAKING CONNECTIONS

Recognize the larger developments and continuities within and across chapters by answering these questions.

1. **ACROSS TIME AND PLACE** Consider the history of the American economy in the twentieth century. Compare the 1970s with other eras: the Great Depression of the 1930s, the industrial boom of the World War II years, and the growth and rising wages in the 1950s and 1960s. Using these comparisons, construct a historical narrative of the period from the 1920s through the 1970s.

2. **VISUAL EVIDENCE** Study the photographs on pages 943 and 959 and the map on page 944. How did the economic downturn of the 1970s affect the lives of ordinary Americans and American culture broadly? What connections can you draw between the two photographs and developments in the global economy and the rise of the Sunbelt?

## MORE TO EXPLORE

Start here to learn more about the events discussed in this chapter.

Jeffrey Hadden and Anson Shupe, *Televangelism: Power and Politics on God's Frontier* (1988). A thought-provoking analysis of Christian broadcasting.

Daniel Horowitz, *Jimmy Carter and the Energy Crisis of the 1970s* (2005). Analysis and documents.

N. E. H. Hull and Peter Charles Hoffer, *Roe v. Wade: The Abortion Rights Controversy in American History* (2001). A sweeping treatment of the controversial decision.

Rick Perlstein, *Nixonland: The Rise of a President and the Fracturing of America* (2008). An excellent overview of the era.

Kirkpatrick Sale, *The Green Revolution: The American Environmental Movement, 1962–1992* (1993). A balanced account of environmentalism.

The Oyez Project at Northwestern University, at **oyez .org/oyez/frontpage**, is an invaluable resource for more than one thousand Supreme Court cases, with audio transcripts, voting records, and summaries.

# TIMELINE

Ask yourself why this chapter begins and ends with these dates and then identify the links among related events.

| 1970 | • Earth Day first observed<br>• Environmental Protection Agency established |
|------|------------------------------------------------------------------------------|
| 1972 | • Equal Rights Amendment passed by Congress<br>• Phyllis Schlafly founds STOP ERA<br>• *Furman v. Georgia* outlaws death penalty<br>• Watergate break-in (June) |
| 1973 | • *Roe v. Wade* legalizes abortion<br>• Endangered Species Act<br>• OPEC oil embargo; gas shortages<br>• Period of high inflation begins<br>• War Powers Act |
| 1974 | • Nixon resigns over Watergate<br>• Congress imposes 55 miles-per-hour speed limit |
| 1975 | • New York nears bankruptcy<br>• "Watergate babies" begin congressional reform |
| 1976 | • Jimmy Carter elected president |
| 1978 | • Proposition 13 reduces California property taxes<br>• *Bakke v. University of California* limits affirmative action<br>• Harvey Milk assassinated in San Francisco |
| 1979 | • Three Mile Island nuclear accident |

**KEY TURNING POINTS:** Based on this timeline, what were the three or four major political turning points of the 1970s? Defend your answer by explaining the impact of the changes.

# Global Capitalism and the End of the American Century

## 1980 to the Present

For historians, the recent past can be a challenge to evaluate and assess. Insufficient time has passed for scholars to weigh the significance of events and to determine which developments will have a lasting effect and which are more fleeting. Nevertheless, the period between the early 1980s and our own day has begun to emerge in the minds of historians with some clarity. Scholars generally agree on the era's three most significant developments: the resurgence of political conservatism, the end of the Cold War, and the globalization of communications and the economy. What *Time* magazine publisher Henry Luce had named the American Century — in his call for the United States to assume global leadership in the decades after World War II — came decisively to an end in the last quarter of the twentieth century and the first decade of the twenty-first. The United States lost its role as the world's dominant economy, faced rising competition from a united Europe and a surging China, and experienced a wide-ranging and divisive internal debate over its own values and priorities. Part 9 remains necessarily a work-in-progress as events continue to unfold; however, through equal parts conflict, struggle, and ingenuity, Americans collectively created a new era in national history after the 1980s, which we consider in terms of the aforementioned three developments:

## Conservative Ascendancy

The 1980s constituted a crucial period in which the forthright conservatism of Ronald Reagan and the New Right was consolidated in the Republican Party and challenged the aggressive liberalism of Lyndon Johnson's Great Society. Under Reagan, the conservative agenda reduced the regulatory power of the federal government, shrank the welfare state created by liberal Democrats during the New Deal and the Great Society, and expanded the military. Evangelical Christians and conservative lawmakers challenged abortion rights, feminism, and gay rights, setting off a "culture war" that sharply divided Americans.

Even as the Reagan coalition brought an end to decades of liberal government activism, much of the legacy of the New Deal was preserved, and in some instances expanded. Medicare, Medicaid, and Social Security survived and grew as a proportion of the federal budget. Conservatives put a stamp on U.S. foreign policy, however, dramatically increasing the defense budget and, under George W. Bush, asserting a new doctrine of "preemptive war" that led to a decades-long war in Iraq. By the presidential election of 2012, national politics seemed as divided as ever. Americans reelected Barack Obama but returned a conservative majority to the House of Representatives. Polls showed that Americans embraced a moderate liberalism on such issues as gay rights and taxes, but the national political system remained mired in stalemate.

## End of the Cold War and Rising Conflict in the Middle East

Under Ronald Reagan, between 1981 and 1989 the United States increased government military spending and returned to the sharp Cold War rhetoric of earlier decades. Yet during the second half of the 1980s, as internal reforms swept through the Soviet Union, Reagan softened his stance measuredly and engaged in productive dialogue with the Soviet leader Mikhail Gorbachev. Then, between 1989 and 1991, the four-decade Cold War came to a stunning halt. The Soviet Union and its satellite communist regimes in Eastern Europe collapsed. The result was, in the words of President George H. W. Bush, a "new world order." Without a credible rival, the United States emerged in the 1990s as the lone military "superpower" in the world. In the absence of a clear Cold War enemy, it intervened in civil wars, worked to disrupt terrorist activities, and provided humanitarian aid—but on a case-by-case basis, guided more by pragmatism than by principle.

The foremost region that occupied U.S. attention was the Middle East, where strategic interest in oil supplies remained paramount. Between 1991 and 2011, U.S. armed forces fought three wars in the region—two in Iraq and one in Afghanistan—and became even more deeply embedded in its politics. The end of the Cold War thus brought a dramatic expansion of the U.S. role in the Middle East and renewed debates at home about the proper American role in the world.

## Globalization and Increasing Social Inequality

The post–World War II expansion of the American economy had ended by the early 1970s. Wages stagnated. Inflation skyrocketed. In the 1980s and 1990s, however, productivity increased, military spending boosted production, and new industries—such as computer technology—emerged. These developments led to renewed economic growth. More and more, though, the economy produced *services* rather than *goods*, which Americans increasingly bought from overseas.

The fall of communism and the end of the Cold War had made possible this global expansion of capitalism, as multinational corporations moved production to low-wage countries and international trade increased. Governments across the world facilitated this process by deregulating financial markets and by creating new trading zones such as the European Union (EU) and the North American Free Trade Agreement (NAFTA).

Conservative tax policies, deindustrialization, the decline of unions, and globalization all contributed to a widening inequality between the wealthiest Americans and the middle class and poor. Between 2007 and 2010, the negative side of global market deregulation became apparent, as Europe and much of North America suffered the worst economic downturn since the Great Depression. Globalization thus brought new economic opportunities and interconnections as well as the potential for renewed economic insecurity.

# Global Capitalism and the End of the American Century 1980 to the Present

## Thematic Understanding

This timeline arranges some of the important events of this period into themes. Consider the entries under "Ideas, Beliefs, and Culture" and "Peopling." What were the major events of the "culture wars," and how did American attitudes and public policy change over the decades between the 1980s and the 2010s? **>**

| | AMERICA IN THE WORLD | POLITICS AND POWER | IDEAS, BELIEFS, AND CULTURE | PEOPLING | WORK, EXCHANGE, AND TECHNOLOGY |
|---|---|---|---|---|---|
| **1980** | • Ronald Reagan begins arms buildup<br><br>• United States arms Contras in Nicaragua<br><br>• Berlin Wall comes down (1989) | • New Right helps elect Ronald Reagan president<br><br>• Iran-Contra scandal (1985–1987)<br><br>• George H. W. Bush elected president (1988) | • HIV/AIDS crisis prompts national conversation about homosexuality<br><br>• Renewed emphasis on material success and the "rich and famous"<br><br>• *Webster v. Reproductive Health Services* (1989) | • Rise in Latino and Asian immigration<br><br>• Californians vote to establish English as official language (1986) | • Recession (1981–1982) followed by strong growth (1982–1987)<br><br>• Reagan tax cut (1981)<br><br>• Apple personal computer introduced (1983)<br><br>• National debt triples (1981–1989) |
| **1990** | • Persian Gulf War (1990–1991)<br><br>• USSR breaks apart; end of Cold War<br><br>• Al Qaeda bombs World Trade Center (1993)<br><br>• UN peacekeeping forces in Bosnia (1992–1995) | • Bill Clinton elected president (1992)<br><br>• Republican resurgence (1994)<br><br>• Welfare reform (1996)<br><br>• Clinton impeached and acquitted (1998–1999) | • Pat Buchanan declares "culture war" (1992)<br><br>• Proposition 209 ends affirmative action in California universities<br><br>• Defense of Marriage Act (1998)<br><br>• WTO protests in Seattle (1999) | • Backlash against "multiculturalism"<br><br>• California bans bilingual education in public schools (1998) | • Internet gains in popularity<br><br>• Recession (1990–1991)<br><br>• NAFTA ratified (1993)<br><br>• Debt reduction under Bill Clinton |
| **2000** | • Al Qaeda attacks World Trade Center and Pentagon (2001)<br><br>• United States and allies invade Afghanistan (2002)<br><br>• United States invades Iraq (2004) | • George W. Bush wins presidency in contested election (2000)<br><br>• USA PATRIOT Act (2002)<br><br>• Barack Obama elected first African American president (2008) | • *Lawrence v. Texas* (2003)<br><br>• Massachusetts becomes first state to legalize same-sex marriage (2004); nine states follow by 2012<br><br>• "War on terror" becomes fixture in American discourse | • New scrutiny of airport passengers after 9/11<br><br>• California, Texas, Hawaii, and New Mexico become "majority-minority" states (where the majority of the population is composed of minorities) | • Crisis in newspaper industry<br><br>• Great Recession (2007–2010)<br><br>• President Bush asks for and receives bank bailout from Congress (2008)<br><br>• Unemployment hits 10 percent |
| **2010** | • Arab Spring (2010–2012)<br><br>• Osama bin Laden killed (2011)<br><br>• Last combat troops withdrawn from Iraq (2011) | • Health-care reform (2010)<br><br>• Tea Party helps Republicans regain control of House of Representatives<br><br>• Barack Obama reelected president (2012) | • Congress and President Obama end "Don't Ask, Don't Tell" policy in U.S. military (2011) | • Obama's 2012 electoral coalition heavily African American, Hispanic, Asian American, female, and young | • Financial industry accounts for largest share of GDP among all industry sectors |

# 30

**CHAPTER**

# Conservative America in the Ascent 1980–1991

The decade of the 1970s saw Americans divided by the Vietnam War, wearied by social unrest, and unmoored by economic drift. As a result, many ordinary citizens developed a deep distrust of the muscular Great Society liberalism of the 1960s. Seizing political advantage amid the trauma and divisions, a revived Republican Party, led by the New Right, offered the nation a fresh way forward: economic deregulation, low taxes, Christian morality, and a reenergized Cold War foreign policy. The election of President Ronald Reagan in 1980 symbolized the ascendance of this new political formula, and the president himself helped shape the era.

The New Right revived confidence in "free markets" and called for a smaller government role in economic regulation and social welfare. Reagan famously said, "Government is not the solution to our problem; government *is* the problem." Like the New Right generally, Reagan was profoundly skeptical of the liberal ideology that had informed American public policy since Franklin D. Roosevelt's New Deal. His presidency combined an economically conservative domestic agenda with aggressive anticommunism abroad. Reagan's foreign policy brought an end to détente—a lessening of tensions—with the Soviet Union (which had begun with Richard Nixon) and then, unexpectedly, a sudden thawing of U.S.-Soviet relations, laying the groundwork for the end of the Cold War.

Reagan defined the conservative ascendancy of the 1980s, but he did not create the New Right groundswell that brought him into office. Grassroots conservative activists in the 1960s and 1970s built a formidable right-wing movement that awaited an opportune political moment to challenge for national power. That moment came in 1980, when Democratic president Jimmy Carter's popularity plummeted as a result of his mismanagement of two national crises. Raging inflation and the Iranian seizure of U.S. hostages in Tehran undid Carter and provided an opening for the New Right, which would shape the nation's politics for the remainder of the twentieth century and the first decade of the twenty-first.

**IDENTIFY THE BIG IDEA**
What factors made the rise of the New Right possible, and what ideas about freedom and citizenship did conservatives articulate in the 1980s?

**1984 Republican National Convention** Ronald Reagan delivers his acceptance speech in this photo from the 1984 Republican National Convention. Reagan's political rise captured the spirit of conservative politics in the late 1970s and 1980s. Ronald Reagan Presidential Library.

# The Rise of the New Right

The Great Depression and World War II discredited the traditional conservative program of limited government at home and diplomatic isolationism abroad. Nevertheless, a right-wing faction survived within the Republican Party. Its adherents continued to oppose the New Deal but reversed their earlier isolationism. In the postwar decades, conservatives pushed for military interventions against communism in Europe, Asia, and the developing world while calling for the broadest possible investigation of subversives at home (Chapter 25).

However, conservatives failed to devise policies that could win the allegiance of American voters in the two decades after World War II. Republicans by and large continued to favor party moderates, such as Dwight Eisenhower, Thomas Dewey, and Nelson Rockefeller. These were politicians, often called liberal Republicans, who supported much of the New Deal, endorsed the containment policy overseas, and steered a middle course through the volatile social and political changes of the postwar era. The conservative faction held out hope, however, that it might one day win the loyalty of a majority of Republicans and remake the party in its image. In the 1960s and 1970s, these conservatives invested their hopes for national resurgence in two dynamic figures: Barry Goldwater and Ronald Reagan. Together, the two carried the conservative banner until the national mood grew more receptive to right-wing appeals.

## Barry Goldwater and Ronald Reagan: Champions of the Right

The personal odyssey of Ronald Reagan embodies the story of New Right Republican conservatism. Before World War II, Reagan was a well-known movie actor as well as a New Deal Democrat and admirer of Roosevelt. However, he turned away from liberalism, partly from self-interest (he disliked paying high taxes) and partly on principle. As head of the Screen Actors Guild from 1947 to 1952, Reagan had to deal with its Communist members, who formed the extreme left wing of the American labor movement. Dismayed by their hard-line tactics and goals, he became a militant anticommunist. After nearly a decade as a spokesperson for the General Electric Corporation, Reagan joined

**UNDERSTAND POINTS OF VIEW**
Why was the New Right disappointed with the Republican Party in the decades after World War II?

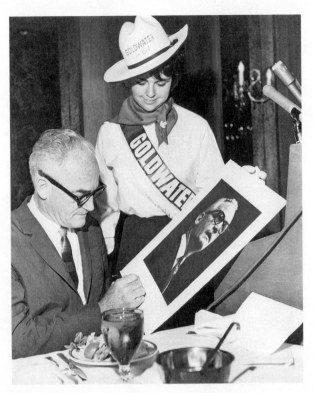

**Barry Goldwater**

Barry Goldwater was a three-term senator from Arizona before he ran for the presidency in 1964 (this photo was taken during the campaign). Goldwater's conservative influence on the Republican Party was considerable and laid the political groundwork for the rise of Ronald Reagan a decade and a half later. © Everett Collection Inc./Alamy.

the Republican Party in the early 1960s and began speaking for conservative causes and candidates.

One of those candidates was archconservative Barry Goldwater, a Republican senator from Arizona. Confident in their power, centrist Republicans did not anticipate that grassroots conservatives could challenge the party's old guard and nominate one of their own for president: Goldwater himself. Understanding how they did so in 1964 brings us closer to comprehending the forces that propelled Reagan to the presidency a decade and a half later. Indeed, Reagan the politician came to national attention in 1964 with a televised speech at the Republican convention supporting Goldwater for the presidency. In a dramatic speech titled "A Time for Choosing," Reagan warned that if we "trade our freedom for the soup kitchen of the welfare state," the nation would "take the first step into a thousand years of darkness."

***The Conscience of a Conservative***   Like Reagan, Goldwater came from the Sunbelt, where citizens embraced a libertarian spirit of limited government and great personal freedom. His 1960 book, **The Conscience of a Conservative**, set forth an uncompromising conservatism. In direct and accessible prose, Goldwater attacked the New Deal state, arguing that "the natural tendency of government [is] to expand in the direction of absolutism." The problem with the Republican Party, as he saw it, was that Eisenhower had been too accommodating to liberalism. When Ike told reporters that he was "liberal when it comes to human problems," Goldwater privately fumed.

*The Conscience of a Conservative* spurred a Republican grassroots movement in support of Goldwater. By distributing his book widely and mobilizing activists at state party conventions, conservatives hoped to create such a groundswell of support that Goldwater could be "drafted" to run for president in 1964, something he reportedly did not wish to do. Meanwhile, Goldwater further enchanted conservatives with another book, *Why Not Victory?*, in which he criticized the containment policy — the strategy of preventing the spread of communism followed by both Democrats and Republicans since 1947 (Chapter 25). It was, he complained, a policy of "timidly refusing to draw our own lines against aggression . . . unmarked by pride or the prospect of victory." Here was a politician saying exactly what conservatives wanted to hear.

**Grassroots Conservatives**   Because moderates dominated the Republican Party leadership, winning the 1964 nomination for Goldwater required conservative activists to build their campaign from the bottom up. They found thousands upon thousands of Americans willing to wear down shoe leather for their political hero. Organizations such as the John Birch Society, Young Americans for Freedom, and the Liberty Lobby supplied an army of eager volunteers. They came from such conservative strongholds as Orange County, California, and the fast-growing suburbs of Phoenix, Dallas, Houston, Atlanta, and other Sunbelt metropolises. A critical boost came in the early spring of 1964, when conservatives outmaneuvered moderates at the state convention of the California Republican Party, which then enthusiastically endorsed Goldwater. The fight had been bruising, and one moderate Republican warned that "sinister forces are at work to take over the whole Republican apparatus in California."

Another spur to Goldwater backers was the appearance of a book by Phyllis Schlafly, who was then a relatively unknown conservative activist from the Midwest. Like Goldwater's own book, Schlafly's *A Choice Not an Echo* accused moderate Republicans of being Democrats in disguise (that is, an "echo" of Democrats). Schlafly, who reappeared in the national spotlight in the early 1970s to help halt the ratification of the Equal Rights Amendment, denounced the "Rockefeller Republicans" of the Northeast and encouraged the party to embrace a defiant conservatism. Contrasting Goldwater's "grassroots Republicans" with Rockefeller's "kingmakers," Schlafly hoped to "forestall another defeat like 1940, 1944, 1948, and 1960," Democratic victories all.

The conservative groundswell won the Republican nomination for Goldwater. However, his strident tone and militarist foreign policy were too much for a nation mourning the death of John F. Kennedy and still committed to liberalism. Democrat Lyndon B. Johnson defeated Goldwater in a historic landslide (Chapter 28). Many believed that Goldwater conservatism would wither and die, but instead the nearly four million volunteers who had campaigned for the Arizona senator swung their support to Ronald Reagan and built toward the future. Skilled conservative political operatives such as Richard Viguerie, a Louisiana-born Catholic and antiabortion activist, applied new computer technology to political campaigning. Viguerie took a list of 12,000 Goldwater contributors and used computerized mailing lists to solicit campaign funds, rally support for conservative causes, and get out the vote on election day. Conservatism was down but not out.

Backed financially by wealthy southern Californians and supported by Goldwaterites, Reagan won California's governorship in 1966 and again in 1970. His impassioned rhetoric supporting limited government and law and order — he vowed to "clean up the mess in Berkeley," referring to campus radicals — won broad support among citizens of the nation's most populous state. More significantly, it made him a force in national politics. His supporters believed that he was in line to succeed Nixon as the next Republican president. The Watergate scandal intervened, however, discrediting Nixon and making Gerald Ford the incumbent. After narrowly losing a campaign against Ford for the Republican presidential nomination in 1976, Reagan was forced to bide his time. When Ford lost to Carter in that year's election, as the party's brightest star Reagan was a near lock to be the nominee in 1980.

## Free-Market Economics and Religious Conservatism

The last phase of Reagan's rise was the product of several additional developments within the New Right. The burgeoning conservative movement increasingly

**PLACE EVENTS IN CONTEXT**
What was the "three-legged stool" of the New Right, and how did each leg develop within the context of the Cold War?

resembled a three-legged stool. Each leg represented an ideological position and a popular constituency: anticommunism, free-market economics, and religious traditionalism. Uniting all three in a political coalition was no easy feat. Religious traditionalists demanded strong government action to implement their faith-based agenda, while economic conservatives favored limited government and free markets. Both groups, however, were ardent anticommunists — free marketeers loathed the state-directed Soviet economy, and religious conservatives despised the "godless" secularism of the Soviet state. In the end, the success of the New Right would come to depend on balancing the interests of economic and moral conservatives.

Since the 1950s, William F. Buckley, the founder and editor of the conservative magazine **National Review**, and Milton Friedman, the Nobel Prize–winning economist at the University of Chicago, had been the most prominent conservative intellectuals. Convinced that "the growth of government must be fought relentlessly," Buckley used the *National Review* to criticize liberal policy. For his part, Friedman became a national conservative icon with the publication of *Capitalism and Freedom* (1962), in which he argued that "economic freedom is . . . an indispensable means toward the achievement of political freedom." Friedman's free-market ideology, along with that of Friedrich von Hayek, another University of Chicago economist, was taken up by wealthy conservatives, who funded think tanks during the 1980s to disseminate market-based public policy ideas. The Heritage Foundation, the American Enterprise Institute, and the Cato Institute issued policy proposals and attacked liberal legislation and the stranglehold of economic regulation they believed it exerted. Followers of Buckley and Friedman envisioned themselves as crusaders, working against what one conservative called "the despotic aspects of egalitarianism."

The most striking addition to the conservative coalition was the **Religious Right**. Until the 1970s, politics was an earthly concern of secondary interest to most fundamentalist and evangelical Protestants. But the perception that American society had become immoral, combined with the influence of a new generation of popular ministers, made politics relevant. Conservative Protestants and Catholics joined together in a tentative alliance, as the Religious Right condemned divorce, abortion, premarital sex, and feminism. The route to a moral life and to "peace, pardon,

purpose, and power," as one evangelical activist said, was "to plug yourself into the One, the Only One [God]."

Charismatic televangelists such as Pat Robertson and Jerry Falwell emerged as the champions of a morality-based political agenda during the late 1970s. Falwell, founder of Liberty University and host of the *Old Time Gospel Hour* television program, established the Moral Majority in 1979. With 400,000 members and $1.5 million in contributions in its first year, it would be the organizational vehicle for transforming the Fourth Great Awakening into a religious political movement. Falwell made no secret of his views: "If you want to know where I am politically," he told reporters, "I thought Goldwater was too liberal." Falwell was not alone. Phyllis Schlafly's STOP ERA, which became Eagle Forum in 1975, continued to advocate for conservative public policy; Focus on the Family was

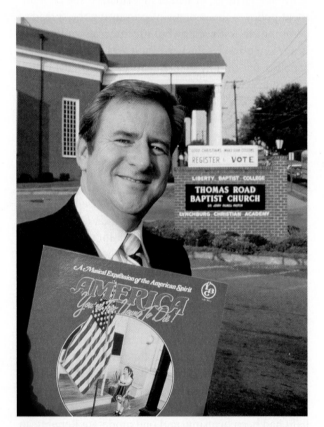

**Jerry Falwell**
The resurgence of evangelical religion in the 1970s was accompanied by a conservative movement in politics known as the Religious Right. Founded in 1979 by televangelist Jerry Falwell, the Moral Majority was one of the earliest Religious Right groups, committed to promoting "family values" and (as the title to the record album he is holding in this photo suggests) patriotism in American society and politics. Wally McNamee/Corbis.

founded in 1977; and a succession of conservative organizations would emerge in the 1980s, including the Family Research Council.

The conservative message preached by Barry Goldwater and Ronald Reagan had appealed to few American voters in 1964. Then came the series of events that undermined support for the liberal agenda of the Democratic Party: the failed war in Vietnam; a judiciary that legalized abortion and pornography, enforced school busing, and curtailed public expression of religion; urban riots; and a stagnating economy. By the late 1970s, the New Right had developed a conservative message that commanded much greater popular support than Goldwater's program had. Religious and free-market conservatives joined with traditional anticommunist hard-liners — alongside whites opposed to black civil rights, affirmative action, and busing — in a broad coalition that attacked welfare-state liberalism, social permissiveness, and an allegedly weak and defensive foreign policy. Ronald Reagan expertly appealed to all of these conservative constituencies and captured the Republican presidential nomination in 1980 (American Voices, p. 978). It had taken almost two decades, but the New Right appeared on the verge of winning the presidency.

## The Carter Presidency

First, the Republican Party had to defeat incumbent president Jimmy Carter. Carter's outsider status and his disdain for professional politicians had made him the ideal post-Watergate president. But his ineffectiveness and missteps as an executive also made him the perfect foil for Ronald Reagan.

Carter had an idealistic vision of American leadership in world affairs. He presented himself as the anti-Nixon, a world leader who rejected Henry Kissinger's "realism" in favor of human rights and peacemaking. "Human rights is the soul of our foreign policy," Carter asserted, "because human rights is the very soul of our sense of nationhood." He established the Office of Human Rights in the State Department and withdrew economic and military aid from repressive regimes in Argentina, Uruguay, and Ethiopia — although, in realist fashion, he still funded equally repressive U.S. allies such as the Philippines, South Africa, and Iran. In Latin America, Carter eliminated a decades-old symbol of Yankee imperialism by signing a treaty on September 7, 1977, turning control of the Panama Canal over to Panama (effective December 31, 1999). Carter's most important efforts came in forging an enduring, although in retrospect limited, peace in the intractable

Arab-Israeli conflict. In 1978, he invited Israeli prime minister Menachem Begin and Egyptian president Anwar el-Sadat to Camp David, where they crafted a "framework for peace," under which Egypt recognized Israel and received back the Sinai Peninsula, which Israel had occupied since 1967.

Carter deplored what he called the "inordinate fear of communism," but his efforts at improving relations with the Soviet Union foundered. His criticism of the Kremlin's record on human rights offended Soviet leader Leonid Brezhnev and slowed arms reduction negotiations. When, in 1979, Carter finally signed the second Strategic Arms Limitations Treaty (SALT II), limiting bombers and missiles, Senate hawks objected. Then, when the Soviet Union invaded Afghanistan that December, Carter suddenly endorsed the hawks' position and treated the invasion as the "gravest threat to world peace since World War II." After ordering an embargo on wheat shipments to the Soviet Union and withdrawing SALT II from Senate consideration, Carter called for increased defense spending and declared an American boycott of the 1980 Summer Olympics in Moscow. In a fateful decision, he and Congress began providing covert assistance to anti-Soviet fighters in Afghanistan, some of whom, including Osama bin Laden, would metamorphose into anti-American Islamic radicals decades later.

**Hostage Crisis**   Carter's ultimate undoing came in Iran, however. The United States had long counted Iran as a faithful ally, a bulwark against Soviet expansion into the Middle East and a steady source of oil. Since the 1940s, Iran had been ruled by Mohammad Reza Shah Pahlavi. Ousted by a democratically elected parliament in the early 1950s, the shah (king) sought and received the assistance of the U.S. Central Intelligence Agency (CIA), which helped him reclaim power in 1953. American intervention soured Iranian views of the United States for decades. Early in 1979, a revolution drove the shah into exile and brought a fundamentalist Shiite cleric, the Ayatollah Ruhollah Khomeini, to power (Shiites represent one branch of Islam, Sunnis the other). When the United States admitted the deposed shah into the country for cancer treatment, Iranian students seized the U.S. embassy in Tehran, taking sixty-six Americans hostage. The captors demanded that the shah be returned to Iran for trial. Carter refused. Instead, he suspended arms sales to Iran and froze Iranian assets in American banks.

For the next fourteen months, the **hostage crisis** paralyzed Carter's presidency. Night after night, humiliating pictures of blindfolded American hostages

## Christianity and Public Life

Modern social-welfare liberalism embodies an ethic of moral pluralism and favors the separation of church and state. Conservative Christians challenge the legitimacy of pluralism and secularism and seek, through political agitation and legal action, to make religion an integral part of public life.

### President Ronald Reagan
### "The Rule of Law Under God"

Reagan's candidacy was strongly supported by Christian conservatives. He delivered these remarks to the National Association of American Evangelicals in 1983.

I want you to know that this administration is motivated by a political philosophy that sees the greatness of America in you, her people, and in your families, churches, neighborhoods, communities — the institutions that foster and nourish values like concern for others and respect for the rule of law under God.

Now, I don't have to tell you that this puts us in opposition to, or at least out of step with, a prevailing attitude of many who have turned to a modern-day secularism, discarding the tried and time-tested values upon which our very civilization is based. No matter how well intentioned, their value system is radically different from that of most Americans. And while they proclaim that they're freeing us from superstitions of the past, they've taken upon themselves the job of superintending us by government rule and regulation. Sometimes their voices are louder than ours, but they are not yet a majority. . . .

Freedom prospers when religion is vibrant and the rule of law under God is acknowledged. When our Founding Fathers passed the First Amendment, they sought to protect churches from government interference. They never intended to construct a wall of hostility between government and the concept of religious belief itself.

Last year, I sent the Congress a constitutional amendment to restore prayer to public schools. Already this session, there's growing bipartisan support for the amendment, and I am calling on the Congress to act speedily to pass it and to let our children pray.

Source: Reprinted with the permission of Simon & Schuster, Inc. from *Speaking My Mind* by Ronald Reagan. Copyright © 1989 Ronald W. Reagan.

### Donald E. Wildmon
### Network Television as a Moral Danger

Wildmon was a Christian minister, a grassroots religious activist, and the founder of the American Family Association.

One night during the Christmas holidays of 1976, I decided to watch television with my family. . . . Not far into the program was a scene of adultery. I reacted to the situation in the manner as I had been taught. I asked one of the children to change channels. Getting involved in the second program, we were shocked with some crude profanity. . . .

As I sat in my den that night, I became angry. I had been disturbed by the deterioration of morals I had witnessed in the media and society during the previous twenty-five years.

This was accompanied by a dramatic rise in crime, a proliferation of pornography, increasingly explicit sexual lyrics in music, increasing numbers of broken homes, a rise in drug and alcohol use among the youth, and various other negative factors. . . .

Realizing that these changes were being brought into the sanctity of my home, I decided I could and would no longer remain silent. . . .

This great struggle is one of values, particularly which ones will be the standard for our society and a base for our system of justice in the years to come. For 200 years our country has based its morals, its sense of right and wrong, on the Christian view of man. The Ten Commandments and the Sermon on the Mount have been our solid foundation. . . .

Television is the most pervasive and persuasive medium we have. At times it is larger than life. It is our only true national medium. Network television is the greatest educator we have. . . .

It is teaching that adultery is an acceptable and approved lifestyle. . . . It is teaching that hardly anyone goes to church, that very few people in our society are Christian or live by Christian principles. How? By simply censoring Christian characters, Christian values, and Christian culture from the programs.

Source: From Donald E. Wildmon, *Home Invaders* (Elgin, IL: Victor Books, 1985). Copyright © 1985. Reprinted by permission of the author.

## A. Bartlett Giamatti

## The Moral Majority as a Threat to Liberty

A. Bartlett Giamatti was the president of Yale University (1978–1986) and subsequently commissioner of Major League Baseball. He offered these remarks to the entering class of Yale undergraduates in 1981.

A self-proclaimed "Moral Majority," and its satellite or client groups, cunning in the use of a native blend of old intimidation and new technology, threaten the values [of pluralism and freedom]. . . .

From the maw of this "morality" come those who presume to know what justice for all is; come those who presume to know which books are fit to read, which television programs are fit to watch. . . . From the maw of this "morality" rise the tax-exempt Savonarolas who believe they, and they alone, possess the "truth." There is no debate, no discussion, no dissent. They know. . . .
What nonsense.

What dangerous, malicious nonsense. . . .

We should be concerned that so much of our political and religious leadership acts intimidated for the moment and will not say with clarity that this most recent denial of the legitimacy of differentness is a radical assault on the very pluralism of peoples, political beliefs, values, forms of merit and systems of religion our country was founded to welcome and foster.

Liberty protects the person from unwarranted government intrusions into a dwelling or other private places. In our tradition the State is not omnipresent in the home. And there are other spheres of our lives and existence, outside the home, where the State should not be a dominant presence.

Freedom extends beyond spatial bounds. Liberty presumes an autonomy of self that includes freedom of thought, belief, expression, and certain intimate conduct.

Source: From Speeches and Articles by and about Presidents of Yale University (RU 65). Manuscripts and Archives, Yale University Library. Used by permission of Manuscripts and Archives, Yale University Library.

## Anthony Kennedy

## The Constitution Protects Privacy

Kennedy, a Roman Catholic, was named to the Supreme Court by Ronald Reagan in 1988. In *Lawrence v. Texas* (2003), which challenged a state antisodomy law, he wrote the opinion for five of the six justices in the majority; Sandra Day O'Connor wrote a concurring opinion.

The question before the Court is the validity of a Texas statute making it a crime for two persons of the same sex to engage in certain intimate sexual conduct.

In Houston, Texas, officers of the Harris County Police Department were dispatched to a private residence in response to a reported weapons disturbance. They entered an apartment where one of the petitioners, John Geddes Lawrence, resided. . . . The officers observed Lawrence and another man, Tyron Garner, engaging in a sexual act. The two petitioners were arrested, held in custody over night, and charged and convicted before a Justice of the Peace.

The complaints described their crime as "deviate sexual intercourse, namely [ . . . ] sex, with a member of the same sex (man)." . . .

We conclude the case should be resolved by determining whether the petitioners were free as adults to engage in the private conduct in the exercise of their liberty under the Due Process Clause of the Fourteenth Amendment to the Constitution.

[The Texas statute in question seeks] to control a personal relationship that, whether or not entitled to formal recognition in the law, is within the liberty of persons to choose without being punished as criminals. . . . The liberty protected by the Constitution allows homosexual persons the right to make this choice. . . .

. . . The petitioners are entitled to respect for their private lives. The State cannot demean their existence or control their destiny by making their private sexual conduct a crime. Their right to liberty under the Due Process Clause gives them the full right to engage in their conduct without intervention of the government. "It is a promise of the Constitution that there is a realm of personal liberty which the government may not enter."

Source: *Lawrence v. Texas*, 539 U.S. 558, 562–563, 567, 571, 579 (2003).

---

### QUESTIONS FOR ANALYSIS

1. Compare the Ronald Reagan and Anthony Kennedy documents. What would Reagan think of the opinion written by Justice Kennedy, his appointee? Given his condemnation of those intent on "subordinating us to government rule and regulation," do you think he would agree with it? Why or why not?

2. According to Wildmon, what should be shown on television, and who should make those decisions? How would Giamatti answer that same question?

3. Consider the different points of view presented here. According to these sources, when should the government police private conduct?

**American Hostages in Iran**
Images of blindfolded, handcuffed American hostages seized by Iranian militants at the U.S. embassy in Tehran in November 1979 shocked the nation and created a foreign policy crisis that eventually cost President Carter his chance for reelection. Alain Mingam/Gamma/Zuma Press.

**PLACE EVENTS IN CONTEXT**
In terms of presidential politics and policy, how successful was Jimmy Carter's term, coming between two Republicans (Nixon and Reagan)?

appeared on television newscasts. An attempt to mount a military rescue in April 1980 had to be aborted because of equipment failures in the desert. Several months later, however, a stunning development changed the calculus on both sides: Iraq, led by Saddam Hussein, invaded Iran, officially because of a dispute over deep-water ports but also to prevent the Shiite-led Iranian Revolution from spreading across the border into Sunni-run Iraq. Desperate to focus his nation's attention on Iraq's invasion, Khomeini began to talk with the United States about releasing the hostages. Difficult negotiations dragged on past the American presidential election in November 1980, and the hostages were finally released the day after Carter left office — a final indignity endured by a well-intentioned but ineffectual president.

**The Election of 1980**  President Carter's sinking popularity hurt his bid for reelection. When the Democrats barely renominated him over his liberal challenger, Edward (Ted) Kennedy of Massachusetts, Carter's approval rating was historically low: a mere 21 percent of Americans believed that he was an effective president. The reasons were clear. Economically, millions of citizens were feeling the pinch from stagnant wages, high inflation, crippling mortgage rates,

and an unemployment rate of nearly 8 percent. In international affairs, the nation blamed Carter for his weak response to Soviet expansion and the Iranians' seizure of American diplomats.

With Carter on the defensive, Reagan remained upbeat and decisive. "This is the greatest country in the world," Reagan reassured the nation in his warm baritone voice. "We have the talent, we have the drive. . . . All we need is the leadership." To emphasize his intention to be a formidable international leader, Reagan hinted that he would take strong action to win the hostages' return. To signal his rejection of liberal policies, he declared his opposition to affirmative action and forced busing and promised to "get the government off our backs." Most important, Reagan effectively appealed to the many Americans who felt financially insecure. In a televised debate with Carter, Reagan emphasized the hardships facing working- and middle-class Americans in an era of stagflation and asked them: "Are you better off today than you were four years ago?"

In November, the voters gave a clear answer. They repudiated Carter, giving him only 41.0 percent of the vote. Independent candidate John Anderson garnered 6.6 percent (with a few minor candidates receiving fractions of a percent), and Reagan won with 50.7 percent of the popular vote (Map 30.1). Moreover, the Republicans elected thirty-three new members of the House of Representatives and twelve new senators,

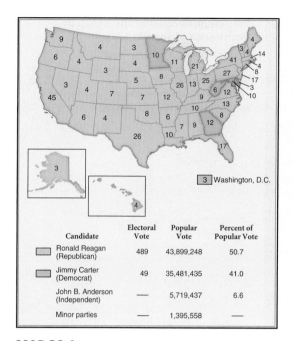

| Candidate | Electoral Vote | Popular Vote | Percent of Popular Vote |
|---|---|---|---|
| Ronald Reagan (Republican) | 489 | 43,899,248 | 50.7 |
| Jimmy Carter (Democrat) | 49 | 35,481,435 | 41.0 |
| John B. Anderson (Independent) | — | 5,719,437 | 6.6 |
| Minor parties | — | 1,395,558 | — |

**MAP 30.1**

**The Presidential Election of 1980**

Ronald Reagan easily defeated Democratic incumbent Jimmy Carter, taking 50.7 percent of the popular vote to Carter's 41.0 percent and winning the electoral vote in all but six states and the District of Columbia. Reagan cut deeply into the traditional Democratic coalition by wooing many southern whites, urban ethnics, and blue-collar workers. More than five million Americans expressed their discontent with Carter's ineffectiveness and Reagan's conservatism by voting for Independent candidate John Anderson, a longtime Republican member of the House of Representatives.

which gave them control of the U.S. Senate for the first time since 1954. The New Right's long road to national power had culminated in an election victory that signaled a new political alignment in the country.

# The Dawning of the Conservative Age

By the time Ronald Reagan took office in 1981, conservatism commanded wider popular support than at any time since the 1920s. As the New Deal Democratic coalition continued to fragment, the Republican Party accelerated the realignment of the American electorate that had begun during the 1960s. Conservatism's ascendancy did more than realign the nation politically. Its emphasis on free markets, low taxes, and individual success shaped the nation's culture and inaugurated a conservative era. Reagan exhorted Americans, "Let

the men and women of the marketplace decide what they want."

## The Reagan Coalition

Reagan's decades in public life, especially his years working for General Electric, had equipped him to articulate conservative ideas in easily understandable aphorisms. Speaking against the growing size and influence of government, Reagan said, "Concentrated power has always been the enemy of liberty." Under his leadership, the core of the Republican Party remained the relatively affluent, white, Protestant voters who supported balanced budgets, opposed government activism, feared communism, and believed in a strong national defense. Reagan Republicanism also attracted middle-class suburbanites and migrants to the Sunbelt states who endorsed the conservative agenda of combating crime and limiting social-welfare spending. Suburban growth in particular, a phenomenon that reshaped metropolitan areas across the country in the 1960s and 1970s, benefitted conservatives politically. Suburban traditions of privatization and racial homogeneity, combined with the amenities of middle-class comfort, made the residents of suburban cities more inclined to support conservative public policies.

This emerging **Reagan coalition** was joined by a large and electorally key group of former Democrats that had been gradually moving toward the Republican Party since 1964: southern whites. Reagan capitalized on the "southern strategy" developed by Richard Nixon's advisors in the late 1960s. Many southern whites had lost confidence in the Democratic Party for a wide range of reasons, but one factor stood out: the party's support for civil rights. When Reagan came to Philadelphia, Mississippi, to deliver his first official speech as the Republican presidential nominee, his ringing endorsement of "states' rights" sent a clear message: he validated twenty-five years of southern opposition to federal civil rights legislation. Some of Reagan's advisors had warned him not to go to Philadelphia, the site of the tragic murder of three civil rights workers in 1964, but Reagan believed the opportunity to launch his campaign on a "states' rights" note too important. After 1980, southern whites would remain a cornerstone of the Republican coalition.

The Religious Right proved crucial to the Republican victory as well. Falwell's **Moral Majority** claimed that it had registered

> **COMPARE AND CONTRAST**
> What different constituencies made up the Reagan coalition, and how would you characterize their regional, geographic, class, and racial composition?

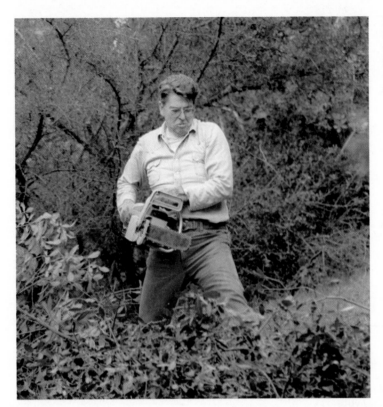

**President Reagan at His Ranch in Southern California**

Images of Reagan quickly became vital for the White House to deliver its message of conservative reform to the American people. This photo was taken by a White House photographer. Ronald Reagan Presidential Library.

two million new voters for the 1980 election, and the Republican Party's platform reflected its influence. That platform called for a constitutional ban on abortion, voluntary prayer in public schools, and a mandatory death penalty for certain crimes. Republicans also demanded an end to court-mandated busing to achieve racial integration in schools, and, for the first time in forty years, opposed the Equal Rights Amendment. Within the Republican Party, conservatism had triumphed.

Reagan's broad coalition attracted the allegiance of another group dissatisfied with the direction of liberalism in the 1970s: blue-collar voters, a high number of Catholics among them, alarmed by antiwar protesters and rising welfare expenditures and hostile to feminist demands. Some observers saw these voters, which many called **Reagan Democrats**, as coming from the "silent majority" that Nixon had swung into the Republican fold in 1968 and 1972. They lived in heavily industrialized midwestern states such as Michigan, Ohio, and Illinois and had been a core part of the Democratic coalition for three decades. Reagan's victory in the 1980s thus hinged on both a revival of right-wing conservative activism and broad dissatisfaction with liberal Democrats—a dissatisfaction that had been building since 1968 but had been interrupted by the post-Watergate backlash against the Republican Party.

## Conservatives in Power

The new president kept his political message clear and simple. "What I want to see above all," he remarked, "is that this country remains a country where someone can always get rich." Standing in the way, Reagan believed, was government. In his first year in office, Reagan and his chief advisor, James A. Baker III, quickly set new governmental priorities. To roll back the expanded liberal state, they launched a three-pronged assault on federal taxes, social-welfare spending, and the regulatory bureaucracy. To prosecute the Cold War, they advocated a vast increase in defense spending and an end to détente with the Soviet Union. And to match the resurgent economies of Germany and Japan, they set out to restore American leadership of the world's capitalist societies and to inspire renewed faith in "free markets."

**Reaganomics**    To achieve its economic objectives, the new administration advanced a set of policies, quickly dubbed **Reaganomics**, to increase the production (and thus the supply) of goods. The theory underlying **supply-side economics**, as this approach was called, emphasized investment in productive enterprises. According to supply-side theorists, the best way to bolster investment was to reduce the taxes paid by corporations and wealthy Americans, who could then use these funds to expand production.

Supply-siders maintained that the resulting economic expansion would increase government revenues and offset the loss of tax dollars stemming from the original tax cuts. Meanwhile, the increasing supply would generate its own demand, as consumers stepped forward to buy ever more goods. Supply-side theory presumed — in fact, gambled — that future tax revenues would make up for present tax cuts. The idea had a growing list of supporters in Congress, led by an ex-professional football player from Buffalo named Jack Kemp. Kemp praised supply-side economics as "an alternative to the slow-growth, recession-oriented policies of the [Carter] administration."

Reagan took advantage of Republican control of the Senate, as well as high-profile allies such as Kemp, to win congressional approval of the 1981 **Economic Recovery Tax Act (ERTA)**, a massive tax cut that embodied supply-side principles. The act reduced income tax rates for most Americans by 23 percent over three years. For the wealthiest Americans — those with millions to invest — the highest marginal tax rate dropped from 70 to 50 percent. The act also slashed estate taxes, levies on inheritances instituted during the Progressive Era to prevent the transmission of huge fortunes from one generation to the next. Finally, the new legislation trimmed the taxes paid by business corporations by $150 billion over a period of five years. As a result of ERTA, by 1986 the annual revenue of the federal government had been cut by $200 billion (nearly half a trillion in 2010 dollars).

David Stockman, Reagan's budget director, hoped to match this reduction in tax revenue with a comparable cutback in federal expenditures. To meet this ambitious goal, he proposed substantial cuts in Social Security and Medicare. But Congress, and even the president himself, rejected his idea; they were not willing to antagonize middle-class and elderly voters who viewed these government entitlements as sacred. As conservative columnist George Will noted ironically, "Americans are conservative. What they want to conserve is the New Deal." After defense spending, Social Security and Medicare were by far the nation's largest budget items; reductions in other programs would not achieve the savings the administration desired. This contradiction between New Right Republican ideology and political reality would continue to frustrate the party into the twenty-first century.

A more immediate embarrassment confronted conservatives, however. In a 1982 *Atlantic* article, Stockman admitted that supply-side theory was based on faith, not economics. To produce optimistic projections of higher tax revenue in future years, Stockman had manipulated the figures. Worse, Stockman told the *Atlantic* reporter candidly that supply-side theory was based on a long-discredited idea: the "trickle-down" notion that helping the rich would eventually benefit the lower and middle classes. Stockman had drawn back the curtain, much to Republicans' consternation, on the flawed reasoning of supply-side theory. But it was too late. The plan had passed Congress, and since Stockman could not cut major programs such as Social Security and Medicare, he had few options to balance the budget.

As the administration's spending cuts fell short, the federal budget deficit increased dramatically. Military spending contributed a large share of the growing **national debt**. But President Reagan remained undaunted. "Defense is not a budget item," he declared. "You spend what you need." To "make America number one again," Reagan and Defense Secretary Caspar Weinberger pushed through Congress a five-year, $1.2 trillion military spending program in 1981. During Reagan's presidency, military spending accounted for one-fourth of all federal expenditures and contributed to rising annual budget deficits (the amount overspent by the government in a single year) and a skyrocketing national debt (the cumulative total of all budget deficits). By the time Reagan left office, the total federal debt had tripled, rising from $930 billion in 1981 to $2.8 trillion in 1989. The rising annual deficits of the 1980s contradicted Reagan's pledge of fiscal conservatism (Figure 30.1).

**Deregulation**   Advocates of Reaganomics asserted that excessive regulation by federal agencies impeded economic growth. **Deregulation** of prices in the trucking, airline, and railroad industries had begun under President Carter in the late 1970s, but Reagan expanded the mandate to include cutting back on government protections of consumers, workers, and the environment. Some of the targeted federal bureaucracies, such as the U.S. Department of Labor, had risen to prominence during the New Deal; others, such as the Occupational Safety and Health Administration (OSHA) and the Environmental Protection Agency (EPA), had been created during the Johnson and Nixon administrations. Although these agencies provided many services to business corporations, they also increased their costs — by protecting the rights of workers, mandating safety improvements in factories, and requiring expensive equipment to limit the release of toxic chemicals into the environment. To reduce the

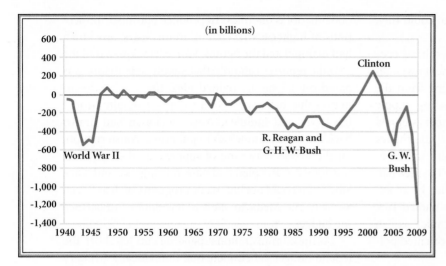

**FIGURE 30.1**

**The Annual Federal Budget Deficit (or Surplus), 1940–2009**

During World War II, the federal government incurred an enormous budget deficit. But between 1946 and 1965, it ran either an annual budget surplus or incurred a relatively small debt. The annual deficits rose significantly during the Vietnam War and the stagflation of the 1970s, but they really exploded between 1982 and 1994, in the budgets devised by the Ronald Reagan and George H. W. Bush administrations, and again between 2002 and 2005, in those prepared by George W. Bush. The Republican presidents increased military spending while cutting taxes, an enjoy-it-now philosophy that transferred costs to future generations of Americans.

reach of federal regulatory agencies, the Reagan administration in 1981 cut their budgets, by an average of 12 percent.

Reagan also rendered regulatory agencies less effective by staffing them with leaders who were opposed to the agencies' missions. James Watt, an outspoken conservative who headed the Department of the Interior, attacked environmentalism as "a left-wing cult." Acting on his free-enterprise principles, Watt opened public lands for use by private businesses — oil and coal corporations, large-scale ranchers, and timber companies. Anne Gorsuch Burford, whom Reagan appointed to head the EPA, likewise disparaged environmentalists and refused to cooperate with Congress to clean up toxic waste sites under a program known as the Superfund. The Sierra Club and other environmental groups aroused enough public outrage about these appointees that the administration changed its position. During President Reagan's second term, he significantly increased the EPA's budget and added acreage to the National Wilderness Preservation System and animals and plants to the endangered species lists.

Ultimately, as these adjustments demonstrate, politics in the United States remained "the art of the possible." Savvy politicians know when to advance and when to retreat. Having attained two of his prime goals — a major tax cut and a dramatic increase in defense spending — Reagan did not seriously attempt to scale back big government and the welfare state. When he left office in 1989, federal spending stood at 22.1 percent of the gross domestic product (GDP) and federal taxes at 19 percent of GDP, both virtually the same as in 1981. In the meantime, though, the federal debt had tripled in size, and the number of government workers had increased from 2.9 to 3.1 million. This outcome — because it cut against the president's rhetoric about balancing budgets and downsizing government — elicited harsh criticism from some conservative commentators. "There was no Reagan Revolution," one conservative noted. A former Reagan aide offered a more balanced assessment: "Ronald Reagan did far less than he had hoped . . . and a hell of a lot more than people thought he would."

**Remaking the Judiciary**   Even if he did not achieve everything many of his supporters desired, Reagan left an indelible imprint on politics, public policy, and American culture. One place this imprint was felt in far-reaching ways was the judiciary, where Reagan and his attorney general, Edwin Meese, aimed at reversing the liberal judicial philosophy that had prevailed since the late 1950s. During his two terms, Reagan appointed 368 federal court judges — most of them with conservative credentials — and three Supreme Court justices: Sandra Day O'Connor (1981), Antonin Scalia (1986), and Anthony Kennedy (1988). Ironically, O'Connor and Kennedy turned out to be far less devoted to New Right conservatism than Reagan and his supporters imagined. O'Connor, the first woman to serve on the Court, shaped its decision making as a swing vote between liberals and conservatives. Kennedy also emerged as a judicial moderate, leaving Scalia as Reagan's only genuinely conservative appointee.

**EXPLAIN CONSEQUENCES**

Why was Reagan unable to reduce federal expenditures as much as many of his supporters had hoped?

**Another Barrier Falls**

In 1981, Sandra Day O'Connor, shown here with Chief Justice Warren Burger, was appointed to the Supreme Court by President Ronald Reagan, the first woman to serve on that body. In 1993, she was joined by Ruth Bader Ginsburg, an appointee of President Bill Clinton. O'Connor emerged as a leader of the moderate bloc on the Court during the 1990s; she retired in 2006. Black Star/Stockphoto.com.

But Reagan also elevated Justice William Rehnquist, a conservative Nixon appointee, to the position of chief justice. Under Rehnquist's leadership (1986–2005), the Court's conservatives took an activist stance, limiting the reach of federal laws, ending court-ordered busing, and endorsing constitutional protection of property rights. However, on controversial issues such as individual liberties, abortion rights, affirmative action, and the rights of criminal defendants, the presence of O'Connor enabled the Court to resist the rightward drift and to maintain a moderate position. As a result, the justices scaled back, but did not usually overturn, the liberal rulings of the Warren and Burger Courts. In the controversial *Webster v. Reproductive Health Services* (1989), for instance, Scalia pushed for the justices to overturn the abortion-rights decision in *Roe v. Wade* (1973). O'Connor refused, but she nonetheless approved the constitutional validity of state laws that limited the use of public funds and facilities for abortions. A more conservative federal judiciary would remain a significant institutional legacy of the Reagan presidency.

**HIV/AIDS**    Another conservative legacy was the slow national response to one of the worst disease epidemics of the postwar decades. The human immunodeficiency virus (HIV), a deadly (though slow-acting) pathogen, developed in Africa when a chimpanzee virus jumped to humans; immigrants carried it to Haiti and then to the United States during the 1970s. In 1981, American physicians identified HIV as a new virus — one that caused a disease known as acquired immunodeficiency syndrome (AIDS). Hundreds of gay men, who were prominent among the earliest carriers of the virus, were dying of AIDS. Within two decades, **HIV/AIDS** had spread worldwide, infected more than 50 million people of both sexes, and killed more than 20 million.

Within the United States, AIDS took nearly a hundred thousand lives in the 1980s — more than were lost in the Korean and Vietnam Wars combined. However, because its most prominent early victims were gay men, President Reagan, emboldened by New Right conservatives, hesitated in declaring a national health emergency. Some of Reagan's advisors asserted that this "gay disease" might even be God's punishment of homosexuals. Between 1981 and 1986, as the epidemic spread, the Reagan administration took little action — worse, it prevented the surgeon general, C. Everett Koop, from speaking forthrightly to the nation about the disease. Pressed by gay activists and prominent health officials from across the country, in Reagan's last years in office the administration finally began to devote federal resources to treatment for HIV and AIDS patients and research into possible vaccines. But the delay had proved costly, inhumane, and embarrassing.

## Morning in America

During his first run for governor of California in 1966, Reagan held a revelatory conversation with a campaign consultant. "Politics is just like the movies," Reagan told him. "You have a hell of an opening, coast for a while, and then have a hell of a close." Reagan indeed had a "hell of an opening": one of the most lavish and expensive presidential inaugurations in American history in 1981 (and another in 1985), showing that he was unafraid to celebrate luxury and opulence, even with millions of Americans unemployed.

Following his spectacular inauguration, Reagan quickly won passage of his tax reduction bill and launched his plan to bolster the Pentagon. But then a long "coasting" period descended on his presidency, during which he retreated on tax cuts and navigated a major foreign policy scandal. Finally, toward the end of his two-term presidency, Reagan found his "hell of

**HIV/AIDS**

The HIV/AIDS epidemic hit the United States in the early 1980s and remained a major social and political issue throughout the decade. Here, AIDS patients and their supporters participate in the 1987 March on Washington for Gay and Lesbian Rights, demanding that the Reagan administration commit more federal resources to finding a cure for the deadly disease. © Bettmann/Corbis.

a close," leaving office as major reforms—which he encouraged from afar—had begun to tear apart the Soviet Union and bring an end to the Cold War. Through all the ups and downs, Reagan remained a master of the politics of symbolism, championing a resurgent American economy and reassuring the country that the pursuit of wealth was noble and that he had the reins of the nation firmly in hand.

Reagan's tax cuts had barely taken effect when he was forced to reverse course. High interest rates set by the Federal Reserve Board had cut the runaway inflation of the Carter years. But these rates—as high as 18 percent—sent the economy into a recession in 1981–1982 that put 10 million Americans out of work and shuttered 17,000 businesses. Unemployment neared 10 percent, the highest rate since the Great Depression. These troubles, combined with the booming deficit, forced Reagan to negotiate a tax increase with Congress in 1982—to the loud complaints of supply-side diehards. The president's job rating plummeted, and in the 1982 midterm elections Democrats picked up twenty-six seats in the House of Representatives and seven state governorships.

**Election of 1984**   Fortunately for Reagan, the economy had recovered by 1983, restoring the president's job approval rating just in time for the 1984 presidential election. During the campaign, Reagan emphasized the economic resurgence, touring the country promoting his tax policies and the nation's new prosperity. The Democrats nominated former vice president Walter Mondale of Minnesota. With strong ties to labor unions, ethnic and racial minority groups, and party leaders, Mondale epitomized the New Deal coalition. He selected Representative Geraldine Ferraro of New York as his running mate—the first woman to run on the presidential ticket of a major political party. Neither Ferraro's presence nor Mondale's credentials made a difference, however: Reagan won a landslide victory, losing only Minnesota and the District of Columbia. Still, Democrats retained their majority in the House and, in 1986, regained control of the Senate.

Reagan's 1984 campaign slogan, "It's Morning in America," projected the image of a new day dawning on a confident people. In Reagan mythology, the United States was an optimistic nation of small towns, close-knit families, and kindly neighbors. "The success story of America," he once said, "is neighbor helping neighbor." The mythology may not have reflected the *actual* nation—which was overwhelmingly urban and suburban, and in which the hard knocks of capitalism held down more than opportunity elevated—but that mattered little. Reagan's remarkable ability to produce

GEORGE FISHER
*Courtesy Arkansas Gazette*

**Presidential Landscaping**

As the cartoon published by the *Arkansas Gazette* illustrates, powerful imagery was also wielded by Reagan's political opponents. Used with permission/ Arkansas Democrat-Gazette, 1984.

positive associations and feelings, alongside robust economic growth after the 1981–1982 recession, helped make the 1980s a decade characterized by both backward-looking nostalgia and aggressive capitalism.

**Return to Prosperity**   Between 1945 and the 1970s, the United States was the world's leading exporter of agricultural products, manufactured goods, and investment capital. Then American manufacturers lost market share, undercut by cheaper and better-designed products from West Germany and Japan. By 1985, for the first time since 1915, the United States registered a negative balance of international payments. It now imported more goods and capital than it exported. The country became a debtor (rather than a creditor) nation. The rapid ascent of the Japanese economy to become the world's second largest was a key factor in this historic reversal (America Compared, p. 988). More than one-third of the American annual trade deficit of $138 billion in the 1980s was from trade with Japan, whose corporations exported huge quantities of electronic goods and made nearly one-quarter of all cars bought in the United States.

Meanwhile, American businesses grappled with a worrisome decline in productivity. Between 1973 and 1992, American productivity (the amount of goods or services per hour of work) grew at the meager rate of 1 percent a year — a far cry from the post–World War II rate of 3 percent. Because managers wanted to cut costs, the wages of most employees stagnated. Further, because of foreign competition, the

number of high-paying, union-protected manufacturing jobs shrank. By 1985, more people in the United States worked for McDonald's slinging Big Macs than rolled out rails, girders, and sheet steel in the nation's steel industry.

A brief return to competitiveness in the second half of the 1980s masked the steady long-term transformation of the economy that had begun in the 1970s. The nation's heavy industries — steel, autos, chemicals — continued to lose market share to global competitors. Nevertheless, the U.S. economy grew at the impressive average rate of 2 to 3 percent per year for much of the late 1980s and 1990s (with a short recession in 1990–1991). What had changed was the direction of growth and its beneficiaries. Increasingly, financial services, medical services, and computer technology — service industries, broadly speaking — were the leading sectors of growth. This shift in the underlying foundation of the American economy, from manufacturing to service, from making *things* to producing *services*, would have long-term consequences for the global competitiveness of U.S. industries and the value of the dollar.

**Culture of Success**   The economic growth of the second half of the 1980s popularized the materialistic values championed by the free marketeers. Every era has its capitalist heroes, but Americans in the 1980s celebrated wealth accumulation in ways unseen since the 1920s. When the president christened self-made entrepreneurs "the heroes for the eighties," he probably had people like Lee Iacocca in mind. Born to Italian

## Yoichi Funabashi

## "Japan and America: Global Partners"

Educated at the University of Tokyo and Keio University, Yoichi Funabashi is a prize-winning journalist who specializes in the U.S.-Japan economic relationship. During the 1980s, he lived in the United States as a columnist (and later bureau chief) for the *Asahi Shimbun*, one of Japan's most important daily newspapers.

As Japan struggled to rebuild itself after World War II, the charismatic Shigeru Yoshida, prime minister during the critical years of 1948 to 1952, called on the country to be a good loser. The Japanese have lost the war, he said, but they must not lose heart. Japan must cooperate with the United States, and pull itself out of misery and disgrace. The Japanese did indeed cooperate willingly with the Allied occupation — with the American (and British) "devils" whom they had been taught for years to despise to the very core of their souls. . . .

Postwar Japan went on to prove that it could indeed be a good loser. Under the new constitution promulgated under the guidance of the occupation, it has developed into a democratic country with a relatively moderate disparity between rich and poor and a stable, smoothly functioning political system. . . .

The Japanese-U.S. relationship has thus come to occupy a truly unique position in world history. Never before has a multiethnic, contract-based society and a homogenous, traditional society joined together to form such a powerful team. As global powers, Japan and the United States combined have a decisive impact on world politics; it follows that their future relations will largely determine the blueprints of multilateral cooperation and world stability in the coming century. . . .

Potential sources of bilateral friction are as numerous as ever: the trade imbalance, market liberalization, growing Japanese investment in the United States, heavy U.S. dependence on Japanese technology, and so on. Occasional outbursts of economic nationalism, or "revisionist" thinking are probably inevitable as the debate over these issues unfolds. . . .

Of far greater concern, however, is that Japanese-U.S. relations now face their gravest challenge since 1945. The end of the Cold War has drastically altered the global geopolitical and geoeconomic context that shaped Japanese-U.S. relations. Both countries now face the urgent need to redefine their relationship to suit the new context. . . .

Before they can build a strong bilateral relationship, Americans and Japanese must outgrow their obsession with being Number One. This psychological adjustment is absolutely necessary for both peoples. Projecting the nature of its own hierarchical society, Japan tends to view the rest of the world, it is said, in terms of ranking. This inclination fosters behavior patterns that are oriented more toward what to *be* than what to *do*. Japan is also overly conscious of itself as a late-starter, having entered modern international society only in the mid-nineteenth century, and this history has made catching up with and outpacing other countries a sort of national pastime. . . . It may be even more difficult for the United States, which dominated the free world during the Cold War, to make the psychological adjustments required to enter into a partnership with Japan that is truly equal.

Source: Yoichi Funabashi, "Japan and America: Global Partners," *Foreign Policy* 86 (Spring 1992): 24–39.

---

### QUESTIONS FOR ANALYSIS

1. Among the "sources of bilateral friction" Funabashi lists the trade imbalance and Japanese investment in the United States. Why would these cause friction?

2. How had the U.S.-Japan relationship changed between 1945 and the 1980s?

---

immigrants and trained as an engineer, Iacocca rose through the ranks to become president of the Ford Motor Corporation. In 1978, he took over the ailing Chrysler Corporation and made it profitable again — by securing a crucial $1.5 billion loan from the U.S.

government, pushing the development of new cars, and selling them on TV. His patriotic commercials in the 1980s echoed Reagan's rhetoric: "Let's make American mean something again." Iacocca's restoration would not endure, however: in 2009, Chrysler declared bankruptcy and was forced to sell a majority stake to the Italian company Fiat.

If Iacocca symbolized a resurgent corporate America, high-profile financial wheeler-dealers also captured Americans' imagination. One was Ivan Boesky, a white-collar criminal convicted of insider trading (buying or selling stock based on information from corporate insiders). "I think greed is healthy," Boesky told a business school graduating class. Boesky inspired the fictional film character Gordon Gekko, who proclaimed "Greed is good!" in 1987's *Wall Street*. A new generation of Wall Street executives, of which Boesky was one example, pioneered the leveraged buyout (LBO). In a typical LBO, a financier used heavily leveraged (borrowed) capital to buy a company, quickly restructured that company to make it appear spectacularly profitable, and then sold it at a higher price.

 To see a movie still from *Wall Street*, along with other primary sources from this period, see *Sources for America's History*.

Americans had not set aside the traditional work ethic, but the Reagan-era public was fascinated with money and celebrity. (The documentary television show *Lifestyles of the Rich and Famous* began its run in 1984.) One of the most enthralling of the era's money moguls was Donald Trump, a real estate developer who craved publicity. In 1983, the flamboyant Trump built the equally flamboyant Trump Towers in New York City. At the entrance of the $200 million apartment building stood two enormous bronze *T*'s, a display of self-promotion reinforced by the media. Calling him "The Donald," a nickname used by Trump's first wife, TV reporters and magazines commented relentlessly on his marriages, divorces, and glitzy lifestyle.

**The Computer Revolution**  While Trump grabbed headlines and made splashy real estate investments, a handful of quieter, less flashy entrepreneurs was busy changing the face of the American economy. Bill Gates, Paul Allen, Steve Jobs, and Steve Wozniak were four entrepreneurs who pioneered the computer revolution in the late 1970s and 1980s (Thinking Like a Historian, p. 990). They took a technology that had been used exclusively for large-scale enterprises — the military and multinational corporations — and made it accessible to individual consumers. Scientists had devised the first computers for military purposes during World War II. Cold War military research subsequently funded the construction of large mainframe computers. But government and private-sector

first-generation computers were bulky, cumbersome machines that had to be placed in large air-conditioned rooms.

Between the 1950s and the 1970s, concluding with the development of the microprocessor in 1971, each generation of computers grew faster and smaller. By the mid-1970s, a few microchips the size of the letter *O* on this page provided as much processing power as a World War II–era computer. The day of the personal computer (PC) had arrived. Working in the San Francisco Bay Area, Jobs and Wozniak founded Apple Computers in 1976 and within a year were producing small, individual computers that could be easily used by a single person. When Apple enjoyed success, other companies scrambled to get into the market. International Business Machines (IBM) offered its first personal computer in 1981, but Apple Corporation's 1984 Macintosh computer (later shortened to "Mac") became the first runaway commercial success for a personal computer.

Meanwhile, two former high school classmates, Gates, age nineteen, and Allen, age twenty-one, had set a goal in the early 1970s of putting "a personal computer on every desk and in every home." They recognized that software was the key. In 1975, they founded the Microsoft Corporation, whose MS-DOS and Windows operating systems soon dominated the software industry. By 2000, the company's products ran nine out of every ten personal computers in the United States and a majority of those around the world. Gates and Allen became billionaires, and Microsoft exploded into a huge company with 57,000 employees and annual revenues of $38 billion. In three decades, the computer had moved from a few military research centers to thousands of corporate offices and then to millions of people's homes. Ironically, in an age that celebrated free-market capitalism, government research and government funding had played an enormous role in the development of the most important technology since television.

> **UNDERSTAND POINTS OF VIEW**
> In what ways did American society embrace economic success and individualism in the 1980s?

# The End of the Cold War

Ronald Reagan entered office determined to confront the Soviet Union diplomatically and militarily. Backed by Republican and Democratic hard-liners alike, Reagan unleashed some of the harshest Cold War rhetoric since the 1950s, labeling the Soviet Union an "evil

## Personal Computing: A Technological Revolution

Considered historically, computers are a strikingly new phenomenon. The ancestors of the first computers were developed in the 1940s using vacuum tubes and transistors. Integrated circuits were introduced in the 1950s and the first microprocessor in the 1970s. Prior to the decade of the 1980s, only the federal government and large corporations and institutions used computers, which were massive in size and expensive to purchase. In the 1980s, inventors and entrepreneurs developed the first "personal" computers, which could fit on desks or tables and were soon within the price range of ordinary families. The computers we know today date from that decade. Another enormous change came in the mid-1990s, when the Internet, whose forerunner was a U.S. Defense Department computer network, became widely available to the public for the first time.

1. **Moore's law, 1965.** *In 1965, the electronics engineer Gordon Moore calculated that the number of transistors on an integrated circuit doubled roughly every two years, meaning that the power of computers was increasing at that rate.*

The complexity for minimum component costs has increased at a rate of roughly a factor of two per year. Certainly over the short term this rate can be expected to continue, if not increase. . . . That means by 1975, the number of components per integrated circuit for minimum cost will be 65,000.

I believe that such a large circuit can be built on a single wafer.

2. **Scene from *2001: A Space Odyssey*, 1968.** *In this scene from an acclaimed science fiction film, a space station's computer system, named HAL, defends itself against an astronaut who is determined to shut down the computer.*

Dave Bowman: Hello, HAL. Do you read me, HAL?
HAL: Affirmative, Dave. I read you.
DB: Open the pod bay doors, HAL.
HAL: I'm sorry, Dave. I'm afraid I can't do that.
DB: What's the problem?
HAL: I think you know what the problem is just as well as I do.
DB: What are you talking about, HAL?
HAL: This mission is too important for me to allow you to jeopardize it.
DB: I don't know what you're talking about, HAL.
HAL: I know that you and Frank were planning to disconnect me, and I'm afraid that's something I cannot allow to happen.
DB: Where the hell did you get that idea, HAL?

HAL: Dave, although you took very thorough precautions in the pod against my hearing you, I could see your lips move.
DB: Alright, HAL. I'll go in through the emergency airlock.
HAL: Without your space helmet, Dave? You're going to find that rather difficult.
DB: HAL, I won't argue with you anymore! Open the door!
HAL: Dave, this conversation can serve no purpose anymore. Goodbye.

3. **Neil Ardley, *World of Tomorrow: School, Work, and Play*, 1981.** *In this book written for teenagers, Neil Ardley speculated about the future of computers.*

Imagine you are living in the future, and are doing a project on Halley's comet. It's quite some time since it last appeared in 1986, and you want to find out when it will again be seen from Earth. You also want to know the results of a space mission to the comet, and find out what the comet is made of.

In the days when the last comet appeared, you would have had to look up Halley's comet in an encyclopedia or a book on astronomy. If you didn't possess these books, you would have gone to the library to get the information. . . .

People still collect books as valuable antiques or for a hobby, but you get virtually all the information you need from the viewscreen of your home computer. The computer is linked to a library — not a library of books but an electronic library where information on every subject is stored in computer memory banks. . . .

Computers will make the world of tomorrow a much safer place. They will do away with cash, so that you need no longer fear being attacked for your money. In addition, you need not worry that your home will be burgled or your car stolen. The computers in your home and car will guard them, allowing only yourself to enter or someone with your permission.

**4. Scene from *Terminator*, 1984.** *A national defense computer network called Skynet decides to exterminate humanity in the film* Terminator.

Reese: There was a war. A few years from now. Nuclear war. The whole thing. All this — [His gesture includes the car, the city, the world.] — everything is gone. Just gone. There were survivors. Here. There. Nobody knew who started it. (pause) It was the machines.

Sarah: I don't understand. . . .

Reese: Defense network computer. New. Powerful. Hooked into everything. Trusted to run it all. They say it got smart . . . a new order of intelligence. Then it saw all people as a threat, not just the ones on the other side. Decided our fate in a microsecond . . . extermination.

**5. Interview with Steve Jobs, February 1, 1985.** *Apple founder Steve Jobs, one of the pioneers of the personal computer, discusses the future of computers and computer networks.*

Question: Why should a person buy a computer?

Steve Jobs: There are different answers for different people. In business, that question is easy to answer: You can really prepare documents much faster and at a higher quality level, and you can do many things to increase office productivity. A computer frees people from much of the menial work. . . . Remember computers are tools. Tools help us do our work better. In education, computers are the first thing to come along since books that will sit there and interact with you endlessly, without judgment. . . .

Question: What will change?

Steve Jobs: The most compelling reason for most people to buy a computer for the home [in the future] will be to link it into a nationwide communications network. We're just in the beginning stages of what will be a truly remarkable breakthrough for most people — as remarkable as the telephone.

**6. Percentage of Americans using the Internet.**

Sources: (1) G. E. Moore, "Cramming More Components onto Integrated Circuits," *Electronics*, April 19, 1965, 114; (2) *2001: A Space Odyssey*, Screenplay by Stanley Kubrick and Arthur C. Clarke (Hawk Films Ltd. and MGM Studios, 1967); (3) Neil Ardley, *World of Tomorrow: School, Work, and Play* (New York: Franklin Watts, 1981), 20–27; (4) *Terminator*, Screenplay by James Cameron and Gale Anne Hurd, Fifth Draft (Pacific Western Productions, Inc., March 11, 1984), 134; (5) *Playboy*, February 1, 1985, 52.

## ANALYZING THE EVIDENCE

1. Compare sources 2 and 4. Anxiety about the extraordinary power of computers has been a regular feature of science fiction, both in writing and in film, since the late 1950s. What do the scenes from these two films tell us about the cultural reactions to computers early in their development?

2. How does source 3 offer a different vision of a future with computers? Why do you think cultural responses to computers tend to swing between extreme anxiety and equally extreme optimism?

3. How does Steve Jobs's assessment of computers in source 5 compare with those in the other documents? Should we trust his judgment more because he is closer to their actual development? Why or why not?

## PUTTING IT ALL TOGETHER

Drawing on the history of personal computers discussed in this chapter, as well as on the documents above, write an essay in which you assess the origin of the personal computer. What cultural reactions and predictions surrounded the computer's birth? What economic and social transformations did it have the potential to unleash? You might also consider a comparison of the Industrial Revolution of the second half of the nineteenth century and the "computer revolution" of the late twentieth century. Are there parallels in how each development transformed American society?

empire" and vowing that it would end up "on the ash heap of history." In a remarkable turnaround, however, by his second term Reagan had decided that this goal would be best achieved by actively cooperating with Mikhail Gorbachev, the reform-minded Russian Communist leader. The downfall of the Soviet Union in 1991 ended the nearly fifty-year-long Cold War, but a new set of foreign challenges quickly emerged.

## U.S.-Soviet Relations in a New Era

When Reagan assumed the presidency in 1981, he broke with his immediate predecessors — Richard Nixon, Gerald Ford, and Jimmy Carter — in Cold War strategy. Nixon regarded himself as a "realist" in foreign affairs. That meant, above all, advancing the national interest without regard to ideology. Nixon's policy of détente with the Soviet Union and China embodied this realist view. President Carter endorsed détente and continued to push for relaxing Cold War tensions. This worked for a time, but the Soviet invasion of Afghanistan empowered hard-liners in the U.S. Congress and forced Carter to take a tougher line — which he did with the Olympic boycott and grain embargo. This was the relationship Reagan inherited in 1981: a decade of détente that had produced a noticeable relaxation of tensions with the communist world, followed by a year of tense standoffs over Soviet advances into Central Asia, which threatened U.S. interests in the Middle East.

**Reagan's Cold War Revival**    Conservatives did not believe in détente. Neither did they believe in the containment policy that had guided U.S. Cold War strategy since 1947. Reagan and his advisors wanted to *defeat*, not merely contain, the Soviet Union. His administration pursued a two-pronged strategy toward that end. First, it abandoned détente and set about rearming America. Reagan's military budgets authorized new weapons systems, dramatically expanded military bases, and significantly expanded the nation's nuclear arsenal. This buildup in American military strength, reasoned Secretary of Defense Caspar Weinberger, would force the Soviets into an arms race that would strain their economy and cause domestic unrest. One of the most controversial aspects of the buildup was Reagan's proposal for a Strategic Defense Initiative — popularly known as "Star Wars" — a satellite-based system that would, theoretically, destroy nuclear missiles in flight. Scientists doubted its viability, and it was never built. The Reagan administration also proposed the Strategic Arms Reduction Talks

(START) with the Soviet Union, in which the United States put forward a plan calculated to increase American advantage in sea- and air-based nuclear systems over the Soviet's ground-based system.

Second, the president supported CIA initiatives to roll back Soviet influence in the developing world by funding anticommunist movements in Angola, Mozambique, Afghanistan, and Central America. To accomplish this objective, Reagan supported repressive, right-wing regimes. Nowhere was this more conspicuous in the 1980s than in the Central American countries of Guatemala, Nicaragua, and El Salvador. Conditions were unique in each country but held to a pattern: the United States sided with military dictatorships and oligarchies if democratically elected governments or left-wing movements sought support from the Soviet Union. In Guatemala, this approach produced a brutal military rule — thousands of opponents of the government were executed or kidnapped. In Nicaragua, Reagan actively encouraged a coup against the left-wing Sandinista government, which had overthrown the U.S.-backed strongman Anastasio Somoza. And in El Salvador, the U.S.-backed government maintained secret "death squads," which murdered members of the opposition. In each case, Reagan blocked Soviet influence, but the damage done to local communities and to the international reputation of the United States, as in Vietnam, was great.

**Iran-Contra**    Reagan's determination to oppose left-wing movements in Central America engulfed his administration in a major scandal during the president's second term. For years, Reagan had denounced Iran as an "outlaw state" and a supporter of terrorism. But in 1985, he wanted its help. To win Iran's assistance in freeing two dozen American hostages held by Hezbollah, a pro-Iranian Shiite group in Lebanon, the administration sold arms to Iran without public or congressional knowledge. While this secret arms deal was diplomatically and politically controversial, the use of the resulting profits in Nicaragua was explicitly illegal. To overthrow the democratically elected **Sandinistas**, whom the president accused of threatening U.S. business interests, Reagan ordered the CIA to assist an armed opposition group called the **Contras** (Map 30.2). Although Reagan praised the Contras as "freedom fighters," Congress worried that the president and other executive branch agencies were assuming war-making powers that the Constitution reserved to the legislature. In 1984, Congress banned the CIA and all other government agencies from providing any military support to the Contras.

### Iran-Contra

The 1987 Iran-Contra congressional hearings, which lasted more than a month and were broadcast on live television, helped to uncover a secret and illegal White House scheme to provide arms to the Nicaraguan Contras. Though Lt. Col. Oliver North (shown here during his testimony before Congress) concocted much of the scheme and was convicted of three felonies, he never served prison time and emerged from the hearings as a populist hero among American conservatives, who saw him as a patriot. © Bettmann/Corbis.

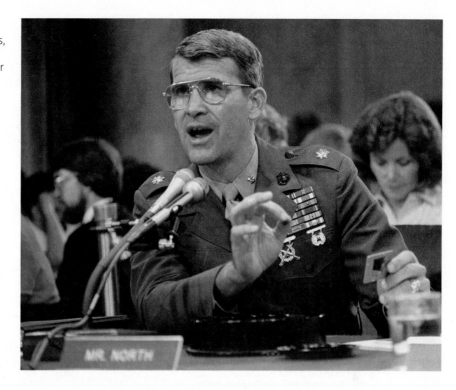

Oliver North, a lieutenant colonel in the U.S. Marines and an aide to the National Security Council, defied that ban. With the tacit or explicit consent of high-ranking administration officials, including the president, North used the profits from the Iranian arms deal to assist the Contras. When asked whether he knew of North's illegal actions, Reagan replied, "I don't remember." The **Iran-Contra affair** not only resulted in the prosecution of North and several other officials but also weakened Reagan domestically — he proposed no bold domestic policy initiatives in his last two years. But the president remained steadfastly engaged in international affairs, where events were unfolding that would bring a dramatic close to the Cold War.

**Gorbachev and Soviet Reform**  The Soviet system of state socialism and central economic planning had transformed Russia from an agricultural to an industrial society between 1917 and the 1950s. But it had done so inefficiently. Lacking the incentives of a market economy, most enterprises hoarded raw materials, employed too many workers, and did not develop new products. Except in military weaponry and space technology, the Russian economy fell further and further behind those of capitalist societies, and most people in the Soviet bloc endured a low standard of living. Moreover, the Soviet invasion of Afghanistan in 1979,

like the American war in Vietnam, turned out to be a major blunder — an unwinnable war that cost vast amounts of money, destroyed military morale, and undermined popular support of the government.

Mikhail Gorbachev, a relatively young Russian leader who became general secretary of the Communist Party in 1985, recognized the need for internal economic reform and an end to the war in Afghanistan. An iconoclast in Soviet terms, Gorbachev introduced policies of *glasnost* (openness) and *perestroika* (economic restructuring), which encouraged widespread criticism of the rigid institutions and authoritarian controls of the Communist regime. To lessen tensions with the United States, Gorbachev met with Reagan in 1985, and the two leaders established a warm personal rapport. By 1987, they had agreed to eliminate all intermediate-range nuclear missiles based in Europe. A year later, Gorbachev ordered Soviet troops out of Afghanistan, and Reagan replaced many of his hardline advisors with policymakers who favored a renewal of détente. Reagan's sudden reversal with regard to the Soviet Union remains one of the most intriguing aspects of his presidency. Many conservatives worried that their cowboy-hero president had been duped by a duplicitous Gorbachev, but Reagan's gamble paid off: the

> **TRACE CHANGE OVER TIME**
>
> How did Reagan's approach to the Soviet Union change between 1981 and 1989?

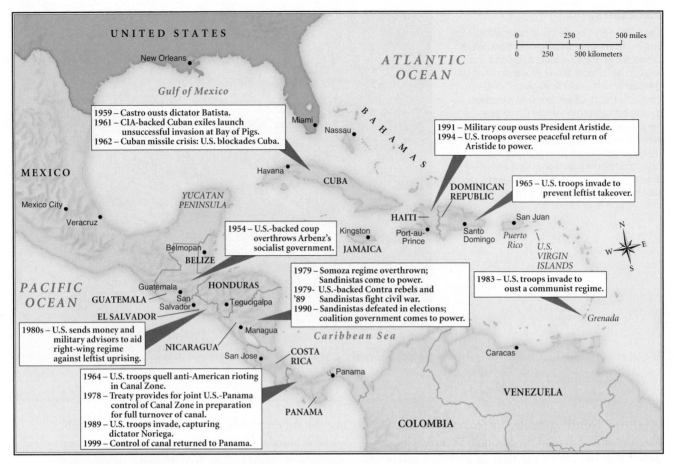

**MAP 30.2**

**U.S. Involvement in Latin America and the Caribbean, 1954–2000**

Ever since the Monroe Doctrine (1823), the United States has claimed a special interest in Latin America. During the Cold War, U.S. foreign policy throughout Latin America focused on containing instability and the appeal of communism in a region plagued by poverty and military dictatorships. Providing foreign aid was one approach to addressing social and economic needs, but the United States frequently intervened with military forces (or by supporting military coups) to remove unfriendly or socialist governments. The Reagan administration's support of the Contra rebels in Nicaragua, some of which was contrary to U.S. law, was one of those interventions.

easing of tensions with the United States allowed the Soviet leader to press forward with his domestic reforms.

As Gorbachev's efforts revealed the flaws of the Soviet system, the peoples of Eastern and Central Europe demanded the ouster of their Communist governments. In Poland, the Roman Catholic Church and its pope — Polish-born John Paul II — joined with Solidarity, the trade union movement, to overthrow the pro-Soviet regime. In 1956 and 1964, Russian troops had quashed similar popular uprisings in Hungary and East Germany. Now they did not intervene, and a series of peaceful uprisings — "Velvet Revolutions" — created a new political order throughout the region. The destruction of the Berlin Wall in 1989 symbolized the end of Communist rule in Central

Europe. Millions of television viewers worldwide watched jubilant Germans knock down the hated wall that had divided the city since 1961 — a vivid symbol of communist repression and the Cold War division of Europe. A new geopolitical order in Europe was in the making.

Alarmed by the reforms, Soviet military leaders seized power in August 1991 and arrested Gorbachev. But widespread popular opposition led by Boris Yeltsin, the president of the Russian Republic, thwarted their efforts to oust Gorbachev from office. This failure broke the dominance of the Communist Party. On December 25, 1991, the Union of Soviet Socialist Republics formally dissolved to make way for an eleven-member Commonwealth of Independent States (CIS). The Russian Republic assumed leadership of the CIS, but

**Reagan and Gorbachev: Fellow Political Revolutionaries**

Both Ronald Reagan and Mikhail Gorbachev changed the political outlook of their nations. As Reagan undermined social-welfare liberalism in the United States, Gorbachev challenged the rigidity of the Communist Party and state socialism in the Soviet Union. Although they remained ideological adversaries, by the mid-1980s the two leaders had established a personal rapport, which helped facilitate agreement on a series of arms reduction measures. © Bettmann/Corbis.

the Soviet Union was no more (Map 30.3). The collapse of the Soviet Union was the result of internal weaknesses of the Communist economy. External pressure from the United States played an important, though secondary, role.

"Nobody — no country, no party, no person — 'won' the cold war," concluded George Kennan, the architect in 1947 of the American policy of containment. The Cold War's cost was enormous, and both sides benefitted greatly from its end. For more than forty years, the United States had fought a bitter economic and ideological battle against that communist foe, a struggle that exerted an enormous impact on American society. Taxpayers had spent some $4 trillion on nuclear weapons and trillions more on conventional arms, placing the United States on a permanent war footing and creating a massive military-industrial complex. The physical and psychological costs were equally high:

radiation from atomic weapons tests, anticommunist witch-hunts, and a constant fear of nuclear annihilation. Of course, most Americans had no qualms about proclaiming victory, and advocates of free-market capitalism, particularly conservative Republicans, celebrated the outcome. The collapse of communism in Eastern Europe and the disintegration of the Soviet Union itself, they argued, demonstrated that they had been right all along.

## A New Political Order at Home and Abroad

Ronald Reagan's role in facilitating the end of the Cold War was among his most important achievements. Overall, his presidency left a mixed legacy. Despite his pledge to get the federal government "off our backs," he could not ultimately reduce its size or scope. Social

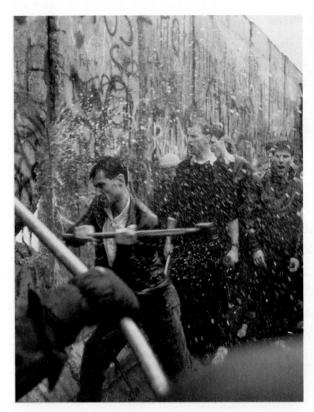

**The Wall Comes Down**

As the Communist government of East Germany collapsed, West Berliners showed their contempt for the wall dividing Berlin by defacing it with graffiti. Then, in November 1989, East and West Berliners destroyed huge sections of the wall with sledgehammers, an act of psychic liberation that symbolized the end of the Cold War. Alexandria Avakian/ Woodfin Camp & Associates.

Security and other entitlement programs remained untouched, and enormous military spending outweighed cuts in other programs. Determined not to divide the country, Reagan did not actively push controversial policies espoused by the Religious Right. He called for tax credits for private religious schools, restrictions on abortions, and a constitutional amendment to permit prayer in public schools, but he did not expend his political capital to secure these measures.

While Reagan failed to roll back the social welfare and regulatory state of the New Deal–Great Society era, he changed the dynamic of American politics. The Reagan presidency restored popular belief that America — and individual Americans — could enjoy increasing prosperity. And his antigovernment rhetoric won many adherents, as did his bold and fiscally aggressive tax cuts. Social-welfare liberalism, ascendant since 1933, remained intact but was now on the defensive — led by Reagan, conservatives had changed the political conversation.

**Election of 1988**   George H. W. Bush, Reagan's vice president and successor, was not beloved by conservatives, who did not see him as one of their own. But he possessed an insider's familiarity with government and a long list of powerful allies, accumulated over three decades of public service. Bush's route to the White House reflected the post-Reagan alignments in American politics. In the primaries, he faced a spirited challenge from Pat Robertson, the archconservative televangelist whose influence and profile had grown during Reagan's two terms. After securing the presidential nomination, which he won largely because of his fierce loyalty to Reagan, Bush felt compelled to select as his vice-presidential running mate an unknown and inexperienced Indiana senator, Dan Quayle. Bush hoped that Quayle would help secure the Christian **"family values"** vote upholding the traditional nuclear family and Christian morality. Robertson's challenge and Quayle's selection showed that the Religious Right had become a major force in Republican politics.

On the Democratic side, Jesse Jackson became the first African American to challenge for a major-party nomination, winning eleven states in primary and caucus voting. However, the much less charismatic Massachusetts governor, Michael Dukakis, emerged as the Democratic nominee. Dukakis, a liberal from the Northeast, proved unable to win back the constituencies Democrats had lost in the 1970s: southern whites, midwestern blue-collar Catholics, and middle-class suburbanites. Indeed, Bush's campaign manager, Lee Atwater, baited Dukakis by calling him a "card-carrying liberal," a not-so-subtle reference to J. Edgar Hoover's 1958 phrase "card-carrying communist." Bush won with 53 percent of the vote, a larger margin of victory than Reagan's in 1980. The election confirmed a new pattern in presidential politics that would last through the turn of the twenty-first century: every four years, Americans would refight the battles of the 1960s, with liberals on one side and conservatives on the other.

**Middle East**   The end of the Cold War left the United States as the world's only military superpower and raised the prospect of what President Bush called a "new world order" dominated by the United States and its European and Asian allies. American officials and diplomats presumed that U.S. interests should prevail in this new environment, but they now confronted an array of regional, religious, and ethnic conflicts that defied easy solutions. None were more pressing or more complex than those in the Middle East — the oil-rich lands stretching from Iran to Algeria. Middle Eastern conflicts would dominate the foreign policy of

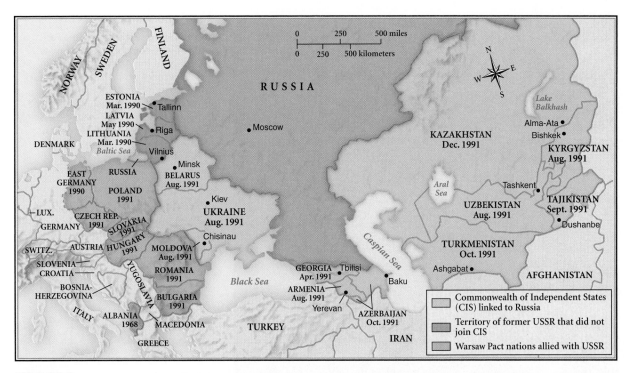

**MAP 30.3**

**The Collapse of the Soviet Union and the Creation of Independent States, 1989–1991**

The collapse of Soviet communism dramatically altered the political landscape of Central Europe and Central Asia. The Warsaw Pact, the USSR's answer to NATO, vanished. West and East Germany reunited, and the nations created by the Versailles treaty of 1919—Estonia, Latvia, Lithuania, Poland, Czechoslovakia, Hungary, and Yugoslavia—reasserted their independence or split into smaller, ethnically defined nations. The Soviet republics bordering Russia, from Belarus in the west to Kyrgyzstan in the east, also became independent states, while remaining loosely bound with Russia in the Commonwealth of Independent States (CIS).

the United States for the next two decades, replacing the Cold War at the center of American geopolitics.

After Carter's success negotiating the 1979 Egypt-Israel treaty at Camp David, there were few bright spots in U.S. Middle Eastern diplomacy. In 1982, the Reagan administration supported Israel's invasion of Lebanon, a military operation intended to destroy the Palestine Liberation Organization (PLO). But when Lebanese militants, angered at U.S. intervention on behalf of Israel, killed 241 American marines, Reagan abruptly withdrew the forces. Three years later, Palestinians living in the Gaza Strip and along the West Bank of the Jordan River—territories occupied by Israel since 1967—mounted an intifada, a civilian uprising against Israeli authority. In response, American diplomats stepped up their efforts to persuade the PLO and Arab nations to accept the legitimacy of Israel and to convince the Israelis to allow the creation of a Palestinian state. Neither initiative met with much success. Unable, or unwilling, to solve the region's most intractable

problems and burdened by a history of support for undemocratic regimes in Middle Eastern countries, the United States was not seen by residents of the region as an honest broker.

**Persian Gulf War** American interest in a reliable supply of oil from the region led the United States into a short but consequential war in the Persian Gulf in the early 1990s. Ten years earlier, in September 1980, the revolutionary Shiite Islamic nation of Iran, headed by Ayatollah Khomeini, came under attack from Iraq, a secular state headed by the dictator Saddam Hussein. The fighting was intense and long lasting—a war of attrition that claimed a million casualties. Reagan supported Hussein with military intelligence and other aid—in order to maintain supplies of Iraqi oil, undermine Iran, and preserve a balance of power in the Middle East. Finally, in 1988, an armistice ended the inconclusive war, with both sides still claiming the territory that sparked the conflict.

**Men—and Women—at War**
Women played visible roles in the Persian Gulf War, comprising approximately 10 percent of the American troops. In the last decades of the twentieth century, increasing numbers of women chose military careers and, although prohibited from most fighting roles, were increasingly assigned to combat zones. Luc Delahaye/ Sipa Press.

Two years later, in August 1990, Hussein went to war to expand Iraq's boundaries and oil supply. Believing (erroneously) that he still had the support of the United States, Hussein sent in troops and quickly conquered Kuwait, Iraq's small, oil-rich neighbor, and threatened Saudi Arabia, the site of one-fifth of the world's known oil reserves and an informal ally of the United States. To preserve Western access to oil, President George H. W. Bush sponsored a series of resolutions in the United Nations Security Council calling for Iraq to withdraw from Kuwait. When Hussein refused, Bush successfully prodded the UN to authorize the use of force, and the president organized a military coalition of thirty-four nations. Dividing mostly along party lines, the Republican-led House of Representatives authorized American participation by a vote of 252 to 182, and the Democratic-led Senate agreed by the close margin of 52 to 47.

The coalition forces led by the United States quickly won the **Persian Gulf War** for the "liberation of Kuwait." To avoid a protracted struggle and retain French and Russian support for the UN coalition, Bush decided against occupying Iraq and removing Saddam Hussein

**IDENTIFY CAUSES**
Why did the United States intervene in the conflicts between Iraq and Iran and between Iraq and Kuwait?

from power. Instead, he won passage of UN Resolution 687, which imposed economic sanctions against Iraq unless it allowed unfettered inspection of its weapons systems, destroyed all biological and chemical arms, and unconditionally pledged not to develop nuclear weapons. The military victory, the low incidence of American casualties, and the quick withdrawal produced a euphoric reaction at home. "By God, we've kicked the Vietnam syndrome once and for all," Bush announced, and his approval rating shot up precipitously. But Saddam Hussein remained a formidable power in the region, and in March 2003, he would become the pretext for Bush's son, President George W. Bush, to initiate another war in Iraq—one that would be much more protracted, expensive, and bloody for Americans and Iraqis alike (Chapter 31).

Thus the end of the Cold War brought not peace, but a new American presence in the Middle East. For half a century, the United States and the Soviet Union had tried to divide the world into two rival economic and ideological blocs: communist and capitalist. The next decades promised a new set of struggles, one of them between a Western-led agenda of economic and cultural globalization and an anti-Western ideology of Muslim and Arab regionalism. Still more post–Cold War shifts were coming into view as well. One was the spectacular emergence of the European Union as a massive united trading bloc, economic engine, and global political force. Another was the equally spectacular economic growth in China, which was just beginning to take off in the early 1990s. The post–Cold War world promised to be a *multi*polar one, with great centers of power in Europe, the United States, and East Asia, and seemingly intractable conflict in the Middle East.

## SUMMARY

This chapter examined two central developments of the years 1980–1991: the rise of the New Right in U.S. politics and the end of the Cold War. Each development set the stage for a new era in American life, one that stretches to our own day. Domestically, the New Right, which had been building in strength since the mid-1960s, criticized the liberalism of the Great Society and the permissiveness that conservative activists associated with feminism and the sexual revolution. Shifting their allegiance from Barry Goldwater to Ronald Reagan, right-wing Americans built a conservative

movement from the ground up and in 1980 elected Reagan president. Advocating free-market economics, lower taxes, and fewer government regulations, Reagan became a champion of the New Right. His record as president was more mixed than his rhetoric would suggest, however. Reagan's initial tax cuts were followed by tax hikes. Moreover, he frequently dismayed the Christian Right by not pursuing their interests forcefully enough — especially regarding abortion and school prayer.

Reagan played a role in the ending of the Cold War. His massive military buildup in the early 1980s strained an already overstretched Soviet economy, which struggled to keep pace. Reagan then agreed to meet with Soviet leader Mikhail Gorbachev in several summits between 1985 and 1987. More important than Reagan's actions, however, were inefficiencies and contradictions in the Soviet economic structure itself. Combined with the forced military buildup and the disastrous war in Afghanistan, these strains led Gorbachev to institute the first significant reforms in Soviet society in half a century. The reforms stirred popular criticism of the Soviet Union, which formally collapsed in 1991.

# CHAPTER REVIEW

**MAKE IT STICK**    Go to **LearningCurve** to retain what you've read.

## TERMS TO KNOW    Identify and explain the significance of each term below.

### Key Concepts and Events

*The Conscience of a Conservative* (p. 975)

*National Review* (p. 976)

**Religious Right** (p. 976)

**hostage crisis** (p. 977)

**Reagan coalition** (p. 981)

**Moral Majority** (p. 981)

**Reagan Democrats** (p. 982)

**supply-side economics (Reaganomics)** (p. 982)

**Economic Recovery Tax Act (ERTA)** (p. 983)

**national debt** (p. 983)

**deregulation** (p. 983)

**HIV/AIDS** (p. 985)

**service industries** (p. 987)

**Sandinistas** (p. 992)

**Contras** (p. 992)

**Iran-Contra affair** (p. 993)

*glasnost* (p. 993)

*perestroika* (p. 993)

**family values** (p. 996)

**Persian Gulf War** (p. 998)

### Key People

**Barry Goldwater** (p. 974)

**Ronald Reagan** (p. 974)

**William F. Buckley** (p. 976)

**Milton Friedman** (p. 976)

**David Stockman** (p. 983)

**Sandra Day O'Connor** (p. 984)

**Mikhail Gorbachev** (p. 993)

**George H. W. Bush** (p. 996)

## REVIEW QUESTIONS
Answer these questions to demonstrate your understanding of the chapter's main ideas.

1. In what ways were the "three-legged stool" components of New Right conservatism compatible? Incompatible?

2. How would you assess the historical importance of Ronald Reagan? What were his most significant legacies, domestically and internationally? Why?

3. Why did the Cold War come to an end when it did? What were the contributing factors?

4. **THEMATIC UNDERSTANDING** Review the events listed on the thematic timeline on page 971. In what ways was the New Right "reactive," responding to liberalism, and in what ways was it "proactive," asserting its own agenda?

## MAKING CONNECTIONS
Recognize the larger developments and continuities within and across chapters by answering these questions.

1. **ACROSS TIME AND PLACE** Compare the two major periods of liberal legislative accomplishment — the New Deal in the 1930s (Chapter 23) and the Great Society in the 1960s (Chapter 28) — with the Reagan era in the 1980s. Did Reagan undo the legislative gains of those earlier eras? What conservative objectives was he able to accomplish, and what limits or obstacles did he encounter?

2. **VISUAL EVIDENCE** Examine the images of Reagan in this chapter (pp. 982, 987, 995). What message do these images convey about Reagan as a person? About his policies? Together, what do they tell us about the image and reality of the Reagan presidency? Do you think that cartoons or photographs are a more accurate source of information for understanding the historical meaning of a particular president and his administration? Why or why not?

## MORE TO EXPLORE
Start here to learn more about the events discussed in this chapter.

Lou Cannon, *President Reagan: The Role of a Lifetime* (2000). A valuable overview of the Reagan presidency.

William Martin, *With God on Our Side: The Rise of the Religious Right in America* (1996).

Lisa McGirr, *Suburban Warriors: The Origins of the New American Right* (2001). Explores the rise of the New Right.

James T. Patterson, *Restless Giant: The United States from Watergate to* Bush v. Gore (2005). Provides a solid analysis of the 1980s and 1990s.

On foreign policy, consult Richard A. Melanson, *American Foreign Policy Since the Vietnam War* (2005), and Raymond Garthoff, *The Great Transition: American-Soviet Relations and the End of the Cold War* (1994).

Two fine Web sites that document various Cold War incidents are the National Security Archive, at **gwu.edu/~nsarchiv**, and the Cold War International History Project, at **wilsoncenter.org/index .cfm?fuseaction=topics.home&topic_id=1409**.

## TIMELINE

Ask yourself why this chapter begins and ends with these dates and then identify the links among related events.

| | |
|---|---|
| **1981** | • Ronald Reagan becomes president<br>• Republicans gain control of Senate<br>• Economic Recovery Tax Act (ERTA) cuts taxes<br>• Military expenditures increase sharply<br>• Reagan cuts budgets of regulatory agencies<br>• Sandra Day O'Connor appointed to the Supreme Court |
| **1981–1989** | • National debt triples<br>• Emergence of New Right think tanks: Heritage Foundation, American Enterprise Institute, and the Cato Institute<br>• United States assists Iraq in war against Iran (1980–1988) |
| **1985** | • Mikhail Gorbachev takes power in Soviet Union |
| **1986** | • Iran-Contra scandal weakens Reagan presidency<br>• William Rehnquist named chief justice |
| **1987** | • United States and USSR agree to limit missiles in Europe |
| **1988** | • George H. W. Bush elected president |
| **1989** | • Destruction of Berlin Wall<br>• "Velvet Revolutions" in Eastern Europe<br>• *Webster v. Reproductive Health Services* limits abortion services |
| **1990–1991** | • Persian Gulf War |
| **1991** | • Dissolution of Soviet Union ends Cold War |

**KEY TURNING POINTS:** Identify some of the key moments in the decline and then end of the Cold War. What part did the United States play in these events, and how did this affect the U.S. role in world affairs more broadly?

# 31
## CHAPTER

# Confronting Global and National Dilemmas
# 1989 to the Present

O n the morning of September 11, 2001, two commercial airliners were deliberately flown into the World Trade Center in lower Manhattan. Millions of Americans, and many more people worldwide, watched live on television and the Internet as the towers burned and collapsed. Simultaneously, a third plane was flown into the Pentagon, and a fourth hijacked plane crashed in rural Pennsylvania. It took Federal Bureau of Investigation officials only a few hours to determine the identity of most of the hijackers, as well as the organization behind the murderous attacks—**Al Qaeda**.

The attacks were made possible by the new era of globalization. Of the nineteen terrorists involved in the hijackings, fifteen were from Saudi Arabia, two were from the United Arab Emirates, one was from Egypt, and one was from Lebanon. Many had trained in Afghanistan, in guerrilla warfare camps operated by Osama bin Laden. Four had gone to flight school in the United States itself. Several had lived and studied in Germany. They communicated with one another and with planners in Afghanistan through e-mail, Web sites, and cell phones. Al Qaeda sympathizers could be found among Muslims from Indonesia to Algeria. The most conspicuous crime of the twenty-first century, which left 2,900 people dead and sent waves of shock and anxiety through the American public, would have been impossible without the openness and interconnectivity that are central features of globalization.

Messages of sympathy and support poured into the United States from nearly every nation. Citizens of fifty-three different countries had perished in the World Trade Center, itself a symbol of the global financial industries. The world, quite literally, stood in shock. The emergence in the Middle East of a radical Muslim movement willing to use terrorism to inflict major damage on the United States and the West testified to the altered realities of global politics. The simple Cold War duality—communism versus capitalism—had for decades obscured regional, ethnic, and religious loyalties and conflicts. Those loyalties and conflicts moved to center stage in an era of globalization.

For Americans, the period between the end of the Cold War and our own day has been defined by twin dilemmas. The first relates to globalization. How would the United States engage in global trade and commerce? How would it relate to emerging nations? How should it confront radical terrorists? The second dilemma relates to domestic politics and the economy. In an era of conservative political dominance, how would the nation manage its cultural conflicts and ensure economic opportunity and security for its citizens? As "profound and powerful forces" shook the world, these were, as the chapter title suggests, Americans' dilemmas in a global society.

**IDENTIFY THE BIG IDEA**

How has globalization affected American politics, economics, and society?

**Energy and the Environment** At the dawn of the twenty-first century, few issues were more critical, in the United States and across the globe, than energy and the environment. This wind farm is an example of the search for non-fossil sources of new energy, a search that is among the many challenges facing the globalized world of our century. Raphael GAILLARDE/Gamma-Rapho via Getty Images.

# America in the Global Economy

On November 30, 1999, more than 50,000 protesters took to the streets of Seattle, Washington, immobilizing a wide swath of the city's downtown. Police, armed with pepper spray and arrayed in riot gear, worked feverishly to clear the clogged streets, get traffic moving, and usher well-dressed government ministers from around the world into a conference hall. Protesters jeered, chanted, and held hundreds of signs and banners aloft. A radical contingent joined the otherwise peaceful march, and a handful of them began breaking the windows of the chain stores they saw as symbols of global capitalism: Starbucks, Gap, Old Navy.

What had aroused such passion in the so-called Battle of Seattle? **Globalization**. The vast majority of Americans never surged into the streets, as had the Seattle protesters who tried to shut down this 1999 meeting of the **World Trade Organization (WTO)**, but no American by the late 1990s could deny that developments in the global economy reverberated at home. In that decade, Americans rediscovered a long-standing truth: the United States was not an island, but was linked in countless different ways to a global economy and society. Economic prosperity in the post–World War II decades had obscured for Americans this fundamental reality (Figure 31.1).

Globalization saw the rapid spread of capitalism around the world, huge increases in global trade and commerce, and a diffusion of communications technology, including the Internet, that linked the world's

**WTO Demonstration, Seattle, 1999**

In November 1999, an estimated 50,000 to 100,000 people from many states and foreign nations staged an effective protest at a World Trade Organization (WTO) meeting in Seattle. The goals of the protesters were diffuse; many feared that the trend toward a system of free (capitalist-run) trade would primarily benefit multinational corporations and would hurt both developing nations and the working classes in the industrialized world. Protests have continued at subsequent meetings of the WTO and the World Bank. Hector Mata/AFP/Getty Images.

**FIGURE 31.1**

**Productivity, Family Income, and Wages, 1970–2004**

This chart tells a complex and not altogether happy story. The median hourly wages of American workers (adjusted for inflation) stagnated between 1970 and 1995. The rise in median family income reflected the increasing proportion of two-earner families, as more married women entered the workforce. The dramatic increases in productivity did not lead to higher wages for workers. Rather, businesses used those gains either to cut prices to compete in the global marketplace or to reward owners, shareholders, and, particularly, corporate executives.

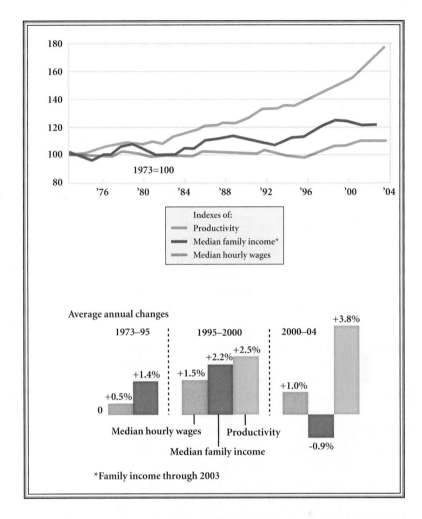

people to one another in ways unimaginable a generation earlier (Thinking Like a Historian, p. 1006). Suddenly, the United States faced a dizzying array of opportunities and challenges, both at home and abroad. "Profound and powerful forces are shaking and remaking our world," said a young President Bill Clinton in his first inaugural address in 1993. "The urgent question of our time is whether we can make change our friend and not our enemy."

An additional question remained, however. In whose interest was the global economy structured? Many of the Seattle activists took inspiration from the five-point "Declaration for Global Democracy," issued by the human rights organization Global Exchange during the WTO's Seattle meeting. "Global trade and investment," the declaration demanded, "must not be ends in themselves but rather the instruments for achieving equitable and sustainable development, including protections for workers and the environment." The declaration also addressed inequality among nations, calling attention to who benefitted from globalization and who did not.

## The Rise of the European Union and China

During the Cold War, the United States and the Soviet Union dominated the global balance of power. These two superpowers oversaw what observers called a bipolar world—two powerful poles, one capitalist and the other communist, around which global geopolitics were organized. Since the early 1990s, however, a multipolar world has emerged—with centers of power in Europe, Japan, China, and the United States, along with rising regional powers such as India and Brazil (America Compared, p. 1008).

In 1992, the nations of Western Europe created the European Union (EU) and moved toward the creation of a single federal state, somewhat like the United States. By the end of the 1990s, the European Union embraced more than twenty countries and 450 million people—the third-largest population in the world, behind China and India—and accounted for a fifth of all global imports and exports. In 2002, the EU introduced a single currency, the euro, which soon rivaled

## Globalization: Its Proponents and Its Discontents

Globalization is perhaps one of the most commonly used, yet least understood, concepts in our modern vocabulary. This chapter has explored how, while there has long been an international, or global, dimension to trade, migration, and other economic activity, there is nevertheless something distinct about the post–Cold War global order. Economic integration and communication networking have created new opportunities for millions of people. Yet those same processes may not benefit all equally. The following documents offer different perspectives on the broad process called globalization.

1. **Interview with Petra Mata, Mexican immigrant to the United States, 2003.** *An immigrant from a low-wage country who was "insourced," Mata worked as a low-paid garment worker until she lost her job in the United States because it was outsourced— sent abroad to workers paid even less.*

My name is Petra Mata. I was born in Mexico. I have completed no more than the sixth grade in school. In 1969, my husband and I came to the U.S. believing we would find better opportunities for our children and ourselves. We first arrived without documents, then became legal, and finally became citizens. For years I moved from job to job until I was employed in 1976 by the most popular company in the market, Levi Strauss & Company. I earned $9.73 an hour and also had vacation and sick leave. Levi's provided me and my family with a stable situation, and in return I was a loyal employee and worked there for fourteen years.

On January 16, 1990, Levi's closed its plant in San Antonio, Texas, where I had been working, leaving 1,150 workers unemployed, a majority of whom were Mexican-American women. The company moved its factory to Costa Rica. . . .

As a result of being laid off, I personally lost my house, my method of transportation, and the tranquility of my home. My family and I had to face new problems. My husband was forced to look for a second job on top of the one he already had. He worked from seven in the morning to six at night. Our reality was very difficult. At that time, I had not the slightest idea what free trade was or meant. . . .

Our governments make agreements behind closed doors without participation from the working persons who are most affected by these decisions — decisions that to my knowledge only benefit large corporations and those in positions of power.

2. **iPhone global supply chain figure, 2011.**

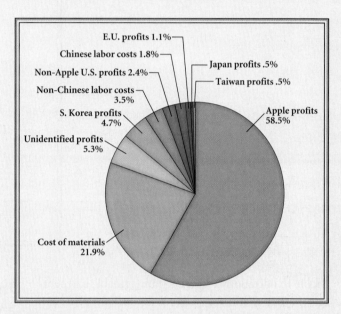

E.U. profits 1.1%
Chinese labor costs 1.8%
Non-Apple U.S. profits 2.4%
Non-Chinese labor costs 3.5%
S. Korea profits 4.7%
Unidentified profits 5.3%
Japan profits .5%
Taiwan profits .5%
Apple profits 58.5%
Cost of materials 21.9%

**FIGURE 31.2**

3. **Seattle Chapter, National Lawyers Guild, "Bringing in an Undemocratic Institution Brings an Undemocratic Response," 2000.**

Many of the businesses that most promote the WTO [World Trade Organization] and its allied institutions rely on undemocratic practices to promote their business interest. In recent years these policies have included not only monopolistic business practices but also outright interference with local governments. Frequently, to promote the interests of business, a militaristic type of government is either promoted, or even created. The effects these governments and their policies have on the citizenry of these nations are disastrous. Farms and forests are ruined and denuded. Low cost toxic waste dumps are created near population centers to service skyrocketing debts. . . .

The WTO was nominally chartered as a dispute resolution organization. The problem is it is an organization with no real oversight or accountability, and a process that favors the most powerful corporations.

## 4. World Trade Organization press release, 2000.

- Extreme poverty is a huge problem. 1.2 billion people survive on less than a dollar a day. A further 1.6 billion, more than a quarter of the world's population, make do with one to two dollars a day.

- To alleviate poverty, developing economies need to grow faster, and the poor need to benefit from this growth. Trade can play an important part in reducing poverty, because it boosts economic growth and the poor tend to benefit from that faster growth.

- The study finds that, in general, living standards in developing countries are not catching up with those in developed countries. But some developing countries are catching up. What distinguishes them is their openness to trade. The countries that are catching up with rich ones are those that are open to trade; and the more open they are, the faster they are converging.

## 5. Stuart Carlson, political cartoon from the *Milwaukee Journal-Sentinel*, 2005.

Stuart Carlson © 2005 Milwaukee Sentinel. Reprinted with permission of UNIVERSAL UCLICK. All rights reserved.

## 6. Former president Bill Clinton, speech at Guildhall, London, 2006.

I spent a lot of time working on globalization when I was president, coming to terms with the fundamental fact of interdependence that goes far beyond economics: open border, easy travel, easy immigration, free flow of money as well as people, products, and services. I tried to figure out how to maximize the dynamism of global interdependence and still broaden its impact in terms of economics and opportunity. The one thing that I am quite sure of is that interdependence is not a choice, it's not a policy, it is the inevitable condition of our time. So, divorce is not an option. . . .

Therefore, the mission of the moment clearly is to build up the positive and reduce the negative forces of global interdependence in a way that enables us to keep score in the right way. Are people going to be better off, will our children have a better chance, will we be more united than divided?

Sources: (1) From *Shafted: Free Trade and America's Working Poor*, by Christine Ahn (Food First Books, 2003). Reprinted by permission of the Institute for Food and Development Policy, 398 60th Street, Oakland, CA 94618.; (2) Kenneth L. Kraemer, Greg Linden, and Jason Dedrick, "Capturing Value in Global Networks: Apple's iPad and iPhone" (Paul Merage School of Business, University of California, Irvine, July 2011). Used by permission of the authors; (3) Seattle Chapter, National Lawyers Guild, "Bringing in an Undemocratic Institution Brings an Undemocratic Response," July 5, 2000, ii, 5; (4) WTO press release, June 13, 2000, quoting a WTO Special Study No. 5, "Trade, Income Disparity, and Poverty," June 2000. Used by permission of the World Trade Organization; (6) collegeofpublicspeaking.co.uk/Clinton-London-2006.html.

### ANALYZING THE EVIDENCE

1. Free trade means that goods can move between countries without restriction or taxation (such as tariffs or duties). Compare sources 1, 3, 5, and 6. How do these different sources explain the effects of freer trade across the globe? How would you interpret the WTO's optimism about free trade alongside Petra Mata's personal experience of displacement?

2. How is increased global communication important to the trade relationships described in source 2? According to source 4, what are some other effects associated with the trade relationships shown here?

3. What tension in globalization is the cartoonist in source 5 attempting to capture? What kind of change over time has the cartoonist identified?

### PUTTING IT ALL TOGETHER

Based on this chapter's discussion of globalization, and using the above documents, write an essay in which you examine the economic effects of recent global integration. In particular, use your essay to define globalization and to outline some of its potential positive and negative effects.

# Global Trade, 1960–2009

One of the major consequences of economic globalization is an increase in trade among nations. The figures below show imports and exports for four of the world's largest economies.

**FIGURE 31.3**
**Imports, 1960–2009**

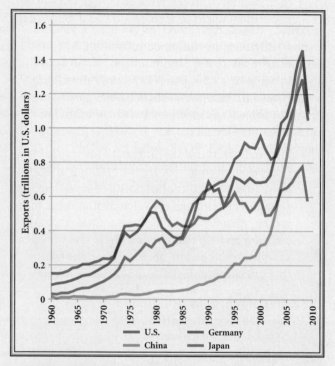

**FIGURE 31.4**
**Exports, 1960–2009**

## QUESTIONS FOR ANALYSIS

1. Notice how U.S. imports rose at roughly the same rate as those of other countries until the 1970s. What accounts for the acceleration of U.S. imports thereafter?

2. China's exports rose spectacularly after the 1990s. Germany increased its exports in this period dramatically as well. What evidence do you see here for increasing competition for the United States in a globalizing economy?

the dollar and the Japanese yen as a major international currency (Map 31.1). Militarily, however, the EU remained a secondary power. An economic juggernaut and trading rival with a suspicion of warfare, the EU presented a number of new dilemmas for American officials.

So did China, a vast nation of 1.3 billion people that was the world's fastest-rising economic power in the first decade of the twenty-first century. Between 2000 and 2008, China *quadrupled* its gross domestic product (GDP). Economic growth rates during those years were consistently near 10 percent—higher than the United States achieved during its periods of

furious economic growth in the 1950s and 1960s. Although still governed by the Communist Party, China embraced capitalism, and its factories produced inexpensive products for export, which Americans eagerly purchased—everything from children's toys and television sets to clothing, household appliances, and video games. To maintain this symbiotic relationship, China deliberately kept its currency weak against the American dollar, ensuring that its exports remained cheap in the United States.

Beneficial to American consumers in the short run, the implications of this relationship for the future may be less promising. Two such implications stand out.

**MAP 31.1**

**Growth of the European Community, 1951–2005**

The European Community (EU) began in the 1950s as a loose organization of Western European nations. Over the course of the following decades, it created stronger common institutions, such as the European Parliament in Strasbourg, the EU Commission in Brussels, and the Court of Justice in Luxembourg. With the collapse of communism, the EU has expanded to include the nations of Eastern and Central Europe. It now includes twenty-eight nations and over 500 million people.

First, as more and more goods that Americans buy are produced in China, the manufacturing base in the United States continues to shrink, costing jobs and adversely affecting communities. Second, China has kept its currency low against the dollar primarily by purchasing American debt. China now owns nearly 25 percent of total U.S. debt, more than any other nation. Many economists believe that it is unwise to allow a single country to wield so much influence over the U.S. currency supply. Should this relationship continue unchanged, Americans may find their manufacturing sector contracting even more severely in the coming decades.

## An Era of Globalization

Americans have long depended on foreign markets to which they export their goods and have long received imported products and immigrants from other countries. But the *intensity* of international exchange has varied over time. The end of the Cold War shattered barriers that had restrained international trade and impeded capitalist development of vast areas of the world. New communications systems—satellites, fiber-optic cables, global positioning networks—were shrinking the world's physical spaces to a degree

unimaginable at the beginning of the twentieth century. Perhaps most important, global financial markets became integrated to an unprecedented extent, allowing investment capital to "flow" into and out of nations and around the world in a matter of moments.

### International Organizations and Corporations

International organizations, many of them created in the wake of World War II, set the rules for capitalism's worldwide expansion. During the final decades of the Cold War, the leading capitalist industrial nations formed the Group of Seven (G7) to manage global economic policy. Russia joined in 1997, creating the **Group of Eight (G8)**. The G8 nations—the United States, Britain, Germany, France, Italy, Japan, Canada, and Russia—largely controlled the major international financial organizations: the World Bank, the International Monetary Fund (IMF), and the General Agreement on Tariffs and Trade (GATT). In 1995, GATT evolved into the World Trade Organization (WTO), with nearly 150 participating nations that regulate and formalize trade agreements with member states.

**EXPLAIN CONSEQUENCES**

What were the major consequences for the United States of the economic rise of China and the European Union?

**COMPARE AND CONTRAST**
What were the potential benefits and risks of globalization to the United States and other countries?

As globalization accelerated, so did the integration of regional economies. To offset the economic clout of the European bloc, in 1993 the United States, Canada, and Mexico signed the **North American Free Trade Agreement (NAFTA).** This treaty, as ratified by the U.S. Congress, envisioned the eventual creation of a free-trade zone covering all of North America. In East Asia, the capitalist nations of Japan, South Korea, Taiwan, and Singapore consulted on economic policy; as China developed a quasi-capitalist economy and became a major exporter of manufactures, its Communist-led government joined their deliberations.

International organizations set the rules, but globalization was made possible by the proliferation of **multinational corporations** (MNCs). In 1970, there were 7,000 corporations with offices and factories in multiple countries; by 2000, the number had exploded to 63,000. Many of the most powerful MNCs were, and continue to be, based in the United States. Walmart, the biggest American retailer, is also one of the world's largest corporations, with 1,200 stores in other nations and more than $400 billion in sales. Apple, maker of the iPhone and iPad, grew spectacularly in the 2000s and now has more than $60 billion annually in global sales. The McDonald's restaurant chain had 1,000 outlets outside the United States in 1980; twenty years later, there were nearly 13,000, and "McWorld" had become a popular shorthand term for globalization.

Globalization was driven by more than a quest for new markets. Corporations also sought ever-cheaper sources of labor. Many American MNCs closed their factories in the United States and outsourced manufacturing jobs to plants in Mexico, Eastern Europe,

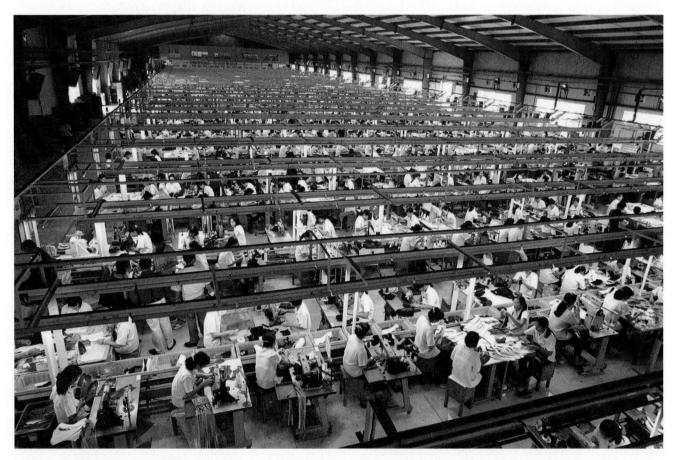

**A Nike Factory in China**
In 2005, Nike produced its shoes and sportswear at 124 plants in China; additional factories were located in other low-wage countries. Most of the Chinese plants were run by subcontractors, who housed the workers — mostly women between the ages of sixteen and twenty-five — in crowded dormitories. The wages were low, about $3 a day, but more than the women could earn if they remained in their rural villages. AP Images.

and especially Asia. The athletic sportswear firm Nike was a prime example. By 2005, Nike had established 700 factories worldwide that employed more than 650,000 workers, most of whom received low wages, endured harsh working conditions, and had no health or pension benefits. Highly skilled jobs were outsourced as well.

**Financial Deregulation**   One of the principal differences between this new era of globalization and previous eras has been the opening of national financial and currency markets to investment from around the world. The United States and Britain led the way. Both countries came under the sway of powerful political forces in the 1980s calling for the total deregulation of banks, brokerage houses, investment firms, and financial markets—letting the free market replace government oversight. Together, the United States and Britain led a quiet revolution in which investment markets around the world were gradually set free.

Financial deregulation led to spectacular profits for investors but produced a more fragile, crash-prone global economy. On the profit side, financial-industry profits in the United States rose from less than 10 percent of total business profits in the 1950s to more than 40 percent beginning in the 1990s. But the costs were becoming clear as well: the bankruptcy of the American savings and loan industry in the 1980s; the "lost decade" in Japan in the 1990s; the near bankruptcy of Russia in the late 1990s and of Argentina in 2001; the 1997 Asian financial crisis, centered in Thailand and Indonesia; and the collapse of nearly the entire global economy in 2008 (p. 1030). These and other episodes dramatized the extraordinary risks that financial globalization has introduced.

## Revolutions in Technology

The technological advances of the 1980s and 1990s changed the character of everyday life for millions of Americans, linking them with a global information and media environment unprecedented in world history. Not since television was introduced to American homes in the years following World War II had technology so profoundly changed the way people lived their lives. Personal computers, cell phones and smartphones, the Internet and the World Wide Web, and other electronic devices and systems altered

**Internet Versus Newspapers**

Between 2000 and 2010, dozens of large and medium-sized newspapers went out of business, their once-robust readership drained away by the convenience of news available for free on the Internet. In 2009, the *Seattle Post-Intelligencer* newspaper ceased print publication and became an online-only news source. In this photo, the paper's news-boxes sit empty, an ominous sign of the struggling newspaper business in the early 2000s. © Bettmann/Corbis.

work, leisure, and access to knowledge in stunning ways. Like unimpeded trade, these advances in communications and personal technologies enhanced globalization.

During the 1990s, personal computers, which had emerged in the late 1970s, grew even more significant with the spread of the Internet and the World Wide Web. Like the computer itself, the Internet was the product of military-based research. During the late 1960s, the U.S. Department of Defense, in conjunction with the Massachusetts Institute of Technology, began developing a decentralized computer network, the **Advanced Research Projects Agency Network (ARPANET)**. The Internet, which grew out of the ARPANET, was soon used by government scientists, academic specialists, and military contractors to exchange data, information, and electronic mail (e-mail). By the 1980s, the Internet had spread to universities, businesses, and the general public.

The debut in 1991 of the graphics-based **World Wide Web** — a collection of servers that allowed access to millions of documents, pictures, and other materials — enhanced the popular appeal and commercial possibilities of the Internet. By 2011, 78 percent of all Americans and more than two billion people worldwide used the Internet to send messages and view information. Businesses used the World Wide Web to sell their products and services; e-commerce transactions totaled $114 billion in 2003, $172 billion in 2005, and neared $500 billion in 2010. The Web proved instantly democratic, providing ordinary people with easy access to knowledge.

## Politics and Partisanship in a New Era

Standing at the podium at the 1992 Republican National Convention, his supporters cheering by the thousands, Patrick Buchanan did not mince words. Buchanan was a former speechwriter for President Richard Nixon and a White House aide to President Ronald Reagan, and despite having lost the nomination for president, he still hoped to shape the party's message to voters. This election, he told the audience — including millions watching on television — "is about what we stand for as Americans." Citing Democratic support for abortion rights and the rights of lesbians and gay men, Buchanan claimed there was "a religious war going on in our country for the soul of America." It was, he emphasized, "a **culture war**."

Buchanan's war was another name for a longstanding political struggle, dating to the 1920s, between religious traditionalists and secular liberals (Chapter 22). This time, however, Americans struggled over these questions in the long shadow of the sixties, which had taken on an exaggerated meaning in the nation's

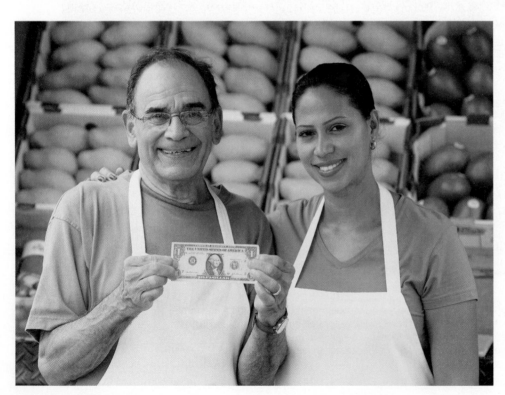

**New Immigrants**

In the early years of the 2000s, more immigrants lived in the United States than at any time since the first decades of the twentieth century. Most came from Asia, Latin America, and Africa. Many, like those pictured here, started small businesses that helped revive the economies of urban and suburban neighborhoods across the country.
© Bettmann/Corbis.

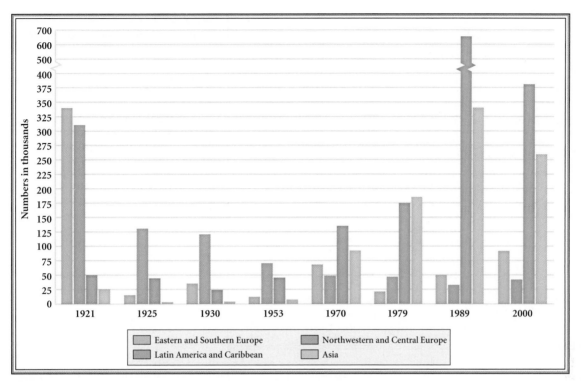

**FIGURE 31.5**

**American Immigration, 1920–2000**

Legislation inspired by nativism slowed the influx of immigrants after 1920, as did the dislocations brought on by economic depression and war in the 1930s and 1940s. Note the high rate of non-European immigration since the 1970s, the result of new eligibility rules in the Immigration Act of 1965 (Chapter 28). The dramatic increase since 1980 in the number of migrants from Latin America and Asia reflects American economic prosperity, traditionally a magnet for migrants, and the rapid acceleration of illegal immigration.

politics. Against the backdrop of globalization, American politics in the 1990s and early 2000s careened back and forth between contests over divisive social issues and concern over the nation's economic future.

## An Increasingly Plural Society

Exact estimates vary, but demographers predict that at some point between 2040 and 2050 the United States will become a "majority-minority" nation: No single ethnic or racial group will be in the numerical majority. This is already the case in California, where in 2010 African Americans, Latinos, and Asians together constituted a majority of the state's residents. As this unmistakable trend became apparent in the 1990s, it fueled renewed debates over ethnic and racial identity and over public policies such as affirmative action.

**New Immigrants**   According to the Census Bureau, the population of the United States grew from 203 million in 1970 to 280 million in 2000 (American Voices, p. 1016). Of that 77-million-person increase, immigrants accounted for 28 million, with legal entrants

numbering 21 million and illegal entrants adding another 7 million (Figure 31.5). As a result, by 2000, 26 percent of California's population was foreign-born, as was 20 percent of New York's and 17 percent each of New Jersey's and Florida's. Relatively few immigrants came from Europe, which had dominated immigration to the United States between 1880 and 1924. The overwhelming majority—some 25 million—now came from Latin America (16 million) and East Asia (9 million) (Map 31.2).

This extraordinary inflow of immigrants was the unintended result of the **Immigration and Nationality Act** of 1965, one of the less well-known but most influential pieces of Great Society legislation. Known as the Hart-Celler Act, the legislation eliminated the 1924 quota system, which had favored Northern Europe. In its place, Congress created a more equal playing field among nations and a slightly higher total limit on immigration. The legislation also included provisions that eased the entry of immigrants who possessed skills in high demand in the United States. Finally, a provision with far-reaching implications was included in the new law: immediate family members of those already

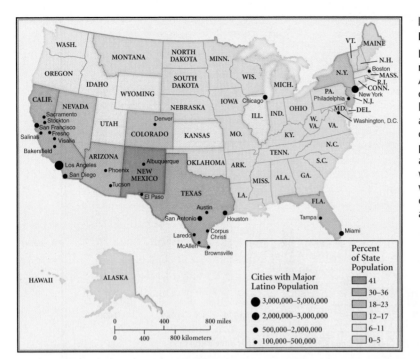

**MAP 31.2**

**Hispanic and Asian Populations, 2000**

In 2000, people of Hispanic descent made up more than 11 percent of the American population, and they now outnumber African Americans as the largest minority group. Asian Americans accounted for an additional 4 percent of the population. Demographers predict that by the year 2050 only about half of the U.S. population will be composed of non-Hispanic whites. Note the high percentage of Hispanics and Asians in California and certain other states.

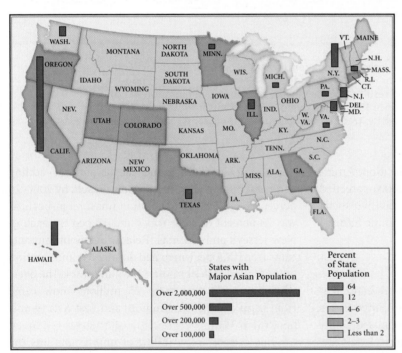

legally resident in the United States were admitted outside of the total numerical limit.

American residents from Latin America and the Caribbean were best positioned to take advantage of the family provision. Millions of Mexicans came to the United States to join their families, and U.S. residents from El Salvador and Guatemala—tens of thousands of whom had arrived seeking sanctuary or asylum

during the civil wars of the 1980s—and the Dominican Republic now brought their families to join them. Nationally, there were now more Latinos than African Americans. Many of these immigrants profoundly shaped the emerging global economy by sending substantial portions of their earnings, called remittances, back to family members in their home countries. In 2006, for instance, workers in the United States sent

$23 billion to Mexico, a massive remittance flow that constituted Mexico's third-largest source of foreign exchange.

Asian immigrants came largely from China, the Philippines, South Korea, India, and Pakistan. In addition, 700,000 refugees came to the United States from Southeast Asia (Vietnam, Laos, and Cambodia) after the Vietnam War. This immigration signaled more than new flows of people into the United States. Throughout much of its history, the United States had oriented itself toward the Atlantic. Indeed, at the end of the nineteenth century, American secretary of state John Hay observed, "The Mediterranean is the ocean of the past; the Atlantic the ocean of the present." He added, presciently, "The Pacific [is] the ocean of the future." By the last decades of the twentieth century, Hay's future had arrived. As immigration from Asia increased, as Japan and China grew more influential economically, and as more and more transnational trade crossed the Pacific, commentators on both sides of the ocean began speaking of the Pacific Rim as an important new region.

**Multiculturalism and Its Critics**   Most new immigrants arrived under the terms of the 1965 law. But those who entered without legal documentation stirred political controversy. After twenty years under the new law, there were three to five million immigrants without legal status. In 1986, to remedy this situation, Congress passed the Immigration Reform and Control Act. The law granted citizenship to many of those who had arrived illegally, provided incentives for employers not to hire undocumented immigrants, and increased surveillance along the border with Mexico. Immigration critics persisted, however. In 1992, Patrick Buchanan, then campaigning for the Republican presidential nomination, warned Americans that their country was "undergoing the greatest invasion in its history, a migration of millions of illegal aliens a year from Mexico." Many states took immigration matters into their own hands. In 1994, for instance, Californians approved Proposition 187, a ballot initiative that barred illegal aliens from public schools, nonemergency care at public health clinics, and all other state social services. The proposed law declared that U.S. citizens have a "right to the protection of their government from any person or persons entering this country unlawfully," but after five years in federal court, the controversial measure was ruled unconstitutional.

 To see a longer excerpt of Proposition 187, along with other primary sources from this period, see *Sources for America's History*.

Debates over post-1965 immigration looked a great deal like conflicts in the early decades of the century. Then, many native-born white Protestants worried that the largely Jewish and Catholic immigrants from Southern and Eastern Europe, along with African American migrants leaving the South, could not assimilate and threatened the "purity" of the nation. Although the conflicts looked the same, the cultural paradigm had shifted. In the earlier era, the *melting pot*—a term borrowed from the title of a 1908 play—became the metaphor for how American society would accommodate its newfound diversity. Some native-born Americans found solace in the melting-pot concept because it implied that a single "American" culture would predominate. In the 1990s, however, a different concept, **multiculturalism**, emerged to define social diversity. Americans, this concept suggested, were not a single people into whom others melted; rather, they comprised a diverse set of ethnic and racial groups living and working together. A shared set of public values held the multicultural society together, even as different groups maintained unique practices and traditions.

Critics, however, charged that multiculturalism perpetuated ethnic chauvinism and conferred preferential treatment on minority groups. Many government policies, as well as a large number of private employers, for instance, continued to support affirmative action programs designed to bring African Americans and Latinos into public- and private-sector jobs and universities in larger numbers. Conservatives argued that such governmental programs were deeply flawed because they promoted "reverse discrimination" against white men and women and resulted in the selection and promotion of less qualified applicants for jobs and educational advancement.

California stood at the center of the debate. In 1995, under pressure from Republican governor Pete Wilson, the regents of the University of California scrapped their twenty-year-old policy of affirmative action. A year later, California voters approved **Proposition 209**, which outlawed affirmative action in state employment and public education. At the height of the 1995 controversy, President Bill Clinton delivered a major speech defending affirmative action. He reminded Americans that Richard Nixon, a Republican president, had endorsed affirmative action, and he concluded by saying the nation should "mend it," not "end it." However, as in the *Bakke* decision of the 1970s (Chapter 29), it was the U.S. Supreme Court that spoke loudest on the subject. In two parallel 2003 cases, the Court invalidated one affirmative action plan at the University of

## Immigration After 1965: Its Defenders and Critics

As we have seen in this chapter, the immigration law passed by Congress in 1965 combined with global developments to shift the flows of people seeking entry to the United States. More and more immigrants came from Latin America, the Caribbean, Asia, and Africa. Immigration has always been politically controversial, but in the 1990s a renewed, and often polarized, debate over immigration emerged.

### John F. Kennedy
### *A Nation of Immigrants*, 1964

This selection is from a revised, and posthumously published, version of a book Kennedy originally published in 1958.

Immigration policy should be generous; it should be fair; it should be flexible. With such a policy we can turn to the world, and to our own past with clean hands and a clean conscience. Such a policy would be a reaffirmation of old principles. It would be an expression of our agreement with George Washington that "The bosom of America is open to receive not only the opulent and respectable stranger, but the oppressed and persecuted of all nations and religions; whom we shall welcome to a participation of all our rights and privileges, if by decency and propriety of conduct they appear to merit the enjoyment."

Source: Nicholas Capaldi, ed., *Immigration: Debating the Issues* (Amherst, NY: Prometheus Books, 1997), 128.

### Roy Beck
### "A Nation of (Too Many) Immigrants?" 1996

Boy Beck is a former journalist who became an activist for immigration reduction.

Since 1970, more than 30 million foreign citizens and their descendants have been added to the local communities and labor pools of the United States. It is the numerical equivalent of having relocated within our borders the entire present population of all Central American countries.

Demographic change on such a massive scale — primarily caused by the increased admission of *legal* immigrants — inevitably has created winners and losers among Americans. Based on opinion polls, it appears that most Americans consider themselves net losers and believe that the United States has become "a nation of too many immigrants."

What level of immigration is best for America, and of real help to the world? Although we often hear that the United States is a nation of immigrants, we seldom ask just what that means. It can be difficult to ask tough questions about immigration when we see nostalgic images of Ellis Island, recall our own families' coming to America, or encounter a new immigrant who is striving admirably to achieve the American dream.

But tough questions about immigration can no longer be avoided as we enter a fourth decade of unprecedentedly high immigration and struggle with its impact on our job markets, on the quality of life and social fabric of our communities, and on the state of the environment. . . .

The task before the nation in setting a fair level of immigration is not about race or some vision of a homogenous white America; it is about protecting and enhancing the United States' unique experiment in democracy for all Americans, including recent immigrants, regardless of their particular ethnicity. It is time to confront the true costs and benefits of immigration numbers, which have skyrocketed beyond our society's ability to handle them successfully.

Source: From *The Case Against Immigration: The Moral, Economic, Social, and Environmental Reasons for Reducing U.S. Immigration Back to Traditional Levels*, by Roy H. Beck (New York: W. W. Norton & Company, 1996). Used by permission of the author.

### Vernon M. Briggs Jr. and Stephen Moore
### "Still an Open Door?" 1994

Two academic policy analysts weigh in on the immigration debate.

Immigrants are certainly not an unmixed blessing. When the newcomers first arrive, they impose short-term costs on the citizenry. Because immigration means more people, they cause more congestion of our highways, a more crowded housing market, and longer waiting lines in stores and hospitals. In states such as California, immigrants' children are heavy users of an already overburdened public school system, and so on. Some immigrants abuse the welfare system, which means that tax dollars from Americans are transferred to immigrant populations. Los Angeles County officials estimate that immigrants' use of county services costs the local government hundreds of millions of dollars each year. . . .

The benefits of immigration, however, are manifold. Perhaps the most important benefit is that immigrants come to the United States with critically needed talents, energies, and ambitions that serve as an engine for economic progress and help the United States retain economic and geopolitical leadership. Because for most of the world's immigrants, America is their first choice, the United States is in a unique position to select the most brilliant and inventive minds from the United Kingdom, Canada, China, Korea, India, Ireland, Mexico, Philippines, Russia, Taiwan, and other nations. Because most immigrants are not poor, tired, huddled masses, but rather are above the average of their compatriots in skill and education levels, the immigration process has a highly beneficial self-selection component, a skimming of the cream of the best workers and top brainpower from the rest of the world.

Source: Vernon M. Briggs Jr. and Stephen Moore, *Still an Open Door? U.S. Immigration Policy and the American Economy* (Washington, DC: The American University Press, 1994).

**President Barack Obama**

## June 15, 2012, Announcement at the White House Rose Garden

In 2012 the president announced a new policy allowing many immigrants to avoid deportation and apply for work authorization.

This morning, Secretary Napolitano [Secretary of Department of Homeland Security] announced new actions my administration will take to mend our nation's immigration policy, to make it more fair, more efficient and more just, specifically for certain young people sometimes called DREAMers.

Now, these are young people who study in our schools, they play in our neighborhoods, they're friends with our kids, they pledge allegiance to our flag. They are Americans in their heart, in their minds, in every single way but one: on paper. They were brought to this country by their parents, sometimes even as infants, and often have no idea that they're undocumented until they apply for a job or a driver's license or a college scholarship.

Put yourself in their shoes. Imagine you've done everything right your entire life, studied hard, worked hard, maybe even graduated at the top of your class, only to suddenly face the threat of deportation to a country that you know nothing about, with a language that you may not even speak.

That's what gave rise to the Dream Act. It says that if your parents brought you here as a child, you've been here for five years and you're willing to go to college or serve in our military, you can one day earn your citizenship. And I've said time and time and time again to Congress that — send me the Dream Act, put it on my desk, and I will sign it right away. . . .

Source: *New York Times*, June 15, 2012.

### QUESTIONS FOR ANALYSIS

1. Compare and contrast the different views on immigration presented here. What are the pros and cons of immigration?

2. Does the debate over immigration depend on whether immigrants are pictured as skilled and educated or unskilled and poor? Explain why it should or shouldn't.

3. The Dream Act that President Obama mentions was stalled in Congress in 2012. What kinds of appeals does he make on behalf of immigrants? How do they compare with Kennedy's remarks?

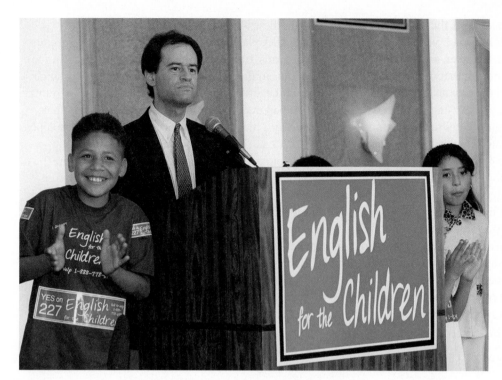

**English Only**

Not everyone was pleased with the new influx of immigrants. Anti-immigrant movements arose in various states, especially those along the Mexican border. In 1998, conservative activist Ron Unz sponsored Proposition 227 in California. The measure, which banned bilingual education in public schools, passed by a wide margin. In this photo, Unz delivers a speech supporting Proposition 227 to an audience in Los Angeles. AP Images.

Michigan but allowed racial preference policies that promoted a "diverse" student body. Thus diversity became the law of the land, the constitutionally acceptable basis for affirmative action. The policy had been narrowed but preserved.

Additional anxieties about a multicultural nation centered on language. In 1998, Silicon Valley software entrepreneur Ron Unz sponsored a California initiative calling for an end to bilingual education in public schools. Unz argued that bilingual education had failed because it did not adequately prepare Spanish-speaking students to succeed in an English-speaking society. The state's white, Anglo residents largely approved of the measure; most Mexican American, Asian American, and civil rights organizations opposed it. When Unz's measure, Proposition 227, passed with a healthy 61 percent majority, it seemed to confirm the limits of multiculturalism in the nation's most diverse state.

**TRACE CHANGE OVER TIME**

How did anti-immigrant sentiment increase between the 1960s and the 1990s, and what sorts of actions were taken by those opposed to immigration?

## Clashes over "Family Values"

If the promise of a multicultural nation was one contested political issue, another was the state of American families. New Right conservatives charged that the "abrasive experiments of two liberal decades," as a Reagan administration report put it, had eroded respect for marriage and what they had called, since the 1970s, "family values." They pointed to the 40 percent rate of divorce among whites and the nearly 60 percent rate of out-of-wedlock pregnancies among African Americans. To conservatives, there was a wide range of culprits: legislators who enacted liberal divorce laws, funded child care, and allowed welfare payments to unmarried mothers, as well as judges who condoned abortion and banished religious instruction from public schools.

**Abortion**   Abortion was central to the battles between feminists and religious conservatives and a defining issue between Democrats and Republicans. Feminists who described themselves as prochoice viewed the issue from the perspective of the pregnant woman; they argued that the right to a legal, safe abortion was crucial to her control over her body and life. Conversely, religious conservatives, who pronounced themselves prolife, viewed abortion from the perspective of the unborn fetus and claimed that its rights trumped those of the mother. That is where the debate had stood since the U.S. Supreme Court's 1973 decision in *Roe v. Wade*.

By the 1980s, fundamentalist Protestants had assumed leadership of the antiabortion movement,

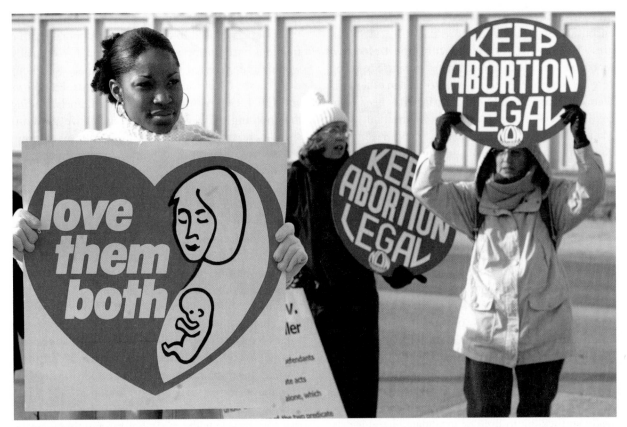

**Activists Protesting Outside the Supreme Court in 2002**

In 2002 the Supreme Court considered a case in which the National Organization for Women (NOW) had challenged the legality of abortion clinic protests, such as those undertaken by Operation Rescue. The activists, and the case itself, demonstrated that the question of abortion remained far from settled, and Americans on all sides of the issue continued to hold passionate opinions. Photo by Mark Wilson/Getty Images.

which became increasingly confrontational and politically powerful. In 1987, the religious activist Randall Terry founded **Operation Rescue**, which mounted protests outside abortion clinics and harassed their staffs and clients. While such vocal protests took shape outside clinics, antiabortion activists also won state laws that limited public funding for abortions, required parental notification before minors could obtain abortions, and mandated waiting periods before any woman could undergo an abortion procedure. Such laws further restricted women's reproductive choices.

**Gay Rights** The issue of homosexuality stirred equally deep passions. As more gay men and women came out of the closet in the years after Stonewall (Chapter 28), they demanded legal protections from discrimination in housing, education, and employment. Public opinion about these demands varied by region, but by the 1990s, many cities and states had banned discrimination on the basis of sexual orientation. Gay

rights groups also sought legal rights for same-sex couples — such as the eligibility for workplace health-care coverage — that were akin to those enjoyed by married heterosexuals. Many of the most prominent national gay rights organizations, such as the Human Rights Campaign, focused on full marriage equality: a legal recognition of same-sex marriage that was on par with opposite-sex marriages.

The Religious Right had long condemned homosexuality as morally wrong, and public opinion remained sharply divided. In 1992, Colorado voters approved an amendment to the state constitution that prevented local governments from enacting ordinances protecting gays and lesbians — a measure that the Supreme Court subsequently overturned as unconstitutional. That same year, however, Oregon voters defeated a more radical initiative that would have

**EXPLAIN CONSEQUENCES**

How did clashes over "family values" alter American politics in the 1990s?

prevented the state from using any funds "to promote, encourage or facilitate" homosexuality. In 1998, Congress entered the fray by enacting the **Defense of Marriage Act**, which allowed states to refuse to recognize gay marriages or civil unions formed in other jurisdictions. More recently, gay marriage has been legalized in eleven states: California, Connecticut, Iowa, Maine, Maryland, Massachusetts, New Hampshire, New York, Vermont, Washington, and Rhode Island.

**Culture Wars and the Supreme Court**   Divisive rights issues increasingly came before the U.S. Supreme Court. Abortion led the way, with abortion rights activists challenging the constitutionality of the new state laws limiting access to the procedure. In *Webster v. Reproductive Health Services* (1989), the Supreme Court upheld the authority of state governments to limit the use of public funds and facilities for abortions. Then, in the important case of *Planned Parenthood of Southeastern Pennsylvania v. Casey* (1992), the Court upheld a law requiring a twenty-four-hour waiting period prior to an abortion. Surveying these and other decisions, a reporter suggested that 1989 was "the year the Court turned right," with a conservative majority ready and willing to limit or invalidate liberal legislation and legal precedents.

This observation was only partly correct. The Court was not yet firmly conservative. Although the *Casey* decision upheld certain restrictions on abortions, it affirmed the "essential holding" in *Roe v. Wade* (1973) that women had a constitutional right to control their reproduction. Justice David Souter, appointed to the Court by President George H. W. Bush in 1990, voted with Reagan appointees Sandra Day O'Connor and Anthony Kennedy to uphold *Roe*. Souter, like O'Connor, emerged as an ideologically moderate justice on a range of issues. Moreover, in a landmark decision, *Lawrence v. Texas* (2003), the Supreme Court limited the power of states to prohibit private homosexual activity between consenting adults and, more recently, in *Windsor v. United States* (2013) declared the Defense of Marriage Act unconstitutional. The Court had crept incrementally, rather than lurched, to the right while signaling its continued desire to remain within the broad mainstream of American public opinion.

## The Clinton Presidency, 1993–2001

The culture wars contributed to a new, divisive partisanship in national politics. Rarely in the twentieth century had the two major parties so adamantly refused to work together. Also rare was the vitriolic rhetoric that politicians used to describe their opponents. The fractious partisanship was filtered through — or, many would argue, created by — the new twenty-four-hour cable news television networks, such as Fox News and CNN. Commentators on these channels, finding that nothing drew viewers like aggressive partisanship, increasingly abandoned their roles as conveyors of information and became entertainers and provocateurs.

That divisiveness was a hallmark of the presidency of William Jefferson Clinton. In 1992, Clinton, the governor of Arkansas, styled himself a New Democrat who would bring Reagan Democrats and middle-class voters back to the party. Only forty-six, he was an energetic, ambitious policy wonk — extraordinarily well informed about the details of public policy. To win the Democratic nomination in 1992, Clinton had to survive charges that he embodied the permissive social values conservatives associated with the 1960s: namely, that he dodged the draft to avoid service in Vietnam, smoked marijuana, and cheated repeatedly on his wife. The charges were damaging, but Clinton adroitly talked his way into the presidential nomination: he had charisma and a way with words. For his running mate, he chose Albert A. Gore, a senator from Tennessee. Gore was about the same age as Clinton, making them the first baby-boom national ticket as well as the nation's first all-southern major-party ticket.

President George H. W. Bush won renomination over his lone opponent, the conservative columnist Pat Buchanan. The Democrats mounted an aggressive campaign that focused on Clinton's domestic agenda: he promised a tax cut for the middle class, universal health insurance, and a reduction of the huge Republican budget deficit. It was an audacious combination of traditional social-welfare liberalism and fiscal conservatism. For his part, Bush could not overcome voters' discontent with the weak economy and conservatives' disgust at his tax hikes. He received only 38.0 percent of the popular vote as millions of Republicans cast their ballots for independent businessman Ross Perot, who won more votes (19.0 percent) than any independent candidate since Theodore Roosevelt in 1912. With 43.7 percent of the vote, Clinton won the election (Map 31.3). Still, there were reasons for him to worry. Among all post–World War II presidents, only Richard Nixon (in 1969) entered the White House with a comparably small share of the national vote.

**New Democrats and Public Policy**   Clinton tried to steer a middle course through the nation's increasingly

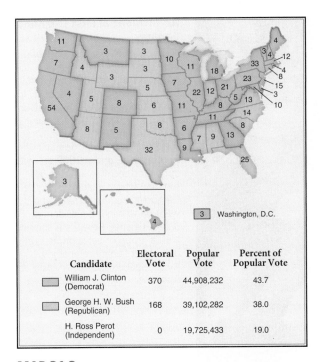

**MAP 31.3**

**The Presidential Election of 1992**

The first national election after the end of the Cold War focused on the economy, which had fallen into a recession in 1991. The first-ever all-southern Democratic ticket of Bill Clinton (Arkansas) and Al Gore (Tennessee) won support across the country but won the election with only 43.7 percent of the popular vote. The Republican candidate, President George H. W. Bush, ran strongly in his home state of Texas and the South, an emerging Republican stronghold. Independent candidate H. Ross Perot, a wealthy technology entrepreneur, polled an impressive 19.0 percent of the popular vote by capitalizing on voter dissatisfaction with the huge federal deficits of the Reagan-Bush administrations.

| Candidate | Electoral Vote | Popular Vote | Percent of Popular Vote |
|---|---|---|---|
| William J. Clinton (Democrat) | 370 | 44,908,232 | 43.7 |
| George H. W. Bush (Republican) | 168 | 39,102,282 | 38.0 |
| H. Ross Perot (Independent) | 0 | 19,725,433 | 19.0 |

major industrialized country that did not provide government-guaranteed health insurance to all citizens. It was an objective that had eluded every Democratic president since Harry Truman.

Recognizing the potency of Reagan's attack on "big government," Clinton's health-care task force—led by First Lady Hillary Rodham Clinton—proposed a system of "managed competition." Private insurance companies and market forces were to rein in health-care expenditures. The cost of this system would fall heavily on employers, and many smaller businesses campaigned strongly against it. So did the health insurance industry and the American Medical Association, powerful lobbies with considerable influence in Washington. By mid-1994, Democratic leaders in Congress declared that the Clintons' universal health-care proposal was dead. Forty million Americans, or 15 percent of the population, remained without health insurance coverage.

More successful was Clinton's plan to reduce the budget deficits of the Reagan-Bush presidencies. In 1993, Clinton secured a five-year budget package that would reduce the federal deficit by $500 billion. Republicans unanimously opposed the proposal because it raised taxes on corporations and wealthy individuals, and liberal Democrats complained because it limited social spending. But shared sacrifice led to shared rewards. By 1998, Clinton's fiscal policies had balanced the federal budget and begun to pay down the federal debt—at a rate of $156 billion a year between 1999 and 2001. As fiscal sanity returned to Washington, the economy boomed, thanks in part to the low interest rates stemming from deficit reduction.

**UNDERSTAND POINTS OF VIEW**

What made President Clinton a "New Democrat," and how much did his proposals differ from traditional liberal objectives?

**The Republican Resurgence**   The midterm election of 1994 confirmed that the Clinton presidency had not produced an electoral realignment: conservatives still had a working majority. In a well-organized campaign, in which grassroots appeals to the New Right dominated, Republicans gained fifty-two seats in the House of Representatives, giving them a majority for the first time since 1954. They also retook control of the Senate and captured eleven governorships. Leading the Republican charge was Representative Newt Gingrich of Georgia, who revived calls for significant tax cuts, reductions in welfare programs, anticrime initiatives, and cutbacks in federal regulations. These initiatives, which Gingrich promoted under the banner of a "**Contract with America**," had been central components

divisive partisanship. On his left was the Democratic Party's weakened but still vocal liberal wing. On his right were party moderates influenced by Reagan-era notions of reducing government regulation and the welfare state. Clinton's "third way," as he dubbed it, called for the new president to tailor his proposals to satisfy these two quite different—and often antagonistic—political constituencies. Clinton had notable successes as well as spectacular failures pursuing this course.

The spectacular failure came first. Clinton's most ambitious social-welfare goal was to provide a system of health care that would cover all Americans and reduce the burden of health-care costs on the larger economy. Although the United States spent a higher percentage of its gross national product (GNP) on medical care than any other nation, it was the only

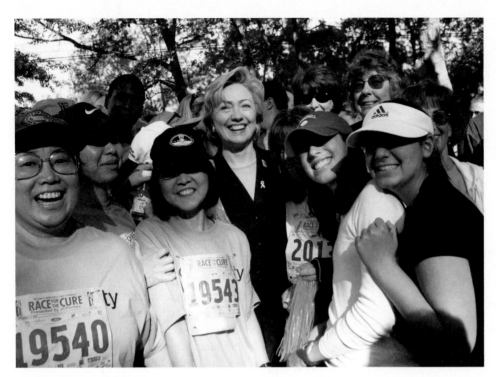

**An Influential First Lady and Senator**

Hillary Clinton was the most influential First Lady since Eleanor Roosevelt. But she had ambitions beyond being a political spouse. In 2000, and again in 2006, she won election to the U.S. Senate from New York. In 2008, she nearly captured the Democratic nomination for president, and in 2009 she was appointed secretary of state by the man who defeated her in the Democratic primaries (and who went on to win the presidency), Barack Obama. Here she is shown with a group of her supporters in one of her Senate campaigns. Photo by David Handschuh/NY Daily News Archive via Getty Images.

of the conservative-backed Reagan Revolution of the 1980s, but Gingrich believed that under the presidency of George H. W. Bush Republicans had not emphasized them enough.

In response to the massive Democratic losses in 1994, Clinton moved to the right. Claiming in 1996 that "the era of big government is over," he avoided expansive social-welfare proposals for the remainder of his presidency and sought Republican support for a centrist New Democrat program. The signal piece of that program was reforming the welfare system, a measure that saved relatively little money but carried a big ideological message. Many taxpaying Americans believed — with some supporting evidence — that the Aid to Families with Dependent Children (AFDC) program encouraged female recipients to remain on welfare rather than seek employment. In August 1996, the federal government abolished AFDC, achieving a long-standing goal of conservatives when Clinton signed the **Personal Responsibility and Work Opportunity Reconciliation Act**. Liberals were furious with the president.

**Clinton's Impeachment** Following a relatively easy victory in the 1996 election, Clinton's second term unraveled when a sex scandal led to his impeachment. Clinton denied having had a sexual affair with Monica Lewinsky, a former White House intern. Independent prosecutor Kenneth Starr, a conservative Republican, concluded that Clinton had committed perjury and obstructed justice and that these actions were grounds

for impeachment. Viewed historically, Americans have usually defined "high crimes and misdemeanors" — the constitutional standard for impeachment — as involving a serious abuse of public trust that endangered the republic. In 1998, conservative Republicans favored a much lower standard because they did not accept Clinton's legitimacy as president. They vowed to oust him from office for lying about an extramarital affair.

On December 19, the House of Representatives narrowly approved two articles of impeachment. Only a minority of Americans supported the House's action; according to a CBS News poll, 38 percent favored impeachment while 58 percent opposed it. Lacking public support, in early 1999 Republicans in the Senate fell well short of the two-thirds majority they needed to remove the president. But like Andrew Johnson, the only other president to be tried by the Senate, Clinton and the Democratic Party paid a high price for his acquittal. Preoccupied with defending himself, the president was unable to fashion a Democratic alternative to the Republicans' domestic agenda. The American public also paid a high price, because the Republicans' vendetta against Clinton drew attention away from pressing national problems.

## Post–Cold War Foreign Policy

Politically weakened domestically after 1994, Clinton believed he could nonetheless make a difference on the international stage. There, post–Cold War developments

**Bill Clinton**

President William (Bill) Clinton returned the Democratic Party to the White House after twelve years under Ronald Reagan and George H. W. Bush. Clinton was best known politically for what he called the *third way*, a phrase that described his efforts to craft policies that appealed to both liberals and moderates in his party. Here he signs the Welfare Reform Act of 1996 (officially the Personal Responsibility and Work Opportunity Reconciliation Act), which brought an end to the federal AFDC program that Democrats had created in 1935. AP Images.

gave him historic opportunities. The 1990s was a decade of stunning change in Europe and Central Asia. A great arc of newly independent states emerged as the Soviet empire collapsed. The majority of the 142 million people living in the former Soviet states were poor, but the region had a sizable middle class and was rich in natural resources, especially oil and natural gas.

Among the challenges for the United States was the question of whether to support the admission of some of the new states into the North Atlantic Treaty Organization (NATO) (Chapter 25). Many observers believed, with some justification, that extending the NATO alliance into Eastern Europe, right up to Russia's western border, would damage U.S-Russian relations. However, Czechoslovakia, Poland, and Hungary were also eager to become NATO members — an outcome that would draw into the Western alliance three nations that Stalin had decisively placed in the Soviet sphere of influence at the close of World War II. Clinton encouraged NATO admission for those three countries but stopped short of advocating a broader expansion of the alliance during his terms in office. Nonetheless, by 2010, twelve new nations — most of them in Eastern Europe — had been admitted to the NATO alliance. Nothing symbolized the end of the Cold War more than the fact that ten of those nations were former members of the Warsaw Pact.

**The Breakup of Yugoslavia**   Two of the new NATO states, Slovenia and Croatia, emerged from an intrac-

table set of conflicts that led to the dissolution of the communist nation of Yugoslavia. In 1992, the heavily Muslim province of Bosnia-Herzegovina declared its independence, but its substantial Serbian population refused to live in a Muslim-run multiethnic state. Slobodan Milosevic, an uncompromising Serbian nationalist, launched a ruthless campaign of "ethnic cleansing" to create a Serbian state. In November 1995, Clinton organized a NATO-led bombing campaign and peacekeeping effort, backed by 20,000 American troops, that ended the Serbs' vicious expansionist drive. Four years later, a new crisis emerged in Kosovo, another province of the Serbian-dominated Federal Republic of Yugoslavia. Again led by the United States, NATO intervened with air strikes and military forces to preserve Kosovo's autonomy. By 2008, seven independent nations had emerged from the wreckage of Yugoslavia.

**America and the Middle East**   No post–Cold War development proved more challenging than the emergence of radical Islamic movements in the Middle East. Muslim nations there had a long list of grievances against the West. Colonialism — both British and French — in the early decades of the twentieth century had been ruthless. A U.S.-sponsored overthrow of Iran's government in 1953 — and twenty-five years of

**PLACE EVENTS IN CONTEXT**

In what specific ways were foreign policy developments during the Clinton presidency evidence of the end of the Cold War?

American support for the Iranian shah—was also a sore point. America's support for Israel in the 1967 Six-Day War and the 1973 Yom Kippur War and its near-unconditional backing of Israel in the 1980s were particularly galling to Muslims. The region's religious and secular moderates complained about these injustices, but many of them had political and economic ties to the West, which constrained their criticism.

This situation left an opening for radical Islamic fundamentalists to build a movement based on fanatical opposition to Western imperialism and consumer culture. These groups interpreted the American presence in Saudi Arabia as signaling new U.S. colonial ambitions in the region. Clinton had inherited from President George H. W. Bush a defeated Iraq and a sizable military force—about 4,000 Air Force personnel—in Saudi Arabia. American fighter jets left Saudi Arabian air bases to fly regular missions over Iraq, enforcing a no-fly zone, where Iraqi planes were

forbidden, and bombing select targets. Clinton also enforced a UN-sanctioned embargo on all trade with Iraq, a policy designed to constrain Saddam Hussein's military that ultimately denied crucial goods to the civilian population. Angered by the continued U.S. presence in Saudi Arabia, Muslim fundamentalists soon began targeting Americans. In 1993, radical Muslim immigrants set off a bomb in a parking garage beneath the World Trade Center in New York City, killing six people and injuring more than a thousand. Terrorists used truck bombs to blow up U.S. embassies in Kenya and Tanzania in 1998, and they bombed the USS *Cole* in the Yemeni port of Aden in 2000.

The Clinton administration knew these attacks were the work of Al Qaeda, a network of radical Islamic terrorists organized by the wealthy Saudi exile Osama bin Laden. In February 1998, bin Laden had issued a call for holy war—a "Jihad against Jews and Crusaders," in which it was said to be the duty of every Muslim to

**Terrorists Bomb USS *Cole***

On October 12, 2000, a radical Muslim group with ties to Al Qaeda detonated a powerful bomb alongside the USS *Cole*, which was refueling in the port of Aden in Yemen. The explosion tore a large hole in the ship's hull, killing seventeen American sailors and injuring thirty-seven others. After repairs costing $250 million, the USS *Cole* returned to active duty in April 2002. AFP/Getty Images.

kill Americans and their allies. After the embassy attacks, Clinton ordered air strikes on Al Qaeda bases in Afghanistan, where an estimated 15,000 radical operatives had been trained since 1990. The strikes failed to disrupt this growing terrorist network, and when Clinton left office, the Central Intelligence Agency (CIA), the State Department, and the Pentagon were well aware of the potential threat posed by bin Laden's followers. That was where things stood on September 10, 2001.

# Into a New Century

In the second decade of the new century, Americans can reflect on two significant developments that have profoundly shaped their own day: the terrorist attack on the United States on September 11, 2001, and the election of the nation's first African American president, Barack Obama, on November 4, 2008. Too little time has passed for us to assess whether either event will be remembered as helping to define the twenty-first century. But both have indelibly marked our present. And both had distinct antecedents and still have profound implications.

## The Ascendance of George W. Bush

The 2000 presidential election briefly offered the promise of a break with the intense partisanship of the final Clinton years. The Republican nominee, George W. Bush, the son of President George H. W. Bush, pre-

sented himself as an outsider, deploring Washington partisanship and casting himself as a "uniter, not a divider." His opponent, Al Gore — Clinton's vice president — was a liberal policy specialist. The election of 2000 would join those of 1876 and 1960 as the closest and most contested in American history. Gore won the popular vote, amassing 50.9 million votes to Bush's 50.4 million, but fell short in the electoral college, 267 to 271. Consumer- and labor-rights activist Ralph Nader ran as the Green Party candidate and drew away precious votes in key states that certainly would have carried Gore to victory.

Late on election night, the vote tally in Florida gave Bush the narrowest of victories. As was their legal prerogative, the Democrats demanded hand recounts in several counties. A month of tumult followed, until the U.S. Supreme Court, voting strictly along conservative/liberal lines, ordered the recount stopped and let Bush's victory stand. Recounting ballots without a consistent standard to determine "voter intent," the Court reasoned, violated the rights of Floridian voters under the Fourteenth Amendment's equal protection clause. As if acknowledging the frailty of this argument, the Court declared that *Bush v. Gore* was not to be regarded as precedent. But in a dissenting opinion, Justice John Paul Stevens warned that the transparently partisan decision undermined "the Nation's confidence in the judge as an impartial guardian of the rule of law."

Although Bush had positioned himself as a moderate, countertendencies drove his administration from the start. His vice president, the uncompromising conservative Richard (Dick) Cheney, became, with Bush's

**The Contested Vote in Florida, 2000**
When the vote recount got under way in Palm Beach, Florida, in 2000, both sides brought out supporters to demonstrate outside the Supervisor of Elections Office, in hopes of influencing the officials doing the counting. In this photograph, supporters of George W. Bush clash with supporters of Al Gore after a rally on November 13, 2000, that had been addressed by Jesse Jackson, the dominant African American figure in the Democratic Party. © Reuters/Corbis.

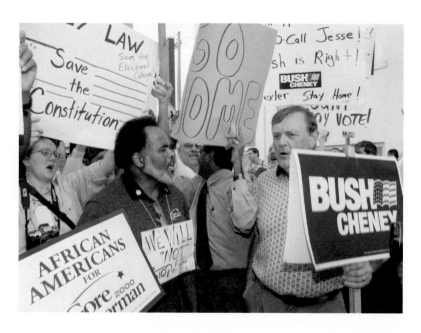

consent, virtually a copresident. Bush also brought into the administration his campaign advisor, Karl Rove, whose advice made for an exceptionally politicized White House. Rove foreclosed the easygoing centrism of Bush the campaigner by arguing that a permanent Republican majority could be built on the party's conservative base. On Capitol Hill, Rove's hard line was reinforced by Tom DeLay, the House majority leader, who in 1995 had declared "all-out war" on the Democrats. To win that war, DeLay pushed congressional Republicans to endorse a fierce partisanship. The Senate, although more collegial, went through a similar hardening process. After 2002, with Republicans in control of both Congress and the White House, bipartisan lawmaking came to an end.

**Tax Cuts**   The domestic issue that most engaged President Bush, as it had Ronald Reagan, was taxes. Bush's **Economic Growth and Tax Relief Act** of 2001 had something for everyone. It slashed income tax rates, extended the earned income credit for the poor, and marked the estate tax to be phased out by 2010. A second round of cuts in 2003 targeted dividend income and capital gains. Bush's signature cuts — those favoring big estates and well-to-do owners of stocks and bonds — skewed the distribution of tax benefits upward (Table 31.1). Bush had pushed far beyond any other postwar president, even Reagan, in slashing federal taxes.

Critics warned that such massive tax cuts would plunge the federal government into debt. By 2006, federal expenditures had

**COMPARE AND CONTRAST**

In what ways was George H. W. Bush a political follower of Ronald Reagan (Chapter 30)? In what ways was he not?

jumped 33 percent, at a faster clip than under any president since Lyndon Johnson. Huge increases in healthcare costs were the main culprit. Two of the largest federal programs, Medicare and Medicaid — health care for the elderly and the poor, respectively — could not contain runaway medical costs. Midway through Bush's second term, the national debt stood at over $8 trillion — much of it owned by foreign investors, who also financed the nation's huge trade deficit. On top of that, staggering Social Security and Medicare obligations were coming due for retiring baby boomers. It seemed that these burdens would be passed on to future generations (Figure 31.6).

**September 11, 2001**   How Bush's presidency might have fared in normal times is another of those unanswerable questions of history. As a candidate in 2000, George W. Bush had said little about foreign policy. He had assumed that his administration would rise or fall on his domestic program. But nine months into his presidency, an altogether different political scenario unfolded. On a sunny September morning, nineteen Islamic terrorists from Al Qaeda hijacked four commercial jets and flew two of them into New York City's World Trade Center, destroying its twin towers and killing more than 2,900 people. A third plane crashed into the Pentagon, near Washington, D.C. The fourth, presumably headed for the White House or possibly the U.S. Capitol, crashed in Pennsylvania when the passengers fought back and thwarted the hijackers. As an outburst of patriotism swept the United States in the wake of the September 11 attacks, George W. Bush proclaimed a "war on terror" and vowed to carry the battle to Al Qaeda.

**TABLE 31.1**

**Impact of the Bush Tax Cuts, 2001–2003**

| Income in 2003 | Taxpayers | Gross Income | Total Tax Cut | % Change in Tax Bill | Tax Bill | Tax Rate |
|---|---|---|---|---|---|---|
| Less than $50,000 | 92,093,452 | $19,521 | $435 | −48% | $474 | 2% |
| $50,000 to 100,000 | 26,915,091 | 70,096 | 1,656 | −21 | 6,417 | 9 |
| $100,000 to 200,000 | 8,878,643 | 131,797 | 3,625 | −17 | 18,281 | 14 |
| $200,000 to 500,000 | 1,999,061 | 288,296 | 7,088 | −10 | 60,464 | 21 |
| $500,000 to 1,000,000 | 356,140 | 677,294 | 22,479 | −12 | 169,074 | 25 |
| $1,000,000 to 10,000,000 | 175,157 | 2,146,100 | 84,666 | −13 | 554,286 | 26 |
| $10,000,000 or more | 6,126 | 25,975,532 | 1,019,369 | −15 | 5,780,926 | 22 |

SOURCE: *New York Times*, April 5, 2006.

**FIGURE 31.6**

**Gross Federal Debt as a Percentage of Gross Domestic Product**

Economists argue that the best measure of a nation's debt is its size relative to the overall economy— that is, its percentage of gross domestic product (GDP). The size of the total U.S. debt declined from its World War II high until the 1980s, when it increased dramatically under President Reagan. Since then, the debt has consistently increased as a percentage of GDP, aside from a small decline under President Clinton's deficit-reduction plans in the mid-1990s. Source: dshort.com.

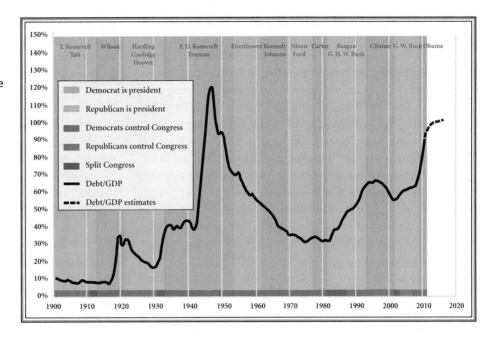

Operating out of Afghanistan, where they had been harbored by the fundamentalist Taliban regime, the elusive Al Qaeda briefly offered a clear target. In October 2001, while Afghani allies carried the ground war, American planes attacked the enemy. By early 2002, this lethal combination had ousted the Taliban, destroyed Al Qaeda's training camps, and killed or captured many of its operatives. However, the big prize, Al Qaeda leader Osama bin Laden, had retreated to a

mountain redoubt. Inexplicably, U.S. forces failed to press the attack, and bin Laden escaped over the border into Pakistan.

**The Invasion of Iraq**   On the domestic side, Bush declared the terrorist threat too big to be contained by ordinary law-enforcement means. He wanted the government's powers of domestic surveillance placed on a wartime footing. With little debate, in 2001 Congress

**September 11, 2001**

Photographers at the scene after a plane crashed into the north tower of New York City's World Trade Center on September 11 found themselves recording a defining moment in the nation's history. When a second airliner approached and then slammed into the building's south tower at 9:03 A.M., the nation knew this was no accident. The United States was under attack. Of the 2,843 people killed on that day, 2,617 died at the World Trade Center. Robert Clark/Institute Artist Management.

passed the **USA PATRIOT Act**, granting the administration sweeping authority to monitor citizens and apprehend suspected terrorists. On the international front, Bush used the war on terror as the premise for a new policy of preventive war. Under international law, only an imminent threat justified a nation's right to strike first. Now, under the so-called Bush doctrine, the United States lowered the bar. It reserved for itself the right to act in "anticipatory self-defense." In 2002, President Bush singled out Iran, North Korea, and Iraq — "an axis of evil" — as the targeted states.

Of the three, Iraq was the preferred mark. Officials in the Pentagon regarded Iraq as unfinished business, left over from the Gulf War of 1991. More grandly, they saw in Iraq an opportunity to unveil America's supposed mission to democratize the world. Iraqis, they believed, would abandon the tyrant Saddam Hussein and embrace democracy if given the chance. The democratizing effect would spread across the Middle East, toppling or reforming other unpopular Arab regimes and stabilizing the region. That, in turn, would secure the Middle East's oil supply, whose fragility Saddam's 1990 invasion of Kuwait had made all too clear. It was the oil, in the end, that was of vital interest to the United States (Map 31.4).

None of these considerations, either singly or together, met Bush's declared threshold for preventive war. So the president reluctantly acceded to the demand by America's anxious European allies that the United States go to the UN Security Council, which demanded that Saddam Hussein allow the return of the UN weapons inspectors expelled in 1998. Saddam surprisingly agreed. Nevertheless, anxious to invade Iraq for its own reasons, the Bush administration geared up for war. Insisting that Iraq constituted a "grave and gathering danger" and ignoring its failure to secure a second, legitimizing UN resolution, Bush invaded in March 2003. America's one major ally in the rush to war was Great Britain. Relations with France and Germany became poisonous. Even neighboring Mexico and Canada condemned the invasion, and Turkey, a key military ally, refused transit permission, ruining the army's plan for a northern thrust into Iraq. As for the Arab world, it exploded in anti-American demonstrations.

Within three weeks, American troops had taken the Iraqi capital. The regime collapsed, and its leaders went into hiding (Saddam Hussein was captured nine months later). But despite meticulous military planning, the Pentagon had made no provision for post-conflict operations. Thousands of poor Iraqis looted

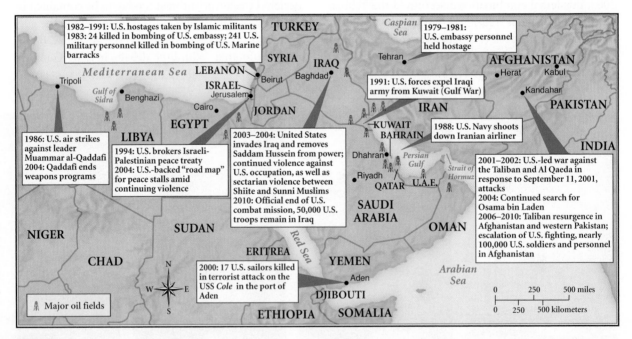

**MAP 31.4**

**U.S. Involvement in the Middle East, 1979–2010**

The United States has long played an active role in the Middle East, driven by the strategic importance of that region and, most important, by America's need to ensure a reliable supply of oil from the Persian Gulf states. This map shows the highlights of that troubled involvement, from the Tehran embassy hostage taking in 1979 to the invasion and current occupation of both Iraq and Afghanistan.

everything they could get their hands on, shattering the infrastructure of Iraq's cities and leaving them without reliable supplies of electricity and water. In the midst of this turmoil, an insurgency began, sparked by Sunni Muslims who had dominated Iraq under Saddam's Baathist regime.

Iraq's Shiite majority, long oppressed by Saddam, at first welcomed the Americans, but extremist Shiite elements soon turned hostile, and U.S. forces found themselves under fire from both sides. With the borders unguarded, Al Qaeda supporters flocked in from all over the Middle East, eager to do battle with the infidel Americans, bringing along a specialty of the jihad: the suicide bomber.

Blinded by their own nationalism, dominant nations tend to underestimate the strength of nationalism in other people. Lyndon Johnson discovered this in Vietnam. Soviet premier Leonid Brezhnev discovered it in Afghanistan. And George W. Bush rediscovered it in Iraq. Although it was hard for Americans to believe, Iraqis of all stripes viewed the U.S. forces as invaders. Moreover, in a war against insurgents, no occupation force comes out with clean hands. In 2004 in Iraq, that painful truth burst forth graphically in photographs showing American guards at Baghdad's **Abu Ghraib prison** abusing and torturing suspected insurgents. The ghastly images shocked the world. For Muslims, they offered final proof of American treachery. At that low point, in 2004, the United States had spent upward of $100 billion. More than 1,000 American soldiers had died, and 10,000 others had been wounded, many maimed for life. But if the United States pulled out, Iraq would descend into chaos. So, as Bush took to saying, the United States had to "stay the course."

**The 2004 Election**   As the 2004 presidential election approached, Rove, Bush's top advisor, theorized that stirring the culture wars and emphasizing patriotism and Bush's war on terror would mobilize conservatives to vote for Bush. Rove encouraged activists to place antigay initiatives on the ballot in key states to draw conservative voters to the polls; in all, eleven states would pass ballot initiatives that wrote bans on gay marriage equality into state constitutions that year. The Democratic nominee, Senator John Kerry of Massachusetts, was a Vietnam hero, twice wounded and decorated for bravery — in contrast to the president, who had spent the Vietnam years comfortably in the Texas Air National Guard. But when Kerry returned from service in Vietnam, he had joined the antiwar group Vietnam Veterans Against the War and in 1971 had delivered a blistering critique of the war to the Senate Armed Services Committee. In the logic of the culture wars, this made him vulnerable to charges of being weak and unpatriotic.

The Democratic convention in August was a tableau of patriotism, filled with waving flags, retired generals, and Kerry's Vietnam buddies. However, a sudden onslaught of slickly produced television ads by a group calling itself Swift Boat Veterans for Truth, falsely charging that Kerry had lied to win his medals, fatally undercut his advantage. Nor did it help that Kerry, as a three-term senator, had a lengthy record that was easily mined for hard-to-explain votes. Republicans tagged him a "flip-flopper," and the accusation, endlessly repeated, stuck. Nearly 60 percent of eligible voters — the highest percentage since 1968 — went to the polls. Bush beat Kerry, with 286 electoral votes to Kerry's 252. In exit polls, Bush did well among voters

**Abu Ghraib**

This image of one of the milder forms of torture experienced by inmates at the Abu Ghraib prison was obtained by the Associated Press in 2003. It shows a detainee bent over with his hands through the bars of a cell while being watched by a comfortably seated soldier. This photograph and others showing far worse treatment administered by sometimes jeering military personnel outraged many in the United States and abroad, particularly in the Muslim world. B.K. Bangash/AP Images.

for whom moral "values" and national security were top concerns. Voters told interviewers that Bush made them feel "safer." Bush was no longer a minority president. He had won a clear, if narrow, popular majority.

## Violence Abroad and Economic Collapse at Home

George Bush's second term was defined by crisis management. In 2005, Hurricane Katrina — one of the deadliest hurricanes in the nation's history — devastated New Orleans. Chaos ensued as floodwaters breached earthen barricades surrounding the city. Many residents remained without food, drinking water, or shelter for days following the storm, and deaths mounted — the final death toll stood at more than 2,000. Initial emergency responses to the catastrophe by federal and local authorities were uncoordinated and inadequate. Because the hardest-hit parts of the city were poor and African American, Katrina had revealed the poverty and vulnerability at the heart of American cities.

The run of crises did not abate after Katrina. Increasing violence and a rising insurgency in Iraq made the war there even more unpopular in the United States. In 2007, changes in U.S. military strategy helped quell some of the worst violence, but the war dragged into its fifth and sixth years under Bush's watch. A war-weary public grew impatient. Then, in 2008, the American economy began to stumble. By the fall, the Dow Jones Industrial Average had lost half its total value, and major banks, insurance companies, and financial institutions were on the verge of collapse. The entire automobile industry was near bankruptcy. Millions of Americans lost their jobs, and the unemployment rate surged to 10 percent. Housing prices dropped by as much as 40 percent in some parts of the country, and millions of Americans defaulted on their mortgages. The United States had entered the worst economic recession since the 1930s, what soon became known as the Great Recession — technically, the recession had begun in 2007, but its major effects were not felt until the fall of 2008.

The 2008 presidential election took shape in that perilous context. In a historically remarkable primary season, the Democratic nomination was contested between the first woman and the first African American to be viable presidential contenders, Hillary Rodham Clinton and Barack Hussein Obama. In a close-fought contest, Obama had emerged by early summer as the nominee.

Meanwhile, the Bush administration confronted an economy in free fall. In September, less than two months before the election, Secretary of the Treasury Henry Paulson urged Congress to pass the Emergency Economic Stabilization Act, commonly referred to as the bailout of the financial sector. Passed in early October, the act dedicated $700 billion to rescuing many of the nation's largest banks and brokerage houses. Between Congress's actions and the independent efforts of the Treasury Department and the Federal Reserve, the U.S. government invested close to $1 trillion in saving the nation's financial system.

## The Obama Presidency

During his campaign for the presidency against Republican senator John McCain, Barack Obama, a Democratic senator from Illinois, established himself as a unique figure in American politics. The son of an African immigrant-student and a young white woman from Kansas, Obama was raised in Hawaii and Indonesia, and he easily connected with an increasingly multiracial and multicultural America. A generation younger than Bill Clinton and George W. Bush, Obama (born in 1961) seemed at once a product of the 1960s, especially civil rights gains, and outside its heated conflicts.

Obama took the oath of office of the presidency on January 21, 2009, amid the deepest economic recession since the Great Depression and with the United States mired in two wars in the Middle East. From the podium, the new president recognized the crises and worried about "a nagging fear that America's decline is inevitable." But Obama also hoped to strike an optimistic tone. Americans, he said, must "begin again the work of remaking America."

**"Remaking America"**   A nation that a mere two generations ago would not allow black Americans to dine with white Americans had elected a black man to the highest office. Obama himself was less taken with this historic accomplishment — which was also part of his deliberate strategy to downplay race — than with developing a plan to deal with the nation's innumerable challenges, at home and abroad. With explicit comparisons to Franklin Roosevelt, Obama used the "first hundred days" of his presidency to lay out an ambitious agenda: an economic stimulus package of federal spending to invigorate the economy; plans to draw down the war in Iraq and refocus American military efforts in Afghanistan; a reform of the nation's health insurance system; and new federal laws to regulate Wall Street.

Remarkably, the president accomplished much of that agenda. The Democratic-controlled Congress

**Barack Obama**

In 2008, Barack Obama became the first African American president in U.S. history. And in 2012, he was reelected to a second term. Here, President Obama and First Lady Michelle Obama walk along Pennsylvania Avenue during his second inauguration. Chip Somodevilla/Getty Images.

elected alongside Obama passed the **American Recovery and Reinvestment Act**, an economic stimulus bill that provided $787 billion to state and local governments for schools, hospitals, and transportation projects (roads, bridges, and rail) — one of the largest single packages of government spending in American history. Congress next passed the Wall Street Reform and Consumer Protection Act, a complex law that added new regulations limiting the financial industry and new consumer protections. Political debate over both measures was heated. Critics on the left argued that Obama and Congress had been too cautious, given the scale of the nation's problems, while those on the right decried both laws as irresponsible government interference in private investment.

Political debate was fiercest, however, over Obama's health insurance reform proposal. Obama encouraged congressional Democrats to put forth their own proposals, while he worked to find Republican allies who might be persuaded to support the first major reform of the nation's health-care system since the introduction of Medicare in 1965. None came forward. Moreover, as debate dragged on, a set of far-right opposition groups, known collectively as the **Tea Party**, emerged. Giving voice to the extreme individualism and antigovernment sentiment traditionally associated with right-wing movements in the United States, the Tea Party rallied Americans against Obama's health-care bill. Despite the opposition, the legislation (officially called the **Patient Protection and Affordable Care Act**) passed,

and Obama signed it into law on March 23, 2010. However, political opposition and the powerful lobbying of the private health insurance industry ensured that the new law contained enough compromises that few could predict its long-term impact.

Following the legislative victories of his first two years in office, President Obama faced a divided Congress. Democrats lost control of the House of Representatives in 2010 and failed to regain it in 2012. With the legislative process stalled, Obama used executive authority to advance his broader, cautiously liberal, agenda. In 2011, for instance, the president repealed the military's "Don't Ask, Don't Tell" policy and ordered that gay men and lesbians be allowed to serve openly in the armed forces. And he made two appointments to the Supreme Court: Sonia Sotomayor in 2009, the first Latina to serve on the high court, and Elena Kagan in 2010. Both Sotomayor and Kagan are committed liberals, though they serve on a Court that has shifted to the right under Chief Justice John Roberts, a George W. Bush appointee.

### War and Instability in the Middle East

Even as he pursued an ambitious domestic agenda, Obama faced two wars in the Middle East that he inherited from his predecessor. Determined to end American occupation of Iraq, the president began in 2010 to draw down

**IDENTIFY CAUSES**

As the nation's first African American president, what kinds of unique challenges did Barack Obama face, and how did these issues impact his presidency?

troops stationed there, and the last convoy of U.S. soldiers departed in late 2011. The nine-year war in Iraq, begun to find alleged weapons of mass destruction, had followed a long and bloody arc to its end. Disengaging from Afghanistan proved more difficult. Early in his first term, the president ordered an additional 30,000 American troops to parts of the country where the Taliban had regained control — a "surge" he believed necessary to avoid further Taliban victories. Securing long-term political stability in this fractious nation, however, has eluded Obama. Leaving with the least damage done was his only viable option, and he pledged to withdraw all U.S. troops by 2014.

Meanwhile, a host of events in the Middle East deepened the region's volatility. In late 2010, a series of multicountry demonstrations and protests, dubbed the Arab Spring, began to topple some of the region's autocratic rulers. Leaders in Egypt, Tunisia, Libya, and Yemen were forced from power by mass movements calling for greater democracy. These movements, which the Obama administration has cautiously supported, continue to reverberate in more than a dozen nations in the Middle East. Not long after the Arab Spring was under way, in May 2011, U.S. Special Forces found and killed Osama bin Laden in Afghanistan, where he had been hiding for many years. Obama received much praise for the tactics that led to the discovery of bin Laden. More controversial has been the president's use of "drone" strikes to assassinate Al Qaeda leaders and other U.S. enemies in the region.

**Climate Change**   American wars and other involvement in the Middle East hinged on the region's centrality to global oil production. Oil is important in another sense, however: its role in climate change. Scientists have known for decades that the production of energy through the burning of carbon-based substances (especially petroleum and coal) increases the presence of so-called greenhouse gases in the atmosphere, warming the earth. Increasing temperatures will produce dramatically new weather patterns and rising sea levels, developments that threaten agriculture, the global distributions of plant and animal life, and whole cities and regions at or near the current sea level. How to halt, or at least mitigate, climate change has been one of the most pressing issues of the twenty-first century.

Arriving at a scientific consensus on climate change has proven easier than developing government policies to address it. This has been especially true in the United States, where oil company lobbyists, defenders of free-market capitalism, and conservatives who deny global warming altogether have been instrumental in

blocking action. For instance, the United States is not a signatory to the major international treaty — the so-called Kyoto Protocol — that is designed to reduce carbon emissions. Legislative proposals have not fared better. Cap-and-trade legislation, so named because it places a cap on individual polluters' emissions but allows those companies to trade for more emission allowances from low polluters, has stalled in Congress. Another proposal, a tax on carbon emissions, has likewise gained little political support. There is little doubt, however, that global climate change, and the role of the United States in both causing and mitigating it, will remain among the most critical questions of the next decades.

**Electoral Shifts**   It remains to be seen how the Obama presidency will affect American politics. From one vantage point, Obama looks like the beneficiary of an electoral shift in a liberal direction. Since 1992, Democrats have won the popular vote in five of the last six presidential elections, and in 2008 Obama won a greater share of the popular vote (nearly 53 percent) than either Clinton (who won 43 percent in 1992 and 49 percent in 1996) or Gore (48 percent in 2000). In his bid for reelection in 2012 against Republican nominee Mitt Romney, Obama won a lower percentage of the popular vote (51 percent) but still won by a comfortable margin of nearly 5 million votes. He won the support of 93 percent of African Americans, 71 percent of Hispanics, 73 percent of Asian Americans, 55 percent of women, and 60 percent of Americans under the age of thirty. His coalition was multiracial, heavily female, and young.

From another vantage point, any electoral shift toward liberalism appears contingent and fragile. Even with Democratic majorities in both houses of Congress that rivaled Franklin Roosevelt's in 1937 and Lyndon Johnson's in 1965, Obama in 2009–2010 was not able to generate political momentum for the kind of legislative advances achieved by those presidential forerunners. The history of Obama's presidency, and of the early twenty-first century more broadly, continues to unfold.

## SUMMARY

This chapter has stressed how globalization — the worldwide flow of capital, goods, and people — entered a new phase after the end of the Cold War. The number of multinational corporations, many of them based in the United States, increased dramatically, and people, goods, and investment capital moved easily across political boundaries. Financial markets, in particular, grew increasingly open and interconnected across the globe. Technological innovations strengthened the American economy and transformed daily life. The computer revolution and the spread of the Internet changed the ways in which Americans shopped, worked, learned, and stayed in touch with family and friends. Globalization facilitated the immigration of millions of Asians and Latin Americans into the United States.

In the decades since 1989, American life has been characterized by the dilemmas presented by the twin issues of globalization and divisive cultural politics. Conservatives spoke out strongly, and with increasing effectiveness, against multiculturalism and what they viewed as serious threats to "family values." Debates over access to abortion, affirmative action, and the legal rights of homosexuals intensified. The terrorist attacks of September 11, 2001, diverted attention from this increasingly bitter partisanship, but that partisanship was revived after President Bush's decision to invade Iraq (a nation not involved in the events of 9/11) in 2003 led to a protracted war. When Barack Obama was elected in 2008, the first African American president in the nation's history, he inherited two wars and the Great Recession, the most significant economic collapse since the 1930s. His, and the nation's, efforts to address these and other pressing issues — including the national debt and global climate change — remain ongoing, unfinished business after Obama's reelection in 2012.

# CHAPTER REVIEW

**MAKE IT STICK**   Go to **LearningCurve** to retain what you've read.

## TERMS TO KNOW   Identify and explain the significance of each term below.

### Key Concepts and Events

Al Qaeda (p. 1002)

globalization (p. 1004)

World Trade Organization (WTO) (p. 1004)

Group of Eight (G8) (p. 1009)

North American Free Trade Agreement (NAFTA) (p. 1010)

multinational corporations (p. 1010)

Advanced Research Projects Agency Network (ARPANET) (p. 1012)

World Wide Web (p. 1012)

culture war (p. 1012)

Immigration and Nationality Act (p. 1012)

multiculturalism (p. 1015)

Proposition 209 (p. 1015)

Operation Rescue (p. 1019)

Defense of Marriage Act (p. 1020)

*Webster v. Reproductive Health Services* (p. 1020)

*Planned Parenthood of Southeastern Pennsylvania v. Casey* (p. 1020)

*Lawrence v. Texas* (p. 1020)

Contract with America (p. 1021)

Personal Responsibility and Work Opportunity Reconciliation Act (p. 1023)

Economic Growth and Tax Relief Act (p. 1026)

USA PATRIOT Act (p. 1028)

Abu Ghraib prison (p. 1029)

American Recovery and Reinvestment Act (p. 1031)

Tea Party (p. 1031)

Patient Protection and Affordable Care Act (p. 1031)

### Key People

Osama bin Laden (p. 1024)

William (Bill) Clinton (p. 1020)

Hillary Rodham Clinton (p. 1022)

Newt Gingrich (p. 1021)

Monica Lewinsky (p. 1023)

George W. Bush (p. 1025)

Saddam Hussein (p. 1028)

Barack Obama (p. 1030)

## REVIEW QUESTIONS    Answer these questions to demonstrate your understanding of the chapter's main ideas.

1. What connections do you see between globalization and the "culture wars" of the 1990s?

2. In what ways has the United States's role in the world changed since the end of the Cold War? In what ways has it remained the same?

3. How did immigration to the United States in the last two decades of the twentieth century and the first decade of the twenty-first benefit the American economy but produce political backlash?

4. **THEMATIC UNDERSTANDING**   Review the events included on the thematic timeline on page 971. In what ways does the period between 1992 (Bill Clinton's election) and 2012 (Barack Obama's reelection) suggest a postliberal era in American politics? In what ways was the conservative resurgence under Reagan preserved, and in what ways was it not?

## MAKING CONNECTIONS    Recognize the larger developments and continuities within and across chapters by answering these questions.

1. **ACROSS TIME AND PLACE**   How would you compare the Iraq War with previous wars in U.S. history? Compare in particular the reasons for entering the war, support for the war abroad and at home, and the outcome of the conflict.

2. **VISUAL EVIDENCE**   What does the photograph on page 1011 convey about the technological and social changes that the digital revolution has wrought on American life?

## MORE TO EXPLORE    Start here to learn more about the events discussed in this chapter.

William Berman, *From the Center to the Edge: The Politics and Policies of the Clinton Presidency* (2001). An in-depth exploration of Clinton's politics and policies.

Richard A. Clarke, *Against All Enemies: Inside America's War on Terror* (2004). A critique of the war on terror from President Clinton's former chief counter-terrorism advisor.

Alfred Eckes Jr. and Thomas Zeilin, *Globalization and the American Century* (2003). Shows that globalization for the United States has a long history, at least to 1898.

Gertrude Himmelfarb, *One Nation, Two Cultures* (1999). A compelling explanation of the divisive politics of the 1990s.

Barack Obama, *Dreams from My Father: A Story of Race and Inheritance* (1995). The president's first memoir makes compelling reading.

See the September 11 Digital Archive at **911digitalarchive.org/** for oral histories and both still and moving images from September 11.

## TIMELINE   Ask yourself why this chapter begins and ends with these dates and then identify the links among related events.

| | |
|---|---|
| **1992** | • Democratic moderate Bill Clinton elected president<br>• *Planned Parenthood of Southeastern Pennsylvania v. Casey* |
| **1993** | • North American Free Trade Agreement (NAFTA)<br>• Clinton budget plan balances federal budget and begins to pay down federal debt |
| **1994** | • Clinton health insurance reform effort fails<br>• Republicans gain control of Congress |
| **1995** | • U.S. troops enforce peace in Bosnia |
| **1996** | • Personal Responsibility and Work Opportunity Reconciliation Act reforms welfare system |
| **1998** | • Bill Clinton impeached by House of Representatives<br>• Defense of Marriage Act |
| **1999** | • Clinton acquitted by Senate<br>• World Trade Organization (WTO) protests |
| **2000** | • George W. Bush wins contested presidential election |
| **2001** | • Bush tax cuts<br>• September 11: Al Qaeda terrorists attack World Trade Center and Pentagon<br>• Congress passes USA PATRIOT Act |
| **2002** | • United States unseats Taliban in Afghanistan<br>• President Bush declares Iran, North Korea, and Iraq an "axis of evil" |
| **2003** | • United States invades Iraq in March |
| **2004** | • Torture at Abu Ghraib prison becomes public<br>• President Bush wins reelection |
| **2007** | • Great Recession begins |
| **2008** | • Barack Obama elected president<br>• American Recovery and Reinvestment Act |
| **2010** | • Patient Protection and Affordable Care Act<br>• "Don't Ask, Don't Tell" military policy on homosexuality ended |
| **2011** | • Osama bin Laden killed by U.S. forces<br>• Last U.S. combat troops withdrawn from Iraq |
| **2013** | • Continued drawdown of U.S. forces in Afghanistan toward planned full exit by 2014 |

**KEY TURNING POINTS:** Based on the timeline, what were the major domestic and foreign policy challenges between the 1990s and 2013?

# Documents

## The Declaration of Independence

### In Congress, July 4, 1776,
### The Unanimous Declaration of the Thirteen United States of America

When in the Course of human events, it becomes necessary for one people to dissolve the political bands which have connected them with another, and to assume among the Powers of the earth, the separate and equal station to which the Laws of Nature and of Nature's God entitle them, a decent respect to the opinions of mankind requires that they should declare the causes which impel them to the separation.

We hold these truths to be self-evident, that all men are created equal, that they are endowed by their Creator with certain unalienable rights, that among these are Life, Liberty, and the pursuit of Happiness. That to secure these rights, Governments are instituted among Men, deriving their just powers from the consent of the governed. That whenever any Form of Government becomes destructive of these ends, it is the Right of the People to alter or to abolish it, and to institute new Government, laying its foundation on such principles and organizing its powers in such form, as to them shall seem most likely to effect their Safety and Happiness. Prudence, indeed, will dictate that Governments long established should not be changed for light and transient causes; and accordingly all experience hath shown, that mankind are more disposed to suffer, while evils are sufferable, than to right themselves by abolishing the forms to which they are accustomed. But when a long train of abuses and usurpations, pursuing invariably the same Object evinces a design to reduce them under absolute Despotism, it is their right, it is their duty, to throw off such Government, and to provide new Guards for their future security. — Such has been the patient sufferance of these Colonies; and such is now the necessity which constrains them to alter their former Systems of Government. The history of the present King of Great Britain is a history of repeated injuries and usurpations, all having in direct object the establishment of an absolute Tyranny over these States. To prove this, let Facts be submitted to a candid world.

He has refused his Assent to Laws, the most wholesome and necessary for the public good.

He has forbidden his Governors to pass Laws of immediate and pressing importance, unless suspended in their operation till his Assent should be obtained; and, when so suspended, he has utterly neglected to attend to them.

He has refused to pass other Laws for the accommodation of large districts of people, unless those people would relinquish the right of Representation in the Legislature, a right inestimable to them and formidable to tyrants only.

He has called together legislative bodies at places unusual, uncomfortable, and distant from the depository of their public Records, for the sole purpose of fatiguing them into compliance with his measures.

He has dissolved Representative Houses repeatedly, for opposing with manly firmness his invasions on the rights of the people.

He has refused for a long time, after such dissolutions, to cause others to be elected; whereby the Legislative powers, incapable of Annihilation, have returned to the People at large for their exercise; the State remaining in the mean time exposed to all the dangers of invasion from without and convulsions within.

He has endeavoured to prevent the population of these States; for that purpose obstructing the Laws of Naturalization of Foreigners; refusing to pass others to encourage their migrations hither, and raising the conditions of new Appropriations of Lands.

He has obstructed the Administration of Justice, by refusing his Assent to Laws for establishing Judiciary powers.

He has made Judges dependent on his Will alone, for the tenure of their offices, and the amount and payment of their salaries.

He has erected a multitude of New Offices, and sent hither swarms of Officers to harass our People, and eat out their substance.

He has kept among us, in times of peace, Standing Armies without the Consent of our legislature.

He has combined with others to subject us to a jurisdiction foreign to our constitution, and unacknowledged by our laws; giving his Assent to their Acts of pretended Legislation:

For quartering large bodies of armed troops among us:

For protecting them, by a mock Trial, from Punishment for any Murders which they should commit on the Inhabitants of these States:

For cutting off our Trade with all parts of the world:

For imposing taxes on us without our Consent:

For depriving us, in many cases, of the benefits of Trial by jury:

For transporting us beyond Seas to be tried for pretended offences:

For abolishing the free System of English Laws in a neighbouring Province, establishing therein an Arbitrary government, and enlarging its Boundaries so as to render it at once an example and fit instrument for introducing the same absolute rule into these Colonies:

For taking away our Charters, abolishing our most valuable Laws, and altering fundamentally the Forms of our Governments:

For suspending our own Legislatures, and declaring themselves invested with Power to legislate for us in all cases whatsoever.

He has abdicated Government here, by declaring us out of his Protection and waging War against us.

He has plundered our seas, ravaged our Coasts, burnt our towns, and destroyed the lives of our people.

He is at this time transporting large armies of foreign mercenaries to compleat the works of death, desolation, and tyranny, already begun with circumstances of Cruelty & perfidy scarcely paralleled in the most barbarous ages, and totally unworthy the Head of a civilized nation.

He has constrained our fellow Citizens taken Captive on the high Seas to bear Arms against their Country, to become the executioners of their friends and Brethren, or to fall themselves by their Hands.

He has excited domestic insurrections amongst us, and has endeavoured to bring on the inhabitants of our frontiers, the merciless Indian Savages, whose known rule of warfare, is an undistinguished destruction of all ages, sexes, and conditions.

In every stage of these Oppressions We have Petitioned for Redress in the most humble terms: Our repeated Petitions have been answered only by repeated injury. A Prince, whose character is thus marked by every act which may define a Tyrant, is unfit to be the ruler of a free people.

Nor have We been wanting in attention to our British brethren. We have warned them from time to time of attempts by their legislature to extend an unwarrantable jurisdiction over us. We have reminded them of the circumstances of our emigration and settlement here. We have appealed to their native justice and magnanimity, and we have conjured them by the ties of our common kindred to disavow these usurpations, which would inevitably interrupt our connections and correspondence. They too have been deaf to the voice of justice and of consanguinity. We must, therefore, acquiesce in the necessity, which denounces our Separation, and hold them, as we hold the rest of mankind, Enemies in War, in Peace Friends.

We, therefore, the Representatives of the United States of America, in General Congress, Assembled, appealing to the Supreme Judge of the world for the rectitude of our intentions, do, in the Name, and by Authority of the good People of these Colonies, solemnly publish and declare, That these United Colonies are, and of Right ought to be FREE AND INDEPENDENT STATES; that they are Absolved from all Allegiance to the British Crown, and that all political connection between them and the State of Great Britain, is and ought to be totally dissolved; and that as Free and Independent States, they have full Power to levy War, conclude Peace, contract Alliances, establish Commerce, and to do all other Acts and Things which Independent States may of right do. And for the support of this Declaration, with a firm reliance on the Protection of Divine Providence, we mutually pledge to each other our Lives, our Fortunes, and our sacred Honor.

### John Hancock

| | | | |
|---|---|---|---|
| Button Gwinnett | George Wythe | James Wilson | Josiah Bartlett |
| Lyman Hall | Richard Henry Lee | Geo. Ross | Wm. Whipple |
| Geo. Walton | Th. Jefferson | Caesar Rodney | Matthew Thornton |
| Wm. Hooper | Benja. Harrison | Geo. Read | Saml. Adams |
| Joseph Hewes | Thos. Nelson, Jr. | Thos. M'Kean | John Adams |
| John Penn | Francis Lightfoot Lee | Wm. Floyd | Robt. Treat Paine |
| Edward Rutledge | Carter Braxton | Phil. Livingston | Elbridge Gerry |
| Thos. Heyward, Junr. | Robt. Morris | Frans. Lewis | Step. Hopkins |
| Thomas Lynch, Junr. | Benjamin Rush | Lewis Morris | William Ellery |
| Arthur Middleton | Benja. Franklin | Richd. Stockton | Roger Sherman |
| Samuel Chase | John Morton | John Witherspoon | Sam'el Huntington |
| Wm. Paca | Geo. Clymer | Fras. Hopkinson | Wm. Williams |
| Thos. Stone | Jas. Smith | John Hart | Oliver Wolcott |
| Charles Carroll of Carrollton | Geo. Taylor | Abra. Clark | |

# The Constitution of the United States of America

## Agreed to by Philadelphia Convention, September 17, 1787
## Implemented March 4, 1789

We the People of the United States, in Order to form a more perfect Union, establish Justice, insure domestic Tranquility, provide for the common defence, promote the general Welfare, and secure the Blessings of Liberty to ourselves and our Posterity, do ordain and establish this Constitution for the United States of America.

## Article I

*Section 1.* All legislative Powers herein granted shall be vested in a Congress of the United States, which shall consist of a Senate and a House of Representatives.

*Section 2.* The House of Representatives shall be composed of Members chosen every second Year by the People of the several States, and the Electors in each State shall have the Qualifications requisite for Electors of the most numerous Branch of the State Legislature.

No Person shall be a Representative who shall not have attained to the Age of twenty-five Years, and been seven Years a Citizen of the United States, and who shall not, when elected, be an Inhabitant of that State in which he shall be chosen.

Representatives and direct Taxes shall be apportioned among the several States which may be included within this Union, according to their respective Numbers, *which shall be determined by adding to the whole Number of free Persons, including those bound to Service for a Term of Years, and excluding Indians not taxed, three fifths of all other Persons.** The actual Enumeration shall be made within three Years after the first Meeting of the Congress of the United States, and within every subsequent Term of ten Years, in such Manner as they shall by Law direct. The Number of Representatives shall not exceed one for every thirty Thousand, but each State shall have at Least one Representative; and *until such enumeration shall be made, the State of New Hampshire shall be entitled to chuse three, Massachusetts eight, Rhode Island and Providence Plantations one, Connecticut five, New York six, New Jersey four, Pennsylvania eight, Delaware one, Maryland six, Virginia ten, North Carolina five, South Carolina five, and Georgia three.*

When vacancies happen in the Representation from any State, the Executive Authority thereof shall issue Writs of Election to fill such Vacancies.

The House of Representatives shall chuse their Speaker and other Officers; and shall have the sole Power of Impeachment.

*Section 3.* The Senate of the United States shall be composed of two Senators from each State, *chosen by the Legislature thereof,*† for six Years; and each Senator shall have one Vote.

*Immediately after they shall be assembled in Consequence of the first Election, they shall be divided as equally as may be into three Classes. The Seats of the Senators of the first Class shall be vacated at the Expiration of the second Year, of the second Class at the Expiration of the fourth Year, and of the third Class at the Expiration of the sixth Year, so that one-third may be chosen every second Year; and if Vacancies happen by Resignation, or otherwise, during the Recess of the Legislature of any State, the Executive thereof may make temporary Appointments until the next Meeting of the Legislature, which shall then fill such Vacancies.*‡

No person shall be a Senator who shall not have attained to the Age of thirty Years, and been nine Years a Citizen of the United States, and who shall not, when elected, be an Inhabitant of that State for which he shall be chosen.

The Vice President of the United States shall be President of the Senate, but shall have no Vote, unless they be equally divided.

The Senate shall chuse their other Officers, and also a President pro tempore, in the absence of the Vice President, or when he shall exercise the Office of President of the United States.

The Senate shall have the sole Power to try all Impeachments. When sitting for that Purpose, they shall be on Oath or Affirmation. When the President of the United States is tried, the Chief Justice shall preside: And no Person shall be convicted without the Concurrence of two-thirds of the Members present.

Judgment in Cases of Impeachment shall not extend further than to removal from Office, and disqualification to hold and enjoy any Office of honor, Trust or Profit under the United States: but the Party convicted shall nevertheless be liable and subject to Indictment, Trial, Judgment and Punishment, according to Law.

*Note:* The Constitution became effective March 4, 1789. Provisions in italics are no longer relevant or have been changed by constitutional amendment.
*Changed by Section 2 of the Fourteenth Amendment.

†Changed by Section 1 of the Seventeenth Amendment.
‡Changed by Clause 2 of the Seventeenth Amendment.

*Section 4.* The Times, Places and Manner of holding Elections for Senators and Representatives, shall be prescribed in each State by the Legislature thereof; but the Congress may at any time by Law make or alter such Regulations, except as to the Places of Chusing Senators.

The Congress shall assemble at least once in every Year, and such Meeting *shall be on the first Monday in December, unless they shall by Law appoint a different Day.**

*Section 5.* Each House shall be the Judge of the Elections, Returns and Qualifications of its own Members, and a Majority of each shall constitute a Quorum to do Business; but a smaller number may adjourn from day to day, and may be authorized to compel the Attendance of absent Members, in such Manner, and under such Penalties, as each House may provide.

Each House may determine the Rules of its Proceedings, punish its Members for disorderly Behavior, and, with the Concurrence of two-thirds, expel a Member.

Each House shall keep a Journal of its Proceedings, and from time to time publish the same, excepting such Parts as may in their Judgment require Secrecy; and the Yeas and Nays of the Members of either House on any question shall, at the Desire of one-fifth of those Present, be entered on the Journal.

Neither House, during the Session of Congress, shall, without the Consent of the other, adjourn for more than three days, nor to any other Place than that in which the two Houses shall be sitting.

*Section 6.* The Senators and Representatives shall receive a Compensation for their Services, to be ascertained by Law, and paid out of the Treasury of the United States. They shall in all Cases, except Treason, Felony and Breach of the Peace, be privileged from Arrest during their Attendance at the Session of their respective Houses, and in going to and returning from the same; and for any Speech or Debate in either House, they shall not be questioned in any other Place.

No Senator or Representative shall, during the Time for which he was elected, be appointed to any civil Office under the Authority of the United States, which shall have been created, or the Emoluments whereof shall have been increased, during such time; and no Person holding any Office under the United States, shall be a Member of either House during his Continuance in Office.

*Section 7.* All Bills for raising Revenue shall originate in the House of Representatives; but the Senate may propose or concur with Amendments as on other Bills.

Every Bill which shall have passed the House of Representatives and the Senate, shall, before it becomes a Law,

*Changed by Section 2 of the Twentieth Amendment.

be presented to the President of the United States; If he approve he shall sign it, but if not he shall return it, with his Objections to that House in which it shall have originated, who shall enter the Objections at large on their Journal, and proceed to reconsider it. If after such Reconsideration two-thirds of that House shall agree to pass the Bill, it shall be sent, together with the Objections, to the other House, by which it shall likewise be reconsidered, and if approved by two-thirds of that House, it shall become a Law. But in all such Cases the Votes of both Houses shall be determined by Yeas and Nays, and the Names of the Persons voting for and against the Bill shall be entered on the Journal of each House respectively. If any Bill shall not be returned by the President within ten Days (Sundays excepted) after it shall have been presented to him, the Same shall be a Law, in like Manner as if he had signed it, unless the Congress by their Adjournment prevent its Return, in which Case it shall not be a Law.

Every Order, Resolution, or Vote to which the Concurrence of the Senate and the House of Representatives may be necessary (except on a question of Adjournment) shall be presented to the President of the United States; and before the Same shall take Effect, shall be approved by him, or being disapproved by him, shall be repassed by two-thirds of the Senate and House of Representatives, according to the Rules and Limitations prescribed in the Case of a Bill.

*Section 8.* The Congress shall have Power To lay and collect Taxes, Duties, Imposts and Excises, to pay the Debts and provide for the common Defence and general Welfare of the United States; but all Duties, Imposts and Excises shall be uniform throughout the United States;

To borrow money on the credit of the United States;

To regulate Commerce with foreign Nations, and among the several States, and with the Indian Tribes;

To establish an uniform Rule of Naturalization, and uniform Laws on the subject of Bankruptcies throughout the United States;

To coin Money, regulate the Value thereof, and of foreign Coin, and fix the Standard of Weights and Measures;

To provide for the Punishment of counterfeiting the Securities and current Coin of the United States;

To establish Post Offices and post Roads;

To promote the Progress of Science and useful Arts, by securing for limited Times to Authors and Inventors the exclusive Right to their respective Writings and Discoveries;

To constitute Tribunals inferior to the supreme Court;

To define and punish Piracies and Felonies committed on the high Seas, and Offenses against the Law of Nations;

To declare War, grant Letters of Marque and Reprisal, and make Rules concerning Captures on Land and Water;

To raise and support Armies, but no Appropriation of Money to that Use shall be for a longer Term than two Years;

To provide and maintain a Navy;

To make Rules for the Government and Regulation of the land and naval Forces;

To provide for calling forth the Militia to execute the Laws of the Union, suppress Insurrections and repel Invasions;

To provide for organizing, arming, and disciplining the Militia, and for governing such Part of them as may be employed in the Service of the United States, reserving to the States respectively, the Appointment of the Officers, and the Authority of training the Militia according to the discipline prescribed by Congress;

To exercise exclusive Legislation in all Cases whatsoever, over such District (not exceeding ten Miles square) as may, by Cession of particular States, and the acceptance of Congress, become the Seat of Government of the United States, and to exercise like Authority over all Places purchased by the Consent of the Legislature of the State in which the Same shall be, for the Erection of Forts, Magazines, Arsenals, dockYards, and other needful Buildings; — And

To make all Laws which shall be necessary and proper for carrying into Execution the foregoing Powers, and all other Powers vested by this Constitution in the Government of the United States, or in any Department or Officer thereof.

*Section 9.* The Migration or Importation of such Persons as any of the States now existing shall think proper to admit, shall not be prohibited by the Congress prior to the Year one thousand eight hundred and eight but a tax or duty may be imposed on such Importation, not exceeding ten dollars for each Person.

The privilege of the Writ of Habeas Corpus shall not be suspended, unless when in Cases of Rebellion or Invasion the public Safety may require it.

No Bill of Attainder or ex post facto Law shall be passed.

*No capitation, or other direct, Tax shall be laid, unless in Proportion to the Census or Enumeration herein before directed to be taken.* *

No Tax or Duty shall be laid on Articles exported from any State.

No Preference shall be given by any Regulation of Commerce or Revenue to the Ports of one State over those of another: nor shall Vessels bound to, or from, one State, be obliged to enter, clear, or pay Duties in another.

No Money shall be drawn from the Treasury, but in Consequence of Appropriations made by law; and a regular Statement and Account of the Receipts and Expenditures of all public Money shall be published from time to time.

*Changed by the Sixteenth Amendment.

No Title of Nobility shall be granted by the United States: And no Person holding any Office of Profit or Trust under them, shall, without the Consent of the Congress, accept of any present, Emolument, Office, or Title, of any kind whatever, from any King, Prince, or foreign State.

*Section 10.* No State shall enter into any Treaty, Alliance, or Confederation; grant Letters of Marque and Reprisal; coin Money; emit Bills of Credit; make any Thing but gold and silver Coin a Tender in Payment of Debts; pass any Bill of Attainder, ex post facto Law, or Law impairing the Obligation of Contracts, or grant any Title of Nobility.

No State shall, without the Consent of the Congress, lay any Imposts or Duties on Imports or Exports, except what may be absolutely necessary for executing its inspection Laws: and the net Produce of all Duties and Imposts, laid by any State on Imports or Exports, shall be for the Use of the Treasury of the United States; and all such Laws shall be subject to the Revision and Control of the Congress.

No State shall, without the Consent of the Congress, lay any duty of Tonnage, keep Troops, or Ships of War in time of Peace, enter into any Agreement or Compact with another State, or with a foreign Power, or engage in War, unless actually invaded, or in such imminent Danger as will not admit of delay.

## Article II

*Section 1.* The executive Power shall be vested in a President of the United States of America. He shall hold his Office during the Term of four Years, and, together with the Vice President, chosen for the same Term, be elected, as follows:

Each State shall appoint, in such Manner as the Legislature thereof may direct, a Number of Electors, equal to the whole Number of Senators and Representatives to which the State may be entitled in the Congress; but no Senator or Representative, or Person holding an Office of Trust or Profit under the United States, shall be appointed an Elector.

*The Electors shall meet in their respective States, and vote by Ballot for two Persons, of whom one at least shall not be an Inhabitant of the same State with themselves. And they shall make a List of all the Persons voted for, and of the Number of Votes for each; which List they shall sign and certify, and transmit sealed to the Seat of the Government of the United States, directed to the President of the Senate. The President of the Senate shall, in the Presence of the Senate and House of Representatives, open all the Certificates, and the Votes shall then be counted. The Person having the greatest Number of Votes shall be the President, if such Number be a Majority of the whole Number of Electors appointed; and if there be more than one who have such Majority, and have an equal Number of Votes, then the House of Representatives shall immediately chuse by*

*Ballot one of them for President; and if no Person have a Majority, then from the five highest on the List the said House shall in like Manner chuse the President. But in chusing the President, the Votes shall be taken by States, the Representation from each State having one Vote; a quorum for this Purpose shall consist of a Member or Members from two thirds of the States, and a Majority of all the States shall be necessary to a Choice. In every Case, after the Choice of the President, the Person having the greatest Number of Votes of the Electors shall be the Vice President. But if there should remain two or more who have equal Votes, the Senate shall chuse from them by Ballot the Vice President.**

The Congress may determine the Time of chusing the Electors, and the Day on which they shall give their Votes; which Day shall be the same throughout the United States.

No Person except a natural born Citizen, or a Citizen of the United States, at the time of the Adoption of this Constitution, shall be eligible to the Office of President; neither shall any Person be eligible to that Office who shall not have attained to the Age of thirty five Years, and been fourteen Years a Resident within the United States.

In Case of the Removal of the President from Office, or of his Death, Resignation, or Inability to discharge the Powers and Duties of the said Office, the same shall devolve on the Vice President, *and the Congress may by Law provide for the Case of Removal, Death, Resignation, or Inability, both of the President and Vice President, declaring what Officer shall then act as President, and such Officer shall act accordingly, until the Disability be removed, or a President shall be elected.†*

The President shall, at stated Times, receive for his Services a Compensation, which shall neither be increased nor diminished during the Period for which he shall have been elected, and he shall not receive within that Period any other Emolument from the United States, or any of them.

Before he enter on the Execution of his Office, he shall take the following Oath or Affirmation: — "I do solemnly swear (or affirm) that I will faithfully execute the Office of President of the United States, and will to the best of my Ability, preserve, protect and defend the Constitution of the United States."

*Section 2.* The President shall be Commander in Chief of the Army and Navy of the United States, and of the Militia of the several States, when called into the actual Service of the United States; he may require the Opinion, in writing, of the principal Officer in each of the executive Departments, upon any Subject relating to the Duties of their respective Offices, and he shall have Power to Grant Reprieves and Pardons for Offences against the United States, except in Cases of Impeachment.

He shall have Power, by and with the Advice and Consent of the Senate, to make Treaties, provided two thirds of the Senators present concur; and he shall nominate, and by and with the Advice and Consent of the Senate, shall appoint Ambassadors, other public Ministers and Consuls, Judges of the supreme Court, and all other Officers of the United States, whose Appointments are not herein otherwise provided for, and which shall be established by Law: but the Congress may by Law vest the Appointment of such inferior Officers, as they think proper, in the President alone, in the Courts of Law, or in the Heads of Departments.

The President shall have Power to fill up all Vacancies that may happen during the Recess of the Senate, by granting Commissions which shall expire at the End of their next Session.

*Section 3.* He shall from time to time give to the Congress Information of the State of the Union, and recommend to their Consideration such Measures as he shall judge necessary and expedient; he may, on extraordinary Occasions, convene both Houses, or either of them, and in Case of Disagreement between them, with Respect to the Time of Adjournment, he may adjourn them to such Time as he shall think proper; he shall receive Ambassadors and other public Ministers; he shall take Care that the Laws be faithfully executed, and shall Commission all the Officers of the United States.

*Section 4.* The President, Vice President and all civil Officers of the United States, shall be removed from Office on Impeachment for, and Conviction of, Treason, Bribery, or other high Crimes and Misdemeanors.

## Article III

*Section 1.* The judicial Power of the United States, shall be vested in one supreme Court, and in such inferior Courts as the Congress may from time to time ordain and establish. The Judges, both of the supreme and inferior Courts, shall hold their Offices during good Behaviour, and shall, at stated Times, receive for their Services a Compensation, which shall not be diminished during their Continuance in Office.

*Section 2.* The judicial Power shall extend to all Cases, in Law and Equity, arising under this Constitution, the Laws of the United States, and Treaties made, or which shall be made, under their Authority; — to all Cases affecting Ambassadors, other public Ministers and Consuls; — to all Cases of admiralty and maritime Jurisdiction; — to Controversies to which the United States shall be a Party; — to Controversies between two or more States; — *between a State and Citizens of another State;‡* — between Citizens of different States; — between Citizens of the same State claiming Lands under

---

*Superseded by the Twelfth Amendment.
†Modified by the Twenty-fifth Amendment.

‡Restricted by the Eleventh Amendment.

Grants of different States, and between a State, or the Citizens thereof, and foreign States, Citizens or Subjects.

In all Cases affecting Ambassadors, other public Ministers and Consuls, and those in which a State shall be Party, the supreme Court shall have original Jurisdiction. In all the other Cases before mentioned, the supreme Court shall have appellate Jurisdiction, both as to Law and Fact, with such Exceptions, and under such Regulations as the Congress shall make.

The trial of all Crimes, except in Cases of Impeachment, shall be by Jury; and such Trial shall be held in the State where said Crimes shall have been committed; but when not committed within any State, the Trial shall be at such Place or Places as the Congress may by Law have directed.

*Section 3.* Treason against the United States, shall consist only in levying War against them, or in adhering to their Enemies, giving them Aid and Comfort. No Person shall be convicted of Treason unless on the Testimony of two Witnesses to the same overt Act, or on Confession in open Court.

The Congress shall have Power to declare the Punishment of Treason, but no Attainder of Treason shall work Corruption of Blood, or Forfeiture except during the Life of the Person attainted.

## Article IV

*Section 1.* Full Faith and Credit shall be given in each State to the public Acts, Records, and judicial Proceedings of every other State. And the Congress may by general Laws prescribe the Manner in which such Acts, Records, and Proceedings shall be proved, and the Effect thereof.

*Section 2.* The Citizens of each State shall be entitled to all Privileges and Immunities of Citizens in the several States.

A Person charged in any State with Treason, Felony, or other Crime, who shall flee from Justice, and be found in another State, shall on demand of the executive Authority of the State from which he fled, be delivered up, to be removed to the State having Jurisdiction of the Crime.

*No Person held to Service or Labour in one State, under the Laws thereof, escaping into another, shall, in Consequence of any Law or Regulation therein, be discharged from such Service or Labour, but shall be delivered up on Claim of the Party to whom such Service or Labour may be due.** 

*Section 3.* New States may be admitted by the Congress into this Union; but no new State shall be formed or erected within the Jurisdiction of any other State; nor any State be formed by the Junction of two or more States, or parts of States, without the Consent of the Legislatures of the States concerned as well as of the Congress.

The Congress shall have Power to dispose of and make all needful Rules and Regulations respecting the Territory or other Property belonging to the United States; and nothing in this Constitution shall be so construed as to Prejudice any Claims of the United States, or of any particular State.

*Section 4.* The United States shall guarantee to every State in this Union a Republican Form of Government, and shall protect each of them against Invasion; and on Application of the Legislature, or of the Executive (when the Legislature cannot be convened) against domestic Violence.

## Article V

The Congress, whenever two-thirds of both Houses shall deem it necessary, shall propose Amendments to this Constitution, or, on the Application of the Legislatures of two-thirds of the several States, shall call a Convention for proposing Amendments, which, in either Case, shall be valid to all Intents and Purposes, as Part of this Constitution, when ratified by the Legislatures of three-fourths of the several States, or by Conventions in three-fourths thereof, as the one or the other Mode of Ratification may be proposed by the Congress; *Provided that no Amendment which may be made prior to the Year One thousand eight hundred and eight shall in any Manner affect the first and fourth Clauses in the Ninth Section of the first Article; and* that no State, without its Consent, shall be deprived of its equal Suffrage in the Senate.

## Article VI

All Debts contracted and Engagements entered into, before the Adoption of this Constitution, shall be as valid against the United States under this Constitution, as under the Confederation.

This Constitution, and the Laws of the United States which shall be made in Pursuance thereof; and all Treaties made, or which shall be made, under the Authority of the United States, shall be the supreme Law of the Land; and the Judges in every State shall be bound thereby, any Thing in the Constitution or Laws of any State to the Contrary notwithstanding.

The Senators and Representatives before mentioned, and the Members of the several State Legislatures, and all executive and judicial Officers, both of the United States and of the several States, shall be bound by Oath or Affirmation, to support this Constitution; but no religious Test shall ever be required as a Qualification to any Office or public Trust under the United States.

*Superseded by the Thirteenth Amendment.

## Article VII

The Ratification of the Conventions of nine States shall be sufficient for the Establishment of this Constitution between the States so ratifying the Same.

Done in Convention by the Unanimous Consent of the States present the Seventeenth Day of September in the Year of our Lord one thousand seven hundred and Eighty seven and of the Independence of the United States of America the Twelfth. In Witness whereof We have hereunto subscribed our Names.

**Go. Washington**
**President and deputy from Virginia**

*New Hampshire*
John Langdon
Nicholas Gilman

*Massachusetts*
Nathaniel Gorham
Rufus King

*Connecticut*
Wm. Saml. Johnson
Roger Sherman

*New York*
Alexander Hamilton

*New Jersey*
Wil. Livingston
David Brearley
Wm. Paterson
Jona. Dayton

*Pennsylvania*
B. Franklin
Thomas Mifflin
Robt. Morris
Geo. Clymer
Thos. FitzSimons
Jared Ingersoll
James Wilson
Gouv. Morris

*Delaware*
Geo. Read
Gunning Bedford jun
John Dickinson
Richard Bassett
Jaco. Broom

*Maryland*
James McHenry
Dan. of St. Thos. Jenifer
Danl. Carroll

*Virginia*
John Blair
James Madison, Jr.

*North Carolina*
Wm. Blount
Richd. Dobbs Spaight
Hu Williamson

*South Carolina*
J. Rutledge
Charles Cotesworth
    Pinckney
Pierce Butler

*Georgia*
William Few
Abr. Baldwin

# Amendments to the Constitution (Including the Six Unratified Amendments)

## Amendment I [1791]*

Congress shall make no law respecting an establishment of religion, or prohibiting the free exercise thereof; or abridging the freedom of speech, or of the press; or the right of the people peaceably to assemble, and to petition the Government for a redress of grievances.

## Amendment II [1791]

A well regulated Militia, being necessary to the security of a free State, the right of the people to keep and bear Arms shall not be infringed.

## Amendment III [1791]

No Soldier shall, in time of peace, be quartered in any house, without the consent of the Owner, nor in time of war, but in a manner to be prescribed by law.

## Amendment IV [1791]

The right of the people to be secure in their persons, houses, papers, and effects, against unreasonable searches and seizures, shall not be violated, and no Warrants shall issue, but upon probable cause, supported by Oath or affirmation, and particularly describing the place to be searched, and the persons or things to be seized.

## Amendment V [1791]

No person shall be held to answer for a capital or otherwise infamous crime, unless on a presentment or indictment of a Grand Jury, except in cases arising in the land or naval forces, or in the Militia, when in actual service in time of War or public danger; nor shall any person be subject for the same offence to be twice put in jeopardy of life or limb; nor shall be compelled in any criminal case to be a witness against himself, nor be deprived of life, liberty, or property, without due process of law; nor shall private property be taken for public use, without just compensation.

## Amendment VI [1791]

In all criminal prosecutions, the accused shall enjoy the right to a speedy and public trial, by an impartial jury of the State and district wherein the crime shall have been committed, which district shall have been previously ascertained by law, and to be informed of the nature and cause of the accusation; to be confronted with the witnesses against him; to have compulsory process for obtaining witnesses in his favor, and to have the Assistance of Counsel for his defence.

## Amendment VII [1791]

In suits at common law, where the value in controversy shall exceed twenty dollars, the right of trial by jury shall be preserved, and no fact tried by a jury, shall be otherwise reexamined in any Court of the United States, than according to the Rules of the common law.

## Amendment VIII [1791]

Excessive bail shall not be required, nor excessive fines imposed, nor cruel and unusual punishments inflicted.

## Amendment IX [1791]

The enumeration in the Constitution, of certain rights, shall not be construed to deny or disparage others retained by the people.

## Amendment X [1791]

The powers not delegated to the United States by the Constitution, nor prohibited by it to the States, are reserved to the States respectively, or to the people.

## *Unratified Amendment*

***Reapportionment Amendment (proposed by Congress September 25, 1789, along with the Bill of Rights)***

*After the first enumeration required by the first article of the Constitution, there shall be one Representative for every thirty thousand, until the number shall amount to one hundred, after which the proportion shall be so regulated by Congress, that there shall be not less than one hundred Representatives, nor less than one Representative for every forty thousand persons, until the number of Representatives shall amount to two hundred; after which the proportion shall be so regulated by Congress, that there shall not be less than two hundred Representatives, nor more than one Representative for every fifty thousand persons.*

## Amendment XI [1798]

The Judicial power of the United States shall not be construed to extend to any suit in law or equity, commenced or prosecuted against one of the United States by Citizens of another State, or by Citizens or subjects of any foreign state.

*The dates in brackets indicate when the amendment was ratified.

## Amendment XII [1804]

The Electors shall meet in their respective States and vote by ballot for President and Vice-President, one of whom, at least, shall not be an inhabitant of the same State with themselves; they shall name in their ballots the person voted for as President, and in distinct ballots the person voted for as Vice-President, and they shall make distinct lists of all persons voted for as President, and of all persons voted for as Vice-President, and of the number of votes for each, which lists they shall sign and certify, and transmit sealed to the seat of government of the United States, directed to the President of the Senate; — the President of the Senate shall, in the presence of the Senate and House of Representatives, open all the certificates and the votes shall then be counted; — The person having the greatest number of votes for President, shall be the President, if such number be a majority of the whole number of Electors appointed; and if no person have such majority, then from the persons having the highest numbers not exceeding three on the list of those voted for as President, the House of Representatives shall choose immediately, by ballot, the President. But in choosing the President, the votes shall be taken by States, the representation from each State having one vote; a quorum for this purpose shall consist of a member or members from two-thirds of the States, and a majority of all the States shall be necessary to a choice. And if the House of Representatives shall not choose a President whenever the right of choice shall devolve upon them, before *the fourth day of March* next following, then the Vice-President shall act as President, as in the case of the death or other constitutional disability of the President.* — The person having the greatest number of votes as Vice-President, shall be the Vice-President, if such number be a majority of the whole number of Electors appointed; and if no person have a majority, then from the two highest numbers on the list, the Senate shall choose the Vice-President; a quorum for the purpose shall consist of two-thirds of the whole number of Senators, and a majority of the whole number shall be necessary to a choice. But no person constitutionally ineligible to the office of President shall be eligible to that of Vice-President of the United States.

## Unratified Amendment

### Titles of Nobility Amendment (proposed by Congress May 1, 1810)

*If any citizen of the United States shall accept, claim, receive or retain any title of nobility or honor or shall, without the consent of Congress, accept and retain any present, pension,*

*office or emolument of any kind whatever, from any emperor, king, prince or foreign power, such person shall cease to be a citizen of the United States, and shall be incapable of holding any office of trust or profit under them, or either of them.*

## Unratified Amendment

### Corwin Amendment (proposed by Congress March 2, 1861)

*No amendment shall be made to the Constitution which will authorize or give to Congress the power to abolish or interfere, within any State, with the domestic institutions thereof, including that of persons held to labor or service by the laws of said State.*

## Amendment XIII [1865]

*Section 1.* Neither slavery nor involuntary servitude, except as a punishment for crime whereof the party shall have been duly convicted, shall exist within the United States, or any place subject to their jurisdiction.

*Section 2.* Congress shall have power to enforce this article by appropriate legislation.

## Amendment XIV [1868]

*Section 1.* All persons born or naturalized in the United States, and subject to the jurisdiction thereof, are citizens of the United States and of the State wherein they reside. No State shall make or enforce any law which shall abridge the privileges or immunities of citizens of the United States; nor shall any State deprive any person of life, liberty, or property, without due process of law; nor deny to any person within its jurisdiction the equal protection of the laws.

*Section 2.* Representatives shall be apportioned among the several States according to their respective numbers, counting the whole number of persons in each State, excluding Indians not taxed. But when the right to vote at any election for the choice of electors for President and Vice-President of the United States, Representatives in Congress, the Executive and Judicial officers of a State, or the members of the Legislature thereof, is denied to any of the *male* inhabitants of such State, being *twenty-one* years of age and citizens of the United States, or in any way abridged, except for participation in rebellion, or other crime, the basis of representation therein shall be reduced in the proportion which the number of such *male* citizens shall bear to the whole number of *male* citizens *twenty-one* years of age in such State.

*Section 3.* No person shall be a Senator or Representative in Congress, or Elector of President and Vice-President, or hold any office, civil or military, under the United States, or under any State, who, having previously taken an oath, as a member of Congress, or as an officer of the United States, or as a member of any State legislature, or as an executive or judicial officer of any State, to support the Constitution of the

---

*Superseded by Section 3 of the Twentieth Amendment.

United States, shall have engaged in insurrection or rebellion against the same, or given aid or comfort to the enemies thereof. Congress may, by a vote of two-thirds of each house, remove such disability.

*Section 4.* The validity of the public debt of the United States, authorized by law, including debts incurred for payment of pensions and bounties for services in suppressing insurrection or rebellion, shall not be questioned. But neither the United States nor any State shall assume or pay any debt or obligation incurred in aid of insurrection or rebellion against the United States, or any claim for the loss or emancipation of any slave; but all such debts, obligations, and claims shall be held illegal and void.

*Section 5.* The Congress shall have power to enforce, by appropriate legislation, the provisions of this article.

## Amendment XV [1870]

*Section 1.* The right of citizens of the United States to vote shall not be denied or abridged by the United States or by any State on account of race, color, or previous condition of servitude —

*Section 2.* The Congress shall have power to enforce this article by appropriate legislation.

## Amendment XVI [1913]

The Congress shall have power to lay and collect taxes on incomes, from whatever source derived, without apportionment among the several States, and without regard to any census or enumeration.

## Amendment XVII [1913]

*Section 1.* The Senate of the United States shall be composed of two Senators from each State, elected by the people thereof, for six years; and each Senator shall have one vote. The electors in each State shall have the qualifications requisite for electors of [voters for] the most numerous branch of the State legislatures.

*Section 2.* When vacancies happen in the representation of any State in the Senate, the executive authority of such State shall issue writs of election to fill such vacancies: Provided, that the Legislature of any State may empower the executive thereof to make temporary appointments until the people fill the vacancies by election as the Legislature may direct.

*Section 3. This amendment shall not be so construed as to affect the election or term of any Senator chosen before it becomes valid as part of the Constitution.*

## Amendment XVIII [1919; repealed 1933 by Amendment XXI]

*Section 1. After one year from the ratification of this article the manufacture, sale, or transportation of intoxicating liquors within, the importation thereof into, or the exportation thereof from the United States and all territory subject to the jurisdiction thereof, for beverage purposes, is hereby prohibited.*

*Section 2. The Congress and the several States shall have concurrent power to enforce this article by appropriate legislation.*

*Section 3. This article shall be inoperative unless it shall have been ratified as an amendment to the Constitution by the legislatures of the several States, as provided by the Constitution, within seven years from the date of the submission thereof to the States by the Congress.*

## Amendment XIX [1920]

*Section 1.* The right of citizens of the United States to vote shall not be denied or abridged by the United States or by any State on account of sex.

*Section 2.* Congress shall have the power to enforce this article by appropriate legislation.

## *Unratified Amendment*

### *Child Labor Amendment*
### *(proposed by Congress June 2, 1924)*

*Section 1. The Congress shall have power to limit, regulate, and prohibit the labor of persons under eighteen years of age.*

*Section 2. The power of the several States is unimpaired by this article except that the operation of State laws shall be suspended to the extent necessary to give effect to legislation enacted by Congress.*

## Amendment XX [1933]

*Section 1.* The terms of the President and Vice-President shall end at noon on the 20th day of January, and the terms of Senators and Representatives at noon on the 3rd day of January, of the years in which such terms would have ended if this article had not been ratified; and the terms of their successors shall then begin.

*Section 2.* The Congress shall assemble at least once in every year, and such meeting shall begin at noon on the 3rd day of January, unless they shall by law appoint a different day.

*Section 3.* If, at the time fixed for the beginning of the term of the President, the President-elect shall have died, the Vice-President-elect shall become President. If a President shall not have been chosen before the time fixed for the beginning of his term, or if the President-elect shall have failed to qualify, then the Vice-President-elect shall act as President until a President shall have qualified; and the Congress may by law provide for the case wherein neither a President-elect nor a Vice-President-elect shall have qualified, declaring who shall then act as President, or the manner in which one who is to act shall be selected, and such person shall act accordingly until a President or Vice-President shall have qualified.

*Section 4.* The Congress may by law provide for the case of the death of any of the persons from whom the House of Representatives may choose a President whenever the right of choice shall have devolved upon them, and for the case of the death of any of the persons from whom the Senate may choose a Vice-President whenever the right of choice shall have devolved upon them.

*Section 5.* Sections 1 and 2 shall take effect on the 15th day of October following the ratification of this article.

*Section 6.* This article shall be inoperative unless it shall have been ratified as an amendment to the Constitution by the Legislatures of three-fourths of the several States within seven years from the date of its submission.

## Amendment XXI [1933]

*Section 1.* The eighteenth article of amendment to the Constitution of the United States is hereby repealed.

*Section 2.* The transportation or importation into any State, Territory, or Possession of the United States for delivery or use therein of intoxicating liquors, in violation of the laws thereof, is hereby prohibited.

*Section 3.* This article shall be inoperative unless it shall have been ratified as an amendment to the Constitution by conventions in the several States, as provided in the Constitution, within seven years from the date of the submission thereof to the States by the Congress.

## Amendment XXII [1951]

*Section 1.* No person shall be elected to the office of the President more than twice, and no person who has held the office of President, or acted as President, for more than two years of a term to which some other person was elected President shall be elected to the office of President more than once. But this article shall not apply to any person holding the office of President when this Article was proposed by the Congress, and shall not prevent any person who may be holding the office of President, or acting as President, during the term within which this Article becomes operative from holding the office of President or acting as President during the remainder of such term.

*Section 2.* This article shall be inoperative unless it shall have been ratified as an amendment to the Constitution by the legislatures of three-fourths of the several States within seven years from the date of its submission to the States by the Congress.

## Amendment XXIII [1961]

*Section 1.* The District constituting the seat of Government of the United States shall appoint in such manner as the Congress may direct: A number of electors of President and Vice-President equal to the whole number of Senators and Representatives in Congress to which the District would be entitled if it were a State, but in no event more than the least populous State; they shall be in addition to those appointed by the States, but they shall be considered for the purposes of the election of President and Vice-President, to be electors appointed by a State; and they shall meet in the District and perform such duties as provided by the twelfth article of amendment.

*Section 2.* The Congress shall have the power to enforce this article by appropriate legislation.

## Amendment XXIV [1964]

*Section 1.* The right of citizens of the United States to vote in any primary or other election for President or Vice-President, for electors for President or Vice-President, or for Senator or Representative in Congress, shall not be denied or abridged by the United States or any State by reason of failure to pay any poll tax or other tax.

*Section 2.* The Congress shall have the power to enforce this article by appropriate legislation.

## Amendment XXV [1967]

*Section 1.* In case of the removal of the President from office or of his death or resignation, the Vice-President shall become President.

*Section 2.* Whenever there is a vacancy in the office of the Vice-President, the President shall nominate a Vice-President who shall take office upon confirmation by a majority vote of both Houses of Congress.

*Section 3.* Whenever the President transmits to the President pro tempore of the Senate and the Speaker of the House of Representatives his written declaration that he is unable to discharge the powers and duties of his office, and until he transmits to them a written declaration to the contrary, such powers and duties shall be discharged by the Vice-President as Acting President.

*Section 4.* Whenever the Vice-President and a majority of either the principal officers of the executive departments or of such other body as Congress may by law provide, transmit to the President pro tempore of the Senate and the Speaker of the House of Representatives their written declaration that the President is unable to discharge the powers and duties of his office, the Vice-President shall immediately assume the powers and duties of the office as Acting President.

Thereafter, when the President transmits to the President pro tempore of the Senate and the Speaker of the House of Representatives his written declaration that no inability exists, he shall resume the powers and duties of his office unless the Vice-President and a majority of either the principal officers of the executive department[s] or of such other body as Congress may by law provide, transmit within four days to the President pro tempore of the Senate and the Speaker of the House of Representatives their written declaration that the President is unable to discharge the powers and duties of his office. Thereupon Congress shall decide the issue, assembling within forty-eight hours for that purpose if not in session. If the Congress, within twenty-one days after receipt of the latter written declaration, or, if Congress is not in session, within twenty-one days after Congress is required to assemble, determines by two-thirds vote of both Houses that the President is unable to discharge the powers and duties of his office, the Vice-President shall continue to discharge the same as Acting President; otherwise, the President shall resume the powers and duties of his office.

## Amendment XXVI [1971]

*Section 1.* The right of citizens of the United States, who are eighteen years of age or older, to vote shall not be denied or abridged by the United States or by any State on account of age.

*Section 2.* The Congress shall have power to enforce this article by appropriate legislation.

## *Unratified Amendment*

***Equal Rights Amendment (proposed by Congress March 22, 1972; seven-year deadline for ratification extended to June 30, 1982)***

*Section 1. Equality of rights under the law shall not be denied or abridged by the United States or by any State on account of sex.*

*Section 2. The Congress shall have the power to enforce, by appropriate legislation, the provisions of this article.*

*Section 3. This amendment shall take effect two years after the date of ratification.*

## *Unratified Amendment*

***District of Columbia Statehood Amendment (proposed by Congress August 22, 1978)***

*Section 1. For purposes of representation in the Congress, election of the President and Vice President, and article V of this Constitution, the District constituting the seat of government of the United States shall be treated as though it were a State.*

*Section 2. The exercise of the rights and powers conferred under this article shall be by the people of the District constituting the seat of government, and as shall be provided by Congress.*

*Section 3. The twenty-third article of amendment to the Constitution of the United States is hereby repealed.*

*Section 4. This article shall be inoperative, unless it shall have been ratified as an amendment to the Constitution by the legislatures of three-fourths of the several states within seven years from the date of its submission.*

## Amendment XXVII [1992]

No law varying the compensation for the services of the Senators and Representatives, shall take effect, until an election of Representatives shall have intervened.

# Appendix

## The American Nation

### Admission of States into the Union

| State | Date of Admission | State | Date of Admission | State | Date of Admission |
|---|---|---|---|---|---|
| 1. Delaware | December 7, 1787 | 18. Louisiana | April 30, 1812 | 35. West Virginia | June 20, 1863 |
| 2. Pennsylvania | December 12, 1787 | 19. Indiana | December 11, 1816 | 36. Nevada | October 31, 1864 |
| 3. New Jersey | December 18, 1787 | 20. Mississippi | December 10, 1817 | 37. Nebraska | March 1, 1867 |
| 4. Georgia | January 2, 1788 | 21. Illinois | December 3, 1818 | 38. Colorado | August 1, 1876 |
| 5. Connecticut | January 9, 1788 | 22. Alabama | December 14, 1819 | 39. North Dakota | November 2, 1889 |
| 6. Massachusetts | February 6, 1788 | 23. Maine | March 15, 1820 | 40. South Dakota | November 2, 1889 |
| 7. Maryland | April 28, 1788 | 24. Missouri | August 10, 1821 | 41. Montana | November 8, 1889 |
| 8. South Carolina | May 23, 1788 | 25. Arkansas | June 15, 1836 | 42. Washington | November 11, 1889 |
| 9. New Hampshire | June 21, 1788 | 26. Michigan | January 26, 1837 | 43. Idaho | July 3, 1890 |
| 10. Virginia | June 25, 1788 | 27. Florida | March 3, 1845 | 44. Wyoming | July 10, 1890 |
| 11. New York | July 26, 1788 | 28. Texas | December 29, 1845 | 45. Utah | January 4, 1896 |
| 12. North Carolina | November 21, 1789 | 29. Iowa | December 28, 1846 | 46. Oklahoma | November 16, 1907 |
| 13. Rhode Island | May 29, 1790 | 30. Wisconsin | May 29, 1848 | 47. New Mexico | January 6, 1912 |
| 14. Vermont | March 4, 1791 | 31. California | September 9, 1850 | 48. Arizona | February 14, 1912 |
| 15. Kentucky | June 1, 1792 | 32. Minnesota | May 11, 1858 | 49. Alaska | January 3, 1959 |
| 16. Tennessee | June 1, 1796 | 33. Oregon | February 14, 1859 | 50. Hawaii | August 21, 1959 |
| 17. Ohio | March 1, 1803 | 34. Kansas | January 29, 1861 | | |

### Presidential Elections

| Year | Candidates | Parties | Percentage of Popular Vote* | Electoral Vote |
|---|---|---|---|---|
| 1789 | **George Washington** | No party designations | | 69 |
| | John Adams† | | | 34 |
| | Other candidates | | | 35 |
| 1792 | **George Washington** | No party designations | | 132 |
| | John Adams | | | 77 |
| | George Clinton | | | 50 |
| | Other candidates | | | 5 |

SOURCES: U.S. Bureau of the Census, *Historical Statistics of the United States, Colonial Times to 1970* (1975); *Statistical Abstract of the United States, 2001*; *Statistical Abstract of the United States, 2006*.

*Prior to 1824, most presidential electors were chosen by state legislators rather than by popular vote. For elections after 1824, candidates receiving less than 1.0 percent of the popular vote have been omitted from this chart. Hence the popular vote does not total 100 percent for all elections.

†Before the Twelfth Amendment was passed in 1804, the electoral college voted for two presidential candidates; the runner-up became vice president.

| Year | Candidates | Parties | Percentage of Popular Vote | Electoral Vote |
|------|-----------|---------|---------------------------|----------------|
| 1796 | **John Adams** | Federalist | | 71 |
| | Thomas Jefferson | Democratic-Republican | | 68 |
| | Thomas Pinckney | Federalist | | 59 |
| | Aaron Burr | Democratic-Republican | | 30 |
| | Other candidates | | | 48 |
| 1800 | **Thomas Jefferson** | Democratic-Republican | | 73 |
| | Aaron Burr | Democratic-Republican | | 73 |
| | John Adams | Federalist | | 65 |
| | Charles C. Pinckney | Federalist | | 64 |
| | John Jay | Federalist | | 1 |
| 1804 | **Thomas Jefferson** | Democratic-Republican | | 162 |
| | Charles C. Pinckney | Federalist | | 14 |
| 1808 | **James Madison** | Democratic-Republican | | 122 |
| | Charles C. Pinckney | Federalist | | 47 |
| | George Clinton | Democratic-Republican | | 6 |
| 1812 | **James Madison** | Democratic-Republican | | 128 |
| | DeWitt Clinton | Federalist | | 89 |
| 1816 | **James Monroe** | Democratic-Republican | | 183 |
| | Rufus King | Federalist | | 34 |
| 1820 | **James Monroe** | Democratic-Republican | | 231 |
| | John Quincy Adams | Independent Republican | | 1 |
| 1824 | **John Quincy Adams** | Democratic-Republican | 30.5 | 84 |
| | Andrew Jackson | Democratic-Republican | 43.1 | 99 |
| | Henry Clay | Democratic-Republican | 13.2 | 37 |
| | William H. Crawford | Democratic-Republican | 13.1 | 41 |
| 1828 | **Andrew Jackson** | Democratic | 56.0 | 178 |
| | John Quincy Adams | National Republican | 44.0 | 83 |
| 1832 | **Andrew Jackson** | Democratic | 54.5 | 219 |
| | Henry Clay | National Republican | 37.5 | 49 |
| | William Wirt | Anti-Masonic | 8.0 | 7 |
| | John Floyd | Democratic | ‡ | 11 |
| 1836 | **Martin Van Buren** | Democratic | 50.9 | 170 |
| | William H. Harrison | Whig | 49.1 | 73 |
| | Hugh L. White | Whig | | 26 |
| | Daniel Webster | Whig | | 14 |
| | W. P. Mangum | Whig | | 11 |
| 1840 | **William H. Harrison** | Whig | 53.1 | 234 |
| | Martin Van Buren | Democratic | 46.9 | 60 |
| 1844 | **James K. Polk** | Democratic | 49.6 | 170 |
| | Henry Clay | Whig | 48.1 | 105 |
| | James G. Birney | Liberty | 2.3 | |
| 1848 | **Zachary Taylor** | Whig | 47.4 | 163 |
| | Lewis Cass | Democratic | 42.5 | 127 |
| | Martin Van Buren | Free Soil | 10.1 | |

‡Independent Democrat John Floyd received the 11 electoral votes of South Carolina; that state's presidential electors were still chosen by its legislature, not by popular vote.

| Year | Candidates | Parties | Percentage of Popular Vote | Electoral Vote |
|------|-----------|---------|----------------------------|----------------|
| 1852 | **Franklin Pierce** | Democratic | 50.9 | 254 |
|      | Winfield Scott | Whig | 44.1 | 42 |
|      | John P. Hale | Free Soil | 5.0 | |
| 1856 | **James Buchanan** | Democratic | 45.3 | 174 |
|      | John C. Frémont | Republican | 33.1 | 114 |
|      | Millard Fillmore | American | 21.6 | 8 |
| 1860 | **Abraham Lincoln** | Republican | 39.8 | 180 |
|      | Stephen A. Douglas | Democratic | 29.5 | 12 |
|      | John C. Breckinridge | Democratic | 18.1 | 72 |
|      | John Bell | Constitutional Union | 12.6 | 39 |
| 1864 | **Abraham Lincoln** | Republican | 55.0 | 212 |
|      | George B. McClellan | Democratic | 45.0 | 21 |
| 1868 | **Ulysses S. Grant** | Republican | 52.7 | 214 |
|      | Horatio Seymour | Democratic | 47.3 | 80 |
| 1872 | **Ulysses S. Grant** | Republican | 55.6 | 286 |
|      | Horace Greeley | Democratic | 43.9 | |
| 1876 | **Rutherford B. Hayes** | Republican | 48.0 | 185 |
|      | Samuel J. Tilden | Democratic | 51.0 | 184 |
| 1880 | **James A. Garfield** | Republican | 48.5 | 214 |
|      | Winfield S. Hancock | Democratic | 48.1 | 155 |
|      | James B. Weaver | Greenback-Labor | 3.4 | |
| 1884 | **Grover Cleveland** | Democratic | 48.5 | 219 |
|      | James G. Blaine | Republican | 48.2 | 182 |
|      | Benjamin F. Butler | Greenback-Labor | 1.8 | |
|      | John P. St. John | Prohibition | 1.5 | |
| 1888 | **Benjamin Harrison** | Republican | 47.9 | 233 |
|      | Grover Cleveland | Democratic | 48.6 | 168 |
|      | Clinton P. Fisk | Prohibition | 2.2 | |
|      | Anson J. Streeter | Union Labor | 1.3 | |
| 1892 | **Grover Cleveland** | Democratic | 46.1 | 277 |
|      | Benjamin Harrison | Republican | 43.0 | 145 |
|      | James B. Weaver | People's | 8.5 | 22 |
|      | John Bidwell | Prohibition | 2.2 | |
| 1896 | **William McKinley** | Republican | 51.1 | 271 |
|      | William J. Bryan | Democratic | 47.7 | 176 |
| 1900 | **William McKinley** | Republican | 51.7 | 292 |
|      | William J. Bryan | Democratic; Populist | 45.5 | 155 |
|      | John C. Wooley | Prohibition | 1.5 | |
| 1904 | **Theodore Roosevelt** | Republican | 57.4 | 336 |
|      | Alton B. Parker | Democratic | 37.6 | 140 |
|      | Eugene V. Debs | Socialist | 3.0 | |
|      | Silas C. Swallow | Prohibition | 1.9 | |
| 1908 | **William H. Taft** | Republican | 51.6 | 321 |
|      | William J. Bryan | Democratic | 43.1 | 162 |
|      | Eugene V. Debs | Socialist | 2.8 | |
|      | Eugene W. Chafin | Prohibition | 1.7 | |

| Year | Candidates | Parties | Percentage of Popular Vote | Electoral Vote |
|------|-----------|---------|---------------------------|----------------|
| 1912 | **Woodrow Wilson** | Democratic | 41.9 | 435 |
|      | Theodore Roosevelt | Progressive | 27.4 | 88 |
|      | William H. Taft | Republican | 23.2 | 8 |
|      | Eugene V. Debs | Socialist | 6.0 | |
|      | Eugene W. Chafin | Prohibition | 1.4 | |
| 1916 | **Woodrow Wilson** | Democratic | 49.4 | 277 |
|      | Charles E. Hughes | Republican | 46.2 | 254 |
|      | A. L. Benson | Socialist | 3.2 | |
|      | J. Frank Hanly | Prohibition | 1.2 | |
| 1920 | **Warren G. Harding** | Republican | 60.4 | 404 |
|      | James M. Cox | Democratic | 34.2 | 127 |
|      | Eugene V. Debs | Socialist | 3.4 | |
|      | P. P. Christensen | Farmer-Labor | 1.0 | |
| 1924 | **Calvin Coolidge** | Republican | 54.0 | 382 |
|      | John W. Davis | Democratic | 28.8 | 136 |
|      | Robert M. La Follette | Progressive | 16.6 | 13 |
| 1928 | **Herbert C. Hoover** | Republican | 58.2 | 444 |
|      | Alfred E. Smith | Democratic | 40.9 | 87 |
| 1932 | **Franklin D. Roosevelt** | Democratic | 57.4 | 472 |
|      | Herbert C. Hoover | Republican | 39.7 | 59 |
|      | Norman Thomas | Socialist | 2.2 | |
| 1936 | **Franklin D. Roosevelt** | Democratic | 60.8 | 523 |
|      | Alfred M. Landon | Republican | 36.5 | 8 |
|      | William Lemke | Union | 1.9 | |
| 1940 | **Franklin D. Roosevelt** | Democratic | 54.8 | 449 |
|      | Wendell L. Willkie | Republican | 44.8 | 82 |
| 1944 | **Franklin D. Roosevelt** | Democratic | 53.5 | 432 |
|      | Thomas E. Dewey | Republican | 46.0 | 99 |
| 1948 | **Harry S. Truman** | Democratic | 49.6 | 303 |
|      | Thomas E. Dewey | Republican | 45.1 | 189 |
|      | J. Strom Thurmond | States' Rights | 2.4 | |
|      | Henry Wallace | Progressive | 2.4 | |
| 1952 | **Dwight D. Eisenhower** | Republican | 55.1 | 442 |
|      | Adlai E. Stevenson | Democratic | 44.4 | 89 |
| 1956 | **Dwight D. Eisenhower** | Republican | 57.6 | 457 |
|      | Adlai E. Stevenson | Democratic | 42.1 | 73 |
| 1960 | **John F. Kennedy** | Democratic | 49.7 | 303 |
|      | Richard M. Nixon | Republican | 49.5 | 219 |
| 1964 | **Lyndon B. Johnson** | Democratic | 61.1 | 486 |
|      | Barry M. Goldwater | Republican | 38.5 | 52 |
| 1968 | **Richard M. Nixon** | Republican | 43.4 | 301 |
|      | Hubert H. Humphrey | Democratic | 42.7 | 191 |
|      | George C. Wallace | American Independent | 13.5 | 46 |

| Year | Candidates | Parties | Percentage of Popular Vote | Electoral Vote |
|------|-----------|---------|---------------------------|----------------|
| 1972 | **Richard M. Nixon** | Republican | 60.7 | 520 |
|      | George S. McGovern | Democratic | 37.5 | 17 |
|      | John G. Schmitz | American | 1.4 | |
| 1976 | **Jimmy Carter** | Democratic | 50.1 | 297 |
|      | Gerald R. Ford | Republican | 48.0 | 240 |
| 1980 | **Ronald W. Reagan** | Republican | 50.7 | 489 |
|      | Jimmy Carter | Democratic | 41.0 | 49 |
|      | John B. Anderson | Independent | 6.6 | 0 |
|      | Ed Clark | Libertarian | 1.1 | |
| 1984 | **Ronald W. Reagan** | Republican | 58.4 | 525 |
|      | Walter F. Mondale | Democratic | 41.6 | 13 |
| 1988 | **George H. W. Bush** | Republican | 53.4 | 426 |
|      | Michael Dukakis | Democratic | 45.6 | 111* |
| 1992 | **Bill Clinton** | Democratic | 43.7 | 370 |
|      | George H. W. Bush | Republican | 38.0 | 168 |
|      | H. Ross Perot | Independent | 19.0 | 0 |
| 1996 | **Bill Clinton** | Democratic | 49 | 379 |
|      | Robert J. Dole | Republican | 41 | 159 |
|      | H. Ross Perot | Reform | 8 | 0 |
| 2000 | **George W. Bush** | Republican | 47.8 | 271 |
|      | Albert Gore | Democratic | 48.4 | 267 |
|      | Ralph Nader | Green | 2.7 | 0 |
| 2004 | **George W. Bush** | Republican | 50.7 | 286 |
|      | John Kerry | Democratic | 48.3 | 252 |
| 2008 | **Barack Obama** | Democratic | 52.9 | 365 |
|      | John McCain | Republican | 45.7 | 173 |
| 2012 | **Barack Obama** | Democratic | 51 | 332 |
|      | Mitt Romney | Republican | 41.2 | 206 |

*One Dukakis elector cast a vote for Lloyd Bentsen.

## Population Growth*

| Year | Population | Percentage Increase | Year | Population | Percentage Increase |
|------|-----------|--------------------|------|-----------|--------------------|
| 1610 | 350 | — | 1820 | 9,638,453 | 33.1 |
| 1620 | 2,300 | 557.1 | 1830 | 12,866,020 | 33.5 |
| 1630 | 4,600 | 100.0 | 1840 | 17,069,453 | 32.7 |
| 1640 | 26,600 | 478.3 | 1850 | 23,191,876 | 35.9 |
| 1650 | 50,400 | 90.8 | 1860 | 31,443,321 | 35.6 |
| 1660 | 75,100 | 49.0 | 1870 | 39,818,449 | 26.6 |
| 1670 | 111,900 | 49.0 | 1880 | 50,155,783 | 26.0 |
| 1680 | 151,500 | 35.4 | 1890 | 62,947,714 | 25.5 |
| 1690 | 210,400 | 38.9 | 1900 | 75,994,575 | 20.7 |
| 1700 | 250,900 | 19.2 | 1910 | 91,972,266 | 21.0 |
| 1710 | 331,700 | 32.2 | 1920 | 105,710,620 | 14.9 |
| 1720 | 466,200 | 40.5 | 1930 | 122,775,046 | 16.1 |
| 1730 | 629,400 | 35.0 | 1940 | 131,669,275 | 7.2 |
| 1740 | 905,600 | 43.9 | 1950 | 150,697,361 | 14.5 |
| 1750 | 1,170,800 | 29.3 | 1960 | 179,323,175 | 19.0 |
| 1760 | 1,593,600 | 36.1 | 1970 | 203,235,298 | 13.3 |
| 1770 | 2,148,100 | 34.8 | 1980 | 226,545,805 | 11.5 |
| 1780 | 2,780,400 | 29.4 | 1990 | 248,709,873 | 9.8 |
| 1790 | 3,929,214 | 41.3 | 2000 | 281,421,906 | 13.2 |
| 1800 | 5,308,483 | 35.1 | 2010 | 308,745,538 | 9.7 |
| 1810 | 7,239,881 | 36.4 | | | |

SOURCES: U.S. Bureau of the Census, *Historical Statistics of the United States, Colonial Times to 1970* (1975); *Statistical Abstract of the United States, 2010.*

*Note: Until 1890, census takers never made any effort to count the Native American people who lived outside their reserved political areas and compiled only casual and incomplete enumerations of those living within their jurisdictions. In 1890, the federal government attempted a full count of the Indian population: the Census found 125,719 Indians in 1890, compared with only 12,543 in 1870 and 33,985 in 1880.

## Immigration by Decade

| Year | Number | Immigrants During this Decade as a Percentage of Total Population | Year | Number | Immigrants During this Decade as a Percentage of Total Population |
|---|---|---|---|---|---|
| 1821–1830 | 151,824 | 1.6 | 1921–1930 | 4,107,209 | 3.9 |
| 1831–1840 | 599,125 | 4.6 | 1931–1940 | 528,431 | 0.4 |
| 1841–1850 | 1,713,251 | 10.0 | 1941–1950 | 1,035,039 | 0.7 |
| 1851–1860 | 2,598,214 | 11.2 | 1951–1960 | 2,515,479 | 1.6 |
| 1861–1870 | 2,314,824 | 7.4 | 1961–1970 | 3,321,677 | 1.8 |
| 1871–1880 | 2,812,191 | 7.1 | 1971–1980 | 4,493,000 | 2.2 |
| 1881–1890 | 5,246,613 | 10.5 | 1981–1990 | 7,338,000 | 3.0 |
| 1891–1900 | 3,687,546 | 5.8 | 1991–2000 | 9,095,083 | 3.7 |
| 1901–1910 | 8,795,386 | 11.6 | **Total** | **32,433,918** | |
| 1911–1920 | 5,735,811 | 6.2 | | | |
| **Total** | **33,654,785** | | 1821–2000 | | |
| | | | **GRAND TOTAL** | **66,088,703** | |

SOURCES: U.S. Bureau of the Census, *Historical Statistics of the United States, Colonial Times to 1970* (1975), part 1, 105–106; *Statistical Abstract of the United States, 2001*.

## Regional Origins

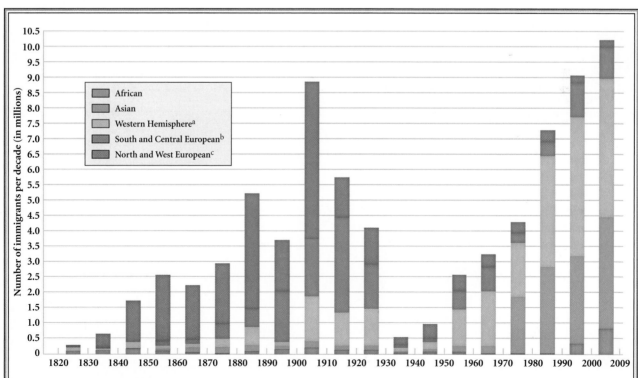

[a] Canada and all countries in South America and Central America.
[b] Italy, Spain, Portugal, Greece, Germany (Austria included, 1938–1945), Poland, former Czechoslovakia (since 1920), former Yugoslavia (since 1920), Hungary (since 1861), Austria (since 1861, except 1938–1945), former USSR (excludes Asian USSR between 1931 and 1963), Latvia, Estonia, Lithuania, Finland, Romania, Bulgaria, Turkey (in Europe), and other European countries not classified elsewhere.
[c] Great Britain, Ireland, Norway, Sweden, Denmark, Iceland, Netherlands, Belgium, Luxembourg, Switzerland, France.
Sources: Stephan Thernstrom, ed., *Harvard Encyclopedia of American Ethnic Groups* (1980), 480; U.S. Bureau of the Census, *Statistical Abstract of the United States, 1991*; U.S. Department of Homeland Security, *Yearbook of Immigration Statistics, 2009*.

# Glossary

**abolitionism:** The social reform movement to end slavery immediately and without compensation that began in the United States in the 1830s. (p. 357)

**Abu Ghraib prison:** A prison just outside Baghdad, Iraq, where American guards were photographed during the Iraq War abusing and torturing suspected insurgents. (p. 1029)

**Adams-Onís Treaty:** An 1819 treaty in which John Quincy Adams persuaded Spain to cede the Florida territory to the United States. In return, the American government accepted Spain's claim to Texas and agreed to a compromise on the western boundary for the state of Louisiana. (p. 243)

*Adkins v. Children's Hospital:* The 1923 Supreme Court case that voided a minimum wage for women workers in the District of Columbia, reversing many of the gains that had been achieved through the groundbreaking decision in *Muller v. Oregon.* (p. 707)

**Advanced Research Projects Agency Network (ARPANET):** A decentralized computer network developed in the late 1960s by the U.S. Department of Defense in conjunction with the Massachusetts Institute of Technology. The Internet grew out of the ARPANET. (p. 1012)

**affirmative action:** Policies established in the 1960s and 1970s by governments, businesses, universities, and other institutions to overcome the effects of past discrimination against specific groups such as racial and ethnic minorities and women. Measures to ensure equal opportunity include setting goals for the admission, hiring, and promotion of minorities; considering minority status when allocating resources; and actively encouraging victims of past discrimination to apply for jobs and other resources. (p. 950)

*The Affluent Society:* A 1958 book by John Kenneth Galbraith that analyzed the nation's successful middle class and argued that the poor were only an "afterthought" in the minds of economists and politicians. (p. 843)

**Agricultural Adjustment Act:** New Deal legislation passed in May 1933 that aimed at cutting agricultural production to raise crop prices and thus farmers' income. (p. 741)

**Al Qaeda:** A network of radical Islamic terrorists organized by Osama bin Laden, who issued a call for holy war against Americans and their allies. Members of Al Qaeda were responsible for the 9/11 terrorist attacks. (p. 1002)

**Alamo:** The 1836 defeat by the Mexican army of the Texan garrison defending the Alamo in San Antonio. Newspapers urged Americans to "Remember the Alamo," and American adventurers, lured by offers of land grants, flocked to Texas to join the rebel forces. (p. 391)

**amalgamation:** A term for racial mixing and intermarriage, almost universally opposed by whites in the nineteenth-century United States. (p. 364)

**America First Committee:** A committee organized by isolationists in 1940 to oppose the entrance of the United States into World War II. The membership of the committee included senators, journalists, and publishers and such well-respected figures as the aviator Charles Lindbergh. (p. 771)

**American, or Know-Nothing, Party:** A political party formed in 1851 that drew on the anti-immigrant and anti-Catholic movements of the 1840s. In 1854, the party gained control of the state governments of Massachusetts and Pennsylvania. (p. 432)

**American Civil Liberties Union:** An organization formed during the Red Scare to protect free speech rights. (p. 713)

**American Colonization Society:** A society founded by Henry Clay and other prominent citizens in 1817. The society argued that slaves had to be freed and then resettled, in Africa or elsewhere. (p. 267)

**American exceptionalism:** The idea that the United States has a unique destiny to foster democracy and civilization on the world stage. (p. 674)

**American Federation of Labor:** Organization created by Samuel Gompers in 1886 that coordinated the activities of craft unions and called for direct negotiation with employers in order to achieve benefits for skilled workers. (p. 570)

**American GI Forum:** A group founded by World War II veterans in Corpus Christi, Texas, in 1948 to protest the poor treatment of Mexican American soldiers and veterans. (p. 877)

**American Indian Movement (AIM):** Organization established in 1968 to address the problems Indians faced in American cities, including poverty and police harassment. AIM organized Indians to end relocation and termination policies and to win greater control over their cultures and communities. (p. 898)

**American Protective Association:** A powerful political organization of militant Protestants, which for a brief period in the 1890s counted more than two million members. In its virulent anti-Catholicism and calls for restrictions on immigrants, the APA prefigured the revived Ku Klux Klan of the 1920s. (p. 600)

**American Recovery and Reinvestment Act:** An economic stimulus bill passed in 2009, in response to the Great Recession, that provided $787 billion to state and local governments for schools, hospitals, and transportation projects. It was one of the largest single packages of government spending in American history. (p. 1031)

**American Renaissance:** A literary explosion during the 1840s inspired in part by Emerson's ideas on the liberation of the individual. (p. 346)

**American System:** The mercantilist system of national economic development advocated by Henry Clay and adopted by John Quincy Adams, with a national bank to manage the nation's financial system; protective tariffs to provide revenue and encourage industry; and a nationally funded network of roads, canals, and railroads. (p. 319)

**American Temperance Society:** A society invigorated by evangelical Protestants in 1832 that set out to curb the consumption of alcoholic beverages. (p. 310)

**American Woman Suffrage Association:** A women's suffrage organization led by Lucy Stone, Henry Blackwell, and others who remained loyal to the Republican Party, despite its failure to include women's voting rights in the Reconstruction Amendments. Stressing the urgency of voting rights for African American men, AWSA leaders held out hope that once Reconstruction had been settled, it would be women's turn. (p. 486)

**anarchism:** The advocacy of a stateless society achieved by revolutionary means. Feared for their views, anarchists became scapegoats for the 1886 Haymarket Square bombing. (p. 568)

**animism:** Spiritual beliefs that center on the natural world. Animists do not worship a supernatural God; instead, they pay homage to spirits and spiritual forces that they believe dwell in the natural world. (p. 17)

**Antifederalists:** Opponents of ratification of the Constitution. Antifederalists feared that a powerful and distant central government would be out of touch with the needs of citizens. They also complained that it failed to guarantee individual liberties in a bill of rights. (p. 207)

**Articles of Confederation:** The written document defining the structure of the government from 1781 to 1788, under which the Union was a confederation of equal states, with no executive and limited powers, existing mainly to foster a common defense. (p. 200)

**artisan republicanism:** An ideology that celebrated small-scale producers, men and women who owned their own shops (or farms). It defined the ideal republican society as one constituted by, and dedicated to the welfare of, independent workers and citizens. (p. 291)

**associated state:** A system of voluntary business cooperation with government. The Commerce Department helped create two thousand trade associations representing companies in almost every major industry. (p. 710)

**Atlanta Compromise:** An 1895 address by Booker T. Washington that urged whites and African Americans to work together for the progress of all. Delivered at the Cotton States Exposition in Atlanta, the speech was widely interpreted as approving racial segregation. (p. 587)

**Atlantic Charter:** A press release by President Roosevelt and British prime minister Winston Churchill in August 1941 calling for economic cooperation, national self-determination, and guarantees of political stability after the war. (p. 772)

**baby boom:** The surge in the American birthrate between 1945 and 1965, which peaked in 1957 with 4.3 million births. (p. 850)

***Bakke v. University of California:*** 1978 Supreme Court ruling that limited affirmative action by rejecting a quota system. (p. 951)

**Bank of the United States:** A bank chartered in 1790 and jointly owned by private stockholders and the national government.

Alexander Hamilton argued that the bank would provide stability to the specie-starved American economy by making loans to merchants, handling government funds, and issuing bills of credit. (p. 218)

**Battle of Little Big Horn:** The 1876 battle begun when American cavalry under George Armstrong Custer attacked an encampment of Sioux, Arapaho, and Cheyenne Indians who resisted removal to a reservation. Custer's force was annihilated, but with whites calling for U.S. soldiers to retaliate, the Native American military victory was short-lived. (p. 533)

**Battle of Long Island (1776):** First major engagement of the new Continental army, defending against 32,000 British troops outside of New York City. (p. 184)

**Battle of Saratoga (1777):** A multistage battle in New York ending with the surrender of British general John Burgoyne. The victory ensured the diplomatic success of American representatives in Paris, who won a military alliance with France. (p. 187)

**Battle of Tippecanoe:** An attack on Shawnee Indians at Prophetstown on the Tippecanoe River in 1811 by American forces headed by William Henry Harrison, Indiana's territorial governor. The governor's troops traded heavy casualties with the confederacy's warriors and then destroyed the holy village. (p. 236)

**Battle of Yorktown (1781):** A battle in which French and American troops and a French fleet trapped the British army under the command of General Charles Cornwallis at Yorktown, Virginia. The Franco-American victory broke the resolve of the British government. (p. 195)

**Bay of Pigs:** A failed U.S.-sponsored invasion of Cuba in 1961 by anti-Castro forces who planned to overthrow Fidel Castro's government. (p. 830)

**Beats:** A small group of literary figures based in New York City and San Francisco in the 1950s who rejected mainstream culture and instead celebrated personal freedom, which often included drug consumption and casual sex. (p. 849)

**Benevolent Empire:** A broad-ranging campaign of moral and institutional reforms inspired by evangelical Christian ideals and endorsed by upper-middle-class men and women in the 1820s and 1830s. (p. 305)

**benevolent masters:** Slave owners who considered themselves committed to the welfare of their slaves. (p. 382)

**Bill of Rights:** The first ten amendments to the Constitution, officially ratified by 1791. The amendments safeguarded fundamental personal rights, including freedom of speech and religion, and mandated legal procedures, such as trial by jury. (p. 216)

**Black Codes:** Laws passed by southern states after the Civil War that denied ex-slaves the civil rights enjoyed by whites, punished vague crimes such as "vagrancy" or failing to have a labor contract, and tried to force African Americans back to plantation labor systems that closely mirrored those in slavery times. (p. 481)

**black nationalism:** a major strain of African American thought that emphasized black racial pride and autonomy. Present in black communities for centuries, it periodically came to the fore, as in Marcus Garvey's pan-Africanist movement in the early twentieth century and in various organizations in the 1960s and 1970s, such as the Nation of Islam and the Black Panther Party. (p. 892)

**Black Panther Party:** A militant organization dedicated to protecting African Americans from police violence, founded in Oakland, California, in 1966 by Huey Newton and Bobby Seale. In the late 1960s the organization spread to other cities, where members undertook a wide range of community-organizing projects, but the Panthers' radicalism and belief in armed self-defense resulted in violent clashes with police. (p. 894)

**black Protestantism:** A form of Protestantism that was devised by Christian slaves in the Chesapeake and spread to the Cotton South as a result of the domestic slave trade. It emphasized the evangelical message of emotional conversion, ritual baptism, communal spirituality, and the idea that blacks were "children of God" and should be treated accordingly. (p. 395)

**"Bleeding Kansas":** Term for the bloody struggle between proslavery and antislavery factions in Kansas following its organization as a territory in the fall of 1854. (p. 433)

**blues:** A form of American music that originated in the Deep South, especially from the black workers in the cotton fields of the Mississippi Delta. (p. 618)

**Bonus Army:** A group of 15,000 unemployed World War I veterans who set up camps near the Capitol building in 1932 to demand immediate payment of pension awards due to be paid in 1945. (p. 738)

**Bretton Woods:** An international conference in New Hampshire in July 1944 that established the World Bank and the International Monetary Fund (IMF). (p. 840)

**Brotherhood of Sleeping Car Porters:** A prominent black trade union of railroad car porters working for the Pullman Company. (p. 873)

***Brown v. Board of Education of Topeka*:** Supreme Court ruling that overturned the "separate but equal" precedent established in *Plessy v. Ferguson* in 1896. The Court declared that separate educational facilities were inherently unequal and thus violated the Fourteenth Amendment. (p. 878)

**Burlingame Treaty:** An 1868 treaty that guaranteed the rights of U.S. missionaries in China and set official terms for the emigration of Chinese laborers to work in the United States. (p. 511)

**Californios:** The elite Mexican ranchers in the province of California. (p. 415)

**carpetbaggers:** A derisive name given by ex-Confederates to northerners who, motivated by idealism or the search for personal opportunity or profit, moved to the South during Reconstruction. (p. 493)

**caucus:** A meeting held by a political party to choose candidates, make policies, and enforce party discipline. (p. 318)

**chattel principle:** A system of bondage in which a slave has the legal status of property and so can be bought and sold. (p. 381)

**chattel slavery:** A system of bondage in which a slave has the legal status of property and so can be bought and sold like property. (p. 40)

**Chicago school:** A school of architecture dedicated to the design of buildings whose form expressed, rather than masked, their structure and function. (p. 608)

**Chicano Moratorium Committee:** Group founded by activist Latinos to protest the Vietnam War. (p. 923)

**Chinese Exclusion Act:** The 1882 law that barred Chinese laborers from entering the United States. It continued in effect until the 1940s. (p. 561)

**Christianity:** A religion that holds the belief that Jesus Christ was himself divine. For centuries, the Roman Catholic Church was the great unifying institution in Western Europe, and it was from Europe that Christianity spread to the Americas. (p. 21)

**"City Beautiful" movement:** A turn-of-the-twentieth-century movement that advocated landscape beautification, playgrounds, and more and better urban parks. (p. 626)

**civic humanism:** The belief that individuals owe a service to their community and its government. During the Renaissance, political theorists argued that selfless service to the polity was of critical importance in a self-governing republic. (p. 20)

**Civil Rights Act of 1866:** Legislation passed by Congress that nullified the Black Codes and affirmed that African Americans should have equal benefit of the law. (p. 481)

**Civil Rights Act of 1875:** A law that required "full and equal" access to jury service and to transportation and public accommodations, irrespective of race. (p. 496)

**Civil Rights Act of 1964:** Law that responded to demands of the civil rights movement by making discrimination in employment, education, and public accommodations illegal. It was the strongest such measure since Reconstruction and included a ban on sex discrimination in employment. (p. 890)

***Civil Rights Cases*:** A series of 1883 Supreme Court decisions that struck down the Civil Rights Act of 1875, rolling back key Reconstruction laws and paving the way for later decisions that sanctioned segregation. (p. 500)

**Civilian Conservation Corps:** Federal relief program that provided jobs to millions of unemployed young men who built thousands of bridges, roads, trails, and other structures in state and national parks, bolstering the national infrastructure. (p. 741)

**classical liberalism, or laissez-faire:** The principle that the less government does, the better, particularly in reference to the economy. (p. 332)

**classical liberalism:** The political ideology of individual liberty, private property, a competitive market economy, free trade, and limited government. The idea being that the less government does, the better, particularly in reference to economic policies such as tariffs and incentives for industrial development. Attacking corruption and defending private property, late-nineteenth-century liberals generally called for elite governance and questioned the advisability of full democratic participation. (p. 498)

**Clayton Antitrust Act:** A 1914 law that strengthened federal definitions of "monopoly" and gave more power to the Justice Department to pursue antitrust cases; it also specified that labor unions could not generally be prosecuted for "restraint of trade," ensuring that antitrust laws would apply to corporations rather than unions. (p. 662)

**closed shop:** A workplace in which a job seeker had to be a union member to gain employment. The closed shop was advocated by craft unions as a method of keeping out lower-wage workers and strengthening the unions' bargaining position with employers. (p. 570)

**coastal trade:** The domestic slave trade with routes along the Atlantic coast that sent thousands of slaves to sugar plantations in Louisiana and cotton plantations in the Mississippi Valley. (p. 380)

**code talkers:** Native American soldiers trained to use native languages to send messages in battle during World War II. Neither the Japanese nor the Germans could decipher the codes used by these Navajo, Comanche, Choctaw, and Cherokee speakers, and the messages they sent gave the Allies great advantage in the battle of Iwo Jima, among many others. (p. 776)

**Coercive Acts:** Four British acts of 1774 meant to punish Massachusetts for the destruction of three shiploads of tea. Known in America as the Intolerable Acts, they led to open rebellion in the northern colonies. (p. 168)

**Cold War liberalism:** A combination of moderate liberal policies that preserved the programs of the New Deal welfare state and forthright anticommunism that vilified the Soviet Union abroad and radicalism at home. Adopted by President Truman and the Democratic Party during the late 1940s and early 1950s. (p. 818)

**collective bargaining:** A process of negotiation between labor unions and employers, which after World War II translated into rising wages, expanding benefits, and an increasing rate of home ownership. (p. 844)

**Columbian Exchange:** The massive global exchange of living things, including people, animals, plants, and diseases, between the Eastern and Western Hemispheres that began after the voyages of Columbus. (p. 43)

**Committee on Public Information:** An organization set up by President Woodrow Wilson during World War I to increase support for America's participation in the war. The CPI was a national propaganda machine that helped create a political climate intolerant of dissent. (p. 690)

**Committee to Defend America By Aiding the Allies:** A group of interventionists who believed in engaging with, rather than withdrawing from, international developments. Interventionists became increasingly vocal in 1940 as war escalated in Europe. (p. 771)

**committees of correspondence:** A communications network established among towns in the colonies, and among colonial assemblies, between 1772 and 1773 to provide for rapid dissemination of news about important political developments. (p. 168)

**Commonwealth System:** The republican system of political economy created by state governments by 1820, whereby states funneled aid to private businesses whose projects would improve the general welfare. (p. 256)

**companionate marriage:** A marriage based on the republican values of equality and mutual respect. Although husbands in these marriages retained significant legal power, they increasingly came to see their wives as loving partners rather than as inferiors or dependents. (p. 258)

**competency:** The ability of a family to keep a household solvent and independent and to pass that ability on to the next generation. (p. 117)

**Compromise of 1850:** Laws passed in 1850 that were meant to resolve the dispute over the status of slavery in the territories. Key elements included the admission of California as a free state and the Fugitive Slave Act. (p. 429)

**Comstock Act:** An 1873 law that prohibited circulation of "obscene literature," defined as including most information on sex, reproduction, and birth control. (p. 585)

**Comstock Lode:** Immense silver ore deposit discovered in 1859 in Nevada that touched off a mining rush, bringing a diverse population into the region and leading to the establishment of boomtowns. (p. 516)

**Congress of Racial Equality (CORE):** Civil rights organization founded in 1942 in Chicago by James Farmer and other members of the Fellowship of Reconciliation (FOR) that espoused nonviolent direct action. In 1961 CORE organized a series of what were called Freedom Rides on interstate bus lines throughout the South to call attention to blatant violations of recent Supreme Court rulings against segregation in interstate commerce. (p. 870)

***The Conscience of a Conservative:*** A 1960 book that set forth an uncompromising conservatism and inspired a Republican grassroots movement in support of its author, Barry Goldwater. (p. 975)

**conscience Whigs:** Whig politicians who opposed the Mexican War (1846–1848) on moral grounds, maintaining that the purpose of the war was to expand and perpetuate control of the national government. (p. 421)

**"consolidated government":** A term meaning a powerful and potentially oppressive national government. (p. 320)

**constitutional monarchy:** A monarchy limited in its rule by a constitution. (p. 87)

**consumer credit:** New forms of borrowing, such as auto loans and installment plans, that flourished in the 1920s but helped trigger the Great Depression. (p. 725)

**consumer revolution:** An increase in consumption in English manufactures in Britain and the British colonies fueled by the Industrial Revolution. Although the consumer revolution raised living standards, it landed many consumers—and the colonies as a whole—in debt. (p. 141)

**containment:** The basic U.S. policy of the Cold War, which sought to contain communism within its existing geographic boundaries. Initially, containment focused on the Soviet Union and Eastern Europe, but in the 1950s it came to include China, North Korea, and other parts of the developing world. (p. 808)

**Continental Association:** An association established in 1774 by the First Continental Congress to enforce a boycott of British goods. (p. 171)

**Continental Congress:** September 1774 gathering of colonial delegates in Philadelphia to discuss the crisis precipitated by the Coercive Acts. The Congress produced a declaration of rights and an agreement to impose a limited boycott of trade with Britain. (p. 169)

**"contrabands":** Slaves who fled plantations and sought protection behind Union lines during the Civil War. (p. 463)

**Contract with America:** Initiatives by Representative Newt Gingrich of Georgia for significant tax cuts, reductions in welfare programs, anticrime measures, and cutbacks in federal regulations. (p. 1021)

**Contras:** An opposition group in Nicaragua that President Reagan ordered the CIA to assist. While Congress banned the CIA and all other government agencies from providing any military support to the Contras, a lieutenant colonel in the U.S. Marines, Oliver North, used the profits from the Iranian arms deal to assist the Contras, resulting in the Iran-Contra affair. (p. 992)

**convict leasing:** Notorious system, begun during Reconstruction, whereby southern state officials allowed private companies to hire out prisoners to labor under brutal conditions in mines and other industries. (p. 495)

**corrupt bargain:** A term used by Andrew Jackson's supporters for the appointment by President John Quincy Adams of Henry Clay as his secretary of state, the traditional stepping-stone to the presidency. Clay had used his influence as Speaker of the House to elect Adams rather than Jackson in the election in 1824. (p. 319)

**counterculture:** A culture embracing values or lifestyles opposing those of the mainstream culture. Became synonymous with hippies, people who opposed and rejected conventional standards of society and advocated extreme liberalism in their sociopolitical attitudes and lifestyles. (p. 918)

**Counter-Reformation:** A reaction in the Catholic Church triggered by the Reformation that sought change from within and created new monastic and missionary orders, including the Jesuits (founded in 1540), who saw themselves as soldiers of Christ. (p. 22)

**Covenant Chain:** The alliance of the Iroquois, first with the colony of New York, then with the British Empire and its other colonies. The Covenant Chain became a model for relations between the British Empire and other Native American peoples. (p. 89)

**covenant of grace:** The Christian idea that God's elect are granted salvation as a pure gift of grace. This doctrine holds that nothing people do can erase their sins or earn them a place in heaven. (p. 62)

**covenant of works:** The Christian idea that God's elect must do good works in their earthly lives to earn their salvation. (p. 62)

**Crédit Mobilier:** A sham corporation set up by shareholders in the Union Pacific Railroad to secure government grants at an enormous profit. Organizers of the scheme protected it from investigation by providing gifts of its stock to powerful members of Congress. (p. 498)

**Crime of 1873:** A term used by those critical of an 1873 law directing the U.S. Treasury to cease minting silver dollars, retire Civil War–era greenbacks, and replace them with notes backed by the gold standard from an expanded system of national banks. (p. 515)

**Crittenden Compromise:** A plan proposed by Senator John J. Crittenden for a constitutional amendment to protect slavery from federal interference in any state where it already existed and for the westward extension of the Missouri Compromise line to the California border. (p. 446)

**Crusades:** A series of wars undertaken by Christian armies between A.D. 1096 and 1291 to reverse the Muslim advance in Europe and win back the holy lands where Christ had lived. (p. 22)

**Cuban missile crisis:** The 1962 nuclear standoff between the Soviet Union and the United States when the Soviets attempted to deploy nuclear missiles in Cuba. (p. 831)

**culture war:** A term used by Patrick Buchanan in 1992 to describe a long-standing political struggle, dating to the 1920s, between religious traditionalists and secular liberals. Social issues such as abortion rights and the rights of lesbians and gay men divided these groups. (p. 1012)

**currency tax:** A hidden tax on the farmers and artisans who accepted Continental bills in payment for supplies and on the thousands of soldiers who took them as pay. Because of rampant inflation, Continental currency lost much of its value during the war; thus, the implicit tax on those who accepted it as payment. (p. 196)

**Dawes Severalty Act:** The 1887 law that gave Native Americans severalty (individual ownership of land) by dividing reservations into homesteads. The law was a disaster for native peoples, resulting over several decades in the loss of 66 percent of lands held by Indians at the time of the law's passage. (p. 532)

**D-Day:** June 6, 1944, the date of the Allied invasion of northern France. D-Day was the largest amphibious assault in world history. The invasion opened a second front against the Germans and moved the Allies closer to victory in Europe. (p. 790)

**Declaration of Independence:** A document containing philosophical principles and a list of grievances that declared separation from Britain. Adopted by the Second Continental Congress on July 4, 1776, it ended a period of intense debate with moderates still hoping to reconcile with Britain. (p. 178)

**Declaratory Act of 1766:** Law issued by Parliament to assert Parliament's unassailable right to legislate for its British colonies "in all cases whatsoever," putting Americans on notice that the simultaneous repeal of the Stamp Act changed nothing in the imperial powers of Britain. (p. 160)

**Defense of Marriage Act:** A law enacted by Congress in 1998 that allowed states to refuse to recognize gay marriages or civil unions formed in other jurisdictions. The Supreme Court ruled that DOMA was unconstitutional in 2013. (p. 1020)

**deindustrialization:** The dismantling of manufacturing—especially in the automobile, steel, and consumer-goods industries—in the decades after World War II, representing a reversal of the process of industrialization that had dominated the American economy from the 1870s through the 1940s. (p. 944)

**deism:** The Enlightenment-influenced belief that the Christian God created the universe and then left it to run according to natural laws. (p. 128)

**demographic transition:** The sharp decline in birthrate in the United States beginning in the 1790s that was caused by changes in cultural behavior, including the use of birth control. The migration of thousands of young men to the trans-Appalachian west was also a factor in this decline. (p. 259)

**deregulation:** The limiting of regulation by federal agencies. Deregulation of prices in the trucking, airline, and railroad industries had begun under President Carter in the late 1970s, and Reagan expanded it to include cutting back on government protections of consumers, workers, and the environment. (p. 950)

**deskilling:** The elimination of skilled labor under a new system of mechanized manufacturing, in which workers completed discrete, small-scale tasks rather than crafting an entire product. With deskilling, employers found they could pay workers less and replace them more easily. (p. 551)

**détente:** The easing of conflict between the United States and the Soviet Union during the Nixon administration, which was achieved by focusing on issues of common concern, such as arms control and trade. (p. 929)

**division of labor:** A system of manufacture that divides production into a series of distinct and repetitive tasks performed by machines or workers. (p. 286)

**dollar diplomacy:** Policy emphasizing the connection between America's economic and political interests overseas. Business would gain from diplomatic efforts in its behalf, while the strengthened American economic presence overseas would give added leverage to American diplomacy. (p. 711)

**domestic slavery:** A term referring to the assertion by Elizabeth Cady Stanton and other female abolitionists that traditional gender roles and legal restrictions created a form of slavery for married women. (p. 370)

**Dominion of New England:** A royal province created by King James II in 1686 that would have absorbed Connecticut, Rhode Island, Massachusetts Bay, Plymouth, New York, and New Jersey into a single, vast colony and eliminated their assemblies and other chartered rights. James's plan was canceled by the Glorious Revolution in 1688, which removed him from the throne. (p. 85)

**domino theory:** President Eisenhower's theory of containment, which warned that the fall of a non-Communist government to communism in Southeast Asia would trigger the spread of communism to neighboring countries. (p. 828)

**draft (conscription):** The system for selecting individuals for conscription, or compulsory military service, first implemented during the Civil War. (p. 452)

***Dred Scott v. Sandford:*** The 1857 Supreme Court decision that ruled the Missouri Compromise unconstitutional. The Court ruled against slave Dred Scott, who claimed that travels with his master into free states and territories made him and his family free. The decision also denied the federal government the right to exclude slavery from the territories and declared that African Americans were not citizens. (p. 433)

**Dunmore's War:** A 1774 war led by Virginia's royal governor, the Earl of Dunmore, against the Ohio Shawnees, who had a long-standing claim to Kentucky as a hunting ground. The Shawnees were defeated and Dunmore and his militia forces claimed Kentucky as their own. (p. 175)

**dust bowl:** A series of dust storms from 1930 to 1941 during which a severe drought afflicted the semiarid states of Oklahoma, Texas, New Mexico, Colorado, Arkansas, and Kansas. (p. 759)

**Earth Day:** An annual event honoring the environment that was first celebrated on April 22, 1970, when 20 million citizens gathered in communities across the country to express their support for a cleaner, healthier planet. (p. 939)

**Economic Growth and Tax Relief Act:** Legislation introduced by President George W. Bush and passed by Congress in 2001 that slashed income tax rates, extended the earned income credit for the poor, and marked the estate tax to be phased out by 2010. (p. 1026)

**Economic Opportunity Act:** 1964 act which created a series of programs, including Head Start to prepare disadvantaged preschoolers for kindergarten and the Job Corps and Upward Bound to provide young people with training and employment, aimed at alleviating poverty and spurring economic growth in impoverished areas. (p. 905)

**Economic Recovery Tax Act (ERTA):** Legislation introduced by President Reagan and passed by Congress in 1981 that authorized the largest reduction in taxes in the nation's history. (p. 983)

**Eisenhower Doctrine:** President Eisenhower's 1957 declaration that the United States would actively combat communism in the Middle East. (p. 829)

**Emancipation Proclamation:** President Abraham Lincoln's proclamation issued on January 1, 1863, that legally abolished slavery in all states that remained out of the Union. While the Emancipation Proclamation did not immediately free a single slave, it signaled an end to the institution of slavery. (p. 464)

**Embargo Act of 1807:** An act of Congress that prohibited U.S. ships from traveling to foreign ports and effectively banned overseas trade in an attempt to deter Britain from halting U.S. ships at sea. The embargo caused grave hardships for Americans engaged in overseas commerce. (p. 234)

***encomienda:*** A grant of Indian labor in Spanish America given in the sixteenth century by the Spanish kings to prominent men. *Encomenderos* extracted tribute from these Indians in exchange for granting them protection and Christian instruction. (p. 234)

**energy crisis:** A period of fuel shortages in the United States after the Arab states in the Organization of Petroleum Exporting

Countries (OPEC) declared an oil embargo in October 1973. (p. 939)

**Enforcement Laws:** Acts passed in Congress in 1870 and signed by President U. S. Grant that were designed to protect freedmen's rights under the Fourteenth and Fifteenth Amendments. Authorizing federal prosecutions, military intervention, and martial law to suppress terrorist activity, the Enforcement Laws largely succeeded in shutting down Klan activities. (p. 499)

**English common law:** The centuries-old body of legal rules and procedures that protected the lives and property of the British monarch's subjects. (p. 159)

**Enlightenment:** An eighteenth-century philosophical movement that emphasized the use of reason to reevaluate previously accepted doctrines and traditions and the power of reason to understand and shape the world. (p. 126)

**Environmental Protection Agency (EPA):** Federal agency created by Congress and President Nixon in 1970 to enforce environmental laws, conduct environmental research, and reduce human health and environmental risks from pollutants. (p. 939)

**environmentalism:** Activist movement begun in the 1960s that was concerned with protecting the environment through activities such as conservation, pollution control measures, and public awareness campaigns. In response to the new environmental consciousness, the federal government staked out a broad role in environmental regulation in the 1960s and 1970s. (p. 939)

**Equal Pay Act (1963):** Law that established the principle of equal pay for equal work. Trade union women were especially critical in pushing for, and winning, congressional passage of the law. (p. 908)

**Equal Rights Amendment (ERA):** Constitutional amendment passed by Congress in 1972 that would require equal treatment of men and women under federal and state law. Facing fierce opposition from the New Right and the Republican Party, the ERA was defeated as time ran out for state ratification in 1982. (p. 952)

**Erie Canal:** A 364-mile waterway connecting the Hudson River and Lake Erie. The Erie Canal brought prosperity to the entire Great Lakes region, and its benefits prompted civic and business leaders in Philadelphia and Baltimore to propose canals to link their cities to the Midwest. (p. 293)

**established church:** A church given privileged legal status by the government. Historically, such established churches in Europe and America were supported by public taxes and were often the only legally permitted religious institutions. (p. 270)

**Ethics in Government Act:** Passed in the wake of the Watergate scandal, the 1978 act forced political candidates to disclose financial contributions and limited the lobbying activities of former elected officials. (p. 948)

**ethnocultural politics:** Refers to the fact that the political allegiance of many American voters was determined less by party policy than by their membership in a specific ethnic or religious group. (p. 340)

**eugenics:** An emerging "science" of human breeding in the late nineteenth century that argued that mentally deficient people should be prevented from reproducing. (p. 594)

**evangelicalism:** The trend in Protestant Christianity that stresses salvation through conversion, repentance of sin, and adherence to scripture; it also stresses the importance of preaching over ritual. (p. 962)

**Executive Order 8802:** An order signed by President Roosevelt in 1941 that prohibited "discrimination in the employment of workers in defense industries or government because of race, creed, color, or national origin" and established the Fair Employment Practices Commission (FEPC). (p. 780)

**Executive Order 9066:** An order signed by President Roosevelt in 1941 that authorized the War Department to force Japanese Americans from their West Coast homes and hold them in relocation camps for the rest of the war. (p. 787)

**Exodusters:** African Americans who walked or rode out of the Deep South following the Civil War, many settling on farms in Kansas in hopes of finding peace and prosperity. (p. 520)

**Fair Deal:** The domestic policy agenda announced by President Harry S. Truman in 1949. Including civil rights, health care, and education reform, Truman's initiative was only partially successful in Congress. (p. 820)

**family values:** Values promoted by the Religious Right, including support for the traditional nuclear family and opposition to same-sex marriage and abortion. (p. 996)

**Farmers' Alliance:** A rural movement founded in Texas during the depression of the 1870s that spread across the plains states and the South. The Farmers' Alliance advocated cooperative stores and exchanges that would circumvent middlemen, and it called for greater government aid to farmers and stricter regulation of railroads. (p. 568)

**fascism:** An authoritarian system of government characterized by dictatorial rule, extreme nationalism, disdain for civil society, and a conviction that imperialism and warfare are the principal means by which nations attain greatness. The United States went to war against fascism when it faced Nazi Germany under Adolf Hitler and Italy under Benito Mussolini during World War II. (p. 768)

**Federal Housing Administration:** An agency established by the Federal Housing Act of 1934 that refinanced home mortgages for mortgage holders facing possible foreclosure. (p. 744)

**Federal Reserve Act:** The central bank system of the United States, created in 1913. The Federal Reserve helps set the money supply level, thus influencing the rate of growth of the U.S. economy, and seeks to ensure the stability of the U.S. monetary system. (p. 661)

**Federalist No. 10:** An essay by James Madison in *The Federalist* (1787–1788) that challenged the view that republican governments only worked in small polities; it argued that a geographically expansive national government would better protect republican liberty. (p. 210)

**Federalists:** Supporters of the Constitution of 1787, which created a strong central government; their opponents, the Antifederalists, feared that a strong central government would corrupt the nation's newly won liberty. (p. 207)

*The Feminine Mystique:* The title of an influential book written in 1963 by Betty Friedan critiquing the ideal whereby women were encouraged to confine themselves to roles within the domestic sphere. (p. 908)

feminism: The ideology that women should enter the public sphere not only to work on behalf of others, but also for their own equal rights and advancement. Feminists moved beyond advocacy of women's voting rights to seek greater autonomy in professional careers, property rights, and personal relationships. (p. 592)

Fetterman massacre: A massacre in December 1866 in which 1,500 Sioux warriors lured Captain William Fetterman and 80 soldiers from a Wyoming fort and attacked them. With the Fetterman massacre the Sioux succeeded in closing the Bozeman Trail, the main route into Montana. (p. 528)

Fifteenth Amendment: Constitutional amendment ratified in 1869 that forbade states to deny citizens the right to vote on grounds of race, color, or "previous condition of servitude." (p. 485)

"Fifty-four forty or fight!": Democratic candidate Governor James K. Polk's slogan in the election of 1844 calling for American sovereignty over the entire Oregon Country, stretching from California to Russian-occupied Alaska and presently shared with Great Britain. (p. 418)

fireside chats: A series of informal radio addresses Franklin Roosevelt made to the nation in which he explained New Deal initiatives. (p. 740)

flapper: A young woman of the 1920s who defied conventional standards of conduct by wearing short skirts and makeup, freely spending the money she earned on the latest fashions, dancing to jazz, and flaunting her liberated lifestyle. (p. 726)

forty-niners: The more than 80,000 settlers who arrived in California in 1849 as part of that territory's gold rush. (p. 425)

Four Freedoms: Identified by President Franklin D. Roosevelt as the most basic human rights: freedom of speech, freedom of religion, freedom from want, and freedom from fear. The president used these ideas of freedom to justify support for England during World War II, which in turn pulled the United States into the war. (p. 771)

Four-Minute Men: Name given to thousands of volunteers enlisted by the Committee on Public Information to deliver short prowar speeches at movie theaters, as part of an effort to galvanize public support for the war and suppress dissent. (p. 690)

Fourteen Points: Principles for a new world order proposed in 1919 by President Woodrow Wilson as a basis for peace negotiations at Versailles. Among them were open diplomacy, freedom of the seas, free trade, territorial integrity, arms reduction, national self-determination, and creation of the League of Nations. (p. 696)

Fourteenth Amendment: Constitutional amendment ratified in 1868 that made all native-born or naturalized persons U.S. citizens and prohibited states from abridging the rights of national citizens, thus giving primacy to national rather than state citizenship. (p. 481)

franchise: The right to vote. Between 1820 and 1860, most states revised their constitutions to extend the vote to all adult white males. Black adult men gained the right to vote with the passage of the Fourteenth Amendment (1868). The Nineteenth Amendment (1920) granted adult women the right to vote. (p. 316)

free silver: A policy of loosening the money supply by expanding federal coinage to include silver as well as gold. Advocates of the policy thought it would encourage borrowing and stimulate industry, but the defeat of Democratic presidential candidate William Jennings Bryan ended the "free silver" movement and gave Republicans power to retain the gold standard. (p. 645)

Freedmen's Bureau: Government organization created in March 1865 to aid displaced blacks and other war refugees. Active until the early 1870s, it was the first federal agency in history that provided direct payments to assist those in poverty and to foster social welfare. (p. 481)

Freedman's Savings and Trust Company: A private bank founded in 1865 that had worked closely with the Freedmen's Bureau and Union army across the South. In June 1874, when the bank failed, Congress refused to compensate its 61,000 depositors, including many African Americans. (p. 497)

Freedom of Information Act: Passed in the wake of the Watergate scandal, the 1974 act gave citizens access to federal records. (p. 948)

freeholds: Land owned in its entirety, without feudal dues or landlord obligations. Freeholders had the legal right to improve, transfer, or sell their landed property. (p. 53)

Freeport Doctrine: The argument presented by Senator Stephen A. Douglas that a territory's residents could exclude slavery by not adopting laws to protect it. (p. 438)

free-soil movement: A political movement that opposed the expansion of slavery. In 1848 the free-soilers organized the Free-Soil Party, which depicted slavery as a threat to republicanism and to the Jeffersonian ideal of a freeholder society, arguments that won broad support among aspiring white farmers. (p. 421)

French Revolution: A 1789 revolution in France that was initially welcomed by most Americans because it abolished feudalism and established a constitutional monarchy, but eventually came to seem too radical to many. (p. 219)

fundamentalism: A term adopted by Protestants, between the 1890s and the 1910s, who rejected modernism and historical interpretations of scripture and asserted the literal truth of the Bible. Fundamentalists have historically seen secularism and religious relativism as markers of sin that will be punished by God. (p. 602)

Gadsden Purchase: A small slice of land (now part of Arizona and New Mexico) purchased by President Franklin Pierce in 1853 for the purpose of building a transcontinental rail line from New Orleans to Los Angeles. (p. 431)

gag rule: A procedure in the House of Representatives from 1836 to 1844 by which antislavery petitions were automatically tabled when they were received so that they could not become the subject of debate. (p. 365)

**gang-labor system:** A system of work discipline used on southern cotton plantations in the mid-nineteenth century in which white overseers or black drivers supervised gangs of enslaved laborers to achieve greater productivity. (p. 388)

**gentility:** A refined style of living and elaborate manners that came to be highly prized among well-to-do English families after 1600 and strongly influenced leading colonists after 1700. (p. 102)

**Ghost Dance movement:** Religion of the late 1880s and early 1890s that combined elements of Christianity and traditional Native American religion. It fostered Plains Indians' hope that they could, through sacred dances, resurrect the great bison herds and call up a storm to drive whites back across the Atlantic. (p. 534)

**Gilded Age:** A term invented in the 1920s describing the late nineteenth century as a period of ostentatious displays of wealth, growing poverty, and government inaction in the face of income inequality. Commentators suggested that this era had been followed by a "Progressive Era" in which citizens mobilized for reform. The chronological line between the "Gilded Age" and the "Progressive Era" remains unclear, since the 1870s and 1880s witnessed mass movements of farmers, industrial laborers, and middle-class women for reform. Historians generally agree, however, that the era after 1900 brought about more laws to address industrial poverty, working conditions, and the power of monopolies and trusts. (p. 638)

*glasnost:* The policy introduced by Soviet president Mikhail Gorbachev during the 1980s that involved greater openness and freedom of expression and that contributed, unintentionally, to the 1991 breakup of the Soviet Union. (p. 993)

**Glass-Steagall Act:** A 1933 law that created the Federal Deposit Insurance Corporation (FDIC), which insured deposits up to $2,500 (and now up to $250,000). The act also prohibited banks from making risky, unsecured investments with customers' deposits. (p. 740)

**globalization:** The spread of political, cultural, and economic influences and connections among countries, businesses, and individuals around the world through trade, immigration, communication, and other means. (p. 1004)

**Glorious Revolution:** A quick and nearly bloodless coup in 1688 in which James II of England was overthrown by William of Orange. Whig politicians forced the new King William and Queen Mary to accept the Declaration of Rights, creating a constitutional monarchy that enhanced the powers of the House of Commons at the expense of the crown. (p. 86)

**gold standard:** The practice of backing a country's currency with its reserves of gold. In 1873 the United States, following Great Britain and other European nations, began converting to the gold standard. (p. 515)

**Granger laws:** Economic regulatory laws passed in some midwestern states in the late 1870s, triggered by pressure from farmers and the Greenback-Labor Party. (p. 566)

**Great Migration:** The migration of over 400,000 African Americans from the rural South to the industrial cities of the North during and after World War I. (p. 694)

**Great Railroad Strike of 1877:** A nationwide strike of thousands of railroad workers and labor allies, who protested the growing power of railroad corporations and the steep wage cuts imposed by railroad managers amid a severe economic depression that had begun in 1873. (p. 565)

**Great Society:** President Lyndon B. Johnson's domestic program, which included civil rights legislation, antipoverty programs, government subsidy of medical care, federal aid to education, consumer protection, and aid to the arts and humanities. (p. 904)

**Greenback-Labor Party:** A national political movement calling on the government to increase the money supply in order to assist borrowers and foster economic growth; "Greenbackers" also called for greater regulation of corporations and laws enforcing an eight-hour workday. (p. 565)

**greenbacks:** Paper money issued by the U.S. Treasury during the Civil War to finance the war effort. (p. 460)

**Group of Eight (G8):** An international organization of the leading capitalist industrial nations: the United States, Britain, Germany, France, Italy, Japan, Canada, and Russia. The G8 largely controlled the world's major international financial organizations: the World Bank, the International Monetary Fund (IMF), and the General Agreement on Tariffs and Trade (GATT). (p. 1009)

**guilds:** Organizations of skilled workers in medieval and early modern Europe that regulated the entry into, and the practice of, a trade. (p. 20)

**Gulf of Tonkin Resolution:** Resolution passed by Congress in 1964 in the wake of a naval confrontation in the Gulf of Tonkin between the United States and North Vietnam. It gave the president virtually unlimited authority in conducting the Vietnam War. The Senate terminated the resolution in 1971 following outrage over the U.S. invasion of Cambodia. (p. 911)

**habeas corpus:** A legal writ forcing government authorities to justify their arrest and detention of an individual. During the Civil War, Lincoln suspended habeas corpus to stop protests against the draft and other anti-Union activities. (p. 454)

**Haitian Revolution:** The 1791 conflict involving diverse Haitian participants and armies from three European countries. At its end, Haiti became a free, independent nation in which former slaves were citizens. (p. 222)

**"hard war":** The philosophy and tactics used by Union general William Tecumseh Sherman, by which he treated civilians as combatants. (p. 470)

**Harlem Renaissance:** A flourishing of African American artists, writers, intellectuals, and social leaders in the 1920s, centered in the neighborhoods of Harlem, New York City. (p. 718)

**Haymarket Square:** The May 4, 1886, conflict in Chicago in which both workers and policemen were killed or wounded during a labor demonstration called by local anarchists. The incident created a backlash against all labor organizations, including the Knights of Labor. (p. 568)

**headright system:** A system of land distribution, pioneered in Virginia and used in several other colonies, that granted land—

usually 50 acres — to anyone who paid the passage of a new arrival. By this means, large planters amassed huge landholdings as they imported large numbers of servants and slaves. (p. 54)

**heresy:** A religious doctrine that is inconsistent with the teachings of a church. (p. 22)

*herrenvolk* **republic:** A republic based on the principle of rule by a master race. To preserve their privileged social position, southern leaders restricted individual liberty and legal equality to whites. (p. 266)

**HIV/AIDS:** A deadly disease that killed nearly a hundred thousand people in the United States in the 1980s. (p. 985)

**Hollywood:** City in the Los Angeles area of California where, by the 1920s, nearly 90 percent of all films in the world were produced. (p. 726)

**Holocaust:** Germany's campaign during World War II to exterminate all Jews living in German-controlled lands, along with other groups the Nazis deemed "undesirable." In all, some 11 million people were killed in the Holocaust, most of them Jews. (p. 792)

**Homestead Act:** The 1862 act that gave 160 acres of free western land to any applicant who occupied and improved the property. This policy led to the rapid development of the American West after the Civil War; facing arid conditions in the West, however, many homesteaders found themselves unable to live on their land. (p. 516)

**Homestead lockout:** The 1892 lockout of workers at the Homestead, Pennsylvania, steel mill after Andrew Carnegie refused to renew the union contract. Union supporters attacked the guards hired to close them out and protect strikebreakers who had been employed by the mill, but the National Guard soon suppressed this resistance and Homestead, like other steel plants, became a non-union mill. (p. 544)

**horizontal integration:** A business concept invented in the late nineteenth century to pressure competitors and force rivals to merge their companies into a conglomerate. John D. Rockefeller of Standard Oil pioneered this business model. (p. 548)

**hostage crisis:** Crisis that began in 1979 after the deposed shah of Iran was allowed into the United States following the Iranian revolution. Iranians broke into the U.S. embassy in Teheran and took sixty-six Americans hostage. The hostage crisis lasted 444 days and contributed to President Carter's reelection defeat. (p. 977)

**House of Burgesses:** Organ of government in colonial Virginia made up of an assembly of representatives elected by the colony's inhabitants. (p. 52)

**House Un-American Activities Committee (HUAC):** Congressional committee especially prominent during the early years of the Cold War that investigated Americans who might be disloyal to the government or might have associated with communists or other radicals. (p. 821)

**household mode of production:** The system of exchanging goods and labor that helped eighteenth-century New England freeholders survive on ever-shrinking farms as available land became more scarce. (p. 120)

**Hull House:** One of the first and most famous social settlements, founded in 1889 by Jane Addams and her companion Ellen Gates Starr in an impoverished, largely Italian immigrant neighborhood on Chicago's West Side. (p. 627)

**Hundred Days:** A legendary session during the first few months of Franklin Roosevelt's administration in which Congress enacted fifteen major bills that focused primarily on four problems: banking failures, agricultural overproduction, the business slump, and soaring unemployment. (p. 740)

**Immigration and Nationality Act:** A 1965 law that eliminated the discriminatory 1924 nationality quotas, established a slightly higher total limit on immigration, included provisions to ease the entry of immigrants with skills in high demand, and allowed immediate family members of legal residents in the United States to be admitted outside of the total numerical limit. (p. 1013)

**indentured servitude:** Workers contracted for service for a specified period. In exchange for agreeing to work for four or five years (or more) without wages in the colonies, indentured workers received passage across the Atlantic, room and board, and status as a free person at the end of the contract period. (p. 54)

**Indian Removal Act of 1830:** Act that directed the mandatory relocation of eastern tribes to territory west of the Mississippi. Jackson insisted that his goal was to save the Indians and their culture. Indians resisted the controversial act, but in the end most were forced to comply. (p. 327)

**Indian Reorganization Act:** A 1934 law that reversed the Dawes Act of 1887. Through the law, Indians won a greater degree of religious freedom, and tribal governments regained their status as semisovereign dependent nations. (p. 756)

**individualism:** Word coined by Alexis de Tocqueville in 1835 to describe Americans as people no longer bound by social attachments to classes, castes, associations, and families. (p. 346)

**Industrial Revolution:** A burst of major inventions and economic expansion based on water and steam power and the use of machine technology that transformed certain industries, such as cotton textiles and iron, between 1790 and 1860. (p. 286)

**Industrial Workers of the World:** An umbrella union and radical political group founded in 1905, dedicated to organizing unskilled workers to oppose capitalism. Nicknamed the Wobblies, it advocated direct action by workers, including sabotage and general strikes. (p. 655)

**inland system:** The slave trade system in the interior of the country that fed slaves to the Cotton South. (p. 380)

*Insular Cases:* A set of Supreme Court rulings in 1901 that declared that the U.S. Constitution did not automatically extend citizenship to people in acquired territories; only Congress could decide whether to grant citizenship. (p. 678)

**internal improvements:** Public works such as roads and canals. (p. 319)

**International Monetary Fund (IMF):** A fund established to stabilize currencies and provide a predictable monetary environment for trade, with the U.S. dollar serving as the benchmark. (p. 840)

**Interstate Commerce Act:** An 1887 act that created the Interstate Commerce Commission (ICC), a federal regulatory agency designed to oversee the railroad industry and prevent collusion and unfair rates. (p. 569)

**Iran-Contra affair:** Reagan administration scandal that involved the sale of arms to Iran in exchange for its efforts to secure the release of hostages held in Lebanon and the redirection — illegal because banned by American law — of the proceeds of those sales to the Nicaraguan Contras. (p. 993)

**Islam:** A religion that considers Muhammad to be God's last prophet. Following the death of Muhammad in A.D. 632, the newly converted Arab peoples of North Africa used force and fervor to spread the Muslim faith into sub-Saharan Africa, India, Indonesia, Spain, and the Balkan regions of Europe. (p. 22)

**Jacobins:** A political faction in the French Revolution. Many Americans embraced the democratic ideology of the radical Jacobins and, like them, formed political clubs and began to address one another as "citizen." (p. 219)

**Jay's Treaty:** A 1795 treaty between the United States and Britain, negotiated by John Jay. The treaty accepted Britain's right to stop neutral ships. In return, it allowed Americans to submit claims for illegal seizures and required the British to remove their troops and Indian agents from the Northwest Territory. (p. 222)

**jazz:** Unique American musical form, developed in New Orleans and other parts of the South before World War I. Jazz musicians developed an ensemble improvisational style. (p. 718)

**Jim Crow:** System of racial segregation in the South that lasted a century, from after the Civil War until the 1960s. (p. 870)

**joint-stock corporation:** A financial organization devised by English merchants around 1550 that facilitated the colonization of North America. In these companies, a number of investors pooled their capital and received shares of stock in the enterprise in proportion to their share of the total investment. (p. 62)

**Judiciary Act of 1789:** Act that established a federal district court in each state and three circuit courts to hear appeals from the districts, with the Supreme Court having the final say. (p. 216)

**Kansas-Nebraska Act:** A controversial 1854 law that divided Indian Territory into Kansas and Nebraska, repealed the Missouri Compromise, and left the new territories to decide the issue of slavery on the basis of popular sovereignty. (p. 432)

**Kerner Commission:** Informal name for the National Advisory Commission on Civil Disorders, formed by the president to investigate the causes of the 1967 urban riots. Its 1968 report warned that "our nation is moving toward two societies, one black, one white, separate and unequal." (p. 863)

**Keynesian economics:** The theory, developed by British economist John Maynard Keynes in the 1930s, that purposeful government intervention in the economy (through lowering or raising taxes, interest rates, and government spending) can affect the level of overall economic activity and thereby prevent severe depressions and runaway inflation. (p. 751)

**King Cotton:** The Confederate belief during the Civil War that their cotton was so important to the British and French economies that those governments would recognize the South as an independent nation and supply it with loans and arms. (p. 456)

**kitchen debate:** A 1959 debate over the merits of their rival systems between U.S. vice president Richard Nixon and Soviet premier Nikita Khrushchev at the opening of an American exhibition in Moscow. (p. 838)

**Knights of Labor:** The first mass labor organization created among America's working class. Founded in 1869 and peaking in strength in the mid-1880s, the Knights of Labor attempted to bridge boundaries of ethnicity, gender, ideology, race, and occupation to build a "universal brotherhood" of all workers. (p. 567)

**Ku Klux Klan:** Secret society that first undertook violence against African Americans in the South after the Civil War but was reborn in 1915 to fight the perceived threats posed by African Americans, immigrants, radicals, feminists, Catholics, and Jews. (p. 499)

**labor theory of value:** The belief that human labor produces economic value. Adherents argued that the price of a product should be determined not by the market (supply and demand) but by the amount of work required to make it, and that most of the price should be paid to the person who produced it. (p. 292)

**laissez faire:** French for "let do" or "leave alone." A doctrine espoused by classical liberals that the less the government does, the better, particularly in reference to the economy. (p. 498)

**land banks:** An institution, established by a colonial legislature, that printed paper money and lent it to farmers, taking a lien on their land to ensure repayment. (p. 107)

**land-grant colleges:** Public universities founded to broaden educational opportunities and foster technical and scientific expertise. These universities were funded by the Morrill Act, which authorized the sale of federal lands to raise money for higher education. (p. 516)

**Lawrence v. Texas:** A 2003 landmark decision by the Supreme Court that limited the power of states to prohibit private homosexual activity between consenting adults. (p. 1020)

**League of Nations:** The international organization bringing together world governments to prevent future hostilities, proposed by President Woodrow Wilson in the aftermath of World War I. Although the League of Nations did form, the United States never became a member state. (p. 697)

**Lend-Lease Act:** Legislation in 1941 that enabled Britain to obtain arms from the United States without cash but with the promise to reimburse the United States when the war ended. The act reflected Roosevelt's desire to assist the British in any way possible, short of war. (p. 771)

**liberal arts:** A form of education pioneered by President Charles W. Eliot at Harvard University, whereby students chose from a range of electives, shaping their own curricula as they developed skills in research, critical thinking, and leadership. (p. 587)

**Liberty League:** A group of Republican business leaders and conservative Democrats who banded together to fight what they called the "reckless spending" and "socialist" reforms of the New Deal. (p. 746)

*Lochner v. New York:* A 1905 Supreme Court ruling that New York State could not limit bakers' workday to ten hours because that violated bakers' rights to make contracts. (p. 649)

**Lodge Bill:** Also known as the Federal Elections Bill of 1890, a bill proposing that whenever 100 citizens in any district appealed for intervention, a bipartisan federal board could investigate and seat the rightful winner. The defeat of the bill was a blow to those seeking to defend African American voting rights and to ensure full participation in politics. (p. 642)

*Lone Wolf v. Hitchcock:* A 1903 Supreme Court ruling that Congress could make whatever Indian policies it chose, ignoring all existing treaties. (p. 532)

**Long Drive:** Facilitated by the completion of the Missouri Pacific Railroad in 1865, a system by which cowboys herded cattle hundreds of miles north from Texas to Dodge City and the other cow towns of Kansas. (p. 519)

**Lost Generation:** The phrase coined by writer Gertrude Stein to refer to young artists and writers who had suffered through World War I and felt alienated from America's mass-culture society in the 1920s. (p. 720)

**Louisiana Purchase:** The 1803 purchase of French territory west of the Mississippi River that stretched from the Gulf of Mexico to Canada. The Louisiana Purchase nearly doubled the size of the United States and opened the way for future American expansion west. The purchase required President Thomas Jefferson to exercise powers not explicitly granted to him by the Constitution. (p. 233)

**Loyalty-Security Program:** A program created in 1947 by President Truman that permitted officials to investigate any employee of the federal government for "subversive" activities. (p. 821)

**machine tools:** Cutting, boring, and drilling machines used to produce standardized metal parts, which were then assembled into products such as textile looms and sewing machines. The rapid development of machine tools by American inventors in the early nineteenth century was a factor in the rapid spread of industrialization. (p. 290)

**management revolution:** An internal management structure adopted by many large, complex corporations that distinguished top executives from those responsible for day-to-day operations and departmentalized operations by function. (p. 546)

**Manhattan Project:** Top-secret project authorized by Franklin Roosevelt in 1942 to develop an atomic bomb ahead of the Germans. The Americans who worked on the project at Los Alamos, New Mexico (among other highly secretive sites around the country), succeeded in producing a successful atomic bomb by July 1945. (p. 793)

**Manifest Destiny:** A term coined by John L. O'Sullivan in 1845 to express the idea that Euro-Americans were fated by God to settle the North American continent from the Atlantic to the Pacific Ocean. (p. 412)

**manumission:** The legal act of relinquishing property rights in slaves. Worried that a large free black population would threaten the institution of slavery, the Virginia assembly repealed Virginia's 1782 manumission law in 1792. (p. 265)

*Marbury v. Madison* (1803): A Supreme Court case that established the principle of judicial review in finding that parts of the Judiciary Act of 1789 were in conflict with the Constitution. For the first time, the Supreme Court assumed legal authority to overrule acts of other branches of the government. (p. 231)

**March on Washington:** Officially named the March on Washington for Jobs and Freedom, on August 28, 1963, a quarter of a million people marched to the Lincoln Memorial to demand that Congress end Jim Crow racial discrimination and launch a major jobs program to bring needed employment to black communities. (p. 886)

**March to the Sea:** Military campaign from September through December 1864 in which Union forces under General Sherman marched from Atlanta, Georgia, to the coast at Savannah. Carving a path of destruction as it progressed, Sherman's army aimed at destroying white southerners' will to continue the war. (p. 470)

**Market Revolution:** The dramatic increase between 1820 and 1850 in the exchange of goods and services in market transactions. The Market Revolution reflected the increased output of farms and factories, the entrepreneurial activities of traders and merchants, and the creation of a transportation network of roads, canals, and railroads. (p. 293)

**married women's property laws:** Laws enacted between 1839 and 1860 in New York and other states that permitted married women to own, inherit, and bequeath property. (p. 371)

**Marshall Plan:** Aid program begun in 1948 to help European economies recover from World War II. (p. 809)

**mass production:** A phrase coined by Henry Ford, who helped to invent a system of mass production of goods based on assembly of standardized parts. This system accompanied the continued deskilling of industrial labor. (p. 551)

**maternalism:** The belief that women should contribute to civic and political life through their special talents as mothers, Christians, and moral guides. Maternalists put this ideology into action by creating dozens of social reform organizations. (p. 589)

**matriarchy:** A gendered power structure in which social identity and property descend through the female line. (p. 15)

*McCulloch v. Maryland* (1819): A Supreme Court case that asserted the dominance of national over state statutes. (p. 241)

**mechanics:** A term used in the nineteenth century to refer to skilled craftsmen and inventors who built and improved machinery and machine tools for industry. (p. 287)

**Medicaid:** A health plan for the poor passed in 1965 and paid for by general tax revenues and administered by the states. (p. 906)

**Medicare:** A health plan for the elderly passed in 1965 and funded by a surcharge on Social Security payroll taxes. (p. 906)

**mercantilism:** A system of political economy based on government regulation. Beginning in 1650, Britain enacted Navigation Acts that controlled colonial commerce and manufacturing for the enrichment of Britain. (p. 45)

**middle class:** An economic group of prosperous farmers, artisans, and traders that emerged in the early nineteenth century. Its rise reflected a dramatic increase in prosperity. This surge in income, along with an abundance of inexpensive mass-produced goods, fostered a distinct middle-class urban culture. (p. 302)

**Middle Passage:** The brutal sea voyage from Africa to the Americas that took the lives of nearly two million enslaved Africans. (p. 94)

**military-industrial complex:** A term President Eisenhower used to refer to the military establishment and defense contractors who, he warned, exercised undue influence over the national government. (p. 841)

**mineral-based economy:** An economy based on coal and metal that began to emerge in the 1830s, as manufacturers increasingly ran machinery fashioned from metal with coal-burning stationary steam engines rather than with water power. (p. 287)

**Minor v. Happersett:** A Supreme Court decision in 1875 that ruled that suffrage rights were not inherent in citizenship and had not been granted by the Fourteenth Amendment, as some women's rights advocates argued. Women were citizens, the Court ruled, but state legislatures could deny women the vote if they wished. (p. 486)

**minstrelsy:** Popular theatrical entertainment begun around 1830, in which white actors in blackface presented comic routines that combined racist caricature and social criticism. (p. 356)

**Minutemen:** Colonial militiamen who stood ready to mobilize on short notice during the imperial crisis of the 1770s. These volunteers formed the core of the citizens' army that met British troops at Lexington and Concord in April 1775. (p. 175)

**Mississippi Freedom Democratic Party:** Party founded in Mississippi during the Freedom Summer of 1964. Its members attempted to attend the 1964 Democratic National Convention in Atlantic City, New Jersey, as the legitimate representatives of their state, but Democratic leaders refused to recognize the party. (p. 890)

**Missouri Compromise:** A series of political agreements devised by Speaker of the House Henry Clay. Maine entered the Union as a free state in 1820 and Missouri followed as a slave state in 1821, preserving a balance in the Senate between North and South and setting a precedent for future admissions to the Union. Most importantly, this bargain set the northern boundary of slavery in the lands of the Louisiana Purchase at the southern boundary of Missouri, with the exception of that state. (p. 269)

**mixed government:** John Adams's theory from *Thoughts on Government* (1776), which called for three branches of government, each representing one function: executive, legislative, and judicial. This system of dispersed authority was devised to maintain a balance of power and ensure the legitimacy of governmental procedures. (p. 198)

**modernism:** A movement that questioned the ideals of progress and order, rejected realism, and emphasized new cultural forms. Modernism became the first great literary and artistic movement of the twentieth century and remains influential today. (p. 595)

**Monroe Doctrine:** The 1823 declaration by President James Monroe that the Western Hemisphere was closed to any further colonization or interference by European powers. In exchange, Monroe pledged that the United States would not become involved in European struggles. (p. 244)

**Montgomery Bus Boycott:** Yearlong boycott of Montgomery's segregated bus system in 1955–1956 by the city's African American population. The boycott brought Martin Luther King Jr. to national prominence and ended in victory when the Supreme Court declared segregated seating on public transportation unconstitutional. (p. 881)

**moral free agency:** The doctrine of free will that was the central message of Presbyterian minister Charles Grandison Finney. It was particularly attractive to members of the new middle class, who had accepted personal responsibility for their lives, improved their material condition, and welcomed Finney's assurance that heaven was also within their grasp. (p. 306)

**Moral Majority:** A political organization established by evangelist Jerry Falwell in 1979 to mobilize conservative Christian voters on behalf of Ronald Reagan's campaign for president. (p. 981)

**Mormonism:** The religion of members of the Church of Jesus Christ of Latter-day Saints, founded by Joseph Smith in 1830. After Smith's death at the hands of an angry mob, Brigham Young led many followers of Mormonism to lands in present-day Utah in 1846. (p. 352)

**Morrill Act:** An 1862 act that set aside 140 million federal acres that states could sell to raise money for public universities. (p. 516)

**muckrakers:** A critical term, first applied by Theodore Roosevelt, for investigative journalists who published exposés of political scandals and industrial abuses. (p. 619)

**Mugwumps:** A late-nineteenth-century branch of reform-minded Republicans who left their party in 1884 to support Democratic presidential candidate Grover Cleveland. Many Mugwumps were classical liberals who denounced corruption and advocated a reduction in government powers and civil service reform. (p. 639)

**Muller v. Oregon:** A 1908 Supreme Court case that upheld an Oregon law limiting women's workday to ten hours, based on the need to protect women's health for motherhood. *Muller* complicated the earlier decision in *Lochner v. New York*, laying out grounds on which states could intervene to protect workers. It divided women's rights activists, however, because some saw its provisions as discriminatory. (p. 652)

**multiculturalism:** The promotion of diversity in gender, race, ethnicity, religion, and sexual preference. This political and social policy became increasingly popular in the United States during the 1980s post–civil rights era. (p. 1015)

**multinational corporations:** Corporations with offices and factories in multiple countries, which expanded to find new markets and cheaper sources of labor. Globalization was made possible by the proliferation of these multinational corporations. (p. 1010)

**Munich Conference:** A conference in Munich held in September 1938 during which Britain and France agreed to allow Germany to annex the Sudetenland—a German-speaking border area of Czechoslovakia—in return for Hitler's pledge to seek no more territory. (p. 770)

**Munn v. Illinois:** An 1877 Supreme Court case that affirmed that states could regulate key businesses, such as railroads and grain elevators, if those businesses were "clothed in the public interest." (p. 514)

**mutual aid society:** An urban aid society that served members of an ethnic immigrant group, usually those from a particular province or town. The societies functioned as fraternal clubs that collected dues from members in order to pay support in case of death or disability. (p. 612)

**My Lai:** The 1968 execution by U.S. Army troops of nearly five hundred people in the South Vietnamese village of My Lai, including a large number of women and children. (p. 928)

**Nation of Islam:** A religion founded in the United States that became a leading source of black nationalist thought in the 1960s. Black Muslims preached an apocalyptic brand of Islam, anticipating the day when Allah would banish the white "devils" and give the black nation justice. (p. 892)

**National American Woman Suffrage Association:** Women's suffrage organization created in 1890 by the union of the National Woman Suffrage Association and the American Woman Suffrage Association. Up to national ratification of suffrage in 1920, the NAWSA played a central role in campaigning for women's right to vote. (p. 592)

**National Association for the Advancement of Colored People (NAACP):** An organization founded in 1910 by leading African American reformers and white allies as a vehicle for advocating equal rights for African Americans, especially through the courts. (p. 655)

**National Association of Colored Women:** An organization created in 1896 by African American women to provide community support. Through its local clubs, the NACW arranged for the care of orphans, founded homes for the elderly, advocated temperance, and undertook public health campaigns. (p. 591)

**National Association of Manufacturers:** An association of industrialists and business leaders opposed to government regulation. In the era of the New Deal, the group promoted free enterprise and capitalism through a publicity campaign of radio programs, motion pictures, billboards, and direct mail. (p. 746)

**National Audubon Society:** Named in honor of antebellum naturalist John James Audubon, a national organization formed in 1901 that advocated for broader government protections for wildlife. (p. 583)

**National Child Labor Committee:** A reform organization that worked (unsuccessfully) to win a federal law banning child labor. The NCLC hired photographer Lewis Hine to record brutal conditions in mines and mills where thousands of children worked. (p. 652)

**National Consumers' League:** Begun in New York, a national progressive organization that encouraged women, through their shopping decisions, to support fair wages and working conditions for industrial laborers. (p. 629)

**national debt:** The cumulative total of all budget deficits. (p. 983)

**National Defense Education Act:** A 1958 act, passed in response to the Soviet launching of the *Sputnik* satellite, that funneled millions of dollars into American universities, helping institutions such as the University of California at Berkeley and the Massachusetts Institute of Technology, among others, become the leading research centers in the world. (p. 842)

**National Interstate and Defense Highways Act:** A 1956 law authorizing the construction of a national highway system. (p. 857)

**National Municipal League:** A political reform organization that advised cities to elect small councils and hire professional city managers who would direct operations like a corporate executive. (p. 624)

**National Organization for Women (NOW):** Women's civil rights organization formed in 1966. Initially, NOW focused on eliminating gender discrimination in public institutions and the workplace, but by the 1970s it also embraced many of the issues raised by more radical feminists. (p. 909)

**National Origins Act:** A 1924 law limiting annual immigration from each country to no more than 2 percent of that nationality's percentage of the U.S. population as it had stood in 1890. The law severely limited immigration, especially from Southern and Eastern Europe. (p. 713)

**National Park Service:** A federal agency founded in 1916 that provided comprehensive oversight of the growing system of national parks. (p. 583)

**National Recovery Administration:** Federal agency established in June 1933 to promote industrial recovery during the Great Depression. It encouraged industrialists to voluntarily adopt codes that defined fair working conditions, set prices, and minimized competition. (p. 741)

*National Review:* A conservative magazine founded by editor William F. Buckley in 1955, who used it to criticize liberal policy. (p. 976)

**National Socialist (Nazi) Party:** German political party led by Adolf Hitler, who became chancellor of Germany in 1933. The party's ascent was fueled by huge World War I reparation payments, economic depression, fear of communism, labor unrest, and rising unemployment. (p. 768)

**National War Labor Board:** A federal agency founded in 1918 that established an eight-hour day for war workers (with time-and-a-half pay for overtime), endorsed equal pay for women, and supported workers' right to organize. (p. 689)

**National Woman Suffrage Association:** A suffrage group headed by Elizabeth Cady Stanton and Susan B. Anthony that stressed the need for women to lead organizations on their own behalf. The NWSA focused exclusively on women's rights — sometimes denigrating men of color, in the process — and took up the battle for a federal women's suffrage amendment. (p. 486)

**National Woman's Party:** A political party founded in 1916 that fought for an Equal Rights Amendment to the U.S. Constitution in the early twentieth century. (p. 695)

**nativist movements:** Antiforeign sentiment in the United States that fueled anti-immigrant and immigration-restriction policies against the Irish and Germans in the 1840s and the 1850s and against other ethnic immigrants in subsequent decades. (p. 310)

**natural rights:** The rights to life, liberty, and property. According to the English philosopher John Locke in *Two Treatises of*

*Government* (1690), political authority was not given by God to monarchs. Instead, it derived from social compacts that people made to preserve their natural rights. (p. 127)

**natural selection:** Charles Darwin's theory that when individual members of a species are born with random genetic mutations that better suit them for their environment—for example, camouflage coloring for a moth—these characteristics, since they are genetically transmissible, become dominant in future generations. (p. 594)

**naturalism:** A literary movement that suggested that human beings were not so much rational agents and shapers of their own destinies as blind victims of forces beyond their control. (p. 594)

**Naturalization, Alien, and Sedition Acts:** Three laws passed in 1798 that limited individual rights and threatened the fledgling party system. The Naturalization Act lengthened the residency requirement for citizenship, the Alien Act authorized the deportation of foreigners, and the Sedition Act prohibited the publication of insults or malicious attacks on the president or members of Congress. (p. 224)

**Navigation Acts:** English laws passed, beginning in the 1650s and 1660s, requiring that certain English colonial goods be shipped through English ports on English ships manned primarily by English sailors in order to benefit English merchants, shippers, and seamen. (p. 83)

**Negro Leagues:** All–African American professional baseball teams where black men could showcase athletic ability and race pride. The leagues thrived until the desegregation of baseball after World War II. (p. 581)

**neo-Europes:** Term for colonies in which colonists sought to replicate, or at least approximate, economies and social structures they knew at home. (p. 40)

**"neomercantilist":** A system of government-assisted economic development embraced by republican state legislatures throughout the nation, especially in the Northeast. This system of activist government encouraged private entrepreneurs to seek individual opportunity and the public welfare through market exchange. (p. 250)

**Neutrality Act of 1935:** Legislation that sought to avoid entanglement in foreign wars while protecting trade. It imposed an embargo on selling arms to warring countries and declared that Americans traveling on the ships of belligerent nations did so at their own risk. (p. 769)

**New Jersey Plan:** Alternative to the Virginia Plan drafted by delegates from small states, retaining the confederation's single-house congress with one vote per state. It shared with the Virginia Plan enhanced congressional powers to raise revenue, control commerce, and make binding requisitions on the states. (p. 206)

**New Left:** A term applied to radical students of the 1960s and 1970s, distinguishing their activism from the Old Left—the communists and socialists of the 1930s and 1940s who tended to focus on economic and labor questions rather than cultural issues. (p. 914)

**New Lights:** Evangelical preachers, many of them influenced by John Wesley, the founder of English Methodism, and George Whitefield, the charismatic itinerant preacher who brought his message to Britain's American colonies. They decried a Christian faith that was merely intellectual and emphasized the importance of a spiritual rebirth. (p. 132)

**"New Look":** The defense policy of the Eisenhower administration that stepped up production of the hydrogen bomb and developed long-range bombing capabilities. (p. 826)

**New Nationalism:** In a 1910 speech, Theodore Roosevelt called for a "New Nationalism" that promoted government intervention to enhance public welfare, including a federal child labor law, more recognition of labor rights, a national minimum wage for women, women's suffrage, and curbs on the power of federal courts to stop reform. (p. 656)

**Newlands Reclamation Act:** A 1902 law, supported by President Theodore Roosevelt, that allowed the federal government to sell public lands to raise money for irrigation projects that expanded agriculture on arid lands. (p. 651)

**1968 Democratic National Convention:** A 1968 convention held in Chicago during which numerous antiwar demonstrators outside the convention hall were tear-gassed and clubbed by police. Inside the convention hall, the delegates were bitterly divided over Vietnam. (p. 921)

**nonimportation movement:** Colonists attempted nonimportation agreements three times: in 1766, in response to the Stamp Act; in 1768, in response to the Townshend duties; and in 1774, in response to the Coercive Acts. In each case, colonial radicals pressured merchants to stop importing British goods. In 1774 nonimportation was adopted by the First Continental Congress and enforced by the Continental Association. American women became crucial to the movement by reducing their households' consumption of imported goods and producing large quantities of homespun cloth. (p. 161)

**North American Free Trade Agreement (NAFTA):** A 1993 treaty that eliminated all tariffs and trade barriers among the United States, Canada, and Mexico. (p. 1010)

**North Atlantic Treaty Organization (NATO):** Military alliance formed in 1949 among the United States, Canada, and Western European nations to counter any possible Soviet threat. (p. 812)

**Northwest Ordinance of 1787:** A land act that provided for orderly settlement and established a process by which settled territories would become the states of Ohio, Indiana, Illinois, Michigan, and Wisconsin. It also banned slavery in the Northwest Territory. (p. 201)

**notables:** Northern landlords, slave-owning planters, and seaport merchants who dominated the political system of the early nineteenth century. (p. 316)

**NSC-68:** Top-secret government report of April 1950 warning that national survival in the face of Soviet communism required a massive military buildup. (p. 813)

**nullification:** The constitutional argument advanced by John C. Calhoun that a state legislature or convention could void a law passed by Congress. (p. 324)

**Old Lights:** Conservative ministers opposed to the passion displayed by evangelical preachers; they preferred to emphasize the importance of cultivating a virtuous Christian life. (p. 132)

**Omaha Platform:** An 1892 statement by the Populists calling for stronger government to protect ordinary Americans. (p. 643)

**open door policy:** A claim put forth by U.S. Secretary of State John Hay that all nations seeking to do business in China should have equal trade access. (p. 679)

**Operation Rescue:** A movement founded by religious activist Randall Terry in 1987 that mounted protests outside abortion clinics and harassed their staffs and clients. (p. 1019)

**Operation Rolling Thunder:** Massive bombing campaign against North Vietnam authorized by President Johnson in 1965; against expectations, it ended up hardening the will of the North Vietnamese to continue fighting. (p. 911)

**Organization of Petroleum Exporting Countries (OPEC):** A cartel formed in 1960 by the Persian Gulf states and other oil-rich developing countries that allowed its members to exert greater control over the price of oil. (p. 938)

**Ostend Manifesto:** An 1854 manifesto that urged President Franklin Pierce to seize the slave-owning province of Cuba from Spain. Northern Democrats denounced this aggressive initiative, and the plan was scuttled. (p. 431)

**The Other America:** A 1962 book by left-wing social critic Michael Harrington, chronicling "the economic underworld of American life." His study made it clear that in economic terms the bottom class remained far behind. (p. 843)

**outwork:** A system of manufacturing, also known as putting out, used extensively in the English woolen industry in the sixteenth and seventeenth centuries. Merchants bought wool and then hired landless peasants who lived in small cottages to spin and weave it into cloth, which the merchants would sell in English and foreign markets. (p. 45)

**Palmer raids:** A series of raids led by Attorney General A. Mitchell Palmer on radical organizations that peaked in January 1920, when federal agents arrested six thousand citizens and aliens and denied them access to legal counsel. (p. 709)

**pan-Africanism:** The idea that people of African descent, in all parts of the world, have a common heritage and destiny and should cooperate in political action. (p. 720)

**Panama Canal:** A canal across the Isthmus of Panama connecting trade between the Atlantic and Pacific oceans. Built by the U.S. Army Corps of Engineers and opened in 1914, the canal gave U.S. naval vessels quick access to the Pacific and provided the United States with a commanding position in the Western Hemisphere. (p. 682)

**Panic of 1819:** First major economic crisis of the United States. Farmers and planters faced an abrupt 30 percent drop in world agricultural prices, and as farmers' income declined, they could not pay debts owed to stores and banks, many of which went bankrupt. (p. 251)

**Panic of 1837:** Second major economic crisis of the United States, which led to hard times from 1837 to 1843. (p. 334)

**Patient Protection and Affordable Care Act:** Sweeping 2010 health-care reform bill championed by President Obama that established nearly universal health insurance by providing subsidies and compelling larger businesses to offer coverage to employees. (p. 1031)

**patriarchy:** A gendered power structure in which social identity and property descend through the male line and male heads of family rule over women and children. (p. 18)

**patronage:** The power of elected officials to grant government jobs and favors to their supporters; also the jobs and favors themselves. (p. 106)

**Peace Corps:** Program launched by President Kennedy in 1961 through which young American volunteers helped with education, health, and other projects in developing countries around the world. (p. 832)

**Pearl Harbor:** A naval base in Pearl Harbor, Hawaii, that was attacked by Japanese bombers on December 7, 1941; more than 2,400 Americans were killed. The following day, President Roosevelt asked Congress for a declaration of war against Japan. (p. 773)

**peasants:** The traditional term for farmworkers in Europe. Some peasants owned land, while others leased or rented small plots from landlords. (p. 18)

**Pendleton Act:** An 1883 law establishing a nonpartisan Civil Service Commission to fill federal jobs by examination. The Pendleton Act dealt a major blow to the "spoils system" and sought to ensure that government positions were filled by trained, professional employees. (p. 638)

**Pennsylvania constitution of 1776:** A constitution that granted all taxpaying men the right to vote and hold office and created a unicameral (one-house) legislature with complete power; there was no governor to exercise a veto. Other provisions mandated a system of elementary education and protected citizens from imprisonment for debt. (p. 198)

**perestroika:** The economic restructuring policy introduced by Soviet president Mikhail Gorbachev during the 1980s that contributed, unintentionally, to the 1991 breakup of the Soviet Union. (p. 993)

**perfectionism:** Christian movement of the 1830s that believed people could achieve moral perfection in their earthly lives because the Second Coming of Christ had already occurred. (p. 352)

**Persian Gulf War:** The 1991 war between Iraq and a U.S.-led international coalition that was sparked by the 1990 Iraqi invasion of Kuwait. A forty-day bombing campaign against Iraq followed by coalition troops storming into Kuwait brought a quick coalition victory. (p. 998)

**Personal Responsibility and Work Opportunity Reconciliation Act:** Legislation signed by President Clinton in 1996 that replaced Aid to Families with Dependent Children, the major welfare program dating to the New Deal era, with Temporary Assistance for Needy Families, which provided grants to the states to assist the poor and which limited welfare payments to two years, with a lifetime maximum of five years. (p. 1022)

**personal-liberty laws:** Laws enacted in many northern states that guaranteed to all residents, including alleged fugitives, the right to a jury trial. (p. 431)

**Philipsburg Proclamation:** A 1779 proclamation that declared that any slave who deserted a rebel master would receive protection, freedom, and land from Great Britain. (p. 190)

**Pietism:** A Christian revival moment characterized by Bible study, the conversion experience, and the individual's personal relationship with God. It began as an effort to reform the German Lutheran Church in the mid-seventeenth century and became widely influential in Britain and its colonies in the eighteenth century. (p. 126)

**Pilgrims:** One of the first Protestant groups to come to America, seeking a separation from the Church of England. They founded Plymouth, the first permanent community in New England, in 1620. (p. 60)

***Planned Parenthood of Southeastern Pennsylvania v. Casey:*** A 1992 Supreme Court case that upheld a law requiring a twenty-four-hour waiting period prior to an abortion. Although the decision upheld certain restrictions on abortions, it affirmed the "essential holding" in *Roe v. Wade* (1973) that women had a constitutional right to control their reproduction. (p. 1020)

**Platt Amendment:** A 1902 amendment to the Cuban constitution that blocked Cuba from making a treaty with any country except the United States and gave the United States the right to intervene in Cuban affairs. The amendment was a condition for U.S. withdrawal from the newly independent island. (p. 678)

***Plessy v. Ferguson:*** An 1896 Supreme Court case that ruled that racially segregated railroad cars and other public facilities, if they claimed to be "separate but equal," were permissible according to the Fourteenth Amendment. (p. 577)

**political machine:** A complex, hierarchical party organization such as New York's Tammany Hall, whose candidates remained in office on the strength of their political organization and their personal relationship with voters, especially working-class immigrants who had little alternative access to political power. (p. 619)

**political machine:** A highly organized group of insiders that directs a political party. As the power of notables waned in the 1820s, disciplined political parties usually run by professional politicians appeared in a number of states. (p. 317)

**Popular Front:** A small but vocal group of Americans who pushed for greater U.S. involvement in Europe. American Communist Party members, African American civil rights activists, and trade unionists, among other members of the Popular Front coalition, encouraged Roosevelt to take a stronger stand against European fascism. (p. 770)

**popular sovereignty:** The principle that ultimate power lies in the hands of the electorate. (p. 179)

**Port Huron Statement:** A 1962 manifesto by Students for a Democratic Society from its first national convention in Port Huron, Michigan, expressing students' disillusionment with the nation's consumer culture and the gulf between rich and poor, as well as a rejection of Cold War foreign policy, including the war in Vietnam. (p. 914)

**"positive good" argument:** An argument in the 1830s that the institution of slavery was a "positive good" because it subsidized an elegant lifestyle for the white elite and provided tutelage for genetically inferior Africans. (p. 386)

**Potsdam Conference:** The July 1945 conference in which American officials convinced the Soviet Union leader Joseph Stalin to accept German reparations only from the Soviet zone, or far eastern part of Germany. The agreement paved the way for the division of Germany into East and West. (p. 807)

**predestination:** The Protestant Christian belief that God chooses certain people for salvation before they are born. Sixteenth-century theologian John Calvin was the main proponent of this doctrine, which became a fundamental tenet of Puritan theology. (p. 22)

**Presidential Commission on the Status of Women:** Commission appointed by President Kennedy in 1961, which issued a 1963 report documenting job and educational discrimination. (p. 909)

**primogeniture:** The practice of passing family land, by will or by custom, to the eldest son. (p. 18)

**Proclamation of Neutrality:** A proclamation issued by President George Washington in 1793, allowing U.S. citizens to trade with all belligerents in the war between France and Great Britain. (p. 219)

**producerism:** The argument that real economic wealth is created by workers who make their living by physical labor, such as farmers and craftsmen, and that merchants, lawyers, bankers, and other middlemen unfairly gain their wealth from such "producers." (p. 566)

**progressivism:** A loose term for political reformers — especially those from the elite and middle classes — who worked to improve the political system, fight poverty, conserve environmental resources, and increase government involvement in the economy. Giving their name to the "Progressive Era," such reformers were often prompted to act by fear that mass, radical protests by workers and farmers would spread, as well as by their desire to enhance social welfare and social justice. (p. 624)

**prohibition:** The ban on the manufacture and sale of alcohol that went into effect in January 1920 with the Eighteenth Amendment. Prohibition was repealed in 1933. (p. 712)

**Proposition 13:** A measure passed overwhelmingly by Californians to roll back property taxes, cap future increases for present owners, and require that all tax measures have a two-thirds majority in the legislature. Proposition 13 inspired "tax revolts" across the country and helped conservatives define an enduring issue: low taxes. (p. 947)

**Proposition 209:** A proposition approved by California voters in 1996 that outlawed affirmative action in state employment and public education. (p. 1015)

**proprietorship:** A colony created through a grant of land from the English monarch to an individual or group, who then set up a form of government largely independent from royal control. (p. 82)

**protective tariff:** A tax or duty on foreign producers of goods coming into or imported into the United States; tariffs gave U.S.

manufacturers a competitive advantage in America's gigantic domestic market. (p. 510)

**Protestant Reformation:** The reform movement that began in 1517 with Martin Luther's critiques of the Roman Catholic Church and that precipitated an enduring schism that divided Protestants from Catholics. (p. 22)

**Public Works Administration:** A New Deal construction program established by Congress in 1933. Designed to put people back to work, the PWA built the Boulder Dam (renamed Hoover Dam) and Grand Coulee Dam, among other large public works projects. (p. 741)

**Pure Food and Drug Act:** A 1906 law regulating the conditions in the food and drug industries to ensure a safe supply of food and medicine. (p. 629)

**Puritans:** Dissenters from the Church of England who wanted a genuine Reformation rather than the partial Reformation sought by Henry VIII. The Puritans' religious principles emphasized the importance of an individual's relationship with God developed through Bible study, prayer, and introspection. (p. 61)

**Quakers:** Epithet for members of the Society of Friends. Their belief that God spoke directly to each individual through an "inner light" and that neither ministers nor the Bible was essential to discovering God's Word put them in conflict with both the Church of England and orthodox Puritans. (p. 82)

**Quartering Act of 1765:** A British law passed by Parliament at the request of General Thomas Gage, the British military commander in America, that required colonial governments to provide barracks and food for British troops. (p. 157)

**race riot:** A term for an attack on African Americans by white mobs, triggered by political conflicts, street altercations, or rumors of crime. In some cases, such "riots" were not spontaneous but planned in advance by a group of leaders seeking to enforce white supremacy. (p. 614)

**Radical Republicans:** The members of the Republican Party who were bitterly opposed to slavery and to southern slave owners since the mid-1850s. With the Confiscation Act in 1861, Radical Republicans began to use wartime legislation to destroy slavery. (p. 463)

**ragtime:** A form of music, apparently named for its "ragged rhythm," that became wildly popular in the early twentieth century among audiences of all classes and races and that ushered in an urban dance craze. Ragtime was an important form of "crossover" music, borrowed from working-class African Americans by enthusiasts who were white and middle class. (p. 617)

**"rain follows the plow":** An unfounded theory that settlement of the Great Plains caused an increase in rainfall. (p. 519)

**Reagan coalition:** A coalition supporting Ronald Reagan that included the traditional core of Republican Party voters, middle-class suburbanites and migrants to the Sunbelt states, blue-collar Catholics, and a large contingent of southern whites, an electorally key group of former Democrats that had been gradually moving toward the Republican Party since 1964. (p. 981)

**Reagan Democrats:** Blue-collar Catholics from industrialized midwestern states such as Michigan, Ohio, and Illinois who were dissatisfied with the direction of liberalism in the 1970s and left the Democratic Party for the Republicans. (p. 982)

**realism:** A movement that called for writers and artists to picture daily life as precisely and truly as possible. (p. 594)

**recall:** A pioneering progressive idea, enacted in Wisconsin, Oregon, California, and other states, that gave citizens the right to remove unpopular politicians from office through a vote. (p. 652)

*reconquista:* The campaign by Spanish Catholics to drive North African Moors (Muslim Arabs) from the European mainland. After a centuries-long effort to recover their lands, the Spaniards defeated the Moors at Granada in 1492 and secured control of all of Spain. (p. 31)

**Reconstruction Act of 1867:** An act that divided the conquered South into five military districts, each under the command of a U.S. general. To reenter the Union, former Confederate states had to grant the vote to freedmen and deny it to leading ex-Confederates. (p. 482)

**Red Scare:** A term for anticommunist hysteria that swept the United States, first after World War I, and led to a series of government raids on alleged subversives and a suppression of civil liberties. (p. 708)

**"Redemption":** A term used by southern Democrats for the overthrow of elected governments that ended Reconstruction in many parts of the South. So-called Redeemers terrorized Republicans, especially in districts with large proportions of black voters, and killed and intimidated their opponents to regain power. (p. 498)

**redemptioner:** A common type of indentured servant in the Middle colonies in the eighteenth century. Unlike other indentured servants, redemptioners did not sign a contract before leaving Europe. Instead, they found employers after arriving in America. (p. 124)

**referendum:** The process of voting directly on a proposed policy measure rather than leaving it in the hands of elected legislators; a progressive reform. (p. 652)

**Regulators:** Landowning protestors who organized in North and South Carolina in the 1760s and 1770s to demand that the eastern-controlled government provide western districts with more courts, fairer taxation, and greater representation in the assembly. (p. 142)

**Religious Right:** Politically active religious conservatives, especially Catholics and evangelical Christians, who became particularly vocal in the 1980s against feminism, abortion, and homosexuality and who promoted "family values." (p. 976)

**"Remember the *Maine*":** After the U.S. battle cruiser *Maine* exploded in Havana harbor, the *New York Journal* rallied its readers to "Remember the *Maine*," galvanizing popular support for the U.S. war against Spain. Evidence of Spanish complicity in the explosion was not found; the likely cause was later found to have been internal to the ship. (p. 675)

**Renaissance:** A cultural transformation in the arts and learning that began in Italy in the fourteenth century and spread through much of Europe. Its ideals reshaped art and architecture and gave rise to civic humanism. (p. 20)

**Report on Manufactures:** A proposal by treasury secretary Alexander Hamilton in 1791 calling for the federal government to urge the expansion of American manufacturing while imposing tariffs on foreign imports. (p. 218)

**Report on the Public Credit:** Alexander Hamilton's 1790 report recommending that the federal government should assume all state debts and fund the national debt — that is, offer interest on it rather than repaying it — at full value. Hamilton's goal was to make the new country creditworthy, not debt-free. (p. 216)

**republic:** A state without a monarch or prince that is governed by representatives of the people. (p. 19)

**republican aristocracy:** The Old South gentry that built impressive mansions, adopted the manners and values of the English landed gentry, and feared federal government interference with their slave property. (p. 386)

**republican motherhood:** The idea that the primary political role of American women was to instill a sense of patriotic duty and republican virtue in their children and mold them into exemplary republican citizens. (p. 259)

**Revenue Act (1942):** An act that expanded the number of people paying income taxes from 3.9 million to 42.6 million. These taxes on personal incomes and business profits paid half the cost of World War II. (p. 775)

**revival:** A renewal of religious enthusiasm in a Christian congregation. In the eighteenth century, revivals were often inspired by evangelical preachers who urged their listeners to experience a rebirth. (p. 129)

**rights liberalism:** The conviction that individuals require government protection from discrimination. This version of liberalism was promoted by the civil rights and women's movements and focused on identities — such as race or gender — rather than the general social welfare of New Deal liberalism. (p. 868)

*Roe v. Wade:* The 1973 Supreme Court ruling that the Constitution protects the right to abortion, which states cannot prohibit in the early stages of pregnancy. The decision galvanized social conservatives and made abortion a controversial policy issue for decades to come. (p. 956)

**Rome-Berlin Axis:** A political and military alliance formed in 1936 between German dictator Adolf Hitler and the Italian dictator Benito Mussolini. (p. 769)

**Roosevelt Corollary:** The 1904 assertion by President Theodore Roosevelt that the United States would act as a "policeman" in the Caribbean region and intervene in the affairs of nations that were guilty of "wrongdoing or impotence" in order to protect U.S. interests in Latin America. (p. 683)

**Roosevelt recession:** A recession from 1937 to 1938 that occurred after President Roosevelt cut the federal budget. (p. 751)

**Root-Takahira Agreement:** A 1908 agreement between the United States and Japan confirming principles of free oceanic commerce and recognizing Japan's authority over Manchuria. (p. 682)

**royal colony:** In the English system, a royal colony was chartered by the crown. The colony's governor was appointed by the crown and served according to the instructions of the Board of Trade. (p. 52)

**Rural Electrification Administration:** An agency established in 1935 to promote nonprofit farm cooperatives that offered loans to farmers to install power lines. (p. 760)

**Rust Belt:** The once heavily industrialized regions of the Northeast and Midwest that went into decline after deindustrialization. By the 1970s and 1980s, these regions were full of abandoned plants and distressed communities. (p. 944)

**Sabbatarian movement:** A movement to preserve the Sabbath as a holy day. These reformers believed that declining observance by Christians of the Sabbath (Sunday) was the greatest threat to religion in the United States. (p. 306)

**salutary neglect:** A term used to describe British colonial policy during the reigns of George I (r. 1714–1727) and George II (r. 1727–1760). By relaxing their supervision of internal colonial affairs, royal bureaucrats inadvertently assisted the rise of self-government in North America. (p. 106)

**Sand Creek massacre:** The November 29, 1864, massacre of more than a hundred peaceful Cheyennes, largely women and children, by John M. Chivington's Colorado militia. (p. 527)

**Sandinistas:** The democratically elected group in Nicaragua that President Reagan accused of threatening U.S. business interests. Reagan attempted to overthrow them by ordering the CIA to assist an armed opposition group called the Contras. (p. 992)

**scalawags:** Southern whites who supported Republican Reconstruction and were ridiculed by ex-Confederates as worthless traitors. (p. 493)

**scientific management:** A system of organizing work developed by Frederick W. Taylor in the late nineteenth century. It was designed to coax maximum output from the individual worker, increase efficiency, and reduce production costs. (p. 552)

**Scopes trial:** The 1925 trial of John Scopes, a biology teacher in Dayton, Tennessee, for violating his state's ban on teaching evolution. The trial created a nationwide media frenzy and came to be seen as a showdown between urban and rural values. (p. 713)

**scorched-earth campaign:** A campaign in the Shenandoah Valley of Virginia by Union general Philip H. Sheridan's troops. The troops destroyed grain, barns, and other useful resources to punish farmers who had aided Confederate raiders. (p. 468)

**Second Bank of the United States:** National bank with multiple branches chartered in 1816 for twenty years. Intended to help regulate the economy, the bank became a major issue in Andrew Jackson's reelection campaign in 1832. (p. 325)

**Second Continental Congress:** Legislative body that governed the United States from May 1775 through the war's duration. It established an army, created its own money, and declared independence once all hope for a peaceful reconciliation with Britain was gone. (p. 176)

**Second Great Awakening:** Unprecedented religious revival that swept the nation between 1790 and 1850; it also proved to be a major impetus for the reform movements of the era. (p. 271)

**Second Hundred Years' War:** An era of warfare beginning with the War of the League of Augsburg in 1689 and lasting until the defeat of Napoleon at Waterloo in 1815. In that time, England fought in seven major wars; the longest era of peace lasted only twenty-six years. (p. 88)

**secret ballot:** Form of voting that allows the voter to enter a choice in privacy without having to submit a recognizable ballot or to voice the choice out loud to others. (p. 393)

**Securities and Exchange Commission:** A commission established by Congress in 1934 to regulate the stock market. The commission had broad powers to determine how stocks and bonds were sold to the public, to set rules for margin (credit) transactions, and to prevent stock sales by those with inside information about corporate plans. (p. 745)

**Sedition Act of 1918:** Wartime law that prohibited any words or behavior that might promote resistance to the United States or help in the cause of its enemies. (p. 691)

**self-made man:** A nineteenth-century ideal that celebrated men who rose to wealth or social prominence from humble origins through self-discipline, hard work, and temperate habits. (p. 304)

**Seneca Falls Convention:** The first women's rights convention in the United States. Held in Seneca Falls, New York, in 1848, it resulted in a manifesto extending to women the egalitarian republican ideology of the Declaration of Independence. (p. 371)

**sentimentalism:** A way of experiencing the world that emphasized emotions and a sensuous appreciation of God, nature, and people. Part of the Romantic movement, it spread to the United States from Europe in the late eighteenth century. (p. 258)

**separate sphere:** A term used by historians to describe the nineteenth-century view that men and women have different gender-defined characteristics and, consequently, that men should dominate the public sphere of politics and economics, while women should manage the private sphere of home and family. (p. 367)

**service industries:** Term that includes food, beverage, and tourist industries, financial and medical service industries, and computer technology industries, which were the leading sectors of U.S. growth in the second half of the 1980s. This pattern represented a shift from reliance on the heavy industries of steel, autos, and chemicals. (p. 987)

**Servicemen's Readjustment Act (1944):** Popularly known as the GI Bill, legislation authorizing the government to provide World War II veterans with funds for education, housing, and health care, as well as loans to start businesses and buy homes. (p. 781)

**sharecropping:** The labor system by which landowners and impoverished southern farmworkers, particularly African Americans, divided the proceeds from crops harvested on the landowner's property. With local merchants providing supplies — in exchange for a lien on the crop — sharecropping pushed farmers into cash-crop production and often trapped them in long-term debt. (p. 491)

**Sharon Statement:** Drafted by founding members of the Young Americans for Freedom (YAF), this manifesto outlined the group's principles and inspired young conservatives who would play important roles in the Reagan administration in the 1980s. (p. 918)

**Shays's Rebellion:** A 1786–1787 uprising led by dissident farmers in western Massachusetts, many of them Revolutionary War veterans, protesting the taxation policies of the eastern elites who controlled the state's government. (p. 204)

***Shelley v. Kraemer:*** A 1948 Supreme Court decision that outlawed restrictive covenants on the occupancy of housing developments by African Americans, Asian Americans, and other minorities. Because the Court decision did not actually prohibit racial discrimination in housing, unfair practices against minority groups continued until passage of the Fair Housing Act in 1968. (p. 857)

**Sheppard-Towner Federal Maternity and Infancy Act:** The first federally funded health-care legislation that provided federal funds for medical clinics, prenatal education programs, and visiting nurses. (p. 709)

**Sherman Antitrust Act:** Landmark 1890 act that forbade anticompetitive business activities, requiring the federal government to investigate trusts and any companies operating in violation of the act. (p. 642)

**Sierra Club:** An organization founded in 1892 that was dedicated to the enjoyment and preservation of America's great mountains (including the Sierra Nevadas) and wilderness environments. Encouraged by such groups, national and state governments began to set aside more public lands for preservation and recreation. (p. 583)

**silent majority:** Term derived from the title of a book by Ben J. Wattenberg and Richard Scammon (called *The Real Majority*) and used by Nixon in a 1969 speech to describe those who supported his positions but did not publicly assert their voices, in contrast to those involved in the antiwar, civil rights, and women's movements. (p. 926)

***Silent Spring:*** Book published in 1962 by biologist Rachel Carson. Its analysis of the pesticide DDT's toxic impact on the human and natural food chains galvanized environmental activists. (p. 939)

***Slaughter-House Cases:*** A group of decisions begun in 1873 in which the Court began to undercut the power of the Fourteenth Amendment to protect African American rights. (p. 500)

**slave society:** A society in which the institution of slavery affects all aspects of life. (p. 388)

**"slavery follows the flag":** The assertion by John C. Calhoun that planters could by right take their slave property into newly opened territories. (p. 428)

**Smoot-Hawley Tariff:** A high tariff enacted in 1930 during the Great Depression. By taxing imported goods, Congress hoped to stimulate American manufacturing, but the tariff triggered retaliatory tariffs in other countries, which further hindered global trade and led to greater economic contraction. (p. 736)

**Social Darwinism:** An idea, actually formulated not by Charles Darwin but by British philosopher and sociologist Herbert Spencer, that human society advanced through ruthless competition and the "survival of the fittest." (p. 594)

**Social Gospel:** A movement to renew religious faith through dedication to public welfare and social justice, reforming both society and the self through Christian service. (p. 600)

**Social Security Act:** A 1935 act with three main provisions: old-age pensions for workers; a joint federal-state system of compensation for unemployed workers; and a program of payments to widowed mothers and the blind, deaf, and disabled. (p. 747)

**social settlement:** A community welfare center that investigated the plight of the urban poor, raised funds to address urgent needs, and helped neighborhood residents advocate on their own behalf. Social settlements became a nationally recognized reform strategy during the Progressive Era. (p. 627)

**socialism:** A system of social and economic organization based on the common ownership of goods or state control of the economy. (p. 351)

**soft power:** The exercise of popular cultural influence abroad, as American radio and movies became popular around the world in the 1920s, transmitting American cultural ideals overseas. (p. 726)

**"Solid South":** The post-Reconstruction goal—achieved by the early twentieth century—of almost complete electoral control of the South by the Democratic Party. (p. 646)

**Sons of Liberty:** Colonists—primarily middling merchants and artisans—who banded together to protest the Stamp Act and other imperial reforms of the 1760s. The group originated in Boston in 1765 but soon spread to all the colonies. (p. 158)

**South Atlantic System:** A new agricultural and commercial order that produced sugar, tobacco, rice, and other tropical and subtropical products for an international market. Its plantation societies were ruled by European planter-merchants and worked by hundreds of thousands of enslaved Africans. (p. 90)

**Southern Christian Leadership Conference (SCLC):** After the Montgomery Bus Boycott, Martin Luther King Jr. and other civil rights leaders formed the SCLC in 1957 to coordinate civil rights activity in the South. (p. 882)

**Specie Circular:** An executive order in 1836 that required the Treasury Department to accept only gold and silver in payment for lands in the national domain. (p. 338)

**spoils system:** The widespread award of public jobs to political supporters after an electoral victory. In 1829, Andrew Jackson instituted the system on the national level, arguing that the rotation of officeholders was preferable to a permanent group of bureaucrats. (p. 318)

*Sputnik:* The world's first satellite, launched by the Soviet Union in 1957. After its launch, the United States funded research and education to catch up in the Cold War space competition. (p. 842)

**squatter:** Someone who settles on land he or she does not own or rent. Many eighteenth-century settlers established themselves on land before it was surveyed and entered for sale, requesting the first right to purchase the land when sales began. (p. 121)

**squatter sovereignty:** A plan promoted by Democratic candidate Senator Lewis Cass under which Congress would allow settlers in each territory to determine its status as free or slave. (p. 424)

**stagflation:** An economic term coined in the 1970s to describe the condition in which inflation and unemployment rise at the same time. (p. 942)

**Stamp Act Congress:** A congress of delegates from nine assemblies that met in New York City in October 1765 to protest the loss of American "rights and liberties," especially the right to trial by jury. The congress challenged the constitutionality of both the Stamp and Sugar Acts by declaring that only the colonists' elected representatives could tax them. (p. 158)

**Stamp Act of 1765:** British law imposing a tax on all paper used in the colonies. Widespread resistance to the Stamp Act prevented it from taking effect and led to its repeal in 1766. (p. 157)

**states' rights:** An interpretation of the Constitution that exalts the sovereignty of the states and circumscribes the authority of the national government. (p. 324)

**States' Rights Democratic Party (Dixiecrats):** A breakaway party of white Democrats from the South, formed for the 1948 election. Its formation shed light on an internal struggle between the civil rights aims of the party's liberal wing and southern white Democrats. (p. 875)

**Stonewall Inn:** A two-day riot by Stonewall Inn patrons after the police raided the gay bar in New York's Greenwich Village in 1969; the event contributed to the rapid rise of a gay liberation movement. (p. 926)

**Stono Rebellion:** Slave uprising in 1739 along the Stono River in South Carolina in which a group of slaves armed themselves, plundered six plantations, and killed more than twenty colonists. Colonists quickly suppressed the rebellion. (p. 101)

**STOP ERA:** An organization founded by Phyllis Schlafly in 1972 to fight the Equal Rights Amendment. (p. 953)

**Student Nonviolent Coordinating Committee (SNCC):** A student civil rights group founded in 1960 under the mentorship of activist Ella Baker. SNCC initially embraced an interracial and nonhierarchical structure that encouraged leadership at the grassroots level and practiced the civil disobedience principles of Martin Luther King Jr. As violence toward civil rights activists escalated nationwide in the 1960s, SNCC expelled nonblack members and promoted "black power" and the teachings of Malcolm X. (p. 882)

**Students for a Democratic Society (SDS):** An organization for social change founded by college students in 1960. (p. 914)

**Sugar Act of 1764:** British law that decreased the duty on French molasses, making it more attractive for shippers to obey the law, and at the same time raised penalties for smuggling. The act enraged New England merchants, who opposed both the tax and the fact that prosecuted merchants would be tried by British-appointed judges in a vice-admiralty court. (p. 155)

**Sunbelt:** Name applied to the Southwest and South, which grew rapidly after World War II as a center of defense industries and nonunionized labor. (p. 862)

**supply-side economics (Reaganomics):** Economic theory that tax cuts for individuals and businesses encourage investment and production (supply) and stimulate consumption (demand) because individuals can keep more of their earnings. In reality, supply-side economics created a massive federal budget deficit. (p. 982)

**Taft-Hartley Act:** Law passed by the Republican-controlled Congress in 1947 that overhauled the 1935 National Labor Relations Act, placing restrictions on organized labor that made it more difficult for unions to organize workers. (p. 819)

**talented tenth:** A term used by Harvard-educated sociologist W. E. B. Du Bois for the top 10 percent of educated African Americans, whom he called on to develop new strategies to advocate for civil rights. (p. 655)

**Tariff of Abominations:** A tariff enacted in 1828 that raised duties significantly on raw materials, textiles, and iron goods. New York senator Van Buren hoped to win the support of farmers in New York, Ohio, and Kentucky with the tariff, but it enraged the South, which had no industries that needed tariff protection and resented the higher cost of imported dutied goods. (p. 320)

**task system:** A system of labor common in the rice-growing regions of South Carolina in which a slave was assigned a daily task to complete and allowed to do as he wished upon its completion. (p. 397)

**tax revolt:** A movement to lower or eliminate taxes. California's Proposition 13, which rolled back property taxes, capped future increases for present owners, and required that all tax measures have a two-thirds majority in the legislature, was the result of one such revolt, inspiring similar movements across the country. (p. 946)

**Tea Act of May 1773:** British act that lowered the existing tax on tea and granted exemptions to the East India Company to make their tea cheaper in the colonies and entice boycotting Americans to buy it. Resistance to the Tea Act led to the passage of the Coercive Acts and imposition of military rule in Massachusetts. (p. 168)

**Tea Party:** A set of far-right opposition groups that emerged during President Obama's first term and gave voice to the extreme individualism and antigovernment sentiment traditionally associated with right-wing movements in the United States. (p. 1031)

**Teapot Dome:** Nickname for scandal in which Interior Secretary Albert Fall accepted $300,000 in bribes for leasing oil reserves on public land in Teapot Dome, Wyoming. It was part of a larger pattern of corruption that marred Warren G. Harding's presidency. (p. 710)

**teenager:** A term for a young adult. American youth culture, focused on the spending power of the "teenager," emerged as a cultural phenomenon in the postwar decades. (p. 847)

**Teller Amendment:** An amendment to the 1898 U.S. declaration of war against Spain disclaiming any intention by the United States to occupy Cuba. The amendment assured the public that the United States would uphold democracy abroad as well as at home. (p. 675)

**Ten Percent Plan:** A plan proposed by President Abraham Lincoln during the Civil War, but never implemented, that would have granted amnesty to most ex-Confederates and allowed each rebellious state to return to the Union as soon as 10 percent of its voters had taken a loyalty oath and the state had approved the Thirteenth Amendment. (p. 480)

**tenancy:** The rental of property. To attract tenants in New York's Hudson River Valley, Dutch and English manorial lords granted long tenancy leases, with the right to sell improvements — houses and barns, for example — to the next tenant. (p. 116)

**tenement:** A high-density, cheap, five- or six-story housing unit designed for working-class urban populations. In the late nineteenth and early twentieth centuries, tenements became a symbol of urban immigrant poverty. (p. 614)

**Tennessee Valley Authority:** An agency funded by Congress in 1933 that integrated flood control, reforestation, electricity generation, and agricultural and industrial development in the Tennessee Valley area. (p. 760)

**Tet offensive:** Major campaign of attacks launched throughout South Vietnam in January 1968 by the North Vietnamese and Vietcong. A major turning point in the war, it exposed the credibility gap between official statements and the war's reality, and it shook Americans' confidence in the government. (p. 919)

**Three Mile Island:** A nuclear plant near Harrisburg, Pennsylvania, where a reactor core came close to a meltdown in March 1979. After the incident at Three Mile Island, no new nuclear plants were authorized in the United States, though a handful with existing authorization were built in the 1980s. (p. 942)

**Title IX:** A law passed by Congress in 1972 that broadened the 1964 Civil Rights Act to include educational institutions, prohibiting colleges and universities that received federal funds from discriminating on the basis of sex. By requiring comparable funding for sports programs, Title IX made women's athletics a real presence on college campuses. (p. 925)

**"To Secure These Rights":** The 1947 report by the Presidential Committee on Civil Rights that called for robust federal action to ensure equality for African Americans. President Truman asked Congress to make all of the report's recommendations — including the abolition of poll taxes and the restoration of the Fair Employment Practices Commission — into law, leading to discord in the Democratic Party. (p. 875)

**toleration:** The allowance of different religious practices. Lord Baltimore persuaded the Maryland assembly to enact the Toleration Act (1649), which granted all Christians the right to follow their beliefs and hold church services. The crown imposed toleration on Massachusetts Bay in its new royal charter of 1691. (p. 62)

**total war:** A form of warfare that mobilizes all of a society's resources—economic, political, and cultural—in support of the military effort. (p. 452)

**town meeting:** A system of local government in New England in which all male heads of households met regularly to elect selectmen, levy local taxes, and regulate markets, roads, and schools. (p. 64)

**Townsend Plan:** A plan proposed by Francis Townsend in 1933 that would give $200 a month (about $3,300 today) to citizens over the age of sixty. Townsend Clubs sprang up across the country in support of the plan, mobilizing mass support for old-age pensions. (p. 747)

**Townshend Act of 1767:** British law that established new duties on tea, glass, lead, paper, and painters' colors imported into the colonies. The Townshend duties led to boycotts and heightened tensions between Britain and the American colonies. (p. 161)

**Trail of Tears:** Forced westward journey of Cherokees from their lands in Georgia to present-day Oklahoma in 1838. Nearly a quarter of the Cherokees died en route. (p. 331)

**transcendentalism:** A nineteenth-century intellectual movement that posited the importance of an ideal world of mystical knowledge and harmony beyond the immediate grasp of the senses. Transcendentalists Ralph Waldo Emerson and Henry David Thoreau called for the critical examination of society and emphasized individuality, self-reliance, and nonconformity. (p. 346)

**transcontinental railroad:** The railway line completed on May 10, 1869, that connected the Central Pacific and Union Pacific lines, enabling goods to move by railway from the eastern United States all the way to California. (p. 508)

**trans-Saharan trade:** The primary avenue of trade for West Africans before European traders connected them to the Atlantic World. Controlled in turn by the Ghana, Mali, and Songhai empires, it carried slaves and gold to North Africa in exchange for salt and other goods. (p. 23)

**Treaty of Ghent:** The treaty signed on Christmas Eve 1814 that ended the War of 1812. It retained the prewar borders of the United States. (p. 241)

**Treaty of Greenville:** A 1795 treaty between the United States and various Indian tribes in Ohio. American negotiators acknowledged Indian ownership of the land, and, in return for various payments, the Western Confederacy ceded most of Ohio to the United States. (p. 226)

**Treaty of Kanagawa:** An 1854 treaty that, in the wake of a show of military force by U.S. Commodore Matthew Perry, allowed American ships to refuel at two ports in Japan. (p. 510)

**Treaty of Paris of 1783:** The treaty that ended the Revolutionary War. In the treaty, Great Britain formally recognized American independence and relinquished its claims to lands south of the Great Lakes and east of the Mississippi River. (p. 196)

**Treaty of Versailles:** The 1919 treaty that ended World War I. The agreement redrew the map of the world, assigned Germany sole responsibility for the war, and saddled it with a debt of $33 billion in war damages. Its long-term impact around the globe—including the creation of British and French imperial "mandates"—was catastrophic. (p. 697)

**Triangle Shirtwaist Fire:** A devastating fire that quickly spread through the Triangle Shirtwaist Company in New York City on March 25, 1911, killing 146 people. In the wake of the tragedy, fifty-six state laws were passed dealing with such issues as fire hazards, unsafe machines, and wages and working hours for women and children. The fire also provided a national impetus for industrial reform. (p. 629)

**tribalization:** The adaptation of stateless peoples to the demands imposed on them by neighboring states. (p. 88)

**tribute:** The practice of collecting goods from conquered peoples. The Aztecs and Incas relied on systems of tribute before they were conquered by Spain; after the conquest, Spanish officials adapted indigenous tribute systems to their own needs by binding Indian labor to powerful men through the *encomienda* and *mita* systems. (p. 8)

**Truman Doctrine:** President Harry S. Truman's commitment to "support free peoples who are resisting attempted subjugation by armed minorities or by outside pressures." First applied to Greece and Turkey in 1947, it became the justification for U.S. intervention into several countries during the Cold War. (p. 809)

**trust:** A small group of associates that hold stock from a group of combined firms, managing them as a single entity. Trusts quickly evolved into other centralized business forms, but progressive critics continued to refer to giant firms like United States Steel and Standard Oil as "trusts." (p. 548)

**U.S. Fisheries Commission:** A federal bureau established in 1871 that made recommendations to stem the decline in wild fish. Its creation was an important step toward wildlife conservation and management. (p. 525)

***U.S. v. Cruikshank:*** A decision in which the Supreme Court ruled that voting rights remained a state matter unless the state itself violated those rights. If former slaves' rights were violated by individuals or private groups, that lay beyond federal jurisdiction. Like the *Slaughter-House Cases*, the ruling undercut the power of the Fourteenth Amendment to protect African American rights. (p. 500)

**"unchurched":** Irreligious Americans, who probably constituted a majority of the population in 1800. Evangelical Methodist and Baptist churches were by far the most successful institutions in attracting new members from the unchurched. (p. 270)

**Underground Railroad:** An informal network of whites and free blacks in the South that assisted fugitive slaves to reach freedom in the North. (p. 362)

**Union League:** A secret fraternal order in which black and white Republicans joined forces in the late 1860s. The League became a powerful political association that spread through the former Confederacy, pressuring Congress to uphold justice for freedmen. (p. 493)

**unions:** Organizations of workers that began during the Industrial Revolution to bargain with employers over wages, hours, benefits, and control of the workplace. (p. 291)

**United Farm Workers (UFW):** A union of farmworkers founded in 1962 by Cesar Chavez and Dolores Huerta that sought to empower the mostly Mexican American migrant farmworkers who faced discrimination and exploitative conditions, especially in the Southwest. (p. 897)

**United Nations:** An international body agreed upon at the Yalta Conference, and founded at a conference in San Francisco in 1945, consisting of a General Assembly, in which all nations are represented, and a Security Council of the five major Allied powers—the United States, Britain, France, China, and the Soviet Union—and seven other nations elected on a rotating basis. (p. 807)

**Universal Negro Improvement Association:** A Harlem-based group, led by charismatic, Jamaican-born Marcus Garvey, that arose in the 1920s to mobilize African American workers and champion black separatism. (p. 719)

**USA PATRIOT Act:** A 2001 law that gave the government new powers to monitor suspected terrorists and their associates, including the ability to access personal information. (p. 1028)

**utopias:** Communities founded by reformers and transcendentalists to help realize their spiritual and moral potential and to escape from the competition of modern industrial society. (p. 349)

**Valley Forge:** A military camp in which George Washington's army of 12,000 soldiers and hundreds of camp followers suffered horribly in the winter of 1777–1778. (p. 189)

**vaudeville:** A professional stage show popular in the 1880s and 1890s that included singing, dancing, and comedy routines; it created a form of family entertainment for the urban masses that deeply influenced later forms, such as radio shows and television sitcoms. (p. 615)

**vertical integration:** A business model in which a corporation controlled all aspects of production from raw materials to packaged products. "Robber barons" or industrial innovators such as Gustavus Swift and Andrew Carnegie pioneered this business form at the end of the Civil War. (p. 547)

**Veterans Administration:** A federal agency that assists former soldiers. Following World War II, the VA helped veterans purchase new homes with no down payment, sparking a building boom that created jobs in the construction industry and fueling consumer spending in home appliances and automobiles. (p. 843)

**vice-admiralty court:** A maritime tribunal presided over by a royally appointed judge, with no jury. (p. 156)

**Vietnamization:** A new U.S. policy, devised under President Nixon in the early 1970s, of delegating the ground fighting to the South Vietnamese in the Vietnam War. American troop levels dropped and American casualties dropped correspondingly, but the killing in Vietnam continued. (p. 927)

**Virginia and Kentucky Resolutions:** Resolutions of 1798 condemning the Alien and Sedition Acts that were submitted to the federal government by the Virginia and Kentucky state legislatures. The resolutions tested the idea that state legislatures could judge the constitutionality of federal laws and nullify them. (p. 225)

**Virginia Plan:** A plan drafted by James Madison that was presented at the Philadelphia Constitutional Convention. It designed a powerful three-branch government, with representation in both houses of the congress tied to population; this plan would have eclipsed the voice of small states in the national government. (p. 205)

**virtual representation:** The claim made by British politicians that the interests of the American colonists were adequately represented in Parliament by merchants who traded with the colonies and by absentee landlords (mostly sugar planters) who owned estates in the West Indies. (p. 157)

**voluntarism:** The funding of churches by their members. It allowed the laity to control the clergy, while also supporting the republican principle of self-government. (p. 270)

**Voting Rights Act of 1965:** Law passed during Lyndon Johnson's administration that empowered the federal government to intervene to ensure minorities' access to the voting booth. (p. 891)

**Wade-Davis Bill:** A bill proposed by Congress in July 1864 that required an oath of allegiance by a majority of each state's adult white men, new governments formed only by those who had never taken up arms against the Union, and permanent disenfranchisement of Confederate leaders. The plan was passed but pocket vetoed by President Abraham Lincoln. (p. 480)

**Wagner Act:** A 1935 act that upheld the right of industrial workers to join unions and established the National Labor Relations Board (NLRB), a federal agency with the authority to protect workers from employer coercion and to guarantee collective bargaining. (p. 747)

**Waltham-Lowell System:** A system of labor using young women recruited from farm families to work in factories in Lowell, Chicopee, and other sites in Massachusetts and New Hampshire. The women lived in company boardinghouses with strict rules and curfews and were often required to attend church. (p. 288)

**War and Peace Democrats:** Members of the Democratic Party that split into two camps over war policy during the Civil War. War Democrats vowed to continue fighting until the rebellion ended, while Peace Democrats called for a constitutional convention to negotiate a peace settlement. (p. 469)

**War Industries Board:** A federal board established in July 1917 to direct military production, including allocation of resources, conversion of factories to war production, and setting of prices. (p. 688)

**War Powers Act (1941):** The law that gave President Roosevelt unprecedented control over all aspects of the war effort during World War II. (p. 773)

**War Powers Act (1973):** A law that limited the president's ability to deploy U.S. forces without congressional approval. Congress passed the War Powers Act in 1973 as a series of laws to fight the abuses of the Nixon administration. (p. 948)

**Warren Court:** The Supreme Court under Chief Justice Earl Warren (1953–1969), which expanded the Constitution's promise of equality and civil rights. It issued landmark decisions in the areas of civil rights, criminal rights, reproductive freedom, and separation of church and state. (p. 930)

**Warsaw Pact:** A military alliance established in Eastern Europe in 1955 to counter the NATO alliance; it included Albania, Bulgaria, Czechoslovakia, East Germany, Hungary, Poland, Romania, and the Soviet Union. (p. 812)

**Watergate:** Term referring to the 1972 break-in at Democratic Party headquarters in the Watergate complex in Washington, D.C., by men working for President Nixon's reelection campaign, along with Nixon's efforts to cover it up. The Watergate scandal led to President Nixon's resignation. (p. 947)

**"waving the bloody shirt":** A term of ridicule used in the 1880s and 1890s to refer to politicians — especially Republicans — who, according to critics, whipped up old animosities from the Civil War era that ought to be set aside. (p. 638)

**Webster v. Reproductive Health Services:** 1989 Supreme Court ruling that upheld the authority of state governments to limit the use of public funds and facilities for abortions. (p. 1020)

**welfare capitalism:** A system of labor relations that stressed management's responsibility for employees' well-being. (p. 708)

**welfare state:** A term applied to industrial democracies that adopt various government-guaranteed social-welfare programs. The creation of Social Security and other measures of the Second New Deal fundamentally changed American society and established a national welfare state for the first time. (p. 747)

**Whigs:** The second national party, the Whig Party arose in 1834 when a group of congressmen contested Andrew Jackson's policies and conduct. The party identified itself with the pre-Revolutionary American and British parties — also called Whigs — that had opposed the arbitrary actions of British monarchs. (p. 332)

**Whiskey Rebellion:** A 1794 uprising by farmers in western Pennsylvania in response to enforcement of an unpopular excise tax on whiskey. (p. 219)

**Williams v. Mississippi:** An 1898 Supreme Court ruling that allowed states to impose poll taxes and literacy tests. By 1908, every southern state had adopted such measures. (p. 645)

**Wilmot Proviso:** The 1846 proposal by Representative David Wilmot of Pennsylvania to ban slavery in territory acquired from the Mexican War. (p. 421)

**Wisconsin Idea:** A policy promoted by Republican governor Robert La Follette of Wisconsin for greater government intervention in the economy, with reliance on experts, particularly progressive economists, for policy recommendations. (p. 652)

**Woman's Christian Temperance Union:** An organization advocating the prohibition of liquor that spread rapidly after 1879, when charismatic Frances Willard became its leader. Advocating suffrage and a host of reform activities, it launched tens of thousands of women into public life and was the first nationwide organization to identify and condemn domestic violence. (p. 589)

**Women's International League for Peace and Freedom:** An organization founded by women activists in 1919; its members denounced imperialism, stressed the human suffering caused by militarism, and proposed social justice measures. (p. 710)

**women's liberation:** A new brand of feminism in the 1960s that attracted primarily younger, college-educated women fresh from the New Left, antiwar, and civil rights movements who sought to end to the denigration and exploitation of women. (p. 924)

**Women's Trade Union League:** A labor organization for women founded in New York in 1903 that brought elite, middle-class, and working-class women together as allies. The WTUL supported union organizing efforts among garment workers. (p. 629)

**Works Progress Administration:** Federal New Deal program established in 1935 that provided government-funded public works jobs to millions of unemployed Americans during the Great Depression in areas ranging from construction to the arts. (p. 749)

**World Bank:** An international bank created to provide loans for the reconstruction of war-torn Europe as well as for the development of former colonized nations in the developing world. (p. 840)

**World Trade Organization (WTO):** International economic body established in 1995 through the General Agreement on Tariffs and Trade to enforce substantial tariff and import quota reductions. (p. 1004)

**World Wide Web:** A collection of interlinked computer servers that debuted in 1991, allowing access by millions to documents, pictures, and other materials. (p. 1012)

**Wounded Knee:** The 1890 massacre of Sioux Indians by American cavalry at Wounded Knee Creek, South Dakota. Sent to suppress the Ghost Dance, soldiers caught up with fleeing Lakotas and killed as many as 300. (p. 534)

**XYZ Affair:** A 1797 incident in which American negotiators in France were rebuffed for refusing to pay a substantial bribe. The incident led the United States into an undeclared war that curtailed American trade with the French West Indies. (p. 223)

**Yalta Conference:** A meeting in Yalta of President Roosevelt, Prime Minister Churchill, and Joseph Stalin in February 1945, in which the leaders discussed the treatment of Germany, the status of Poland, the creation of the United Nations, and Russian entry into the war against Japan. (p. 806)

**yellow journalism:** A derogatory term for newspapers that specialize in sensationalistic reporting. Yellow journalism is associated with the inflammatory reporting by the Hearst and Pulitzer newspapers leading up to the Spanish-American War in 1898. (p. 619)

**Yellowstone National Park:** Established in 1872 by Congress, Yellowstone was the United States's first national park. (p. 525)

**Young Americans for Freedom (YAF):** The largest student political organization in the country, whose conservative members defended free enterprise and supported the war in Vietnam. (p. 915)

**Young Lords Organization:** An organization that sought self-determination for Puerto Ricans in the United States and in the Caribbean. Though immediate victories for the YLO were few, their dedicated community organizing produced a generation of leaders and awakened community consciousness. (p. 894)

**Young Men's Christian Association:** Introduced in Boston in 1851, the YMCA promoted muscular Christianity, combining evangelism with athletic facilities where men could make themselves "clean and strong." (p. 580)

**Zimmerman telegram:** A 1917 intercepted dispatch in which German foreign secretary Arthur Zimmerman urged Mexico to join the Central Powers and promised that if the United States entered the war, Germany would help Mexico recover Texas, New Mexico, and Arizona. Published by American newspapers, the telegram outraged the American public and help precipitate the move toward U.S. entry in the war on the Allied side. (p. 686)

**zoot suits:** Oversized suits of clothing in fashion in the 1940s, particularly among young male African Americans and Mexican Americans. In June 1943, a group of white sailors and soldiers in Los Angeles, seeking revenge for an earlier skirmish with Mexican American youths, attacked anyone they found wearing a zoot suit in what became known as the zoot suit riots. (p. 783)

# Index

sheep, 254, 515
*Sheik, The* (movie), 704
**Sheldon, Charles,** 600
*Shelley v. Kraemer* (1948), 857, 879(*m*)
Shelterbelts program, 760
Shenandoah National Park, 761
Shenandoah Valley region, 124, 124(*i*)
    Civil War in, 449, 450(*m*), 468
**Shepherd, William G.,** on Triangle fire, 630
Sheppard-Towner Federal Maternity and
        Infancy Act (1921), 709, 710
**Sheridan, Philip H.,** 468
**Sherman, Roger,** Declaration of
        Independence and, 178
**Sherman, William Tecumseh,** 467, 470(*i*),
        535
    march through Confederacy, 468, 469,
        470–471, 471(*m*), 472–473
    Native Americans and, 528
    on secession, 470
Sherman Antitrust Act (1890), 642, 650,
        662, 662(*t*)
Shiite Muslims
    in Iran, 977, 980, 997
    in Iraq, 1029
Shiloh, battle at, 445(*i*), 452, 453(*m*), 459
ships and shipping. *See also* canals; navies;
        Navy (U.S.); Royal Navy (England)
    American, 255
    Barbary pirates and, 231
    British seizures of, 219
    British textile industry and, 287
    in Civil War, 452
    colonial, 103, 201
    expansion of, 84
    Hawaii and, 510
    in Japan, 510, 511(*i*)
    Portuguese, 25
    privateering and, 223
    slave ships and, 94(*i*)
    transatlantic, 301
    whaling, 303(*i*)
    in World War I, 686
    in World War II, 775(*i*)
**Shiras, George,** 649(*i*)
shocks, economic, 721
shoe industry, 255, 286
shopping centers, 725
shopping malls, 860–862
"Short Narrative of My Proceedings"
        (Randolph), 68–69
Shoshone people, 10(*m*), 15, 233, 417
*Show and Extravagance* (Street), 555
Siberia, ancient migration from, 8, 9(*m*)
Sicily, in World War II, 790, 790(*m*)
Siegel-Cooper Department Store, 575(*i*)
Sierra Club, 583, 939, 984
Sierra Leone, 25, 97
    free blacks in, 264–265
Sierra Nevada mountains, 425, 761

"Significance of the Frontier in American
        History, The" (Turner), 535
**Sigourney, Lydia,** 327
silent majority, Nixon and, 929–932, 948
*Silent Spring* (Carson), 939, 940
Silk Road, 22, 29(*m*)
silver, 325
    in Americas, 27(*i*), 42, 45
    discoveries in West, 515, 516–517,
        517(*m*)
    free silver and, 645, 647
    vs. gold standard, 515, 645
Silver Legion, 714
**Simpson, Jerry,** 644
**Simpson, W. J.,** 390
Sinai Peninsula, 977
**Sinclair, Upton,** 629, 629(*i*), 748(*m*)
Singer Manufacturing Company, 548, 553(*i*)
Singer Sewing Machine Company, 291
single-sex higher education, 588
Sino-Japanese War (1894–1895), 678
Sioux Indians, 15, 233, 407, 414(*m*), 525, 531
    Ghost Dance and, 534
    reservation for, 526, 533, 534(*m*), 898
    resistance by, 526–527, 528, 532
    society of, 417
    at Wounded Knee, 898–899
**Sipkins, Henry,** 267
**Sirhan Sirhan,** 921
*Sister Carrie* (Dreiser), 603
sit-down strikes, 749(*i*)
sit-ins, civil rights movement and, 882
**Sitting Bull** (Lakota Sioux chief), 532, 534
Six-Day War (1967), 938, 1024
Six Nations (Iroquois), 90, 164
*Six Sermons on . . . Intemperance* (Lyman
        Beecher), 368
Sixteenth Amendment (1913), 660, 662(*t*)
skilled workers, 307, 544, 550–553, 558,
        567, 569–570
skyscrapers, 608–609, 609(*i*)
**Slater, Samuel,** 287
*Slaughter-House Cases,* 500
slaughterhouses, 519, 547
slave catchers, 362, 429, 431
Slave Coast, 24–25
slave codes, 55, 361
slave owners. *See also* planters and
        plantations
    in Alabama, 393
    free blacks as, 402
    Indians as, 327, 464
    in South, 383, 388–389, 395, 446
"Slave Power" conspiracy, 421, 436, 463
slave society, South as, 388
slave states, 269, 269(*m*), 363(*m*), 378,
        379(*m*)
slave trade
    abolition in District of Columbia, 429
    abolition of Atlantic, 267

Africa, Africans, and, 24(*m*), 29–30,
        92–96, 93(*m*)
    in Atlantic region, 23–25, 35, 90–92,
        93(*m*), 266, 378, 394
    coastal system of, 380
    congressional regulation of, 206
    domestic, 378–383
    end of (1808), 229–230
    inland system of, 380–381, 381(*i*)
    profits in, 92
    sugar and, 22
*Slave Trader, Sold to Tennessee* (Miller),
        381(*i*)
"slavery follows the flag" (Calhoun), 428
slaves and slavery, 434–435. *See also*
        abolition and abolitionism; African
        Americans; Middle Passage; runaway
        slaves
    abolition issue and, 159–160, 360–363
    advertising of, 98(*i*)
    in Africa, 29–30
    African influences on, 395–396, 397
    aristocratic republicanism and, 264–269
    on Atlantic islands, 28
    banned north of Ohio River, 201
    in Barbados, 91
    Black Codes and, 481
    in Brazil, 35
    chattel slavery and, 40, 381
    in Chesapeake, 96
    Civil War and, 444, 449, 452, 462–463,
        464
    Compromise of 1850 and, 428–430,
        429(*m*)
    Constitution on, 206–207
    as "contrabands," 463
    cotton and, 376, 377(*i*), 388
    culture of, 395–397, 396(*i*)
    defense of, 266, 268–269, 282, 364(*i*),
        386–388
    Dutch and, 59
    economic role of, 90–103
    emancipation and, 463–464
    evangelicalism and, 271–272
    extension of, 378, 407, 446–447
    families of, 377(*i*), 382, 397, 398, 399(*i*)
    forced migration of (1790–1860), 380(*f*)
    Franklin on, 128
    free labor and, 384–385
    free-soil movement and, 421
    gang-labor system of, 388, 397
    Haitian revolt and, 223
    housing for, 400(*i*)
    Indians and, 17, 18, 90, 327
    kinship ties and, 397, 398
    as labor, 397
    Lincoln and, 437–438
    literacy and, 337
    marriages of, 382, 397
    Mexican War and, 421, 422–423

from India, 289
mills and, 254
tariffs for, 512
technology for, 254, 287–288, 290–291
U.S. production in, 289(t)
in Waltham, Massachusetts, 288–290
women in, 254, 285(i), 288–290, 293
Thailand, financial crisis in, 1011
**Thayendanegea.** *See* Brant, Joseph
(Thayendanegea)
**Thayer, Webster,** 708(i), 709
theater, 356
O'Neill plays in, 721
vaudeville, 359, 541, 615
Yiddish, 612
*Their Eyes Were Watching God* (Hurston),
761
theology. *See also* Christianity; *specific groups*
of Shakers, 349–350
Twain on, 595
therapy, for marriage, 961
thermonuclear weapons, 813
**Theyanoguin, Hendrick Peters,** 137(i)
**Thieu, Nguyen Van,** 929
Third Great Awakening (1880–1900), 275
Third International (Comintern), 708
third way, of Clinton, Bill, 1023(i)
Third World, 826
decolonization in (1943–1990), 895(m)
Thirteenth Amendment (1865), 371(i), 470,
480, 484(t), 504
*Thirty Seconds over Tokyo* (movie), 782
**Thistlewood, Thomas,** 96
**Thompson, Florence,** 760(i)
**Thompson, James G.,** 873
**Thoreau, Henry David,** 299, 347, 363, 438
**Thornton, Big Mama,** 848
**Thorpe, Jim,** 582(i)
*Thoughts on Female Education* (Rush), 259
*Thoughts on Government* (John Adams),
198, 210
"Thoughts on Indian Affairs" (Bradstreet),
164
three-fifths clause, 207, 208, 225
Three Mile Island, nuclear accident at
(1979), 942
*Three Soldiers, The* (Dos Passos), 720
**Thurmond, J. Strom,** 819, 820, 820(m),
891, 892, 923
Tidewater region, 383–386
revivalism in, 133–134
in Revolutionary War, 195
Tijuana, as vice town, 712–713
**Tilden, Samuel J.,** 500–501
Tilden Park, 761
**Till, Emmett,** 880
**Tillman, Ben (Pitchfork),** 645
**Tillman, Juliann Jane,** 275(i)
Timbuktu, 25, 94
time zones, establishment of, 513(m)

Tin Pan Alley, 617
tinplate, 287
**Tipler, Charles S.,** on disease in Civil War,
458
Tippecanoe, Battle of, 236
Title IX (1972), 925
**Tito, Josip Broz,** 814
**Titus** (runaway), 192
Titusville, Pennsylvania, petroleum in, 547
Tlaxcala, 32
Tlingit Indians, 16, 17(i)
"To Secure These Rights" (1946), 875, 896
*Toast, The,* 220(i)
tobacco and tobacco industry
in Chesapeake region, 54
English tobacco colonies and, 47–52
labor for, 96
planters and, 266, 386
slavery and, 266
in Virginia, 81(i)
Tobago, 196
**Tocqueville, Alexis de**
*Democracy in America,* 248, 314, 317
individualism and, 346
on Jackson, 329
"Letter to Louis de Kergorlay," 317
**Tojo, Hideki,** 768, 773. *See also* Japan;
World War II
Tokyo (Edo), 510, 795
toleration. *See* religious toleration
Toleration Act (Maryland, 1649), 52
toll roads, 255, 293
**Tompkins, Daniel,** 307
**Tooker, John,** 459
**Toomer, Jean,** 718
**Toplitzky, Nathan,** 563
**Torbert, James,** 388
**Toriello, Guillermo,** 811
Toronto, 236
**Torrey, Samuel,** 64(i)
**Tortillott, Jane Gould,** 413
Tortola, 53
torture, of Iraqi prisoners, 1029
total war
Civil War as, 452, 460
World War II as, 767(i)
totem poles, 16
**Toth, Susan Allen,** 852–853
Tougaloo university, 493
tourism
in Indian Country, 531
railroad, 508, 525
in West, 760
working-class, 584
town meetings, in New England, 64
towns. *See* cities and towns
**Townsend, Francis,** 747, 748(m)
**Townsend, Hannah** and **Mary,** 361(i)
**Townsend, John,** 439
Townsend Clubs, 747

Townsend Plan, 747
**Townshend, Charles,** 110, 157, 160–162,
160(t)
Townshend Act (1767), 161, 171(t)
repeal of, 166
Toynbee Hall (London), 628
Tract Society, 275
**Tracy, Spencer,** 782
trade. *See also* commerce; exports; slave
trade
in Africa, 23–25, 24(m)
with Africa, 28–29
American, 8
American silver and, 42
Arab, 19
with Asia, 510
with China, 251(i)
in Civil War, 449
colonial, 84–85, 152
Crusades and, 22
Dutch, 58
English, 45–46, 84–85
Eurasian, 29(m)
Eurasian and European colonies
(c. 1770), 154(m)
European Union and, 999
expansion of, 842
external duties on, 161
French, 58
with French West Indies, 223
global, 576, 699, 1005, 1008(f), 1009–
1011
Indian, 15, 16–17, 48(m), 56, 417
interregional, 296, 297
Italian, 20, 28
with Japan, 431, 510
with Latin America, 510
Mississippi River and, 232
New York City and, 301
in Northern Europe, 20
paper money and, 110
as political weapon (1763–1776), 166(f)
Portuguese, 25–28
along Santa Fe Trail, 416
with South America, 301
in South Carolina, 82
in Spanish America, 42
Supreme Court on, 707
trans-Saharan, 23–25, 24(m)
transatlantic, 103
transcontinental railroad and, 508
Western European, 19–20
in World War I, 685–686
trade associations, 710
trade deficit, colonial, 141
trade routes, across Sahara, 23–25, 24(m)
trade unions, 565, 567, 569–570. *See also*
labor unions
African Americans in, 871–872
middle-class expansion and, 844–845

Whigs (England), 332

whipping, of slaves, 362, 388, 389(i)

**Whipple, Henry,** 526

whiskey, taxation on, 219

Whiskey Rebellion, 219, 221, 222(i), 231

Whiskey Ring scandal, 498

**Whistler, Henry,** journal of, 57

**White, Dan,** 957

**White, Edward Douglas,** 649(i)

**White, Harry Dexter,** 820

**White, Hugh L.,** 334

**White, John,** 47(i), 48(i)

**White, William Allen,** 771

White Citizens' Councils, 878

white-collar workers, 302, 549

white flight, 931(i)

White House Conference on Dependent
    Children (1909), 652, 662(t)

White League, 499

White Man's Party (Grimes County, Texas),
    646

white primary, 646, 871

"white slavery," 626, 626(i), 627

white supremacy. *See also* Ku Klux Klan;
    race and racism
    in 1930s, 714
    challenges to, 884–885
    Democrats and, 645–646
    slavery and, 266, 391
    in South, 282, 444, 462, 499

**Whitefield, George,** 115(i), 129–132,
    132(i), 134, 271

whites. *See also* Anglos
    affirmative action and, 951
    Atlanta Compromise and, 587–588
    challenging supremacy of, 884–885
    in Chesapeake region, 55(f)
    depictions of Indians, 530–531, 531(i)
    identity and equality of, 102–103
    as Loyalists, 174
    in Middle Atlantic region, 122
    in South, 376, 383–391
    voting rights for male, 257, 257(m), 316,
        393

"whites only" drinking fountains, 870, 870(i)

**Whiteside, James A.** (1803–1861), and
    family, 394(i)

**Whitfield, Donald,** 912

**Whitman, Walt,** 291, 348
    on slavery in territories, 423

**Whitney, Eli,** 290, 290(i)

Who, the (musical group), 918

wholesale prices, from 1869 to 1913, 546(f)

*Why Is There No Socialism in the United
    States?* (Sombart), 555

*Why Not Victory?* (Goldwater), 975

"Why We Fight" (documentaries), 782

**Whyte, William,** 842, 859

widows, assistance for, 748–749

**Wigfall, Louis,** 394

**Wild, John Caspar,** 256(i)

*Wild One, The* (movie), 848

Wild West, 530(i)

Wilderness, Battle of the, 467, 469(m)

Wilderness Preservation Act (1964), 907(t)

Wilderness Society, 939

wildlife, 525
    protection of, 583, 651

**Wildmon, Donald E.,** 978

**Wilkes, John,** 152

**Wilkinson, Eliza,** 199

**Wilkinson, James,** 233

**Wilkinson, Jemima,** 275

**Will, George,** 983

Willamette Valley, Oregon, 412, 413

**Willard, Emma Hart,** 276

**Willard, Frances,** 589

**Willard, John,** 260

**William of Orange,** 85(m), 86, 87(i), 88

**Williams, Roger,** 62

**Williams, Tim,** 898(i)

*Williams v. Mississippi* (1898), 645

**Willkie, Wendell,** 771

Willow Grove (amusement park), 617

**Wilmot, David,** 421

Wilmot Proviso (1846), 421, 463

**Wilson, Hawkins,** 382

**Wilson, Tessie Hickam,** 785

**Wilson, Woodrow** (1856–1924), 636, 714
    banking and, 661–662
    election of 1912 and, 656–660, 660(i),
        660(m)
    election of 1916, 686
    foreign policy of, 672, 683–684
    Fourteen Points of, 668, 696–697
    illness of, 699, 708
    labor and, 662
    Mexico and, 683–684
    neutrality policy of, 669, 685
    New Freedom and, 657
    as president (1913–1921), 542, 636, 672
    progressivism and, 662(t)
    trusts and, 662
    Versailles treaty and, 697, 697(i), 698, 699
    woman suffrage and, 695, 696
    World War I and, 686, 690

wind erosion, dust bowl and, 759

Windows operating system, 989

*Windsor v. United States* (2013), 1020

Windward Coast, 97

**Winthrop, James,** 207

**Winthrop, John,** 61–62, 67

Wisconsin, 201, 293, 330
    Fugitive Slave Act and, 431
    political reforms in, 652

Wisconsin Idea, 652

**Wise, John,** 127, 131

**Wise, Stephen S.,** on Triangle fire, 630

witchcraft, Puritans and, 63–64

wives. *See* married women

Wobblies. *See* Industrial Workers of the
    World

**Wolde-Giorghis, Hailou,** 876

**Wolfe, James,** 138

**Wollstonecraft, Mary,** 199(i), 259

Wolof people, 97

*Woman in the Nineteenth Century* (Fuller),
    347

woman suffrage, 257–258, 485–487, 486(i)
    Roosevelt, Theodore, and, 656
    World War I and, 695–696

Woman's Christian Temperance Union
    (WCTU), 589–591, 590(i), 636

*Woman's Exponent,* 521

*Woman's Work, A* (Sloan), 595(i)

women. *See also* abortion and abortion
        rights; feminism; gender and gender
        issues; girls; women's rights
    abolitionism and, 362, 365–366, 370–371
    affirmative action and, 951
    African American, 924–925
    African American organizations of,
        591–592
    antislavery movement and (1837–1838),
        370(m)
    athletics for, 925
    in Benevolent Empire, 305, 336
    in Chesapeake region, 55(f)
    in Chinese factories, 1010(i)
    Christianity and, 963
    in civil rights movement, 890(i)
    in Civil War, 456, 456(i), 461–462,
        472–473
    in clothing industry, 305
    in Congress, 686
    consumer culture and, 577, 724
    in corporations, 550
    as Daughters of Liberty, 161–162
    domesticity of, 850
    education for, 260, 263(i), 276, 495, 588,
        589(i)
    families and, 851–855
    as feminists, 592
    as flappers, 704, 705(i), 726
    Fourierism and, 351
    freedwomen's work and, 490–491
    in Great Depression, 728–729
    higher education and, 925
    as homesteaders, 520–521
    in household economy, 116–117
    immigrant, 310, 559
    as indentured servants, 55
    Indian, 12, 15, 227, 417
    Indian removal and, 327
    industrialization and, 584–585
    in Klan, 716(i), 717
    labor of, 118, 119(i)
    labor unions and, 567, 570, 629
    legal marriage rights of, 117
    marriage and, 258, 260–261

## About the authors

**James A. Henretta** is Professor Emeritus of American History at the University of Maryland, College Park. His publications include *"Salutary Neglect": Colonial Administration under the Duke of Newcastle; The Origins of American Capitalism*; and an edited volume, *Republicanism and Liberalism in America and the German States, 1750–1850*. His most recent publication is a long article, "Charles Evans Hughes and the Strange Death of Liberal America," in *Law and History Review*, derived from his ongoing research on the liberal state in America, and in particular New York, 1820–1975.

**Eric Hinderaker** is Professor of History and Director of Graduate Studies at the University of Utah. His research explores early modern imperialism, relations between Europeans and Native Americans, and comparative colonization. His publications include *The Two Hendricks: Unraveling a Mohawk Mystery*, which won the Dixon Ryan Fox Prize; *Elusive Empires: Constructing Colonialism in the Ohio Valley, 1673–1800*; and, with Peter C. Mancall, *At the Edge of Empire: The Backcountry in British North America*. He is currently working on two books, one about the Boston Massacre and another, with Rebecca Horn, on patterns of European colonization in the Americas.

**Rebecca Edwards** is Eloise Ellery Professor of History at Vassar College, where she teaches courses on the Civil War era, the West, environmental history, and the history of women and gender roles. She is the author of, among other publications, *Angels in the Machinery: Gender in American Party Politics from the Civil War to the Progressive Era; New Spirits: Americans in the "Gilded Age," 1865–1905*; and the essay "Women's and Gender History" in *The New American History*. She is currently researching the connections between westward expansion, high frontier fertility, and nineteenth-century political ideologies.

**Robert O. Self** is Professor of History at Brown University. His research focuses on urban history, American politics, and the post-1945 United States. He is the author of *American Babylon: Race and the Struggle for Postwar Oakland*, which won four professional prizes, including the James A. Rawley Prize from the Organization of American Historians, and *All in the Family: The Realignment of American Democracy Since the 1960s*. He is currently at work on a book about the centrality of houses, cars, and children to family consumption in the twentieth-century United States.

# How to Analyze Primary Sources

In their search for an improved understanding of the past, historians look for new evidence — written documents or visual artifacts. When they encounter a written or visual primary source, historians ask certain key questions. You should ask these questions too. Sometimes historians can't be certain about the answer, but they always ask the question.

## Analyzing a written document

- Who wrote the document? Is it a specific person or someone whose identity you can merely infer from the context of the document (for example, a parent writing to a child, a traveler writing home)?
- When and where was it written?
- Why was the document written? Is there a clear purpose, or are multiple interpretations possible?
- Who was, or who might have been, its intended audience?
- What point of view does it reflect?
- What can the document tell us about the individual who produced it and the society from which he or she came?

## Analyzing a visual source

- Who made the image or artifact, and how was it made?
- When and where was the image or artifact made?
- Who paid for or commissioned it? How can you tell?
- For what audience might it have been intended? Where might it have originally been displayed or used?
- What message or messages is it trying to convey?
- How could it be interpreted differently depending on who viewed or used it?
- What can this visual source tell us about the individual who produced it and the society from which he or she came?